West Academic Publishing's Law School Advisory Board

JESSE H. CHOPER
Professor of Law and Dean Emeritus,
University of California, Berkeley

JOSHUA DRESSLER
Distinguished University Professor, Frank R. Strong Chair in Law
Michael E. Moritz College of Law, The Ohio State University

YALE KAMISAR
Professor of Law Emeritus, University of San Diego
Professor of Law Emeritus, University of Michigan

MARY KAY KANE
Professor of Law, Chancellor and Dean Emeritus,
University of California, Hastings College of the Law

LARRY D. KRAMER
President, William and Flora Hewlett Foundation

JONATHAN R. MACEY
Professor of Law, Yale Law School

ARTHUR R. MILLER
University Professor, New York University
Formerly Bruce Bromley Professor of Law, Harvard University

GRANT S. NELSON
Professor of Law, Pepperdine University
Professor of Law Emeritus, University of California, Los Angeles

A. BENJAMIN SPENCER
Earle K. Shawe Professor of Law,
University of Virginia School of Law

JAMES J. WHITE
Robert A. Sullivan Professor of Law Emeritus,
University of Michigan

CLASS ACTIONS
AND OTHER MULTI-PARTY LITIGATION

CASES AND MATERIALS

Fourth Edition

■ ■ ■

Robert H. Klonoff
Jordan D. Schnitzer Professor of Law
Dean of the Law School, 2007–2014
Lewis & Clark Law School

AMERICAN CASEBOOK SERIES®

The publisher is not engaged in rendering legal or other professional advice, and this publication is not a substitute for the advice of an attorney. If you require legal or other expert advice, you should seek the services of a competent attorney or other professional.

American Casebook Series is a trademark registered in the U.S. Patent and Trademark Office.

© West, a Thomson business, 2000, 2006
© 2012 Thomson Reuters
© 2017 LEG, Inc. d/b/a West Academic
    444 Cedar Street, Suite 700
    St. Paul, MN 55101
    1-877-888-1330

West, West Academic Publishing, and West Academic are trademarks of West Publishing Corporation, used under license.

Printed in the United States of America

ISBN: 978-1-63459-926-9

This book is dedicated to my family and to the many jurists and scholars who have thought and written about class actions. Without the support, patience, and understanding of the former, and the creativity and insights of the latter, this book would not have been possible.

PREFACE

This casebook addresses class actions and other multi-party litigation, principally in federal courts. It is designed for courses in class actions and complex litigation, as well as other courses with a substantial class action component, such as mass torts. Originally published in 2000, and revised in 2006 and 2012, this fourth edition contains substantial updates, including major recent Supreme Court and federal courts of appeals decisions, an expanded treatment of multidistrict litigation, and a new section on third-party financing.

In addition to teaching class actions and complex litigation, I have served as counsel in scores of class actions, including highly publicized securities fraud, mass tort, employment discrimination, antitrust, and consumer class actions. I have also served as a class expert in numerous cases, including the BP oil spill case (Deepwater Horizon), the National Football League Concussion case, and the Volkswagen Clean Diesel case. Moreover, I have served as the academic member of the Federal Civil Rules Advisory Committee since 2011 (second term expires in 2017), and also served on the Committee's Class Action Subcommittee. And I served as an Associate Reporter for the American Law Institute's project, *Principles of the Law of Aggregate Litigation*. I have endeavored to write a textbook that is rich in theory but at the same time is relevant to the real world of aggregate litigation practice.

Throughout this casebook, I have adopted editorial conventions that have led to certain modifications of the source documents. I have included citations within excerpted materials only to the extent that such citations served some pedagogical purpose (often to permit the reader to follow up on a particular point of law, but sometimes because the use of the authority is, for one reason or another, interesting or provocative). For U.S. Supreme Court cases, I provide only the United States Reporter cite if it is available. If it is not available, I cite to the Supreme Court Reporter. Citation form may vary from the excerpted source, *e.g.*, long- versus short-form. I have reflected my edits to excerpted materials by using three asterisks, as opposed to ellipses (ellipses in excerpted materials set forth in this casebook were present in the originals). I have included references to denial of *certiorari* only in cases in which the denial occurred in 2013 or later. I have noted when emphasis has been added to a source; if no notation is provided, the emphasis was in the original. On occasion, I have made minor typeface modifications to headings in excerpted materials for purposes of presentation. In the Table of Cases, I provide the name of a case and the pages in the book where the case appears. I do not distinguish between different opinions by the same court or different courts for the same case. This enables the student to easily find all discussions relevant to a particular case.

I am grateful for the invaluable assistance I received on all four editions of this casebook. In addition to the many people who reviewed or assisted with the first, second, and third editions of this text (and who were acknowledged therein), I wish to recognize the contributions of those who worked on this latest edition: Jacob Abbott, Evan Christopher, Max Goins, Christina Helregel, Ben Pepper, Elisabeth Rennick, and Daniel Walker.

It goes without saying that the statements and conclusions in this text are mine alone (or those of the judges or authors whose writings are excerpted).

I also wish to acknowledge the following copyright holders (listed in alphabetical order) who gave me permission to reprint excerpts from their copyrighted materials. (Apart from granting me permission to reprint excerpts in this book, the copyright holders have reserved all of their rights.)

ACKNOWLEDGMENTS

Absmeier, Mike, Note, *The Professional Objector and Revised Rule 23: Protecting Voice Rights While Limiting Objector Abuse*, 24 Rev. Litig. 609 (2005). As originally published in The Review of Litigation. Copyright © 2005 Mike Absmeier. Reprinted with permission of the author.

American Law Institute, *Complex Litigation: Statutory Recommendations and Analysis* (1994). Copyright © 1994 the American Law Institute. Reproduced with the permission of the Institute.

American Law Institute, *Principles of the Law of Aggregate Litigation* (2010). Copyright © 2010 the American Law Institute. Reproduced with the permission of the Institute.

Anderson, Lloyd C., *The Approval and Interpretation of Consent Decrees in Civil Rights Class Action Litigation*, 1983 U. Ill. L. Rev. 579 (1983). Copyright © 1983 University of Illinois Law Review. Reprinted with permission of the University of Illinois Law Review.

Borden, Catherine R., Lee, Emery G. III & Williams, Margaret S., *Centripetal Forces: Multidistrict Litigation and Its Parts*, 75 La. L. Rev. 425 (2014). Copyright © 2014 Catherine R. Borden, Emery G. Lee III, and Margaret S. Williams. Reprinted with permission of the authors.

Brandt, Elizabeth B., *Fairness to the Absent Members of a Defendant Class: A Proposed Revision of Rule 23*, 1990 BYU L. Rev. 909. Copyright © 1990 Elizabeth B. Brandt. Reprinted with permission of the author.

Brunet, Edward, *Class Action Objectors: Extortionist Free Riders or Fairness Guarantors*, 2003 U. Chi. Legal F. 403 (2003). Copyright © 2003 University of Chicago Legal Forum. Originally appearing in the University of Chicago Legal Forum, Vol. 2003. Reprinted with permission from the University of Chicago Legal Forum and the University of Chicago Law School.

Bucklo, Hon. Elaine & Meites, Thomas R., *What Every Judge Should Know About a Rule 23 Settlement (But Probably Isn't Told)*, 41 Litigation 1 (2015). This article originally appeared in Litigation, Volume 41, Number 3, Spring 2015. Copyright © 2015 the American Bar Association. Reproduced with permission.

Burbank, Stephen B., Farhang, Sean & Kritzer, Herbert M., *Private Enforcement*, 17 Lewis and Clark L. Rev. 637 (2013). Copyright © 2013 Stephen B Burbank, Sean Farhang and Herbert M. Kritzer. Reprinted with permission of the authors.

Burch, Elizabeth C., *Financiers as Monitors in Aggregate Litigation*, pp. 8–13, Georgia Law Advocate Magazine: Vol. 48: Iss. 1, Article 3. (2014). Copyright © 2014 Elizabeth C. Burch & Advocate. A version of this article originally appeared in the New York University Law Review, Volume 87, 2012. Reprinted with permission from the University of Georgia School of Law and its alumni magazine Advocate.

Burns, Jean W., *Decorative Figureheads: Eliminating Class Representatives in Class Actions*, 42 Hastings L.J. 165 (1990). Copyright © 1990 University of California, Hastings College of the Law. Reprinted with permission of the Hastings Law Journal.

Coffee, John C., Jr., *Class Wars: The Dilemma of the Mass Tort Class Action.* Copyright © 1995 John C. Coffee and the Columbia Law Review. Reprinted with permission of the author and the Columbia Law Review.

Coffee, John C., Jr., *You Just Can't Get There from Here: A Primer on Wal-Mart v. Dukes*, 80 U.S.L.W. 93 (2011). Copyright © 2011 John C. Coffee. Reprinted with permission of the author.

Cohen, Anne E., *Mass Tort Litigation after* Amchem ALI–ABA Course of Study Matters, Civil Practice and Litigation Techniques in the Federal Courts, (1998). Copyright © 1998 the American Law Institute. Reproduced with the permission of American Law Institute–American Bar Association Continuing Professional Education.

Comment, *Capacity and Class Actions Under Federal Rule 23.2*, 61 B.U. L. Rev. 713 (1981). Copyright © 1981 Keith Higgins. Reprinted with permission of the author. Originally published in the Boston University Law Review.

Comment, *Federal Rule of Civil Procedure 23(a)(3) Typicality Requirement: The Superfluous Prerequisite to Maintaining a Class Action*, 42 Ohio St. L.J. 797 (1981). Copyright © Olger Twyner C. III and the Ohio State Law Journal. Reprinted with permission of the author and the Ohio State Law Journal.

Comment, *Mandatory Notice and Defendant Class Actions: Resolving the Paradox of Identity Between Plaintiffs and Defendants*, 40 Emory L.J. 611 (1991). Copyright © 1991 Debra J. Libby. Reprinted with permission of the author.

Cooper, Edward H., *The (Cloudy) Future of Class Actions*, 30 Ariz. L. Rev. 923 (1998). Copyright © 1998 Edward H. Cooper and the Arizona Law Review. Reprinted with permission of the author and the Arizona Law Review.

Davis, Mary J., *Toward the Proper Role for Mass Tort Class Actions*, 77 Or. L. Rev. 157 (1998). Copyright © 1998 Mary J. Davis. Reprinted with permission of the author.

Dodge, Jaime, *Facilitative Judging: Organizational Design in Mass-Multidistrict Litigation*, 64 Emory L.J. 329 (2014). Copyright © 2014 Jaime Dodge. Reprinted with permission of the author.

Downs, Howard M., *Federal Class Actions: Diminished Protection for the Class and the Case for Reform*, 73 Neb. L. Rev. 646 (1994). Copyright © 1994 Nebraska Law Review. Reprinted with permission of the Nebraska Law Review.

Drake, Hon. W. Homer & Strickland, Christopher, *Chapter 11 Reorganizations*, Thomson/West (2d ed. 2002). Copyright © 2002 Thomson Reuters. Reprinted with the permission of Thomson Reuters.

Duke Law Center for Judicial Studies, *Standards and Best Practices for Large and Mass-Tort MDLs*, https://law.duke.edu/sites/default/files/centers/judicialstudies/duke_compendium_appendix-final.pdf (last visited Dec. 21, 2016). Reproduced with the permission of the Duke Law Center for Judicial Studies.

Ebert, Robert T., Epley, Leslie A. & Plevin, Mark D., *Pre-Packaged Asbestos Bankruptcies: A Flawed Solution*, 44 S. Tex. L. Rev. 883 (2003). Copyright © 2003 Robert T. Ebert, Leslie A. Epley, Mark D. Plevin and the South Texas Law Review. Reprinted with permission of the authors and the South Texas Law Review.

Erichson, Howard M. & Zipursky, Benjamin C., *Consent Versus Closure*, 96 Cornell L. Rev. 265 (2011). Copyright © 2011 Cornell Law Review. Reprinted with permission of the Cornell Law Review.

Feinberg, Kenneth R., *Creative Use of ADR: The Court–Appointed Special Settlement Master*, 59 Alb. L. Rev. 881 (1996). Copyright © 1996 Albany Law Review. Reprinted with permission of the Albany Law Review. This article originally appeared in the *Albany Law Review*, Volume 59, 1996.

Fisch, Jill E., *Class Action Reform: Lessons from Securities Litigation*, 39 Ariz. L. Rev. 533 (1997). Copyright © 1997 Jill E. Fisch and the Arizona Law Review. Reprinted with permission of the author and the Arizona Law Review.

Fiss, Owen M., *The Political Theory of the Class Action*, 53 Wash. & Lee L. Rev. 21 (1996). Copyright © 1996 Owen M. Fiss. Reprinted with permission of the author.

Freer, Richard D., *Exodus from and Transformation of American Civil Litigation*, 65 Emory L.J. 1491 (2016). Copyright © 1996 Richard D. Freer. Reprinted with permission of the author.

George, Tracey E. & Williams, Margaret S., *Who Will Manage Complex Civil Litigation? The Decision to Transfer and Consolidate Multidistrict Litigation*, 10 J. Empirical Legal Stud. 424 (2013). Copyright © 2013 Cornell Law School and Wiley Subscription Services, Inc. Reprinted with permission of the authors, the Journal of Empirical Legal Studies, and Wiley Subscription Services, Inc.

Gerard, Robert B. & Johnson, Scott M., *The Role of the Objector in Class Action Settlements: A Case Study of the General Motors Truck "Side Saddle" Fuel Tank Litigation*, 31 Loy. L.A. L. Rev. 409 (1998). Copyright © 1998 Robert B. Gerard and Scott M. Johnson. Reprinted with the permission of the authors.

Greenberg, Jack, *Civil Rights Class Actions: Procedural means of Obtaining Substance*, 39 Ariz. L. Rev. 575 (1997). Copyright © 1997 Jack Greenberg and the Arizona Law Review. Reprinted with permission of the author and the Arizona Law Review.

Harkins, John G., Jr., *Federal Rule 23—The Early Years*, 39 Ariz. L. Rev. 705 (1997). Copyright © 1997 John G. Harkins, Jr. and the Arizona Law Review. Reprinted with permission of the author and the Arizona Law Review.

Hart, Melissa, *Will Employment Discrimination Class Actions Survive?*, 37 Akron L. Rev. 813 (2004). Copyright © 2004, Akron Law Review, The University of Akron Law School. Reprinted with permission of the Akron Law Review.

Hazard, Geoffrey C., Jr. & Hodes, W. William, *The Law of Lawyering : A Handbook on the Model Rules of Professional Conduct* (3d ed. 2011 supplement). Copyright © 1997 Wolters Kluwer Law & Business/Aspen Publishers. Reprinted with permission of Wolters Kluwer Law & Business/Aspen Publishers.

Hensler, Deborah R. & Peterson, Mark A., *Understanding Mass Personal Injury Litigation: A Socio–Legal Analysis*, 59 Brook. L. Rev. 961 (1993). Copyright © 1993 Brooklyn Law Review. Reprinted with permission of the Brooklyn Law Review.

Issacharoff, Samuel, *Private Claims, Aggregate Rights*, 2008 Sup. Ct. Rev. 183 (2008). Copyright © 2008 the University of Chicago. Reprinted with permission of the author, the Supreme Court Review, and the University of Chicago.

Koniak, Susan P., *Feasting While the Widow Weeps*: Georgine v. AMCHEM Products, Inc., 80 Cornell L. Rev. 1045 (1995). Copyright © 1995 Cornell Law Review. Reprinted with permission of the Cornell Law Review.

Landers, Jonathan M., *Of Legalized Blackmail and Legalized Theft: Consumer Class Actions and the Substance Procedure Dilemma*, 47 S. Cal. L. Rev. 842 (1974), reprinted with the permission of the Southern California Law Review.

Leubsdorf, John, *Class Actions at the Cloverleaf*, 39 Ariz. L. Rev. 453 (1997). Copyright © 1997 John Leubsdorf and the Arizona Law Review. Reprinted with permission of the author and the Arizona Law Review.

Mabey, Ralph R. & Zisser, Peter A., *Improving Treatment of Future Claims: The Unfinished Business Left by the Manville Amendments*, 69 Am. Bankr. L.J. 487 (1995). Copyright © 1995 American Bankruptcy Law Journal. Reprinted with permission of the American Bankruptcy Law Journal.

Maclin, Alan H., "Strategies and Options for Defending Class Actions (With Case Resources)," *The Practical Litigator*, Vol. 9, No. 5 (Sept. 1998). Copyright 1998 the American Law Institute. Reproduced with the permission of American Law Institute–American Bar Association Continuing Professional Education.

Malveaux, Suzette M., *Class Actions at the Crossroads: An Answer to Wal–Mart v. Dukes*, 5 Harv. L. & Pol'y Rev. at 11 (2011). Copyright © Harvard Law & Policy Review. Reprinted with permission of the Harvard Law & Policy Review.

Matthews, Mary E., *Derivative Suits and the Similarly Situated Shareholder Requirement*, 8 DePaul Bus. L.J. 1 (1995). Copyright © Mary E.

Matthews and DePaul Business & Commercial Law Journal. Reprinted with permission of the author and the DePaul Business & Commercial Law Journal.

McGuire, Bartlett H., *The Death Knell for Eisen: Why the Class Action Should Include an Assessment of the Merits*, 168 F.R.D. 366 (1996). Copyright © Barlett H. McGuire and Thomson Reuters. Reprinted with permission of the author and Thomson Reuters.

Menkel–Meadow, Carrie, *When Dispute Resolution Begets Disputes of Its Own: Conflicts Among Dispute Professionals*, 44 UCLA L. Rev. 1871 (1997). Copyright © 1997 Carrie Menkel–Meadow. Reprinted with permission of the author.

Minow, Martha, *Judge for the Situation: Judge Jack Weinstein, Creator of Temporary Administrative Agencies*, 97 Colum. L. Rev. 2010 (1997). Copyright © 1997 Martha Minow and the Columbia Law Review. Reprinted with permission of the author and the Columbia Law Review.

Morawetz, Nancy, *Bargaining, Class Representation, and Fairness*, 54 Ohio St. L.J. 1 (1993). Copyright © 1993 Nancy Morawetz and the Ohio State Law Journal. Reprinted with permission of the author and the Ohio State Law Journal.

Nagareda, Richard, *In the Aftermath of the Mass Tort Class Action*, 85 Geo. L.J. 295 (1996). Reprinted with permission of the publisher, Georgetown Law Journal a 1996.

Nagareda, Richard, *Class Certification in the Age of Aggregate Proof*, 84 N.Y.U. L. Rev. 97 (2009). Copyright © 2009 New York University Law Review. Reprinted with permission of the New York University Law Review.

Newberg, Herbert, & Conte, Alba, Newberg on Class Actions, (4th ed. 2002). Copyright © 2002 Thomson Reuters. Reprinted with permission of Thomson Reuters.

Note, *Class Actions in the Asbestos Context: Balancing the Due Process Considerations Implicated by the Right to Opt Out*, 70 Tex. L. Rev. 211 (1991). Copyright © 1991 Steve Baughman and the Texas Law Review Association. Reprinted with permission of the author and the Texas Law Review Association.

Note, *Class Certification in Mass Accident Cases Under Rule 23(b)(1)*, 96 Harv. L. Rev. 1143 (1983). Copyright © 1983 Harvard Law Review. Reprinted with permission of the Harvard Law Review.

Note, *Developments in the Law: Multiparty Litigation in the Federal Courts*, 71 Harv. L. Rev. 874 (1958). Copyright © 1983 Harvard Law Review. Reprinted with permission of the Harvard Law Review.

Phillips, Carter G., Schaerr, Gene C. & Abraham, Anil K., *Rescuing Multidistrict Litigation From the Altar of Expediency*, 1997 BYU L. Rev. 821. Copyright © 1997 Carter G. Phillips, Gene C. Schaerr, Anil K. Abraham and Brigham Young University Law Review. Reprinted with permission of the authors.

Redish, Martin H., Julian, Peter & Zyontz, Samantha, *Cy Pres Relief and the Pathologies of the Modern Class Action: A Normative and Empirical analysis*, 62 Fla. L. Rev. 617 (2010). Copyright © 2010 Martin H. Redish, Peter Julian, Samantha Zyontz and the Florida Law Review. Reprinted with permission of the authors and the Florida Law Review.

Resnick, Alan N., *Bankruptcy as a Vehicle for Resolving Enterprise–Threatening Mass Tort Liability*, 148 U. Pa. L. Rev. 2045 (2000). Copyright © 2000 University of Pennsylvania Law Review. Reprinted with permission of the University of Pennsylvania Law Review.

Rice, Joseph F. & Davis, Nancy Worth, *The Future of Mass Tort Claims: Comparison of Settlement Class Action to Bankruptcy of Mass Tort Claims*, 50 S.C. L. Rev. 405 (1999). Copyright © Joseph F. Rice and Nancy Worth Davis and the South Carolina Law Review. Reprinted with permission of the authors and the South Carolina Law Review.

Rowe, Thomas D., Jr., *1367 and All That: Recodifying Federal Supplemental Jurisdiction*, 74 Ind. L.J. 53 (1998). (Copyright © 1998 by the Trustees of Indiana University. Reprinted with permission.)

Schuck, Peter H., Reprinted by permission of the publisher from AGENT ORANGE ON TRIAL: MASS TOXIC DISASTERS IN THE COURTS, ENLARGED EDITION, by Peter H. Schuck, pp. 259–260, 295–296, Cambridge, Mass.: The Belknap Press of Harvard University Press, Copyright © 1986, 1987 by Marcy Schuck, Trustee.

Schuck, Peter H., *Mass Torts: An Institutional Evolutionist Perspective*, 80 Cornell L. Rev. 941 (1995). Copyright © 1995 Cornell Law Review. Reprinted with permission of the Cornell Law Review.

Schwarzer, William, Hirsch, Alan & Sussman, Edward, *Judicial Federalism: A Proposal to Amend the Multidistrict Litigation Statute to Permit Discovery Coordination of Large–Scale Litigation Pending in State and Federal Courts*, 73 Tex. L. Rev. 1529 (1995). Copyright © 1995 Edward Sussman and the Texas Law Review Association. Reprinted with permission of the author and the Texas Law Review Association.

Sherman, Edward, *The MDL Model for Resolving Complex Litigation if a Class Action is Not Possible*, 82 Tul. L. Rev. 2205 (2008). Copyright © 2008 Edward Sherman. Reprinted with permission of the author.

Silver, Charles & Baker, Lynn A., *Mass Lawsuits and the Aggregate Settlement Rule*, 32 Wake Forest L. Rev. 773 (1997). Copyright © Wake Forest Law Review. Reprinted with permission of the Wake Forest Law Review.

Silver, Charles & Miller, Geoffrey P., *The Quasi–Class Action Method of Managing Multi–District Litigations: Problems and a Proposal*, 63 Vand. L. Rev. 107 (2010). Copyright © Vanderbilt Law Review. Reprinted with permission of the Vanderbilt Law Review.

Solovy, Jerold, Chorvat, Timothy, Stern, Avidan & Feinberg, David, "*Strategies for Defending a Class Action*," in LITIGATION & RESOLUTION OF COMPLEX CLASS ACTIONS (Glasser LegalWorks 1998). Copyright © 1998 Glass Legal-Works.

Spiegel, S. Arthur, *Settling Class Actions*, 62 U. Cin. L. Rev. 1565 (1994). Copyright © 1994 University of Cincinnati Law Review. Reprinted with the permission of the University of Cincinnati Law Review.

Steinberg, David E., *The Motion to Transfer and the Interests of Justice*, 66 Notre Dame L. Rev. 443 (1990). Copyright © Notre Dame Law Review. Reprinted with permission of the Notre Dame Law Review.

Walker, Laurens & Monahan, John, *Sampling Damages*, 83 Iowa L. Rev. 545 (1998). Copyright © 1998 Laurens Walker and John Monahan. Reprinted with permission of the authors.

Weigel, Stanley A., *The Judicial Panel on Multidistrict Litigation, Transferor Courts and Transferee Courts*, 78 F.R.D. 575 (1978). Copyright © 1978 Thomson Reuters. Reprinted with permission of Thomson Reuters.

Weinstein, Jack B., *The Future of Class Actions in Mass Tort Cases: A Roundtable Discussion*, 66 Fordham L. Rev. 1657 (1998). Copyright © 1998 Jack B. Weinstein. Reprinted with permission of the author.

Woolley, Patrick, *Mass Tort Litigation and the Seventh Amendment Reexamination Clause*, 83 Iowa L. Rev. 499 (1998). Copyright © 1998 Patrick Woolley. Reprinted with permission of the author.

Woolley, Patrick, *Rethinking the Adequacy of Adequate Representation*, 75 Tex. L. Rev. 571 (1997). Copyright © 1997 Patrick Woolley and the Texas Law Review Association. Reprinted with permission of the author and the Texas Law Review Association.

Wright, Charles, A., *Class Actions*, 47 F.R.D. 169 (1970). Copyright © 1970 Thomson Reuters. Reprinted with permission of Thomson Reuters.

Wright, Charles A., Miller, Arthur R., & Kane, Mary Kay, *Federal Practice and Procedure*, (3d ed. 2005). Copyright © 2005 Thomson Reuters. Reprinted with permission of Thomson Reuters.

SUMMARY OF CONTENTS

PREFACE v
ACKNOWLEDGMENTS vii
SUMMARY OF CONTENTS xv
TABLE OF CASES xxxiii
TABLE OF SECONDARY AUTHORITIES li

CHAPTER 1. INTRODUCTION AND HISTORY 1
Sec.
A. Themes of This Casebook 1
B. Perspectives on Class Actions 7
C. Historical Overview 16

CHAPTER 2. CLASS CERTIFICATION: THRESHOLD REQUIREMENTS AND RULE 23(a) 35
Sec.
A. Threshold Requirements 35
B. Explicit Requirements—Rule 23(a) 72

CHAPTER 3. CLASS CERTIFICATION: RULE 23(b) 159
Sec.
A. Rule 23(b)(1) 159
B. Rule 23(b)(2) 190
C. Rule 23(b)(3) 211

CHAPTER 4. LITIGATING A CLASS ACTION 253
Sec.
A. Initial Strategic Considerations in Prosecuting and Defending a Class Action 253
B. Certification Decision 266
C. Class Action Discovery 307
D. Summary Judgment Motions 336
E. Judicial Control of Proceedings 339
F. Trial Structure and Evidentiary Issues 350

CHAPTER 5. NOTICE OF CLASS CERTIFICATION, "OPT-OUT" RIGHTS, AND COMMUNICATIONS WITH CLASS MEMBERS 371
Sec.
A. Notice of Class Certification and "Opt-Out" Rights 371
B. Communications With Class Members 389

CHAPTER 6. MULTI-JURISDICTIONAL CLASS ACTIONS 399
Sec.
A. General Considerations 399
B. Personal Jurisdiction and Choice-of-Law Issues 407

CHAPTER 7. CIVIL PROCEDURE DOCTRINES WITH SPECIAL CLASS ACTION IMPLICATIONS 431

Sec.
A. Statute of Limitations Issues in Class Actions 431
B. Issues Relating to Diversity Jurisdiction 442
C. Res Judicata and Collateral Estoppel 463
D. Federal Relations With State Courts in the Class Action Context 504

CHAPTER 8. RESOLUTION AND FUNDING OF CLASS ACTIONS 529

Sec.
A. Class Action Settlements 529
B. Class Action Remedies 614
C. Attorneys' Fees in Class Actions 632
D. Third-Party Litigation Financing 649
E. Alternative Dispute Resolution 668

CHAPTER 9. APPELLATE REVIEW 697

Sec.
A. Interlocutory Appellate Review of Class Certification Decisions 697
B. Appeal From Final Judgment 709
C. Standards of Review on Appeal From Class Certification 719

CHAPTER 10. SPECIAL FOCUS ON MASS TORT, EMPLOYMENT DISCRIMINATION, AND SECURITIES FRAUD CLASS ACTIONS 723

Sec.
A. Mass Tort Class Actions 725
B. Employment Discrimination Class Actions 783
C. Securities Fraud Class Actions 836

CHAPTER 11. DEFENDANT CLASS ACTIONS, DERIVATIVE SUITS, AND SUITS INVOLVING UNINCORPORATED ASSOCIATIONS 889

Sec.
A. Defendant Class Actions 889
B. Shareholder Derivative Suits 915
C. Suits Involving Unincorporated Associations 941

CHAPTER 12. MULTIDISTRICT LITIGATION 953

Sec.
A. Overview and Statistics 953
B. How MDL Works 957
C. The Administration and Resolution of MDL Cases 973
D. Policy and Reform Issues 992
E. MDL Case Study: The *VW Clean Diesel* Litigation 1001
F. Coordination of Federal and State Claims 1004

CHAPTER 13. MISCELLANEOUS AGGREGATION DEVICES 1015
Sec.
A. Aggregation Devices Under the Federal Rules of
   Civil Procedure.. 1015
B. Additional Aggregation Devices 1109
C. Potential New Directions: Aggregate Settlement Without the
   Class Mechanism 1147
D. Afterword 1154

APPENDIX A: FEDERAL RULE OF CIVIL PROCEDURE 23..................... 1157
APPENDIX B: CLASS ACTION FAIRNESS ACT OF 2005 1163
INDEX... 1179

TABLE OF CONTENTS

PREFACE v
ACKNOWLEDGMENTS.. vii
SUMMARY OF CONTENTS xv
TABLE OF CASES xxxiii
TABLE OF SECONDARY AUTHORITIES.. li

CHAPTER 1. INTRODUCTION AND HISTORY 1
Sec.
A. Themes of This Casebook 1
    1. The Importance of Class Actions... 1
    2. Approach of This Casebook... 2
    3. Recurring Questions and Concerns...................................... 4
B. Perspectives on Class Actions 7
    Owen M. Fiss, The Political Theory of the Class Action 7
    La Mar v. H & B Novelty & Loan Co. 10
    Jonathan M. Landers, Of Legalized Blackmail and Legalized Theft: Consumer Class Actions and the Substance–Procedure Dilemma 11
    Stephen B. Burbank, Sean Farhang & Herbert M. Kritzer, Private Enforcement... 14
    Notes and Questions... 15
C. Historical Overview 16
    1. Echoes From the Past... 16
       Notes and Questions... 17
    2. The Old Federal Equity Rules... 17
       Charles A. Wright, Arthur R. Miller & Mary K. Kane, Federal Practice and Procedure... 18
       Notes and Questions... 19
    3. Original Rule 23 19
       John G. Harkins, Jr., Federal Rule 23—The Early Years........... 20
       Notes and Questions... 22
       Zechariah Chafee, Jr., The Thomas M. Cooley Lectures: Some Problems of Equity 22
       Notes and Questions... 23
    4. Modern Rule 23 23
       Charles A. Wright, Class Actions 23
       Notes and Questions... 27
    5. Amended Rule 23 and the Class Action Fairness Act 27
       Notes and Questions... 29
    6. Contemporary Judicial Views on Class Actions........................... 30
       Rahman v. Chertoff... 30
       Klay v. Humana, Inc... 31
       Notes and Questions... 33

CHAPTER 2. CLASS CERTIFICATION: THRESHOLD REQUIREMENTS AND RULE 23(a) 35
Sec.
A. Threshold Requirements 35
    1. A Definable Class 35

		Manual for Complex Litigation (Fourth) 36
		In re Teflon Prods. Liab. Litig. 37
		Notes and Questions 41
		Mullins v. Direct Digital, LLC 44
		Notes and Questions 53
	2.	The Proposed Representatives' Membership in the Class 54
		Harriston v. Chi. Tribune Co. 54
		Notes and Questions 56
	3.	A Live Controversy (Mootness Considerations) 58
		Rocky v. King 58
		Notes and Questions 62
		Campbell–Ewald Co. v. Gomez 63
		Notes and Questions 69
	4.	Standing Issues in Class Actions 70
B.	Explicit Requirements—Rule 23(a) 72
	1.	Numerosity 73
		Zeidman v. J. Ray McDermott & Co. 73
		Patrykus v. Gomilla 78
		Notes and Questions 80
		Problem 86
	2.	Commonality 86
		Wal–Mart Stores, Inc. v. Dukes 87
		Notes and Questions 99
		Problem 102
	3.	Typicality 103
		Taylor v. Safeway Stores, Inc. 104
		Notes and Questions 106
		Marcus v. BMW of N. Am., LLC 107
		Notes and Questions 111
		Problem 115
	4.	Adequacy of Representation 115
		Hansberry v. Lee 117
		Notes and Questions 121
		Black v. Rhone–Poulenc, Inc. 123
		Notes and Questions 124
		Kaplan v. Pomerantz 128
		Notes and Questions 133
		Robin v. Doctors Officenters Corp. 135
		Notes and Questions 137
		Jean W. Burns, *Decorative Figureheads: Eliminating Class Representatives in Class Actions* 143
		Notes and Questions 147
		Problem 147
		Gomez v. Ill. State Bd. of Educ. 147
		Dubin v. Miller 149
		Notes and Questions 152
		Problem 155
		Barbara J. Rothstein & Thomas E. Willging, *Managing Class Action Litigation: A Pocket Guide for Judges* 156
		Notes and Questions 157
		Oxendine v. Williams 157
		Notes and Questions 158

CHAPTER 3. CLASS CERTIFICATION: RULE 23(b) 159

Sec.
A. Rule 23(b)(1) 159
  1. Rule 23(b)(1)(A) Actions 160
    In re Dennis Greenman Sec. Litig. 161
    Notes and Questions 163
    In re Telectronics Pacing Sys., Inc., Accufix Atrial "J" Leads Prod. Liab. Litig. 166
  Notes and Questions 169
  Problem 171
  2. Rule 23(b)(1)(B) Actions 171
    Ortiz v. Fibreboard Corp. 172
    Notes and Questions 182
    Doe v. Karadzic 184
    Notes and Questions 187
    Problem 190
B. Rule 23(b)(2) 190
  1. Core Considerations 191
    Walters v. Reno 191
    Notes and Questions 193
  2. Relevance of Type of Relief Sought 197
    Wal–Mart Stores, Inc. v. Dukes 198
    Notes and Questions 203
  3. The "Necessity" Requirement 207
    Dionne v. Bouley 207
    Notes and Questions 211
    Problem 211
C. Rule 23(b)(3) 211
  1. Predominance 212
    Brown v. Cameron–Brown Co. 212
    Notes and Questions 215
    McManus v. Fleetwood Enters., Inc. 219
    Notes and Questions 223
  2. Superiority 231
    Sonmore v. Checkrite Recovery Servs., Inc. 233
    Notes and Questions 237
    Notes and Questions 244
    Notes and Questions 246
    In re Domestic Air Transp. Antitrust Litig. 247
    Notes and Questions 250
    Problem 251

CHAPTER 4. LITIGATING A CLASS ACTION 253
Sec.
A. Initial Strategic Considerations in Prosecuting and Defending a Class Action 253
  1. Plaintiffs' Strategic Considerations 253
    Herbert Newberg & Alba Conte, *Newberg on Class Actions* 253
  2. Defendant's Strategic Considerations 259
    Jerold Solovy, Timothy Chorvat, Avidan Stern & David Feinberg, "Strategies for Defending a Class Action," In *Litigation & Resolution of Complex Class Actions* 259
    Alan H. Maclin, *Strategies and Options for Defending Class Actions* 260
  3. Issues Common to Both Sides: Need to Review Local Rules 264

		Problem 265
B.	Certification Decision 266
	1.	Core Principles 266
		Manual for Complex Litigation (Fourth) 266
		Notes and Questions 267
		Amgen Inc. v. Conn. Ret. Plans & Trust Funds 272
		Notes and Questions 278
		Comcast Corp. v. Behrend 281
		Notes and Questions 288
		Am. Honda Motor Co., Inc. v. Allen 289
		Notes and Questions 292
		Problem 293
	2.	Additional Certification Issues 293
		Bing v. Roadway Express, Inc. 293
		Notes and Questions 295
		Notes and Questions 298
		Manual for Complex Litigation (Fourth) 298
		Notes and Questions 299
		Pruitt v. Allied Chem. Corp. 302
		Notes and Questions 306
C.	Class Action Discovery 307
	1.	Pre-Certification Discovery 307
		Hart v. Nationwide Mut. Fire Ins. Co. 308
		Notes and Questions 310
		In re Rail Freight Surcharge Antitrust Litig. 312
		Notes and Questions 313
		Borskey v. Medtronics, Inc. 319
		Notes and Questions 321
		Nat'l Org. for Women, Inc. v. Sperry Rand Corp. 321
		Notes and Questions 325
		Baldwin & Flynn v. Nat'l Safety Assocs. 326
		Laborers Local 17 Health & Benefit Fund v. Philip Morris, Inc. 328
		Notes and Questions 331
	2.	Post-Certification Discovery 332
		Brennan v. Midwestern United Life Ins. Co. 332
		Manual for Complex Litigation (Fourth) 334
		Notes and Questions 335
		Problem 335
D.	Summary Judgment Motions 336
	Cowen v. Bank United 336
	Notes and Questions 337
E.	Judicial Control of Proceedings 339
	1.	Role of the Judge 339
		Martha Minow, *Judge for the Situation: Judge Jack Weinstein, Creator of Temporary Administrative Agencies* 339
		Manual for Complex Litigation (Fourth) 345
		Notes and Questions 346
	2.	Rule 23(d)(1)(A) 347
		Charles A. Wright, Arthur R. Miller & Mary K. Kane, *Federal Practice and Procedure* 347
	3.	Other Provisions of Rule 23(d)(1) 348
F.	Trial Structure and Evidentiary Issues 350
	1.	Seventh Amendment Issues 351

		Mullen v. Treasure Chest Casino, LLC 353
		Melissa Hart, Will Employment Discrimination Class Actions Survive? 356
		Notes and Questions 358
	2.	Due Process Issues: Aggregate Proof and Trial Structure 359
		Tyson Foods, Inc. v. Bouaphakeo 361
		Notes and Questions 368

CHAPTER 5. NOTICE OF CLASS CERTIFICATION, "OPT-OUT" RIGHTS, AND COMMUNICATIONS WITH CLASS MEMBERS 371

Sec.

A. Notice of Class Certification and "Opt-Out" Rights 371
    1. Notice and Opt-Out Rights in Classes Certified Under Rule 23(b)(3) 372
       Eisen v. Carlisle & Jacquelin 372
       Manual for Complex Litigation (Fourth) 375
       Notes and Questions 375
       Problem 376
    2. Costs, Timing, Form, and Content of Notice in Class Actions Certified Under Rule 23(b)(3) 378
       Oppenheimer Fund, Inc. v. Sanders 379
       Notes and Questions 382
       Manual for Complex Litigation (Fourth) 384
       Notes and Questions 384
    3. The Right to Make an Appearance in Rule 23(b)(3) Class Actions 385
    4. Notice and Opt-Out Rights in Class Actions Certified Under Rules 23(b)(1) or 23(b)(2) 386
    5. Notice to Class Members of Decertification 387
       Culver v. City of Milwaukee 387
       Notes and Questions 389
B. Communications With Class Members 389
    1. Contacts With Potential Class Members Before a Class Action Is Filed 389
    2. Communications With Potential Class Members Between Filing and Class Certification 390
       Gulf Oil Co. v. Bernard 391
       Notes and Questions 393
       Cox Nuclear Med., Inc. v. Gold Cup Coffee Serv., Inc. 394
       Notes and Questions 395
    3. Communications With Class Members After Class Certification 396
       Haffer v. Temple Univ. 396
       Notes and Questions 398

CHAPTER 6. MULTI-JURISDICTIONAL CLASS ACTIONS 399

Sec.

A. General Considerations 399
    Califano v. Yamasaki 399
    Notes and Questions 402
    Alabama v. Blue Bird Body Co. 403
    Notes and Questions 406
B. Personal Jurisdiction and Choice-of-Law Issues 407
    Phillips Petroleum Co. v. Shutts 407

	Notes and Questions	412
	In re Rhone–Poulenc Rorer, Inc.	414
	In re Copley Pharm., Inc., "Albuterol" Prod. Liab. Litig.	419
	Castano v. Am. Tobacco Co.	421
	Notes and Questions	426

CHAPTER 7. CIVIL PROCEDURE DOCTRINES WITH SPECIAL CLASS ACTION IMPLICATIONS 431

Sec.

A. Statute of Limitations Issues in Class Actions 431
   Armstrong v. Martin Marietta Corp. 431
   Notes and Questions 438
   Problem 441
B. Issues Relating to Diversity Jurisdiction 442
   1. Aggregation of Claims for Purposes of Jurisdictional Amount 444
      Exxon Mobil Corp. v. Allapattah Servs., Inc. 444
      Notes and Questions 448
   2. Determining Citizenship for Diversity Purposes 449
   3. Broadening the Scope of Federal Diversity 451
      Notes and Questions 458
C. *Res Judicata* and Collateral Estoppel 463
   1. Claim Preclusion (*Res Judicata*) in the Class Action Context 463
      McDowell v. Brown 464
      Notes and Questions 469
      Johnson v. General Motors Corp. 473
      Notes and Questions 475
      Patrick Woolley, Rethinking the Adequacy of Adequate Representation 480
      Notes and Questions 482
   2. Issue Preclusion (Collateral Estoppel) in the Class Action Context 483
      Premier Elec. Constr. Co. v. Nat'l Elec. Contractors Ass'n, Inc. 484
      Notes and Questions 492
      Smith v. Bayer Corp. 492
      Notes and Questions 500
      Problem 503
D. Federal Relations With State Courts in the Class Action Context 504
   1. Overview of the Issues 504
      In re Gen. Motors Corp. Pick-Up Truck Fuel Tank Prods. Liab. Litig. 504
      Notes and Questions 509
   2. Full Faith and Credit 509
      Matsushita Elec. Indus. Co. v. Epstein 509
      Epstein v. MCA, Inc. 514
      Notes and Questions 520
   3. The "*Rooker–Feldman*" Doctrine 522
      Kamilewicz v. Bank of Bos. Corp. 522
      Notes and Questions 526

CHAPTER 8. RESOLUTION AND FUNDING OF CLASS ACTIONS 529

Sec.

A. Class Action Settlements 529
   1. Interested Participants 529
   2. Negotiation of Class Action Settlements 535

Nancy Morawetz, *Bargaining, Class Representation, and Fairness* 535
John C. Coffee, Jr., *Class Wars: The Dilemma of the Mass Tort Class Action* 538
Notes and Questions 542
S. Arthur Spiegel, *Settling Class Actions* 544
Hon. Elaine Bucklo & Thomas R. Meites, *What Every Judge Should Know About a Rule 23 Settlement (But Probably Isn't Told)* 546
Notes and Questions 549

3. Settlement Certification 550
Amchem Prods., Inc. v. Windsor 550
Notes and Questions 562
Ortiz v. Fibreboard Corp. 563
Notes and Questions 563

4. Procedural Considerations in Assessing Class Action Settlements 565
Zimmer Paper Prods., Inc. v. Berger & Montague, P.C. 566
Notes and Questions 572
Manual for Complex Litigation (Fourth) 576
Notes and Questions 576

5. Substantive Considerations in Approving Class Action Settlements 579
Reynolds v. Beneficial Nat'l Bank 579
In re Nat'l Football League Players Concussion Injury Litig. ... 585
Notes and Questions 597
Lazy Oil Co. v. Witco Corp. 601
Notes and Questions 605

6. Dismissal of Class Claims Prior to Class Certification 605
7. The Class Action Fairness Act and Settlement Issues 606
Notes and Questions 607
8. Proposed Rule Changes Dealing With Settlement 608
Notes And Questions 609
9. Final Thoughts on Settlement 610
Susan P. Koniak, *Feasting While the Widow Weeps: Georgine v. Amchem Products, Inc.* 610
Notes and Questions 612

B. Class Action Remedies 614
1. Equitable Relief 614
Jack Greenberg, *Civil Rights Class Actions: Procedural Means of Obtaining Substance* 614
Lloyd C. Anderson, *The Approval and Interpretation of Consent Decrees in Civil Rights Class Action Litigation* 620
Notes and Questions 621
2. Damages 623
Notes and Questions 624
In re BankAmerica Corp. Sec. Litig. 625
Notes and Questions 631

C. Attorneys' Fees in Class Actions 632
Manual for Complex Litigation (Fourth) 632
In re Thirteen Appeals Arising Out of the San Juan Dupont Plaza Hotel Fire Litig. 636
Notes and Questions 644

D. Third-Party Litigation Financing 649

  1. Class Action Context 649
    Deborah R. Hensler, Third-Party Financing Of Class
    Action Litigation In The United States: Will The Sky Fall? 649
  2. The Non-Class Aggregation Context 657
    Elizabeth Chamblee Burch, Financiers As Monitors In
    Aggregate Litigation 657
  3. Disclosure of Funders 665
    Natto Iyela Gbarabe v. Chevron Corp. 665
    Notes And Questions 667
E. Alternative Dispute Resolution 668
  1. The Promise of ADR in Class Actions 668
    Carrie Menkel–Meadow, When Dispute Resolution Begets
    Disputes of Its Own: Conflicts Among Dispute Professionals .. 668
    Kenneth R. Feinberg, Creative Use of ADR: The Court-
    Appointed Special Settlement Master 669
    Notes and Questions 673
  2. Individual Arbitration in Lieu of Class Actions 675
    AT&T Mobility LLC v. Concepcion 676
    Notes and Questions 687
    Am. Express Co. v. Italian Colors Rest. 688
    Notes and Questions 695

CHAPTER 9. APPELLATE REVIEW 697
Sec.
A. Interlocutory Appellate Review of Class Certification Decisions 697
  1. Background to Rule 23(f) 697
  2. Rule 23(f) 701
    Advisory Committee Notes to 1998 Amendment to Federal
    Rule of Civil Procedure 23 701
    Chamberlan v. Ford Motor Co. 702
    Notes and Questions 706
B. Appeal From Final Judgment 709
  1. Intervention for Purposes of Appeal 709
    United Airlines, Inc. v. McDonald 709
    Notes and Questions 712
  2. Appeal by Unnamed Class Members After Settlement 714
    Devlin v. Scardelletti 714
    Notes and Questions 718
  3. Mootness of Class Representative's Claim 719
C. Standards of Review on Appeal From Class Certification 719
  Yokoyama v. Midland Nat'l Life Ins. Co. 719
  Notes and Questions 722

CHAPTER 10. SPECIAL FOCUS ON MASS TORT, EMPLOYMENT
  DISCRIMINATION, AND SECURITIES FRAUD CLASS ACTIONS .. 723
Sec.
  John Leubsdorf, Class Actions at the Cloverleaf 723
A. Mass Tort Class Actions 725
  1. Overview 725
    Deborah R. Hensler & Mark A. Peterson, Understanding
    Mass Personal Injury Litigation: A Socio–Legal Analysis 727
    Notes and Questions 734
  2. A Historical Review: The Courts' Treatment of Mass Tort
    Class Actions 735

		In re Rhone–Poulenc Rorer, Inc.	737
		Castano v. Am. Tobacco Co.	742
		Amchem Prods., Inc. v. Windsor	747
		Ortiz v. Fibreboard Corp.	747
		Manual for Complex Litigation (Fourth)	747
		Notes and Questions	749
	3.	Other Issues in Mass Tort Class Actions	755
		Carlough v. Amchem Prods., Inc.	756
		John C. Coffee, Jr., *Class Wars: The Dilemma of the Mass Tort Class Action*	760
		Notes and Questions	762
		In re Fibreboard Corp.	764
		Cimino v. Raymark Indus., Inc.	769
		Laurens Walker & John Monahan, *Sampling Damages*	774
		Notes and Questions	777
		Problem	778
	4.	Mass Tort Reform	779
		Peter H. Schuck, *Mass Torts: An Institutional Evolutionist Perspective*	779
		Notes and Questions	780
		Notes and Questions	783
B.	Employment Discrimination Class Actions		783
	1.	Applicability of Rule 23 to Title VII Suits	785
		E. Tex. Motor Freight Sys., Inc. v. Rodriguez	785
		Notes and Questions	789
		Johnson v. Montgomery Cnty. Sheriff's Dep't	791
		Wal–Mart Stores, Inc. v. Dukes	794
		Notes and Questions	794
		Hoffman v. R.I. Enters., Inc.	798
		Notes and Questions	799
		Notes and Questions	802
		Notes and Questions	806
		Cooper v. Federal Reserve Bank	807
		Notes and Questions	812
	2.	Employment Discrimination Suits Not Subject to Rule 23	813
		Hoffmann–La Roche Inc. v. Sperling	813
		Notes and Questions	820
		Shushan v. Univ. of Colo.	821
		Notes and Questions	827
		Thiessen v. Gen. Elec. Capital Corp.	827
		Notes and Questions	835
		Problem	836
C.	Securities Fraud Class Actions		836
	1.	Materiality and Reliance in 10b–5 Class Actions	837
		Basic, Inc. v. Levinson	837
		Amgen Inc. v. Conn. Ret. Plans & Trust Funds	844
		Notes and Questions	844
	2.	Loss Causation and Class Certification	857
		Erica P. John Fund, Inc. v. Halliburton Co.	857
		Notes and Questions	861
	3.	Securities Class Action Reform	862
		Notes and Questions	864
		Greebel v. FTP Software, Inc.	866
		Notes and Questions	869

In re Oxford Health Plans, Inc., Sec. Litig. 871
Notes and Questions 875
In re Milestone Scientific Sec. Litig. 878
Notes and Questions 883
Notes and Questions 886
Problem 888

CHAPTER 11. DEFENDANT CLASS ACTIONS, DERIVATIVE SUITS, AND SUITS INVOLVING UNINCORPORATED ASSOCIATIONS 889

Sec.
A. Defendant Class Actions 889
   1. Overview of Rule 23 Considerations 890
      Thillens, Inc. v. Cmty. Currency Exch. Ass'n 890
      Notes and Questions 896
   2. Additional Issues Involving Adequacy of Defendant Class Representatives 900
      Coal. for Econ. Equity v. Wilson 900
      Notes and Questions 902
      La Mar v. H & B Novelty & Loan Co. 903
      Notes and Questions 905
   3. Special Problems Under Rule 23(b)(2) 905
      Henson v. E. Lincoln Township 905
      Notes and Questions 913
B. Shareholder Derivative Suits 915
   1. Nature of Injury Required 916
      Bagdon v. Bridgestone/Firestone, Inc. 916
      Notes and Questions 919
   2. Recurring Themes in Rule 23.1 Litigation 920
      Blasband v. Rales 920
      Notes and Questions 924
      Garber v. Lego 925
      Notes and Questions 931
   3. Similarities to Rule 23 932
      Deleo v. Swirsky 935
      Notes and Questions 938
C. Suits Involving Unincorporated Associations 941
   1. Applicability of Rule 23.2 When an Unincorporated Association Can Sue as a "Jural Entity" in State Court 944
      Northbrook Excess and Surplus Ins. Co. v. Med. Malpractice Joint Underwriting Ass'n 944
      Notes and Questions 947
   2. Prior Existence of Association 948
   3. Applicability of Rule 23(a) and Rule 23(b) to Analysis of Certification Under Rule 23.2 948

CHAPTER 12. MULTIDISTRICT LITIGATION 953

Sec.
A. Overview and Statistics 953
   Multidistrict Litigation Act 954
   Richard D. Freer, *Exodus from and Transformation of American Civil Litigation* 956
   Edward F. Sherman, *The MDL Model for Resolving Complex Litigation If a Class Action Is Not Possible* 956
B. How MDL Works 957

	1.	The Role of The MDL Panel 957
		Stanley A. Weigel, *The Judicial Panel on Multidistrict Litigation, Transferor Courts and Transferee Courts*............. 957
		Notes and Questions.. 959
	2.	Standards for Transfer 960
		In re Multi-Piece Rim Prods. Liab. Litig. 960
		Margaret S. Williams & Tracey E. George, *Who Will Manage Complex Civil Litigation?*... 963
		Notes and Questions.. 967
	3.	Selection of Transferee Judge.. 969
		In re Silicone Gel Breast Implants Prods. Liab. Litig. 969
		Jaime Dodge, *Facilitative Judging: Organizational Design in Mass-Multidistrict Litigation* 971
		Notes and Questions.. 972
C.	The Administration and Resolution of MDL Cases 973	
	1.	Settlements 973
		Howard M. Erichson & Benjamin C. Zipursky, *Consent Versus Closure* 973
		Notes and Questions.. 975
	2.	Remand and Trial Issues 976
		Catherine R. Borden, Emery G. Lee III & Margaret S. Williams, *Centripetal Forces: Multidistrict Litigation and its Parts* 976
		Notes and Questions.. 977
		Lexecon, Inc. v. Milberg Weiss Bershad Hynes & Lerach 977
		Notes and Questions.. 983
	3.	Bellwether Trials in MDL Proceedings 987
		Eldon E. Fallon, Jeremy T. Graybill & Robert Pitard Wynne, *Bellwether Trials In Multidistrict Litigation* 987
		Notes and Questions.. 992
D.	Policy and Reform Issues... 992	
	1.	Overview of Policy Concerns 992
		Elizabeth Chamblee Burch, *Judging Multidistrict Litigation* . 992
		Notes and Questions.. 999
	2.	Best Practices 1000
		Standards and Best Practices for Large and Mass-Tort MDLs... 1000
		Notes and Questions.. 1001
E.	MDL Case Study: The *VW Clean Diesel* Litigation 1001	
	Problem 1003	
F.	Coordination of Federal and State Claims 1004	
	1.	Informal Coordination 1004
		Manual for Complex Litigation (Fourth).................................. 1004
		Notes and Questions.. 1008
	2.	Proposed Formal Federal-State Coordination.......................... 1008
		Complex Litigation: Statutory Recommendations and Analysis.. 1008
		William W. Schwarzer, Alan Hirsch & Edward Sussman, *A Proposal to Amend the Multidistrict Litigation Statute to Permit Discovery Coordination of Large-Scale Litigation Pending in State and Federal Court* 1010
		Notes and Questions.. 1012

CHAPTER 13. MISCELLANEOUS AGGREGATION DEVICES 1015

Sec.

A. Aggregation Devices Under the Federal Rules of Civil Procedure 1015
    1. Permissive Joinder 1015
        Guedry v. Marino 1016
        DIRECTV, Inc. v. Adrian 1019
        Notes and Questions 1022
        Problem 1027
    2. Compulsory Joinder 1027
        Iron Workers Local Union No. 17 Ins. Fund v. Philip Morris, Inc. 1029
        Kescoli v. Babbitt 1035
        Notes and Questions 1040
        Shimkus v. Gersten Co. 1044
        Notes and Questions 1048
    3. Impleader 1049
        Tiesler v. Martin Paint Stores, Inc. 1052
        Notes and Questions 1053
    4. Interpleader 1058
        Federal Interpleader Act 1059
        State Farm Fire & Casualty Co. v. Tashire 1059
        6247 Atlas Corp. v. Marine Ins. Co. 1064
        Notes and Questions 1068
    5. Intervention 1071
        Johnson v. City of Dallas 1072
        Mausolf v. Babbitt 1075
        Notes and Questions 1082
        Woolen v. Surtran Taxicabs, Inc. 1085
        Notes and Questions 1091
        Problem 1092
        Martin v. Wilks 1093
        Notes and Questions 1097
    6. Consolidation 1099
        Daybrook Fisheries, Inc. v. Am. Marine Constr., Inc. 1100
        Malcolm v. Nat'l Gypsum Co. 1102
        Notes and Questions 1107

B. Additional Aggregation Devices 1109
    1. Transfers Under 28 U.S.C. § 1404 1109
        Hoffman v. Blaski 1110
        Notes and Questions 1113
    2. Bankruptcy 1116
        W. Homer Drake, Jr. & Christopher S. Strickland, *Chapter 11 Reorganizations* 1117
        Ralph R. Mabey & Peter A. Zisser, *Improving Treatment of Future Claims: The Unfinished Business Left by the Manville Amendments* 1118
        Notes and Questions 1120
        Alan N. Resnick, *Bankruptcy as a Vehicle for Resolving Enterprise-Threatening Mass Tort Liability* 1121
        Joseph F. Rice & Nancy Worth Davis, *The Future of Mass Tort Claims: Comparison of Settlement Class Action to Bankruptcy Treatment of Mass Tort Claims* 1123
        Notes and Questions 1126
        Marl D. Plevin, Robert T. Ebert & Leslie A. Epley, *Pre-Packaged Asbestos Bankruptcies: A Flawed Solution* 1126

	Samuel Issacharoff, Private Claims, Aggregate Rights	1133
	Notes & Questions	1135
	In re Dow Corning Corp.	1135
	Notes and Questions	1142
	In re Joint E. and S. Dist. Asbestos Litig.	1144
	Notes and Questions	1146
C.	Potential New Directions: Aggregate Settlement Without the Class Mechanism	1147
	Charles Silver & Lynn A. Baker, Mass Lawsuits and the Aggregate Settlement Rule	1148
	Notes and Questions	1149
	Principles of the Law of Aggregate Litigation	1149
	Principles of the Law of Aggregate Litigation	1151
	Howard M. Erichson & Benjamin C. Zipursky, Consent Versus Closure	1152
	Notes and Questions	1154
D.	Afterword	1154
	Developments in the Law: Multiparty Litigation in the Federal Courts	1154
	Edward H. Cooper, The (Cloudy) Future of Class Actions	1156
APPENDIX A: FEDERAL RULE OF CIVIL PROCEDURE 23		1157
APPENDIX B: CLASS ACTION FAIRNESS ACT OF 2005		1163
INDEX		1179

TABLE OF CASES

The principal cases are in bold type. Cases cited or discussed in the text are in roman type. References are to pages. Cases cited in principal cases and within other quoted materials are not included.

6247 Atlas Corp. v. Marine Ins. Co., 155 F.R.D. 454 (S.D.N.Y.1994), **1064**

Abbot v. Lockheed Martin Corp., 725 F.3d 803 (7th Cir. 2013), 43
Abdallah v. Coca–Cola Co., 133 F.Supp.2d 1364 (N.D.Ga.2001), 623
Abdullah v. Acands, Inc., 30 F.3d 264 (1st Cir. 1994), 1025
Abell v. Potomac Ins. Co., 858 F.2d 1104 (5th Cir. 1988), 856
Abron v. Black & Decker (United States) Inc., 654 F.2d 951 (4th Cir. 1981), 57
Acevedo v. Allsup's Convenience Stores, Inc., 600 F.3d 516 (5th Cir. 2010), 1026
Activision Securities Litigation, In re, 1986 WL 15339 (N.D. Cal. 1986), 900
Adams v. Robertson, 520 U.S. 83, 117 S. Ct. 1028, 137 L.Ed.2d 203 (1997), 478
Adamson v. Bowen, 855 F.2d 668 (10th Cir. 1988), 194
Adams Public School Dist. v. Asbestos Corp., Ltd., 7 F.3d 717 (8th Cir. 1993), 440
Affiliated Ute Citizens of Utah v. United States, 406 U.S. 128, 92 S.Ct. 1456, 31 L.Ed.2d 741 (1972), 226, 853
Agent Orange Product Liability Litigation, In re (Ivy v. Diamond Shamrock Chemicals Co.), 996 F.2d 1425 (2d Cir. 1993), 758
Agent Orange Product Liability Litigation, In re, 611 F.Supp. 1396 (E.D.N.Y. 1985), 339
Agent Orange Product Liability Litigation, In re, 544 F.Supp. 808 (E.D.N.Y. 1982), 1056
Agent Orange Product Liability Litigation, In re, 635 F.2d 987 (2d Cir. 1980), 428
Agent Orange Product Liability Litigation, In re, 506 F.Supp. 737 (E.D.N.Y. 1979), 339
Agent Orange Product Liability Litigation MDL No. 381, In re, 818 F.2d 145 (2d Cir. 1987), 736
A.H. Robins Co., Inc., In re, 880 F.2d 709 (4th Cir. 1989), 58, 737
A.H. Robins Co., Inc. v. Piccinin, 788 F.2d 994 (4th Cir. 1986), 1143
Air Liquide America, L.P. v. Process Service Corp., 2004 WL 325143 (E.D. La. 2004), 1057
Airline Ticket Commission Antitrust Litigation, In re, 307 F.3d 679 (8th Cir. 2002), 628
Akerman v. Oryx Communications, Inc., 609 F.Supp. 363 (S.D.N.Y. 1984), 898
Alabama v. Blue Bird Body Co., Inc., 573 F.2d 309 (5th Cir. 1978), 351, **403**
Albers v. Guthy–Renker Corp., 2004 WL 540697 (9th Cir. 2004), 57
Alcantar v. Hobart Service, 800 F.3d 1047 (9th Cir. 2015), 278

Alcoholic Beverages Litigation, In re, 95 F.R.D. 321 (E.D.N.Y. 1982), 143
Alexander v. Fulton County, Ga., 207 F.3d 1303 (11th Cir. 2000), 1022
Alkire v. Irving, 330 F.3d 802 (6th Cir. 2003), 82
Allegheny Child Care Academy v. Klein, 2003 WL 23112776 (W.D. Pa. 2003), 1069
Allen v. Marshall Field & Co., 93 F.R.D. 438 (N.D. Ill. 1982), 820
Alliance to End Repression v. Rochford, 565 F.2d 975 (7th Cir. 1977), 44
Allison v. Citgo Petroleum Corp., 151 F.3d 402 (5th Cir. 1998), 197, 203, 802
Amalgamated Workers Union of Virgin Islands v. Hess Oil Virgin Islands Corp., 478 F.2d 540 (3d Cir. 1973), 232
Amchem Products, Inc. v. Windsor, 521 U.S. 591, 117 S.Ct. 2231, 138 L.Ed.2d 689 (1997), 6, 106, 140, 194, 235, 244, 470, 542, **550**, **747**, 762
American Airlines, Inc. v. Block, 905 F.2d 12 (2d Cir. 1990), 1070
American Express Co. v. Italian Colors Restaurant, 133 S. Ct. 2304 (2013), 687, **688**
American Honda Motor Co., Inc. v. Allen, 600 F.3d 813 (7th Cir. 2010), **289**
American Honda Motor Co., Inc. Dealers Relations Litigation, In re, 979 F.Supp. 365 (D.Md.1997), 232, 440
American Medical Systems, Inc., In re, 75 F.3d 1069 (6th Cir. 1996), 270, 402, 700, 749
American Pipe & Const. Co. v. Utah, 414 U.S. 538, 94 S.Ct. 756, 38 L.Ed.2d 713 (1974), 349, 438
American Trucking Ass'n, Inc. v. New York State Thruway Authority, 795 F.3d 351 (2d Cir. 2015), 1043
Ameritech Ben. Plan Committee v. Communication Workers of America, 220 F.3d 814 (7th Cir. 2000), 913
Amgen Inc. v. Conn. Ret. Plans & Trusts Funds, 133 S.Ct. 1184 (2013), **272, 844**
Analytical Surveys, Inc. Securities Litigation, In re, WL 406332 (S.D. Ind. 2001), 939
Anderson v. Hackett, 646 F.Supp.2d 1041 (S.D. Ill. 2009), 456
Anderson v. Merrill Lynch Pierce Fenner & Smith, Inc., 521 F.3d 1278 (10th Cir. 2008), 887
Anderson v. United States Dept. of Housing & Urban Development, 554 F.3d 525 (5th Cir. 2008), 295
Andrews v. Bechtel Power Corp., 780 F.2d 124 (1st Cir. 1985), 82, 307
Anthony v. Small Tube Mfg. Corp., 535 F.Supp.2d 506 (E.D. Pa. 2007), 455

Appleton Elec. Co. v. Graves Truck Line, Inc., 635 F.2d 603 (7th Cir. 1980), 900

Appleyard v. Wallace, 754 F.2d 955 (11th Cir. 1985), 112

Ardrey v. United Parcel Service, 798 F.2d 679 (4th Cir. 1986), 805

Arenson v. Whitehall Convalescent & Nursing Home, Inc., 164 F.R.D. 659 (N.D. Ill. 1996), 227

Argo v. Hills, 425 F.Supp. 151 (E.D.N.Y. 1977), 383

Arizona Dairy Products Litigation, In re, 1975 WL 966 (D. Ariz. 1975), 375

Armstrong v. Martin Marietta Corp., 138 F.3d 1374 (11th Cir. 1998), **431**, 700, 707

Arnold v. United Artists Theatre Circuit, Inc., 158 F.R.D. 439 (N.D. Cal. 1994), 203

Aronson v. Lewis, 473 A.2d 805 (Del. Supr. 1984), 915, 931

Aronson v. McKesson HBOC, Inc., 79 F.Supp.2d 1146 (N.D. Cal. 1999), 877

Arreola v. Godinez, 546 F.3d 788 (7th Cir. 2008), 122

Asbestos Litigation, In re, 134 F.3d 668 (5th Cir. 1998), 564

Asbestos Litigation, In re, 90 F.3d 963 (5th Cir. 1996), 413

Asbestos Products Liability Litigation (No. VI), In re, 771 F.Supp. 415 (Jud. Pan. Mult. Lit. 1991), 968

Asbestos School Litigation, In re, 104 F.R.D. 422 (E.D. Pa. 1984), 426

Asbestos Workers Local No. 23 Pension Fund ex rel. Norcross v. United States, 303 F.Supp.2d 551 (M.D. Pa. 2004), 1068

Ashcroft v. Iqbal, 556 U.S. 662, 129 S.Ct. 1937, 173 L.Ed.2d 868 (2009), 258

Askew v. Sheriff of Cook County, Illinois, 568 F.3d 632 (7th Cir. 2009), 1043

Association to Protect Hammersley, Eld, & Totten Inlets v. Taylor Resources, Inc., 299 F.3d 1007 (9th Cir. 2002), 1043

AT&T Mobility LLC v. Concepcion, 563 U.S. 333, 131 S.Ct. 1740, 179 L.Ed.2d 742 (2011), **676**

Audette v. Sullivan, 1992 WL 220910 (W.D. Mich. 1992), 484

Auerbach v. Bennett, 47 N.Y.2d 619, 419 N.Y.S.2d 920, 393 N.E.2d 994 (N.Y. 1979), 932

B., Inc. v. Miller Brewing Co., 663 F.2d 545 (5th Cir. 1981), 442

Bagdon v. Bridgestone/Firestone, Inc., 916 F.2d 379 (7th Cir. 1990), **916**

Bailey v. Great Lakes Canning, Inc., 908 F.2d 38 (6th Cir. 1990), 577

Baker v. Wade, 769 F.2d 289 (5th Cir. 1985), 349

Baldridge v. SBC Communications, Inc., 404 F.3d 930 (5th Cir. 2005), 709

Baldwin & Flynn v. National Safety Associates, 149 F.R.D. 598 (N.D. Cal. 1993), **326**

Ballard v. Advance America, 349 Ark. 545, 79 S.W.3d 835 (Ark. 2002), 718

BankAmerica Corp. Sec. Litigation, In re, 775 F.3d 1060 (2015), **625**

Bank of New York Derivative Litigation, In re, 320 F.3d 291 (2d Cir. 2003), 925

Bank of the West v. Estate of Leo, 231 F.R.D. 386 (D. Ariz. 2005), 1056

Barnes v. American Tobacco Co., 161 F.3d 127 (3d Cir. 1998), 194

Barnhill v. Florida Microsoft Anti–Trust Litigation, 905 So.2d 195 (Fla. App. 3 Dist. 2005), 718

Bartelson v. Dean Witter & Co., 86 F.R.D. 657 (E.D. Pa. 1980), 57

Basch v. Ground Round, Inc., 139 F.3d 6 (1st Cir. 1998), 439

Basic Inc. v. Levinson, 485 U.S. 224 (1988), 224, **837**

Bateson v. Magna Oil Corp., 414 F.2d 128 (5th Cir. 1969), 925

Bausch & Lomb, Inc. Securities Litigation, In re, 941 F.Supp. 1352 (W.D.N.Y. 1996), 441

Beal v. Midlothian Independent School Dist. 070908 of Ellis County, 2002 WL 1033085 (N.D. Tex. 2002), 143

Beattie v. CenturyTel, Inc., 511 F.3d 554 (6th Cir. 2007), 237

Beeson v. Med–1 Solutions, LLC, 2009 WL 3242105 (S.D. Ind. 2009), 384

Begier v. IRS, 496 U.S. 53, 110 S. Ct. 2258, 110 L.Ed.2d 46 (1990), 1135

Belcher v. Shoney's, Inc., 927 F.Supp. 249 (M.D. Tenn. 1996), 820

Bell v. Ascendant Solutions, Inc., 422 F.3d 307 (5th Cir. 2005), 224

Bell v. Hershey Co., 557 F.3d 953 (8th Cir. 2009), 458

Bellas v. CBS, Inc., 201 F.R.D. 411 (W.D. Pa. 2000), 211

Bell Atlantic Corp. v. Bolger, 2 F.3d 1304 (3d Cir. 1993), 939

Bell Atlantic Corp. v. Twombly, 550 U.S. 544, 127 S.Ct. 1955, 167 L.Ed.2d 929 (2007), 258

Bemis Co., Inc., In re, 279 F.3d 419 (7th Cir. 2002), 797

Bentkowski v. Marfuerza Compania Maritima, S. A., 70 F.R.D. 401 (E.D. Pa. 1976), 242

Berger v. Compaq Computer Corp., 279 F.3d 313 (5th Cir. 2002), 127

Berger v. Compaq Computer Corp., 257 F.3d 475 (5th Cir. 2001), 126, 127

Berger v. Xerox Corp. Retirement Income Guarantee Plan, 338 F.3d 755 (7th Cir. 2003), 203

Bevemet Metais, Ltda., v. Gallie Corp., 3 F.R.D. 352 (S.D.N.Y. 1942), 1057

Biben v. Card, 1986 WL 1199 (W.D. Mo. 1986), 141

Bierman v. Marcus, 246 F.2d 200 (3d Cir. 1957), 1069

Bing v. Roadway Exp., Inc., 485 F.2d 441 (5th Cir. 1973), **293**

Birmingham Steel Corp. v. Tennessee Valley Authority, 353 F.3d 1331 (11th Cir. 2003), 127

Bishop v. Committee on Professional Ethics & Conduct of Iowa State Bar Ass'n, 686 F.2d 1278 (8th Cir. 1982), 57

Bivens Gardens Office Bldg., Inc. v. Barnett Banks of Florida, Inc., 140 F.3d 898 (11th Cir. 1998), 919

TABLE OF CASES

Black v. Rhone–Poulenc, Inc., 173 F.R.D. 156 (S.D.W.Va.1996), 44, **123**

Blackie v. Barrack, 524 F.2d 891 (9th Cir. 1975), 270

Black Panther Party v. Smith, 661 F.2d 1243, 213 U.S. App. D.C. 67 (D.C. Cir. 1981), 264

Blades v. Monsanto Co., 400 F.3d 562 (8th Cir. 2005), 218

Blair v. Equifax Check Services, Inc., 181 F.3d 832 (7th Cir. 1999), 707

Blake Partners, Inc. v. Orbcomm, Inc., 2008 WL 2277117 (D.N.J. 2008), 869

Blasband v. Rales, 971 F.2d 1034 (3d Cir. 1992), **920**

Blood Reagents Antitrust Litigation, In re, 783 F.3d 183 (3d Cir. 2015), 292

Blue Chip Stamps v. Manor Drug Stores, 421 U.S. 723, 95 S.Ct. 1917, 44 L.Ed.2d 539 (1975), 886

Blum v. Schlegel, 150 F.R.D. 38 (W.D.N.Y. 1993), 1084

Blum v. Yaretsky, 457 U.S. 991, 102 S.Ct. 2777, 73 L.Ed.2d 534 (1982), 56, 1084

Board of Educ. of Tp. High School v. Climatemp, Inc., 1981 WL 2033 (N.D. Ill. 1981), 232

Bogard v. Cook, 586 F.2d 399 (5th Cir. 1978), 475

Boggess v. Hogan, 410 F.Supp. 433 (N.D. Ill. 1975), 939

Boggs v. Divested Atomic Corp., 141 F.R.D. 58 (S.D. Ohio 1991), 160

Bolton v. Gramlich, 540 F.Supp. 822 (S.D.N.Y. 1982), 940

Borskey v. Medtronics, 1998 WL 122602 (E.D. La. 1998), **319**

Bowling v. Pfizer, Inc., 143 F.R.D. 141 (S.D. Ohio 1992), 152

Brand Name Prescription Drugs Antitrust Litigation, In re, 115 F.3d 456 (7th Cir. 1997), 712, 719

Brazil v. Dell, 585 F. Supp. 2d 1158 (N.D. Cal. 2008), 42

Brennan v. Midwestern United Life Ins. Co., 450 F.2d 999 (7th Cir. 1971), **332**

Bright v. United States, 603 F.3d 1273 (Fed. Cir. 2010), 439

Brinkerhoff v. Rockwell Intern. Corp., 83 F.R.D. 478 (N.D. Tex. 1979), 325

Briseno v. ConAgra Foods, Inc., 844 F.3d 1121 (9th Cir. 2017), 53

Brown v. American Honda, 522 F.3d 6 (1st Cir. 2008), 218

Brown v. Cameron–Brown Co., 92 F.R.D. 32 (E.D. Va. 1981), **212**

Brown v. Nucor Corp., 785 F.3d 895 (4th Cir. 2015), 102

Brown v. Plata, 563 U.S. 493, 131 S.Ct. 1910, 179 L.Ed.2d 969 (2011), 33

Brown v. Ticor Title Ins. Co., 982 F.2d 386 (9th Cir. 1992), 478

Browning v. Yahoo! Inc., 2007 WL 4105971 (N.D. Cal. 2007), 575

Bruschi v. Brown, 876 F.2d 1526 (11th Cir. 1989), 837

Buckeye Check Cashing, Inc. v. Cardegna, 546 U.S. 440, 126 S.Ct. 1204, 163 L.Ed.2d 1038 (2006), 687

Buford v. H & R Block, Inc., 168 F.R.D. 340 (S.D.Ga.1996), 243

Bullard v. Burlington Northern Santa Fe Ry. Co., 535 F.3d 759 (7th Cir. 2008), 458

Bureerong v. Uvawas, 167 F.R.D. 83 (C.D. Cal. 1996), 1084

Burghart v. Landau, 821 F.Supp. 173 (S.D.N.Y. 1993), 919

Butler v. Sears, Roebuck & Co. 702 F.3d 359 (7th Cir. 2012), 70

Butler v. Suffolk Cnty., 289 F.R.D. 80 (E.D.N.Y. 2013), 204

Burke v. Ruttenberg, 317 F.3d 1261 (11th Cir. 2003), 646

Busby v. JRHBW Realty, Inc., 513 F.3d 1314 (11th Cir. 2008), 152

Byrd v. Aaron's Inc., 784 F.3d 154 (3d Cir. 2015), 53

Califano v. Yamasaki, 442 U.S. 682, 99 S.Ct. 2545, 61 L.Ed.2d 176 (1979), **399**

California Public Employees' Retirement System v. Chubb Corp., 127 F.Supp.2d 572 (D.N.J. 2001), 870

California Public Employees Retirement System v. Moody's Corp., 2009 WL 3809816 (N.D. Cal. 2009), 453

California Rural Legal Assistance, Inc. v. Legal Services Corp., 917 F.2d 1171 (9th Cir. 1990), 58

Cammer v. Bloom, 711 F.Supp. 1264 (D.N.J. 1989), 855

Campbell v. Ewald Co. v. Gomez, 136 S. Ct. 663, 193 L.Ed.2d 571 (2016), **63**

Campbell v. First American Title Ins. Co., 269 F.R.D. 68 (D. Me. 2010), 42

Carlough v. Amchem Products, Inc., 158 F.R.D. 314 (E.D. Pa. 1993), 762

Carlough v. Amchem Products, Inc., 834 F.Supp. 1437 (E.D. Pa. 1993), **756**

Carnegie v. Household Intern., Inc., 376 F.3d 656 (7th Cir. 2004), 562

Caroline C. By & Through Carter v. Johnson, 174 F.R.D. 452 (D. Neb. 1996), 171

Carr v. Wilson–Coker, 203 F.R.D. 66 (D. Conn. 2001), 122

Carriere v. Cominco Alaska, Inc., 823 F.Supp. 680 (D. Alaska 1993), 1055

Carson v. Merrill Lynch, Pierce, Fenner & Smith Inc., 1998 WL 34076402 (W.D. Ark. 1998), 870

Carter v. West Pub. Co., 1999 WL 376502 (M.D. Fla. 1999), 805

Carvalho v. Equifax Information Services, LLC, 588 F.Supp.2d 1089 (N.D. Cal. 2008), 338

Casale v. Kelly, 257 F.R.D. 396 (S.D.N.Y. 2009), 134

Castano v. American Tobacco Co., 84 F.3d 734 (5th Cir. 1996), 226, 229, 270, 299, 352, **421**, 700, **742**

Castano v. American Tobacco Co., 162 F.R.D. 112 (E.D. La. 1995), 700

Castano v. American Tobacco Co., 160 F.R.D. 544 (E.D. La. 1995), 427

Catfish Antitrust Litigation, In re, 826 F.Supp. 1019 (N.D. Miss. 1993), 406

Cathode Ray Tube (CRT) Antitrust Litigation, In re, 281 F.R.D. 531 (N.D. Cal. 2012), 609
Catholic Social Services, Inc. v. I.N.S., 232 F.3d 1139 (9th Cir. 2000), 439
Cavanaugh, In re, 306 F.3d 726 (9th Cir. 2002), 884
CBC Companies, Inc., In re, 181 F.R.D. 380 (N.D. Ill. 1998), 125
CE Design Ltd. v. King Architectural Metals, Inc., 637 F.3d 721 (7th Cir. 2011), 135
Cendant Corp. Litigation, In re, 264 F.3d 201 (3d Cir. 2001), 884
Cendant Corp. Securities Litigation, In re, 404 F.3d 173 (3d Cir. 2005), 646
Central Tools, Inc. v. Mitutoyo Corp., 381 F.Supp.2d 71 (D.R.I. 2005), 1041
Central Wesleyan College v. W.R. Grace & Co., 6 F.3d 177 (4th Cir. 1993), 296, 426
CGC Holding Co., LLC v. Broad & Cassel, 773 F.3d 1076 (10th Cir. 2014), 227
Chadbourne & Park LLP v. Troice, 134 S.Ct. 1058, 188 L.Ed.2d 88 (2014), 887
Chamberlan v. Ford Motor Co., 402 F.3d 952 (9th Cir. 2005), **702**
Chase Manhattan Bank, N.A. v. Aldridge, 906 F.Supp. 866 (S.D.N.Y. 1995), 1057
Chavez v. Netflix, Inc., 75 Cal. Rptr. 3d 413 (Cal. App. 1 Dist. 2008), 575
Chen v. Allstate Ins. Co., 819 F.3d 1136 (9th Cir. 2016), 69
Chlorine & Caustic Soda Antitrust Litigation, In re, 116 F.R.D. 622 (E.D. Pa. 1987), 237
Christiana Mortg. Corp. v. Delaware Mortg. Bankers Ass'n, 136 F.R.D. 372 (D. Del. 1991), 83
Christopher v. Brusselback, 302 U.S. 500, 58 S.Ct. 350, 82 L.Ed. 388 (1938), 19
Church v. Consolidated Freightways, Inc., 137 F.R.D. 294 (N.D. Cal. 1991), 827
Churchill Village, L.L.C. v. General Electric, 361 F.3d 566 (9th Cir. 2004), 719
Cimino v. Raymark Industries, Inc., 151 F.3d 297 (5th Cir. 1998), **769**
Cimino v. Raymark Industries, Inc., 1989 WL 253889 (E.D. Tex. 1989), 765
City of (see name of city)
Clark v. McDonald's Corp., 213 F.R.D. 198 (D.N.J. 2003), 913
Clarke v. Ford Motor Co., 228 F.R.D. 631 (E.D. Wis. 2005), 389
Clement v. Occidental Chemical Corp., 699 So.2d 1110 (La. App. 5 Cir. 1997), 754
CLRB Hanson Industries, LLC v. Weiss & Associates, PC, 465 F. App'x 617 (9th Cir. 2002), 608
CMS Energy Erisa Litigation, In re, 225 F.R.D. 539 (E.D. Mich. 2004), 161
Coalition for Economic Equity v. Wilson, 1996 WL 788376 (N.D. Cal. 1996), **900**
Coates v. Johnson & Johnson, 756 F.2d 524 (7th Cir. 1985), 805
Coburn v. DaimlerChrysler Services North America, L.L.C., 2005 WL 736657 (N.D. Ill. 2005), 268
Coburn v. 4–R Corp., 77 F.R.D. 43 (E.D. Ky. 1977), 735

Coca–Cola Bottling Co. of Elizabethtown, Inc. v. Coca–Cola Co., 95 F.R.D. 168 (D. Del. 1982), 82
Coffey v. Freeport McMoran Copper & Gold, 581 F.3d 1240 (10th Cir. 2009), 456
Cohen v. Beneficial Indus. Loan Corp., 337 U.S. 541, 69 S.Ct. 1221, 93 L.Ed. 1528 (1949), 697, 698
Cohen v. Young, 127 F.2d 721 (6th Cir. 1942), 939
Coleman v. Block, 562 F.Supp. 1353 (D.N.D. 1983), 43
Coleman v. Union Carbide Corp., 2013 WL 5461855 (S.D. W.Va. 2013), 171
Coleman v. Watt, 40 F.3d 255 (8th Cir. 1994), 43
College of Dental Surgeons of Puerto Rico v. Connecticut General Life Ins. Co., 585 F.3d 33 (1st Cir. 2009), 461
Columbia Health Services of El Paso, Inc. v. Columbia/HCA Healthcare Corp., 1996 WL 812934 (W.D. Tex. 1996), 897
Comcast Corp. v. Behrend, 133 S. Ct. 1426 (2013), 229, **281**, 289
Committee of Blind Vendors of District of Columbia v. District of Columbia, 695 F.Supp. 1234 (D.D.C. 1988), 83
Community Bank of Northern Virginia, In re, 418 F.3d 277 (3d Cir. 2005), 549, 1109
Connecticut v. Moody's Corp., 664 F.Supp.2d 196 (D. Conn. 2009), 457
Constar International Inc. Securities Litigation, In re, 585 F.3d 774 (3d Cir. 2009), 856
Cooper v. Federal Reserve Bank of Richmond, 467 U.S. 867, 104 S.Ct. 2794, 81 L.Ed.2d 718 (1984), 483, **807**
Cooper v. Southern Co., 390 F.3d 695 (11th Cir. 2004), 205
Coopers & Lybrand v. Livesay, 437 U.S. 463, 98 S.Ct. 2454, 57 L.Ed.2d 351 (1978), 698, 709
Copley Pharmaceutical, Inc., In re, 161 F.R.D. 456 (D. Wyo. 1995), 229, 352, **419**
Copley Pharmaceutical, Inc., In re, 158 F.R.D. 485 (D.Wyo. 1994), 163
Corber v. Xanodyne Pharmaceuticals, Inc., 771 F.3d 1218 (9th Cir. 2004), 462
Cordes & Co. Financial Services, Inc. v. A.G. Edwards & Sons, Inc., 502 F.3d 91 (2d Cir. 2007), 217, 300
Corrugated Container Antitrust Litigation, In re, 756 F.2d 411 (5th Cir. 1985), 484
Coughlin v. Rogers, 130 F.3d 1348 (9th Cir. 1997), 1025
County of (see name of county)
Countrywide Fin. Corp. Mortg. Lending Practices, In re, 708 F.3d 704 (6th Cir. 2013), 102
Cowen v. Bank United, 70 F.3d 937 (7th Cir. 1995), **336**
Cox Nuclear Medicine v. Gold Cup Coffee Services, Inc., 214 F.R.D. 696 (S.D. Ala. 2003), **394**
CP Nat. Corp. v. Bonneville Power Admin., 928 F.2d 905 (9th Cir. 1991), 1040, 1042
Crasto v. Kaskel's Estate, 63 F.R.D. 18 (S.D.N.Y. 1974), 238
Crazy Eddie Securities Litigation, In re, 135 F.R.D. 39 (E.D.N.Y. 1991), 426

Creative Montessori Learning Ctrs. v. Ashford Gear LLC, 662 F.3d 913 (7th Cir. 2011), 153, 600
Crosby v. Bowater Inc. Retirement Plan for Salaries Employees of Great Northern Paper, Inc., 382 F.3d 587 (6th Cir. 2004), 57
Crow v. California Dept. of Human Resources, 325 F.Supp. 1314 (N.D. Cal. 1970), 160
Crowder v. Lash, 687 F.2d 996 (7th Cir. 1982), 475, 483
Crown, Cork & Seal Co., Inc. v. Parker, 462 U.S. 345, 103 S.Ct. 2392, 76 L.Ed.2d 628 (1983), 438
Cullen v. New York State Civil Service Commission, 435 F.Supp. 546 (E.D.N.Y. 1977), 349
Culver v. City of Milwaukee, 277 F.3d 908 (7th Cir. 2002), 116, 127, **387**
Cummings v. Connell, 316 F.3d 886 (9th Cir. 2003), 140
Cunningham v. Municipality of Metropolitan Seattle, 751 F.Supp. 885 (W.D. Wash. 1990), 1042
Curley v. Brignoli, Curley & Roberts Associates, 915 F.2d 81 (2d Cir. 1990), 947, 948

Daniels v. Witco Corp., 877 So.2d 1011 (La. App. Ct. 2004), 754
Dare v. Knox County, 457 F.Supp.2d 52 (D. Me. 2006), 578
Dart Cherokee Basin Operating Co., LLC v. Owens, 135 S. Ct. 547 (2014), 459
Daubert v. Merrell Dow Pharmaceuticals, Inc., 509 U.S. 579, 113 S.Ct. 2786, 125 L.Ed.2d 469 (1993), 288
David v. Signal Intern., LLC, 257 F.R.D. 114 (E.D. La. 2009), 331
David v. Signal Intern., LLC, 588 F.Supp.2d 718 (E.D.La.2008), 331
Davis v. Comed, Inc., 619 F.2d 588 (6th Cir. 1980), 932
Davis v. Southern Bell Tel. & Tel. Co., 1993 WL 593999 (S.D. Fla. 1993), 227
Day v. NLO, Inc., 144 F.R.D. 330 (S.D. Ohio 1992), 166
Day v. Sebelius, 227 F.R.D. 668 (D.Kan.2005), 1084, 1085
Daybrook Fisheries, Inc. v. American Marine Const., 1998 WL 748586 (E.D. La. 1998), **1100**
DeBoer v. Mellon Mortg. Co., 64 F.3d 1171 (8th Cir. 1995), 572
Deepwater Horizon, In re, 739 F.3d 790 (5th Cir. 2014), 753
Delco Wire & Cable Co. v. Keystone Roofing Co., 80 F.R.D. 428 (E.D. Pa. 1978), 1055
DeLeo v. Swirsky, 2002 WL 989526 (N.D. Ill. 2002), **935**
DeMasi v. Weiss, 669 F.2d 114 (3d Cir. 1982), 700
Denney v. Deutsche Bank AG, 443 F.3d 253 (2d Cir. 2006), 70, 578
Dennis v. Kellogg Co., 2013 WL 6055326 (S.D. Cal. 2013), 609
Dennis Greenman Securities Litigation, In re, 829 F.2d 1539 (11th Cir. 1987), **161**, 190

Dennings v. Clearwire Corp., 928 F. Supp. 2d 1270 (W.D. Wash. 2013), 609
Dennison v. Carolina Payday Loans, Inc., 2008 WL 5484559 (D.S.C. 2008), 455
Detroit, City of v. Grinnell Corp., 495 F.2d 448 (2d Cir. 1974), 577
Devlin v. Scardelletti, 536 U.S. 1, 122 S.Ct. 2005, 153 L.Ed.2d 27 (2002), 577, **714**, 940
Dewey v. Volkswagen Aktiengesellschaft, 681 F.3d 170 (3d Cir. 2012), 140
D'Hondt v. Digi Intern. Inc., 1997 WL 405668 (D. Minn. 1997), 877
Diet Drugs, In re, 582 F.3d 524 (3d Cir. 2009), 648
Diet Drugs (Phentermine/Fenfluramine/ Dexfenfluramine) Products Liability Litigation, In re, 431 F.3d 141 (3d Cir. 2005), 471
Dionne v. Bouley, 757 F.2d 1344 (1st Cir. 1985), **207**
DIRECTV, Inc. v. Adrian, 2004 WL 1146122 (N.D. Ill. 2004), **1019**
DIRECTV, Inc. v. Essex, 2002 U.S. Dist. LEXIS 26923 (W.D. Wash. 2002), 1023
DIRECTV, Inc. v. Imburgia, 136 S. Ct. 463 (2015), 695
DIRECTV, Inc. v. Patel, 2003 WL 22669031 (N.D. Ill. 2003), 1023
Disability Rights Council of Greater Washington v. Washington Metropolitan Area Transit Authority, 239 F.R.D. 9 (D.D.C. 2006), 207
Disabled American Veterans v. United States Dept. of Veterans Affairs, 783 F.Supp. 187 (S.D.N.Y. 1992), 464
Disabled Rights Action Committee v. Las Vegas Events, Inc., 375 F.3d 861 (9th Cir. 2004), 1041
Dixon v. Edwards, 290 F.3d 699 (4th Cir. 2002), 1041
D.L. v. District of Columbia, 713 F.3d 120 (D.C. Cir. 2013), 102
Doe v. Karadzic, 192 F.R.D. 133 (S.D.N.Y. 2000), **184**
Doe v. Miller, 216 F.R.D. 462 (S.D. Iowa 2003), 160
Domestic Air Transp. Antitrust Litigation, In re, 148 F.R.D. 297 (N.D. Ga. 1993), 250, 598
Domestic Air Transp. Antitrust Litigation, In re, 137 F.R.D. 677 (N.D. Ga. 1991), **247**, 406
Donald J. Trump Casino Securities Litigation–Taj Mahal Litigation, In re, 7 F.3d 357 (3d Cir. 1993), 849
Donnelly v. Glickman, 159 F.3d 405 (9th Cir. 1998), 1083
Dow Corning Corp., In re, 211 B.R. 545 (Bkrtcy. E.D. Mich. 1997), 972
Dow Corning Corp., In re, 113 F.3d 565 (6th Cir. 1997), 1143
Dow Corning Corp., In re, 1996 WL 511646 (E.D. Mich. 1996), 1142
Dow Corning Corp., In re, 86 F.3d 482 (6th Cir. 1996), **1135**
Doyel v. McDonald's Corp., 2009 WL 350627 (E.D. Mo. 2009), 311
DPR Const., Inc. v. IKEA Property, Inc., 2005 WL 1667778 (E.D. Va. 2005), 1043

Table of Cases

D.R. Horton, Inc. v. NLRB, 737 F.3d 344 (5th Cir. 2013), 696

Drexel Burnham Lambert Group, Inc., In re, 960 F.2d 285 (2d Cir. 1992), 1146

DTD Enterprises, Inc. v. Wells, 130 S.Ct. 7, 175 L.Ed.2d 300 (2009), 383

Dubin v. Miller, 132 F.R.D. 269 (D. Colo. 1990), **149**

Duffy v. Si–Sifh Corp., 726 So.2d 438 (La. App. 4 Cir. 1999), 500

Dugan v. Lloyds TSB Bank, PLC, 2013 WL 1703375 (N.D. Cal. 2013), 204

Dukes v. Wal–Mart Stores, Inc., 603 F.3d 571 (9th Cir. 2010), 197

Dura Pharmaceuticals, Inc. v. Broudo, 544 U.S. 336, 125 S.Ct. 1627, 161 L.Ed.2d 577 (2005), 857

Easter v. American West Financial, 381 F.3d 948 (9th Cir. 2004), 762

East Texas Motor Freight System Inc. v. Rodriguez, 431 U.S. 395, 97 S.Ct. 1891, 52 L.Ed.2d 453 (1977), 56, **785**

E.E.O.C. v. D.H. Holmes Co., Ltd., 556 F.2d 787 (5th Cir. 1977), 797

E.E.O.C. v. Pemco Aeroplex, Inc., 383 F.3d 1280 (11th Cir. 2004), 797

E.E.O.C. v. Waffle House, Inc., 534 U.S. 279, 122 S.Ct. 754, 151 L.Ed.2d 755 (2002), 797

Eisen v. Carlisle & Jacquelin, 417 U.S. 156, 94 S.Ct. 2140, 40 L.Ed.2d 732 (1974), 269, **372**, 379

Ellis v. Costco Wholesale Corp., 657 F.3d 970 (9th Cir. 2011), 102

Emrich v. Touche Ross & Co., 846 F.2d 1190 (9th Cir. 1988), 453

Epic Systems Corp. v. Lewis, 2017 WL 125664 (U.S. Jan. 13, 2017), 696

Epstein v. MCA, Inc., 179 F.3d 641 (9th Cir. 1999), **514**

Equal Employment Opportunity Commission v. D. H. Holmes Co., Ltd., 556 F.2d 787 (5th Cir. 1977), 797

Erica P. John Fund, Inc. v. Halliburton Co., 563 U.S. 804, 131 S. Ct. 2179 (2011), 224, **857**

Erie R. Co. v. Tompkins, 304 U.S. 64, 58 S.Ct. 817, 82 L.Ed. 1188 (1938), 924

Esden v. Bank of Boston, 5 F.Supp.2d 214 (D. Vt. 1998), 265

Esler v. Northrop Corp., 86 F.R.D. 20 (W.D. Mo. 1979), 82, 84

Ethylene Propylene Diene Monomer (EPDM) Antitrust Litigation, In re, 256 F.R.D. 82 (D.Conn.2009), 293

Eubank v. Pella Corp., 753 F.3d 718 (7th Cir. 2014), 33, 139, 600

Eubanks v. Billington, 110 F.3d 87, 324 U.S.App.D.C. 41 (D.C. Cir. 1997), 350, 387

Evans v. Jeff D., 475 U.S. 717, 106 S.Ct. 1531, 89 L.Ed.2d 747 (1986), 598

Ex parte (see name of party)

Exxon Mobil Corp. v. Allapattah Services, Inc., 545 U.S. 546 (2005), **444**, 1026, 1057

Exxon Shipping Co. v. Baker, 554 U.S. 471, 128 S.Ct. 2605, 171 L.Ed.2d 570 (2008), 625

Falcon v. Philips Electronics North America Corp., 2008 WL 4820527 (2d Cir. 2008), 127

Federal Deposit Ins. Corp. v. Loube, 134 F.R.D. 270 (N.D. Cal. 1991), 1056

Federal Exp. Corp. v. Holowecki, 552 U.S. 389, 128 S.Ct. 1147, 170 L.Ed.2d 10 (2008), 800

Federal Sav. & Loan Ins. Corp. v. Huttner, 265 F.Supp. 40 (N.D. Ill. 1967), 160

Federal Skywalk Cases, In re, 93 F.R.D. 415 (W.D. Mo. 1982), 164, 735

Federative Republic of Brazil, United States v., 784 F.3d 86 (2d Cir. 2014), 1071

Feinstein v. Firestone Tire & Rubber Co., 535 F.Supp. 595 (S.D.N.Y. 1982), 142

Fellows v. Universal Restaurants, Inc., 701 F.2d 447 (5th Cir. 1983), 800

Fibreboard Corp., In re, 893 F.2d 706 (5th Cir. 1990), **764**

Fidelity Bankers Life Ins. Co. v. Wedco, Inc., 102 F.R.D. 41 (D. Nev. 1984), 1082

Fields v. Wolfson, 41 F.R.D. 329 (S.D.N.Y. 1967), 157

Financial Guar. Ins. Co. v. City of Fayetteville, Ark., 749 F.Supp. 934 (W.D. Ark. 1990), 1071

First Alabama Bank of Montgomery, N.A. v. Martin, 425 So.2d 415 (Ala. 1982), 413

Fisher v. Bristol–Myers Squibb Co., 181 F.R.D. 365 (N.D. Ill. 1998), 232

FleetBoston Financial Corp. Securities Litigation, In re, 253 F.R.D. 315 (D.N.J. 2008), 85

Flight Safety Technologies, Inc. Securities Litigation, In re, 231 F.R.D. 124 (D. Conn. 2005), 870

Folding Carton Antitrust Litigation, In re, 744 F.2d 1252 (7th Cir. 1984), 251

Folding Carton Antitrust Litigation, In re, 88 F.R.D. 211 (N.D. Ill. 1980), 251

Forbush v. J.C. Penney Co., Inc., 994 F.2d 1101 (5th Cir. 1993), 194

Ford Motor Co. Bronco II Product Liability Litigation, In re, 177 F.R.D. 360 (E.D. La. 1997), 414

Ford Motor Co. Vehicle Paint Litigation, In re, 182 F.R.D. 214 (E.D. La. 1998), 226

Forest Conservation Council v. United States Forest Service, 66 F.3d 1489 (9th Cir. 1995), 1083

Fortner v. Thomas, 983 F.2d 1024 (11th Cir. 1993), 475

Foulke v. Dugan, 212 F.R.D. 265 (E.D. Pa. 2002), 1053

Fradkin v. Ernst, 98 F.R.D. 478 (N.D. Ohio 1983), 933

Frahm v. Equitable Life Assur. Soc. of United States, 137 F.3d 955 (7th Cir. 1998), 238

Franklin v. Barry, 909 F.Supp. 21 (D.D.C. 1995), 161

Franklin v. General Elec. Co., 1977 WL 15390 (W.D. Va. 1977), 232

Freeland v. Iridium World Communications, Ltd., 233 F.R.D. 40 (D.D.C. 2006), 857

Freeman v. Blue Ridge Paper Products, Inc., 551 F.3d 405 (6th Cir. 2008), 458

Fresh America Corp. v. Wal–Mart Stores, Inc., 393 F.Supp.2d 411 (N.D. Tex. 2005), 1069

Friedman v. Quest Energy Partners LP, 261 F.R.D. 607 (W.D. Okla. 2009), 877
Friends of the Earth, Inc. v. Laidlaw Environmental Services (TOC), Inc., 528 U.S. 167, 120 S.Ct. 693, 145 L.Ed.2d 610 (2000), 63
Froud v. Anadarko E & P Co. Ltd. Partnership, 607 F.3d 520 (8th Cir. 2010), 461
Fujishima v. Board of Ed., 460 F.2d 1355 (7th Cir. 1972), 207
Fuller v. Home Depot Services, LLC, 2007 WL 2345257 (N.D. Ga. 2007), 455

Gabel, Petition of, 350 F.Supp. 624 (C.D. Cal. 1972), 164
Gap Stores Securities Litigation, In re, 79 F.R.D. 283 (N.D.Cal.1978), 896, 899
Garber v. Lego, 11 F.3d 1197 (3d Cir. 1993), **925**
Gardner v. Westinghouse Broadcasting Co., 437 U.S. 478, 98 S.Ct. 2451, 57 L.Ed.2d 364 (1978), 699
Gates v. Rohm & Haas Co., 655 F.3d 255 (3d Cir. 2011), 195, 300
Gayle v. Warden Monmouth Cnty. Corr. Inst., 838 F.3d 297 (3d Cir. 2016), 211
Gelb v. American Tel. & Tel. Co., 150 F.R.D. 76 (S.D.N.Y. 1993), 203
General American Life Ins. Co. Sales Practices Litigation, In re, 302 F.3d 799 (8th Cir. 2002), 718
General Motors Corp. Pick–Up Truck Fuel Tank Products Liability Litigation, In re, 134 F.3d 133 (3d Cir. 1998), **504**
General Tel. Co. of the Northwest, Inc. v. Equal Employment Opportunity Commission, 446 U.S. 318, 100 S.Ct. 1698, 64 L.Ed.2d 319 (1980), 796
General Telephone Co. of Southwest v. Falcon, 457 U.S. 147, 102 S.Ct. 2364, 72 L.Ed.2d 740 (1982), 106, 270, 308, 789
Georgine v. Amchem Products, Inc., 83 F.3d 610 (3d Cir. 1996), 550
Georgine v. Amchem Products, Inc., 878 F.Supp. 716 (E.D. Pa. 1994), 762
Georgine v. Amchem Products, Inc., 157 F.R.D. 246 (E.D. Pa. 1994), 762
Geraghty v. United States Parole Com'n, 719 F.2d 1199 (3d Cir. 1983), 402
Gibbs v. Buck, 307 U.S. 66, 59 S.Ct. 725, 83 L.Ed. 1111 (1939), 942
Gilmore v. Bayer Corp., 2009 WL 4789406 (S.D. Ill. 2009), 452
Gintis v. Bouchard Transp. Co., Inc., 596 F.3d 64 (1st Cir. 2010), 752
Goldberger v. Integrated Resources, Inc., 209 F.3d 43 (2d Cir. 2000), 646
Goldman v. Belden, 754 F.2d 1059 (2d Cir. 1985), 850
Gomez v. Illinois State Bd. of Educ., 117 F.R.D. 394 (N.D. Ill. 1987), **147**
Gordon, Town of v. Great American Ins. Co., Inc., 331 F.Supp.2d 1357 (M.D. Ala. 2004), 1056
Grant ex rel. Family Eldercare v. Gilbert, 324 F.3d 383 (5th Cir. 2003), 63
Gray v. H.A.S., 18 F.Supp.2d 1320 (M.D. Ala. 1998), 450

Greebel v. FTP Software, Inc., 939 F.Supp. 57 (D. Mass. 1996), **860**
Green v. Wolf Corp., 406 F.2d 291 (2d Cir. 1968), 237, 350
Greenspan v. Brassler, 78 F.R.D. 130 (S.D.N.Y. 1978), 125
Green Tree Financial Corp. v. Bazzle, 539 U.S. 444, 123 S.Ct. 2402, 156 L.Ed.2d 414 (2003), 687
Gregory v. Finova Capital Corp., 442 F.3d 188 (4th Cir. 2006), 242
Gregory v. Hershey, 51 F.R.D. 188 (E.D. Mich. 1970), 160
Grimes v. Mazda North American Operations, 355 F.3d 566 (6th Cir. 2004), 1056
Grogan v. Garner, 806 F.2d 829 (8th Cir. 1986), 919
Gross v. FBL Financial Services, Inc., ___ U.S. ___, 129 S.Ct. 2343, 174 L.Ed.2d 119 (2009), 785
Groves v. Ins. Co. of North America, 433 F.Supp. 877 (E.D. Pa. 1977), 349
Gruber v. Price Waterhouse, 776 F.Supp. 1044 (E.D.Pa.1991), 854
Guarantee Co. of North America v. Pinto, 208 F.R.D. 470 (D. Mass. 2002), 1055
Guedry v. Marino, 164 F.R.D. 181 (E.D. La. 1995), **1016**
Guenther v. Pacific Telecom, Inc., 123 F.R.D. 341 (D. Or. 1987), 933
Gulf Oil Co. v. Bernard, 452 U.S. 89 (1981), **391**
Gutierrez v. Johnson & Johnson, 523 F.3d 187 (3d Cir. 2008), 708
Guzman v. VLM, Inc., 2008 WL 597186 (E.D.N.Y. 2008), 821

Haffer v. Temple University, 115 F.R.D. 506 (E.D. Pa. 1987), **396**
Haley v. Medtronic, Inc., 169 F.R.D. 643 (C.D. Cal. 1996), 242, 246
Hall v. Bio–Medical Application, Inc., 671 F.2d 300 (8th Cir. 1982), 264
Halliburton Co. v. Erica P. John Fund, Inc., 134 S. Ct. 2398 (2014), 224, 844
Halsted Video, Inc. v. Guttillo, 115 F.R.D. 177 (N.D. Ill. 1987), 934
Hammond v. Stamps.com, Inc., 844 F.3d 909 (10th Cir. 2016), 459
Hanley v. First Investors Corp., 151 F.R.D. 76 (E.D. Tex. 1993), 1025
Hanlon v. Chrysler Corp., 150 F.3d 1011 (9th Cir. 1998), 216
Hannaford Bros. Co. Customer Data Security Breach Litigation, In re, 564 F.3d 75 (1st Cir. 2009), 454, 458
Hansberry v. Lee, 311 U.S. 32 (1940), 5, 116, **117**
Harik v. California Teachers Ass'n, 326 F.3d 1042 (9th Cir. 2003), 82
Harrington v. City of Albuquerque, 222 F.R.D. 505 (D.N.M. 2004), 58
Harrison v. Great Spring Waters of America, Inc., 1997 WL 469996 (E.D.N.Y. 1997), 113
Harriston v. Chicago Tribune Co., 992 F.2d 697 (7th Cir. 1993), **54**

Hart v. Nationwide Mut. Fire Ins. Co., 270 F.R.D. 166 (D. Del. 2010), **308**
Hartman v. Duffey, 19 F.3d 1459, 305 U.S.App. D.C. 256 (D.C. Cir. 1994), 57
Heffner v. Blue Cross & Blue Shield of Alabama, Inc., 443 F.3d 1330 (11th Cir. 2006), 195
Heller Financial, Inc. v. Prudential Ins. Co. of America, 371 F.3d 944 (7th Cir. 2004), 1069
Hemenway v. Peabody Coal Co., 159 F.3d 255 (7th Cir. 1998), 439
Hemi Grp., LLC v. City of N.Y., 559 U.S. 1 (2010), 227
Henson v. East Lincoln Tp., 814 F.2d 410 (7th Cir. 1987), **905**
Herbst v. Able, 47 F.R.D. 11 (S.D.N.Y. 1969), 232
Hernandez v. Alexander, 152 F.R.D. 192 (D. Nev. 1993), 83
Hernandez v. Motor Vessel Skyward, 61 F.R.D. 558 (S.D. Fla. 1973), 164
Herron v. Beck, 693 F.2d 125 (11th Cir. 1982), 475
Hertz Corp. v. Friend, 559 U.S. 77 (2010), 455
Hewlett–Packard Co. v. Intelco Medical Systems, Inc., 1991 WL 70883 (N.D. Ill. 1991), 1056
Hicks v. Stanley, 2005 WL 2757792 (S.D.N.Y. 2005), 578
Hidalgo-Velez v. San Juan Asset Management, 758 F.3d 98 (1st Cir. 2014), 887
Hilao v. Estate of Marcos, 103 F.3d 767 (9th Cir. 1996), 360
Hill v. BASF Wyandotte Corp., 782 F.2d 1212 (4th Cir. 1986), 1025
Hillson Partners Ltd. Partnership v. Adage, Inc., 42 F.3d 204 (4th Cir. 1994), 849
Hiser v. Franklin, 94 F.3d 1287 (9th Cir. 1996), 475
Hoffman v. Blaski, 363 U.S. 335, 80 S.Ct. 1084, 4 L.Ed.2d 1254 (1960), **1110**
Hoffman v. R.I. Enterprises, Inc., 50 F.Supp.2d 393 (M.D. Pa. 1999), **798**
Hoffmann–La Roche Inc. v. Sperling, 493 U.S. 165, 110 S.Ct. 482, 107 L.Ed.2d 480 (1989), **813**
Hohider v. United Parcel Service, Inc., 574 F.3d 169 (3d Cir. 2009), 301
Holden v. Burlington Northern, Inc., 665 F.Supp. 1398 (D. Minn. 1987), 576
Holland v. Steele, 92 F.R.D. 58 (N.D. Ga. 1981), 84
Homestead Title of Pinellas, Inc. v. United States, 2005 WL 1221865 (M.D. Fla. 2005), 1069
Horizon/CMS Healthcare Corp. Securities Litigation, In re, 3 F.Supp.2d 1208 (D.N.M. 1998), 875
Hum v. Dericks, 162 F.R.D. 628 (D. Hawai'i 1995), 82
Hunt v. United States Tobacco Co., 538 F.3d 217 (3d Cir. 2008), 226
Hussain v. Boston Old Colony Ins. Co., 311 F.3d 623 (5th Cir. 2002), 1070
Hydrogen Peroxide Antitrust Litigation, In re, 552 F.3d 305 (3d Cir. 2008), 258, 269, 279, 289

IKO Roofing Shingle Products Liability Litigation, In re, 757 F.3d 599 (7th Cir. 2014), 230
Ikonen v. Hartz Mountain Corp., 122 F.R.D. 258 (S.D. Cal. 1988), 113, 246
Impervious Paint Industries, Inc. v. Ashland Oil, 508 F.Supp. 720 (W.D. Ky. 1981), 398
Indianapolis Colts v. Mayor & City Council of Baltimore, 733 F.2d 484 (7th Cir. 1984), 1070
Ingram Barge Co., In re, 2007 WL 148647 (E.D. La. 2007), 456
Initial Public Offering Securities Litigation, In re, 226 F.R.D. 186 (S.D.N.Y. 2005), 543
Initial Public Offerings Securities Litigation, In re, 471 F.3d 24 (2d Cir. 2006), 269, 271, 289, 855
In re (see name of party)
Insolia v. Philip Morris Inc., 186 F.R.D. 547 (W.D. Wis. 1999), 1023
Ins. Brokerage Antitrust Litigation, In re, 579 F.3d 241 (3d Cir. 2009), 563
Integra Realty Resources, Inc., In re, 354 F.3d 1246 (10th Cir. 2004), 914
International Broth. of Teamsters, Local 734 Health & Welfare Trust Fund v. Philip Morris Inc., 196 F.3d 818 (7th Cir. 1999), 754
International Painters & Allied Trades Industry Pension Fund v. Calabro, 312 F.Supp.2d 697 (E.D. Pa. 2004), 1068
Intown Properties Management, Inc. v. Wheaton Van Lines, Inc., 271 F.3d 164 (4th Cir. 2001), 1109
Iron Workers Local Union No. 17 Ins. Fund & its Trustees v. Philip Morris Inc., 182 F.R.D. 512 (N.D. Ohio 1998), **1029**
Itel Securities Litigation, In re, 89 F.R.D. 104 (N.D. Cal. 1981), 897

Jackson v. Johns–Manville Sales Corp., 750 F.2d 1314 (5th Cir. 1985), 429
Jackson v. Motel 6 Multipurpose, Inc., 130 F.3d 999 (11th Cir. 1997), 700
Jackson v. New York Telephone Co., 163 F.R.D. 429 (S.D.N.Y. 1995), 820, 827
Jackson Lockdown/MCO Cases, In re, 568 F.Supp. 869 (E.D. Mich. 1983), 475
Jackson Nat. Life Ins. Co. v. Cabrera, 2002 WL 31190163 (9th Cir. 2002), 1069
Jefferson–Pilot Ins. Co. v. Short, 346 F.Supp.2d 825 (M.D.N.C. 2004), 1068
Jenkins v. BellSouth Corp., 491 F.3d 1288 (11th Cir. 2007), 708
Jenkins v. Raymark Industries, Inc., 782 F.2d 468 (5th Cir. 1986), 86, 737, 764
Jenson v. Eveleth Taconite Co., 139 F.R.D. 657 (D. Minn. 1991), 58
Jenson v. Fiserv Trust Co., 2007 WL 4163889 (9th Cir. 2007), 227
Jerry Enterprises of Gloucester County, Inc. v. Allied Beverage Group, L.L.C., 178 F.R.D. 437 (D.N.J. 1998), 122
Johnson v. Advance America, 549 F.3d 932 (4th Cir. 2008), 455
Johnson v. City of Dallas, Tex., 155 F.R.D. 581 (N.D. Tex. 1994), **1072**
Johnson v. General Motors Corp., 598 F.2d 432 (5th Cir. 1979), **473**

TABLE OF CASES xli

Johnson v. Manhattan Ry. Co., 289 U.S. 479, 53 S.Ct. 721, 77 L.Ed. 1331 (1933), 1109

Johnson v. Montgomery County Sheriff's Dept., 99 F.R.D. 562 (M.D. Ala. 1983), **791**

Johnson v. Moore, 80 Wash.2d 531, 496 P.2d 334 (Wash. 1972), 413

Johnson v. Nextel Communications Inc., 780 F.3d 128 (2d Cir. 2015), 426

Johnson v. Shreveport Garment Co., 422 F.Supp. 526 (W.D. La. 1976), 104

Joint Eastern & Southern Dist. Asbestos Litigation, In re, 14 F.3d 726 (2d Cir. 1993), **1144**

Joint Eastern & Southern Districts Asbestos Litigation, In re, 769 F.Supp. 85 (E.D.N.Y. 1991), 1113

Jones–Bey v. Caso, 535 F.2d 1360 (2d Cir. 1976), 475

Joseph v. Wiles, 223 F.3d 1155 (10th Cir. 2000), 226, 856

Joshlin v. Gannett River States Pub. Corp., 152 F.R.D. 577 (E.D. Ark. 1993), 264

Joy v. North, 692 F.2d 880 (2d Cir. 1982), 920

Juris v. Inamed Corp., 685 F.3d 1294 (11th Cir. 2012), 140, 378, 564

Kamen v. Kemper Financial Services, Inc., 500 U.S. 90, 111 S.Ct. 1711, 114 L.Ed.2d 152 (1991), 924

Kamilewicz, Ex parte, 700 So.2d 340 (Ala. 1997), 527

Kamilewicz v. Bank of Boston Corp., 92 F.3d 506 (7th Cir. 1996), **522**

Kamilewicz v. Bank of Boston Corp., 100 F.3d 1348 (7th Cir. 1996), 527

Kanawi v. Bechtel Corp., 254 F.R.D. 102 (N.D. Cal. 2008), 165

Kanter v. Barella, 388 F.Supp.2d 474 (D.N.J. 2005), 931

Kaplan v. Pomerantz, 132 F.R.D. 504 (N.D. Ill. 1990), **128**

Karvaly v. eBay, Inc., 245 F.R.D. 71 (E.D.N.Y. 2007), 575

Katrina Canal Breaches Litigation, In re, 628 F.3d 185 (5th Cir. 2010), 182

Katrina Canal Litigation Breaches, In re, 524 F.3d 700 (5th Cir. 2008), 457

Katz v. Gerardi, 552 F.3d 558 (7th Cir. 2009), 888

Kaufman v. Allstate New Jersey Ins. Co., 561 F.3d 144 (3d Cir. 2009), 454, 456

Kedra v. City of Philadelphia, 454 F.Supp. 652 (E.D. Pa. 1978), 1025

Keele v. Wexler, 149 F.3d 589 (7th Cir. 1998), 57

Kenwin Shops, Inc. v. Bank of Louisiana, 1999 WL 294800 (S.D.N.Y. 1999), 986

Kern v. Siemens Corp., 393 F.3d 120 (2d Cir. 2004), 821

Kernan v. Holiday Universal, Inc., 1990 WL 289505 (D. Md. 1990), 242

Kerner v. City & Cnty. of Denver, 2013 WL 1222394 (D. Colo. 2013), 204

Kescoli v. Babbitt, 101 F.3d 1304 (9th Cir. 1996), **1035**

Key v. Gillette Co., 782 F.2d 5 (1st Cir. 1986), 152

Kim v. Dial Service Intern., Inc., 1997 WL 5902 (S.D.N.Y. 1997), 441

King v. Livent, Inc., 36 F.Supp.2d 187 (S.D.N.Y. 1999), 870

King Fisher Marine Service, Inc. v. 21st Phoenix Corp., 893 F.2d 1155 (10th Cir. 1990), 1056, 1057

Kircher v. Putnam Funds Trust, 547 U.S. 633, 126 S.Ct. 2145, 165 L.Ed.2d 92 (2006), 886

Kirkpatrick v. J.C. Bradford & Co., 827 F.2d 718 (11th Cir. 1987), 934

Kirschner Medical Corp. Securities Litigation, In re, 139 F.R.D. 74 (D. Md. 1991), 414

Kitzmiller v. Dover Area School Dist., 229 F.R.D. 463 (M.D. Pa. 2005), 1085

Klay v. Humana, Inc., 382 F.3d 1241 (11th Cir. 2004), **31**, 217, 244, 429

Klotz v. Superior Elec. Products Corp., 498 F.Supp. 1099 (E.D. Pa. 1980), 1054

Knight v. Lavine, 2013 WL 427880 (E.D. Va. 2013), 102

Kohen v. Pacific Investment Management Co., 571 F.3d 672 (7th Cir. 2009), 70

Korwek v. Hunt, 827 F.2d 874 (2d Cir. 1987), 439

Kourtis v. Cameron, 419 F.3d 989 (9th Cir. 2005), 1098

Kramer v. Scientific Control Corp., 534 F.2d 1085 (3d Cir. 1976), 153

Kriendler v. Chemical Waste Management, Inc., 877 F.Supp. 1140 (N.D. Ill. 1995), 153

Krueger v. New York Telephone Co., 163 F.R.D. 433 (S.D.N.Y. 1995), 270

Krupski v. Costa Crociere S. p. A., 130 S.Ct. 2485 (2010), 441

Kumho Tire Co., Ltd. v. Carmichael, 526 U.S. 137, 119 S.Ct. 1167, 143 L.Ed.2d 238 (1999), 290

Kurczi v. Eli Lilly & Co., 160 F.R.D. 667 (N.D. Ohio 1995), 152, 153, 241

Kurth v. Arcelormittal USA, Inc., 2009 WL 3346588 (N.D. Ind. 2009), 456

Kuzmickey v. Dunmore Corp., 420 F.Supp. 226 (E.D. Pa. 1976), 934

Laborers Local 17 Health & Benefit Fund v. Philip Morris, Inc., 191 F.3d 229 (2d Cir. 1999), 755

Laborers Local 17 Health & Ben. Fund v. Philip Morris, 1998 WL 241279 (S.D.N.Y. 1998), **328**

Labovitz v. Washington Times Corp., 172 F.3d 897, 335 U.S.App.D.C. 296 (D.C. Cir. 1999), 919

Lake v. First Nationwide Bank, 156 F.R.D. 615 (E.D. Pa. 1994), 231

La Mar v. H & B Novelty & Loan Co., 489 F.2d 461 (9th Cir. 1973), **10**, 163, **903**

Lamphere v. Brown University, 553 F.2d 714 (1st Cir. 1977), 267

Lance v. Dennis, 546 U.S. 459, 126 S.Ct. 1198, 163 L.Ed.2d 1059 (2006), 527

Landry v. Price Waterhouse Chartered Accountants, 123 F.R.D. 474 (S.D.N.Y. 1989), 114

Lane v. Page, 250 F.R.D. 634 (D.N.M. 2007), 870

Langley v. Coughlin, 715 F.Supp. 522 (S.D.N.Y. 1989), 441

Langner v. Brown, 1996 WL 709757 (S.D.N.Y. 1996), 113

Laramore v. Illinois Sports Facilities Authority, 1993 WL 45959 (N.D. Ill. 1993), 197

Larson v. Dumke, 900 F.2d 1363 (9th Cir. 1990), 932

LASA Per L'Industria Del Marmo Societa Per Azioni of Lasa, Italy v. Alexander, 414 F.2d 143 (6th Cir. 1969), 1054

Latham v. Stein, 2010 WL 3294722 (D.S.C. 2010), 865

Lazy Oil Co. v. Witco Corp., 166 F.3d 581 (3d Cir. 1999), **601**

Ledbetter v. Goodyear Tire & Rubber Co., Inc., 550 U.S. 618, 127 S.Ct. 2162, 167 L.Ed.2d 982 (2007), 807

Lehman v. Revolution Portfolio L.L.C., 166 F.3d 389 (1st Cir. 1999), 1056

Leimbach v. Allen, 976 F.2d 912 (4th Cir. 1992), 1068

Leist v. Shawano County, 91 F.R.D. 64 (E.D. Wis. 1981), 899

Lemon v. International Union of Operating Engineers, Local No. 139, AFL–CIO, 216 F.3d 577 (7th Cir. 2000), 197

Lenon v. St. Paul Mercury Ins. Co., 136 F.3d 1365 (10th Cir. 1998), 1026

Lerner v. Haimsohn, 126 F.R.D. 64 (D. Colo. 1989), 125

Levell v. Monsanto Research Corp., 191 F.R.D. 543 (S.D. Ohio 2000), 748

Lewis v. Anselmi, 564 F.Supp. 768 (S.D.N.Y. 1983), 920

Lewis v. City of Chicago, Ill., 560 U.S. 205, 130 S.Ct. 2191, 176 L.Ed.2d 967 (2010), 807

Lewis v. Curtis, 671 F.2d 779 (3d Cir. 1982), 933

Lewis v. Epic Systems Corp. 823 F.3d 1147 (7th Cir. 2016), 696

Lewis v. Ward, 2003 WL 22461894 (Del. Ch. 2003), 925

Lexecon Inc. v. Milberg Weiss Bershad Hynes & Lerach, 523 U.S. 26, 118 S.Ct. 956, 140 L.Ed.2d 62 (1998), **977**

Leysoto v. Mama Mia I., Inc., 255 F.R.D. 693 (S.D. Fla. 2009), 240

Leyva v. Buley, 125 F.R.D. 512 (E.D. Wash. 1989), 197

Leyva v. Medline Indus. Inc., 716 F.3d 510 (9th Cir. 2013), 231

Liberty Mut. Group v. Hillman's Sheet Metal & Certified Welding, Inc., 168 F.R.D. 90 (D. Me. 1996), 1085

Liberty Mut. Ins. Co. v. Treesdale, Inc., 419 F.3d 216 (3d Cir. 2005), 1048

Liddell v. Board of Educ. of City of St. Louis, State of Mo., 567 F.Supp. 1037 (E.D. Mo. 1983), 599

Ligon v. City of N.Y., 288 F.R.D. 72, 77 (S.D.N.Y. 2013), 203

LILCO Securities Litigation, In re, 111 F.R.D. 663 (E.D.N.Y. 1986), 426

Lloyd v. City of Philadelphia, 121 F.R.D. 246 (E.D. Pa. 1988), 172

Local 703, I.B. of T. Grocery & Food Emps. Welfare Fund v. Regions Fin. Corp., 762 F.3d 1248 (11th Cir. 2014), 877

London v. Wal–Mart Stores, Inc., 340 F.3d 1246 (11th Cir. 2003), 139

Long John Silver's Restaurants, Inc. v. Cole, 514 F.3d 345 (4th Cir. 2008), 820

Lujan v. Defenders of Wildlife, 504 U.S. 555, 112 S.Ct. 2130, 119 L.Ed.2d 351 (1992), 63

Lummis v. White, 629 F.2d 397 (5th Cir. 1980), 1070

Lusted v. San Antonio Independent School Dist., 741 F.2d 817 (5th Cir. 1984), 295

Luther v. Countrywide Home Loans Servicing LP, 533 F.3d 1031 (9th Cir. 2008), 888

Lynch v. Rank, 604 F.Supp. 30 (N.D.Cal.1984), 402

Magana v. Platzer Shipyard, Inc., 74 F.R.D. 61 (S.D. Tex. 1977), 606

Maher v. Zapata Corp., 714 F.2d 436 (5th Cir. 1983), 939

Maine v. Director, United States Fish & Wildlife Service, 262 F.3d 13 (1st Cir. 2001), 1082

Malack v. BDO Seidman, LLP, 617 F.3d 743 (3d Cir. 2010), 856

Malchman v. Davis, 588 F.Supp. 1047 (S.D.N.Y. 1984), 139

Malchman v. Davis, 706 F.2d 426 (2d Cir. 1983), 577

Malcolm v. National Gypsum Co., 995 F.2d 346 (2d Cir. 1993), **1102**

Maldonado v. Ochsner Clinic Foundation, 493 F.3d 521 (5th Cir. 2007), 195

Management Television Systems, Inc. v. National Football League, 52 F.R.D. 162 (E.D. Pa. 1971), 949

Mangual v. Rotger–Sabat, 317 F.3d 45 (1st Cir. 2003), 1082

MannPaller Foundation, Inc. v. Econometric Research, Inc., 644 F.Supp. 92 (D.D.C. 1986), 919

Mantolete v. Bolger, 767 F.2d 1416 (9th Cir. 1985), 311

Marcus v. BMW of North America, LLC, 687 F.3d 583 (3d Cir. 2012), 81, **107**

Marek v. Lane, 134 S. Ct. 8 (2013), 631

Marine Asbestos Cases, In re, 265 F.3d 861 (9th Cir. 2001), 165

Marino v. Ortiz, 484 U.S. 301, 108 S. Ct. 586, 98 L.Ed.2d 629 (1988), 713

Marrone v. Philip Morris USA, Inc., 2004 WL 2050485 (Ohio App. 9 Dist. 2004), 143

Marseilles Hydro Power, LLC v. Marseilles Land & Water Co., 299 F.3d 643 (7th Cir. 2002), 1054

Martens v. Smith Barney, Inc., 181 F.R.D. 243 (S.D.N.Y. 1998), 673

Martin v. Wilks, 490 U.S. 755, 109 S.Ct. 2180, 104 L.Ed.2d 835 (1989), 1048, **1093**

Martinez–Mendoza v. Champion Intern. Corp., 340 F.3d 1200 (11th Cir. 2003), 127

Marx v. Montgomery, 632 So.2d 1315 (Miss. 1994), 413

Masonite Corp. Hardboard Siding Products Liability Litigation, In re, 170 F.R.D. 417 (E.D. La. 1997), 241

Table of Cases

Masters v. Wilhelmina Model Agency, Inc., 473 F.3d 423 (2d Cir. 2007), 608
Matrixx Initiatives, Inc. v. Siracusano, 563 U.S. 27 (2011), 258, 851, 865
Matsushita Elec. Indus. Co., Ltd. v. Epsten, 516 U.S. 367, 116 S.Ct. 873, 134 L.Ed.2d 6 (1996), **509**
Matter of (see name of party)
Mattes v. ABC Plastics, Inc., 323 F.3d 695 (8th Cir. 2003), 1053
Mattoon v. City of Pittsfield, 128 F.R.D. 17 (D. Mass. 1989), 215
Mausolf v. Babbitt, 85 F.3d 1295 (8th Cir. 1996), **1075**
McAdams v. McCord, 584 F.3d 1111 (8th Cir. 2009), 857
McBride v. Galaxy Carpet Mills, Inc., 920 F.Supp. 1278 (N.D. Ga. 1995), 402
McClain v. Lufkin Industries, Inc., 519 F.3d 264 (5th Cir. 2008), 205
McCurdy v. Wedgewood Capital Management Co., Inc., 1999 WL 554590 (E.D. Pa. 1999), 1054
McDonald v. Pension Plan of NYSA–ILA Pension Trust Fund, 320 F.3d 151 (2d Cir. 2003), 268
McDonald v. Santa Fe Trail Transp. Co., 427 U.S. 273, 96 S.Ct. 2574, 49 L.Ed.2d 493 (1976), 784
McDonnell Douglas Corp. v. Green, 411 U.S. 792, 93 S.Ct. 1817, 36 L.Ed.2d 668 (1973), 803
McDonnell Douglas Corp. v. United States Dist. Court for Central Dist. of California, 523 F.2d 1083 (9th Cir. 1975), 163
McDowell v. Brown, 5 Vet. App. 401 (1993), **464**
McFarland v. Folsom, 854 F.Supp. 862 (M.D. Ala. 1994), 1043
McGowan v. Faulkner Concrete Pipe Co., 659 F.2d 554 (5th Cir. 1981), 152
McGuire v. International Paper Co., 1994 WL 261360 (S.D. Miss. 1994), 43, 125
McIntyre v. Household Bank, 2004 WL 2958690 (N.D. Ill. 2004), 113
McLaughlin v. American Tobacco Co., 522 F.3d 215 (2d Cir. 2008), 226, 300
McMahon Books, Inc. v. Willow Grove Associates, 108 F.R.D. 32 (E.D. Pa. 1985), 247
McManus v. Fleetwood Enterprises, Inc., 320 F.3d 545 (5th Cir. 2003), 206, **219**
M.D. ex rel. Stukenberg v. Perry, 675 F.3d 832 (5th Cir. 2012), 102
Meadows v. Pacific Inland Securities Corp., 36 F.Supp.2d 1240 (S.D. Cal. 1999), 900
Mejdrech v. Met–Coil Systems Corp., 319 F.3d 910 (7th Cir. 2003), 301, 752
Melton ex rel. Dutton v. Carolina Power & Light Co., 283 F.R.D. 280 (D.S.C. 2012), 42
Mendez v. Teachers Ins. & Annuity Ass'n & College Retirement Equities Fund, 982 F.2d 783 (2d Cir. 1992), 1070
Merck & Co., Inc. Securities, Derivative & ERISA Litigation, In re, 2009 WL 331426 (D.N.J. 2009), 189
Merrill Lynch, Pierce, Fenner & Smith Inc. v. Dabit, 547 U.S. 71, 126 S.Ct. 1503, 164 L.Ed.2d 179 (2006), 886

Mertens v. Abbott Laboratories, 99 F.R.D. 38 (D.N.H. 1983), 215
Messner v. Northshore University HealthSystem, 669 F.3d 802 (7th Cir. 2012), 42
Methyl Tertiary Butyl Ether (MTBE) Products Liability Litigation, In re, 241 F.R.D. 435 (S.D.N.Y. 2007), 753
Methyl Tertiary Butyl Ether ('MTBE') Products Liability Litigation, In re, 209 F.R.D. 323 (S.D.N.Y. 2002), 307
Meyer v. Portfolio Recovery Assocs., LLC, 707 F.3d 1036 (9th Cir. 2012), 134
Meyer v. U.S. Tennis Ass'n, 297 F.R.D. 75 (S.D.N.Y. 2013), 102
Milestone Scientific Securities Litigation, In re, 187 F.R.D. 165 (D.N.J. 1999), **878**
Miller v. Baltimore Gas & Elec. Co., 202 F.R.D. 195 (D. Md. 2001), 205
Miller v. Nat'l Wildlife Federation, 1987 WL 488717 (Va. Cir. Ct. 1987), 413
Miller v. Register & Tribune Syndicate, Inc., 336 N.W.2d 709 (Iowa 1983), 932
Milliken v. Bradley, 433 U.S. 267, 97 S.Ct. 2749, 53 L.Ed.2d 745 (1977), 622
Mississippi ex rel. Hood v. AU Optronics Corp., 134 S. Ct. 736, 187 L.Ed.2d 654 (2014), 461
Mitsubishi Motors Corp. v. Soler Chrysler–Plymouth, Inc., 473 U.S. 614, 105 S.Ct. 3346, 87 L.Ed.2d 444 (1985), 690
Modafinil Antitrust Litigation, In re, 837 F.3d 238 (3d Cir. 2016), 86
Monumental Life Ins. Co., In re, 365 F.3d 408 (5th Cir. 2004), 237
Mooney v. Aramco Services Co., 54 F.3d 1207 (5th Cir. 1995), 835
Moore v. Napolitano, 926 F. Supp. 2d 8 (D.D.C. 2013), 204
Moore v. New York Cotton Exchange, 270 U.S. 593, 46 S.Ct. 367, 70 L.Ed. 750 (1926), 1022
Moran v. Household Intern., Inc., 490 A.2d 1059 (Del. Ch. 1985), 919
Morris v. Ernst & Young, LLP, 834 F.3d 975 (9th Cir. 2016), 696
Morrison v. National Australia Bank Ltd., 561 U.S. 247, 130 S.Ct. 2869, 177 L.Ed.2d 535 (2010), 862
Mosley v. General Motors Corp., 497 F.2d 1330 (8th Cir. 1974), 1022
Motor Fuel Temp. Sales Practices Litigation, In re, 292 F.R.D. 652 (D. Kan. 2013), 204
Mullen v. Treasure Chest Casino, LLC, 186 F.3d 620 (5th Cir. 1999), 57, **353**
Mullins v. Direct Digital, LLC, 795 F.3d 654 (2015), **44**, 233
Multi–Piece Rim Products Liability Litigation, In re, 464 F.Supp. 969 (Jud. Pan. Mult. Lit. 1979), **960**
Murray v. Sevier, 50 F.Supp.2d 1257 (M.D. Ala. 1999), 947

Nagy v. Jostens, Inc., 91 F.R.D. 431 (D. Minn. 1981), 383
Nassau County Strip Search Cases, In re, 461 F.3d 219 (2d Cir. 2006), 300

National Accident Ins. Underwriters, Inc. v. Citibank, FSB, 333 F.Supp.2d 720 (N.D. Ill. 2004), 1069

National Asbestos Workers Medical Fund v. Philip Morris, Inc., 2000 WL 1424931 (E.D.N.Y. 2000), 707

National Asbestos Workers Medical Fund v. Philip Morris, Inc., 86 F.Supp.2d 137 (E.D.N.Y. 2000), 438

National Football League Players Concussion Injury Litigation, In re, 821 F.3d 410 (3d Cir. 2016), 140, **585**, 753

National Football League Players Concussion Injury Litigation, In re, 775 F.3d 570 (3d Cir. 2014), 708

National Football League Players Concussion Injury Litigation, In re, 307 F.R.D. 351, 423 (E.D. Penn. 2015), 578

National Licorice Co. v. N.L.R.B., 309 U.S. 350, 60 S.Ct. 569, 84 L.Ed. 799 (1940), 1042

National Organization for Women, Farmington Valley Chapter v. Sperry Rand Corp., 88 F.R.D. 272 (D. Conn. 1980), **321**

National Organization For Women, Inc. v. Scheidler, 172 F.R.D. 351 (N.D. Ill. 1997), 42

Natto Iyela Gbarabe v. Chevron Corp., 2016 WL 4154849 (2016), **665**

Navigant Consulting, Inc., Securities Litigation, In re, 275 F.3d 616 (7th Cir. 2001), 715

N.C. Right to Life, Inc. v. Bartlett, 1998 U.S. Dist. LEXIS 6443 (E.D.N.C. 1998), 914

Neale v. Volvo Cars of N. America, LLC, 794 F.3d 353 (3d Cir. 2015), 70

Nelson v. Quimby Island Reclamation Dist. Facilities Corp., 491 F.Supp. 1364 (N.D. Cal. 1980), 1055

Newby v. Enron Corp., 338 F.3d 467 (5th Cir. 2003), 503

Newsom v. Norris, 888 F.2d 371 (6th Cir. 1989), 295

Newton v. Merrill Lynch, Pierce, Fenner & Smith, Inc., 259 F.3d 154 (3d Cir. 2001), 226

New York News, Inc. v. Kheel, 972 F.2d 482 (2d Cir. 1992), 1084

Nilsen v. York County, 382 F.Supp.2d 206 (D. Me. 2005), 578

No. 84 Employer–Teamster Joint Council Pension Trust Fund v. America West Holding Corp., 320 F.3d 920 (9th Cir. 2003), 850

Northbrook Excess & Surplus Ins. Co. v. Medical Malpractice Joint Underwriting Ass'n of Massachusetts, 900 F.2d 476 (1st Cir. 1990), **944**

Northern Dist. of California "Dalkon Shield" IUD Products Liability Litigation, In re, 521 F.Supp. 1188 (N.D. Cal. 1981), 736

Northwestern Nat. Bank of Minneapolis v. Fox & Co., 102 F.R.D. 507 (S.D.N.Y. 1984), 899

Oatis v. Crown Zellerbach Corp., 398 F.2d 496 (5th Cir. 1968), 798

O'Connor v. Boeing North American, Inc., 180 F.R.D. 359 (C.D. Cal. 1997), 170

Oil Spill by Oil Rig Deepwater Horizon in Gulf of Mexico, on Apr. 20, 2010, In re, 910 F. Supp. 2d 891 (E.D. La. 2012), 753

Oil Spill by Oil Rig Deepwater Horizon, 295 F.R.D. 112 (E.D. La. 2013), 753

Olden v. Gardner, 294 F. App'x 210 (6th Cir. 2008), 605

Olden v. LaFarge Corp., 383 F.3d 495 (6th Cir. 2004), 752

O'Neil v. Appel, 165 F.R.D. 479 (W.D. Mich. 1996), 57

Online DVD-Rental Antitrust Litigation, 779 F.3d 934 (9th Cir. 2015), 607

Oppenheimer Fund, Inc. v. Sanders, 437 U.S. 340, 98 S.Ct. 2380, 57 L.Ed.2d 253 (1978), 308, **379**

Oran v. Stafford, 226 F.3d 275 (3d Cir. 2000), 850

Oregon Laborers–Employers Health & Welfare Trust Fund v. Philip Morris Inc., 185 F.3d 957 (9th Cir. 1999), 755

Orthopedic Bone Screw Products Liability Litigation, In re, 1995 WL 428683 (E.D. Pa. 1995), 1024

Ortiz v. Fibreboard Corp., 527 U.S. 815, 119 S.Ct. 2295, 144 L.Ed.2d 715 (1999), 6, 16, **172**, 189, 359, 413, 470, 479, 542, **563**, **747**, 762, 780, 1120, 1144

Oscar Private Equity Investments v. Allegiance Telecom, Inc., 487 F.3d 261 (5th Cir. 2007), 271

Oskoian v. Canuel, 269 F.2d 311 (1st Cir. 1959), 942

O'Sullivan v. Countrywide Home Loans, Inc., 319 F.3d 732 (5th Cir. 2003), 216

Ouellette v. International Paper Co., 86 F.R.D. 476 (D. Vt. 1980), 111

Oxendine v. Williams, 509 F.2d 1405 (4th Cir. 1975), **157**

Oxford Health Plans, Inc. Securities Litigation, In re, 182 F.R.D. 42 (S.D.N.Y. 1998), **871**

Paige v. California, 102 F.3d 1035 (9th Cir. 1996), 699

Painewebber Ltd. Partnerships Litigation, In re, 147 F.3d 132 (2d Cir. 1998), 350

Paramount Pictures, United States v., 334 U.S. 131, 68 S.Ct. 915, 92 L.Ed. 1260 (1948), 172

Parker v. Time Warner Entertainment Co., L.P., 331 F.3d 13 (2d Cir. 2003), 311

Parnes v. Gateway 2000, Inc., 122 F.3d 539 (8th Cir. 1997), 848

Parsons v. Ryan, 289 F.R.D. 513 (D. Ariz. 2013), 102, 204

Paskuly v. Marshall Field & Co., 646 F.2d 1210 (7th Cir. 1981), 441

Passa v. Derderian, 308 F.Supp.2d 43 (D.R.I. 2004), 1116

Patterson v. McLean Credit Union, 491 U.S. 164 (1989), 784

Patrykus v. Gomilla, 121 F.R.D. 357 (N.D. Ill. 1988), **78**

Pearl v. Allied Corp., 102 F.R.D. 921 (E.D. Pa. 1984), 142

Pearson v. NBTY, 772 F.3d 778 (7th Cir. 2014), 600

Peck v. General Motors Corp., 894 F.2d 844 (6th Cir. 1990), 919

Pederson v. Louisiana State University, 213 F.3d 858 (5th Cir. 2000), 84

Percodani v. Riker–Maxson Corp., 51 F.R.D. 263 (S.D.N.Y. 1970), 157

Perdue v. Kenny A. ex rel. Winn, 559 U.S. 542, 130 S.Ct. 1662, 176 L.Ed.2d 494 (2010), 648

Perez–Funez v. I.N.S., 611 F.Supp. 990 (C.D. Cal. 1984), 403

Peters v. National R.R. Passenger Corp., 966 F.2d 1483, 296 U.S. App. D.C. 202 (D.C. Cir. 1992), 376

Petition of (see name of party)

PetSmart, Inc. Securities Litigation, In re, 61 F.Supp.2d 982 (D. Ariz. 1999), 851

Pettway v. American Cast Iron Pipe Co., 494 F.2d 211 (5th Cir. 1974), 360

Philadelphia Elec. Co. v. Anaconda American Brass Co., 43 F.R.D. 452 (E.D. Pa. 1968), 350

Philip Morris Inc. v. National Asbestos Workers Medical Fund, 214 F.3d 132 (2d Cir. 2000), 700

Philippine American Life Ins. v. Raytheon Aircraft Co., 2003 WL 23484637 (D. Kan. 2003), 1057

Phillips v. Joint Legislative Committee on Performance & Expenditure Review of State of Mississippi, 637 F.2d 1014 (5th Cir. 1981), 83

Phillips Petroleum Co. v. Shutts, 472 U.S. 797, 105 S.Ct. 2965, 86 L.Ed.2d 628 (1985), 5, 104, 204, 237, **407**, 460, 477, 527

Phipps v. Wal–Mart Stores, Inc., 792 F.3d 637 (6th Cir. 2015), 439

Pizza Time Theatre Securities Litigation, In re, 112 F.R.D. 15 (N.D. Cal. 1986), 414

Plummer v. American Institute of Certified Public Accountants, 97 F.3d 220 (7th Cir. 1996), 622

Plywood Anti–Trust Litigation, In re, 76 F.R.D. 570 (E.D. La. 1976), 241

Poleon, Anderson v. General Motors Corp., 1999 WL 1289473 (D. Virgin Islands 1999), 1024

Police & Fire Retirement Systems of Detroit v. IndyMac MBS, Inc., 721 F.3d 95 (2d Cir. 2013), 871

Polypropylene Carpet Antitrust Litigation, In re, 178 F.R.D. 603 (N.D. Ga. 1997), 406

Poptech, LP v. Stewardship Inv. Advisors, LLC, 2010 WL 4365669 (D. Conn. 2010), 870

Poulos v. Caesars World, Inc., 379 F.3d 654 (9th Cir. 2004), 227

Powers v. Hamilton County Public Defender Com'n, 501 F.3d 592 (6th Cir. 2007), 216

Premier Elec. Const. Co. v. National Elec. Contractors Ass'n, Inc., 814 F.2d 358 (7th Cir. 1987), **484**

Preston v. Tenet Healthsystem Memorial Medical Center, Inc. (Preston I), 485 F.3d 804 (5th Cir. 2007), 455

Preston v. Tenet Healthsystem Memorial Medical Center, Inc. (Preston II), 485 F.3d 793 (5th Cir. 2007), 455

Price v. Wilmington Trust Co., 730 A.2d 1236 (Del. Ch. 1997), 125

Prissert v. Emcore Corp., 2010 U.S. Dist. LEXIS 86598 (D.N.M. 2010), 869

Probe v. State Teachers' Retirement System, 780 F.2d 776 (9th Cir. 1986), 264

Professional Management Associates, Inc. v. Coss, 598 N.W.2d 406 (Minn. App. 1999), 925

Provenz v. Miller, 102 F.3d 1478 (9th Cir. 1996), 850

Provident Tradesmens Bank & Trust Co. v. Patterson, 390 U.S. 102, 88 S.Ct. 733, 19 L.Ed.2d 936 (1968), 1040, 1042

Prudential Ins. Co. America Sales Practice Litigation Agent Actions, In re, 148 F.3d 283 (3d Cir. 1998), 112

Pruitt v. Allied Chemical Corp., 85 F.R.D. 100 (E.D. Va. 1980), **302**, 737

Public School Retirement System of Missouri v. United States, 227 F.R.D. 502 (W.D. Mo. 2005), 1069

P.V. ex rel. Valentin v. School Dist. of Phila., 289 F.R.D. 227 (E.D. Pa. 2013), 203

Radcliffe v. Experian Information Solutions Inc., 715 F.3d 1157 (9th Cir. 2013), 138, 600

Raftery v. Mercury Finance Co., 1997 WL 529553 (N.D. Ill. 1997), 883

Rahman v. Chertoff, 530 F.3d 622 (7th Cir. 2008), **30**, 44

Raie v. Cheminova, Inc., 336 F.3d 1278 (11th Cir. 2003), 439

Rail Freight Fuel Surcharge Antitrust Litigation, In re, 258 F.R.D. 167 (D.D.C. 2009), **312**

Ranchers Cattlemen Action Legal Fund United Stockgrowers of America v. United States Dept. of Agriculture, 2005 WL 1719211 (9th Cir. 2005), 1083

Randle v. Spectran, 129 F.R.D. 386 (D. Mass. 1988), 414

Randleman v. Fidelity National Title Ins. Co., 646 F.3d 347 (6th Cir. 2011), 43

Rannis v. Recchia, 2010 WL 2124096 (9th Cir. 2010), 83

Rappaport v. Katz, 62 F.R.D. 512 (S.D.N.Y. 1974), 44

Rathborne v. Rathborne, 508 F.Supp. 515 (E.D. La. 1980), 934

Rattray v. Woodbury County, Iowa, 253 F.R.D. 444 (N.D. Iowa 2008), 126

Razorfish, Inc. Securities Litigation, In re, 143 F.Supp.2d 304 (S.D.N.Y. 2001), 877

R & D Business Systems v. Xerox Corp., 150 F.R.D. 87 (E.D. Tex. 1993), 384

Reab v. Electronic Arts, Inc., 214 F.R.D. 623 (D. Colo. 2002), 575

Reeb v. Ohio Dept. of Rehabilitation & Correction, 435 F.3d 639 (6th Cir. 2006), 197

Redman v. RadioShack Corp., 768 F.3d 622 (7th Cir. 2014), 600, 607

Regents of University of California v. Credit Suisse First Boston (USA), Inc., 482 F.3d 372 (5th Cir. 2007), 226

Reilly v. Ceridian Corp., 664 F.3d 38 (3d Cir. 2011), 70

Remijas v. Neiman Marcus Group, LLC, 794 F.3d 688 (7th Cir. 2015), 70

Ren–Dan Farms, Inc. v. Monsanto Co., 952 F.Supp. 370 (W.D. La. 1997), 450
Repetitive Stress Injury Litigation, In re, 11 F.3d 368 (2d Cir. 1993), 1107
Republic of Bolivia v. Philip Morris Companies, Inc., 39 F.Supp.2d 1008 (S.D. Tex. 1999), 1114
Republic of Philippines v. Pimentel, 553 U.S. 851, 128 S.Ct. 2180, 171 L.Ed.2d 131 (2008), 1028
Retirement Systems of Ala. v. J.P. Morgan Chase & Co., 386 F.3d 419 (2d Cir. 2004), 503
Reynolds v. Beneficial Nat. Bank, 288 F.3d 277 (7th Cir. 2002), 154, **579**
Reynolds v. Rick's Mushroom Service, Inc., 2003 WL 22741335 (E.D. Pa. 2003), 1055
Rhone–Poulenc Rorer, Inc., Matter of, 51 F.3d 1293 (7th Cir. 1995), 5, 271, 351, **414**, 700, **737**
Ridgeway v. Flagstar Corp., 1994 WL 525553 (N.D. Cal. 1994), 622
Rikos v. Proctor & Gamble Co., 799 F.3d 497 (6th Cir. 2015), 278
R.J. Reynolds Tobacco Co. v. Engle, 672 So.2d 39 (Fla. Dist. Ct. App. 1996), 754
Roach v. T.L. Cannon Corp., 778 F.3d 401 (2d Cir. 2015), 231
Robbins v. Yamaha Motor Corp., 98 F.R.D. 36 (M.D. Pa. 1983), 1054
Robert F. Booth Trust v. Crowley, 687 F.3d 314 (7th Cir. 2012), 940
Roberts v. Texaco, Inc., 979 F.Supp. 185 (S.D.N.Y. 1997), 623
Robidoux v. Celani, 987 F.2d 931 (2d Cir. 1993), 85
Robin v. Doctors Officenters Corp., 686 F.Supp. 199 (N.D. Ill. 1988), **135**
Robinson v. Cheetah Transp., 2006 WL 3322580 (W.D. La .2006), 455
Robinson v. Fountainhead Title Group Corp., 447 F.Supp.2d 478 (D. Md. 2006), 900
Robinson v. Lattimore, 946 F.2d 1566, 292 U.S. App. D.C. 86 (D.C. Cir. 1991), 475
Robinson v. Metro–North Commuter R.R. Co., 267 F.3d 147 (2d Cir. 2001), 197
Robinson v. Texas Auto. Dealers Ass'n, 387 F.3d 416 (5th Cir. 2004), 218
Robinson v. U–Haul Co., 785 F.Supp. 1378 (D. Alaska 1992), 1055
Rocky v. King, 900 F.2d 864 (5th Cir. 1990), **58**
Rodriguez, In re, 695 F.3d 360 (5th Cir. 2012), 43
Rodriguez v. Department of the Treasury, 108 F.R.D. 360 (D.D.C. 1985), 311
Rodriguez v. Disner, 688 F.3d 645 (9th Cir. 2012), 600
Rodriguez v. West Publishing Corp., 563 F.3d 948 (9th Cir. 2009), 137, 544, 600
Roginsky v. Richardson–Merrell, Inc., 378 F.2d 832 (2d Cir. 1967), 188
Rogosin v. Steadman, 71 F.R.D. 514 (S.D.N.Y. 1976), 939
Roper v. Consurve, Inc., 578 F.2d 1106 (5th Cir. 1978), 606
Roseville Employees' Retirement System, City of v. Textron Inc., 2009 WL 4545161 (D.R.I. 2009), 877
Rothenberg v. Security Management Co., Inc., 667 F.2d 958 (11th Cir. 1982), 932
Rozenboom v. Van Der Moolen Holding, N.V., 2004 WL 816440 (S.D.N.Y. 2004), 877
Ruggiero v. American Bioculture, Inc., 56 F.R.D. 93 (S.D.N.Y. 1972), 938

Sac & Fox Nation of Missouri v. Norton, 240 F.3d 1250 (10th Cir. 2001), 1041
Salomon Analyst Metromedia Litigation, In re, 544 F.3d 474 (2d Cir. 2008), 225
San Francisco Unified School Dist. v. W.R. Grace & Co., 44 Cal.Rptr.2d 305 (Cal. App. 1 Dist.1995), 297
Santiago v. City of Philadelphia, 72 F.R.D. 619 (E.D. Pa. 1976), 194
Satterfield v. Simon & Schuster, Inc., 569 F.3d 946 (9th Cir. 2009), 575
Saulic v. Symantec Corp., 596 F.Supp.2d 1323 (C.D. Cal. 2009), 240
Scardelletti v. Debarr, 265 F.3d 195 (4th Cir. 2001), 576
Schaffner v. Chemical Bank, 339 F.Supp. 329 (S.D.N.Y. 1972), 232
Schleicher v. Wendt, 618 F.3d 679 (7th Cir. 2010), 225
Schlesinger v. Reservists Committee to Stop the War, 418 U.S. 208, 94 S.Ct. 2925, 41 L.Ed.2d 706 (1974), 56
School Asbestos Litigation, In re, 789 F.2d 996 (3d Cir. 1986), 188, 216, 426, 736
Schwab v. Erie Lackawanna R. Co., 438 F.2d 62 (3d Cir. 1971), 1057
Schwartz v. Celestial Seasonings, Inc., 178 F.R.D. 545 (D. Colo. 1998), 126
Schwarzschild v. Tse, 69 F.3d 293 (9th Cir. 1995), 338
Scrap Metal Antitrust Litigation, In re, 527 F.3d 517 (6th Cir. 2008), 218
Seagate Technologies Securities Litigation, In re, 115 F.R.D. 264 (N.D. Cal. 1987), 914
Seagate Technology II Securities Litigation, In re, 156 F.R.D. 229 (N.D. Cal. 1994), 857
Seagate Technology II Securities Litigation, In re, 843 F.Supp. 1341 (N.D. Cal. 1994), 856
Sears v. Likens, 912 F.2d 889 (7th Cir. 1990), 919
S.E.C. v. Bilzerian, 378 F.3d 1100, 363 U.S. App. D.C. 143 (D.C. Cir. 2004), 1041
Securities & Exchange Commission v. Dresser Industries, Inc., 628 F.2d 1368, 202 U.S. App. D.C. 345 (D.C. Cir. 1980), 1084
Security Ins. Co. of Hartford v. Schipporeit, Inc., 69 F.3d 1377 (7th Cir. 1995), 1083
Segal v. Fifth Third Bank, N.A., 581 F.3d 305 (6th Cir. 2009), 887
Sembach v. McMahon College, Inc., 86 F.R.D. 188 (S.D. Tex. 1980), 942, 948
Serrano v. 180 Connect, Inc., 478 F.3d 1018 (9th Cir. 2007), 454
SG Cowen Securities Corp. v. United States Dist. Court for Northern Dist. of CA, 189 F.3d 909 (9th Cir. 1999), 865
Shady Grove Orthopedic Associates, P.A. v. Allstate Ins. Co., 559 U.S. 393, 130 S.Ct. 1431, 176 L.Ed.2d 311 (2010), 521

Shady Grove Orthopedic Associates, P.A. v. Allstate Ins. Co., 549 F.3d 137 (2d Cir. 2008), 521

Shelton v. Bledsoe, 775 F.3d 554 (3d Cir. 2015), 54

Shelton v. Pargo, Inc., 582 F.2d 1298 (4th Cir. 1978), 606

Shields v. Barrow, 58 U.S. 130, 17 How. 130 (1854), 1042

Shimkus v. Gersten Companies, 816 F.2d 1318 (9th Cir. 1987), **1044**

Shin v. Cobb County Bd. of Educ., 248 F.3d 1061 (11th Cir. 2001), 707

Shook v. El Paso County, 386 F.3d 963 (10th Cir. 2004), 196

Shore v. Parklane Hosiery Co., Inc., 606 F.2d 354 (2d Cir. 1979), 349

Shores v. Sklar, 647 F.2d 462 (5th Cir. 1981), 856

Shushan v. University of Colorado at Boulder, 132 F.R.D. 263 (D. Colo. 1990), **821**

Sierra Club v. Espy, 18 F.3d 1202 (5th Cir. 1994), 1082

Sierra Club v. Watt, 608 F.Supp. 305 (E.D. Cal. 1985), 1042

Silber v. Mabon, 18 F.3d 1449 (9th Cir. 1994), 376

Silicone Gel Breast Implants Products Liability Litigation, In re, 793 F.Supp. 1098 (Jud. Pan. Mult. Lit. 1992), **969**

Simer v. Rios, 661 F.2d 655 (7th Cir. 1981), 216

Simon II Litigation, In re, 211 F.R.D. 86 (E.D.N.Y. 2002), 188

Slack v. Stiner, 358 F.2d 65 (5th Cir. 1966), 441

Slanina v. William Penn Parking Corp., Inc., 106 F.R.D. 419 (W.D. Pa. 1984), 264

Smalls v. Advance America, 2008 WL 4177297 (D.S.C. 2008), 455

Smilow v. Southwestern Bell Mobile Systems, Inc., 323 F.3d 32 (1st Cir. 2003), 218, 237

Smith v. Bayer Corp., 564 U.S. 299, 131 S.Ct. 2368, 180 L.Ed.2d 341 (2011), **492**, 813

Smith v. North American Rockwell Corp. Tulsa Div., 50 F.R.D. 515 (N.D. Okla. 1970), 349

Smith v. Pennington, 352 F.3d 884 (4th Cir. 2003), 439

Smith v. Swormstedt, 57 U.S. (16 How.) 288 (1853), 19, 889

Sokaogon Chippewa Community v. Babbitt, 214 F.3d 941 (7th Cir. 2000), 1082

Sokolski v. Trans Union Corp., 178 F.R.D. 393 (E.D.N.Y. 1998), 441

Sollenbarger v. Mountain States Tel. & Tel. Co., 121 F.R.D. 417 (D.N.M. 1988), 383

Sondel v. Northwest Airlines, Inc., 56 F.3d 934 (8th Cir. 1995), 501

Sonmore v. CheckRite Recovery Services, Inc., 206 F.R.D. 257 (D. Minn. 2001), **233**

Spectrum Brands, Inc., In re, 2007 WL 1483633 (N.D. Ga. 2007), 865

Spokeo, Inc. v. Robins, 136 S. Ct. 1540, 194 L.Ed.2d 635 (2016), 71

Stambaugh v. Kansas Dept. of Corrections, 151 F.R.D. 664 (D. Kan. 1993), 58

Standard Fire Ins.Co. v. Knowles, 568 U.S. 558, 133 S. Ct. 1345, 185 L.Ed.2d 439 (2013), 458

Stanford v. Tennessee Val. Authority, 18 F.R.D. 152 (M.D. Tenn. 1955), 1108

Stanley v. United States Steel Co., 2008 WL 4225781 (E.D. Mich. 2008), 578

Star Gas Securities Litigation, In re, 2005 WL 818617 (D. Conn. 2005), 877

Stastny v. Southern Bell Tel. & Tel. Co., 628 F.2d 267 (4th Cir. 1980), 806

State v. (see opposing party)

State Farm Fire & Cas. Co. v. Tashire, 386 U.S. 523, 87 S.Ct. 1199, 18 L.Ed.2d 270 (1967), **1059**

State Farm Mut. Auto. Ins. Co. v. Campbell, 538 U.S. 408, 123 S.Ct. 1513, 155 L.Ed.2d 585 (2003), 625

Staton v. Boeing Co., 327 F.3d 938 (9th Cir. 2003), 647

Steinmetz v. Bache & Co., Inc., 71 F.R.D. 202 (S.D.N.Y.1976), 232

Stephenson v. Dow Chemical Co., 346 F.3d 19 (2d Cir. 2003), 756

Stephenson v. Dow Chemical Co., 273 F.3d 249 (2d Cir. 2001), 140, 470, 755

Stevens v. Lowder, 643 F.2d 1078 (5th Cir. 1981), 919

Stewart v. Abraham, 275 F.3d 220 (3d Cir. 2001), 85

Stewart v. Winter, 669 F.2d 328 (5th Cir. 1982), 311

Stewart Coach Industries, Inc. v. Moore, 512 F.Supp. 879 (S.D. Ohio 1981), 919

St. Jude Medical, Inc., In re, 425 F.3d 1116 (8th Cir. 2005), 414

Stolt–Nielsen S.A. v. AnimalFeeds International Corp., 559 U.S. 662, 130 S.Ct 1758, 176 L.Ed. 2d 605 (2010), 687

Stolz v. United Broth. of Carpenters & Joiners of America, Local Union No. 971, 620 F.Supp. 396 (D. Nev. 1985), 949

Stoneridge Inv. Partners, LLC v. Scientific–Atlanta, 552 U.S. 148, 128 S.Ct. 761, 169 L.Ed.2d 627 (2008), 225, 226, 861

Strykers Bay Neighborhood Council, Inc. v. City of New York, 695 F.Supp. 1531 (S.D.N.Y. 1988), 83

Stuart v. Hewlett–Packard Co., 66 F.R.D. 73 (E.D. Mich. 1975), 232

Suffolk, County of v. Long Island Lighting Co., 907 F.2d 1295 (2d Cir. 1990), 350

Suffolk, County of v. Long Island Lighting Co., 710 F.Supp. 1422 (E.D.N.Y. 1989), 347

Sugar Industry Antitrust Litigation, In re, 73 F.R.D. 322 (E.D. Pa. 1976), 384

Sullivan v. DB Investments, 667 F.3d 273 (3d Cir. 2011), 430

Sun Oil Co. v. Wortman, 486 U.S. 717, 108 S.Ct. 2117, 100 L.Ed.2d 743 (1988), 413

Supreme Tribe of Ben Hur v. Cauble, 255 U.S. 356, 41 S.Ct. 338, 65 L.Ed. 673 (1921), 448, 449

Susquehanna Corp. v. Korholz, 84 F.R.D. 316 (N.D. Ill. 1979), 939

Swann v. Charlotte–Mecklenburg Bd. of Ed., 402 U.S. 1, 91 S.Ct. 1267, 28 L.Ed.2d 554 (1971), 622

Swanson v. Citibank, N.A., 614 F.3d 400 (7th Cir. 2010), 258

Swartz v. Deutsche Bank AG, 2008 WL 534535 (W.D. Wash. 2008), 865
Sweet v. Bermingham, 65 F.R.D. 551 (S.D.N.Y. 1975), 934
Syngenta Crop Protection, Inc. v. Henson, 537 U.S. 28, 123 S.Ct. 366, 154 L.Ed.2d 368 (2002), 756
System Federation No. 91 v. Reed, 180 F.2d 991 (6th Cir. 1950), 23
Szabo v. Bridgeport Machines, Inc., 249 F.3d 672 (7th Cir. 2001), 269, 271

Talley v. Leo J. Shapiro & Associates, Inc., 713 F.Supp. 254 (N.D. Ill. 1989), 311
Tanoh v. Dow Chemical Co., 561 F.3d 945 (9th Cir. 2009), 458
Tardiff v. Knox County, 365 F.3d 1 (1st Cir. 2004), 237
Taylor v. Safeway Stores, Inc., 524 F.2d 263 (10th Cir. 1975), **104**
Taylor v. Sturgell, 553 U.S. 880, 128 S.Ct. 2161, 171 L.Ed.2d 155 (2008), 1098
Teamsters Local 445 Freight Div. Pension Fund v. Bombardier Inc., 546 F.3d 196 (2d Cir. 2008), 279
Teflon Products Liability Litigation, In re, 254 F.R.D. 354 (S.D. Iowa 2008), **37**, 142
Telectronics Pacing Systems, Inc., In re, 172 F.R.D. 271 (S.D. Ohio 1997), **166**, 427
Tellabs, Inc. v. Makor Issues & Rights, Ltd., 551 U.S. 308, 127 S.Ct. 2499, 168 L.Ed.2d 179 (2007), 864
Temple v. Synthes Corp., Ltd., 498 U.S. 5, 111 S.Ct. 315, 112 L.Ed.2d 263 (1990), 1043
Temple v. Synthes Corp., 498 U.S. 5, 111 S.Ct. 315, 112 L.Ed.2d 263 (1990), 1043
Tetracycline Cases, In re, 107 F.R.D. 719 (W.D. Mo. 1985), 299
Texas Dept. of Community Affairs v. Burdine, 450 U.S. 248, 101 S.Ct. 1089, 67 L.Ed.2d 207 (1981), 803
Thiessen v. General Electric Capital Corp., 267 F.3d 1095 (10th Cir. 2001), **827**
Thillens, Inc. v. Community Currency Exchange Ass'n of Illinois, Inc., 97 F.R.D. 668 (N.D. Ill. 1983), **890**
Thirteen Appeals Arising Out of San Juan Dupont Plaza Hotel Fire Litigation, In re, 56 F.3d 295 (1st Cir. 1995), **636**
Thorn v. Jefferson–Pilot Life Ins. Co., 445 F.3d 311 (4th Cir. 2006), 197
Thorogood v. Sears, Roebuck & Co., 624 F.3d 842 (7th Cir. 2010), 311
Ticor Title Ins. Co. v. Brown, 511 U.S. 117, 114 S.Ct. 1359, 128 L.Ed.2d 33 (1994), 204, 478
Tiesler v. Martin Paint Stores, Inc., 76 F.R.D. 640 (E.D. Pa .1977), **1052**
Tilley v. TJX Companies, Inc., 345 F.3d 34 (1st Cir. 2003), 708, 913, 914
Torres v. Shalala, 48 F.3d 887 (5th Cir. 1995), 402
Town of (see name of town)
Toyota Motor Corp. Unintended Acceleration Marketing, Sales Practices, & Products Liability Litigation, In re, 785 F. Supp. 2d 925 (C.D. Cal. 2011), 286

Triggs v. John Crump Toyota, Inc., 154 F.3d 1284 (11th Cir. 1998), 450
Truck–a–Tune, Inc. v. Re, 856 F.Supp. 77 (D. Conn. 1993), 1070
Tunstall v. Brotherhood of Locomotive Firemen & Enginemen, 148 F.2d 403 (4th Cir. 1945), 942
Tylka v. Gerber Products Co., 178 F.R.D. 493 (N.D. Ill. 1998), 223
Tyson Foods, Inc. v. Bouaphakeo, 136 S. Ct. 1036, 194 L.Ed.2d 124 (2016), 70, 231, **361**, 778

UFCW Local 1776 v. Eli Lilly & Co., 620 F.3d 121 (2d Cir. 2010), 226
Unger v. Amedisys Inc., 401 F.3d 316 (5th Cir. 2005), 224, 855
Uniondale Beer Co., Inc. v. Anheuser–Busch, Inc., 117 F.R.D. 340 (E.D.N.Y. 1987), 134
Unisys Corp. Securities Litigation, In re, 2000 WL 1367951 (E.D. Pa .2000), 851
United Airlines, Inc. v. McDonald, 432 U.S. 385, 97 S.Ct 2464, 53 L.Ed.2d 423 (1977), **709**
United National Ins. Corp. v. Jefferson Downs Corp., 220 F.R.D. 456 (M.D. La. 2003), 1055
United States v. (see opposing party)
United States Foodservice Inc. Pricing Litigation, In re, 729 F.3d 108 (2d Cir. 2013), 430
United States Industries, Inc. v. Anderson, 579 F.2d 1227 (10th Cir. 1978), 919
United States Trust Co. of New York v. Alpert, 10 F.Supp.2d 290 (S.D.N.Y. 1998), 1071
Universal Access, Inc. Securities Litigation, In re, 209 F.R.D. 379 (E.D. Tex. 2002), 870
Urethane Antitrust Litigation, In re, 768 F.3d 1245 (10th Cir. 2014), 231

Valentino v. Carter–Wallace, Inc., 97 F.3d 1227 (9th Cir. 1996), 232, 352
Vallario v. Vandehey, 554 F.3d 1259 (10th Cir. 2009), 271
Valley Drug Co. v. Geneva Pharmaceuticals, Inc., 350 F.3d 1181 (11th Cir. 2003), 140
Vancouver Women's Health Collective Soc. v. A.H. Robins Co., Inc., 820 F.2d 1359 (4th Cir. 1987), 376
Vaszlavik v. Storage Technology Corp., 175 F.R.D. 672 (D. Colo. 1997), 805
Vega v. T–Mobile USA, Inc., 564 F.3d 1256 (11th Cir. 2009), 81, 87, 271
Verizon New England v. Maine Public Utilities Com'n, 229 F.R.D. 335 (D. Me. 2005), 1082
Vermont v. Homeside Lending, Inc., 175 Vt. 239, 826 A.2d 997 (Vt. 2003), 527
Vickers v. Trainor, 546 F.2d 739 (7th Cir. 1976), 207
Vietnam Veterans Against the War v. Benecke, 63 F.R.D. 675 (W.D. Mo. 1974), 41
Vinole v. Countrywide Home Loans, Inc., 571 F.3d 935 (9th Cir. 2009), 258, 268
Visa Check/Mastermoney Antitrust Litigation, In re, 297 F.Supp.2d 503 (E.D.N.Y. 2003), 578
Visendi v. Bank of America, N.A., 733 F.3d 863 (9th Cir. 2013), 461
VMS Ltd. Partnership Securities Litigation, In re, 1995 WL 355722 (N.D. Ill. 1995), 376

Wade v. Danek Medical, Inc., 5 F.Supp.2d 379 (E.D. Va. 1998), 440

Waldo v. Lakeshore Estates, Inc., 433 F.Supp. 782 (E.D. La. 1977), 393

Wallace v. Louisiana Citizens Property Ins. Corp., 444 F.3d 697 (5th Cir. 2006), 1116

Wal-Mart Stores, Inc. v. Dukes, 564 U.S. 338, 131 S.Ct 2541, 180 L.Ed.2d 374 (2011), 5, 27, 86, **87**, 99, 106, 196, **198**, 230, 269, 271, 289, 359, 439, 476, 480, **794**, 967, 1023, 1085, 1109

Walters v. Reno, 145 F.3d 1032 (9th Cir. 1998), **191**

Warfarin Sodium Antitrust Litigation, In re, 391 F.3d 516 (3d Cir. 2004), 430, 563

Warnell v. Ford Motor Co., 189 F.R.D. 383 (N.D. Ill. 1999), 805

Waters v. Barry, 711 F.Supp. 1125 (D.D.C. 1989), 141

Watson v. Fort Worth Bank & Trust, 487 U.S. 977, 108 S.Ct. 2777, 101 L.Ed.2d 827 (1988), 806

Wausau Ins. Companies v. Gifford, 954 F.2d 1098 (5th Cir. 1992), 1070

Weaver v. Nestle USA, Inc., 2008 WL 5453734 (N.D. Cal. 2008), 455

Weaver v. Reagan, 701 F.Supp. 717 (W.D. Mo. 1988), 84

Webcraft Technologies, Inc. v. Alden Press, Inc., 228 U.S.P.Q. 182 (N.D. Ill. 1985), 914

Weber v. Goodman, 9 F.Supp.2d 163 (E.D.N.Y. 1998), 143

Weight Watchers of Philadelphia, Inc. v. Weight Watchers Intern., 53 F.R.D. 647 (E.D.N.Y. 1971), 347

Weight Watchers of Philadelphia, Inc. v. Weight Watchers Intern., Inc., 455 F.2d 770 (2d Cir. 1972), 349

Wein v. Master Collectors, Inc., 1995 WL 550475 (N.D. Ga. 1995), 154

Weiss v. Regal Collections, 385 F.3d 337 (3d Cir. 2004), 268

Weltz v. Lee, 199 F.R.D. 129 (S.D.N.Y. 2001), 877

West v. Carfax, Inc., 2009 WL 5064143 (Ohio App. 11 Dist. 2009), 575

West v. Randall, 29 F.Cas. 718 (C.C.D.R.I. 1820), 941

Wetzel v. Liberty Mut. Ins. Co., 508 F.2d 239 (3d Cir. 1975), 194

Whirlpool Corp. Front-Loading Washer Products Liability Litigation, In re, 722 F.3d 838 (6th Cir. 2013), 70, 230

White v. Alabama, 74 F.3d 1058 (11th Cir. 1996), 572

White v. National Football League, 836 F.Supp. 1458 (D. Minn. 1993), 599

Wichita & Affiliated Tribes of Oklahoma v. Hodel, 788 F.2d 765, 252 U.S. App. D.C. 140 (D.C.Cir. 1986), 1041

Wiener v. Dannon Co., Inc., 255 F.R.D. 658 (C.D. Cal. 2009), 106

Wilderness Society, The v. Kane County, Utah, 581 F.3d 1198 (10th Cir. 2009), 1043

Will v. United States, 389 U.S. 90, 88 S.Ct. 269, 19 L.Ed.2d 305 (1967), 700

William S. v. Gill, 536 F.Supp. 505 (N.D. Ill. 1982), 1053

Williams v. Jani-King of Philadelphia, 837 F.3d 314 (3d Cir. 2016), 278

Williams v. MGM-Pathe Communications Co., 129 F.3d 1026 (9th Cir. 1997), 608

Williams v. Mohawk Industries, Inc., 568 F.3d 1350 (11th Cir. 2009), 205

Williams v. United States Dist. Court, 658 F.2d 430 (6th Cir. 1981), 393

Wisconsin Dept. of Corrections v. Schacht, 524 U.S. 381, 118 S.Ct. 2047, 141 L.Ed.2d 364 (1998), 459

Wolfert ex rel. Estate of Wolfert v. Transamerica Home First, Inc., 439 F.3d 165 (2d Cir. 2006), 470

Woolen v. Surtran Taxicabs, Inc., 684 F.2d 324 (5th Cir. 1982), **1085**

Worlds of Wonder Securities Litigation, In re, 1990 WL 61951 (N.D. Cal. 1990), 414

Wright v. Collins, 766 F.2d 841 (4th Cir. 1985), 475

Wright v. Dougherty County, Ga., 358 F.3d 1352 (11th Cir. 2004), 1109

Wyandotte Nation v. City of Kansas City, Kansas, 214 F.R.D. 656 (D. Kan. 2003), 172

Wyatt By & Through Rawlins v. Poundstone, 169 F.R.D. 155 (M.D. Ala. 1995), 125

Wyatt ex rel. Rawlins v. Poundstone, 169 F.R.D. 155 (M.D. Ala. 1995), 125

Yang v. Odom, 392 F.3d 97 (3d Cir. 2004), 439

Yocupicio v. PAE Group, LLC, 795 F.3d 1057 (9th Cir. 2015), 463

Yokoyama v. Midland Nat. Life Ins. Co., 594 F.3d 1087 (9th Cir. 2010), **719**

Yorkshire v. United States I.R.S., 26 F.3d 942 (9th Cir. 1994), 1084

Zachery v. Texaco Exploration & Production, Inc., 185 F.R.D. 230 (W.D. Tex. 1999), 205

Zarate v. Younglove, 86 F.R.D. 80 (C.D. Cal. 1980), 349

Zeidman v. J. Ray McDermott & Co., Inc., 651 F.2d 1030 (5th Cir. 1981), **73**

Zemel Family Trust v. Philips Intern. Realty Corp., 205 F.R.D. 434 (S.D.N.Y .2002), 114

Zimmer Paper Products, Inc. v. Berger & Montague, P.C., 758 F.2d 86 (3d Cir. 1985), **566**

Zinser v. Accufix Research Institute, Inc., 253 F.3d 1180 (9th Cir. 2001), 170, 748

Zurn Pex Plumbing Products Liability Litigation, In re, 644 F.3d 604 (8th Cir. 2011), 293

Zylstra v. Safeway Stores, Inc., 578 F.2d 102 (5th Cir. 1978), 153

TABLE OF SECONDARY AUTHORITIES

Principal authorities are in bold.

Absmeier, Note, The Professional Objector and Revised Rule 23: Protecting Voice Rights While Limiting Objector Abuse, 24 Rev. Litig. 609 (2005), 533

American Bar Association, Model Jury Instructions: Employment Litigation (2d ed. 2005), 803

American Bar Association's Revised Model Business Corporation Act, 931

American Jurisprudence (Second), Federal Courts § 2004 (1996), 232

American Law Institute, Complex Litigation: Statutory Recommendations and Analysis (1994), 986, **1008**, 1026, 1049, 1058, 1071, 1099, 1147

American Law Institute, Principles of the Law of Aggregate Litigation (2010), 2, 472, 500, 543, 563, 572, 577, 578, 764, **1149**, **1151**

American Law Institute, Principles of Corporate Governance, 931

Anderson, The Approval and Interpretation of Consent Decrees in Civil Rights Class Action Litigation, 1983 U. Ill. L. Rev. 579 (1983), **620**

Andrews, The Personal Jurisdiction Problem Overlooked in the National Debate About "Class Action Fairness" 58 SMU L. Rev. 1313 (2005), 460

Annotation, Consumer Class Actions Based on Fraud or Misrepresentation, 53 A.L.R.3d 834 (1996), 223

Bainbridge & Gulati, How Do Judges Maximize? (The Same Way Everyone Else Does—Boundedly): Rules of Thumb in Securities Fraud Opinions, 51 Emory L.J. 83 (2002), 849

Bechtle, Administration in the MDL Transferee Court, 10 No. 2 Andrews Class Actions Litig. Rep. 26 (2003), 959

Bechtle, Multidistrict Litigation: A Judicial Perspective, For the Defense (2003), 959

Beeson, Top 15 High Court Class Action Rulings of the Past 15 Years, LAW 360 (June 29, 2015), 34

Blackwell, Securities Loophole in Need of Repair, Wash.Times (Aug. 25, 1997), 885

Boland & Liazos, The Class Action Fairness Act—Three Years Later and Counting, 9 Class Action Litig. Report 395 (2008), 455

Bone, Tyson Foods and the Future of Statistical Adjudication, 95 N.C. L. Rev. ___ (forthcoming 2017), 369

Bone & Evans, Class Certification and the Substantive Merits, 51 Duke L.J. 1251 (2002), 280

Borden, Lee, and Williams, Centripetal Forces: Multidistrict Litigation and its Parts, 75 La. L. Rev. 425 (2014), **976**

Brandt, Fairness to the Absent Members of a Defendant Class: A Proposed Revision of Rule 23, 1990 BYU L. Rev. 909 (1990), 899

Bronte, Carving at the Joint: The Precise Function of Rule 23(c)(4), 62 DePaul L. Rev. 745 (2013), 300

Brunet, Class Action Objectors: Extortionist Free Riders or Fairness Guarantors, 2003 U. Chi. Legal F. 403 (2003), 1092

Bucklo & Meites, What Every Judge Should Know About a Rule 23 Settlement (But Probably Isn't Told) 41 Litig. 18 (2015), 546

Burbank, Sean Farhang & Herbert M. Kritzer, Private Enforcement, 17 Lewis & Clark L. Rev. 637 (2013), 7, **14**

Burch, Financiers As Monitors In Aggregate Litigation, 48 Georgia Law Advocate 1 (2014), **657**

Burch, Judging Multidistrict Litigation, 90 N.Y.U. L. Rev. 71 (2015), **992**

Burch & Williams, Repeat Players in Multidistrict Litigation: The Social Network, ___ Cornell L. Rev. ___ (forthcoming 2017), 953

Burns, Decorative Figureheads: Eliminating Class Representatives in Class Actions, 42 Hastings L.J. 165 (1990), 63, **143**

Cabraser, The Class Abides: Class Actions and the "Roberts Court", 48 Akron L. Rev. 757 (2015), 288

Cabraser, The Class Action Counterreformation, 57 Stan. L. Rev. 1475 (2005), 1024, 1109

Chafee, Jr., The Thomas M. Cooley Lectures: Some Problems of Equity (1950), Univ. of Michigan Law School, **22**

Changelo, Reconciling Class Action Certification with the Civil Rights Act of 1991, 36 Colum. J.L. and Soc. Probs. 133 (2003), 359

Clermont, Solving the Puzzle of Transnational Class Actions, 90 Ind. L.J. Supp. 69 (2015), 473

Clermont & Eisenberg, CAFA Judicata: A Tale of Waste and Politics, 156 U. Pa. L. Rev. 1553 (2008), 30

Clopton, Transnational Class Actions in the Shadow of Preclusion, 90 Ind. L.J. 1387 (2015), 473

Coffee, A Primer on *Wal-Mart v. Dukes*, 80 U.S.L.W. 93 (2011), 795, 801

Coffee, Class Wars: The Dilemma of the Mass Tort Class Action, 95 Colum. L. Rev. 1343 (1995), 154, 183, 530, **538**, **760**, 972

Coffee, The Regulation of Entrepreneurial Litigation: Balancing Fairness and Efficiency in the Large Class Action, 54 U. Chi. L. Rev. 877 (1987), 503

Coffee & Heur, Class Certification: Developments Over the Last Five Years 2005–2010, 11 Class Action Litig. Report: Special Report (2010), 861

Cohen, Mass Tort Litigation After *Amchem*, ALI–ABA Course on Civil Practice and Litigation Techniques in the Federal Courts 269 (1998), 726

Comment, A Catalyst for Reforming Self-Transfer in Multidistrict Litigation: Lexecon, Inc. v. Milberg Weiss, 72 St. John's L. Rev. 623 (1998), 985

Comment, Attorney's Fees and Reversionary Fund Settlements in Small Claims Consumer Class Actions, 50 UCLA L. Rev. 879 (2003), 608

Comment, Bifurcation of Liability and Damages in Rule 23(b)(3) Class Actions: History, Policy, Problem, and a Solution, 36 Sw. L.J. 743 (1982), 358

Comment, Capacity and Class Actions Under Federal Rule 23.2, 61 B.U. L. Rev. 713 (1981), 950

Comment, Catch–23(b)(1)(B): The Dilemma of Using the Mandatory Class Action to Resolve the Problem of the Mass Tort Case, 40 Emory L.J. 665 (1991), 183

Comment, Compulsory Joinder of Classes Under Rule 19, 58 U. Chi. L. Rev. 1453 (1991), 1048

Comment, Defendant Class Actions: The Failure of Rule 23 and a Proposed Solution, 38 UCLA L. Rev. 223 (1990), 889, 914

Comment, Defendant Class Certification: The Difficulties Under Rule 23(b)(2) and the Rule 65(d) Solution, 8 N.Ill.U. L. Rev. 143 (1987), 914

Comment, Federal Rule of Civil Procedure 23(a)(3) Typicality Requirement: The Superfluous Prerequisite to Maintaining a Class Action, 42 Ohio St. L.J. 797 (1981), 115

Comment, Fraud-on-the-Market Theory and Thinly-Traded Securities Under Rule 10b–5: How Does A Court Decide If a Stock Market Is Efficient?, 25 Wake Forest L. Rev. 223 (1990), 855

Comment, Getting Title VII Back on Track: Leaving *Allison* Behind for the Robinson Line, 17 BYU J. Pub. L. 411 (2003), 359

Comment, Maintaining Standing in a Shareholder Derivative Action, 28 U.C. Davis L. Rev. 343 (2004), 925

Comment, Mandatory Notice and Defendant Class Actions: Resolving the Paradox of Identity Between Plaintiffs and Defendants, 40 Emory L.J. 611 (1991), 898

Comment, Rebutting the *Levinson* Presumption of Reliance: The Consistency and Relevancy of Enquiring Into a Plaintiff's Conduct in Certain Rule 10b–5 Fraud on the Market Cases, 61 U. Colo. L. Rev. 625 (1990), 853

Comment, Regulation Through Litigation 304 (W. Kip Viscusi, ed. 2002), 183

Comment, The Fraud-Created-The-Market Theory: The Presumption of Reliance in the Primary Issue Context, 60 U. Cin. L. Rev. 495 (1991), 856

Comment, The Judicial Panel on Multidistrict Litigation: Time for Rethinking, 140 U. Pa. L. Rev. 711 (1991), 953

Committee on Rules of Practice and Procedure of the Judicial Conference of the United States, Preliminary Draft of Proposed Amendments to the Federal Rules of Appellate, Bankruptcy, Civil and Criminal Procedure (Aug. 2016), 609, 709

Cooper, The (Cloudy) Future of Class Actions, 40 Ariz. L. Rev. 923 (1998), **1156**

Cover, For James Wm. Moore: Some Reflections on a Reading of the Rules, 84 Yale L.J. 718 (1975), 723

Daly & Etzold, 2015 Securities Litigation Study (Pricewaterhouse Coopers LLP 2016), 864

Dam, Class Action Notice: Who Needs It?, 1974 S. Ct. Rev. 97, 375

Dansider, The Next Big Thing for Litigators, 37 Md. B.J. 12 (July/Aug. 2004), 754

Davis, Toward the Proper Role for Mass Tort Class Actions, 77 Or. L. Rev. 157 (1998), 781

Dayton, The Myth of Alternative Dispute Resolution in the Federal Courts, 76 Iowa L. Rev. 889 (1991), 674

Delgado, Fairness and Formality: Minimizing the Risk of Prejudice in Alternative Dispute Resolution, 1985 Wis. L. Rev. 1359 (1985), 674

Delikat & Kleiner, Comparing Litigation and Arbitration of Employment Disputes: Do Claimants Better Vindicate Their Rights in Litigation?, 6 A.B.A. Litig. Sec. Conflict Mgmt. 1 (2003), 675

Developments in the Law: Multiparty Litigation in the Federal Courts, 71 Harv. L. Rev. 874 (1958), **1154**

Developments in the Law: Class Actions, 89 Harv. L. Rev. 1318 (1976), 624

Developments in the Law—The Paths of Civil Litigation, 113 Harv. L. Rev. 1827 (2000), 647

Dodge, Facilitative Judging: Organizational Design in Mass-Multidistrict Litigation, 64 Emory L.J. 329 (2014), **971**

Downs, Federal Class Actions: Diminished Protection for the Class and the Case for Reform, 73 Neb. L. Rev. 646 (1994), 530, 574, 613

Drahozal, Arbitration Costs and Forum Accessibility: Empirical Evidence, 41 U. Mich. J.L. Reform 813 (2007–2008), 674

Drake & Strickland, Chapter 11 Reorganizations (Thomson/West, 2d ed. 2002), **1117**

Eisenberg & Hill, Arbitration & Litigation of Employment Claims: An Empirical Comparison, 58 Disp. Res. J. 44 (Nov. 2003–Jan. 2004), 675

Eisenberg & Miller, Attorneys' Fees in Class Action Settlements: 1993–2008 (2009), 648

Elhauge, How Italian Colors Guts Private Antitrust Enforcement by Replacing It with Ineffective Forms of Arbitration, 38 Fordham Int'l L.J. 771 (2015), 696

Erichson, Informal Aggregation: Procedural and Ethical Implications of Coordination Among Counsel in Related Lawsuits, 50 Duke L.J. 381 (2000), 1008

Erichson & Zipursky, Consent Versus Closure, 96 Cornell L. Rev. 265 (2011), 973, 1152

Fallon, Graybill & Wynne, Bellwether Trials in Multidistrict Litigation, 82 Tul L. Rev. 2323 (2008), 987

Feinberg, Lecture, 56 Ala. L. Rev. 543 (2004), 674

Feinberg, Creative Use of ADR: The Court-Appointed Special Settlement Master, 59 Alb. L. Rev. 881 (1996), 669

Feinberg, Reporting from the Front Line—One Mediator's Experience With Mass Torts, 31 Loy. L.A. L. Rev. 359 (1998), 783

Ferrara, Abikoff & Gansler, Shareholder Derivative Litigation (1995), 932

Finegan, Five Key Considerations for a Successful International Notice Program, 78 Class Action Litig. Report 2611 (2010), 376

Finegan, On Demand Media Could Change the Future of Best Practicable Notice, 9 Class Action Litig. Report 307 (2008), 385

Fisch, Class Action Reform: Lessons from Securities Litigation, 39 Ariz. L. Rev. 533 (1997), 877

Fiss, Against Settlement, 93 Yale L.J. 1073 (1984), 4, 674

Fiss, The Political Theory of the Class Action, 53 Wash. & Lee L. Rev. 21 (1996), 7

Fitzpatrick, Do Class Action Lawyers Make Too Little?, 158 U. Pa. L. Rev. 2043 (2010), 648

Fitzpatrick, The End of Class Actions?, 57 Ariz. L. Rev. 161, 163 (2015), 696

Fletcher, The Comparative Rights Indispensable Sovereigns, 40 Gonz. L. Rev. 1 (2005), 1041

Fletcher, The Structure of Standing, 98 Yale L.J. 221 (1988), 72

Freer, Avoiding Duplicative Litigation: Rethinking Plaintiff Autonomy and the Court's Roles in Defining the Litigation Unit, 50 U. Pitt. L. Rev. 809 (1989), 503

Freer, Exodus from and Transformation of American Civil Litigation, 65 Emory L.J. 1491 (2016), 956

Freer, Interlocutory Review of Class Action Certification Decisions: A Preliminary Empirical Study of Federal and State Experience, 35 W. St. U. L. Rev. 13 (2007), 709

Friedenthal, Kane & Miller, Civil Procedure (4th ed. 2005), 483, 1043, 1057

Gerard & Johnson, The Role of the Objector in Class Action Settlements: A Case Study of the General Motors Truck "Side Saddle" Fuel Tank Litigation, 31 Loy. L.A. L. Rev. 409 (1998), 530

Greenberg, Civil Rights Class Actions: Procedural Means of Obtaining Substance, 39 Ariz. L. Rev. 575 (1997), 614

Grillo, The Mediation Alternative: Process Dangers for Women, 100 Yale L.J. 1545 (1991), 674

Gulliver, Takeaways from Decisions Following Campbell-Ewald, LAW 360 (Aug. 9, 2016), 69

H.R. 1927—Fairness in Class Action Litigation & Furthering Asbestos Claim Transparency Act of 2016, 72

Hancock, Calif. Court Mandates Disclosure of Third-Party Funding in Class Actions, LAW.COM (Jan. 24, 2017), 667

Harkins, Jr., Federal Rule 23—The Early Years, 39 Ariz. L. Rev. 705 (1997), 20

Hart, Will Employment Discrimination Class Actions Survive?, 37 Akron L. Rev. 813 (2004), 27, 356, 621

Haudek, The Settlement and Dismissal of Stockholder's Actions, Part II: The Settlement, 23 Sw. L.J. 765 (1969), 939

Hazard, The Futures Problem, 148 U.Pa. L. Rev. 1901 (2000), 763

Hazard, Gedid & Sowle, An Historical Analysis of the Binding Effect of Class Suits, 146 U. Pa. L. Rev. 1849 (1998), 17, 121, 463

Hazard & Hodes, The Law of Lawyering: A Handbook on the Model Rules of Professional Conduct (3d ed. 2011 supplement), 396

Henderdon, Reconciling the Juridical Links Doctrine with the Federal Rules of Criminal Procedure and Article III, 67 U. Chi. L. Rev. 1347 (2000), 898

Hensler, As Time Goes By: Asbestos Litigation After Amchem and Ortiz, 80 Tex. L. Rev. 1899 (2002), 564

Hensler, Class Action Dilemmas: Pursuing Public Goals for Private Gain, RAND Institute for Civil Justice 28 (1999), 27

Hensler, Third-Party Financing of Class Action Litigation In The United States: Will The Sky Fall?, 63 DePaul L. Rev. 499 (2014), 649

Hensler & Peterson, Understanding Mass Personal Injury Litigation: A Socio–Legal Analysis, 59 Brook. L. Rev. 961 (1993), 727, 752

Herr, Multidistrict Litigation (1986), 954

Herrmann, Self-Transfers Gone After "*Lexecon*"?, N.Y.L.J. (Nov. 23, 1998), 986

Herrmann, To MDL or Not to MDL? A Defense Perspective, Litigation (Summer 1988), 968

Hermann, Ritz, & Larson, Statewide Coordinated Proceedings: State Court Analogues to the Federal MDL Process (2004), 1000

Herzog, Fraud Created the Market: An Unwise and Unwarranted Extension of Section 10(b) and Rule 10b–5, 63 Geo. Wash. L. Rev. 359 (1995), 856

Hilsee, Global Class Actions: Lasting Peace or Ticking Time Bombs, 11 Class Action Litig. Report 394 (2010), 376

Hilsee, Nationwide Class Actions: Shine a Light on (Another) Bad Notice, 9 Class Action Litig. Report 113 (2008), 385

Hilsee, Wheatman & Intrepido, Do You Really Want Me to Know My Rights, The Ethics Behind Due Process in Class Action Notice Is More Than Just Plain Language: A Desire to Actually Inform, 18 Geo. J. Legal Ethics 1359 (2005), 385

Howard, Arbitrating Claims of Employment Discrimination, What Really Does Happen? What Really Should Happen?, Disp. Res. J. 40 (Oct.–Dec.2005), 675

Issacharoff, Class Action Conflicts, 30 U.C. Davis L. Rev. 805 (1997), 183

Issacharoff, Governance and Legitimacy in the Law of Class Actions, 1999 Sup. Ct. Rev. 337 (1999), 154

Issacharoff, Private Claims, Aggregate Rights, 2008 Sup. Ct. Rev. 183 (2008), **1133**

Issacharoff, "Shocked": Mass Torts and Aggregate Asbestos Litigation After Amchem and Ortiz, 80 Tex. L. Rev. 1925 (2002), 564

Issacharoff, The Vexing Problem of Reliance in Consumer Class Actions, 74 Tul. L. Rev. 1633 (2000), 227

Issacharoff, When Substance Mandates Procedure: Martin v. Wilks and the Rights of Vested Incumbents in Civil Rights Consent Decrees, 77 Cornell L. Rev. 189 (1992), 1098

Issacharoff & Klonoff, The Public Value of Settlement, 78 Fordham L. Rev. 1177 (2009), 4, 623, 674

Kahan & Silberman, Matsushita and Beyond: The Role of State Courts in Class Actions Involving Exclusive Federal Claims, 1996 Sup. Ct. Rev. 219 (1996), 520

Kahan & Silberman, The Inadequate Search for "Adequacy" in Class Actions: A Critique of Epstein v. MCA, Inc., 73 N.Y.U. L. Rev. 765 (1998), 473

Kane, Of Carrots and Sticks: Evaluating the Role of the Class Action Lawyer, 66 Tex. L. Rev. 385 (1987), 531, 612

Kennedy, The Supreme Court Meets the Bride of Frankenstein: *Phillips Petroleum Co. v. Shutts* and the State Multistate Class Action, 334 U. Kan. L. Rev. 255 (1985), 482

Kinsella & Gorman, Reality Check: The State of New Media Options for Class Action Notice, 11 Class Action Litig. Report 187 (2010), 576

Klement, Who Should Guard the Guardians? A New Approach for Monitoring Class Action Lawyers, 21 Rev. Litig. 25 (2002), 542

Klock, What Will It Take to Label Participation in a Deceptive Scheme to Defraud Buyers of Securities a Violation of Section 10(b)? The Disastrous Result and Reasoning of *Stoneridge*, 58 Kan. L. Rev. 309 (2009), 861

Klonoff, Antitrust Class Actions: Chaos in the Courts, 11 Stan. J.L. Bus. and Fin. 1 (2005), 219

Klonoff, Class Actions for Monetary Relief Under Rule 23(b)(1)(A) and (B): Does Due Process Require Notice and Opt-Out Rights?, 82 Geo. Wash. L. Rev. 798 (2014), 183, 387

Klonoff, Class Actions in the Year 2026: A Prognosis, 65 Emory L.J. 1569 (2016), 33, 114, 350, 575, 600, 609, 848

Klonoff, Class Actions Part II: A Respite from the Decline, 92 N.Y.U. L. Rev. ___ (forthcoming October 2017), 102, 795

Klonoff, The Adoption of a Class Action Rule: Some Issues for Mississippi to Consider, 24 Miss. C. L. Rev., 261 (2005), 413, 452

Klonoff, The Decline of Class Actions, 90 Wash. U. L. Rev. 729 (2013), 30, 42, 83, 102, 204, 216, 227, 302, 709

Klonoff, The Judiciary's Flawed Application of Rule 23's "Adequacy of Representation" Requirement, 2004 Mich. St. L. Rev. 671 (2004), 115, 125, 133, 135, 152, 600

Klonoff & Herrman, The Class Action Fairness Act: An Ill–Conceived Approach to Class Settlements, 80 Tul. L. Rev. 1695 (2006), 608

Klonoff, Hermann & Harrison, Making Class Actions Work: The Untapped Potential of the Internet, 69 U. Pitt. L. Rev. 727 (2008), 385, 575

Koniak, Feasting While the Widow Weeps: Georgine v. Amchem Products, Inc., 80 Cornell L. Rev. 1045 (1995), 482, **610**

Koniak, How Like a Winter? The Plight of Absent Class Members Denied Adequate Representation, 79 Notre Dame L. Rev. 1787 (2004), 473

Koniak & Cohen, Under Cloak of Settlement, 82 Va. L. Rev. 1051 (1996), 614

Kozel & Rosenberg, Solving the Nuisance-Value Settlement Problem: Mandatory Summary Judgment, 90 Va. L. Rev. 1849 (2004), 338

Kramer, Class Actions and Jurisdictional Boundaries: Choice of Law in Complex Litigation, 71 N.Y.U. L. Rev. 547 (1996), 426

Krebs, Comcast v. Behrend: The Class Action Channel Is Still Scrambled, 16 Duq. Bus. L.J. 83 (2013), 288

Kyle, The Mechanics of Motion Practice Before the Judicial Panel on Multidistrict Litigation, 175 F.R.D. 589 (1997), 953

Landers, Of Legalized Blackmail and Legalized Theft: Consumer Class Actions and the Substance–Procedure Dilemma, 47 S. Cal. L. Rev. 842 (1974), **11**

Langevoort, Theories, Assumptions, and Securities Regulation: Market Efficiency Revisited, 140 U. Pa. L. Rev. 851 (1992), 854

Lawyers Look to the Future of Toxic Torts, See New Claims, New Plaintiffs, New Defendants, 24 Toxics L. Reporter 1331 (2009), 754

Lee & Willging, Fed. Judicial Ctr., Impact of the Class Action Fairness Act on the Federal Courts; Preliminary Findings from Phase Two's Pre-CAFA Sample of Diversity Class Actions (Nov. 2008), 458

Lee & Willging, Fed. Judicial Ctr., The Impact of the Class Action Fairness Act of 2005 on the Federal Courts: Fourth Interim Report to the Judicial Conference Advisory Committee on Civil Rules (Apr. 2008), 458, 751, 821

Leubsdorf, Class Actions at the Cloverleaf, 39 Ariz. L. Rev. 453 (1997), 6, **723**

Levy, Complex Multidistrict Litigation and the Federal Courts, 40 Fordham L. Rev. 41 (1971), 967

Lewis & Norman, Litigating Employment Discrimination and Civil Rights Cases (2005), 798, 803

Lieberman & Henry, Lessons from the Alternative Dispute Resolution Movement, 53 U. Chi. L. Rev. 424 (1986), 668

Lilly, Modeling Class Actions: The Representative Suit as an Analytical Tool, 81 Neb. L. Rev. 1008 (2003), 17, 900

Lindemann & Grossman, Employment Discrimination Law (4th ed. 2007, Supp. 2009), 794, 800

Loss, Securities Regulation (2d ed. 1961), 836

Lopatka & Smith, Class Action Professional Objectors: What to Do About Them?, 39 Fla. St. U. L. Rev. 865 (2012), 609

Louisell & Hazard, Pleading and Procedure: State and Federal (1962), 941

Mabey & Zisser, Improving Treatment of Future Claims: The Unfinished Business Left by the Manville Amendments, 69 Am. Bankr. L. J. 487 (1995), **1118**

Macey & Miller, The Plaintiffs' Attorney's Role in Class Action and Derivative Litigation: Economic Analysis and Recommendations for Reform, 58 U. Chi. L. Rev. 1 (1991), 125, 612, 924

Maclin, Strategies and Options for Defending Class Actions, Practical Litigator (Sept. 1998), **260**

Main, Traditional Equity and Contemporary Procedure, 78 Wash. L. Rev. 429 (2003), 19

Maltby, Employment Arbitration and Workplace Justice, 38 U.S.F. L. Rev. 105 (2003), 675

Malveaux, Class Actions at the Crossroads: An Answer to *Wal-Mart v. Dukes*, 5 Harv. L. & Policy Rev. 375 (2011) 476, 802, 803

Malveaux, Front Loading and Heavy Lifting: How Pre-Dismissal Discovery Can Address the Detrimental Effect of *Iqbal* on Civil Rights Cases, 14 Lewis & Clark L. Rev. 65 (2010), 258

Malveaux, How Goliath Won: The Future Implications of Dukes v. Wal-Mart, 106 NW. U. L. Rev. Colloquy 34 (2011), 801

Malveaux, Is It the "Real Thing"? How Coke's One-Way Binding Arbitration May Bridge the Divide Between Litigation and Arbitration, 2009 J. Disp. Resol. 77 (2009), 675

Malveaux, Statutes of Limitations: A Policy Analysis in the Context of Reparations Litigation, 74. Geo. Wash. L. Rev. 68 (2005), 438

Malveaux & Webber, Making It Happen: Class Certification in Employment Discrimination Cases, The Employee Advocate 51 (Fall 2002), 359

Manual for Complex Litigation, Federal Judicial Center (various editions), 2, **36**, 41, 42, 264, 265, **266**, 280, **298**, 315, 318, 331, **334**, 338, **345**, 372, **375**, 383, **384**, 386, **576**, 577, 598, 606, 608, 632, 645, **747**, 972, 985, 986, **1004**

Marcus, Confronting the Consolidation Conundrum, 1995 BYU L. Rev. 879, 1109

Matthews, Derivative Suits and the Similarly Situated Shareholder Requirement, 8 DePaul Bus. L. J. 1 (1995), 935

McGovern, Resolving Mature Mass Tort Litigation, 69 B. U. L. Rev. 659 (1989), 751

McGovern, Rethinking Cooperation Among Judges in Mass Tort Litigation, 44 UCLA L. Rev. 1851 (1997), 1008

McGuire, The Death Knell for *Eisen*: Why the Class Action Analysis Should Include and Assessment of the Merits, 168 F.R.D. 366 (1996), 280

McKenzie, The Mass Tort Bankruptcy: A Pre-History, 5 J. Tort L. 59 (2012), 1135

McNamara, Reexamining the Seventh Amendment Argument Against Issue Certification, 34 Pace L. Rev. 1041 (2014), 359

Menkel-Meadow, Ethics and the Settlement of Mass Torts: When the Rules Meet the Road, 80 Cornell L. Rev. 1159 (1995), 534

Menkel-Meadow, When Dispute Begets Resolution Disputes of its Own: Conflicts Among Dispute Professionals, 44 UCLA L. Rev. 1871 (1997), **668**

Miller, Conflicts of Interest in Class Action Litigation: An Inquiry Into the Appropriate Standard, 2003 U. Chi. Legal F. 581 (2003), 142

Miller, Review of the Merits in Class Action Certification, 33 Hofstra L. Rev. 51 (2004), 270

Miller & Crump, Jurisdiction and Choice of Law in Multistate Class Actions After Petroleum v. Shutts, 96 Yale L.J. 1 (1986), 460, 503

Minow, Judge for the Situation: Judge Jack Weinstein, Creator of Temporary Administrative Agencies, 97 Colum. L. Rev. 2010 (1997), **339**

Monaghan, Antisuit Injunctions and Preclusion Against Nonresident Class Members, 98 Colum. L. Rev 1148 (1998), 473

Moore, Moore's Federal Practice (various editions), 916, 941, 949

Moore, Moore's Federal Rules Pamphlet (various editions), 1041

Morawetz, Bargaining, Class Representation, and Fairness, 54 Ohio St. L.J. 1 (1993), **535**

Morrison, The Inadequate Search for "Adequacy" in Class Actions: A Brief Rejoinder to Professors Kahan and Silberman, 735 N.Y.U. L. Rev. 1179 (1998), 116

Mullenix, Back to the Futures: Privatizing Future Claims Resolution, 148 U. Pa. L. Rev. 1919 (2000), 763

Mullenix, Class Actions, Personal Jurisdiction, and Plaintiffs' Due Process: Implications for Mass Tort Litigation, 28 U.C. Davis L. Rev. 871 (1995), 413

Mullenix, Class Actions in the Gulf South Symposium: Abandoning the Federal Class Action Ship: Is There Smoother Sailing for Class Actions in Gulf Waters?, 74 Tul. L. Rev. 1709 (2000), 777

Mullenix, Getting to *Shutts*, 46 U. Kan. L. Rev. 727 (1998), 478

Mullenix, Mass Tort as Public Law Litigation: Paradigm Misplaced, 88 Nw. U. L. Rev. 579 (1994), 778

Mullenix, Nine Lives: The Punitive Damage Class, 58 U. Kan. L. Rev. 845 (2010), 188

Mullenix, Standing and Other Dispositive Motions After *Amchem* and *Ortiz*: The Problem of "Logically Antecedent" Inquiries, 2004 Mich. St. L. Rev. 703 (2004), 763

Mullenix & Stewart, The September 11th Victim Compensation Fund: Fund Approaches to Resolving Mass Tort Litigation, 9 Conn. Ins. L.J. 121 (2002/2003), 783

Murdock, Corporate Governance, The Role of Special Litigation Committees, 68 Wash. L. Rev. 79 (1993), 932

Murphy, The Intersystem Class Settlement: Of Comity, Consent and Collusion, 47 U. Kan. L. Rev. 413 (1999), 520

Nagareda, Class Certification in the Age of Aggregate Proof, 84 N.Y.U. L. Rev. 97 (2009), 100

Nagareda, In the Aftermath of the Mass Tort Class Action, 85 Geo. L.J. 295 (1996), 782

Nagareda, Punitive Damage Class Actions and the Baseline of Tort, 36 Wake Forest L. Rev. 943 (2001), 188

Newberg & Conte, Newberg on Class Actions (various editions), 240, **253**

Newman, Herrmann & Ritts, Basic Truths: The Implications of the Fraud-on-the-Market Theory for Evaluating the "Misleading" and "Materiality" Elements of Securities Fraud Claims, 20 J. Corp. L. 571 (1995), 848

Note, Abuse in Plaintiff Class Action Settlements: The Need for a Guardian During Pretrial Settlement Negotiations, 84 Mich. L. Rev. 308 (1985), 530, 612

Note, "Adrift on an Unchartered Sea": A Survey of Section 1404(a) Transfer in the Federal System, 67 N.Y.U. L. Rev. 612 (1992), 1114

Note, Capacity and Class Actions Under Federal Rule 23.2, 61 B.U. L. Rev. 713 (1981), 950

Note, *Castano v. American Tobacco Co.*: Class Treatment of Mass Torts is Going Up in Smoke, 24 N. Ky. L. Rev. 673 (1997), 428

Note, Certification of Defendant Classes Under Rule 23(b)(2), 84 Colum. L. Rev. 1371 (1984), 914, 920, 921, 914

Note, Class Actions in the Asbestos Context: Balancing the Due Process Considerations Implicated by the Right to Opt Out, 70 Tex. L. Rev. 211 (1991), 318

Note, Class Certification in Mass Accident Cases Under Rule 23(b)(1), 96 Harv. L. Rev. 1143 (1983), 164

Note, Class Standing and the Class Representative, 94 Hav. L. Rev. 1637 (1981), 72

Note, Compulsory Party Joinder and Tribal Sovereignty Immunity: A Proposal to Modify Federal Courts' Application of Rule 19 To Cases Involving Absent Tribes As "Necessary" Parties, 56 Okla. L. Rev. 931 (2003), 1041

Note, Consent Waivers in Non-Class Aggregate Settlements: Respecting Risk Preference in a Transactional Adjudication Model, 22 Geo. J. Legal Ethics 677 (2009), 1154

Note, Constrained Individualism in Group Litigation: Requiring Class Members to Make a Good Cause Showing Before Opting Out of a Federal Class Action, 100 Yale L.J. 745 (1990), 378

Note, Defendant Class Actions, 91 Harv. L. Rev. 630 (1978), 897

Note, Developments in the Law: Class Actions, 89 Harv. L. Rev. 1318 (1976), 307, 335

Note, Developments in the Law: Multiparty Litigation in the Federal Courts, 71 Harv. L. Rev. 874 (1958), 1051

Note, Due Process: Accuracy or Opportunity? 65. S. Cal. L. Rev. 2705 (1992), 482

Note, Evading Friendly Fire: Achieving Class Certification After the Civil Act of 1991, 100 Colum. L. Rev. 1847 (2000), 359

Note, Fast and Loose Litigants in Court: Carnegie v. Household International, Inc., and the End of Settlement Classes, 84 Tex. L. Rev. 541 (2005), 563

Note, In-Kind Class Action Settlements, 109 Harv. L. Rev. 810 (1996), 599

Note, Locating Investment Asymmetries and Optimal Deterrence in the Mass Tort Class Action, 117 Harv. L. Rev. 2665 (2004), 734

Note, Mechanical and Constitutional Problems in the Certification of Mandatory Multistate Mass Tort Class Actions Under Rule 23, 49 Brook. L. Rev. 517 (1983), 165

Note, Notice and the Protection of Class Members' Interests, 69 S. Cal. L. Rev. 1121 (1996), 574

Note, Offensive Assertion of Collateral Estoppel by Persons Opting Out of a Class, 31 Hastings L.J. 1189 (1980), 492

Note, On the Outside Seeking In: Must Intervenors Demonstrate Standing to Join a Lawsuit?, 52 Duke L.J. 455 (2002), 1082

Note, Opt-In Class Action Under the FLSA, EPA, and ADEA: What Does It Mean to be "Similarly Situated"?, 38 Suffolk U. L. Rev. 95 (2004), 827

Note, Rule 24(a) Intervention of Right: Why the Federal Courts Should Require Standing to Intervene, 36 Loy. L. A. L. Rev. 527 (2002), 1082

Note, Securities Fraud or Mere Puffery: Refinement of the Corporation Puffery Defense, 51 Vand. L. Rev. 1049 (1998), 849

Note, Settlement Class Actions and "Mere-Exposure" Future Claimants: Problems in Mass Toxic Tort Liability, 47 Drake L. Rev. 113 (1998), 763

Note, Severance Packages: Judicial Use of Federal Rule of Civil Procedure 23(c)(4)(A), 91 Geo. L.J. 219 (2002), 302

Note, Standing on Its Head: The Problem of Future Claimants in Mass Tort Class Actions, 77 Tex. L. Rev. 215 (1998), 763

Note, The Due Process Right to Opt Out of a Class Action, 73 N.Y.U. L. Rev. 480 (1998), 377

Note, The "Need Requirement": A Barrier to Class Actions Under Rule 23(b)(2), 67 Geo. L.J. 1211 (1979), 207

Note, The Path to Preclusion: Federal Injunctive Relief Against Nationwide Classes in State Court, 54 Duke L.J. 221 (2004), 503

Note, The Plight of the Private Securities Litigation Reform Act in the Post-Enron Era: The Ninth Circuit's Interpretation of Materiality in *Employer-Teamster v America West*, 2004 BYU L. Rev. 863 (2004), 850

Note, The Rules Enabling Act and the Limits of Rule 23, 111 Harv. L. Rev. 2294 (1998), 562

Note, The September 11 Victim Compensation Fund: Legislative Justice Sui Generis, 59 N.Y.U. Ann. Surv. Am. L. 513 (2004), 783

Note, There is Always a Need: The Necessity Doctrine and Class Certification Against Government Agencies, 103 Mich. L. Rev. 1018 (2005), 207

Note, When Futures Fight Back: For Long–Latency Injury Claimants in Mass Tort Class Actions, Are Asymptomatic Subclasses the Cure to the Disease?, 72 Fordham L. Rev. 1219 (2004), 763

Note, Wielding the Sledgehammer: Legislative Solutions for Class Action Jurisdictional Reform, 75 N.Y.U L. Rev. 507 (2000), 502, 503

Note, Which Came First, The Fraud of the Market: Is the Fraud-Created-the-Market Theory Valid Under Rule 10b–5?, 69 Fordham L. Rev. 2611 (2001), 856

Note, Who Can Tell the Futures? Protecting Settlement Class Action Members Without Notice, 85 Va. L. Rev. 531 (1999), 116

Note, Why Bankruptcy "Related To" Jurisdiction Should Not Reach Mass Tort Nondebtor Codefendants, 73 N.Y.U.L. Rev. 1627 (1998), 1144

Oquendo, Six Degrees of Separation: From Derivative Suits to Shareholders Class Actions, 48 Wake Forest L. Rev. 643 (2013), 940

Ostolaza & Hartmann, The Judicial Panel on Multidistrict Litigation and Coordinating Multijurisdicitional Disputes, 16 No. 4 Prac. Litigation 23 (2005), 959, 1000

Ovington, IV, SLUSA Preclusion of State Law Investor Class Actions, 34 Rev. Banking & Fin. L. 36 (2014), 888

Page, Introduction: Reexamining the Standards for Certification of Antitrust Class Actions, 21 Antitrust 53 (2007), 219

Painter, Responding to a False Alarm: Federal Preemption of State Securities Fraud Causes of Action, 84 Cornell L. Rev. 1 (1998), 885

Parkinson, Comcast Corp v. Behrend and Chaos on the Ground, 81 U. Chi. L. Rev. 1213 (2014), 288

Pasquale, Combustion Engineering: Setting Limits on Pre-Packaged Asbestos Bankruptcies, 24–Feb. Am. Bankr. Inst. J. 36 (2005), 1135

Perino, Class Action Chaos: The Theory of the Core and an Analysis of Opt-Out Rights in Mass Tort Class Actions, 46 Emory L.J. 85 (1997), 412

Petts, Hildbold, & Kim, Recent Developments in Related-To Jurisdiction Under Pacor, 29 Am. Bankr. Inst. L. Rev. 22 (2010), 1143

Phillips, Schaerr & Abraham, Rescuing Multidistrict Litigation From the Altar of Expediency, 1997 BYU L. Rev. 821 YR, 985

Piar, The Uncertain Future of Title VII Class Actions After the Civil Rights Acts of 1991, 2001 BYU L. Rev. 305 (2001), 358, 813

Plevin, Ebert & Epley, Pre-Packaged Asbestos Bankruptcies: A Flawed Solution, 44 S. Tex. L. Rev. 883 (2003), 1126

Redish, Julian & Zyontz, Cy Pres Relief and the Pathologies of the Modern Class Action: A Normative and Empirical Analysis, 62 Fla. L. Rev. 617 (2010), 632

Redish & Kastanek, Settlement Class Actions, the Case-or-Controversy Requirement, and the Nature of the Adjudicatory Process, 73 U. Chi. L. Rev. 545 (2006), 563

Resnick, Bankruptcy as a Vehicle for Resolving Enterprise-Threatening Mass Tort Liability, 148 U. Pa. L. Rev. 2045 (2000), 1121

Resnick, Lessons in Federalism from the 1960s Class Action Rules and the 2005 Class Action Fairness Act, 156 U. Pa. L. Rev. 1929 (2008), 29

Rhodes, The Judicial Panel on Multidistrict Litigation: Time for Rethinking, 140 U. Pa. L. Rev. 711 (1991), 985

Rice & Davis, The Future of Mass Tort Claims: Comparison of Settlement Class Action to Bankruptcy Treatment of Mass Tort Claims, 50 S.C. L. Rev. 405 (1999), 1123

Richey, Tilted Scales of Justice? The Consequences of Third-Party Financing of American Litigation, 63 Emory L.J. 489 (2013), 667

Richman, Transnational Class Actions and Judgment Recognition, 11 Class Action Litig. Report 583 (2010), 376

Richmond, Class Actions and Ex Parte Communications: Can We Talk?, 69 Mo. L. Rev. 813 (2003), 398

Rivlin & Potts, Proposed Rule Changes to Federal Civil Procedure May Introduce New Challenges in Environmental Class Action Litigation, 27 Harv. Envtl. L. Rev. 519 (2003), 27

Robinson & Calcagnie, To Join an MDL . . . Or Not, 37 Trial 7 (2001), 968

Rosenberg, The Causal Connection in Mass Exposure Cases: A "Public Law" Vision of the Tort System, 97 Harv. L. Rev. 849 (1984), 763, 778

Rosenberg, The Regulatory Advantage of Class Action, in Regulation Through Litigation 244 (W. Kip Viscusi, ed. 2002), 183

Ross, Do Conflicts Between Class Members Vitiate Class Action Securities Fraud Suits?, 70 St. John's L. Rev. 209 (1996), 857

Rothstein & Willging, Managing Class Action Litigation: A Pocket Guide for Judges, Federal Judicial Center (3d ed. 2010), **156**

Rowe, 1367 and All That: Recodifying Federal Supplemental Jurisdiction, 74 Ind. L.J. 53 (1998), 443

Rutherglen, Better Late Than Never: Notice and Opt-Out at the Settlement Stage of Class Actions, 71 N.Y.U. L. Rev. 258 (1996), 470

Rutledge, Whither Arbitration?, 6 Geo. J.L. & Pub. Pol'y 549 (2008), 675

Saks & Blanck, Justice Improved: The Unrecognized Benefits of Aggregation and Sampling in the Trial of Mass Torts, 44 Stan. L. Rev. 815 (1992), 778

Schlanger, The Courts: Beyond the Hero Judge: Institutional Reform Litigation as Litigation, 97 Mich. L. Rev. 1994 (1999), 623

Schuck, Agent Orange on Trial: Mass Toxic Disasters in the Courts (1987), 347

Schuck, Mass Torts: An Institutional Evolutionist Perspective, 80 Cornell L. Rev. 941 (1995), **779**

Schwartz, First the Spill Then the Lawsuits, NYTimes.com, June 10, 2010, 753

Schwartz, Mandatory Arbitration and Fairness, 84 Notre Dame L. Rev. 1247 (2008–2009), 674

Schwarzer, Hirsch & Sussman, A Proposal to Amend the Multidistrict Litigation Statute to Permit Discovery Coordination of Large-Scale Litigation Pending in State and Federal Court, 73 Tex. L. Rev. 1529 (1995), **1010**

Schwarzer, Weiss & Hirsch, Judicial Federalism in Action: Coordination of Litigation in State and Federal courts, 78 Va. L. Rev. 1689 (1992), 1013

Sharkey, CAFA Settlement Notice Provision: Optimal Regulatory Policy?, 156 U. Pa. L. Rev. 101 (2008), 607

Shaw, Class Ascertainability, 124 Yale L.J. 2354 (2015), 54

Shepherd, Ideal Versus Reality in Third-Party Litigation Financing, 8 J.L. Econ. & Pol'y 593 (2012), 667

Sherman, American Class Actions: Significant Features and Developing Alternatives in Foreign Legal Systems, 215 F.R.D. 130 (2003), 27

Sherman, Class Actions and Duplicative Litigation, 62 Ind. L.J. 507 (1987), 250

Sherman, The MDL Model for Resolving Complex Litigation if a Class Action is Not Possible, 82 Tul. L. Rev. 2205 (2008), 3, **956**

Shreve & Raven–Hansen, Understanding Civil Procedure (4th ed. 2009), 622, 1052

Silver, Comparing Class Actions and Consolidations, 10 Rev. Litig. 495 (1991), 1109

Silver, Due Process and the Lodestar Method: You Can't Get There From Here, 74 Tul. L. Rev. 1809 (2000), 646

Silver & Baker, Mass Lawsuits and the Aggregate Settlement Rule, 32 Wake Forest L. Rev. 733 (1997), **1148**

Simpson & Perra, Defendant Class Actions, 32 Conn. L. Rev. 1319 (2000), 902

Solomon, Post–Spokeo, Standing Challenges Remain Unpredictable, LAW 360 (Oct. 26, 2016), 72

Solovy, Chorvat, Stern, & Feinberg, "Strategies for Defending a Class Action," in Litigation & Resolution of Complex Class Actions (Glasser Legal Works 1998), **259**

Special Project, The Remedial Process in Institutional Reform Litigation, 78 Colum. L. Rev. 784 (1978), 153

Spiegel, Settling Class Actions, 62 U. Cin. L. Rev. 1565 (1994), **544**

Spier, Settlement With Multiple Plaintiffs: The Role of Insolvency, 18 J.L. Econ. & Org. 295 (2002), 1120

Standards and Best Practices for Large and Mass Tort MDLs, Duke Law Center for Judicial Studies (2014), **1000**

Starykh & Boettrich, Recent Trends in Securities Class Action Litigation: 2015 Full-Year Review (NERA Economic Consulting 2016), 864

Steinberg, The Motion to Transfer and the Interest of Justice, 66 Notre Dame L. Rev. 443 (1990), 1114

Steiner & Upsahl, Attorney Communications in Class Litigation, 115 Banking L.J. 430 (1998), 398

Steinman, Our Class Action Federalism: *Erie* and the Rules Enabling Act After Shady Grove, 86 Notre Dame L. Rev. 1131 (2011), 522

Steinman, The Effects of Case Consolidation on the Procedural Rights of Litigants: What They Are, What They Might Be Part 1: Justiciability and Jurisdiction (Original and Appellate), 42 UCLA L. Rev. 717 (1995), 1109

Stern & McCallum, The Private Securities Litigation Reform Act: Ten Years After, 38 Rev. Sec. & Commodities Reg. 789 (2005), 864

Stout, Are Stock Markets Costly Casinos? Disagreement, Market Failure, and Securities Regulation, 81 Va. L. Rev. 611 (1995), 854

Strauch & Weber, "Multi-District Litigation," Business and Commercial Litigation in Federal Courts (1998), 232

Swanson, Juggling Shareholder Rights and Strike Suits in Derivative Litigation: The ALI Drops the Ball, 77 Minn. L. Rev. 1339 (1993), 931, 932

Swanzey, Using Class Actions to Litigate Mass Torts: Is There Justice for the Individual?, 11 Geo. J. Legal Ethics 421 (1998), 783

Symeonides, Introduction: The ALI's Complex Litigation Project: Commencing the National Debate, 54 La. L. Rev. 843 (1994), 1013

Symposium, (multiple authors), Pondering *Iqbal*, 14 Lewis & Clark L. Rev. 3 (2010), 258

Taylor, Defendant Class Actions Under Rule 23(b)(2): Resolving the Language Dilemma, 40 U. Kan. L. Rev. 77 (1991), 914

Tidmarsh, The Story of *Hansberry*: The Foundation for Modern Class Actions, Civil Procedure Stories 217 (Kevin M. Clermont ed., 2004), 121

Tobias, Standing to Intervene, 1991 Wisc. L. Rev. 415, 1082

Trends: Communication Technology Poses Novel Notification Issues, 11 Class Action Litig. Report 183 (2010), 575

Tribe, Trial By Mathematics: Precision and Ritual in the Legal Process, 84 Harv. L. Rev. 1329 (1971), 778

Vairo, Class Action Fairness Act of 2005; With Commentary and Analysis (Matthew Bender 2005), 449, 451, 607

Walker, A Model Plan to Resolve Federal Class Action Cases by Jury Trial, 88 Va. L. Rev. 405 (2002), 369

Walker & Monahan, Sampling Damages, 83 Iowa L. Rev. 545 (1998), **774**

Wasserman, Transnational Class Actions and Interjurisdictional Preclusion, 86 Notre Dame L. Rev. 313 (2011), 862

Weigel, The Judicial Panel on Multidistrict Litigation, Transferor Courts and Transferee Courts, 78 F.R.D. 575 (1977), **957**

Weinstein, Preliminary Reflections on Administration of Complex Litigations, 1 Cardozo L. Rev. 1 (2009), 347

Weinstein, Revision of Procedure: Some Problems in Class Actions, 9 Buff. L. Rev. 433 (1960), 232, 726

Weinstein, The Future of Class Actions in Mass Tort Cases: A Roundtable Discussion, 66 Fordham L. Rev. 1657 (1998), 726

Weinstein & Schwartz, Notes from the Cave: Some Problems of Judges in Dealing with Class Action Settlements, 163 F.R.D. 39 (1995), 534, 599, 613

Weiss & Beckerman, Let the Money Do The Monitoring: How Institutional Investors Can Reduce Agency Costs in Securities Class Actions, 104 Yale L.J. 2053 (1995), 875, 884

Werner, Note, The Viability and Strategic Significance of Class Action Alternatives Under CAFA's Mass Action Provisions, 103 Geo. L.J. 465 (2015), 463

Wheaton, Representation Suits Involving Numerous Litigants, 19 Cornell L.Q. 399 (1934), 19

Willging, Hooper & Niemic, Class Actions and the Rulemaking Process: An Empirical Analysis of Rule 23 to Address the Rulemaking Challenges, 71 N.Y.U. L. Rev. 74 (1996), 268

Willging, Hooper & Niemic, Fed. Judicial Ctr., Empirical Study of Class Actions in Four Federal District Courts: Final Report to the Advisory Committee on Civil Rules (1996), 621

Willging & Wheatman, Fed. Judicial Ctr., Attorney Reports on the Impact of Amchem and Ortiz on Choice of a Federal or State Forum in Class Action Litigation (2004), 461, 648

Williams & George, Who Will Manage Complex Civil Litigation?, 10 J. Empirical Legal Stud. 424 (2013), **963**

Winter, The Metaphor of Standing and the Problem of Self-Governance, 40 Stan. L. Rev. 1341 (1988), 72

Wolff, Preclusion in Class Action Litigation, 105 Colum. L. Rev. 717 (2005), 813

Wood, Redrafting Reverse Removal: Four Recommendations to Improve the American Law Institute's Complex Litigation Project, 44 Case W. Res. L. Rev. 1129 (1995), 1013

Woolley, Mass Tort Litigation and the Seventh Amendment Reexamination Clause, 83 Iowa L. Rev. 499 (1998), 358

Woolley, Rethinking the Adequacy of Adequate Representation, 75 Tex. L. Rev. 571 (1997), 121, **480**

Woolley, The Availability of Collateral Attack for Inadequate Representation in Class Suits, 79 Tex. L. Rev. 383 (2000), 473

Wright, Class Actions, 47 F.R.D. 169 (1970), **23**

Wright & Colussi, The Successful Use of the Class Action Device in the Management of the Skywalks Mass Tort Litigation, 52 UMKC L. Rev. 141 (1984), 735

Wright & Miller, Federal Practice and Procedure (2nd ed. 1995), 1057

Wright, Miller & Kane, Federal Practice and Procedure (various editions), **18**, 189, **347**, 350, 614, 902, 940, 949, 1048, 1056, 1057, 1058

Yeazell, From Medieval Group Litigation to the Modern Class Action (1987), 16, 17

CLASS ACTIONS
AND OTHER MULTI-PARTY LITIGATION

CASES AND MATERIALS

Fourth Edition

CHAPTER 1

INTRODUCTION AND HISTORY

■ ■ ■

A. THEMES OF THIS CASEBOOK

1. THE IMPORTANCE OF CLASS ACTIONS

This casebook focuses on one of the most important and dynamic areas of modern federal civil practice—aggregate-party litigation, particularly class actions under Federal Rule of Civil Procedure 23. In the nearly half century since modern Rule 23 was adopted in 1966, class actions have grown to dominate the civil litigation landscape in a manner unexpected by all but Rule 23's most ardent supporters and most vehement critics. Not only do practitioners attempt to use the class action device to address a vast range of subject areas, but the stakes in such cases may be exponentially higher than the stakes in traditional, one-on-one litigation. Class actions (and other party-aggregation devices) are powerful and pervasive instruments of social change. Indeed, some have said they are *too* powerful—a concern that explains numerous attempts in recent years to curtail the permissible uses of the class action device.

Any list of the most important civil litigation matters in recent decades would include a large number of class actions and other multi-party lawsuits. Examples include school desegregation, asbestos, Agent Orange, breast implants, tobacco, employment discrimination, environmental disasters, prescription drugs, sports injuries, securities fraud, and defective automobiles. These cases are important because the rights and remedies of vast numbers of people (sometimes in the millions) may be determined in a single proceeding or series of proceedings. Not surprisingly, these cases raise a host of procedural and constitutional issues. For example, can such cases be tried efficiently and fairly, given their size? How can the law ensure that those who purport to represent the interests of both themselves and absent class members are adequate to the task? How can a court ensure that class action dismissals and settlements do not end up benefiting counsel and the defendants at the expense of the class members? And, absent a class action, how can corporations and other defendants be held accountable when they injure large numbers of people but those injuries are too small to warrant individual lawsuits?

The merits of various class actions, as well as the procedures underlying the use of the class action device, have sharply divided courts, legislators, and commentators. Many of the underlying legal issues have required Supreme Court resolution. Legislators have repeatedly proposed—and in certain instances adopted—legislation changing the way that class actions and other multi-party cases are handled. The Class Action Fairness Act of 2005 is a contemporary example of sweeping legislative reform. Commentators have written hundreds of articles in the past several years. Issues regarding the roles of courts and parties in adjudication are never far below the surface of any class action dispute. Highlights of these judicial, legislative, and scholarly debates appear throughout this casebook.

One notable feature of multi-party litigation is that new issues are constantly arising. Thus, although the basic principles of aggregate-party litigation are discernible, and are illustrated in this casebook, many issues are unsettled. As a result, a number of cutting-edge issues are ripe for scholarly writing and debate. At the same time, the existence of many unsettled issues means that creative lawyering can make a real difference in litigating these cases. This casebook provides the essential materials for effective advocacy in multi-party cases.

2. APPROACH OF THIS CASEBOOK

General Approach. In many ways, this is a traditional casebook. The principal materials are excerpts from court decisions. On many of the issues, however, there are no "leading" cases or even any representative appellate decisions, because the issues are unsettled. Thus, in contrast to many casebooks, this text contains a number of opinions by trial courts. At the same time, with the availability (since 1998) of discretionary review of class certification decisions under Federal Rule of Civil Procedure 23(f), this edition of the casebook contains many more appellate decisions than earlier editions of the book. Furthermore, because the field of aggregate-party litigation has generated an unusually wide variety of secondary materials, this casebook includes a rich selection of thoughtful articles from leading scholars, judges, and practitioners. First, this text repeatedly cites and quotes from the Committee Notes of the Advisory Committee on Civil Rules (the group of judges, lawyers, and academics who study and recommend to the Supreme Court changes to the rules of civil procedure). (The author has been the academic member of the Committee since 2011, with his second three-year term expiring in 2017.) Second, the text frequently cites and quotes from the *Manual for Complex Litigation (Fourth)*, published by the Federal Judicial Center. The Manual synthesizes recommendations of judges, lawyers, and academics for addressing difficult issues in cases involving multiple parties or other complexities). The Fourth and most recent edition of the Manual was published in 2004. A third source referenced frequently herein, one that has been cited extensively by courts and commentators, is *Principles of the Law of Aggregate Litigation*, approved by the American Law Institute (ALI) in May 2009 and published in May 2010. The author served as an Associate Reporter for the ALI project, with primary responsibility for the chapter on settlements and attorneys' fees.

An understanding of how the requirements of Rule 23 have been interpreted by the courts, and how those issues play out during litigation, is essential to any meaningful consideration of the cutting-edge theoretical and policy issues in this exciting field. After addressing those crucial threshold issues, much of the text focuses on ethics, theory, policy, and reform. And because the author has personally litigated or served as in expert in well over 100 class actions, issues of litigation strategy also appear throughout the book.

Although the primary focus of the casebook is on class actions, there are numerous other devices for adjudicating multi-party disputes. These include permissive and compulsory joinder, impleader, interpleader, consolidation, and intervention, all of which are set forth in the Federal Rules of Civil Procedure. Additional devices for adjudicating multi-party cases, set forth in various federal statutes, include: transfers pursuant to the multidistrict litigation (MDL) statute; transfers for the convenience of the parties and witnesses and in the interests of justice; and transfers pursuant to the Bankruptcy Code. Courts may also use informal devices to coordinate and manage multi-party suits pending in more than one jurisdiction. These devices are not only important on their own, but also critical to understanding class actions, since a major issue in many class actions is whether a class action is superior to other methods for resolving the case. The MDL device (which can be used in both non-class and classwide litigation) is especially important for a course on complex litigation. MDL has been the subject of numerous articles in recent years, and it has figured prominently in most of the high-profile class actions of the last decade.

It is important to note that, to the extent that recent judicial decisions and legislative enactments have limited the availability of class actions in certain kinds of cases, non-class methods of adjudicating or resolving complex cases have become increasingly important. For example, in 2007, pharmaceutical defendant Merck & Co. agreed to pay $4.85 billion to an estimated 47,000 plaintiffs to settle claims of injury allegedly caused by Merck's since-recalled Vioxx pain medication. *See, e.g.*, Edward F. Sherman, *The MDL Model for Resolving Complex Litigation if a Class Action is Not Possible*, 82 Tul. L. Rev. 2205, 2213–16 (2008). Because courts found the Vioxx personal injury claims inappropriate for class action treatment, the parties had to construct the settlement agreement using MDL but without the benefit of Rule 23's framework.

The author believes that aggregate-party litigation is best taught by letting students evaluate the merits of various approaches. For example, throughout the book both majority and dissenting judicial opinions are often included, and students are frequently asked to evaluate which approach to a particular problem is more consistent with the text of the pertinent rules or statutes or with public policy and basic principles of fairness. The book also contains numerous hypothetical problems, so that students can apply the legal principles and address the policy and ethical concerns set forth in the materials.

Finally, the casebook attempts to provide materials from all perspectives. It does not take any philosophical position on the wisdom of class actions or other multi-party devices. Nor does it present its own agenda or proposals for reform. Instead, it provides the raw materials for students and professors to debate these important questions.

Structure of the Casebook. The issues surrounding class actions and other multi-party litigation are complex, unsettled, and provocative. This casebook captures the essence of these issues, so that the reader will have the tools to make a meaningful contribution to class action theory and practice. The remainder of this chapter raises several recurring questions and concerns in this area of law before providing a theoretical and historical framework. Chapters 2 to 5 focus on the structure of Rule 23 and how it is litigated in practice. The casebook next raises significant issues relating to class actions that may involve the laws of multiple jurisdictions

(Chapter 6), civil procedure doctrines that play out in interesting ways in the class action context (Chapter 7), class action resolutions—including settlement, remedies, attorneys' fees, alternative dispute resolution, and arbitration (Chapter 8), and appeals in class actions (Chapter 9).

Chapter 10 focuses on three particular substantive areas of class action practice: mass torts, employment discrimination, and securities fraud. The purpose of this chapter is not only to introduce students to three important areas of class action litigation, but also to explore the extent to which Rule 23's requirements are trans-substantive—that is, whether the Rule applies in the same way regardless of the substantive claims at issue. To the extent that courts and legislators may have created rules that apply only (or primarily) to certain kinds of class actions, the question arises why such limitations have been imposed. Are there, for example, lessons that can be drawn from mass tort cases that should be applied in securities or employment cases?

The casebook then turns to three types of "class" suits that do not fit the traditional model of Rule 23—defendant class actions, derivative suits under Rule 23.1, and suits involving unincorporated associations under Rule 23.2 (Chapter 11). The casebook then focuses on MDL procedures (Chapter 12). Finally, the casebook discusses a variety of other non-class aggregation devices, such as joinder, impleader, interpleader, intervention, consolidation, bankruptcy, informal federal-state cooperation, and non-class aggregate settlements (Chapter 13).

3. RECURRING QUESTIONS AND CONCERNS

This casebook highlights numerous recurring themes that arise in aggregate-party litigation. These include the following:

What Is a Class? A fundamental question that underlies many disputes, but which is often never explicitly addressed, is just what a class *is* in a class action. Is a class simply a convenient way to refer to a collection of individuals? Or is a class an entity unto itself—analogous perhaps to a corporation or unincorporated association—that has legal status apart from its individual members? Courts and commentators often have unstated assumptions about this core issue that color their assessment of other issues, such as the role of class representatives, discovery against absent class members, and the determination of causation and damages.

The "Day-In-Court" Ideal and Aggregate Realities. Courts and commentators have long struggled to reconcile traditional notions of individualized adjudication, in which litigants are promised their day in court, with the recognition that, to avoid overwhelming the judicial system, some form of aggregation and aggregate settlement may be necessary to resolve the claims of large numbers of people with similar claims. *Compare, e.g.*, Owen Fiss, *Against Settlement*, 93 Yale L.J. 1073, 1075 (1984) (arguing that, "[l]ike plea bargaining, settlement is a capitulation to the conditions of mass society and should be neither encouraged nor praised"), *with* Samuel Issacharoff & Robert H. Klonoff, *The Public Value of Settlement*, 78 Fordham L. Rev. 1177, 1179 (2009) (challenging Professor Fiss's characterization of plaintiffs as systematically disadvantaged in a legal system that encourages settlement, and contending that "the ability of a legal system

The Crucial Question of Adequacy. Class actions are premised on the expectation that a few persons may litigate the issues of many others who are not before the court, thereby avoiding the need for repetitious litigation. To preserve fairness, however, the Supreme Court has recognized—at least since *Hansberry v. Lee*, 311 U.S. 32 (1940) (*see* Chapter 2(B)(4)(a))—that the claims of absent class members will not be extinguished by class action litigation if their interests were not adequately represented by the class representatives. Rule 23(a)(4) and Rule 23(g) also require adequate class counsel. Fundamental questions arise: What does it mean to be an adequate class representative? What does it mean to be adequate counsel for the class? Is there a due process basis for requiring adequacy of representation?

The Importance of Notice (and the Possibility of Appearance). A core theme in class action jurisprudence is the importance of notice. In *Phillips Petroleum Co. v. Shutts*, 472 U.S. 797 (1985) (*see* Chapter 6(B)), the Supreme Court emphasized the importance of notifying absent class members that their rights are going to be adjudicated. *Shutts* even raised the possibility that an absent class member may have a due process right to be present and participate in the litigation.

The Aspiration of Empowerment. Courts and commentators have often recognized that the class action device permits those who are less powerful to band together and—using lawyers as their champions—seek redress of grievances that would go unremedied if each litigant had to litigate alone.

Getting Out—or No Exit. Despite the strength of the notion that class actions may empower the weak, courts and commentators have also recognized that individual litigants often wish to disassociate themselves from aggregate litigation. Rule 23, however, permits litigants to "opt out" in only certain kinds of class actions. Again, the *Shutts* case (and the subsequent case of *Wal-Mart Stores, Inc. v. Dukes*, 564 U.S. 338 (2011)) raised the possibility that absent class members may, at least in some circumstances, be entitled to "opt out" of *any* class action seeking significant money damages. The issue is complicated, however, and credible policy arguments can be made to support different sides of the ongoing debate.

The Threat of Coercion. Counterbalancing the notion of empowerment is the concern that those who oppose class actions may be coerced into settling meritless cases because the stakes are too high to risk going to trial. This concern has caused some courts to reject class certification in part because of concern that defendants would be "blackmailed" into accepting settlement. For a widely cited example, *see In re Rhone–Poulenc Rorer, Inc.*, 51 F.3d 1293 (7th Cir. 1995) (Posner, J.), excerpted in Chapters 6(B) and 10(A)(2)(c).

The Possibility of Conflict and Collusion—A Tool for Whom? Again, despite the notion of the class action as a tool of empowerment, courts and commentators have voiced concerns about the role of class action counsel. Some have noted the possibility that class counsel may have incentives (in terms of attorneys' fees and potentially differing political or social agendas) that put them at odds with the interests of the classes they purport to represent. This tension has caused longstanding concerns about the application of rules of professional responsibility in aggregate litigation. Others have noted the risk that class counsel may collude with defendants to reach settlements that profit class counsel and also benefit the defendants, but harm some or all of the class members whom class counsel are supposed to represent. The concern is that defendants care only about the total amount that they pay, thereby pitting class members against class lawyers in allocating the settlement funds. Two significant Supreme Court decisions, *Amchem Products, Inc. v. Windsor*, 521 U.S. 591 (1997) (*see* Chapter 8(A)(3)), and *Ortiz v. Fibreboard Corp.*, 527 U.S. 815 (1999) (*see* Chapter 3(A)(2)), invalidated sweeping class action settlements in which objectors alleged that class members had been treated unfairly because of collusive deals between class counsel and the defendants. A number of federal circuit court cases have similarly struck down settlements deemed to be collusive.

The Conundrum of Manageability. Courts and commentators have long debated how class actions can be fairly and capably managed. Courts have experimented with unusual means of trying such cases, and commentators have filled pages of academic journals and practice books with proposals for adjudicating multi-party cases in a single trial. Courts have also attempted, with mixed success, to split off issues for "partial" class certification, in recognition that some cases cannot be addressed on a classwide basis for all issues. Furthermore, courts have struggled with the possibility of splitting trials into more manageable segments in hopes of bringing order to the chaos, while attempting to be mindful of the constitutional concerns such trial plans may present.

The Impact of Procedure on Substance. Judges and scholars have often debated whether, and to what extent, aggregate litigation actually changes the substance of the claims being litigated. *See, e.g., Amchem*, 521 U.S. at 613 ("Rule 23's requirements must be interpreted in keeping with * * * the Rules Enabling Act, which instructs that rules of procedure 'shall not abridge, enlarge or modify any substantive right[.]' "). Some have claimed that Rule 23 has changed the substantive rights of parties or absent class members and that such changes may exceed the courts' power to impose and interpret rules of procedure.

The Impact of Substance on Procedure. At the same time, courts and commentators have questioned whether the substance being adjudicated in multi-party litigation has fundamentally changed the rules of aggregation. Some have openly questioned whether a separate law of class actions has developed for mass torts, securities, employment, and the like, and whether legislation or court-made doctrines have become so specialized in some areas that it is wrong to speak of Rule 23 as being "trans-substantive" (*i.e.*, applicable in the same manner regardless of the underlying substantive claims). *See* John Leubsdorf, *Class Actions at the Cloverleaf*, 39 Ariz. L. Rev. 453 (1997).

What Are the Alternatives and When Should They Be Used? Rule 23 explicitly calls for consideration of alternatives to class treatment by requiring courts to assess whether joinder of parties is "impracticable" and, in some circumstances, whether class treatment is "superior" to alternatives. Thus, courts and commentators routinely discuss Rule 23's interplay with other forms of party aggregation, such as joinder or consolidation.

Furthermore, commentators have made numerous proposals to modify the rules of party aggregation to address perceived needs, and those proposals have engendered significant debate. One important potential alternative is relief through government enforcement. If an administrative agency has jurisdiction to seek enforcement based on the facts at issue, should a class action be rejected as unnecessary? *See* Stephen B. Burbank, Sean Farhang & Herbert M. Kritzer, *Private Enforcement*, 17 Lewis & Clark L. Rev. 637 (2013).

Where Should the Case Be Heard? Courts and commentators have engaged in considerable debate over the propriety of multistate class actions being brought in state court. Some have expressed concerns over class counsel's ability to forum shop for particular state courts in which to file nationwide class actions. Others have fought to keep class actions in state court for fear that overburdened federal courts would hesitate to certify cases involving the laws of different states—to the detriment of plaintiffs alleging injuries in a variety of circumstances. In response, Congress enacted the Class Action Fairness Act of 2005 (CAFA), which provides a jurisdictional basis to remove most multistate class actions to federal court.

B. PERSPECTIVES ON CLASS ACTIONS

OWEN M. FISS, THE POLITICAL THEORY OF THE CLASS ACTION
53 Wash. & Lee L. Rev. 21, 21–25 (1996).

Courts are not self-starting. Their proceedings must be initiated by some outside agency, and it is that agency, not the courts, who will conduct the factual investigation, devise the discovery program, select and examine witnesses, write the legal briefs, and monitor the implementation of the remedy. Who might play that role?

When the remedy for violation of a legal norm consists of jail or some other form of punishment and the judicial proceeding is considered a criminal one, the power of initiation is exclusively in the hands of an officer of the state, for example, the attorney general or district attorney. Victims of crimes cannot commence criminal proceedings, and over the years the Supreme Court has been reluctant to grant individual citizens any power to review or otherwise superintend the government's decision to commence a criminal prosecution.

The situation is entirely different in the civil context. There the purpose is not to punish for a past violation, but to compensate for past injuries or to stop future violations, and the remedy sought is damages or an injunction rather than a fine or imprisonment. For such proceedings, the power of initiation has been allocated to two different agencies: public officers and private citizens. In my judgment, the class action can be understood best as a fusion of both of these agencies.

Civil suits initiated by private citizens may serve their private purposes. Imagine a price-fixing agreement among stockbrokers and a suit by one of the investors for an injunction to prevent price-fixing in the future or to recover damages for the harm inflicted. The suit may vindicate or protect the individual rights of the investor. However, a public purpose also may be served by this very same suit in the sense that, if successful, it will bring the brokers' behavior into accord with antitrust law. An injunction against price-fixing in the future clearly would have that effect, but so would an award of damages to the investor. The damage award would force the stockbrokers to internalize the costs of their wrongdoing and, through the operation of ordinary principles of deterrence, discourage future violations by the defendants and other brokers.

In many instances, there is no need to disentangle the private and public purposes of a citizen-initiated lawsuit. The citizen furthers the public interest by pursuing private ends. However, there is a category of cases—of increasing importance in the modern times—when the two purposes become distinct. This occurs when the harm to an individual citizen is not sufficient to give that citizen a good reason to bring a lawsuit, yet the aggregate harm to society is quite considerable. Once again consider a price-fixing agreement. This time the agreement involves stockbrokers who handle small transactions. The damage inflicted on an individual investor may be seventy dollars, but the aggregate damage inflicted on all the investors—numbering in the millions—is sixty million dollars. In such an instance, the legal system could be relatively indifferent as to whether the seventy dollars is ever collected, but not at all indifferent to the public ramifications of the defendants' action because of the enormous social loss incurred.

To some extent, such situations can be handled by suits brought by public officers. If the public interest is great and the private interest relatively trivial, then the attorney general should be able to sue the stockbrokers. While we have a strong tradition, dating from the late nineteenth century, that authorizes government-initiated civil suits as an alternative to criminal prosecution, we have been reluctant to make it the only available alternative for dealing with such cases. * * * [T]he unwillingness to make the government-initiated lawsuit the only civil option in these situations may be rooted in misgivings with the official system of governance and how public officials discharge their duties. The issue is one of accountability. The power vested in the attorney general is discretionary, and there are fears that discretion might be abused because of corruption or that the needs of certain sections of society—for example, the politically powerless—might be systematically slighted. As a result, the idea of the private attorney general has emerged. The power of initiation is vested in the individual citizen, but the function of the suit is the same as one brought by the attorney general, namely, to vindicate the public interest.

How is such a citizen-initiated lawsuit to be financed? The suit might be brought in the name of some individual citizen, but the work is going to be done by lawyers. While the term "private attorney general" is usually applied to the plaintiffs, it is the lawyers who, in reality, fulfill that role, and they must be compensated for their time and effort. Indeed, going even further, the level of compensation must be high enough to make it worthwhile for the best and the brightest to undertake such ventures. Because we in the United States operate under a rule that does not award attorney's fees to the victor, there is no separate award for fees, and that means that the lawyer for the plaintiff must be paid out of the damages collected by the plaintiff from the defendant if the suit is successful. When the damage award is sixty million dollars, there is more than enough to go around;

there would be an army of lawyers prepared to handle that case on a contingent fee basis, but not when the award is seventy dollars.

Our response to this dilemma, like all things American, has been both varied and pragmatic. One approach has been to relax the American rule on attorney's fees when the named plaintiff is acting as a private attorney general. In such a case there can be a separate award of attorney's fees to compensate the lawyers who served in that role for their time and effort. In some jurisdictions, this change was wrought by the courts alone; at the federal level, it took the enactment of a statute. Most of the federal fee shifting statutes are asymmetrical; defendants receive attorney's fees only upon a special showing, for example, that the litigation was brought in bad faith, while plaintiffs receive the fees for their attorneys simply on condition that they prevail.

A second approach has been to create a separate corps of lawyers that might act as private attorneys general and then to pay them out of funds that come from the public itself, sometimes in the form of tax revenue, but most often out of private donations. This has led to the emergence of an entire panoply of organizations—the NAACP, ACLU, Natural Resources Defense Council, Legal Services Corporation, Center for Law & Social Policy, Equal Rights Associates—that provide lawyers to serve as private attorneys general.

The third, and perhaps most imaginative, solution to the problem of funding the private attorney general is the class action. In essence, the class action allows the named plaintiff to collect not just the seventy dollars—the amount the plaintiff was injured—but rather the sixty million dollars—the damages due to all investors. Most of that award would be paid to the investors, but a hefty chunk—perhaps as much as six million dollars (10 percent) or even twenty million dollars (33 1/3 percent)—would go to the lawyers for the plaintiff. The lawyers would be paid from the common fund they created.

In short, the class action could be viewed as a device to fund the private attorney general and is able to play that role because of the aggregation of the claims of a large number of persons who have similar or identical claims, none of which—standing alone—would justify the suit. The person who brings the suit is referred to as "the named plaintiff," and the others are referred to as "the unnamed members of the class." The named plaintiff acts on behalf of the unnamed members of the class, and to more fully understand the dilemmas created by the class action we must consider the impact the action of the named plaintiff will have upon the rights of the class.

A victory by the named plaintiff will preclude any further action on their claims by the unnamed members of the class. This seems relatively straightforward. The unnamed members of the class will have no reason whatsoever to pursue their claims because, by hypothesis, their claims have been paid or honored and, in any event, the most elementary fairness would require that result. The defendants should not have to pay twice.

But what should happen if, as indeed is possible, the named plaintiff loses the suit? The general rule is to bar the unnamed members of the class from any further action, but the reasons for that rule are far from clear.

One notion, perhaps more appropriate to gambling than to litigation, assumes that the risks of the defendant should be symmetrical. If the defendant loses, the loss is big; so if the defendant wins, the win also should be big. Alternatively, the rule might be based on a fear of wearing down the defendant—after winning one case, the defendant might have to mount a second defense, then a third, and so forth. Admittedly, the size of the claim is too small to assume that one named plaintiff after another will bring suit on an individual basis, but there are no obvious reasons why the first person to bring a class action should be the only one able to do so.

Whatever its rationale, the rule foreclosing the claims of the unnamed members of the class on the contingency of a loss by the named plaintiff has become well entrenched and gives rise to the central normative tension in the class action: a conflict with the principle that promises to each person a day in court before his or her claim is foreclosed. At a superficial level, this tension has been resolved by conceiving the class action as a form of representative action because, to be precise, the legal system does not guarantee that every person will have a day in court, but only that the interest of each person will be represented in court. It is fairly well established that if I appoint an agent to represent my interest and that agent brings a lawsuit on my behalf and then loses, I will not be able to sue again.

The class action is in fact a representative lawsuit—as noted, the named plaintiff is bringing a suit on behalf of all the unnamed members of the class—but it employs a peculiar concept of representation: self-appointment. Contrary to the situation where I appoint someone as my agent, in the class action the named plaintiff appoints himself or herself as the representative of the class. Self-appointment is not unheard of in the world of politics and other social domains. Indeed, it is quite commonplace in political situations where there is a radical shift in regimes. The persons who gathered in Philadelphia in the summer of 1787 to draft the United States Constitution appointed themselves to represent the people. * * * Yet there is no denying that self-appointment is an anomalous form of representation, only justified, if at all, by the most exceptional circumstances. The use of it in the class action reveals the truly exceptional—perhaps even revolutionary—character of that procedural device.

* * *

LA MAR v. H & B NOVELTY & LOAN CO.
United States Court of Appeals, Ninth Circuit, 1973.
489 F.2d 461.

Before ELY and SNEED, CIRCUIT JUDGES, and SWEIGERT, DISTRICT JUDGE [N.D. Cal., by designation].

SNEED, CIRCUIT JUDGE.

* * * The emergence of the class action inescapably forces consideration of the characteristics of the judicial and administrative processes because its features in many instances are derived from both. In a broad sense, fixing the outer limits of permissible class actions involves the determination of the extent to which proceedings within the judiciary will be permitted to resemble in function the administrative process.

It is obvious to even the casual observer that the two processes have features in common and that there is no bright line between them. Judges, for example, bring to their tasks the same informed judgment about the society within which their rulings operate as do administrators. Also those in executive positions frequently find themselves involved, either in a formal or informal setting, in passing judgment on particular claims presented on the basis of a substantially circumscribed record.

Nonetheless, the archetypes are distinguishable and it is in the interest of the judiciary, as well as the executive, to recognize and maintain these distinctions. There is no need to dwell on them at great length. It is enough to observe that the judicial process generally is concerned with discrete complaints of injury by one or a very small number of alleged wrongdoers. Those invoking the aid of the courts generally have in mind particular relief which can be provided by the court in a relatively easy and expeditious manner. The passivity of the judiciary is underscored by its dependence on the evidence provided by the parties and the relatively narrow scope of possible resolutions of the controversy imposed by the applicable rules of law which it must observe. The attorneys for the parties function in a manner compatible with this structure. The method by which evidence is introduced and the type of evidence that is permissible are rigidly controlled. The forums within which persuasion may be attempted are fixed and the methods of persuasion limited and to a degree quite formal. Finally, and of particular importance to class actions, the attorneys are restrained in their pursuit of clients. While the limits of these restraints continue to perplex the profession, which must function in a world in which advertising and salesmanship are omnipresent, no one will deny that restraints do and should exist. All perceive that they are congruent with the fundamentally passive role of the judiciary.

The administrative process, on the other hand, frequently need not await the specific complaint. It can initiate, *sua sponte*, steps designed to correct perceived evils in accordance with the authority provided it by legislative action or delegation from higher executive authority. Traditionally it represents large and imprecise interests which, at the highest level of abstraction, are designated "the public interest." * * *

* * *

JONATHAN M. LANDERS, OF LEGALIZED BLACKMAIL AND LEGALIZED THEFT: CONSUMER CLASS ACTIONS AND THE SUBSTANCE–PROCEDURE DILEMMA

47 S. Cal. L. Rev. 842, 845–48, 857–58, 860 (1974).

To consumerists, the consumer class action is an inviting procedural device to cope with frauds causing small damages to large groups. The slight loss to the individual, when aggregated in the coffers of the wrongdoer, results in gains which are both handsome and tempting. The alternatives to the class action—private suits or governmental actions—have been so often found wanting in controlling consumer frauds that not even the ardent critics of class actions seriously contend that they are truly effective. The consumer class action, when brought by those who have no other avenue of legal redress, provides restitution to the injured, and deterrence of the wrongdoer. Since both of these objectives are, at least partially, goals of the legal system itself, the class action device cannot be all bad.

There is, however, another side of the coin. One can perceive the legal system as set up from a functional point of view to deter the bringing of small claims. Just as consumers have no effective redress within the legal system for small injuries in the absence of the class action device, business concerns are similarly afflicted. The business confronted with unpaid accounts or minor damage claims of a few dollars or even a few hundred dollars is no more able to sue than is the consumer. Many businesses regularly "write off" such small claims, and others turn such claims over to collection agencies which may retain 50 percent of an account in fees. Even those states which have small claims courts frequently prevent business use of the courts either by absolute prohibition, or by such methods as limiting the maximum number of suits which can be filed within a year. Hence, one might argue that in an increasingly complex, impersonal, and interdependent society, there will be an ever increasing number of small grievances and minor disputes, and that such matters are better handled by allowing the loss to lie where it falls than by trying to reallocate the loss through the legal system. In the case of widespread or recurrent situations, a combination of governmental action, criminal penalties, and remedial legislation could be employed.

The consumer class action, as already noted, is seen as the savior for remedying instances of small injuries to large numbers of persons, and it has unquestionably been used in this role numerous times under Rule 23. It is not very clear, however, that the rule was ever intended to serve such a purpose. The Advisory Committee has stated that subsection 23(b)(3)

> encompasses those cases in which a class action would achieve economies of time, effort, and expense, and promote uniformity of decision as to persons similarly situated.

Such a statement, standing alone, tends to suggest that the draftsmen conceived of the rule as an advanced joinder device to include in a single action all persons of a definable group in a situation where absent the class action at least a portion of the group both could and would sue as individuals. * * * Moreover, the Advisory Committee may have given substance to such an interpretation by its examples of the kinds of class action cases which would be "approved" under the new rule. The cases cited by the Committee involved relatively high individual losses of from several hundred to several thousand dollars, small classes of from a few hundred to at most one thousand individuals, and readily identifiable class members. In sum, the Advisory Committee discussion is at least consistent with the view that the class action was basically a joinder device which would be used where the individual cases would otherwise be brought separately. Significantly, this literal reading of the Committee's class action comments would support the preclusion of class actions for large groups suing for small amounts. The dominant characteristic of such suits is that they do not involve combinations of persons who would sue anyway, but rather are actions on behalf of persons who, absent the class remedy, would not sue at all. In effect, then, the class action has not simply made an old remedy more efficient; in a realistic sense it has created a new remedy where none existed.

The Advisory Committee did make a passing reference to the class action by numerous individuals seeking small damages. Under Rule 23(b)(3), the court must find the class action to be superior to other methods of handling the dispute, and one of the factors to be considered is the interest of the individual members in controlling their own actions. The Advisory Committee addressed itself to this individual interest criterion as follows:

> The interests of individuals in conducting separate lawsuits may be so strong as to call for denial of a class action. On the other hand, these interests may be theoretic rather than practical; the class may have a high degree of cohesion and prosecution of the action through representatives would be quite unobjectionable, *or the amounts at stake for individuals may be so small that separate suits would be impracticable.*

Whether or not the Committee contemplated that such suits would be brought when *all* class members had such small claims, when damages were just a few dollars, and when there were hundreds of thousands of class members is shrouded in mystery. In any event, the draftsmen gave no evidence that they conceived of Rule 23 as the kind of broad instrument for social justice which has been suggested by the apologists for the class action. At the very least, one would have expected so distinguished a group as the Advisory Committee to furnish more evidence of such a significant and far-reaching goal than a passing reference, without supporting examples, which was not even included within the Committee's discussion of the purpose of the rule. Interestingly, however, * * * this "passing reference" has rapidly mushroomed into a dominant area of litigation under Rule 23. The vast difference between consumer class actions and the kind of joinder cases suggested by the Advisory Committee should, however, have caused courts to waive the yellow flag of caution before the class action express.

* * *

Perhaps the best indication of the remedial nature of the class action lies in the arguments of the proponents of such actions. They argue that the consumer's existing rights require provisions for effective enforcement, because impliedly the usual individual action for damages is inadequate, and they speak of the great need for deterrence and of restoration of ill-gotten gains. These are precisely the types of arguments that are frequently heard in the legislative halls during the debates on consumer legislation and, particularly, on the appropriate remedial provisions to be attached to the legislation. However, they are not the kinds of arguments which courts should be considering under the guise of formulating rules of procedure. Indeed, [it has been argued] that it is irrelevant whether there is even to be restitution at all, and that the funds garnered in the class might just as well be distributed on a random basis to those in the telephone directory. While such a method might be desirable, it is seriously doubtful whether the rulemaking authority was ever intended to authorize a court to reach such a result by rule. * * *

***

STEPHEN B. BURBANK, SEAN FARHANG & HERBERT M. KRITZER, PRIVATE ENFORCEMENT
17 Lewis & Clark L. Rev. 637, 662, 667 (2013)

***

A. The Potential Advantages of Private Enforcement

In assessing the potential advantages and disadvantages of private enforcement regimes, we draw on the substantial literature debating their wisdom, which is always, explicitly or implicitly, evaluating them in relation to public enforcement. This literature is largely characterized by advocacy either for or against private enforcement. Aside from advocacy, we believe that the arguments on each side highlight dimensions of private enforcement that are useful to weigh when considering whether to deploy this enforcement strategy. * * * [W]e also believe that many of the arguments are context-dependent, with their relative importance likely to vary across specific policy domains and political, legal, and institutional environments.

On the positive side of the ledger, relative to administrative implementation, private enforcement regimes can: (1) multiply resources devoted to prosecuting enforcement actions; (2) shift the costs of regulation off of governmental budgets and onto the private sector; (3) take advantage of private information to detect violations; (4) encourage legal and policy innovation; (5) emit a clear and consistent signal that violations will be prosecuted, providing insurance against the risk that a system of administrative implementation will be subverted; (6) limit the need for direct and visible intervention by the bureaucracy in the economy and society; and (7) facilitate participatory and democratic governance.

***

B. The Potential Disadvantages of Private Enforcement

The foregoing account of private enforcement regimes as an effective form of policy intervention is heatedly contested. A contending line of arguments not only doubts whether private litigation can advance statutory policy goals, but, in its strongest form, suspects that private litigation may actually discourage compliance efforts. This perspective is characterized by the following core arguments: private enforcement regimes (1) empower judges, who lack policy expertise, to make policy; (2) tend to produce inconsistent and contradictory doctrine from courts; (3) weaken the administrative state's capacity to articulate a coherent regulatory scheme by preempting administrative rulemaking; (4) usurp prosecutorial discretion; (5) discourage cooperation with regulators and voluntary compliance; (6) weaken oversight of policy implementation by the legislative and executive branches; and (7) lack democratic legitimacy and accountability.

* * *

NOTES AND QUESTIONS

1. Professor Fiss focuses on the class action device as a way to permit private parties to serve public purposes. What other mechanisms besides private-party litigation could be used to vindicate the rights of those whose claims are litigated in class actions?

2. What is the thrust of the Ninth Circuit's distinction in *La Mar* between the administrative process and the judicial process? When reviewing materials throughout this casebook, consider the extent to which such distinctions make sense, given the realities of modern aggregate adjudication.

3. Professor Landers argues that class actions have not been an unblemished success. Is there merit in the view that consumers—and others who suffer minor injuries that would never be litigated in the absence of party-aggregation devices—should simply take their lumps?

4. Based on the discussion by Professor Burbank and his co-authors, should public enforcement regimes defer more frequently to class actions and other private litigation? Or should public enforcement generally be the preferred method?

5. When studying each party-aggregation device discussed in the chapters that follow, consider the following questions:

• Does the aggregation device serve to protect the plaintiff, the defendant, a third party, or all of the above?

• To what extent does the aggregation device promote efficiency and avoid conflicting and overlapping cases in front of multiple judges?

• In addition to judicial efficiency, what other potential benefits are achieved through the aggregation device?

• To what extent does the device, through its particular requirements, limit or undercut judicial efficiency?

• To what extent is the device being used not to promote efficient adjudication, but instead to obtain *dismissal* of the action?

• To what extent does the device give the court authority to *compel* aggregation?

• What costs are incurred through the use of the device?

• How does the existence and utilization of the device change incentives for bringing an action?

• How do the attorneys involved in the case—or those hoping to become involved—benefit or suffer from the use of the aggregation device?

• To what extent does the device depend on the ability and incentives of the existing parties to raise issues of concern?

• Have the courts developed rules that provide adequate guidance to litigants about how the device should be used in practice?

With respect to each of the questions identified above, consider to what extent the answer depends on the underlying substantive claim(s) at issue in the litigation.

C. HISTORICAL OVERVIEW

1. ECHOES FROM THE PAST

As the Supreme Court noted in *Ortiz v. Fibreboard Corp.*, 527 U.S. 815 (1999), the modern class action rule has a long pedigree:

> Although representative suits have been recognized in various forms since the earliest days of English law, class actions as we recognize them today developed as an exception to the formal rigidity of the necessary parties rule in equity, as well as from the bill of peace, an equitable device for combining multiple suits. The necessary parties rule in equity mandated that "all persons materially interested, either as plaintiffs or defendants in the subject matter of the bill ought to be made parties to the suit, however numerous they may be." But because that rule would at times unfairly deny recovery to the party before the court, equity developed exceptions, among them one to cover situations "where the parties are very numerous, and the court perceives, that it will be almost impossible to bring them all before the court; or where the question is of general interest, and a few may sue for the benefit of the whole; or where the parties form a part of a voluntary association for public or private purposes, and may be fairly supposed to represent the rights and interests of the whole. . . ." From these roots, modern class action practice emerged in the 1966 revision of Rule 23. In drafting Rule 23(b), the Advisory Committee sought to catalogue in "functional" terms "those recurrent life patterns which call for mass litigation through representative parties."

Id. at 832–33 (citations omitted). For an interesting historical account of group litigation, *see* Stephen C. Yeazell, *From Medieval Group Litigation to the Modern Class Action* 268–77 (Yale Univ. Press 1987). In his book, which was cited in the *Ortiz* Court's discussion of the history of Rule 23, Professor Yeazell traced the history of Anglo-American group litigation across three broad periods: medieval (twelfth to fifteenth centuries), early modern (sixteenth and seventeenth centuries), and modern (eighteenth century forward).

Even in medieval times, Yeazell recounted, group litigation existed in some form, but early on, it "generated no theory [or] legal doctrine * * *." *Id.* In the early modern period, however, Chancery courts began to articulate legal doctrines for group litigation, which resulted in a "narrower range of litigation"—relative to the medieval period—in terms of both substantive law and limitations on which groups were susceptible of representation. *Id.* "At the same time, the legal order developed a set of very rough principles that explained how these groups could appear in court * * *." *Id.* Finally, in the "modern" period, starting in the 1700s, the idea of representative litigation faced perhaps its greatest challenge. Professor Yeazell explained: "The primacy of individual autonomy comes into fundamental conflict with any practice of group litigation, and since 1700[,] lawyers have therefore wrestled with the task of finding a justification for a procedure that seems to violate a basic tenet of the legal system." *Id.*

NOTES AND QUESTIONS

1. In light of Professor Yeazell's contention that procedural rules are informed by their social settings, consider how the social context of modern America is reflected in contemporary group litigation. Have advances in communications or other technology made group litigation more or less efficient, manageable, or fair? In examining the following materials, consider whether Rule 23 and the other aggregate litigation devices addressed in this casebook are up to the task of resolving the disputes that modern society places before federal courts.

2. Professor Yeazell has stated that "[r]epresentative litigation must find some justification for its departure from the path of individualism," but the justification that "[t]he modern class action * * * has found is * * * so powerful that if extended to its maximum reach, it would transform the face of litigation and the adjudicatory system." Yeazell, *From Medieval Group Litigation to the Modern Class Action, supra*, at 268–77. As a result, he concluded, limiting principles must be identified. This search for limiting principles to control the potentially undesirable consequences of aggregate litigation is a major theme of this text.

3. For additional commentary on the history of group litigation, *see* Geoffrey C. Hazard, Jr. et al., *An Historical Analysis of the Binding Effect of Class Suits*, 146 U. Pa. L. Rev. 1849, 1861–63 (1998). *See also* Graham C. Lilly, *Modeling Class Actions: The Representative Suit as an Analytic Tool*, 81 Neb. L. Rev. 1008, 1013–14 (2003) (noting that "[t]raditionally, legal historians have traced the roots of the class action to the Bill of Peace, which originated in seventeenth-century English chancery courts," and that Professor Yeazell challenges that view "by mustering historical evidence that group litigation developed gradually as an outgrowth of communal harms within English Feudal social structures").

2. THE OLD FEDERAL EQUITY RULES

Class lawsuits have been a part of American jurisprudence for more than a century and a half. The rules governing such actions, however, have changed over time. From 1842 through 1912, class actions in federal court were governed by Equity Rule 48:

EQUITY RULE 48 (1842)

Where the parties on either side are very numerous, and cannot, without manifest inconvenience and oppressive delays in the suit, be all brought before it, the Court in its discretion may dispense with making all of them parties, and may proceed in the suit, having sufficient parties before it to represent all the adverse interests of the plaintiffs and the defendants in the suit properly before it. But, in such cases, the decree shall be without prejudice to the rights and claims of all the absent parties.

* * *

In 1912, Equity Rule 38 supplanted Equity Rule 48:

EQUITY RULE 38 (1912)

When the question is one of common or general interest to many persons constituting a class so numerous as to make it impracticable to bring them all before the court, one or more may sue or defend for the whole.

CHARLES A. WRIGHT, ARTHUR R. MILLER & MARY K. KANE, FEDERAL PRACTICE AND PROCEDURE

Thomson West (3d ed. 2005) Vol. 7A § 1751, at 15–17.

Although the English practice was to treat a class action judgment as binding on everyone in the group, there was considerable uncertainty in the United States as to the *res judicata* effect on nonparty class members. Federal Equity Rule 48, in force between 1842 and 1912, recited the usual prerequisites for a class action, gave the court discretion to dispense with requiring that all interested persons be named as parties, authorized the court to proceed to judgment when a sufficient number of persons representing all the interests of the class were before the court, and concluded with the statement: "But, in such cases, the decree shall be without prejudice to the rights and claims of the absent parties." This passage seemed to limit the binding effect of a class action adjudication to those class members actually named and present before the court. Nonetheless, since one of the principal purposes of allowing class suits was to prevent the multiplicity of actions involving common questions and to obtain a final determination of the issues raised, this sentence occasionally was ignored and the judgment was declared binding on all members of the group. For example, in *Smith v. Swormstedt*, [57 U.S. (16 How.) 288 (1853)], the Supreme Court, without mentioning Equity Rule 48, announced a proposition contrary to the rule when it said [in discussing the reach of a judgment in a class action] that "the decree binds all of them the same as if all were before the court." In other instances, however, especially if the court felt that the absentees had not been adequately represented or had not been given a fair hearing of the common issues, Equity Rule 48 was used to prevent the judgment from prejudicing those who had not been before the court.

In 1912, Equity Rule 38 replaced Equity Rule 48 and omitted the sentence in the earlier rule dealing with the effect of a class action on those not before the court. Although this omission removed the express limitation upon the effect of a representative suit, it did not necessarily solve the question whether binding absent class members was consistent with due process and the notion of a right to a day in court. As a result, there continued to be confusion and uncertainty as to the application of a final decree in a class suit.

Then in 1921, in *Supreme Tribe of Ben–Hur v. Cauble* [255 U.S. 356 (1921)], the Supreme Court left little doubt as to its belief in the desirability of binding unnamed members of a class. It stated:

> If the federal courts are to have the jurisdiction in class suits to which they are obviously entitled, the decree when rendered must bind all of the class properly represented. * * *

In a later case, however, the Supreme Court, without citing *Ben–Hur*, revived some of the doubt by limiting the effect of Equity Rule 38 to cases affecting the absentees' interests in property within the territorial jurisdiction of the court. [*Christopher v. Brusselback*, 302 U.S. 500 (1938).]

* * *

NOTES AND QUESTIONS

1. Compare Equity Rule 38 to Equity Rule 48. What is the practical significance, if any, of each change from the earlier rule to the latter? With respect to the binding effect of class action judgments, note the impact of *Smith v. Swormstedt*, 57 U.S. (16 How.) 288 (1853), on the courts' interpretation of Equity Rule 48. Is there any value to a rule that permits one person to sue as the representative of others, but does not prevent absent (*i.e.*, represented) parties within the defined class, who were not actually named as litigants, from later bringing suit on the same claim?

2. Class action practice across the United States at the time of Equity Rules 38 and 48 was conducted under a variety of state equity rules that differed from jurisdiction to jurisdiction. For a summary of the variations, and of the issues those rules presented, *see, e.g.*, Carl C. Wheaton, *Representation Suits Involving Numerous Litigants*, 19 Cornell L.Q. 399 (1934).

3. ORIGINAL RULE 23

In 1937, the Supreme Court of the United States promulgated the Federal Rules of Civil Procedure, which, among other things, unified the rules of law and equity in the federal courts. (For a brief history of the merger of law and equity, *see* Thomas O. Main, *Traditional Equity and Contemporary Procedure*, 78 Wash. L. Rev. 429 (2003)). Those rules became effective September 16, 1938, and contained a new rule for class actions—Rule 23. Although Rule 23 has undergone a complete transformation since 1938, a basic understanding of the 1938 rule is important for the student of modern class actions.

RULE 23 (1938)

a. Representation. If persons constituting a class are so numerous as to make it impracticable to bring them all before the court, such of them, one or more, as will fairly insure the adequate representation of all may, on behalf of all, sue or be sued, when the character of the right sought to be enforced for or against the class is

> (1) joint, or common, or secondary in the sense that the owner of a primary right refuses to enforce that right and a member of the class thereby becomes entitled to enforce it;
>
> (2) several, and the object of the action is the adjudication of claims which do or may affect specific property involved in the action; or
>
> (3) several, and there is a common question of law or fact affecting the several rights and a common relief is sought.

b. [Related to derivative actions by shareholders and, in the 1966 revision, carried forward as Rule 23.1. *See* Chapter 11(B).]

c. Dismissal or Compromise. A class action shall not be dismissed or compromised without the approval of the court. If the right sought to be enforced is one defined in paragraph (1) of subdivision (a) of this rule notice of the proposed dismissal or compromise shall be given to all members of the class in such manner as the court directs. If the right is one defined in paragraphs (2) or (3) of subdivision (a) notice shall be given only if the court requires it.

JOHN G. HARKINS, JR., FEDERAL RULE 23—THE EARLY YEARS
39 Ariz. L. Rev. 705, 705–09 (1997).

Before we turn to the content of the 1938 Rule 23, we might take note of a key principle which guided the drafting process. The drafters understood that the rules which they would propose should be rules of procedure only, not rules which would cause changes in substantive rights. In the context of class actions, where the rights of those not before the court might be affected, this principle had obvious importance. The result was said to be an attempt to categorize the types of cases which might proceed as class actions, based on the existing practice. One could describe the proposed Rule 23, therefore, as primarily an attempt to codify, not to reform.

One other background point may be worthy of note. The 1938 Rules abolished the distinction between actions at law and those in equity, creating instead a single form of civil action. The class action device had previously been exclusively the province of equity, which may have influenced its development in subtle ways. From 1938 forward, any such mystique was lost and the scope of debate about the proper use and function of the class device was, it would seem, widened.

* * *

A number of important concepts are embedded in the introductory portion of subdivision (a) [of the 1938 Rule 23]. There must be a "class" and its members must be "so numerous as to make it impracticable to bring them all before the court." One or more of the members of the class may sue or be sued on behalf of all only if the representative or representatives "will fairly insure the adequate representation of all." And since the words "sue or be sued" are used, there can be plaintiff classes and defendant classes. The matter of notice is considered only in subdivision (c) and then only in a very limited context. All of the Rule 23(a) concepts, except adequacy of representation, had been articulated in Equity Rule 38; and adequacy of representation was a well understood, if unwritten, prerequisite to class status under Rule 38.

A categorization of acceptable classes—described in terms of the character of the interests to be litigated—occurs in the three numbered paragraphs of subdivision (a). The organizing theme, according to Professor Moore [author and principal supporter of the 1938 version of Rule 23], was the "jural relationships" among the members of the class. The three classes were described by Professor Moore as, respectively, a "true" class, a "hybrid" class and a "spurious" class.

In a "true" or (a)(1) class, the rights sought to be enforced were shared rights—the "jural relationship"—and joinder of all members of the class would be required to adjudicate those rights. The (a)(1) class action was thus a substitute for mandatory joinder where the members of the class were so numerous as to make such joinder impracticable. In the case of the "hybrid" or (a)(2) class, while the rights of the class members might be several and not joint, those rights would relate to some specific property, often a fund, over which the court would assume what would be (or at least would be akin to) *in rem* jurisdiction. The jural relationship would arise from the fact that the members of the class had "several" (rather than joint) interests involving some distinct property and the interests of all of them with respect to that property might be affected by the outcome of the litigation.

In the "spurious" class under (a)(3), if there was any "jural relationship," it was a fiction created to justify bringing together those who had no prior relationship whatsoever. What would join the members of an (a)(3) class together was the happenstance (and not a relationship) that determination of their "several" rights would depend at least in part on resolution of a common question of law or fact, and then only if it were further supposed that the members would seek common relief. In this case, allowing the action to proceed as a class action would serve (imperfectly) as a kind of permissive joinder mechanism [*see infra* Chapter 13(A)(1)] by which strangers might come together to litigate. It might be added that if the new rule was a codification, there was plenty of precedent for the first two types of classes; but the same could not so easily be said of the third category. Indeed, doubt was expressed that the bringing together of simple money damage claims, bound only by a common question, could be considered a proper class at all.

In practice, identification of the members of a class of the "true" and "hybrid" categories was relatively straightforward since a relationship of some sort would have existed among the members prior to the institution of the litigation. Moreover, representation and adequacy of representation (except perhaps in the context of a defendant class) also seemed to be less of an issue in these types of class actions compared with the (a)(3) variety, perhaps again based on the fact of the preexisting relationship. And the nature of the rights at stake in (a)(1) and (a)(2) litigation made it appropriate (perhaps one could say necessary) that all members of the class be bound by the judgment, whereas in the case of an (a)(3) class, the prevailing view (as noted below) was that absent members of the class would not be bound until they actually appeared of record in the action.

* * *

Most of the interesting issues under the 1938 version of Rule 23 arose in the context of the spurious class action under (a)(3). A large part of the discussion centered on what came to be known as one way intervention. To understand that phrase, one should first recall that the rule did not explain who would be bound by a judgment in a class action. And as a corollary, it said nothing about how an absent class member could take advantage of a judgment favorable to his or her interest. Moreover, the only reference in the rule to notice was in the context of a compromise or dismissal; and as to an (a)(3) action, even notice of a compromise or dismissal was to be given only if the court required it.

Consider also the belief that the Constitution requires some form of notice and an opportunity to be heard as the normal minimal safeguard afforded one whose interests might be the subject of a judgment. Although there was certainly precedent (and perhaps a rationale) among the so-called association and common fund cases for the proposition that a judgment in a class action could be binding on absent class members who had received no personal notice, no justification seemed to exist for such a result in the case of strangers bound together only by a "common question" affecting their several rights.

Against this background, it was generally understood that if a plaintiff class action under (a)(3) ended in victory for the defendant, the judgment would not bind absent class members who had not intervened and to whom no notice had been sent. Subject to statute of limitations issues, the absent class member could still sue on his or her claim. The other side of the coin was that absent class members would not obtain the advantage of a ruling favorable to their claims unless they intervened. This led to the practice of giving notice to absent class members of a favorable verdict and allowing them to intervene to make a claim before the judgment for the named plaintiff became final. Thus, "one way intervention" was born. * * * The absent class member was given the opportunity and a means to bind the defendant to a result adverse to the defendant; but the successful defendant had no reciprocal right to bind absent members of a plaintiff class.

* * *

NOTES AND QUESTIONS

1. What would a litigant have to show to bring an action under the 1938 version of Rule 23? Compare that rule to Equity Rules 48 and 38. What is the practical significance, if any, of each change?

2. Is there merit to classifying different class actions according to the rights that are at stake?

3. Why might the drafters of original Rule 23 have believed that class members in "spurious" class actions should be bound only if they join the litigation, whereas class members in "true" and "hybrid" class actions should be bound without opportunity for exclusion?

The 1938 version of Rule 23 had a significant impact on the dockets of federal courts.

ZECHARIAH CHAFEE, JR., THE THOMAS M. COOLEY LECTURES: SOME PROBLEMS OF EQUITY
University of Michigan Law School, at 199–200 (1950).

* * * [In 1938], a flood of reported cases under Rule 23 began. * * * In 1941 an able article in the *University of Chicago Law Review* by Kalven and Rosenfield [8 U. Chi. L. Rev. 684] hailed the class-suits device as a great improvement over corporate reorganization committees. The result is that class suits come rushing at us from all directions, not only in old-fashioned areas of business and insurance law but in litigation under the Securities Exchange Act, in claims for private injuries caused by monopolistic violations of the antitrust laws, in claims for overtime pay, in attacks on the validity of patents, and so on, with no breathing spell in sight. The situation [was] * * * tangled and bewildering * * *.

* * *

[End of Excerpt]

Eventually, Rule 23, as adopted in 1938, proved unworkable for the courts. In an influential 1966 law review article, a reporter for the revision of Rule 23 explained why a change was deemed necessary. *See* Benjamin Kaplan, *Continuing Work of the Civil Committee: 1966 Amendments of the Federal Rules of Civil Procedure (I)*, 81 Harv. L. Rev. 356 (1967). The article observed that, "[i]n the wash of more than [a] quarter-century's experience, [the original, 1938 version of] Rule 23 did not come out very well." *Id.* at 380. Professor Kaplan explained that the original Rule 23 categories

> were not helpful and on occasion they seemed to distract attention from the real issues. * * * Some cases classified by the courts as spurious seemed suitable, at least on surface inspection, for judgments having full binding effect. * * * On the other hand, there were instances of courts classifying actions as true or attributing consequences to them seemingly following from such a classification where * * * it was hard to see why the rights were not "several." * * * The class-action device, then, had become snarled. * * *

Id. at 381–85.

NOTES AND QUESTIONS

1. One case cited by Professor Kaplan in his 1967 article was *System Federation No. 91 v. Reed*, 180 F.2d 991 (6th Cir. 1950). In *Reed*, the Sixth Circuit described some of the difficulties courts had experienced with the 1938 class action rule:

> Much confusion has been created by the use of the nomenclature applied to class actions as true, spurious, or hybrid. "The task of pigeonholing operative facts into one of the three categories as of 'true,' 'hybrid,' or 'spurious' suit has baffled both courts and commentators." * * * Moreover, the classification, in Rule 23(a), of the rights to be enforced as common and joint, or several, gives rise to other difficulties. It may not always be a simple problem to tell when a right is common or when several. Whether there should be a distinction between suits involving plaintiff classes and defendant classes has likewise been suggested. The question as to when the decree is *res judicata* upon members of a class represented but not appearing in the action presents further difficulties.

Id. at 996 (citations omitted).

2. When studying modern Rule 23 in the next section and elsewhere, consider whether the new rule effectively responds to the concerns raised by Kaplan and others.

4. MODERN RULE 23

Rule 23 was completely revised in 1966. Since then, Rule 23 has remained in largely the same form. This section describes the 1966 Rule, while the next section describes subsequent modifications to Rule 23.

CHARLES A. WRIGHT, CLASS ACTIONS
47 F.R.D. 169, 170–73, 174, 176–82, 185 (1970).

As originally adopted in 1938, Rule 23 made a bold and well-intentioned attempt to encourage more frequent use of class actions. The rule made this procedure available in actions for legal relief as well as in those that were historically equitable, and it sought to give guidance on the kind of cases for which class treatment was appropriate. But * * * a quarter century of experience demonstrated very serious defects in the original rule. Accordingly in 1966 the rule was extensively amended. The amended rule * * * sought to substitute functional tests for the conceptualisms of the old rule. In addition, it sought to provide better guidance on the measures that may be taken by the court in managing the class action. Unfortunately the new rule, though generously described as "complicated," still "tends to ask more questions than it answers." * * * [Moreover,] the amended rule is in jeopardy from those who embrace it too enthusiastically just as it is from those who approach it with distaste. Admonitions that the amended rule "should be given a liberal rather than a restrictive interpretation" and that "if there is to be an error made, let it be in favor and not against the maintenance of the class action" convey a receptive spirit. But if they encourage courts to allow maintenance of class actions in controversies that are unmanageable by this device, the rule may come into disrepute even for the cases to which it is well suited. It may well be that "it will take a generation or so before we can fully appreciate the scope, the virtues, and the vices of the new Rule 23." * * *

* * *

For the class to be large enough to permit a class suit, impossibility of joinder is not required. Extreme difficulty or impracticability of joinder is sufficient. * * * The requirement of a numerous class is intended to protect members of a small class from being deprived of their rights without a day in court, and in a particular case this object should be weighed in the light of the situation that exists.

Adequacy of representation is essential. The representative must not hold interests that conflict with those of the class he seeks to represent. The adequacy of representation should be scrutinized with particular care where suit is brought, as the rule has always permitted, against a class of defendants. Plaintiffs must not be allowed to succumb to the temptation to name as representatives of the defendant class persons whose defense will be less zealous.

* * *

It has frequently been said that a sufficient number of members of the class must appear as parties to insure a fair representation of the class, but it has increasingly come to be recognized that the quality of the representation is more important than numbers, and that even a single representative of the class may be enough.

* * *

Under the old rule the limited effect given the judgment in the "spurious" action was in contrast to a "true" class suit, in which all the members of the class were bound, and the "hybrid" class suit, where the members of the class were bound only as to rights, if any, in the property involved. But this was not the only respect in which important consequences turned on the label applied to the class suit. Such matters as jurisdiction, venue, intervention, and tolling of the statute of limitations were all thought to vary depending on which kind of class suit was involved.

This was the most serious defect in the old rule, and was of much more consequence than the anomaly of a class suit that did not bind the class. If matters of importance turn on the classification given a particular suit, then it is vital that it be clearly understood which classification applies. The fact was that the task of determining which label was appropriate for a particular suit "baffled both courts and commentators." * * * Cases challenging racial discrimination provided a particularly striking example. Some courts thought this a "true" class action, others called it "spurious," while most simply said that it was a permissible class action and avoided the unrewarding task of further identification.

The principal reason for rewriting Rule 23 in 1966 was to get away from the conceptually-defined categories of the old rule. The new rule does describe categories of cases that may be appropriate for class treatment, and procedural consequences may depend on which category is involved, but the new categories are described functionally rather than conceptually. Inevitably there is some overlap among the categories. Because there are three categories in the new rule, just as there were in the old, there has been some tendency to suppose that the old names, "true," "hybrid," and "spurious," may still be used, though with their definitions in the rule altered. This is not only wrong but dangerously wrong. Nothing in the new rule corresponds to the former "spurious" class action, since it is expected that the judgment in a class action under the new rule will bind all members of the class, except those who have been expressly excluded. Nor do any of the clauses of new Rule 23(b) correspond with the old "true" or "hybrid" class actions. The new rule must be approached on its own pragmatic terms, rather than with preconceptions derived from the old conceptual categories.

Rule 23(b)(1) permits a class action where this is necessary to avoid possible adverse effects on the opponents of the class or on absent members of the class. The party opposing the class would be prejudiced if inconsistent results in individual adjudications establish incompatible standards of conduct to which he must adhere, as in a suit by taxpayers to invalidate municipal action or in a suit involving the rights and duties of riparian owners. Individual members of the class would be prejudiced if adjudications in individual actions would "as a practical matter" impair their ability to protect their interests, as in a suit to compel reorganization of a fraternal association or a suit by stockholders to compel declaration of a dividend.

Rule 23(b)(2) permits a class action where the party opposing the class has acted or refused to act on grounds generally applicable to the class. It is intended primarily for civil rights cases, though there may well be other kinds of cases that will fall within it. It is expressly limited to cases in which "final injunctive relief or corresponding declaratory relief with respect to the class as a whole" will be appropriate, and thus deliberately excludes actions for damages, in which it might otherwise be asserted that a party's denial of fault, and refusal to pay claims against it, was a refusal to act on a ground generally applicable to a class.

The most complicated and controversial portion of the 1966 revision is Rule 23(b)(3). This authorizes a class action where the only justification for such a procedure is the presence of common questions of law or fact.

Though this bears a superficial resemblance to the old "spurious" action, the "spurious" action was not really a class action at all while a suit under (b)(3) is a class action in all respects. The court has discretion whether to allow a (b)(3) action. Before permitting it to be maintained the court must find that the questions of law or fact common to the members of the class predominate over any questions affecting only individual members, and that a class action is superior to other available methods for the fair and efficient adjudication of the controversy. The rule itself lists four factors that the court is to consider, among others, in determining whether a class action is superior to other methods.

Predictions that not "very many actions" would be allowed to proceed under (b)(3) have proved quite ill-founded. The great bulk of reported cases in which class actions have been allowed under the revised rule have been (b)(3) actions. This device has been especially useful in cases involving securities frauds, where individual investors allegedly injured are in a poor position to seek redress, either because they do not know enough or because the cost of suit is disproportionate to each individual claim. * * *

If the court permits a (b)(3) class action to be maintained, it must direct to the members of the class the best notice practicable under the circumstances, including individual notice to all members who can be identified through reasonable effort. This notice is crucial to the whole scheme of (b)(3). * * *

* * *

The notice to the absentee in a (b)(3) action advises him of his rights in the action, including the right if he wishes to appear through his counsel, that he will be excluded from the class if he so requests by a date and procedure specified in the notice, and that the judgment will include him if he has not requested exclusion.

Critical to the entire operation of the revised rule is the effect of the judgment. It is clearly contemplated that every judgment in every class action will bind all of the members of the class, except for those who have asked to be excluded in a (b)(3) action. The rule does not say this. It says only that the judgment "shall include and describe those whom the court finds to be members of the class," and who have not asked to be excluded from a (b)(3) action. This recognizes that a court conducting an action cannot predetermine its *res judicata* effect, and that this can be tested only in a subsequent action. It recognizes, too, that even a party named in the judgment will not be bound if he has been denied due process of law. But the rule is intended to provide due process to absentees and it plainly contemplates that they will be bound.

The absentee has an absolute right to be excluded from a (b)(3) action. If he does, and the judgment ultimately is favorable to the class, he should not be entitled to rely on it as collateral estoppel, in those jurisdictions that have departed from the requirement of mutuality for estoppel. To permit him to do this would make a mockery of the (b)(3) procedure, and would restore in a different form the "one way" intervention that the amended rule was expressly intended to preclude. Notions of collateral estoppel are not so inexorable that a party who has affirmatively obtained exclusion from a judgment need be allowed later to claim the benefits of the judgment.

The court is required to make a determination as early as is practicable [now, at "an early practicable time," (Rule 23(c)(1)(A))] whether the action can be maintained as a class action. This is especially important with (b)(3) actions but it is required for all. This is a tentative determination, and may be altered later if events indicate that this would be wise.

* * *

NOTES AND QUESTIONS

1. What does a litigant have to show to bring an action under the modern version of Rule 23? Compare modern Rule 23 to original Rule 23, Equity Rule 48, and Equity Rule 38. Which principles remain? Which concepts were added? Which were deleted? What is the practical significance of each change?

2. As noted in the excerpts from both Professor Kaplan and Professor Wright, the rewriting of Rule 23 was a response, in part, to dissatisfaction with the classification scheme of original Rule 23. Later chapters will examine whether the classification scheme of modern Rule 23, as amended, provides sufficient guidance to courts and practitioners about the circumstances in which class actions are appropriate.

3. Since Professor Wright published his article in 1970, many of his conclusions have stood the test of time. For example, as discussed in Chapter 3, although Professor Wright's conclusion that Rule 23(b)(2) "deliberately excludes actions for damages" has been hotly contested among the circuits, the Supreme Court has, in *Wal-Mart Stores, Inc. v. Dukes*, 564 U.S. 338 (2011), come close to affirming his conclusion. *See id.* at 366 ("We need not decide in this case whether there are any forms of 'incidental' monetary relief that are consistent with * * * Rule 23(b)(2) * * * and that comply with the Due Process Clause"). Additionally, Professor Wright's perception that Rule 23(b)(3) class suits are the "most complicated and controversial" continues to be shared by many commentators. *See, e.g.*, Deborah R. Hensler et al., *Class Action Dilemmas: Pursuing Public Goals for Private Gain* 49–50 (Rand 2000); Melissa Hart, *Will Employment Discrimination Class Actions Survive?*, 37 Akron L. Rev. 813, 816 (2004); Kenneth S. Rivlin & Jamaica D. Potts, *Proposed Rule Changes to Federal Civil Procedure May Introduce New Challenges in Environmental Class Action Litigation*, 27 Harv. Envtl. L. Rev. 519, 525–26 (2003).

It also remains true, almost five decades after Professor Wright's initial observations, that most cases in which class certification is granted are certified under Rule 23(b)(3). Class actions arising under the other three subdivisions of Rule 23—(b)(1)(A), (b)(1)(B), and (b)(2)—are less frequent. *See, e.g.*, Edward F. Sherman, *American Class Actions: Significant Features and Developing Alternatives in Foreign Legal Systems*, 215 F.R.D. 130, 134 (2003) ("Today, a very high percentage of American class actions are Rule 23(b)(3) class actions."); Hensler et al., *Class Action Dilemmas: Pursuing Public Goals for Private Gain*, *supra*, at 52 (noting prevalence of damages actions under Rule 23(b)(3)).

5. AMENDED RULE 23 AND THE CLASS ACTION FAIRNESS ACT

Various rule changes and legislation (some significant, some less so) have been adopted since the promulgation of the 1966 version of Rule 23.

a. 1998 Amendments

On December 1, 1998, the 1966 version of Rule 23 underwent its most significant amendment to that point with the addition of subdivision 23(f). That subdivision—which is discussed in detail in Chapter 9—permits appellate courts to grant discretionary review of decisions granting or denying class certification, even if the district court has not certified the ruling for interlocutory review under 28 U.S.C. § 1292(b). Rule 23(f) has facilitated the development of a significant body of federal appellate case law concerning the certification requirements of Rule 23.

b. 2003 Amendments

In June 2002, the Judicial Conference's Committee on Rules of Practice and Procedure approved amendments to two subdivisions of Rule 23, as well as the addition of two new subsections. *See* Rule 23(c) (amended to replace the directive that a court make the class certification determination "as soon as practicable" with the more flexible "at an early practicable time"); 23(e) (amended to provide more detailed criteria for courts to use in evaluating class settlements); 23(g) (newly added to provide standards for appointment of class counsel); and 23(h) (added to provide criteria for awards of attorneys' fees and nontaxable costs). These amendments, which are described below, took effect on December 1, 2003.

Amended Rule 23(c) addresses the time frame for determining whether the court should certify a class. It also addresses class notice, including the addition of a notice provision that explicitly deals with (b)(1) and (b)(2) class actions. *See* Chapter 4(B)(1)(a) and Chapter 5(A)(4).

Amended Rule 23(e) spells out, in greater detail than prior Rule 23(e), the procedure for reviewing proposed settlements, requiring court approval for voluntary dismissal or settlement of the claims, issues, or defenses of a *certified* class, but not for the dismissal or compromise of an *uncertified* class. Amended Rule 23(e)(1) requires the court, in a certified class action, to "direct notice in a reasonable manner to all class members who would be bound by the proposal." Amended Rule 23(e)(2) provides that, "[i]f the proposal would bind class members, the court may approve it only after a hearing and on finding that it is fair, reasonable, and adequate." Amended Rule 23(e)(3) directs the parties to identify any side agreements made in connection with a proposed settlement. Amended Rule 23(e)(4) establishes that the court may condition approval of a settlement on providing a new opportunity for class members to exclude themselves from a (b)(3) class settlement after expiration of the initial opt-out period. Amended Rule 23(e)(5) describes the right to object to a proposed settlement and requires court approval for withdrawal of an objection. *See* Chapter 8(A)(4).

Amended Rule 23(g) focuses on class counsel. It provides that class counsel must fairly represent the class, a concept that was already embodied in Rule 23(a)(4)'s adequacy requirement and then-existing case law. In addition, amended Rule 23(g) establishes a formal requirement that class counsel be appointed upon certification of a class. *See* Chapter 2(B)(4)(c)(ii).

Amended Rule 23(h) establishes a general procedure for dealing with attorneys' fee requests (motions for fee awards, objections to the motion, hearings and findings, and referral to a special master or magistrate judge). *See* Chapter 8(C).

c. Subsequent Legislative Action and Rule Amendments

The Class Action Fairness Act of 2005 significantly expanded the jurisdiction of federal courts over class actions and imposed new restrictions on certain kinds of class-action settlements, including so-called coupon settlements. These important changes are described in detail in later chapters. *See* Chapters 7(A)(b)(3) (jurisdiction) & 8(A)(7) (settlements).

In 2007, the Court adopted housekeeping amendments, modifying subdivision 23(d)(2) (clarifying the judicial power to alter or amend orders "from time to time" over the course of the litigation), along with making non-substantive stylistic changes to Rule 23 and other Federal Rules. Finally, in 2009, Rule 23(f)'s deadline to petition for interlocutory appeal was changed from 10 days to 14 days, in keeping with general changes in the Federal Rules of Civil Procedure, which aim to simplify the way timing and filing deadlines are calculated.

d. Proposed Changes to Rule 23

In August 2016, the Committee on Practice and Procedure published a request for comments on proposed amendments to Rule 23:

- http://www.sefinanciallitigation.com/2016/10/federal-rules-advisory-committee-proposes-amendments-to-rule-governing-class-actions-in-federal-court/ *(containing link to PDF of the request for comments).*

- The proposed rules deal primarily with class settlements, including "frontloading" of information for the judge's initial review of the settlement; facts and circumstances that the court should consider in reviewing the fairness of a settlement; and provisions designed to deter meritless objections by serial objectors. In addition, the proposed rule changes clarify that electronic notice may suffice (without notice by first-class mail) in some circumstances. These proposed amendments are mentioned later in the text when relevant.

e. 2017 Proposed Legislation

At the time this text went to press, the Fairness in Class Actions Litigation Act of 2017, H.R. 985, 115th Cong. (2017), had passed the House of Representatives and was pending in the Senate. The bill has elicited sharp criticism from many commentators, and if enacted would have a major impact on the class action device.

NOTES AND QUESTIONS

1. Professor Judith Resnik, in an article titled *Lessons in Federalism from the 1960s Class Action Rule and the 2005 Class Action Fairness Act*, 156 U. Pa. L. Rev. 1929 (2008), suggests that both the revision of Rule 23 in 1966, and the enactment of CAFA in 2005, were prompted by concerns about state courts (albeit very different concerns):

> In the 1960s, Rule 23 was redrafted to expand class action opportunities for claimants in the federal courts. By easing access, rulemakers wanted to maximize the enforcement of federal rights, which they perceived to be under-protected in state courts, especially when state

actors were charged with discrimination. * * * [Similarly, when CAFA was enacted in 2005,] the purpose was, once again, to offer an alternative to state courts perceived by then to have over-protected rights for various kinds of plaintiffs.

Id. at 1930. When studying CAFA later in this course, particularly in Chapters 7 and 8, consider whether the Act strikes an appropriate balance between state and federal interests.

2. Professors Clermont and Eisenberg reviewed all the published cases in federal courts involving disputes over CAFA during the first two and a half years of the Act's existence. Kevin M. Clermont & Theodore Eisenberg, *CAFA Judicata: A Tale of Waste and Politics*, 156 U. Pa. L. Rev. 1553 (2008). They note that "CAFA has produced a lot of litigation in its short life," *id.* at 1553, which they attribute in part to an "especially poor job" by Congress in drafting CAFA's "vague and ambiguous" provisions. *Id.* at 1567. In their view, "most of the judicial activity" during the study period "was socially wasteful litigation [that] emphasized transitional efforts to interpret sloppily drafted provisions." *Id.* at 1553. CAFA continues to generate extensive litigation, and it has had profound consequences. *See* Robert H. Klonoff, *The Decline of Class Actions*, 90 Wash. U. L. Rev. 729, 745 (2013) (discussing CAFA's "enormous impact in shifting most class actions to federal court"). Its impact is explored later. *See* Chapters 7(B) & 8(A)(7).

6. CONTEMPORARY JUDICIAL VIEWS ON CLASS ACTIONS

RAHMAN V. CHERTOFF
United States Court of Appeals, Seventh Circuit, 2008.
530 F.3d 622.

Before EASTERBROOK, CHIEF JUDGE, and KANNE and TINDER, CIRCUIT JUDGES.

EASTERBROOK, CHIEF JUDGE.

[A group of United States citizens, each of whom had been detained multiple times upon reentering the country, sued to challenge the governmental policies that allegedly resulted in their "repeated, lengthy and abusive border detentions" in violation of their rights under the Fourth and Fifth Amendments. Plaintiffs pointed to two primary government policies. First, they alleged that the "Terrorist Screening Database"—a list of more than 200,000 names maintained by the Federal Bureau of Investigation—was over-inclusive and inaccurate, as shown by the repeated border searches and detentions of plaintiffs despite the fact that they had never been connected with terrorism in any way. Second, plaintiffs alleged that defendants had "repeatedly misidentif[ied]" as potential security threats U.S. citizens whose names were similar or identical to names in the database. The district court certified two classes under Rule 23(b)(2): a "Primary Traveler Class" consisting of "[a]ll US citizens who now are and/or in the future will be subjected to detentions upon reentry to the US as a result of defendants' contested policies, practices and customs"; and a "Family Detainee Class" of persons subjected to the same contested policies "because they are a family member of and traveling with a member of the primary traveler class." Defendants appealed the district court's decision to certify the classes, and the Seventh Circuit reversed the district court.]

* * *

The classes certified in this case are equivalent to a class of "all persons in the United States who have been, or ever will be, stopped without probable cause." * * * Improper arrests are best handled by individual suits for damages (and potentially through the exclusionary rule), not by a structural injunction designed to make every error by the police an occasion for a petition to hold the officer (and perhaps the police department as a whole) in contempt of court. Just so with stops at the border. * * *

The classes here are so ambulatory that plaintiffs might as well have proposed a class comprising "We the People of the United States." The expansive nature of that class (and of the two classes actually certified) shows that the case presents issues more suited to resolution by the democratic process than to adjudication. How much time returning travelers should spend cooling their heels at the border, while agents try to determine whether they are who they claim to be, and have been where they claim to have been, are legislative or executive questions. The political process is receptive to citizens who are abused by bureaucrats. The FBI and Department of Homeland Security have agreed to implement many of the Inspector General's suggestions (though not as many, or as fast, as plaintiffs think they should). * * *

Plaintiffs are entitled to relief that will redress any discrete wrong done them. That can be accomplished without certifying a class. * * * Decisions favorable to particular plaintiffs will have their effect in the normal way: through the force of precedent. If this seems a modest vision of the judiciary's role, we answer that modesty is the best posture for the branch that knows the least about protecting the nation's security and that lacks the full kit of tools possessed by the legislative and executive branches. * * *

REVERSED AND REMANDED.

* * *

KLAY v. HUMANA, INC.
United States Court of Appeals, 11th Circuit, 2004.
382 F.3d 1241.

Before TJOFLAT, BIRCH, and GOODWIN [(9th Cir.), by designation], CIRCUIT JUDGES.

TJOFLAT, CIRCUIT JUDGE.

This is a [class action case involving] almost all doctors versus almost all major health maintenance organizations (HMOs), coming before us for the third time in as many years; there have been twenty-one published orders and opinions in this case from various federal courts. The plaintiffs are a putative class of all doctors who submitted at least one claim to any of the defendant HMOs between 1990 and 2002. They allege that the defendants conspired with each other to program their computer systems to systematically underpay physicians for their services. We affirm the district court's certification of the plaintiffs' federal claims * * *.

* * *

* * * [W]e hold that the district court acted well within its discretion in concluding that it would be better to handle this case as a class action instead of clogging the federal courts with innumerable individual suits litigating the same issues repeatedly. The defendants have failed to point to any specific management problems—aside from the obvious ones that are intrinsic in large class actions—that would render a class action impracticable in this case.

Moving beyond the factors enumerated in [Rule 23], the defendants offer two additional reasons why a class action is inferior to a host of individual suits in resolving these disputes. First, they maintain that "a single jury, in a single trial, should not decide the fate of the managed care industry." Courts have occasionally found the impact that a class action suit could potentially have on an industry to be a persuasive reason to prohibit a class action from proceeding. * * * We find such reasoning unpersuasive and contrary to the ends of justice. This trial is not about the managed care industry; it is about whether several large HMOs conspired to systematically underpay doctors. The issue is not whether managed care is wrong, but whether particular managed care companies failed to live up to their agreements. The plaintiffs are seeking nothing more than the compensatory damages to which they are contractually entitled, and the treble damages to which they are statutorily entitled.

We have nothing but the defendants' conclusory, self-serving speculations to support their claim that this trial could devastate the managed care industry. * * * More importantly, however, if their fears are truly justified, the defendants can blame no one but themselves. It would be unjust to allow corporations to engage in rampant and systematic wrongdoing, and then allow them to avoid a class action because the consequences of being held accountable for their misdeeds would be financially ruinous. We are courts of justice, and can give the defendants only that which they deserve; if they wish special favors such as protection from high—though deserved—verdicts, they must turn to Congress.

Second, the defendants contend that a class action creates "unfair and coercive pressures on [them]" to settle that are unrelated to the merits of the plaintiffs' claims. * * * Mere pressure to settle is not a sufficient reason for a court to avoid certifying an otherwise meritorious class action suit.

* * *

Moreover, while affirming certification may induce some defendants to settle, overturning certification may create similar "hydraulic" pressures on the plaintiffs, causing them to either settle or—more likely—abandon their claims altogether. Because one of the parties will generally be disadvantaged regardless of how a court rules on certification, this factor should not be weighed.

For the reasons articulated above, we affirm the district court's grants of class certification as to all [federal] claims * * *.

Given the number of parties involved in this case, it threatens to degenerate into a Hobbesian war of all against all. Nevertheless, we feel that the district court—a veritable Leviathan—will be able to prevent the parties from regressing to a state of nature. One can only hope that, on remand, the proceedings will be short, though preferably not nasty and brutish.

SO ORDERED.

NOTES AND QUESTIONS

1. What core themes regarding aggregate litigation are illustrated by the excerpts from *Rahman* and *Klay*? Can *Rahman* and *Klay* be reconciled? What common ground, if any, do they share?

2. *Rahman* and *Klay* arose in quite different legal contexts—national security and civil RICO, respectively. From the excerpts provided, do the particular substantive areas of law at issue appear to play a role in the courts' decisions?

3. Judge Richard Posner of the Seventh Circuit is one of the country's most thoughtful and influential judges in the class action area. In a 2014 opinion for the Seventh Circuit, he discussed both the theoretical underpinnings and the practical limitations of the class action device:

> The class action is an ingenious procedural innovation that enables persons who have suffered a wrongful injury, but are too numerous for joinder of their claims alleging the same wrong committed by the same defendant or defendants to be feasible, to obtain relief as a group, a class as it is called. The device is especially important when each claim is too small to justify the expense of a separate suit, so that without a class action there would be no relief, however meritorious the claims. * * *

> The class action is a worthwhile supplement to conventional litigation procedure [citing numerous law review articles] * * *. Class actions are the brainchildren of the lawyers who specialize in prosecuting such actions, and in picking class representatives they have no incentive to select persons capable or desirous of monitoring the lawyers' conduct of the litigation. * * *

Eubank v. Pella Corp., 753 F.3d 718, 719–20 (7th Cir. 2014). As Judge Posner's opinion suggests, class action jurisprudence often reflects a tension between the utility of class actions and their potential for abuse if courts do not carefully monitor the proceedings.

4. Class action issues are frequently complicated, and thus it is not surprising that a relatively small number of judges, such as Judge Posner, appear frequently as authors of (or dissenters in) class action opinions. *See* Robert H. Klonoff, *Class Actions in the Year 2026: A Prognosis*, 65 Emory L.J. 1569, 1635–41 (2016) (listing the most influential class action judges, including Judges Posner and Easterbrook of the Seventh Circuit, Judge Scirica of the Third Circuit, Judge Tjoflat of the Eleventh Circuit, and Justice Ginsburg and the late Justice Scalia of the U.S. Supreme Court).

5. In the area of structural reform, it is almost a given that many cases are best handled on a classwide basis. For instance, in *Brown v. Plata*, 563 U.S. 493 (2011), the Supreme Court upheld the district court's ruling that a prison population limit was necessary to remedy violations of the prisoners' Eighth Amendment rights. The litigation consisted of two class actions on behalf of almost 160,000 California inmates. Importantly, the majority did not even consider the possibility that the litigation might be ill-suited for a class action.

NYU law professor Sam Issacharoff has stated, referring to *Brown v. Plata*, that "[t]he most significant class action case from the [Supreme Court] may be one that no one has ever heard of." Ed Beeson, *Top 15 High Court Class Action Rulings of the Past 15 Years*, LAW 360 (June 29, 2015), http://www.law360.com/articles/671772/. Issacharoff noted that the case was an example of the "[c]lass action [device] working as it should." *Id.*

Chapter 2

Class Certification: Threshold Requirements and Rule 23(a)

■ ■ ■

Rule 23(a) contains several explicit requirements, each of which must be satisfied before a class action can be certified. Courts have also identified additional threshold requirements that must also be satisfied for class treatment to be appropriate. This chapter addresses these various requirements.

A. THRESHOLD REQUIREMENTS

This section discusses several threshold requirements that must be satisfied before a class may properly be certified: (1) a definable class (including the requirement of some courts that the identification of class members be administratively feasible); (2) the representative's membership in the class; and (3) a claim that is live, not moot (including cases dealing with efforts to moot class actions through offers of judgment to the class representatives). These considerations were long viewed as "implicit" in Rule 23, although the first one noted above is now explicitly referenced (but not explained) in the Rule, and the second is arguably set forth as well (*see infra*). These requirements have generated extensive controversy and litigation.

Another issue discussed in this section is whether, under Article III of the U.S. Constitution, a class action may go forward when a significant number of the unnamed class members allegedly suffered no injury. Several recent cases have addressed standing in the class certification context.

1. A DEFINABLE CLASS

For many years, the primary focus in assessing class definition was whether there was an objective test for determining who is in the class. For instance, a class defined as individuals who have been "mistreated" by the police is very vague. As a related matter, courts looked at whether the proposed definition constituted a fail-safe class—where the definition turns on the merits so that someone who loses the case is not in the class (*e.g.*, all employees who were discriminated against on the basis of their race). In recent years, some courts have also focused on whether there is an administratively feasible way to identify class members. This text refers to the latter issue as "heightened ascertainability." This section addresses both issues.

a. An Objective Class Definition

It is critical to define a class properly. Without a precise, workable class definition, a court cannot determine who is in the class and thus bound by the judgment. Modern Rule 23 was amended in 2003 to reflect this priority. Rule 23(c)(1)(B) states that "[a]n order that certifies a class action must define the class and the class claims, issues, or defenses * * *." Despite this new language, however, neither the amended Rule nor the accompanying Advisory Committee Notes set forth what criteria courts should use when determining whether a class has been properly defined. Indeed, the governing principles are difficult to articulate and to apply consistently. Consider whether the following authorities provide useful guidance.

MANUAL FOR COMPLEX LITIGATION (FOURTH)
Federal Judicial Center (2004) § 21.222.

Defining the class is of critical importance because it identifies the persons (1) entitled to relief, (2) bound by a final judgment, and (3) entitled under Rule 23(c)(2) to the "best notice practicable" in a Rule 23(b)(3) action. The definition must be precise, objective, and presently ascertainable. For example, the class may consist of those persons and companies that purchased specified products or securities from the defendants during a specified period, or it may consist of all persons who sought employment or who were employed by the defendant during a fixed period.

Although the identity of individual class members need not be ascertained before class certification, the membership of the class must be ascertainable. Because individual class members must receive the best notice practicable and have an opportunity to opt out, and because individual damage claims are likely, Rule 23(b)(3) actions require a class definition that will permit identification of individual class members, while Rule 23(b)(1) or (b)(2) actions may not. An identifiable class exists if its members can be ascertained by reference to objective criteria. The order defining the class should avoid subjective standards (*e.g.*, a plaintiff's state of mind) or terms that depend on resolution of the merits (*e.g.*, persons who were discriminated against). The order should use objective terms in defining persons to be excluded from the class, such as affiliates of the defendants, residents of particular states, persons who have filed their own actions, or members of another class.

A class may be defined to include individuals who may not become part of the class until later. Such "future claimants" are primarily a feature of those mass tort actions involving latent injury. * * * Apart from mass tort cases, membership in a Rule 23(b)(3) class ordinarily should be ascertainable when the court enters judgment. There is no need to identify every individual member at the time of certification of a Rule 23(b)(2) class action for injunctive relief as long as the court can determine at any given time whether a particular individual is a member of the class. * * *

The court should also consider whether the class definition captures all members necessary for efficient and fair resolution of common questions of fact and law in a single proceeding. If the definition fails to include a substantial number of persons with claims similar to those of the class members, the definition of the class may be questionable. A broader class action definition or separate class might be more appropriate. If the class definition includes people with similar claims but divergent interests or positions, subclasses with separate class representatives and counsel might suffice.

The applicable substantive law and choice of law considerations may also affect the appropriate scope of the class. The difficulties posed by these considerations are likely to be compounded in nationwide or multistate class action litigation raising state law claims or defenses. Differences in applicable law and the number of divergent interests may lead a court to decline to certify a class.

The class definition should describe the operative claims, issues, or defenses, such as injury resulting from securities fraud or denial of employment on account of race. The relevant time should be included in the class definition. The relevant time, often referred to as the "class period," is, for example, the period during which members of the proposed class incurred the claimed injury. The order should delineate how the class representatives meet the commonality and typicality requirements of Rule 23(a). In a Rule 23(b)(3) case, defining the class and the class claims in the order helps confirm that class treatment is superior to other available methods for the fair and efficient adjudication of the controversy.

* * *

IN RE TEFLON PRODS. LIAB. LITIG.
United States District Court, Southern District of Iowa, 2008.
254 F.R.D. 354.

LONGSTAFF, SENIOR DISTRICT JUDGE.

The Court has before it plaintiffs' motion for class certification, filed August 4, 2008.

* * *

BACKGROUND

[P]laintiffs seek certification of twenty-three classes of persons who acquired cookware coated with DuPont's "Teflon" product. Plaintiffs allege that in producing and marketing its Teflon and unbranded, non-stick cookware coatings ("NSCC"), DuPont made false, misleading and deceptive representations regarding the safety of its product. They also claim that DuPont knew or should have known about potential risks attendant in using cookware containing its coating, and failed to disclose this information to consumers.[3]

The following relevant facts are accepted as true as alleged in [the Complaint]. Scientists in DuPont's Jackson Laboratory invented Teflon in 1938. DuPont first began selling Teflon commercially in 1946, and the product became a popular component of cookware in the 1960s. To date, billions of cookware products coated with Teflon have been sold world-wide.

---

[3] DuPont has sold its NSCC products under a variety of brand names during the time periods at issue in this litigation, including Teflon, Silverstone, and Autograph. DuPont also has sold its NSCC on an "unbranded" basis to cookware companies that do not want to pay a licensing fee to use the DuPont trademark. In all, DuPont sells its non-stick coatings to approximately 120 different houseware manufacturers. It is important to note that DuPont does not manufacturer cookware—only the coating used on other manufacturers' cookware. * * *

Various studies have shown that DuPont's NSCC can decompose at temperatures within the realm of "normal use," potentially releasing a synthetic chemical known as perfluorooctanoic acid ("PFOA"). Exposure to PFOA * * * may cause a flu-like condition known as "polymer fume fever."

In addition, blood sample data obtained by the Environmental Protection Agency ("EPA") caused the Agency to conclude that PFOA has the ability to cross the human placenta, potentially leading to birth defects. * * *

DuPont has been aware of potential health hazards from the use of NSCC since the 1950s or 1960s, but has represented to consumers that its product is completely safe. * * * DuPont has never disclosed the symptoms of polymer fume fever directly to consumers, nor has it suggested to consumers that there are any potential health risks from the use of its NSCC.

It is important to note that none of the proposed class representatives alleges that he or she has been injured from the use of DuPont NSCC. Rather, in each of the purported class actions, plaintiffs seek recovery solely for economic damage * * *.

Plaintiffs now move to certify the following class definition, with appropriate state-specific modifications:[7]

All persons who obtained ownership of cookware in State ___, within the State's applicable statute of limitations or repose of ___ years, and who fall within any of the following subclasses:

Sub–Class 1. All purchasers of cookware containing DuPont branded non-stick coating labeled with the DuPont trade names known as Teflon, Autograph, or Silverstone * * * who continue to possess the cookware, cookware packaging, or other documentation of the cookware.

Sub–Class 2. All purchasers of brands, makes, product lines, and/or models of cookware containing DuPont non-stick coating, whether branded with DuPont tradenames or not, and who continue to possess the cookware. The following manufacturers' or distributors' brands, makes, product lines, and/or models of cookware meet these criteria during the following time frames:

[The definition listed 22 brands of cookware, each with an associated time frame], and/or models of cookware admitted by DuPont to contain a DuPont non-stick cookware coating.

Sub–Class 3. All purchasers or owners of cookware coated with DuPont non-stick coating who do not qualify as members of Sub–Class 1 or 2.

* * *

APPLICABLE LAW AND DISCUSSION
* * *

The burden is on the party seeking certification to satisfy [Rule 23(a)'s requirements of (1) numerosity, (2) commonality, (3) typicality, and (4) adequate representation]. * * *

---

[7] This is the revised definition submitted during the hearing, and in plaintiffs' posthearing submission.

In addition to the above factors, numerous courts also have recognized * * * that the class definition [must be] drafted to ensure that membership is "capable of ascertainment under some objective standard;" and [] that all class representatives are in fact members of the proposed class.

Because the class definition is at the heart of any decision on certification, the Court will begin its analysis by considering these "implicit" factors.

1. Sufficiency of Class Definition

A well-crafted class definition must ensure that the Court can determine objectively who is in the class, and therefore, bound by the ultimate ruling. The Court should not be required to resort to speculation, or engage in lengthy, individualized inquiries in order to identify class members.

As set forth above, plaintiffs' revised class definition is divided into three sub-classes. Unfortunately for plaintiffs, however, the newly-created sub-classes do little to ease the Court's concerns regarding ascertainability. Each sub-class is addressed in turn, below.

a. Sub–Class One

Sub-class one covers individuals who purchased NSCC labeled with the Teflon, Autograph, or Silverstone trademarks, and who continue to possess the cookware, cookware packaging, or other documentation of the cookware. Individuals in this sub-class must have *purchased* their cookware in the state covered by the particular complaint, within the state's statute of limitations period.

Few proposed representatives have been able to meet this definition. As illustrated by the "Cookware Summary" in Defendant's Exhibit 9, plaintiffs produced documentation identifying the cookware for less than 8% of the items submitted for consideration. Packaging, literature and/or labels were available for only 5.6% of the items collected. Furthermore, the proposed representatives did not know the date or state of purchase for 22.2 and 32.4 percent of the items, respectively.

Accordingly, the proposed representative's own testimony, coupled with the cookware item itself, were the only evidence available to establish membership in sub-class one in the vast majority of cases. Neither have been shown to be particularly reliable.[13]

For example, proposed Texas sub-class one representative Kimberly Cowart testified in her deposition that she did not know whether the pan upon which she bases her claims against DuPont in fact has a Teflon nonstick coating, but *simply believes* it must be Teflon "[b]ecause when I purchased the pan, I would have only purchased it if it had said Teflon." She testified further that she did not recall purchasing her pan, did not remember anything about the packaging that came with the pan, and knew only that she purchased it "more than five years ago."

Similar to Ms. Cowart, proposed New York sub-class one representative Gary Frechter believed his pan to be a Teflon-coated product because:

---

[13] As demonstrated by the product photographs contained in Defendant's Exhibit 12, many of the pans submitted by proposed representatives had no visible product markings or labels. Even those containing a brand marker could not be identified as containing a Teflon coating, however, due to uncertainties regarding the year in which the product was manufactured and/or purchased.

"It is older than the rest, and I thought it was Teflon because [my wife and I] looked for Teflon products." When questioned further, however, Mr. Frechter indicated he could not ensure his pan actually contained a non-stick coating, and could not identify the place or even decade of purchase. [The court also cited deposition testimony in which the] proposed New Jersey sub-class one representative testified she "believed" her Wearever pan had Teflon coating because in the past, she specifically looked for pans with Teflon coating; [the] proposed Massachusetts sub-class one representative testified she believed her Copco pan had Teflon coating because "it's very old, and I don't recall it being any other options besides Teflon 35, 40 years ago."

b. Sub–Class Two

Sub-class two includes purchasers of certain NSCC that was not necessarily sold with a DuPont trademark, but was sold under a brand name believed to contain Teflon coating during the time-frame at issue. During the hearing, plaintiffs contend[ed] that they and/or DuPont can establish with relative certainty which brands of cookware were made with DuPont non-stick coating during certain time periods, and that those brands are incorporated into the definition of sub-class two. DuPont vigorously disputes the reliability of the third-party manufacturer records, however. Furthermore, deposition testimony of various cookware manufacturers' representatives shows that it is virtually impossible to identify a brand of non-stick coating based on a visual examination of the item of cookware. Lastly, membership in this class necessarily requires a plaintiff to pinpoint the date on which he or she purchased the item of cookware. As demonstrated in DuPont's Cookware Summary, the proposed class representatives were unable to recall this information almost one-fourth of the time.

c. Sub–Class Three

Lastly, sub-class three includes: "All purchasers or owners of cookware coated with DuPont non-stick coating who do not qualify as members of Sub–Class 1 or 2." This "catch-all" sub-class theoretically includes anyone who *believes* he or she has *ever* owned or purchased an item of cookware containing DuPont nonstick coating, regardless of whether an objective basis exists to support that belief. Notably, an individual does not even need to possess the pan to assert a claim under this sub-class.

Proposed Illinois sub-class 3 representative Paula Bardwell is illustrative of these individuals. Ms. Bardwell conceded in her deposition that she did not know either the specific type of non-stick coating used on any of her three pieces of cookware or the date(s) on which she purchased the cookware. Nor did she have the original packaging to ensure the non-stick coating was manufactured by DuPont. In fact, when questioned further by defense counsel, Ms. Bardwell admitted she was unsure whether she in fact purchased the cookware in the State of Illinois.

d. Conclusion Regarding Sufficiency of Definition

In short, too many infirmities exist in the present class definitions to ensure the Court can determine objectively who is in the class, without resort to speculation. As argued by DuPont, many class representatives mistakenly believe their product contained Teflon coating—even when they were informed the particular brand of cookware at issue never used Teflon.

Others believe *all* non-stick coating is from DuPont, shedding further doubt on the feasibility of ensuring membership with objective certainty.

* * *

Accordingly, the Court finds that the revised definition submitted by plaintiffs fails to provide an objective basis to determine several facts significant to establishing membership: 1) whether the cookware item in fact contains DuPont non-stick coating; 2) whether the item was purchased or obtained in some other manner; and 3) if purchased, whether the item was purchased in the state at issue within the applicable statute of limitations period. Without a clear basis for determining this information, plaintiffs' class definition necessarily fails.

* * *

NOTES AND QUESTIONS

1. Given the importance of class definition, why did the drafters of Rule 23 and the 2003 amendments fail to spell out specific requirements for defining the class? If Rule 23 were being amended again to address the issue, what requirements would a drafter want to include?

2. The plaintiffs in *In re Teflon* proposed three subclasses in response to the court's concern about certifying a single class. How permissive should a court be in allowing proponents of class treatment to modify class definitions to correct actual or potential problems? Does the court's ability to revise the class definition provide any tactical advantage to the proponents of a class action?

3. Should the adequacy of a class definition turn on the type of relief sought? For instance, as stated in the *Manual for Complex Litigation (Fourth)*, should a court be more permissive in approving a class definition when a case involves injunctive relief, as opposed to damages? Or should this distinction be irrelevant? Should it matter whether the class members are entitled to "opt out"—that is, to refuse to proceed as part of the class?

4. Based on the court's decision, why is it important to have a well-defined class?

5. A problem that some plaintiffs have had in drafting class action complaints is using class definitions that turn on class members' state of mind. In *Vietnam Veterans Against the War v. Benecke*, 63 F.R.D. 675 (W.D. Mo. 1974), the plaintiffs moved to certify a class defined as "persons who attend or participate or who wish to attend or participate in any public assembly or demonstration in Kansas City, Missouri held by citizens' groups or organizations whose political or social views conflict with those of the officials in the government or the Kansas City, Missouri Police Department." *Id.* at 678. In refusing to certify the class, the court reasoned:

> The definition of the class is based upon such a general and indefinite state of mind, encompassing a kaleidoscopic variety of mental positions which could be included, that there is no rational or reasonable process of defining and determining the extent and character of the class, and what individuals are in the class or not in it. Even assuming that all persons in the Kansas City, Missouri "area" (and those who may in the future be in the area), with vaguely described political or social philosophies could be identified, a determination of those who might act in a manner subjecting them to arrest * * * or to

surveillance by the Kansas City, Missouri Police Department is practically impossible. More than normal speculation is required for definition of the alleged class relied upon by the plaintiffs.

Id. at 680.

On the other hand, in *National Organization For Women, Inc. v. Scheidler*, 172 F.R.D. 351 (N.D. Ill. 1997), the court addressed the defendant's argument that the plaintiff class was unascertainable. Defendants noted that the definition included "all women who are not NOW members who have used or may use the services of women's health centers that provide abortions." *Id.* at 355. The court remedied the problem by modifying the definition based on language in the plaintiffs' reply brief. The court then certified a class defined as "the class of women who are not NOW members and whose rights to the services of women's health centers in the United States at which abortions are performed have been or will be interfered with by defendants' unlawful activities." *Id.* at 359. Was the defendant's argument—that membership in the class turned on class members' state of mind—a legitimate one? Did the court's revised definition solve the problem?

6. Why is it important, as the *Manual for Complex Litigation (Fourth)* states, that the class definition not exclude a substantial number of persons with claims similar to those asserted by the class?

7. For a discussion of the approach taken by some courts in granting plaintiffs no leeway or second chances to adequately define a class, *see* Robert H. Klonoff, *The Decline of Class Actions*, 90 Wash. U. L. Rev. 729, 761–68 (2013).

8. Another potentially difficult class definition issue is the so-called fail-safe class, which is "defined so that whether a person qualifies as a member depends on whether the person has a valid claim." *Messner v. Northshore Univ. HealthSystem*, 669 F.3d 802, 825 (7th Cir. 2012). "Such a class definition is improper because a class member either wins or, by virtue of losing, is defined out of the class and is therefore not bound by the judgment." *Id.*

Courts have the discretion to amend a fail-safe class definition. *See, e.g., Campbell v. First Am. Title Ins. Co.*, 269 F.R.D. 68, 73–74 (D. Me. 2010) ("A court may, in an exercise of its discretion, revise a proposed class definition to avoid the problem of a fail-safe class."). Yet many courts have denied class certification at least in part because of fail-safe class concerns. *See, e.g., Brazil v. Dell*, 585 F. Supp. 2d 1158, 1167 (N.D. Cal. 2008) (granting motion to strike class allegations where class definition included all persons who purchased Dell computer products that "Dell falsely advertised"); *Melton ex rel. Dutton v. Carolina Power & Light Co.*, 283 F.R.D. 280, 288–89 (D.S.C. 2012) (denying certification of class defined to include "those who own property encumbered by Defendant's transmission line easements, where Defendant has installed fiber optic cable which it has then used for general telecommunications purposes 'without the right to do so'"). In *Melton*, the district court noted: "It is better *** when practical and possible, to refine the class definition before flatly denying class certification on that basis." *Id.* at 289. In the case before it, however, the *Melton* court concluded that because the proposed class also failed the requirements of commonality, predominance, and superiority, it would be "impractical and unnecessary to undertake an effort to revise the potentially impermissible class definition." *Id.*

Ultimately, the greatest challenge may lie in determining whether the flaws of a particular proposed class definition are merely semantic (and thus potentially correctible), or instead are symptomatic of individual issues that threaten to make class certification untenable. For example, in *Randleman v. Fidelity National Title Ins. Co.*, 646 F.3d 347 (6th Cir. 2011), the Sixth Circuit affirmed the decertification of "an improper fail-safe class" where the class definition "only included those who [were] 'entitled to relief.'" *Id.* at 352. The court also found that the lower court did not abuse its discretion in finding a lack of predominance because plaintiffs had "defined the class and presented their claim in a manner that requires substantial, individual inquiries * * *." *Id.* at 353.

In 2013, the Seventh Circuit discussed the challenges inherent in differentiating between a permissible class definition and an overly broad fail-safe class:

> A decision on a class definition should not, in principle, influence the merits of the case. All class definitions allude to the merits, in that they assume either implicitly or explicitly that the defendant's conduct has adversely affected the defined group of people. We do not worry that certifying a class in such cases somehow prevents the defendant from proving that it is not liable for unlawful conduct. The class definition is a tool of case management. It settles the question who the adversaries are, and so it enables the defendant to gauge the extent of its exposure to liability and it alerts excluded parties to consider whether they need to undertake separate actions in order to protect their rights. What it does not tell us is who will win the case.

Abbott v. Lockheed Martin Corp., 725 F.3d 803, 810 (7th Cir. 2013) (Wood, J.); *see also In re Rodriguez*, 695 F.3d 360, 369–70 (5th Cir. 2012) (explaining that Fifth Circuit precedent does not prohibit fail-safe classes).

9. Consider whether a sufficiently definite class exists in each of the following circumstances:

    a. Plaintiffs allege contamination of a river system from a paper company's discharge of dioxin and sue on behalf of a class of: "[A]ll present or former business owners and operators such as commercial fishermen, bait and tackle shop owners, boat sales and boating equipment businesses whose business premises are located and affected by the contaminated river system." *McGuire v. Int'l Paper Co.*, 1994 WL 261360, at *2 (S.D. Miss. 1994).

    b. Plaintiff alleges a violation of his constitutional rights when his car was seized by the Little Rock, Arkansas Police Department, and sues on behalf of "others who are similarly situated." *Coleman v. Watt*, 40 F.3d 255, 259 (8th Cir. 1994).

    c. Plaintiffs, certain North Dakota farmers, allege that the Farmers Home Administration (FmHA) violated their constitutional rights by refusing to allow applications for deferment of loans, terminating funds for necessary living and operating expenses, and subjecting farmers to a biased and unconstitutional appeals process, and sue on behalf of "all persons who currently have or will acquire FmHA farmer program loans within North Dakota." *Coleman v. Block*, 562 F. Supp. 1353, 1356 (D.N.D. 1983).

    d. Plaintiffs claim that certain rules imposed by the Clerk of the City of New York "in conjunction with his officiating at civil weddings—namely those dealing with appropriate attire and the exchange of rings—violate their rights to privacy and free expression."

Rappaport v. Katz, 62 F.R.D. 512, 513 (S.D.N.Y. 1974). They sue on behalf of a class consisting of "all persons who wish and are legally entitled to be married by [the defendant]." *Id.*

e. Plaintiffs sue on behalf of proposed class members residing, present, or located in Chicago, Illinois, "who engage or have engaged in lawful political, religious, educational or social activities and who, as a result of these activities, have been within the last five years, are now, or hereafter may be, subjected to or threatened by alleged infiltration, physical or verbal coercion, photographic, electronic, or physical surveillance, summary punishment, harassment, or dossier collection, maintenance, and dissemination by [law enforcement officials] or their agents." *Alliance to End Repression v. Rochford*, 565 F.2d 975, 976 (7th Cir. 1977).

f. Plaintiffs sue on behalf of "all persons or other entities, who or which sustained damage as a result of the leak of toxic gas from the [defendant's] facility * * * on February 15, 1996." *Black v. Rhone–Poulenc, Inc.*, 173 F.R.D. 156, 158 (S.D. W. Va. 1996).

g. "Plaintiffs seek to represent * * * citizens who have been delayed in reentering the United States from abroad as a result of watch lists maintained by the Department of Homeland Security." *Rahman v. Chertoff*, 530 F.3d 622, 623 (7th Cir. 2008). They propose two classes under Rule 23(b)(2): a "Primary Traveler Class" consisting of "[a]ll US citizens who now are and/or in the future will be subjected to detentions upon reentry to the U.S. as a result of defendants' contested policies, practices and customs"; and a "Family Detainee Class" of persons subjected to the same contested policies "because they are a family member of and traveling with a member of the primary traveler class." *Id.* at 625; *see also* 244 F.R.D. 443, 446–50 (N.D. Ill. 2007) (district court opinion).

b. Heightened Ascertainability

In addition to requiring an objective class definition, some courts also require that plaintiffs demonstrate a reliable and administratively feasible mechanism for identifying class members (a requirement often referred to as "heightened ascertainability"). Other courts (including the decision below) have rejected "heightened ascertainability" as a separate requirement.

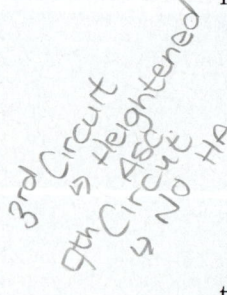

MULLINS V. DIRECT DIGITAL, LLC
United States Court of Appeals, Seventh Circuit, 2015.
795 F.3d 654.

Before BAUER, KANNE, and HAMILTON, CIRCUIT JUDGES.

HAMILTON, CIRCUIT JUDGE.

We * * * address whether Rule 23(b)(3) imposes a heightened "ascertainability" requirement as the Third Circuit and some district courts have held recently. *See, e.g.*, *Carrera v. Bayer Corp.*, 727 F.3d 300 (3d Cir. 2013). In this case, the plaintiff alleges consumer fraud by the seller of a dietary supplement, and the district court certified a plaintiff class. The court found that the proposed class satisfies the explicit requirements of Rule 23(a) and (b)(3), and the court rejected defendant's argument that Rule 23(b)(3) implies a heightened ascertainability requirement.

We affirm. * * *

* * *

I. *Factual and Procedural Background*

Plaintiff Vince Mullins sued defendant Direct Digital, LLC for fraudulently representing that its product, Instaflex Joint Support, relieves joint discomfort. He alleges that statements on the Instaflex labels and marketing materials—"relieve discomfort," "improve flexibility," "increase mobility," "support cartilage repair," "scientifically formulated," and "clinically tested for maximum effectiveness"—are fraudulent because the primary ingredient in the supplement (glucosamine sulfate) is nothing more than a sugar pill and there is no scientific support for these claims. Mullins asserts that Direct Digital is liable for consumer fraud under the Illinois Consumer Fraud and Deceptive Business Practices Act, and similar consumer protection laws in nine other states.

Mullins moved to certify a class of consumers "who purchased Instaflex within the applicable statute of limitations of the respective Class States for personal use until the date notice is disseminated." The district court certified the class under Rule 23(b)(3).

[We granted interlocutory review under Rule 23(f).]

II. *Analysis*

A. *The Established Meaning of "Ascertainability"*

We begin with the current state of the law in this circuit. Rule 23 requires that a class be defined, and experience has led courts to require that classes be defined clearly and based on objective criteria. When courts wrote of this implicit requirement of "ascertainability," they trained their attention on the adequacy of the class definition itself. They were not focused on whether, given an adequate class definition, it would be difficult to identify particular members of the class.

This "weak" version of ascertainability has long been the law in this circuit. * * *

The language of this well-settled requirement is susceptible to misinterpretation, though, which may explain some of the doctrinal drift described below. To understand its established meaning, it's better to focus on the three common problems that have caused plaintiffs to flunk this requirement.

First, classes that are defined too vaguely fail to satisfy the "clear definition" component. * * * Vagueness is a problem because a court needs to be able to identify who will receive notice, who will share in any recovery, and who will be bound by a judgment. To avoid vagueness, class definitions generally need to identify a particular group, harmed during a particular time frame, in a particular location, in a particular way. * * *

Second, classes that are defined by subjective criteria, such as by a person's state of mind, fail the objectivity requirement. * * *

Third, classes that are defined in terms of success on the merits—so-called "fail-safe classes"—also are not properly defined. Defining the class in terms of success on the merits is a problem because "a class member either wins or, by virtue of losing, is defined out of the class and is therefore not bound by the judgment." This raises an obvious fairness problem for the defendant: the defendant is forced to defend against the class, but if a plaintiff loses, she drops out and can subject the defendant to another round of litigation. The key to avoiding this problem is to define the class so that membership does not depend on the liability of the defendant.

The class definition in this case complies with this settled law and avoids all of these problems. It is not vague. It identifies a particular group of individuals (purchasers of Instaflex) harmed in a particular way (defrauded by labels and marketing materials) during a specific period in particular areas. The class definition also is not based on subjective criteria. It focuses on the act of purchase and Direct Digital's conduct in labeling and advertising the product. It also does not create a fail-safe class. If Direct Digital prevails, *res judicata* will bar class members from re-litigating their claims.

Direct Digital argues, however, that we should demand more. It urges us to adopt a new component to the ascertainability requirement that goes beyond the adequacy of the class definition itself. Drawing on recent decisions by the Third Circuit, Direct Digital argues that class certification should be denied if the plaintiff fails to show a reliable and administratively feasible way to determine whether a particular person is a member of the class. And, Direct Digital continues, affidavits from putative class members are insufficient as a matter of law to satisfy this requirement.

* * *

B. *The Recent Expansion of "Ascertainability"*

To understand the genesis of Direct Digital's argument, we briefly summarize the law of the Third Circuit, which has adopted this more stringent version of ascertainability. The Third Circuit's innovation began with *Marcus v. BMW of North America, LLC*, 687 F.3d 583 (3d Cir. 2012), where the court vacated certification of a poorly defined class. The decisive portion of the opinion certainly seems sound, but the opinion went on to caution that on remand, if defendants' records would not identify class members, the district court should not approve a method relying on "potential class members' say so," and the opinion said that reliance on class members' affidavits might not be "proper or just." The opinion did not explain this new requirement other than to cite an easily distinguishable district court decision.

Since *Marcus,* the court has applied this heightened ascertainability requirement in several more cases. * * *

As it stands now, the Third Circuit's test for ascertainability has two prongs: (1) the class must be "defined with reference to objective criteria" (consistent with long-established law discussed above), and (2) there must be "a reliable and administratively feasible mechanism for determining whether putative class members fall within the class definition." * * *

This second requirement sounds sensible at first glance. Who could reasonably argue that a plaintiff should be allowed to certify a class whose members are impossible to identify? In practice, however, some courts have used this requirement to erect a nearly insurmountable hurdle at the class certification stage in situations where a class action is the only viable way to pursue valid but small individual claims.

The demands of this heightened requirement are most apparent from the Third Circuit's discussion of self-identification by affidavit. It has said that affidavits from putative class members cannot satisfy the stringent ascertainability requirement. * * * Direct Digital urges us to adopt this rule and to reverse the certification order here because the only method for identifying class members proposed by Mullins in the district court was self-identification by affidavit.

We decline to do so. The Third Circuit's approach in *Carrera,* which is at this point the high-water mark of its developing ascertainability doctrine, goes much further than the established meaning of ascertainability and in our view misreads Rule 23. *Carrera* and cases like it have given four policy reasons for requiring more than affidavits from putative class members. We address each one below and find them unpersuasive.

In general, we think imposing this stringent version of ascertainability does not further any interest of Rule 23 that is not already adequately protected by the Rule's explicit requirements. On the other side of the balance, the costs of imposing the requirement are substantial. The stringent version of ascertainability effectively bars low-value consumer class actions, at least where plaintiffs do not have documentary proof of purchases, and sometimes even when they do. Accordingly, we conclude that the district court here did not abuse its discretion by deferring until later in the litigation decisions about more detailed aspects of ascertainability and the management of any claims process. * * *

We now turn to the policy concerns identified by the courts that have embraced this heightened ascertainability requirement. * * *

1. *Administrative Convenience*

Some courts have argued that imposing a stringent version of ascertainability "eliminates serious administrative burdens that are incongruous with the efficiencies expected in a class action by insisting on the easy identification of class members." * * * It does this by ensuring that the court will be able to identify class members without "extensive and individualized fact-finding or mini-trials."

This concern about administrative inconvenience is better addressed by the explicit requirements of Rule 23(b)(3), which requires that the class device be "superior to other available methods for fairly and efficiently adjudicating the controversy." One relevant factor is "the likely difficulties in managing a class action." Fed. R. Civ. P. 23(b)(3)(D).

The superiority requirement of Rule 23(b)(3) is clarified by substantial case law. Imposing a stringent version of ascertainability because of concerns about administrative inconvenience renders the manageability criterion of the superiority requirement superfluous. It also conflicts with the well-settled presumption that courts should not refuse to certify a class merely on the basis of manageability concerns. * * *

A reader might fairly ask whether there is any practical difference between addressing administrative inconvenience as a matter of ascertainability versus as a matter of superiority. In fact, there is. When administrative inconvenience is addressed as a matter of ascertainability, courts tend to look at the problem in a vacuum, considering only the administrative costs and headaches of proceeding as a class action. * * * But when courts approach the issue as part of a careful application of Rule 23(b)(3)'s superiority standard, they must recognize both the costs *and benefits* of the class device. * * *

Rule 23(b)(3)'s superiority requirement, unlike the freestanding ascertainability requirement, is comparative: the court must assess efficiency with an eye toward "other available methods." In many cases where the heightened ascertainability requirement will be hardest to satisfy, there realistically is no other alternative to class treatment. * * *

This does not mean, of course, that district courts should automatically certify classes in these difficult cases. But it does mean that before refusing to certify a class that meets the requirements of Rule 23(a), the district court should consider the alternatives as Rule 23(b)(3) instructs rather than denying certification because it may be challenging to identify particular class members. District courts have considerable experience with and flexibility in engineering solutions to difficult problems of case management.

In addition, a district judge has discretion to (and we think normally should) wait and see how serious the problem may turn out to be after settlement or judgment, when much more may be known about available records, response rates, and other relevant factors. And if a problem is truly insoluble, the court may decertify the class at a later stage of the litigation.

If faced with what appear to be unusually difficult manageability problems at the certification stage, district courts have discretion to insist on details of the plaintiff's plan for notifying the class and managing the action. In conducting this inquiry, district courts should consider also whether the administrative burdens can be eased by the procedures set out in Rule 23(c) and (d) [involving various types of orders for conducting the action]. * * *

Under this comparative framework, refusing to certify on manageability grounds alone should be the last resort. * * *

On the other hand, if courts look only at the cost side of the equation and fail to consider administrative solutions like those available under Rule 23(c) and (d), courts will err systematically against certification. * * * The stringent version of ascertainability invites precisely this type of systemic error.

2. *Unfairness to Absent Class Members*

Courts also have asserted that the heightened ascertainability requirement is needed to protect absent class members. If the identities of absent class members cannot be ascertained, the argument goes, it is unfair to bind them by the judicial proceeding. A central premise of this argument is that class members must receive actual notice of the class action so that they do not lose their opt-out rights.

We believe that premise is mistaken. For Rule 23(b)(3) classes, Rule

23(c)(2)(B) requires the "best notice that is practicable under the circumstances, including individual notice to all members who can be identified through reasonable effort." The rule does not insist on actual notice to all class members in all cases. It recognizes it might be *impossible* to identify some class members for purposes of actual notice. While actual individual notice may be the ideal, due process does not always require it. * * *

When class members' names and addresses are known or knowable with reasonable effort, notice can be accomplished by first-class mail. When that is not possible, courts may use alternative means such as notice through third parties, paid advertising, and/or posting in places frequented by class members, all without offending due process. * * * Due process simply does not require the ability to identify all members of the class at the certification stage.

More broadly, the stringent version of ascertainability loses sight of a critical feature of class actions for low-value claims like this one. In these cases, "only a lunatic or a fanatic" would litigate the claim individually, so opt-out rights are not likely to be exercised by anyone planning a separate individual lawsuit. When this is true, it is particularly important that the types of notice that courts require correspond to the value of the absent class members' interests. * * *

The heightened ascertainability approach upsets this balance. It comes close to insisting on actual notice to protect the interests of absent class members, yet overlooks the reality that without certification, putative class members with valid claims would not recover anything at all. * * * When it comes to protecting the interests of absent class members, courts should not let the perfect become the enemy of the good.

3. *Unfairness to Bona Fide Class Members*

The third concern offered to justify the heightened ascertainability requirement is the interests of class members with valid claims. Courts have expressed concern that if class members are identified only by their own affidavits, individuals without a valid claim will submit erroneous or fraudulent claims and dilute the share of recovery for true class members. * * *

* * *

We see two problems with using these concerns to impose the heightened ascertainability standard. First, in practice, the risk of dilution based on fraudulent or mistaken claims seems low, perhaps to the point of being negligible. We are aware of no empirical evidence that the risk of dilution caused by inaccurate or fraudulent claims in the typical low-value consumer class action is significant. In most cases, the expected recovery is so small that we question whether many people would be willing to sign affidavits under penalty of perjury saying that they purchased the good or service. In this case, for example, the value of each claim is approximately $70 (the retail price). Direct Digital has provided no evidence, and we have found none, that claims of this magnitude have provoked the widespread submission of inaccurate or fraudulent claims.

We could be wrong, of course, about this empirical prediction. Suppose people are more willing to file inaccurate or fraudulent claims for low-value recoveries than we suspect. Even then, the risk of dilution appears small because only a tiny fraction of eligible claimants ever submit claims for compensation in consumer class actions. * * * Any participation rate less than 100 percent leaves unclaimed funds in the pot, whether it is a judgment award or a settlement fund. When there are unclaimed funds, the addition of a fraudulent or inaccurate claim typically does not detract from a bona fide class member's recovery because the non-deserving claimant merely takes from unclaimed funds, not the deserving class member. It is of course theoretically possible that the total sum claimed by non-deserving claimants exceeds the total amount of unclaimed funds, in which case there would be dilution, but given the low participation rates actually observed in the real world, this danger is not so great that it justifies denying class certification altogether, at least without empirical evidence supporting the fear. * * *

We recognize that the risk of mistaken or fraudulent claims is not zero. But courts are not without tools to combat this problem during the claims administration process. They can rely, as they have for decades, on claim administrators, various auditing processes, sampling for fraud detection, follow-up notices to explain the claims process, and other techniques tailored by the parties and the court to take into account the size of the claims, the cost of the techniques, and an empirical assessment of the likelihood of fraud or inaccuracy. * * * Relying on concerns about what are essentially claim administration issues to deny certification and to prevent any recovery on valid claims upsets the balance a district judge must consider. In the face of such empirical uncertainty, a district judge has discretion to say let's wait until we know more and see how big a problem this turns out to be.

The second problem with this dilution argument is that class certification provides the only meaningful possibility for bona fide class members to recover anything at all. Keep in mind what's at stake. If the class is certified and fraudulent or inaccurate claims actually cause dilution, then deserving class members still receive something. But if class certification is denied, they will receive nothing, for they would not have brought suit individually in the first place. To deny class certification based on fear of dilution would in effect deprive bona fide class members of any recovery as a means to ensure they do not recover too little.

This stringent approach has far-reaching consequences, too. By "focusing on making absolutely certain that compensation is distributed only to those individuals who were actually harmed," the heightened ascertainability requirement "has ignored an equally important policy objective of class actions: deterring and punishing corporate wrongdoing." * * *

When faced with this counterargument, courts applying the heightened ascertainability approach have tended to emphasize that the plaintiff has the burden to satisfy Rule 23 and that the deterrence concern is therefore irrelevant. * * * With respect, that response begs an important question. Why are affidavits from putative class members deemed *insufficient as a matter of law* to satisfy this burden? In other words, no one disputes that the plaintiff carries the burden; the decisive question is whether certain evidence is sufficient to meet it. * * *

If not disputed, self-serving affidavits can support a defendant's motion for summary judgment, for example, and defendants surely will be entitled to a fair opportunity to challenge self-serving affidavits from plaintiffs. We are aware of only one type of case in American law where the testimony of one witness is legally insufficient to prove a fact. *See* U.S. Const., Art. III, § 3, cl. 1 ("No person shall be convicted of treason unless on the testimony of two witnesses to the same overt act, or on confession in open court."). There is no good reason to extend that rule to consumer class actions.

Given the significant harm caused by immunizing corporate misconduct, we believe a district judge has discretion to allow class members to identify themselves with their own testimony and to establish mechanisms to test those affidavits as needed.

4. *Due Process Interest of the Defendant*

Finally, courts have said the heightened ascertainability requirement is needed to protect a defendant's due process rights. Relying on cases about a defendant's right to "present every available defense," these courts have argued that the defendant must have a similar right to challenge the reliability of evidence submitted to prove class membership. * * *

We agree with the due process premise but not the conclusion. A defendant has a due process right to challenge the plaintiffs' evidence at any stage of the case, including the claims or damages stage. That does not mean a court cannot rely on self-identifying affidavits, subject as needed to audits and verification procedures and challenges, to identify class members. To see why, separate the two claims about a defendant's interest. It is certainly true that a defendant has a due process right not to pay in excess of its liability and to present individualized defenses if those defenses affect its liability. It does not follow that a defendant has a due process right to a *cost-effective* procedure for challenging every individual claim to class membership. * * * And we should not underestimate the ability of district courts to develop effective auditing and screening methods tailored to the individual case.

Whether a defendant's due process interest is violated depends on the nature of the class action, the plaintiff's theory of recovery, and the defendant's opportunity to contest liability and the amount of damages it owes. The due process question is not whether the identity of class members can be ascertained with perfect accuracy at the certification stage but whether the defendant will receive a fair opportunity to present its defenses when putative class members actually come forward. A district court can tailor fair verification procedures to the particular case, and a defendant may need to decide how much it wants to invest in litigating individual claims.

To see why this due process argument does not justify the heightened ascertainability requirement, consider three types of class actions. The first type is where the total amount of damages can be determined in the aggregate. A leading treatise provides an example:

> Assume a class of employees has a $50 million pension fund with each employee's share determinable only by a complex formula concerning age, years in service, retirement age, etc. Further assume that the fund's trustee simply transfers the full $50 million

to her own personal account. In a case for conversion or fraud, the class would have to demonstrate damage to show liability. They could make that showing simply by demonstrating the aggregate damage the class has suffered—the amount the defendant converted. Individual damages could be worked out later or in subsequent proceedings.

Newberg on Class Actions § 12:2 (footnote omitted). In this situation, the identity of particular class members does not implicate the defendant's due process interest at all. The addition or subtraction of individual class members affects neither the defendant's liability nor the total amount of damages it owes to the class. * * *

The second type of class action is where the total amount of damages cannot be determined in the aggregate, but there is a common method of determining individual damages. (Most consumer fraud class actions fit this model.) The same treatise provides this example:

> Now assume that [the] same class of current employees is statutorily entitled to overtime wages at time and a half after 40 hours work/week but that the defendant employer has never paid such overtime. In a case alleging violation of the statute, it may be sufficient to demonstrate that the defendant failed to pay overtime without assessing a full aggregate liability. There would be a common method for showing individual damages—a simple formula could be applied to each class member's employment records—and that would be sufficient for the predominance and superiority requirements to be met.

Newberg on Class Actions § 12:2 (footnote omitted). In this situation, the defendant's due process interest is implicated because the calculation of each class member's damages affects the total amount of damages it owes to the class. That's why the method of determining damages must match the plaintiff's theory of liability and be sufficiently reliable. It's also why the defendant must be given the opportunity to raise individual defenses and to challenge the calculation of damages awards for particular class members.

But neither of these requirements has any necessary connection to the heightened ascertainability requirement. Whether putative class members self-identify by affidavits simply does not matter. Suppose an employee files an affidavit falsely claiming that she worked 60 hours a week when in fact she worked only 50, or suppose a person files an affidavit falsely claiming to have been an employee. In either case, so long as the defendant is given a fair opportunity to challenge the claim to class membership and to contest the amount owed each claimant during the claims administration process, its due process rights have been protected.

The third type of class action is where the defendant's liability can be determined on a class-wide basis, but aggregate damages cannot be established and there is no common method for determining individual damages. In this situation, courts often bifurcate the case into a liability phase and a damages phase. * * *

* * *

As long as the defendant is given the opportunity to challenge each class member's claim to recovery during the damages phase, the defendant's due process rights are protected.

In sum, the concern about protecting a defendant's due process rights does not justify the heightened ascertainability requirement. * * *

Ultimately, we decline Direct Digital's invitation to adopt a heightened ascertainability requirement. * * *

C. *Commonality*

[The court also found that commonality was satisfied.]

AFFIRMED.

* * *

NOTES AND QUESTIONS

1. As the court noted in *Mullins*, the courts are divided on whether heightened ascertainability is a separate requirement for class certification. *Mullins* concluded that it is not, but the court presented the reasoning of courts that reach the opposite approach. Which approach is most consistent with the text of Rule 23? With the policy of the rule?

2. Although the Third Circuit was one of the first courts to apply heightened ascertainability, it has retreated from its own rigid approach. In *Byrd v. Aaron's, Inc.*, 784 F.3d 154 (3d Cir. 2015), the court reversed a denial of class certification on heightened ascertainability grounds. The case alleged damages from spyware installed on leased computers. The putative class members included purchasers or lessees of the computers, along with their "household members." The court held that the inclusion of "household members" should not derail certification because " 'household members' is a phrase that is easily defined and not, as Defendants argue, inherently vague." *Id.* at 170–71. The court criticized defendants for "seiz[ing] upon [the] lack of precision [in the case law] by invoking the ascertainability requirement with increasing frequency in order to defeat class certification." *Id.* at 162. It noted that the doctrine was "narrow" and that "[i]f defendants intend to challenge ascertainability, they must be exacting in their analysis * * *." *Id.* at 165.

3. What kinds of cases would be most directly impacted by a heightened ascertainability requirement? What kinds of cases likely would not be impacted significantly?

4. The *Mullins* court indicated that heightened ascertainability concerns can be addressed under Rule 23(b)(3)'s superiority requirement. Is the court merely substituting terminology but ending up with the same result? Or is the Seventh Circuit's approach substantively different from the Third Circuit's (and if so, how)?

5. In *Briseno v. ConAgra Foods, Inc.*, 844 F.3d 1121 (9th Cir. 2017), the Ninth Circuit refused to adopt the Third Circuit's approach to ascertainability. It thus rejected the defendant's argument that a putative class must demonstrate that there is an "administratively feasible way to determine who is in the class." *Id.* at 1124–25. The court declined to recognize "a threshold 'ascertainability' prerequisite to certification," *id.* at 1124 n.4, and expressly eschewed the term "ascertainability" itself, noting that "courts ascribe widely varied meanings to that term." *Id.* at 1124 n.3. Rather, the court explained,

"we * * * address[] the types of alleged definitional deficiencies other courts have referred to as 'ascertainability' issues * * * through analysis of Rule 23's enumerated requirements." *Id.* at 1124 n.4.

6. In a 2015 decision, the Third Circuit held that "ascertainability is not a requirement for certification of a (b)(2) class seeking only injunctive and declaratory relief." *Shelton v. Bledsoe*, 775 F.3d 554, 563 (3d Cir. 2015). The court explained: "The ascertainability requirement ensures that the procedural safeguards necessary for litigation as a (b)(3) class are met, but it need not (and should not) perform the same function in (b)(2) litigation." *Id.* at 562. Rule 23(b)(2) and (b)(3) classes are discussed in Chapter 3.

7. For an excellent scholarly treatment of ascertainability, *see* Geoffrey C. Shaw, *Class Ascertainability*, 124 Yale L.J. 2354 (2015).

8. On February 9, 2017, as this text was going to press, Congressman Bob Goodlatte introduced H.R. 985, a bill that would have sweeping implications for class actions. Among other things, section 1718 of the bill would codify (and arguably go beyond) the Third Circuit's approach to ascertainability, making that approach the law in all federal courts.

2. THE PROPOSED REPRESENTATIVES' MEMBERSHIP IN THE CLASS

A second threshold requirement for class certification is that the class representatives actually be members of the class. The requirement of class membership is set forth in the introductory language of Rule 23(a). *See* Fed. R. Civ. P. 23(a) ("*One or more members of a class* may sue or be sued as representative parties on behalf of all members only if" the four requirements of Rule 23(a) are satisfied) (emphasis added). The following case applies this requirement.

HARRISTON V. CHI. TRIBUNE CO.
United States Court of Appeals, Seventh Circuit, 1993.
992 F.2d 697.

Before MANION and ROVNER, CIRCUIT JUDGES, and ESCHBACH, SENIOR CIRCUIT JUDGE.

MANION, CIRCUIT JUDGE.

The Chicago Tribune Company ("Tribune"), an Illinois corporation that publishes and distributes the *Chicago Tribune* newspaper, employed Octavia Harriston ("Harriston"), a black woman, from 1965 to 1989. Over the years she received a number of promotions and pay increases. After receiving some critical performance appraisals, she brought a discrimination action against the Tribune, Charles Brumback, John Sloan, and Vincent Riordan ("Defendants"). [The district court denied class certification and granted summary judgment in favor of defendants.] We affirm.

* * *

The Tribune hired Harriston in 1965 as a part-time, voluntary advertisement taker. During the next fifteen years of Harriston's career with the Tribune, she was promoted to various positions within the Advertising Department. * * *

In 1984, George Veon, the Tribune's Vice President of Employee Relations, asked Harriston whether she wanted to transfer from the Retail Advertising Department to the Employee Relations Department and become the EEO/Employment Manager. As EEO/Employment Manager, she would be responsible for hiring new employees, on-campus college recruiting, filing EEO (Equal Employment Opportunity) reports, and handling discrimination charges and lawsuits. The new position would be a promotion for Harriston, from a grade nine to a grade thirteen. She would be the first black person to hold the position. The people who held the position before her were white.

Harriston reluctantly accepted the position, which she considered a "great challenge" and a "major opportunity." Her hesitance stemmed from her concern that she was not qualified for the job. * * *

* * *

In April 1987, John Sloan replaced Veon as the Vice President of Employee Relations. Sloan found Harriston's work performance as EEO/Employment Manager unsatisfactory, mainly because she lacked the skills a human resources manager needed. Sloan thought Harriston better suited for the work done in the Advertising Department. * * *

[Sloan informed Harriston about an opening in the Advertising Department, which Harriston accepted, effective June 1987, at a salary $2,000.00 greater than she had made as the EEO/Employment Manager.]

* * * Ronald Williams, a black man, replaced Harriston as the EEO/Employment Manager. Unlike Harriston, Williams had considerable experience in the area of human resources * * *.

In June 1988, after working as a Senior Sales Representative for one year, Harriston received her first performance appraisal. [Her supervisor] gave her a "satisfactory" rating, but criticized her sales level. * * *

* * *

* * * In May 1989, [her supervisor] sent Harriston a memorandum expressing his displeasure with her sales performance and requested her to inform him how she planned to improve. * * * Harriston, however, failed to respond to the memorandum. Instead, she submitted a letter of resignation in June 1989. In the letter, she alleged age and race discrimination. * * *

* * *

* * * Harriston argues that the district court erred in denying her motion for class certification. She moved for class certification on behalf of all black people who had been excluded from management positions at the Tribune * * *.

* * * To have standing to sue as a class representative, the plaintiff "must be part of the class and 'possess the same interest and suffer the same injury' as the class members." *E. Tex. Motor Freight Sys., Inc. v. Rodriguez*, 431 U.S. 395, 403 (1977) (quoting *Schlesinger v. Reservists Comm. to Stop the War*, 418 U.S. 208, 216 (1974)). * * *

Harriston did not demonstrate that she was a member of the class she purported to represent. She brought her motion on behalf of all blacks whom the Tribune had failed to promote to management positions. Yet, the

Tribune promoted her to the management position of EEO/Employment Manager, and she has not pointed to one specific promotion to a management position that the Defendants denied her. Consequently, because Harriston was not a member of the class she describes, the district court properly denied her motion for class certification. *See Blum v. Yaretsky*, 457 U.S. 991, 999 (1982); *Rodriguez*, 431 U.S. at 403–04.

* * *

[The court also upheld the lower court's decision granting summary judgment in favor of the defendants, rejecting, *inter alia*, the plaintiff's argument that her demotion from management was based on discrimination.]

NOTES AND QUESTIONS

1. In articulating the rule that a class representative must be a member of the class he or she purports to represent, the *Harriston* court cites two Supreme Court cases, *Reservists* and *Rodriguez*. *Reservists* was a constitutional (*i.e.*, Article III) standing case, not a Rule 23 case, but it is often quoted by courts applying Rule 23. The case involved a suit by a class of citizens and taxpayers challenging the eligibility of a member of Congress to serve in the Armed Forces Reserve. Although the case articulated the principle that a person lacks standing as a class representative unless he or she belongs to the proposed class, the ultimate conclusion was that *the entire class* lacked standing: the class members alleged an injury that was too abstract—namely, the concern that members of Congress would be subject to undue Executive Branch influence by serving as reservists. *See Schlesinger v. Reservists Comm. to Stop the War*, 418 U.S. 208, 220–23 (1974). The class representatives in *Reservists* were clearly part of the class they sought to represent. *See id.* at 216–17.

In *East Texas Motor Freight Systems, Inc. v. Rodriguez*, 431 U.S. 395 (1977) (*see* Chapter 10(B)(1)(a)), however, although the Court quoted from *Reservists*, it analyzed the named representatives' membership in the class as an aspect of Rule 23(a). *Rodriguez* held that because the named plaintiffs in an employment discrimination suit lacked the qualifications for the job positions at issue, they "were not members of the class of discriminatees they purported to represent" and thus "were not proper class representatives under [Rule] 23(a)." *Rodriguez*, 431 U.S. at 403. After finding that the evidence established that the named plaintiffs were not class members, the Court began its analysis of Rule 23(a)(4)—adequacy of representation—by stating, "[a]part from the named plaintiffs' evident lack of class membership, the record * * * disclosed at least two *other* strong indications that they would not 'fairly and adequately protect the interests of the class.'" *Id.* at 404–05 (quoting Rule 23(a)(4)) (emphasis added). Thus, the Court addressed the plaintiffs' standing only in the context of Rule 23(a)(4). Are there any circumstances in which a "representative" could be adequate, yet not be a member of the class?

2. The *Harriston* court also cited *Blum v. Yaretsky*, 457 U.S. 991 (1982), at the end of its standing analysis. *Blum*, like *Reservists*, approached the issue of a class representative's membership in the class as one of constitutional standing. The *Blum* Court articulated the governing principles as follows:

> It is axiomatic that the judicial power conferred by Art. III may not be exercised unless the plaintiff shows "that he personally has suffered some actual or threatened injury as a result of the putatively

illegal conduct of the defendant." * * * It is not enough that the conduct of which the plaintiff complains will injure *someone*. The complaining party must also show that he is within the class of persons who will be concretely affected.

457 U.S. at 999. Is there any argument that Harriston met this requirement? Given that the plaintiff in *Harriston* was claiming discrimination by the Tribune, should she be disqualified from representing others claiming discrimination as well, simply because her theory of discrimination (*i.e.*, discrimination at the management level) is different? To be sure, Harriston *was* promoted to management, whereas the proposed class members were not, but Harriston claimed that she was transferred out of a management position because of discrimination. Are the theories so different that Harriston could not properly represent the class? *Cf. Abron v. Black & Decker, Inc.*, 654 F.2d 951, 955–73 (4th Cir. 1981) (Murnaghan, J., dissenting) (rejecting argument that, in discrimination suit, class representative must assert precisely same theory or form of discrimination as proposed class members).

3. Following *Reservists* and *Rodriguez*, the lower courts have taken a variety of approaches as to how a representative's lack of membership in the class should be analyzed.

a. Some courts, like *Reservists, Harriston*, and *Blum*, analyze the issue as part of Article III standing. *See, e.g., Albers v. Guthy–Renker Corp.*, 92 F. App'x. 497, 500 (9th Cir. 2004) (where plaintiffs had not attended seminars or purchased securities in putative class action alleging that defendants sold fraudulent securities, plaintiffs did not suffer same injury as putative class members and were therefore not members of class); *Crosby v. Bowater Inc. Ret. Plan for Salaried Employees of Great N. Paper, Inc.*, 382 F.3d 587 (6th Cir. 2004) (where an employee benefit plan participant brought a class action on behalf of similarly situated plan participants and beneficiaries for equitable relief that "could only benefit members of the class other than" himself, he could not maintain a class action because he did not have a justiciable claim); *Keele v. Wexler*, 149 F.3d 589 (7th Cir. 1998); *Hartman v. Duffey*, 19 F.3d 1459, 1469 (D.C. Cir. 1994) (both holding that to satisfy standing requirement in lawsuit brought as class action, class representative must possess same interest and suffer same injury as individuals he or she seeks to represent).

b. Other courts, like *Rodriguez*, view class membership as a component of the "adequacy" of class representatives under Rule 23(a)(4) (*see* Chapter 10(B)(1)(a)). *See, e.g., Bishop v. Committee on Prof'l Ethics & Conduct of the Iowa State Bar Ass'n*, 686 F.2d 1278, 1289 (8th Cir. 1982) (non-practicing attorney was inadequate representative for suit by Iowa attorneys since he did not "possess the same interest" or "suffer the same injury" as class members); *O'Neil v. Appel*, 165 F.R.D. 479, 493 (W.D. Mich. 1996) ("The bedrock requirement of adequacy is that the named representative be a member of the class.").

c. Other courts view class membership as a component of the "typicality" of the class representatives under Rule 23(a)(3) (see Chapter 2(B)(3)). *See, e.g., Mullen v. Treasure Chest Casino, LLC*, 186 F.3d 620, 625 (5th Cir. 1999) (typicality "focuses on the similarity between the named plaintiffs' legal and remedial theories and the theories of those whom they purport to represent"); *Bartelson v. Dean Witter & Co.*, 86 F.R.D. 657, 668–69 (E.D. Pa. 1980) (a white female could not represent a class of African–Americans and other minorities because her claims were not typical of those of class members).

d. Other courts view a representative's lack of class membership as being relevant to the "commonality" requirement of Rule 23(a)(2) (*see* Section

2(B)(2) of this chapter). *See, e.g., Cal. Rural Legal Assistance, Inc. v. Legal Servs. Corp.*, 917 F.2d 1171, 1175 (9th Cir. 1990).

e. Still other courts view class membership as an "implicit" requirement separate and apart from Rule 23(a) and Article III constitutional standing. *See, e.g., Harrington v. City of Albuquerque*, 222 F.R.D. 505, 509 (D.N.M. 2004) ("In addition to the four explicit prerequisites enumerated in Fed. R. Civ. P. 23(a), courts have established two additional, implicit requirements for class certification [including membership in the class]."); *In re A.H. Robins Co., Inc.*, 880 F.2d 709, 728 (4th Cir. 1989) ("Though not specified in the Rule, establishment of a class action implicitly requires both that there be an identifiable class and that the plaintiff or plaintiffs be a member of such class."); *Stambaugh v. Kan. Dep't of Corr.*, 151 F.R.D. 664, 671 (D. Kan. 1993) ("Essential, but implied, prerequisites are that a defined or identifiable class exists and that the class representatives are members of the class."); *Jenson v. Eveleth Taconite Co.*, 139 F.R.D. 657, 659–60 (D. Minn. 1991) ("As a preliminary matter, plaintiffs must establish that a defined class exists and that the class representatives fall within the class. If these implicit requirements are fulfilled, plaintiffs must satisfy the explicit requirements of Rule 23 * * *.").

Which one of these approaches is the most analytically sound?

4. Standing is a potentially important issue in many class actions. The issue of standing is discussed in Section (A)(4) of this chapter.

3. A LIVE CONTROVERSY (MOOTNESS CONSIDERATIONS)

Another threshold requirement (subject to various exceptions) is that the class representative's claim must be live, not moot. The doctrine of mootness, like standing, is complicated, and its intricacies are beyond the scope of this casebook. Nevertheless, the following cases illustrate the issues that can arise. As they demonstrate, mootness can occur because of changed factual circumstances. In addition, defendants have tried to create mootness by tendering payment of the amount at issue to the class representative.

a. Mootness Because of Changed Circumstances

ROCKY V. KING
United States Court of Appeals, Fifth Circuit, 1990.
900 F.2d 864.

Before JOHNSON, WILLIAMS, and GARWOOD, CIRCUIT JUDGES.

GARWOOD, CIRCUIT JUDGE.

Plaintiff-appellant Robert G. Rocky (Rocky) brought this suit against defendant-appellee John T. King, *et al.* (King), for alleged violations of the federally protected rights of Rocky and similarly situated inmates who worked in the fields at the Louisiana State Penitentiary in Angola, Louisiana (Angola). Rocky appeals the district court's denial of class certification and grant of summary judgment in favor of King.

FACTS AND PROCEEDINGS BELOW

Rocky, *pro se*, filed his claim, pursuant to 42 U.S.C. § 1983, on November 8, 1983, in the form of a class action in which only injunctive and declaratory relief were requested. At that time, Rocky was an inmate at Angola and was assigned to work in the field lines there. Such inmates work in the fields two times per day for periods up to four hours in length. Angola provides drinking water but not toilet facilities for the field workers. Thus, the field workers typically urinate or defecate in the fields or attempt to refrain from doing so until they return from the fields. Moreover, Angola apparently does not provide toilet paper and hand-washing facilities for the inmates to cleanse themselves while in the fields, although the inmates are allowed to wash their hands before eating their meals indoors. Rocky claims that these practices cause a variety of medical problems to the field workers, such as the spread of certain diseases or parasites, and violate the inmates' constitutional rights of privacy and of freedom from cruel and unusual punishment, as well as certain federal regulations.

On April 9, 1984, Angola officials removed Rocky from field work because of eye surgery and temporarily assigned him to light duty indoors. These officials continually renewed Rocky's temporary status until that status became permanent primarily because of Rocky's glaucoma. As a result, Rocky has not worked in the fields since April 9, 1984. [On May 10, 1984, Rocky filed a *pro se* motion for class certification, which the court denied five days later. The district court subsequently granted the defendant's motion for summary judgment, based on the magistrate's recommendation.]

* * *

DISCUSSION

The threshold question in this case is whether Rocky's complaint presents a justiciable controversy under the constitutional case-or-controversy requirement. *See* U.S. Const. art. III, § 2, cl. 1. In support of King's second motion for summary judgment, King asserted * * * that Rocky's claim was moot. The mootness doctrine requires that the controversy posed by the plaintiff's complaint be "live" not only at the time the plaintiff files the complaint but also throughout the litigation process. *See United States Parole Comm'n v. Geraghty*, 445 U.S. 388, 397 (1980) (quoting Monaghan, *Constitutional Adjudication: The Who and When*, 82 Yale L.J. 1363, 1384 (1973), defining mootness as "the doctrine of standing set in a time frame"). The magistrate, however, found this issue to be immaterial, granting summary judgment for King on the merits of Rocky's claim. Although both parties refer in passing to the question of mootness in their appellate briefs, it is unclear whether either of the parties has specifically raised this issue on appeal. Nevertheless, "[s]triking at the very heart of federal subject matter jurisdiction, a mootness issue quite clearly can be raised *sua sponte* if not addressed by the parties." *Sannon v. United States*, 631 F.2d 1247, 1250 (5th Cir. 1980).

* * * [A]lthough Rocky's claim challenges the field conditions, Rocky has not been a field worker since April 9, 1984. Moreover, Rocky did not file his motion for class certification until May 10, 1984, and the district court denied that motion on May 15, 1984. Thus, Rocky was not a field worker at either the time this motion was filed or denied. The facts of this case raise the question whether this Court may review the district court's denial of class certification and grant of summary judgment on the merits where the named plaintiff's individual claim has become moot prior to his filing of a motion for class certification and the district court's denial of that motion.

On appeal, Rocky asserts that his individual claim is not moot because, although he is no longer a field worker, the diseases and parasites spread among the field workers may be transferred to the other inmates through direct contact with the workers or through eating the food on which they have urinated or defecated. Nevertheless, even broadly interpreting Rocky's original *pro se* complaint, Rocky clearly filed his complaint as a class action on behalf of those inmates similarly incarcerated who were working in the fields of Angola and challenged the legality of the conditions of confinement only with respect to those workers. Although Rocky's complaint alleged that Angola's failure to provide toilet and hand-washing facilities caused harm to field workers, it did not allege that these practices harmed in any manner those inmates not working in the fields. Thus, Rocky's individual claim for injunctive and declaratory relief became moot when he was removed from the fields on April 9, 1984.

An action is moot where (1) the controversy is no longer live or (2) the parties lack a personal stake in its outcome. The first aspect of the mootness doctrine is not at issue in the present case because the controversy over the conditions of confinement with respect to the Angola field workers apparently is "live" with respect to those inmates at Angola currently working in the fields for whom Rocky seeks to be the representative. The present case, however, concerns the second aspect of mootness—*i.e.*, whether Rocky's no longer retaining a personal stake in the substantive aspects of this controversy renders this action moot. The purpose of the personal-stake requirement is to assure that the dispute involves "sharply presented issues in a concrete factual setting and self-interested parties vigorously advocating opposing positions."

On several occasions in recent years, the United States Supreme Court has addressed the application of the personal-stake requirement in the class action context. For example, in *Sosna v. Iowa*, 419 U.S. 393 (1975), the Court held that, even though the named plaintiff's individual claim had become moot after proper certification of a class, the class action was not rendered moot. *Sosna* reasoned that when the district court certified the class, that class "acquired a legal status separate from the interest asserted by" the named plaintiff. Thus, so long as the controversy is still live with respect to some members of the class at the time the appellate court reviews the case, and the named plaintiff had a personal stake in the action at the time the class was properly certified, the class action is not moot. Moreover, so long as the named plaintiff remains an adequate class representative, pursuant to Fed. R. Civ. P. 23(a), the named plaintiff may continue to represent the interests of the class on appeal. *Sosna* obviously is distinguishable from the present case because here when the district court denied Rocky's motion for class certification Rocky's individual claim had already become moot, having become so even before he had filed that motion.

In *United States Parole Comm'n v. Geraghty*, the named plaintiff, while in prison, brought an action challenging the legality of certain federal parole guidelines. The district court subsequently denied class certification and granted summary judgment for the defendants on the merits. While the action was on appeal, however, the named plaintiff was released from prison. The Supreme Court held that, even though the named plaintiff's individual substantive claim had become moot after the denial of class certification, the action was not rendered moot for the limited purpose of challenging the district court's denial of class certification. So long as the named plaintiff continues vigorously to advocate the right to certify a class, the named plaintiff retains a sufficient personal stake in posing such a procedural challenge. * * *

To support this holding, the *Geraghty* Court relied on the "relation back" doctrine. Under that doctrine, to determine whether the named plaintiff has a personal stake in challenging class certification denial, a court must examine the named plaintiff's personal stake at the time the district court denied the motion for class certification. Because the named plaintiff in *Geraghty* was not released from prison until shortly before appeal of the district court's denial of class certification and grant of summary judgment in favor of the defendants, the Court found that the named plaintiff's alleged

> "injury continued up to and beyond the time the District Court denied class certification. We merely hold that when a District Court erroneously denies a procedural motion, which, if correctly decided, would have prevented the action from becoming moot, an appeal lies from the denial and the corrected ruling 'relates back' to the date of the original denial.
>
> ". . . The 'relation back' principle, a traditional equitable doctrine applied to class certification claims . . ., serves logically to distinguish this case from the one brought a day after the prisoner is released. . . . *If the named plaintiff has no personal stake in the outcome at the time class certification is denied, relation back of appellate reversal of that denial would not prevent mootness of the action.*"

Thus, *Geraghty* also is distinguishable from the present case. In *Geraghty*, it was crucial that the named plaintiff's individual claim became moot *after* the denial of class certification; therefore, the named plaintiff had a personal stake in the outcome of the action at the time of denial. In the present case, however, Rocky's individual claim became moot *before* the denial of class certification (indeed before he moved for class certification).

* * *

Applying the Supreme Court's analysis in *Geraghty* * * *, we first must determine whether Rocky may challenge the district court's denial of his motion for class certification. Because Rocky was no longer a field worker when the district court ruled on his motion for class certification, Rocky's individual claim, which was only for injunctive and declaratory relief in respect to Angola field work conditions, clearly had then already become moot. Because Rocky had no personal stake in the case when the district court denied class certification, it is also not appropriate for this Court to reach Rocky's challenge to the district court's grant of summary judgment for King on the merits. Even if Rocky is correct in his contention that the district court erred in denying class certification, nevertheless relation back of appellate reversal of that denial would not prevent mootness of the action. Thus, we hold that Rocky does not meet the personal-stake requirement even for the limited purpose of appealing the district court's denial of class certification because his individual claim had become moot when that ruling was made.

The Supreme Court has carved out a narrow exception to the general rule that a named plaintiff must have a personal stake in the outcome of the case at the time the district court rules on class certification. More specifically, where a claim is "capable of repetition, yet evading review," an appellate court may review the propriety of a ruling on class certification, even though the named plaintiff's individual claim became moot after the suit was filed but prior to the district court's ruling on the class certification issue. For example, in *Gerstein v. Pugh*, 420 U.S. 103 (1975), named plaintiffs challenged the conditions of their pretrial detention. Even though the named plaintiffs apparently were no longer in custody awaiting trial when the district court certified them as representatives of a class of pretrial detainees, the court held that this narrow exception applied to such an inherently transitory claim because there was no indication that "any given individual, named as plaintiff would be in pretrial custody long enough for a district judge to certify the class."

This narrow exception as applied to the transitory claims in *Gerstein* is inapplicable in the present case. Unlike the named plaintiffs in *Gerstein*, Rocky is challenging conditions of long-term, not short-term, confinement. Hundreds of inmates at Angola apparently work in the fields and could file a claim identical to that filed by Rocky. There is no indication that Angola officials will remove such inmates from field work before a district court rules on class certification in order to render that claim moot.

Rocky also suggests that his claim is "capable of repetition, yet evading review" because he potentially could be returned to the fields due to a single disciplinary infraction or another physician's reaching a different conclusion about Rocky's glaucoma. The magistrate found no indication in the record that Rocky's glaucoma will change or that Angola officials will reassign Rocky to field work for any other reason. In light of the speculative nature of Rocky's assertion that he may be returned to the fields in the future, we concur with the magistrate's assessment of the record and find the narrow exception for claims "capable of repetition, yet evading review" also to be inapplicable on this ground. * * *

For the foregoing reasons, the judgment of the district court is reversed and remanded with instructions to dismiss the case as moot.

NOTES AND QUESTIONS

1. Is there any real concern about whether Rocky would be a vigorous representative, particularly if he were represented by able counsel? Would he be any less vigorous than the class representative in *Geraghty*—a man free from the prison about which he complained? Can a representative who lacks a live claim *ever* be an effective class representative? If so, should such a person be allowed to remain a representative? Under what circumstances?

2. What policies underlie the mootness doctrine? Are those policies served in *Rocky*?

3. Could *Rocky* have been decided on the ground that plaintiff was not a member of the class of "inmates who worked in the fields" at the Angola facility? What is the difference between the membership requirement and the mootness doctrine?

4. The Fifth Circuit concluded that the potential for future harm was too speculative for Rocky to retain standing, thereby mooting his claim against King. The courts also conduct a similar inquiry when determining standing—*i.e.*, whether plaintiffs have suffered an injury in fact. An injury in fact is defined as "an invasion of a legally protected interest [that] is (a) concrete and particularized, * * * and (b) actual or imminent, not 'conjectural' or 'hypothetical.'" *Lujan v. Defenders of Wildlife*, 504 U.S. 555, 560 (1992).

5. What are the differences between standing and mootness? In *Friends of the Earth, Inc. v. Laidlaw Environmental Services, Inc.*, 528 U.S. 167 (2000), the Supreme Court noted several distinctions between the doctrines. Specifically, standing and mootness impose the burden of proof on different parties (plaintiffs have the burden of proving standing, while defendants have the burden of proving mootness); are not subject to the same exceptions (*i.e.*, "capable of repetition, yet evading review" applies to mootness only); and are justified by different policy rationales (*i.e.*, standing promotes judicial economy, whereas mootness often undermines it). 528 U.S. at 190–92. *See, e.g., Grant ex rel. v. Gilbert*, 324 F.3d 383 (5th Cir. 2003) (conducting separate inquiries as to whether named plaintiff had initial standing to bring certain claims on behalf of class and whether claim was moot).

6. For a critical analysis of the Supreme Court's class-action mootness case law, *see* Jean W. Burns, *Decorative Figureheads: Eliminating Class Representatives in Class Actions*, 42 Hastings L.J. 165, 168–72 (1990).

7. In the following case, the Supreme Court resolved a circuit split on whether an offer of judgment to the named plaintiffs under Fed. R. Civ. P. 68 moots the case.

b. "Pick Off" and Mootness

CAMPBELL–EWALD CO. v. GOMEZ
Supreme Court of the United States, 2016.
136 S. Ct. 663.

JUSTICE GINSBURG delivered the opinion of the Court.

Is an unaccepted offer to satisfy the named plaintiff's individual claim sufficient to render a case moot when the complaint seeks relief on behalf of the plaintiff and a class of persons similarly situated? This question, on which Courts of Appeals have divided, was reserved in *Genesis Healthcare Corp. v. Symczyk*, 133 S. Ct. 1523, 1528, 1529, n.4 (2013). We hold today, in accord with Rule 68 of the Federal Rules of Civil Procedure, that an unaccepted settlement offer has no force. Like other unaccepted contract offers, it creates no lasting right or obligation. With the offer off the table, and the defendant's continuing denial of liability, adversity between the parties persists.

* * *

I

The Telephone Consumer Protection Act (TCPA or Act), 47 U.S.C. § 227(b)(1)(A)(iii), prohibits any person, absent the prior express consent of a telephone-call recipient, from "mak[ing] any call . . . using any automatic telephone dialing system . . . to any telephone number assigned to a paging service [or] cellular telephone service." A text message to a cellular telephone, it is undisputed, qualifies as a "call" within the compass of § 227(b)(1)(A)(iii). For damages occasioned by conduct violating the TCPA, § 227(b)(3) authorizes a private right of action. A plaintiff successful in such an action may recover her "actual monetary loss" or $500 for each violation, "whichever is greater." Damages may be trebled if "the defendant willfully or knowingly violated" the Act.

Petitioner Campbell–Ewald Company (Campbell) is a nationwide advertising and marketing communications agency. Beginning in 2000, the United States Navy engaged Campbell to develop and execute a multimedia recruiting campaign. In 2005 and 2006, Campbell proposed to the Navy a campaign involving text messages sent to young adults, the Navy's target audience, encouraging them to learn more about the Navy. The Navy approved Campbell's proposal, conditioned on sending the messages only to individuals who had "opted in" to receipt of marketing solicitations on topics that included service in the Navy. In final form, the message read:

> "Destined for something big? Do it in the Navy. Get a career. An education. And a chance to serve a greater cause. For a FREE Navy video call [phone number]."

Campbell then contracted with Mindmatics LLC, which generated a list of cellular phone numbers geared to the Navy's target audience—namely, cellular phone users between the ages of 18 and 24 who had consented to receiving solicitations by text message. In May 2006, Mindmatics transmitted the Navy's message to over 100,000 recipients.

Respondent Jose Gomez was a recipient of the Navy's recruiting message. Alleging that he had never consented to receiving the message, that his age was nearly 40, and that Campbell had violated the TCPA by sending the message (and perhaps others like it), Gomez filed a class-action complaint in the District Court for the Central District of California in 2010. On behalf of a nationwide class of individuals who had received, but had not consented to receipt of, the text message, Gomez sought treble statutory damages, costs, and attorney's fees, also an injunction against Campbell's involvement in unsolicited messaging.

Prior to the agreed-upon deadline for Gomez to file a motion for class certification, Campbell proposed to settle Gomez's individual claim and filed an offer of judgment pursuant to Federal Rule of Civil Procedure 68.[61]

---

[1] Federal Rule of Civil Procedure 68 provides, in relevant part:

(a) Making an Offer; Judgment on an Accepted Offer. At least 14 days before the date set for trial, a party defending against a claim may serve on an opposing party an offer to allow judgment on specified terms, with the costs then accrued. If, within 14 days after being served, the opposing party serves written notice accepting the offer, either party may then file the offer and notice of acceptance, plus proof of service. The clerk must then enter judgment.

(b) Unaccepted Offer. An unaccepted offer is considered withdrawn, but it does not preclude a later offer. Evidence of an unaccepted offer is not admissible except in a proceeding to determine costs.

* * *

Campbell offered to pay Gomez his costs, excluding attorney's fees, and $1,503 per message for the May 2006 text message and any other text message Gomez could show he had received, thereby satisfying his personal treble-damages claim. Campbell also proposed a stipulated injunction in which it agreed to be barred from sending text messages in violation of the TCPA. The proposed injunction, however, denied liability and the allegations made in the complaint, and disclaimed the existence of grounds for the imposition of an injunction. The settlement offer did not include attorney's fees, Campbell observed, because the TCPA does not provide for an attorney's-fee award. Gomez did not accept the settlement offer and allowed Campbell's Rule 68 submission to lapse after the time, 14 days, specified in the Rule.

Campbell thereafter moved to dismiss the case pursuant to Federal Rule of Civil Procedure 12(b)(1) for lack of subject-matter jurisdiction. No Article III case or controversy remained, Campbell urged, because its offer mooted Gomez's individual claim by providing him with complete relief. Gomez had not moved for class certification before his claim became moot, Campbell added, so the putative class claims also became moot. The District Court denied Campbell's motion. * * *

* * *

The Court of Appeals for the Ninth Circuit * * * agreed that Gomez's case remained live. * * *

We granted certiorari * * *.

II

Article III of the Constitution limits federal-court jurisdiction to "cases" and "controversies." U.S. Const. art. III, § 2. * * * "If an intervening circumstance deprives the plaintiff of a 'personal stake in the outcome of the lawsuit,' at any point during litigation, the action can no longer proceed and must be dismissed as moot.". A case becomes moot, however, "only when it is impossible for a court to grant any effectual relief whatever to the prevailing party." "As long as the parties have a concrete interest, however small, in the outcome of the litigation, the case is not moot."

In *Genesis Healthcare,* the Court considered a collective action brought by Laura Symczyk, a former employee of Genesis HealthCare Corp. Symczyk sued on behalf of herself and similarly situated employees for alleged violations of the Fair Labor Standards Act of 1938, 29 U.S.C. § 201 *et seq.* In that case, as here, the defendant served the plaintiff with an offer of judgment pursuant to Rule 68 that would have satisfied the plaintiff's individual damages claim. Also as here, the plaintiff allowed the offer to lapse by failing to respond within the time specified in the Rule. But unlike the case Gomez mounted, Symczyk did not dispute in the lower courts that Genesis HealthCare's offer mooted her individual claim. Because of that failure, the *Genesis Healthcare* majority refused to rule on the issue. Instead, the majority simply assumed, without deciding, that an offer of complete relief pursuant to Rule 68, even if unaccepted, moots a plaintiff's claim. * * *

(d) Paying Costs After an Unaccepted Offer. If the judgment that the offeree finally obtains is not more favorable than the unaccepted offer, the offeree must pay the costs incurred after the offer was made.

JUSTICE KAGAN, writing in dissent, explained that she would have reached the threshold question and would have held that "an unaccepted offer of judgment cannot moot a case." She reasoned:

"When a plaintiff rejects such an offer—however good the terms—her interest in the lawsuit remains just what it was before. And so too does the court's ability to grant her relief. An unaccepted settlement offer—like any unaccepted contract offer—is a legal nullity, with no operative effect. * * *

We now adopt JUSTICE KAGAN'S analysis * * *. Accordingly, we hold that Gomez's complaint was not effaced by Campbell's unaccepted offer to satisfy his individual claim.

As earlier recounted, Gomez commenced an action against Campbell for violation of the TCPA, suing on behalf of himself and others similarly situated. Gomez sought treble statutory damages and an injunction on behalf of a nationwide class, but Campbell's settlement offer proposed relief for Gomez alone, and it did not admit liability. Gomez rejected Campbell's settlement terms and the offer of judgment.

Under basic principles of contract law, Campbell's settlement bid and Rule 68 offer of judgment, once rejected, had no continuing efficacy. Absent Gomez's acceptance, Campbell's settlement offer remained only a proposal, binding neither Campbell nor Gomez. Having rejected Campbell's settlement bid, and given Campbell's continuing denial of liability, Gomez gained no entitlement to the relief Campbell previously offered. In short, with no settlement offer still operative, the parties remained adverse; both retained the same stake in the litigation they had at the outset.

The Federal Rule in point, Rule 68, hardly supports the argument that an unaccepted settlement offer can moot a complaint. An offer of judgment, the Rule provides, "is considered withdrawn" if not accepted within 14 days of its service. Fed. Rule Civ. Proc. 68(a), (b). The sole built-in sanction: "If the [ultimate] judgment . . . is not more favorable than the unaccepted offer, the offeree must pay the costs incurred after the offer was made." Rule 68(d).

* * *

* * * [W]hen the settlement offer Campbell extended to Gomez expired, Gomez remained emptyhanded; his TCPA complaint, which Campbell opposed on the merits, stood wholly unsatisfied. Because Gomez's individual claim was not made moot by the expired settlement offer, that claim would retain vitality during the time involved in determining whether the case could proceed on behalf of a class. While a class lacks independent status until certified, a would-be class representative with a live claim of her own must be accorded a fair opportunity to show that certification is warranted.

* * *

In sum, an unaccepted settlement offer or offer of judgment does not moot a plaintiff's case, so the District Court retained jurisdiction to adjudicate Gomez's complaint. That ruling suffices to decide this case. We need not, and do not, now decide whether the result would be different if a defendant deposits the full amount of the plaintiff's individual claim in an account payable to the plaintiff, and the court then enters judgment for the plaintiff in that amount. That question is appropriately reserved for a case in which it is not hypothetical.

* * *

For the reasons stated, the judgment of the Court of Appeals for the Ninth Circuit is affirmed, and the case is remanded for further proceedings consistent with this opinion.

It is so ordered.

JUSTICE THOMAS, concurring in the judgment.

The Court correctly concludes that an offer of complete relief on a claim does not render that claim moot. But, in my view, the Court does not advance a sound basis for this conclusion. The Court rests its conclusion on modern contract law principles and a recent dissent concerning Federal Rule of Civil Procedure 68. I would rest instead on the common-law history of tenders. That history—which led to Rule 68—demonstrates that a mere offer of the sum owed is insufficient to eliminate a court's jurisdiction to decide the case to which the offer related. I therefore concur only in the judgment.

I

The text of Article III's case-or-controversy requirement, that requirement's drafting history, and our precedents do not appear to provide sufficiently specific principles to resolve this case. When faced with such uncertainty, it seems particularly important for us to look to how courts traditionally have viewed a defendant's offer to pay the plaintiff's alleged damages. That history—which stretches from the common law directly to Rule 68 and modern settlement offers—reveals one unbroken practice that should resolve this case: A defendant's offer to pay the plaintiff—without more—would not have deprived a court of jurisdiction. Campbell–Ewald's offers thus do not bar federal courts from continuing to hear this case.

A

Modern settlement procedure has its origins in the law of tenders, as refined in the 18th and 19th centuries. As with much of the early common law, the law of tenders had many rigid formalities. These formalities make clear that, around the time of the framing, a mere offer of relief was insufficient to deprive a court of jurisdiction.

At common law, a prospective defendant could prevent a case from proceeding, but he needed to provide substantially more than a bare offer. A "mere proposal or proposition" to pay a claim was inadequate to end a case. Nor would a defendant's "readiness and an ability to pay the money" suffice to end a case. Rather, a prospective defendant needed to provide a "tender"—an offer to pay the entire claim before a suit was filed, accompanied by "actually produc[ing]" the sum "at the time of tender" in an "unconditional" manner.

Furthermore, in state and federal courts, a tender of the amount due was deemed "an admission of a liability" on the cause of action to which the tender related, so any would-be defendant who tried to deny liability could not effectuate a tender. * * * The tender had to offer and actually deliver complete relief. And an offer to pay less than what was demanded was not a valid tender.

Even when a potential defendant properly effectuated a tender, the case would not necessarily end. At common law, a plaintiff was entitled to "deny that [the tender was] sufficient to satisfy his demand" and accordingly "go on to trial."

This history demonstrates that, at common law, a defendant or prospective defendant had to furnish far more than a mere offer of settlement to end a case. This history also demonstrates that courts at common law would not have understood a mere offer to strip them of jurisdiction.

B

Although 19th-century state statutes expanded the common-law-tender regime, the law retained its essential features. These changes, for example, allowed defendants to offer a tender "during the pendency of an action," as well as before it commenced. Statutes also expanded the right of tender to cover types of actions in which damages were not certain.

Nevertheless, state statutes generally retained the core of the common-law tender rules. Most critically for this case, a mere offer remained insufficient to end a lawsuit. Like the common-law tender rules, state statutes recognized that plaintiffs could continue to pursue litigation by rejecting an offer.

C

The offer-of-judgment procedure in Rule 68 was modeled after a provision in the New York Field Code that was enacted in the mid-19th century. That code abrogated many of the common-law formalities governing civil procedure. Among its innovations, the code allowed defendants in any cause of action to make an offer in writing to the plaintiff proposing to accept judgment against the defendant for a specified sum. The plaintiff could accept the offer, which would end the litigation, or reject the offer, in which case the offer was considered withdrawn without any admission of liability by the defendant.

In 1938, Rule 68 was adopted as part of the Federal Rules of Civil Procedure, and has subsisted throughout the years without material changes.
* * *

D

In light of the history discussed above, a rejected offer does not end the case. And this consistent historical practice demonstrates why Campbell–Ewald's offers do not divest a federal court of jurisdiction to entertain Gomez's suit. Campbell–Ewald made two settlement offers after Gomez sued—one filed with the District Court under Rule 68 and one freestanding settlement offer. But with neither of these offers did the company make payment; it only declared its intent to pay. Because Campbell–Ewald only offered to pay Gomez's claim but took no further steps, the court was not deprived of jurisdiction.

II

Although the Court reaches the right result, I cannot adopt its reasoning. Building on the dissent in *Genesis Healthcare Corp. v. Symczyk,* the Court relies on principles of contract law that an unaccepted offer is a legal nullity. But the question here is not whether Campbell–Ewald's offer formed an enforceable contract. The question is whether its continuing offer of complete relief eliminated the case or controversy required by Article III. * * * I believe that we must resolve the meaning of "case" and "controversy" in Article III by looking to "the traditional, fundamental limitations upon the powers of common-law courts" because "cases" and "controversies" "have virtually no meaning except by reference to that tradition."

* * *

[Dissenting opinion by CHIEF JUSTICE ROBERTS, with whom JUSTICE SCALIA and JUSTICE ALITO join, is omitted.]

[Dissenting opinion by JUSTICE ALITO is omitted.]

NOTES AND QUESTIONS

1. The Court in *Campbell–Ewald* leaves open the question of whether a tender can moot a claim if the money is actually paid. What are the arguments in favor of mootness in that circumstance? Assuming that such a payment *would* moot the class representative's claim, does that mean that the representative can no longer pursue classwide claims?

2. In his dissent, Chief Justice Roberts opined that the case was moot because Campbell–Ewald offered the full value of the claim. Justice Alito endorsed Chief Justice Roberts's reasoning and also emphasized that there was no dispute that Campbell–Ewald had the capacity and willingness to pay. Are the points made by the dissents valid?

3. In *Chen v. Allstate Ins. Co.*, 819 F.3d 1136 (9th Cir. 2016), the Ninth Circuit held that the deposit of funds in an escrow account pursuant to Rule 68 did not moot the plaintiff's case or prevent the plaintiff from seeking class certification. The case, like *Campbell–Ewald,* was filed under the Telephone Consumer Protection Act. The suit alleged that Allstate violated the Act by making unsolicited, automated calls to class members' cellular phones. After *Campbell–Ewald* was decided, Allstate deposited $20,000, purportedly in full settlement of the claims of the class representative (Florencio Pacleb), in an escrow account. The funds were to remain in that account pending an order of the district court directing the escrow agent to pay the funds to Pacleb, requiring Allstate to refrain from making non-emergency calls to Pacleb in the future, and dismissing the case as moot. The Ninth Circuit held for two reasons that that tactic did not moot the class claims. First, even if the district court entered judgment on Pacleb's individual claims, Pacleb would still be allowed under Ninth Circuit precedent to seek class certification. Second, even if such a ploy could moot the entire action, the Ninth Circuit held that it would not direct that the money be paid to Pacleb before Pacleb had had a full opportunity to move for class certification. According to the court, mootness does not occur until full relief has been received, not merely when it has been offered. The court relied in language in *Campbell–Ewald* that "*a would-be class representative with a live claim of her own must be accorded a fair opportunity to show that certification is warranted.*" *Id.* at 1147 (citing *Campbell–Ewald*) (emphasis added by Ninth Circuit). The court noted that its approach was also consistent with other cases and treatises discussing mootness, and with two district court cases post-*Campbell–Ewald* that had likewise refused to moot a case before the class representative had had a fair opportunity to litigate class certification.

4. For a discussion of other federal court decisions construing *Campbell–Ewald, see* Colleen Carey Gulliver, *Takeaways from Decisions Following* Campbell-Ewald, LAW 360 (Aug. 9, 2016), www.law360.com/articles/826450/takeaways-from-decisions-following-campbell-ewald. The article concludes that "[t]he overwhelming majority of circuit and district courts have held that tendering full relief to a named plaintiff will not moot a class action before the named plaintiff is given the opportunity to attempt certification." *Id.* Yet the article notes that there is authority holding that a pre-certification tender to the plaintiff of the amount of the claim will moot both the individual and class claims. Clearly, *Campbell–Ewald* has not completely settled the issues involving mootness and tendering of relief to named plaintiffs.

4. STANDING ISSUES IN CLASS ACTIONS

A controversial issue is whether, under Article III of the U.S. Constitution, a class action may go forward when the class representatives, or a significant number of unnamed class members, have allegedly suffered no injury. This issue has received significant attention from courts and commentators.

a. Case Law

In recent years, defendants have challenged "no-injury" classes, relying on the "case or controversy" requirement of Article III. They have argued that, even if the named plaintiffs have standing, Article III is violated if a substantial number of unnamed class members cannot allege injury. Some courts have rejected the argument, holding that a class action go forward if at least one named plaintiff has standing. *See, e.g., Neale v. Volvo Cars of N. Am., LLC*, 794 F.3d 353, 364 (3d Cir. 2015); *Kohen v. Pac. Inv. Mgmt. Co.*, 571 F.3d 672, 676 (7th Cir. 2009). Other courts, however, have held that all (or the vast majority of) class members must have standing. *See, e.g., Denney v. Deutsche Bank AG*, 443 F.3d 253, 264 (2d Cir. 2006).

This Article III issue was litigated in two consumer class actions: *In re Whirlpool Corp. Front-Loading Washer Prods. Liab. Litig.*, 722 F.3d 838 (6th Cir. 2013) and *Butler v. Sears, Roebuck & Co.* 702 F.3d 359 (7th Cir. 2012), *vacated*, 133 S. Ct. 2768 (2013), *judgment reinstated*, 727 F.3d 796 (7th Cir. 2013). In both cases, purchasers of washing machines alleged that the machines were defective because they were susceptible to mold growth. Defendants argued that most class members had not experienced the mold problem, and therefore the suit violated Article III. Both the Sixth Circuit and the Seventh Circuit rejected defendants' argument. The Supreme Court denied certiorari in both cases. *Glazer*, 134 S. Ct. 1277; *Butler*, 134 S. Ct. 1277.

A similar issue often arises in data breach class actions brought against companies that have compromised customers' personal information. For example, in *Remijas v. Neiman Marcus Group, LLC*, 794 F.3d 688, 696–97 (7th Cir. 2015), the Seventh Circuit held that the plaintiffs—customers who had used payment cards at the defendant's stores prior to a large data breach—had Article III standing, even though only some class members alleged subsequent fraudulent charges. On the other hand, the Third Circuit held in *Reilly v. Ceridian Corp.*, 664 F.3d 38, 46 (3d Cir. 2011), that the plaintiffs lacked standing without a showing that the compromised data at issue was actually used to cause financial injury.

In the 2016 Term, the Supreme Court decided two cases in which "no-injury" issues were raised. In *Tyson Foods, Inc. v. Bouaphakeo*, 136 S. Ct. 1036 (2016), a wage-and-hour suit claiming unpaid overtime, the petitioner raised (as one of two questions presented) the issue of "[w]hether a class action may be certified or maintained under Rule 23(b)(3), or a collective action certified or maintained under the Fair Labor Standards Act (FLSA), when the class contains hundreds of members who were not injured and have no legal right to any damages." Petition for Writ of Certiorari at i, *Tyson Foods*, 136 S. Ct. 1036 (2016) (No. 14-1146). Although the Court did address a separate question of whether statistical evidence was properly admitted in the case (*see* Chapter 4(F)(2)), it did not address the Article III question. Instead, the Court concluded that "the question whether uninjured class members may recover is one of great importance," but it was not "a question yet fairly presented [in *Tyson Foods*], because the damages award has not yet been disbursed, nor does the record indicate how it will be disbursed." *Tyson Foods*, 136 S. Ct. at 1050.

In *Spokeo, Inc. v. Robins*, 136 S. Ct. 1540 (2016), the focus was on whether the class representative alleged cognizable injury under Article III. Plaintiff Robins filed a putative class action under the Fair Credit Reporting Act (FCRA), 15 U.S.C. § 1681(a), claiming that the website known as "Spokeo" posted inaccurate information about him, thereby harming his prospects for finding work. The defendant argued that Robins had not suffered actual injury but was merely speculating about possible harm. The district court dismissed the case for lack of standing, but the Ninth Circuit reversed, holding that Robins had adequately alleged that his statutory rights had been violated, and that he had a personalized interest in the handling of his credit information.

In a 6–2 opinion, the Supreme Court reversed the Ninth Circuit's finding of standing. The majority reasoned that the Ninth Circuit erred in focusing solely on particularity and not on concreteness, since both are elements of Article III standing. According to the Supreme Court, in assessing whether alleged injury is concrete, a court may consider both tangible and intangible injuries. But the fact that Congress has "identif[ied] and elevat[ed]" intangible interests "does not mean that a plaintiff automatically satisfies the injury-in-fact requirement whenever a statute grants a person a statutory right and purports to authorize that person to sue to vindicate that right." *Spokeo*, 136 S. Ct. at 1549. At the same time, even a "risk of real harm" can satisfy the concreteness requirement. *Id*. As the Court noted by way of example, "the law has long permitted recovery by certain tort victims even if their harms may be difficult to prove or measure." *Id*.

Turning to Robins's particular situation, the Court noted that a credit reporting agency's consumer information "may be entirely accurate," or may be inaccurate in an immaterial way, such as "an incorrect zip code." *Id*. at 1550. The Court thus remanded the case to the Ninth Circuit to consider, in the first instance, whether the alleged injury was sufficiently concrete. (Justice Thomas joined the majority, but wrote separately to elaborate on how standing requirements apply to different types of rights.)

Justice Ginsburg, joined by Justice Sotomayor, dissented. According to the dissent, there was no need for a remand because Robins had alleged not an incorrect zip code but "misinformation about his education, family situation, and economic status, inaccurate representations that could affect his fortune in the job market." *Id*. at 1556 (Ginsburg, J., dissenting).

It is important to note that the focus of *Spokeo* is on statutory damages. The Court did not make broad pronouncements about standing in class actions. Nor did *Spokeo* address the question of whether, in a class action, all or most class members must allege Article III injury, or whether it is sufficient for standing purposes that at least one class representative has alleged particularity and concreteness.

Thus, neither *Tyson Foods* nor *Spokeo* provides the last word regarding how Article III applies in the context of a class action.

Post-*Spokeo* cases have adopted a variety of approaches, with some holding that a mere allegation of a violation of a federal or state statute is sufficient for Article III standing, but with others holding violations of intangible rights under a statute do not confer standing. For a discussion of these cases, *see* Ronnie Solomon, *Post*-Spokeo, *Standing Challenges Remain Unpredictable*, LAW 360 (Oct. 26, 2016), www.law360.com/articles/854898/post-spokeo-standing-challenges-remain-unpredictable. As the article concludes, "*Spokeo* standing challenges * * * is an area of the law still in flux."

b. Legislative Efforts

Congressmen Bob Goodlatte and Trent Franks introduced H.R. 1927, the "Fairness in Class Action Litigation and Furthering Asbestos Claim Transparency Act of 2016." H.R. 1927, 114th Cong. § 1 (2016). The proposed Act contains controversial language requiring proof of common injury of "the same type and scope" as that suffered by the class representatives:

> No Federal court shall certify any proposed class seeking monetary relief for personal injury or economic loss unless the party seeking to maintain such a class action affirmatively demonstrates that each proposed class member suffered the same type and scope of injury as the named class representative or representatives.

H.R. 1927 § 2(a).

Read literally, the legislation could have far-reaching consequences. For example, the law could be used to foreclose class certification in many consumer product cases. It is frequently the case that a product with a propensity to fail works fine for some consumers but not for others. Indeed, wholly apart from consumer cases, there are many kinds of cases in which a class could include members who arguably have not suffered injury. Not surprisingly, H.R. 1927 has generated significant controversy, with liberal groups condemning the proposal and the business community supporting it.

H.R. 1927 came before the full House for a vote on January 8, 2016, passing by a vote of 211–188 (mainly along party lines). *H.R. 1927—Fairness in Class Action Litigation & Furthering Asbestos Claim Transparency Act of 2016*, Congress.gov, https://www.congress.gov/bill/114th-congress/house-bill/1927/actions (last visited Feb. 6, 2017).

Congressman Goodlatte reintroduced a similar bill on February 9, 2017, as this text was going to press. It contains language regarding standing that is virtually identical to that in H.R. 1927.

c. Commentary

For those interested in exploring the nuances of standing, *see, e.g.*, William A. Fletcher, *The Structure of Standing*, 98 Yale L.J. 221 (1988); Steven L. Winter, *The Metaphor of Standing and the Problem of Self-Governance*, 40 Stan. L. Rev. 1371 (1988); Note, *Class Standing and the Class Representative*, 94 Harv. L. Rev. 1637 (1981).

B. EXPLICIT REQUIREMENTS—RULE 23(a)

In addition to the threshold criteria, there are four explicit criteria under Rule 23(a) that must be met. The four prerequisites of Rule 23(a) are key battlegrounds in the struggle over class certification. Two of these elements, numerosity and commonality, focus mainly upon the class as a whole; the other two, typicality and adequacy, focus mainly on the proposed representatives. The labels commonly applied to these elements have some definitional force—a class must be numerous; it must present at least one common question; the representative(s) must have claims typical of those of the class; and those representing the class must perform that task adequately. Yet despite the long pedigree of many of these elements (see Chapter 1(C)), and decades of litigation under the 1966 version of Rule 23, the nature and contours of the Rule 23(a) prerequisites remain somewhat elusive.

1. NUMEROSITY

Rule 23(a)(1) states that "[o]ne or more members of a class may sue or be sued as representative parties on behalf of all members only if: (1) the class is so numerous that joinder of all members is impracticable * * *." This requirement—known in the case law as "numerosity"—is at the very core of the concept of a class action. If only a few people wish to litigate common issues, there is no need to have fewer still stand in as representatives for the rest. Class actions conjure up, quite properly, mental images of numerous claimants.

Because the notion of numerosity is so fundamental, most class actions are not instituted unless a large number of class members would be involved if a class were certified. As a result, it is not surprising that defendants often concede numerosity, especially when the proposed class is large and widely dispersed. Nonetheless, the numerosity requirement has led to a substantial body of law, and in some circumstances a plaintiff's burden in establishing numerosity may be more difficult than one might expect. This subsection focuses on some of the key issues that courts have addressed under Rule 23(a)(1).

ZEIDMAN V. J. RAY MCDERMOTT & CO.
United States Court of Appeals, Fifth Circuit, 1981.
651 F.2d 1030.

Before THORNBERRY, RANDALL, and TATE, CIRCUIT JUDGES.

RANDALL, CIRCUIT JUDGE.

This appeal is brought by the two named plaintiffs in a suit filed as a class action but never certified as such. The court declined to certify the class because of the absence of sufficient evidence to meet the numerosity requirement of Federal Rule of Civil Procedure 23(a)(1). The plaintiffs submitted additional evidence on numerosity shortly after the court's refusal to certify the class, but on the same day as the plaintiffs submitted this evidence the defendants tendered to the plaintiffs the full amount of their personal claims. The district court did not consider the additional evidence submitted by the plaintiffs; instead, the court dismissed the entire action for mootness on the basis of the defendants' tender in the absence of a certified class.

The plaintiffs first argue that the district court abused its discretion by declining to find Rule 23(a)(1) to have been satisfied with respect to their purported classes (groups consisting of most non-professional and non-institutional investors who sold certain nationally-traded stock and [call options] within given periods of time) on the basis of evidence before the court at the time of its decision (an estimate of the total number of shares and calls traded during the relevant periods). The plaintiffs then argue that the district court erred by refusing to consider their additional evidence on the question of numerosity; they contend that the action should not have been dismissed for mootness upon the defendants' tender of their personal claims.

Based on our reading of the district court's initial decision, which we find left the plaintiffs' motion for class certification pending before the court, we hold that the district court did not abuse its discretion by declining at that time to certify the class, but we hold that the court did err by dismissing the case and refusing to consider the plaintiffs' additional evidence. We reverse the judgment of the district court dismissing this case and remand the case to the district court for proceedings consistent with this opinion.

I. The Procedural Background Leading To This Appeal

Fred Zeidman and Steven Youngelson instituted this suit on August 26, 1977 against J. Ray McDermott & Co., Inc. (McDermott), Smith Barney, Harris Upham & Co., Inc. (Smith Barney), and four of McDermott's principal officers. The litigation arises out of a highly publicized tender offer contest for control of Babcock & Wilcox Co. (B & W) that took place in mid–1977 between McDermott (whose investment banker was Smith Barney) and United Technologies Corp. (UTC). During the battle for control of B & W, Zeidman sold (on August 8) 1,000 shares of B & W common stock and Youngelson sold (on August 9) four 100–share call options for B & W common stock; both plaintiffs sold their securities at a price substantially below that eventually offered by McDermott in its final and successful tender offer.

Suing on behalf of themselves and other investors who sold B & W stock and options during this period, the plaintiffs alleged in their complaint that the defendants had engaged, during the course of the tender offer contest, in an unlawful scheme to manipulate downward the market price of B & W securities by issuing false and misleading information. According to the plaintiffs, the purpose of this alleged scheme was to frustrate a competing tender offer previously made by UTC, to coerce the B & W Board of Directors into recommending a subsequent McDermott tender offer, and eventually to effect a takeover by McDermott of B & W.

Since this appeal involves the denial of class action certification and not the merits of the plaintiffs' claims, we need not examine these allegations in any great detail. However, certain dates and events in the plaintiffs' complaint form the limits of the class that the plaintiffs seek to represent and are therefore relevant at this time.

The illegal scheme alleged by the plaintiffs begins on March 30, 1977; the plaintiffs allege that open market purchases begun by McDermott on that date were a tender offer within the meaning of [the securities laws,] but that McDermott made no attempt to comply with [the requirement to file a proper schedule, Schedule 13D, with the Securities and Exchange Commission showing that McDermott was making substantial open-market purchases of stock]. * * * On August 9, 1977, Dow Jones reported in a

Broad Tape [news] release that McDermott had denied reports that it might make a tender offer for B & W stock. The plaintiffs allege that this release was materially misleading, since McDermott in fact was planning to make a tender offer; the plaintiffs further allege that the release was based on information provided to a Dow Jones reporter by McDermott's chief public relations officer, and that McDermott made no attempt to correct the misleading impression created by the release. Three days after this news report—on August 12, 1977—McDermott formally announced a tender offer for B & W stock. At this point an open tender offer battle commenced, with McDermott and UTC quickly outbidding each other until McDermott made its successful bid on August 23.

On November 25, 1977, the plaintiffs moved to certify their suit as a class action. Their motion requested certification with respect to a class consisting of the plaintiffs and all other persons similarly situated "who were between March 29, 1977 and August 14, 1977 beneficial owners of Babcock & Wilcox Company shares or Babcock & Wilcox Company calls and who sold such shares or calls between March 29, 1977 and August 14, 1977" and who sustained losses on such sales by reason of the illegal scheme alleged in the plaintiffs' complaint. This class was subsequently divided by the plaintiffs into two subclasses: first, those investors who sold their B & W stock or calls between March 29 and August 8 (represented by Youngelson); and second, those investors who sold their B & W stock or calls between August 9 and August 11 (represented by Zeidman). The event that divides these two classes is the Dow Jones Broad Tape release of August 9, on which only the Zeidman class is alleged to have relied.

In February 1978 the parties submitted memoranda addressing the question of class certification. * * * Neither the plaintiffs nor the defendants dealt with [numerosity] in any great detail in their memoranda. In order to meet the numerosity requirement of Rule 23(a)(1), the plaintiffs did no more than to allege the numbers of shares that were traded during the time periods involved; in particular, the plaintiffs asserted that almost 6,000,000 B & W shares were sold between March 30 and August 8, 1977, and that approximately 666,000 shares of B & W stock and at least 14,100 "shares of B & W underlying calls" were sold between August 9 and August 11, 1977. In response, the defendants argued that the important figure was not the total number of *shares* traded, but was instead the total number of *investors* who made those trades, since only the latter figure represents the total number of potential plaintiffs. * * *

The district court issued its decision on the class certification question on June 28, 1978. The court found that each prerequisite other than numerosity had been satisfactorily established by the plaintiffs, but that there was insufficient evidence in the record to determine whether the numerosity requirement had been met. * * *

[The district court determined that institutional and professional investors could not be included in the class.] * * * Since the plaintiffs' numerosity evidence consisted only of the number of shares that had been traded in each time frame, and since the presumably large group composed of all institutional and professional investors had been excluded from the potential classes, the [district] court held that the plaintiffs had not introduced sufficient evidence of numerosity.

While the court refused to find in favor of the plaintiffs on the numerosity issue, however, it did not find to the contrary that numerosity did not exist in this case. Instead, the court seems to have left the issue open. After discussing the numerosity question, the court concluded:

> Consequently, this aspect of the class certification will remain open until sufficient additional evidence of numerosity is introduced into the record to allow a ruling on this issue.

* * *

As a result of this decision, the plaintiffs commenced the compilation of certain documentary evidence on numerosity and the preparation of a memorandum specifically addressed to that issue. This additional evidence and memorandum were filed in the district court on July 6, 1978—approximately one week after the court's initial opinion on class certification. The plaintiffs relied for their new analysis on several published sources for stock exchange data. * * * Based on figures reported in these sources, the plaintiffs made the following estimates:

(1) during the Youngelson class period (May 11–August 8, 1977), 3,466 round-lot trades involving under 1,000 shares averaged 272 shares and accounted for 88% of total sale executions;

(2) during the three-day Zeidman class period (August 9–11, 1977), 567 round-lot trades involving under 1,000 shares averaged 318 shares and accounted for 80% of total sale executions; and

(3) 5 major "retail" brokerage firms sold many more shares than they purchased during the two class periods.

The plaintiffs argued that a sufficiently large number of non-professional and non-institutional investors must have sold B & W securities during the two class periods because of the extremely large number of small trades in those periods, since institutional and professional investors rarely trade in small amounts. The plaintiffs further argued that while the plaintiffs' losses come from the *sale* of securities, professional and institutional investors would primarily have been *purchasing* securities during these periods, since the largest percentage of such trading would likely be done by arbitrageurs who purchase stock in anticipation of a tender offer. * * * Finally, the plaintiffs submitted figures from a survey of B & W shareholders prepared by B & W and dated April 15, 1977; the survey showed that there were 23,380 individual B & W shareholders holding an average of 149 shares and at least some of whom resided in every state in the nation.

[Because the defendants tendered to the plaintiffs the full amount of their claims promptly after this new evidence was submitted, the district court did not consider the new numerosity evidence, but instead dismissed the case as moot.]

* * *

III. Did The District Court Abuse Its Discretion By Refusing To Find "Numerosity" On The Basis Of Evidence Submitted To It Before Its Initial Decision Of June 28?

The plaintiffs argue that the district court abused its discretion by requiring additional evidence on numerosity; according to the plaintiffs, the court should have found numerosity on the basis of the evidence initially submitted to it. In order to address this contention we must first consider the nature of the question the district court was called upon to decide. * * * In order to satisfy his burden with respect to [numerosity], a plaintiff must ordinarily demonstrate some evidence or reasonable estimate of the number of purported class members. However, this does not mean that the actual number of class members is the determinative question, for "[t]he proper focus [under Rule 23(a)(1)] is not on numbers alone, but on whether joinder of all members is practicable in view of the numerosity of the class and all other relevant factors." Thus, a number of facts other than the actual or estimated number of purported class members may be relevant to the "numerosity" question; these include, for example, the geographical dispersion of the class, the ease with which class members may be identified, the nature of the action, and the size of each plaintiff's claim. It is not surprising, therefore, that no definitive pattern has emerged under Rule 23(a)(1) in terms of the number of purported class members. Indeed, classes with as few as twenty-five or thirty members have been certified by some courts.

We must emphasize, however, that this issue is—as are other questions involved in the decision to certify a class action—left to the sound discretion of the district court. Because the certification of a class action has such a great effect on the district court's control of litigation before it, and because certification involves substantial fact questions, we will not reverse a district court's decision on class certification absent an abuse of its discretion.

The evidence submitted to the district court before its initial decision on class certification consisted only of the number of shares traded during the periods involved in the plaintiffs' two purported classes: the plaintiffs alleged that almost 6,000,000 shares of B & W stock were traded during the time-span of the Youngelson class and that 666,000 shares of B & W stock and at least 14,100 "shares of B & W underlying calls" were traded during the time-span of the Zeidman class. The plaintiffs' discussion of these figures in their initial memorandum on class certification is brief, but their argument seems to have relied on a common-sense assumption. In particular, the plaintiffs appear to have presumed that *any* class composed of the sellers of a nationally traded security during a period in which hundreds of thousands or even millions of shares of the security were traded must necessarily be "so numerous that joinder of all members is impracticable." This assumption is indeed a reasonable one, since it is difficult to imagine any such class composed of a small number of sellers, and since the class would in all likelihood be geographically dispersed and difficult to identify. As one would expect, therefore, the prerequisite expressed in Rule 23(a)(1) is generally assumed to have been met in class action suits involving nationally traded securities. * * * Indeed, a number of courts have found the numerosity requirement to have been met with respect to a purported class of purchasers or sellers of nationally traded securities on the basis of evidence similar to that initially offered by the plaintiffs in this case.[6]

---

[6] Some courts, however, have found the numerosity requirement *not* to have been met with respect to a purported class of purchasers or sellers of nationally traded securities on the basis of evidence similar to that initially offered by the plaintiffs in this case.

Although the evidence initially submitted by the plaintiffs would ordinarily seem adequate to meet the numerosity requirement in a securities case, two factors distinguish this case from the more common cases such as those cited above. In the first place, the plaintiffs do not seek to represent *all* investors who purchased B & W securities during the periods at issue; the district court excluded from the plaintiffs' purported classes the undeniably significant group composed of "the arbitrage community" and other "large institutional or professional" investors, and the plaintiffs do not contest this exclusion on appeal. What the district court had to decide, therefore, was whether the remaining class composed only of *non-institutional* and *non-professional* investors met the numerosity requirement.

In the second place, the district court did not find that the numerosity requirement had not been met by the plaintiffs, but instead left the question open pending submission of additional evidence. * * * [T]he district court's initial decision on class certification found the record inadequate to make any determination with regard to numerosity until evidence on the size of the excluded groups were introduced, and then properly gave the plaintiffs an opportunity to submit such evidence.

Viewed in this light, we cannot say that the district court's initial decision on class certification was an abuse of its discretion. Where an admittedly large and potentially dominant group is excluded from a plaintiff's purported class, it is obviously difficult to estimate the numerosity of the plaintiff's class absent some evidence of the size either of the excluded group or of the remaining class. Thus, some courts have indeed refused to find numerosity on the basis of evidence similar to that initially introduced by the plaintiffs, in situations where—as here—the plaintiffs have introduced no evidence as to the size of a particular subclass of securities buyers or sellers which they seek to represent. We conclude therefore that the district court did not abuse its discretion by holding the numerosity issue open pending submission of additional evidence on the role of professional and institutional investors in the market for B & W securities.

* * *

[The court held that the district court should not have dismissed for mootness based on tender to the named plaintiffs of the amount of their personal claims. Thus, the court remanded the case so that the district court could consider, *inter alia*, plaintiffs' additional evidence on the issue of numerosity.]

PATRYKUS V. GOMILLA
United States District Court, Northern District of Illinois, 1988.
121 F.R.D. 357.

CONLON, DISTRICT JUDGE.

Plaintiffs Allen Patrykus, Richard Babel, and John Doe ("class representatives") brought [a civil rights] action * * * for declaratory and injunctive relief and for damages, individually and on behalf of all others similarly situated ("plaintiff class" or "class members"). * * *

The class representatives move for certification of the class pursuant to Fed. R. Civ. P. 23. For the reasons that follow, plaintiffs' motion is granted.

BACKGROUND

The class representatives sue on behalf of a purported class that is defined as follows:

> ... [A]ll persons who were subjected to any of the unlawful seizures, detentions, searches, use of excessive force and interrogations and photographing performed by agents of the Northeastern Metropolitan Group and the Chicago Police Department during a raid at Carol's Speakeasy on September 12, 1985.

Plaintiff class members allegedly were subjected to the same unconstitutional course of conduct by agents of the Northeastern Metropolitan Group ("NEMEG defendants"), which is a statutorily created inter-governmental drug enforcement agency, and by officers of the Chicago Police Department ("Chicago Police defendants").

Approximately 50 persons were present at Carol's Speakeasy ("Carol's"), a Chicago bar primarily frequented by homosexual and bisexual men, when ten NEMEG defendants entered through several doors. Shortly thereafter, seven Chicago Police defendants entered Carol's and stood guard at the doors. The defendants did not have warrants for the arrest or search of any class member; plaintiffs claim they were behaving lawfully and provided no probable or reasonable cause, suspicion, or any other legal justification, for the seizures, detentions, searches and interrogations alleged. Plaintiffs believe that defendants possessed only a single arrest warrant for a bartender at Carol's.

Plaintiffs further allege that the NEMEG defendants told class members that they could not leave the bar, and forced all of them to lie face down on the floor for periods of approximately one to three hours. During the raid, the NEMEG defendants allegedly subjected class members to homosexual slurs. The Chicago Police defendants stood by during the events alleged.

Each class member allegedly was subjected to a pat-down search and a search of personal effects, was compelled to reveal detailed personal information and was photographed. While class members were on the floor, the NEMEG defendants allegedly searched Carol's membership files, which contained information about some of the class members.

Plaintiffs seek declaratory judgment that the defendants' conduct deprived them of their constitutional rights to be free from unreasonable searches and seizures, excessive force, and invasion of their privacy, to equal protection of the laws and to freedom of association. They seek an injunction directing defendants to return all personal information and photographs or to insure destruction of these materials. They also seek a list of any persons or agencies that were furnished information about class members derived from the raid on Carol's. Finally, $50,000 in compensatory damages and an additional $50,000 in punitive damages are sought on behalf of each class member in each of five claims for relief, in addition to attorneys' fees and costs.

DISCUSSION

* * *

I. Requirements of Fed. R. Civ. P. 23(a)

1. Numerosity

A proposed class must be so numerous that joinder of all members is impracticable. The complaint need not allege the exact number or identity of class members. The court is entitled to make common sense assumptions in order to support a finding of numerosity. In addition to estimating the number of class members, the court considers judicial economy and the ability of class members to institute individual suits.

Plaintiffs assert that the class defined in their consolidated complaint, comprised of approximately 50 persons, is sufficiently large to render joinder of all class members impracticable. Plaintiffs rely on *Swanson v. American Consumer Industries*, 415 F.2d 1326, 1333 n.9 (7th Cir. 1969) (class of 151 held sufficient, but 40 would have been acceptable); *Rosario v. Cook County*, 101 F.R.D. 659, 661 (N.D. Ill. 1983) (class of 20 held sufficient); *Dale Electronics v. R.C.L. Electronics, Inc.*, 53 F.R.D. 531, 534 (D.N.H. 1971) (class of 13 held sufficient). Plaintiffs further contend that the nature of the relief sought, primarily a declaration of unconstitutionality and an injunction compelling the return of unlawfully seized materials, weighs heavily in favor of a finding of impracticability. Finally, plaintiffs argue that the potential stigma of bringing a claim for occurrences in a gay bar is likely to discourage potential class members from proceeding individually or in their own names.

Defendants distinguish *Swanson* and *Dale Electronics* on the ground that the plaintiffs have not alleged that the class is geographically disbursed and, further, that the substantial damage claim here makes joinder practicable. Defendants contend that *Rosario* is inapposite because "future class members cannot exist."

The individual circumstances of a case must be considered in determining whether joinder is impracticable. A relatively small group may form a class if other considerations make joinder impracticable. The present geographical disbursement of persons who all happened to be at the same Chicago bar on an evening almost three years ago is not known. More importantly, there is an unusual factor in this case that must be considered: the potential social prejudice against homosexuals, or against persons who associate with homosexuals, that may deter class members from suing in their own names. Nor is there any reason to burden the judicial system, as defendants suggest, with 50 "John Doe" lawsuits arising out of the same incident. Accordingly, the numerosity requirement of Rule 23 is satisfied.

[The court found that the other requirements for class certification were also satisfied.]

NOTES AND QUESTIONS

1. The *Patrykus* court stated in the above excerpt that "[t]he court is entitled to make common sense assumptions in order to support a finding of numerosity." Under such an approach, could one argue as a matter of common sense that the class in *Zeidman* was sufficiently numerous and geographically

diverse to warrant a finding of numerosity? If the district court in *Zeidman* had found numerosity based on plaintiffs' initial evidence, would that finding have been an abuse of discretion? Or would the appellate court have upheld *that* result as well? Put another way, can the Fifth Circuit's opinion be explained as being based on deference to the district court?

2. Consider the Eleventh Circuit's approach to the question in *Vega v. T–Mobile USA, Inc.*, 564 F.3d 1256 (11th Cir. 2009). There, the appellate court reversed a district court's holding that the numerosity requirement was met by a class of the defendant's Florida employees, who allegedly were improperly denied sales commissions. Despite testimony that the company had thousands of sales employees nationwide, the record contained no evidence of the number of sales employees in Florida who were members of the class. While clarifying that "a plaintiff need not show the precise number of members in the class," the appellate court nonetheless held that the plaintiff must make "some showing, affording the district court the means to make a supported factual finding, that the class actually certified meets the numerosity requirement." *Id.* at 1267 (citation and internal quotation marks omitted). The appellate court explained:

> Yes, T–Mobile is a large company, with many retail outlets, and, as such, it might be tempting to assume that the number of retail sales associates the company employed in Florida during the relevant period can overcome the generally low hurdle presented by Rule 23(a)(1). However, a plaintiff still bears the burden of establishing every element of Rule 23, and a district court's factual findings must find support in the evidence before it. In this case, the district court's inference of numerosity for a Florida-only class without the aid of a shred of Florida-only evidence was an exercise in sheer speculation. Accordingly, the district court abused its discretion by finding the numerosity requirement to be satisfied with respect to a Florida-only class when the record is utterly devoid of any showing that the certified class of T–Mobile sales representatives "in Florida" is "so numerous that joinder of all members is impracticable."

Id. at 1267–68 (citations omitted). Is the *T–Mobile* court's approach more like that of the court in *Zeidman* or the court in *Patrykus*? Does the Eleventh Circuit take common sense assumptions into account? How much discretion does a district court have under the *T–Mobile* approach?

3. For another recent example of the increasingly rigorous approach to numerosity, *see* Chapter 2(B)(3)(b), *Marcus v. BMW of North America, LLC*, 687 F.3d 583 (3d Cir. 2012), in which the Third Circuit reversed the district court's certification of a (b)(3) class in a case alleging product defects in a certain type of tire. The *Marcus* court found the Eleventh Circuit's decision in *Vega* (discussed above) to be "particularly instructive," 687 F.3d at 595, and concluded that, as in *Vega*, the district court had erred in finding the plaintiff had satisfied Rule 23(a)(1). *Id.* at 597. As the Third Circuit explained: "When a plaintiff attempts to certify both a nationwide class and a state-specific subclass, * * * evidence that is sufficient to establish numerosity with respect to the nationwide class is not necessarily sufficient to establish numerosity with respect to the state-specific subclass." *Id.* at 595. It thus concluded:

> Given the complete lack of evidence specific to BMWs purchased or leased in New Jersey with Bridgestone ["run-flat tires," or "RFTs"] that have gone flat and been replaced, the District Court's numerosity ruling crossed the line separating inference and speculation. BMW is a large company that sells and leases many cars throughout

the country, many with RFTs. But the Court did not certify a nationwide class of BMW owners and lessees with any brand of RFTs. It certified a New Jersey class of owners and lessees with Bridgestone RFTs that have gone flat and been replaced. It is tempting to assume that the New Jersey class meets the numerosity requirement based on the defendant companies' nationwide presence. But the only fact with respect to numerosity proven by a preponderance of the evidence is that [plaintiff] himself is a member of the proposed class. "[I]f there are no members of the class other than the named representatives, then Rule 23(a)(1) obviously has not been satisfied." * * * Accordingly, we hold that the District Court abused its discretion by finding the numerosity requirement to be satisfied with respect to the New Jersey class.

Id. at 597.

4. Is the *Patrykus* court persuasive in holding that a class of 50 is sufficiently numerous to satisfy the numerosity requirement? What about the cases cited in *Patrykus*, which held that classes as small as 13 or 20 were sufficient? In light of such cases, can the result in *Zeidman* be justified? Is there any doubt that the class in *Zeidman* included *at least* 13 members?

5. As both *Zeidman* and *Patrykus* make clear, geographic dispersion of the proposed class is a very important factor in assessing the impracticability of joinder. *Accord, e.g., Coca–Cola Bottling Co. v. Coca–Cola Co.*, 95 F.R.D. 168, 175 (D. Del. 1982) ("[C]ourts have often held that geographic dispersion renders joinder impracticable.") (citing examples); *cf., e.g., Andrews v. Bechtel Power Corp.*, 780 F.2d 124, 132 (1st Cir. 1985) (upholding denial of class certification in part because the 49 potential class members "all liv[ed] in southeastern Massachusetts—and, therefore, could join or be joined in a suit of named parties"). Why does geographic location of class members play a role in the Rule 23(a)(1) analysis? Given that the *Patrykus* court found that the geographic disbursement of the class was not known, should the court have ruled that plaintiffs failed to meet their burden of showing numerosity? Given the context of the case (involving alleged civil rights violations at a Chicago bar), is it not reasonable to assume, unlike in *Zeidman*, that most of the class members are from the same geographic region (*i.e.*, the Chicago metropolitan area)?

6. In finding that joinder was impracticable, the *Patrykus* court relied in part upon the "social prejudice against homosexuals" that could deter the filing of individual claims. Should it be sufficient to show impracticability that individual class members may have reasons why they would not sue except as part of a class action? If so, what other examples come to mind that would permit a small group to pursue a class action?

7. Courts have differed widely in assessing the number of potential class members needed to satisfy numerosity. As one court has stated, "[c]ourts have certified classes with as few as thirteen members, and have denied certification of classes with over three hundred members." *Hum v. Dericks*, 162 F.R.D. 628, 634 (D. Haw. 1995) (citing authorities). *See also Alkire v. Irving*, 330 F.3d 802, 820 (6th Cir. 2003) (numerosity not satisfied where defendant's records indicated that there were only nine putative class members and plaintiffs' speculation that there were "hundreds" was "highly improbable"); *Harik v. California Teachers Ass'n*, 326 F.3d 1042, 1051 (9th Cir. 2003) (denying certification of classes comprising seven, nine, and ten members); *Esler v. Northrop Corp.*, 86 F.R.D. 20, 34 (W.D. Mo. 1979) ("[G]enerally classes of forty or more persons

have been certified, while those of less than twenty-five have not been certified."). Some courts have emphasized that it is erroneous to focus on mere numbers alone. *See, e.g., Phillips v. Joint Legislative Comm. on Performance & Expenditure Review*, 637 F.2d 1014, 1022 (5th Cir. 1981) (court must look at numbers in view of "all other relevant factors"); *Hernandez v. Alexander*, 152 F.R.D. 192, 194 (D. Nev. 1993) ("[I]n some instances, joinder may be impracticable even where the relative size of the potential class is small."); *see also* Robert H. Klonoff, *The Decline of Class Actions*, 90 Wash. U. L. Rev. 729, 768, 771 (2013) (contrasting courts that have made numerosity overly demanding with those that have "been willing to apply common sense, make reasonable assumptions, and permit plaintiffs to develop additional evidence when their existing evidence is deficient"). The Ninth Circuit recently upheld certification of a class of 20 when the defendant had "aggressively urged at least one class member to opt out" and the record contained indications that the defendant might have been the cause of 31 other opt-outs. *Rannis v. Recchia*, 2010 WL 2124096, at *5 (9th Cir. 2010). What sort of case involving 13 class members would be sufficiently numerous for purposes of certification? What type of case involving 300 members would *not* satisfy numerosity?

8. Some courts have held that the socioeconomic status of the proposed class members is relevant to numerosity. For example, in *Committee of Blind Vendors v. District of Columbia*, 695 F. Supp. 1234 (D.D.C. 1988), *rev'd on other grounds*, 28 F.3d 130 (D.C. Cir. 1994), the court addressed whether a class of 63 blind vendors satisfied numerosity. In holding that it did, the court noted that "[t]he relatively meager financial resources of the individual vendors countenance[d] against requiring individual actions." 695 F. Supp. at 1242. By contrast, in *Strykers Bay Neighborhood Council, Inc. v. City of New York*, 695 F. Supp. 1531, 1538 (S.D.N.Y. 1988), the court held that a group of 32 families seeking construction of low-income housing was insufficient to satisfy numerosity, reasoning in part:

> Plaintiffs' only argument going to the impracticability of joinder is that plaintiffs are largely poor and cannot afford to bring their own actions. This, however, is not persuasive since plaintiffs can combine their resources, limited as they may be, and hire one lawyer to represent their common claims. Moreover, the prospects for *pro bono* representation in a case like the present one appear excellent.

Can *Committee of Blind Vendors* and *Strykers Bay Neighborhood Council* be reconciled with each other?

9. Some courts have discounted the significance of the number of proposed class members by opining that "it is likely that not all the proposed class members will seek to join the suit." *Christiana Mortgage Corp. v. Delaware Mortgage Bankers Ass'n*, 136 F.R.D. 372, 378 (D. Del. 1991) (citation omitted). Should such reasoning govern the numerosity analysis? Or should a court assume, in cases where putative class members may exclude themselves or "opt out," that all or most proposed class members may remain in the suit?

10. The *Zeidman* court suggests that when the size of a potential class is unclear, a court does not err in holding that plaintiffs have failed to establish numerosity. By contrast, in another case handed down the same year, the same court of appeals that decided *Zeidman* found, contrary to a district court's holding, that numerosity was satisfied in a discrimination case precisely because "neither party [could] even count how many [class members] there [were], let alone identify all of them." *Phillips v. Joint Legislative Comm. on Performance*

& *Expenditure Review*, 637 F.2d 1014, 1022 (5th Cir. 1981). Are these decisions necessarily in conflict with one another?

11. Some courts have found Rule 23(a)(1) more easily satisfied "when the individual claims are for small amounts of damages." *Esler v. Northrop Corp.*, 86 F.R.D. 20, 34 (W.D. Mo. 1979). Joinder is conceivably more impracticable because plaintiffs have less incentive to participate in such litigation. Should the amount of the typical class member's claim have any bearing on whether a court finds joinder to be impracticable?

12. Consistent with an argument made by plaintiffs in *Patrykus*, many courts have held that Rule 23(a)(1) is more easily satisfied when injunctive relief is sought. *See, e.g., Holland v. Steele*, 92 F.R.D. 58 (N.D. Ga. 1981). This is especially true—as was *not* the case in *Patrykus*—when relief is sought on the basis of future as well as present class members. *Holland*, 92 F.R.D. at 63 (class suit seeking access to court and counsel for present and future inmates of particular jail); *see also Weaver v. Reagen*, 701 F. Supp. 717, 721 (W.D. Mo. 1988) (numerosity found in suit seeking relief for at least 61 present class members and unknown number of future AIDS victims who were denied Medicaid coverage for drug AZT), *aff'd as modified*, 886 F.2d 194 (8th Cir. 1989). Should courts be more liberal in evaluating Rule 23(a)(1) when injunctive relief or future claimants are involved?

13. In *Pederson v. Louisiana State Univ.*, 213 F.3d 858 (5th Cir. 2000), the court addressed a class action claiming that Louisiana State University had discriminated against women in connection with intercollegiate athletics by, *inter alia*, denying them equal opportunity to participate in intercollegiate sports and denying them equal opportunity for athletic scholarships. The district court provisionally certified a class, but then decertified the class after the close of evidence at trial on the ground that plaintiffs had failed to establish numerosity. Relying on *Zeidman*, the Fifth Circuit reversed, reasoning:

> At trial, [plaintiffs] established that a number of current LSU female students had a desire to try out for varsity soccer or fast-pitch softball. [Defendants] admit that eight people showed up for varsity soccer tryouts. These eight, however, do not constitute the sum total of class members. The class consists of all "female students enrolled at LSU since 1993 and any time thereafter" who wish to participate. Plaintiffs established that, around the time of trial, well over 5,000 young women were playing soccer or fast-pitch softball at the high school level in Louisiana. They also established that many former members of a Baton Rouge soccer club received scholarships to play intercollegiate soccer. As [defendants] point out, these women, because they are not students at LSU, are not members of the putative class. However, considering the talent pool in Louisiana established by these figures and the number of LSU students who come from Louisiana, [plaintiffs] have established that numerous future female LSU students will desire to try out for varsity soccer and fast-pitch softball. To satisfy the numerosity prong, "a plaintiff must ordinarily demonstrate some evidence or reasonable estimate of the number of purported class members." *Zeidman v. J. Ray McDermott & Co.*, 651 F.2d 1030, 1038 (5th Cir. 1981).

* * *

Our independent review of the record satisfies us that the numerosity prong has been satisfied. Because the district court failed to identify specific findings that led it to conclude that the numerosity prong had not been satisfied, we can only conclude that its assessment of the evidence was clearly erroneous and, therefore, that it abused its discretion in declining finally to certify the putative class on the ground of lack of numerosity. Accordingly, we vacate the district court's decertification order.

Pederson, 213 F.3d at 868–69. Was the Fifth Circuit correct that, under *Zeidman*, the district court had abused its discretion? Notably, Chief Judge King, who authored *Zeidman* (under her former name, Judge Randall), was on the panel in *Pederson* and joined the court's opinion.

14. In *Robidoux v. Celani*, 987 F.2d 931 (2d Cir. 1993), the Second Circuit vacated the judgment of a district court that refused to certify a class challenging defendant Vermont Department of Social Welfare's failure to timely process public assistance applications. Because the defendant was responsible, in part, for plaintiffs' inability to determine which application delays were attributable to the defendant and which to plaintiffs, the Second Circuit concluded that it was an abuse of discretion for the district court to find that numerosity had not been satisfied:

> [Plaintiffs] presented documentary evidence of delays in 22 to 133 cases per month, depending on the month and whether the assistance sought was Food Stamps or ANFC [Aid to Needy Families with Children Program]. Other government benefits cases have held that class representatives who presented similar numbers of potential class members satisfied the numerosity requirement. * * *
>
> The Department contends on appeal, however, that not all of the delayed cases included in the figures provided to the court can be attributed to Departmental fault. The Department argues that the figures included cases in which applications were delayed by applicants themselves (for example, those in which the application did not provide the necessary information to the Department). The Department conceded at oral argument that it does not keep records of the reasons for the delays and so cannot provide an exact number of persons delayed by applicant fault. Plaintiffs have presented documentary evidence of delays in a sufficient number of cases to meet the numerosity requirement. The Department cannot prevail by claiming that delays are due to applicant fault and meanwhile fail to document its claim. * * * Furthermore, the Department's own report concluded that the delays were caused by the increase in applications, not applicants' delays. * * *

Robidoux, 987 F.2d at 936. Is the Second Circuit's reasoning persuasive? Does it matter which party created the delay, so long as common sense indicates that there were between 22 and 133 cases of delay per month?

15. In *In re FleetBoston Fin. Corp. Sec. Litig.*, 253 F.R.D. 315 (D.N.J. 2008), the district court applied the Third Circuit's holding in *Stewart v. Abraham*, 275 F.3d 220, 226–27 (3d Cir. 2001), which stated that numerosity is generally satisfied with 40 or more class members. According to the district court, those 40 class members must be genuine plaintiffs with standing to sue:

> Numerosity is not an abstract concept: the requirement for at least 40 class members articulated * * * in *Stewart* can be met only by "real" plaintiffs, each of which has standing to sue. The benchmark number cannot be satisfied by a group of 40 or more entities having no standing, since the sum of forty zeros is still a zero. * * * Indeed,

finding otherwise would make a mockery of the Third Circuit's 40–plus requirement, since—if such an interpretation is adopted—a showing of one "real" [plaintiff] and thirty-nine "non-plaintiffs" would still meet the benchmark.

Id. at 350. Does this approach make sense? Should the court decide the issue of standing for unnamed class members before deciding numerosity?

16. In 2016, the Third Circuit offered an extensive discussion of how a court should assess the impracticability of joinder:

> We have not had occasion to list relevant factors that are appropriate for district court judges to consider when determining whether joinder would be impracticable. We do so now. This non-exhaustive list includes: judicial economy, the claimants' ability and motivation to litigate as joined plaintiffs, the financial resources of class members, the geographic dispersion of class members, the ability to identify future claimants, and whether the claims are for injunctive relief or for damages.

In re Modafinil Antitrust Litigation, 837 F.3d 238, 252–53 (3d Cir. 2016). Applying these criteria, the court held that the district court erred in finding numerosity with respect to a class consisting of 22 members. In dissent, Judge Rendell opined that the majority erred in second guessing the careful analysis of the district court. Because the case involved such a small class, it is unclear whether the majority ruling will have a significant impact in cases involving a significantly larger number of class members.

17. Should Rule 23(a)(1) be amended to provide more explicit criteria for determining numerosity? If so, what should be the components of such a rule?

PROBLEM

Plaintiffs, three individuals from different states who suffer from a rare blood disorder, have sued their health insurance carrier, Coverage, Inc. ("Coverage"), on behalf of themselves and others similarly situated, alleging that Coverage improperly refused to pay for expensive experimental surgery that is the only hope for correcting the disorder. Scientists believe that the disorder is linked to high quantities of alcohol consumption. Plaintiffs estimate that there are about 1,000 individuals across the country who suffer from the same disorder. They cannot state, however, how many of these individuals also have policies with Coverage. Based on these facts, is numerosity satisfied? What arguments can be made to the contrary?

2. COMMONALITY

Rule 23(a)(2) states that members of a class may sue as representatives only if "there are questions of law or fact common to the class * * *." This requirement, which applies to all class actions under the Federal Rules, is referred to as "commonality."

From the adoption of the 1966 version of Rule 23 until the Supreme Court's 2011 opinion in *Wal–Mart Stores, Inc. v. Dukes*, 564 U.S. 338 (2011), most courts had found that commonality was not difficult to satisfy. *See, e.g., Jenkins v. Raymark Indus. Inc.*, 782 F.2d 468, 472 (5th Cir. 1986) (noting that the "threshold of commonality is not high"). Under this liberal approach, commonality was far less rigorous than the predominance standard of Rule 23(b)(3), which requires that common issues predominate over individual issues.

Yet even prior to *Dukes*, courts had occasionally applied Rule 23(a)(2) more rigorously. *See, e.g.*, *Vega v. T–Mobile USA, Inc.*, 564 F.3d 1256, 1269 (11th Cir. 2009) (Rule 23(a)(2) "demands significant[] * * * analytical rigor and precision; backing into the requisite findings, and relying on a reviewing court to connect the dots, is not enough").

In 2011, the Supreme Court rendered a landmark decision interpreting Rule 23(a)(2).

WAL–MART STORES, INC. V. DUKES[†]

Supreme Court of the United States, 2011.
564 U.S. 338.

JUSTICE SCALIA delivered the opinion of the Court.

We are presented with one of the most expansive class actions ever. The District Court and the Court of Appeals approved the certification of a class comprising about one and a half million plaintiffs, current and former female employees of petitioner Wal–Mart who allege that the discretion exercised by their local supervisors over pay and promotion matters violates Title VII by discriminating against women.[††]

* * *

I

A

Petitioner Wal–Mart is the Nation's largest private employer. It operates four types of retail stores throughout the country: Discount Stores, Supercenters, Neighborhood Markets, and Sam's Clubs. Those stores are divided into seven nationwide divisions, which in turn comprise 41 regions of 80 to 85 stores apiece. Each store has between 40 and 53 separate departments and 80 to 500 staff positions. In all, Wal–Mart operates approximately 3,400 stores and employs more than one million people.

Pay and promotion decisions at Wal–Mart are generally committed to local managers' broad discretion, which is exercised "in a largely subjective manner." Local store managers may increase the wages of hourly employees (within limits) with only limited corporate oversight. As for salaried employees, such as store managers and their deputies, higher corporate authorities have discretion to set their pay within preestablished ranges.

Promotions work in a similar fashion. Wal–Mart permits store managers to apply their own subjective criteria when selecting candidates as "support managers," which is the first step on the path to management. Admission to Wal–Mart's management training program, however, does

---

[†] The portion of *Dukes* excerpted here involves the Court's treatment of Rule 23(a)(2), an issue that divided the Court 5–4. The Court's discussion of Rule 23(b)(2), which was unanimous, is set out in Chapter 3(B). *Dukes* is also discussed in connection with aggregate proof (Chapter 4(F)(2)(a)); class certification (Chapter 4(B)(1)(b)(i)); and employment class actions, (Chapter 10(B)). [Ed.]

[††] Title VII of the Civil Rights Act of 1964, as amended, 42 U.S.C. § 2000e–1 *et seq.*, prohibits employment discrimination based on "race, color, religion, sex, or national origin." *See also infra* Chapter 10(B) on employment discrimination class actions. [Ed.]

require that a candidate meet certain objective criteria, including an above–average performance rating, at least one year's tenure in the applicant's current position, and a willingness to relocate. But except for those requirements, regional and district managers have discretion to use their own judgment when selecting candidates for management training. Promotion to higher office—*e.g.*, assistant manager, co–manager, or store manager—is similarly at the discretion of the employee's superiors after prescribed objective factors are satisfied.

B

The named plaintiffs in this lawsuit, representing the 1.5 million members of the certified class, are three current or former Wal–Mart employees who allege that the company discriminated against them on the basis of their sex by denying them equal pay or promotions, in violation of Title VII of the Civil Rights Act of 1964, 78 Stat. 253, as amended, 42 U.S.C. § 2000e–1 *et seq.*

Betty Dukes began working at a Pittsburgh, California, Wal–Mart in 1994. She started as a cashier, but later sought and received a promotion to customer service manager. After a series of disciplinary violations, however, Dukes was demoted back to cashier and then to greeter. Dukes concedes she violated company policy, but contends that the disciplinary actions were in fact retaliation for invoking internal complaint procedures and that male employees have not been disciplined for similar infractions. Dukes also claims two male greeters in the Pittsburgh store are paid more than she is.

Christine Kwapnoski has worked at Sam's Club stores in Missouri and California for most of her adult life. She has held a number of positions, including a supervisory position. She claims that a male manager yelled at her frequently and screamed at female employees, but not at men. The manager in question "told her to 'doll up,' to wear some makeup, and to dress a little better."

The final named plaintiff, Edith Arana, worked at a Wal–Mart store in Duarte, California, from 1995 to 2001. In 2000, she approached the store manager on more than one occasion about management training, but was brushed off. Arana concluded she was being denied opportunity for advancement because of her sex. She initiated internal complaint procedures, whereupon she was told to apply directly to the district manager if she thought her store manager was being unfair. Arana, however, decided against that and never applied for management training again. In 2001, she was fired for failure to comply with Wal–Mart's timekeeping policy.

These plaintiffs, respondents here, do not allege that Wal–Mart has any express corporate policy against the advancement of women. Rather, they claim that their local managers' discretion over pay and promotions is exercised disproportionately in favor of men, leading to an unlawful disparate impact on female employees, *see* 42 U.S.C. § 2000e–2(k). And, respondents say, because Wal–Mart is aware of this effect, its refusal to cabin its managers' authority amounts to disparate treatment, *see* § 2000e–2(a).††††

* * *

Importantly for our purposes, respondents claim that the discrimination to which they have been subjected is common to *all* Wal–Mart's female employees. The basic theory of their case is that a strong and uniform "corporate culture" permits bias against women to infect, perhaps subconsciously, the discretionary decisionmaking of each one of Wal–Mart's thousands of managers—thereby making every woman at the company the victim of one common discriminatory practice. Respondents therefore wish to litigate the Title VII claims of all female employees at Wal–Mart's stores in a nationwide class action.

C

* * * Under Rule 23(a), the party seeking certification must demonstrate, first, that: "(1) the class is so numerous that joinder of all members is impracticable, (2) there are questions of law or fact common to the class, (3) the claims or defenses of the representative parties are typical of the claims or defenses of the class, and (4) the representative parties will fairly and adequately protect the interests of the class."

* * *

* * * [R]espondents moved the District Court to certify a plaintiff class consisting of "[a]ll women employed at any Wal–Mart domestic retail store at any time since December 26, 1998, who have been or may be subjected to Wal–Mart's challenged pay and management track promotions policies and practices." As evidence that there were * * * "questions of law or fact common to" all the women of Wal–Mart, as Rule 23(a)(2) requires, respondents relied chiefly on three forms of proof: statistical evidence about pay and promotion disparities between men and women at the company, anecdotal reports of discrimination from about 120 of Wal–Mart's female employees, and the testimony of a sociologist, Dr. William Bielby, who conducted a "social framework analysis" of Wal–Mart's "culture" and personnel practices, and concluded that the company was "vulnerable" to gender discrimination. * * *

Wal–Mart unsuccessfully moved to strike much of this evidence. It also offered its own countervailing statistical and other proof in an effort to defeat Rule 23(a)'s requirements of commonality, typicality, and adequate representation. * * *

* * *

[The district court certified a nationwide class of female Wal–Mart employees. On the (a)(2) issue, it noted that "Wal–Mart raised a number of challenges to Plaintiffs' evidence of commonality but concluded that, in fact, most of these objections related *not* to * * * commonality but to the ultimate merits of the case and 'thus should properly be addressed by a jury considering the merits' rather than a judge considering class certification." 509 F.3d at 1168, 1177–78 (9th Cir. 2007) (quoting district court).

---

†††† Title VII provides remedies for both "disparate treatment," *i.e.*, intentional discrimination, as well as for "'disparate impact," *i.e.*, where a facially non-discriminatory practice or policy nonetheless produces a discriminatory effect. [Ed.]

The Ninth Circuit panel endorsed this analysis. *Id.* The Court of Appeals, rehearing the case en banc, affirmed in substantial part. As to Rule 23(a)(2), it held that "Plaintiffs' factual evidence, expert opinions, statistical evidence, and anecdotal evidence provide sufficient support *to raise the common question* whether Wal–Mart's female employees nationwide were subjected to a *single set of corporate policies* (not merely a number of independent discriminatory acts) that may have worked to unlawfully discriminate against them in violation of Title VII." *Id.* Judge Ikuta, joined by four other judges, dissented, reasoning that the class failed to meet, *inter alia*, the commonality requirement of 23(a)(2), because "[n]one of plaintiffs' evidence is probative of company–wide discrimination." *Id.* at 640 (Ikuta, J., dissenting). In the dissent's view, "[e]very piece of evidence merely purport[ed] to support another," and "the plaintiffs' circular presentation cannot conceal the fact that they have failed to offer any significant proof of a company–wide policy of discrimination * * *." *Id.* at 640–41. *See also id.* at 652 (Kozinski, C.J., dissenting) ("the half–million members of the majority's approved class * * * have little in common but their sex and this lawsuit.").]

* * *

II

* * *

A

The crux of this case is commonality—the rule requiring a plaintiff to show that "there are questions of law or fact common to the class." Rule 23(a)(2).[5] That language is easy to misread, since "[a]ny competently crafted class complaint literally raises common 'questions.'" Richard Nagareda, *Class Certification in the Age of Aggregate Proof*, 84 N.Y.U. L. Rev. 97, 131–132 (2009). For example: Do all of us plaintiffs indeed work for Wal–Mart? Do our managers have discretion over pay? Is that an unlawful employment practice? What remedies should we get? Reciting these questions is not sufficient to obtain class certification. Commonality requires the plaintiff to demonstrate that the class members "have suffered the same injury." This does not mean merely that they have all suffered a violation of the same provision of law. Title VII, for example, can be violated in many ways—by intentional discrimination, or by hiring and promotion criteria that result in disparate impact, and by the use of these practices on the part of many different superiors in a single company. Quite obviously, the mere claim by employees of the same company that they have suffered a Title VII injury, or even a disparate–impact Title VII injury, gives no cause to believe that all their claims can productively be litigated at once. Their claims must depend upon a common contention—for example, the assertion of discriminatory bias on the part of the same supervisor.

---

[5] We have previously stated in this context that "[t]he commonality and typicality requirements of Rule 23(a) tend to merge. Both serve as guideposts for determining whether under the particular circumstances maintenance of a class action is economical and whether the named plaintiff's claim and the class claims are so interrelated that the interests of the class members will be fairly and adequately protected in their absence. Those requirements therefore also tend to merge with the adequacy-of-representation requirement, although the latter requirement also raises concerns about the competency of class counsel and conflicts of interest." *General Telephone Co. of Southwest v. Falcon*, 457 U.S. 147, 157–58, n.13 (1982). In light of our disposition of the commonality question, however, it is unnecessary to resolve whether respondents have satisfied the typicality and adequate-representation requirements of Rule 23(a).

That common contention, moreover, must be of such a nature that it is capable of classwide resolution—which means that determination of its truth or falsity will resolve an issue that is central to the validity of each one of the claims in one stroke.

> "What matters to class certification . . . is not the raising of common 'questions'—even in droves—but, rather the capacity of a classwide proceeding to generate common *answers* apt to drive the resolution of the litigation. Dissimilarities within the proposed class are what have the potential to impede the generation of common answers." Nagareda, *supra*, at 132.

Rule 23 does not set forth a mere pleading standard. A party seeking class certification must affirmatively demonstrate his compliance with the Rule—that is, he must be prepared to prove that there are *in fact* sufficiently numerous parties, common questions of law or fact, etc. We recognized in *Falcon*[, 457 U.S. 147 (1982),] that "sometimes it may be necessary for the court to probe behind the pleadings before coming to rest on the certification question," and that certification is proper only if "the trial court is satisfied, after a rigorous analysis, that the prerequisites of Rule 23(a) have been satisfied." Frequently that "rigorous analysis" will entail some overlap with the merits of the plaintiff's underlying claim. That cannot be helped. " '[T]he class determination generally involves considerations that are enmeshed in the factual and legal issues comprising the plaintiff's cause of action.' " *Id.* at 160.††††

In this case, proof of commonality necessarily overlaps with respondents' merits contention that Wal–Mart engages in a *pattern or practice* of discrimination.[7] That is so because, in resolving an individual's Title VII claim, the crux of the inquiry is "the reason for a particular employment decision," *Cooper v. Federal Reserve Bank of Richmond*, 467 U.S. 867, 876 (1984). Here respondents wish to sue about literally millions of employment decisions at once. Without some glue holding the alleged *reasons* for all those decisions together, it will be impossible to say that examination of all the class members' claims for relief will produce a common answer to the crucial question *why was I disfavored*.

B

This Court's opinion in *Falcon* describes how the commonality issue must be approached. There an employee who claimed that he was deliberately denied a promotion on account of race obtained certification of a class comprising all employees wrongfully denied promotions and all applicants wrongfully denied jobs. We rejected that composite class for lack of commonality and typicality, explaining:

---

†††† The issue of evidentiary proof of the class certification requirements is discussed in Chapter 4(B)(1)(b)(i). [Ed.]

[7] In a pattern-or-practice case, the plaintiff tries to "establish by a preponderance of the evidence that . . . discrimination was the company's standard operating procedure[,] the regular rather than the unusual practice." *Teamsters v. United States*, 431 U.S. 324, 358 (1977); *see also Franks v. Bowman Transp. Co.*, 424 U.S. 747, 772 (1976). If he succeeds, that showing will support a rebuttable inference that all class members were victims of the discriminatory practice, and will justify "an award of prospective relief," such as "an injunctive order against the continuation of the discriminatory practice."

"Conceptually, there is a wide gap between (a) an individual's claim that he has been denied a promotion [or higher pay] on discriminatory grounds, and his otherwise unsupported allegation that the company has a policy of discrimination, and (b) the existence of a class of persons who have suffered the same injury as that individual, such that the individual's claim and the class claim will share common questions of law or fact and that the individual's claim will be typical of the class claims." *Id.* at 157–58.

Falcon suggested two ways in which that conceptual gap might be bridged. First, if the employer "used a biased testing procedure to evaluate both applicants for employment and incumbent employees, a class action on behalf of every applicant or employee who might have been prejudiced by the test clearly would satisfy the commonality and typicality requirements of Rule 23(a)." Second, "[s]ignificant proof that an employer operated under a general policy of discrimination conceivably could justify a class of both applicants and employees if the discrimination manifested itself in hiring and promotion practices in the same general fashion, such as through entirely subjective decisionmaking processes." We think that statement precisely describes respondents' burden in this case. The first manner of bridging the gap obviously has no application here; Wal–Mart has no testing procedure or other companywide evaluation method that can be charged with bias. The whole point of permitting discretionary decisionmaking is to avoid evaluating employees under a common standard.

The second manner of bridging the gap requires "significant proof" that Wal–Mart "operated under a general policy of discrimination." That is entirely absent here. Wal–Mart's announced policy forbids sex discrimination, and * * * the company imposes penalties for denials of equal employment opportunity. The only evidence of a "general policy of discrimination" respondents produced was the testimony of Dr. William Bielby, their sociological expert. * * * Bielby testified that Wal–Mart has a "strong corporate culture," that makes it " 'vulnerable' " to "gender bias." He could not, however, "determine with any specificity how regularly stereotypes play a meaningful role in employment decisions at Wal–Mart. At his deposition . . . Dr. Bielby conceded that he could not calculate whether 0.5 percent or 95 percent of the employment decisions at Wal–Mart might be determined by stereotyped thinking." The parties dispute whether Bielby's testimony even met the standards for the admission of expert testimony under Federal Rule of [Evidence] 702 and our *Daubert* case, *see Daubert v. Merrell Dow Pharmaceuticals, Inc.*, 509 U.S. 579 (1993).††††† The District Court concluded that *Daubert* did not apply to expert testimony at the certification stage of class-action proceedings. We doubt that is so, but even if properly considered, Bielby's testimony does nothing to advance respondents' case. "[W]hether 0.5 percent or 95 percent of the employment decisions at Wal–Mart might be determined by stereotyped thinking" is the essential question on which respondents' theory of commonality depends. If Bielby admittedly has no answer to that question, we can safely disregard what he has to say. It is worlds away from "significant proof" that Wal–Mart "operated under a general policy of discrimination."

---

††††† In *Daubert*, the Court held that district courts must serve a gate-keeping function by ensuring that expert testimony is reliable before it can be admitted into evidence. The question of *Daubert*'s applicability at the class certification stage is discussed in Chapter 4(B)(1)(b)(ii). [Ed.]

C

The only corporate policy that the plaintiffs' evidence convincingly establishes is Wal–Mart's "policy" of *allowing discretion* by local supervisors over employment matters. On its face, of course, that is just the opposite of a uniform employment practice that would provide the commonality needed for a class action; it is a policy *against having* uniform employment practices. It is also a very common and presumptively reasonable way of doing business—one that we have said "should itself raise no inference of discriminatory conduct," *Watson v. Fort Worth Bank & Trust*, 487 U.S. 977, 990 (1988).

To be sure, we have recognized that, "in appropriate cases," giving discretion to lower-level supervisors can be the basis of Title VII liability under a disparate-impact theory—since "an employer's undisciplined system of subjective decisionmaking [can have] precisely the same effects as a system pervaded by impermissible intentional discrimination." But the recognition that this type of Title VII claim "can" exist does not lead to the conclusion that every employee in a company using a system of discretion has such a claim in common. To the contrary, left to their own devices most managers in any corporation—and surely most managers in a corporation that forbids sex discrimination—would select sex-neutral, performance–based criteria for hiring and promotion that produce no actionable disparity at all. Others may choose to reward various attributes that produce disparate impact—such as scores on general aptitude tests or educational achievements. And still other managers may be guilty of intentional discrimination that produces a sex-based disparity. In such a company, demonstrating the invalidity of one manager's use of discretion will do nothing to demonstrate the invalidity of another's. A party seeking to certify a nationwide class will be unable to show that all the employees' Title VII claims will in fact depend on the answers to common questions.

Respondents have not identified a common mode of exercising discretion that pervades the entire company—aside from their reliance on Dr. Bielby's [testimony] that we have rejected. In a company of Wal–Mart's size and geographical scope, it is quite unbelievable that all managers would exercise their discretion in a common way without some common direction. Respondents attempt to make that showing by means of statistical and anecdotal evidence, but their evidence falls well short.

The statistical evidence consists primarily of regression analyses performed by Dr. Richard Drogin, a statistician, and Dr. Marc Bendick, a labor economist. Drogin conducted his analysis region-by-region, comparing the number of women promoted into management positions with the percentage of women in the available pool of hourly workers. After considering regional and national data, Drogin concluded that "there are statistically significant disparities between men and women at Wal–Mart . . . [and] these disparities . . . can be explained only by gender discrimination." Bendick compared work-force data from Wal–Mart and competitive retailers and concluded that Wal–Mart "promotes a lower percentage of women than its competitors."

Even if they are taken at face value, these studies are insufficient to establish that respondents' theory can be proved on a classwide basis. In *Falcon*, we held that one named plaintiff's experience of discrimination was insufficient to infer that "discriminatory treatment is typical of [the employer's employment] practices." 457 U.S. at 158. A similar failure of inference arises here. * * * A regional pay disparity, for example, may be attributable to only a small set of Wal–Mart stores, and cannot by itself establish the uniform, store-by-store disparity upon which the plaintiffs' theory of commonality depends.

There is another, more fundamental, respect in which respondents' statistical proof fails. Even if it established (as it does not) a pay or promotion pattern that differs from the nationwide figures or the regional figures in *all* of Wal–Mart's 3,400 stores, that would still not demonstrate that commonality of issue exists. Some managers will claim that the availability of women, or qualified women, or interested women, in their stores' area does not mirror the national or regional statistics. And almost all of them will claim to have been applying some sex-neutral, performance–based criteria—whose nature and effects will differ from store to store. In the landmark case of ours which held that giving discretion to lower–level supervisors can be the basis of Title VII liability under a disparate–impact theory, the plurality opinion *conditioned* that holding on the corollary that merely proving that the discretionary system has produced a racial or sexual disparity *is not enough*. "[T]he plaintiff must begin by identifying the specific employment practice that is challenged." *Watson*, 487 U.S., at 994. * * * That is all the more necessary when a class of plaintiffs is sought to be certified. Other than the bare existence of delegated discretion, respondents have identified no "specific employment practice"—much less one that ties all their 1.5 million claims together. Merely showing that Wal–Mart's policy of discretion has produced an overall sex–based disparity does not suffice.

Respondents' anecdotal evidence suffers from the same defects, and in addition is too weak to raise any inference that all the individual, discretionary personnel decisions are discriminatory. In *Teamsters v. United States*, 431 U.S. 324 (1977), in addition to substantial statistical evidence of company-wide discrimination, the Government (as plaintiff) produced about 40 specific accounts of racial discrimination from particular individuals. That number was significant because the company involved had only 6,472 employees, of whom 571 were minorities, and the class itself consisted of around 334 persons. The 40 anecdotes thus represented roughly one account for every eight members of the class. Moreover, the Court of Appeals noted that the anecdotes came from individuals "spread throughout" the company who "for the most part" worked at the company's operational centers that employed the largest numbers of the class members. Here, by contrast, respondents filed some 120 affidavits reporting experiences of discrimination—about 1 for every 12,500 class members—relating to only some 235 out of Wal–Mart's 3,400 stores. More than half of these reports are concentrated in only six States (Alabama, California, Florida, Missouri, Texas, and Wisconsin); half of all States have only one or two anecdotes; and 14 States have no anecdotes about Wal–Mart's operations at all. Even if every single one of these accounts is true, that would not demonstrate that the entire company "operate[s] under a general policy of discrimination," which is what respondents must show to certify a companywide class.[9]

The dissent misunderstands the nature of the foregoing analysis. It criticizes our focus on the dissimilarities between the putative class members on the ground that we have "blend[ed]" Rule 23(a)(2)'s commonality requirement with Rule 23(b)(3)'s inquiry into whether common questions "predominate" over individual ones. That is not so. We quite agree that for purposes of Rule 23(a)(2) " '[e]ven a single [common] question' " will do. We consider dissimilarities not in order to determine (as Rule 23(b)(3) requires) whether common questions *predominate*, but in order to determine (as Rule 23(a)(2) requires) whether there *is* "[e]ven a single [common] question." And there is not here. Because respondents provide no convincing proof of a companywide discriminatory pay and promotion policy, we have concluded that they have not established the existence of any common question.[10]

* * *

The judgment of the Court of Appeals is

Reversed.

JUSTICE GINSBURG, with whom JUSTICE BREYER, JUSTICE SOTOMAYOR, and JUSTICE KAGAN join, [dissenting in relevant part].

* * * Whether the class the plaintiffs describe meets the specific requirements of Rule 23(b)(3) is not before the Court, and I would reserve that matter for consideration and decision on remand. The Court, however, disqualifies the class at the starting gate, holding that the plaintiffs cannot cross the "commonality" line set by Rule 23(a)(2). In so ruling, the Court imports into the Rule 23(a) determination concerns properly addressed in a Rule 23(b)(3) assessment.

I

A

Rule 23(a)(2) establishes a preliminary requirement for maintaining a class action: "[T]here are questions of law or fact common to the class." The Rule "does not require that all questions of law or fact raised in the litigation be common;" indeed, "[e]ven a single question of law or fact common to the members of the class will satisfy the commonality requirement," Richard Nagareda, *The Preexistence Principle and the Structure of the Class Action*, 103 Colum. L. Rev. 149, 176, n.110 (2003). A "question" is ordinarily understood to be "[a] subject or point open to controversy." American Heritage Dictionary 1483 (3d ed. 1992). Thus, a "question" "common to the

---

[9] The dissent says that we have adopted "a rule that a discrimination claim, if accompanied by anecdotes, must supply them in numbers proportionate to the size of the class." That is not quite accurate. A discrimination claimant is free to supply as few anecdotes as he wishes. But when the claim is that a company operates under a general policy of discrimination, a few anecdotes selected from literally millions of employment decisions prove nothing at all.

[10] For this reason, there is no force to the dissent's attempt to distinguish *Falcon* on the ground that in that case there were " 'no common questions of law or fact' between the claims of the lead plaintiff and the applicant class." Here also there is nothing to unite all of the plaintiffs' claims, since (contrary to the dissent's contention) the same employment practices do not "touch and concern all members of the class."

class" must be a dispute, either of fact or of law, the resolution of which will advance the determination of the class members' claims.[3]

B

The District Court, recognizing that "one significant issue common to the class may be sufficient to warrant certification," found that the plaintiffs easily met that test. Absent an error of law or an abuse of discretion, an appellate tribunal has no warrant to upset the District Court's finding of commonality. The District Court certified a class of "[a]ll women employed at any Wal–Mart domestic retail store at any time since December 26, 1998." The named plaintiffs, led by Betty Dukes, propose to litigate, on behalf of the class, allegations that Wal–Mart discriminates on the basis of gender in pay and promotions. They allege that the company "[r]eli[es] on gender stereotypes in making employment decisions such as . . . promotion[s] [and] pay." Wal–Mart permits those prejudices to infect personnel decisions, the plaintiffs contend, by leaving pay and promotions in the hands of "a nearly all male managerial workforce" using "arbitrary and subjective criteria." Further alleged barriers to the advancement of female employees include the company's requirement, "as a condition of promotion to management jobs, that employees be willing to relocate." Absent instruction otherwise, there is a risk that managers will act on the familiar assumption that women, because of their services to husband and children, are less mobile than men.

Women fill 70 percent of the hourly jobs in the retailer's stores but make up only "33 percent of management employees." "[T]he higher one looks in the organization the lower the percentage of women." The plaintiffs' "largely uncontested descriptive statistics" also show that women working in the company's stores "are paid less than men in every region" and "that the salary gap widens over time even for men and women hired into the same jobs at the same time."

The District Court identified "systems for . . . promoting in-store employees" that were "sufficiently similar across regions and stores" to conclude that "the manner in which these systems affect the class raises issues that are common to all class members." The selection of employees for promotion to in-store management "is fairly characterized as a 'tap on the shoulder' process," in which managers have discretion about whose shoulders to tap. Vacancies are not regularly posted; from among those employees satisfying minimum qualifications, managers choose whom to promote on the basis of their own subjective impressions.

Wal–Mart's compensation policies also operate uniformly across stores, the District Court found. The retailer leaves open a $2 band for every position's hourly pay rate. Wal–Mart provides no standards or criteria for setting wages within that band, and thus does nothing to counter unconscious bias on the part of supervisors.

Wal–Mart's supervisors do not make their discretionary decisions in a vacuum. The District Court reviewed means Wal–Mart used to maintain a

---

[3] The Court suggests Rule 23(a)(2) must mean more than it says. If the word "questions" were taken literally, the majority asserts, plaintiffs could pass the Rule 23(a)(2) bar by "[r]eciting . . . questions" like "Do all of us plaintiffs indeed work for Wal–Mart?" Sensibly read, however, the word "questions" means disputed issues, not any utterance crafted in the grammatical form of a question.

"carefully constructed . . . corporate culture," such as frequent meetings to reinforce the common way of thinking, regular transfers of managers between stores to ensure uniformity throughout the company, monitoring of stores "on a close and constant basis," and "Wal–Mart TV," "broadcas[t] . . . into all stores."

The plaintiffs' evidence, including class members' tales of their own experiences,[4] suggests that gender bias suffused Wal–Mart's company culture. Among illustrations, senior management often refer to female associates as "little Janie Qs." One manager told an employee that "[m]en are here to make a career and women aren't." A committee of female Wal–Mart executives concluded that "[s]tereotypes limit the opportunities offered to women."

Finally, the plaintiffs presented an expert's appraisal to show that the pay and promotions disparities at Wal–Mart "can be explained only by gender discrimination and not by . . . neutral variables." Using regression analyses, their expert, Richard Drogin, controlled for factors including, *inter alia*, job performance, length of time with the company, and the store where an employee worked.[5] The results, the District Court found, were sufficient to raise an "inference of discrimination."

C

The District Court's identification of a common question, whether Wal–Mart's pay and promotions policies gave rise to unlawful discrimination, was hardly infirm. The practice of delegating to supervisors large discretion to make personnel decisions, uncontrolled by formal standards, has long been known to have the potential to produce disparate effects. Managers, like all humankind, may be prey to biases of which they are unaware.[6] The risk of discrimination is heightened when those managers are predominantly of one sex, and are steeped in a corporate culture that perpetuates gender stereotypes.

* * *

We have held that "discretionary employment practices" can give rise to Title VII claims, not only when such practices are motivated by discriminatory intent but also when they produce discriminatory results. *See Watson v. Fort Worth Bank & Trust*, 487 U.S. 977, 988, 991 (1988). In *Watson*,

---

[4] The majority purports to derive from *Teamsters v. United States*, 431 U.S. 324 (1977), a rule that a discrimination claim, if accompanied by anecdotes, must supply them in numbers proportionate to the size of the class. *Teamsters*, the Court acknowledges, instructs that statistical evidence alone may suffice; that decision can hardly be said to establish a numerical floor before anecdotal evidence can be taken into account.

[5] The Court asserts that Drogin showed only average differences at the "regional and national level" between male and female employees. In fact, his regression analyses showed there were disparities within stores. The majority's contention to the contrary reflects only an arcane disagreement about statistical method—which the District Court resolved in the plaintiffs' favor. Appellate review is no occasion to disturb a trial court's handling of factual disputes of this order.

[6] An example vividly illustrates how subjective decisionmaking can be a vehicle for discrimination. Performing in symphony orchestras was long a male preserve. Goldin and Rouse, *Orchestrating Impartiality: The Impact of "Blind" Auditions on Female Musicians*, 90 Am. Econ. Rev. 715, 715–16 (2000). In the 1970's orchestras began hiring musicians through auditions open to all comers. Reviewers were to judge applicants solely on their musical abilities, yet subconscious bias led some reviewers to disfavor women. Orchestras that permitted reviewers to see the applicants hired far fewer female musicians than orchestras that conducted blind auditions, in which candidates played behind opaque screens.

as here, an employer had given its managers large authority over promotions. An employee sued the bank under Title VII, alleging that the "discretionary promotion system" caused a discriminatory effect based on race. Four different supervisors had declined, on separate occasions, to promote the employee. Their reasons were subjective and unknown. The employer, we noted "had not developed precise and formal criteria for evaluating candidates"; "[i]t relied instead on the subjective judgment of supervisors."

Aware of "the problem of subconscious stereotypes and prejudices," we held that the employer's "undisciplined system of subjective decisionmaking" was an "employment practic[e]" that "may be analyzed under the disparate impact approach."

The plaintiffs' allegations state claims of gender discrimination in the form of biased decisionmaking in both pay and promotions. The evidence reviewed by the District Court adequately demonstrated that resolving those claims would necessitate examination of particular policies and practices alleged to affect, adversely and globally, women employed at Wal–Mart's stores. Rule 23(a)(2), setting a necessary but not a sufficient criterion for class–action certification, demands nothing further.

II

A

The Court gives no credence to the key dispute common to the class: whether Wal–Mart's discretionary pay and promotion policies are discriminatory. "What matters," the Court asserts, "is not the raising of common 'questions,' " but whether there are "[d]issimilarities within the proposed class" that "have the potential to impede the generation of common answers." (quoting Nagareda, *Class Certification in the Age of Aggregate Proof*, 84 N.Y.U. L. Rev. 97, 132 (2009)).

The Court blends Rule 23(a)(2)'s threshold criterion with the more demanding criteria of Rule 23(b)(3), and thereby elevates the (a)(2) inquiry so that it is no longer "easily satisfied."[7] Rule 23(b)(3) certification requires, in addition to the four 23(a) findings, determinations that "questions of law or fact common to class members predominate over any questions affecting only individual members" and that "a class action is superior to other available methods for . . . adjudicating the controversy."

The Court's emphasis on differences between class members mimics the Rule 23(b)(3) inquiry into whether common questions "predominate" over individual issues. And by asking whether the individual differences "impede" common adjudication, the Court duplicates 23(b)(3)'s question whether "a class action is superior" to other modes of adjudication. Indeed, Professor Nagareda, whose "dissimilarities" inquiry the Court endorses, developed his position in the context of Rule 23(b)(3). * * * "The Rule

---

[7] The Court places considerable weight on *General Telephone Co. of Southwest v. Falcon*, 457 U.S. 147 (1982). That case has little relevance to the question before the Court today. The lead plaintiff in *Falcon* alleged discrimination evidenced by the company's failure to promote him and other Mexican–American employees and failure to hire Mexican–American applicants. There were "no common questions of law or fact" between the claims of the lead plaintiff and the applicant class. The plaintiff-employee alleged that the defendant-employer had discriminated against him intentionally. The applicant class claims, by contrast, were "advanced under the 'adverse impact' theory," appropriate for facially neutral practices. "[T]he only commonality [wa]s that respondent is a Mexican–American and he seeks to represent a class of Mexican–Americans." Here the same practices touch and concern all members of the class.

23(b)(3) predominance inquiry" is meant to "tes[t] whether proposed classes are sufficiently cohesive to warrant adjudication by representation." If courts must conduct a "dissimilarities" analysis at the Rule 23(a)(2) stage, no mission remains for Rule 23(b)(3).

Because Rule 23(a) is also a prerequisite for Rule 23(b)(1) and Rule 23(b)(2) classes, the Court's "dissimilarities" position is far reaching. Individual differences should not bar a Rule 23(b)(1) or Rule 23(b)(2) class, so long as the Rule 23(a) threshold is met. For example, in *Franks v. Bowman Transp. Co.*, 424 U.S. 747 (1976), a Rule 23(b)(2) class of African–American truck drivers complained that the defendant had discriminatorily refused to hire black applicants. We recognized that the "qualification[s] and performance" of individual class members might vary. "Generalizations concerning such individually applicable evidence," we cautioned, "cannot serve as a justification for the denial of [injunctive] relief to the entire class."

B

The "dissimilarities" approach leads the Court to train its attention on what distinguishes individual class members, rather than on what unites them. Given the lack of standards for pay and promotions, the majority says, "demonstrating the invalidity of one manager's use of discretion will do nothing to demonstrate the invalidity of another's."

Wal–Mart's delegation of discretion over pay and promotions is a policy uniform throughout all stores. The very nature of discretion is that people will exercise it in various ways. A system of delegated discretion, *Watson* held, is a practice actionable under Title VII when it produces discriminatory outcomes. A finding that Wal–Mart's pay and promotions practices in fact violate the law would be the first step in the usual order of proof for plaintiffs seeking individual remedies for company-wide discrimination. *Teamsters v. United States*, 431 U.S. 324, 359 (1977). That each individual employee's unique circumstances will ultimately determine whether she is entitled to backpay or damages, § 2000e–5(g)(2)(A) (barring backpay if a plaintiff "was refused . . . advancement . . . for any reason other than discrimination"), should not factor into the Rule 23(a)(2) determination.

* * *

The Court errs in importing a "dissimilarities" notion suited to Rule 23(b)(3) into the Rule 23(a) commonality inquiry. I therefore cannot join Part II of the Court's opinion.

NOTES AND QUESTIONS

1. As Justice Scalia's opinion noted, the Court granted *certiorari* in *Dukes* after a divided (6–5) *en banc* Ninth Circuit decision. Wal–Mart sought review on two questions. The first was whether claims for monetary relief could be certified under Rule 23(b)(2) and, if so, under what circumstances. Petition for Writ of Certiorari at i, *Wal–Mart Stores, Inc. v. Dukes*, 564 U.S. 338 (2011) (No. 10-277). The second was "[w]hether the certification order conforms to the requirements of Title VII, the Due Process Clause, the Seventh Amendment, the Rules Enabling Act, and Federal Rule of Civil Procedure 23." *Id.* The Court granted review on the first question, and that portion of the opinion is set forth in Chapter 3. It denied review on the second question, but it instructed the parties to brief and argue a second question of its own: "Whether the class certification ordered under Rule 23(b)(2) was consistent with Rule 23(a)." Since

Wal–Mart's petition made only brief reference to Rule 23(a)'s requirements, why would the Court add its own question that focused solely on Rule 23(a)? Moreover, why might the Court have chosen to base its Rule 23(a) holding on commonality, as opposed to typicality under (a)(3) or adequacy of representation under (a)(4)?

2. To what extent was the plaintiffs' failure to prove the existence of common issues in *Dukes* a function of Wal–Mart's—and the class's—sheer size? Justice Scalia, writing for the majority, states that "[i]n a company of Wal–Mart's size and geographical scope, it is quite unbelievable that all managers would exercise their discretion in a common way without some common direction." 564 U.S. at 356.

3. Justice Ginsburg argued in her dissent that, "[i]f courts must conduct a 'dissimilarities' analysis at the Rule 23(a)(2) stage, no mission remains for Rule 23(b)(3)." *Id.* at 376 (Ginsburg, J., dissenting in part). When considering 23(b)(3) later in this course, *see* Chapter 3(C)(1), consider what a Rule 23(b)(3) "predominance" analysis should look like after *Dukes*.

4. Both the majority and the dissent quoted Professor Richard Nagareda's article, *Class Certification in the Age of Aggregate Proof*, 84 N.Y.U. L. Rev. 97 (2009). It is rare for the Court to pay such close attention to the views of a particular commentator. The fact that it did so in *Dukes* stands as a tribute to Professor Nagareda, who tragically passed away in October 2010, while the case was pending before the Supreme Court. Although the Justices agreed on the significance of Professor Nagareda's work, they differed sharply as to its import. In a passage cited by both the majority and dissent, Nagareda wrote:

> By its terms, Rule 23 speaks of common "questions" that "predominate" over individual ones and of action by the defendant on grounds that "apply generally to the class" so as to warrant relief "respecting the class as a whole." The overarching picture is one of some decisive degree of similarity across the proposed class. But * * * what really matters to class certification—what courts are actually attempting to discern with regard to replicated proof, for instance—is primarily the opposite: not similarity at some unspecified level of generality but, rather, dissimilarity that has the capacity to undercut the prospects for joint resolution of class members' claims through a unified proceeding. * * * [T]he question of whether a proposed class exhibits some fatal dissimilarity is the proper inquiry for class certification. By contrast, the question of whether the class exhibits some fatal similarity—a failure of proof as to all class members on an element of their cause of action—is properly engaged as a matter of summary judgment.
>
> The formulation of Rule 23 in terms of predominant common "questions" and generally applicable misconduct obscures the crucial line between dissimilarity and similarity within the class. The existence of common "questions" does not form the crux of the class certification inquiry, at least not literally * * * Any competently crafted class complaint literally raises common "questions." What matters to class certification, however, is not the raising of common "questions"—even in droves—but, rather, the capacity of a class-wide proceeding to generate common *answers* apt to drive the resolution of the litigation. Dissimilarities within the proposed class are what have the potential to impede the generation of common answers.

*** The language in Rule 23(b)(3) tends to obscure this point, however, by asking whether "questions of law or fact common to class members predominate over any questions affecting only individual [class] members." Heaps of similarities do not overcome dissimilarities that would prevent common resolution.

The language of Rule 23(b)(2) tends toward similar confusion. The insight of the rule is not simply that class treatment is appropriate when the defendant has engaged in a course of conduct that is similar at some unspecified level of generality. Rather, the crux of the rule in actual operation today consists of the indivisible nature of the injunctive or declaratory remedy warranted—the notion that the conduct is such that it can be enjoined or declared unlawful only as to all of the class members or as to none of them. Here, again, what matters is not similarity arising from the defendant's conduct but rather dissimilarity that has the capacity to undercut the indivisible character of an appropriate remedy.

Nagareda, *supra*, 84 N.Y.U. L. Rev. at 131–33 (footnotes omitted). Which *Dukes* opinion—the majority or the dissent—correctly interprets Nagareda's argument?

5. Must a case present multiple common issues in order to satisfy commonality? Although the Court in *Dukes* did not need to resolve the issue, given its conclusion that not even one common issue was presented, both the majority and the dissent "agree[d] that for purposes of Rule 23(a)(2), '[e]ven a single [common] question' will do." 564 U.S. at 359 (majority opinion; citation omitted); *accord* 564 U.S. at 369 (Ginsburg, J., dissenting in part).

6. Rule 23(a)(2)'s requirement of "questions of law or fact common to the class" is echoed by Federal Rules of Civil Procedure 20(a) (permissive joinder of parties), 24(b) (permissive intervention), and 42 (consolidation of trials or issues); and by the Multi-District Litigation statute, 28 U.S.C. § 1407, all of which employ very similar language. *See* Fed. R. Civ. P. 20(a)(1)(B); 20(a)(2)(B) (requiring a "question of law or fact common to all" plaintiffs or defendants in order for multiple parties' claims to be permissively joined); Fed. R. Civ. P. 24(b)(1)(B) (allowing court to "permit anyone to intervene who *** has a claim or defense that shares with the main action a common question of law or fact"); Fed. R. Civ. P. 42(a)(2) (allowing court to consolidate trials "[i]f actions before the court involve a common question of law or fact"); 28 U.S.C. § 1407(a) (providing, *inter alia*, that "[w]hen civil actions involving one or more common questions of fact are pending in different districts, such actions may be transferred to any district for coordinated or consolidated pretrial proceedings").

Does this similarity in language mean that *Dukes* should apply to permissive joinder, permissive intervention, consolidation, and MDL proceedings, as well as class certification? *See also* Chapters 13(A)(1) (discussing Rule 20 joinder as a non-class aggregation device); 13(A)(5) (Rule 24 intervention); 13(A)(6) (Rule 42 consolidation); & Chapter 12 (MDL statute).

7. In the wake of *Dukes,* courts must grapple with the question of whether the case should be limited to its particular facts and context. Put another way, should *Dukes* be read broadly, such that the rigorous analysis prescribed for commonality in that case applies in equal measure to all class actions? Or is the Rule 23 procedural holding so entangled with the Title VII substantive law that the effects of *Dukes* are likely to be limited to certain categories of employment discrimination cases?

Thus far, the weight of authority in the federal circuits has concluded that the *Dukes* commonality standard applies to all types of class actions—regardless of the substantive nature of the claims and the Rule 23(b) subsection under which certification is sought. Moreover, *Dukes* has been widely understood as having raised the threshold for commonality (although the precise degree to which it did so—and its effect on any particular case—remain matters of debate). *See also* Robert H. Klonoff, *The Decline of Class Actions*, 90 Wash. U. L. Rev. 729, 773–80 (2013). Post *Dukes*, several courts of appeals have rejected class certification based on the commonality standard articulated by the Supreme Court. *See, e.g., D.L. v. District of Columbia*, 713 F.3d 120 (D.C. Cir. 2013) (reversing class certification of Individuals with Disabilities Education Act claims on commonality grounds); *M.D. ex rel. Stukenberg v. Perry*, 675 F.3d 832, 839–46 (5th Cir. 2012) (reversing grant of certification and noting that "[a]lthough the district court's analysis may have been a reasonable application of pre-*Wal–Mart* precedent, the *Wal–Mart* decision has heightened the standards for establishing commonality under Rule 23(a)(2)"); *Ellis v. Costco Wholesale Corp.*, 657 F.3d 970, 974–75 (9th Cir. 2011); *In re Countrywide Fin. Corp. Mortg. Lending Practices*, 708 F.3d 704, 708 (6th Cir. 2013) ("The district court did not abuse its discretion in finding that *Dukes* forecloses the instant proposed class from establishing commonality.").

To be sure, *Dukes* has not prevented class actions from being certified, even under subsections (b)(1) and (b)(2). For cases that have distinguished *Dukes* and found commonality met, *see, e.g., Knight v. Lavine*, 2013 WL 427880, at *3 (E.D. Va. 2013) (certifying class under (b)(1) and (b)(2) in ERISA case where "[t]he issues of commonality in this case are quite different from [*Dukes*]," because "each Plaintiff allege[d] the same conduct constituted the same breach of fiduciary duty by the same individuals"); *Parsons v. Ryan*, 289 F.R.D. 513, 521 (D. Ariz. 2013) (certifying (b)(2) class of prisoners alleging 8th Amendment violations due to defendant's health care policy; court noted that the "lack of commonality in [*Dukes*] contrasts with this case, where all inmates are subjected to Defendants' actions or lack thereof, because [Defendants] have the sole responsibility for health care policy" in the prison), *aff'd*, 754 F.3d 657 (9th Cir. 2014); *see also Meyer v. U.S. Tennis Ass'n*, 297 F.R.D. 75, 85 (S.D.N.Y. 2013) (certifying (b)(3) class involving alleged violations of state and federal labor laws, explaining that "[n]othing in *Dukes* is inconsistent with this Court's conclusion with respect to commonality"); *Brown v. Nucor Corp.*, 785 F.3d 895, 901 (4th Cir. 2015) ("At the very least, *Wal-Mart* recalibrated and sharpened the lens through which a court examines class certification decisions under Rule 23(a)(2), an impact plainly manifested by the number of certifications overturned in its wake."); Robert H. Klonoff, *Class Actions Part II: A Respite from the Decline*, 92 N.Y.U. L. Rev. ___ (forthcoming October 2017), *available at* http://papers.ssrn.com/sol3/papers.cfm?abstract_id=2881484 (noting that *Dukes* has not had the major adverse consequences that many plaintiffs' attorneys had feared).

Problem

Plaintiffs are four prisoners at the Harwood Federal Prison who claim that security guards have violated their constitutional rights by engaging in cruel and inhumane treatment. They sue on behalf of themselves and other prisoners similarly situated. Plaintiff Smith claims that Harwood guards frequently beat him, causing serious physical injuries. Plaintiff Jones claims that guards falsely spread rumors that he was a "snitch," and then looked the other way while other prisoners assaulted him. Plaintiff Frye claims that prison guards destroyed his incoming and outgoing mail and refused to put through telephone calls from his attorney. Finally, plaintiff Butler claims that he was forced to endure long periods of solitary confinement for no reason whatsoever, and that he was deprived of food or water during those periods. The theory of the suit is that the guards were unhappy with their wages and benefits and thus decided to mistreat the inmates until their demands were met. Based upon these facts, is commonality satisfied?

3. TYPICALITY

Rule 23(a)(3) requires, as a prerequisite to class certification, that "the claims or defenses of the representative parties [be] typical of the claims or defenses of the class * * *." As noted earlier, whereas numerosity and commonality focus mostly on the proposed class, Rule 23(a)(3)'s typicality and Rule 23(a)(4)'s adequacy focus mostly on the proposed representatives.

As discussed below, the typicality requirement has long puzzled courts and commentators. Some courts have reasoned that this requirement merely duplicates commonality or adequacy. Other courts, however, have found that the typicality requirement contains separate criteria that must be satisfied. Indeed, a fair number of cases have held that the failure to satisfy typicality is fatal to class certification. In reviewing the following materials, consider whether the typicality requirement does indeed contain substance and, if so, what core concerns typicality is designed to address.

In confronting typicality and, thereafter, adequacy, it is important to note an apparent anomaly in the case law. Proponents of a class action cannot be expected to present evidence of their own failure to satisfy typicality or adequacy. Thus, opponents of a proposed class action are left to make such arguments. In reviewing the following materials, consider whether opponents are credible in purporting to express concerns about the typicality or adequacy of class representatives or counsel. Do opponents of class certification really *want* typical and adequate class representatives and class counsel? Or would they really prefer *ineffective* representatives who present *atypical* claims? Do defendants need to ensure that class representatives are adequate and typical in order to protect any defense verdict against attack by class members? Consider the views of one court, made in the context of a discussion of adequacy:

> Because only another court can determine the *res judicata* effect of a final judgment, a judgment purporting to bind absent parties whose interests have been represented with dubious effectiveness acquires a particularly suspect character. The doubt as to adequacy of representation, and therefore binding effect, may give rise to new suits on the same subject matter by absent class members against the same defendants. The very likelihood of the new actions, even if they are decided against the class on *res judicata* grounds, defeats the historical purpose of the class action, to prevent a multiplicity of suits. Attempting to bind absent parties without adequate representation, then, not only prejudices the absent class members, but also fails to provide a safe harbor in which the party adverse to the class can rest. The protection of the judgment is merely illusory. If the Court has substantial doubt as to the adequacy of representation, it should act pursuant to its protective responsibility to deny or revoke class certification.

Johnson v. Shreveport Garment Co., 422 F. Supp. 526, 533 (W.D. La. 1976), *aff'd*, 577 F.2d 1132 (5th Cir. 1978); *see also Phillips Petroleum Co. v. Shutts*, 472 U.S. 797, 805 (1985) ("Whether it wins or loses on the merits, [defendant] has a distinct and personal interest in seeing the entire plaintiff class bound by *res judicata* just as [it] is bound."). This same analysis applies to typicality. Defendants have an interest in ensuring that the judgment will not be attacked on the ground that the representatives were atypical and that, accordingly, certification of the class violated Rule 23(a)(3). Is the judicial system well served by allowing opponents to raise issues of typicality and adequacy? If not the opponents, then who can be relied upon to raise those issues?

a. Whether the Typicality Requirement Has Independent Meaning

TAYLOR V. SAFEWAY STORES, INC.
United States Court of Appeals, Tenth Circuit, 1975.
524 F.2d 263.

Before LEWIS, CHIEF JUDGE, and BREITENSTEIN and BARRETT, CIRCUIT JUDGES.

LEWIS, CHIEF JUDGE.

This appeal originates from a suit charging Safeway Stores, Inc. of Colorado with discriminatory employment practices in violation of 42 U.S.C. § 2000e *et seq.* [Title VII] and 42 U.S.C. § 1981. The plaintiff Taylor filed this suit on behalf of himself and those "Negro persons who are employed, have been employed, or might have been in the past or will in the future be employed by Safeway . . . in its various wholesale, retail, and distribution centers throughout . . . Colorado."

Taylor was hired by Safeway to work at its Denver frozen food warehouse on December 1, 1968. Three weeks later Taylor was discharged, ostensibly because of his inadequate job performance. * * *

* * * [T]he district court [tentatively certified a class action, but subsequently] * * * held that under Rule 23(a)'s typicality requirement, Taylor's class claim should be limited to "a class of Negroes employed at the frozen food warehouse in the Denver distribution center."

After a trial on the merits, the district court concluded that Safeway had not discriminated against Taylor individually in its initial failure to hire him, in his job training, or in its refusal to transfer him to a retail store. The court found, however, that Taylor's discharge from the frozen food warehouse had been racially motivated. The evidence indicated that Taylor's immediate supervisor at the warehouse had an adverse attitude towards blacks and had manipulated Taylor's work assignments in such a manner as to influence negatively his production averages. On the individual claim, the court awarded Taylor back pay and attorney's fees, but refused to reinstate him. Finding no merit in Taylor's class claim, the court refused to award attorney's fees.

Taylor appeals those rulings adverse to him. We affirm the rulings of the district court in part, reverse in part, and remand.

[The court first held that reversal of Taylor's individual claims was required because of certain erroneous rulings relating to Taylor's damages.]

* * *

We next turn our attention to Taylor's class claims. Prior to the trial, Safeway challenged the ability of Taylor to represent a class of all "Negro persons who are employed, have been employed, or might have been in the past or will in the future" be employed by Safeway in its wholesale, retail, and distribution facilities throughout Colorado for failure to meet the prerequisites of Rule 23(a). The district court determined that Taylor had not met the typicality requirement of Rule 23(a)(3) as defined by *White v. Gates Rubber Co.*, 53 F.R.D. 412 [(D.Colo. 1971)], where the district court ruled that the typicality prerequisite required a class action plaintiff to "demonstrate that other members of the class he purports to represent (actual, not hypothetical complainants) have suffered the same (or similar) grievances of which he complains."

* * * [T]he district court [ultimately] found that at most, Taylor had only established that his grievances were typical of a class of Negro employees situated at Safeway's frozen food warehouse in Denver, thus effectively narrowing the original class claim made by Taylor.

* * *

Rule 23(a)(3) has been the subject of various judicial interpretations since it first appeared in the 1966 amendments to the Federal Rules of Civil Procedure,[5] which can be partially explained by the failure of the advisory committee to articulate the meaning of the Rule 23(a) prerequisites. The courts have not only failed to give Rule 23(a)(3) a commonly accepted meaning, but have been accused of giving it no independent meaning at all or merely making it duplicative of other Rule 23(a) prerequisites. The guiding rationale for many of the judicial interpretations of the typicality requirement has been the historical nexus between subsections (a)(3) and (a)(4); both of these subsections were derived from a common phrase in the original [1938 version of] Rule 23 [*see* Chapter 3(C)(3)] requiring "one or more (representatives), as will fairly insure the adequate representation of all. . . ." Because of its source in the original rule, subsection (a)(3) should logically deal with the adequacy of representation, but due to the broad language of subsection (a)(4) that a representative must "fairly and adequately" represent the class, it is difficult to attach a meaning to (a)(3) that is not included or does not overlap somewhat with subsection (a)(4).

It was against this backdrop that the district court in *White* determined that the typicality requirement "must be given an independent meaning" or otherwise there was no need to have included it as a prerequisite of Rule 23(a). The district court in *White* ruled that subsection (a)(3) at least requires that class-action plaintiffs establish that "there is in fact a class needing representation." *White* has not been alone in attempting to

---

[5] *See, e.g., Rosado v. Wyman*, 322 F. Supp. 1173, 1193 (E.D.N.Y.) (the typicality requirement was "designed to buttress the fair representation requirement in Rule 23(a)(4)"), *aff'd on other grounds*, 437 F.2d 619 (2d Cir. 1970), *aff'd*, 402 U.S. 991 (1971); *Cohen v. D.C. Nat'l Bank*, 59 F.R.D. 84, 89 (D.D.C. 1972) (typicality is satisfied when there is a lack of adversity between the representatives and the absent class members); *Taliaferro v. State Council of Higher Educ.*, 372 F. Supp. 1378, 1387 (E.D. Va. 1974) (typicality requires that the disputed issue occupy a similar degree of centrality to the claim of the representative as to that of the other class members) * * *.

give the typicality requirement an independent meaning and requiring the plaintiff to establish the existence of a class.

We accept *White*'s compelling reasoning that subsection (a)(3) must have a meaning independent of the other provisions of Rule 23(a). Any inquiry into typicality under Rule 23(a)(3) requires a comparison of the claims or defenses of the representative with the claims or defenses of the class. Since the burden is on the plaintiff to establish the prerequisites of Rule 23, it is not unreasonable to require the plaintiff to establish the existence of a class as preliminary to the court's comparison of claims and defenses. The *White* definition of typicality has done no more than verbalize an implicit requirement of subsection (a)(3); therefore, we must conclude that this definition is correct.

Next, we must examine whether the trial court correctly applied subsection (a)(3) to the present case. The trial court found that Taylor had failed to present evidence of any discriminatory employment practices by Safeway outside of the frozen food warehouse and limited his class action to individuals employed at the warehouse. Since Taylor has failed to show the existence of any discriminatory employment practices by Safeway outside the frozen food warehouse or the existence of any similarly aggrieved Safeway employee outside the warehouse, the trial court had no alternative than to limit his class claim to warehouse employees.

* * *

Notes and Questions

1. Is the *Taylor* court persuasive in attempting to give meaning to the typicality requirement? Or is that court's definition nothing more than a restatement of adequacy and commonality (or perhaps one of the threshold requirements discussed earlier in Part (A)(1) of this chapter)? Is the test for typicality in *Taylor* clear? Is it simple to apply? Do the cases cited in footnote five of *Taylor* provide any additional guidance?

2. The Supreme Court has suggested that the adequacy, typicality, and commonality inquiries will often overlap, both factually and conceptually:

> The adequacy-of-representation requirement "tend[s] to merge" with the commonality and typicality criteria of Rule 23(a), which "serve as guideposts for determining whether . . . maintenance of a class action is economical and whether the named plaintiff's claim and the class claims are so interrelated that the interests of the class members will be fairly and adequately protected in their absence."

Amchem Prods., Inc. v. Windsor, 521 U.S. 591, 626 n.20 (1997) (quoting *General Tel. Co. v. Falcon*, 457 U.S. 147, 157 n.13 (1982)); *accord Wal–Mart Stores, Inc. v. Dukes*, 564 U.S. 338, 349 n.5 (2011). Is this analysis instructive? If one accepts this premise, could any specific meaning be given to typicality that distinguishes it from commonality and adequacy?

3. For a case where certification turned on the typicality requirement, see *Wiener v. Dannon Co., Inc.*, 255 F.R.D. 658 (C.D. Cal. 2009). There, the named plaintiff sought to bring a class action for various state law violations, alleging Dannon had made deceptive and unsubstantiated claims regarding the health benefits of three of its dairy products—Activia, DanActive, and Activia Light. The court found that the putative class met every requirement for certification under Rule 23(b)(3), save one: Wiener, who had only purchased

one of the three products, could not satisfy the typicality requirement to represent the proposed class of "California residents that purchased DanActive, Activia, or Activia Light." *Id.* at 666. Because the class claims would require proof of distinct misrepresentations, at least with respect to both Activia and DanActive, "the evidence needed to prove Wiener's claims involving Activia * * * is not probative of the claims of unnamed class members who purchased DanActive[.]" *Id.* at 667. In particular, the court said, "while [Wiener] has an incentive to prove the alleged deception surrounding Dannon's claims that Activia aids digestion, [s]he has no incentive to go further and prove the alleged deception surrounding Dannon's claims that DanActive strengthens the immune system." *Id.* Because Wiener was the only representative for the proposed class, the court denied certification. Presumably, this concern would not have existed had there been a separate representative for each product.

As a practical matter, do courts need to worry that named plaintiffs will have inadequate incentives to bring forward evidence that proves the claims of absent class members but not the claims of the named plaintiffs? What, if any, incentives would drive class counsel to investigate all claims thoroughly and present the best possible evidence?

b. Application of the Typicality Requirement

MARCUS V. BMW OF N. AM., LLC

United States Court of Appeals, Third Circuit, 2012.
687 F.3d 583.

AMBRO, CIRCUIT JUDGE.

This class action involves run-flat tires ("RFTs"). As their name suggests, they can "run" while "flat." Even if an RFT suffers a total and abrupt loss of air pressure from a puncture or other road damage, the vehicle it is on remains stable and can continue driving for 50 to 150 miles at a speed of up to 50 miles per hour.

Jeffrey Marcus leased a BMW convertible equipped with four Bridgestone RFTs. Unfortunately, he experienced four "flat" tires during his three-year lease. In each case, the RFT worked as intended. Even though the tire lost air pressure, Marcus was able to drive his car to a BMW dealer to have the tire replaced. Unsatisfied nonetheless, Marcus sued Bridgestone Corporation, Bridgestone Americas Tire Operations, LLC ("BATO") (together "Bridgestone"), and BMW of North America, LLC ("BMW"), asserting consumer fraud, breach of warranty, and breach of contract claims. Among other things, he claims that Bridgestone RFTs are "defective" because they: (1) are "highly susceptible to flats, punctures and bubbles, and ... fail at a significantly higher rate than radial tires or other run-flat tires;" (2) cannot be repaired, only replaced, "in the event of a small puncture;" and (3) are "exorbitantly priced." He also claims RFT-equipped BMWs cannot be retrofitted to operate with conventional, non-run-flat tires, and that "many service stations do not sell" Bridgestone RFTs, making them difficult to replace. He faults BMW and Bridgestone for failing to disclose these "defects."

The District Court certified Marcus's suit under Federal Rule of Civil Procedure 23(b)(3) as an opt-out class action brought on behalf of all purchasers and lessees of certain model-year BMWs equipped with Bridgestone RFTs sold or leased in New Jersey with tires that "have gone flat and been replaced." * * * We * * * vacate the District Court's certification order and remand for proceedings consistent with this opinion.

I. FACTUAL AND PROCEDURAL BACKGROUND

In July 2007, Jeffrey Marcus (a New York resident) leased a 2007 BMW 328ci from an authorized BMW dealership in Ramsey, New Jersey. The convertible first caught his eye at another dealership in South Hampton, New York. He saw the car on the showroom floor and, interest piqued, picked up a brochure. Aside from visiting the dealership, picking up the brochure, and riding in a friend's 328ci as a passenger, Marcus claims he "absolutely [did] not" do any other research on BMW vehicles or RFTs before leasing his car.

As noted, Marcus suffered four "flat" tires during his three-year lease. Each time he experienced a flat, he drove his car to a BMW dealership in New York and had the tire replaced. BMW then billed Marcus between $350 to $390 for parts, labor, fees, and taxes. After his first flat, Marcus purchased a road-hazard warranty for about $400, which covered at least some of the replacement costs for flat tires two through four.

Marcus's first two flat tires were not available for inspection in this lawsuit. Dealer records show that a nail punctured the first tire and the second was replaced due to a "blown out bubble." Marcus's third tire was replaced because he ran over a chunk of metal "the size of a finger," according to his own expert, and his fourth because he ran over another sharp object that tore and gouged the tire and damaged the sidewall. The parties' experts agree that the third and fourth tires could not have been repaired, and that any tire (run-flat or conventional) would have been damaged, if not destroyed, under the circumstances. They also agree on two other, more general propositions: (1) a tire can "go flat" or fail for a wide variety of reasons and not be a "defective" tire; and (2) to determine properly and accurately the cause of any particular tire failure, a careful and thorough examination of that tire is necessary.

The parties dispute what Marcus knew about RFTs and RFT-equipped BMWs before leasing his car and, more importantly, what other purchasers and lessees *could* have known. To "provide a market and consumer perspective" on RFTs and BMWs, BMW presented the expert report and testimony of William Pettit. He concluded that "[a]n abundance of [RFT] information exists in the public domain extolling the safety and convenience benefits and discussing potential downsides." He pointed to BMW and Bridgestone documents (*e.g.,* their press releases and marketing brochures), as well as information from the public domain (*e.g.,* articles in publications like *Consumer Reports, BusinessWeek, The Wall Street Journal,* and *The New York Times*).

To take but a few examples, BMW boasts in its brochures that "should you get a flat, you can still travel up to 150 miles at 50 mph, thanks to [the 2007 BMW 3 Series Convertible's] standard run-flat tires," "so you can drive off a busy highway, out of a dangerous area, or just continue on your journey on a rainy night." In several other places, its brochures mention that the car comes equipped with RFTs and that, "[d]ue to low-profile tires, wheels, tires and suspension parts are more susceptible to road hazard and consequential damages." * * * In addition, the BMW Owner's Manual for the 328i warns drivers that, "[f]or safety reasons, BMW recommends that damaged Run–Flat Tires be replaced rather than repaired." * * *

Marcus disputes BMW's and Bridgestone's openness about RFTs, the information available in the public domain, and whether this information is sufficient to provide consumers with notice about the downsides of Bridgestone RFTs. He offers internal BMW and Bridgestone documents—such as emails, research reports and marketing surveys—to show that the defendants were aware that many other consumers were as displeased with RFTs as he was.

After his second flat tire, Marcus sued BMW and Bridgestone. In his Amended Class Action Complaint, he asserts claims against BMW and Bridgestone: (1) on behalf of a nationwide class, for breach of implied warranty in violation of the Magnuson Moss Warranty Act ("MMWA"); and (2) on behalf of a New Jersey sub-class for (a) consumer fraud in violation of the New Jersey Consumer Fraud Act ("NJCFA"), (b) breach of implied warranty, (c) breach of contract, and (d) breach of the implied covenant of good faith and fair dealing. He also asserts a claim on behalf of the New Jersey sub-class for breach of express warranty against BMW.

The District Court denied Marcus's motion for class certification with respect to the nationwide class, but granted the motion with respect to the New Jersey sub-class. * * *

* * *

[The court found that the class definition was not sufficiently precise, that plaintiff failed to offer an administratively feasible method for identifying class members, and that there was insufficient evidence to establish numerosity; it also found that commonality *was* satisfied.]

C. Typicality

The concepts of typicality and commonality are closely related and often tend to merge. "Both serve as guideposts for determining whether under the particular circumstances maintenance of a class action is economical and whether the named plaintiff's claim and the class claims are so interrelated that the interests of the class members will be fairly and adequately protected in their absence." Typicality, however, derives its independent legal significance from its ability to "screen out class actions in which the legal or factual position of the representatives is markedly different from that of other members of the class even though common issues of law or fact are present."

To determine whether a plaintiff is markedly different from the class as a whole, we consider the attributes of the plaintiff, the class as a whole, and the similarity between the plaintiff and the class. This comparative analysis addresses[:]

> three distinct, though related, concerns: (1) the claims of the class representative must be generally the same as those of the class in terms of both (a) the legal theory advanced and (b) the factual circumstances underlying that theory; (2) the class representative must not be subject to a defense that is both inapplicable to many

members of the class and likely to become a major focus of the litigation; and (3) the interests and incentives of the representative must be sufficiently aligned with those of the class.

If a plaintiff's claim arises from the same event, practice or course of conduct that gives rises to the claims of the class members, factual differences will not render that claim atypical if it is based on the same legal theory as the claims of the class.

The District Court found that Marcus is typical of the class, because "[w]hat is crucial to the typicality analysis here is that Marcus and the class members purportedly suffered harm from the same alleged course of conduct: the defendants failed to disclose defects in their products, misrepresented or omitted important information about the products, and made promises about the products that were not true." BMW and Bridgestone argue that the Court erred in its finding for three reasons. First, Marcus performed very little research before leasing his car, whereas the average BMW purchaser or lessee performs significant research prior to purchase or lease. Second, Marcus leased only one model BMW with one kind of Bridgestone RFT, yet he seeks to represent a class composed of people with other model-year BMWs and Bridgestone tire types. According to Bridgestone, Marcus's claims potentially cover 49 different tire designs of varying specifications, including size, load rating, and model type. Third, New York law—not New Jersey law—applies to Marcus's claims and, as a result, Marcus is subject to unique defenses that do not apply to all members of the proposed class. We see no abuse of discretion behind any of these arguments.

First, even if there are marked differences in the amounts of research class members performed, these differences by themselves do not render Marcus's claims atypical. * * * [I]f a class member knew about the alleged "defects" prior to purchase or lease, then that knowledge could break the proximate cause link between the alleged defect and any damages suffered. Determining whether a class member had such knowledge requires an individualized inquiry. That creates a predominance problem. If Marcus knew of the defects prior to his lease, then he would risk having the causal link between the defendants' conduct and his damages broken. If that were so, he would be unable to represent fairly the interests of class members who did not have such knowledge. That would create a typicality problem. But Marcus may be in a better position than other potential class members because he did not do significant research before leasing his car. That fact may distinguish him from other class members, but it does not prejudice his ability to protect absent class members' interests fairly and adequately.

The fact that Marcus leased only one model BMW with one kind of Bridgestone RFT also does not pose a typicality problem. When a class includes purchasers of a variety of different products, a named plaintiff that purchases only one type of product satisfies the typicality requirement if the alleged misrepresentations or omissions apply uniformly across the different product types. The parties agree that different tire models and sizes, and different vehicles, have different performance characteristics, compositions, designs, purposes, and uses. But Marcus alleges that the problems with Bridgestone RFTs—that they are highly susceptible to road hazard damage, unrepairable, expensive, difficult to purchase, and that a vehicle cannot be converted for use of conventional tires—are uniform and apply to all 2006–2009 BMW vehicles equipped with Bridgestone RFTs.

As we discuss below with respect to predominance, the District Court did not abuse its discretion when finding that a defect making Bridgestone RFTs highly susceptible to road hazard damage will show itself in a substantially similar way across the various tire models and sizes at issue here. Nor is there any indication that BMW's and Bridgestone's representations differed significantly depending on the model-year BMW or specification of Bridgestone RFT. Therefore, the fact that Marcus leased only one model BMW with one kind of Bridgestone RFT does not pose a typicality problem.

Finally, "[i]t is well-established that a proposed class representative is not 'typical' under Rule 23(a)(3) if 'the representative is subject to a unique defense that is likely to become a major focus of the litigation.'" "Other courts of appeals emphasize, as do we, the challenge presented by a defense unique to a class representative—the representative's interests might not be aligned with those of the class, and the representative might devote time and effort to the defense at the expense of issues that are common and controlling for the class." Here, BMW and Bridgestone argue that New York law, not New Jersey law, applies to Marcus's claims and, along with it, certain unique defenses. For example, they claim that New York law, unlike New Jersey law, requires privity of contract in order to pursue a claim for breach of implied warranty.

* * * But even if New York, rather than New Jersey, law applies to Marcus's claims, BMW and Bridgestone have failed to demonstrate how any defenses unique to Marcus's claims will become a major focus of the litigation. * * *

[The court went on to hold, however, that the district court did not adequately support its finding that common issues predominated over individual issues for purposes of Rule 23(b)(3).]

NOTES AND QUESTIONS

1. What was the typicality issue in *Marcus*? How did the court resolve it? Is the court's reasoning persuasive.

2. Like *Marcus*, many courts do not impose a very rigorous analysis in determining whether factual differences between class representatives and unnamed class members defeat typicality. For example, in *Ouellette v. International Paper Co.*, 86 F.R.D. 476 (D. Vt. 1980), a federal district court in Vermont was faced with two putative classes involving alleged discharges by a paper mill. One class challenged the discharge of waste into a lake, while the other class challenged the discharge of pollutants into the air. The court ultimately concluded that a water class, but not the air class, should be certified. Nonetheless, the court had no difficulty finding that typicality was satisfied for both classes:

> Defendant, relying on its depositions of plaintiffs, argues that they do not all allege the same kinds of damage they claim on behalf of the classes they purport to represent. According to defendant this proves as a matter of logic that plaintiffs' claims are not typical. But

defendant appears to misapprehend the nature of rule 23(a)(3)'s requirement. Although the Advisory Committee's notes do little to illuminate this aspect of the rule, decisional law has made clear that whether or not it has independent significance the importance of the typicality requirement lies in assuring that the named plaintiffs will adequately represent those who are unnamed. Differences in the degree of harm suffered, or even in the ability to prove damages do not vitiate the typicality of a representative's claims. Typicality, therefore, should be evaluated in terms of the plaintiffs' claims as to liability.

With this in mind, we find the named plaintiffs' claims typical of the classes they seek to represent. Proof of defendant's liability for the alleged pollution of the air and Lake Champlain will benefit all members of the proposed classes; that the damages, if any, may reach a *de minimis* level at some point among the class members does not make the named plaintiffs' claims atypical.

Id. at 490.

3. Similarly, in *Appleyard v. Wallace*, 754 F.2d 955 (11th Cir. 1985), the named plaintiffs—who had been denied Medicaid nursing home benefits—alleged that Alabama's Medicaid nursing home admissions criteria violated plaintiffs' statutory and constitutional rights. Those criteria required applicants for nursing home benefits to show that they needed medical care that could be provided only in a nursing home. The district court denied certification on the ground that the differences in the medical conditions of the named plaintiffs prevented any named plaintiff from having "typical" claims. In reversing the district court, the Eleventh Circuit held:

In this case the district court was concerned by the "vast factual differences surrounding the medical condition of each of the named Plaintiffs." These factual distinctions, however, have little or no relevance to the relief requested by the plaintiffs. In their complaint the plaintiffs asked that the court (1) declare the level of care criteria invalid, (2) order reinstatement of the previous criteria pending development of new criteria * * *, (3) declare the policies and customs of the defendants invalid, and (4) enjoin the defendants from determining any member of the class to be ineligible for benefits without full compliance with applicable federal law. It does not appear that the factual differences surrounding the medical conditions of the various plaintiffs would preclude the district court from determining whether the plaintiffs are entitled to the relief they seek. The similarity of the legal theories shared by the plaintiffs and the class at large is so strong as to override whatever factual differences might exist and dictate a determination that the named plaintiffs' claims are typical of those of the members of the putative class.

Id. at 958.

4. Likewise, in *In re Prudential Ins. Co. of America Sales Practice Litigation*, 148 F.3d 283 (3d Cir. 1998), the court upheld the district court's ruling that typicality was satisfied in a case involving a class of more than eight million Prudential Life Insurance policyholders who allegedly were victims of fraudulent sales practices by Prudential's sales personnel. In reaching its decision, the court reasoned:

> The named plaintiffs, as well as the members of the proposed class, all have claims arising from the fraudulent scheme perpetrated by Prudential. That overarching scheme is the linchpin of the [complaint], regardless whether each class member alleges a churning claim [*i.e.*, convincing customers to use the cash value of policies to buy new policies], a vanishing premium claim [*i.e.*, falsely telling the customer that after a certain number of payments, the value of the policy would generate sufficient income to maintain the policy for the remainder of the insured's life], [a fraudulent] investment plan claim, or some other injury falling within the category of "other sales" claims. "Commentators have noted that cases challenging the same unlawful conduct which affects both the named plaintiffs and the putative class usually satisfy the typicality requirement irrespective of the varying fact patterns underlying the individual claims." Consequently, the factual distinctions among and between the named plaintiffs and the 8 million putative class members do not defeat a finding of typicality. "[E]ven relatively pronounced factual differences will generally not preclude a finding of typicality where there is a strong similarity of legal theories" or where the claim arises from the same practice or course of conduct.

Id. at 311.

5. Not all courts are so lenient. An example of a rigorous approach to typicality is *Ikonen v. Hartz Mountain Corp.*, 122 F.R.D. 258 (S.D. Cal. 1988). In *Ikonen*, named plaintiffs asserted that their pets were poisoned (and showed such symptoms as tremors, hyper-salivation, diarrhea, vomiting, ataxia and seizures) when "Blockade," a flea and tick spray made by defendant, was applied to the animals' skin. Many of the pets died or suffered neurological and physical injuries. The court found that typicality was lacking because:

> [E]ach animal will have been injured in different ways and to different degrees by Blockade. Each pet owner, for purposes of emotional distress claims, will have been affected in different ways and to different degrees by the loss of their pets. It would be necessary to decide whether Blockade proximately caused such harm in each individual case. * * * Plaintiffs thus have not met the requirement of typicality * * *.

Id. at 263. How might one construct an argument that typicality was satisfied in *Ikonen*?

6. One issue under typicality is whether the class representative would be subject to unique defenses that could harm the class. For example, if a plaintiff in an employment discrimination case had been caught stealing from the company, and if the company claimed that conduct was the reason for the termination, that class representative would have a potential typicality problem. Many courts have been reluctant to find typicality violated based on unique differences. *See, e.g., Harrison v. Great Spring Waters of Am., Inc.*, 1997 WL 46996 (E.D.N.Y. 1996) (typicality satisfied even though defendant planned to raise defenses that would prevent plaintiff from recovering (or impact the damages she could recover); *Langner v. Brown*, 1996 WL 709757 (S.D.N.Y. 1996) (class representative who served on board of directors of a corporation that was a defendant in the case (and that was allegedly mismanaged) was not atypical of class members who had no management role in the company).

Not all courts, however, have taken such a narrow view of the "unique defenses" concept. For example, in *McIntyre v. Household Bank*, 2004 WL

2958690 (N.D. Ill. 2004), plaintiff filed a putative class-action suit claiming that defendant's credit card lending practices violated federal and state law. The court held that the plaintiff failed to satisfy the typicality requirement because defendant had an argument that plaintiff's claim was barred by the statute of limitations. The court reasoned that the focus at trial on the timeliness of plaintiff's claims would "divert resources" from the prosecution of other class members' claims. According to the court, " 'even an arguable defense peculiar to the named plaintiff or a small subset of the plaintiff class may destroy the required typicality of the class * * *.' " *Id.* at *6. *See also, e.g., Zemel Family Trust v. Philips Int'l Realty Corp.*, 205 F.R.D. 434 (S.D.N.Y. 2002) (class representative atypical in case alleging a false and misleading proxy statement where class representative had himself previously been involved in conduct similar to that alleged); *Landry v. Price Waterhouse Chartered Accountants*, 123 F.R.D. 474, 475–77 (S.D.N.Y. 1989) (class representatives in securities fraud case atypical because of alleged lack of reliance on defendant or on the market's integrity). Can these cases be reconciled? Under what circumstances should unique defenses defeat typicality?

7. The author has noted that defendants have not taken full advantage of the typicality requirement and are likely to rely on it more heavily in the coming years in challenging class certification. *See* Robert H. Klonoff, *Class Actions in the Year 2026: A Prognosis*, 65 Emory L.J. 1569, 1614–17 (2016).

8. Consider the following proposal:

To avoid future confusion, rule 23 should be amended either to eliminate or to define precisely the typicality requirement. The National Conference of Commissioners on Uniform State Laws has drafted a proposed rule which would eliminate the typicality requirement. Section 1 of [the 1976] Uniform Class Action Act provides:

One or more members of a class may sue or be sued as representative parties on behalf of all in a class action if:

(1) the class is so numerous or so constituted that joinder of all members, whether or not otherwise required or permitted, is impracticable; and

(2) there is a question of law or fact common to the class.

The adequate representation requirement appears in section 2(b) of the Act: "The court may certify an action as a class action, if it finds that . . . the representative parties fairly and adequately will protect the interests of the class."

The proposal would protect absent class members and sustain the viability of the class action without imposing a typicality requirement. It would not pose any substantial problems since most courts have treated the typicality requirement along with one of the other requirements of rule 23. Thus, the typicality requirement is unnecessary. Further, the other three prerequisites of rule 23 are adequate safeguards to protect class members.

* * * All reasonable attempts to give the typicality requirement independent meaning have resulted in duplication of the other requirements. Therefore, the more reasonable alternative would be to eliminate the typicality requirement from rule 23.

Comment, *Federal Rule of Civil Procedure 23(a)(3) Typicality Requirement: The Superfluous Prerequisite to Maintaining a Class Action*, 42 Ohio St. L.J. 797, 810–11 (1981). Should the typicality requirement be abandoned? Is there any way to define the typicality requirement to give it meaning separate from commonality and adequacy?

PROBLEM

Plaintiffs Adamson, Bailey, and Cagney were shareholders in General Medicines, Inc. General Medicines had announced six months ago that its drug Cholestlow could substantially reduce cholesterol when taken regularly. Based on that announcement, Adamson and Bailey each purchased 1,000 shares of the stock. Adamson believed the truth of the announcement and based her decision to purchase on that information. Bailey, by contrast, was a scientist at the National Institutes of Health and knew, based on his training and the ingredients of Cholestlow, that the claims were a hoax. Nonetheless, he firmly believed that the company's stock would soar for many months, if not years, until someone uncovered the hoax. Cagney purchased 1,000 shares of General Medicines stock at the same time as Adamson and Bailey. He did not see the announcement, however, and instead purchased the stock merely because he had used Cholestlow and his cholesterol levels had fallen.

Much to the disappointment of the three plaintiff shareholders, a disgruntled former employee of General Medicines went public three weeks after the announcement and revealed, based on internal documents, that there was no scientific basis for General Medicines' claims. As a result, General Medicines' stock price declined 75 percent within hours of the revelation.

Plaintiffs want to sue for securities fraud (*see* Chapter 10(C)), claiming that the value of their stock fell when the company revealed the truth. Should plaintiffs' counsel propose each of these plaintiffs as a class representative? What factors should play a role? What typicality challenges, if any, can General Medicines make as to each plaintiff? What responses do plaintiffs have? As a strategic matter, should General Medicines mount a typicality attack against any of the proposed class representatives?

4. ADEQUACY OF REPRESENTATION

Under Rule 23(a)(4), a court must find, as a prerequisite to class certification, that "the representative parties will fairly and adequately protect the interest of the class." Although the Rule speaks only of the adequacy of the "parties," courts had long extended the 23(a)(4) analysis to the attorneys representing the proposed class representatives. This interpretation is now reinforced by Rule 23(g), added in 2003, which requires the court to appoint class counsel who can "fairly and adequately represent the interest of the class." Fed. R. Civ. P. 23(g)(1)(B). *See* discussion of Rule 23(g) later in this chapter at Part (B)(4)(c).

A large body of case law has developed articulating the standards for adequacy. *See generally* Robert H. Klonoff, *The Judiciary's Flawed Application of Rule 23's "Adequacy of Representation" Requirement*, 2004 Mich. St. L. Rev. 671 (2004). It is not surprising that the issue of adequacy has been frequently litigated: Because the actions of named representatives and class counsel will have direct and lasting implications on the claims and interests of unnamed class members, court supervision of the adequacy of class representatives and counsel is, in the view of many, "essential" to the fair functioning of the class action device. Alan B. Morrison, *The Inadequate Search for "Adequacy" in Class Actions: A Brief Reply to Professors Kahan and Silberman*, 73 N.Y.U. L. Rev. 1179, 1186–87 (1998).

In a Seventh Circuit decision, Judge Posner summarized why class actions inherently raise adequacy issues:

> The class action is an awkward device, requiring careful judicial supervision, because the fate of the class members is to a considerable extent in the hands of [one or more plaintiffs] whom the other members of the class may not know and who may not be able or willing to be an adequate fiduciary of their interests. Often the class representative has a merely nominal stake * * * and the real plaintiff in interest is then the lawyer for the class, who may have interests that diverge from those of the class members. The lawyer for the class is not hired by the members of the class and his fee will be determined by the court rather than by contract with paying clients. The cases have remarked [on] the danger that the lawyer will sell out the class in exchange for the defendant's tacit agreement not to challenge the lawyer's fee request.
>
> Rule 23 tries to minimize the potential abuses of the class action device in two principal ways, first by insisting that the class be reasonably homogeneous [as determined by Rule 23(a)(2) and Rule 23(b)], and second by insisting that the class representative be shown to be an adequate representative of the class. These are often and here related controls because if the class is heterogeneous, the representative is unlikely to be able to offer representation to all members * * *.
>
> * * *
>
> For purposes of determining whether the class representative is an adequate representative of the members of the class, the performance of the class lawyer is inseparable from that of the class representative. This is so because even when the class representative has some stake * * * it is usually very small in relation to the stakes of the class as a whole, magnifying the role of the class lawyer and making him [or] * * * her realistically a principal. Indeed *the* principal.

Culver v. City of Milwaukee, 277 F.3d 908, 910–11, 913 (7th Cir. 2002).

This section focuses on issues involving the adequacy of class representatives and the adequacy of class counsel.

a. Historical Basis for the Adequacy Requirement

Although it arises out of state court and thus does not involve federal class action rules, *Hansberry v. Lee*, 311 U.S. 32 (1940), is widely viewed as "the seminal Supreme Court case on adequate representation * * *." Note, *Who Can Tell the Futures? Protecting Settlement Class Action Members Without Notice*, 85 Va. L. Rev. 531, 562 (1999). Like many landmark cases, *Hansberry* is difficult to digest, but the patient reader will understand the value of the effort.

HANSBERRY V. LEE
Supreme Court of the United States, 1940.
311 U.S. 32.

JUSTICE STONE delivered the opinion of the Court.

The question is whether the Supreme Court of Illinois, by its adjudication that petitioners in this case [the Hansberrys and others who allegedly conspired with them] are bound by a judgment rendered in an earlier litigation to which they were not parties, has deprived them of the due process of law guaranteed by the Fourteenth Amendment.

Respondents [residents of the neighborhood at issue] brought this suit in the Circuit Court of Cook County, Illinois, to enjoin the breach by petitioners of an agreement restricting the use of land within a described area of the City of Chicago, which was alleged to have been entered into by some five hundred of the landowners. The agreement stipulated that for a specified period no part of the land should be "sold, leased to or permitted to be occupied by any person of the colored race," and provided that it should not be effective unless signed by the "owners of 95 per centum of the frontage" within the described area. The bill of complaint set up that the owners of 95 per cent of the frontage had signed; that respondents are owners of land within the restricted area who have either signed the agreement or acquired their land from others who did sign; and that petitioners Hansberry, who are Negroes, have, with the alleged aid of the other petitioners and with knowledge of the agreement, acquired and are occupying land in the restricted area formerly belonging to an owner who had signed the agreement.

To the defense that the agreement had never become effective because owners of 95 per cent of the frontage had not signed it, respondents pleaded that that issue was *res judicata* by the decree in an earlier suit [*Burke v. Kleiman*]. [The Hansberrys responded] that they were not parties to that suit or bound by its decree, and that denial of their right to litigate, in the present suit, the issue of performance of the condition precedent to the validity of the agreement would be a denial of due process of law guaranteed by the Fourteenth Amendment. It does not appear, nor is it contended[,] that any of petitioners is the successor in interest to or in privity with any of the parties in the earlier suit.

The circuit court, after a trial on the merits, found that owners of only about 54 per cent of the frontage had signed the agreement, and that the only support of the judgment in the *Burke* case was a false and fraudulent stipulation * * * that owners of 95 per cent had signed. But it ruled that the issue of performance of the condition precedent to the validity of the agreement was *res judicata* as alleged and entered a decree for respondents. The Supreme Court of Illinois affirmed. * * *

The Supreme Court of Illinois, upon an examination of the record in [*Burke*] found that [*Burke*] * * * was brought by a landowner in the restricted area * * * in behalf of herself and other property owners in like situation, against four named individuals who had acquired or asserted an interest in a plot of land formerly owned by another signer of the agreement; that upon stipulation of the parties in that suit that the agreement had been signed by owners of 95 per cent of all the frontage, the court had adjudged that the agreement was in force, that it was a covenant running with the land and binding all the land within the described area in the hands of the parties to the agreement and those claiming under them including defendants, and had entered its decree restraining the breach of the agreement by the defendants and those claiming under them, and that the appellate court had affirmed the decree. It found that the stipulation was untrue but held, contrary to the trial court, that it was not fraudulent or collusive. * * *

From this the Supreme Court of Illinois concluded in the present case that [*Burke*] was a "class" or "representative" suit and that in such a suit "where the remedy is pursued by a plaintiff who has the right to represent the class to which he belongs, other members of the class are bound by the results in the case unless it is reversed or set aside on direct proceedings"; that petitioners in the present suit were members of the class represented by the plaintiffs in the earlier suit and consequently were bound by its decree which had rendered the issue of performance of the condition precedent to the restrictive agreement *res judicata*, so far as petitioners are concerned. The court thought that the circumstance that the stipulation in the earlier suit that owners of 95 per cent of the frontage had signed the agreement was contrary to the fact as found in the present suit did not militate against this conclusion since the court in the earlier suit had jurisdiction to determine the fact as between the parties before it and that its determination, because of the representative character of the suit, even though erroneous, was binding on petitioners until set aside by a direct attack on the first judgment.

* * * [W]hen the judgment of a state court, ascribing to the judgment of another court the binding force and effect of *res judicata*, is challenged for want of due process it becomes the duty of this Court to examine the course of procedure in both litigations to ascertain whether the litigant whose rights have thus been adjudicated has been afforded such notice and opportunity to be heard as are requisite to the due process which the Constitution prescribes.

It is a principle of general application in Anglo–American jurisprudence that one is not bound by a judgment *in personam* in a litigation in which he is not designated as a party or to which he has not been made a party by service of process. A judgment rendered in such circumstances is not entitled to the full faith and credit which the Constitution and statute of the United States, 28 U.S.C. § 687, prescribe, and judicial action enforcing it against the person or property of the absent party is not that due process which the Fifth and Fourteenth Amendments requires.

To these general rules there is a recognized exception that, to an extent not precisely defined by judicial opinion, the judgment in a "class" or "representative" suit, to which some members of the class are parties, may bind members of the class or those represented who were not made parties to it.

The class suit was an invention of equity to enable it to proceed to a decree in suits where the number of those interested in the subject of the litigation is so great that their joinder as parties in conformity to the usual rules of procedure is impracticable. Courts are not infrequently called upon to proceed with causes in which the number of those interested in the litigation is so great as to make difficult or impossible the joinder of all because some are not within the jurisdiction or because their whereabouts is unknown or where if all were made parties to the suit its continued abatement by the death of some would prevent or unduly delay a decree. In such cases where the interests of those not joined are of the same class as the interests of those who are, and where it is considered that the latter fairly represent the former in the prosecution of the litigation of the issues in which all have a common interest, the court will proceed to a decree.

It is evident that the considerations which may induce a court thus to proceed, despite a technical defect of parties, may differ from those which must be taken into account in determining whether the absent parties are bound by the decree or, if it is adjudged that they are, in ascertaining whether such an adjudication satisfies the requirements of full faith and credit. Nevertheless, there is scope within the framework of the Constitution for holding in appropriate cases that a judgment rendered in a class suit is *res judicata* as to members of the class who are not formal parties to the suit. Here, as elsewhere, the Fourteenth Amendment does not compel state courts or legislatures to adopt any particular rule for establishing the conclusiveness of judgments in class suits; nor does it compel the adoption of the particular rules thought by this court to be appropriate for the federal courts. With a proper regard for divergent local institutions and interests, this Court is justified in saying that there has been a failure of due process only in those cases where it cannot be said that the procedure adopted, fairly insures the protection of the interests of absent parties who are to be bound by it.

It is familiar doctrine of the federal courts that members of a class not present as parties to the litigation may be bound by the judgment where they are in fact adequately represented by parties who are present, or where they actually participate in the conduct of the litigation in which members of the class are present as parties, or where the interest of the members of the class, some of whom are present as parties, is joint, or where for any other reason the relationship between the parties present and those who are absent is such as legally to entitle the former to stand in judgment for the latter.

In all such cases, so far as it can be said that the members of the class who are present are, by generally recognized rules of law, entitled to stand in judgment for those who are not, we may assume for present purpose that such procedure affords a protection to the parties who are represented, though absent, which would satisfy the requirements of due process and full faith and credit. Nor do we find it necessary for the decision of this case to say that, when the only circumstance defining the class is that the determination of the rights of its members turns upon a single issue of fact or law, a state could not constitutionally adopt a procedure whereby some of the members of the class could stand in judgment for all, provided that the procedure were so devised and applied as to insure that those present are of the same class as those absent and that the litigation is so conducted as to insure the full and fair consideration of the common issue. We decide only that the procedure and the course of litigation sustained here by the plea of *res judicata* do not satisfy these requirements.

The restrictive agreement did not purport to create a joint obligation or liability. If valid and effective its promises were the several obligations of the signers and those claiming under them. The promises ran severally to every other signer. It is plain that in such circumstances all those alleged to be bound by the agreement would not constitute a single class in any litigation brought to enforce it. Those who sought to secure its benefits by enforcing it could not be said to be in the same class with or represent those whose interest was in resisting performance, for the agreement by its terms imposes obligations and confers rights on the owner of each plot of land who signs it. If those who thus seek to secure the benefits of the agreement were rightly regarded by the state Supreme Court as constituting a class, it is evident that those signers or their successors who are interested in challenging the validity of the agreement and resisting its performance are not of the same class in the sense that their interests are identical so that any group who had elected to enforce rights conferred by the agreement could be said to be acting in the interest of any others who were free to deny its obligation.

Because of the dual and potentially conflicting interests of those who are putative parties to the agreement in compelling or resisting its performance, it is impossible to say, solely because they are parties to it, that any two of them are of the same class. Nor without more, and with the due regard for the protection of the rights of absent parties which due process exacts, can some be permitted to stand in judgment for all.

It is one thing to say that some members of a class may represent other members in a litigation where the sole and common interest of the class in the litigation, is either to assert a common right or to challenge an asserted obligation. It is quite another to hold that all those who are free alternatively either to assert rights or to challenge them are of a single class, so that any group, merely because it is of the class so constituted, may be deemed adequately to represent any others of the class in litigating their interests in either alternative. Such a selection of representatives for purposes of litigation, whose substantial interests are not necessarily or even probably the same as those whom they are deemed to represent, does not afford that protection to absent parties which due process requires. The doctrine of representation of absent parties in a class suit has not hitherto been thought to go so far. Apart from the opportunities it would afford for the fraudulent and collusive sacrifice of the rights of absent parties, we think that the representation in this case no more satisfies the requirements of due process than a trial by a judicial officer who is in such situation that he may have an interest in the outcome of the litigation in conflict with that of the litigants.

The plaintiffs in [*Burke*] sought to compel performance of the agreement in behalf of themselves and all others similarly situated. They did not designate the defendants in the suit as a class or seek any injunction or other relief against others than the named defendants, and the decree which was entered did not purport to bind others. In seeking to enforce the agreement the plaintiffs in that suit were not representing the petitioners here whose substantial interest is in resisting performance. The defendants in the first suit were not treated by the pleadings or decree as representing others or as foreclosing by their defense the rights of others; and, even though nominal defendants, it does not appear that their interest in defeating the contract outweighed their interest in establishing its validity. For a court in this situation to ascribe to either the plaintiffs or defendants the performance of such functions on behalf of petitioners here, is to attribute to them a power that it cannot be said that they had assumed to exercise, and a responsibility which, in view of their dual interests it does not appear that they could rightly discharge.

Reversed.

JUSTICE MCREYNOLDS, JUSTICE ROBERTS and JUSTICE REED concur in the result.

NOTES AND QUESTIONS

1. Why does *Hansberry* say that adequate representation is a critical component of due process? In what ways did the *Burke* plaintiff fail to provide adequate representation?

2. Some commentators have read *Hansberry* as holding that adequacy is *all* that is constitutionally required to satisfy due process in the class action context. *See* Patrick Woolley, *Rethinking the Adequacy of Adequate Representation*, 75 Tex. L. Rev. 571, 571 n.2 (1997) (collecting examples of such commentators' opinions). Does *Hansberry* support this reading? Professor Woolley does not believe so:

> The *Hansberry* Court simply did not address the issue. The Court held only that it was a violation of due process to bind to a judgment an individual who has not been adequately represented. Adequate representation is necessary; it may or may not be sufficient.

Id. at 574. Is Professor Woolley correct? Later chapters will focus on whether, in various circumstances, notice of the proceeding, a right to opt out of a class, and the ability to participate in the proceeding are also components of due process.

3. Although the 1938 version of Rule 23 had been adopted at the time the *Hansberry* case was decided, the Court did not refer to Rule 23 in its decision. Why not?

4. What criteria, if any, did the *Hansberry* Court provide for evaluating the adequacy of representation?

5. For a useful discussion of case law leading up to *Hansberry*, see Geoffrey C. Hazard, Jr., et al., *An Historical Analysis of the Binding Effect of Class Suits*, 146 U. Pa. L. Rev. 1849 (1998). For an informative account of the facts and circumstances surrounding *Hansberry*, see Jay Tidmarsh, *The Story of Hansberry: The Foundation for Modern Class Actions, in* Civil Procedure Stories 217 (Kevin M. Clermont ed., 2004).

6. Can an unnamed member of a class bring a lawsuit after judgment has been rendered to challenge the adequacy of representation? If the class member was absent from trial and did not have the opportunity to raise adequacy objections at the district court level or on appeal, should a court's ruling that the adequacy requirement had been met at class certification in the original lawsuit preclude the class member from raising objections in a collateral attack? Professor Woolley argues that collateral attacks in such circumstances are deeply entrenched in the law and are essential to protecting the interests of absent class members:

> Requiring class members to raise objections during the class suit to the adequacy of the representation would be a major step away from the representative model, which is, as [*Phillips Petroleum Co.*

v.] Shutts [472 U.S. 797 (1985), *see* Chapter 6(B)] recognized, at the heart of Rule 23. Such a requirement would impose on absent class members a significant obligation inconsistent with a pure representative model. Absent class members could no longer, as *Shutts* put it, "sit back and allow the litigation to run its course." Instead, they would have to raise any objections to the adequacy of the representation *before* the litigation ended. Failure to do so would leave them with no protection against inadequate representation as they would be foreclosed from raising the issue in any other forum. In essence, a requirement that absent class members raise adequacy objections in the class suit itself would create a hybrid procedural device: a class suit which would be only *partly* representative. Put another way, a requirement that absent class members raise adequacy objections in the class suit itself or forfeit the objections would shift the responsibility of protecting the interests of class members from "the court and named plaintiffs," where *Shutts* stated it lay, to the class members themselves.

Patrick Woolley, *The Availability of Collateral Attack for Inadequate Representation in Class Suits*, 79 Tex. L. Rev. 383, 398–99 (2000). *See also, e.g., Stephenson v. Dow Chem. Co.*, 273 F.3d 249 (2d Cir. 2001) (permitting collateral attack by two plaintiffs covered by settlement of Agent Orange claims), *aff'd in part, vacated in part*, 539 U.S. 111 (2003). For further exploration of these issues, see Chapter 7(C)(1)(b)(iii).

7. Does a trial court have an independent duty to ensure that the named plaintiffs and counsel adequately represent the interests of the absent class members? *Compare Carr v. Wilson–Coker*, 203 F.R.D. 66 (D. Conn. 2001) (court declined to conduct adequacy analysis because defendant did not dispute the issue), *with Jerry Enterprises, Inc. v. Allied Beverage Grp., L.L.C.*, 178 F.R.D. 437, 446 n.4 (D.N.J. 1998) (refusing to find counsel adequate, even in the absence of a challenge by defendants); *see generally* Robert H. Klonoff, *The Judiciary's Flawed Application of Rule 23's "Adequacy of Representation" Requirement*, 2004 Mich. St. L. Rev. 671, 680 (arguing that courts should consider adequacy of representation regardless of whether defendants raise the issue). Does an appellate court have a duty to address adequacy if the issue is not raised on appeal?

8. In *Arreola v. Godinez*, 546 F.3d 788 (7th Cir. 2008), the plaintiff sued on behalf of himself and a putative class of inmates allegedly subjected to unconstitutional mistreatment due to "the Jail's policy of denying crutches in certain areas of the Jail to the inmates who live there." *Id.* at 790. Plaintiff had left the jail prior to filing suit. In evaluating plaintiff's adequacy, the court concluded that, although plaintiff had a concrete stake in his damages claim, his interest in prospective relief was "too tenuous * * * to permit an award of injunctive relief on his individual claims." *Id.* at 799. The court found the likelihood that plaintiff would "return to the Jail and will once again be suffering from a lower-extremity fracture requiring crutches" to be "too speculative to support a right to an injunction on his part." *Id.* Thus, "[t]he district court did not abuse its discretion in declining to certify Arreola as the representative for an injunctive-relief class." *Id.* Assuming no other problems, would Arreola have adequately represented the interests of other inmates under these circumstances, despite the slim chance that he would suffer from the same treatment again? How, under the analysis in *Arreola*, could a class ever seek the requested injunctive relief?

b. Adequacy of Class Representatives

i. Competence

BLACK v. RHONE–POULENC, INC.
United States District Court, Southern District of West Virginia, 1996.
173 F.R.D. 156.

HADEN, CHIEF JUDGE.

Pending is Plaintiffs' motion for class certification. The Court conditionally GRANTS the motion.

I. Factual Background

Defendant is a New York corporation doing business in Kanawha County, West Virginia. Plaintiffs are putative class representatives of persons seeking redress for events that occurred on February 15, 1996. A fire broke out at Rhone–Poulenc's Institute, West Virginia plant on that date (hereinafter the "Fire"). During the Fire, a cloud of toxic substances * * * was released into the atmosphere.

* * * [T]he public was ordered to shelter-in-place and certain thoroughfares were closed temporarily. Some individuals suffered physical injuries from exposure to the chemicals. Most suffered only inconvenience and emotional distress.

* * * The Amended Complaint contains four counts alleging claims for (1) strict liability pursuant to *Restatement (Second) of Torts* § 519 (1977); (2) general strict liability or, in the alternative, negligence; (3) intentional infliction of emotional distress; and (4) negligent infliction of emotional distress. The complaint seeks compensatory and punitive damages as well as equitable relief requiring Defendant's submission to regular independent safety audits.

Plaintiffs have moved now for class certification. This relief is vigorously opposed by Defendant. According to Plaintiffs, the proposed class should consist of "all persons or other entities, who or which sustained damage as a result of the leak of toxic gas from the Institute, West Virginia facility of [Defendant] on February 15, 1996."

II. DISCUSSION

* * *

* * * "[T]he two factors that are now predominantly recognized as the basic guidelines for the Rule 23(a)(4) prerequisite [as to representative plaintiffs] are (1) absence of conflict and (2) assurance of vigorous prosecution." * * *

Defendant does not contend there is any significant conflict between the representatives and the potential class members. Rather, it focuses on the element of vigor. Defendant asserts the representative Plaintiffs are inadequate, in part, because "their knowledge of and involvement in this case [is] limited to having been told by their counsel that they had been selected to testify about what happened [to them]." Defendant rightly also asserts some of the Plaintiffs, *inter alia*, (1) did not know they were class representatives until shortly before or during their depositions; (2) had no idea what the duties of a class representative were; and (3) never read the amended complaint.

While Defendant's assertions are troubling, they are not a wholly accurate portrayal of the class representatives. For instance, while Plaintiff Billy K. Evans suggested he would have grave difficulty making decisions for other class members, he also testified in response to how he perceived his responsibilities as a class representative:

> To attempt to create a climate where something beneficial may come out of this lawsuit for not only myself but for the entire * * * community, the people that live in that community, to prevent any future shelter in place or being imprisoned in your own home in your own community without permission, and to attempt to prevent the fear that I feel of this company negligently loosing a poison in the community[.]

Plaintiff Harris testified his role as class representative essentially would consist of being a "mediator, consultant, liaison and confidant." He testified his "overall objective [was] to see that there is a safer environment in th[e] * * * area."

Plaintiff Edna Contreras read certain documents in the case and indicated an adequate understanding of her responsibilities, stating her attorney "would get in touch with [her] and the others to find out what [they thought and] where [they stood] on the different issues" arising in the case.

While some of the representative Plaintiffs demonstrated less than a complete understanding of their responsibilities and of the technical legal issues, that alone does not bar conditional certification. The Court can direct remedial action to correct the problem.

Plaintiffs' counsel is instructed to explain again to the putative representatives (1) the particulars of this action, including the contents of the amended complaint and the Court's prior rulings; (2) the costs and benefits to be derived from the case; (3) the responsibilities and potential consequences of being a representative Plaintiff; and (4) the fashion in which the litigation likely will proceed from this point. Should any of the representatives express discomfort or significant confusion on these issues, class counsel should act quickly to remedy the problem by realigning the proposed representatives and by promptly informing the Court and opposing counsel.

Counsel is further directed to (1) immediately apprise the representative Plaintiffs of all filings and make such available for inspection; and (2) inform the Court of the class action experience and practice areas of [out-of-state] attorneys [representing plaintiffs] who shall, in addition to local counsel, endorse all pleadings.

[The court concluded that all of the other requirements for class certification were met.]

NOTES AND QUESTIONS

1. Does the *Black* court's approach properly address the concerns about the adequacy of the proposed class representatives? Is it realistic to believe that plaintiffs' counsel will inform the court of problems involving adequacy?

Given the representatives' lack of knowledge about their duties and the allegations in the complaint, should the court have removed them as representatives?

2. What level of knowledge should a court require of a proposed class representative? Should that knowledge relate to his or her own facts, the circumstances of other class members, the legal proceedings, or some combination of such factors? Is it really important for named plaintiffs to be knowledgeable if able counsel is involved? Cases differ on this issue. *Compare, e.g., In re CBC Cos., Inc.*, 181 F.R.D. 380, 384 (N.D. Ill. 1998) (fact that class representative "was out of contact with her lawyers for nearly eight months" did not make her inadequate, because "this case as all class actions is prosecuted by lawyers" and "[t]here is no argument that anyone was harmed by the temporary lack of contact between [the representative] and her lawyers"), and *Lerner v. Haimsohn*, 126 F.R.D. 64, 67 (D. Colo. 1989) ("[A]s long as the plaintiffs, as class representatives, know something about the case, even though they are not knowledgeable of the complaint's specific allegations, the class should be certified"), *with McGuire v. International Paper Co.*, 1994 WL 261360, at *5 (S.D. Miss. 1994) (class representatives were inadequate where they "seem[ed] to lack familiarity with their suit" and were "not able to articulate the class they seek to represent"), and *Greenspan v. Brassler*, 78 F.R.D. 130, 133–34 (S.D.N.Y. 1978) (plaintiff was inadequate because he displayed "an alarming unfamiliarity with the suit"; he could not "identify any of the defendants [except for one]"; and was "[un]aware of certain elements of the complaint").

3. Some commentators believe that an inquiry into a class representative's intellect and knowledge of the claims does not make sense and should be abandoned. *See, e.g.*, Jonathan R. Macey & Geoffrey P. Miller, *The Plaintiffs' Attorney's Role in Class Action and Derivative Litigation: Economic Analysis and Recommendations for Reform*, 58 U. Chi. L. Rev. 1, 93–94 (1991) ("In large-scale, small-claim litigation, the courts should forthrightly acknowledge that the named plaintiff is a figurehead and should accordingly prohibit any inquiry by the defendant into the named plaintiff's intellect, educational achievements, or understanding of the case."). Should courts adopt this view? *See* Robert H. Klonoff, *The Judiciary's Flawed Application of Rule 23's "Adequacy of Representation" Requirement*, 2004 Mich. St. L. Rev. 671, 682–84 (2004) (empirical study of 10 year period finding that only 2.4 percent of cases ruling on adequacy held representatives inadequate because of incompetence or lack of knowledge).

4. How committed should the named representative be to the case? Does a representative's skepticism about the merits of some of the claims asserted make him or her inadequate?

5. How much weight should a court give to a representative's physical or mental disabilities? For example, if a named plaintiff is physically incapable of attending the trial from beginning to end, should he or she be deemed inadequate? How should adequacy be determined if a class is composed of a group of persons with mental disabilities? *See, e.g., Wyatt ex rel. Rawlins v. Poundstone*, 169 F.R.D. 155, 165 (M.D. Ala. 1995) (certifying class of mentally disabled residents of state facilities after finding the two mentally disabled representatives adequate; court said that representatives were articulate and that their parents spoke on their behalf); *Price v. Wilmington Trust Co.*, 730 A.2d 1236, 1239 (Del. Ch. 1997) (citing several "cases in which courts have certified individuals despite the existence of medical conditions which raised questions as to the representative's ability adequately to represent the class").

6. Should a class representative be deemed inadequate because the amount of his or her personal claim (and thus personal stake in the action) is small?

7. Which side should bear the burden on the issue of adequacy? Courts have diverged. *See* Klonoff, *supra*, at 676–77. Consider the following:

> What constitutes adequate representation is a question of fact that depends on the circumstances of each case. Criteria for assessing adequacy of representation include whether the plaintiff has common interests with the class members and whether the representative will vigorously prosecute the interests of the class through qualified counsel. The plaintiff has the initial burden to show facts to support a finding that it will adequately protect the interests of the class. Once the plaintiff has made a *prima facie* showing of adequate representation, the burden shifts to the defendant. Absent evidence to the contrary, a presumption of adequate representation is invoked. Any doubt regarding adequacy of representation should be resolved in favor of [] upholding the class, subject to later possible reconsideration, or the creation of subclasses initially.

Schwartz v. Celestial Seasonings, Inc., 178 F.R.D. 545, 552 (D. Colo. 1998). Is this "shifting-burdens" scheme workable? Should doubts about adequacy be resolved in favor of the representative, or against? *See, e.g.*, *Berger v. Compaq Computer Corp.*, 257 F.3d 475, 481 (5th Cir. 2001) (discussing conflict among courts and holding that "[a]dequacy is for the plaintiffs to demonstrate; it is not up to defendants to disprove * * * adequacy").

8. In some instances, courts blur the distinction between adequacy of class counsel and that of the class representatives. For instance, in *Rattray v. Woodbury County, IA*, 253 F.R.D. 444 (N.D. Iowa 2008), *aff'd*, 614 F.3d 831 (8th Cir. 2010), both the district court and the Eighth Circuit found that plaintiffs failed to satisfy the adequacy standard. Although both courts spoke about the adequacy of the representatives, both cited conduct of counsel, not conduct of the representatives. The initial complaint in *Rattray* alleged that the County had a policy of performing strip searches on all arrestees accused of a serious misdemeanor, regardless of whether reasonable suspicion existed to justify a particular search. 614 F.3d at 833. The district court found that these allegations should have alerted plaintiff's counsel to the potential for class certification much earlier in the litigation, and the Eighth Circuit agreed:

> * * * Rattray's initial complaint, at a minimum, forecasts that a broad strip search policy was in effect at the county jail. * * * Accepting that these allegations were made in good faith, Rattray and her counsel knew when she filed the complaint in February 2007 that a potential class existed, or at least that there was reason to investigate the matter promptly. Yet Rattray did not amend her complaint to assert a class action on behalf of other arrestees until October 2007.
>
> Even beyond that lapse in time, the district court was most concerned about the nearly six-month period from the filing of the amended complaint to the filing of the motion to certify the class. Including this delay, over fourteen months passed between the filing of the initial complaint and the motion to certify. Rattray's failure to move to certify with alacrity undermines confidence in the zeal with which she would represent the interests of absent class members. A failure of the putative class representative to assure the court that it

will vigorously pursue the interests of class members is a sufficient basis to deny certification.

Id. at 835–36 (citations omitted). Should class representatives be held accountable for the actions of class counsel? This is an important point: A finding that only the representatives are inadequate leaves existing counsel free to remain in the case and substitute new class representatives.

9. In *Birmingham Steel Corp. v. Tennessee Valley Authority*, 353 F.3d 1331 (11th Cir. 2003), the Eleventh Circuit held that the district court, after finding the named plaintiffs inadequate, abused its discretion in decertifying the class without affording an opportunity for a new class representative to be substituted. *Id.* at 1333. The court emphasized that, at the time the finding of inadequacy was made, "discovery had been completed, numerous pretrial motions had been resolved, and the case was ready for trial * * *." *Id.* at 1342. *Compare Culver v. City of Milwaukee*, 277 F.3d 908, 912–13 (7th Cir. 2002) (upholding decertification without leaving open case for counsel to find new representative, where there was no evidence that any class member "ha[d] any interest beyond that of a curious onlooker in pursuing th[e] litigation"). Assuming the correctness of *Birmingham Steel*, should a similar opportunity be afforded when the finding of inadequacy occurs early in the lawsuit, before significant discovery or pre-trial rulings?

In *Falcon v. Philips Electronics North America Corp.*, 304 F. App'x 896 (2d. Cir. 2008), the Second Circuit upheld the district court's refusal to allow plaintiff to conduct further discovery to identify a substitute class representative, where the original representative was deemed inadequate under Rule 23(a)(4). The court noted that the original plaintiff could not " 'plausibly argue that she never considered that, as someone who neither purchased nor retained a defective Philips television set, she might not adequately represent a class of persons consisting of those who did' " purchase and retain defendant's television sets, and that "[t]he deadlines for both class certification discovery and merits discovery ha[d] come and gone" by the time plaintiff sought to reopen class discovery to look for a new class representative. *Id.* at 898 (quoting district court). Ultimately, is the adequacy problem in *Falcon* that of the class representative or of class counsel?

10. Must a named plaintiff be able to prevail on his or her own claim in order to be an adequate class representative? *See Martinez–Mendoza v. Champion Int'l Corp.*, 340 F.3d 1200, 1215–16 (11th Cir. 2003) ("[A] plaintiff's capacity to act as representative of the class is not *ipso facto* terminated when he loses his case on the merits. * * * Consequently, even after finding against plaintiffs on the merits, the court should have determined whether the class action could be maintained, and whether the plaintiffs could represent that class."). Is *Martinez–Mendoza* correct?

11. The Private Securities Litigation Reform Act of 1995, 109 Stat. 737 (PSLRA), provides a process for appointing a class representative in securities class actions. The statute requires the court to appoint, as lead plaintiff, the plaintiff with the greatest financial stake in the relief sought, as long as he or she meets the requirements of Rule 23. In *Berger v. Compaq Computer Corp.*, 257 F.3d 475 (5th Cir. 2001), the court initially held that the PSLRA heightened the requirements of Rule 23(a)(4) and mandated a lead plaintiff who would actually manage the litigation as opposed to having the litigation directed by counsel. In a *per curiam* denial of rehearing, however, *Berger v. Compaq Computer Corp.*, 279 F.3d 313 (5th Cir. 2002), the court stated that the

23(a)(4) standards remain the same in PSLRA cases. For more discussion of the PSLRA, see Chapter 10(C)(2)(a).

ii. *Honesty and Good Character*

KAPLAN V. POMERANTZ
United States District Court, Northern District of Illinois, 1990.
132 F.R.D. 504.

ROVNER, DISTRICT JUDGE.

I. INTRODUCTION

[This is a securities fraud case. Plaintiff is the administrator of his wife's estate. His wife purchased certain securities, which are the subject of the lawsuit at issue.] Pending is defendants' motion for decertification of the class. For the reasons stated below, [defendants'] motion is granted.

II. FACTS

Plaintiff filed this class action securities fraud lawsuit on September 18, 1989. * * * On May 22, 1990, * * * the Court certified a class with respect to two of the three counts of the complaint.

Defendants now argue that decertification is appropriate because plaintiff gave false answers in his deposition with respect to his involvement in other lawsuits and his wife's ownership of other stocks. The precise language and the context of the testimony at issue is significant, and the Court therefore sets forth the relevant passages in detail:

Q. What assets does your wife's estate have?

A. What assets? Well, the stocks.

Q. Fifty shares of [defendant] Gaylord stock; is that correct?

A. Yes.

Q. Does the estate hold other stocks?

MR. SIMON [plaintiff's counsel]: Objection. I direct the witness not to answer that question.

Q. Does the—did your wife hold other stocks before her death?

MR. SIMON: Objection, same instruction.

Q. Mr. Kaplan, do you know what assets your wife held before her death?

A. No; just the stocks.

Q. Do you know what stocks she held before her death?

A. I knew she had this (Indicating).

MR. SIMON: "This," meaning Exhibit 3.

THE WITNESS: The 50 shares of Gaylord.

Q. Do you know if she held any other securities?

MR. SIMON: Objection. We've gone through this route before.

MR. JOHNSON [defendants' counsel, conducting the deposition]: My question now is whether he knows if she held any.

MR. SIMON: It's the same subject matter, Mr. Johnson, phrased in an artfully different way.

MR. JOHNSON: Are you instructing him not to answer?

MR. SIMON: Yes, I am.

* * *

Q. Mr. Kaplan, are you refusing to answer that question on the grounds—on the basis of your counsel's directive?

A. Yes.

Q. Do you know, apart from securities, if your wife had any other assets that are part of her estate?

A. No. There is [sic] no other assets.

* * *

Q. Mr. Kaplan, is it correct that the only assets that your wife held before her death of any kind were 50 shares of Gaylord stock?

A. Well, my lawyer said I shouldn't answer that question.

Q. No. Your lawyer did not say you shouldn't answer that question.

MR. SIMON: If you know the answer as to what assets she had, answer it.

THE WITNESS: Besides these 50 shares, I don't know.

MR. SIMON: That's the answer.

Q. She may have held assets; you don't know what they are?

MR. SIMON: Objection. That calls for speculation and guesswork.

* * *

Q. Mr. Kaplan, have you made any attempts to find out whether your wife held any assets other than the 50 shares of Gaylord stock before her death?

* * *

A. I looked through papers.

Q. What papers did you look through?

A. Any papers I had at home.

Q. What kind of papers?

A. All kinds, I guess.

Q. You mean, financial records?

A. Yes, any kind of records at all.

Q. Can you describe them any better than that, what kind of records there were at home?

A. Not really.

* * *

Q. From your review of your papers at home, did you learn that your wife held no other assets other than the 50 shares of Gaylord stock?

A. The only thing she owned was the 50 shares of Gaylord.

* * *

Q. Mr. Kaplan, do you know if your wife held any other assets other than the 50 shares of Gaylord stock?

A. I don't know.

* * *

Q. If she did hold other assets, you didn't find any records of those other assets in your search; is that correct?

A. Yes.

Q. Do you know of any other security purchase that your wife had ever made?

A. No, I don't know.

Q. Had she discussed seeing a lawyer with anyone else at that time; do you know?

A. I don't know. I don't know.

Q. Had she discussed Gaylord stock with anyone else at that time?

A. I don't know that answer either.

* * *

Q. Have you ever been a party to a lawsuit before, Mr. Kaplan?

A. No.

Q. Have you ever given testimony before?

A. No.

Q. Was your wife ever party to a lawsuit?

A. No.

Q. Did your wife ever give testimony?

A. No.

Q. This was the only stock, as far as you know, that your wife ever owned; correct?

A. Correct.

Defendants claim that portions of plaintiff's deposition [regarding whether he was ever a party to another lawsuit] are contradicted by the undisputed facts that on October 6, 1989, plaintiff filed suit in the U.S. District Court for the Central District of California against Medstone International, Inc., and other defendants, and on November 9, 1989, he filed an action in the U.S. District Court for the District of Connecticut against Finevest Foods, Inc., and other defendants. Plaintiff filed both of these cases in his capacity as administrator of his wife's estate, and both cases include allegations of securities fraud. In both cases, plaintiff is represented by one of the same law firms which represents him in this case.

[Defendants also claim that plaintiff gave false testimony about his wife's ownership of stock other than Gaylord stock.]

III. ANALYSIS

Defendant[s] argue[] that plaintiff's answers in the deposition warrant decertification of the class because they call into question plaintiff's credibility * * *. Plaintiff responds that the answers were not false and that any inconsistencies do not relate to the merits of the action and are so minor that decertification is not warranted.

* * *

With respect to the first issue, defendants argue that plaintiff lied by denying involvement in any other lawsuits when he was, at the time of his testimony, a plaintiff in two other securities fraud class actions. Plaintiff responds as follows:

> [D]efendants' attack upon Mr. Kaplan's veracity is based upon a twisted mischaracterization of his deposition testimony in this case. In their attempt to impugn Mr. Kaplan's honesty, defendants have focused on answers to deposition questions that they have taken out of context and have ignored his answers to other questions. Defendants' accusation that Mr. Kaplan was not truthful in answering "no" when he was asked whether he had "ever been a party to a lawsuit before" is entirely unfounded. Mr. Kaplan's answer was truthful. He had never been a party to a lawsuit before the initiation of this action. . . . [The other two actions] were filed *after* the complaint in this action was filed on September 18, 1989. Defendants' accusation that "[i]n late June, defendants' counsel learned that Mr. Kaplan's answer was not true" is thus not only false, but is belied by defendants' own submission to the Court here [identifying the other lawsuits]. Neither of the experienced defense counsel who interrogated Mr. Kaplan at his deposition here, in fact, asked Mr. Kaplan anything about his involvement in current litigation. Mr. Kaplan answered truthfully and honestly that he had never been a party to a lawsuit before he filed this action in September 1989.

The problem with this response is that it ignores the actual language of the question and answer at issue. Defendants' counsel did not ask plaintiff whether he had ever been a party to a lawsuit "before he filed this action," and plaintiff did not answer that he had never been a party to a lawsuit "before he filed this action." The question was "*have* you ever been a party to a lawsuit before?" and the answer was "no." There is no reasonable interpretation of this question and answer other than that plaintiff was asked whether he had ever been a party to another lawsuit at any time prior to the time that the question was asked, and that plaintiff denied that he had. * * * The Court can reach no other conclusion than that plaintiff gave a false answer and that plaintiff's counsel acquiesced in that false answer.

The second issue is whether plaintiff gave false testimony as to whether his wife held stocks other than the Gaylord stock. Plaintiff concedes that he knew at the time of the deposition that his wife had owned other stocks, but claims that at the time of his wife's death, the only stock he knew of was the Gaylord stock. Plaintiff's counsel explain his deposition answers as follows:

> [D]efendants have twisted and mischaracterized Mr. Kaplan's deposition testimony and have ignored his answers to other questions. Defendants fail to note that prior to the deposition questions and answers that they cite, Mr. Kaplan unambiguously testified in response to two separate questions that his wife and her estate owned not just Gaylord stock but other "stocks":
>
> Q. What assets does your wife's estate have?
> A. What assets? Well, the stocks.
> Q. Mr. Kaplan, do you know what assets your wife held before her death?
> A. No; just the stocks.
>
> This testimony negates any implication that Mr. Kaplan was lying about the content of his wife's estate.

* * *

* * * [T]his response ignores the plain language of the deposition testimony. * * * [P]laintiff did not say that his wife held "other stocks"; he answers only that his wife held "the stocks." Because the only stocks which were ever discussed were the Gaylord stocks, and because in other places plaintiff testified that the only assets were the Gaylord stocks, the only reasonable interpretation of this testimony is that it referred to "the Gaylord stocks." This is particularly true when, for instance, the first passage is considered in light of the follow-up questions:

Q. What assets does your wife's estate have?
A. What assets? Well, the stocks.
Q. Fifty shares of Gaylord stock; is that correct?
A. Yes.
Q. Does the estate hold other stocks?

MR. SIMON [plaintiff's counsel]: Objection. I direct the witness not to answer that question.

This passage leaves no doubt that when plaintiff said his wife's estate's assets were "the stocks," he was referring only to the Gaylord stocks. * * *

Similarly, plaintiff's contention that he was testifying only as to what he knew at the time of his wife's death, rather than what he knew at the time of the deposition, is untenable. There simply is no support in the transcript for such an interpretation. * * *

In light of these instances of false deposition testimony, the Court cannot in good conscience allow this case to continue as a class action with plaintiff serving as the class representative. A plaintiff's honesty and integrity are important considerations in allowing him to represent a class. In this case, plaintiff's statements go beyond minor inconsistencies. Plaintiff may be correct in asserting that the subjects of his statements are of marginal relevance to this lawsuit; nonetheless, they evince a willingness to give intentionally false and misleading testimony in an effort to further his interests in this litigation. Under these circumstances, allowing him to prosecute this case as a class action would not be fair to the Court, to the defendants, or to the other individuals whose interests plaintiff purports to represent.

Plaintiff argues that even if his credibility has been called into question to some extent, that does not warrant decertification of the class. Plaintiff argues that in considering the adequacy of representation, courts consider two factors: "(a) the plaintiff's attorney must be qualified, experienced, and generally able to conduct the proposed litigation, and (b) the plaintiff must not have interests antagonistic to the class." A plaintiff with credibility problems, however, does have interests "antagonistic to the class." * * *

The * * * class shall therefore be decertified. * * *

NOTES AND QUESTIONS

1. In addition to finding the class representative inadequate, and based upon the same analysis, the *Kaplan* court found that the representative failed to satisfy the typicality requirement. The court also found plaintiff's counsel inadequate on the ground that he was "at least a silent accomplice in, and at most encourag[ing], plaintiff's false testimony." *Kaplan*, 132 F.R.D. at 511. The court faulted counsel for his failure to make "defendants aware of the true facts * * *." *Id.* According to the court, "[t]his behavior constitute[d] an alternative reason for the Court's conclusion that the adequacy of representation prong of Rule 23 has not been satisfied." *Id.* The issue of the adequacy of class counsel is discussed later in this chapter at Part (B)(4)(c).

2. Many courts have been more reluctant than the *Kaplan* court to find a disqualifying lack of candor. *See* Robert H. Klonoff, *The Judiciary's Flawed Application of Rule 23's "Adequacy of Representation" Requirement*, 2004 Mich. St. L. Rev. 671, 685 (2004) (only four cases out of 763 that ruled on adequacy during 10-year sample period found representatives inadequate because of ethical violations, lack of honesty, or character flaws). For example, in *Biben v. Card*, 1986 WL 1199 (W.D. Mo. 1986), another securities fraud suit, the court stated:

> Defendants also label the named plaintiffs as inadequate class representatives because of alleged credibility problems. Specifically, defendants point to inconsistencies in the deposition testimonies of the proposed class representatives and their brokers. Citations to the broker's depositions are made to counter the assertions of the named plaintiffs that they did not know that [the stock in question] was a highly speculative investment but that they did rely on [the company's] financial statements (or the market reaction thereto). * * * Defendants' search for perfect class representatives is doomed to failure—which of course is the desired result. Defendants simply have not convinced me that the named plaintiffs are likely guilty of any dishonesty that would seriously taint their proposed representative status. Even if they did know of some of the risks involved in [the stock], this knowledge may well have been possessed by the class members generally. Certainly, that the class representatives and their brokers do not recall some of the events surrounding the trading

in [the] stock similarly is to a certain degree to be expected and does not establish the existence of deliberate falsehoods. Most importantly, such variances in memory do not support a conclusion that the named plaintiffs would sacrifice the interests of the class * * *.

Id. at *8. Which approach makes more sense—the one taken in *Kaplan* or in *Biben*?

3. Should the moral character of the named plaintiff be relevant in determining adequacy? What if the named plaintiff has a prior felony conviction? Does it depend on the particular crime committed? Does it depend on when the crime occurred and on the person's post-conviction conduct? *See, e.g., Meyer v. Portfolio Recovery Assocs., LLC*, 707 F.3d 1036, 1042 (9th Cir. 2012) (district court did not abuse its discretion in finding that a class representative was not disqualified on adequacy grounds because of convictions for deceptive conduct, where such convictions were from more than 10 years ago and "Meyer had since taken positive steps in his life, including graduation from the University of California").

What if the representative has been found liable for civil fraud? In *Uniondale Beer Co. v. Anheuser–Busch, Inc.*, 117 F.R.D. 340 (E.D.N.Y. 1987), an antitrust class action, the court held that three representatives—one who had written bad checks, one who was a defendant in an unrelated lawsuit, and one who was the subject of a cease and desist order for an unrelated environmental action—were not disqualified from being class representatives. The court found that defendants' arguments regarding "allegations of misconduct in unrelated actions" were " 'grasping at straws.' " *Id.* at 343. Would absent class members want such plaintiffs as class representatives? Should it matter whether the alleged misconduct is related to the subject of the lawsuit at issue?

4. In *Casale v. Kelly*, 257 F.R.D. 396 (S.D.N.Y. 2009), plaintiffs brought a class action against the New York City Police Department and others, alleging that defendants had violated the Fourth, Fifth, and Fourteenth Amendment rights of the putative class by continuing to enforce two provisions of a loitering law that had been declared unconstitutional decades earlier. The district court certified classes under Rule 23(b)(2) and (b)(3), rejecting, among other arguments, defendants' contention that the two proposed class representatives, Casale and Garcia, were inadequate:

> Named plaintiffs are not flawless individuals. * * * Casale has a history of mental illness, and Garcia has spent time in correctional facilities as a result of drug use. However, * * * plaintiffs have demonstrated admirable dedication to the pursuit of this lawsuit. Casale sought out representation and has pursued his claims *despite* a fear of retaliation. Garcia reviewed the complaint twice before attending his deposition *despite* difficulties reading. Casale declared that he decided to pursue the lawsuit "because [h]e felt that what happened to [him] was a grave injustice and it is something that * * * shouldn't be happening to people. It shouldn't be allowed to continue." Plaintiffs' knowledge of the suit is also more than sufficient to allow them to serve as class representatives, particularly in light of their professed dedication to the case and the assistance of experienced advocates.
>
> Frankly put, defendants' assault on named plaintiffs' capability to represent the interests of similarly situated individuals is disrespectful and blatantly self-serving. It is irrelevant that Casale suffers from depression and believes he has suffered incidents of paranoia. It is also irrelevant that Garcia was once hospitalized with chest pains

or had a test result indicating a possibility of untreated diabetes. It is further irrelevant that both named plaintiffs were unaware of potential liability for defendants' fees and costs, particularly as plaintiffs' counsel are likely paying the costs of this action. And the fact that Garcia did not know [the judge's] name is only interesting to defendants' counsel. What is relevant is that these characteristics and ailments are typical of individuals who tend to be victims of the enforcement of unconstitutionally vague statutes—the vagabonds, the homeless, and the destitute—who often lack the resources to enforce their rights. If individuals like Casale and Garcia were ineligible to represent a class, the claims of those even worse off would inevitably go unheard. Therefore, named plaintiffs meet the adequacy requirement of Rule 23(a)(4).

257 F.R.D. at 412–13. Are there any circumstances in which class representatives should be deemed inadequate because they do not know the name of the judge or other basic facts involving the lawsuit? Should plaintiffs' medical conditions ever affect adequacy? How should a court decide whether a representative is adequate under such circumstances? Consider *CE Design Ltd. v. King Architectural Metals, Inc.*, 637 F.3d 721, 727–28 (7th Cir. 2011), where the Seventh Circuit vacated a class certification order because, *inter alia*, the named plaintiff had a "credibility problem" that rendered it potentially inadequate. Judge Posner nonetheless cautioned: "We don't want to be misunderstood * * * as extending an invitation to defendants to try to derail legitimate class actions by conjuring up trivial credibility problems * * *." *Id.* at 728.

5. What standards should a court apply in assessing whether allegations of misconduct render a class representative inadequate?

iii. Conflicts of Interest

The most common reason for courts to find class representatives inadequate is that they have interests that conflict with those of other class members. *See* Robert H. Klonoff, *The Judiciary's Flawed Application of Rule 23's "Adequacy of Representation" Requirement*, 2004 Mich. St. L. Rev. 671, 687 (2004) (more than half of cases finding class representatives inadequate during 10-year period studied based their decision on the existence of conflicts). As the following case illustrates, however, it is often difficult for defendants to show that an alleged conflict is disqualifying.

ROBIN V. DOCTORS OFFICENTERS CORP.
United States District Court, Northern District of Illinois, 1988.
686 F. Supp. 199.

CONLON, DISTRICT JUDGE.

BACKGROUND

This consolidated securities litigation arises from a public offering of the common stock of defendant Doctors Officenters Corporation ("DOC") in December, 1983. Plaintiffs are purchasers of DOC stock who allegedly purchased their shares in reliance on a prospectus issued by DOC on December 7, 1983. They contend that the prospectus contained material omissions and misleading statements, thereby constituting federal securities and common law fraud violations.

In the first complaint plaintiffs named as defendants DOC, FMP (a medical partnership that owned DOC stock) and six individuals who served as directors and officers of DOC. Plaintiffs filed a second action against the law firm of Katten, Muchin & Zavis, DOC's counsel in connection with the public offering, as well as six individual directors and officers. Plaintiffs filed the third case against Arthur Young & Company, the accounting firm that audited the financial statements included in the December 7, 1983 prospectus. Steiner Diamond [& Co., Inc.], the managing underwriter for the public offering, was not named as a defendant in any of the three cases.

[The court first granted Defendants' motion to join Steiner Diamond as a third-party defendant potentially liable for contribution.]

II. DEFENDANTS' MOTION TO DECERTIFY THE CLASS

Defendants jointly move to decertify the class on the grounds that * * * the class representatives' relationships with Steiner Diamond [described below] present a conflict of interest * * *. For the reasons that follow, defendants' motion to decertify the class is denied.

* * *

(1) Adequacy of the Class Representatives

Defendants contend that plaintiffs' business and social relationships with Steiner Diamond and its principals render them incapable of objectively evaluating class claims against Steiner Diamond. They argue that if Steiner Diamond is joined as a third-party defendant, plaintiffs will not be able to prosecute their claims without exposing the principals of Steiner Diamond to judgment. Because no one can gauge the impact of the conflict on the effectiveness of the class representatives, defendants suggest that plaintiffs should not be permitted to prosecute their claims as a class action.

Plaintiffs argue that Steiner Diamond has been potentially liable to the defendants for contribution since the inception of this action. They reason that they would not have filed this action against any of the defendants if they had been concerned about Steiner Diamond's potential exposure. As evidence of their vigorous prosecution of the claims, the named plaintiffs assert that they have sustained $300,000 in damages and have expended over $15,000 to date in this litigation, in addition to their personal time and attention. They maintain that disclosure of the fact that Steiner Diamond was not named as an original defendant in the class notice is the appropriate remedy rather than decertification of the class.

The court's primary concern in determining the adequacy of representation is whether the class representative has a common interest with the class and has vigorously prosecuted its interests. A representative cannot adequately protect the class if his interests are antagonistic to or in conflict with the interests of those he represents. Representation is inadequate where the class representative fails to name as a defendant a party with whom he has a continuing business relationship, despite the fact that the party is liable to the class. Where the conflict is merely a potential one, however, the class may be maintained by adding at least one representative who has neither a business nor a social relationship with the putative defendant. The burden is on the party opposing class certification to demonstrate that representation will be inadequate.

The history of this litigation supports plaintiffs' contention that they have vigorously prosecuted the class' common claims against the defendants. It appears, however, that members of the class may have an interest in suing Steiner Diamond as well as those defendants already named in this action. Nevertheless, the alleged conflict does not dictate decertification of the class.

In granting plaintiffs' motion to certify the class, the court considered the identical arguments in opposition and determined that neither the personal nor professional relationships between Steiner Diamond and the named plaintiffs created a conflict of interest. Specifically, the court noted that numerous absent class members also used Steiner Diamond's brokerage services. The court also rejected the argument that the representatives' personal relationships with Steiner Diamond's principals, Robert Steiner or Terry Diamond, render the representation inadequate. It determined that the identity of the claims of the representatives and absent class members was not defeated by the fact that certain absent members may elect to pursue a claim against Steiner Diamond. In their present motion, defendants do not offer additional facts to establish any conflict of interest; they argue that the actual joinder of Steiner Diamond as a third-party defendant warrants re-examination of the adequacy of representation.

At this stage of the litigation, the court is not persuaded that the joinder of Steiner Diamond creates a conflict that renders representation of the class inadequate. Any potential conflict may be prevented by means other than decertification of the class. First, * * * the notice to the class shall disclose that Steiner Diamond, the managing underwriter for the offering at issue, is not a defendant for purposes of recovery by the class. Second, the order of class certification shall be amended to require the addition of at least one representative, together with his or her legal counsel, who is not a social or business acquaintance of Steiner Diamond or its principals. The attorney then may decide whether the class should name Steiner Diamond as a defendant in the main action. This approach ensures that the interests of all absent class members will be fairly and adequately represented.

* * *

CONCLUSION

* * * Defendants' joint motion to decertify the plaintiff class is denied. The class is ordered to select an additional representative with his or her own legal counsel within 30 days; neither the representative nor his or her counsel may be a business or social acquaintance of Steiner Diamond or its principals. * * *

NOTES AND QUESTIONS

1. Is the requirement that another representative and separate counsel be added—one without a relationship with Steiner Diamond—a sufficient response to the purported conflict? How will "[t]he class" (*see* above excerpt) choose such a representative?

2. Incentive payments to class representatives can raise conflicts. In *Rodriguez v. West Publ'g Corp.*, 563 F.3d 948 (9th Cir. 2009), a class of law stu-

dents alleged that bar preparation course providers violated the federal antitrust laws. The parties settled, but several class-member objectors challenged the settlement on appeal. They were particularly concerned with the impact on the settlement of certain incentive agreements—entered into prior to litigation between class counsel and five of the seven class representatives—that obligated class counsel to seek incentive awards for each of the five representatives, with the amount contingent upon the final settlement or verdict in the case. *Id.* at 957. The Ninth Circuit found that the agreements created conflicts among those representatives, their counsel, and the rest of the class. Nonetheless, it upheld approval of the settlement, finding Rule 23(a)(4) satisfied because two of the class representatives (who were separately represented) did *not* have incentive agreements. According to the court, "[t]he adequacy-of-representation requirement is satisfied as long as one of the class representatives is an adequate class representative." 563 F.3d at 961 (citation and internal quotation marks omitted).

In *Radcliffe v. Experian Information Solutions Inc.*, 715 F.3d 1157 (9th Cir. 2013), the Ninth Circuit reversed the district court's certification of a settlement class on adequacy grounds stemming from $5,000 incentive payments to class representatives under the settlement. The Ninth Circuit acknowledged that it had previously approved class settlements that included incentive awards. *Id.* at 1161. This case was different, however, because

> [U]nlike the incentive awards that we have approved before, these awards were conditioned on the class representatives' support for the settlement. These conditional incentive awards caused the interests of the class representatives to diverge from the interests of the class because the settlement agreement told class representatives that they would not receive incentive awards unless they supported the settlement. Moreover, the conditional incentive awards significantly exceeded in amount what absent class members could expect to get upon settlement approval. Because these circumstances created a patent divergence of interests between the named representatives and the class, we conclude that the class representatives and class counsel did not adequately represent the absent class members, and for this reason the district court should not have approved the class-action settlement.

Id. at 1161.

3. The *Robin* court's decision does not discuss the precise nature of the relationship between the named representatives and Steiner Diamond. Should it make a difference whether the relationship is primarily or exclusively social, as opposed to business? What about a family relationship?

4. A conflict may also arise because of a class representative's relationship with class counsel. As one court explained:

> Objectors [to the proposed class settlement] contend that the named plaintiffs are inadequate representatives because of their relationship to class counsel. Plaintiff Nathan Malchman is the brother of class co-counsel Irving Malchman. Plaintiff Conway is the sister of the chauffeur of Milton Gould, a senior partner of Shea & Gould [which was serving as class counsel]. Plaintiff Louis Stone is a personal friend of class co-counsel Stanley Kaufman. * * *
>
> There is some authority for the argument that a plaintiff who is a close relative of the attorney may be disqualified as a representative

of the class. The theory is that such a relationship may result in an improper settlement. *See Susman v. Lincoln Am. Corp.*, 561 F.2d 86, 90–91 (7th Cir. 1977). In that case class action status was denied because plaintiff was the brother of the attorney. However in *Fischer v. ITT*, 72 F.R.D. 170 (E.D.N.Y. 1976), the court allowed a class action to proceed where the plaintiff was the father of the attorney. The court analyzed the cases and found that the "touchstone" for denial of class action status was the question of whether the plaintiff had an interest in the attorney's fee.

There is no indication that any of the plaintiffs in the present litigation have an interest in the attorneys' fees or that plaintiffs have acted in any manner other than as normal and proper plaintiffs in a class action. Moreover, one of [the] plaintiffs * * * has no relationship with any of plaintiffs' attorneys.

It is, of course, a matter of common experience in class actions that the named plaintiffs are often people of very little sophistication in financial or legal matters. It is almost always the attorneys who make the litigation decisions, determine strategy, and negotiate settlement terms. In practical fact, the quality of the attorneys is frequently the most important factor in determining the quality of representation.

Malchman v. Davis, 588 F. Supp. 1047, 1057–58 (S.D.N.Y. 1984), *aff'd on other grounds*, 761 F.2d 893 (2d Cir. 1985). Is the standard applied by the court rigorous enough to ensure that the relationship between the class representatives and class counsel will not harm absent class members? Are problems caused by close familial or other relationships sufficient to raise adequacy concerns even when the plaintiff has no claim to, or interest in, the attorneys' fees? *See also London v. Wal–Mart Stores, Inc.*, 340 F.3d 1246, 1249, 1255 (11th Cir. 2003) (where named plaintiff was class counsel's stockbroker and "close friend" since high school, and class counsel's fee far exceeded any individual class member's recovery, court held named plaintiff was inadequate).

5. In *Eubank v. Pella Corp.*, 753 F.3d 718 (7th Cir. 2014), the court reversed a district court's approval of a class settlement on multiple grounds related to adequacy:

The settlement should have been disapproved on multiple grounds. To begin with, it was improper for the lead class counsel to be the son-in-law of the lead class representative. Class representatives are * * * fiduciaries of the class members, and fiduciaries are not allowed to have conflicts of interest without the informed consent of their beneficiaries, which was not sought in this case. Only a tiny number of class members would have known about the family relationship between the lead class representative and the lead class counsel—a relationship that created a grave conflict of interest; for the larger the fee award to class counsel, the better off [the class representative's] daughter and son-in-law would be financially—and (which sharpened the conflict of interest) by a lot. They may well have had an acute need for an infusion of money, in light not only of [lead class counsel's] ethical embroilment, which cannot help his practice, but also of the litigation against him by his former law partners and his need for money to finance his new firm. The appellees * * * point out that [the lead class representative] was one of five class representatives, and the other four didn't have a conflict of interest. But the four other *original* class representatives had opposed the settlement, whereupon they had been replaced by new named plaintiffs—selected by the conflicted lead class counsel.

Id. at 723–24. The court further noted, *inter alia*, that the settlement terms were one-sided in favor of the defendant, the settlement was overvalued by the parties and the court below, and the notice sent to class members was "incomplete and misleading," *id.* at 728. Thus, the court found that "almost every danger sign in a class action settlement that our court and other courts have warned district judges to be on the lookout for was present in this case." *Id.* at 728 (citing cases).

6. An important potential for conflict arises when the claims of named plaintiffs differ materially from those of the class members. In *Amchem Prods., Inc. v. Windsor*, 521 U.S. 591 (1997) (*see* Chapter 8(A)(3)), for example, the putative class included individuals who had been exposed to asbestos and had already suffered injury and those who were exposed but had not yet suffered injury. The Court found that already-injured plaintiffs could not adequately represent those who had suffered no injury: "[F]or the currently injured, the critical goal is generous immediate payments. That goal tugs against the interest of exposure-only plaintiffs in ensuring an ample, inflation-protected fund for the future." 521 U.S. at 626. Could the conflict cited in *Amchem* have been resolved by appointing class representatives who had not manifested injury? What about by dividing the class into two subclasses—the injured and non-injured? *See, e.g., In re Nat'l Football League Players Concussion Injury Litig.*, 821 F.3d 410, 432 (3d Cir. 2016) (finding that creating "two subclasses of players [the injured and the non-injured] guarded against any *Amchem* conflict of interest," and rejecting objectors' adequacy challenge), *cert. denied*, 137 S. Ct. 591 (Dec. 12, 2016); *see also Juris v. Inamed Corp.*, 685 F.3d 1294, 1323–24 (11th Cir. 2012) (stating that "*Amchem* and *Ortiz* appear to hold that Rule 23(a)(4) calls for *some type* of adequate structural protection, which would include, but may not necessarily require, formally designated subclasses," but declining to hold that "the *due process* concept of adequate representation is so rigid and inflexible as to demand formal subclasses" in this instance, a mandatory limited fund case involving allegedly defective silicone breast implants). For another class action where already-injured plaintiffs were held inadequate to represent the interests of those who had not yet manifested injury, *see Stephenson v. Dow Chem. Co.*, 273 F.3d 249 (2d Cir. 2001), *aff'd in part and vacated in part*, 539 U.S. 111 (2003) (discussed in Chapter 10(A)(3)(a)(i)); *see also Dewey v. Volkswagen Aktiengesellschaft*, 681 F.3d 170, 188–90 (3d Cir. 2012) (reversing district court's certification of a class because adequacy requirement not met where interests of representatives "aligned in opposing directions" to those of another group of class members).

7. How definite must a conflict of interest between the named plaintiffs and class members be for the named plaintiffs to be deemed inadequate? Are speculative or potential conflicts enough? *See, e.g., Cummings v. Connell*, 316 F.3d 886, 896 (9th Cir. 2003) ("The Union [defendant] produced no evidence that class members actually possess opposing views regarding the pursuit of the punitive remedy. Without some evidence of an actual conflict, the district court did not abuse its discretion by granting class certification."). In *Valley Drug Co. v. Geneva Pharms. Inc.*, 350 F.3d 1181, 1189 (11th Cir. 2003), the Eleventh Circuit concluded: "[T]he existence of minor conflicts alone will not defeat a party's claim to class certification: the conflict must be a 'fundamental' one going to the specific issues in controversy. A fundamental conflict exists

where some party members claim to have been harmed by the same conduct that benefitted other members of the class." Is this standard sound?

8. In *Waters v. Barry*, 711 F. Supp. 1125, 1127 (D.D.C. 1989), plaintiffs filed a class action challenging a Washington, D.C. curfew statute making it illegal for persons under age 18 to be on the streets of D.C. between 11 p.m. and 6 a.m. The class consisted, among others, of all minors subject to the law and their parents. Defendants argued that the class representatives were not adequate because "not all members [of the class] oppose the curfew * * *." *Id.* at 1131. The court rejected the argument:

> The Court agrees that the proposed class will inevitably include individuals who favor the curfew. In matters of this type, involving a class of this size, differences of opinion are unavoidable. Nevertheless, diversity of opinion within a class does not defeat class certification.
>
> The circumstances of this particular case augment the Court's conclusion that the interests of the class are not *antagonistic* to those of the named plaintiffs. Should the plaintiffs succeed in their challenge to the Act, those members of the class who favor the curfew will not be affected in the least; they may still unilaterally obey the Act's time limits and thereby further each of [the Act's] objectives * * *. The "conflict" or "antagonism" present here is thus largely theoretical; it is fundamentally different from the situation in which a successful class suit would somehow alter the rights or obligations of the dissenting class members.

Id. at 1131–32. Does the court's analysis withstand scrutiny? When should differences between class representatives and absent class members render a class representative inadequate? Can such a conflict always be dealt with by simply appointing additional class representatives?

9. An interesting issue arose in *Biben v. Card*, 1986 WL 1199 (W.D. Mo. 1986), namely, whether the class representatives were inadequate on the ground that they had dismissed certain broker-defendants in a securities fraud suit. The court rejected the adequacy challenge, but found the issue to be a close one:

> In candor, the questions surrounding the deletion of [E.F.] Hutton [and its brokers as defendants in the consolidated *Biben* complaint] strike me as the most serious obstacle to class certification, in particular because no adequate explanation for that decision has been presented. In the absence of any development of documentation of nationwide fault by Hutton, however, it would seem that the possible omitted claims would be individualized ones against particular Hutton brokers. As opposed to the presently named defendants whose alleged misconduct in disseminating written misrepresentations would have affected the entire class (by undermining the integrity of the market and artificially inflating the price of [the defendant company's] stock), the Hutton brokers would not likely have had such classwide impact. The class members would necessarily have dealt with different brokers, many of whom were unaffiliated with Hutton. The joinder of Hutton and/or its brokers, consequently, would cause undue and unnecessary complications in the litigation. Moreover, the interests of class members *vis-a-vis* Hutton (or non-Hutton brokers for that matter) can be safeguarded by the use of a class notice that clearly indicates that claims against brokers that have been asserted

by some * * * shareholders are not involved in this litigation and that any such claims must be pursued outside the context of the present case. With a degree less certainty than in my other rulings, therefore, I conclude that the Hutton problem does not render the named plaintiffs inadequate representatives of the proposed class.

Id. at *9. Given its concern, was the court correct in rejecting arguments that the class representatives were inadequate? What are the interests at stake? Does the proposed notice adequately protect those interests? What is the likelihood that class members will pursue their own separate claims against defendants who are not named in the class action?

10. Does the current approach taken by courts adequately address the conflicts of interest issues that commonly arise in class action litigation? *See* Geoffrey P. Miller, *Conflicts of Interest in Class Action Litigation: An Inquiry Into the Appropriate Standard*, 2003 U. Chi. Legal F. 581, 582–83 (2003) (arguing that current standards are inadequate and proposing that "a conflict of interest should be deemed impermissible if a reasonable plaintiff, operating under a veil of ignorance as to his or her role in the class, would refuse consent to the arrangement").

iv. *Omitting or Deleting Claims to Make Class Certification More Viable*

In *Pearl v. Allied Corp.*, 102 F.R.D. 921 (E.D. Pa. 1984), a case alleging injuries from foam insulation in private homes, plaintiffs filed an amended complaint that sought a medical monitoring fund and punitive damages, but that deleted their earlier claims for personal injuries and breach of express warranty. The court found that plaintiffs were inadequate representatives because, to improve chances of obtaining class certification, they had jeopardized the class members' chances of later bringing the deleted claims. Specifically, under the *res judicata* principle that a litigant must bring in one action all claims arising from the same transaction or occurrence, "class members whose claims would be abandoned by the plaintiffs may find themselves precluded * * * from asserting those claims in subsequent actions." *Id.* at 924. Accord, e.g., *Feinstein v. Firestone Tire & Rubber Co.*, 535 F. Supp. 595, 606 (S.D.N.Y. 1982) ("[A] serious question of adequacy of representation arises when the class representatives profess themselves willing * * * to assert on behalf of the class" only breach of warranty claims involving allegedly defective tires, and not claims for "death, injury, accident related property damage, or other consequential damage * * * ."); *In re Teflon Prods. Liab. Litig.*, 254 F.R.D. 354, 366–68 (S.D. Iowa 2008) (holding that named plaintiffs did not satisfy Rule 23(a)(4) because they had "abandon[ed] their original claims for medical monitoring, and expressly disavow[ed] any current claim for personal injury," and the possibility that a subsequent court could determine that the claims were barred by *res judicata* "prevent[ed] the named plaintiffs' interests from being fully aligned with those of the class"). (Chapter 7(C)(1) contains a detailed treatment of *res judicata* in the class action context.)

Were plaintiffs in *Pearl* and *Teflon Products* inadequate because they deleted certain claims to improve the chances of class certification? Would they have been inadequate had they not brought personal injury or breach of warranty claims initially? Is a representative who decides to bring only limited claims always subject to challenge on adequacy grounds? Although the analysis in *Pearl*, *Feinstein*, and *Teflon Products* was premised upon conflicts between class representatives and unnamed class members, does that analysis make sense? Could it be argued that the representatives and class members share a preference for bringing at least some claims on a class basis, since all (or at least most) class members likely would not bring individual claims in the absence of a class? In other words, is a class action involving *some* claims better than no lawsuits at all? Some courts have rejected the *Pearl/Feinstein/Teflon Products* approach, holding that limiting a class action to only certain claims does not reflect inadequacy of representation. *See, e.g., Marrone v. Philip Morris, USA, Inc.*, 2004 WL 2050485 (Ohio App. 2004) (rejecting adequacy attack premised on fact that plaintiffs in tobacco case sued only for economic damages and not personal injury damages; court reasoned that because class was so limited, individual class members were free to file separate personal injury claims).

v. Ability and Willingness of the Representative to Finance the Lawsuit

In most cases, a plaintiff is not expected to advance the costs of litigation in order to be deemed adequate. As one court has explained:

> Although a few courts have thought it appropriate in certain situations to scrutinize the moving party's ability to pay before certifying a class, most courts have not adopted such a practice. In general, the courts have shunned such inquiries, especially where, as here, the attorneys representing the plaintiffs have indicated a willingness to advance all costs of litigation, and defendants have not disputed their ability to do so.

In re Alcoholic Beverages Litig., 95 F.R.D. 321, 326 (E.D.N.Y. 1982). *But see, e.g., Beal v. Midlothian Indep. Sch. Dist.*, 2002 WL 1033085, at *6 (N.D. Tex. 2002) ("all that is required" to establish a representative's adequacy is to provide proof that the representatives "have committed the necessary funds to prosecute [the] action"); *cf. Weber v. Goodman*, 9 F. Supp. 2d 163 (E.D.N.Y. 1998) (finding both the class representative and class counsel inadequate because the representative had not agreed to advance any of the costs of litigation).

vi. Attacks on the Adequacy Standard

JEAN W. BURNS, DECORATIVE FIGUREHEADS: ELIMINATING CLASS REPRESENTATIVES IN CLASS ACTIONS
42 Hastings L.J. 165, 165, 180–86, 190–191, 194–96, 202 (1990).

The role of the class representative in class actions has become something of an enigma. On a doctrinal level, the Supreme Court at times has treated the named plaintiff as a pivotal figure in the class lawsuit, with the fate of the entire action rising or falling with the status of the representative. Yet, at other times the Court in effect has reduced the representative to nothing more than a figurehead with little or no function. On a practical level, both courts and commentators increasingly acknowledge that the latter view is closer to reality: the named plaintiff plays almost no role in the actual prosecution of the class action, leaving this function for the class attorney.

* * *

* * * [T]he class action simply does not function like the traditional private-rights lawsuit around which most common law jurisprudence and practice has developed. The class action may have some similarity with the traditional lawsuit, in that the class representative occupies the position of a traditional plaintiff or defendant, but that similarity is merely superficial. * * *

First and foremost, unlike the traditional model of litigation, which involves a dispute between two private individuals with unitary interests, the class action is fundamentally a device to resolve the problems of a group of individuals. The class action is not an application of rights, duties, and remedies to an individual case brought by a particular person seeking his day in court. * * * A single action or practice of a corporation or governmental agency may affect hundreds or thousands of people. The class action permits the affected group to challenge the activity and to aggregate (and to some extent average) their individual circumstances and interests in seeking relief. In doing so, moreover, the class action frequently seeks to vindicate a political or social "right" (what some term a "public right") rather than simply the "private right" envisioned by the traditional litigation model.

A second major difference between the class action and the traditional litigation model lies in the role of the client. In traditional litigation, the lawsuit is party-initiated and party-controlled: the disgruntled client hires a lawyer to pursue the client's claim, and the client monitors the lawyer's activities in prosecuting the lawsuit. The class action, in contrast, typically is not initiated or controlled by the class representative. In most class actions, the class attorney first finds the class claim and *then* seeks out a client to be the class representative. The class attorney may use a "professional" class representative; he may find the "client" through an informal * * * network of referrals among class action attorneys; he may engage in nationwide advertising to solicit a class representative. In addition, the class attorney may switch from one class representative to another as the case progresses and different characteristics in the class representative are needed. Regardless of how the class representative is chosen, the class attorney typically makes the decision to initiate the suit, even in those cases in which the representative brings the claim to the lawyer's attention. Furthermore, unlike the client in a traditional lawsuit, the class representative has little or no control over the conduct of litigation once the class action has begun. * * *

This reversal of the traditional attorney-client roles in class actions stems from a number of factors. In part, the economics of the class litigation dictate the change. Unlike the traditional lawsuit, in which the client usually has a larger financial stake than his attorney, the class attorney has a larger stake in the form of attorney fees than the individual class member, who typically is going to recover a modest sum, at best. * * * Furthermore, once the class action has begun, the class representative, having a relatively small financial stake in the lawsuit, is unlikely to invest much time or effort in monitoring the litigation. Instead, the attorney, who has the greater financial interest, will make the litigation decisions unfettered by an intruding client. The class attorney may even seek out a compliant class representative to avoid client intrusion. And even if a class representative wishes to take an active role in the case, he may not be able to do so. Many important decisions in a class action involve complex, procedural matters—decisions that have low visibility but demand a high level of sophistication and expertise to understand and monitor.

The class action also differs from traditional private-rights litigation in that there is not always a unity of interest on the class side of the case. Rather, because the judge frequently can choose between a range of remedies in a class action (unlike the traditional lawsuit in which the remedy typically is derived from the substantive violation), class members may hold differing views on litigation objectives and particularly on remedies or terms of settlement. * * *

Finally, the role of the judge is significantly different in class litigation than in the traditional two-party lawsuit. While in the traditional lawsuit the judge plays only a passive, neutral role, the judge in the class action typically takes on a more activist role in supervising and guiding the litigation. In part, judges in class actions are responding to a perceived need to protect absent class members, some of whom may have a conflict of interest with the named plaintiff or class counsel; in part, the complexity of the class action may dictate a more active judicial involvement. * * *

* * *

Thus, class action practice confirms what class action doctrine has recognized only sporadically: The class lawsuit and the class representative do not function according to the traditional private-rights model. Unlike the traditional client, the class representative plays little part in initiating or shaping the case. Instead, the class attorney controls the litigation, presenting the *class* claims; the representative provides no more than an anecdotal example of the class claim. Furthermore, unlike traditional private-rights litigation, the class action carries with it substantial risk of a conflict of interest between the class representative and some segment of the class. Because of this potential conflict and the complexity of class litigation, judges have naturally assumed, and ultimately been charged with, more activist roles than those taken in traditional litigation.

* * *

Given the confused state of class action doctrine and the diluted if not nonexistent role actually played by the class representative, we must ask: Do we really need the class representative? * * *

* * *

Without the class representative, the court's focus in a class action properly will shift to the class. And without the illusion of a traditional lawsuit, there is a greater chance that courts will recognize that the doctrines developed in the traditional nonclass cases cannot be simply transplanted into the class action. Instead, courts might begin the long overdue task of constructing a class action jurisprudence specifically tailored to address the peculiar problems of class litigation. Courts might focus directly on questions such as: Under what circumstances should we permit a class action to be brought or continued? How can we assure that there will be some meaningful supervision of the class lawyer? How can we increase the likelihood that conflicts within the class will be brought to the court's attention? How should we handle settlements by less than all members of the class?

The existence of the class representative not only masks these real problems, it also wastes judicial and lawyer resources on phantom issues. * * *

* * *

But how, our skeptic asks, will a district court be certain that the proposed class claim is concrete? If he does nothing else, the class representative assures the court that it is not deciding an abstract and theoretical question. Without a class representative, the class attorney becomes a roving ideological plaintiff, free to interfere in matters that do not concern him and about which those directly affected have not complained.

While concreteness is certainly a valid concern, it can be assured without resurrecting the class representative. Specifically, it can be assured by requiring that the class attorney present to the district court some "exemplary class members" during the certification process. These exemplary class members would demonstrate that: (1) the class issue presented in the complaint indeed had arisen in specific, concrete instances; (2) there are class members who want the issue resolved; and (3) there are class members who can fulfill any necessary jurisdictional or administrative requirements. Moreover, the district court could adjust the number of exemplary class members required to match the complexity and breadth of the claims in the particular case. The exemplary class members, however, would not be named plaintiffs, and the fate of the action would not depend on the continued vitality of their particular claims.

Our skeptic may ask about supervision of the class attorney. Is it not likely that some class representatives provide some monitoring of the class attorney, and is this not beneficial? Indeed, we do not permit the class attorney to be the class representative precisely to avoid giving the class attorney undue control over the class lawsuit.

* * *

* * * Under my proposal, the district court would require the class attorney present to the court "class monitors" as part of the class certification process. The job of these monitors would be to supervise the activities of the class lawyer during the various stages of litigation. These class monitors need not be members of the class, and therefore need not be the same persons who are presented as exemplary class members. In many cases, the most effective monitor may be a nonmember organization with a special interest in the subject matter of the lawsuit. Whether a class member or not, the class monitor should possess certain key qualities such as the time and sophistication (including knowledge of the economic realities and substantive merits of the claims) to supervise actively the class attorney in the planning and decision-making involved in the lawsuit.

NOTES AND QUESTIONS

1. Does Professor Burns's proposal have merit? What problems, if any, would result if class representatives were eliminated?

2. What are the merits and drawbacks of eliminating class representatives and relying solely on class counsel, without even having the exemplary class members or monitors suggested by Professor Burns?

PROBLEM

Plaintiffs are two employees of Universal Rent-A-Car who suffer from epilepsy and who claim that Universal has engaged in discrimination in violation of the Americans With Disabilities Act (ADA). They seek to represent a class of Universal employees with disabilities, claiming that the company systematically pays less to individuals with disabilities than to people without disabilities with comparable skills and qualifications. One of the class representatives, Don Waller, is African–American and also claims that Universal engaged in racial discrimination. Waller failed to attend two scheduled deposition dates because he was ill (unrelated to his epilepsy). On neither occasion did he notify anyone in advance that he would not be attending. When he did attend on the third occasion, he could not explain any of the technical requirements for a class action, had never heard of the Americans With Disabilities Act, had never read the complaint, and could not provide the name of the lawyer representing the class. He did, however, testify that he wanted his "day in court to advance the rights of Universal employees throughout the country who are being mistreated because of their disabilities and their race." Judy Minerow, the other class representative, testified falsely at her deposition that she had never received a year-end bonus, even though she had received such bonuses on three occasions. She also testified that she had never before sued under the ADA, when in fact she had sued two previous employers. What arguments can be made that Waller and Minerow are adequate representatives? What arguments can be made to the contrary?

c. Adequacy of Class Counsel

Issues relating to the adequacy of class counsel had long been litigated under Rule 23(a)(4), along with the adequacy of the proposed class representatives. Now, however, following the 2003 revisions to Rule 23, subsection (g) provides a specific set of criteria for courts to apply in determining whether the attorneys in a putative class action will provide adequate legal representation to the class.

The two main cases in this section address the issue prior to the adoption of Rule 23(g), but the courts' analyses remain directly relevant to the adequacy of counsel analysis under 23(g). *See also* Chapter 4(B)(4)(d) (discussing disputes over selection of lead counsel under Rule 23(g)).

GOMEZ v. ILL. STATE BD. OF EDUC.
United States District Court, Northern District of Illinois, 1987.
117 F.R.D. 394.

ZAGEL, DISTRICT JUDGE.

Plaintiffs Jorge Gomez, Marisa Gomez, Efrain Carmona, Alina Carmona, Maria Huerta, Juan Huerta, Cristina Calderon and Jaime Escobedo filed this action requesting class certification, and seeking declaratory and injunctive relief to enjoin the defendants' alleged violations of the Equal Educational Opportunities Act of 1974 (the "EEOA"), the fourteenth amendment and Title VI of the Civil Rights Act of 1964. The defendants subsequently moved to dismiss the complaint pursuant to Fed. R. Civ. P. 12(b)(6). Judge Bua dismissed the action * * * without ruling upon the plaintiffs' request for class certification, and the plaintiffs appealed.

On appeal, the Seventh Circuit affirmed the dismissals of the plaintiffs' claims under the fourteenth amendment and Title VI, but reversed and remanded the dismissals of the plaintiffs' claims under the EEOA and the regulations promulgated pursuant to Title VI. * * * [T]he case was reassigned here. Before the court [is] the plaintiffs' motion for class certification under Fed. R. Civ. P. 23(b)(2) * * *.

I. STATEMENT OF FACTS

* * *

In their complaint, the plaintiffs allege that they have been deprived of the right to equal educational opportunities as the result of the defendants' violations of the EEOA and the regulations promulgated pursuant to Title VI. The plaintiffs[] allege, *inter alia*, that the defendants have [failed to promulgate proper guidelines and failed to ensure compliance with federal and state law].

* * *

II. DISCUSSION

* * *

Adequacy of Representation

Adequate representation is the foundation of all representative actions, and embodies the due process requirement that each litigant is entitled to his day in court. "Because a class action judgment would bind absent class members, strict enforcement of [subsection (a)(4)] is vitally necessary in order to ensure 'that protection to absent parties which due process requires.' " Thus, due process requires that absent class members be adequately represented in order to prevent a collateral attack on the judgment.

* * *

Adequacy of Counsel

The defendants do not take issue with the adequacy of plaintiffs' counsel. Nevertheless, due to the existence of constitutional concerns the Court is obligated to ensure that the case is in the care of competent counsel.[11] Indeed, the Court's obligation to inquire into the adequacy of representation does not end with the motion for certification, but is continuing in order to ensure that due process is satisfied at all stages of the proceeding.

---

[11] We therefore decline to adopt the reasoning that competence will be presumed if a party opposing a motion for class certification fails to challenge the adequacy of counsel. The rationale for this rejection is obvious: the focus of this reasoning is on the *opponent*. We believe that the focus should be on the *absentee members*, and therefore that such an inquiry must be made regardless of the opponent's actions.

Factors involved in an examination of the adequacy of counsel include: the nature of the relationship between the named plaintiffs and counsel; counsel's experience in handling the type of litigation involved; counsel's motivation; counsel's support staff; and counsel's other professional commitments.

Plaintiffs' counsel, the Mexican American Legal Defense and Educational Fund, Inc. (MALDEF), is a national civil rights legal organization which has advocated and defended the rights of Hispanics in many civil rights cases, often in the context of class actions. MALDEF has offices in six cities spread throughout the continental United States, and employs two attorneys in its regional office in Chicago.

Where, as here, attorneys have been found to be adequate in the past, it is persuasive evidence that they will be adequate again. There is no indication that the relationship between any of the named plaintiffs and MALDEF is such that it would undermine counsel's impartiality toward all of the class members in prosecuting this action. Nor is there any evidence that counsel's motivation in bringing this suit as a class action is improper,[12] or that counsel has other professional commitments which are antagonistic to, or which would detract from, its efforts to secure a favorable decision for the class in this case. Indeed, we note that counsel, after the plaintiffs' complaint was initially dismissed, successfully appealed the dismissal to the Seventh Circuit and since has zealously prosecuted the action in this Court. Counsel's performance in this action also indicates that counsel possesses adequate resources to represent the class competently. We find, therefore, that counsel is adequate.

[The court found that the other requirements for certification were satisfied.]

DUBIN V. MILLER
United States District Court, District of Colorado, 1990.
132 F.R.D. 269.

NOTTINGHAM, DISTRICT JUDGE.

[Plaintiff alleged that the defendants, certain officers and directors of a Colorado corporation that eventually declared bankruptcy, engaged in a fraudulent scheme to inflate the price of the corporation's stock. Defendants moved to decertify a class that had been previously certified under procedures available prior to 2003 that allowed a court to "conditionally" certify a class action.]

The case's initial year of life was consumed by procedural wrangling and rule 12 motions practice. During this period plaintiff filed one amended complaint, and defendants filed motions to dismiss, first, the original complaint and then the amended complaint. Plaintiff also filed a motion to certify the class described in the amended complaint. On June 23, 1986, Judge Carrigan dismissed all claims arising under state law, leaving only the claim for violation of rule 10b–5. On December 3, 1986, he denied the motion to certify the class on the ground that, premised as it was on an amended complaint which he had partially dismissed, the motion was

---

[12] For example, the defendants do not claim that the plaintiffs have brought this suit as a class action in order to pressure them [defendants] into settling * * *.

moot. He also ordered plaintiff to file (1) a second amended complaint re-articulating the remaining claim under rule 10b–5 and (2) a motion for class certification, if plaintiff still wished to pursue a claim on behalf of a class.

It took plaintiff over three months to do *anything* in response to Judge Carrigan's order of December 3, 1986. On March 19, 1987, he filed his Second Amended Class Action Complaint and Jury Demand—one day after Judge Carrigan had entered an order directing him to show cause why the case should not be dismissed for failure to prosecute it. Still, he did not file a motion seeking certification of the class for another few months—June 2, 1987. Because of requests for extension of time filed by both sides, the next six months were consumed in briefing the motion and setting (then re-setting) a hearing.

Judge Carrigan conditionally certified a Fed. R. Civ. P. 23(b)(3) class action on January 29, 1988. * * *

Despite Judge Carrigan's admonition [to move the case quickly to trial], the case proceeded no more expeditiously after his ruling than it had before. The named plaintiff's deposition was not concluded until August of 1988. The case was set for a 15-day trial to a jury to commence on October 2, 1989. Seventeen days before trial (September 15, 1989), defendants moved to decertify the class. Five days before trial (September 27, 1989), plaintiff responded to the motion by filing his own motion to bifurcate the trial in order to have the liability issues tried separately from the defenses of the statute of limitations and reliance, which plaintiff conceded might be applicable to his claims. *He still had filed no motion to give any notice to the class.*

On September 27, 1989, because of a conflicting criminal trial, Judge Carrigan vacated the trial date. Not until October 20, 1989, *eighteen days after trial had originally been scheduled to commence*, did plaintiff file a motion seeking court approval of the notice he proposed to send to class members, alerting them to the pendency of a class action. On November 8, 1989, Judge Carrigan entered an order approving the proposed notice. Plaintiff then proceeded to give notice to the class members, despite the pendency of defendants' motion to decertify the class.

It is against this background that I must consider defendants' arguments [to decertify the class] * * *.

Rule 23(a)(4): Adequacy of Representation

[The court found that plaintiff was not an adequate class representative.]

Adequacy of representation also requires that counsel for the class fulfill a fiduciary obligation to the class * * *. Counsel for plaintiff allude to "extensive and successful participation in securities fraud class actions" and list all such actions in which counsel has been involved. This experience is undoubtedly important, but the court is surely entitled to consider what has been done in the case before it in order to evaluate whether counsel has adequately represented the class. This case's unusual procedural history affords a full opportunity to do so.

I am not satisfied that counsel for plaintiff have fulfilled their responsibilities. For example, in addition to the insufficiently-explained absence of [one former director from the case as a defendant], plaintiff has failed to name two other [corporate] directors as defendants, one of whom * * * was a director during 45 months of the 50–month class period. This raises serious questions concerning the conduct of the litigation. The failure to join all responsible parties as defendants further supports the finding that plaintiff and counsel do not adequately represent the class.

More serious is plaintiff's delay in providing notice to the class members and in pursuing the class issues throughout the litigation. Rule 23(c)(2) requires that the best notice practicable be given to class members. Class members need to be alerted to their rights to opt out, to intervene and meaningfully participate in the pending class action, or to object to the adequacy of representation. This notice should go out as promptly as circumstances permit.

Plaintiff and counsel have not complied with the requirement to pursue their action with dispatch and to request notice to the class as promptly as circumstances permitted. Although plaintiff initially proceeded properly (by requesting class certification on February 6, 1986, the complaint having been filed October 1, 1985), interest seems to have waned after Judge Carrigan, having dismissed large parts of the amended complaint, ordered plaintiff to file a new complaint and motion to certify the class, if a class action was still desired. It took six months, and an intervening order threatening dismissal for failure to prosecute, for plaintiff to file the new complaint and motion. More critically, the court conditionally certified the class on January 29, 1988. It was not until October 20, 1989, 21 months after certification, 18 days after the original trial had been scheduled, and four years after the case had been filed, that plaintiff moved for court approval to send notice to the class.

Plaintiff seeks to explain the extraordinary delay in moving for notice to the class by portraying it as part of a considered, deliberate strategy to avoid needless expense in the circumstances presented here. The argument is that, since Judge Carrigan had only conditionally certified the class, it would have been imprudent of plaintiff to move for notice until after final certification. Plaintiff also points to one case permitting notice after trial and entry of judgment, ignoring the suggestion in the case itself that such delayed notice is the rare exception.

I am not persuaded by plaintiff's explanation, in light of the sequence of events here. Plaintiff could have moved for notice at any time, and, if he truly wished to avoid needless expense, he could have asked Judge Carrigan in this motion to review discovery and other events subsequent to the order of conditional certification and to confirm that the case could proceed as a class action. He did not do so. Instead, he waited until defendants had filed motions for decertification based partly on his failure to give notice. He responded in two ways. First, he moved to bifurcate the trial, so that it could proceed without notice to the class. Second, *while the motion to decertify was pending*, he not only moved for notice to the class, but also proceeded to assume the expense of giving notice, never once bringing to Judge Carrigan's attention his concern that he would incur needless expense if the court withdrew its conditional certification—a concern which should have been heightened by the filing of the motion for decertification. I therefore infer that plaintiff's delay in moving for notice to the class was hardly the result of a deliberate, sound strategy to avoid the potentially-needless expense of giving notice; the timing of the motion for notice can only be viewed as part of an ill-conceived, scrambling and belated attempt to blunt one of the better arguments made in the motions to decertify the class. It fully supports the finding that plaintiff and his counsel are not adequate class representatives.

* * *

NOTES AND QUESTIONS

1. Is *Gomez* correct that a court should assess the adequacy of class counsel even if defendants fail to raise the issue? *See* Robert H. Klonoff, *The Judiciary's Flawed Application of Rule 23's "Adequacy of Representation" Requirement*, 2004 Mich. St. L. Rev. 671, 689–90 (discussing numerous cases finding counsel adequate solely because defendants did not object). What criteria does the *Gomez* court use to evaluate the adequacy of counsel? Can *Dubin* be reconciled with *Gomez*? What facts were most significant to the *Dubin* court?

2. Challenging the adequacy of counsel is normally very difficult. *See* Klonoff, *supra*, 2004 Mich. St. L. Rev. at 689 (noting that out of 687 cases ruling on adequacy of counsel during 10-year sample period, only 31 found counsel inadequate; author gives numerous examples of poorly reasoned, conclusory decisions). Nonetheless, isolated cases in addition to *Dubin* have found class counsel inadequate based on their conduct in the case at issue. *See, e.g., Key v. Gillette Co.*, 782 F.2d 5, 7 (1st Cir. 1986) (counsel found inadequate after failing to present expert testimony in understandable way and because of otherwise "lackluster" performance in current case); *McGowan v. Faulkner Concrete Pipe Co.*, 659 F.2d 554, 559 (5th Cir. 1981) (counsel's failure to file timely motion for class certification or to conduct discovery for more than two years demonstrated lack of competence); *Kurczi v. Eli Lilly & Co.*, 160 F.R.D. 667, 679 (N.D. Ohio 1995) (counsel inadequate because he "failed to research legal issues adequately and to construct thoughtful pleadings" and "proved to be incapable of handling the workload involved in processing the extensive discovery material"). Should there be some heightened minimal level of competence (beyond mere bar membership in good standing) required of attorneys who seek appointment as class counsel?

3. Consider whether the following matters should be relevant to the adequacy of class counsel:

  a. An attorney's reputation and prior experience in class action litigation? *See, e.g., Bowling v. Pfizer, Inc.*, 143 F.R.D. 141, 160 (S.D. Ohio 1992) (counsel who had not litigated prior cases involving heart valves was adequate because counsel had substantial experience in class actions and mass tort suits and had obtained special counsel with expertise in area).

  b. An attorney's allegedly improper solicitation of named plaintiffs in past cases? *See Busby v. JRHBW Realty, Inc.*, 513 F.3d 1314, 1323–24 (11th Cir. 2008) (noting that only the most egregious solicitation violations would warrant denial of certification and that the appropriate remedy in most cases would be disciplinary action against the attorney and notice to the class).

c. Whether class counsel has been found guilty in other cases of ethical violations or violations of other court rules? *See, e.g., Kriendler v. Chem. Waste Mgmt., Inc.*, 877 F. Supp. 1140, 1160 (N.D. Ill. 1995) (violation of local rule requiring filing of written contingent fee agreement did not render counsel inadequate).

4. Confronted with class counsel misconduct that "demonstrated a lack of integrity that cast[] serious doubt on their trustworthiness as representatives of the class," the Seventh Circuit announced an adequacy standard that makes it easier to contest adequacy. *See Creative Montessori Learning Ctrs. v. Ashford Gear LLC*, 662 F.3d 913, 917 (7th Cir. 2011). As Judge Posner wrote for the court, misconduct that "creates a serious doubt that counsel will represent the class loyally" renders representation inadequate. *Id.* at 918. The Seventh Circuit criticized the standard applied by the district court—that only the "most egregious misconduct" could ever arguably justify denial of class status—because it would "condone, and by condoning invite, unethical conduct." *Id.*

5. Conflicts of interest between attorneys and class members may lead to a finding that counsel is inadequate. *See, e.g., Zylstra v. Safeway Stores, Inc.*, 578 F.2d 102, 104 (5th Cir. 1978) ("[A]ttorneys who are partners or spouses of named plaintiffs, or who themselves are members of the class of plaintiffs should be subject to a *per se* rule of disqualification under [the canons of ethics] and should not be permitted to serve as counsel for the class."); *Kramer v. Scientific Control Corp.*, 534 F.2d 1085, 1090–92 (3d Cir. 1976) (to the same effect); *Kurczi v. Eli Lilly & Co.*, 160 F.R.D. 667, 679 (N.D. Ohio 1995) (by representing individual plaintiffs in parallel state court action, counsel put "potential class members * * * at risk that counsel will trade off the interests of certain of its clients to the detriment of other clients"). What standards should a court apply in finding an alleged conflict sufficiently serious to hold that counsel is inadequate? Is *any* conflict enough? Must the conflict violate applicable ethical rules?

6. Should the decision concerning whether to find counsel inadequate depend upon when the issue is raised? In *Kramer, supra*, Judge Rosenn addressed this issue in the context of alleged conflicts of interest:

> Where it is possible for the class to obtain substitute counsel without substantially prejudicing the interests of the class or substantially delaying the action, the district court should disqualify counsel. There may be cases that have progressed so far and are so complex that requiring substitution of counsel would substantially delay the termination of the litigation and substantially harm the interests of the class members. In such instances, the district court may allow the litigation to proceed to termination without change in representative or counsel. The choice, in my view, lies in the informed discretion of the district court.

Kramer, 534 F.2d at 1094 (Rosenn, J., concurring). Does Judge Rosenn's analysis make sense? Does the failure to substitute counsel when there is a problem invite collateral litigation by unhappy class members if the defendant wins?

7. Do special adequacy issues arise in the context of public-interest attorneys? One article has noted that "the professional group rights litigator who controls the litigation may, either intentionally or inadvertently, subordinate to his own interests those of the class members." Special Project, *The Remedial Process in Institutional Reform Litigation*, 78 Colum. L. Rev. 784, 877 (1978). Is this concern warranted?

8. Although a proposed class representative's lack of familiarity with the case may support a claim that he or she is inadequate, the client's lack of familiarity is also occasionally cited to show the inadequacy of class counsel. As one court explained in finding class counsel inadequate:

> Even after the court has granted a motion to withdraw presented by three attorneys, Plaintiff remains represented by six attorneys. However, Plaintiff was not given the opportunity to review the complaint before it was filed, nor was she aware of the court where the complaint was initially filed, nor did she know that the case had been transferred to this court, nor did she know anything about the progression of the case. The court is concerned about counsel's failure to keep the [Plaintiff] apprised as to the basic events of this lawsuit, and especially in conjunction with Plaintiff's apparent disinterest in following the progression of the action, the breakdown of communication between counsel and Plaintiff strongly suggests that the putative class would not be adequately represented.

Wein v. Master Collectors, Inc., 1995 WL 550475, at *4 (N.D. Ga. 1995). Is this attack on class counsel legitimate? Whose job is it to ensure that the class representatives are informed—class counsel's or the proposed class representative's? Notably, the *Wein* court also found the proposed class representative inadequate because "she does not understand even her own claim, much less that of the putative class as a whole, and she has abandoned the prosecution of this claim entirely to her attorneys." *Id.*

9. One practice that has received significant scholarly attention is the so-called reverse auction. In *Reynolds v. Beneficial Nat'l Bank*, 288 F.3d 277 (7th Cir. 2002), Judge Posner explained:

> [A reverse auction is] the practice whereby the defendant in a series of class actions picks the most ineffectual class lawyers to negotiate a settlement with in the hope that the district court will approve a weak settlement that will preclude other claims against the defendant. The ineffectual lawyers are happy to sell out a class they anyway can't do much for in exchange for generous attorneys' fees, and the defendants are happy to pay generous attorneys' fees since all they care about is the bottom line—the sum of the settlement and the attorneys' fees—and not the allocation of money between the two categories of expense.

Id. at 282–83. Does a reverse auction constitute inadequate representation by class counsel? If so, why? How can the court avoid such a problem? *See generally* John C. Coffee, *Class Wars: The Dilemma of the Mass Tort Class Action*, 95 Colum. L. Rev. 1343 (1995) (discussing ways of avoiding reverse auctions); Samuel Issacharoff, *Governance and Legitimacy in the Law of Class Actions*, 1999 Sup. Ct. Rev. 337 (discussing class action governance problems, including reverse auctions).

10. In light of the foregoing materials, what standards should be applied to determine adequacy of class representatives and counsel? Should the proper inquiry focus upon whether a potential disqualifier would be relevant to absent plaintiffs? To future persons attempting to challenge a class judgment? Should the inquiry focus upon whether such a factor would so obviously disqualify a party or lawyer that no reasonable person could disagree? Should the benefit of the doubt be in favor of class treatment? In favor of protecting the interests of unrepresented absent parties?

PROBLEM

Two attorneys have brought identical class action suits in the same federal court claiming that the Keater Corporation has discharged dangerous substances from its chemical manufacturing plant, resulting in a higher-than-average incidence of cancer among the surrounding residents. The attorneys have agreed to consolidate the cases and to allow the court to choose one attorney to represent the class.

The first attorney, Joe Gillup, graduated from law school only two years ago. He has a Ph.D. in chemistry and specializes in environmental cases. He has never before handled a class action, never taken a case to trial, and never litigated against a firm of more than three lawyers. (Keater's counsel, Roper & Fromm, is the largest—500 lawyers—and most prominent law firm in the state.) Gillup is a sole practitioner, and his staff consists of a secretary and a part–time paralegal. He is committed to environmental causes and believes that Keater has engaged in egregious misconduct.

The second attorney, John Parker, is the senior partner in the state's premier plaintiffs' firm. He has tried 12 class actions and settled close to 100. His firm has 40 lawyers, all of whom were on law review and most of whom held prestigious judicial clerkships. Parker has little, if any, knowledge of chemistry, but is known to hire only the best experts to assist in his cases. Parker's wife is a partner at Roper & Fromm, but Parker has opposed the Roper firm in several cases. Recently, Parker was disciplined by the state bar for withholding critical documents in a case and falsely asserting in an affidavit that no such documents existed. Several other serious ethical charges involving document destruction are pending against him. In the last year, Parker settled a number of asbestos cases for more than $40 million. Since that time, he has spent half his time in his villa in France, delegating much of his caseload to others at his firm.

Which attorney should the court select to represent the class (and why)?

d. Disputes Over Selection of Lead Class Counsel

Subsection 23(g), which was added to Rule 23 as part of the 2003 amendments, makes explicit the court's responsibilities in appointing lead class counsel. Subdivision 23(g)(1) provides that "Unless a statute provides otherwise, a court must appoint class counsel." The Rule goes on to enumerate four specific factors the court "must consider," *see* 23(g)(1)(A)(i)–(iv), and then adds that the court "may" also "consider any other matter pertinent to counsel's ability to fairly and adequately represent the interests of the class * * *." Rule 23(g)(1)(B).

Prior to the 2003 amendments, Rule 23 did not explicitly cover the appointment process. Courts, however, generally considered class counsel's qualifications under the adequacy of representation requirement of Rule 23(a)(4), generally looking to the types of factors now spelled out in 23(g). To a large extent, then, 23(g) simply codified the preexisting case law in this area.

In the following excerpt, written as a guide for the district court judge hearing a class action, the authors (including federal judge Rothstein) explain several general approaches to the appointment of class counsel.

Barbara J. Rothstein & Thomas E. Willging, Managing Class Action Litigation: A Pocket Guide for Judges

Federal Judicial Center (3d ed. 2010), at 7–8.

There are at least five approaches to selection of counsel in class action litigation. * * *

A. Single-lawyer model

In the typical class action, the lawyer who filed the case will be the only logical choice for appointment as class counsel. That lawyer may have investigated the case independently or may have spoken with government regulators, investigative journalists, or other public information sources. In those cases, the task of selecting counsel consists of determining that the filing attorney satisfies Rule 23(g) standards, that is, has the requisite knowledge of the substantive law, class action legal experience, and financial and staff resources to represent the class adequately. That attorney, of course, must not have a conflict of interest with the class.

B. Private ordering

In high-stakes, high-profile class action litigation, entrepreneurial plaintiff attorneys often compete to play the lead role. This competition may be heightened when the case piggybacks on a case investigated and perhaps litigated or prosecuted by a governmental entity. Nonetheless, substantial resources may be necessary to finance the expenses of the litigation. Most often, attorneys in such cases attempt to resolve the competition by "private ordering," that is, by agreeing to divide the labor, expenses, and fees. To safeguard the interests of the class and to prevent unnecessary litigation and overstaffing, you may want to review those agreements (which will be subject to disclosure upon settlement in any event).

C. Selection by the judge

In the absence of private ordering, you will have to select among competing counsel by reviewing submissions based on the factors identified in Rule 23(g)(1)(C). That section explicitly permits you to include in the order of appointment "provisions about the award of attorney fees or nontaxable costs." Few judges have unilaterally imposed strict limits on fees in the order of appointment. Consider, however, requesting that counsel submit *ex parte* or under seal a proposed budget for fees in the case. The budget would serve as an *ex ante* record of the projected time and expense the case might require; judicial review of a proposed fee award at the end of the case would still be necessary, but would most likely be easier.

D. Empowered plaintiff model

As mentioned earlier, Rule 23(g) presents explicit criteria and a procedure for appointing counsel to represent the class. For securities class actions [discussed in Chapter 10(C)], the Private Securities Litigation Reform Act (PSLRA) directs you to employ a special procedure for selecting an "empowered" lead plaintiff (presumptively one with sizable claims), who, in turn, has the right to select and retain class counsel, subject to your approval.

E. Competitive bidding

In a very narrow set of cases, a few courts have used competitive bidding to select counsel. After an intensive study, a task force in the Third Circuit concluded that competitive bidding "should be an exception to the rule that qualified counsel can be selected either by private ordering or by judicial selection of qualified counsel * * *." *Third Circuit Task Force Report on Selection of Counsel*, 74 Temp. L. Rev. 689, 741 (2001).

NOTES AND QUESTIONS

1. Of the five approaches set out by the *Pocket Guide for Judges*, which, if any, seems most likely to ensure that the interests of the class members are adequately represented?

2. Both prior to and following the addition of Rule 23(g), courts have sometimes appointed joint lead counsel or a multi-member group of attorneys. *See, e.g., Fields v. Wolfson*, 41 F.R.D. 329 (S.D.N.Y. 1967). Occasionally, the court will restrain other attorneys representing members of the class from interfering with the litigation in order to discourage duplicative efforts. *See, e.g., Percodani v. Riker–Maxson Corp.*, 51 F.R.D. 263 (S.D.N.Y. 1970) (prohibiting attorney other than lead counsel from moving for summary judgment), *aff'd*, 442 F.2d 457 (2d Cir. 1971). Courts must also be careful, however, not to impair the ability of attorneys who are not lead counsel to represent their clients.

e. Adequacy of Pro Se Litigants

Should *pro se* prisoners have the right to file class actions on behalf of other prisoners? That question presents peculiar issues relating to "adequacy of counsel." Consider the following case.

OXENDINE V. WILLIAMS
United States Court of Appeals, Fourth Circuit, 1975.
509 F.2d 1405.

Before BUTZNER, RUSSELL, and FIELD, CIRCUIT JUDGES.

PER CURIAM.

Seeking injunctive relief and damages for alleged deprivation of constitutional rights, Craig M. Oxendine brought this *pro se* class action under 42 U.S.C. § 1983 for himself and all other inmates of the Caswell County Unit of the North Carolina Department of Correction. He alleged five constitutional violations: (1) inmates are denied adequate medical treatment; (2) living conditions are so crowded and unsanitary as to constitute a threat to their health; (3) inmates are denied sufficient clean clothing; (4) inmates are denied reasonable access to the courts; and (5) inmates are not allowed physical contact with their families. After considering affidavits submitted by both parties, the district court granted summary judgment for the defendant against Oxendine and the class consisting of "all inmates incarcerated at the Caswell County Unit."

Oxendine's request for an injunction against prison policies that affect all inmates places this class action under Fed. R. Civ. P. 23(b)(2). A judgment against him may prevent the other inmates from later raising the same claims. Fed. R. Civ. P. 23(c)(2). It follows that unless he can "fairly and adequately protect the interest of the class," he may not represent it.

Fed. R. Civ. P. 23(a)(4). Ability to protect the interests of the class depends in part on the quality of counsel, and we consider the competence of a layman representing himself to be clearly too limited to allow him to risk the rights of others. Neither Oxendine nor any other prisoner has assigned error to the class aspect of this case, but it is plain error to permit this imprisoned litigant who is unassisted by counsel to represent his fellow inmates in a class action.

[The court proceeded to address Oxendine's individual claims.]

NOTES AND QUESTIONS

1. Did the *Oxendine* court adopt a *per se* rule that a *pro se* litigant cannot be adequate class counsel? What would be the justification for such a rule?

2. Should a *per se* rule apply in *pro se* cases even if no lawyer is willing to take the case? Assuming that a *pro se* plaintiff is knowledgeable about basic legal principles, should he or she be permitted to represent others similarly situated? Would this constitute the unauthorized practice of law?

CHAPTER 3

CLASS CERTIFICATION: RULE 23(b)

■ ■ ■

Chapter 2 focused on the threshold requirements for class certification, as well as the requirements under Rule 23(a). In addition to satisfying all of those requirements, however, a proposed class action must satisfy at least one of the subsections of Rule 23(b).

Recall from Chapter 1 that Rule 23(b) has three subdivisions, and that one of those subdivisions—23(b)(1)—is further broken down into two additional parts, denoted (A) and (B). Rule 23(b)(1)(A) permits a class action when a party opposing the class would otherwise face individual adjudications that would pose a risk of creating incompatible standards of conduct. Rule 23(b)(1)(B) permits a class action when individual litigation otherwise risks the ability of class members to protect their rights or interests, such as when a defendant has only a limited fund available to satisfy the claims of many claimants. Rule 23(b)(2) provides that a class may be certified when a party opposing the class has acted (or refused to act) in the same manner toward a definable group, thus making it appropriate to render declaratory or injunctive relief to that group. Finally, Rule 23(b)(3) permits a class to be certified when one or more questions of law or fact common to a group of litigants "predominate" over any individualized issues that would have to be litigated and, in light of all relevant circumstances, adjudication of the lawsuit as a class action would be the fairest and most efficient manner of resolving the controversy. This chapter focuses on the requirements of Rule 23(b).

A. RULE 23(b)(1)

As noted above, Rule 23(b)(1) has two subdivisions—(b)(1)(A) and (b)(1)(B)—and satisfying either one (in addition to Rule 23(a)) is sufficient to permit a class action to be certified. Rule 23(b)(1)(A) focuses on the party *opposing* the class—typically the defendant—and authorizes a class action if:

> [P]rosecuting separate actions by or against individual class members would create a risk of * * * inconsistent or varying adjudications with respect to individual class members that would establish incompatible standards of conduct for the party opposing the class[.]

Rule 23(b)(1)(B), by contrast, focuses on protecting the class members. It authorizes a class action if:

> [P]rosecuting separate actions by or against individual class members would create a risk of * * * adjudications with respect to individual class members that, as a practical matter, would be dispositive of the interests of the other members not parties to the

individual adjudications or would substantially impair or impede their ability to protect their interests[.]

This section addresses a variety of issues arising under Rules 23(b)(1)(A) and (b)(1)(B). Such actions are much less common than actions under Rules 23(b)(2) or (b)(3). Nonetheless, the legal issues have been as challenging (and sometimes as contentious) as those raised under Rules 23(b)(2) and (b)(3).

1. RULE 23(b)(1)(A) ACTIONS

ADVISORY COMMITTEE NOTES TO 1966 AMENDMENT TO RULE 23(b)(1)(A)

One person may have rights against, or be under duties toward, numerous persons constituting a class, and be so positioned that conflicting or varying adjudications in lawsuits with individual members of the class might establish incompatible standards to govern his conduct. The class action device can be used effectively to obviate the actual or virtual dilemma which would thus confront the party opposing the class. The matter has been stated thus: "The felt necessity for a class action is greatest when the courts are called upon to order or sanction the alteration of the *status quo* in circumstances such that a large number of persons are in a position to call on a single person to alter the *status quo*, or to complain if it is altered, and the possibility exists that [the] actor might be called upon to act in inconsistent ways." * * * To illustrate: Separate actions by individuals against a municipality to declare a bond issue invalid or condition or limit it, to prevent or limit the making of a particular appropriation or to compel or invalidate an assessment, might create a risk of inconsistent or varying determinations. In the same way, individual litigations of the rights and duties of riparian owners, or of landowners' rights and duties respecting a claimed nuisance, could create a possibility of incompatible adjudications. Actions by or against a class provide a ready and fair means of achieving unitary adjudication.

a. Core Principles

Rule 23(b)(1)(A) has been used to certify classes in a wide variety of factual circumstances. Examples include: a suit to enjoin state officers from terminating unemployment compensation without a hearing (*see Crow v. Cal. Dep't of Human Res.*, 325 F. Supp. 1314 (N.D. Cal. 1970), *rev'd on other grounds*, 490 F.2d 580 (9th Cir. 1973), *vacated*, 420 U.S. 917 (1975)); an action for a declaratory judgment with respect to an insurance company's liability on an illegally declared dividend (*see Fed. Sav. & Loan Ins. Corp. v. Huttner*, 265 F. Supp. 40 (N.D. Ill. 1967), *aff'd on other grounds*, 401 F.2d 58 (7th Cir. 1968)); an action seeking a declaration of eligibility for deferments under the Selective Service Act (*see Gregory v. Hershey*, 51 F.R.D. 188 (E.D. Mich. 1970)); a case seeking injunctive relief against radioactive plant emissions (*see Boggs v. Divested Atomic Corp.*, 141 F.R.D. 58 (S.D. Ohio 1991)); a case by convicted sex offenders challenging the constitutionality of a state statute prohibiting them from living within 2,000 feet of a school or child-care facility (*see Doe v. Miller*, 216 F.R.D. 462 (S.D. Iowa 2003)); a case by participants of an employee savings and incentive plan against fiduciaries for failing to provide information bearing on the value of company stocks and to manage plan assets prudently (*see In re CMS Energy ERISA Litig.*, 225 F.R.D. 539 (E.D. Mich. 2004)); and an action brought by Hispanic prisoners in the District of Columbia's correctional facilities, challenging the constitutionality of the District's policy of denying alien prisoners transfers to minimum-security facilities (*see Franklin v. Barry*, 909 F. Supp. 21 (D.D.C. 1995)). Courts have imposed limits on Rule 23(b)(1)(A), however. Consider the following.

IN RE DENNIS GREENMAN SEC. LITIG.
United States Court of Appeals, Eleventh Circuit, 1987.
829 F.2d 1539.

Before HILL and JOHNSON, CIRCUIT JUDGES, and HENLEY, SENIOR CIRCUIT JUDGE [(8th Cir.), by designation].

HENLEY, SENIOR CIRCUIT JUDGE.

This is an appeal from a final district court judgment certifying a class action and approving a settlement in a complex securities fraud case. The plaintiffs are victims of a fraud perpetrated by Dennis Greenman, a securities seller. The defendants are brokerage firms that employed Greenman while he was conducting the fraud as well as others who might be liable for Greenman's actions. Appellants, some alleged victims of Greenman, contend that the district court erred in certifying the class for settlement purposes pursuant to Fed. R. Civ. P. 23(b)(1). For reasons to be stated, we reverse.

Greenman conducted the fraud over a period of almost four years beginning in mid-1977 as a broker for or associate of three different brokerage firms: Merrill Lynch, Pierce, Fenner & Smith Incorporated (Merrill Lynch), Paine Webber Jackson & Curtis, Inc. (Paine Webber), and Barclay Financial Corp. (Barclay). Greenman represented himself as operating a riskless, highly profitable computer-driven arbitrage system. In actuality, he was investing the funds in high risk options trading and lost substantial sums of money. Greenman also converted funds to his own use. He concealed the fraud by diverting the genuine account statements to false post office box addresses and forwarding fictitious account statements. Investors who sought to withdraw funds from their accounts were paid with other investors' funds in a "Ponzi" type scheme. Over 600 people participated in the scheme either dealing directly with Greenman or investing through other participants. They invested approximately $86 million, of which they lost over $50 million.

In April of 1981, the Securities and Exchange Commission filed a complaint against Greenman, Barclay, and its principals seeking injunctive relief and the appointment of a receiver. The district court issued an injunction against Greenman and appointed a receiver to collect and distribute the investors' assets under the custody or control of Greenman, Barclay, or A.G. Becker. The receiver found that the investors' funds were commingled to the extent that specific ownership could not be traced. * * * [The court ordered interim distributions of] $17,280,681.76, which represented a 35% return of net investments to investors with net losses.

Subsequent to the SEC's disclosure of the fraud, numerous suits were filed on behalf of investors. Among the suits, a complaint was filed on behalf of all people and entities who lost investments. The class action complaint named as defendants: Greenman, Paine Webber, Barclay, A.G. Becker, Inc., and various officers of Paine Webber and Barclay. The plaintiffs alleged violations of [federal and state securities laws, as well as common law claims. Plaintiffs sought compensatory and punitive damages.]

After receiving advice from counsel and conducting hearings, the district court consolidated and stayed the individual suits and certified a class action pursuant to Fed. R. Civ. P. 23(b)(1). * * *

After a year and a half of discovery, the parties began to seek a settlement. * * * The parties reached an agreement. Adherence to the agreement was conditioned upon the district court certifying a class action pursuant to Rule 23(b)(1). The district court certified a class for settlement purposes pursuant to Rule 23(b)(1) and approved the settlement.

In certifying the class, the district court * * * emphasized the special circumstances of the case. * * * [T]he district court feared that individual actions would cause the defendants to face incompatible standards of conduct or create for them inconsistent adjudications. * * *

A group of plaintiffs, named the *Baer* plaintiffs, brought this appeal challenging the district court's class certification under Rule 23(b)(1). Appellants contend that the class should have been certified pursuant to Rule 23(b)(3) to allow class members to opt out.

* * *

* * * We note that the propriety of certification under the various subsections [of Rule 23(b)] is quite controversial and not well defined. At stake are the nature of the notice to be given to class members and their right to opt out from or refuse to be part of the class. Notice of options must be given only in the (b)(3) case. Fed. R. Civ. P. 23(c)(2). Members of a (b)(3) class, but not those of a (b)(1) class, may choose to opt out and not be bound by the judgment. Fed. R. Civ. P. 23(c)(3). These practical differences affect the ability of plaintiffs to bring class actions as well as their attractiveness to defendants. Applying the various subsections of Rule 23(b) requires a balance between an individual's due process rights and the judiciary's need to expedite the orderly resolution of conflict.

* * *

As a threshold consideration to certification under sub-part A [of Rule 23(b)(1)], it must be ascertained that separate actions would result if the class was not certified pursuant to Rule 23(b)(1). It is clear in this case that separate actions would be filed if the class was not certified pursuant to Rule 23(b)(1). At the time the district court first certified the class, twenty-five separate actions were pending. Indeed, the appellants bring this appeal for the purpose of prosecuting or being able to prosecute their own actions. Consequently, this threshold concern is satisfied.

The identity of judicial action that creates "inconsistent or varying adjudications" is not clear. Many courts confronting the issue have held that Rule 23(b)(1)(A) does not apply to actions seeking compensatory damages. These courts reason that inconsistent standards for future conduct are not created because a defendant might be found liable to some plaintiffs and not to others. Implicit in these decisions is the view that only actions seeking declaratory or injunctive relief can be certified under this section. Underlying is the concern that if compensatory damage actions can be certified under Rule 23(b)(1)(A), then all actions could be certified under the section, thereby making the other sub-sections of Rule 23 meaningless, particularly Rule 23(b)(3).

Albeit reluctantly, we must agree. Although sound criticism exists for this interpretation, the Advisory Committee Notes support the proposition that (b)(1)(A) certification is for cases seeking injunctive and declaratory relief. The relevant Note states that the section is proper in suits to invalidate a bond issue, to declare the rights and duties of riparian owners or landowners, or to abate a common nuisance. Since the plaintiffs sought compensatory damages, the district court erred by certifying the class pursuant to (b)(1)(A).

* * *

[In addition to reversing the district court's certification ruling under Rule 23(b)(1)(A), the court held that the district court also erred in certifying a class under Rule 23(b)(1)(B).]

NOTES AND QUESTIONS

1. The *Dennis Greenman* court ruled that, for Rule 23(b)(1)(A) to apply, it is necessary that separate adjudications "would" otherwise result. Is that standard consistent with the language of Rule 23(b)(1)(A)? How confident should a court be about the risk of multiple adjudications?

2. In ruling that Rule 23(b)(1)(A) is limited to cases seeking declaratory and injunctive relief, the *Dennis Greenman* court is in the majority. *See, e.g., La Mar v. H & B Novelty & Loan Co.*, 489 F.2d 461, 466 (9th Cir. 1973) (actions involving money damages will "[i]nfrequently, if ever" qualify under Rule 23(b)(1)(A)); *In re Copley Pharm., Inc., "Albuterol" Prods. Liab. Litig.*, 158 F.R.D. 485, 490 (D. Wyo. 1994) (refusing to certify Rule 23(b)(1)(A) class of plaintiffs who allegedly suffered injuries (or death) using defendant's prescription medication for respiratory disorders; although plaintiffs sought declaratory relief, their "central" claim was for "monetary" damages).

Indeed, even if declaratory relief is sought, Rule 23(b)(1)(A) certification will be denied if the requested relief is simply a declaration that defendants are liable to plaintiffs for damages. For example, in *McDonnell Douglas Corp. v. United States District Court*, 523 F.2d 1083 (9th Cir. 1975), plaintiffs sought class certification under Rule 23(b)(1)(A) in an air crash case seeking damages and a declaration of defendants' liability. In reversing the district court's order granting class certification, the court of appeals held:

> The district court found [that Rule 23(b)(1)(A)'s requirements were] met in this case because if separate actions were maintained, defendants might be held liable in some actions but not in others. This conclusion is untenable. * * *
>
> * * * [A] judgment that defendants were liable to one plaintiff would not require action inconsistent with a judgment that they were not liable to another plaintiff. By paying the first judgment, defendants could act consistently with both judgments. *The declaratory relief sought by plaintiffs does not alter this conclusion. They seek only*

a declaration of liability. They have not specified, and we cannot discern, what obligations such a declaration would impose upon defendants that a judgment for damages would not.

Id. at 1086 (emphasis added). Did the *McDonnell Douglas* court construe Rule 23(b)(1)(A) appropriately?

3. The *Dennis Greenman* court acknowledged that "sound criticism" exists for the view that Rule 23(b)(1)(A) cannot be used to certify actions involving compensatory damages. Consider the following:

> [I]f various fact finders reach inconsistent conclusions about the same set of facts, the defendant (and others in similar circumstances) is left without any guidance concerning the legality of its conduct, which may serve important legitimate aims. * * * [D]efendants and plaintiffs alike have compelling interests in consistent liability determinations, interests that can and should be addressed. Therefore, certifying (b)(1)(A) classes to promote these interests, even in cases in which there is no danger of conflicting equitable decrees, is fully compatible with the language and policy of the rule.

Note, *Class Certification in Mass Accident Cases Under Rule 23(b)(1)*, 96 Harv. L. Rev. 1143, 1154–55 (1983). If the approach of the Harvard Note were applied, under what circumstances would a proposed action that satisfies Rule 23(a) *not* satisfy Rule 23(b)(1)(A)? Would the other provisions of Rule 23(b) be rendered superfluous?

4. Consistent with the Harvard Note, some older cases rejected the view that Rule 23(b)(1)(A) is improper in cases seeking primarily or exclusively monetary damages. *See, e.g., Hernandez v. Motor Vessel Skyward*, 61 F.R.D. 558 (S.D. Fla. 1973) (certifying Rule 23(b)(1)(A) class in suit alleging food poisoning on cruise ship), *aff'd*, 507 F.2d 1278 (5th Cir. 1975); *In re Gabel*, 350 F. Supp. 624 (C.D. Cal. 1972) (certifying liability issues relating to airplane crash). In *In re Federal Skywalk Cases*, 93 F.R.D. 415 (W.D. Mo. 1982), *vacated on other grounds*, 680 F.2d 1175 (8th Cir. 1982), the court certified a class under Rule 23(b)(1)(A) of persons who allegedly suffered physical, mental, or property damage as a result of the collapse of two skywalks (*i.e.*, elevated pedestrian walkways) in the lobby of the Hyatt Regency Hotel in Kansas City, Missouri in July of 1981, a disaster that killed 114 people. The court reasoned as follows:

> Rule 23(b)(1)(A) directs the Court to consider whether multiple individual suits aimed at determining any or all defendants' liability for compensatory and punitive damages would have an adverse effect on those defendants. The subdivision provides that a class action may be maintained if the prosecution of separate actions by individual members of the class would create a risk of "inconsistent or varying adjudications with respect to individual members of the class which would establish incompatible standards of conduct for the party opposing the class." Thus, in order to consider Rule 23(b)(1)(A) as a proper vehicle for resolving the liability issues, there must be a risk that separate actions will, in fact, be tried if a class action is not certified.

> Given the nature of the personal injury and punitive damage claims filed in this litigation, this Court would be embarking on utter naivete if it concluded that there was not a substantial likelihood of multiple suits being tried. Not all claimants will be mollified by the amounts offered in settlement, since they have expressed an avowed

determination to try to punish those defendants, if any, which were responsible for the tragic events of July 17[, 1981]. While this Court wholeheartedly encourages the continued settlement of legitimate claims, and is mindful that the vast majority of claims may be settled, it cannot, in good conscience, allow a minority of claimants to take any or all defendants to trial time and time again until a compensatory or punitive damage judgment is obtained.

Though no defendant has expressly moved this Court to certify a Rule 23(b)(1)(A) class action in order to protect it from successive punitive damage awards or from inconsistent adjudications on the liability issues, the Court believes that Rule 23(b)(1)(A) certification is necessary as a ready and fair means of achieving unitary adjudication. One or more of the defendants risk being faced with incompatible standards of conduct if varying or inconsistent adjudications with respect to individual members of the class were obtained on the issues of liability for compensatory or punitive damages. * * *

Since a Rule 23(b)(1)(A) class action on the issues of liability for compensatory and punitive damages offers economy of effort and uniformity of result without imposing undue debilitation of the procedural or substantive safeguards of members of the class or of persons defending against the class action, this Court concludes that a Rule 23(b)(1)(A) class action on the issues of liability for compensatory and punitive damages must be certified.

93 F.R.D. at 423–24. Does the court's rationale make sense given that no defendant sought class certification?

Which approach—the district court opinion in *Skywalk* or the Eleventh Circuit's opinion in *Dennis Greenman*—is more consistent with the text of Rule 23(b)(1)(A)? With the Advisory Committee Notes? With the overall structure and policies of Rule 23(b)? *See* Note, *Mechanical and Constitutional Problems in the Certification of Mandatory Multistate Mass Tort Class Actions Under Rule 23*, 49 Brook. L. Rev. 517, 531–33 (1983) (criticizing district court opinion in *Skywalk*).

5. Although Rule 23(b)(1)(A) and (B) classes are not common, one major area in which courts have found those provisions applicable is litigation involving the Employee Retirement Income Security Act ("ERISA"), 29 U.S.C. §§ 1001 *et seq. See, e.g., Kanawi v. Bechtel Corp.*, 254 F.R.D. 102, 111 (N.D. Cal. 2008) (observing that "[m]ost ERISA class action cases are certified under Rule 23(b)(1)" and certifying the case before it under Rule 23(b)(1)(A)).

b. Medical Monitoring

The following case addresses Rule 23(b)(1)(A) in the context of a medical monitoring claim. *See, e.g., In re Marine Asbestos Cases*, 265 F.3d 861, 866 (9th Cir. 2001) (identifying typical elements of a claim for recovery of medical monitoring costs as requiring plaintiff to prove: (1) plaintiff was significantly exposed to a proven hazardous substance through the defendant's negligence; (2) that exposure proximately caused plaintiff to suffer a significantly increased risk of contracting a serious latent disease; (3) that increased risk makes periodic diagnostic medical examinations reasonably necessary; and (4) monitoring and testing programs exist which make the early detection and treatment of the disease possible and beneficial). Medical monitoring is often sought when a plaintiff has been exposed to a potentially dangerous substance and, while not manifesting signs of injury, is concerned that he or she may do so in the future.

One court has provided the following discussion of this kind of claim:

> Relief in the form of medical monitoring may be by a number of means. First, a court may simply order a defendant to pay a plaintiff a certain sum of money. The plaintiff may or may not choose to use that money to have his medical condition monitored. Second, a court may order the defendants to pay the plaintiffs' medical expenses directly so that a plaintiff may be monitored by the physician of his choice. * * *
>
> However, a court may also establish an elaborate medical monitoring program of its own, managed by court-appointed[,] court-supervised trustees, pursuant to which the plaintiff is monitored by particular physicians and the medical data produced is utilized for group studies. In this situation, a defendant, of course, would finance the program as well as being required by the court to address issues as they develop during the program administration. * * *

Day v. NLO, Inc., 144 F.R.D. 330, 335–36 (S.D. Ohio 1992), *vacated in part on other grounds*, 5 F.3d 154 (6th Cir. 1993). Before analyzing the case below, consider how one might argue in favor of or against certifying a medical monitoring claim under Rule 23(b)(1)(A).

IN RE TELECTRONICS PACING SYS., INC., ACCUFIX ATRIAL "J" LEADS PROD. LIAB. LITIG.

United States District Court, Southern District of Ohio, 1997.
172 F.R.D. 271.

SPIEGEL, SENIOR DISTRICT JUDGE.

BACKGROUND

A. The Parties

This is a products liability action concerning pacemakers containing the Accufix Atrial "J" Lead. Plaintiffs in this action are recipients of the Accufix Atrial "J" Lead Pacemaker Model 330–801 and Model 329–701 ("J" Lead).

Defendant, TPLC, Incorporated ("TPLC"), is a Delaware corporation engaged in the business of designing, manufacturing, and marketing medical devices including the Accufix Atrial "J" Lead pacemakers at issue in this case. They manufactured the "J" Lead pacemakers Models 330–801 and 329–701 from 1988 until 1994. Defendant, Telectronics Pacing Systems, Incorporated ("TPSI"), is also a Delaware corporation. TPSI's sole business is to hold certain industrial property rights, real estate and the equity interest in TPLC.

* * *

B. The "J" Lead Controversy

A pacemaker is a device that uses electrical impulses to reproduce or regulate the rhythms of the heart. It is driven by a battery and connected to the heart by leads and electrodes.

The heart pacing system at issue consists of three main parts: a pulse generator, leads, and a programmer. Pacemaker Models 330–801 and 329–701 utilize a retention wire to hold the atrial lead in the shape of a "J." * * *

The retention wire is encased in polyurethane insulation and bends back and forth within the system. The bending has caused the retention wire to break in some instances and poke through the polyurethane. The retention wire is not electrically active in the pacing circuit. Consequently, it has nothing to do with the conduction of the electrical signal or the operation of the pacing system. A fracture, however, can cause serious injury to the heart or blood vessels if it pokes through the polyurethane.

Approximately 25,000 pacemakers with "J" Leads were implanted in hearts of United States residents. Between December 1988 and February 1993, TPLC received reports of at least seven fractures of "J" Lead retention wires. On October 21, 1994, TPLC notified the Food and Drug Administration ("FDA") that it was recalling all unsold leads. Telectronics' President, James W. Dennis, then sent a letter to all doctors on November 3, 1994, notifying them that TPLC was voluntarily recalling all un-implanted Accufix Atrial "J" Lead pacemakers, Models 330–801 and 329–701.

By August 1996, TPLC had received notice of at least thirty-two injuries due to fractures, including six deaths. Additionally, eight others have died while having their lead extracted. On February 10, 1995, TPLC estimated the incidence of suspected fracture at 12%. Other TPLC documents indicate that the fracture rate may be as high as 20%.

In response to the fracture problem, TPLC has done three things to control the situation. First, TPLC has established the Accufix Research Institute ("ARI") to manage the lead recall. The ARI communicates with doctors and patients concerning patient management recommendations. ARI is conducting a Multi–Center study ("MCS") involving twelve hospitals to monitor a subset of leads over time. ARI analyzes the data from the MCS to assess the risk of injury from the "J" wire fracture as well as the risk of injury from lead extraction.

Secondly, TPLC formed a Physicians Advisory Committee ("PAC") to provide advice concerning clinical management of lead patients. The PAC reviews information from the MCS and other sources. The PAC then makes recommendations to the ARI concerning patient care.

Upon the PAC's recommendation, Telectronics sent a letter to doctors advising them that implantees should receive screening for fractures every six months. The letter stated [that because fluoroscopic screening could detect lead fractures before those fractures injured patients, Telectronics recommended such screening for all patients implanted with the relevant pacemakers].

* * *

Finally, TPLC has agreed to "reimburse reasonable unreimbursed medical expenses for screening and lead extraction that are consistent with patient management guidelines."

C. Procedural History

Plaintiffs, Elise and Eugene Owens, filed the lead action in this case on February 13, 1995, alleging injury due to a defective "J" Lead. Plaintiffs allege that it was TPLC's negligent manufacture or design of the "J" Lead that causes the retention wire to fracture. * * *

* * * On July 20, 1995, Plaintiffs filed an Amended and Consolidated Master Class Action Complaint asserting thirteen [common law] claims for relief * * *.

The Court initially certified a worldwide class of all "J" Lead implantees for the common issues of medical monitoring, negligence, strict liability, fraud, misrepresentation, and breach of warranty. * * * On July 16, 1996, the Court granted [TPLC's] motion to reconsider and decertified this case as a class action (hereinafter Decertification Order).

D. Class Structure

Plaintiffs have now filed a Renewed Motion for Class Certification. * * *

* * * Plaintiffs propose one nationwide subclass for all medical monitoring claims. It is defined as follows:

> * * * all persons who have had the Accufix atrial "J" pacemaker leads, Model 330–801 and Model 329–701 placed in their bodies whose leads have not been explanted and who seek the establishment of a medical monitoring and research program.

The medical monitoring program which Plaintiffs seek would provide diagnostic testing for each class member [and] conduct research on better methods of detecting fractured leads and determine safer methods for removing the fractured leads.

[The court first found that the medical monitoring class satisfied Rule 23(a).]

* * *

III.

Elements of Rule 23(b) and Medical Monitoring Class

* * *

A. Class Certification of Medical Monitoring Pursuant to Rule 23(b)(1)(A).

Rule 23(b)(1)(A) states that class certification is proper if separate actions "would create a risk of inconsistent or varying adjudications with respect to individual members of the class which would establish incompatible standards of conduct for the party opposing the class. . . ." Fed. R. Civ. P. 23(b)(1)(A). "The phrase 'incompatible standards of conduct' is thought to refer to the situation where different results in separate actions would impair the opposing party's ability to pursue a uniform continuing course of conduct." Charles A. Wright, Arthur R. Miller & Mary K. Kane, 7A *Federal Practice & Procedure*, § 1773 at 431 (2d ed. 1986) (citing cases). * * *

The medical monitoring claim here is an ideal candidate for class certification pursuant to Rule 23(b)(1)(A) because separate adjudications would impair TPLC's ability to pursue a single uniform medical monitoring program. Presently, TPLC is conducting a research program which is investigating the cause of the fractures, looking for better ways to detect the fractures and seeking safer methods of extracting the damaged leads. Plaintiffs seek the establishment of a medical monitoring program which would include diagnostic testing and research. TPLC asserts that medical monitoring beyond that recommended by TPLC's Physicians' Advisory Committee is not warranted. TPLC's research program is a uniform benefit to the class of "J" lead implantees as a whole. Any judicially-imposed modification of this program would then, by necessity, affect all of the "J" lead implantees. Furthermore, separate judicial orders pertaining to medical monitoring could require TPLC to institute differing types of monitoring programs which TPLC would have to reconcile.

TPLC argues that the recommendations of the Physicians' Advisory Committee are subject to approval by the FDA. TPLC insists that "the Court [will] have to reconcile its involvement in a medical monitoring program with FDA's statutorily mandated oversight function. . . . The potential for unnecessary conflict and expense with no patient benefit is readily apparent, with TPLC caught in an impossible position between the judicial and executive branches of government." Whether FDA regulations preempt or otherwise limit state law tort claims for medical monitoring goes to the merits of the class claims and must be determined at a later date.

However, individual adjudication of implantees' claims for medical monitoring would not alleviate TPLC's fear of conflicting standards of medical monitoring imposed by the judicial branch and executive branch. In fact, the danger of courts imposing conflicting duties upon Telectronics would only be compounded if the question of medical monitoring is not certified as a class action pursuant to Rule 23(b)(1)(A). Presently, there are over 400 individual actions consolidated before this Court by the Judicial Panel for Multidistrict Litigation. [*See* Chapter 12 (discussing the JPML)]. Certainly, a large number of similar cases are pending in state courts across the country. Thus, TPLC could still face multiple and conflicting orders rendered from different courts regarding the scope and necessity of a medical monitoring program which may also conflict with FDA imposed requirements. Accordingly, the Court CERTIFIES the medical monitoring sub-class under Rule 23(b)(1)(A).

* * *

[The court also found that certification of a medical monitoring class was proper under Rule 23(b)(3).]

* * *

NOTES AND QUESTIONS

1. Is *Telectronics Pacing Systems* consistent with the reasoning of *Dennis Greenman*?

2. Compare *O'Connor v. Boeing North American, Inc.*, 180 F.R.D. 359 (C.D. Cal. 1997), in which plaintiffs alleged, *inter alia*, that defendants released hazardous waste during nuclear testing between the 1950s and the 1980s. Plaintiffs claimed that they and the members of the class were at an increased risk of developing cancer, and they sought a fund to establish a medical monitoring program to ensure early detection of diseases resulting from exposure to the hazardous waste. The court refused to certify a Rule 23(b)(1)(A) class, reasoning:

> The Court * * * finds that certification of the Class under 23(b)(1)(A) is inappropriate in this case. Plaintiffs have failed to establish how separate actions in this case will create a risk of "inconsistent adjudications . . . which would establish incompatible standards of conduct" for Defendants. * * * Defendants will not be required to treat all members of the Class alike, because all class members may not qualify for relief in the form of medical monitoring and may not qualify for the additional compensatory, punitive, and exemplary damages that Plaintiffs also seek. Individual issues, such as exposure level, family history, and other risk factors, will dictate whether class members will qualify for the medical monitoring program Plaintiffs propose, which includes not only examinations, but treatment of diseases as well. * * * Therefore, because Plaintiffs have not shown the Court a risk of separate actions establishing incompatible standards of conduct for the Defendants, the Court finds that the class cannot be maintained under Rule 23(b)(1)(A).

Id. at 377. The court distinguished *Telectronics Pacing Systems* as follows:

> Although the court in that case certified a class for a medical monitoring claim under 23(b)(1)(A), the defendant in that case had already established a medical monitoring program for diagnostic testing and research, such that "[a]ny judicially-imposed modification of th[e] program" would affect all class members. Furthermore, the medical monitoring class sought to establish a medical monitoring claim, rather than seek medical monitoring as a form of relief based on a different claim. Thus, if the class prevailed on their claim, the defendant would necessarily be required to treat all class members alike, as all class members would then be eligible for the medical monitoring program by virtue of winning their medical monitoring claim. Finally, court ordered medical monitoring would have to be reconciled with the FDA's statutorily mandated oversight function, a non-issue in the current case.

Id. at 377 n.22. Is the *O'Connor* court's distinction between the two cases persuasive?

3. The *O'Connor* court suggested that a Rule 23(b)(1)(A) class is not appropriate if numerous individualized issues are involved. As discussed in Section (C)(1) of this chapter, Rule 23(b)(3) requires common issues to predominate over individual issues. Is the *O'Connor* court correct that the number of individual issues involved should be relevant under Rule 23(b)(1)(A)?

4. In *Zinser v. Accufix Research Institute, Inc.*, 253 F.3d 1180, 1193–95 (9th Cir.), *opinion amended on denial of reh'g*, 273 F.3d 1266 (9th Cir. 2001), the court focused on the "incompatible standards of conduct" language in Rule 23(b)(1)(A), upholding the district court's denial of class certification. Because the plaintiffs sought the creation of a medical monitoring fund and not a medical monitoring program, the court concluded that the nature of the relief

sought was primarily monetary and thus did not risk incompatible standards of *conduct*.

5. *Zinser* is certainly not an encouraging case for plaintiffs seeking a medical monitoring class under Rule 23(b)(1)(A). Moreover, plaintiffs have not fared much better in seeking medical monitoring classes under Rules 23(b)(1)(B), (b)(2), or (b)(3). Indeed, the court in *Coleman v. Union Carbide Corp.*, 2013 WL 5461855, at *41 (S.D. W. Va. 2013), stated that "[n]o circuit court of appeals has ever approved certification of a medical monitoring class action."

PROBLEM

Several female patients at the Hastings Regional Center, a state-supported mental health care facility, filed suit against the facility alleging that they, and other female patients similarly situated, were victims of numerous assaults and rapes by male patients. They claim that the facility violated the female patients' constitutional rights by failing to provide adequate protection to female patients and failing to remedy the situation in the face of repeated complaints. The suit sought only declaratory and injunctive relief, including the implementation of policies for monitoring patient conduct and for pre-admission screenings. In the actual case raising these facts, the court refused to certify a class under Rule 23(b)(1)(A), although it did grant certification under other subdivisions of Rule 23(b). *See Caroline C. v. Johnson*, 174 F.R.D. 452 (D. Neb. 1996). In its analysis of (b)(1)(A), the court reasoned that "plaintiffs have submitted no evidence indicating that [a danger of incompatible standards of conduct for the defendant] exists," and thus failed to satisfy their burden under Rule 23(b)(1)(A). *Id.* at 468. What kind of evidence could have been sought to establish a basis for certification under (b)(1)(A)?

2. RULE 23(b)(1)(B) ACTIONS

ADVISORY COMMITTEE NOTES TO 1966 AMENDMENT TO RULE 23(b)(1)(B)

This clause takes in situations where the judgment in a nonclass action by or against an individual member of the class, while not technically concluding the other members, might do so as a practical matter. The vice of an individual action would lie in the fact that the other members of the class, thus practically concluded, would have had no representation in the lawsuit. In an action by policy holders against a fraternal benefit association attacking a financial reorganization of the society, it would hardly have been practical, if indeed it would have been possible, to confine the effects of a validation of the reorganization to the individual plaintiffs. Consequently a class action was called for with adequate representation of all members of the class. For much the same reason actions by shareholders to compel the declaration of a dividend[,] the proper recognition and handling of redemption or preemption rights, or the like (or actions by the corporation for corresponding declarations of rights), should ordinarily be conducted as class actions, although the matter has been much obscured by the insistence that each shareholder has an individual claim. The same reasoning applies to an action which charges a breach of trust by an indenture trustee or other fiduciary similarly affecting the members of a large class of security holders or other beneficiaries, and which requires an accounting or like measures to restore the subject of the trust.

In various situations an adjudication as to one or more members of the class will necessarily or probably have an adverse practical effect on the interests of other members who should therefore be represented in the lawsuit. This is plainly the case when claims are made by numerous persons against a fund insufficient to satisfy all claims. A class action by or against representative members to settle the validity of the claims as a whole, or in groups, followed by separate proof of the amount of each valid claim and proportionate distribution of the fund, meets the problem. The same reasoning applies to an action by a creditor to set aside a fraudulent conveyance by the debtor and to appropriate the property to his claim, when the debtor's assets are insufficient to pay all creditors' claims. Similar problems, however, can arise in the absence of a fund either present or potential. A negative or mandatory injunction secured by one of a numerous class may disable the opposing party from performing claimed duties toward the other members of the class or materially affect his ability to do so. An adjudication as to movie "clearances and runs" [see *United States v. Paramount Pictures*, 334 U.S. 131, 144 n.6 (1948), for an explanation of "clearances and runs"], nominally affecting only one exhibitor would often have practical effects on all the exhibitors in the same territorial area. Assuming a sufficiently numerous class of exhibitors, a class action would be advisable.

* * *

[End of Excerpt]

Rule 23(b)(1)(B) has been used under various factual scenarios. Rule 23(b)(1)(B) certification may be appropriate in actions involving labor relations, governmental policies, and trustees' fiduciary obligations, where other people's rights may be implicated by any individual lawsuit. *See, e.g.*, *Lloyd v. City of Phila.*, 121 F.R.D. 246, 247–52 (D. Pa. 1988) (provisionally certifying class seeking to enjoin enforcement of compulsory union membership requirement, because requirement's unconstitutionality would dispose of absent class members' rights); *Wyandotte Nation v. City of Kansas City*, 214 F.R.D. 656, 664–65 (D. Kan. 2003) (federally recognized tribe's pursuit of declaratory relief, recovery of possession of real property, and monetary damages from over 1,362 defendants would implicate rights of absent class members of defendant class). The most common use of Rule 23(b)(1)(B), however, is in the so-called limited fund lawsuit, as described below.

ORTIZ V. FIBREBOARD CORP.
Supreme Court of the United States, 1999.
527 U.S. 815.

JUSTICE SOUTER delivered the opinion of the Court.

This case turns on the conditions for certifying a mandatory settlement class on a limited fund theory under Federal Rule of Civil Procedure 23(b)(1)(B). We hold that applicants for contested certification on this rationale must show that the fund is limited by more than the agreement of the parties, and has been allocated to claimants belonging within the class by a process addressing any conflicting interests of class members.

I.

Like *Amchem Products, Inc. v. Windsor*, 521 U.S. 591 (1997) [*see* Chapter 8(A)(3)], this case is a class action prompted by the elephantine mass of asbestos cases * * *. In 1967, one of the first actions for personal asbestos injury was filed in the United States District Court for the Eastern District of Texas against a group of asbestos manufacturers. * * *

Respondent Fibreboard Corporation was a defendant in the 1967 action. Although it was primarily a timber company, from the 1920's through 1971 the company manufactured a variety of products containing asbestos, mainly for high-temperature industrial applications. As the tide of asbestos litigation rose, Fibreboard found itself litigating on two fronts. On one, plaintiffs were filing a stream of personal injury claims against it, swelling throughout the 1980's and 1990's to thousands of new claims for compensatory damages each year. On the second front, Fibreboard was battling for funds to pay its tort claimants. From May, 1957, through March, 1959, respondent Continental Casualty Company had provided Fibreboard with a comprehensive general liability policy with limits of $1 million per occurrence, $500,000 per claim, and no aggregate limit. Fibreboard also claimed that respondent Pacific Indemnity Company had insured it from 1956 to 1957 under a similar policy. [In 1990, a California state court held that Continental and Pacific were liable for indemnification costs prior to the policies' expiration dates, as well as for defense costs.] The insurance companies appealed.

With asbestos case filings continuing unabated, and its secure insurance assets almost depleted, Fibreboard in 1988 began a practice of "structured settlement," paying plaintiffs 40 percent of the settlement figure up front with the balance contingent upon a successful resolution of the coverage dispute.[2] By 1991, however, the pace of filings forced Fibreboard to start settling cases entirely with the assignments of its rights against Continental, with no initial payment. * * *

Meanwhile, * * * Fibreboard approached a group of leading asbestos plaintiffs' lawyers, offering to discuss a "global settlement" of its asbestos personal-injury liability. * * *

In February 1993, after Continental had lost on both issues at the trial level, and thus faced the possibility of practically unbounded liability, it too joined the global settlement negotiations. Because Continental conditioned its part in any settlement on a guarantee of "total peace," ensuring no unknown future liabilities, talks focused on the feasibility of a mandatory class action, one binding all potential plaintiffs and giving none of them any choice to opt out of the certified class. Negotiations continued throughout the spring and summer of 1993, but the difficulty of settling both actually pending and potential future claims simultaneously led to an agreement in early August to segregate and settle an inventory of some 45,000 pending claims, being substantially all those filed by one of the plaintiffs' firms negotiating the global settlement. The settlement amounts per claim were higher than average, with one-half due on closing and the remainder

---

[2] Because Fibreboard's insurance policy with Continental expired in 1959, before the global settlement [at issue in this case,] the settlement value of claims by victims exposed to Fibreboard's asbestos prior to 1959 was much higher than for victims exposed after 1959, where the only right of recovery was against Fibreboard itself.

contingent upon either a global settlement or Fibreboard's success in the coverage litigation. This agreement provided the model for settling inventory claims of other firms.

With the insurance companies' appeal of the consolidated coverage case set to be heard on August 27, the negotiating parties faced a motivating deadline, and about midnight before the argument, in a coffee shop in Tyler, Texas, the negotiators finally agreed upon $1.535 billion as the key term of a "Global Settlement Agreement." $1.525 billion of this sum would come from Continental and Pacific, in the proportion established by the California trial court in the coverage case, while Fibreboard would contribute $10 million, all but $500,000 of it from other insurance proceeds. The negotiators also agreed to identify unsettled present claims against Fibreboard and set aside an as-then unspecified fund to resolve them, anticipating that the bulk of any excess left in that fund would be transferred to class claimants. The next day, as a hedge against the possibility that the Global Settlement Agreement might fail, plaintiffs' counsel insisted as a condition of that agreement that Fibreboard and its two insurers settle the coverage dispute by what came to be known as the "Trilateral Settlement Agreement." The two insurers agreed to provide Fibreboard with funds eventually set at $2 billion to defend against asbestos claimants and pay the winners, should the Global Settlement Agreement fail to win approval.

On September 9, 1993, as agreed, a group of named plaintiffs filed an action in the United States District Court for the Eastern District of Texas, seeking certification for settlement purposes of a mandatory class comprising three groups: all persons with personal injury claims against Fibreboard for asbestos exposure who had not yet brought suit or settled their claims before the previous August 27; those who had dismissed such a claim but retained the right to bring a future action against Fibreboard; and "past, present and future spouses, parents, children, and other relatives" of class members exposed to Fibreboard asbestos. The class did not include claimants with actions presently pending against Fibreboard or claimants "who filed and, for cash payment or some other negotiated value, dismissed claims against Fibreboard, and whose only retained right is to sue Fibreboard upon development of an asbestos-related malignancy." The complaint pleaded personal injury claims against Fibreboard, and, as justification for class certification, relied on the shared necessity of ensuring insurance funds sufficient for compensation. After Continental and Pacific had obtained leave to intervene as party-defendants, the District Court provisionally granted class certification, enjoined commencement of further separate litigation against Fibreboard by class members, and appointed a guardian *ad litem* to review the fairness of the settlement to the class members.

As finally negotiated, the Global Settlement Agreement provided that in exchange for full releases from class members, Fibreboard, Continental, and Pacific would establish a trust to process and pay class members' asbestos personal injury and death claims. Claimants seeking compensation would be required to try to settle with the trust. If initial settlement attempts failed, claimants would have to proceed to mediation, arbitration, and a mandatory settlement conference. Only after exhausting that process could claimants go to court against the trust, subject to a limit of $500,000 per claim, with punitive damages and prejudgment interest barred. Claims resolved without litigation would be discharged over three years, while judgments would be paid out over a 5- to 10-year period. The Global Settlement Agreement also contained spendthrift provisions to conserve the trust, and provided for paying more serious claims first in the event of a shortfall in any given year.

After an extensive campaign to give notice of the pending settlement to potential class members, the District Court allowed groups of objectors, including petitioners here, to intervene. After an 8-day fairness hearing, the District Court certified the class [under Rule 23(b)(1)(B)] and approved the settlement as "fair, adequate, and reasonable," under Rule 23(e). * * * [It cited] the risk that Fibreboard might lose or fare poorly on appeal of the coverage case or lose the assignment-settlement dispute, leaving it without funds to pay all claims. * * * It found both the "disputed insurance asset liquidated by the $1.535 billion Global Settlement," and, alternatively, "the sum of the value of Fibreboard plus the value of its insurance coverage," as measured by the insurance funds' settlement value, to be relevant "limited funds."

On appeal, the Fifth Circuit affirmed both as to class certification and adequacy of settlement. * * *

Shortly thereafter, this Court decided *Amchem* and proceeded to vacate the Fifth Circuit's judgment and remand for further consideration in light of that decision. [*See* Chapter 8(A)(3).] On remand, the Fifth Circuit again affirmed, in a brief *per curiam* opinion, distinguishing *Amchem* on the grounds that the instant action proceeded under Rule 23(b)(1)(B) rather than (b)(3), and did not allocate awards according to the nature of the claimant's injury. * * *

* * *

III.

A.

Rule 23(b)(1)(B) speaks from a vantage point within the class, [from which the Advisory Committee] spied out situations where lawsuits conducted with individual members of the class would have the practical if not technical effect of concluding the interests of the other members as well, or of impairing the ability of the others to protect their own interests. [In each of the examples cited in the relevant Advisory Committee Note,] the shared character of rights claimed or relief awarded entails that any individual adjudication by a class member disposes of, or substantially affects, the interests of absent class members.

[The Court described various early limited fund actions.]

* * *

B.

The cases forming [the] pedigree of the limited fund class action as understood by the drafters of Rule 23 have a number of common characteristics, despite the variety of circumstances from which they arose. The points of resemblance are not necessarily the points of contention resolved in the particular cases, but they show what the Advisory Committee must have assumed would be at least a sufficient set of conditions to justify binding absent members of a class under Rule 23(b)(1)(B), from which no one has the right to secede.

The first and most distinctive characteristic is that the totals of the aggregated liquidated claims and the fund available for satisfying them, set definitely at their maximums, demonstrate the inadequacy of the fund to pay all the claims. The concept driving this type of suit was insufficiency, which alone justified the limit on an early feast to avoid a later famine. * * *

Second, the whole of the inadequate fund was to be devoted to the overwhelming claims. It went without saying that the defendant or estate or constructive trustee with the inadequate assets had no opportunity to benefit himself or claimants of lower priority by holding back on the amount distributed to the class. The limited fund cases thus ensured that the class as a whole was given the best deal; they did not give a defendant a better deal than *seriatim* litigation would have produced.

Third, the claimants identified by a common theory of recovery were treated equitably among themselves. The cases assume that the class will comprise everyone who might state a claim on a single or repeated set of facts, invoking a common theory of recovery, to be satisfied from the limited fund as the source of payment. * * *

* * *

C.

The Advisory Committee, and presumably the Congress in approving subdivision (b)(1)(B), must have assumed that an action with these characteristics would satisfy the limited fund rationale cognizable under that subdivision. The question remains how far the same characteristics are necessary for limited fund treatment. While we cannot settle all the details of a subdivision (b)(1)(B) limited fund here * * *, there are good reasons to treat these characteristics as presumptively necessary, and not merely sufficient, to satisfy the limited fund rationale for a mandatory action. At the least, the burden of justification rests on the proponent of any departure from the traditional norm.

It is true, of course, that the text of Rule 23(b)(1)(B) is on its face open to a more lenient limited fund concept, just as it covers more historical antecedents than the limited fund. But the greater the leniency in departing from the historical limited fund model, the greater the likelihood of abuse in ways that will be apparent when we apply the limited fund criteria to the case before us. The prudent course, therefore, is to presume that when subdivision (b)(1)(B) was devised to cover limited fund actions, the object was to stay close to the historical model. * * *

To begin with, the Advisory Committee looked cautiously at the potential for creativity under Rule 23(b)(1)(B), at least in comparison with Rule 23(b)(3). Although the committee crafted all three subdivisions of the Rule in general, practical terms, without the formalism that had bedeviled the original Rule 23, the Committee was consciously retrospective with intent to codify pre-Rule categories under Rule 23(b)(1), not forward-looking as it was in anticipating innovations under Rule 23(b)(3). Thus, the Committee intended subdivision (b)(1) to capture the " 'standard' " class actions recognized in pre-Rule practice.

Consistent with its backward look under subdivision (b)(1), as commentators have pointed out, it is clear that the Advisory Committee did not contemplate that the mandatory class action codified in subdivision (b)(1)(B) would be used to aggregate unliquidated tort claims on a limited fund rationale. None of the examples cited in the Advisory Committee Notes or by [the reporter for the Advisory Committee in a contemporaneous law review article] remotely approach what was then described as a "mass accident" case. While the Advisory Committee focused much attention on the amenability of Rule 23(b)(3) to such cases, the Committee's debates are silent about resolving tort claims under a mandatory limited fund rationale under Rule 23(b)(1)(B). * * *

The Rules Enabling Act underscores the need for caution. As we said in *Amchem*, no reading of the Rule can ignore the Act's mandate that "rules of procedure 'shall not abridge, enlarge or modify any substantive right,' " *Amchem*, 521 U.S. at 613, (quoting 28 U.S.C. § 2072(b)). Petitioners argue that the Act has been violated here, asserting that the Global Settlement Agreement's priorities of claims and compromise of full recovery abrogated the state law that must govern this diversity action under 28 U.S.C. § 1652. Although we need not grapple with the difficult choice-of-law and substantive state-law questions raised by petitioners' assertion, we do need to recognize the tension between the limited fund class action's *pro rata* distribution in equity and the rights of individual tort victims at law. Even if we assume that some such tension is acceptable under the Rules Enabling Act, it is best kept within tolerable limits by keeping limited fund practice under Rule 23(b)(1)(B) close to the practice preceding its adoption.

Finally, if we needed further counsel against adventurous application of Rule 23(b)(1)(B), the Rules Enabling Act and the general doctrine of constitutional avoidance would jointly sound a warning of the serious constitutional concerns that come with any attempt to aggregate individual tort claims on a limited fund rationale. [The Court noted a potential Seventh Amendment problem (see Chapter 4(F)(1)), as well as potential due process issues (see Chapter 7(C)(1)(b)), if the Fifth Circuit's approach were affirmed, because the result was a mandatory settlement of money damages with no right of the class members to opt out of the class.]

IV.

The record on which the District Court rested its certification of the class for the purpose of the global settlement did not support the essential premises of mandatory limited fund actions. It failed to demonstrate that the fund was limited except by the agreement of the parties, and it showed exclusions from the class and allocations of assets at odds with the concept of limited fund treatment and the structural protections of Rule 23(a) * * *.

A.

The defect of certification going to the most characteristic feature of a limited fund action was the uncritical adoption by both the District Court and the Court of Appeals of figures agreed upon by the parties in defining the limits of the fund and demonstrating its inadequacy. When a district court, as here, certifies for class action settlement only, the moment of certification requires "heightene[d] attention" to the justifications for binding the class members. This is so because certification of a mandatory settlement class, however provisional technically, effectively concludes the proceeding save for the final fairness hearing. * * *

We have already alluded to the difficulties facing limited fund treatment of huge numbers of actions for unliquidated damages arising from mass torts, the first such hurdle being a computation of the total claims. It is simply not a matter of adding up the liquidated amounts, as in the models of limited fund actions. Although we might assume *arguendo* that prior judicial experience with asbestos claims would allow a court to make a sufficiently reliable determination of the probable total, the District Court here apparently thought otherwise, concluding that "there is no way to predict Fibreboard's future asbestos liability with any certainty." Nothing turns on this conclusion, however, since there was no adequate demonstration of the second element required for limited fund treatment, the upper limit of the fund itself, without which no showing of insufficiency is possible.

The "fund" in this case comprised both the general assets of Fibreboard and the insurance assets provided by the two policies. As to Fibreboard's assets exclusive of the contested insurance, the District Court and the Fifth Circuit concluded that Fibreboard had a then-current sale value of $235 million that could be devoted to the limited fund. While that estimate may have been conservative, at least the District Court heard evidence and made an independent finding at some point in the proceedings. The same, however, cannot be said for the value of the disputed insurance.

The insurance assets would obviously be "limited" in the traditional sense if the total of demonstrable claims would render the insurers insolvent, or if the policies provided aggregate limits falling short of that total; calculation might be difficult, but the way to demonstrate the limit would be clear. Neither possibility is presented in this case, however. Instead, any limit of the insurance asset here had to be a product of potentially unlimited policy coverage discounted by the risk that Fibreboard would ultimately lose the coverage dispute litigation. This sense of limit as a value discounted by risk is of course a step removed from the historical model, but even on the assumption that it would suffice for limited fund treatment, there was no adequate finding of fact to support its application here. Instead of undertaking an independent evaluation of potential insurance funds, the District Court (and, later, the Court of Appeals), simply accepted the $2 billion Trilateral Settlement Agreement figure as representing the maximum amount the insurance companies could be required to pay tort victims, concluding that "[w]here insurance coverage is disputed, it is appropriate to value the insurance asset at a settlement value."

Settlement value is not always acceptable, however. One may take a settlement amount as good evidence of the maximum available if one can assume that parties of equal knowledge and negotiating skill agreed upon the figure through arms-length bargaining, unhindered by any considerations tugging against the interests of the parties ostensibly represented in the negotiation. But no such assumption may be indulged in this case, or probably in any class action settlement with the potential for gigantic fees.

In this case, certainly, any assumption that plaintiffs' counsel could be of a mind to do their simple best in bargaining for the benefit of the settlement class is patently at odds with the fact that at least some of the same lawyers representing plaintiffs and the class had also negotiated the separate settlement of 45,000 pending claims, the full payment of which was contingent on a successful global settlement agreement or the successful resolution of the insurance coverage dispute (either by litigation or by agreement, as eventually occurred in the Trilateral Settlement Agreement). Class counsel thus had great incentive to reach any agreement in the global settlement negotiations that they thought might survive a Rule 23(e) fairness hearing, rather than the best possible arrangement for the substantially unidentified global settlement class. * * *

We do not, of course, know exactly what an independent valuation of the limit of the insurance assets would have shown. * * * But objecting and unidentified class members alike are entitled to have the issue settled by specific evidentiary findings independent of the agreement of defendants and conflicted class counsel.

B.

The explanation of need for independent determination of the fund has necessarily anticipated our application of the requirement of equity among members of the class. There are two issues, the inclusiveness of the class and the fairness of distributions to those within it. On each, this certification for settlement fell short.

The definition of the class excludes myriad claimants with causes of action, or foreseeable causes of action, arising from exposure to Fibreboard asbestos. While the class includes those with present claims never filed, present claims withdrawn without prejudice, and future claimants, it fails to include those who had previously settled with Fibreboard while retaining the right to sue again "upon development of an asbestos related malignancy," plaintiffs with claims pending against Fibreboard at the time of the initial announcement of the Global Settlement Agreement, and the plaintiffs in the "inventory" claims settled as a supposedly necessary step in reaching the global settlement. The number of those outside the class who settled with a reservation of rights may be uncertain, but there is no such uncertainty about the significance of the settlement's exclusion of the 45,000 inventory plaintiffs and the plaintiffs in the unsettled present cases, estimated by the Guardian *Ad Litem* at more than 53,000 as of August 27, 1993. It is a fair question how far a natural class may be depleted by prior dispositions of claims and still qualify as a mandatory limited fund class, but there can be no question that such a mandatory settlement class will not qualify when in the very negotiations aimed at a class settlement, class counsel agree to exclude what could turn out to be as much as a third of the claimants that negotiators thought might eventually be involved, a substantial number of whom class counsel represent.

Might such class exclusions be forgiven if it were shown that the class members with present claims and the outsiders ended up with comparable benefits? The question is academic here. On the record before us, we cannot speculate on how the unsettled claims would fare if the Global Settlement were approved, or under the Trilateral Settlement. As for the settled inventory claims, their plaintiffs appeared to have obtained better terms than the class members. They received an immediate payment of 50 percent of a settlement higher than the historical average, and would get the remainder if the global settlement were sustained (or the coverage litigation resolved, as it turned out to be by the Trilateral Settlement Agreement); the class members, by contrast, would be assured of a 3-year payout for claims settled, whereas the unsettled faced a prospect of mediation followed by arbitration as prior conditions of instituting suit, which would even then be subject to a recovery limit, a slower payout and [other] limitations * * *. Finally, as discussed below, even ostensible parity between settling nonclass plaintiffs and class members would be insufficient to overcome the failure to provide the structural protection of independent representation as for subclasses with conflicting interests.

On the second element of equity within the class, the fairness of the distribution of the fund among class members, the settlement certification is likewise deficient. Fair treatment in the older cases was characteristically assured by straightforward *pro rata* distribution of the limited fund. While equity in such a simple sense is unattainable in a settlement covering present claims not specifically proven and claims not even due to arise, if at all, until some future time, at the least such a settlement must seek equity by providing for procedures to resolve the difficult issues of treating such differently situated claimants with fairness as among themselves.

First, it is obvious after *Amchem* that a class divided between holders of present and future claims (some of the latter involving no physical injury and to claimants not yet born) requires division into homogeneous subclasses under Rule 23(c)(4)(B), with separate representation to eliminate conflicting interests of counsel. * * * No such procedure was employed here, and the conflict was as contrary to the equitable obligation entailed by the limited fund rationale as it was to the requirements of structural protection applicable to all class actions under Rule 23(a)(4).

Second, the class included those exposed to Fibreboard's asbestos products both before and after 1959. The date is significant, for that year saw the expiration of Fibreboard's insurance policy with Continental, the one which provided the bulk of the insurance funds for the settlement. Pre-1959 claimants accordingly had more valuable claims than post-1959 claimants, the consequence being a second instance of disparate interests within the certified class. * * *

* * *

C.

A third contested feature of this settlement certification that departs markedly from the limited fund antecedents is the ultimate provision for a fund smaller than the assets understood by the Court of Appeals to be available for payment of the mandatory class members' claims; most notably, Fibreboard was allowed to retain virtually its entire net worth. Given our treatment of the two preceding deficiencies of the certification, there is of course no need to decide whether this feature of the agreement would alone be fatal to the Global Settlement Agreement. To ignore it entirely, however, would be so misleading that we have decided simply to identify the issue it raises, without purporting to resolve it at this time.

Fibreboard listed its supposed entire net worth as a component of the total (and allegedly inadequate) assets available for claimants, but subsequently retained all but $500,000 of that equity for itself.[34] On the face of it, the arrangement seems irreconcilable with the justification of necessity in denying any opportunity for withdrawal of class members whose jury trial rights will be compromised, whose damages will be capped, and whose payments will be delayed. With Fibreboard retaining nearly all its net worth, it hardly appears that such a regime is the best that can be provided for class members. * * *

* * *

The judgment of the Court of Appeals, accordingly, is reversed, and the case is remanded for further proceedings consistent with this opinion.

JUSTICE BREYER, with whom JUSTICE STEVENS joins, dissenting.

* * *

II.

* * *

Th[is] case falls within [Rule 23(b)(1)(B)'s] language as long as there was a significant "risk" that the total assets available to satisfy the claims of the class members would fall well below the likely total value of those claims, for in such circumstances the money would go to those claimants who brought their actions first, thereby "substantially impair[ing]" the "ability" of later claimants "to protect their interests." And the District Court found there was indeed such a "risk."

Conceptually speaking, that "risk" was no different from the risk inherent in a classic pre-Rules "limited fund" case. Suppose a broker agrees to invest the funds of 10 individuals who each give the broker $100. The broker misuses the money, and the customers sue. (1) Suppose their claims total $1,000, but the broker's total assets amount to $100. (2) Suppose the same broker has no assets left, but he does have an insurance policy worth $100. (3) Suppose the broker has both $100 in assets and a $100 insurance policy.

The first two cases are classic limited fund cases. The third case simply combines the first two, and that third case is the case before us.

Of course the value of the insurance policies in our case is not as precise as the $100 in my example, nor was it certain at the time of settlement. But that uncertainty makes no difference. It was certain that the insurance policies' value was limited. And that limitation was created by the likelihood of an independent judicial determination of the meaning of words in the policy, in respect to which the merits or value of the underlying tort claims against Fibreboard were beside the point.

Nor does it matter that the value of the insurance policies in our case might have fluctuated over time. Long before the Federal Rules of Civil

---

[34] We need not decide here how close to insolvency a limited fund defendant must be brought as a condition of class certification. While there is no inherent conflict between a limited fund class action under Rule 23(b)(1)(B) and the Bankruptcy Code, it is worth noting that if limited fund certification is allowed in a situation where a company provides only a *de minimis* contribution to the ultimate settlement fund, the incentives such a resolution would provide to companies facing tort liability to engineer settlements similar to the one negotiated in this case would, in all likelihood, significantly undermine the protections for creditors built into the Bankruptcy Code. * * *

Procedure, courts permitted actions by one group of insurance policy holders to bind all policy holders, even where the group proceeded against an insurance-company-administered fund that fluctuated over time.

Neither does it matter that the insurance policies *might* be worth much more money *if* the California court decided the coverage dispute in Fibreboard's favor. A trust worth, say, $1 million (faced with $2 million in claims) is a limited fund, despite the possibility that a company whose stock it holds *might* strike oil and send the value of the trust skyrocketing. Limitation is a matter of present value, which takes appropriate account of such future possibilities.

* * *

[End of Excerpt]

NOTES AND QUESTIONS

1. What elements were identified by the *Ortiz* majority as classic aspects of a limited fund class action? Is each element necessary? Is any element independently sufficient?

2. How could the district court have legitimately structured this case as a limited fund class action? Did the Supreme Court leave open the possibility of restructuring the class on remand?

3. As noted in *Ortiz*, one use of a "limited fund" class action is to avoid bankruptcy. Was the Supreme Court correct to conclude that use of a limited fund settlement when the defendant makes only a small contribution would undermine the Bankruptcy Code and the protections it gives to creditors? The propriety of using Rule 23(b)(1)(B) to avoid bankruptcy is discussed in Chapter 13(B)(2).

4. The *Ortiz* majority expressed concern that Fibreboard was able to retain most of its net worth, but did not base its ruling on that ground. Even Justice Breyer was concerned about this aspect of the settlement, noting (in a portion of his dissent not excerpted above) that it "raise[d] a more difficult question" than the other two conditions for a limited fund discussed by the majority. 527 U.S. at 881 (Breyer, J., dissenting). Ultimately, he concluded that a strict requirement that the whole of the fund be used to satisfy the claims should be "relax[ed] * * * where its basic purpose is met, *i.e.*, where there is no doubt that 'the class as a whole was given the best deal' * * *." *Id.* When, if at all, should a defendant in a limited fund settlement context be permitted to retain most (or even all) of its net worth? Does Justice Breyer's dissenting opinion provide a workable test?

5. In *In re Katrina Canal Breaches Litigation*, 628 F.3d 185 (5th Cir. 2010), the Fifth Circuit reversed the district court's certification of a settlement class under Rule 23(b)(1)(b), finding, *inter alia*, that the proposed settlement agreement "fail[ed] to meet [the third] 'essential premise[] of mandatory limited fund actions' identified by the Supreme Court in *Ortiz*." *Id.* at 194 (citation omitted). The Fifth Circuit explained:

> The class members in this case suffered a wide variety of injuries, ranging from property damage to personal injury and death, and no method is specified for how these different claimants will be treated *vis-a-vis* each other. * * * [T]he settlement provides for the appointment of a special master to "provide to the Court a recommended disposition and protocol with regard to the remaining [settlement fund],

and treatment of Claims of Class members." This arrangement simply punts the difficult question of equitable distribution from the court to the special master, without providing any more clarity as to how fairness will be achieved. The lack of any "procedures to resolve the difficult issues of treating such differently situated claimants with fairness as among themselves" leads us to reverse the district court's order certifying this class.

Id. at 193–94 (alterations in original).

6. Commentators have noted similarities between class actions under Rule 23(b)(1)(B) and compulsory joinder under Rule 19 (discussed in Chapter 13(A)(2)), as well as between (b)(1)(B) classes and interpleader (discussed in Chapter 13(A)(4)). *See, e.g.*, Comment, *Catch–23(b)(1)(B): The Dilemma of Using the Mandatory Class Action to Resolve the Problem of the Mass Tort Case*, 40 Emory L.J. 665, 702 & n.151 (1991).

7. What are the benefits of a mandatory limited fund class action? *See* David Rosenberg, *The Regulatory Advantage of Class Action*, in Regulation Through Litigation 244, 244–49 (W. Kip Viscusi ed., 2002) (arguing, *inter alia*, that such actions provide "the more cost-effective means of adjudicating mass production torts," maximize economies of scale by spreading and reducing the cost of litigation, and achieve optimal tort deterrence). What are the detriments? *See, e.g.*, *Comment*, Regulation Through Litigation 304 (W. Kip Viscusi, ed. 2002) (arguing that "by bringing massive numbers of citizens under the governance of mandatory class actions, [Rosenberg] would advance the efforts of * * * [activist] judges through recreating an elitist form of the agency model within the court system"); Samuel Issacharoff, *Class Action Conflicts*, 30 U.C. Davis L. Rev. 805, 821 (1997) (describing "tremendous strategic incentives for collusion" in limited fund class actions because "the rights of non-participants can be extinguished without notice or an opportunity to get out from under a prospective court decree").

8. Whose interests are mandatory limited fund class actions designed to protect? *See* John C. Coffee, Jr., *Class Wars: The Dilemma of the Mass Tort Class Action*, 95 Colum. L. Rev. 1343, 1382–83 (1995) (arguing that "in reality" such actions protect "defendants against the 'danger' that high stakes individual claimants, dissatisfied with the terms of the settlement class, will opt out," while "the existence of substantial opt outs may be the best evidence that the original settlement was inadequate (and possibly collusive)"). What is the counterargument that a mandatory limited fund class protects class members, particularly future claimants?

9. The *Ortiz* decision foreshadows a number of issues that will appear repeatedly in this text, including the problems presented when both present and future claimants are involved; the difficulties raised in settling large mass tort cases; the conflicts that can occur when class counsel represent class members with differing interests; the issues that arise when rules of procedure have the potential effect of abridging or modifying the rights of class members; the potential tension between a (b)(1)(B) class and bankruptcy; and the potential Seventh Amendment and due process issues that may surface in the class action context.

10. The Court in *Ortiz* noted potential due process concerns in aggregating personal injury tort claims in a Rule 23(b)(1)(B) limited fund class action. Nonetheless, it did not decide the case on that basis. For a discussion of the various approaches taken by courts in addressing claims for monetary relief under Rule 23(b)(1)(A) and (b)(1)(B), *see* Robert H. Klonoff, *Class Actions for*

Monetary Relief Under Rule 23(b)(1)(A) and (B): Does Due Process Require Notice and Opt-Out Rights?, 82 Geo. Wash. L. Rev. 798 (2014).

DOE V. KARADZIC
United States District Court, Southern District of New York, 2000.
192 F.R.D. 133.

LEISURE, DISTRICT JUDGE.

Plaintiffs in this class action seek compensatory and punitive damages for acts of genocide, including murder, rape, torture, and other torts, allegedly committed in Bosnia–Herzegovina by individuals under the command and control of defendant Radovan Karadzic. * * * Thereafter, plaintiffs S. Kadic *et al.* (the "Kadic plaintiffs") sought decertification of the plaintiff class or, alternatively, certification of one or more subclasses. For the following reasons, the motion to decertify is granted. * * *

BACKGROUND
* * *

By Opinion and Order dated December 2, 1997, the Court granted the Doe plaintiffs' motion to certify the case as a limited fund class action, pursuant to Federal Rule of Civil Procedure 23(b)(1)(B). At the time, the Kadic plaintiffs did not oppose certification. As per the December 2, 1997 Order, the class consists of "all people who suffered injury as a result of rape, genocide, summary execution, arbitrary detention, disappearance, torture or other cruel, inhuman or degrading treatment inflicted by Bosnian–Serb Forces under the command and control of defendant between April 1992 and the present."

Following the certification order, however, the Kadic plaintiffs began a full-fledged campaign to withdraw from the mandatory class. On October 23, 1998, the Court denied their motion to opt out of the class. Thereafter, on January 7, 1999, the Court refused the Kadic plaintiffs' request for reconsideration of its previous ruling and declined to certify the issue for an interlocutory appeal.

Despite these efforts, the litigation continued to move forward. * * * However, on March 19, 1999, the Kadic plaintiffs moved for decertification of the plaintiff class, pursuant to Fed. R. Civ. P. 23(c)(1), on the ground that the class no longer satisfied the basic requirements of Rule 23. Alternatively, they requested certification of one or more subclasses, pursuant to Fed. R. Civ. P. 23(c)(4)(B) [now 23(c)(5)].

While the two motions were pending before this Court, on June 23, 1999, the United States Supreme Court issued its decision in *Ortiz v. Fibreboard Corp.*, 527 U.S. 815 (1999). * * * Because Justice Souter's well-reasoned opinion in *Ortiz* provides the Court with a new starting point for determining the appropriateness of class certification on a Rule 23(b)(1)(B) limited fund rationale, this Court must again "engage in a 'rigorous analysis' of whether the conditions for maintaining a class action have been satisfied."

DISCUSSION

* * *

[T]his Court must reexamine the appropriateness of class certification on a limited fund rationale based on the guidelines set forth in *Ortiz*. * * * Thus, the Court must evaluate whether the Doe plaintiffs have satisfied the evidentiary burden necessary to establish the existence of a limited fund.

* * *

III. Necessary Characteristics of a Rule 23(b)(1)(B) Class Action

* * *

* * * [T]he paradigm suit under Rule 23(b)(1)(B) is the limited fund class action, in which " 'claims are made by numerous persons against a fund insufficient to satisfy all claims.' " * * *

* * * [W]hile the Rule speaks to the "risk of impairment" of future claims, courts have long recognized that "the meaning of subsection (b)(1)(B) is not as broad as it seems." Undoubtedly, nearly every potentially large judgment risks depletion of the defendant's assets and thus creates a risk that adjudication could "as a practical matter be dispositive of the interests of the other members not parties to the adjudications or substantially impair or impede their ability to protect their interests." Fed. R. Civ. P. 23(b)(1)(B).

Accordingly, *Ortiz* confirmed that mandatory class treatment under a limited fund rationale must be confined to a narrow category of cases. * * * Since *Ortiz*, the lower federal courts have followed the High Court in declining to certify putative (b)(1)(B) classes that fail to conform to the traditional pedigree.

With these precedents in mind, this Court too must carefully scrutinize these characteristics as they apply to the situation at hand. Of particular relevance is the question of whether the parties can provide specific evidence supporting the existence of a limited fund. Based on the language in *Ortiz*, any substantial deviation from the classic limited fund class action would compel decertification. At the very least, "the burden of justification rests on the proponent of any departure from the traditional norm." *Ortiz*, 527 U.S. at 817.

IV. Specific Evidence of the Inadequacy of the Fund to Satisfy All Claims

"The first and most distinctive characteristic [of the limited fund pedigree] is that the totals of the aggregated liquidated claims and the fund available for satisfying them, set definitely at their maximums, demonstrate the inadequacy of the fund to pay all the claims." *Id.* * * * To guide future certification decisions, the Court articulated a requirement that the parties present "evidence on which the district court may ascertain the limit and the insufficiency of the fund, with support in findings of fact following a proceeding in which the evidence is subject to challenge." Upon hearing such evidence, the district court must make an independent finding regarding the "the upper limit of the fund itself, without which no showing of insufficiency is possible." * * *

A. Scope of the Fund

Before determining whether the so-called "fund" is a "limited" one, the Court must first ascertain the parameters of the "fund" at issue in this case. The Doe plaintiffs submit that the amount potentially available to satisfy a judgment in this case is the defendant's current net wealth, an assumption upon which the Court originally certified the plaintiff class. This comports with the Supreme Court's recognition that a defendant's assets "would obviously be 'limited' in the traditional sense if the total of demonstrable claims would render [him] insolvent." *Ortiz*, 527 U.S. at 851.

Yet, in contrast to the traditional limited fund class action, the defendant here is neither a corporation with limited liability nor "a fixed and limited fund in danger of depletion," but rather an individual, living person subject to *in personam* claims. Any judgment against the defendant will be enforceable against him for at least twenty years, and any assets subsequently discovered by the plaintiffs or earned by the defendant will be subject to the judgment. Hence, the Doe plaintiffs must establish not only that the defendant's current net worth is insufficient to satisfy a potential judgment, but also a "substantial probability" that the defendant will be unable to pay such claims over the life of the judgment.

B. Evidentiary Requirement

Based on the above definition of the "fund" at stake in this litigation, the Court must conclude that there can be "no adequate finding of fact to support [the] application [of Rule 23(b)(1)(B)] here." *Ortiz*, 527 U.S. at 851. As the Kadic plaintiffs correctly point out, there has been no fact-finding inquiry to examine evidence supporting certification under Rule 23(b)(1)(B). Neither discovery nor hearings were ever conducted. Nor was any evidence obtained or considered, with the single exception of defendant's own self-serving, unsworn assertion that he could not afford to defend the action in the United States.[13] Aside from the Doe plaintiffs' "*ipse dixit* assertion that such a certification is needed," there is no indication of defendant's true financial status. Because there is no credible evidence before the Court regarding the amount or whereabouts of defendant's assets—not to mention his future earning potential—it is impossible to make an "independent valuation" of the limit of the so-called "fund."

The Doe plaintiffs urge the Court to ignore the requirement of formal evidentiary findings on the grounds that such findings are both unnecessary and impractical, given the unique circumstances of this litigation. They note that defendant's instruction to his attorneys not to participate further in District Court proceedings renders it unlikely that additional evidence would be adduced through such a process, and cite the Kadic plaintiffs' admission that defendant has "refus[ed] to comply with document requests expressly seeking documentation as to the whereabouts, types and amounts of his assets." This failure to obey various discovery

---

[13] In a letter to the Court, defendant stated, "'I do not have the financial resources to bring witnesses for my defense to the U.S. for either depositions, or trial.'" *Doe v. Karadzic*, 176 F.R.D. 458, 462 (S.D.N.Y. 1997) (quoting Letter from Radovan Karadzic to the Court, dated February 28, 1997). Relying on this declaration, the Court originally certified the class on the "assum[ption] that defendant could not satisfy even a fraction of the monetary judgments that could be entered against him." *Id.*

directives, they argue, would entitle them to an order, pursuant to Fed. R. Civ. P. 37(b)(2)(A), establishing the existence of a limited fund.

The Court finds these arguments unavailing. It may well be true that, as the Doe plaintiffs have long suggested, "a potential judgment is likely to total in excess of $10 billion, and there are very few individuals on the face of the earth who have such resources." Nevertheless, *Ortiz* unequivocally proclaims that "objecting and unidentified class members alike are entitled to have the issue settled by specific evidentiary findings independent of the agreement of defendants and conflicted class counsel." *Ortiz*, 527 U.S. at 853. * * * [I]n the case at hand, there is no credible evidence whatsoever concerning the whereabouts or amount of defendant's assets or the lack thereof.

The Doe plaintiffs' second argument has somewhat more merit, for defendant's defiance of numerous court orders may indeed entitle them to a decree establishing the existence of a limited fund. [Where a party fails to obey a discovery order, the court in which the action is pending may determine that the facts shall be deemed established for purposes of the case under Rule 37(b)(2)(A).] To be sure, defendant has consistently refused to comply with his discovery obligations, thereby impeding the plaintiffs' access to evidence that might enable them to make the necessary showing of inadequate assets. However, this Court is unaware of any precedent for a Rule 23(b)(1)(B) certification based on such an order, and therefore will not entertain such a request in the absence of a formal motion.

* * * Finally, any argument that certification might be appropriate without specific district court findings is implausible in light of *Ortiz*.

In sum, under the standard articulated by *Ortiz*, the Doe plaintiffs have not satisfied their burden of "defining the limits of the fund and demonstrating its inadequacy." *Ortiz*, 527 U.S. at 848. * * * [T]he Doe plaintiffs "did not make their 'limited fund' claim with much force, submitting little evidence." Their attorneys even concede that defendant may have assets hidden in various locations, including perhaps the United States. In short, there is insufficient evidence for the Court to make a finding on whether or not a limited fund exists. Given this substantial deficiency, the Court need not consider whether the putative class action conforms to the second and third traditional characteristics identified by *Ortiz*, as the first factor alone is enough to convince the Court that certification under Rule 23(b)(1)(B) is inappropriate.

Accordingly, the Court shall grant the Kadic plaintiffs' motion to decertify the plaintiff class. * * *

NOTES AND QUESTIONS

1. What was the proposed limited fund involved in *Karadzic?* What did the court rely upon in determining that the requirements of a limited fund class were not satisfied?

2. The *Karadzic* court conceded that very few people could satisfy a judgment exceeding $10 billion. 192 F.R.D. at 143. A footnote in the court's opinion provides further support for this proposition:

> According to Forbes, as of April 30, 1999, there were 32 individuals worldwide worth more than $10 billion. *See 200 Global Billionaires,*

Forbes, July 15, 1999, at 158–228; James Cox, *Technology, Stock Market Click for World's Richest*, U.S.A. Today, June 21, 1999, at 2A.

Karadzic, 192 F.R.D. at 143 n.15. Given this type of information, and given the evidentiary obstacles pointed out by the *Doe* plaintiffs, is the court's insistence on "specific evidentiary findings" reasonable?

3. In 1986, the Third Circuit decertified a mandatory, nationwide class of school districts seeking punitive damages from 50 defendants associated with the asbestos industry. *See In re Sch. Asbestos Litig.*, 789 F.2d 996 (3d Cir. 1986). The mandatory class included only school districts, not other governmental entities or other property owners, and also did not include punitive damages for personal injury claimants. The Third Circuit noted that the trial court had not relied upon a formal limited fund theory, because plaintiffs had not presented any evidence that the defendants' available assets would be insufficient to pay all claims, although the proponents of the class asserted "the very real possibility" that the late-coming plaintiffs would be unable to receive punitive damages if a future court decided that the defendants had already been punished enough in earlier cases (a theory sometimes referred to as "overkill," *see, e.g., Roginsky v. Richardson–Merrell, Inc.*, 378 F.2d 832, 839 (2d Cir. 1967) (Friendly, J.)). The Third Circuit, in *School Asbestos Litigation*, held that such a possibility was insufficient to support the existence of a limited fund pursuant to Rule 23(b)(1)(B), and also noted that other jurisdictions did not then recognize the overkill theory. Even assuming that plaintiffs could provide proof of a limited fund, the court held that class certification would still be inappropriate because the proposed class—which, as noted above, included only certain categories of plaintiffs—was under-inclusive:

> * * * [B]ecause all awards must come from the same defendants, a mandatory class predicated on a potential legal limit to punitive damages would logically include all litigants who seek such awards. From that standpoint, the (b)(1)(B) class certified here is under-inclusive with the result that separate actions by those who should properly be included in the class will go forward. However, the suppression of such separate actions is described in the advisory committee note as "the [reason] for and the principal key to the propriety and value" of a 23(b)(1) class.

Id. at 1006. Is this reasoning consistent with *Ortiz*? *See generally* Richard A. Nagareda, *Punitive Damage Class Actions and the Baseline of Tort*, 36 Wake Forest L. Rev. 943 (2001) (arguing that mandatory limited fund classes for resolving punitive damages violate *Ortiz* and may serve the interests of class counsel more than class members); *see also* Linda Mullenix, *Nine Lives: The Punitive Damage Class*, 58 U. Kan. L. Rev. 845, 850 (2010) (concluding that "the Supreme Court is extremely unlikely" to create an exception to *Ortiz* for punitive damage classes).

4. In *In re Simon II Litigation*, 211 F.R.D. 86 (E.D.N.Y. 2002), *rev'd*, 407 F.3d 125 (2d Cir. 2005), the district court certified a punitive damages class under Rule 23(b)(1)(B) in a nationwide class action by smokers, reasoning that, because there is a constitutional limit on punitive damages, the failure to certify a mandatory class "creates a potential first-in-time problem where the first plaintiffs may recover vast sums while others who arrive later are left with a depleted fund against which they cannot recover." 211 F.R.D. at 190. The district court ordered that the trial proceed in three stages: (1) "a class-wide determination of liability and estimated total value of national undifferentiated compensatory harm to all members of the class"; (2) (assuming a verdict on

phase one favorable to plaintiffs) a determination "whether the defendants engaged in conduct warranting punitive damages"; and (3) (if the answer to #2 is affirmative) a determination of "the amount of punitive damages to be awarded the class and how the damages will be allocated, on a disease-by-disease basis." *Id.* at 100. The same jury would decide all of these questions. The Second Circuit, however, reversed the district court's certification order, finding that the putative class failed to satisfy the first characteristic of a "limited fund" class articulated in *Ortiz*, namely, "a 'fund' with a definitely ascertained limit." 407 F.3d at 137 (quoting *Ortiz v. Fibreboard Corp.*, 527 U.S. 815, 841 (1999)). According to the Second Circuit, the constitutional limit on punitive damages

> is a theoretical one, unlike any of those in the cases cited in *Ortiz*, where the fund was either an existing *res* or the total of defendants' assets available to satisfy claims. The fund here is—in essence—postulated, and for that reason it is not easily susceptible to proof, definition, or even estimation, by any precise figure. It is therefore fundamentally unlike the classic limited funds of the historical antecedents of Rule 23. Not only is the upper limit of the proposed fund difficult to ascertain, but the record in this case does not evince a likelihood that any given number of punitive awards to individual claimants would be constitutionally excessive, either individually or in the aggregate, and thus overwhelm the available fund. * * * Without evidence indicating either the upper limit or the insufficiency of the posited fund, class plaintiffs cannot demonstrate that individual plaintiffs would be prejudiced if left to pursue separate actions without having their interests represented in this suit, as Rule 23(b)(1)(B) would require.

407 F.3d at 138. Was the Second Circuit's approach compelled by *Ortiz*?

5. As the Advisory Committee Notes reflect, Rule 23(b)(1)(B) is sometimes utilized outside the context of limited fund cases. The critical fact in such cases is that an action by an individual class member would, as a practical matter, directly impact the rights and interests of other class members. One leading treatise notes the following examples: suits by affected class members challenging the validity of a statute; suits seeking to enjoin a nuisance; and suits in which an entire class is claiming that a defendant breached a contract. 7AA Charles A. Wright, Arthur R. Miller & Mary K. Kane, *Federal Practice and Procedure* § 1774, at 38–40 (3d ed. 2005).

6. As with Rule 23(b)(1)(A) (*see* Chapter 3(A)(1)(a)), Rule 23(b)(1)(B) has been found applicable in ERISA cases, particularly ERISA "stock drop" cases. In such cases, pension fund beneficiaries allege a breach of fiduciary duty by a plan's management after the plan's value drops due to corporate malfeasance, such as misrepresentations that artificially inflate a stock price. *See, e.g., In re Merck & Co., Inc. Sec., Derivative & ERISA Litig.*, 2009 WL 331426, at *11 (D.N.J. 2009) (finding certification under Rules 23(b)(1(A) and 23(b)(1)(B) appropriate in ERISA stock drop class action). The *Merck* court rejected defendants' argument that 23(b)(1)(B) was confined to "limited fund" cases, which it stated "are but one species of the genus of Rule 23(b)(1)(B) cases." 2009 WL 331426, at *10 (citing *Ortiz v. Fibreboard Corp.*, 527 U.S. 815, 834 (1999)). The ERISA provision under which plaintiffs brought suit "expressly empower[ed]" the court "to provide relief by removing a fiduciary," such as the defendants; and thus, if plaintiffs' claims were to proceed individually, "and one court removed a Plan fiduciary, this would be, as a practical matter, dispositive of the

interests of the other Plan members in that particular regard." 2009 WL 331426, at *10.

7. One important limitation under Rule 23(b)(1)(B) case law is that "the possibility that an action will have either precedential or *stare decisis* effect on [class members in] later cases is not sufficient to satisfy Rule 23(b)(1)(B)." *In re Dennis Greenman Sec. Litig.*, 829 F.2d 1539, 1546 (11th Cir. 1987) (citing cases). What is the purpose of such a limitation? Are there instances in which adverse precedent in a suit by an individual class member would so impact other members of the class that Rule 23(b)(1)(B) certification should be allowed?

PROBLEM

Plaintiff Sharon Wish filed a class action complaint against Interneuron Pharmaceutical, Inc. ("Interneuron") for damages resulting from her use of a diet drug prescription medication combination commonly known as "Fen/Phen." She claims that she suffered serious heart valve damage from the medication and therefore requires ongoing treatment. The class includes those who have already suffered injuries from Fen/Phen and users of the drug whose injuries have not yet developed. Under a proposed settlement, Interneuron agreed to deposit $15 million into a settlement fund, along with all of its remaining insurance policies (estimated to be worth $28 million). Interneuron would remain an ongoing operation, but would be required to make biannual payments to the fund based on 15 percent of certain royalty proceeds and on seven percent of gross sales of all Interneuron products. Such payments would occur for seven years, or until the payments totaled $55 million. If, at the end of seven years, the $55 million figure were not reached, Interneuron would be required to distribute either stock or cash to the fund to meet the shortfall. Distribution of proceeds to the class would be handled by a claims resolutions procedure administered by the court. In arguing in favor of certifying a class under Rule 23(b)(1)(B) for purposes of settlement, plaintiffs' counsel and defense counsel claimed that, were the Fen/Phen litigation to continue, it would exhaust all of Interneuron's insurance proceeds and other assets. They also argued that only by settling could Interneuron continue to develop products and thereby generate revenue. At the time of settlement, there was very little data available from trial judgments or eve-of-trial settlements to assess what an individual Fen/Phen plaintiff might recover.

In what ways does this settlement address the problems cited in *Ortiz*? What arguments could be advanced by those class members who object to the proposed settlement? Should the court accept or reject the settlement?

B. RULE 23(b)(2)

Rule 23(b)(2) addresses situations where the primary relief sought is classwide declaratory or injunctive relief. The drafters envisioned that the subdivision would be used heavily in civil rights cases, but various other kinds of cases may also qualify for (b)(2) certification. In recent years, Rule 23(b)(2) has generated a number of difficult and controversial issues.

ADVISORY COMMITTEE NOTES TO 1966 AMENDMENT TO RULE 23(b)(2)

This subdivision is intended to reach situations where a party has taken action or refused to take action with respect to a class, and final relief of an injunctive nature or of a corresponding declaratory nature, settling the legality of the behavior with respect to the class as a whole, is appropriate. Declaratory relief "corresponds" to injunctive relief when as a practical matter it affords injunctive relief or serves as a basis for later injunctive relief. The subdivision does not extend to cases in which the appropriate final relief relates exclusively or predominantly to money damages. Action or inaction is directed to a class within the meaning of this subdivision even if it has taken effect or is threatened only as to one or a few members of the class, provided it is based on grounds which have general application to the class.

Illustrative are various actions in the civil-rights field where a party is charged with discriminating unlawfully against a class, usually one whose members are incapable of specific enumeration. Subdivision (b)(2) is not limited to civil-rights cases. Thus an action looking to specific or declaratory relief could be brought by a numerous class of purchasers, say retailers of a given description, against a seller alleged to have undertaken to sell to that class at prices higher than those set for other purchasers, say retailers of another description, when the applicable law forbids such a pricing differential. So also a patentee of a machine, charged with selling or licensing the machine on condition that purchasers or licensees also purchase or obtain licenses to use an ancillary unpatented machine, could be sued on a class basis by a numerous group of purchasers or licensees, or by a numerous group of competing sellers or licensors of the unpatented machine, to test the legality of the "tying" condition.

1. CORE CONSIDERATIONS

WALTERS V. RENO

United States Court of Appeals, Ninth Circuit, 1998.
145 F.3d 1032.

Before GOODWIN and REINHARDT, CIRCUIT JUDGES, and KING, SENIOR DISTRICT JUDGE [(D. Haw.), by designation].

REINHARDT, CIRCUIT JUDGE.

The plaintiffs brought suit against the government on behalf of themselves and similarly situated noncitizens, seeking declaratory and injunctive relief on the ground that the administrative procedures used by the INS [Immigration and Naturalization Service] to obtain final orders under the document fraud provisions of the Immigration and Naturalization Act of 1990 ("INA" or "the Act") violated their rights to procedural due process. Under § 274C of the Act, 8 U.S.C. § 1324c, the INS may issue an unappealable final order against an alien who has been accused of document fraud if the alien does not request a hearing in writing within 60 days of receiving the notice of intent to fine ("the fine notice") and the notice of rights/waiver ("the rights/waiver notice") forms. Such an order renders the alien deportable and permanently excludable. Deportation is automatic, except in narrowly limited circumstances. If the alien signs a statement waiving his rights with respect to the document fraud charges, including his right to a hearing, the INS will immediately issue an unappealable final order assessing a fine and requiring the alien to cease and desist from his wrongful conduct, but the ultimate result that ordinarily will follow soon thereafter will be the issuance of an order of deportation.

In their complaint, the plaintiffs contend that despite the dramatic immigration consequences for those charged with violating the document fraud provisions of the INA, the forms served on aliens in connection with these charges are dense and written in complex, legal language. The plaintiffs allege that on account of the confusing nature of the forms, aliens in document fraud proceedings are not adequately informed of the steps they must take in order to contest the charges brought against them and thus do not learn how to obtain a hearing on them. Moreover, they allege, they do not learn the true consequences of failing to request that hearing. They also challenge the general procedures by which the forms are presented to them. The plaintiffs moved to certify a class of approximately 4,000 aliens who had been or were subject to final orders, and moved for the entry of a preliminary injunction, summary judgment, a permanent injunction, and an order requiring the INS to reopen each plaintiff's document fraud case and provide hearings if necessary.

In March 1996, Judge Coughenour certified the plaintiffs as a class with the following characteristics:

> All non-citizens who have or will become subject to a final order under § 274C of the Immigration and Naturalization Act because they received notice forms that did not adequately advise them of their rights, of the consequences of waiving their rights or of the consequences of failing to request a hearing.

Under the district court's order, an individual alien can establish his status as a class member by attesting that he did not understand either his rights in the document fraud proceedings or the consequences of waiving his rights. In the same order, Judge Coughenour ruled on summary judgment that the procedures and forms used by the INS in document fraud cases are unconstitutional because they deny aliens their rights to due process of law. The court also granted permanent injunctive relief; the terms of the injunction were to be decided after the parties submitted proposals to the court.

In October 1996, Judge Coughenour entered final judgment in favor of the plaintiffs and granted a permanent injunction requiring the INS to take a variety of actions to remedy the constitutional violations. According to the terms of the injunction, the INS must: (1) revise the two misleading forms (the fine notice and the rights/waiver notice); (2) send notice to possible class members at their last known addresses, and, through a publicity campaign that must include specific attempts to contact all class members inside and outside of the country, publicize the opportunity for class members to reopen their document fraud proceedings; (3) refrain from deporting noncitizens on the basis of § 274C final orders that were entered without a hearing until class members have the opportunity to pursue reopening procedures; (4) reopen § 274C proceedings for each class member who was subject to a § 274C final order, unless the government can show that alien received adequate notice; (5) parole or make other arrangements for class members outside the United States to pursue reopened proceedings; and (6) recharge any alien charged with deficient forms who failed to request a hearing but has not yet been subjected to a final order, unless the government can show that the alien received adequate notice.

III. CLASS CERTIFICATION

* * *

Rule 23(b)(2) Certification

* * *

* * * [T]he district court found certification proper because the plaintiffs claimed that the INS's practices in document fraud proceedings were violative of due process. The forms and procedures in question were used by the INS in document fraud cases on a nationwide basis. Further, the plaintiffs sought injunctive, not monetary relief.

With respect to certification under Rule 23(b)(2), the government's primary objection appears to be that certifying this class does not further the purposes of Rule 23. * * * [T]he government points to the individual proceedings that will result from the district court's injunction as evidence that judicial efficiency will actually be undermined by the class action. While the government correctly observes that numerous individual administrative proceedings may flow from the district court's decision, it fails to acknowledge that the district court's decision eliminates the need for individual litigation regarding the constitutionality of INS's official forms and procedures. Absent a class action decision, individual aliens across the country could file complaints against the INS in federal court, each of them raising precisely the same legal challenge to the constitutionality of the § 274C forms. Contrary to the government's assertion, therefore, class certification in this case is entirely proper in light of the general purposes of Rule 23, avoiding duplicative litigation.

We note that with respect to 23(b)(2) in particular, the government's dogged focus on the factual differences among the class members appears to demonstrate a fundamental misunderstanding of the rule. Although common issues must predominate for class certification under Rule 23(b)(3), no such requirement exists under 23(b)(2). It is sufficient if class members complain of a pattern or practice that is generally applicable to the class as a whole. Even if some class members have not been injured by the challenged practice, a class may nevertheless be appropriate.

Moreover, the claims raised by the plaintiffs in this action are precisely the sorts of claims that Rule 23(b)(2) was designed to facilitate. As the Advisory Committee Notes explain, 23(b)(2) was adopted in order to permit the prosecution of civil rights actions.

[The court also upheld the district court's ruling that the INS's procedures violated the aliens' due process rights.]

NOTES AND QUESTIONS

1. To what extent does the class certification in *Walters* promote the purposes of Rule 23? Are those benefits outweighed by the individualized issues that remain under the district court's injunction?

2. Does the relief granted by the district court in *Walters* meet the class definition, or is that relief either under-inclusive or over-inclusive?

3. The *Walters* court stated that Rule 23(b)(2), unlike Rule 23(b)(3) (discussed later in Part (C)(1) of this chapter), does not require that common issues predominate over individual issues. Courts have overwhelmingly agreed with that position. *See, e.g., Forbush v. J.C. Penney Co.*, 994 F.2d 1101, 1105 (5th Cir. 1993) ("[T]he question of whether common issues 'predominate' over individual ones has no place in determining whether a class should be certified under 23(b)(2)."); *Adamson v. Bowen*, 855 F.2d 668, 676 (10th Cir. 1988) (same).

4. Some courts, however, have evaluated the impact of individualized issues even under Rule 23(b)(2). Consider, for example, *Barnes v. American Tobacco Co.*, 161 F.3d 127 (3d Cir. 1998), in which the Third Circuit faced the argument that a district court had erred in refusing to certify, under Rule 23(b)(2), a claim by Pennsylvania smokers for medical monitoring. After performing an exhaustive analysis of how proof of entitlement to monitoring would have to be submitted by each class member, and after assessing the extent to which individualized issues would permeate the proofs at trial, the Third Circuit affirmed the district court's ruling, finding that the class lacked "cohesiveness":

> Recently, the Supreme Court reexamined the requirement for Rule 23 certification in the context of mass tort class actions. In *Amchem Products, Inc. v. Windsor*, 521 U.S. 591 (1997), [the issue] was 'whether [the] proposed classes [were] sufficiently cohesive to warrant adjudication by representation.' * * *
>
> While *Amchem* involved a Rule 23(b)(3) class action, the cohesiveness requirement enunciated by both this court and the Supreme Court extends beyond Rule 23(b)(3) class actions. Indeed, a (b)(2) class may require more cohesiveness than a (b)(3) class. This is so because in a (b)(2) action, unnamed members are bound by the action without the opportunity to opt out.
>
> While 23(b)(2) class actions have no predominance or superiority requirements, it is well established that the class claims must be cohesive. Discussing the requirements for 23(b)(2) classes in *Wetzel v. Liberty Mutual Insurance Co.*, 508 F.2d 239 (3d Cir. 1975), we noted, "[b]y its very nature, a (b)(2) class must be cohesive as to those claims tried in the class action. . . . Because of the cohesive nature of the class, Rule 23(c)(3) [which specifies that the judgment shall describe all members of the class] contemplates that all members of the class will be bound. Any resultant unfairness to the members of the class was thought to be outweighed by the purposes behind class actions: eliminating the possibility of repetitious litigation and providing small claimants with a means of obtaining redress for claims too small to justify individual litigation." * * *
>
> In *Santiago* [*v. City of Philadelphia*, 72 F.R.D. 619, 628 (E.D. Pa. 1976)], the court recognized two reasons why courts must determine whether a proposed (b)(2) class implicates individual issues. First, unnamed members with valid individual claims are bound by the action without the opportunity to withdraw and may be prejudiced by a negative judgment in the class action. "Thus, the court must ensure that significant individual issues do not pervade the entire action because it would be unjust to bind absent class members to a negative decision where the class representatives's claims present different in-

dividual issues than the claims of the absent members present." Second, "the suit could become unmanageable and little value would be gained in proceeding as a class action . . . if significant individual issues were to arise consistently."

Id. at 142–43. Is the *Barnes* court's approach to evaluating a Rule 23(b)(2) class action inconsistent with the Ninth Circuit's approach in *Walters*? When studying Rule 23(b)(3) in the pages that follow, assess whether there is a difference between determining if common issues predominate over individual issues (the Rule 23(b)(3) "predominance" inquiry) and determining if the class is "cohesive"—the *Barnes* approach under Rule 23(b)(2). What point is being made by the *Wetzel* court, quoted in the *Barnes* decision? What about the *Santiago* case? Do these authorities support the *Barnes* court's analysis? Is there any basis in the text of Rule 23(b)(2) for a "cohesiveness" requirement? *See also, e.g., Gates v. Rohm & Haas Co.*, 2011 WL 3715817, at *11 (3d Cir. 2011) (noting that, although "[t]he requirements of predominance and superiority for maintaining a class action under Rule 23(b)(3) are less stringent than the cohesiveness requirement of Rule 23(b)(2) * * * the two inquiries are similar"); *Maldonado v. Ochsner Clinic Found.*, 493 F.3d 521, 524 (5th Cir. 2007) (upholding denial of class certification under (b)(2) where "individualized issues * * * overwhelm class cohesiveness"); *Heffner v. Blue Cross & Blue Shield of Ala., Inc.*, 443 F.3d 1330, 1333 (11th Cir. 2006) (treating the "class as a whole" language in (b)(2) as having an effect similar to the predominance standard of (b)(3) by holding that, because "each plaintiff must prove reliance" on information provided by the ERISA plan administrator, "final injunctive or declaratory relief [is] inappropriate for the class as a whole").

5. Courts are also divided over whether Rule 23(b)(2) contains a manageability requirement, an issue touched upon in the *Barnes* court's quotation from *Santiago*, above. As one federal circuit court explained:

> The district court also looked to a manageability requirement in applying Rule 23(b)(2): it found that the "breadth [of relief] [made] the proposed class action not manageable with [the] court's limited jurisdiction." The circuits do not speak with one voice on whether courts may look to manageability considerations in evaluating Rule 23(b)(2) class certification. The Fourth Circuit, for example, has held that "issues such as class action manageability are properly committed to the district court's discretion, because that court generally has a greater familiarity and expertise with the practical and primarily factual problems of administering a lawsuit than does a court of appeals." *Lowery v. Circuit City Stores, Inc.*, 158 F.3d 742, 757 (4th Cir. 1998). The court also stated that, "in exercising the 'broad discretion' to decide whether to allow a suit to proceed as a class action, some courts have ruled it is appropriate to take account of considerations not expressly addressed in Rule 23, including manageability in Rule 23(b)(2) cases." The *Lowery* court went on to hold that since "efficiency is one of the primary purposes of class action procedure, . . . in appropriate circumstances a district court may exercise its discretion to deny certification if the resulting class action would be unmanageable or cumbersome."
>
> According to the Fifth Circuit, however, in *Forbush v. J.C. Penney Co., Inc.*, 994 F.2d 1101, 1105 (5th Cir. 1993), "questions of man-

ageability and judicial economy are . . . irrelevant to 23(b)(2) class actions." The Ninth Circuit reached a similar conclusion in *Elliott v. Weinberger*, 564 F.2d 1219, 1229 (9th Cir. 1977) * * *.

We agree with the *Lowery* court. Elements of manageability and efficiency are not categorically precluded in determining whether to certify a 23(b)(2) class. While Rule (b)(2) classes for injunctive relief are usually easier to manage than damages class actions, courts also need to look to whether the class is amenable to uniform group remedies. The vehicle of class action litigation must ultimately satisfy practical as well as purely legal considerations.

Shook v. El Paso Cnty. Bd. of Cnty. Comm'rs, 386 F.3d 963, 972–73 (10th Cir. 2004).

Chief Judge Tacha dissented, reasoning:

* * * I find that the standard rules of statutory construction lead to a result contrary to that reached by the majority. Rule 23(b)(3) explicitly has a manageability criterion. *See* Fed. R. Civ. P. 23(b)(3)(D). Rule 23(b)(2) does not. Standard rules of construction, then, lead to the conclusion that manageability is not a criterion for Rule 23(b)(2) classes. *See O'Gilvie v. United States*, 519 U.S. 79, 96 (1996) ("When the legislature uses certain language in one part of the statute and different language in another, the court assumes different meanings were intended.") (internal citation omitted).

The majority counters that Rule 23(b)'s language is merely permissive, allowing the district court to consider Rule 23(b)(3) criteria in a Rule 23(b)(2) class. *See* Fed. R. Civ. P. 23(b) ("An action *may* be maintained as a class action if the prerequisites [are met.]") (emphasis added). Such a reading, however, simply ignores the entire structure of Rule 23(b). The majority's reading collapses the differences between a Rule 23(b)(1), (b)(2) and (b)(3) class, allowing a district court to consider any criteria under any of the subsections for any type of class. Such a reading is not in line with the structure of Rule 23(b) and is thus contrary to standard statutory construction. *See United States v. Rodgers*, 461 U.S. 677, 706 (1983) ("The word 'may,' when used in a statute, usually implies some degree of discretion[, but] [t]his common-sense principle of statutory construction . . . can be defeated by indications of legislative intent to the contrary or by obvious inferences from the structure and purpose of the statute."). Rule 23(b) clearly envisions the different subsections and their concomitant criteria applying distinctly to different types of class actions.

I find, therefore, the Fifth and Ninth Circuits' approach more persuasive. As such, I respectfully dissent from the manageability section of the majority's opinion.

Id. at 974–75. *See also Wal–Mart Stores, Inc. v. Dukes*, 564 U.S. 338, 362–63 (2011) ("When a [(b)(2)] class seeks an indivisible injunction benefitting all its members at once, there is no reason to undertake a case-specific inquiry into whether class issues predominate or whether [a] class action is a superior method of adjudicating the dispute. Predominance and superiority are self-evident."); *see also infra* Chapter 3(B)(2). Which approach in *Shook* is more persuasive: the majority's or the dissent's? Is the issue purely one of statutory construction? To what extent should the purposes underlying Rule 23(b)(2) be considered?

2. RELEVANCE OF TYPE OF RELIEF SOUGHT

The Advisory Committee Notes specifically caution that Rule 23(b)(2) does not apply to cases in which the relief sought "predominantly" consists of money damages. As the Notes suggest, a major purpose of Rule 23(b)(2) was to authorize civil rights class actions seeking equitable relief. Following the adoption of Rule 23(b)(2), and continuing well into the 1990s, courts often certified civil rights and other institutional, structural reform actions against governmental and non-governmental entities under (b)(2), even if significant damages were sought in addition to injunctive relief. *See, e.g.*, *Leyva v. Buley*, 125 F.R.D. 512 (E.D. Wash. 1989) (although "monetary damages element [was] not *de minimis*," certification under (b)(2) was still appropriate because "the injunctive relief sought appear[ed] to be equally important"); *Laramore v. Ill. Sports Facilities Auth.*, 1993 WL 45959 (N.D. Ill. 1993).

In 1991, Congress enacted legislation making compensatory and punitive damages available in Title VII employment discrimination cases. This new legislation led to a split among circuits over the availability of monetary damages in (b)(2) class actions. Most circuits, relying on the Fifth Circuit's decision in *Allison v. Citgo Petroleum Corp.*, 151 F.3d 402 (5th Cir. 1998), had endorsed the rule that claims for money damages could be certified under Rule 23(b)(2) only if the damages were "incidental" to injunctive or declaratory relief. *See, e.g.*, *Reeb v. Ohio Dep't of Rehab. & Corr.*, 435 F.3d 639, 651 (6th Cir. 2006); *Thorn v. Jefferson–Pilot Life Ins. Co.*, 445 F.3d 311, 330 n.25 (4th Cir. 2006); *Lemon v. Int'l Union of Operating Eng'rs*, 216 F.3d 577, 580–81 (7th Cir. 2000). The Second Circuit, by contrast, in *Robinson v. Metro–North Commuter Railroad*, 267 F.3d 147 (2d Cir. 2001), articulated an "ad hoc approach" for determining, case by case, whether injunctive or declaratory relief predominated, based on "the relative importance of the remedies sought, given all of the facts and circumstances of the case." *Id.* at 164 (citation and internal quotation marks omitted). And the Ninth Circuit, in a decision that was reversed by the Supreme Court (in the opinion featured below), stated yet another test, under which, to be certified under Rule 23(b)(2), a class could only seek monetary damages if they were not " 'superior [in] strength, influence, or authority' to injunctive and declaratory relief." *Dukes v. Wal–Mart Stores, Inc.*, 603 F.3d 571, 616 (9th Cir. 2010) (*en banc*), *rev'd*, 564 U.S. 338 (2011).

Despite their different formulations, however, most courts agreed on two basic premises. First, courts took as their interpretive starting point the Advisory Committee Notes' statement that class certification under (b)(2) "does not extend to cases in which the appropriate final relief relates exclusively or *predominantly* to money damages" (emphasis added). While courts developed a variety of tests, all of the tests focused on what it meant for monetary damages to "predominate" in a given case. Second, the courts consistently held that backpay, long considered an "equitable" remedy, could be awarded in a (b)(2) class action. *See, e.g.*, *Allison v. Citgo Petroleum Corp.*, 151 F.3d 402, 415 (5th Cir. 1998) ("Back pay, of course, ha[s] long been recognized as an equitable remedy under Title VII." (citation omitted)). While backpay clearly involves the payment of money, courts indulged the well-recognized legal fiction that backpay is distinct from money damages, thus allowing class plaintiffs to seek backpay in (b)(2) class actions.

In 2011, the Supreme Court granted review to resolve the proper approach for (b)(2) cases involving money as well as injunctive or other equitable relief.

WAL–MART STORES, INC. V. DUKES[†]
Supreme Court of the United States, 2011.
564 U.S. 338.

JUSTICE SCALIA delivered the opinion of the Court.[††]

* * * The District Court and the Court of Appeals approved the certification of a class comprising about one and a half million plaintiffs, current and former female employees of petitioner Wal–Mart who allege that the discretion exercised by their local supervisors over pay and promotion matters violates Title VII by discriminating against women. In addition to injunctive and declaratory relief, the plaintiffs seek an award of backpay. We consider whether the certification of the plaintiff class was consistent with * * * [Rule 23(b)(2)].

* * *

The named plaintiffs in this lawsuit, representing the 1.5 million members of the certified class, are three current or former Wal–Mart employees who allege that the company discriminated against them on the basis of their sex by denying them equal pay or promotions, in violation of Title VII of the Civil Rights Act of 1964, 78 Stat. 253, as amended, 42 U.S.C. § 2000e–1 *et seq.* * * * [Plaintiffs'] complaint seeks injunctive and declaratory relief, punitive damages, and backpay. It does not ask for compensatory damages.

* * *

[In addition to meeting the requirements of Rule 23(a)], the proposed class must satisfy at least one of the three requirements listed in Rule 23(b). Respondents rely on Rule 23(b)(2), which applies when "the party opposing the class has acted or refused to act on grounds that apply generally to the class, so that final injunctive relief or corresponding declaratory relief is appropriate respecting the class as a whole."

Invoking these provisions, respondents moved the District Court to certify a plaintiff class consisting of " '[a]ll women employed at any Wal–Mart domestic retail store at any time since December 26, 1998, who have been or may be subjected to Wal–Mart's challenged pay and management track promotions policies and practices.' " * * * Wal–Mart * * * contended that respondents' monetary claims for backpay could not be certified under Rule 23(b)(2), first because that Rule refers only to injunctive and declaratory relief, and second because the backpay claims could not be manageably tried as a class without depriving Wal–Mart of its right to present certain

---

[†] The facts in *Dukes* are set forth in Chapter 2(B)(2), and should be reviewed in connection with the (b)(2) issues discussed in this section. [Ed.]

[††] Although the Justices split 5–4 in the section of *Dukes* addressing Rule 23(a)(2) commonality, this section of the Court's opinion—on the Rule 23(b)(2) issue—was unanimous. [Ed.]

statutory defenses. With one limitation not relevant here, the District Court granted respondents' motion and certified their proposed class.

A divided en banc Court of Appeals substantially affirmed the District Court's certification order. * * * With respect to the Rule 23(b)(2) question, the Ninth Circuit held that respondents' backpay claims could be certified as part of a (b)(2) class because they did not "predominat[e]" over the requests for declaratory and injunctive relief, meaning they were not "superior in strength, influence, or authority" to the nonmonetary claims.

* * *

III

We * * * conclude that respondents' claims for backpay were improperly certified under Federal Rule of Civil Procedure 23(b)(2). Our opinion in *Ticor Title Ins. Co. v. Brown*, 511 U.S. 117, 121 (1994) (per curiam) expressed serious doubt about whether claims for monetary relief may be certified under that provision. We now hold that they may not, at least where (as here) the monetary relief is not incidental to the injunctive or declaratory relief.

A

Rule 23(b)(2) allows class treatment when "the party opposing the class has acted or refused to act on grounds that apply generally to the class, so that final injunctive relief or corresponding declaratory relief is appropriate respecting the class as a whole." One possible reading of this provision is that it applies *only* to requests for such injunctive or declaratory relief and does not authorize the class certification of monetary claims at all. We need not reach that broader question in this case, because we think that, at a minimum, claims for *individualized* relief (like the backpay at issue here) do not satisfy the Rule. The key to the (b)(2) class is "the indivisible nature of the injunctive or declaratory remedy warranted—the notion that the conduct is such that it can be enjoined or declared unlawful only as to all of the class members or as to none of them." Richard Nagareda, *Class Certification in the Age of Aggregate Proof*, 84 N.Y.U. L. Rev. 97, 132 (2009). In other words, Rule 23(b)(2) applies only when a single injunction or declaratory judgment would provide relief to each member of the class. It does not authorize class certification when each individual class member would be entitled to a *different* injunction or declaratory judgment against the defendant. Similarly, it does not authorize class certification when each class member would be entitled to an individualized award of monetary damages.

That interpretation accords with the history of the Rule. Because Rule 23 "stems from equity practice" that pre-dated its codification, *Amchem Products, Inc. v. Windsor*, 521 U.S. 591, 613 (1997), in determining its meaning we have previously looked to the historical models on which the Rule was based, *Ortiz v. Fibreboard Corp.*, 527 U.S. 815, 841–45 (1999). As we observed in *Amchem*, "[c]ivil rights cases against parties charged with unlawful, class-based discrimination are prime examples" of what (b)(2) is meant to capture. In particular, the Rule reflects a series of decisions involving challenges to racial segregation—conduct that was remedied by a single classwide order. In none of the cases cited by the Advisory Committee as examples of (b)(2)'s antecedents did the plaintiffs combine any claim for individualized relief with their classwide injunction. *See* Advisory Committee's Note, 39 F.R.D. 69, 102 (1966) (citing cases) * * *.

Permitting the combination of individualized and classwide relief in a (b)(2) class is also inconsistent with the structure of Rule 23(b). Classes certified under (b)(1) and (b)(2) share the most traditional justifications for class treatment—that individual adjudications would be impossible or unworkable, as in a (b)(1) class, or that the relief sought must perforce affect the entire class at once, as in a (b)(2) class. For that reason these are also mandatory classes: The Rule provides no opportunity for (b)(1) or (b)(2) class members to opt out, and does not even oblige the District Court to afford them notice of the action. Rule 23(b)(3), by contrast, is an "adventuresome innovation" of the 1966 amendments, framed for situations "in which 'class-action treatment is not as clearly called for.'" It allows class certification in a much wider set of circumstances but with greater procedural protections. Its only prerequisites are that "the questions of law or fact common to class members predominate over any questions affecting only individual members, and that a class action is superior to other available methods for fairly and efficiently adjudicating the controversy." And unlike (b)(1) and (b)(2) classes, the (b)(3) class is not mandatory; class members are entitled to receive "the best notice that is practicable under the circumstances" and to withdraw from the class at their option.

Given that structure, we think it clear that individualized monetary claims belong in Rule 23(b)(3). The procedural protections attending the (b)(3) class—predominance, superiority, mandatory notice, and the right to opt out—are missing from (b)(2) not because the Rule considers them unnecessary, but because it considers them unnecessary *to a (b)(2) class*. When a class seeks an indivisible injunction benefitting all its members at once, there is no reason to undertake a case-specific inquiry into whether class issues predominate or whether [a] class action is a superior method of adjudicating the dispute. Predominance and superiority are self-evident. But with respect to each class member's individualized claim for money, that is not so—which is precisely why (b)(3) requires the judge to make findings about predominance and superiority before allowing the class. Similarly, (b)(2) does not require that class members be given notice and opt-out rights, presumably because it is thought (rightly or wrongly) that notice has no purpose when the class is mandatory, and that depriving people of their right to sue in this manner complies with the Due Process Clause. In the context of a class action predominantly for money damages we have held that absence of notice and opt-out violates due process. *See Phillips Petroleum Co. v. Shutts*, 472 U.S. 797, 812 (1985). While we have never held that to be so where the monetary claims do not predominate, the serious possibility that it may be so provides an additional reason not to read Rule 23(b)(2) to include the monetary claims here.

B

Against that conclusion, respondents argue that their claims for backpay were appropriately certified as part of a class under Rule 23(b)(2) because those claims do not "predominate" over their requests for injunctive and declaratory relief. They rely upon the Advisory Committee's statement that Rule 23(b)(2) "does not extend to cases in which the appropriate final relates *exclusively or predominantly* to money damages." The negative implication, they argue, is that it *does* extend to cases in which the appropriate final relief relates only partially and nonpredominantly to money damages. Of course it is the Rule itself, not the Advisory Committee's description of it, that governs. And a mere negative inference does not in our view suffice to establish a disposition that has no basis in the Rule's text, and that does obvious violence to the Rule's structural features. The mere "predominance" of a proper (b)(2) injunctive claim does nothing to justify elimination of Rule 23(b)(3)'s procedural protections: It neither establishes the superiority of *class* adjudication over *individual* adjudication nor cures the notice and opt-out problems. We fail to see why the Rule should be read to nullify these protections whenever a plaintiff class, at its option, combines its monetary claims with a request—even a "predominating request"—for an injunction.

Respondents' predominance test, moreover, creates perverse incentives for class representatives to place at risk potentially valid claims for monetary relief. In this case, for example, the named plaintiffs declined to include employees' claims for compensatory damages in their complaint. That strategy of including only backpay claims made it more likely that monetary relief would not "predominate." But it also created the possibility (if the predominance test were correct) that individual class members' compensatory-damages claims would be *precluded* by litigation they had no power to hold themselves apart from. If it were determined, for example, that a particular class member is not entitled to backpay because her denial of increased pay or a promotion was *not* the product of discrimination, that employee might be collaterally estopped from independently seeking compensatory damages based on that same denial. That possibility underscores the need for plaintiffs with individual monetary claims to decide *for themselves* whether to tie their fates to the class representatives' or go it alone—a choice Rule 23(b)(2) does not ensure that they have.

The predominance test would also require the District Court to reevaluate the roster of class members continually. The Ninth Circuit recognized the necessity for this when it concluded that those plaintiffs no longer employed by Wal–Mart lack standing to seek injunctive or declaratory relief against its employment practices. The Court of Appeals' response to that difficulty, however, was not to eliminate *all* former employees from the certified class, but to eliminate only those who had left the company's employ by the date the complaint was filed. That solution has no logical connection to the problem, since those who have left their Wal–Mart jobs *since* the complaint was filed have no more need for prospective relief than those who left beforehand. As a consequence, even though the validity of a (b)(2) class depends on whether "final injunctive relief or corresponding declaratory relief is appropriate respecting the class *as a whole*," about half the members of the class approved by the Ninth Circuit have no claim for injunctive or declaratory relief at all. Of course, the alternative (and logical) solution of excising plaintiffs from the class as they leave their employment may have struck the Court of Appeals as wasteful of the District Court's time. Which indeed it is, since if a backpay action were properly certified for class treatment under *(b)(3)*, the ability to litigate a plaintiff's backpay claim as part of the class would not turn on the irrelevant question whether she is still employed at Wal–Mart. What follows from this, however, is not that some arbitrary limitation on class membership should be imposed but that the backpay claims should not be certified under Rule 23(b)(2) at all.

Finally, respondents argue that their backpay claims are appropriate for a (b)(2) class action because a backpay award is equitable in nature. The latter may be true, but it is irrelevant. The Rule does not speak of "equitable" remedies generally but of injunctions and declaratory judgments. As Title VII itself makes pellucidly clear, backpay is neither. *See* 42 U.S.C. § 2000e–5(g)(2)(B)(i) and (ii) (distinguishing between declaratory and injunctive relief and the payment of "backpay," *see* § 2000e–5(g)(2)(A)).

C

In *Allison v. Citgo Petroleum Corp.*, 151 F.3d 402, 415 (5th Cir. 1998), the Fifth Circuit held that a (b)(2) class would permit the certification of monetary relief that is "incidental to requested injunctive or declaratory relief," which it defined as "damages that flow directly from liability to the class *as a whole* on the claims forming the basis of the injunctive or declaratory relief." In that court's view, such "incidental damage should not require additional hearings to resolve the disparate merits of each individual's case; it should neither introduce new substantial legal or factual issues, nor entail complex individualized determinations." We need not decide in this case whether there are any forms of "incidental" monetary relief that are consistent with the interpretation of Rule 23(b)(2) we have announced and that comply with the Due Process Clause. Respondents do not argue that they can satisfy this standard, and in any event they cannot. Contrary to the Ninth Circuit's view, Wal–Mart is entitled to individualized determinations of each employee's eligibility for backpay. Title VII includes a detailed remedial scheme. If a plaintiff prevails in showing that an employer has discriminated against him in violation of the statute, the court "may enjoin the respondent from engaging in such unlawful employment practice, and order such affirmative action as may be appropriate, [including] reinstatement or hiring of employees, with or without backpay . . . or any other equitable relief as the court deems appropriate." § 2000e–5(g)(1). But if the employer can show that it took an adverse employment action against an employee for any reason other than discrimination, the court cannot order the "hiring, reinstatement, or promotion of an individual as an employee, or the payment to him of any backpay." § 2000e–5(g)(2)(A).

We have established a procedure for trying pattern-or-practice cases that gives effect to these statutory requirements. When the plaintiff seeks individual relief such as reinstatement or backpay after establishing a pattern or practice of discrimination, "a district court must usually conduct additional proceedings . . . to determine the scope of individual relief." *Teamsters*, [431 U.S. 324, 361 (1977)]. At this phase, the burden of proof will shift to the company, but it will have the right to raise any individual affirmative defenses it may have, and to "demonstrate that the individual applicant was denied an employment opportunity for lawful reasons."

The Court of Appeals believed that it was possible to replace such proceedings with Trial by Formula. A sample set of the class members would be selected, as to whom liability for sex discrimination and the backpay owing as a result would be determined in depositions supervised by a master. The percentage of claims determined to be valid would then be applied to the entire remaining class, and the number of (presumptively) valid claims thus derived would be multiplied by the average backpay award in the sample set to arrive at the entire class recovery—without further individualized proceedings. We disapprove that novel project. Because the Rules Enabling Act forbids interpreting Rule 23 to "abridge, enlarge or modify any substantive right," 28 U.S.C.§ 2072(b), a class cannot be certified on the premise that Wal–Mart will not be entitled to litigate its statutory defenses to individual claims. And because the necessity of that litigation will prevent backpay from being "incidental" to the classwide injunction, respondents' class could not be certified even assuming, *arguendo*, that "incidental" monetary relief can be awarded to a 23(b)(2) class.

* * *

The judgment of the Court of Appeals is *Reversed.*

NOTES AND QUESTIONS

1. What test for (b)(2) remedies did the Court endorse? Is it the test articulated by the Fifth Circuit in *Allison v. Citgo Petroleum Corp.*, 151 F.3d 402 (5th Cir. 1998), which is discussed in part III-C of *Dukes* above? Or is it something even more restrictive?

2. The Court in *Dukes* reserved the question "whether there are any forms of 'incidental' monetary relief that are consistent with the interpretation of Rule 23(b)(2) we have announced and that comply with the Due Process Clause." 564 U.S. at 366. For some examples of the wide range of cases in which courts had previously certified (b)(2) classes, see, e.g., *Berger v. Xerox Corp. Ret. Income Guarantee Plan*, 338 F.3d 755, 764 (7th Cir. 2003) (where monetary relief is "the direct, anticipated consequence of [declaratory relief], rather than something unrelated to it, the suit can be maintained under Rule 23(b)(2)"); *Arnold v. United Artists Theatre Circuit, Inc.*, 158 F.R.D. 439 (N.D. Cal. 1994) (primary relief requested was injunctive where plaintiffs sought order requiring theaters to modify facilities pursuant to Americans With Disabilities Act, although plaintiffs also sought minimum statutory damages under state statute); *Gelb v. Am. Tel. & Tel. Co.*, 150 F.R.D. 76, 77–78 (S.D.N.Y. 1993) (injunctive relief predominated where plaintiffs sought order prohibiting misleading advertising and disclosure of telephone company's rate structure, as well as minimal damages to individual calling card holders).

3. To date, the Supreme Court has not had occasion to answer the question left open in *Dukes*: whether "any forms of 'incidental' monetary relief" can be sought in a (b)(2) class. From the post-*Dukes* case law, however, it is fair to say that *Dukes*'s holding on this point has sharpened the distinction between those cases that are compatible with (b)(2) and those that must be brought under (b)(3). In short, courts have heeded *Dukes*'s admonition that "individualized monetary claims belong in Rule 23(b)(3)."

Specifically, courts have remained willing to certify (b)(2) classes in cases seeking truly group-wide injunctive relief. See, e.g., *Ligon v. City of N.Y.*, 288 F.R.D. 72, 77 (S.D.N.Y. 2013) (certifying (b)(2) class seeking preliminary injunctive relief against allegedly unconstitutional search and seizure program by NYPD); *P.V. ex rel. Valentin v. Sch. Dist. of Phila.*, 289 F.R.D. 227, 235–36 (E.D. Pa. 2013) (certifying (b)(2) class challenging alleged policy of transferring autistic students in violation of Individuals with Disabilities Education Act and related statutes; court noted that "Plaintiffs mainly seek systemic relief that will provide the opportunity for greater parental involvement to all putative class members in making decisions that allegedly affect the educational placement of their children"); *Parsons v. Ryan*, 289 F.R.D. 513, 524 (D. Ariz. 2013) (certifying (b)(2) class of prisoners alleging 8th Amendment violations due to defendant's health care policy where the relief sought "would not lie in providing specific care to specific inmates"; "[r]ather, the level of care and resources would be raised for all inmates"), *aff'd*, 754 F.3d 657 (9th Cir. 2014).

On the other hand, many cases that might have been certified under Rule 23(b)(2) prior to *Dukes* are now apt to be certified (if at all) only under (b)(3). *See, e.g., Moore v. Napolitano*, 926 F. Supp. 2d 8, 12 (D.D.C. 2013) (certifying (b)(3) class in Title VII and § 1981 case alleging a pattern and practice of racial discrimination by U.S. Secret Service in promoting African–American Special Agents); *Kerner v. City & Cnty. of Denver*, 2013 WL 1222394, at *5 (D. Colo. 2013) (certifying (b)(3) class of job applicants who alleged that the governmental defendants' employment test had a disparate impact on black and Hispanic applicants, in violation of Title VII).

Other courts have continued to take a "hybrid" approach, certifying monetary or individualized claims under (b)(3) and injunctive or declaratory claims under (b)(2) in the same case. *See, e.g., Butler v. Suffolk Cnty.*, 289 F.R.D. 80, 102–03 (E.D.N.Y. 2013) (certifying injunctive class under (b)(2) and damages class under (b)(3)); *In re Motor Fuel Temp. Sales Practices Litig.*, 292 F.R.D. 652, 675–76 (D. Kan. 2013) (certifying classes for injunctive relief under Rule 23(b)(2) and classes for liability issues under Rules (b)(3) and (c)(4)); *Dugan v. Lloyds TSB Bank, PLC*, 2013 WL 1703375, at *5–6 (N.D. Cal. 2013) (certifying nationwide "damages/declaratory relief class" under (b)(3) and California-only "injunction/restitution class" under (b)(2)).

4. As discussed later, the Supreme Court has long hinted that a mandatory class (*i.e.*, one without a right to opt out) may never be appropriate for monetary damages claims. *See* Chapter 7(C)(1)(b)(ii); *Phillips Petroleum Co. v. Shutts*, 472 U.S. 797, 811 n.3 (1985); *Ticor Title Ins. Co. v. Brown, cert. dismissed as improvidently granted*, 511 U.S. 117 (1994). Did the fact that (b)(2) is a mandatory class influence the Court's analysis in *Dukes*?

5. Although dissenting in *Dukes* on the separate issue of commonality under Rule 23(a)(2) (*see* Chapter 2(B)(2)), Justice Ginsburg (joined by Justices Breyer, Sotomayor, and Kagan) stated explicitly that she agreed with the majority that "[t]he class in this case * * * should not have been certified under Federal Rule of Civil Procedure 23(b)(2)," because "[t]he plaintiffs, alleging discrimination in violation of Title VII, seek monetary relief that is not merely incidental to any injunctive or declaratory relief that might be available." 564 U.S. at 367–68 (Ginsburg, J., concurring in part and dissenting in part). Because the Court's (b)(2) holding can be viewed as significantly restricting civil rights class actions, is it surprising that the four liberal justices would join the majority on this issue? Importantly, at the time *Dukes* was decided, the lower federal courts had universally approved of bringing backpay claims under Rule 23(b)(2). *See* Robert H. Klonoff, *The Decline of Class Actions*, 90 Wash. U. L. Rev. 729, 789 (2013).

6. Assume that, in order to secure (b)(2) certification, a class representative eschews damages even though class members suffered injury for which one could seek compensatory damages. In that circumstance, is the representative open to claims of inadequacy under Rule 23(a)(4)? The Court did not squarely address that issue in *Dukes*, but it did observe that:

> Respondents' predominance test * * * creates perverse incentives for class representatives to place at risk potentially valid claims for monetary relief. In this case, for example, the named plaintiffs

declined to include employees' claims for compensatory damages in their complaint. That strategy of including only backpay claims made it more likely that monetary relief would not "predominate." But it also created the possibility (if the predominance test were correct) that individual class members' compensatory-damages claims would be *precluded* by litigation they had no power to hold themselves apart from. If it were determined, for example, that a particular class member is not entitled to backpay because her denial of increased pay or a promotion was *not* the product of discrimination, that employee might be collaterally estopped from independently seeking compensatory damages based on that same denial. That possibility underscores the need for plaintiffs with individual monetary claims to decide *for themselves* whether to tie their fates to the class representatives' or go it alone—a choice Rule 23(b)(2) does not ensure that they have.

564 U.S. at 364; *see also Cooper v. Southern Co.*, 390 F.3d 695, 721 (11th Cir. 2004) (abandoning damages claims to increase likelihood of (b)(2) certification raises concerns whether "the named plaintiffs would adequately represent the interests of other putative class members"); *Zachery v. Texaco Exploration & Prod., Inc.*, 185 F.R.D. 230 (W.D. Tex. 1999) (same); *Miller v. Baltimore Gas & Elec. Co.*, 202 F.R.D. 195, 203 (D. Md. 2001) (denying named plaintiff's motion for leave to amend class complaint to drop claims for compensatory and punitive damages, and concluding that motion "raises serious questions regarding the ability of the named plaintiffs to represent the putative class adequately"). In *McClain v. Lufkin Industries, Inc.*, 519 F.3d 264 (5th Cir. 2008), the Fifth Circuit cited with approval the *Zachery* opinion and held that denial of certification was appropriate because the plaintiffs had omitted claims for compensatory and punitive damages. *Id.* at 283; *see also* Chapter 2(B)(4)(b)(iv) (discussing similar issue regarding adequacy of representation).

7. In *Allison, supra*, the Fifth Circuit panel majority also addressed the question of whether the district court erred in refusing to certify a "hybrid" class—*i.e.*, a Rule 23(b)(2) class for declaratory and injunctive relief and a Rule 23(b)(3) class for compensatory and punitive damages. The *Allison* court affirmed the district court's rejection of that approach. As to damages, the court found that individual issues—*e.g.*, the nature of discrimination alleged, how each plaintiff was affected, and what kinds of medical treatment for emotional distress each plaintiff received—outweighed the common issues. *See infra* Chapter 3(C) (discussing Rule 23(b)(3) criteria). As to the concept of a class trial solely on the claims for declaratory and injunctive relief, the court determined that certification under (b)(2) likewise was unwarranted. *See Allison*, 151 F.3d at 422–25 (explaining Seventh Amendment right-to-jury-trial concerns raised by prospect of bifurcated jury trial); *but see id.* at 434 (noting, in denying petition for rehearing, that panel was not "called upon to decide whether the district court would have abused its discretion if it had elected to bifurcate liability issues that are common to the class and to certify for class determination those [discrete] liability issues"); *see generally* Chapter 4(F)(1) (discussing Seventh Amendment issues relating to bifurcated trials).

In *Williams v. Mohawk Industries, Inc.*, 568 F.3d 1350 (11th Cir. 2009), a class of employees alleged that Mohawk had engaged in racketeering activity by hiring illegal aliens, thereby depressing the employees' wages. The Eleventh Circuit, after finding that the district court had erred in rejecting class certification under Rule 23(b)(3), instructed the district court on remand to evaluate the propriety of certifying a hybrid ((b)(2) and (b)(3)) class:

*** The district court declined to certify a hybrid class because allowing many individual suits for liability and monetary relief followed by judicial resolution of class-wide equitable relief would be "overly cumbersome, confusing, and highly inefficient." This inefficiency dissolves if the district court determines common issues predominate and certifies a class under subsection (b)(3). The definition of the hybrid class under subsection (b)(2) would be confined to current employees of Mohawk because only those members of the employees' proposed class have standing to seek injunctive relief. If the employees succeed in establishing the liability of Mohawk in their suit for damages under subsection (b)(3), the district court would consider whether to fashion equitable relief under subsection (b)(2).

568 F.3d at 1360 (citation omitted).

Does the Court's opinion in *Dukes* leave open the possibility of a hybrid approach to class certification in certain cases? Such an approach would not have worked in *Dukes* itself, because the Court found as a separate issue that the class did not satisfy Rule 23(a)(2) and thus could not be certified under any subdivision of Rule 23(b).

8. An interesting application of Rule 23(b)(2) can be found in *McManus v. Fleetwood Enters., Inc.*, 320 F.3d 545 (5th Cir. 2003), which is featured in the section on Rule 23(b)(3) below. In that case, plaintiffs filed a class suit against a motor home manufacturer alleging that, contrary to representations that the motor homes could tow 3,500 pounds, the vehicles in fact could not do so without the addition of supplemental brakes. The suit sought certification under both (b)(2) and (b)(3). With respect to (b)(2), plaintiffs sought injunctive relief to compel the manufacturer to provide information to class members about the towing limitations of the homes and to supply supplemental brakes to each class member. The Fifth Circuit held that (b)(2) certification was not appropriate, reasoning:

> The McManuses' lawsuit is markedly different from the paradigm Rule 23(b)(2) class action. First, the ordinary relief for their lawsuit would be money damages, not injunctive relief.
>
> Second, Fleetwood sold its motor homes over a limited period of time to a limited number of purchasers and does not have an ongoing relationship with its purchasers. Third, Fleetwood would have to prove *individual* relief, based on the various models of motor homes, to each individual plaintiff having purchased a motor home between 1994 and 1999, as opposed to a "uniform group remedy."
>
> These sharp differences make the class-wide injunctive relief contemplated under Rule 23(b)(2) inappropriate to the case. We could find no case where injunctive relief was awarded under comparable circumstances. This result is unsurprising because damages would be the superior remedy, especially considering that some class members may already own, or have no need for, supplemental brakes. We emphasize that otherwise inappropriate injunctive relief does not become appropriate for class treatment merely because the more permissive Rule 23(b)(2), as opposed to (b)(3), contemplates injunctive relief.

Id. at 553–54. Did the court correctly apply Rule 23(b)(2)? Should courts evaluate the suitability of injunctive relief in deciding whether to certify a class?

See Chapter 4(B)(1)(b)(i) (discussing whether courts may look at merits in deciding class certification). If the superior remedy was damages, why did plaintiffs pursue an alternative classwide injunctive relief remedy? Does *Dukes* shed any light on the correctness of the Fifth Circuit's holding in *McManus*?

3. THE "NECESSITY" REQUIREMENT

If one person sues, for example, a state government to enjoin its enforcement of a law and prevails, the resulting decree may provide relief to all persons who would be subject to that law. If so, is a class action necessary? The question of "necessity" has given some courts pause, and some have refused to certify a class when a successful suit by an individual would inure to the benefit of those similarly situated. Most courts, however, have rejected the necessity requirement, finding that "if the prerequisites and conditions of Rule 23 have been met, 'a court may not deny class status because there is no "need" for it.'" *Vickers v. Trainor*, 546 F.2d 739, 747 (7th Cir. 1976) (quoting *Fujishima v. Bd. of Educ.*, 460 F.2d 1355, 1360 (7th Cir. 1972)); *see also, e.g., Disability Rights Council of Greater Washington v. Washington Metro. Area Transit Auth.*, 239 F.R.D. 9, 23 (D.D.C. 2006) ("As numerous courts have observed, whether certification is 'necessary' is not a question Rule 23 directs courts to consider." (citations omitted)). Commentators have criticized the "necessity" doctrine as well. For example, one commentator notes:

> [E]limination [of the necessity requirement] is consistent with the purpose of Rule 23 to allow class actions when the specified criteria are met. Elimination of the requirement also recognizes that in most cases the burdens associated with a Rule 23(b)(2) class action are not severe, and that the benefits resulting from a (b)(2) class certification often outweigh the costs.

Note, *The "Need Requirement": A Barrier to Class Actions Under Rule 23(b)(2)*, 67 Geo. L.J. 1211, 1236 (1979); *see also* Note, *There is Always a Need: The "Necessity Doctrine" and Class Certification Against Government Agencies*, 103 Mich. L. Rev. 1018, 1021 (2005) (urging rejection of necessity doctrine because of "the inability of plaintiffs to invoke offensive nonmutual collateral estoppel against government agencies" and because of "the tendency of agencies to decline to apply adverse circuit court rulings to nonlitigants, a practice known as 'nonacquiescence'").

There are a few notable exceptions, however. A case purporting to take an intermediate position is set forth below.

DIONNE V. BOULEY
United States Court of Appeals, First Circuit, 1985.
757 F.2d 1344.

Before CAMPBELL, CHIEF JUDGE, BOWNES, CIRCUIT JUDGE, and PEREZ–GIMENEZ, DISTRICT JUDGE [(D.P.R.), by designation].

CAMPBELL, CHIEF JUDGE.

This case concerns the constitutionality of the post-judgment garnishment procedure of Rhode Island. It raises the question whether Rhode Island law provides adequate notice to a judgment debtor whose property is attached of any right he may have under state or federal law to have his property exempted from attachment, and of the means for claiming such exemption, and whether Rhode Island affords an adequate opportunity for a prompt hearing at which the question of exemption can be determined. The United States District Court for the District of Rhode Island, in a comprehensive opinion, held that current procedures were constitutionally insufficient. It enjoined defendant Gerard Bouley, Chief Clerk of the District Courts of the State of Rhode Island, from issuing writs of attachment thereunder. We modify and affirm.

I. FACTS

On July 26, 1982, plaintiff Rose Dionne was the losing party in an action of eviction brought against her by her landlord * * *. The judgment included an order that she pay one month's rent, a sum of $550. Pursuant to the judgment, an execution was issued against Dionne, which was returned to the state court marked "unsatisfied." Thereafter, the judgment creditor obtained a writ of attachment from the clerk of the state court * * * and served the writ on Dionne's bank. As a result, the bank "froze" her bank account on August 13, 1982.

At the time this occurred, Rhode Island law permitted any creditor who was unable to execute his judgment to file a second "debt on judgment" action against the debtor and to attach the debtor's property as security for this second suit. Dionne's bank account was attached pursuant to a suit of this nature filed by the creditor * * * in which the creditor sought another money judgment in the amount of $551.80 plus costs of $50. Dionne was served with process in this second action on August 17, 1982. That same day, she received notice from her bank that one of her checks had been returned for insufficient funds and that the bank was imposing a $5 service charge for the check's return. On calling the bank to inquire about this, Dionne was told that her funds had been attached.

Dionne's checking account contained $601 when it was attached, most of which consisted of social security benefits paid to her and her four minor children, with a small portion of the account being attributable to her wages. Under federal law, social security benefits are not subject to "attachment, garnishment, or other legal process. . . ." Other exemptions, federal and state, also exist which might have pertained to some or all [of] Dionne's monies in this account. Dionne, who was solely responsible for the support of herself and her children, was unaware of, and was not provided with notice of, any procedures through which she could challenge the attachment or raise a claim that some or all of the property was exempt.

According to the parties' stipulations it was the practice of the state district court to issue blank writs of attachment upon request, with the name of the clerk and the seal already affixed, to creditors or their attorneys. No motion to attach was required with these, the writ being simply served directly on the trustee (*i.e.*, bank, employer). The parties also stipulated that there was no required hearing or notice of any possible hearing, either before or after the writ of attachment was issued and served, and that there was no notice to the judgment debtor of any possible defenses or exemption claims.

A short time after learning of the attachment, on September 14, 1982, Dionne brought this action in the federal district court challenging the constitutionality of the post-judgment garnishment procedure in the state district court system. She asserted causes of action under 42 U.S.C. § 1983 for alleged violation of the due process and supremacy clauses of the federal Constitution. Dionne criticized the state's failure to have provided her with a prompt notice of the attachment that would have informed her of the existence of the state and federal exemptions and the means for her to claim them. She further criticized the lack of any specific provision in Rhode Island law for a hearing, either prior to the attachment or immediately following the issuance and service of the writ, at which any exemptions could be claimed. She requested declaratory and injunctive relief, and class certification.

* * *

In November 1982, Dionne moved to certify a class of all judgment debtors in Rhode Island who might have been subject in the future to post-judgment attachment procedures and whose funds might have been exempt in whole or in part under state or federal statutory exemptions. Defendant opposed this motion. On March 18, 1983, the district court denied certification on the ground that any injunctive relief awarded "would inure to the benefit of all those similarly situated, and would be identical regardless of whether or not the action is maintained as a class action."

Thereafter, Dionne moved for summary judgment, most of the above facts having been previously stipulated by the parties. On March 23, 1984, the district court issued its opinion and order, declaring the challenged procedure unconstitutional and issuing the requested injunction. * * *

* * *

VI. CLASS CERTIFICATION

On cross-appeal, plaintiff challenges the denial of class certification. She claims the district court erred in applying a "necessity requirement" to deny her petition for class certification under Fed. R. Civ. P. 23(b)(2).

* * *

The "necessity requirement" challenged by plaintiff refers to a practice, followed by several circuits, of denying class certification under Rule 23(b)(2), when a class is not needed to obtain the same relief. In *Galvan v. Levine*, 490 F.2d 1255 (2d Cir. 1973), one of the leading cases in this area, plaintiffs were two Puerto Ricans who were adversely affected by a policy of the New York State Industrial Commission denying unemployment compensation benefits to persons who left the New York labor market area and moved to an area of persistent, high unemployment. Plaintiffs alleged that, as applied, this policy was used to bar Puerto Ricans who, like themselves, worked in largely seasonal jobs in New York and returned to Puerto Rico when without work there. They moved for class certification under Fed. R. Civ. P. 23(b)(2). The district court denied the motion. In an opinion by Judge Friendly, the Second Circuit affirmed, holding that a class action was unnecessary:

> [I]nsofar as the relief sought is prohibitory, an action seeking declaratory or injunctive relief against state officials on the ground of unconstitutionality of a statute or administrative practice is the

archetype of one where class action designation is largely a formality, at least for the plaintiffs. As we have recently noted, what is important in such a case for the plaintiffs or, more accurately, for their counsel, is that the judgment runs to the benefit not only of the named plaintiffs but of all others similarly situated, as the judgment did here. The state has made it clear that it understands the judgment to bind it with respect to all claimants[;] indeed even before the entry of the judgment it withdrew the challenged policy even more fully than the court ultimately directed and stated it did not intend to reinstate the policy.

[*Galvan, supra,*] 490 F.2d at 1261. Other courts have followed this approach. However, some circuits have refused. And the approach has been criticized by some commentators.

We agree with those circuits which deny Rule 23(b)(2) certification where it is a formality or otherwise inappropriate. However, we prefer not to speak of a "necessity requirement," since this suggests some kind of mechanical classification, whereas the justification for denying class certification rests on the particular circumstances. One factor that a court may properly take into account is the fact—if it be a fact—that the same relief can, for all practical purposes, be obtained through an individual injunction without the complications of a class action. But this does not mean that "certification of a (b)(2) class action is purely discretionary, or that the Rule requires showing a special need apart from what can be found in traditional equity and declaratory judgment jurisprudence." The language of Rule 23(b)(2) is reasonably clear: whether the action should be maintained as a class action depends on the *appropriateness* of injunctive or corresponding declaratory relief with respect to the class as a whole. Thus, when the same relief can be obtained without certifying a class, a court may be justified in concluding that class relief is not "appropriate."

There may, however, be situations where a class certification under Rule 23(b)(2) will arguably be unnecessary, but where other considerations may render a denial of certification improper. This could be the case, for example, where there is a danger that the individual claim might be moot, where the good faith of the loser cannot be fairly presumed, or where class certification does not impose any significant burden on the court. In sum, we do not accept the concept of a strict "necessity requirement" under Rule 23(b)(2); rather, in cases like this where the district court denies certification, we shall look to the discretion that the district court enjoys under the rule to deny class certification should it reasonably determine that class relief is not "appropriate."

Here we find no abuse of discretion in the court's denial of class certification on the ground that any injunctive or declaratory relief will inure to the benefit of all those similarly situated. The injunction forbids the defendant, as Chief Clerk of the District Court of the State of Rhode Island, "from issuing Writs of Attachment pursuant to the existing forms and procedures insofar as they are inconsistent with this opinion." While apparently some writs may have been issued shortly after this injunction, the practice has now ceased and we understood at appellate argument that the Chief Clerk is issuing no more writs in any post-judgment attachment cases. Under the circumstances, we see no practical need for class certification. Plaintiff's claim was not moot, and plaintiff was represented by an attorney from Rhode Island Legal Services, Inc., an office that can be expected to maintain an ongoing interest in seeing that the decree is enforced. The court could reasonably assume the good faith of a defendant such as the Chief Clerk of a state court especially given his express willingness to follow the court's injunction. There is some precedent in this circuit for non-class relief in cases of this type.

[On the merits, the court agreed, for the most part, with the district court's holding that the challenged procedures violated plaintiff's due process rights.]

NOTES AND QUESTIONS

1. How is the *Dionne* court's approach different from a "necessity" rule?

2. For a summary of the various approaches to the necessity doctrine, *see Gayle v. Warden Monmouth Cnty. Corr. Inst.*, 838 F.3d 297 (3d Cir. 2016) (ultimately adopting the First Circuit's approach in *Dionne*).

3. Should class certification be denied if relief in an individual action would achieve the same result? What would be the practical impact of adopting such a rule?

4. Why would a plaintiff go through the difficulty and expense of pursuing a class action if relief would inure to the benefit of those similarly situated even without a class?

5. Is the "necessity" rule limited to (b)(2) classes? *See Bellas v. CBS, Inc.*, 201 F.R.D. 411, 418 (W.D. Pa. 2000) (noting absence of "any case law which applies the necessity doctrine to any motion for class certification other than those brought under Rule 23(b)(2)"). Most, but not all, cases limit the "necessity" rule to cases seeking injunctive relief and do not apply it to suits for damages. *See id.* at 417–18 (discussing case law). Should the doctrine apply only to suits under (b)(2)? Should it apply only to suits not involving monetary relief?

PROBLEM

Plaintiff Cynthia Jones is a resident at the Pineville Nursing Home. She claims, on behalf of a class of residents, that conditions at the facility are deplorable and raise serious health and safety concerns. She seeks certification of a class under Rule 23(b)(2). In addition to seeking an order requiring that the health and safety problems be corrected and that proper health and safety standards be maintained in the future, she also seeks nominal compensatory damages (for discomfort and inconvenience) and substantial punitive damages. Excluded from the class are those who have suffered actual physical injuries. Should a (b)(2) class be certified?

C. RULE 23(b)(3)

Subsection (b)(3) was viewed by the drafters of the 1966 revision to Rule 23 as that rule's most innovative feature, and in the decades since 1966, Rule 23(b)(3) has been used across numerous substantive areas—securities fraud, mass torts, consumer protection, employment discrimination, civil rights, antitrust, environmental law, and others—with varied results. This section describes the basic elements of the inquiry under Rule 23(b)(3).

Rule 23(b)(3) states that a class action:

> may be maintained if Rule 23(a) is satisfied and if: * * * (3) the court finds that the questions of law or fact common to class members predominate over any questions affecting only individual members, and that a class action is superior to other available methods for fairly and efficiently adjudicating the controversy. The matters pertinent to these findings include: (A) the class members' interests in individually controlling the prosecution or defense of separate actions; (B) the extent and nature of any litigation concerning the controversy already begun by or against class members; (C) the desirability or undesirability of concentrating the litigation of the claims in the particular forum; and (D) the likely difficulties in managing a class action.

Rule 23(b)(3) requires a court to make two separate inquiries: (i) Do the common issues "predominate" over issues affecting only individual members? (ii) Is class treatment of the action "superior" to other alternative methods for adjudicating the controversy? As illustrated below, these two inquiries have generated substantial litigation.

1. PREDOMINANCE

Courts have struggled for almost half a century to describe what it means for common questions to "predominate" over questions affecting only individual members of a proposed class.

a. Core Analysis

BROWN V. CAMERON–BROWN CO.
United States District Court, Eastern District of Virginia, 1981.
92 F.R.D. 32.

WARRINER, DISTRICT JUDGE.

Named plaintiffs in the present suit have moved the Court to certify the suit as a class action under Fed. R. Civ. P. 23(b)(3). Plaintiffs are fourteen mortgagors who assert that, as a condition to obtaining residential mortgage loans, each was required by their prospective mortgagee to make monthly installments to an "escrow account" of 1/12 the estimated annual amount for local tax levys, insurance premiums and other obligations associated with their property. They seek to represent a class of all borrowers similarly situated. Plaintiffs claim that until the levies come due and the mortgagee makes the payments the escrowed funds are either co-mingled with the mortgagees' general funds or put to other profitable uses without an accounting being made to the mortgagors for interest earned, or otherwise providing mortgagors with a pecuniary benefit for use of their money.

The crux of plaintiff's complaint is that the periodic installments are placed into "escrow accounts" which are put to profitable use by the mortgagees for their own benefit without either paying interest on the escrow accounts or "capitalizing" the payments to reduce the outstanding principle of the loan itself. They assert the above practices are concerted and violate [federal and state] antitrust laws as a part of an ongoing conspiracy originating in the 1960's to eliminate the "capitalization" method of accounting for mortgage escrow payments, that the effect of this conspiracy has been a less competitive market in which mortgage loans with escrow payments subject to "capitalization" are unobtainable, and that plaintiffs have been and continue to be injured thereby.

The [35 remaining] defendants * * * comprise a variety of different types of lending institutions operating under numerous statutes and regulations, both federal and State. Defendants assert that the business practices and loan policies of the several institutions vary between the institutions and even between loans within each institution, depending on a variety of factors including: conditions on the secondary market, internal policy, [and] federal and State statutes and regulations. [The court had previously denied certification under Rule 23(b)(2); this opinion addresses plaintiffs' proposal for certification under Rule 23(b)(3).]

* * *

III.

Plaintiffs' burden under 23(b)(3) is to assure the Court that use of the class action device will achieve the economies of time, effort and expense contemplated by the Rule, without sacrificing procedural fairness or bringing about other undesirable results. Subdivision (b)(3) contemplates a dual test: First, questions of law or fact common to the members of the class must predominate over questions affecting individual members; and, second, the court must be satisfied that a class action is superior to other available methods for the fair and efficient adjudication of the controversy. The rule also suggests a non-exhaustive list of four factors that the court is to consider in making its determination.

1. Predominance of Common Questions

The issue of predominance is often treated by the courts in conjunction with their 23(a)(2) analysis. The focus of the 23(b)(3) requirement, however, is different. Whereas (a)(2) addresses the issue of whether Rule 23 has any applicability at all to the lawsuit, (b)(3) addresses the issue of whether Rule 23 certification will have practical utility in the suit, considering the facts, substantive law, procedural due process, and fundamental fairness. The Advisory Committee notes that only where questions common to the class predominate over questions affecting individual members will the court be able to achieve the economies of time contemplated by the Rule.

Professor Moore suggests that the predominance analysis involves two stages, not necessarily distinguished in practice. He states:

> [1] Once the threshold determination has been made that common questions predominate sufficiently to support overall class treatment, [2] the predominance criterion acts as a guide to the judge in molding and defining the action. At this juncture the standard assumes its more pragmatic aspect, as a test whether potential subclasses or other subdivisions can be useful. Here it is appropriate to consider simply the degree to which the common questions may be decisive of the issues to be dealt with in the separate

phases of the action, in order to judge the efficiency of the arrangement.

3B James B. Moore, *Moore's Federal Practice*, § 23.45(2), at 23–333 (2d ed. 1980). This view comports with the fact that courts tend to approach the problem of predominance, in both the antitrust and the related securities frauds fields, from a perspective of "the severability of the issues of liability and damages—whether the asserted statutory violations can be effectively adjudicated in a class proceeding independent from the proceeding in which individual damages would be assessed." Damages always require individual proofs and the crucial element in a court's analysis will be whether the "liability" issues (discussed below) are so closely linked to the "damage" issue that severability is not practicable.

Courts, in their consideration of this issue, have generally rejected quantitative tests comparing the amount of time and attention required to settle the common questions with that needed for the resolution of individual issues, although such considerations are relevant during the court's analysis of the superiority issue. Similarly, an outcome determinative test has been rejected as well. A valid concern at this stage is whether the class action will splinter into individual trials suggesting that common questions do not predominate over individual questions and that a class action would be inappropriate.

Private antitrust actions, though usually brought under (b)(3), are accorded no presumption on the issue of predominance. Courts are in agreement that a plaintiff in such an action must prove three elements to succeed: (1) violation of the antitrust laws; (2) direct injury to the plaintiff from each violation; and (3) damages sustained by the plaintiff. * * *

* * *

A. Violation

There is general agreement that a conspiracy allegation as to violation of the antitrust laws involves common questions as to the class and plaintiffs' proof in this action will generally be the same as to all defendants.

B. Fact of Injury or Impact

In numerous cases where certification has been questioned on the predominance issue, the court's resolution of the issue of liability usually has been the determining factor as to whether certification will be granted. Generally, where a court finds liability to be a question common to the class it holds 23(b)(3) satisfied.

* * *

As a practical matter, where plaintiffs have been affected by a concerted practice effecting a common course of conduct, the proofs necessary to establish "the fact of injury" or "impact" will be essentially the same for each member of the class notwithstanding the rule that such an issue is individual to each plaintiff. As to the present case, proof as to the existence, implementation and effect of the alleged conspiracy appear to be the same for each class member. Accordingly, the evidence necessary to prove liability of the defendants, *i.e.*, violation and impact, would appear to be sufficiently similar as to all members of the class to permit resolution within the class action process.

C. Damages

*** [C]ourts have recognized that individual damage questions will not be held to predominate to the preclusion of a class action where liability has been found to be common to the class, where the issues of liability and individual damages can be treated separately, or where damages are susceptible to mathematical or formula calculation.

* * *

As to the present case, the proof plaintiffs' representatives would have to present to establish the existence, implementation, and effect of a conspiracy would be essentially common to the entire class constituting a "common thread of evidence which would correspond to evidence which would otherwise be introduced by absent class members." Such individual defenses as may exist would not appear sufficient to predominate over the common questions affecting the class as a whole. Establishing a conspiracy in this case, though not the gravamen of the case, will be a crucial and most difficult aspect of the case to prove. The present case may present facts which are particularly suited to severance of the violation issue as failure on that point would be entirely dispositive of the rest of the case.

To satisfy the issue of the fact of injury, plaintiffs would need to prove a causal tie between the violation and some loss resulting from that violation. If defendants did conspire to eliminate the capitalization method of accounting and to offer only the escrow method, without interest being paid to the plaintiff class, the fact of injury, if any, would be essentially identical as to each class member. * * *

As to damages, the plaintiffs appear to be correct in their assertion that damages could be determined mathematically or through a formula in a relatively simple procedure, which they themselves have suggested. * * * Accordingly, the court should rule that the issues common to the plaintiff class predominate over questions affecting individual members of the class, namely, that questions of conspiracy are common questions, the issue of impact, though individualized[,] will in fact involve proof common to the entire class and that such individual questions as are involved in the determination of damages will be subject to mathematical or formula proofs.

[The court also found that class treatment would be superior to alternatives, and certified the action under Rule 23(b)(3).]

NOTES AND QUESTIONS

1. Because neither Rule 23(b)(3) nor its Advisory Committee Notes provide a definition of "predominance," courts and commentators have wrestled with what the predominance determination requires. How did the *Brown* court interpret the "predominance" requirement? Consider some alternative approaches that other courts have used:

a. Some courts have stated that, although adjudication of common questions need not resolve the entire litigation, common questions predominate if resolution of such questions at least signals the beginning of the end of the litigation. *See, e.g., Mattoon v. City of Pittsfield*, 128 F.R.D. 17, 20 (D. Mass. 1989) ("[C]ommon issues are predominant only if their resolution would 'provide a definite signal of the beginning of the end.'" (quoting *Mertens v. Abbott Labs*, 99 F.R.D. 38, 41 (D.N.H. 1983))).

b. Other courts have found that common questions may predominate if resolution of the litigation as a whole is materially advanced by resolving the common questions. *See, e.g.*, *In re Sch. Asbestos Litig.*, 789 F.2d 996, 1010 (3d Cir. 1986) ("There may be cases in which class resolution of one issue or a small group of them will so advance the litigation that they may fairly be said to predominate."); *see also Hanlon v. Chrysler Corp.*, 150 F.3d 1011, 1022 (9th Cir. 1998) ("When common questions present a significant aspect of the case and they can be resolved for all members of the class in a single adjudication, there is clear justification for handling the dispute on a representative rather than on an individual basis."); *Powers v. Hamilton Cnty. Pub. Defender Comm'n*, 501 F.3d 592, 619 (6th Cir. 2007) (the "predominance requirement is met if [a] common question is at the heart of the litigation").

c. Still other courts have resisted attempts to define the predominance inquiry in terms of quantity or quality of issues. Like the court in *Brown*, they have found that the issue should be a decision by a trial court, based upon consideration of how the case actually would be litigated. In *Simer v. Rios*, 661 F.2d 655, 672 (7th Cir. 1981), for example, the Seventh Circuit noted:

> The notion of predominance in the class action analysis is a relatively impalpable concept. Several alternative analytical frameworks attempting to give substantive content to the concept have been articulated in various lines of cases. Most courts have looked to economies in trying the case as a class action. At the extremes the analyses have ranged from whether the total time trying both common issues and separate issues would be less than trying all issues separately to whether the total time spent trying common issues would be greater than time spent on trial of individual issues. These analyses are plainly inadequate. The former would render the "predominance" requirement nugatory since if at least one issue could be tried in common the requirement would be satisfied. As to the latter approach, it would unduly block class actions from going forward because only the most complex of common questions would require more litigation time than a series of individual trials.

In place of some mathematical calculus, the *Simer* court suggested that a predominance analysis should first "focus * * * on the substantive elements of plaintiffs' cause of action and inquire into the proof necessary for the various elements," then "inquire into the form that trial on these issues would take." *Id*. Moreover, apparently suggesting that the "predominance" and "superiority" analyses of Rule 23(b)(3) tend to merge, *Simer* further noted that "[a]t this point [in the analysis] it also becomes necessary to examine the procedural devices and alternatives available in trying class actions. This discussion interfaces with many aspects of the issue of manageability * * *." *Id.*; *see also O'Sullivan v. Countrywide Home Loans, Inc.*, 319 F.3d 732, 738 (5th Cir. 2003) ("Determining whether legal issues common to the class predominate over individual issues requires that the court inquire how the case will be tried[, which] entails identifying the substantive issues that will control the outcome, assessing which issues will predominate, and then determining whether the issues are common to the class" (citation omitted)); Robert H. Klonoff, *The Decline of Class Actions*, 90 Wash. U.L. Rev. 729, 792 (2013) (noting judicial trend of finding an absence of predominance after identifying "significant individualized issues," and "without carefully *weighing* those individualized issues against the common issues").

d. In *Klay v. Humana, Inc.*, 382 F.3d 1241 (11th Cir. 2004), the Eleventh Circuit observed that:

> "Whether an issue predominates can only be determined after considering what value the resolution of the class-wide issue will have in each class member's underlying cause of action." *Rutstein v. Avis Rent–A–Car Sys. Inc.*, 211 F.3d 1228, 1234 (11th Cir. 2000). Common issues of fact and law predominate if they "have a direct impact on every class member's effort to establish liability and on every class member's entitlement to injunctive and monetary relief." *Ingram v. Coca–Cola Co.*, 200 F.R.D. 685, 699 (N.D. Ga. 2001). Where, after adjudication of the classwide issues, plaintiffs must still introduce a great deal of individualized proof or argue a number of individualized legal points to establish most or all of the elements of their individual claims, such claims are not suitable for class certification under Rule 23(b)(3). *See Perez v. Metabolife Int'l, Inc.*, 218 F.R.D. 262, 273 (S.D. Fla. 2003) (declining class certification in part because "any efficiency gained by deciding the common elements will be lost when separate trials are required for each class member in order to determine each member's entitlement to the requested relief").
>
> An alternate formulation of this test was offered in *Alabama v. Blue Bird Body Co.*, 573 F.2d 309 (5th Cir. 1978). In that case, we observed that if common issues truly predominate over individualized issues in a lawsuit, then "the addition or subtraction of any of the plaintiffs to or from the class [should not] have a substantial effect on the substance or quantity of evidence offered." *Id.* at 322. Put simply, if the addition of more plaintiffs to a class requires the presentation of significant amounts of new evidence, that strongly suggests that individual issues (made relevant only through the inclusion of these new class members) are important. *Id.* ("If such addition or subtraction of plaintiffs does affect the substance or quantity of evidence offered, then the necessary common question might not be present."). If, on the other hand, the addition of more plaintiffs leaves the quantum of evidence introduced by the plaintiffs as a whole relatively undisturbed, then common issues are likely to predominate.

Klay, 382 F.3d at 1255.

Do any of these formulations (including the discussion in *Brown*) provide a workable analytical framework for addressing the question of predominance? What factors should enter into a court's decision as to whether common issues predominate over individual ones? Could the rule be more specific? If so, how should it be rewritten?

2. Predominance issues arise frequently in antitrust class actions. Some courts are receptive to certifying antitrust cases. For example, in *Cordes & Co. Financial Services v. A.G. Edwards & Sons, Inc.*, 502 F.3d 91 (2d Cir. 2007), plaintiffs alleged a conspiracy to fix the spreads charged by underwriters in certain initial public offerings. The district court had denied class certification, finding, *inter alia*, that plaintiffs failed to meet Rule 23(b)(3)'s predominance requirement because they did not offer evidence establishing that antitrust injury could be proven by a method common to the class. *Id.* at 95. The Second Circuit reversed and remanded, finding that at least two common questions existed: "(1) all factual and legal questions that must be resolved to determine

whether the defendants violated Section 1 of the Sherman Act; and (2) all factual and legal questions that must be resolved to decide whether, assuming a plaintiff paid supracompetitive prices, that payment was caused by the defendants' antitrust violation and constitutes the kind of injury with which the antitrust laws are concerned." *Id.* at 108. While not "discount[ing] the possibility that the individual questions raised by injury-in-fact might * * * predominate over the * * * common questions," *id.*, the Second Circuit nonetheless remanded, directing the district court to reconsider the predominance question. *See also In re Scrap Metal Antitrust Litig.*, 527 F.3d 517 (6th Cir. 2008) ("[W]here there are individual variations in damages, the requirements of Rule 23(b)(3) are satisfied if the plaintiffs can establish that the defendants conspired to interfere with the free-market pricing structure."); *Smilow v. Sw. Bell Mobile Sys., Inc.*, 323 F.3d 32, 38–41 (1st Cir. 2003) (where class of wireless telephone customers challenged identical form contract, faced same waiver defense, and "individual factual determinations [regarding damages could] be accomplished using computer records, clerical assistance, and objective criteria," common issues predominated).

Other circuits have been less receptive to finding antitrust injury to be susceptible of common proof. For instance, in *Blades v. Monsanto Co.*, 400 F.3d 562 (8th Cir. 2005), farmers who bought genetically modified corn and soybean seed brought an antitrust action, alleging a price-fixing conspiracy between the holder of patents for genes used to develop the seeds and the patent licensees. The Eighth Circuit affirmed the district court's denial of (b)(3) certification on the grounds that the farmers could not prove classwide injury with proof common to the class. The district court reasoned as follows:

> In sum, after carefully considering all the evidence submitted during the class certification hearing, I am convinced that the impact of defendants' alleged antitrust violations cannot be shown on a classwide basis with common proof. Instead, it is a highly individualized, fact-intensive inquiry that necessarily requires consideration of factors unique to each potential class member. The variety of [genetically modified] seeds purchased, geographic location, growing conditions and the terms of purchase are all relevant to a determination of impact and cannot be shown with common proof on a class-wide basis.
> * * *

Id. at 571. The Eighth Circuit affirmed the district court's holding that "neither the existence of a conspiracy to fix prices, nor the existence of some resultant harm constitute questions common to the class." *Id.* at 566. Similarly, in *Robinson v. Texas Automobile Dealers Ass'n*, 387 F.3d 416 (5th Cir. 2004), the Fifth Circuit reversed the certification of a class of more than one million consumers who purchased automobiles in Texas. It held that plaintiffs' theory—that every class member suffered antitrust injury by paying a tax in addition to the negotiated price of the car—was incorrect because some consumers likely "negotiate[d] with an eye to the 'bottom line' "; that is, they negotiated a lower price for the vehicle to account for the extra cost of the tax. *Id.* at 423. As a result, the court would "have to hear evidence *regarding each purported class member and his transaction*" in order to determine who had been injured, so common questions did not predominate. *Id.* at 424; *see also Brown v. Am. Honda*, 522 F.3d 6, 28–29 (1st Cir. 2008) (holding that even if plaintiffs could show that defendants' actions reduced the number of lower-priced Canadian automobiles in the U.S. market and that the reduction raised recommended retail prices in the U.S., they would still have to show that each class member suffered injury by paying more than he or she would have absent defendants' actions, in light of individual negotiations).

For a discussion of conflicting antitrust case law, *see* Robert H. Klonoff, *Antitrust Class Actions: Chaos in the Courts*, 11 Stan. J.L. Bus. & Fin. 1, 21–25 (2005). *See also* William H. Page, Introduction: *Reexamining the Standards for Certification of Antitrust Class Actions*, 21 Antitrust 53 (Summer 2007).

3. As noted in *Brown*, a number of courts have ruled that class certification under Rule 23(b)(3) cannot be defeated solely on the ground that class members' damages will have to be determined on an individualized basis after adjudication of liability on a classwide basis. That issue is discussed in detail in Section (C)(1)(b)(v) of this chapter.

b. Other Recurring Themes in the Predominance Inquiry

i. Fraud and Related Claims

Plaintiffs often seek certification under Rule 23(b)(3) in cases involving fraud or other claims analogous to fraud. Defendants often contend, in response, that because plaintiffs have been exposed to differing representations, individual issues relating to what representations were made to each plaintiff will predominate over any common issues. Moreover, defendants often argue that the materiality of the statements at issue will differ from plaintiff to plaintiff based on the information that was available to each plaintiff at the time of the representation. Defendants contend that reliance will be inherently individualized, since it will depend on the information available to each plaintiff and whether each plaintiff actually (and, when legally required, reasonably) relied upon the representations at issue. Indeed, the debate was presaged in Rule 23(b)(3)'s Advisory Committee Notes, which state:

> [A] fraud perpetrated on numerous persons by the use of similar misrepresentations may be an appealing situation for a class action, and it may remain so despite the need, if liability is found, for separate determination of the damages suffered by individuals within the class. On the other hand, although having some common core, a fraud case may be unsuited for treatment as a class action if there was material variation in the representation[s] made or in the kinds or degrees of reliance by the persons to whom they were addressed.

It is therefore hardly surprising that courts have reached differing results with respect to certification of claims sounding in fraud. One example is set forth below.

McManus v. Fleetwood Enters., Inc.
United States Court of Appeals for the Fifth Circuit, 2003.
320 F.3d 545.

Before EMILIO M. GARZA and CLEMENT, CIRCUIT JUDGES, and HUDSPETH, DISTRICT JUDGE [(W.D. Tex., by designation)].

CLEMENT, CIRCUIT JUDGE.

The district court certified a subclass of plaintiffs who purchased Class A motor homes in Texas from defendant Fleetwood Enterprises, Inc., a California corporation, between 1994 and 1999. Representative plaintiffs Donnie and June McManus allege that Fleetwood misrepresented the towing capacity of its motor homes. They seek injunctive relief under Federal Rule of Civil Procedure 23(b)(2) and, in the alternative, damages under Rule 23(b)(3). The district court abused its discretion in certifying the class under Rule 23(b)(3), except with regard to the McManuses' claim for breach of implied warranty of merchantability. * * * We affirm in part, and reverse and remand in part.

I. FACTS AND PROCEEDINGS

The McManuses purchased a Fleetwood motor home in Texas in 1997, with the intention of towing a Jeep Cherokee behind it. Donnie McManus noticed a tag affixed to the wardrobe door stating that the motor home could tow 3,500 pounds, and the sales representative assured him that the motor home would be able to tow a Jeep Cherokee. The wardrobe door tag was titled "CARRYING CAPACITY" and it listed various statistics, including an entry reading "GTW *3500 LBS*." The tag explained:

> GTW (Gross Towed Weight): means the maximum permissible loaded weight of a trailer or car that this motor home has been designed to tow. This cannot be increased by changing the trailer hitch.

The bottom of the tag stated in large, bold print:

> CONSULT OWNER'S MANUAL FOR WEIGHING
> INSTRUCTIONS AND TOWING GUIDELINES

A Fleetwood engineer contacted Fleetwood's chassis manufacturers in 1994 and discovered that, according to the chassis manufacturers, the motor homes would require supplemental brakes to safely tow 3,500 pounds. * * * The engineer concluded in a company memorandum, "To assure safe operation of our products, the wardrobe door tag, owners manual and advertising material should reflect two GCW's [gross combination weight], one for towed loads without brakes and one for towed loads with brakes."

The McManuses allege that the representation that the motor home could safely *tow* 3,500 pounds amounted to a representation that it could safely *brake* while towing 3,500 pounds. Their complaint asserts the following five claims: (1) violation California's Consumers Legal Remedies Act, Cal. Civ. Code §§ 1750–1784; (2) breach of express warranty; (3) breach of implied warranty of merchantability under California's Song–Beverly Consumer Warranty Act, Cal. Civ. Code § 1792; (4) negligent misrepresentation; and (5) fraudulent concealment. They seek [in addition to injunctive relief under (b)(2)] * * * money damages under Rule 23(b)(3).

Fleetwood counters, in short, that the wardrobe tag was accurate because it said nothing about supplemental brakes, and because it conspicuously led the consumer to a paper trail that would reveal the relevant information. The tag directed the consumer to the motor home owner's manual, which directed the consumer to the chassis manufacturer's manual containing the relevant towing limitations.

The district court [certified a Texas-only class under (b)(2) and (b)(3)]. * * * As a preliminary determination in deciding that the Rule 23 class action prerequisites were met, the district court also concluded, contrary to the McManuses' assertions, that Texas law would govern the dispute instead of California law.

II. DISCUSSION

The McManuses now concede that Texas law governs the dispute, so the only issue for this interlocutory appeal is the propriety of the district court's certification decision, which we review for abuse of discretion.

* * *

* * * We consider the district court's decision under Rule 23(b)(3) * * *.

A. Certification is only proper under Rule 23(b)(3) for the McManuses' claim for breach of implied warranty of merchantability

* * * Fleetwood argues that the common questions of fact do not predominate over individual matters. In particular, Fleetwood asserts that since each of the plaintiffs' claims requires a showing of reliance on the alleged misrepresentation, the district court abused its discretion in certifying the class under Rule 23(b)(3). The McManuses respond that the district court may presume classwide reliance because the same information—that the motor homes could tow 3,500 pounds—was given to all of the class members.

1. *Reliance may not be presumed under Texas law.*

The McManuses rely upon *Life Ins. Co. of Southwest v. Brister*, 722 S.W.2d 764 (Tex. App. 1986) and *Reserve Life Ins. Co. v. Kirkland*, 917 S.W.2d 836 (Tex. App. 1996) for the proposition that Texas law permits a class-wide presumption of reliance. In each case, the appellate court determined that the proposed class members had a "sufficient community of interest," *Brister*, 722 S.W.2d at 774, to justify certification under Texas Rule of Civil Procedure 42 [the Texas class action rule]. The result was premised on the view that Texas courts "should err in favor and not against the maintenance of the class action since the class certification order is always subject to modification should later developments during the course of the trial so require." The Texas Supreme Court has since overruled those cases, explicitly "reject[ing] this approach of certify now and worry later." *Southwestern Refining Co. v. Bernal*, 22 S.W.3d 425, 435 (Tex. 2000).

The *Bernal* court emphasized that "[p]rocedural devices may 'not be construed to enlarge or diminish any substantive rights or obligations of any parties to any civil action.'" In a particularly instructive post-*Bernal* case, the Texas Supreme Court held that issues of reliance defeated the predominance requirement of [the Texas class action rule] in a class action alleging, among other things, that advertising for dental office management software was false and misleading:

> [T]he 20,000 class members in the present case are held to the same standards of proof of reliance—and for that matter all the other elements of their claims—that they would be required to meet if each sued individually. This does not mean, of course, that reliance or other elements of their causes of action cannot be

proved class-wide with evidence generally applicable to all class members; class-wide proof is possible when class-wide evidence exists. But evidence insufficient to prove reliance in a suit by an individual does not become sufficient in a class action simply because there are more plaintiffs. Inescapably individual differences cannot be concealed in a throng. The procedural device of a class action eliminates the necessity of adducing the same evidence over and over again in a multitude of individual actions; it does not lessen the quality of evidence required in an individual action or relax substantive burdens of proof.

Henry Schein, Inc. v. Stromboe, 102 S.W.3d 675, [693–94] (Tex. 2002).

We note additionally that neither *Brister* nor *Kirkland* speaks to the *substantive* standard of proof of the underlying causes of action; those cases are concerned only with the *procedural* standard to justify certification under *Texas* procedural law. Since we are bound to follow *Federal* Rule of Civil Procedure 23, not Texas' corresponding [rule], *Brister* and *Kirkland* are not instructive to the issue. As *Bernal* and *Henry Schein* make clear, Texas law does not permit the type of presumed reliance urged by the McManuses.

2. *Reliance issues are fatal to a Rule 23(b)(3) class for claims of fraudulent concealment and negligent misrepresentation.*

"Claims for money damages in which individual reliance is an element are poor candidates for class treatment, at best. We have made that plain." Here, it is undisputed that class members would only be entitled to relief under theories of fraudulent concealment or negligent misrepresentation if they could show they relied on the alleged misrepresentation. Reliance will vary from plaintiff to plaintiff, depending on the circumstances surrounding the sale. For instance, Donnie McManus testified at his deposition that he read the wardrobe door tag and asked the salesperson about the towing capacity. June McManus testified that she did not read the tag, nor did she draw any conclusion as to whether the motor home would be able to tow a Jeep Cherokee. The individual reliance issues are apparent even as between the two representative plaintiffs. Other potential class members certainly may have read the wardrobe door tag as Fleetwood reads it—as being silent on the issue of supplemental brakes—and certainly some class members may have actually *known* at the time of purchase that supplemental brakes would be needed. At this point in the litigation, the McManuses have failed to show that these potential variables are sufficiently uniform to justify class treatment, and we conclude that the district court abused its discretion in finding that questions of fact common to the class were predominant, for purposes of Rule 23(b)(3), with respect to the McManuses' claims for fraudulent inducement and negligent misrepresentation.

3. *The McManuses' claim, under Rule 23(b)(3), for breach of express warranty requires reliance and is inappropriate for class treatment.*

The McManuses argue that their claim for breach of express warranty does not require a showing of reliance, thereby avoiding the variable factual circumstances explained above. We disagree. Under Texas law, an express warranty is created when a seller makes a representation or promise "which relates to the goods and becomes part of the *basis of the bargain.*

..." Tex. Bus. & Com. Code Ann. § 2.313 (emphasis added). There is a split of authority as to whether that wording (from the U.C.C.) is meant to dispense with the common law's requirement of reliance in express warranty cases. The Texas Supreme Court has concluded that " '[b]asis of the bargain' loosely reflects the common-law express warranty requirement of reliance," and that therefore an express warranty claim "requires *a form of reliance.*" *Am. Tobacco Co., Inc. v. Grinnell*, 951 S.W.2d 420, 436 (Tex. 1997) (emphasis added). That court has recently characterized a breach of express warranty claim as requiring reliance "*to a certain extent.*" *Henry Schein*, 102 S.W.3d at [693] (emphasis added).

Although the precise level of reliance required under Texas law to recover for breach of express warranty is unclear, purchasers who understood the towing limitations, or who did not read or consider the wardrobe door tag, cannot be said to have relied on the allegedly misleading wardrobe tag to *any* extent. Thus, the McManuses have failed to show that the representations were part of the "basis of the bargain" to such a uniform extent that class certification is appropriate under Rule 23(b)(3) for the breach of express warranty claim.

[The court found that the district court did not abuse its discretion in certifying a claim for breach of implied warranty of merchantability, which does not require a showing of reliance. The court also found that Rule 23(b)(2) certification was improper.]

NOTES AND QUESTIONS

1. The *McManus* court provided a claim-by-claim analysis of whether reliance barred a class action under Rule 23(b)(3). Note that the court purported to analyze the underlying substantive law closely in order to determine whether, given the factual allegations, reliance would be a necessary element of the proofs. Is that analysis persuasive? How could the plaintiff respond to the holdings concerning fraudulent concealment, negligent misrepresentation, and express warranty?

2. As noted earlier, courts have reached differing results as to whether claims analogous to fraud can be certified under Rule 23(b)(3). *See generally* Annotation, *Consumer Class Actions Based on Fraud or Misrepresentation*, 53 A.L.R. 3d 834 (1996) (summarizing case law). One potential solution to the problem of potentially individualized fraud issues is to sue under a statute that does not require individualized proof of the elements of fraud, and to claim that the representations were uniform. In *Tylka v. Gerber Products Co.*, 178 F.R.D. 493 (N.D. Ill. 1998), for example, plaintiffs sued under, *inter alia*, the Illinois Consumer Fraud and Deceptive Business Practices Act. The court certified a class action under Rule 23(b)(3) on that claim, finding that materiality was judged under the consumer fraud statute by an objective standard and that the statute did not require proof of individual reliance. Against defendant's claims that the representations differed over time, the court responded:

> [T]he class members were subject to standardized conduct. Gerber's ads, although varied according to geography and medium, allegedly carried the same message: misrepresentation of the quality and ingredients in Gerber's second and third-stage baby food products. Further, Gerber does not argue that the class Plaintiffs relied on any individual representations or communications. All allegedly fraudulent

representations were conveyed through widely circulated and generalized advertisements.

Id. at 499.

3. Reliance in securities cases is discussed in detail in Chapter 10(C). These notes provide a brief overview of the subject. Courts have developed several doctrines that address circumstances under which class treatment may be accorded to a fraud suit. One doctrine, approved by the Supreme Court in *Basic Inc. v. Levinson*, 485 U.S. 224 (1988) (*see* Chapter 10(C)(1)), addresses both misrepresentations and omissions. Under the "*Basic* presumption," in a well-developed securities market (in which there are numerous buyers and sellers of a defendant company's stock and numerous analysts and professionals to analyze and trade in the stock), courts are willing to presume that all relevant information is synthesized and valued in the stock's current price. Thus, a buyer or seller of stock may be presumed to have relied on the integrity of the market in making a purchase or sale, and a defendant may be found liable for misrepresentations or omissions that were material—that is, those that influenced (or, in the case of omitted information, would have influenced) the price of the stock. This is so regardless of whether a particular buyer or seller proves that he or she actually relied on—or even received—a particular misrepresentation. In 2014, the Supreme Court considered whether the *Basic* presumption should be overruled, but ultimately declined to do so. *See Halliburton Co. v. Erica P. John Fund, Inc.*, 134 S. Ct. 2398 (2014) (discussed in Ch. 10).

4. The *Basic* doctrine is commonly referred to as the "fraud-on-the-market" theory. *See Unger v. Amedisys Inc.*, 401 F.3d 316, 322 (5th Cir. 2005) (explaining that "fraud-on-the-market" theory is "based on the hypothesis that, in an open and developed securities market, the price of a company's stock is determined by the available material information regarding the company and its business" and that "[m]isleading statements will therefore defraud purchasers of stock even if the purchasers do not directly rely on the misstatements"). Some cases have held that, to obtain a presumption of classwide reliance under the fraud-on-the-market theory, plaintiffs must make an evidentiary showing of market efficiency at the class certification stage. *Id.* ("To support this rebuttable presumption, a securities plaintiff must prove, *inter alia*, that the security at issue is traded in an 'efficient market.' "). In *Bell v. Ascendant Solutions, Inc.*, 422 F.3d 307, 313 (5th Cir. 2005), the Fifth Circuit "joined several * * * sister circuits in applying 'rigorous, though preliminary, standards of proof to the market efficiency determination,' and [it] * * * set forth various factors utilized by courts to decide whether a stock trades in an efficient market." *Id.* at 313. In *Bell*, where the plaintiffs—who carry the burden of demonstrating (b)(3) predominance—failed to make "any serious effort to show market efficiency," the Fifth Circuit held that the district court did not abuse its discretion in denying (b)(3) certification. *Id.* at 316.

In a 2011 case, however, the Supreme Court held that the Fifth Circuit erred in requiring securities fraud plaintiffs to prove "loss causation" at the class certification stage in order to meet the predominance requirement of Rule 23(b)(3). *Erica P. John Fund, Inc. v. Halliburton Co.*, 563 U.S. 804 (2011). Following circuit precedent, the Fifth Circuit determined that plaintiffs, to avail themselves of the *Basic* presumption, "needed to prove that the decline in [defendant's] stock was 'because of the correction to a prior misleading statement' and 'that the subsequent loss could not otherwise be explained by some additional factors revealed then to the market.' " *Id.* at 2185 (quoting 597 F.3d 330, 336 (5th Cir. 2010)). The Supreme Court reversed, in a unanimous opinion by

Chief Justice Roberts, concluding that the Fifth Circuit's requirement of proving loss causation at the class certification stage was "not justified by *Basic* or its logic." *Id.* The Court distinguished between "reliance," which it also termed "transaction causation," on the one hand, and "loss causation" on the other:

> * * * Under *Basic*'s fraud-on-the-market doctrine, an investor presumptively relies on a defendant's misrepresentation if that "information is reflected in [the] market price" of the stock at the time of the relevant transaction. Loss causation, by contrast, requires a plaintiff to show that a misrepresentation that affected the integrity of the market price also caused a subsequent economic loss. * * * According to the Court of Appeals, however, an inability to prove loss causation would prevent a plaintiff from invoking the rebuttable presumption of reliance. Such a rule contravenes *Basic*'s fundamental premise—that an investor presumptively relies on a misrepresentation so long as it was reflected in the market price at the time of his transaction. The fact that a subsequent loss may have been caused by factors other than the revelation of a misrepresentation has nothing to do with whether an investor relied on the misrepresentation in the first place, either directly or presumptively through the fraud-on-the-market theory. Loss causation has no logical connection to the facts necessary to establish the efficient market predicate to the fraud-on-the-market theory.

Id. at 2186. In so holding, the Court resolved a circuit split "as to whether securities fraud plaintiffs must prove loss causation in order to obtain class certification." *Id.* at 2184 (citations omitted); *see also, e.g., In re Salomon Analyst Metromedia Litig.*, 544 F.3d 474, 483 (2d Cir. 2008) (not requiring investors to prove loss causation at class certification stage); *Schleicher v. Wendt*, 618 F.3d 679, 687 (7th Cir. 2010) (same).

How does the *Basic* presumption affect who may be held liable for securities fraud? In *Stoneridge Investment Partners LLC v. Scientific–Atlanta*, 552 U.S. 148 (2008), plaintiffs alleged that Charter Communications entered into a series of fraudulent transactions with Scientific–Atlanta whereby Scientific–Atlanta enabled Charter to create the appearance that Charter had higher revenues. The value of plaintiffs' Charter shares fell dramatically when Charter later disclosed the improprieties. The plaintiffs did not allege that Scientific–Atlanta had made direct misrepresentations that affected the share price; rather, they alleged that Scientific–Atlanta's actions caused the misrepresentations made by Charter. They argued that the *Basic* presumption should satisfy the reliance element of their claim against Scientific–Atlanta, despite the lack of public misrepresentations, because Scientific–Atlanta's actions indirectly affected the price of the shares.

The Court disagreed, holding that the *Basic* presumption did not apply without a public statement by the defendant. *Id.* at 160. In an opinion by Justice Kennedy, the Court explained that were it otherwise, plaintiffs would be able to use securities law to impose liability on "the whole marketplace in which the issuing company does business." *Id.* It also noted that "[i]t was Charter, not [Scientific–Atlanta], that misled its auditor and filed fraudulent financial statements; nothing [Scientific–Atlanta] did made it necessary or inevitable for Charter to record the transactions as it did." *Id.* at 161. As a result, Scientific–Atlanta's actions were "too remote [from the stockholders' losses] to satisfy the requirement of reliance." *Id.*

5. A second doctrine, announced in *Affiliated Ute Citizens v. United States*, 406 U.S. 128 (1972), addresses material omissions. Under the "*Ute* presumption," a plaintiff is excused from proving reliance upon material omissions (the theory being that it is very difficult for someone to prove reliance upon what he or she did *not* hear). The Supreme Court restated the *Ute* presumption in *Stoneridge Investment Partners LLC v. Scientific–Atlanta*, 552 U.S. 148 (2008): "[I]f there is an omission of a material fact by one with a duty to disclose, the investor to whom the duty was owed need not provide specific proof of reliance." *Id.* at 159; accord, e.g., *Regents of Univ. of Cal. v. Credit Suisse First Bos., Inc.*, 482 F.3d 372, 383–84 (5th Cir. 2007); *Joseph v. Wiles*, 223 F.3d 1155, 1162 (10th Cir. 2000); *Newton v. Merrill Lynch, Pierce, Fenner & Smith, Inc.*, 259 F.3d 154, 175 (3d Cir. 2001).

6. Reliance issues under *Basic* also have arisen outside the securities context. Most courts have rejected the proposition that the *Basic* presumption should apply outside the area of securities fraud suits. See *In re Ford Motor Co. Vehicle Paint Litig.*, 182 F.R.D. 214, 221 (E.D. La. 1998) (collecting state and federal cases and stating, "this Court's research reveals that the vast majority of states have never adopted a rule allowing reliance to be presumed in common law fraud cases, and some states have expressly rejected such a proposition. * * * Moreover, the vast majority of federal courts have refused to recognize such a presumption in common law fraud cases when the controlling state has not expressly adopted such a rule."); *Hunt v. U.S. Tobacco Co.*, 538 F.3d 217, 228 (3d Cir. 2008) (holding *Basic* inapplicable in a case involving antitrust allegations against a smokeless tobacco company because the plaintiff did "not allege that Smokeless made a misrepresentation to an efficient market; rather, he alleges that Smokeless concealed the inefficiency of the market [caused by Smokeless's anticompetitive conduct] for Smokeless's product"). Under what circumstances might extension of the *Basic* doctrine be warranted?

In *McLaughlin v. American Tobacco Co.*, 522 F.3d 215 (2d Cir. 2008), plaintiffs argued that the *Basic* presumption should apply to their RICO claims that tobacco companies falsely advertised that light cigarettes were less harmful to smokers' health than full-flavored cigarettes. *Id.* at 220, 223. The plaintiffs argued that they "relied upon the public's general sense that Lights were healthier than full-flavored cigarettes, whether or not individual plaintiffs were actually aware of defendants' alleged misrepresentation." *Id.* at 223–24. The Second Circuit reversed the district court's certification of the class. *Id.* at 221. It held the *Basic* presumption inapplicable on the facts because the cigarette market was not as efficient as the securities market; it noted, in particular, that sales of Light cigarettes did not decrease after the publication of a major report detailing the hazards of Lights. *Id.* at 224. Looking at reliance without the *Basic* presumption, the court found that because class members might have smoked light cigarettes for reasons other than the defendants' advertisements, "reliance [was] too individualized to admit of common proof." *Id.* at 226. The court did not, however, "adopt the Fifth Circuit's blanket rule that 'a fraud class action cannot be certified when individual reliance will be an issue.'" *Id.* at 224 (quoting *Castano v. Am. Tobacco Co.*, 84 F.3d 734, 745 (5th Cir. 1996)). It cited the Advisory Committee Notes as support for the proposition that fraud claims are sometimes suitable for class certification. *McLaughlin*, 522 F.3d at 225.

Following up on *McLaughlin*, in *UFCW Local 1776 v. Eli Lilly & Co.*, 620 F.3d 121 (2d Cir. 2010), the Second Circuit reversed the district court's certification of a class of third-party payors for prescription drugs who alleged that the defendant drug manufacturer's misrepresentations to prescribing doctors directly caused financial injury to the class in the form of higher prices. *Id.* at 123. The district court had distinguished *McLaughlin*, finding that "reliance could be proven for the class because the alleged fraud was 'directed through mailings and otherwise at doctors who relied, causing damages in overpayments by plaintiffs.' " *Id.* at 130 (quoting district court's opinion). "This, the district court concluded, could appropriately be shown by generalized proof, in contrast to the more abstract 'fraud on the market' theory rejected in *McLaughlin*." *Id.* The Second Circuit reversed, finding that, as in *McLaughlin*, too many individual variables existed for the plaintiffs' claims to be susceptible of generalized, classwide proof. *Id.* at 132–37.

7. The *Ute* presumption also has been addressed outside the securities context. *See, e.g., Davis v. S. Bell Tel. & Tel. Co.*, 1993 WL 593999, at *11 (S.D. Fla. 1993) (holding, based on the *Ute* presumption, that plaintiffs' state-law fraud claims against the defendant phone company could be adjudicated as a class action, notwithstanding the fact that plaintiffs had to prove reliance and damages, because "[p]roof of reliance should be a simple matter," given that "reliance is presumed where the misrepresentation at issue arises from material omissions"). Should the *Ute* presumption permit Rule 23(b)(3) certification for fraud claims? What limits, if any, should be imposed? *See Poulos v. Caesars World, Inc.*, 379 F.3d 654, 667 (9th Cir. 2004) (holding that even if *Ute* applies outside the securities context, it is limited to cases "primarily alleg[ing] omissions").

8. The existence of reliance issues does not necessarily defeat class certification, even absent a presumption of reliance. Some courts have been willing to find that even if individual questions of reliance exist, certification may still be appropriate under Rule 23(b)(3). In *Arenson v. Whitehall Convalescent & Nursing Home, Inc.*, 164 F.R.D. 659 (N.D. Ill. 1996), for example, the court certified a class involving, *inter alia*, common law fraud, finding that "[e]ven for [a] common law fraud claim, which requires proof of reliance, '[i]t is well established that individual issues of reliance do not thwart class actions.' " *Id.* at 666. Similarly, in *Jenson v. Fiserv Trust Co.*, 256 F. App'x 924 (9th Cir. 2007), the court found that reliance could be "infer[red]" where the defendant told each prospective investor that it would get a high yield from the investment. *Id.* at 926. How would the *McManus* court respond to these decisions? Would Rule 23(b)(3) benefit from a black-letter provision explicitly permitting—or prohibiting—certification of class actions sounding in fraud? For further discussion of this issue, *see* Samuel Issacharoff, *The Vexing Problem of Reliance in Consumer Class Actions*, 74 Tul. L. Rev. 1633 (2000) (arguing that most proposed consumer class actions should be allowed to proceed as class actions notwithstanding issues of reliance). *But see* Robert H. Klonoff, *The Decline of Class Actions*, 90 Wash. U. L. Rev. 729, 793 (2013) ("Many courts have adopted essentially a *per se* view that fraud suits involving questions of individual reliance are not suitable for class certification.").

9. In *CGC Holding Co., LLC v. Broad & Cassel*, 773 F.3d 1076, 1089, 1095 (10th Cir. 2014), the Tenth Circuit affirmed certification of a (b)(3) class alleging civil claims under the Racketeer Influenced and Corrupt Organizations Act ("RICO"). Under 18 U.S.C. § 1964(c), a civil cause of action exists for "[a]ny person injured in his business or property by reason of" a violation of RICO's prohibitions. Courts have read the "by reason of" language in § 1964(c) to require a civil RICO plaintiff to plead and prove "that a RICO predicate offense not only was a 'but for' cause of his injury, but was the proximate cause as well." *Hemi Grp., LLC v. City of N.Y.*, 559 U.S. 1, 9 (2010) (citation and

internal quotation marks omitted). In a fraud case, causation is usually shown through proof of reliance on a misrepresentation, and because reliance is often an individualized issue, courts have frequently found RICO classes unfit for class certification. In *Broad & Cassel*, however, the Tenth Circuit found that the case before it was indeed certifiable based on the allegations presented:

> In practice, efforts to certify classes based on causes of action that require an element of causation, including RICO, often turn on whether the class can demonstrate that reliance is susceptible to generalized proof.
>
> * * * In terms of Rule 23 doctrine, individualized issues of reliance often preclude a finding of predominance. But that is not always the case. * * * For example, where circumstantial evidence of reliance can be found through generalized, classwide proof, then common questions will predominate and class treatment is valuable in order to take advantage of the efficiencies essential to class actions. Under certain circumstances, therefore, it is beneficial to permit a commonsense inference of reliance applicable to the entire class to answer a predominating question as required by Rule 23. In the RICO context, class certification is proper when "causation can be established through an inference of reliance where the behavior of plaintiffs and the members of the class cannot be explained in any way other than reliance upon the defendant's conduct." * * * Cases involving financial transactions, such as this one, are the paradigmatic examples of how the inference operates as an evidentiary matter. * * *

773 F.3d at 1081, 1089–90. The court stressed the narrowness of its holding in a footnote, stating that the inference of reliance it found permissible was "limited to transactional situations—almost always financial transactions—where it is sensible to assume that rational economic actors would not make a payment unless they assumed that they were receiving some form of the promised benefit in return," and noting that "[t]his inference would not be appropriate in most RICO class actions." *Id.* at 1091 n.9. Is the Tenth Circuit correct in holding that an inference of reliance is proper in certain kinds of RICO cases? Is the court persuasive in characterizing its approach as a narrow one? Should the court have rejected an inference of reliance altogether in RICO cases and instead have ruled that a presumption of reliance is not permissible outside of the securities fraud area?

ii. *Personal Injury Claims*

Another recurring theme involves the suitability of personal injury claims for certification under Rule 23(b)(3). Again, the Advisory Committee Notes to Rule 23(b)(3) address the propriety of class certification of such claims:

> A "mass accident" resulting in injuries to numerous persons is ordinarily not appropriate for a class action because of the likelihood that significant questions, not only of damages but of liability and defenses to liability, would be present, affecting the individuals in different ways. In these circumstances an action conducted nominally as a class action would degenerate in practice into multiple lawsuits separately tried.

Are there "mass accidents" (such as airplane crashes) that would be appropriate for class certification? This issue is explored in depth in a later discussion of mass torts (see Chapter 10(A)).

iii. Individualized Defenses

Courts also have struggled over the extent to which the existence of individualized defenses to each class member's claims should defeat predominance. This has arisen with greatest frequency in mass tort cases. *See, e.g., Castano v. Am. Tobacco Co.*, 84 F.3d 734 (5th Cir. 1996) (decertifying nationwide class of persons addicted to nicotine because of, *inter alia*, existence of numerous individualized defenses); *In re Copley Pharm.*, 161 F.R.D. 456 (D. Wyo. 1995) (reaffirming class certification of mass tort case notwithstanding defendants' claim of numerous individualized defenses). How could the existence of individual defenses make certification under Rule 23(b)(3) inappropriate? Would the possibility of such problems suggest any strategies for defense counsel in a potential class action? What about for plaintiffs' counsel? This issue is addressed in detail in the context of mass tort cases (see Chapter 10(A)(3)(b)), as well as employment cases (*see* Chapter 10(B)(1)(d)).

iv. Proposed Class Actions Involving Numerous Jurisdictions' Laws

Serious predominance issues—often fatal to class certification—are also raised in cases involving the application of laws of more than one jurisdiction. Those issues are explored in Chapter 6(B).

v. Predominance and Individualized Damages

The Supreme Court's decision in *Comcast Corp. v. Behrend*, 133 S. Ct. 1426 (2013), which is set out in Chapter 4, has led to an increased focus by litigants on whether individualized damages defeat predominance. In *Comcast*, the Court held that an antitrust class action had been improperly certified where the plaintiffs' economic model fell "far short of establishing that damages are capable of measurement on a classwide basis." *Id.* at 1433. Plaintiffs had conceded that, without classwide proof of damages, certification would not be proper. Notably, the dissent in *Comcast* emphasized that, because of plaintiffs' concession, the majority opinion "should not be read to require, as a prerequisite to certification, that damages attributable to a classwide injury be measurable on a class-wide basis." *Id.* at 1436 (Ginsburg & Breyer, J.J., dissenting) (citation and internal quotation marks omitted). The dissent stated that the majority opinion "br[oke] no new ground on the standard for certifying a class action under [Rule] 23(b)(3)." The dissent explained:

> Recognition that individual damages calculations do not preclude class certification under Rule 23(b)(3) is well nigh universal. Legions of appellate decisions across a range of substantive claims are illustrative. [Citations omitted]. Antitrust cases, which typically involve common allegations of antitrust violation, antitrust impact, and the fact of damages, are classic examples. As this Court has rightly observed, "[p]redominance is a test readily met" in actions alleging "violations of the antitrust laws."

Id. at 1437.

The Seventh Circuit, in an opinion by Judge Easterbrook, rejected a sweeping reading of *Comcast* and *Wal–Mart Stores, Inc. v. Dukes*, 564 U.S. 338 (2011), that would preclude class certification in every case involving individualized damages calculations:

> The [district] court read [*Comcast* and *Dukes*] to require proof "that the plaintiffs will experience a common damage and that their claimed damages are not disparate." Elsewhere the district court wrote that "commonality of damages" is essential. If this is right, then class actions about consumer products are impossible * * *.
>
> Yet *Wal–Mart* has nothing to do with commonality of damages. It dealt instead with the need for conduct common to members of the class, and it concerned Rule 23(a)(2) rather than Rule 23(b)(3). * * * *Comcast*, by contrast, does discuss the role of injury under Rule 23(b)(3), though not in the way the district court thought. Plaintiffs filed an antitrust suit and specified four theories of liability. The district judge certified a class limited to one of these four. The plaintiffs' damages expert, however, estimated harm starting with the assumption that all four theories had been established. The Court held that this made class treatment inappropriate: without a theory of loss that matched the theory of liability, the class could not get anywhere. That would be equally true in a suit with just one plaintiff. In antitrust law, damages are limited to the sort of injury that flows from unlawful conduct. * * * It is essential to distinguish the encouraged injuries (to producers, from competition) from the forbidden ones (to consumers, from monopoly). That requires matching the theory of liability to the theory of damages. * * *
>
> Plaintiffs in our litigation have two theories of damages that match their theory of liability. * * *
>
> * * *
>
> (The first and second are alternatives: they imply the same gross compensation to the class as a whole, and to award both remedies would be double counting.) But neither approach runs afoul of *Comcast*: both the * * * remedies match the theory of liability, as *Comcast* requires.
>
> * * *
>
> * * * The district court denied plaintiffs' motion to certify under a mistaken belief that "commonality of damages" is legally indispensable. With that error corrected, the district court can proceed using the proper standards.

In re IKO Roofing Shingle Prods. Liab. Litig., 757 F.3d 599, 602–03 (7th Cir. 2014) (citations omitted). Other circuits have similarly read *Comcast* as not foreclosing certification in a case where damages are individualized. *See, e.g., In re Whirlpool Corp. Front-Loading Washer Prods. Liab. Litig.*, 722 F.3d 838, 860 (6th Cir. 2013) ("Where determinations on liability and damages have been bifurcated, *see* Fed. R. Civ. P. 23(c)(4), the decision in

Comcast * * * has limited application."), *cert. denied*, 134 S. Ct. 1277 (2014); *Leyva v. Medline Indus. Inc.*, 716 F.3d 510, 514 (9th Cir. 2013) ("[T]he presence of individualized damages cannot, by itself, defeat class certification under Rule 23(b)(3)."); *Roach v. T.L. Cannon Corp.*, 778 F.3d 401, 407 (2d Cir. 2015) ("[T]he Court did not hold that proponents of class certification must rely upon a classwide damages model to demonstrate predominance." (citing cases)); *In re Urethane Antitrust Litig.*, 768 F.3d 1245, 1257–58 (10th Cir. 2014) ("*Comcast* did not rest on the ability to measure damages on a class-wide basis.")

In *Tyson Foods, Inc. v. Bouaphakeo*, 136 S. Ct. 1036 (2016), the Supreme Court cast further doubt on the correctness of interpreting *Comcast* to require proof of classwide damages to satisfy predominance. There, the Court stated:

> The predominance inquiry "asks whether the common, aggregation-enabling, issues in the case are more prevalent or important than the non-common, aggregation-defeating, individual issues." When "one or more of the central issues in the action are common to the class and can be said to predominate, the action may be considered proper under Rule 23(b)(3) even though other important matters will have to be tried separately, *such as damages* or some affirmative defenses peculiar to some individual class members."

Id. at 1045 (emphasis added; citations omitted). In light of this language, defendants will have great difficulty arguing that *Comcast* changed the rules governing predominance and individualized damages.

2. SUPERIORITY

In addition to predominance, Rule 23(b)(3) requires a court addressing a motion for class certification to assess whether class treatment is "superior to other available methods for the fair and efficient adjudication of the controversy." But what criteria are supposed to assist the court in determining whether one form of dispute resolution is "superior" to another? Should efficiency be the benchmark? Some notion of justice or fairness? Or some other criterion? The following materials explore the "superiority" requirement.

According to the district court in *Lake v. First Nationwide Bank*, 156 F.R.D. 615, 625 (E.D. Pa. 1994):

> The superiority finding requires at a minimum (1) an informed consideration of alternative available methods of adjudication of each issue, (2) a comparison of the fairness to all whose interests may be involved between such alternative methods and a class action, and (3) a comparison of the efficiency of adjudication of each method. The interests that should be taken into account include those of the judicial system, the putative class, the instant plaintiffs and defendant and their attorneys, and the general public.

Does this formulation of the superiority requirement provide useful guidance? Is it grounded in Rule 23(b)(3)?

a. Superior to What?—Alternatives to Class Treatment

What alternatives should be considered in performing a superiority analysis? In particular circumstances, courts have determined that it may be appropriate to consider, for example:

- Individual actions (which may create collateral estoppel). *See, e.g., Fisher v. Bristol–Myers Squibb Co.*, 181 F.R.D. 365, 373–74 (N.D. Ill. 1998);
- Test cases. *See, e.g., In re Am. Honda Motor Co., Inc. Dealer Relations Litig.*, 979 F. Supp. 365 (D. Md. 1997);
- Intervention by a government entity. *See, e.g., Stuart v. Hewlett Packard Co.*, 66 F.R.D. 73, 77–78 (E.D. Mich. 1975) (intervention by Equal Employment Opportunity Commission would avoid manageability problems of class action);
- Joinder under Rules 19 and 20. *See, e.g., Bd. of Educ. of Twp. High Sch. Dist. No. 214 v. Climatemp, Inc.*, 1981 WL 2033 (N.D. Ill. 1981); *see also* Chapter 13(A)(2) and (1), respectively;
- Liberal intervention under Rule 24 for those similarly interested. *See, e.g., Herbst v. Able*, 47 F.R.D. 11, 17 (S.D.N.Y. 1969), *amended by* 49 F.R.D. 286 (S.D.N.Y. 1970) (deciding to permit class action treatment); *see also* Chapter 13(A)(5);
- Consolidation under Rule 42(a). *See, e.g., Steinmetz v. Bache & Co., Inc.*, 71 F.R.D. 202, 206 (S.D.N.Y. 1976); *see also* Chapter 13(A)(6);
- Multidistrict Litigation. *See, e.g., Valentino v. Carter–Wallace, Inc.*, 97 F.3d 1227, 1235 (9th Cir. 1996) ("[T]here has been no showing why the class mechanism is superior to alternative methods of adjudication, particularly when coupled with the discovery coordination that is made possible by the [Judicial Panel on Multidistrict Litigation] consolidation."); *see also* Chapter 12;
- An action in an administrative forum. *See, e.g., Franklin v. Gen. Elec. Co.*, 24 Fed. R. Serv. 2d 115 (W.D. Va. 1977) (EEOC action would adequately protect rights of purported class members and avoid waste of judicial resources and risk of inconsistent adjudications). *But see, e.g., Amalgamated Workers Union of the Virgin Islands v. Hess Oil Virgin Islands Corp.*, 478 F.2d 540, 542–45 (3d Cir. 1973) (availability of administrative remedies irrelevant to superiority inquiry); and
- An action in another judicial forum. *See, e.g., Schaffner v. Chem. Bank*, 339 F. Supp. 329, 335 (S.D.N.Y. 1972) (determining that state-court action was superior to federal class action).

For discussion of benefits, disadvantages, and considerations in choosing among multidistrict litigation, consolidation, and class actions, *see, e.g.,* 1 John L. Strauch & Robert C. Weber, "Multi-District Litigation," *Business and Commercial Litigation in Federal Courts* § 11.3 (1998); *see also* 32B Am. Jur. 2d. *Federal Courts* § 2004 (1996 & Cum. Supp. 2005) (compiling citations to cases presenting alternatives to class action method); Jack B. Weinstein, *Revision of Procedure: Some Problems in Class Actions*, 9 Buff. L. Rev. 433, 438–54 (1960) (discussing alternatives to class actions). For a case relying on the superiority inquiry as a basis for adopting a separate, heightened "ascertainability" standard, see *Mullins v. Direct Digital, LLC*, 795 F.3d 654 (7th Cir. 2015), set out in Chapter 2(A)(1)(b).

b. Superiority—Factors Considered

i. *Generally*

In making an assessment of superiority, a trial court is directed to examine at least four factors. *See* Rule 23(b)(3)(A)–(D). According to the Advisory Committee's Notes:

> In this connection the court should inform itself of any litigation actually pending by or against the individuals. The interests of individuals in conducting separate lawsuits may be so strong as to call for denial of a class action. On the other hand, these interests may be theoretical rather than practical; the class may have a high degree of cohesion and prosecution of the action through representatives would be quite unobjectionable, or the amounts at stake for individuals may be so small that separate suits would be impracticable. The burden that separate suits would impose on the party opposing the class, or upon the court calendars, may also fairly be considered. * * *
>
> Also pertinent is the question of the desirability of concentrating the trial of the claims in the particular forum by means of a class action, in contrast to allowing the claims to be litigated separately in forums to which they would ordinarily be brought. Finally, the court should consider the problems of management which are likely to arise in the conduct of a class action.

Each of the four factors is discussed below. Initially, however, consider the following case, which focuses upon factors (A) and (D).

SONMORE V. CHECKRITE RECOVERY SERVS., INC.
United States District Court, District of Minnesota, 2001.
206 F.R.D. 257.

ALSOP, SENIOR DISTRICT JUDGE.

Plaintiffs Eric L. Sonmore ("Sonmore") and Jennifer M. Rodine ("Rodine") filed suit in this Court alleging that Defendant, Jon R. Hawks, Ltd. ("Hawks, Ltd."), Defendant Jon R. Hawks ("Jon Hawks"), and Defendant CheckRite Recovery Services, Inc. ("CheckRite"), sometimes collectively referred to as "Defendants," violated the Fair Debt Collection Practices Act, 15 U.S.C. § 1692, *et seq.* ("FDCPA"). This matter comes before the Court on Plaintiffs' motion for an Order certifying a class of similarly situated consumers in relation to Plaintiffs' claims against Hawks, Ltd. and Jon Hawks, sometimes collectively referred to as "Defendants Hawks." For the reasons stated below, the Court will deny Plaintiffs' motion for class certification.

I. BACKGROUND

* * * Hawks, Ltd. is a Minnesota corporation and Jon Hawks, an attorney, is its sole officer and shareholder. Hawks, Ltd. acts as a debt collector for CheckRite. Defendants Hawks and CheckRite regularly send debt collection form letters to debtors and are debt collectors under 15 U.S.C.

§ 1692a(6). Plaintiffs allege that Defendants' respective debt collection letters violate the FDCPA in various ways.

This suit stems specifically from separate collection letters Defendants sent to each Plaintiff to collect on Plaintiffs' dishonored checks that were written for their personal use: a two dollar check written by Sonmore to purchase gasoline and a thirty dollar check written by Rodine to purchase food at a restaurant. The checks were dishonored because Plaintiffs had insufficient funds to cover the amounts of the checks in their respective checking accounts.

When Plaintiffs failed to pay the amounts CheckRite alleged they owed, CheckRite referred collection of Plaintiffs' dishonored checks to Defendants Hawks. Defendants Hawks sent both Plaintiffs a substantially identical letter. Plaintiffs contend that the letters violate the FDCPA because in sending the mass-generated form letters, Defendants Hawks were not actually acting as attorneys and because the letters do not state the amounts Plaintiffs owe CheckRite.

Agreeing that material facts were not in dispute regarding the claims, Plaintiffs and Defendants Hawks filed cross motions for summary judgment on the portions of the Complaint pertaining to Defendants Hawks * * *. The Court granted Plaintiffs' motion for summary judgment on these claims finding that, as a matter of law, Defendants Hawks violated the FDCPA.

Plaintiffs moved to certify a class consisting of all consumers that, according to Defendants Hawks' records, reside in the State of Minnesota and within one year from the date of the filing of Plaintiffs' Complaint (November 28, 2000) were sent letters seeking to collect on a debt incurred for a personal, family, or household purpose that were materially identical to the letters Defendants Hawks sent to Plaintiffs. Defendants Hawks oppose Plaintiffs' motion.

II. DISCUSSION

* * *

[The court first determined that although plaintiffs had satisfied Rules 23(a)(1)–(3), they failed the test of adequacy. The Court found that plaintiffs lacked adequate financial incentives to pursue class remedies because, having prevailed on their individual claims, "Sonmore and Rodine [were] in a position to immediately recover the very same amount of statutory damages that they [could] recover if they were to pursue the action as representatives of a class." The Court was also concerned about whether plaintiffs were sufficiently responsible to serve as class representatives, given that both had bounced checks.]

C. Federal Rule of Civil Procedure 23(b)

* * *

1. Predominance

* * *

It is readily apparent in this action that determining the propriety of Defendants Hawks' form letter and Jon Hawks' standard procedures for sending that form letter will predominate over any questions affecting only individual class members. Jon Hawks's course of conduct with respect to his involvement in the mass mailing of debt collection letters is accentuated by uniformity and, thus, any individualized claim pertaining to whether he acted as a lawyer in a meaningful way with respect to a given debt is minimized. The issues involved are common to all class members, thus the Court finds that Plaintiffs have satisfied Rule 23(b)(3)'s predominance criteria.

2. Superiority

There is no bedrock standard upon which a Court determines that a class action is "superior to other available methods for the fair and efficient adjudication of the controversy." Fed. R. Civ. P. 23(b)(3). Upon consideration of Rule 23(b)(3)'s nonexhaustive list of pertinent factors, however, the Court will deny Plaintiffs' motion for class certification because class action treatment is not a superior method for adjudicating the proposed class members' claims. Factors that weighed particularly heavy in the Court's determination in this regard include 23(b)(3)(A) and (D). Thus, they are discussed below.

(i) Rule 23(b)(3)(A)

Rule 23(b)(3)(A) invites a court to evaluate "the interest of members of the class in individually controlling the prosecution or defense of separate actions." "In setting out Rule 23(b)(3)'s factors for a court to consider, it was 'anticipated that in each case, courts would "consider the interests of individual members of the class in controlling their own litigations." ' " [*Amchem Prods., Inc. v. Windsor*, 521 U.S. 591, 616 (1997).] Defendants Hawks argue, and the Court agrees, that class treatment would be detrimental to absent class members because it would substantially limit their recovery.

A debt collector who violates the FDCPA is liable to a debtor plaintiff for statutory damages in an amount not to exceed $1,000. *See* 15 U.S.C. § 1692k(a)(2)(A). When a suit is maintained as a class action, however, absent class members may only be awarded statutory damages equaling "such amount as the court may allow . . . without regard to a minimum individual recovery, not to exceed the lessor of $500,000 or 1 per centum of the net worth of the debt collector." 15 U.S.C. § 1692k(a)(2)(B)(ii).

Plaintiffs and Defendants Hawks offer conflicting arguments regarding Defendants Hawks' net worth. Defendants Hawks claim a negative net worth, while Plaintiffs assert their net worth is substantially higher. The actual net worth of Defendants Hawks is not determinative in this matter, because the FDCPA places a $500,000 cap on class recovery. Based on Plaintiffs' definition of the estimated class, there would be approximately 20,000 absent class members. Thus, if $500,000 is less than one percent of Defendants Hawks' net worth, [then] each absent class member stands to recover a maximum of twenty-five dollars. Such an award is shockingly low when compared to the statutory damages of up to $1,000 that each class member may be eligible to receive in an individual suit.

Additionally, it is virtually certain that Defendants Hawks' actual net worth is something far less than $50 million, which makes one percent of their net worth the maximum amount available to the class. Thus, absent class members' damages would be even more paltry than twenty-five dollars in this case. For example, although Plaintiffs assert that Defendants

Hawks failed to produce accurate net worth information during discovery, they estimate that Jon Hawks' net worth is $300,000. Under this scenario, the entire class would be entitled to, at most, $3,000 from Jon Hawks. Thus, each of the estimated 20,000 persons would be eligible for a maximum recovery of fifteen cents.

The maximum potential award of statutory damages if this action were maintained as a class action is "clearly relevant" to consideration of Rule 23(b)(3)(A). *Bryant* [*v. Bonded Accounts Serv./Check Recovery, Inc.*, 208 F.R.D. 251 (D. Minn. 2000)]. The FDCPA's cap on class action damages, combined with the large number of putative class members, causes an unacceptably large discrepancy in the amount of available damages. By certifying the class, the court would ensure a *de minimis* monetary recovery for class members, which constitutes a substantial reduction in what class members may otherwise be entitled [to] by pursuing their claims individually. Because plaintiffs [pursuing] an action individually are eligible to recover a maximum of $1,000, while absent class members in this case are eligible for a maximum of merely twenty-five dollars, the Court finds that the interest of class members in individually controlling the prosecution of their claims prevails over any efficiency objectives that may be achieved through management of the litigation as a class action. Thus, Plaintiffs have failed to establish that a class action is a superior method for adjudicating claims regarding Defendants Hawks' conduct and form letter.

(ii) Rule 23(b)(3)(D)

Inquiry into the superiority of class action treatment under Rule 23(b)(3) also requires a court to consider the manageability of such treatment. The Court is mindful that dismissal for management reasons is not favored. Under Rule 23(b)(3)(D), however, "[m]anageability is a real issue," and the Court is unconvinced that management of a class action in this situation is a tenable, not to mention a "superior," method of litigating the prospective class members' claims. Thus, taken in the context of the Court's other concerns about superiority and findings regarding adequacy, the Court is persuaded that class action treatment is not a superior method for adjudicating these potential claims.

Unfortunately, this Court's experience with class actions involving class members whose financial circumstances make it difficult to ascertain their identities or their present whereabouts convinces this Court that a class action is not a superior vehicle to provide an appropriate remedy in this situation. The Court anticipates tremendous difficulty and only limited success in notifying [prospective] class members of the class action and their rights to opt out and recover a potentially greater damage award under the FDCPA if they proceed individually. The Court also anticipates difficulty in ensuring that class members who do not opt out actually receive their damages awards. It is the Court's experience that the benefits of such a class action would inure, if at all, to class counsel and the designated recipient of class funds that the Court is unable to distribute to class members. Thus, the Court finds that presentation of individualized claims in separate proceedings would be superior to the vehicle of a class action.

In sum, having closely examined the Rule 23 factors that Plaintiffs must satisfy, the Court finds that the proposed class should not be certified, and the Court will deny Plaintiffs' motion.

NOTES AND QUESTIONS

1. Why did the *Sonmore* court find that superiority was not satisfied? Is its reasoning persuasive? Would class members' right to opt out of the class eliminate some of the court's concerns? The court responded that it was "unconvinced by [the opt-out] argument for many reasons, including many of the same concerns discussed * * * pertaining to manageability." *Sonmore*, 206 F.R.D. at 266 n.5.

2. If plaintiffs have already prevailed on their individual claims, should that interfere with their ability to serve as class representatives?

3. Are there circumstances in which plaintiffs may satisfy all of Rule 23(a) and the predominance inquiry of Rule 23(b)(3), but nevertheless fail superiority?

ii. Rule 23(b)(3)(A)—Interest in Individual Control of Litigation

The first of the factors listed in Rule 23(b)(3) is "the class members' interests in individually controlling the prosecution or defense of separate actions." Class actions are often justified on the ground that they permit the aggregation of claims of a group of people who may be similarly wronged, where each injured person's limited damages would make individual litigation cost-prohibitive. In *In re Chlorine and Caustic Soda Antitrust Litigation*, 116 F.R.D. 622 (E.D. Pa. 1987), for example, the court found that superiority was satisfied in an antitrust suit because " 'a large number of individuals may have been injured, although no one person may have been damaged to a degree which would have induced him to institute litigation solely on his own behalf.' " *Id.* at 627 (quoting *Green v. Wolf Corp.*, 406 F.2d 291, 296 (2d Cir. 1968)). Courts have labeled such situations "negative value" suits. *See, e.g., In re Monumental Life Ins. Co.*, 365 F.3d 408, 411 n.1 (5th Cir. 2004) (citing *Phillips Petroleum Co. v. Shutts*, 472 U.S. 797, 809 (1985)). In *Tardiff v. Knox Cnty.*, 365 F.3d 1 (1st Cir. 2004), the First Circuit analyzed superiority in a case brought by arrestees who alleged that they were improperly strip searched in pre-arraignment jail facilities. Specifically, the First Circuit affirmed the district court's certification under (b)(3), noting:

> Whether the law should encourage the bringing of very small claims that would otherwise not be brought is a different matter; lawsuits serve purposes beyond compensation, and the balance of cost and benefit varies from case to case. It is enough for the superiority determination here that for most strip search claimants, class status here is not only the superior means, but probably the only feasible one * * * to establish liability and perhaps damages.

Id. at 7.

Similarly, in *Smilow v. Southwestern Bell Mobile Systems, Inc.*, 323 F.3d 32 (1st Cir. 2003), the court stated that "[t]he class certification prerequisites should be construed in light of the underlying objectives of class actions. Rule 23(b)(3) is intended to be a less stringent requirement than Rule 23(b)(1) or (b)(2). The core purpose of Rule 23(b)(3) is to vindicate the claims of consumers and other groups of people whose individual claims would be too small to warrant litigation." *Id.* at 41; *see also Beattie v. Cen-*

turyTel, Inc., 511 F.3d 554, 567 (6th Cir. 2007) (finding superiority requirement satisfied in suit alleging "deceptive billing practices" because "individual suits would yield only a small amount of damages," and thus "[s]uch a small possible recovery would not encourage individuals to bring suit, thereby making a class action a superior mechanism for adjudicating this dispute"). In light of the materials set forth above, is it true that Rule 23(b)(3) is "less stringent" than other provisions of Rule 23(b), as the *Smilow* court maintained? Should the amount in controversy for each individual play a role in how the strictures of Rule 23(b)(3) are interpreted?

Litigants, however, occasionally try to certify class actions in situations involving significant damage claims by each individual plaintiff. In such cases, a court may believe that aggregation is unnecessary, inasmuch as lawyers will have adequate incentives to pursue individual suits. Moreover, the court may find that each potential litigant may have a much greater desire to direct the course of the litigation personally when damages may be significant. *See, e.g., Frahm v. Equitable Life Assurance Soc'y*, 137 F.3d 955, 957 (7th Cir. 1998) (observing that "[i]ndividual rather than class litigation is the best way to resolve person-specific contentions when the stakes are large enough to justify individual suits"). The same individuals may also desire personal control because of (i) a concern that litigation in one forum, as opposed to another, will disadvantage their claims relative to others' or (ii) a concern (for example, in a multi-jurisdictional class action) that class treatment will not account for favorable local differences in applicable law.

One example of Rule 23(b)(3)(A) in action is *Crasto v. Estate of Kaskel*, 63 F.R.D. 18 (S.D.N.Y. 1974). In *Crasto*, plaintiffs were shareholders in 360 East 72nd Street Owners Incorporated ("the Corporation"), a co-operative apartment building located in Manhattan, New York. Plaintiffs sued on behalf of a class of all persons who had purchased, held, or been allocated shares in the Corporation. They alleged that defendants, including the sponsor of the cooperative, had made oral and written representations to plaintiffs in violation of federal and state securities laws and the common law. The securities, which were sold as shares in the cooperative, involved the rights to occupy the apartments at 360 East 72nd Street.

Plaintiffs' complaints alleged that the defendants falsely represented to the class that the co-operative plan would be offered only to New York state residents, that the plan would not become effective until 35 percent of the tenants had purchased shares in the Corporation, that the requisite 35 percent was lawfully obtained by the Sponsor, that no claims or lawsuits were threatened or pending against the Sponsor or its agent in connection with the plan, and that federal and New York state income tax deductions would be available to the shareholders. Records indicated that while approximately 298 persons had purchased, held, or been allocated, shares in the Corporation, 151 people had agreed to settle their claims with defendants, leaving 147 potential class members.

The district court found that common questions of law or fact did not predominate over individual questions because the defendants' representations to individual plaintiffs varied substantially. The court further found that the class action device was not superior to other available methods of adjudication because "the members of the class have a strong interest in individually controlling the prosecution of their claims":

> [T]his is not the typical securities action in which no more than a person's investment in a corporation's stock is at stake. Here, most, if not all, of the class members bought a home. The basic interest of all the class members is not necessarily in recovering their investments or damages. We cannot say that the ends sought or the strategy adopted by the class representatives will be shared by all members of the class whose individual monetary interests may be transcended by other considerations. Since all members of the class who do not request exclusion will be bound by the judgment, important individual interests may be lost if these actions proceed on a class basis. Thus, some class members may prefer not to litigate at all but to attempt to reach an amicable agreement with defendants, which will guarantee the security of their homes while making recompense for any wrongs they have suffered. Others may wish to move out of the building, sell their shares and attempt to collect damages from defendants.
>
> Where the claims involved "vitally affect a significant aspect of the lives of the claimants . . . [and] there is a wide range of choice of the strategy and tactics" in the litigation, the court is justified in finding that each class member has a legitimate interest in individually litigating his claim. Here, since the claims, in many cases, involve the purchase of homes, a significant aspect of the class members' lives is vitally affected. Moreover, the possible strategies the class members might adopt vary greatly.
>
> The class members' strong interest in controlling their own destiny in this litigation is evidenced by the large numbers of nonparty class members who have already agreed to settle their claims with defendants and appear likely to opt out.
>
> In addition, there appears to be no question that the class members have both the resources and the inclination to vindicate their rights on an individual basis. The apartments involved were luxury units, located in one of the most fashionable areas of New York City, and the class members' initial investments ranged from $11,000 to $85,000, with yearly maintenance charges of $1,370 to $10,000. The issues raised by these actions have been discussed at length by the shareholders at meetings of the Corporation, amid some bickering and bitterness among the members of the class. Thus, the shareholders are well aware of their rights and have sufficient resources to retain counsel and litigate themselves. The presence of strong disagreement within the class is yet another reason why these actions should proceed on an individual basis.
>
> Finally, this is not a case in which the damage suffered by each class member is too small to justify individual action, thereby making a class action the only means available for vindicating the claims of the class. On the contrary, here, each shareholder's claim, whether for rescission or damages, is for a substantial

amount of money and more than sufficient to enable him to bring his own action.

We find, therefore, that a class action is not superior to other means available for adjudicating these controversies, *i.e.*, individual actions by the class members. The resources of the court can best be utilized by employing the liberal provisions in the Federal Rules of Civil Procedure for multi-party litigation, including permissive joinder, intervention and consolidation.

Id. at 24–25.

What factors did the *Crasto* court deem relevant to the inquiry under Rule 23(b)(3)(A)? What arguments could be made to *support* class certification in *Crasto*?

Some courts have found class certification not superior in cases involving significant potential statutory damages and little or no actual harm to plaintiffs. For instance, in *Leysoto v. Mama Mia I., Inc.*, 255 F.R.D. 693 (S.D. Fla. 2009), the court declined to certify a proposed class of 46,000 people who concededly had suffered no actual economic injury, concluding that the "sole benefit of certification would be the *threat* of ruinous damages for the purposes of settlement" against a defendant with only $40,000 in net assets. *Id.* at 699; *see also Saulic v. Symantec Corp.*, 596 F. Supp. 2d 1323 (C.D. Cal. 2009) (superiority requirement not met where defendants' potential liability "would be enormous and completely out of proportion to any harm plaintiff suffered").

In discussing the relevance of the potential magnitude of recovery in evaluating superiority, one commentator notes:

> The interest in prosecuting individual suits has not been particularly significant in most Rule 23(b)(3) actions, because most of them have been based on violations of the antitrust and securities laws, and have involved significant numbers of small individual claimants relative to costs of litigation. In these cases the dictates of judicial economy and the economic disadvantages of individual suits have generally outweighed any interest in individual litigation.

2 Herbert B. Newberg & Alba Conte, Newberg on Class Actions § 4.29, at 262 (4th ed. 2002). Should the magnitude of the potential recovery play a role in the Rule 23(b)(3)(A) analysis? In what way(s)? Newberg and Conte continue:

> In other cases, especially in mass tort cases, the growing awareness of the need to fashion a means for unitary adjudication at least for material liability issues affecting a multiplicity of related suits, together with recent decisions upholding the offensive use of collateral estoppel without mutuality of parties, has led to similar discounting of the significance of interest in individual litigation.

Id. Should a desire on behalf of the judicial system to adjudicate the "material liability issues" of mass tort (or other) cases in a single, "unitary adjudication" play any role in the analysis under Rule 23(b)(3)(A)? How could one formulate a contrary argument? Does the potential availability of offensive non-mutual collateral estoppel weigh in favor of or against class treatment when viewed through the lens of Rule 23(b)(3)(A)?

What weight should a court attach to potential class members' desires to litigate their claims on their own? Should a court certify a case as a class action under Rule 23(b)(3) if most members of the potential class do not want a class action? Under what circumstances (if any)?

Should a *defendant's* interest in litigating each case individually bear any weight in the Rule 23(b)(3)(A) analysis?

iii. Rule 23(b)(3)(B)—Extent and Nature of Pending Litigation

Rule 23(b)(3)(B) requires a certifying court to consider "the extent and nature of any litigation concerning the controversy already begun by or against class members." This rule has been interpreted to call for a variety of different assessments. Consider the following excerpts:

(i) In *In re Plywood Antitrust Litigation*, 76 F.R.D. 570, 587 (E.D. La. 1976), an antitrust action, the court stated:

> Because of the transfer of all actions to this Court for pretrial proceedings under 28 U.S.C. Section 1407 [*see* Chapter 12], all of the actions commenced by the members of any of the proposed classes are already before us. Thus, the factors listed in Rule 23(b)(3)(B) and 23(b)(3)(C) need no further exposition. Indeed, the Judicial Panel recognized that the conflicting class allegations in the complaints was a basic reason for centralizing all actions in this district.

(ii) In *In re Masonite Corp. Hardboard Siding Products Liability Litigation*, 170 F.R.D. 417, 426 (E.D. La. 1997), an action attempting to certify a nationwide class action against Masonite for allegedly defective siding:

> If the court finds that several other actions already are pending and that a clear threat of multiplicity and a risk of inconsistent adjudications actually exist, a class action may not be appropriate since, unless the other suits can be enjoined, which is not always feasible, a Rule 23 proceeding only might create one more action.

Noting that another nationwide class action had previously been brought in state court in Alabama, the court observed: "Today plaintiffs' counsel seeks to create one more national litigation class action in the name of the same set of plaintiffs. One wonders how judicial economy (or any other policy) is thereby served." *Id.*

(iii) In *Kurczi v. Eli Lilly & Co.*, 160 F.R.D. 667, 680 (N.D. Ohio 1995), a products liability action relating to a drug:

> [I]n the instant case, at least four of the five named plaintiffs in this action are also plaintiffs in a parallel state court action. The state court action alleges the same causes of action and same injuries against the same defendants. Accordingly, this Court finds that this consideration weighs against the superiority of a class action.

(iv) In *Kernan v. Holiday Universal, Inc.*, 1990 WL 289505, at *6 (D. Md. 1990), a case involving claims of race discrimination against a chain of health spas:

> [T]here has been no mention of similar litigation which affects the proposed class action in any significant way, and accordingly, this factor favors class certification under subsection (b)(3).

(v) In *Haley v. Medtronic, Inc.*, 169 F.R.D. 643, 652 (C.D. Cal. 1996), a products liability action against the manufacturer of pacemaker leads:

> In the instant case, there are currently twenty-five other pending lawsuits. Because all of these lawsuits involve the same basic theories and claims of liability, it seems probable that the Court will indeed be able to enjoin these other cases if the plaintiffs do not opt out of the class. Thus, because the Court will probably not encounter a problem in terms of not being able to enjoin other litigation, this factor also slightly weighs in favor of granting class certification.

(vi) In *Bentkowski v. Marfuerza Compania Maritima, S.A.*, 70 F.R.D. 401 (E.D. Pa. 1976), an action by passengers on a cruise ship for alleged water and food poisoning during their voyage:

> [S]o far as this Court is aware, there have been only two suits brought involving the operative facts of the present case. [One case] resulted in a settlement of $130.00. The second suit * * * has been transferred to this Court pending the outcome of the class action litigation. The Court finds that the scarcity of individually instituted suits indicates that in this respect there are no significant barriers to class certification in the instant case.

Id. at 404–05. The court further observed:

> [I]t is believed that there is a dependent relationship between this consideration [of Fed. R. Civ. P. 23(b)(3)(B)] and Fed. R. Civ. P. 23(b)(3)(A). That is, the fact that there are a dearth of other suits pending tends to show that potential class members do not have a great interest in the individual prosecution of their causes of action. Those cases which find that individual lawsuits are superior are usually beset with a number of pending lawsuits at the time the class is sought to be certified.

Id. at 405 n.10.

(vii) In *Gregory v. Finova Capital Corp.*, 442 F.3d 188, 191 (4th Cir. 2006), a securities fraud suit brought against a bankrupt defendant, the court held that a bankruptcy forum was superior to a class action proceeding:

> The bankruptcy court must decide the matters raised in the adversary proceeding in order to determine the validity and priority of [the] creditors' claims. It would be inefficient and needlessly duplicative to allow the class action to go forward when the adversary proceeding will likely adjudicate this controversy in the normal course of [the defendant's] bankruptcy. The adversary proceeding presents no danger of unfairness due to disparate results because it, like the class action, will yield a single result for all of

the noteholders. Also, the adversary proceeding will avoid many of the expenses and complexities associated with having the class action and the adversary proceeding pending simultaneously. * * * For these reasons, the class action cannot be considered the superior method for the fair and efficient adjudication of the controversy.

(viii) In *Buford v. H & R Block, Inc.*, 168 F.R.D. 340 (S.D. Ga. 1996), *aff'd mem.*, 117 F.3d 1433 (11th Cir. 1997), an action by customers of a tax preparer alleging that the defendant's program for providing loans to customers in anticipation of their tax refunds (the "RAL" program) violated federal law, and seeking certification of a nationwide class, the court stated:

> This Court has knowledge of five relevant pending putative class actions. *Basile v. H & R Block, Inc.* is a pending action in the Philadelphia Court of Common Pleas. The *Basile* plaintiff is seeking to certify a Pennsylvania class but there has been no ruling on the motion for certification. Two cases, *Beckett v. H & R Block, Inc.*, and *Peterson v. H & R Block, Inc.*, are pending in the Cook County, Illinois state court system. Both are attempting to certify national classes. *Mitchell v. H & R Block, Inc.*, is pending either in the Northern District of Alabama or it may have been remanded to the state court system in Birmingham. The plaintiff in that case is attempting to certify an Alabama class. *Rizzo v. H & R Block, Inc.* is pending in the Western District of Missouri. That case, which was filed subsequent to this case, is the only other case which asserts a RICO claim and is attempting to certify a Rule 23(b)(2) class as opposed to a Rule 23(b)(3) class. The parties in that case are now involved in the briefing stages pertaining to the motion for certification.
>
> There are three other tangentially relevant cases. *Cades v. H & R Block, Inc.* was pending in the District of South Carolina. The plaintiff in that case pressed Truth in Lending Act and National Bank Act claims regarding the RAL program. The district court apparently granted summary judgment without ruling on the motion for certification. The decision of the court was affirmed. * * * In two other cases, federal courts refused to certify classes challenging Defendants' RAL program.
>
> After examining the status of these cases, this Court finds that it currently is in the most advanced position to decide the propriety of class certification of these claims and that factor (B) does not operate to preclude certification of the class.

168 F.R.D. at 362. With respect to the two federal actions in which class certification had been denied, the court found that they were "without guiding value" because one court "made no findings of fact or conclusions of law other than a perfunctory denial of the Rule 23 motion," while the other "appeared to be based largely upon the district court's view of the merits of the action as well as upon the inability of [plaintiffs'] counsel to shoulder the costs of notice." *Id.* at 362 n.11.

NOTES AND QUESTIONS

1. What different meanings do the courts above ascribe to Rule 23(b)(3)(B)? Are the courts consistent? Is the *Plywood* court correct in concluding that because the various plywood antitrust cases had been consolidated before it, Rule 23(b)(3)(B) should play no role in its superiority analysis?

2. Does Rule 23(b)(3)(B) presume that duplicative litigation is an evil to be avoided? What risks are created by duplicative litigation? Might there be countervailing benefits?

3. Should it matter to the analysis under Rule 23(b)(3)(B) whether the other litigation being evaluated is class litigation, as opposed to one or more individual suits?

4. Note that *Masonite* and *Haley* both consider the issue of enjoining other pending litigation. Is there any difference in their approaches to this issue? Does it matter if the other litigation is pending in state court rather than federal court? *See* Chapter 7(C)(2)(b) (discussing Anti-Injunction Act).

5. Compare clauses (A) and (B) of Rule 23(b)(3). What concerns are reflected by each clause? How do those concerns affect the decision of whether to certify a class? Is the *Bentkowski* court's (*see* example (vi) above) analysis of the relationship between (A) and (B) convincing?

iv. Rule 23(b)(3)(C)—Desirability or Undesirability of Concentrating Litigation in a Particular Forum

Rule 23(b)(3)(C) requires a court considering class treatment to assess "the desirability or undesirability of concentrating the litigation of the claims in the particular forum." In *Klay v. Humana, Inc.*, 382 F.3d 1241 (11th Cir. 2004), the Eleventh Circuit summarized the state of the law relating to this factor as follows:

> Once the plaintiffs establish that common issues of fact and law predominate over individualized issues, there are typically three main reasons why it is desirable to litigate multiple parties' claims in a single forum. First, class actions "offer[] substantial economies of time, effort, and expense for the litigants . . . as well as for the [c]ourt." Holding separate trials for claims that could be tried together "would be costly, inefficient, and would burden the court system" by forcing individual plaintiffs to repeatedly prove the same facts and make the same legal arguments before different courts. Where predominance is established, this consideration will almost always mitigate in favor of certifying a class.
>
> Second, as the Supreme Court has recognized in a related context, class actions often involve "an aggregation of small individual claims, where a large number of claims are required to make it economical to bring suit. The plaintiff's claim may be so small, or the plaintiff so unfamiliar with the law, that he would not file suit individually. . . ." *Phillips Petroleum Co. v. Shutts*, 472 U.S. 797, 813 (1985); *see also Amchem Prods., Inc. v. Windsor*, 521 U.S. 591, 617 (1997) (noting that, in enacting Rule 23(b)(3), "the Advisory Committee had dominantly in mind vindication of 'the rights of groups of people who individually would be without effective strength to bring their opponents into court at all.' "). This

consideration supports class certification in cases where the total amount sought by each individual plaintiff is small in absolute terms. It also applies in situations where, as here, the amounts in controversy would make it unlikely that most of the plaintiffs, or attorneys working on a contingency fee basis, would be willing to pursue the claims individually. This is especially true when the defendants are corporate behemoths with a demonstrated willingness and proclivity for drawing out legal proceedings for as long as humanly possible and burying their opponents in paperwork and filings.

Third, it is desirable to concentrate claims in a particular forum when that forum has already handled several preliminary matters. In this case, various individual claims were consolidated before the district court by the Panel on Multidistrict Litigation, and the court has done a fine job in addressing a wide range of pretrial motions. While such extensive work is by no means necessary for us to conclude that concentration of the claims in a class action in a single forum is desirable, in this case it is impossible to overlook the significant efforts that have already been put into these proceedings. Consequently, the most common factors for assessing whether it is desirable for the plaintiffs' claims to be litigated in a single forum point to class certification in this case.

There are also several reasons courts commonly cite as to why it is particularly undesirable to litigate a class's claims in a single judicial forum. Perhaps most importantly, we assess whether the potential damages available in a class action are grossly disproportionate to the conduct at issue. Where the defendant's alleged behavior is deliberate or intentional, we have had no problem allowing class actions to proceed. Where defendants are being sued for statutory damages for unintentional acts under a strict liability standard, however, courts take a harder look at whether a defendant deserves to be subject to potentially immense liability. Similar reasoning applies where damages are being sought for technical violations of a "complex regulatory scheme, subject to different reasonable interpretations." In cases where "the defendants' potential liability would be enormous and completely out of proportion to any harm suffered by the plaintiff," we are likely to find that individual suits, rather than a single class action, are the superior method of adjudication.

* * *

At least one district court in our circuit has suggested that, in considering whether it is desirable to have all putative class members' claims litigated in a single forum, we should consider whether the theories under which they seek relief are "immature"—that is, relatively new or innovative. * * *

None of our cases has ever held the "maturity" of a tort to be a proper consideration in the certification decision. Without delving into whether the plaintiffs' claims in this case are sufficiently new or innovative to count as an "immature" tort * * *, we reject this as a legitimate consideration in making a "superiority" determination. There is no reason why, even with so-called "immature torts," district and circuit courts cannot make the necessary determinations under Rule 23 based on the pleadings and whatever evidence has been gathered through discovery. Moreover, there is no basis in Rule 23 for arbitrarily foreclosing plaintiffs from pursuing innovative theories through the vehicle of a class action lawsuit. Particularly when the considerations discussed at the beginning of this Section would preclude most plaintiffs from individually litigating their personal claims, a class action may be the only way that most people can have their rights—even "innovative" or "immature" rights—enforced. Furthermore, if an "immature tort" truly raises a variety of new or complicated legal questions, then those questions constitute significant common issues of law. Their resolution in a single class-action forum would greatly foster judicial efficiency and avoid unnecessary, repetitious litigation. * * *

Klay, 382 F.3d at 1270–72.

NOTES AND QUESTIONS

1. In *Ikonen v. Hartz Mountain Corp.*, 122 F.R.D. 258 (S.D. Cal. 1988), plaintiffs sued Hartz after using its "Blockade" flea-and-tick spray on their pets. Plaintiffs contended that the spray poisoned animals when applied to the skin. Rejecting plaintiffs' motion for certification of a nationwide Rule 23(b)(3) class action on numerous grounds, the *Ikonen* court noted with respect to Rule 23(b)(3)(C) that:

> Relevant to this consideration are the number of other cases involving Blockade poisoning filed in the Southern District of California, whether potential class members live here, whether witnesses, evidence, or documentation exists here, and whether, because of the diverse citizenship of potential claimants, it would be convenient to other class members to hold the trials here.
>
> One other case involving Blockade poisoning has been filed here. The potential class members are strewn across the United States, since Hartz apparently marketed Blockade nationally. Witnesses and evidence on each class member will thus also be scattered across the country. It is therefore inevitable that conducting a class action here will inconvenience many potential class members.

122 F.R.D. at 266. How does this approach compare to the discussion in *Klay*?

2. In *Haley v. Medtronic, Inc.*, 169 F.R.D. 643, 653 (C.D. Cal. 1996), the products liability action against the manufacturer of pacemaker leads mentioned in the preceding subsection, the court also found that Rule 23(b)(3)(C) considerations militated against certification:

> In this case, where the potential plaintiffs are located across the country and where the witnesses and the particular evidence will also be found across the country, plaintiffs have failed to establish any particular reason why it would be especially efficient for this Court to hear such a massive class action lawsuit. Indeed, plaintiffs have not even established that the vast majority of the individual lawsuits that have been filed—or that will be filed—should be brought in the Central District of California. Absent such evidence, it seems clear

that this factor indicates that class action treatment is inappropriate in the instant circumstances.

Does this approach seem more in keeping with *Klay* or *Ikonen*?

3. Consider also *McMahon Books, Inc. v. Willow Grove Associates*, 108 F.R.D. 32 (E.D. Pa. 1985), an action in which a tenant and former tenant in a shopping mall moved for class certification of their RICO case against the mall owners. With respect to Rule 23(b)(3)(C), the court found that the (b)(3)(C) factor

> weighs in favor of class certification. If a class were certified, all the tenants who fail to opt out of the class would have their claims litigated in this forum. Litigation of all the claims in this forum would be more efficient than dispersed litigation. The activity that forms the subject matter of these claims took place in this forum, and this forum would appear to be the most convenient one for all concerned parties to litigate the claims. If a class were not certified, some plaintiffs might sue in other forums. Any such cases might be transferred back to this forum pursuant to 28 U.S.C. § 1404 [transfer for the convenience of the parties, witnesses, etc.—discussed in Chapter 13(B)(1)]. Thus, failure to certify a class would not necessarily lead to dispersed litigation. Nevertheless, class certification would further desirable concentration of the litigation of these claims in this forum and avoid possible future delays in determining transfer motions and similar interlocutory rulings.

Id. at 41.

Given *McMahon Books* and the various other approaches discuseed above, how should a court apply Rule 23(b)(C) in assessing superiority?

4. Should a court be empowered to deny class certification under Rule 23(b)(3)(C) solely on the ground that it would be undesirable to concentrate litigation of the claims before that court?

5. Should a court, in evaluating a potential class action under Rule 23(b)(3)(C), consider whether it believes itself to be institutionally competent to adjudicate such claims? Should it consider whether its docket will permit efficient adjudication of the proposed class action?

6. The *Klay* court addresses the theory of whether a class should be denied certification because the legal theory at issue is "immature." For a discussion of that theory, *see* Chapter 10(A)(4)(b).

v. Rule 23(b)(3)(D)—Manageability Issues

Rule 23(b)(3)(D) requires a court addressing class certification to consider "the likely difficulties in managing a class action." The following case addressed arguments that the proposed class was unmanageable.

In re Domestic Air Transp. Antitrust Litig.
United States District Court, Northern District of Georgia, 1991.
137 F.R.D. 677.

Shoob, District Judge.

[Plaintiffs brought a nationwide antitrust class action against several major domestic airlines and against Airline Tariff Publishing Company ("ATPC"), alleging that from January 1, 1988 through 1991, the defendants agreed not to engage in price competition with any defendant airline on routes to or from that defendant's hub airport. Plaintiffs also alleged that defendants had misused the computerized fare information system provided by ATPC as a tool for their conspiracy. The court found that the issue of defendants' conspiracy, its impact on individual class members, and calculation of each class member's damages were susceptible to generalized proof common to all members of the class. The proof included documents, fact testimony, and expert testimony relating to the relevant market and the impact of defendants' alleged behavior. Finding that common issues predominated, the court turned to the issue of superiority.]

B. Superiority

In addition to finding that common questions predominate over individual inquiries, in certifying a class under Rule 23(b)(3), the Court must find that the class action vehicle is superior to other available methods for adjudication. In making its determination the Court must find that difficulties in management will not render this action improper for certification.

Defendants insist that this case will be unmanageable as a class action because the proposed class will number in the millions and will involve over 400 million transactions, requiring "mini-trials" for millions of purchasers. The Court cannot deny certification, however, merely because the number of plaintiffs makes the proceeding complex or difficult. The Court admits that it has been most concerned about the manageability of this action; however, "difficulties in management are of significance only if they make the class action a *less* 'fair and efficient' method of adjudication than other available techniques."

The Court finds a class action the *only* fair method of adjudication for plaintiffs. The individual claims of many class members are so small that the cost of individual litigation would be far greater than the value of those claims. Thus, if this case is not certified as a class action, a majority of class members would likely abandon their claims even if it can be proven that defendants have conspired to fix prices of domestic air transportation. Justice Douglas, concurring in *Eisen v. Carlisle & Jacquelin*, 417 U.S. 156 (1974), recognized the necessity of a class action in a case such as this:

> [A] class action serves not only the convenience of the parties but also prompt, efficient judicial administration. . . . [Plaintiffs may be] consumers whose claims may seem *de minimis* but who alone have no practical recourse for either remuneration or injunctive relief. . . . The class action is one of the few legal remedies the small claimant has against those who command the *status quo*.

Either the case proceeds as a class action or it is over. While the action involves an enormous class of claimants, the Court will not preclude plaintiffs from pursuing their remedies under the civil antitrust laws unless the only conclusion the Court is able to reach is that the action is unmanageable.

At the Court's request, plaintiffs submitted a preliminary plan for the administration of class member claims. Included in the preliminary plan is plaintiffs' estimate that the class will number close to 12.5 million purchasers. Plaintiffs' preliminary plan, while lacking in detail, evidences a keen understanding of the steps necessary to process claims. In addition, manageability will be enhanced by the considerable experience of counsel and the inclusion of accounting firms specializing in class litigation. Computers can index and control vast quantities of textual data and scanners are available to enter data automatically into the computer. These are resources that have only recently become available and that courts must be willing to employ to resolve the dilemma of the massive antitrust case.

At this juncture, the Court finds that the size of the class and number of damage claims do not present insurmountable manageability problems. While the number of possible claimants is staggering, defendants should not be permitted to avoid responsibility for the magnitude of their alleged conspiracy. Plaintiffs have come forward with sufficient evidence of formulaic approaches to the measure of damages. The calculation of individual damages for class members, therefore, does not make this case unmanageable as a class action.

Defendants' second attack on the superiority of the class action is that the enormous number of class members would make individual notice [required under Rule 23(c)(2)—see Chapter 5(A)(2)] to each impossible, as the cost would be prohibitive. Defendants contend that many of the class members are not readily identifiable and, therefore, plaintiffs cannot direct individual notice to all class members, in violation of Rule 23(c)(2).

In a case certified pursuant to Rule 23(b)(3), notice must be given to the members of the class and an opportunity must be given to them to opt out of the class. Rule 23(c)(2) requires the "best notice practicable under the circumstances, including individual notice to all members who can be identified through reasonable effort." Rule 23 does not mandate individual notice; instead, it requires that "[t]he notice must be such as is reasonably calculated to reach interested parties and apprise them of the pendency of the action." *See Mullane v. Cent. Hanover Bank & Trust Co.*, 339 U.S. 306, 314 (1950).

Where the names and addresses of class members are known, individual notice to each is required. However, in this action, the identity of each class member, defined as a purchaser of domestic airline passenger tickets, is not yet known and at least for the purpose of initial class notice, cannot be known. Defendants acknowledge that their records do not reflect the addresses of all passengers, nor do they list all actual purchasers of airline tickets. * * *

* * * Plaintiffs assert that the best notice practicable in this case may be publication notice. The class traffic includes 23 hub locations. Publication notice, therefore, could be given in a newspaper of general circulation in each of those 23 locations. In addition, as has been done in many other cases, publication notice could be given in various national publications such as *USA Today*, the national edition of *The Wall Street Journal*, and various magazines and business publications (*e.g., Newsweek, Business Week*, etc.).

Each of the defendant airlines places in the seat pocket of its aircraft a magazine for the passengers. Plaintiffs suggest that notice could also be included in those magazines which would be likely to reach a large segment of the class. Likewise, since many members of the class purchase their airline tickets either through travel agents or at airline ticket offices or counters, it would also be possible to place notices at each of those locations, including individual notices that could be handed to, or torn off from placards by, interested class members.

Plaintiffs contend that it is also possible in a reasonable manner to obtain as a result of the publication notice, a list that would identify at least some class members by name and address. The publication notice could provide an address and/or an "800" telephone number with which class members could communicate in order to identify themselves and obtain additional information concerning the class action.

The Court finds that the notice requirement of Rule 23 does not presently render this action unmanageable. Plaintiffs have offered an abundance of information concerning the possibility of notice. This discussion does not represent the Court's final determination concerning the adequacy of notice; a separate hearing will be held to determine the method and content of class notice.

* * *

In certifying the class, the Court recognizes its right, at a later date, to create subclasses to enhance manageability and to appoint special masters. In addition, the Court will continue to review and monitor the manageability of this action in light of evidentiary developments throughout the course of this litigation. At this juncture, the Court finds that difficulties in management resulting from the large number of potential claims do not make the class action a less fair and efficient method than other available techniques.

* * *

NOTES AND QUESTIONS

1. The *Domestic Air Transportation* case later settled. *See In re Domestic Air Transp. Antitrust Litig.*, 148 F.R.D. 297 (N.D. Ga. 1993). Could it have been adjudicated in a trial format? How would such a trial have been structured?

2. One commentator contends that:

> A class action should not be found unmanageable without exploring the procedural devices available for bringing it in line. These include subclassing and trial of subclass issues separately [*see* Chapter 4(B)(2)(d)], bifurcating liability and damages, using a fluid recovery [see Chapter 8(B)(2)], devising an objective formula for determining individual damages, issuing orders under Rule 23(d) to "prevent undue repetition or complication in the presentation of evidence or argument," appointing a special master for difficult evidentiary matters, use of litigation committees or surrogates to receive claims and proof of eligibility for individual damages, and trying certain issues first in anticipation of furthering settlement.

Edward Sherman, *Class Actions and Duplicative Litigation*, 62 Ind. L.J. 507, 516–17 (1987). Is Professor Sherman correct in placing a duty on the court to assess whether procedural steps could be taken to alleviate manageability problems? Or should the burden be on the proponent of class treatment to suggest methods of addressing potential problems?

3. In *In re Folding Carton Antitrust Litigation*, 88 F.R.D. 211, 216 (N.D. Ill. 1980), the court observed that " '[d]ismissal for management reasons, in view of the public interest involved in class actions, should be the exception rather than the rule.' " Does this view comport with the text of Rule 23(b)(3)? With the allocation of the burden of persuasion at the class certification stage? What arguments support this view?

4. Manageability issues often play a significant role in decisions relating to certification of multi-jurisdictional and mass tort class actions under Rule 23(b)(3). For explorations of those issues, see Chapters 6 and 10(A), respectively.

vi. Tools for Addressing Predominance or Manageability Problems

Courts have struggled with issues relating to whether either subclassing under Rule 23(c)(5) or limited class certification under Rule 23(c)(4) can reduce or eliminate predominance or manageability problems in proposed Rule 23(b)(3) class actions. Those issues are explored in Chapter 4(B)(2).

PROBLEM

A group of 40 children were injured on a Ferris wheel at the Nebraska State Fair. After the Ferris wheel stopped and the children unfastened their belts, the wheel suddenly moved again, throwing most of the children from their seats. The complaint alleges a design defect as the cause of the accident. The manufacturer of the Ferris wheel—the defendant in the case—claims that operator negligence was the cause. Three children suffered major injuries and likely will be paralyzed for life. Numerous children suffered broken arms or legs. Others suffered no physical injuries but were extremely upset by the incident. The parents of one of the paralyzed children seek certification of a class under Rule 23(b)(3). Because the manufacturer is a resident of Wyoming, the suit was brought in federal court based on diversity. The judge assigned to the case is new to the federal bench and has asked his law clerk to address the pros and cons of certification under (b)(3) versus other methods for resolving the case. What is the correct advice?

Now change the facts. Assume that 60 similar accidents have occurred throughout the country (involving approximately 2,400 children) and that the plaintiff seeks certification of a nationwide class. Is the advice the same? If not, how is it different?

CHAPTER 4

LITIGATING A CLASS ACTION

■ ■ ■

Understanding the requirements of Rule 23 is only the first step in successfully prosecuting or defending a class action. A host of other litigation-related issues—explored in this chapter—can ultimately make the difference between victory and defeat for a class action practitioner. An understanding of these issues is also essential for those wishing to engage in meaningful theoretical or policy analysis relating to class actions. This chapter focuses on strategic litigation considerations; certification decision mechanics; certification options (*e.g.*, partial certification, tentative certification, subclasses); discovery; case management and summary judgment; and trial issues (trial structure, Seventh Amendment, and due process).

A. INITIAL STRATEGIC CONSIDERATIONS IN PROSECUTING AND DEFENDING A CLASS ACTION

The following excerpts consider the wide variety of strategic considerations that class action attorneys must address. As these excerpts reveal, such strategic evaluations necessarily require a comprehensive knowledge of the legal principles governing class actions. Moreover, these discussions illustrate that plaintiffs' and defendants' views about the applicable principles and strategies vary greatly.

1. PLAINTIFFS' STRATEGIC CONSIDERATIONS

HERBERT NEWBERG & ALBA CONTE, NEWBERG ON CLASS ACTIONS
(4th ed. 2002) §§ 6.1–6.9.

Before filing a class complaint, plaintiff's counsel should consider several factors in order to achieve the most advantageous litigation posture. * * *

* * * [B]efore a class complaint is filed, plaintiff's counsel should consider the advantages of a class action, who should be the class representative, whether a single plaintiff or multiple class plaintiffs should be joined, which defendants should be sued and for what claims, which forum should be chosen, how large the class scope should be, what the settlement possibilities are without filing a lawsuit, and what fee arrangements with class representatives should be negotiated.

Advantages of Class Actions From the Plaintiff's Standpoint

At the outset, it is important for a plaintiff and his or her counsel to consider the advantages and limitations of proceeding in the class action forum.

* * *

Selecting the Plaintiffs for Class Representatives

* * *

Standing Aspects

As in any individual or class action, the plaintiff should meet proper standing requirements to pursue the litigation.

Conflicts with Other Class Members

In order to be an adequate representative within the meaning of Rule 23(a)(4), it is necessary that the named plaintiff have no conflicts with other class members with respect to the issues in controversy.

Thus, when a choice of plaintiffs is available, selection of a class representative with the least vulnerability to challenge for conflict of interest is desirable.

Commonality of Legal Controversy

The class representative should ordinarily be the person who has the lowest number of individual issues. This choice will * * * diminish the likelihood of individual defenses being raised concerning claims of the plaintiff that are not common to the class . . . * * *

* * *

Best Factual Case for Proving Liability

Ideally, * * * the plaintiff having the strongest factual case of proving liability should be selected. In complex litigation * * * the plaintiff may have limited knowledge of the facts concerning the defendant's activities, yet the plaintiff may be a completely adequate representative of the class by virtue of obtaining qualified legal counsel and prosecuting the case vigorously.

* * *

Broad Scope of Claims Common to Class

A class complaint may set forth one or more claims common to a class. To the extent possible, class representatives should be selected who possess standing individually to raise the broadest scope of claims common to the class. * * * Counsel for the class, however, should take care not to make the scope of a class for damage claims so broad that it raises the specter of unmanageability. * * *

Single or Multiple Class Representatives

A single plaintiff is adequate to represent a class of persons, even a very large class. Sometimes, when the opportunity is available, the joinder of additional plaintiffs as joint class representatives may have certain advantages. For example, if the claims of one or more plaintiffs are likely to become moot during the course of the litigation, additional plaintiffs whose claims may remain viable may obviate any challenge on the ground of mootness. * * * The court may decide that only some of the aspiring representatives are suitable and reject others due to unique defenses, lack of interest, or other reasons. * * * It should be stressed, however, that several class representatives are unnecessary—one will do, even with a small individual claim, as a fully qualified class representative. * * *

* * *

Selecting Parties [as] Defendant[s]

Careful attention must be focused on decisions regarding which parties should be joined as defendants. * * * A joining of more defendants means lining up more adversaries and more potential challenges, and possibly delays and continuances during the course of the litigation. On the other hand, more defendants may mean the availability of larger settlement opportunities for the class and added dissension among defense counsel. * * *

Joinder of Claims

Federal and State Claims

Frequently, allegedly illegal activities may give rise to claims under both federal and state law, or under several alternative theories of liability, or affecting a group of persons as well as individuals.

Some theories are cognizable within federal jurisdiction, while others may be pursued only in state courts. Still others are amenable to concurrent jurisdiction. When both federal and state claims may be available, the class plaintiff in federal court may join state claims, arising from the same common nucleus of facts, under [supplemental] jurisdiction. Alternatively, state claims may be joined under diversity of citizenship jurisdictional statutes when the necessary prerequisites are present. In either case, the class representative should consider the advantages and disadvantages of joining federal and state claims in a single class complaint. * * *

Different Theories of Liability

One also must consider whether to join additional claims for different theories of liability leading to approximately the same relief. Often this joinder may be advantageous when the precise theory of liability that may be applicable is subject to uncertainty or when the class possesses several related claims. On the other hand, * * * [a] longer complaint may afford additional opportunities for challenge by the defendants concerning the impropriety of certifying a class action and may also give rise to feelings by the court of management difficulties. * * *

* * *

Choice of Forum

* * * [T]he plaintiffs should select a forum that may give them an advantage over one more convenient to the defendants. Weight given by the courts to the plaintiff's choice of forum in a class action is sometimes less than that given in an action not brought as a class action, because class members are often located over a broad geographical area, and in instances when a multiplicity of actions is likely, convenience of the defendants takes on added importance in choice of forum. In instances when a multiplicity of actions is not likely, as when individual claims are small, or when no other class actions are pending, the plaintiff's choice of forum is entitled to its customary weight. The defendants, of course, always have the option, in

appropriate circumstances, of moving to transfer to a more convenient forum.

Class Scope

In filing a class action, one must consider how broadly or narrowly to define the scope of the class in terms of geographical distribution and the range of claims to be litigated. In actions seeking primarily declaratory or injunctive relief, one may safely sue on behalf of as broad a class of persons as are affected by the controversy. * * * On the other hand, in a class action for damages under Rule 23(b)(3) * * * individual notice must be sent at the plaintiff's expense to all class members who can be identified through reasonable effort. * * * [T]he expense of notice relative to the size of the plaintiff's claim and pocketbook may mandate the bringing of a class complaint of narrower scope than one that would include the entire universe of potentially affected persons.

* * *

Settlement Considerations

Often overlooked by counsel is the possibility of a favorable settlement with the defendant, either for the individual claims of the plaintiff or for the claims of the class, before the filing of a class complaint. * * *

Fee Arrangements with Class Representatives or Class Members

Fee arrangements between counsel and the class representative or class members vary among different law firms and various locations. Often the plaintiff's counsel will undertake class litigation on a contingent fee basis, with or without an initial retainer. Attorney fees may be authorized by statute to be recovered from the losing party or may be awarded from a common fund. Fees from absent class members, in the event of successful litigation, are subject to court determination. * * *

* * *

[End of Excerpt]

In addition to those mentioned by Newberg and Conte, other considerations for plaintiffs include:

Whether to Pursue a Class Action. As addressed briefly by Newberg and Conte, a threshold decision is whether to pursue a class action at all. In some cases, the most desirable aspects of class litigation can be achieved with other procedural devices, such as joinder of multiple related lawsuits (*see* Fed. R. Civ. P. 20; Chapter 13(A)(1)), permissive intervention (*see* Fed. R. Civ. P. 24(b); Chapter 13(A)(5)), consolidation (*see* Fed. R. Civ. P. 42(a); Chapter 13(A)(6)), or pretrial coordination under the Multi-District Litigation statute (*see* 28 U.S.C. § 1407; Chapter 12). Another possibility may be a test case with potential *res judicata* or collateral estoppel effects (*see* Chapter 7(C)).

In certain cases, however, a class action offers a significant advantage over other procedural devices: If a class is certified, the plaintiff class may be able to insist on settlement terms far more favorable than what could be obtained in an individual suit. Importantly, however, this bargaining advantage is accompanied by a substantial expansion of class counsel's responsibilities. By filing a class action suit, plaintiffs' counsel becomes a fiduciary to all potential members of the class.

Where to Bring Suit. The often-critical decision of where to file a putative class action is discussed in the previous excerpt. Several developments, however, have added new complexities to the decision.

Until recently, conventional wisdom held that plaintiffs' attorneys preferred state court, while defense attorneys preferred federal court. State court judges (many of whom are elected) were sometimes perceived as being more willing than their federal counterparts to certify sprawling class actions in the face of potential management issues. This perception prompted legislative efforts—culminating in The Class Action Fairness Act of 2005 ("CAFA")—to transfer most interstate class actions to federal court. The upshot of CAFA's impact is that now, in many cases, plaintiffs' counsel will not be able to maintain a class action in state court, because CAFA allows defendants in most class actions of significant size to remove the case to federal court unless the action fits within one of CAFA's relatively narrow exceptions. *See* Chapter 7(B)(3)(c) (discussing CAFA's exceptions). If removal is inevitable, counsel may simply forgo state courts in the first instance, focusing instead on whether the law of a particular federal circuit is more hospitable to the lawsuit's ultimate chances of success. In such a situation, to the extent that there is a choice between federal circuits in which to litigate (which is often the case with multistate class actions), plaintiffs' counsel may seek to file suit in a federal district court within a circuit whose class action law is seen as most favorable.

Moreover, even if a class action falls within one of CAFA's exceptions (thereby remaining in state court), plaintiffs' counsel might still prefer a federal forum. For example, litigating in state court may require the class to give up potentially viable federal claims, since the assertion of a federal claim will allow the defendant to remove the case to federal court.

How to Define the Class. Although the class definition will often be contested by defendants, and may end up being modified by the court, plaintiffs have the first opportunity to offer a definition of their proposed class. A broadly defined class may have pecuniary or tactical advantages. On the other hand, a class may be defined so broadly, or so vaguely, as to bring about its own undoing. For example, an expansive nationwide class action suit may entail so many individualized issues—such as complicated choice-of-law issues—that the court would be compelled to deny class certification. *See* Chapter 6(B) (discussing choice-of-law issues in class litigation). Additionally, under CAFA, the scope of the class may affect plaintiffs' ability to remain in state court. A more limited statewide class, in which only one state's law controls, may have a better chance of certification. *See* Chapter 7(B)(3) (discussing CAFA and its exceptions). Likewise, a class that is defined more narrowly in terms of the number of people and time period involved may be more suitable for certification than an unwieldy class involving hundreds of thousands (or even millions) of people.

When to Move for Class Certification. As discussed in Section (B)(1)(a) of this chapter, many jurisdictions—both federal and state—have specific rules on when a plaintiff must move for class certification. Absent such a rule, plaintiffs' counsel must decide when to move for class certification.

This decision will depend in part on whether, absent discovery, the defendant is likely to possess evidence showing individualized issues (*e.g.*, evidence showing that class members suffered various types of injuries at different times). If discovery will permit defendant to make a better showing against the suitability of class certification, then plaintiff may prefer to seek an early certification ruling. It is important to note, however, that the decision on when to move for a decision on class certification does not lie exclusively with plaintiffs' counsel. Certainly, in most cases it is the plaintiffs who move for certification, but several courts have ruled that Rule 23 contains no *per se* rule that defendants may not seek a ruling on class certification, and in fact defendants have sometimes done so. *See, e.g.*, *Vinole v. Countrywide Home Loans, Inc.*, 571 F.3d 935, 939–41 (9th Cir. 2009); *see also* Chapter 4(B)(1)(a), *infra* (discussing timing of class certification decision).

Complying with Pleading Requirements. Another consideration for plaintiffs is how to comply with the more rigorous pleading standard established by the Supreme Court in *Bell Atlantic Corp. v. Twombly*, 550 U.S. 544 (2007), and *Ashcroft v. Iqbal*, 556 U.S. 662 (2009). *Twombly* held that, for a plaintiff's complaint to survive a motion to dismiss for failure to state a claim upon which relief can be granted, the complaint must contain sufficient "[f]actual allegations * * * to raise a right to relief above the speculative level," and noted that "a formulaic recitation of the elements of a cause of action will not do." 550 U.S. at 555. The Court explained that plaintiffs are required to plead "enough facts to state a claim to relief that is plausible on its face." *Id.* at 570. In *Iqbal*, the Court elaborated, explaining that, "[w]hile legal conclusions can provide the framework of a complaint, they must be supported by factual allegations." 556 U.S. at 679. Importantly, *Iqbal* also clarified that *Twombly*'s holding "expounded the pleading standard for all civil actions * * *." *Id.* at 684 (citations and internal quotation marks omitted).

Although the implications of the "plausibility" standard are not limited to class actions, some concerns expressed in *Twombly* (which was itself a putative class action) apply with particular force in the class action context. *See, e.g.*, *In re Hydrogen Peroxide Antitrust Litig.*, 552 F.3d 305, 310 (3d Cir. 2008) (citing *Twombly* for the proposition that "certain antitrust class actions may present prime opportunities for plaintiffs to exert pressure upon defendants to settle weak claims"). The plausibility standard has generated a range of views as to both its meaning and its fairness to litigants. *See, e.g.*, Symposium, *Pondering* Iqbal, 14 Lewis & Clark L. Rev. 3 (2010), including Suzette M. Malveaux, *Front Loading and Heavy Lifting: How Pre-Dismissal Discovery Can Address the Detrimental Effect of* Iqbal *on Civil Rights Cases*, 14 Lewis & Clark L. Rev. 65 (2010). As an example of lower courts struggling with this line of cases, see *Swanson v. Citibank, N.A.*, 614 F.3d 400 (7th Cir. 2010), in which a Seventh Circuit panel disagreed over whether *Twombly* and *Iqbal* mandated dismissal.

For a recent case in which the Supreme Court applied the pleading requirements of *Twombly* and *Iqbal* to a securities fraud class action complaint, *see Matrixx Initiatives, Inc. v. Siracusano*, 563 U.S. 27 (2011). *Matrixx* presented the question whether a plaintiff could state a claim for securities fraud based on the defendant pharmaceutical company's "failure to disclose reports of adverse events associated with a product if the reports do not disclose a statistically significant number of adverse events." *Id.* at 30. The defendant argued that the complaint did not adequately allege that defendant "made a material representation or omission or that it acted with scienter because the complaint [did] not allege that [defendant] knew of a statistically significant number of adverse events requiring disclosure." *Id.* The Court, however, in a unanimous opinion by Justice Sotomayor, declined to draw a bright-line rule requiring a "statistically significant" number of adverse event reports for a misrepresentation to be "material." *Id.* at 30–31. Rather, after considering the totality of the allegations in plaintiffs' complaint, the Court concluded that the allegations sufficed "to raise a 'reasonable expectation that discovery will reveal evidence' satisfying the materiality requirement, and to 'allo[w] the court to draw the reasonable inference that the defendant is liable for the misconduct alleged.'" *Id.* at 46 (quoting, respectively, *Twombly*, 550 U.S. at 556; and *Iqbal*, 556 U.S. at 678). It should be noted that, in addition to the requirements of Rule 12(b)(6), the plaintiffs in *Matrixx* also had to (and did) meet the heightened pleading requirements of the Private Securities Litigation Reform Act of 1995, 109 Stat. 737, discussed in Chapter 10(C)(2)(a).

At bottom, *Twombly* and *Iqbal* present new challenges to plaintiffs' counsel—and corresponding opportunities for defendants' counsel—at the earliest stages of class action lawsuits. But the *Matrixx* case suggests that those decisions might not be quite the sea change that defendants had assumed.

2. DEFENDANT'S STRATEGIC CONSIDERATIONS

The following materials discuss strategic considerations from the defendant's perspective. It should be noted that defendants, like plaintiffs, must consult any applicable local court rules.

JEROLD SOLOVY, TIMOTHY CHORVAT, AVIDAN STERN & DAVID FEINBERG, "STRATEGIES FOR DEFENDING A CLASS ACTION," IN LITIGATION & RESOLUTION OF COMPLEX CLASS ACTIONS

Glasser Legal Works (1998) at 31–36.

One * * * strategic choice that defendants often confront in the early stages of a class action is whether to pursue a defense on the merits before class certification is resolved.

* * *

The advantage of moving for a judgment before certification is obviously to dispose of the named plaintiffs' claims with a minimum of expense. * * * [By doing so,] the defendant can effectively moot the issue of class certification. Without any claims, the named plaintiffs cannot bring any action, let alone a class action.

While the plaintiff's counsel, or another attorney, could elect to try again on behalf of a different plaintiff, a dismissal of an action also can undermine the viability of such successor suits. While the proposed class members will not be legally precluded from seeking individual relief in successor suits, the dismissal of the named plaintiffs' claim will, as a practical matter, deter the individual actions. * * *

The disadvantage to the defendant of filing a merits-based motion before certification is that an order dismissing an action before certification is only binding on the named plaintiffs and will not have preclusive effect with respect to the other putative class members. This could potentially require the defendant to stave off a series of individual claims brought by members of the proposed class.

* * *

* * * [C]lass certification may be advantageous to a defendant because any subsequent judgment will bind the entire class. Thus, defense counsel should consider the strategic consequences of opposing class certification before embarking on such a course of action. Defense counsel should carefully weigh the chances of succeeding on the merits, the likelihood that individual plaintiffs would sue, and the expense of a class action suit versus the expense of individual actions. * * *

On the other hand, defeating a motion for class certification can destroy the plaintiff's counsel's incentive to pursue the case, even where an individual plaintiff's case remains pending. * * *

* * *

ALAN H. MACLIN, STRATEGIES AND OPTIONS FOR DEFENDING CLASS ACTIONS
Practical Litigator (September 1998), at 37–59.

When a class action case comes in the door, what should you, as defense counsel, do first? As with any lawsuit, you must consider strategy early, and be prepared to reconsider actions and strategy as developments occur. * * *

FORUM CONSIDERATIONS: REMOVAL, TRANSFER, AND MULTIDISTRICT LITIGATION

One of the factors that will seriously affect how you proceed in a class action is the jurisdiction in which the case is filed. In some cases, it may be to your advantage to have the case transferred, or to point out any jurisdictional defects.

Case Filed in State Court

If the case has been filed in state court, is removal an option?[†] If you intend to oppose certification vigorously, it may be wise to consider removal to federal court, given recent decisions by the Supreme Court and several courts of appeals directing district courts to apply Rule 23 certification requirements more rigorously.

* * *

Case Filed in Federal Court

If the case has been filed in federal court, analyze whether the court will assert subject matter jurisdiction over the claims. If the basis is diversity, [determine whether in fact diversity jurisdiction exists].

[†] The Class Action Fairness Act of 2005 (CAFA), discussed in detail in Chapter 7(B)(3), makes it more likely that the answer to this question is "yes." [Ed.]

* * *

Transfer

Is the case a good candidate for transfer of venue and would that help your client? Generally, you would apply the same transfer analysis to a class action as to any other kind of case. *See* 28 U.S.C. § 1404(a) (action may be transferred to another district where it could have been brought "[f]or the convenience of parties and witnesses, in the interest of justice"). [*See* Chapter 13(B)(2)].

[The author also discusses a procedure for the transfer of cases by the Panel on Multidistrict Litigation for pretrial proceedings. (*See* discussion of multidistrict litigation in Chapter 12.)]

INSURANCE COVERAGE OR OTHER INDEMNITY OBLIGATIONS

The existence of insurance or some other indemnity obligation can affect the nature and extent of a defendant's liability. Thus, it may be in the defendant's interest to seek contribution, indemnification, and to raise cross-claims.

* * *

SCHEDULING AND DISCOVERY

Scheduling and discovery are subject to local rules, and the requirements can vary considerably. For example, * * * [s]ome jurisdictions * * * require plaintiffs to file their motion for class certification within 90 days after the action is filed.

* * *

Bifurcation Between Class and Merits

To limit the burden and possible exposure of discovery, a defendant may consider requesting that discovery be bifurcated between class discovery and merits discovery.

When Is Bifurcation a Good Idea for the Defendant?

Bifurcation is particularly helpful to a defendant with strong defenses to class certification, but who is in a weaker position on the merits. This is because it allows discovery on the class certification issues to take place without exposing the defendant to any burdensome and potentially risky discovery on the merits. A motion to stay discovery will accomplish the same result.

There will naturally be some fine distinctions between class and merits discovery, and counsel for the parties will have to attempt to work out any disagreements based on the particular facts of the case.

Discovery Considerations for Defendant During Pretrial Period

Commentators tend to agree that timing is crucial for both the defendant and the plaintiff. Specifically, the defendant's discovery, and the burden imposed upon the defendant, will be affected by its decision to attack the class, merits, or both. After the defendant makes this choice, it can attempt to affect the timing of discovery to relieve its burden. * * *

* * *

DISPOSITIVE MOTIONS

An important consideration with dispositive motions in class action litigation is when to file them. In some instances, it may be appropriate to file a dispositive motion before reaching the merits.

Resolution of Named Plaintiff's Claims Before Class Determination

A defendant may wish to push resolution on the merits with respect to the named plaintiff only, with class issues to be decided later. Bifurcating between named plaintiffs and the class may be desirable for a defendant if the named plaintiffs have a weak case on the merits, and class certification is either a strong possibility or poses a great risk, burden, or expense to the defendant. * * * Of course any resulting dismissal of the case would be without prejudice to the putative class, and plaintiffs' counsel may need only to find another class representative to challenge the defendant in another lawsuit. * * *

However, the grounds for the dispositive motion decision may effectively preclude any subsequent actions with different named plaintiffs, * * * where the district court's reasoning applies equally to other potential class members.

OPPOSING CLASS CERTIFICATION

Whether to oppose class certification is an important decision that depends on the facts of the particular case. On the one hand, successfully opposing class certification may result in abandonment of the case altogether or very limited exposure on individual claims. On the other hand, successful opposition to class certification may subject the defendant to multiple individual lawsuits and defending a class action suit may be less expensive than defending multiple lawsuits. Thus, class certification may, under rare circumstances, be advantageous to the defendant—especially the defendant with strong arguments on the merits—because a subsequent judgment will bind the entire class.

* * *

IS A QUICK SETTLEMENT COST-EFFECTIVE?

Plaintiffs must bear the cost of notifying class members when a Rule 23(b)(3) class is certified. * * * If the records identifying class members are in the possession of the defendant, the defendant may be ordered to make those records available to plaintiffs. * * *

Negotiated Settlement

Frequently, costs of class notice are borne by the defendant in a negotiated settlement. In a Rule 23(b)(3) class, the court must order that "the best notice practicable under the circumstances" be given to class members, "including individual notice to all members who can be identified through reasonable effort." Rule 23(c)(2). "Practicable" in this context also provides some wiggle room, and there are no bright-line tests regarding what types of notice satisfy these requirements.

TRIAL CONSIDERATIONS

If there is no way to avoid going to trial, you have to consider the most convenient and cost-effective way to try the case.

Split Trials and Consolidation Issues

Consolidation is an appropriate method when there are many actions pending in different districts and the proof of liability will be difficult and complex (for example, a national antitrust price-fixing scheme). The defendant [often] has a right to a jury trial and, generally, the same jury should be retained.

Pilot/Lead/Bellwether/Test Cases

These cases are a good solution when the claims of the parties in the test case are typical in substance of the class, so that adjudication of one case will resolve principal claims and defenses for the class (for example, a securities action, in which evidence will be essentially the same). A few tips:

- Adjudicating the merits of these claims is usually determinative, either by agreement, *stare decisis* or collateral estoppel, of the remaining, untried claims;
- The defendant should be alert to the choice of representative, because the plaintiff will attempt to choose the most straightforward plaintiff; and
- It may be wise for a defendant to push for this alternative early because the defendant could use it as a reason to limit discovery to "bellwether" plaintiffs.

* * *

Proof of Claim

Once liability is determined, the defendant may want to have proofs of claim issued to class members. Since this would be the only method of participating in the recovery, the defendant should try to ensure that a mandatory response or bar date, beyond which the court will not receive the form, is inserted into the form.

Existence of Common or Unique Defenses

The existence of unique defenses may suggest that a motion for decertification of the class would be appropriate.

CONCLUSION

The division between class certification issues and the underlying merits of the plaintiffs' claims calls for some special strategizing in class action litigation. This division also affects the basics of discovery, pretrial practice, and settlement. This article sets out some of the basics. Be sure to research how the courts in your jurisdiction handle these topics.

* * *

3. ISSUES COMMON TO BOTH SIDES: NEED TO REVIEW LOCAL RULES

Counsel for all parties must review the local rules of the court in which a putative class action suit is filed, and take care to adhere to filing requirements. For example, numerous federal courts have local rules that plaintiffs must file motions for class certification within a specified time after filing their complaint.† Although many of these local rules allow the district court to extend or modify these deadlines, counsel must notify the court promptly of any potential delays. Some courts have "strictly constru[ed]" such rules in order "to expedite resolution of class certification issues for the benefit of the Court, the potential class members, and the parties as well." *Joshlin v. Gannett River States Publ'g Corp.*, 152 F.R.D. 577, 578 (E.D. Ark. 1993); *see also Black Panther Party v. Smith*, 661 F.2d 1243, 1279 (D.C. Cir. 1981) (affirming refusal to grant extension of time to file motion for class certification, which was sought 11 days after 90-day deadline had expired, and noting that "the status of class actions should be determined quickly"), *vacated on other grounds*, 458 U.S. 1118 (1982); *Hall v. Bio–Med. Application, Inc.*, 671 F.2d 300, 302–03 (8th Cir. 1982) (upholding strict application of time limit for motion).

Other courts, however, have excused noncompliance with local rules as a matter of discretion. For example, in *Slanina v. William Penn Parking Corp.*, 106 F.R.D. 419, 422 (W.D. Pa. 1984), the court found that the search for a potential class representative took more time than the local rule permitted because some members of the proposed class feared reprisals as a result of the proposed litigation. In addition, the court found that counsel's caution in seeking a proper named representative also delayed the plaintiffs' motion. Given these circumstances, the court found that plaintiffs had filed their motion for class certification as soon as was practicable, as was then required by Rule 23. *See also Probe v. State Teachers' Ret. Sys.*, 780 F.2d 776, 780 (9th Cir. 1986) (untimely motion permissible because of lack of prejudice to defendants).

The *Manual for Complex Litigation (Fourth)* notes a tension between local rules and the requirements of Rule 23:

> Some local rules specify a short period within which the plaintiff must file a motion to certify a class action. Such rules, however, may be inconsistent with Rule 23(c)(1)(A)'s emphasis on the parties' obligation to present the court with sufficient information to support an informed decision on certification. Parties need sufficient time to develop an adequate record.

---

† *See, e.g.*, D. Vt. Local Rule 23(c)(1) ("Within 90 days after filing a class action complaint, unless the period is extended on motion for good cause, the plaintiff must move for a determination under Fed. R. Civ. P. 23(c)(1), as to whether the case is to be maintained as a class action."); N.D. Tex. Local Rule 23.2 ("Within 90 days of filing a class action complaint, or at such other time as the presiding judge by order directs, an attorney for the plaintiff must move for certification."); *see also, e.g.*, M.D. Pa. Local Rule 23.3 (90 days); M.D.N.C. Local Rule 23.1(b) (90 days); M.D. Fla. Local Rule 4.04(b) (90 days); N.D. Ga. Local Rule 23.1(B) (90 days); *cf.* S.D. Ohio Local Rule 23.3 ("In all cases with class action allegations, the parties shall include in their Fed. R. Civ. P. 26(f) [discovery conference] report proposed deadlines * * * for filing a motion to certify a class, as well as a proposed date for class action determination."). [Ed.]

Manual for Complex Litigation (Fourth) § 21.133 (2004).

The 2003 amendment to Rule 23(c)(1)—directing the court to determine the propriety of class certification "at an early practicable time," rather than "as soon as practicable"—was designed in part to provide the parties more time to gather information necessary for the class certification determination. *See* 2003 Advisory Committee Notes to Rule 23(c)(1)(A).

Some courts have responded to amended Rule 23(c)(1)(A) by amending their local rules. For example, in the Southern District of Florida, Local Rule 23.1(3)'s requirement that plaintiffs file their class certification motion within 90 days of filing the complaint has been deleted in recognition that pursuant to the federal rule, "a Court may defer the decision on whether to certify a class if it is prudent to do so." Comments to the 2004 Amendment to S.D. Fla. Local Rule 23.1(3).

Local rules may also require that plaintiffs plead specific facts tending to support the complaint's class action allegations. For example, in federal court in Vermont, Local Rule 23.1 requires that in any case sought to be maintained as a class action, the class action allegations must, *inter alia*, (a) specify the provision or provisions of Federal Rule of Civil Procedure 23(b) under which the class should be certified, (b) specify or estimate the size of the class, (c) contain appropriate allegations justifying plaintiff's claim to be an adequate representative of the class, and (d) specify the questions of law and fact claimed to be common to the class. *See* D. Vt. R. 23.1. Class certification may be denied if the complaint fails to comply with the rule. *Esden v. Bank of Bos.*, 5 F. Supp. 2d 214, 218 (D. Vt. 1998) (denying without prejudice plaintiff's motion to certify class, and allowing plaintiff to file amended complaint, where "the required allegations are scattered throughout [plaintiff's] memoranda in support of the Motion for Class Certification, [but] the complaint fails to meet these Local Rule 23.1 requirements").

PROBLEM

(A) Jonathan Li, a prominent civil rights practitioner in Elmsville, a large city in a medium-sized state, receives a visit from three local residents, all originally from El Salvador, about improper traffic stops. They report that the local police (and, on a couple of occasions, the state police) have repeatedly pulled them over on major streets and subjected them to harassment and interrogation. They report that several Latino friends have been similarly mistreated, and they explain that they believe that Latinos are being "targeted for harassment" by the police.

One of the three potential plaintiffs is not a United States citizen and is concerned about playing a visible role in a prominent suit. A second plaintiff has had three prior speeding tickets in the last month from other parts of the state. The third potential plaintiff has served as a class representative in two prior class actions (securities fraud and consumer fraud) and recovered about $1,000 in each case. All three potential plaintiffs have little income to devote to a lawsuit.

There are potential civil rights claims for damages and injunctive relief under both federal and state law, although only federal law allows punitive damages. Li has only three lawyers in his firm, and has never handled a civil rights class action without bringing in co-counsel.

What issues does Li need to address prior to filing suit?

(B) Assume that Li brings the case, using all three potential plaintiffs as class representatives. He files federal and state claims in state court under the state equivalents to Rule 23(b)(2) and 23(b)(3), seeking compensatory and punitive damages, as well as injunctive relief. He brings the suit on behalf of Latinos of driving age throughout the state and sues all local and state police departments throughout the state. Li decides not to associate co-counsel because he believes he is competent to handle the lawsuit. Additionally, he can make a lot of money from the case and does not want to have to divide it with other lawyers.

What issues should Li address now that he has filed suit?

(C) The various police departments hire Althea Johnson of the firm of Light & Corran. Johnson knows the following facts not known to Li:

• Several of the police chiefs across the state have previously been sued successfully for violating the civil rights of African–Americans.

• Numerous internal documents of the state police contain racial and ethnic slurs regarding African–Americans, Latinos, and other minority groups.

• Several Latino police officers from Elmsville have heard comments supporting plaintiffs' claim that Latinos are being targeted for harassment in that city. Although these officers do not want to "make waves," they will tell the truth if questioned.

What issues should Johnson consider?

B. CERTIFICATION DECISION

It is difficult to overstate the importance of the class certification decision in class litigation. The value and success of a case will frequently rise or fall significantly based on whether a court permits it to proceed as a class action. Despite the high stakes, courts normally have significant discretion in deciding motions to certify class actions.

This section explores a number of important issues relating to the class certification decision—procedural and substantive considerations underlying the decision itself, tentative certification (as distinct from "conditional certification," which is discussed in Section (B)(2)(b) of this chapter), and the possibility of subclasses or partial certification.

1. CORE PRINCIPLES

a. Timing of the Class Certification Decision

Rule 23(c)(1) instructs district courts to address class certification "at an early practicable time." This language was added in 2003 to replace the phrase "as soon as practicable." *See* Rule 23(c)(1)(A).

MANUAL FOR COMPLEX LITIGATION (FOURTH)
Federal Judicial Center (2004) § 21.133.

Federal Rule of Civil Procedure 23(c)(1) directs the court to determine "at an early practicable time" whether to certify an action as a class action. The "early practicable time" is when the court has sufficient information to decide whether the action meets the certification criteria of Rules 23(a) and (b). The timing of the certification decision deserves discussion early in the case, often at the initial scheduling conference where the judge and counsel can address the issues bearing on certification and can establish a schedule for the work necessary to permit an informed ruling on the class certification motion. Appropriate timing will vary with the circumstances of the case, although an early resolution is generally desirable.

Precertification discovery may be necessary. The court may rule on motions pursuant to Rule 12, Rule 56, or other threshold issues before deciding on certification; however, such rulings bind only the named parties. Most courts agree, and Rule 23(c)(1)(A) reflects, that such precertification rulings on threshold dispositive motions are proper, and one study found a substantial rate of precertification rulings on motions to dismiss or for summary judgment. Precertification rulings frequently dispose of all or part of the litigation.

Efficiency and economy are strong reasons for a court to resolve challenges to personal or subject-matter jurisdiction before ruling on certification. The judge should direct counsel to raise such challenges before filing motions to certify. Similarly, courts should rule early on motions to dismiss, challenging whether the plaintiffs have stated a cause of action. Early resolution of these questions may avoid expense for the parties and burdens for the court and may minimize use of the class action process for cases that are weak on the merits. In unusual cases, involuntary precertification dismissal may unfairly affect the interests of members of the proposed class. For example, in a case in which the filing was accompanied by extensive publicity, but where the dismissal had little publicity, individual members of the proposed class may rely on the pendency of the class action to toll [the statute of] limitations. If the risk of unfair prejudice is present, some form of notice under Rule 23(d)(2) may be appropriate.

NOTES AND QUESTIONS

1. Rule 23(c)(1) does not set concrete guidelines for determining the issue of class certification. As a result, most appellate courts have permitted district courts to exercise broad discretion over the issue of timing. As the First Circuit explained in *Lamphere v. Brown University*, 553 F.2d 714, 718–19 (1st Cir. 1977):

> Given the inexhaustible variety of cases, we think the issue must in most imaginable circumstances be entrusted to the district court during the trial. [Former] Rule 23(c)(1) specifically calls for a decision on the class issue as early as practicable in the litigation, and also provides for reconsideration of the decision as the case progresses. The underlying theme is flexibility; different cases call for different approaches. In retrospect we may, with our 20–20 hindsight vision, conclude that the court committed some reversible error, but we lack the foresight to announce guidelines.

Consider whether justice would be better served by the adoption of more stringent rules governing the timing of class certification decisions. If so, what kinds of rules would be appropriate? Recall, as noted earlier in this chapter, that many district courts have, in fact, adopted rules containing a presumption that motions for class certification must be filed within a certain time after the plaintiff files suit, absent good cause for an extension.

As the 2003 Advisory Committee Notes explain, there are "many valid reasons that may justify deferring the initial certification decision." Advisory Committee Note to Rule 23(c)(1)(A). The Notes refer to the possible need for "controlled discovery into the 'merits,'" pre-certification dispositive motions, and designation of class counsel. *See also Weiss v. Regal Collections*, 385 F.3d 337, 348 n.17 (3d Cir. 2004) (noting that change in rule was "necessary for sound judicial administration"); *Coburn v. DaimlerChrysler Serv. N. Am., L.L.C.*, 2005 WL 736657, at *7 n.5 (N.D. Ill. 2005) (noting that change in rule provides additional flexibility in court's ability to determine when certification decision should be made). Although delay in the certification decision is often necessary, the Advisory Committee Notes also emphasize that courts must actively manage cases to ensure that any such delay is truly justified. *See* Advisory Committee Note to Rule 23(c)(1)(A).

2. May an individual who successfully brings his own individual suit then seek to bring a class action on behalf of those similarly situated? In *McDonald v. Pension Plan of the NYSA–ILA Pension Trust Fund*, 320 F.3d 151 (2d Cir. 2003), a retiree who prevailed in his individual suit against a plan administrator for violating ERISA subsequently sought classwide relief. The district court refused to grant the relief, finding the "'attempt to transform what was clearly an individual claim into a class claim after a favorable decision on the merits troubling.'" *Id*. at 161–62 (quoting district court). On appeal, recognizing the importance of notifying a defendant early in the litigation of its potential exposure, the Second Circuit held that "the district court's decisions neither to certify a class nor to afford relief to beneficiaries who were not parties involved no abuse of discretion." *Id*. at 162.

3. There is little solid empirical data concerning the rapidity with which motions for certification are filed and ruled upon. One Federal Judicial Center study, however, provides a snapshot of these issues in four judicial districts (N.D. Cal., S.D. Fla., N.D. Ill., and E.D. Pa.) concerning class actions resolved between 1992 and 1994. Thomas E. Willging, Laural L. Hooper & Robert J. Niemic, *Class Actions and the Rulemaking Process: An Empirical Analysis of Rule 23 to Address the Rulemaking Challenges*, 71 N.Y.U. L. Rev. 74 (1996). The study found that the median time for plaintiffs to file motions to certify—or courts to act *sua sponte* concerning certification—ranged from 3.1 months to 4.3 months after the filing of the complaint, and that 75 percent of the motions or orders were filed within a period of 6.5 to 16.3 months after the filing of the complaint. *See id*. at 102.

4. Although plaintiffs ordinarily raise the issue of class certification by motion, defendants may raise the issue as well under certain circumstances. For example, in *Vinole v. Countrywide Home Loans, Inc.*, 571 F.3d 935 (9th Cir. 2009), the Ninth Circuit held that the district court did not abuse its discretion in granting the defendant's motion to *deny* class certification before the plaintiffs had filed a motion seeking certification. The court of appeals found that "[n]othing in the plain language of Rule 23(c)(1)(A) either vests the plaintiffs with the exclusive right to put the class certification issue before the district court or prohibits a defendant from seeking early resolution of the class certification question." *Id*. at 939–40 (citing cases). To be sure, in most cases it is the plaintiff who moves for class certification, not the defendant who moves to deny certification. Additionally, an important ground for the holding in *Vinole* was that plaintiffs had "adequate time in which to conduct discovery related to the question of class certification," so that plaintiffs were not prejudiced by the timing of the district court's ruling. *Id*. at 942. Other examples of

cases in which defendants moved to deny class certification are noted in the section of this chapter on class certification discovery, Section (C)(1).

Is it fair to permit a defendant to raise the issue of class certification? Under what circumstances? What should a plaintiff do under such circumstances? Should the legal burden of persuasion vary depending on which side is the moving party?

b. Merits Inquiry and Expert Testimony

In *Wal–Mart Stores, Inc. v. Dukes*, 564 U.S. 338 (2011), the Supreme Court endorsed what by that point had become the consensus view in federal courts—namely, that the district court has a duty to conduct a "rigorous analysis" of the Rule 23 requirements at the certification stage, based on actual evidence and not on mere allegations. As the Court noted, "[f]requently that 'rigorous analysis' will entail some overlap with the merits of the plaintiff's underlying claim. That cannot be helped." *Id.* at 351. The Court explained: "Rule 23 does not set forth a mere pleading standard." *Id.* at 350. Rather, "[a] party seeking class certification must affirmatively demonstrate his compliance with the Rule—that is, he must be prepared to prove that there are *in fact* sufficiently numerous parties, common questions of law or fact, etc." *Id.*

Moreover, even before the Court decided *Dukes*, most circuits had already reached similar conclusions. *See, e.g., In re Hydrogen Peroxide Antitrust Litig.*, 552 F.3d 305 (3d Cir. 2008); *In re Initial Pub. Offering Secs. Litig.*, 471 F.3d 24 (2d Cir. 2006); *Szabo v. Bridgeport Machs., Inc.*, 249 F.3d 672 (7th Cir. 2001). For many years, however, there was significant uncertainty as to the proper scope of the court's analysis at the class certification stage—in particular, the relationship between the merits of the underlying claims and the requirements of Rule 23.

i. *The Relevance of Merits to Class Certification*

The debate over the propriety of inquiring into the merits at the class certification stage arose from a statement in *Eisen v. Carlisle & Jacquelin*, 417 U.S. 156 (1974). The specific question before the Supreme Court in *Eisen* was whether the district court could shift the cost of giving notice to absent class members from the plaintiff to the defendants, based on a preliminary hearing in which the district court found that such cost-shifting was justified because the plaintiff was "more than likely" to prevail on his claims. *Id.* at 169 (quoting district court). The district court analogized the situation to the law of preliminary injunctions, which generally requires an assessment of the likelihood of a party's success on the merits. Although much of Justice Powell's opinion for the Supreme Court focused on the issue of what notice must be given under Rule 23(c)(2) to absent class members regarding their right to opt out of the class (a topic discussed in Chapter 5), the Court also found that the district court had overstepped the bounds of Rule 23 by inquiring into the substantive merits of Eisen's claims in order to shift the cost of notice. *Id.* at 177. Most importantly for present purposes, the Court wrote: "We find nothing in either the language or history of Rule 23 that gives a court any authority to conduct a preliminary inquiry into the merits of a suit in order to determine whether it may be maintained as a class action." *Id.* at 177–78.

Although *Eisen* was based in part on the Court's concern "that a preliminary determination of the merits may result in substantial prejudice to a defendant," *id.* at 178, post-*Eisen* case law reveals that the *Eisen* rule was usually invoked by *plaintiffs* as an argument that a court should address class certification without extensive consideration of "merits" issues. One early example of a plaintiff-friendly invocation of *Eisen* was *Blackie v. Barrack*, 524 F.2d 891 (9th Cir. 1975), in which the Ninth Circuit rejected defendants' challenge to class certification, stating:

> * * * [N]either the possibility that a plaintiff will be unable to prove his allegations, nor the possibility that the later course of the suit might unforeseeably prove the original decision to certify the class wrong, is a basis for declining to certify a class which apparently satisfies the Rule. * * * The Court made clear in [*Eisen*] that [the class certification] determination does not permit or require a preliminary inquiry into the merits; thus, the district judge is necessarily bound to some degree of speculation by the uncertain state of the record on which he must rule. * * *

Id. at 900–01. *Blackie* exemplified a permissive approach to the class certification decision, under which doubts relating to certification should be resolved in favor of granting class status, and under which plaintiffs' pleadings, taken as true, could largely determine whether a class should be certified.

In *General Telephone Co. v. Falcon*, 457 U.S. 147 (1982), the Supreme Court again confronted the issue of the extent to which district courts should scrutinize the merits at the class certification stage. The Court explained: "Sometimes the issues are plain enough from the pleadings to determine whether the interests of the absent parties are fairly encompassed within the named plaintiff's claim, and sometimes it may be necessary for the court to probe behind the pleadings before coming to rest on the certification question." *Id.* at 160. It concluded "that a Title VII class action, like any other class action, may only be certified if the trial court is satisfied, after a rigorous analysis, that the prerequisites of Rule 23(a) have been satisfied." *Id.* at 161.

Notwithstanding *Falcon*, during the 1980s and 1990s, certain federal district courts, following the apparent signal of appellate decisions like *Blackie*, refused to probe behind the pleadings when deciding class certification. *See, e.g., Krueger v. N.Y. Tel. Co.*, 163 F.R.D. 433, 438 (S.D.N.Y. 1995) ("The Court should not resolve any material factual disputes in the process of determining whether plaintiffs have provided a reasonable basis for their assertions." (citation omitted)); *see generally, e.g.*, Geoffrey P. Miller, *Review of the Merits in Class Action Certification*, 33 Hofstra L. Rev. 51, 52–63 (2004) (describing various lower courts' evolving interpretations of *Eisen*).

By the mid-1990s, however, a definitive shift had begun to occur at the federal appellate level. In *Castano v. American Tobacco Co.*, 84 F.3d 734 (5th Cir. 1996), the Fifth Circuit reversed a district court's certification of a nationwide class including "[a]ll nicotine-dependent persons in the United States" who had used the defendants' tobacco products, holding that the lower court had mistakenly "believed that it could not go past the pleadings for the certification decision." *Id.* at 737, 744; *see also In re Am. Med.*

Sys., Inc., 75 F.3d 1069, 1079 (6th Cir. 1996) (reversing district court's certification of product liability class and stating that "[a] class is not maintainable as a class action by virtue of its designation as such in the pleadings"); *In re Rhone–Poulenc Rorer, Inc.*, 51 F.3d 1293, 1299 (7th Cir. 1995) (Posner, J.) (decertifying class on grounds that included "the demonstrated great likelihood that the plaintiffs' claims, despite their human appeal, lack legal merit"); Chapters 6(B) and 10(A).

The shift was highlighted in 2001 in a much-cited case, *Szabo v. Bridgeport Machines, Inc.*, 249 F.3d 672 (7th Cir. 2001) (Easterbrook, J.). In *Szabo*, which was cited favorably by the Supreme Court in *Dukes*, the Seventh Circuit found that the lower court had erroneously conflated the standard for class certification under Rule 23 with the standard for resolving a Rule 12(b)(6) motion to dismiss for failure to state a claim. The Seventh Circuit explained:

> The reason why judges accept a complaint's factual allegations when ruling on motions to dismiss under Rule 12(b)(6) is that a motion to dismiss tests the legal sufficiency of a pleading. Its *factual* sufficiency will be tested later—by a motion for summary judgment under Rule 56, and if necessary by trial. By contrast, an order certifying a class usually is the district judge's last word on the subject; there is no later test of the decision's factual premises (and, if the case is settled, there could not be such an examination even if the district judge viewed the certification as provisional). Before deciding whether to allow a case to proceed as a class action, therefore, a judge should make whatever factual and legal inquiries are necessary under Rule 23.

249 F.3d at 675–76. *Szabo* flatly rejected the district court's reliance on *Eisen*, at least insofar as the lower court had understood *Eisen* to preclude any inquiry that touches on "merits" issues at the certification stage.

Numerous courts around the country embraced the *Szabo* approach. *See, e.g., In re Initial Pub. Offering Secs. Litig.* ("*IPO*"), 471 F.3d 24, 27 (2d Cir. 2006) (concluding that "the fact that a Rule 23 requirement might overlap with an issue on the merits does not avoid the court's obligation to make a ruling as to whether the requirement is met, although such a circumstance might appropriately limit the scope of the court's inquiry at the class certification stage"); *Oscar Private Equity Invs. v. Allegiance Telecom, Inc.*, 487 F.3d 261, 267 (5th Cir. 2007) ("the plain text of Rule 23 requires the court to 'find,' not merely assume, the facts favoring class certification"); *Vallario v. Vandehey*, 554 F.3d 1259, 1265–67 (10th Cir. 2009) (adopting *IPO* analysis); *Vega v. T–Mobile USA, Inc.*, 564 F.3d 1256, 1266 (11th Cir. 2009) (same).

Predictably, in *Wal–Mart Stores, Inc. v. Dukes*, 564 U.S. 338 (2011), the Supreme Court confirmed *Szabo*'s reading of *Eisen*. The majority opinion in *Dukes* stated that "[t]he class determination generally involves considerations that are enmeshed in the factual and legal issues comprising the plaintiff's cause of action." *Id.* at 351 (citations and internal quotation marks omitted). To eliminate any doubt about how *Eisen* should be interpreted, the Court added this footnote to the sentence just quoted:

> A statement in one of our prior cases, *Eisen v. Carlisle & Jacquelin*, 417 U.S. 156, 177 (1974), is sometimes mistakenly

cited to the contrary: "We find nothing in either the language or history of Rule 23 that gives a court any authority to conduct a preliminary inquiry into the merits of a suit in order to determine whether it may be maintained as a class action." But in that case, the judge had conducted a preliminary inquiry into the merits of a suit, not in order to determine the propriety of certification under Rules 23(a) and (b) (he had already done that), but in order to shift the cost of notice required by Rule 23(c)(2) from the plaintiff to the defendants. To the extent the quoted statement goes beyond the permissibility of a merits inquiry for any other pretrial purpose, it is the purest dictum and is contradicted by our other cases.

Id. at 351 n.6. *Dukes* thus appeared to confirm the approach to Rule 23 certification that had already taken hold in many of the circuits. Two years later, however, the Supreme Court returned to the issue and addressed it in far more depth.

AMGEN INC. v. CONN. RET. PLANS & TRUST FUNDS
Supreme Court of the United States, 2013.

133 S. Ct. 1184.

JUSTICE GINSBURG delivered the opinion of the Court.

This case involves a securities-fraud complaint filed by Connecticut Retirement Plans and Trust Funds (Connecticut Retirement) against biotechnology company Amgen Inc. and several of its officers (collectively, Amgen). Seeking class-action certification under Federal Rule of Civil Procedure 23, Connecticut Retirement invoked the "fraud-on-the-market" presumption endorsed by this Court in *Basic Inc. v. Levinson*, 485 U.S. 224, 108 (1988), and recognized most recently in *Erica P. John Fund, Inc. v. Halliburton Co.*, 131 S. Ct. 2179 (2011). The fraud-on-the-market premise is that the price of a security traded in an efficient market will reflect all publicly available information about a company; accordingly, a buyer of the security may be presumed to have relied on that information in purchasing the security.

Amgen has conceded the efficiency of the market for the securities at issue and has not contested the public character of the allegedly fraudulent statements on which Connecticut Retirement's complaint is based. Nor does Amgen here dispute that Connecticut Retirement meets all of the class-action prerequisites stated in Rule 23(a): (1) the alleged class "is so numerous that joinder of all members is impracticable"; (2) "there are questions of law or fact common to the class"; (3) Connecticut Retirement's claims are "typical of the claims . . . of the class"; and (4) Connecticut Retirement will "fairly and adequately protect the interests of the class."

The issue presented concerns the requirement stated in Rule 23(b)(3) that "the questions of law or fact common to class members predominate over any questions affecting only individual members." Amgen contends that to meet the predominance requirement, Connecticut Retirement must do more than plausibly *plead* that Amgen's alleged misrepresentations and misleading omissions materially affected Amgen's stock price. According to Amgen, certification must be denied unless Connecticut Retirement *proves* materiality, for immaterial misrepresentations or omissions, by definition, would have no impact on Amgen's stock price in an efficient market.

While Connecticut Retirement certainly must prove materiality to prevail on the merits, we hold that such proof is not a prerequisite to class certification. Rule 23(b)(3) requires a showing that *questions* common to the class predominate, not that those questions will be answered, on the merits, in favor of the class. Because materiality is judged according to an objective standard, the materiality of Amgen's alleged misrepresentations and omissions is a question common to all members of the class Connecticut Retirement would represent. The alleged misrepresentations and omissions, whether material or immaterial, would be so equally for all investors composing the class. As vital, the plaintiff class's inability to prove materiality would not result in individual questions predominating. Instead, a failure of proof on the issue of materiality would end the case, given that materiality is an essential element of the class members' securities-fraud claims. As to materiality, therefore, the class is entirely cohesive: It will prevail or fail in unison. In no event will the individual circumstances of particular class members bear on the inquiry.

Essentially, Amgen, also the dissenters from today's decision, would have us put the cart before the horse. To gain certification under Rule 23(b)(3), Amgen and the dissenters urge, Connecticut Retirement must first establish that it will win the fray. But the office of a Rule 23(b)(3) certification ruling is not to adjudicate the case; rather, it is to select the "metho[d]" best suited to adjudication of the controversy "fairly and efficiently."

I

A

This case involves the interaction between federal securities-fraud laws and Rule 23's requirements for class certification. To obtain certification of a class action for money damages under Rule 23(b)(3), a plaintiff must satisfy Rule 23(a)'s above-mentioned prerequisites of numerosity, commonality, typicality, and adequacy of representation * * * and must also establish that "the questions of law or fact common to class members predominate over any questions affecting only individual members, and that a class action is superior to other available methods for fairly and efficiently adjudicating the controversy." To recover damages in a private securities-fraud action under § 10(b) of the Securities Exchange Act of 1934, 48 Stat. 891, as amended, 15 U.S.C. § 78j(b), and Securities and Exchange Commission Rule 10b–5, 17 CFR § 240.10b–5, a plaintiff must prove "(1) a material misrepresentation or omission by the defendant; (2) scienter; (3) a connection between the misrepresentation or omission and the purchase or sale of a security; (4) reliance upon the misrepresentation or omission; (5) economic loss; and (6) loss causation." * * *

"Reliance," we have explained, "is an essential element of the § 10(b) private cause of action" because "proof of reliance ensures that there is a proper connection between a defendant's misrepresentation and a plaintiff's injury." * * * "The traditional (and most direct) way" for a plaintiff to demonstrate reliance "is by showing that he was aware of a company's statement and engaged in a relevant transaction * * * based on that specific misrepresentation." We have recognized, however, that requiring proof of direct reliance "would place an unnecessarily unrealistic evidentiary burden on [a] plaintiff who has traded on an impersonal market." Accordingly, in *Basic* the Court endorsed the "fraud-on-the-market" theory, which permits certain Rule 10b–5 plaintiffs to invoke a rebuttable presumption of reliance on material misrepresentations aired to the general public.

The fraud-on-the-market theory rests on the premise that certain well-developed markets are efficient processors of public information. In such markets, the "market price of shares" will "reflec[t] all publicly available information." Few investors in such markets, if any, can consistently achieve above-market returns by trading based on publicly available information alone, for if such above-market returns were readily attainable, it would mean that market prices were not efficiently incorporating the full supply of public information. * * *

In *Basic,* we held that if a market is shown to be efficient, courts may presume that investors who traded securities in that market relied on public, material misrepresentations regarding those securities. This presumption springs from the very concept of market efficiency. If a market is generally efficient in incorporating publicly available information into a security's market price, it is reasonable to presume that a particular public, material misrepresentation will be reflected in the security's price. Furthermore, it is reasonable to presume that most investors—knowing that they have little hope of outperforming the market in the long run based solely on their analysis of publicly available information—will rely on the security's market price as an unbiased assessment of the security's value in light of all public information. Thus, courts may presume that investors trading in efficient markets indirectly rely on public, material misrepresentations through their "reliance on the integrity of the price set by the market." "[T]he presumption," however, is "just that, and [can] be rebutted by appropriate evidence." * * *

* * * Absent the fraud-on-the-market theory, the requirement that Rule 10b–5 plaintiffs establish reliance would ordinarily preclude certification of a class action seeking money damages because individual reliance issues would overwhelm questions common to the class. The fraud on the market theory, however, facilitates class certification by recognizing a rebuttable presumption of classwide reliance on public, material misrepresentations when shares are traded in an efficient market.

B

In its complaint, Connecticut Retirement alleges that Amgen violated § 10(b) and Rule 10b–5 through certain misrepresentations and misleading omissions regarding the safety, efficacy, and marketing of two of its flagship drugs. According to Connecticut Retirement, these misrepresentations and omissions artificially inflated the price of Amgen's stock at the time Connecticut Retirement and numerous other securities buyers purchased the stock. When the truth came to light, Connecticut Retirement asserts, Amgen's stock price declined, resulting in financial losses to those who purchased the stock at the inflated price. In its answer to Connecticut Retirement's complaint, Amgen conceded that "[a]t all relevant times, the market for [its] securities," which are traded on the NASDAQ stock exchange, "was an efficient market"; thus, "the market for Amgen's securities promptly digested current information regarding Amgen from all publicly available sources and reflected such information in Amgen's stock price."

The District Court granted Connecticut Retirement's motion to certify a class action under Rule 23(b)(3) on behalf of all investors who purchased Amgen stock between the date of the first alleged misrepresentation and the date of the last alleged corrective disclosure. * * *

Amgen raised two arguments on appeal [under Rule 23(f)]. First, Amgen contended that the District Court erred by certifying the proposed class without first requiring Connecticut Retirement to prove that Amgen's alleged misrepresentations and omissions were material. Second, Amgen argued that the District Court erred by refusing to consider certain rebuttal evidence that[,] * * * in Amgen's view, demonstrated that the market was well aware of the truth regarding its alleged misrepresentations and omissions at the time the class members purchased their shares.

The Court of Appeals rejected both contentions. * * *

* * *

We granted Amgen's petition for certiorari to resolve a conflict among the Courts of Appeals over whether district courts must require plaintiffs to prove, and must allow defendants to present evidence rebutting, the element of materiality before certifying a class action under § 10(b) and Rule 10b–5. * * *

II

A

The only issue before us in this case is whether Connecticut Retirement has satisfied Rule 23(b)(3)'s requirement that "questions of law or fact common to class members predominate over any questions affecting only individual members." Although we have cautioned that a court's class-certification analysis must be "rigorous" and may "entail some overlap with the merits of the plaintiff's underlying claim," *Wal–Mart Stores, Inc. v. Dukes*, 564 U.S. 338, 351 (2011), Rule 23 grants courts no license to engage in free-ranging merits inquiries at the certification stage. Merits questions may be considered to the extent—but only to the extent—that they are relevant to determining whether the Rule 23 prerequisites for class certification are satisfied. * * *

Bearing firmly in mind that the focus of Rule 23(b)(3) is on the predominance of common *questions,* we turn to Amgen's contention that the courts below erred by failing to require Connecticut Retirement to prove the materiality of Amgen's alleged misrepresentations and omissions before certifying Connecticut Retirement's proposed class. As Amgen notes, materiality is not only an element of the Rule 10b–5 cause of action; it is also an essential predicate of the fraud-on-the-market theory. * * * That theory, Amgen correctly observes, is premised on the understanding that in an efficient market, all publicly available information is rapidly incorporated into, and thus transmitted to investors through, the market price. Because immaterial information, by definition, does not affect market price, it cannot be relied upon indirectly by investors who, as the fraud-on-the-market theory presumes, rely on the market price's integrity. Therefore, the fraud-on-the-market theory cannot apply absent a *material* misrepresentation or omission. And without the fraud-on-the-market theory, the element of reliance cannot be proved on a classwide basis through evidence common to the class. It thus follows, Amgen contends, that materiality must be proved before a securities-fraud class action can be certified.

Contrary to Amgen's argument, the key question in this case is not whether materiality is an essential predicate of the fraud-on-the-market theory; indisputably it is. Instead, the pivotal inquiry is whether proof of materiality is needed to ensure that the *questions* of law or fact common to the class will "predominate over any questions affecting only individual members" as the litigation progresses. Fed. R. Civ. P. 23(b)(3). For two reasons, the answer to this question is clearly "no."

First, because "[t]he question of materiality * * * is an objective one, involving the significance of an omitted or misrepresented fact to a reasonable investor," materiality can be proved through evidence common to the class. Consequently, materiality is a "common questio[n]" for purposes of Rule 23(b)(3). * * *

Second, there is no risk whatever that a failure of proof on the common question of materiality will result in individual questions predominating. Because materiality is an essential element of a Rule 10b–5 claim, Connecticut Retirement's failure to present sufficient evidence of materiality to defeat a summary-judgment motion or to prevail at trial would not cause individual reliance questions to overwhelm the questions common to the class. Instead, the failure of proof on the element of materiality would end the case for one and for all; no claim would remain in which individual reliance issues could potentially predominate.

* * *

Because the question of materiality is common to the class, and because a failure of proof on that issue would not result in questions "affecting only individual members" predominating, Fed. R. Civ. P. 23(b)(3), Connecticut Retirement was not required to prove the materiality of Amgen's alleged misrepresentations and omissions at the class certification stage. This is not a case in which the asserted problem—*i.e.*, that the plaintiff class cannot prove materiality—"exhibits some fatal dissimilarity" among class members that would make use of the class-action device inefficient or unfair. Instead, what Amgen alleges is "a fatal similarity—[an alleged] failure of proof as to an element of the plaintiffs' cause of action." Such a contention is properly addressed at trial or in a ruling on a summary-judgment motion. The allegation should not be resolved in deciding whether to certify a proposed class. * * *

It is so ordered.

[Concurring opinion by JUSTICE ALITO and dissenting opinion by JUSTICE SCALIA are omitted.]

JUSTICE THOMAS, with whom JUSTICE KENNEDY joins, and with whom JUSTICE SCALIA joins except for Part I–B, dissenting.

I

The Court today allows plaintiffs to obtain certification of securities-fraud class actions without proof that common questions predominate over individualized questions of reliance, in contravention of Federal Rule of Civil Procedure 23(b)(3). The Court does so by all but eliminating materiality as one of the predicates of the fraud-on-the-market theory, which serves as an alternative mode of establishing reliance. * * *

* * * Because a securities-fraud plaintiff invoking *Basic*'s fraud-on-the-market presumption to satisfy Rule 23(b)(3) should be required to prove each of the predicates of that theory at certification in order to demonstrate that questions of reliance are common to the class, I respectfully dissent.

A

* * *

If a plaintiff opts to show reliance through fraud on the market, *Basic* is clear that the plaintiff must show the following predicates in order to prevail: (1) an efficient market, (2) a public statement, (3) that the stock was traded after the statement was made but before the truth was revealed, and (4) the materiality of the statement. Both the Court and respondent agree that materiality is a necessary component of fraud on the market. * * * The materiality of a specific statement is, therefore, essential to the fraud-on-the-market presumption, which in turn enables a plaintiff to prove reliance.

B

* * *

* * * [T]he Court asserts that materiality—by its own admission an essential predicate to invoking fraud on the market—need not be established at certification because it will ultimately be proved at the merits stage. This assertion is an express admission that parties *will not know* at certification whether reliance is an individual or common question.

* * *

It is the Court, not Amgen, that "would have us put the cart before the horse," by jumping chronologically to the § 10(b) merits element of materiality. But Rule 23, as well as common sense, requires class certification issues to be addressed first. * * * A plaintiff who cannot prove materiality does not simply have a claim that is " 'dead on arrival' " at the merits; he has a class that should never have arrived at the merits at all because it failed Rule 23(b)(3) certification from the outset. Without materiality, there is no fraud-on-the-market presumption, questions of reliance remain individualized, and Rule 23(b)(3) certification is impossible. And the fact that evidence of materiality goes to both fraud on the market at certification and an independent merits element is no issue; *Wal–Mart* expressly held that a court at certification may inquire into questions that also have later relevance on the merits. The Court reverses that inquiry, effectively saying that certification may be put off until later because an adverse merits determination will retroactively wipe out the entire class. However, a plaintiff who cannot prove materiality cannot prove fraud on the market and, thus, cannot demonstrate that the question of reliance is susceptible of a classwide answer.

The fact that a statement may prove to be material at the merits stage does not justify conflating the doctrinally independent (and distinct) elements of materiality and reliance. The Court's error occurs when, instead of asking whether the element of *reliance* is susceptible to classwide proof, the Court focuses on whether *materiality* is susceptible to classwide proof. * * * The result is that the Court effectively equates § 10(b) materiality with fraud-on-the-market materiality and elides reliance as a § 10(b) element. But a plaintiff seeking certification under Rule 23 bears the burden of proof with regard to all the elements of a § 10(b) claim, which includes materiality *and* reliance. * * * If the elements of fraud on the market are not proved at certification, a plaintiff has failed to carry his burden of establishing that questions of individualized reliance will not predominate, without which the plaintiff class cannot obtain certification. * * * It is only by establishing all of the elements of the fraud-on-the-market presumption that reliance can be proved on a classwide basis. Therefore, if a plaintiff wishes to use *Basic*'s presumption to prove that reliance is a common question, he must establish the entire presumption, including materiality, at the class certification stage.

* * *

II

The majority's approach is, thus, doctrinally incorrect under *Basic*. * * *

III

I, thus, would reverse the judgment of the Ninth Circuit and hold that a plaintiff invoking the fraud-on-the-market presumption bears the burden to establish all the elements of fraud on the market at certification, including the materiality of the alleged misstatement.

NOTES AND QUESTIONS

1. Can the majority's approach in *Amgen* be reconciled with its statements in *Dukes* about the relevance of evidence bearing on the merits? What is the majority's reason for finding that Amgen's approach would "put the cart before the horse"? Why did Justice Thomas and Justice Kennedy disagree?

2. Following *Amgen*, several circuits have emphasized that class certification is not the place to decide the merits. For instance, in *Rikos v. Proctor & Gamble Co.*, 799 F.3d 497, 523 (6th Cir. 2015), the Sixth Circuit reasoned that evidence proffered by P & G "affect[ed] *only* the merits of this case, not predominance" and thus should not have been considered at the certification stage. (Emphasis added). Similarly, in *Alcantar v. Hobart Service*, 800 F.3d 1047, 1053 (9th Cir. 2015), the Ninth Circuit concluded that "the district court erred in denying class certification because it evaluated the merits rather than focusing on whether the questions presented—meritorious or not—were common to the class." And in *Williams v. Jani–King of Philadelphia*, 837 F.3d 314, 322 (3d Cir. 2016), the Third Circuit refused to answer Jani–King's first question on appeal (" 'Do the system controls inherent in a franchise relationship make a franchisor the employer of its franchise owners under Pennsylvania's multi-factor employment test?' ") because that question "ask[ed the court] to weigh in on the merits of the Plaintiffs' claims *now*." (Emphasis added).

3. The Third Circuit stated in *In re Hydrogen Peroxide Antitrust Litigation*, 552 F.3d 305, 320 (3d Cir. 2008), that the standard of proof for Rule 23 issues is the preponderance of the evidence standard. The Second Circuit has reached a similar conclusion. *See Teamsters Local 445 Freight Div. Pension Fund v. Bombardier, Inc.*, 546 F.3d 196, 202 (2d Cir. 2008) (holding "that the preponderance of the evidence standard applies to evidence proffered to establish Rule 23's requirements"). Given the stakes at class certification, should some other standard apply?

In *Dukes*, the Supreme Court clarified that "[a] party seeking class certification * * * must be prepared to prove that there are *in fact* sufficiently numerous parties, common questions of law or fact, etc.," 564 U.S. at 350, but did not specify a standard of proof.

4. *Amgen* made clear that, at the class certification stage, district courts are forbidden from assessing whether plaintiffs are likely to win the case. At most, courts can look at the merits if they overlap with class certification requirements. Some commentators, however, have argued expressly that the district court *should* make a preliminary assessment of the merits at class certification, even if there is no overlap with the class certification requirements. For instance, Bartlett H. McGuire argues:

> The dynamics of class action litigation would be dramatically altered if the courts, in making their class action rulings, were free to consider the merits of the underlying claims. The merits could be assessed by an analysis of prior judgments or test cases, especially in mass tort litigation where individual claims are large enough to be pursued. In small-claim cases where individual litigation is uneconomic, the courts could undertake an inquiry similar to that conducted in a preliminary injunction hearing. In some situations—*e.g.*, where only a handful of individual cases have been pursued—a combination of the two approaches might be appropriate. * * * If the courts were thus free to make preliminary assessments of the merits:
>
> 1. There would be far less risk of creating litigation where none should exist. Class treatment could be denied in cases that were frivolous or had little possibility of succeeding on the merits. However, litigation might still be created, properly, where the court found substantial merit to claims that would be too small to pursue on an individual basis.
>
> 2. Faced with the requirement of showing that their claims had substantial merit, plaintiffs' attorneys would be less likely to negotiate pre-certification settlements that are vulnerable to rejection because "[t]he case was simply settled too quickly with too little development on the merits."
>
> 3. Fortified by rulings that their claims had substantial merit, the attorneys for class representatives would be less likely, after class certification, to settle strong claims on the cheap; and lawyers for unnamed class members would have additional ammunition for challenging settlements that appeared to be inadequate.
>
> 4. Although defendants would still be faced with economic pressure to settle class actions, the preliminary assessment of the merits would preclude certification of the weakest class action claims, where the pressures to settle are particularly unfair.

5. In mature mass tort cases that were found to have substantial merit, the courts might be encouraged to find creative ways of invoking the class action procedure.

6. The issue of hearings on the merits would no longer generate the splits in authority and inconsistencies in approach that have plagued our class-action jurisprudence for almost 30 years.

Bartlett H. McGuire, *The Death Knell for* Eisen: *Why the Class Action Analysis Should Include an Assessment of the Merits*, 168 F.R.D. 366, 374–75 (1996). Should courts—wholly apart from assessing the requirements of Rule 23—be permitted or required to make a preliminary inquiry into the merits of plaintiffs' claims in ruling on class certification? Under what circumstances? How would such an approach affect discovery costs prior to the class certification hearing? Should the approach advocated by McGuire apply at least when the claims appear to be frivolous?

Professors Bone and Evans similarly advocate that courts take account of the substantive merits in assessing class certification:

> In the modest form of our proposal, the trial judge would review the evidence and determine whether the legal and factual issues on which the parties rely to support (or oppose) commonality, typicality, predominance, and other Rule 23 certification requirements are in fact viable. In addition, the judge would consider evidence, not just allegations, when mapping the path of the lawsuit and predicting which issues—those common to the class or specific to individual class members—are likely to consume the bulk of litigation time and resources. Finally, the judge in our proposal would weigh the evidence on both sides—not only evidence supporting the plaintiffs' prima facie case, but also the defendant's rebuttal evidence and, when relevant, any evidence relating to affirmative defenses.
>
> Under our more ambitious proposal, the judge would conduct the same evidentiary review, but that review would not be limited to Rule 23's certification requirements. Instead, the judge would make a general assessment of the strength of the plaintiffs' case as a whole and certify a case only if the case met a threshold "likelihood of success" standard.

Robert G. Bone & David S. Evans, *Class Certification and the Substantive Merits*, 51 Duke L.J. 1251, 1278 (2002). How do the inquiries (modest and more ambitious) proposed by Professors Bone and Evans compare to the standards adopted by the Supreme Court in *Amgen*? Is such a proposal fair to plaintiffs? Should plaintiffs have to show a "likelihood of success" before being permitted to proceed?

5. The *Manual for Complex Litigation (Fourth)* § 21.21 observes:

> A hearing under Federal Rule of Civil Procedure 23(c) is a routine part of the certification decision. The nature and scope of the disputed issues relating to class certification bear on the kind of hearing the judge should conduct. An evidentiary hearing may be necessary in a challenge to the factual basis for a class action. Disputed facts material to deciding certification may be narrowed or eliminated by stipulations, requests for admission, affidavits, or declarations. The parties should submit a statement of stipulated facts and identify disputed facts relevant to Rule 23 issues * * *. When there is disagreement over the legal standards but not over the facts material to the

certification decision, the court may rely on the parties' stipulations of fact, affidavits, declarations, and relevant documents to establish the factual record. In such a case, a hearing may be limited to argument over whether the certification requirements are met. A hearing is appropriate, even if the parties jointly move for certification of a class for settlement and for approval of the settlement class. A hearing ensures a full record, particularly if it is unclear that the certification standards are met or if there are likely to be objections to the settlement.

An evidentiary hearing to resolve disputed facts relevant to the certification decision should not be a mini-trial on the merits of the class or individual claims. Instead, the parties should present facts and arguments to let the judge determine the nature of the claims and defenses and how they will be presented at trial, whether there are common issues that can be tried on a class-wide basis, and whether those common issues predominate and class treatment is a superior method of resolving them. * * *

If the parties have submitted a trial plan to aid the judge in determining whether certification standards are met, the certification hearing provides an opportunity to examine the plan and its feasibility.

* * *

After the hearing, the court should enter findings of fact and conclusions of law addressing each of the applicable criteria of Rule 23. Failure to make such findings may result in reversal or remand for further proceedings after interlocutory appeal under Rule 23(f).

Does the *Manual* simply articulate the *Amgen* approach? If not, how do the two approaches differ?

ii. Expert Testimony (Comcast)

COMCAST CORP. V. BEHREND
Supreme Court of the United States, 2013.
133 S. Ct. 1426

JUSTICE SCALIA delivered the opinion of the Court.

The District Court and the Court of Appeals approved certification of a class of more than 2 million current and former Comcast subscribers who seek damages for alleged violations of the federal antitrust laws. We consider whether certification was appropriate under Federal Rule of Civil Procedure 23(b)(3).

I

Comcast Corporation and its subsidiaries, petitioners here, provide cable-television services to residential and commercial customers. From 1998 to 2007, petitioners engaged in a series of transactions that the parties have described as "clustering," a strategy of concentrating operations within a particular region. The region at issue here, which the parties have referred to as the Philadelphia "cluster" or the Philadelphia "Designated Market Area" (DMA), includes 16 counties located in Pennsylvania, Delaware, and New Jersey. Petitioners pursued their clustering strategy by acquiring competitor cable providers in the region and swapping their own systems outside the region for competitor systems located in the region. * * * As a result of nine clustering transactions, petitioners' share of subscribers in the region allegedly increased from 23.9 percent in 1998 to 69.5 percent in 2007.

The named plaintiffs, respondents here, are subscribers to Comcast's cable-television services. They filed a class-action antitrust suit against petitioners, claiming that petitioners entered into unlawful swap agreements, in violation of § 1 of the Sherman Act, and monopolized or attempted to monopolize services in the cluster, in violation of § 2. Petitioners' clustering scheme, respondents contended, harmed subscribers in the Philadelphia cluster by eliminating competition and holding prices for cable services above competitive levels.

Respondents sought to certify a class under Federal Rule of Civil Procedure 23(b)(3). That provision permits certification only if "the court finds that the questions of law or fact common to class members predominate over any questions affecting only individual members." The District Court held, and it is uncontested here, that to meet the predominance requirement respondents had to show (1) that the existence of individual injury resulting from the alleged antitrust violation (referred to as "antitrust impact") was "capable of proof at trial through evidence that [was] common to the class rather than individual to its members"; and (2) that the damages resulting from that injury were measurable "on a class-wide basis" through use of a "common methodology."[2]

Respondents proposed four theories of antitrust impact: First, Comcast's clustering made it profitable for Comcast to withhold local sports programming from its competitors, resulting in decreased market penetration by direct broadcast satellite providers. Second, Comcast's activities reduced the level of competition from "overbuilders," companies that build competing cable networks in areas where an incumbent cable company already operates. Third, Comcast reduced the level of "benchmark" competition on which cable customers rely to compare prices. Fourth, clustering increased Comcast's bargaining power relative to content providers. Each of these forms of impact, respondents alleged, increased cable subscription rates throughout the Philadelphia DMA.

The District Court accepted the overbuilder theory of antitrust impact as capable of classwide proof and rejected the rest. Accordingly, in its certification order, the District Court limited respondents' "proof of antitrust impact" to "the theory that Comcast engaged in anticompetitive clustering conduct, the effect of which was to deter the entry of overbuilders in the Philadelphia DMA."[3]

The District Court further found that the damages resulting from overbuilder-deterrence impact could be calculated on a classwide basis. To establish such damages, respondents had relied solely on the testimony of

---

[2] Respondents sought certification for the following class: "All cable television customers who subscribe or subscribed at any times since December 1, 1999, to the present to video programming services (other than solely to basic cable services) from Comcast, or any of its subsidiaries or affiliates in Comcast's Philadelphia cluster."

[3] The District Court did not hold that the three alternative theories of liability failed to establish antitrust impact, but merely that those theories could not be determined in a manner common to all the class plaintiffs. The other theories of liability may well be available for the plaintiffs to pursue as individual actions. Any contention that the plaintiffs should be allowed to recover damages attributable to all four theories in this class action would erroneously suggest one of two things—either that the plaintiffs may *also* recover such damages in individual actions or that they are precluded from asserting those theories in individual actions.

Dr. James McClave. Dr. McClave designed a regression model comparing actual cable prices in the Philadelphia DMA with hypothetical prices that would have prevailed but for petitioners' allegedly anticompetitive activities. The model calculated damages of $875,576,662 for the entire class. As Dr. McClave acknowledged, however, the model did not isolate damages resulting from any one theory of antitrust impact. The District Court nevertheless certified the class.

A divided panel of the Court of Appeals affirmed. On appeal, petitioners contended the class was improperly certified because the model, among other shortcomings, failed to attribute damages resulting from overbuilder deterrence, the only theory of injury remaining in the case. The court refused to consider the argument because, in its view, such an "attac[k] on the merits of the methodology [had] no place in the class certification inquiry." The court emphasized that, "[a]t the class certification stage," respondents were not required to "tie each theory of antitrust impact to an exact calculation of damages." According to the court, it had "not reached the stage of determining on the merits whether the methodology is a just and reasonable inference or speculative." Rather, the court said, respondents must "assure us that if they can prove antitrust impact, the resulting damages are capable of measurement and will not require labyrinthine individual calculations." In the court's view, that burden was met because respondents' model calculated "supra-competitive prices regardless of the type of anticompetitive conduct."

We granted certiorari.[4]

II

The class action is "an exception to the usual rule that litigation is conducted by and on behalf of the individual named parties only." *Califano v. Yamasaki*, 442 U.S. 682, 700–01 (1979). To come within the exception, a party seeking to maintain a class action "must affirmatively demonstrate his compliance" with Rule 23. *Wal–Mart Stores, Inc. v. Dukes*, 564 U.S. 338, 350 (2011). The Rule "does not set forth a mere pleading standard." Rather, a party must not only "be prepared to prove that there are *in fact* sufficiently numerous parties, common questions of law or fact," typicality of claims or defenses, and adequacy of representation, as required by Rule 23(a). The party must also satisfy through evidentiary proof at least one of the provisions of Rule 23(b). The provision at issue here is Rule 23(b)(3), which requires a court to find that "the questions of law or fact common to class members predominate over any questions affecting only individual members."

Repeatedly, we have emphasized that it " 'may be necessary for the court to probe behind the pleadings before coming to rest on the certifica-

---

[4] The question presented reads: "Whether a district court may certify a class action without resolving whether the plaintiff class had introduced admissible evidence, including expert testimony, to show that the case is susceptible to awarding damages on a class-wide basis." Respondents contend that petitioners forfeited their ability to answer this question in the negative because they did not make an objection to the admission of Dr. McClave's testimony under the Federal Rules of Evidence. *See Daubert v. Merrell Dow Pharmaceuticals, Inc.*, 509 U.S. 579 (1993). Such a forfeit would make it impossible for petitioners to argue that Dr. McClave's testimony was not "admissible evidence" under the Rules; but it does not make it impossible for them to argue that the evidence failed "to show that the case is susceptible to awarding damages on a class-wide basis." Petitioners argued below, and continue to argue here, that certification was improper because respondents had failed to establish that damages could be measured on a classwide basis. That is the question we address here.

tion question,' and that certification is proper only if 'the trial court is satisfied, after a rigorous analysis, that the prerequisites of Rule 23(a) have been satisfied.'" Such an analysis will frequently entail "overlap with the merits of the plaintiff's underlying claim." That is so because the "class determination generally involves considerations that are enmeshed in the factual and legal issues comprising the plaintiff's cause of action."

The same analytical principles govern Rule 23(b). If anything, Rule 23(b)(3)'s predominance criterion is even more demanding than Rule 23(a). Rule 23(b)(3), as an "adventuresome innovation," is designed for situations "in which class-action treatment is not as clearly called for." That explains Congress's addition of procedural safeguards for (b)(3) class members beyond those provided for (b)(1) or (b)(2) class members (*e.g.*, an opportunity to opt out), and the court's duty to take a "close look" at whether common questions predominate over individual ones.

III

Respondents' class action was improperly certified under Rule 23(b)(3). By refusing to entertain arguments against respondents' damages model that bore on the propriety of class certification, simply because those arguments would also be pertinent to the merits determination, the Court of Appeals ran afoul of our precedents requiring precisely that inquiry. And it is clear that, under the proper standard for evaluating certification, respondents' model falls far short of establishing that damages are capable of measurement on a classwide basis. Without presenting another methodology, respondents cannot show Rule 23(b)(3) predominance: Questions of individual damage calculations will inevitably overwhelm questions common to the class. This case thus turns on the straightforward application of class-certification principles; it provides no occasion for the dissent's extended discussion of substantive antitrust law.

A

We start with an unremarkable premise. If respondents prevail on their claims, they would be entitled only to damages resulting from reduced overbuilder competition, since that is the only theory of antitrust impact accepted for class-action treatment by the District Court. It follows that a model purporting to serve as evidence of damages in this class action must measure only those damages attributable to that theory. If the model does not even attempt to do that, it cannot possibly establish that damages are susceptible of measurement across the entire class for purposes of Rule 23(b)(3). Calculations need not be exact, but at the class-certification stage (as at trial), any model supporting a "plaintiff's damages case must be consistent with its liability case, particularly with respect to the alleged anticompetitive effect of the violation." And for purposes of Rule 23, courts must conduct a "rigorous analysis" to determine whether that is so.

The District Court and the Court of Appeals saw no need for respondents to "tie each theory of antitrust impact" to a calculation of damages. That, they said, would involve consideration of the "merits" having "no place in the class certification inquiry." That reasoning flatly contradicts our cases requiring a determination that Rule 23 is satisfied, even when that requires inquiry into the merits of the claim. The Court of Appeals simply concluded that respondents "provided a method to measure and quantify damages on a classwide basis," finding it unnecessary to decide "whether the methodology [was] a just and reasonable inference or speculative." Under that logic, at the class-certification stage *any* method of measurement is acceptable so long as it can be applied classwide, no matter how arbitrary the measurements may be. Such a proposition would reduce Rule 23(b)(3)'s predominance requirement to a nullity.

B

There is no question that the model failed to measure damages resulting from the particular antitrust injury on which petitioners' liability in this action is premised.[5] The scheme devised by respondents' expert, Dr. McClave, sought to establish a "but for" baseline—a figure that would show what the competitive prices would have been if there had been no antitrust violations. Damages would then be determined by comparing to that baseline what the actual prices were during the charged period. The "but for" figure was calculated, however, by assuming a market that contained none of the four distortions that respondents attributed to petitioners' actions. In other words, the model assumed the validity of all four theories of antitrust impact initially advanced by respondents: decreased penetration by satellite providers, overbuilder deterrence, lack of benchmark competition, and increased bargaining power. At the evidentiary hearing, Dr. McClave expressly admitted that the model calculated damages resulting from "the alleged anticompetitive conduct as a whole" and did not attribute damages to any one particular theory of anticompetitive impact.

This methodology might have been sound, and might have produced commonality of damages, if all four of those alleged distortions remained in the case. But as Judge Jordan's partial dissent pointed out:

> [B]ecause the only surviving theory of antitrust impact is that clustering reduced overbuilding, for Dr. McClave's comparison to be relevant, his benchmark counties must reflect the conditions that would have prevailed in the Philadelphia DMA but for the alleged reduction in overbuilding. In all respects unrelated to reduced overbuilding, the benchmark counties should reflect the actual conditions in the Philadelphia DMA, or else the model will identify 'damages' that are not the result of reduced overbuilding, or, in other words, that are not the certain result of the wrong.

The majority's only response to this was that "[a]t the class certification stage we do not require that Plaintiffs tie each theory of antitrust impact to an exact calculation of damages, but instead that they assure us that if they can prove antitrust impact, the resulting damages are capable of measurement and will not require labyrinthine individual calculations." But such assurance is not provided by a methodology that identifies damages that are not the result of the wrong. For all we know, cable subscribers in Gloucester County may have been overcharged because of petitioners' alleged elimination of satellite competition (a theory of liability that is not capable of classwide proof); while subscribers in Camden County may have paid elevated prices because of petitioners' increased bargaining power vis-à-vis content providers (another theory that is not capable of classwide proof); while yet other subscribers in Montgomery County may have paid

---

[5] The dissent is of the view that what an econometric model proves is a "question of fact" on which we will not "undertake to review concurrent findings . . . by two courts below in the absence of a very obvious and exceptional showing of error." To begin with, neither of the courts below found that the model established damages attributable to overbuilding alone. Second, while the data contained within an econometric model may well be "questions of fact" in the relevant sense, what those data prove is no more a question of fact than what our opinions hold. And finally, even if it were a question of fact, concluding that the model here established damages attributable to overbuilding alone would be "obvious[ly] and exceptional[ly]" erroneous.

rates produced by the combined effects of multiple forms of alleged antitrust harm; and so on. The permutations involving four theories of liability and 2 million subscribers located in 16 counties are nearly endless.

In light of the model's inability to bridge the differences between supra-competitive prices in general and supra-competitive prices attributable to the deterrence of overbuilding, Rule 23(b)(3) cannot authorize treating subscribers within the Philadelphia cluster as members of a single class.[6] Prices whose level above what an expert deems "competitive" has been caused by factors unrelated to an accepted theory of antitrust harm are not "anticompetitive" in any sense relevant here. "The first step in a damages study is the translation of the *legal theory of the harmful event* into an analysis of the economic impact *of that event*." Federal Judicial Center, Reference Manual on Scientific Evidence 432 (3d ed. 2011) (emphasis added). The District Court and the Court of Appeals ignored that first step entirely.

The judgment of the Court of Appeals for the Third Circuit is reversed.

* * *

JUSTICE GINSBURG and JUSTICE BREYER, with whom JUSTICE SOTOMAYOR and JUSTICE KAGAN join, dissenting.

Today the Court reaches out to decide a case hardly fit for our consideration. On both procedural and substantive grounds, we dissent.

I

This case comes to the Court infected by our misguided reformulation of the question presented. For that reason alone, we would dismiss the writ of certiorari as improvidently granted.

Comcast sought review of the following question: "[W]hether a district court may certify a class action without resolving 'merits arguments' that bear on [Federal Rule of Civil Procedure] 23's prerequisites for certification, including whether purportedly common issues predominate over individual ones under Rule 23(b)(3)." We granted review of a different question: "Whether a district court may certify a class action without resolving *whether the plaintiff class has introduced admissible evidence*, including expert testimony, to show that the case is susceptible to awarding damages on a class-wide basis." ([E]mphasis added).

Our rephrasing shifted the focus of the dispute from the District Court's Rule 23(b)(3) analysis to its attention (or lack thereof) to the admissibility of expert testimony. The parties, responsively, devoted much of their briefing to the question whether the standards for admissibility of expert evidence set out in Federal Rule of Evidence 702 and *Daubert v. Merrell Dow Pharmaceuticals, Inc.*, 509 U.S. 579 (1993), apply in class certification proceedings. Indeed, respondents confirmed at oral argument that they understood our rewritten question to center on admissibility, not Rule 23(b)(3).

As it turns out, our reformulated question was inapt. To preserve a claim of error in the admission of evidence, a party must timely object to or

---

[6] We might add that even if the model had identified subscribers who paid more solely because of the deterrence of overbuilding, it still would not have established the requisite commonality of damages unless it plausibly showed that the extent of overbuilding (absent deterrence) would have been the same in all counties, or that the extent is irrelevant to effect upon ability to charge supra-competitive prices.

move to strike the evidence. Fed. R. Evid. 103(a)(1). In the months preceding the District Court's class certification order, Comcast did not object to the admission of Dr. McClave's damages model under Rule 702 or *Daubert*. Nor did Comcast move to strike his testimony and expert report. Consequently, Comcast forfeited any objection to the admission of Dr. McClave's model at the certification stage. At this late date, Comcast may no longer argue that respondents' damages evidence was inadmissible.

Comcast's forfeiture of the question on which we granted review is reason enough to dismiss the writ as improvidently granted. The Court, however, elects to evaluate whether respondents "failed to show that the case is susceptible to awarding damages on a class-wide basis." To justify this second revision of the question presented, the Court observes that Comcast "argued below, and continue[s] to argue here, that certification was improper because respondents had failed to establish that damages could be measured on a classwide basis." And so Comcast did, in addition to endeavoring to address the question on which we granted review. By treating the first part of our reformulated question as though it did not exist, the Court is hardly fair to respondents.

* * * The Court's newly revised question, focused on predominance, phrased only after briefing was done, left respondents without an unclouded opportunity to air the issue the Court today decides against them. And by resolving a complex and fact-intensive question without the benefit of full briefing, the Court invites the error into which it has fallen.

II

[The dissent explained why the majority opinion should not be read to require that damages be provable on a classwide basis. *See also* Chapter 3(C)(1)(b) (discussing this issue). [Ed.]]

* * *

The oddity of this case, in which the need to prove damages on a classwide basis through a common methodology was never challenged by respondents, is a further reason to dismiss the writ as improvidently granted. The Court's ruling is good for this day and case only. In the mine run of cases, it remains the "black letter rule" that a class may obtain certification under Rule 23(b)(3) when liability questions common to the class predominate over damages questions unique to class members.

* * *

[The dissent also took issue with the majority's reading of the substantive antitrust law. [Ed.]]

* * *

Because the parties did not fully argue the question the Court now answers, all Members of the Court may lack a complete understanding of the model or the meaning of related statements in the record. The need for focused argument is particularly strong here where, as we have said, the underlying considerations are detailed, technical, and fact-based. The Court departs from our ordinary practice, risks inaccurate judicial decisionmaking, and is unfair to respondents and the courts below. For these reasons, we would not disturb the Court of Appeals' judgment and, instead, would dismiss the writ as improvidently granted.

* * *

NOTES AND QUESTIONS

1. Is the dissent correct that the majority opinion broke no new ground? Subsequent to *Comcast*, several courts have addressed whether *Comcast* eliminated the longstanding rule that individualized damages did not defeat predominance. Most courts held that *Comcast* did not eliminate that rule. The Supreme Court in *Tyson Foods* further clarified that individualized damages do not, standing alone, defeat predominance. *See* Chapter 3(C)(1)(b).

2. As the dissent in *Comcast* noted, the Court granted certiorari on a different question than the one on which Comcast had actually sought review. Similarly, in *Dukes*, the Court also reformulated the question presented, as discussed in Chapter 2(B)(2). Does the Court's apparent inclination to formulate specific questions regarding class certification suggest anything about the majority's views on class actions generally?

3. How is the question that the Court decided different from the question that the Court formulated when it granted certiorari?

4. For various views on *Comcast*, *see, e.g.*, Alex Parkinson, Comcast Corp v. Behrend *and Chaos on the Ground*, 81 U. Chi. L. Rev. 1213, 1258 (2014) (stating that "how *Comcast* is interpreted will dictate the course of Rule 23(b)(3) jurisprudence for years to come"); Elizabeth J. Cabraser, *The Class Abides: Class Actions and the "Roberts Court"*, 48 Akron L. Rev. 757, 768 (2015) (forecast of "widespread implications [of *Comcast*] for the future of class certification * * * has not materialized"); Joseph Krebs, Comcast v. Behrend: *The Class Action Channel Is Still Scrambled*, 16 Duq. Bus. L.J. 83, 104 (2013) ("While *Comcast* has obviously been one more step in Justice Scalia's movement to end what he believe[d] is the blight of class actions, it only serves to scramble the class action channel.").

iii. Expert Testimony (Daubert)

Subsumed within the general question of the standard by which Rule 23's requirements should be applied is the issue of expert testimony. Parties routinely provide expert opinions at class certification purporting to show that issues relating to the merits would—or would not—be susceptible of classwide proof. A plaintiff in a consumer fraud case, for example, might offer an expert to show that all of the products implicated by the proposed class definition are materially identical, so that individual issues would not arise relating to different designs or models. Or a defendant in an environmental disaster case might offer an expert to show that, because there are multiple potential causes of a given disease, isolating whether the defendant's conduct caused a particular plaintiff to contract the disease would require individual assessments of each potential class member, making classwide adjudication impossible.

How should a district court evaluate expert testimony proffered at the time of class certification to address the elements of Rule 23? Students who have already taken an evidence class will be familiar with *Daubert v. Merrell Dow Pharmaceuticals, Inc.*, 509 U.S. 579 (1993), in which the Supreme Court recognized that trial courts must serve an important gatekeeping function, prescribed by Federal Rule of Evidence 702, by ensuring that proffered scientific expert testimony is both relevant and reliable.

Should this gatekeeping begin at class certification—that is, should a court deciding whether to certify a class exclude from consideration expert evidence that is irrelevant or unreliable? The question of how a district court should balance *Daubert*'s requirements and Rule 23's class certification provisions played an important part in the analysis in several of the cases discussed in the previous subsection. *See, e.g., In re Hydrogen Peroxide Antitrust Litig.*, 552 F.3d 305, 323 (3d Cir. 2008) ("Expert opinion with respect to class certification, like any matter relevant to a Rule 23 requirement, calls for rigorous analysis." (citation omitted)); *In re Initial Pub. Offering Secs. Litig.*, 471 F.3d 24, 42 (2d Cir. 2006) ("A district judge is to assess all of the relevant evidence admitted at the class certification stage and determine whether each Rule 23 requirement has been met, just as the judge would resolve a dispute about any other threshold prerequisite for continuing a lawsuit.").

Although it did not decide the issue, the Supreme Court in *Wal-Mart Stores, Inc. v. Dukes*, 564 U.S. 338 (2011), strongly suggested that *Daubert* does apply at the class certification stage:

> * * * The parties dispute whether [plaintiffs' expert's] testimony even met the standards for the admission of expert testimony under [Federal Rule of Evidence] 702 and our *Daubert* case. The District Court concluded that *Daubert* did not apply to expert testimony at the certification stage of class-action proceedings. *We doubt that is so*, but even if properly considered, [plaintiffs' expert's] testimony does nothing to advance respondents' case. * * *

Id. at 354 (emphasis added). As noted in the previous subsection, the Supreme Court had raised the possibility of further addressing the issue of *Daubert* and class certification in *Comcast Corp. v. Behrend*, 133 S. Ct. 1426 (2013), where it granted *certiorari* on the question "[w]hether a district court may certify a class action without resolving whether the plaintiff class has introduced admissible evidence, including expert testimony, to show that the case is susceptible to awarding damages on a class-wide basis." *Id.* at 1435 (Ginsburg & Breyer, J.J., dissenting). As it turned out, however, Comcast was found to have waived its *Daubert* argument by not raising it in the courts below, leaving the question unanswered.

For an analysis of *Daubert* and the role of expert testimony in the context of class certification, consider the following case.

AM. HONDA MOTOR CO., INC. V. ALLEN
United States Court of Appeals, Seventh Circuit, 2010.
600 F.3d 813.

Before POSNER, EVANS, and TINDER, CIRCUIT JUDGES.

PER CURIAM.

American Honda Motor Company and Honda of America Manufacturing (collectively "Honda") seek leave to appeal the district court's grant of class certification pursuant to Federal Rule of Civil Procedure 23(f). Specifically, Honda asks us to resolve whether the district court must conclusively rule on the admissibility of an expert opinion prior to class certification in this case because that opinion is essential to the certification decision. * * *

Plaintiffs are purchasers of Honda's Gold Wing GL1800 motorcycle; they allege that the motorcycle has a design defect that prevents the adequate dampening of "wobble," that is, side-to-side oscillation of the front steering assembly about the steering axis. In other words, they claim that the defect makes the steering assembly shake excessively and they want Honda to fix the problem. Plaintiffs moved for class certification pursuant to Rule 23(b)(3). To demonstrate the predominance of common issues, they relied heavily on a report prepared by Mark Ezra, a motorcycle engineering expert. Ezra's report opined that motorcycles should "by [their] design and manufacture exhibit[] decay of any steering oscillations sufficiently and rapidly so that the rider neither reacts to nor is frightened by such oscillations." Assuming that human reaction time to wobble is 1/2 to 3/4 of a second, Ezra opined that wobble should decay, or dissipate, to 37% of its original amplitude within 3/4 of a second to ensure that riders do not perceive and react to the oscillations. This standard, which Ezra devised himself and characterizes as "reasonable," was published in the June 2004 edition of the *Journal of the National Academy of Forensic Engineers*. After testing one used GL1800 serviced to factory condition, Ezra concluded that it failed to meet his wobble decay standard. He also concluded that his standard could be achieved in the GL1800 motorcycle by replacing the regular ball bearings in the steering assembly with tapered ones.

Honda moved to strike the report pursuant to *Daubert v. Merrell Dow Pharms., Inc.*, 509 U.S. 579 (1993), arguing that Ezra's wobble decay standard was unreliable because it was not supported by empirical testing, was not developed through a recognized standard-setting procedure, was not generally accepted in the relevant scientific, technical, or professional community, and was not the product of independent research.† In the alternative, Honda argued that even if the standard was reliable, Ezra did not reliably apply it to this case because he only tested one motorcycle and did not account for variables that could affect the wobble decay rate.

The district court concluded that it was proper to decide whether the report was admissible prior to certification because "most of Plaintiffs' predominance arguments rest upon the theories advanced by Mr. Ezra." * * * [The district] court then concluded, "Viewing all of the arguments together, the court has definite reservations about the reliability of Mr. Ezra's wobble decay standard. Nevertheless, the court declines to exclude the report in its entirety at this early stage of the proceedings." The court denied Honda's motion to exclude "without prejudice," and granted Plaintiffs' motion for class certification in part, certifying two classes of individuals who purchased GL1800s.

In *Szabo v. Bridgeport Machs., Inc.*, 249 F.3d 672, 676 (7th Cir. 2001), we held that a district court must make whatever factual and legal inquiries are necessary to ensure that requirements for class certification are satisfied before deciding whether a class should be certified, even if those considerations overlap the merits of the case. And in *West v. Prudential Sec.*,

---

† *Daubert* directed federal courts to evaluate the relevance and reliability of expert testimony by assessing the expert's reasoning or methodology with reference to general scientific principles, including whether the theory or methodology: (1) can be tested; (2) has been subjected to peer review and publication; (3) has a known error rate; and (4) is generally accepted within the "relevant scientific community." 509 U.S. at 589–95. A subsequent case, *Kumho Tire Co., Ltd. v. Carmichael*, 526 U.S. 137 (1999), extended *Daubert* to apply to "all expert testimony," not "only to 'scientific' testimony." *Id.* at 147. [Ed.]

Inc., 282 F.3d 935, 938 (7th Cir. 2002), we held that a plaintiff cannot obtain class certification just by hiring a competent expert. We emphasized, "A district judge may not duck hard questions by observing that each side has some support. . . . Tough questions must be faced and squarely decided, if necessary by holding evidentiary hearings and choosing between competing perspectives." But we have not yet specifically addressed whether a district court must resolve a *Daubert* challenge prior to ruling on class certification if the testimony challenged is integral to the plaintiffs' satisfaction of Rule 23's requirements.

* * *

We hold that when an expert's report or testimony is critical to class certification, as it is here, a district court must conclusively rule on any challenge to the expert's qualifications or submissions prior to ruling on a class certification motion. That is, the district court must perform a full *Daubert* analysis before certifying the class if the situation warrants. If the challenge is to an individual's qualifications, a court must make that determination "by comparing the area in which the witness has superior knowledge, skill, experience, or education with the subject matter of the witness's testimony." The court must also resolve any challenge to the reliability of information provided by an expert if that information is relevant to establishing any of the Rule 23 requirements for class certification.

* * * The district court acknowledged Honda's concerns about the reliability of Ezra's testimony and largely agreed with them. It expressed reservations about Ezra's failure to "establish the minimal amplitude required for a rider to detect an oscillation," his failure to "verif[y] whether a lesser or greater percentage of decay would also provide an appropriate margin of safety," the fact that his wobble decay standard was developed "to assist with a lawsuit and was not conceived through the logical flow of independent research," the questionable peer-review process that his article underwent, the engineering community's lack of acceptance of his proposed standard, and his test sample size of one used GL1800. Yet the district court ultimately declined, without further explanation, "to exclude the report in its entirety at this early stage of the proceedings."

* * * The court's effective statement of admissibility here is not even conclusory; it leaves open the questions of what portions of Ezra's testimony it may have decided (or will decide) to exclude, whether Ezra reliably applied the standard to the facts of the case, and, ultimately, whether Plaintiffs have satisfied Rule 23(b)(3)'s predominance requirement. As a result, the district court never actually reached a conclusion about whether Ezra's expert report was reliable enough to support Plaintiffs' class certification request. Instead it denied Honda's motion to exclude without prejudice and noted that the case was in an "early stage of the proceedings." This was not sufficient. Indeed, it was an abuse of discretion. * * *

As we have explained, a district court must make the necessary factual and legal inquiries and decide all relevant contested issues prior to certification. The district court's actions here were more akin to the "provisional" approach that we rejected in *Szabo*. Ezra's testimony is necessary to show that Plaintiffs' claims are capable of resolution on a class-wide basis and that the common defect in the motorcycle predominates over the class members' individual issues. Therefore, by failing to clearly resolve the issue of its admissibility before certifying the class, the district court erred.

* * *

The "theory" here is Ezra's wobble decay standard, and, as the district court thoroughly enumerated, there are many reasons to harbor "definite reservations" about its reliability. Ezra originally developed the standard for use in a mid-1980s lawsuit in which he testified as an expert against Honda and subsequently published it in a journal article aimed at forensic engineers who testify as experts on motorcycle instability, *see* Mark A.M. Ezra, *Forensic Engineering Investigation of Motorcycle Instability Induced Crashes*, 21 J. Nat'l Acad. Forensic Eng'rs 69, 80–84 (2004) (discussing seven common "attacks by opposing counsel," including "You Did What While Testing the Motorcycle?!", and instructing future experts to "be ready to defend in simple lay terms the standard [they have] proposed and relied upon in evaluating the motorcycle and its reasonableness"). Despite its publication, there is no indication that Ezra's wobble decay standard has been generally accepted by anyone other than Ezra. * * *

Even if we were to assume that Ezra's standard is generally accepted by mere virtue of its publication in a peer-reviewed journal, its reliability remains in question. Ezra has never conducted any rider confidence studies to determine when motorcycle riders perceive wobble, or performed any tests to determine the minimal wobble amplitude at which riders detect oscillation. His report merely deemed "reasonable" his proposed standard, relying solely on his own previous (and similarly unsupported) assessment of the same for support. The "principles and methodology" underlying his findings, then, are questionable at best. * * *

Without Ezra's testimony, * * * Plaintiffs are not only unable to support their theory that all GL1800 motorcycles use ball bearings that fail to adequately dampen wobble, they are also unable to demonstrate that their wobble claim sufficiently predominates as to warrant class certification under Rule 23(b)(3).

We therefore * * * VACATE the district court's denial of Honda's motion to strike and its order certifying a class, and REMAND for proceedings consistent with this opinion.

NOTES AND QUESTIONS

1. Consistent with *American Honda*, the Third Circuit has held that "a plaintiff cannot rely on challenged expert testimony, when critical to class certification, to demonstrate conformity with Rule 23 unless plaintiff also demonstrates, and the trial court finds, that the expert testimony satisfies the standard set out in *Daubert*." *In re Blood Reagents Antitrust Litig.*, 783 F.3d 183, 187 (3d Cir. 2015).

2. *American Honda* held that, "when an expert's report or testimony is critical to class certification, as it is here, a district court must conclusively rule on any challenge to the expert's qualifications or submissions prior to ruling on a class certification motion." 600 F.3d at 815–16. Thus, *American Honda* does not mandate that *Daubert* hearings always precede class certification, but rather only "when an expert's report or testimony is critical to class certification."

3. Should analysis of expert evidence at class certification, where necessary, be as searching as it is at summary judgment or at trial?

4. Notwithstanding *American Honda* and *Hydrogen Peroxide*, the issue of *Daubert*'s relevance at class certification is still evolving. *See, e.g., In re Zurn Pex Plumbing Prods. Liab. Litig.*, 644 F.3d 604, 612 (8th Cir. 2011) (affirming district court's application of a " 'tailored' *Daubert* analysis" that "[r]eject[ed] both parties' extreme positions" and "examined the reliability of the expert opinions in light of the available evidence and the purpose for which they were offered"). The *Zurn Pex* court distinguished *American Honda*, pointing out that *American Honda* involved "expert conclusions based on flawed methodology and a sample size of one," whereas no party in *Zurn Pex* had argued that either side's expert testimony was "similarly flawed." 644 F.3d at 611–12.

Are the standards set out in these cases appropriate? What further refinements, if any, are required?

PROBLEM

In *In re Ethylene Propylene Diene Monomer (EPDM) Antitrust Litigation*, 256 F.R.D. 82 (D. Conn. 2009), the court granted class certification and refused to weigh the parties' competing testimony:

> * * * In essence, the defendants are asking the court to determine which multiple regression model [for proving classwide damages] is most accurate, which is ultimately a merits decision. The real question before this court is whether the plaintiffs have established a workable multiple regression equation, not whether plaintiffs' model actually works, because the issue at class certification is not which expert is the most credible, or the most accurate modeler, but rather have the plaintiffs demonstrated that there is a way to prove a classwide measure of damages through generalized proof.

Id. at 100–01. Does the court's analysis comport with the case law discussed above?

2. ADDITIONAL CERTIFICATION ISSUES

a. Court's Obligation to Rule/Class Actions by Implication

BING V. ROADWAY EXPRESS, INC.
United States Court of Appeals, Fifth Circuit, 1973.
485 F.2d 441.

Before THORNBERRY, AINSWORTH, and RONEY, CIRCUIT JUDGES.

THORNBERRY, CIRCUIT JUDGE.

[Plaintiff Bing brought a race discrimination claim against defendant Roadway Express. The district court found the company liable, and Roadway appealed. The Fifth Circuit affirmed and remanded for remedial proceedings. The district court then awarded classwide relief, and Roadway again appealed.]

* * *

The district court's failure to rule whether this case was a class action apparently escaped the attention of all the parties in the proceedings below. Nowhere in the record do we find a motion by plaintiff–appellant that his cause be determined a class action, and likewise missing from the record is any objection by defendants–appellees that it would be improper to frame this suit as a class action. Roadway raises this issue for the first time on appeal, and presents this court with a novel question: Can a class action exist without a formal, explicit determination by the court? For the reasons stated below we conclude that in this case we may infer that the trial court approved the class action nature of this lawsuit.

It was apparent from the beginning that Bing intended his suit to be a class action. The action was brought by Bing on behalf of himself and "all others similarly situated." He complained that Roadway's no-transfer rule discriminated against himself and "all others similarly situated," and his complaint alleged that the union's regulations and policy were discriminatory toward Negroes and prevented "Negroes from having equal employment. . . ." For relief he asked the court to enjoin the union from "discriminating against petitioner and others similarly situated," [and] to award him damages and all other relief that was just or required. Thus * * * Bing alleged harm to a class and requested relief for a class.

Although the complaint must have notified Roadway and the union that Bing sought class relief, the record reveals no objection to, or motion to dismiss because of, the class nature of this action. We infer from the record's silence that all parties to the action knew of its class nature and acquiesced in it.

We infer that the trial court also believed the suit to be a class action. After this court remanded the case for remedial proceedings, Bing moved to amend his complaint. In its order denying the motion to amend, the court said, "[t]his case was originally filed as a class action. . . ." The court described the amendment in a manner that indicated awareness and approval of the action's class nature:

> By such amendment the plaintiff seeks to specify certain members of the class for the purpose of presenting their claims for differential back pay and seniority rights.

The court in that order went on to express misgivings about the appropriateness of awarding back pay in a class action. Furthermore, the court indicated that defendant–appellee Roadway also believed the action to be a class action. "The defendant has filed a brief in opposition to the plaintiff's motion to amend arguing that relief in a class action is proper only for general and future relief."

The judgment rendered by the trial court indicates that the suit retained its class nature throughout the proceedings below. It recited that Bing had brought the action on behalf of himself and all black employees of Roadway. It enjoined Roadway and the union "from engaging in any act or practice at the Roadway Express, Inc., Atlanta, Georgia facilities which has the purpose or effect of discriminating against any individual because of his race or color." * * * In other words, the court enjoined present and future discrimination against Roadway's black employees and thus gave relief that was aimed at a class of people. Such relief is in keeping with the thesis that the trial court believed the suit to be a class action.

We conclude that the trial court implicitly determined that this suit would be maintained as a class action. * * * To say that this is not a class action would be to ignore the substance of the proceedings below in favor of an excessively formalistic adherence to the Federal Rules of Civil Procedure. * * *

* * *

NOTES AND QUESTIONS

1. *Bing* relied heavily on the fact that the complaint sought classwide relief. If a complaint seeks classwide relief, a district court is obligated to address that claim, precisely to avoid the ambiguity resolved in *Bing*. When a complaint seeks relief only on behalf of an individual plaintiff and is not timely amended to assert a claim for classwide relief, courts have refused to allow the action to proceed as a class action. *See, e.g., Lusted v. San Antonio Indep. Sch. Dist.*, 741 F.2d 817, 821 (5th Cir. 1984) ("[I]f [plaintiffs] decide to bring a class action, it must be brought and identified as such, and the predicate for class action relief must be carefully laid. In the meantime, [Lusted's] victory is for her alone to taste and enjoy." (citation omitted)).

2. *Bing* has never been overruled. Can its holding, however, be squared with contemporary appellate standards relating to the need for a "rigorous analysis" of class certification?

3. Can a court, on its *own* initiative, transform an individual action into a class action at the judgment stage? In *Newsom v. Norris*, 888 F.2d 371 (6th Cir. 1989), the plaintiffs were prisoners who had served as "inmate advisors"— inmates who assisted other inmates in disciplinary proceedings. After being denied reappointment to advisor positions, the plaintiffs claimed that they had been punished for exercising their First Amendment rights by criticizing the chairman of the disciplinary board. The magistrate who heard the case not only granted an injunction reinstating the plaintiffs, but also required the defendants to create a training program for inmate advisors. The district court affirmed in all respects. On appeal, the Sixth Circuit affirmed the court's reinstatement of the four individual plaintiffs but disagreed with respect to the district court's *de facto* certification of a remedial class:

> Although a trial "court may suggest that relief to a definable class would be appropriate, . . . it cannot convert an individual action into a class action on its own motion." * * * In the instant case, the trial court's *sua sponte* action in mandating the appellants to submit a remedial training plan for Disciplinary Board members and inmate advisors and in certifying the proceeding as a class action constituted error, particularly under circumstances where those issues were not joined by the complaint nor developed by the proof and, consequently, that part of the district court's order must be vacated.

Id. at 380–82. Would the outcome in *Newsom* have been the same if plaintiffs had sought leave to obtain classwide relief? What if the magistrate had allowed the defendant to supplement the record to address classwide issues?

4. In *Anderson v. United States Department of HUD*, 554 F.3d 525 (5th Cir. 2008), a class of public housing residents who had been displaced by Hurricane Katrina sued the state and federal housing agencies, seeking (i) an order enjoining the demolition of a building the residents had occupied before Katrina, and (ii) monetary damages. The district court dismissed those claims but nonetheless certified a class based on "'claims dealing with the administration and issuance of vouchers to displaced public housing tenants.'" *Id.* at 528 (quoting district court). On interlocutory appeal, however, the Fifth Circuit

held that the lower court had abused its discretion, given that the plaintiffs' complaint had not mentioned the voucher program, but instead was based on "a totally different course of conduct[.]" *Id.* at 529. In so holding, the Fifth Circuit stated: "The district court's authority to certify a class under Rule 23 does not permit it to structure a class around claims not pled." *Id.* Is the Fifth Circuit's approach persuasive?

b. Conditional Certification

Prior to the 2003 amendments to Rule 23, courts were also allowed to certify classes on a "conditional" basis, and could alter, amend or conditionally certify "before the decision on the merits." Those provisions were modified in the 2003 amendments. As the 2003 Advisory Committee Notes to Rule 23 explain:

> Subdivision (c)(1)(C) reflects two amendments. The provision that a class certification "may be conditional" is deleted. A court that is not satisfied that the requirements of Rule 23 have been met should refuse certification until they have been met. The provision that permits alteration or amendment of an order granting or denying class certification is amended to set the cut-off point at final judgment rather than "the decision on the merits." This change avoids the possible ambiguity in referring to "the decision on the merits." Following a determination of liability, for example, proceedings to define the remedy may demonstrate the need to amend the class definition or subdivide the class. In this setting the final judgment concept is pragmatic. It is not the same as the concept used for appeal purposes, but it should be flexible, particularly in protracted litigation.

Why is a court given broad discretion to alter or amend its certification decision prior to final judgment? Given that amended Rule 23 still allows a court to exercise its discretion to alter or amend the certification ruling, this chapter uses the term "tentative" certification, rather than "conditional" certification.

For an interesting perspective, consider *Central Wesleyan College v. W.R. Grace & Co.*, 6 F.3d 177 (4th Cir. 1993), decided under the prior rule. In that case, the Fourth Circuit held—despite some misgivings—that the district court had not abused its discretion in conditionally certifying a nationwide class of colleges and universities who sued a group of asbestos producers for the costs of removing asbestos from their properties as required by federal law. According to the Fourth Circuit, the district court:

> * * * exercised its discretion under [the pre-2003 version of] Fed. R. Civ. P. 23(c)(1) and 23(c)(4)(A) to certify the class conditionally for a "Phase One certification procedure" on eight common issues. The [district] court identified these issues as (1) whether defendants knew or had reason to know of the health hazards of asbestos (the "state of the art" issue); (2) whether certain categories of asbestos products (fireproofing, acoustical ceiling sprays, thermal insulation) are friable, or are capable of becoming friable as defined by federal regulations, and therefore, must at some

time be removed;† (3) whether defendants' asbestos products can release asbestos fiber in the course of foreseeable use, including maintenance, renovation, and demolition; (4) whether defendants participated in conspiratorial activities, either industrywide or within segments of the industry; (5) whether defendants failed adequately to test their products for fiber release potential; (6) whether defendants failed to warn users of the potential hazards of their products; (7) whether defendants breached a duty of due care in selling friable asbestos products for use in colleges; and (8) whether defendants' conduct justifies the imposition of punitive damages. The [district] court characterized these questions as "primarily factual," but noted that if separate state laws needed to be applied to these questions, subclasses of plaintiffs could be formed.

Id. at 184. While stating that it was "not unsympathetic to defendants' arguments" against conditionally certifying the class, the Fourth Circuit nonetheless concluded:

* * * The limited certification adopted here was both authorized by the Rule and encouraged by circuit precedent as a valuable tool in addressing mass tort litigation. It would be premature to say that the plaintiff is not correct in its assessment of this lawsuit as an opportunity "to assist in resolving asbestos litigation nationwide" and to avoid some of the "enormous waste of resources" that could accompany individual litigation.

Id. at 186. The court went on to caution, however:

* * * This enormous undertaking is fraught with potential problems that may well offset the advantages that the class mechanism might afford. Should such a situation develop, class certification may have to be reconsidered. * * * As this litigation proceeds, the district court must make certain that manageability and other types of problems do not overwhelm the advantages of conditional certification. Should such concerns render the class mechanism ineffective, the district court must be prepared to use its considerable discretion to decertify the class, either on a defendant's motion, or *sua sponte*. If, for example, so many colleges and universities opt out of the voluntary class that it no longer promises to achieve economies of scale on common issues, the district court should reconsider its conditional certification. * * * If manageability problems with presenting the eight common issues to a jury prove intractable, the court also should consider decertification. If just some of those issues seem to the district court upon reflection not to lend themselves to class treatment, the district court should decertify them.

---

† As the court explained earlier in its opinion, " '[f]riable' * * * asbestos products [are those] that 'when dry, can be crumbled, pulverized, or reduced to powder by hand pressure.'" 6 F.3d at 181 (quoting 40 C.F.R. § 61.141). Whether asbestos-containing material is friable is important because "[t]he physical danger to persons occupying a building containing asbestos begins when asbestos fibers become airborne," and "[r]espirable asbestos fibers may be released from friable asbestos-containing materials when these materials are disturbed." *San Francisco Unified Sch. Dist. v. W.R. Grace & Co.*, 37 Cal. App. 4th 1318, 1325 (1995) (citation omitted). [Ed.]

* * *

> Our acknowledgement of concern about the manageability of this litigation is not intended to forecast its demise. Rather it is to reinforce the point that the course of this litigation is not set and that the district court retains considerable discretion to react to events as they unfold. The course chosen by the district court deserves the chance to succeed in resolving issues of unquestioned importance in this litigation, and it is to be expected that counsel, who have ably argued this appeal, will proceed in that spirit. The district court for its part proceeded with caution in its conditional certification order, and accordingly, did not abuse its discretion in the limited step that it took.

Id. at 186, 189–90.

NOTES AND QUESTIONS

1. Given the assumption in *Central Wesleyan* that class certification may facilitate settlement, was the court correct in placing so much reliance on the district court's ability to decertify in light of later developments? Is it proper to certify a class in order to facilitate a settlement?

2. The *Manual for Complex Litigation (Fourth)* observes:

> Rule 23(c)(1)(C) makes clear that an action should be certified only if it meets Rule 23's requirements. However, Rule 23(c)(1)(C) permits later alteration or amendment of an order granting or denying class certification. Nevertheless, decertifying or redefining an expansive class, certified on insufficient information, may unnecessarily cost the parties substantial time and expense and add to the court's load. In a federal question case, the pendency of class action allegations tolls the statute of limitations. Individuals removed from a narrowed class after receiving notice that they were included may be entitled to notice that the statute of limitations has now begun to run against them. If the judge expands a class definition in a Rule 23(b)(3) case, those added members must receive notice and an opportunity to opt out, adding expense and effort.

Manual for Complex Litigation (Fourth) § 21.133 (2004). Based on the *Manual*'s observations, under what circumstances should a court alter or amend an order granting or denying class certification? What concerns, if any, have the 2003 amendments eliminated? What approach makes more sense—that of the *Central Wesleyan* court or that of amended Rule 23?

c. Certification of Specific Issues

MANUAL FOR COMPLEX LITIGATION (FOURTH)
Federal Judicial Center (2004) § 21.24.

Rule 23(c)(4)(A) [current Rule 23(c)(4)] permits a class to be certified for specific issues or elements of claims raised in the litigation. Selectively used, this provision may enable a court to achieve the economies of class action treatment for a portion of a case, the rest of which may either not qualify under Rule 23(a) or may be unmanageable as a class action. A court may certify a Rule 23(b)(3) class for certain claims, allowing class members to opt out, while creating a non-opt-out Rule 23(b)(1) or (b)(2) class for other claims. Certification of an issues class is appropriate only if it permits fair presentation of the claims and defenses and materially advances the disposition of the litigation as a whole. If the resolution of an issues class leaves a large number of issues requiring individual decisions, the certification may not meet this test. * * *

* * *

An issues-class approach contemplates a bifurcated trial where the common issues are tried first, followed by individual trials on questions such as proximate causation and damages. A bifurcated trial must adequately present to the jury applicable defenses and be solely a class trial on liability. * * *

Before certifying an issues class under Rule 23(d), the judge should be satisfied that common questions are sufficiently separate from other issues and that a severed trial will not infringe any party's constitutional right to a jury trial and will permit all the parties fairly to present the claims and defenses.

NOTES AND QUESTIONS

1. When a court uses Rule 23(c)(4) to certify only limited issues for class treatment, it must decide whether to consider the Rule 23(a) and (b) requirements in light of the entire case, or only in light of the particular issues for which certification is proposed. One approach to this question is that taken in *Castano v. American Tobacco Co.*, 84 F.3d 734 (5th Cir. 1996), where the Fifth Circuit rejected the district court's attempt to utilize current Rule 23(c)(4) to try "core liability" and punitive damages on a classwide basis:

> Severing the defendants' conduct from reliance under [R]ule 23(c)(4) does not save the class action. A district court cannot manufacture predominance through the nimble use of subdivision (c)(4). The proper interpretation of the interaction between subdivisions (b)(3) and (c)(4) is that a cause of action, as a whole, must satisfy the predominance requirement of (b)(3) and that (c)(4) is a housekeeping rule that allows courts to sever the common issues for a class trial. Reading [R]ule 23(c)(4) as allowing a court to sever issues until the remaining common issue predominates over the remaining individual issues would eviscerate the predominance requirement of [R]ule 23(b)(3); the result would be automatic certification in every case where there is a common issue, a result that could not have been intended.

Id. at 745 n.21. In contrast to *Castano*, in *In re Tetracycline Cases*, 107 F.R.D. 719 (W.D. Mo. 1985), the court determined that it should limit its inquiry to the issues for which certification is proposed:

> If the requirement under [former] Rule 23(c)(4)(A) [current Rule 23(c)(4)] was not only that there be one or more issues which met the [R]ule 23(a) tests for commonality, typicality and adequacy of representation, but also that those issues "predominate," in the usual Rule 23(b) sense, when compared with *all* the issues in the case, there would obviously be no need or place for [R]ule 23(c)(4)(A). Reference to the general rules of construction suggests that any interpretation which makes a federal rule superfluous is to be avoided. I believe,

accordingly, that the appropriate meaning of Rule 23(b)'s predominance requirement, as applied in the context of a partial class certification request under Rule 23(c)(4)(A), is simply that the issues covered by the request be such that their resolution (as a class matter) will materially advance a disposition of the litigation as a whole. In applying this test the court must obviously consider the nature of the other potential issues in the litigation; but, to me at least, the ultimate analytical process followed in that regard is quite different than in the usual application of this part of Rule 23(b).

Id. at 727. Is the Fifth Circuit correct? Or is the district court in *Tetracyline* more persuasive in maintaining instead that Rule 23(c)(4)(A) *does* limit the rigor of a court's Rule 23(b)(3) predominance inquiry (but that this result is acceptable because the court must still perform a "superiority" analysis with respect to the structure of the resulting proposed class action)?

2. The Second Circuit has also taken a different view than *Castano* regarding how Rule 23(c)(4) and Rule 23(b)(3) may work together when determining the propriety of specific-issue certification. *See In re Nassau Cnty. Strip Search Cases*, 461 F.3d 219, 226–27 (2d Cir. 2006) (declining to follow *Castano* and stating that "[e]ven if the common questions do not predominate over the individual questions so that class certification of the entire action is warranted, Rule 23 authorizes the district court in appropriate cases to isolate the common issues under Rule 23(c)(4)(A) and proceed with class treatment of those particular issues"); *Cordes & Co. Fin. Serv., Inc. v. A.G. Edwards & Sons, Inc.*, 502 F.3d 91, 108–09 (2d Cir. 2007) (confirming approach taken in *Nassau County*); *McLaughlin v. Am. Tobacco Co.*, 522 F.3d 215, 234 (2d Cir. 2008) (noting that Rule 23(c)(4) may be applied if the resolution of the issue certified "would * * * materially advance the litigation").

3. The Fifth Circuit itself appears to have retreated from *Castano*, and its view is now arguably consistent with cases such as *Nassau County et al. See* Patricia Bronte, *Carving at the Joint: The Precise Function of Rule 23(c)(4)*, 62 DePaul L. Rev. 745, 745–46 (2013) (citing post-*Castano* Fifth Circuit authority and arguing that there is no longer a circuit conflict).

4. How, if at all, can Rule 23(b)(3) and Rule 23(c)(4)(A) be reconciled? Section 2.02 of the American Law Institute's *Principles of the Law of Aggregate Litigation* undertakes to clarify the issue certification inquiry, recommending that a court exercise its discretion to authorize issue certification "if the court determines that resolution of the common issue would * * * materially advance the resolution of multiple civil claims by addressing the core of the dispute in a manner superior to other realistic procedural alternatives * * *." *Id.* at § 2.02(a)(1). Elaborating on the meaning of the key phrase "materially advance," a comment to § 2.02 explains:

> As a matter of broad generalization, accumulated experience with the class-action device suggests that aggregate treatment of a common issue will materially advance the resolution of multiple civil claims more frequently when the issue concerns "upstream" matters focused on the generally applicable conduct of those opposing the claimants in the litigation, as distinct from "downstream" matters focused on those claimants themselves.

§ 2.02 cmt. a (citation omitted). Is § 2.02's articulation of the standard for determining whether to certify issues classes clear? Is it persuasive? Is the ALI approach more in keeping with that of the Fifth Circuit in *Castano*, or of the Second Circuit in *Nassau County*? *See also Gates v. Rohm & Haas Co.*, 2011

WL 3715817, at *15 (3d Cir. 2011) (endorsing ALI approach, under which a court, in deciding whether to certify an issue class, considers several non-exclusive factors including "the impact partial certification will have on the constitutional and statutory rights" of the parties, "the repercussions certification of an issue(s) class will have on the effectiveness and fairness of resolution of [the] remaining issues," and "the efficiencies to be gained by granting partial certification in light of realistic procedural alternatives"); *Hohider v. United Parcel Serv., Inc.*, 574 F.3d 169, 200–02 (3d Cir. 2009) (listing considerations relevant to propriety of issue certification under Rule 23(c)(4), including "the type of claim(s) and issue(s)," "the overall complexity of the case," "the substantive law underlying the claim(s)," and "the potential preclusive effect [of] resolution of the proposed issues class").

5. The Seventh Circuit, in a decision by Judge Posner, held that the district court properly certified a class in a case alleging groundwater contamination by a noxious solvent (TCE). *Mejdrech v. Met–Coil Sys. Corp.*, 319 F.3d 910 (7th Cir. 2003). The district court certified (and the court of appeals upheld certification of) two issues: (1) "whether [defendant] leaked TCE in violation of law," and (2) "whether the TCE reached the soil and groundwater beneath the homes of the class members." *Id.* at 911. The Seventh Circuit acknowledged that, after resolution of these common questions, "[t]he individual class members will still have to prove the fact and extent of their individual injuries." *Id.* at 912. Nonetheless, without citing Rule 23(c)(4), the Seventh Circuit agreed with the district court that there was no proper argument against class certification "other than one based on a general distaste for the class-action device." *Id.* Specifically, the court reasoned:

> The suit seeks injunctive and monetary relief under federal and Illinois environmental law. Mindful that not only the amount but the fact of damage might vary from class member to class member, the district judge limited class treatment to what he described as "the core question, *i.e.*, whether or not and to what extent [Met–Coil] caused contamination of the area in question." Whether a particular class member suffered any legally compensable harm and if so in what dollar amount are questions that the judge reserved for individual hearings if and when Met–Coil is determined to have contaminated the soil and water under the class members' homes in violation of federal or state law.
>
> We think the district judge's determination was reasonable, indeed right. Rather than parse the subdivisions of Rule 23 as the district judge (appropriately) did, we merely point out that class action treatment is appropriate and is permitted by Rule 23 when the judicial economy from consolidation of separate claims outweighs any concern with possible inaccuracies from their being lumped together in a single proceeding for decision by a single judge or jury. Often, and as it seems to us here, these competing considerations can be reconciled in a "mass tort" case by carving at the joint of the parties' dispute. If there are genuinely common issues, issues identical across all the claimants, issues moreover the accuracy of the resolution of which is unlikely to be enhanced by repeated proceedings, then it makes good sense, especially when the class is large, to resolve those issues in one fell swoop while leaving the remaining, claimant-specific issues to individual follow-on proceedings. The questions whether Met–Coil leaked TCE in violation of law and whether the

TCE reached the soil and groundwater beneath the homes of the class members are common to all the class members.

Id. at 911. Was the Seventh Circuit in effect applying (c)(4) even though it did not say so? Is the court's reasoning limited to pollution cases? *See id.* at 910 (granting review on "the appropriateness of class action treatment in pollution cases"). If so, why should pollution cases be treated differently than, for example, personal injury cases? More basically, in light of the materials set forth in this casebook, is Judge Posner correct in stating that "class action treatment is appropriate * * * when the judicial economy from consolidation of separate claims outweighs any concern with possible inaccuracies from their being lumped together in a single proceeding for decision by a single judge or jury"?

6. For a discussion of the genesis of Rule 23(c)(4), *see* Note, *Severance Packages: Judicial Use of Federal Rule of Civil Procedure 23(c)(4)(A)*, 91 Geo. L.J. 219 (2002). For a discussion of how the Seventh Amendment's Reexamination Clause complicates "issue class" certification, *see* Robert H. Klonoff, *The Decline of Class Actions*, 90 Wash. U. L. Rev. 729, 812–15 (2013).

d. Subclasses

PRUITT V. ALLIED CHEM. CORP.
United States District Court, Eastern District of Virginia, 1980.
85 F.R.D. 100.

MERHIGE, DISTRICT JUDGE.

* * *

Plaintiffs [in a mass tort case alleging that Allied Chemical Corp. discharged toxic effluents associated with the manufacture of the chemical Kepone into the Chesapeake Bay] seek the certification of the following class:

> All persons * * * who are residents of the Commonwealth of Virginia or the State of Maryland and whose livelihood or income is derived from, or dependent upon, the catching, taking, buying, selling, processing, packing, packaging, or distributing of seafood from the Chesapeake Bay, the James River, their tributaries, and adjacent water areas.

For the reasons which follow, the Court deems it inappropriate to certify the proposed class as a single class. Rather, the Court must divide the proposed class into distinct subclasses for certification so as to facilitate a manageable and fair adjudication of the plaintiffs' claims.

[The court first addressed the Rule 23(a) factors and found that each was satisfied except Rule 23(a)(4), which was complicated by potential conflicts between Virginia and Maryland watermen (and which was resolved by its subclassing and definitions of the class, below). The court rejected certification under Rules 23(b)(1) and (b)(2), and then turned to Rule 23(b)(3).]

The first requirement for bringing a subsection (b)(3) class action is that the Court finds that questions of law and fact common to the class as a whole predominate over questions affecting only subgroups or individuals within the class. The parties are in apparent agreement that the questions of Allied's responsibility for the Kepone pollution of Virginia and Maryland waterways, the pollution's effect on marine life, and the measures necessary to ameliorate the pollutant's harmful effect, are common to all of the members of the proposed class. Defendant Allied argues, however, that plaintiffs' suit entails a multitude of individual determinations inapplicable to the class as a whole, which predominate over the common issues. Allied cites four separate categories of questions which affect only certain members of the proposed class: (1) differing theories of causation and liability, (2) differing defenses, (3) individualized damages determination, and (4) choice of law difficulties.

Initially, plaintiffs have asserted several causes of action against Allied, including trespass, nuisance, negligence, and statutory violations. Allied contends that no single cause of action may be asserted by the class as a whole or by any easily defined subgroup of the class. For example, Allied points out that a cause of action for trespass requires a showing of some property interest in the property trespassed upon—a showing which may be met by the lessees of oysterbeds, but certainly not by packagers and processors of seafood. A cause of action for a private nuisance requires the same kind of showing of a property interest to establish an interference with the use and enjoyment of that property. Plaintiffs' negligence claims entail a showing of foreseeability and proximate causation which may vary across the class. Allied may be held to have foreseen damage to fishermen by its discharge of pollutants into the James River, but may not be held responsible for anticipating harm to those plaintiffs whose livelihoods are further removed from the direct harvesting of the marine life, such as packagers and restauranteurs. Similarly, Allied argues that a showing of proximate cause would necessarily involve varying degrees of direct harm from the pollution depending upon the plaintiffs' locations along the affected waterways, and the varying impact of the publicity surrounding the Kepone pollution, depending upon each plaintiff's location and livelihood. Plaintiffs asserting statutory remedies must establish not only a violation of the relevant statutes, but also their membership in the class protected by that statute; a showing which may not inure to the benefit of the class as a whole.

Secondly, just as causation and liability questions may vary among the class members, so may the defenses to the various causes of action. For example, Allied's proposed defense of intervening causes, more particularly of [the governor of Virginia's] closure of certain sections of the James River and Chesapeake Bay, will apply only to those plaintiffs located in the areas affected by the respective intervening cause.

Thirdly, any defense of a plaintiff's failure to mitigate damages will have to be determined on an individual basis. The plaintiffs' damages will also require individual showings of losses which Allied argues will reduce a class action to a series of innumerable mini-trials. * * *

Lastly, Allied points to the variety of locations and occupations represented by the plaintiffs as posing conflicts of law problems within the class. The Court may be required to assert admiralty jurisdiction over those plaintiffs who engage in traditional maritime activities, which under the precedent in this circuit may not include but a small fraction of the proposed class. Determinations of the applicability of admiralty jurisdiction will also depend upon such individualized considerations as the situs of the business injury and the scope of the particular maritime activity affected. A choice between federal maritime tort law and non-maritime tort law may further divide the class. Finally, the presence of both Virginia and Maryland residents may involve the Court in choices of state law as well.

Defendant Allied contends that these questions affecting only varying subgroups of the proposed class predominate over the questions common to all class members. The Court concurs. * * *

* * * [A] showing by the watermen of Allied's pollution of the James River and Chesapeake Bay would not establish that Allied is liable to the plaintiffs as a result of that pollution. * * * [T]he issues relevant to liability, *i.e.*, injury and damages, may vary from class member to class member as detailed above.

A finding that common questions of law or fact do not predominate over the questions affecting only individuals within the class does not, however, end the Court's inquiry. Subsection (c)(4) of Rule 23 provides that:

> When appropriate (A) an action may be brought or maintained as a class action with respect to particular issues, or (B) a class may be divided into subclasses and each subclass treated as a class, and the provisions of this rule shall then be construed and applied accordingly.

Rule 23(c)(4) requires the Court to consider employment of these restructuring measures where an apparently unmanageable class action could be converted to a manageable one. This subsection provides the Court with the flexibility and the authority to "treat common things in common and to distinguish the distinguishable."

Having found that the individual questions of foreseeability of harm and impact of pollution, of intervening cause defenses, and of choices of applicable law predominate over questions common to the entire class, the Court must determine whether the proposed class may be subdivided under (c)(4) so that well-defined subclasses may present common questions concerning Allied's liability for the subclasses' damages. The Court has concluded that six distinguishable subclasses within plaintiffs' proposed class merit separate class action treatment due to the predominance of common questions among their respective members.

The first subclass consists of all proposed class members directly involved with the harvesting of seafood from the James River, Chesapeake Bay and adjacent waterways. This group would include commercial fishermen, crabbers, clammers, shell-fishermen, oyster tongers, lessees of oyster beds, and employees of same, all of whom earn their livelihood by catching seafood and selling their catches to the commercial seafood industry. This subclass shares common questions of Allied's foreseeability of harm and the impact on business from the pollution and publicity surrounding it, as all its members are directly involved in the catching and selling of seafood from the affected waterways. The applicability or nonapplicability of admiralty jurisdiction as well as of maritime or non-maritime tort law should be uniform throughout the entire subclass. Because of the additional problems regarding choice of state law, Maryland or Virginia, in addition to the Court's aforementioned skepticism concerning the adequacy of representation of the Maryland plaintiffs' interest by the named plaintiffs, the Court deems it prudent to exclude all plaintiffs who reside in Maryland from this and all other subclasses. Finally, because of the potential intervening cause defense based on [the governor's] closures of parts of the James River and Chesapeake Bay, the Court will further halve this subclass of fishermen into classes comprised of those affected by the closure orders and those unaffected by them.

Another distinguishable subclass of plaintiffs consists of businessmen whose livelihoods are more indirectly involved with the catching of seafood. This group would consist of boat owners, captains and crewmen, tackle owners and bait owners, marina owners and operators, and employees of the same, all of whom earn part or all of their livelihood by offering their services or equipment, for sale or hire, to persons who attempt to catch seafood in the affected waters. As with the subclasses of fishermen, this group should be further divided according to the applicability or nonapplicability of Allied's defense involving the closure of parts of the James River and Chesapeake Bay. When divided as such, these two subclasses would present common questions regarding causation and impact, foreseeability of harm, and applicable law, which would predominate over any questions of fact or law affecting only particular members of the subclasses.

Another group which the Court has found distinguishable from other class members consists of businessmen in the seafood industry who purchase seafood caught in the waters affected by the pollution and who process, prepare or otherwise distribute the seafood to the public or to others in the commercial seafood industry. The class members represented in this subclass would be seafood wholesalers and retailers, seafood processors and packagers, distributors, and restauranteurs, and the employees of same, whose livelihoods are based in whole or in part on the purchase for resale to the public or for distribution of seafood from the affected waterways. Because these seafood dealers and restauranteurs may have been variously affected by the closure of the James River and Chesapeake Bay to fishermen from whom seafood is purchased, this group will also be divided into two subclasses of those affected and those unaffected by the closure orders. Again, questions of the foreseeability of harm to these businessmen situated further along in the chain of commercial seafood marketing, as well as the questions of applicable law and causation, should be uniform throughout these two subclasses.

The Court acknowledges that the lines of demarcation between these six subclasses are not as clear as the Court may have indicated. The pleadings and discovery taken on the matter of class certification have revealed that many members of the latter two subclasses of dealers and distributors were also involved directly in the catching of the seafood, and therefore would qualify for representation in one of the two subclasses of fishermen. Similarly, many members of the two subclasses of fishermen were also participants in the distribution, preparation or sale to the public of the seafood caught, and would thereby qualify for representation in one of the two subclasses of dealers and distributors. Such cross-overs do not, however, preclude certification of the individual subclasses, as those plaintiffs belonging to more than one subclass may be represented in more than one, or may opt out of however many subclasses they choose.

The subclasses as delineated above present, individually, common issues of recovery for any damage sustained from Allied's discharge of pollution into the James River. While there still exist several questions affecting only individuals within the subclasses, the Court is of the view that the questions common to the members of each subclass predominate over the questions that divide them. Subsection (b)(3) of Rule 23 requires only that the common questions outweigh the individual questions; they need not be dispositive of the entire litigation. The presence of issues concerning individual plaintiffs' damages and the defenses thereto, however, requires the Court to employ the second device under Rule 23(c)(4) of bifurcating the class actions here certified between liability issues and damage issues. Severing these issues will allow each class to establish, if they can, Allied's liability to the class as a whole, while reserving the proof and computation of individual plaintiffs' damages, as well as any defenses such as failure to mitigate damages, for a later proceeding. This procedure, often referred to as a partial class action, was recommended in the Advisory Committee's Note accompanying the 1966 amendments of Rule 23, and has been utilized by federal courts in class actions where, as here, the advantages and economies to be achieved by a single adjudication of common issues recommends class action treatment of those issues.

* * *

There still remain some judicial housekeeping matters regarding the certification of the six subclasses of plaintiffs. As noted above, the Maryland class members are excluded from these class actions for reasons of manageability and the potential for antagonistic interests within the subclasses. * * *

The Court's certification order, which in any event is tentative, will be further conditioned on (1) a showing of each subclass' satisfaction of Rule 23(a) prerequisites, particularly those of numerosity and adequacy of representation, and (2) a showing by the representative parties in each subclass of their ability to finance the cost of notice to absent class members required by Rule 23(c)(2). While the Court finds the proposed class action to have satisfied Rule 23(a) prerequisites, that determination may not necessarily compel a finding that the subclasses individually satisfy those requirements. Because the class has been significantly subdivided and the issues thereby refined, satisfaction of the prerequisites of numerosity and adequacy of representation, as well as of commonality and typicality, must be reestablished for the benefit of each subclass to be certified. A showing by class representatives of their ability to finance notice to the class members [required by Rule 23(c)(2)—see Chapter 2(B)(4)(b)(v) & Chapter 5(A)(2)(a)] is necessary to the end that the Court be assured of an effective notification to class members of the pendency of these actions and their opportunity to exclude themselves from a judgment therein.

An appropriate order shall issue.

NOTES AND QUESTIONS

1. How did the court in *Pruitt* envision the case being tried? What practical difficulties were presented, and how should the court have addressed each such problem at trial? Based on the claims presented, would the court have been justified in simply denying class certification? What arguments can be

made that the court's approach of dividing the class into subclasses was an abuse of discretion? What arguments can be made that the court acted within its discretion?

2. Is the *Pruitt* court correct that a class member can simultaneously be a member of more than one subclass? How would such an approach work in practice? What complications might arise?

3. In Note, *Developments in the Law: Class Actions*, 89 Harv. L. Rev. 1318, 1479 (1976), the author provides the following rationale for subclassing:

> By dividing a class, a judge may be able to redefine the responsibilities of class attorneys and named plaintiffs in terms of the interests of distinct and relatively unified portions of a class. The * * * likelihood that diverse absentee interests will be presented to the court [may therefore] increase.

In addition to the reason noted, are there other reasons why a court may wish to impose subclasses? Are there reasons why a defendant would or would not want subclasses? Are there reasons why class representatives and their attorneys would or would not want subclasses?

4. When subclasses are proposed, each subclass must independently satisfy Rule 23(a)(1). *See* Rule 23(c)(5) (each subclass must be treated as a separate class for purposes of Rule 23 requirements); *see also In re Methyl Tertiary Butyl Ether ("MTBE") Prods. Liab. Litig.*, 209 F.R.D. 323, 351 (S.D.N.Y. 2002) (each subclass must meet all requirements of Rule 23(a) and one category of 23(b)); *Andrews v. Bechtel Power Corp.*, 780 F.2d 124, 132 (1st Cir. 1985) (subclasses failed to satisfy numerosity because members of each subclass lived in the same area and could be easily joined). Is there a legitimate rationale for the requirement that each subclass comply with Rules 23(a) and (b)?

5. If subclasses are utilized, should separate counsel be secured? If one accepts the premise that, in some cases, class actions are largely lawyer-driven so that class representatives do not significantly influence either the overall strategy or the presentation of evidence at trial, how can potentially divergent subclass interests be advanced *without* separate lawyers?

e. Class Certification for Purposes of Settlement

If parties to litigation jointly request class certification so that they may settle their dispute and resolve the maximum number of claims possible, should a court relax its scrutiny of whether class certification is appropriate? *See* Chapter 8(A)(3) (discussing "settlement certification").

C. CLASS ACTION DISCOVERY

1. PRE-CERTIFICATION DISCOVERY

This subsection explores issues raised by class certification discovery. It asks, first, if discovery is required before a court rules on whether to certify a class action. It then discusses the possible subjects of such discovery, as well as the trial court's control over the issues and process. (As background, it may be useful to review Fed. R. Civ. P. 26 through 37, which govern discovery in federal cases, including class actions.)

a. Is Discovery Necessary?

The Supreme Court has instructed that a class "may only be certified if the trial court is satisfied, after a rigorous analysis," that the relevant provisions of Rule 23 have been met. *Gen. Tel. Co. v. Falcon*, 457 U.S. 147, 161 (1982). Moreover, the Court has observed that "discovery often has been used to illuminate issues upon which a district court must pass in deciding whether a suit should proceed as a class action under Rule 23, such as numerosity, common questions, and adequacy of representation." *Oppenheimer Fund, Inc. v. Sanders*, 437 U.S. 340, 351 n.13 (1978). Other authorities cited in the previous section noted that discovery often is not only appropriate but essential to the determination of issues relating to class certification. Yet, as further noted in the previous section, the Supreme Court in *Falcon* hinted that, in particular cases, it may be appropriate for a district court to certify a class action based solely on the pleadings. The Court noted that "[s]ometimes the issues are plain enough from the pleadings to determine whether the interests of the absent parties are fairly encompassed within the named plaintiff's claim * * *." 457 U.S. at 160. How does a court determine whether discovery is necessary?

HART V. NATIONWIDE MUT. FIRE INS. CO.
United States District Court, District of Delaware, 2010.
270 F.R.D. 166.

FARNAN, DISTRICT JUDGE.

Pending before the Court is Plaintiff Geneyne Hart's Motion To Compel Production Of Documents. * * * For reasons to be discussed, Plaintiff's Motion will be granted in part and denied in part * * *.

I. Background

Plaintiff Geneyne Hart ("Plaintiff") is a Delaware resident and insured of Defendant Nationwide Mutual Fire Insurance Company ("Defendant"). * * * Plaintiff alleges that on March 7, 2007, she was, through no fault of her own, involved in an automobile collision in which her vehicle was struck by another vehicle. Plaintiff alleges that she sustained serious injuries and that she sought medical treatment from various providers. Specifically, Plaintiff alleges that medical records detailing her diagnosis and treatment plan were submitted to Defendant, and that she was treated for a lumbar sprain at Delaware Pain & Spine and Dynamic Therapy on April 19, May 3, May 17, and June 14, 2007. Plaintiff alleges that, although the treatments were reasonable and necessary, Defendant refused to make full and prompt payments and reduced payments because "[t]he amount allowed is based on provider charges within the provider's geographic region."

On October 29, 2007, Plaintiff filed this proposed class action on behalf of herself and all others similarly situated. In a nine-count Complaint, Plaintiff alleges that Defendant committed various statutory and common law violations, including *inter alia*, breaches of insurance contracts, bad faith breaches of insurance contracts, breaches of the duty of fair dealing, common law fraud, consumer fraud, unjust enrichment, and racketeering activity in connection with Defendant's denial of benefits under Personal

Injury Protection ("PIP") coverage, issued as part of Defendant's auto insurance contracts pursuant to [Delaware statute].

II. Motion To Compel

A. Parties' Contentions

* * * Plaintiff asks the Court to enter an order compelling Defendant to provide (1) all of Defendant's PIP files from October 29, 2002 to the present, (2) all documents, correspondence, memoranda and emails responsive to Plaintiff's requests, (3) all information concerning the decision to engage and disengage use of bill reduction software, and (4) a privilege log for withheld documents. * * * Plaintiff maintains that discovery of the [PIP] files is needed for preparation of the class certification motion, and that the files are needed to show numerosity of the proposed class, commonality and typicality of the proposed members' claims, and the amount of damages.

In response, Defendant contends that Plaintiff is seeking information that exceeds the scope of pre-certification discovery, and that Plaintiff's attempt to discover files and documents so unrelated to her individual claims must be rejected. Defendant contends providing Plaintiff access to all PIP files is not warranted because the fact that Plaintiff needs to review them is itself inconsistent with the existence of a certifiable class. * * *

B. Discussion

Federal Rule of Civil Procedure 26 provides that the "[p]arties may obtain discovery regarding any nonprivileged matter that is relevant to any party's claim or defense." Fed. R. Civ. P. 26(b)(1). As long as the information sought is reasonably calculated to lead to the discovery of admissible evidence, it is discoverable, even if it is ultimately not admissible at trial. *Id.* District courts have considerable discretion regarding discovery. With regard to pre-certification discovery in putative class actions, "[t]ypically district courts will allow discovery relevant to determining whether the requirements of Rule 23(a) are satisfied and whether the action is maintainable under one of the categories listed in Rule 23(b)."[1]

The Court will not compel Defendant to produce all of its PIP files from October 29, 2002 to the present. Such a voluminous and far-reaching request of documents is, in the Court's view, significantly broader than is necessary for Plaintiff to research the numerosity, typicality, and commonality of the proposed class, and to prepare its class certification motion. As previously noted, Plaintiff is entitled to relevant discovery to determine if the requirements of Rule 23 are satisfied, and the Court would entertain a more narrowly tailored request for Defendant's PIP files. For example, the parties could consider production of a representative sample of Defendant's PIP files which would provide Plaintiff with enough information to make its certification arguments without being unduly burdensome on Defendant.

---

[1] Discovery in this action has not been bifurcated, but the parties agreed to engage in preliminary discovery on * * * certification issues, and agreed that there may be an overlap between certification issues and those going to the merits.

* * *

III. Motion For Protective Order Regarding Time Frame Of Discovery

A. Parties' Contentions

By its motion, Defendant asks the Court to enter a protective order limiting the time frame on which Plaintiff can obtain discovery of Defendant's claim review practices. * * * Defendant contends that, although Plaintiff is challenging its practice of reducing charges after a pricing review by third party system vendor Mitchell Medical, the pricing review function was not enabled until February 14, 2005. * * *

Plaintiff responds that Defendant's use of bill review software is relevant to Plaintiff's claim of bad faith handling of PIP claims. According to Plaintiff, Defendant used such software in Delaware until 2001, re-engaged such software around February 2005 (approximately the same time Defendant settled a Delaware class action related to PIP claims), and then disengaged the use of such software again after this litigation commenced. Plaintiff further disputes Defendant's contention that it is attempting to extend the scope of discovery, and contends that Defendant has not shown that good cause exists for entry of a protective order.

* * *

C. Discussion

The Court will deny Defendant's Motion for two reasons. First, as previously noted, the Court recognizes that information concerning Defendant's practices and procedures in the payment of PIP claims prior to 2004–2005, particularly Defendant's decision to repeatedly engage and re-engage bill review software, is potentially relevant to Plaintiff's bad faith allegations. Second, Defendant has not met its burden of demonstrating good cause exists for entry of a protective order. Although Defendant's Motion is premised on the general contention that Plaintiff is seeking unreasonably broad discovery, Defendant has not demonstrated that it will suffer a clearly defined and serious injury if a protective order is not entered.

* * *

V. Conclusion

For the reasons discussed, the Court will grant in part and deny in part Plaintiff's Motion To Compel Production Of Documents, and deny Defendant's Motion For Protective Order Regarding Time Frame of Discovery * * *.

* * *

NOTES AND QUESTIONS

1. What was the basis for the *Hart* court's ruling? Was the court too willing to order that voluminous documents be produced prior to the class certification decision? Or was the material sought by the plaintiff limited and justified?

As *Hart* reflects, in many cases the vast majority of pertinent documents belong to the defendant, not to the plaintiff. As Judge Posner explained in another case:

In most class action suits, * * * there is far more evidence that plaintiffs may be able to discover in defendants' records (including emails, the vast and ever-expanding volume of which has made the cost of discovery soar) than vice versa. For usually the defendants' conduct is the focus of the litigation and it is in their records, generally much more extensive than the plaintiffs' (especially when as in a consumer class action the plaintiffs are individuals rather than corporations or other institutions), that the plaintiffs will want to rummage in quest of smoking guns.

Thorogood v. Sears, Roebuck & Co., 624 F.3d 842, 849–50 (7th Cir. 2010). Do the points raised by Judge Posner suggest that courts should impose strict limits on discovery sought by plaintiffs? Or do they suggest that plaintiffs have a legitimate need for broad discovery?

2. Should a court be permitted to *deny* class certification or dismiss class allegations without granting a plaintiff any discovery? Under what circumstances? *See Mantolete v. Bolger*, 767 F.2d 1416, 1424 (9th Cir. 1985) (noting that the test is whether "discovery is likely to produce substantiation of the class allegations"). Several cases have allowed dismissal of class claims without discovery. *See, e.g., Stewart v. Winter*, 669 F.2d 328, 331–32 (5th Cir. 1982); *Rodriguez v. Dept. of Treasury*, 108 F.R.D. 360, 361–62 (D.D.C. 1985); *see also, e.g., Talley v. Leo J. Shapiro & Assocs., Inc.*, 713 F. Supp. 254, 257–58 (N.D. Ill. 1989) (dismissing certain class allegations without discovery on grounds of standing, but refusing to dismiss other class allegations without discovery). Other courts, however, have held that failure to allow pre-certification discovery was an abuse of discretion. *See, e.g., Parker v. Time Warner Entm't Co.*, 331 F.3d 13, 21–22 (2d Cir. 2003) (vacating district court's denial of (b)(2) and (b)(3) class certification following denial of pre-certification discovery, and noting that "it is likely that minimal class discovery must be conducted in order to provide the court with the factual information necessary to decide whether or not to certify a Rule 23(b)(2) class").

3. In *Doyel v. McDonald's Corp.*, 2009 WL 350627 (E.D. Mo. 2009), a class of McDonald's employees in Missouri sued the company for unpaid wages and maintaining inaccurate records. In denying defendant's motion to dismiss the class allegations before discovery had taken place, the court stated: "Striking plaintiffs' class action allegations prior to discovery and the class certification stage is a rare remedy, appropriate where the complaint itself demonstrates that the requirements for maintaining a class action cannot be met." *Id.* at *5. At the same time, the court expressed skepticism regarding plaintiffs' ultimate chances of success, opining that, "[g]oing forward, plaintiffs will likely have difficulty proving classwide injury with proof common to the class * * *." *Id.* at *6. Would it be appropriate in such a situation for the court to simply dismiss the class claims without allowing discovery at all? Why or why not?

4. Of course, even without formal discovery, parties often submit evidentiary materials at the certification stage, and courts often consider such materials in rendering decisions on certification. How might such evidence be gathered, and what might it include?

b. **Scope of Discovery**

i. *Limiting Discovery to Class Certification Issues*

a) *"Class" Versus "Merits" Discovery*

IN RE RAIL FREIGHT SURCHARGE ANTITRUST LITIG.
United States District Court, District of Columbia, 2009.
258 F.R.D. 167.

JOHN M. FACCIOLA, UNITED STATES MAGISTRATE JUDGE.

Now pending before the Court is Defendants' Motion for Phased Discovery. Defendants propose a Case Management Order that provides for class discovery before class certification and merits discovery. Plaintiffs propose an alternative order that provides for class certification at the conclusion of all fact discovery. The issue now before this Court is whether bifurcated discovery is appropriate.

I. Background.

Defendants are the four largest Class I railroads[†] based in the United States. Plaintiffs are eighteen businesses from multiple districts that allege that defendants * * * violated federal antitrust laws by conspiring to fix and maintain the prices of rail freight transportation services through the use of Rail Fuel Surcharges. * * * Plaintiffs claim that defendants implemented a uniform Rail Fuel Surcharge program by which they fixed and imposed artificially high surcharges that exceeded their increased fuel costs and generated billions of dollars of profits. Plaintiffs claim that defendants agreed to maintain the established rates and took other collective actions to enforce their conspiracy. * * *

II. Summary of the Arguments.

* * * Defendants argue that phased discovery facilitates early resolution of the class certification issue and reduces the burden of the subsequent merits discovery. * * * Primarily, plaintiffs argue that class certification and merits evidence are indistinguishable. The "information about the nature of the claims on the merits and the proof that they require is important to deciding certification." * * *

* * *

III. Analysis.

* * * [T]he evidence plaintiffs need for certification purposes is closely intertwined with the merits evidence. * * * To satisfy th[e] "predominance" requirement [of Rule 23(b)(3)], plaintiffs must secure evidence concerning "Defendants' adoption of the fuel surcharge program, how it was imposed, and the Defendants' purposes in doing so" which bears directly on the element of common impact. In essence, the scope of defendants' alleged conspiracy is indistinguishable from its operation. Plaintiffs need evidence concerning the operation of the conspiracy—evidence defendants classify

---

[†] "Class I" railroads are the category of freight railroad companies with the greatest operating revenues, as classified by the Surface Transportation Board according to federal regulations. *See* 49 C.F.R. § 1201. [Ed.]

as "merits-based"—to establish the scope of the conspiracy. In turn, plaintiffs need evidence of the scope of the conspiracy to prove common impact and thereby satisfy Rule 23's "predominance" requirement.

Here, the alleged conspiracy's operation and scope are so closely intertwined that it would be an "arbitrary insistence . . . that thwarts the informed judicial assessment that the current class certification practice emphasizes" to insist that one be classified as "certification evidence" and the other as "merits evidence." * * *

* * * Bifurcated discovery fails to promote judicial economy when it requires "ongoing supervision of discovery." If bifurcated, this Court would likely have to resolve various needless disputes that would arise concerning the classification of each document as "merits" or "certification" discovery. * * * Furthermore, the continued need for supervision and the increased number of disputes would further delay the case proceedings. * * *

In this case, the need for the Court to facilitate a resolution is especially strong. * * * Even if plaintiffs' proposed class is not certified, discovery into merits-based evidence is not necessarily wasted; the information "may be valued circumstantial evidence" if litigation continues absent certification. *Manual For Complex Litigation (Fourth)* § 21.14. At this stage, "there is no reason to believe that denial of class certification will terminate this litigation." Eighteen individual businesses from multiple districts have alleged claims against defendants. Each business independently sought judicial relief before four businesses moved to consolidate the cases.

* * *

This discussion is not to say that untrammeled and unlimited discovery is appropriate before the issue of class certification is addressed. Plaintiffs will have to concede that what may be a king's ransom will have been spent on discovery that may never be used if [the district court] denies class certification or narrows the nature of the class. * * * Instead, I intend to allow an initial period of discovery, after which the parties will have to brief the certification issue. * * * I appreciate that this is a compromise but I can only hope that like any compromise it will displease both sides equally. It is my goal to avoid creating the new discovery disputes that would arise by instituting a new criterion—relevance to certification—on top of the requirements for discoverability outlined in the Federal Rules of Civil Procedure. I also would like to see the issue of certification resolved as quickly as it can be to bring certainty to the litigation and avoid wasting resources on discovery that turns out to be irrelevant. * * *

Accordingly, * * * I will order counsel to meet and confer in the next ten days to ascertain whether they can jointly agree to a schedule for all the remaining events to take place in the case[.] * * * If the parties cannot agree, each side will have to file proposed schedules fourteen days from the date of this Order. * * *

NOTES AND QUESTIONS

1. The *Rail Freight Surcharge* case provides an interesting example of a class discovery issue in the wake of *Hydrogen Peroxide* (a 2008 decision) and the other cases discussed in Section (B)(1)(b)(i) of this chapter. Those cases

emphasized the evidentiary burden on the party seeking certification, cautioning district courts against drawing artificial distinctions between merits and certification issues when applying the Rule 23 requirements. How are these rulings reflected in the *Rail Freight Surcharge* court's analysis? How do they affect the discovery strategies of the parties?

Does imposing an initial discovery period, followed by a ruling on certification, make sense? Is a necessary consequence of the *Hydrogen Peroxide* line of cases a presumption against bifurcation of class discovery? Or are there still circumstances where bifurcated discovery should be preferred? What factors should weigh in the district court's decision?

2. There is some tension between a defendant's argument at the discovery stage that merits issues are not relevant to class certification, and subsequent argument at the class certification stage that certification should be denied because the plaintiffs have made an insufficient showing to withstand a rigorous analysis of whether Rule 23 is satisfied. Likewise, a plaintiff who argues that extensive merits discovery is necessary prior to the class certification determination may face judicial skepticism if he or she then argues that the court is precluded from engaging in a rigorous evidentiary assessment at class certification. How should counsel for each side approach these issues? When might *defendants* in a putative class action want merits discovery to take place before the certification decision?

3. The first edition of the *Manual for Complex Litigation*, published in 1977, "recommended that no discovery on the merits be permitted during the discovery of the class action issue, except as is relevant to the class [certification] determination." *Id.* at § 1.40. When the second edition was published in 1985, the *Manual* was more equivocal regarding the advisability of bifurcated discovery, stating that "[o]ften, * * * bifurcating [between class and merits] discovery * * * will be counterproductive." *Id.* at § 30.12. "Discovery relating to 'class issues,'" the *Manual (Second)* continued, "is not always distinguishable from other discovery." *Id.* The third edition, published in 1995, added that "[b]ifurcating class and merits discovery can at times be more efficient and economical (particularly when the merits discovery would not be used if class certification were denied), but can result in duplication and unnecessary disputes among counsel over the scope of discovery." *Id.* at § 30.12. The *Manual (Third)* further acknowledged that "[d]iscovery relating to class issues may overlap substantially with merits discovery." *Id.* Accordingly, the *Manual (Third)* emphasized the desirability of the district court's calling "for a specific discovery plan from the parties, identifying the depositions and other discovery contemplated and the subject matter to be covered." *Id.*

Most recently, in 2004, the *Manual* issued yet a fourth discussion of bifurcation of class and merits discovery:

> Courts often bifurcate discovery between certification issues and those related to the merits of the allegations. * * * There is not always a bright line between the two. Courts have recognized that information about the nature of the claims on the merits and the proof that they require is important to deciding certification. Arbitrary insistence on the merits/class discovery distinction sometimes thwarts the informed judicial assessment that current class certification practice emphasizes.
>
> Allowing some merits discovery during the precertification period is generally more appropriate for cases that are large and likely to continue even if not certified. On the other hand, in cases that are

unlikely to continue if not certified, discovery into aspects of the merits unrelated to certification delays the certification decision and can create extraordinary and unnecessary expense and burden. If merits discovery is stayed during the precertification period, the judge should provide for lifting the stay after deciding the certification motion.

It is often useful under Rule 26(f) to require a specific and detailed precertification discovery plan from the parties. The plan should identify the depositions and other discovery contemplated, as well as the subject matter to be covered and the reason it is material to determining the certification inquiry under Rule 23.

Manual for Complex Litigation (Fourth) § 21.14 (2004). Does this discussion provide useful guidance? How, if at all, does this approach contrast with those set forth in earlier editions of the *Manual*? Which of the various approaches makes the most sense?

In light of decisions like *Hydrogen Peroxide* and *Szabo*, discussed earlier in this chapter, is there a need for a Fifth Edition of the *Manual* to revisit yet again the issue of bifurcated class and merits discovery?

4. Assuming that a district court decides to bifurcate discovery among "class" and "merits" issues, how should it determine whether a particular discovery request seeks information relating to one, as opposed to the other? For example:

a. A plaintiff in a sex discrimination case requests discovery relating to the policies or procedures that were in place during a given period.

b. A defendant in a securities fraud case requests discovery relating to what information a plaintiff relied upon in making an investment decision (reliance being one of the elements of a fraud claim).

c. A plaintiff in a product liability suit seeks production of all documents relating to claims of any sort of harm by other users of the particular drug at issue.

d. In depositions of plaintiffs in a suit involving potential exposure to a toxic substance, a defendant asks questions about a plaintiff's lifestyle, and, in particular, about the plaintiff's exposure to other potentially toxic substances.

In each of the examples above, how could the proponent of discovery argue that the information sought addresses issues relating to certification? How could the opponent contend that the discovery relates solely to merits issues?

b) Permissible Areas of Inquiry

What is the actual content of pre-certification discovery? What do the parties seek to learn through the discovery process at this early juncture? The *Manual for Complex Litigation (Fourth)* provides some guidance:

Numerosity. Determining whether the proposed class is sufficiently numerous for certification is usually straightforward. Affidavits, declarations, or even reasonable estimates in briefs are often sufficient to establish the approximate size of the class and whether joinder might be a practical and manageable alternative to class action litigation.

Commonality. Identifying common questions typically requires examining the parties' claims and defenses, identifying the type of proof the parties expect to present, and deciding the extent to which there is a need for individual, as opposed to common, proof. * * *

* * *

Typicality. Deciding typicality requires determining whether the named plaintiff's claim arises from the same course of events and involves legal arguments similar to those of each class member. The court must also establish that the proposed class representative's claims are not subject to defenses that do not apply to other members of the class. Discovery may be necessary to determine if the plaintiff's claim is atypical, although discovery may not be necessary if the pleadings or readily available information reveals that a named plaintiff's claim is idiosyncratic.

Adequacy of representation. The named plaintiffs must show that the proposed action will fairly and adequately protect the interests of the class. They must first demonstrate that class counsel is qualified, experienced, and able to conduct the litigation in the interests of the class. That also is part of the showing required for appointment of class counsel under Rule 23(g). * * *

Plaintiffs also must show that the named representatives have no substantial interests antagonistic to those of proposed class members and that the representatives share the desire to prosecute the action vigorously. A trial plan can help to identify distinct claims that may demand separate representation or a denial of certification. * * * Proposed class members' interests may differ from those of the named representatives for a variety of reasons. Different state law may apply to different class members. In a mass tort case, those with present injuries have different interests than those who have been exposed to the injurious substance but have not yet manifested injury. Those with severe injuries may have different interests than those with slight injuries.

The proponents of certification sometimes attempt to meet Rule 23's adequacy-of-representation requirements by suing for only one type of relief, such as an injunction, on behalf of the class. In that case, the named plaintiffs may be inadequate representatives for class members who also have existing damage claims. Discovery may be needed to identify any appropriate remedies not included in the proposed class claims.

* * *

Precertification inquiries into the named parties' finances or the financial arrangements between the class representatives and their counsel are rarely appropriate, except to obtain information necessary to determine whether the parties and their counsel have the resources to represent the class adequately. Ethics rules permit attorneys to advance court costs and expenses of litigation, the repayment of which may be contingent on the outcome of the matter. * * *

Rule 23(b)(1)(B). In addition to satisfying the Rule 23(a) criteria, a Rule 23(b)(1)(B) non-opt-out "limited fund" class must overcome a high threshold set by the Supreme Court. * * * First, the judge must find that there is a limited fund. The evidence must prove that the value of class claims exceeds the proven value of the fund. Next, the judge must find that there would be equitable treatment of all claimants * * *. Finally, the judge must find that payment of the claims would exhaust the limited fund or that failure to exhaust the fund would be justified. * * * Certifying a Rule 23(b)(1)(B) class ordinarily will call for extensive factual findings showing that the standards have been met, which may require extensive discovery.

Rule 23(b)(2). The Rule 23(b)(2) class action applies when class-wide injunctive or declaratory relief is necessary to redress group injuries, such as infringements on civil rights, and is commonly relied on by litigants seeking institutional reform through injunctive relief. Because a Rule 23(b)(2) class action does not permit opting out, it presumes that the class is homogenous and therefore cohesive. That presumption can be destroyed by showing individualized issues as to liability or remedy.

* * *

* * * Discovery may be necessary to show the existence of underlying state law preconditions for such claims as medical monitoring. * * *

When a proposed class seeks both injunctive relief and damages, the judge may have to make findings as to the relative importance of the damage claims and decide whether to provide class members notice and an opportunity to opt out. * * *

Rule 23(b)(3). Rule 23(b)(3) maintainability requires the judge to determine that common questions predominate over individualized ones and that class action treatment is superior to other available methods for the fair and efficient adjudication of the controversy.

* * *

Precertification discovery may be needed to assist the judge in distinguishing the individual from the common elements of the claims, issues, and defenses, and in deciding the extent to which the need for individual proof outweighs the economy of receiving common proof. A trial plan addressing each element of the claims can help to identify the nature and extent of the individualized proof required.

To analyze superiority, the judge will need information from the parties about alternative approaches to the claims of the proposed class and the defenses they will face. Discovery may be needed to determine the extent to which individual potential class members have an interest in separate actions, inconsistent with class treatment. * * *

The judge must decide whether the proposed Rule 23(b)(3) class will be manageable. For the most part, courts determine manageability by reviewing affidavits, declarations, trial plans, and choice-of-law analyses that counsel present. Discovery may be needed to determine whether a need for individual proof will hinder the fair presentation of common questions to the finder of fact and whether class members can be identified without making numerous fact-intensive inquiries. * * *

Manual for Complex Litigation (Fourth) § 21.14 (2004).

Countless cases have addressed particularized requests for pre-certification discovery relating to various elements of Rules 23(a) and (b). Although appellate courts may police the outer boundaries of pre-certification discovery, the issue generally rests within the broad, informed discretion of the trial court.

Review the following examples of discovery requests, taken from actual class action litigation, and consider how proponents and opponents of the discovery requests would argue whether they are relevant to class certification issues and whether they are unduly burdensome:

1. *Plaintiffs' Discovery*:

   a. Interrogatory [general]. If the defendant contends that the proposed class representatives' claims are not typical of the claims of members of the class as defined, state the basis for the contention.

   b. Interrogatory [general]. If the defendant denies that the issues in the complaint are common to the claims of all members of the proposed class, identify which issues are not common and explain why they are not common.

   c. Interrogatory [general]. If the defendant contends that there is any method of resolving the dispute between class members and defendant that is more manageable than a class action, identify that method and explain why it is more manageable than a class action.

   d. Request for Production [employment discrimination case]. All documents reflecting the procedures and criteria for assigning, training, assisting, evaluating, transferring, giving supervisory duties to, promoting, increasing salary of, disciplining, and discharging employees.

   e. Request for Production [employment discrimination case]. All documents reflecting or referring to any and all correspondence between the defendant and either the Equal Employment Opportunity Commission or the [State] Human Relations Commission, regarding allegations of [age/race/gender/national origin/religious] discrimination.

   f. Interrogatory [employment discrimination case]. Identify each former employee of defendant who was discharged or terminated by defendant at any time since [the date of adoption of the alleged discriminatory policy or practice], and state as to each: (a) name, address, sex, age, race, national origin, and religion; (b) position held; (c) duties and responsibilities of position; and (d) date of discharge.

2. *Defendant's Discovery*:

a. Interrogatory [general]. State every fact relied upon by you or the putative plaintiff class supporting your contention that a class action is the superior method of adjudicating this controversy.

b. Interrogatory [general]. State every fact relied upon by you or the putative plaintiff class supporting your contention that the named plaintiffs and class counsel will adequately, zealously, and competently protect the interests of the class, including, without limitation, your financial ability, and your experience with similar cases.

c. Interrogatory [general]. Describe the efforts by the proposed class representatives and class counsel to do any of the following: inform class members of the issues and progress of the class action; solicit members' views regarding the issues and progress of the class action; determine whether the views expressed by the putative class representatives and class counsel reflect the views of the majority of the members of the class; identify dissent; or address or accommodate divergent views.

d. Interrogatory [general]. With respect to the purported class, provide the following: (a) identify all persons known to you or your attorneys who are or may be a member of the class; (b) describe all procedures you or your attorneys will use to identify the members of the class; (c) state the time and expense you estimate will be required to identify the members of the class; and (d) identify any experts, consultants and other individuals whom you have employed to assist you in identifying members of the class.

e. Interrogatory [securities fraud case]. Identify each person with whom you consulted regarding your business or financial affairs between [year] and the present.

f. Request for Production [securities fraud case]. All communications between any member of the putative plaintiff class and [any of the defendants] or any third party referring or relating to actual or potential purchases or sales of [the defendant corporation's] stock.

ii. *Other Limitations on the Scope of Discovery*

BORSKEY V. MEDTRONICS, INC.
United States District Court, Eastern District of Louisiana, 1998.
1998 WL 122602.

FALLON, DISTRICT JUDGE.

Before the Court is plaintiffs' motion to compel responses to discovery. For the following reasons, plaintiffs' motion is HEREBY DENIED. * * *

I. BACKGROUND

Between 1993 and 1994 plaintiffs in these consolidated actions were all allegedly implanted with a SynchroMed Implantable Infusion Pump or a Reservoir Pump ("the pumps") manufactured, designed, promoted, distributed and sold by defendant, Medtronic, Inc. ("Medtronic"). Plaintiffs aver that they required the use of the pain medication Demerol, which was placed inside their pumps. Plaintiffs assert, and defendant does not appear to dispute, that Demerol was not a drug approved by the Food and Drug Administration ("FDA") for use in the pumps. Plaintiffs charge that Demerol caused the pumps to fail, requiring plaintiffs to have their pumps surgically removed. Plaintiffs filed suit, seeking recovery under several theories of liability. * * * In addition, plaintiffs seek class certification [of a nationwide class]. Defendants objected to much of plaintiffs' class certification discovery, and plaintiffs moved to compel.

II. PLAINTIFFS' MOTION TO COMPEL

* * *

In furtherance of their attempt to certify [the] class, plaintiffs filed Interrogatories and Requests for Production. Defendant objected to several of these discovery requests, reasoning that plaintiffs sought information pertaining to a class for which they could not possibly be certified. Defendant argues that any class plaintiffs could be certified to represent would be limited to those potential plaintiffs with the alleged characteristics of the named plaintiffs, namely (1) Louisiana residents (2) implanted with Medtronic pump models 8615 or 8611H whose pumps (3) failed in connection with the administration of (4) Demerol and (5) [who] have had their pumps surgically explanted. Plaintiffs moved to compel discovery on a broader class, maintaining that they are entitled to discovery of information pertaining to the potential class [for which they seek certification], namely (1) all U.S. residents who have had (2) any Medtronic Implantable Infusion Pump system surgically implanted which (3) failed in connection with the use of Demerol or any other non-approved drug, even if (4) the device has not been removed. Most of the discovery dispute revolves around the issue of the proper scope of the potential class for which plaintiffs are entitled to discovery.

In deciding whether plaintiffs' discovery requests were proper, the Court must ascertain whether the "information sought appears reasonably calculated to lead to the discovery of admissible evidence." Fed. R. Civ. P. 26. Whether the evidence uncovered could be admissible is determined by the contours of the potential class plaintiffs might represent under Fed. R. Civ. P. 23.

The Court finds that plaintiffs at this point cannot show that they could be entitled to represent a class larger than (1) Louisiana residents (2) implanted with Medtronic pump models 8615 or 8611H whose pump has (3) already failed in connection with the administration of (4) Demerol. Therefore, the Court will exercise its "broad discretion" in limiting "precertification discovery to evidence that, in its sound judgment, would be 'necessary or helpful' to the certification decision," and will limit discovery to potential plaintiffs meeting the above four criteria.

It appears to the Court that in no event could named plaintiffs represent a class consisting of non-Louisiana residents. * * * The "Fifth Circuit . . . has stated that federal district courts should not certify national classes in mass tort cases that arise under state law." *In re Masonite Corp. Hardboard Siding Prod. Liab. Litig.*, 170 F.R.D. 417, 421 (E.D. La. 1997). As to the other issues—whether the drug causing the alleged pump failure was Demerol or some other non-FDA approved drug and whether the pumps at issue must be limited to a certain model(s)—the Court's ruling is not intended to be final. If after discovery limited to the above criteria the plaintiffs appear to warrant certification, the Court will consider ordering additional discovery regarding a potentially expanded class. However, at this point plaintiffs' entitlement to class certification for even the most limited category of plaintiffs is by no means obvious. Therefore, before the Court fully releases the hounds of discovery to flush out the entire spectrum of possible plaintiffs, the Court finds it prudent to focus the spotlight on those criteria that the named plaintiffs allegedly possess.

* * *

NOTES AND QUESTIONS

1. What types of limitations on discovery are illustrated by the *Borskey* decision? Were those limitations reasonably applied?

2. The court suggested that it might entertain requests for additional discovery if plaintiffs could show a basis for class certification as a result of the initial, more limited discovery. Does the court's approach to possible additional discovery make sense?

NAT'L ORG. FOR WOMEN, INC. v. SPERRY RAND CORP.
United States District Court, District of Connecticut, 1980.
88 F.R.D. 272.

CLARIE, CHIEF JUDGE.

This case involves alleged employment discrimination by the defendant, Sperry Univac, against the [individual] plaintiff, [Susan] Madison, and also against members of the plaintiff [association], National Organization for Women (NOW). The plaintiffs have also brought this action on behalf of a class of employees, and prospective employees, who claim to have been injured by the employment practices of the defendant. There has been no determination regarding class certification at this juncture.

The defendant has moved to compel disclosure of the full membership list of NOW. The plaintiffs have moved to compel answers to interrogatories and production of documents, both of which are allegedly necessary for the purpose of class certification. Both motions are granted, as modified by the Court. The questions presented will be discussed separately, beginning with the defendant's motion.

* * *

I. Defendant's Motion To Compel an Answer to an Interrogatory

Facts

On November 15, 1978, the defendant served on NOW a series of interrogatories including, at paragraph three, a request that NOW supply "the names, sex, race, current address, occupation and present employer of each and every member of the National Organization for Women, [Farmington Valley Chapter]." The defendant indicated that this information is discoverable under Rule 26(b) of the Federal Rules of Civil Procedure in that it is relevant and not privileged. The relevancy of the information, claims the defendant, is derived from NOW's allegation that a number of its members are aggrieved by certain practices followed by Sperry Univac. Finally, the defendant argues that any privilege regarding the information at issue was waived by NOW due to its initial decision to bring this action.

The defendant's position is rebutted by NOW's claim of privilege, based upon the first amendment's protection of associational rights. This privilege requires particular protection in the case at bar, NOW argues, due to the potential for "retaliation against Chapter members by the defendant or other employers. . . ." NOW denies that its status as a plaintiff should result in a finding of waiver. Finally, NOW claims that the information sought is not relevant in that the individual members of NOW are not plaintiffs, rather, it is the Farmington Valley Chapter of NOW which is the plaintiff in this action.

Discussion of the Law

On the question of relevancy, the stance taken by each party is too extreme to be sustained. NOW argues that none of the information requested is relevant to this action, yet the complaint clearly alleges that the defendant's actions caused injury to members of NOW. It further alleges that, "NOW has members who are, have been, have sought, or are interested in seeking employment with defendant Sperry Univac and have been and are aggrieved by the sex-based and race-based discriminatory actions of the defendant." Notwithstanding the grammatical deficiencies of this charge, it does contain allegations of injury to four classes of individuals who are members of NOW: (1) those members who are employed by Sperry Univac, (2) those who were employed by Sperry Univac, and (3) those members who did attempt or (4) who may attempt to obtain employment at Sperry Univac. NOW proposes to identify individual members of the class "after a class is certified."[3] This position presupposes that certification is assured, but there is no basis for such an understanding. If a class is not certified, NOW can only go forward in this case by establishing that some of its members were injured, as alleged in the complaint. Therefore, the defendant's claim of relevance is, in part, persuasive.

NOW has alleged sexual and racial discrimination against some of its members. In order adequately to prepare its defense against these allegations, the defendant is entitled to discover the name, sex, race, current address, and occupation of every member of NOW, Farmington Valley Chapter, who is a current employee of the defendant, who was an employee of the defendant, and who was interested, or who claims that they may be interested, in seeking employment with the defendant. The defendant is not entitled to the requested information regarding any other member of NOW, since no injury to other members has been alleged. Further, the request for information regarding the present employers of the injured members is denied, at least at this stage, since the occupation of those members will be made known to the defendant.

Plaintiff NOW has raised the issue of privilege, based upon the first amendment's protection of associational rights. This privilege is designed

---

[3] NOW cites the case of *Brinkerhoff v. Rockwell International Corp.*, 83 F.R.D. 478 (N.D. Tex. 1979), in support of its claim that information regarding unnamed members of a class is not relevant. In that case, however, discovery was denied because the defendant sought to obtain information regarding people who had in no way assented to participation in the action. In the case at bar, there is no indication that NOW has brought suit on behalf of members who object to being represented by the association.

to protect members of groups from harassment and intimidation. *Bates v. City of Little Rock*, 361 U.S. 516 (1960); *NAACP v. Alabama*, 357 U.S. 449 (1958); *Bursey v. United States*, 466 F.2d 1059, 1083 (9th Cir. 1972). Further, NOW rejects the defendant's assertion that, whatever privilege NOW may have held, its status as a plaintiff amounts to a waiver of that privilege. * * *

* * * In the instant case, NOW has alleged that the defendant is guilty of a variety of harassing tactics, all of which were summarized in a concluding sentence of one paragraph in the complaint, "Defendant and its agents and employees have created an extremely unpleasant work environment for Ms. Madison." The allegations, if true, describe intolerable practices which must be prevented from recurring. However, there are substantial differences between the difficulties presently alleged by NOW and [the threats of physical coercion and other public hostility] which confronted the NAACP in Alabama in 1958. This is an important factor in weighing the infringement upon first amendment rights versus the defendant's right to prepare an adequate defense.

Finally, some consideration must be given to the defendant's argument that NOW, by entering this action as a plaintiff, has waived its associational privacy rights. This Court is not of the opinion that one's status as a plaintiff results in full waiver of associational privacy rights, yet it is evident that these rights have been given the fullest protection in those cases where they were claimed by defendants. NOW has assiduously pursued this action and it seeks substantial recovery from the defendant. * * * Fairness dictates that NOW, as a plaintiff, cannot realistically hope to pursue this suit in a risk-free atmosphere.

The foregoing serves to justify some infringement on the associational privacy rights of the members of NOW. However, those individuals have not completely sacrificed their privacy rights, simply by bringing this action. The defendant only requires the information at issue in order to prepare an adequate defense; that information cannot be used for any other purpose. Therefore, the Court finds that the defendant may discover the name, sex, race, current address, and occupation of every member of NOW, Farmington Valley Chapter, who is a current or former employee of the defendant, or who was, or may be, interested in seeking employment with the defendant. Further, the information revealed to defendant's counsel may not be communicated to any other person, including members of the defendant corporation, except upon further application to and specific order of this Court, subject to the contempt powers of the Court.

II. Plaintiffs' Motion to Compel Discovery

Facts

On December 22, 1978, the plaintiffs filed twenty-six interrogatories and six requests for production of documents. The defendant answered the first interrogatory and objected to the remaining twenty-five. Objections were also lodged against the requests for production of documents, excepting request number one and part of request number two.

The plaintiffs argue that broad discovery is essential in order that the Court may reach an accurate decision on the issue of class certification.

Comprehensive discovery, claim the plaintiffs, will reveal a pattern of discrimination carried on by the defendant. The information requested by the plaintiffs is stated to be "general policy information which should be available in some central way." The defendant's opposition to the proposed discovery is based on claims that the requests are overly broad and burdensome, they are irrelevant to the issue of class certification, and some of the material sought represents impermissible inquiries into privileged or confidential areas.

This suit is, as yet, in the pre-certification stage. If class certification is eventually denied, the suit can only go forward with a relatively few plaintiffs: (1) Susan C. Madison and (2) the Farmington Valley Chapter of NOW, as it represents those of its members injured by the defendant. Despite this possibility, the plaintiffs seek pre-certification discovery which could reach into some three hundred Sperry Rand plant facilities across the country, which could involve the personnel files of some thirty-five thousand employees. This could result, says the defendant, in an expenditure of approximately three million dollars. The plaintiffs have countered with the argument that the defendant's conclusions are the result of an exaggerated misconstruction of the interrogatories. There is some basis for this position. Interrogatory number twenty-two, for example, seeks discovery of any allegations, by employees, of sexual or racial discrimination. Instead of offering to supply copies of any applicant or employee complaints which may have been formally filed, the defendant suggests that the interrogatory can only be answered by a series of one-to-three hour interviews with eleven thousand supervisory and personnel representatives, at a cost of over five hundred thousand dollars. This type of misconstruction, however, is the exception rather than the rule. Further, the plaintiffs are adamant regarding their intention to extend their inquiries into every Sperry Rand facility. Such an approach inevitably would lead to an unnecessary magnification of cost and effort.

The plaintiffs have offered a list of information easily available to the defendant which the plaintiffs will accept as full or partial answers to interrogatories. Nonetheless, even this reduced list will result in an expenditure, by the *plaintiffs'* calculations, of three hundred thousand dollars. The plaintiffs have not supplied the Court with any affidavits regarding the source of their calculations, the defendant's basic estimates were carefully researched, and even if the plaintiffs' partisan figure of three hundred thousand dollars is correct, it nonetheless represents a very heavy burden on the defendant to satisfy initially the claims of one single employee.

Discussion of the Law
* * *

The [pre-certification] discovery permitted must be sufficiently broad in order that the plaintiffs have a realistic opportunity to meet the requirements [of Rule 23]; at the same time, the defendant must be protected from discovery which is overly burdensome, irrelevant, or which invades privileged or confidential areas. Discovery is not to be used as a weapon, nor must discovery on the merits be completed precedent to class certification. Unnecessarily broad discovery will not benefit either party. To spend either three million or three hundred thousand dollars, in order to move a mountain of documents and statistics from the defendant's facilities to the plaintiffs' offices, would be, in this pre-certification context, a wasteful and unjustifiable action.

To simply deny the requested discovery would force the plaintiffs to redesign their interrogatories, the results of which might then be subjected to new challenges by the defendant. * * * Consequently, after reviewing the plaintiffs' interrogatories and weighing the competing considerations of relevance, privilege, and undue burden, the Court finds that the following information is discoverable by the plaintiffs:

(1) Each of the twenty-four subsequent interrogatories shall be limited in application to three Sperry Rand facilities: the Sperry Univac Division facility located in Windsor, Connecticut, one Sperry Univac facility located in New Jersey, and one Sperry Univac facility located in Pennsylvania.[8] At this time, information regarding individual employees is only discoverable as it relates to those at management level.

[The court addressed each of the other discovery requests in turn, limiting the requests as it believed necessary in light of the considerations it noted above.]

* * *

NOTES AND QUESTIONS

1. What limitations on pre-certification discovery are illustrated in the *NOW* decision? Are the court's limitations reasonable? What other approaches could the court have taken to balance the various interests at stake?

2. In footnote three of the *NOW* decision, the court addressed *Brinkerhoff v. Rockwell International Corp.*, 83 F.R.D. 478 (N.D. Tex. 1979). In *Brinkerhoff*, defendants accused of employment discrimination sought discovery of the names of all class members in the putative class action. In holding that plaintiff was not required to identify the putative class members, the court reasoned:

> Defendants have failed to show why they need the names of these putative class members to defend against Plaintiff's claims of numerosity and commonality. Nor do defendants show a need to know the names of these women to evaluate the typicality of their claims. Defendants only need to know what the claims are, not who made them, to assess the similarity of those claims and plaintiff's claims. Typicality requires "that the claims or the defenses of the class 'resemble' or 'exhibit the essential characteristics of' those of the representatives." Resemblance and characteristics of a claim can be evaluated without knowing the identity of the claimant.
>
> * * *
>
> The court acknowledges defendants' need to know the general nature of the claims in order to argue plaintiff's claim is not typical and is peculiar. But defendants can obtain this information by taking

---

[8] The New Jersey and Pennsylvania facilities described are those facilities at which plaintiff Susan C. Madison applied for transfers. The discovery which is thus allowed should be sufficient to show a pattern of discrimination, if one exists, for purposes of class certification. At the same time, if class certification is denied, the named plaintiffs will be in possession of material which will be relevant for purposes of preparing their case, yet which will not have been assembled at great expense to the defendant.

plaintiff's deposition and asking her to describe the nature of the claims of the putative class members. The court is relying on plaintiff's representation she does not intend to present the putative class members at the class certification hearing unless those members have been identified to defendants. If plaintiff can prove the need for class action treatment without using the names of these putative class members, defendants can certainly defend against class certification without knowing the names of the putative class members.

Id. at 480–81. Did the *NOW* court accurately distinguish *Brinkerhoff*? Could the defendant in *NOW* have distinguished *Brinkerhoff* on other grounds? Could the *NOW* plaintiffs have argued more forcefully that the same considerations that motivated the court in *Brinkerhoff* should cause the *NOW* court to deny defendant's request for discovery?

iii. Discovery Directed to Absent Plaintiffs

BALDWIN & FLYNN V. NAT'L SAFETY ASSOCS.
United States District Court, Northern District of California, 1993.
149 F.R.D. 598.

LANGFORD, CHIEF MAGISTRATE JUDGE.

* * *

BACKGROUND

National Safety Associates [NSA] is a multilevel direct sales organization. Its products are household air and water filtration systems. One pays a fee to become a dealer or independent distributor. A dealer/distributor can advance and earn income through either one's own sales to the public or through the sales made by others recruited into the marketing program.

Plaintiffs [members of a direct sales organization for household air and water filtration systems] describe this as a "pyramid sales scheme." Members benefit from sales to others in the distribution chain, as well as retail sales to the public.

NSA says it has existed for twenty years. Plaintiffs say that it has existed in its present form only since 1986, at its present volume since 1988.

State regulators have accused NSA of fraud. It has settled with such regulators in ten states, having paid fines and penalties of $500,000.

In this lawsuit, plaintiffs claim violations of federal securities laws, RICO, and make pendent state law claims for fraud, unfair competition and false advertising.

DISCOVERY DISPUTE

Defendants wish to take the depositions of at least 15–20 of 44 unnamed class members. A Motion for Class Certification has been filed April 2, 1993, for hearing July 30, 1993.

Defendants say plaintiffs at one point were willing for defendant to depose 15 unnamed plaintiffs, half to be selected by each side. Plaintiffs deny this.

Defendants say this is not the usual securities fraud case, which is most often based on claims in a written prospectus. Defendants oppose class certification because they say that each plaintiff may have received a different "pitch" from a different person. Multiple speakers may number as many as 100. Many of the speakers may have been independent contractors, not agents of NSA. Plaintiffs may have relied on different aspects of the NSA presentations.

The defendant wants the court to hear from as many plaintiffs as possible, through their deposition transcripts, to decide whether the putative class members share common questions of law and fact.

It is critical to NSA's * * * Opposition to Class Certification to be able to demonstrate that each independent distributor relied on unique and separate aspects of the NSA proposition, or in fact relied on statements of other putative class members whose statements are not attributable to NSA.

* * *

APPLICABLE LAW

* * *

Defendants must have leave of court to take depositions of members of a putative class, other than the named class members—after first showing that discovery is both necessary and for a purpose other than taking undue advantage of class members. The burden is heavy to justify asking questions by interrogatories, even heavier to justify depositions. * * *

Plaintiffs say that the 42 putative class members are dispersed across the United States. The court should consider the need for efficiency and economy before ordering discovery.

A court may find that pre-certification discovery is needed; the extent of pre-certification discovery is at the discretion of the trial court; where the propriety of class certification cannot be fairly determined without discovery, it is an abuse of discretion to deny it.

Plaintiffs say that the allegations of the complaint and supporting declarations provide enough information to permit the court to decide whether to certify the class.

ANALYSIS

* * * Defendants are seeking depositions of anywhere from 12 to 20 of the unnamed plaintiffs in the as yet uncertified class. They say they need to provide evidence for the court that plaintiffs' claims do not have the common issues of fact and law required by Rule 23(a)(2) of Federal Rules of Civil Procedure for their case to be certified as a class action. Defendants claim that this case is not based on written materials, but on verbal inducements. Therefore, each plaintiff may have relied on a different "pitch" from a different person.

A court may not require plaintiffs to prove their case in order to be certified as a class. * * *

Plaintiffs in their complaint cite as sources of misrepresentation: promotional seminars, audio-tapes, videos, scripted telephone presentations, written promotional materials and other promotional efforts which NSA used to recruit dealer/distributors. Plaintiffs also offer examples of written promotional materials extolling the good life which NSA has brought to some of its dealer/distributors.

Plaintiffs have provided ample documentation of written and scripted materials upon which they relied before joining NSA. Any oral representations which might be revealed in plaintiffs' depositions would be only minor additions to the overwhelming volume of evidence of NSA's recruitment techniques.

Defendants have failed to demonstrate the need for depositions of unnamed class members. The motion of defendants to compel depositions of unnamed class members is DENIED.

* * *

LABORERS LOCAL 17 HEALTH & BENEFIT FUND V. PHILIP MORRIS, INC.
United States District Court, Southern District of New York, 1998.
1998 WL 241279.

DOLINGER, MAGISTRATE JUDGE.

Plaintiffs, consisting of nine employee benefit trust funds, have filed these parallel class action lawsuits to seek relief for purported fraud and other tortious conduct by the six principal domestic cigarette manufacturers and related defendants. The gist of the case is found in the plaintiffs' assertion that, for many decades, defendants concealed crucial information about the dangers of cigarette smoking and other exposure to tobacco products, and that, as a result, the plaintiff funds and other, similarly situated funds were required to pay gargantuan medical benefits to treat tobacco-related illnesses suffered by fund beneficiaries. The implication is that, had the pertinent information been disclosed, the funds would have undertaken different, and perhaps more aggressive, anti-smoking programs and perhaps other steps to limit such costs. The relevant injury, then, is to the "plaintiffs' infrastructure and financial stability."

The parties have commenced discovery that is directed to plaintiffs' recently filed motions for class certification [seeking certification under Rules 23(b)(2) and (3)]. Although merits discovery has not been stayed, it is the understanding of the parties, with the acquiescence of the court, that such discovery should be held in abeyance at present, at least until pending motions to remand a number of parallel suits have been disposed of by [the district court.]

Defendants claim that * * * discovery, in the form of interrogatories, document requests and depositions, is necessary in order to permit them to explore the degree of commonality, or lack thereof, among class members on the issue of reliance and, apparently, the extent and nature of their injury. Defendants argue that such information is required to assist them in resisting the class certification motion, specifically with regard to the existence of common questions, the predominance of such questions and the typicality of the named plaintiffs' claims.

The courts have frequently noted the "inevitable tension in the discovery of nonrepresentative class members because of the conflict between the competing interests of the absent class members in remaining passive and the defendant in having the ability to ascertain necessary information for its defense." Such discovery is not *per se* unavailable, although it is generally disfavored and will therefore not be permitted unless (1) the defendant demonstrates a clear need for the information for trial of those aspects pertinent to the class claims, (2) the court is satisfied that the discovery requests are narrowly tailored to their purpose and (3) the discovery is not intended to, and will not, impose undue burdens on the absent class members. The requirement of tailoring has also led a number of courts to deem document requests and interrogatories as preferable to depositions of class members.

In this case defendants argue that they need to explore the knowledge of individual class members as to smoking hazards during the pertinent period, the steps that those members took in reliance on that knowledge, and the extent to which they were misled by the alleged withholding of defendants' scientific data, that is, what the members did or failed to do because of their ignorance of the assertedly withheld information. All of this discovery is said to be needed in order to contest plaintiffs' class-action motion, presumably on the basis that the extent of each class member's knowledge and reliance is unique to that member, and hence that individual issues predominate over issues common to the purported class. Defendants also suggest that they may seek to contest the typicality of the named plaintiffs' claims.

In assessing defendants' assertion of need, we note that there are already nine named plaintiff funds from which defendants may obtain discovery of this nature. If, as appears altogether likely, each fund relied to a differing degree on the absence of the allegedly withheld information about the dangers of smoking, those differences may be apparent from discovery of those plaintiffs. We also note that, as defined by plaintiffs, the common issues on which they rely for certification are almost all concerned with the activities of the defendants rather than of the plaintiffs. This suggests that, insofar as relevant to the question of the predominance of common issues, there will not be much dispute between plaintiffs and defendants that the precise degree to which each class member relied will differ.[3]

In response, defendants assert that the nine plaintiffs do not constitute a sufficiently large universe to develop the necessary data. Moreover, they may also be heard to argue that the extent of the difference in reliance among class members will be relevant in assessing both the appropriateness of class certification and the choice of the current class representatives as typical of the class.

Defendants' argument about the need for a larger universe for discovery purposes is made in conclusory terms and without any specifics or evidentiary grounding. Moreover, defendants seek both written discovery—interrogatories and document production—and a deposition campaign that, by defendants' terms, would yield as many as fifty depositions of absent class members, in addition to their planned discovery of the nine class representatives and others, and they do so without concrete explanation for the size of this proposed expedition.

Despite the generality of defendants' presentation, it is not entirely unpersuasive. There is no question that plaintiffs allege conduct by defendants that was common to all of the plaintiffs, that is, the withholding of

---

[3] In fairness to defendants, however, at oral argument plaintiffs' counsel declined to concede that the precise form and extent of reliance varies among class members.

data and misrepresentations to the public at large. Nonetheless, the balance of the case concerns the class members' reactions to that conduct, and those responses are likely to have varied. If so, opposition to the certification motion will likely focus on both the degree of such variation and its significance for adjudicating plaintiffs' claims. It is also plausible that, in seeking to block certification, defendants will legitimately desire to delve into the typicality of the named plaintiffs' claims.

Given this focus, the discovery related to the certification motion will also center on reliance issues and perhaps on the significant distinctions, if there be any, between the relevant circumstances of the nine plaintiffs and the other class members. In view of that conclusion, we cannot say that the interest of the defendants in obtaining some information pertinent to these matters from some of the non-plaintiff class members is unjustified[6] or reflective of any bad-faith motives. Moreover, since the class members here are not the typical members of a plaintiff class—individuals with small claims and presumably limited means—but rather are organized entities providing financial and other benefits to members of their constituencies under pre-existing collective bargaining agreements, there is less concern that some controlled discovery will be unduly burdensome or imperil the maintenance of the class.

There does remain, however, a serious question as to the extent and scope of any discovery to be undertaken by the defendants. As noted, their current plans are both generally stated and seemingly very broad in scope. We are not prepared, at this stage and on the current record, to approve the extent of the discovery that they seek.

For present purposes, defendants may select a total of ten class members from the lists either already provided or soon to be provided by the plaintiffs, and may request documents from those members reflecting such matters as the nature of the class member's constituency (that is, the type of work done by the beneficiaries of the fund), the nature of the fund's activities that were purportedly affected by the defendants' alleged misconduct, and the degree and nature of the alleged effect, as well as any indication that the fund was already aware of the information purportedly withheld by defendants. Whether follow-up discovery from these members, particularly the use of narrative interrogatories or short depositions, will be permitted in preparation for opposing the class certification motion will depend on whether defendants can make a showing that specific further inquiry is warranted.

CONCLUSION

For the reasons noted, we approve a limited document request by defendants directed to ten non-plaintiff members for the purpose of preparing to respond to the certification motion. Our analysis is limited to that purpose, and is not intended to suggest any views as to the propriety of discovery addressed to class members concerning the merits of the case.

---

[6] I note that defendants' argument about typicality could be made in any case, and thus could be viewed as proving too much, since it would justify discovery of class members in virtually all cases. That said, we note that in many cases there will be little, if any, real question about the named plaintiffs' typicality, or else the facts pertinent to that question will be readily apparent from the face of the complaint or discovery directed solely to the named plaintiffs. That is not the case here, since the uniqueness of each fund's pertinent activities is neither self-evident nor likely to be learned solely from the plaintiff funds.

NOTES AND QUESTIONS

1. Based on *Baldwin & Flynn* and *Laborers Local 17 Health and Benefit Fund*, under what circumstances is it permissible to take discovery from absent potential class members? Why should such absent persons be afforded more protection from discovery than named class members? Are the approaches in *Baldwin & Flynn* and *Laborers Local 17 Health and Benefit Fund* consistent with each other? If not, how do they differ?

2. As a matter of strategy, is it better for defendants to seek extensive discovery from unnamed class members, hoping the court will "split the baby," or to draft carefully limited requests in an effort to appear reasonable? Do *Baldwin & Flynn* and *Laborers Local 17 Health and Benefit Fund* shed any light on this strategy decision? Similarly, are plaintiffs better off agreeing to *some* discovery against unnamed class members or opposing all such discovery?

3. *The Manual for Complex Litigation (Fourth)* suggests ways in which courts can limit pre-certification discovery of putative class members upon a proper showing:

> If precertification discovery of unnamed class members is appropriate, the court should consider imposing limits beyond those contemplated by the Federal Rules of Civil Procedure. Such limits might include the scope, subject matter, number, and time allowed for depositions, interrogatories, or other discovery directed to class representatives or unnamed class members, and might limit the period for completing certification-related discovery.

Manual for Complex Litigation (Fourth) § 21.14 (2004). How should a court decide which, if any, of these limitations is appropriate in a particular case?

4. In *David v. Signal Intern., LLC*, 257 F.R.D. 114 (E.D. La. 2009), the plaintiffs alleged that putative class members had been trafficked into the United States from India and other foreign countries and subjected to forced labor at defendant Signal International's post-Hurricane Katrina operations in Mississippi and Texas. The district court had previously denied defendants' motion to dismiss the claims—including violations of RICO, the Thirteenth Amendment, and the federal Trafficking Victims Protection Act. *See* 588 F. Supp. 2d 718 (E.D. La. 2008). Plaintiffs, after moving for class certification under Rules 23(b)(2) and (b)(3), sought a protective order precluding discovery on their current immigration status, post-termination employment status, and current addresses, arguing that such discovery was not relevant to the class members' substantive claims or the requirements of Rule 23. 257 F.R.D. at 122. Defendants argued, *inter alia*, that information as to the class members' current immigration status would allow them to test the plaintiffs' credibility and thus their adequacy as class representatives. *Id.* at 124. The court agreed with plaintiffs, finding the protective order necessary, "as 'it is entirely likely that any undocumented [litigant] forced to produce documents related to his or her immigration status will withdraw from the suit rather than produce such documents and face . . . potential deportation.'" *Id.* at 122 (citation omitted; alteration in original). The court found that "such examination would impose an undue burden on private enforcement of employment discrimination laws," and that "defendants' opportunity to test the credibility of plaintiffs does not outweigh the public interest in allowing employees to enforce their rights." *Id.* at 124. Is the court's ruling fair to the defendants? Was the court correct in imposing a balancing test to assess the need for discovery?

2. POST-CERTIFICATION DISCOVERY

Discovery issues frequently arise even after class certification has been granted. In most respects (aside from magnitude), the discovery disputes that accompany class actions resemble those in traditional, one-on-one litigation. Yet one recurring issue, already presaged in the preceding subsection, occurs only in class litigation—merits discovery directed to absent class members.

BRENNAN V. MIDWESTERN UNITED LIFE INS. CO.
United States Court of Appeals, Seventh Circuit, 1971.
450 F.2d 999.

Before SWYGERT, CHIEF JUDGE, and CUMMINGS and STEVENS, CIRCUIT JUDGES.

SWYGERT, CHIEF JUDGE.

The issue on this appeal is whether in a class action under Rule 23, Fed. R. Civ. P., those identifiable absent members of the representative plaintiff's class who received notice of the pendency of the suit and neither elected to be excluded nor entered an appearance may be required to submit to discovery under Rules 33 and 34, Fed. R. Civ. P., on pain of dismissal of their claims with prejudice for failure to respond. * * *

* * *

* * * Movants contend that absent class members are not "parties" to a suit and are consequently not subject to the "party" discovery procedures provided by Rules 33 and 34, Fed. R. Civ. P. Movants argue that Rule 23, Fed. R. Civ. P., contemplates an adversary contest involving only the representative member of a class, with all other members of the class being permitted passively to await the outcome of the principal suit, and that it is inconsistent with the purpose of Rule 23 to require any affirmative action from absent class members before the conclusion of the representative suit. While the question is a difficult one and there is some merit in movants' arguments, we hold that absent class members may, under certain circumstances, be required to submit to discovery under Rules 33 [Interrogatories to Parties] and 34 [Production of Documents and Things and Entry Upon Land For Inspection and Other Purposes] and that the sanctions of Rule 37 [Sanctions For Failure to Make Disclosure or Cooperate in Discovery] are available to compel compliance with such discovery orders.

Note should be made initially that there is a paucity of recorded precedent in this area. A few district courts have indicated that some form of discovery may be required of class members. Professor Moore has noted that, "A court may * * * give a dual or an additional notice, under [Rule 23](d)(2) to class members who do not opt out and require them to take some affirmative action as a condition of ultimate recovery." 3B J. Moore, *Federal Practice* ¶ 23.55, at 23–1161 (2d ed. 1969).

Rule 23 in terms does not speak of discovery from class members, but the spirit of the rule would seem to encompass such procedure particularly when subsection (d) is considered. *See* Professor Moore's observation, *supra*. We do not believe there is any real inconsistency between Rule 23's general policy of permitting absent class members to remain outside the principal action and our holding that in appropriate cases absent class members may be required to submit to discovery. It is true that an absent class member is given a "free ride" under Rule 23 and has no duty to actively engage in the prosecution of the action. Yet the absent class member's interests are identical with those of the named plaintiff and his rights and liabilities are adjudicated in the principal suit. If discovery from the absent member is necessary or helpful to the proper presentation and correct adjudication of the principal suit, we see no reason why it should not be allowed so long as adequate precautionary measures are taken to insure that the absent member is not misled or confused. While absent class members should not be required to submit to discovery as a matter of course, if the trial judge determines that justice to all parties requires that absent parties furnish certain information, we believe that he has the power to authorize the use of the Rules 33 and 34 discovery procedures.

The record shows that the district judge had valid reasons from the standpoint of preparing the case for trial for ordering the discovery in this case. The requests were not designed solely to determine the identity and amount of the class members' claims, but were also directed at obtaining information relating to certain defenses raised by Midwestern in the principal trial. Counsel for the named plaintiff admitted that the information sought by Midwestern was relevant to its claim that it was not liable to the class. Moreover, movants impliedly concede that the discovery was proper by their argument that Midwestern could have proceeded with its pretrial discovery under Rules 30 [Depositions Upon Oral Examination] and 31 [Depositions Upon Written Questions], Fed. R. Civ. P., to which the sanctions of Rule 45, Fed. R. Civ. P. [Subpoena], are applicable. Finally, there is nothing in the record to suggest that the discovery procedures were used as a tactic to take undue advantage of the class members or as a stratagem to reduce the number of claimants.

Movants argue, with some persuasiveness, that the initial notice under Rule 23(c)(2) which informed the class members that, unless they indicated a desire to be excluded, they would be included in the action which the named plaintiff and her counsel would prosecute on their behalf is inconsistent with a subsequent requirement that the absent class members furnish discovery information. Movants contend that the initial notice implied that class members could remain passive throughout the principal proceeding, and that consequently a subsequent requirement that a class member take some affirmative action is not only likely to create confusion in his mind but contradicts the implied understanding by which he elected to participate in the suit. The initial notice, however, in no way suggested that subsequent directions from the court could be ignored; and there can be little question about the adequacy of the subsequent notices concerning the discovery orders and the consequences of failure to supply the required information. It is not disputed that movants and those similarly situated received actual notice of the show-cause order and counsel's letter transmitting a copy to them. Nor is it disputed that they had previously received notice of the orders requiring the discovery and counsel's communications relating to the necessity for compliance. Moreover, even if movants had an initial impression that no action on their part was required to join the class and thereby participate in a recovery, if any, that impression should have been completely dispelled by the subsequent orders of the court and the efforts of counsel for the named plaintiff to get a response to those orders.

* * *

In summary, we hold that absent members of a class who receive notice of the pendency of the class suit may be subjected to the party discovery procedures permitted under the Federal Rules. Before ordering such discovery, a trial court must be assured that the requested information is actually needed in preparation for trial and that discovery devices are not used to take unfair advantage of "absent" class members. Moreover, adequate notice must be given so that such persons are fully informed of the discovery order and the possible consequences of their noncompliance with it. In this case both requirements were observed. * * *

STEVENS, CIRCUIT JUDGE (dissenting).

Movants were not parties to the litigation in which the district court purported to adjudicate their rights. They were not involuntary parties because they were not served with process. None of them became voluntary parties by entering an appearance or taking any other affirmative action.

* * *

* * * [M]ovants were unwilling or unable to respond to the discovery orders. In my opinion, they had a right to request exclusion from the class as an alternative to responding; they were never advised of any such right, and no such request was made on their behalf. They had no representative in court to advocate protection of their separate interests, whatever they may have been, in not divulging the requested information. * * *

* * * In this case movants' interest in avoiding the sanction of dismissal with prejudice—as opposed to the possible sanction of exclusion from the class—was a matter of indifference to the representative plaintiff. For that reason, which is entirely unrelated to the skill of counsel, movants were not adequately represented by any party to the case. * * *

* * *

MANUAL FOR COMPLEX LITIGATION (FOURTH)
Federal Judicial Center (2004) § 21.41.

Post-certification discovery directed at individual class members (other than named plaintiffs) should be conditioned on a showing that it serves a legitimate purpose. * * * One of the principal advantages of class actions over massive joinder or consolidation would be lost if all class members were routinely subjected to discovery. Most courts limit discovery against unnamed class members, but do not forbid it altogether. In setting appropriate limits, a judge should inquire whether the information sought from absent class members is available from other sources and whether the proposed discovery will require class members to obtain personal legal counsel or technical advice from an expert. Some courts have held that class members are not parties for the purpose of discovery by interrogatories, but may be required to respond to a questionnaire approved by the court. Others have permitted limited numbers of interrogatories upon a showing of need, limited the number of class members to whom interrogatories may be directed, limited the scope of the discovery to a brief, nonmandatory questionnaire relating to common issues, or have imposed on defendants the added cost of mailing otherwise permissible interrogatories to absent members of a plaintiff class. Deposing absent class members requires greater justification than written discovery.

* * *

NOTES AND QUESTIONS

1. For additional discussion and suggestions as to when discovery of absent class members might be permissible, *see* Note, *Developments in the Law: Class Actions*, 89 Harv. L. Rev. 1318, 1444–48 (1976) (arguing that, "[a]s a basic principle, discovery of absentees should be discouraged because of the potential for abuse," and that a defendant should first be "required * * * to seek the necessary information from the class representative," but noting that "limited discovery" might be appropriate where "the defendant establishes to the satisfaction of the court that discovery of absentees is essential for the prosecution of his case"). The Note also suggests that a "key consideration" in the discovery balance is "the substantiality of the class member's claim." *Id.* at 1448.

2. *Brennan*, the *Manual for Complex Litigation (Fourth)*, and the Harvard Note discussed in note 1 all point out that discovery against absent class members can be used by defendants for abusive purposes. What kinds of abuse may arise?

3. Should merits discovery against absent class members be allowed? If so, under what circumstances? The *Manual* asserts that courts require greater justification to allow depositions than to allow written discovery of absentees. Should that be the case? The Harvard Note asserts (in a portion not quoted in note 1) that more discovery should be allowed from class members who actively participate in the case. Should the level of participation be relevant? What, if any, other factors should be relevant?

4. If an absent class member refuses to comply with court-authorized discovery, what should be the appropriate sanction? Dismissal of the class member's claims with prejudice? Exclusion from the class?

5. Do *Brennan* and the *Manual* provide concrete guidance to trial courts as to when discovery against absent class members should be allowed? How compelling are then-Judge (subsequently Justice) Stevens's arguments in dissent in *Brennan*? How much of the debate turns on the adequacy of representation?

6. In the context of absent class members, should courts be more liberal in allowing merits discovery than pre-certification discovery?

PROBLEM

You represent the named plaintiff, Juanita Jones, in a putative class action. The complaint alleges that the defendant, Lumberboard, Inc., manufactured defective hardboard siding that rotted, causing damage to the houses of Jones and the other class members. What discovery would you request to establish a basis for class certification? If you were representing Lumberboard, what discovery would you want to enable you to defeat class certification? What merits discovery would you want from unnamed class members?

D. SUMMARY JUDGMENT MOTIONS

What is the impact on pending class action allegations when a court grants summary judgment to the defendant before ruling on class certification? Consider the following.

COWEN v. BANK UNITED
United States Court of Appeals, Seventh Circuit, 1995.
70 F.3d 937.

Before POSNER, CHIEF JUDGE, and CUDAHY and MANION, CIRCUIT JUDGES.

POSNER, CHIEF JUDGE.

The Truth in Lending Act requires lenders covered by the Act to disclose to the borrower at the time of making the loan not only the interest rate but also any "finance charge," defined as a charge that is payable directly or indirectly by the borrower and imposed directly or indirectly by the lender as an incident to or condition of the loan. 15 U.S.C. § 1605(a); 12 C.F.R. § 226.4(a). The concern behind this specific requirement is that a lender might try to make the interest rate look lower than it really is by charging part of the interest in the form of fees for services rendered in connection with the closing of the loan. One form this abuse might take—an example of indirect imposition—would be to hire an agent to perform a service in the making of the loan that the lender would normally perform and reflect in the interest rate, and to bill the borrower for the cost of the service, thus concealing part of the interest expense of the loan. * * * The plaintiffs accuse the defendant, Bank United of Texas, of [this conduct].

The plaintiffs borrowed money from the bank in order to refinance their home, on which they had two mortgages that they wanted to replace with a single mortgage from Bank United. The proceeds of the loan secured by this mortgage therefore went to the prior mortgagees to pay off their mortgages. The title insurance company that handled the closing hired an overnight courier to carry Bank United's checks to the mortgagees. The courier's fee was $14, which the title company charged to the plaintiffs. The bank did not disclose the fee on the Truth in Lending disclosure form that it furnished the plaintiffs, and the plaintiffs claim that the omission violated the Act because the fee was really a finance charge. By using an overnight courier rather than the mails the title company actually saved the plaintiffs money, because the extra expense was less than the interest saved by paying off the two mortgages sooner. So the plaintiffs incurred no loss—in fact received a windfall gain—as a result of the bank's alleged violation of the Act. Ordinarily one cannot seek damages (other than, in some cases, punitive damages) unless one has suffered a loss, but the Truth in Lending Act allows a monetary recovery even if the failure to disclose the charge caused the borrower no harm. 15 U.S.C. § 1640(a)(2).

* * *

* * * [A] suit for $14 (or $24—for the plaintiffs contend that a $10 assignment fee should also have been disclosed) may seem a quixotic project. Not so. First of all, the plaintiffs, if they win, would be entitled to statutory damages of $1000 without any proof of injury, because 15 U.S.C. § 1640(a)(2)(A) allows the recovery of twice the finance charge up to $1000,

and the finance charge here exceeded $500 (by quite a bit—$45,027.32, to be exact). Second, and more important, the plaintiffs are attempting to sue on behalf of a class of similarly situated customers of Bank United. The bank elected to move for summary judgment before the district judge decided whether to certify the suit as a class action. This is a recognized tactic, and does not seem to us improper. It is true that Rule 23(c)(1) of the civil rules requires certification as soon as practicable, which will usually be before the case is ripe for summary judgment. But "usually" is not "always," and "practicable" allows for wiggle room. Class actions are expensive to defend. One way to try to knock one off at low cost is to seek summary judgment before the suit is certified as a class action. A decision that the claim of the named plaintiffs lacks merit ordinarily, though not invariably, disqualifies the named plaintiffs as proper class representatives. The effect is to moot the question whether to certify the suit as a class action unless the lawyers for the class manage to find another representative. They could not here because the ground on which the district court threw out the plaintiff's claims [*see* below] would apply equally to any other member of the class. After granting the defendant's motion for summary judgment, therefore, and since (as was predictable, given the district judge's ground) no one stepped forward to pick up the spear dropped by the named plaintiffs, the judge denied the motion for class certification.

When the procedure that we have just described is followed, the defendant loses the preclusive effect on subsequent suits against him of class certification but saves the added expense of defending a class action and may be content to oppose the members of the class one by one, as it were, by moving for summary judgment, every time he is sued, before the judge presiding over the suit decides whether to certify it as a class action. If we reverse, the plaintiffs will be able to renew their motion for class certification; that is no doubt why they appealed the adverse judgment in this ostensibly trivial case.

[On the merits, the court held that the district court properly granted summary judgment because the courier fee was not a finance charge and the assignment fee was in fact disclosed.]

NOTES AND QUESTIONS

1. When would a defense attorney want to seek summary judgment before challenging class certification? When would he or she want to challenge the class issues first? Was the strategy adopted by the defense in *Cowen* a sound one?

2. In *Cowen*, the Seventh Circuit defended Bank United's use of summary judgment to avoid class certification, while recognizing Rule 23(c)(1)'s requirement that the certification decision be made "as soon as practicable." Rule 23(c)(1) has since been amended, requiring the certification decision to be made "at an early practicable time" (*see* discussion in Section (B)(1)(a) of this chapter). The Advisory Committee Notes to Rule 23(c)(1) state that the timing of the certification decision may be influenced by the fact that the "party opposing the class may prefer to win dismissal or summary judgment as to the individual plaintiffs without certification and without binding the class that might have been certified." This practice is not unusual:

> Most courts agree, and Rule 23(c)(1)(A) reflects, that such precertification rulings on threshold dispositive motions are proper, and one

study found a substantial rate of precertification rulings on motions to dismiss or for summary judgment.

Manual for Complex Litigation (Fourth) § 21.133 (2004). Should courts encourage parties to file dispositive motions prior to the decision on class certification? If so, under what circumstances? Should precertification consideration of summary judgment be mandatory, as a way of preventing plaintiffs from extracting nuisance-value settlements for meritless claims? *See* Randy J. Kozel & David Rosenberg, *Solving the Nuisance–Value Settlement Problem: Mandatory Summary Judgment*, 90 Va. L. Rev. 1849 (2004).

3. One issue that appellate courts have addressed is whether, when a defendant in a putative class action obtains summary judgment after a class is certified but before notice has been sent, the defendant can require plaintiff to notify the class. In *Schwarzschild v. Tse*, 69 F.3d 293 (9th Cir. 1995), the district court granted class certification and then granted defendants' summary judgment motion before notice of class certification was sent. The court (in a split decision) held that, by obtaining summary judgment, the defendants had forfeited their right to have notice of class certification sent to the class:

> [W]hen defendants obtain summary judgment before the class has been properly certified or before notice has been sent, they effectively waive their right to have notice circulated to the class under Rule 23(c)(2); in such cases, the district court's decision binds only the named plaintiffs. The defendants' novel interpretation of Rule 23(c) ignores its purpose, development, and text. Given that notice would serve no purpose in this case save to require the plaintiffs to engage in a costly and unnecessary exercise, we decline to apply Rule 23(c)(2) in a manner that is clearly contrary to the intent of its framers.

Id. at 297. Under the facts of *Schwarzschild*, should defendants have received the benefits of a classwide victory, given that a class had already been certified? Or should they be deemed to have waived that right by seeking summary judgment before notice had been sent?

4. If a trial court concludes—after a class has been certified but before notice has been sent—that summary judgment should be granted in favor of defendants, should it (i) issue its ruling before notifying the class, or (ii) withhold its ruling and send out notice?

5. In *Carvalho v. Equifax Information Services, LLC*, 588 F. Supp. 2d 1089 (N.D. Cal. 2008), the named plaintiff sought to represent a class of consumers, claiming the defendant credit reporting agencies had violated California and federal law by not adequately investigating disputed credit information. In response to plaintiff's motion for class certification, defendants moved for summary judgment and requested that the court consider that motion first because it was potentially dispositive. *Id.* at 1091. The court agreed, noting that under Ninth Circuit precedent, it was within the district court's discretion to rule on summary judgment first "[w]here the defendant assumes the risk that summary judgment in his favor will have only stare decisis [as opposed to *res judicata*] effect on the members of the putative class * * *." *Id.* at 1091 n.1 (citation and internal quotation marks omitted). The court went on to grant summary judgment for the defendants and accordingly denied plaintiff's motion for class certification as moot. 588 F. Supp. 2d at 1100. The abuse of discretion standard of review means, as a practical matter, that a district court's decision with respect to the sequence of ruling on summary judgment and class certification issues will rarely be reversed on appeal. What factors should guide the district court's exercise of its discretion in these cases?

E. JUDICIAL CONTROL OF PROCEEDINGS

1. ROLE OF THE JUDGE

What is the judge's role in class action litigation? Rule 23 obviously contemplates substantial court involvement in proceedings, principally as the guardian of the rights of absent plaintiffs during the course of class litigation. But how should the role be defined? Dean Minow addresses that question through the example of Senior United States District Court Judge Jack Weinstein of the Eastern District of New York, one of the most well-known class action judges of all time.

MARTHA MINOW, JUDGE FOR THE SITUATION: JUDGE JACK WEINSTEIN, CREATOR OF TEMPORARY ADMINISTRATIVE AGENCIES
97 Colum. L. Rev. 2010, 2012–33 (1997).

I. Getting Hold of the Whole Problem

Lawyers and judges are familiar with the narrowing effects of litigation. Pleading rules, pre-trial conferences, and increasingly managerial roles for judges usually point in the direction of reducing the issues for trial and streamlining the dispute before the court. * * * A very different approach, and one frequently pursued by Judge Weinstein, uses the powers of the court to expand the lawsuit to encompass more of the actors and institutions involved in a given problem.

* * *

Judge Weinstein's conduct in the *Agent Orange* litigation [*In re "Agent Orange" Prod. Liab. Litig.*, 506 F. Supp. 737 (E.D.N.Y. 1979), *rev'd*, 635 F.2d 987 (2d Cir. 1980); *In re "Agent Orange" Prod. Liab. Litig.*, 611 F. Supp. 1396 (E.D.N.Y. 1985), *aff'd in part and rev'd in part*, 818 F.2d 179 (2d Cir. 1987), *on remand*, 689 F. Supp. 1250 (E.D.N.Y. 1988)] provides [an] example of his commitment to embrace the whole situation rather than use litigation to narrow the issues. This litigation, a consolidation of more than 600 cases, alleged that Vietnam veterans and their family members wrongfully suffered injuries due to exposure to a chemical substance produced by companies under contract to the United States and used in conducting the war. Judge Weinstein took over the case from another judge, and quickly adopted a commitment to a wide lens and inclusive party structure for the case—a sharp departure from the approach taken by the judge previously assigned to the case. Judge Weinstein sought to keep the United States government as a party in the case, involve more defendants, and include within the scope of the suit all potential claimants, including children not yet born. The case ultimately involved approval of a class action despite difficulties identifying all of the individual plaintiffs. It ended with a monetary settlement, approved by Judge Weinstein and affirmed by the Court of Appeals for the Second Circuit, which established a structure for processing the claims of individual plaintiffs.

Especially in complex tort cases, Judge Weinstein has repeatedly structured suits as efforts to achieve "total peace," and therefore approved plans to include potential future claims. * * * In complex tort cases, civil rights cases, and other contexts, Judge Weinstein's search for global resolutions has involved six distinctive elements: (1) he has sought prospective as well as compensatory solutions; (2) he has permitted the involvement of multiple parties and tried to keep seemingly marginal parties in the suits; (3) he has included potential reforms of political and economic systems within the ambit of analysis in individual cases; (4) he has managed cases actively; (5) he has appointed additional court officers and given them unusual powers not only to find facts, but also to hold meetings and devise plans for the future treatment of the problems behind the suits; and (6) he and his court-appointed officers have used community-wide hearings and other such devices to promote extensive debate and participation in deliberating the issues at hand.

* * *

Judge Weinstein's underlying vision conceives of the judiciary as an institution primarily connected with, and obliged to serve, the larger community. * * * Even those who share this vision may be skeptical that a federal court has the tools to pursue total justice, much less to engage in that pursuit through a participatory process involving large numbers of individuals and groups. Judge Weinstein's techniques of innovation, thus, deserve attention not only in their own terms, but as tentative means to pursue his ambitious vision.

II. Inventive Procedural Techniques

To maintain the involvement of a broad range of individuals and institutions in particular lawsuits, Judge Weinstein has devised creative rulings on a range of technical procedural issues * * *. These individual rulings show erudition and a willingness to stretch, if not defy, existing rules; they also reflect Judge Weinstein's larger vision of global resolution and total peace. * * * Judge Weinstein's inclusive approach is aspirational and proceeds even when imperfectly achieved. His gifts of persuasion and pressure reflect not only personal traits, but also a strategy for producing inclusive results. His court's actions often set in motion the equivalent of a temporary administrative agency, and the technical rulings necessary to accomplish this act of creation underscore Judge Weinstein's brilliance, creativity, and audacity.

A. Technical Rulings

Judge Weinstein's technical rulings often depart from the common practice of courts to use procedural rules to sift, narrow, curb, or avoid altogether the lawsuits brought before them. * * *

* * * Judge Weinstein experimented with innovative choice-of-law rules in the *Agent Orange* case. There, no single trial could proceed with all of the plaintiffs and defendants if the laws of different states and nations had to apply to each particular claim, based on the plaintiffs' and defendants' locations and contacts. Moreover, a strange kind of unfairness would ensue if soldiers who had received the same exposure to *Agent Orange*, with the same injuries, were to obtain different court judgments based on the happenstance of their home states.

Judge Pratt, who first presided over the case, concluded that federal common law should apply, and thus permitted a unified trial, but the court of appeals reversed in an interlocutory appeal. Judge Weinstein was left with the apparent morass posed by more than 600 consolidated cases involving multiple state and national laws applicable to 2.4 million veterans, their families (including children not-yet born), and soldiers from Australia and New Zealand. [Judge Weinstein] * * * declared that *any* state court would look to a "national consensus law" on manufacturers' liability, relevant defenses, and damages. Thus, [he] reasoned that his federal court must do the same. * * * He treated his own announcement of national consensus law as a provisional ruling to guide the parties' thinking. He thus insulated his reasoning from further appellate review pending the case's denouement. * * *

* * *

B. The Personal as Powerful

No small measure of Judge Weinstein's innovative success depends on his personal powers and techniques. Most obvious is his stance as an active judge. A litigant in Judge Weinstein's court must expect the judge to take initiative in shaping the suit, to establish strict and quick time lines for the litigation, to explore innovative substantive norms, to appoint masters, to work with magistrates, and to devise expert panels to move discovery, pretrial scheduling, and fact-finding along, while promoting settlement throughout the process. * * *

* * * Judge Weinstein has been known to act "as if he were dealing not with a case at law, but rather with a political problem that required a political solution transcending the legal conflict between plaintiffs and defendants." To do so, he has introduced, or emphasized, uncertainty about the legal and factual issues in order to encourage the parties to settle, while also often involving broader sectors of the community in hearings on the fairness of proposed settlements, or potential plans for community change. These strategies at times make the judge himself seem more threatening and unpredictable to the parties than the opposing parties seem to each other, while at other times they make the judge seem like a person who understands how much people want to participate and be heard.

C. Creator of Temporary Administrative Agencies

* * *

Judges like Judge Weinstein engage in action that does more than resemble the creation of administrative agencies. Creation of claims processing facilities, use of public hearings, and consultation with community members and experts amount to the establishment of uniquely temporary and contextually specific administrative processes. These devices are framed around the parties to a litigation. The court, and the adjunct actors employed by the court, perform the work of processing claims under simplified procedures and management, seeking to fulfill party expectations swiftly. * * *

* * * [Although] it is fair to point to the similarities between these judicially created claims procedures and legislatively created administrative agencies, the differences between the two are * * * striking. Two important differences divide court-created administration systems from established administrative agencies: (1) the fact of court creation rather than legislative or executive authorization, and (2) their temporary, collapsible struc-

ture as compared to the more enduring, and at times entrenched, bureaucratic nature of traditional administrative agencies. The first invites intense scrutiny and potentially fatal objection on Article III and separation-of-powers grounds; the second may offer an intriguing challenge to other forms of administration. Both are, in my view, valuable contributions to American law and politics.

1. *Separation of Powers*—If a federal court, rather than the legislative or executive branches, creates an administrative agency, it is fair to inquire into the potential breach of separation-of-powers requirements and bounded authority for the judiciary. Has the court strayed into the domain of the executive to enforce the law or taken over the task of the legislature to devise prospective rules and establish governmental agencies? Have appointed judges stepped into the fray reserved for elected officials? * * *

* * *

Three modest defenses can be offered on behalf of * * * judges who use judicial resources to respond to such social problems despite inaction by the elected branches. The first is precisely the inaction of the elected branches: The vacuum created by their inaction leaves judges with properly filed, concrete claims, requiring some sort of response. * * *

Judicial action actually may trigger action by the other branches, and thereby promote the vision of overlapping and checking branches of government that lies behind the separation of powers. * * *

Second, judicial action may be defended here as continuous, rather than discontinuous, with other forms of adjudication. * * * [A]ll judicial action requires appropriations and expenditures of public funds, ranging from the salaries of judges and clerks to outlays for paper and computer disks. Enforcement of the simplest damages award requires the use of personnel to process forms and, at times, to execute liens on property. There is no sharp line separating the tasks of adjudication and the tasks of implementing the law. * * *

Third, exposure and defense of the boundaries between the branches are necessary for reasoned debate: The initiative of someone like Judge Weinstein can generate public debate and analysis to sharpen understandings of separation of powers, a crucial element of our governmental structure. * * *

2. *Temporary Administration*—An administrative agency established by the legislature or the executive may have an endpoint or sunset provision terminating its existence, but this is not the common practice. Instead, such administrative agencies, once established, tend to endure and require massive efforts to trim them, much less to close them down. The administrative processes established by courts, in contrast, have very specific time limitations, even if they endure for several years. * * *

Many observers of bureaucracies emphasize their self-perpetuating tendencies and their capacity to redefine tasks to justify the continuation of the bureaucracy itself. In this light, self-limiting administrative initiatives offer real benefits in terms of cost savings and accountability. * * *

III. Critiques and Responses

Judge Jack Weinstein exemplifies public law judging, with all the virtues and vices of that phenomenon. He exhibits bold, pragmatic responsiveness to complex problems. He combines brilliant technical and deft personal abilities to manage polycentric disputes. But he treats rules like pipe cleaners to be bent or tossed aside. And his personal powers risk extending to the point of insulating his own actions from review or limitation. Quite aside from objections based on separation-of-powers concerns, Judge Weinstein can be criticized for using his personal strengths to produce settlements, rather than to declare and enforce the law; to impose his own views, rather than to shepherd fair negotiations among the parties; and to shield his actions from review by higher courts. These are serious and weighty objections that help to highlight occasions where even those who hold him in the utmost regard may conclude that he has misstepped.

A. Supervising Settlements vs. Declaring the Law

When a judge uses the structure of a federal court to grab the whole of complex problems, negotiated settlements are more likely results than trials. If done repeatedly and systematically, this use of the court tilts away from its function of declaring the law and toward its role in resolving disputes. * * *

* * * The practical concern, which is weighty, involves how to assure that settlements are fair—that weaker, less well funded parties are not perpetually induced to forgo good claims because of the sheer costs of litigating and living with uncertainty. Judicial guidance through pre-trial conferences and supervision of settlements, especially in the context of class actions, should provide some check, but then confidence in the judge becomes the central point of contention—and this is precisely the concern raised by the second objection.

B. The Person of the Judge

The objection actually comes in two versions: first, reliance on the person of the judge exposes litigants, and society, to risks of abuse of power; and, second, decisions that depend upon the brilliance and compassion of even an exceptional person may inspire other, less talented people to impose their personal views through the office of the judge. The underlying ideal could be called "separation of persons" from the office of the judge. Somehow, the role of the impartial arbiter who is obligated to interpret the law is supposed to confine and constrain individual discretion, preference, and politics. As applied to Judge Weinstein, this ideal supports an objection: Judge Weinstein allegedly has abused his power, or, even if he has not, he inspires others to act in ways that might produce abuses of power. Instead of such conduct, proceeds the objection, all judges should be limited to settled routines. Otherwise, broad powers exercised by a person with whose values one agrees would remain available to be exercised by someone with less agreeable values. Moreover, the role of the judge should be designed for the ordinary, not the extraordinary person.

* * *

C. Unreviewable Discretion

The one remaining check provided by the system against abusive behavior by an active judge is the possibility of appellate review. Of course, a thoughtful trial judge can shield many judgments from review by clothing them in factual findings or other matters left to trial court discretion. Subject then to the "abuse of discretion" standard, only truly egregious decisions will be overturned.

Once again, the *Agent Orange* case provides an illustration—and it is one that presses the limits of acceptability. Judge Weinstein issued many "tentative" rulings in the case, such as his notion of "national consensus law" to handle the choice-of-law problem, yet none of these rulings remained subject to review once the case ended in settlement. This, I believe, should not provide great cause for concern precisely because the settlement erased all of those rulings: They have no binding force in that, or any subsequent, case. However, such rulings undoubtedly affected the settlement process; and * * * assuring the availability of an independent judge should the case proceed to trial might help both the appearance and assurance of fairness in future cases. In addition, where the settlement resolves a class action, appellate review of the trial judge's requisite approval provides a potential means to check abuse.

More worrisome is the basic problem that no reviewing court is likely to want to undo the settlement of a sprawling, messy case. Some comfort against this prediction is afforded by the actual behavior of the Court of Appeals for the Second Circuit in the *Agent Orange* case, which reformulated aspects of the trial court's reasoning. Yet, appellate handling of subsequent claims, filed in state court but moved through extraordinary procedural maneuvers to Judge Weinstein's court and merged there into the settlement, seems very much an abdication of independent review. The reviewing courts approved the remarkable use of the All Writs Act to remove a newly filed Texas state court case to federal court—despite the absence of independently existing grounds for federal jurisdiction. The predictable transfer of the case to Judge Weinstein's chambers ensured that no fresh judicial eyes would deal with the merits of the newly filed claims. Instead, those claims were absorbed in the preexisting settlement, with the rubber stamp of the Second Circuit.

Perhaps, ironically, the most reassuring defense of Judge Weinstein comes from the pattern of reversals that earned him the nickname, "reversible Jack." Frequent reversals by the appellate courts indicate some degree of review, although inevitably only a small portion of cases end up on appeal. At the same time, frequent reversals should not be understood as a measure of a trial judge's incompetence. Never to be reversed is not a badge of honor. If the law is ever to grow and respond to changing circumstances, trial judges need to push and stretch it. Those closest to the situations presented in court especially need to test the settled patterns of case law and practice against more immediate perceptions of what justice requires. Moreover, it is "reversible Jack" who helps judges, lawyers, and students understand precisely the contingent boundaries of the law. In this way, reversed trial court decisions teach the same way that dissenting opinions do. The presence and publication of rejected positions educate the entire community about the range of concerns that could be raised, about the lines of arguments rejected at least temporarily, and about avenues for decision that could open in the future.

If Judge Weinstein did not exist, law professors would have to invent him, but we could never convince students that such a smart, learned, creative, and iconoclastic person actually served as a judge. A legal system filled with Judge Weinsteins, however, would be unimaginable, and probably undesirable. At the same time, a legal system without him would be deeply impoverished.

MANUAL FOR COMPLEX LITIGATION (FOURTH)
Federal Judicial Center (2004) § 10.13.

Effective judicial management generally has the following characteristics:

• *It is active.* The judge anticipates problems before they arise rather than waiting passively for counsel to present them. Because the attorneys may become immersed in the details of the case, innovation and creativity in formulating a litigation plan frequently will depend on the judge.

• *It is substantive.* The judge becomes familiar at an early stage with the substantive issues in order to make informed rulings on issue definition and narrowing, and on related matters, such as scheduling, bifurcation and consolidation, and discovery control.

• *It is timely.* The judge decides disputes promptly, particularly those that may substantially affect the course or scope of further proceedings. Delayed rulings may be costly and burdensome for litigants and will often delay other litigation events. The parties may prefer that a ruling be timely rather than perfect.

• *It is continuing.* The judge periodically monitors the progress of the litigation to see that schedules are being followed and to consider necessary modifications of the litigation plan. Interim reports may be ordered between scheduled conferences.

• *It is firm, but fair.* Time limits and other controls and requirements are not imposed arbitrarily or without considering the views of counsel, and they are revised when warranted. Once established, however, schedules are met, and, when necessary, appropriate sanctions are imposed * * * for derelictions and dilatory tactics.

• *It is careful.* An early display of careful preparation sets the proper tone and enhances the court's credibility and effectiveness with counsel.

The judge's role is crucial in developing and monitoring an effective plan for the orderly conduct of pretrial and trial proceedings. Although elements and details of the plan will vary with the circumstances of the particular case, each plan must include an appropriate schedule for bringing the case to resolution. Case-management plans ordinarily prescribe a series of procedural steps with firm dates to give direction and order to the case as it progresses through pretrial proceedings to summary disposition or trial. * * *

* * *

NOTES AND QUESTIONS

1. What admirable qualities does Dean Minow see in Judge Weinstein's bold manner of dealing with multi-party litigation? What risks does she identify? Should Judge Weinstein serve as a model for class action judging? What effects would such an approach have on the federal judiciary? On the development of class action law?

2. Some commentators have been considerably less measured than Dean Minow in their assessments of Judge Weinstein, and in particular his handling of the *Agent Orange* litigation. For example, Professor Schuck observed:

> On one view, Weinstein flagrantly abused his exalted position. He pushed the parties here, pulled them there, reformulated legal doctrine, self-consciously used procedural rules to shape desired substantive outcomes, emphasized one thing to the PMC [Plaintiffs' Management Committee] and another to the chemical companies, employed special masters to do as agents what he as principal knew he should not do directly (for example, communicating with each side *ex parte*), articulated his views of the merits publicly, and used evidentiary rulings to decide fundamental factual disputes. In a sense, he played a massive game of chicken in which he made highly questionable decisions while working for a settlement that would render them invulnerable to appeal. Through these stratagems, he transformed the court from the essentially reactive, umpirelike institution that [District Judge George Pratt, the prior *Agent Orange* judge] embodied into that of an active, engaged policymaker.
>
> On another view, however, Weinstein's extraordinary moves were no more than was demanded by an extraordinary case like *Agent Orange*. His legal innovations—his propensity to "make things up as he goes along"—can be seen as the quintessential work of the common-law judge, "working the law pure" as it is applied to unforeseen cases in unprecedented circumstances, devising judicial solutions in an area of policy in which legislatures have been content to permit the courts to take the lead. * * *

* * *

> In *Agent Orange*, Judge Weinstein's problem-solving decisions imaginatively reconceptualized and reconstructed tort law for mass exposures, combining its traditional features with an innovative public law design. That eclecticism, however, combined some of the most worrisome features of each approach. By preserving traditional tort concepts—for example, each litigant's right to an individualized adjudication of specific causation and damages—he hoped to draw upon tort law's distinctive moral integrity and coherence, an important source of legitimacy. But those concepts were prohibitively expensive and manifestly unworkable in the context of a case like *Agent Orange*, as Weinstein fully appreciated. He therefore tried to graft several elements of a new species, the public law remedy, onto the traditional tort law stock.
>
> The resulting hybrid, however, engendered new difficulties even as it boldly grappled with old ones. It sacrificed individual litigants'

interests to collective ones. It relied heavily upon inevitably flawed, limited epidemiological techniques. It exalted and personalized the judge's role in controlling, directing, and terminating the litigation. It created a dependency upon massive class actions and upon the motives of the financiers and lawyers who support and manage them. It further weakened the already attenuated relationship between lawyers and clients. It resorted to procedural shortcuts and necessarily crude, categorical distributions. It encouraged "nuisance suits." More generally, it attempted to shoehorn an aggregative, probabilistic, policy-oriented methodology into legal forms designed to express individualistic, moralistic, corrective justice values. In *Agent Orange*, Weinstein's approach ended up compromising and distorting both the new methodology and the old forms—and did so at an extremely high cost.

Peter H. Schuck, *Agent Orange on Trial: Mass Toxic Disasters in the Courts* 259–60, 295–96 (1987). What is the appropriate role for the judge in the face of a mass tort like the *Agent Orange* litigation? What are the consequences of taking a proactive approach to such cases, as opposed to relying on more traditional techniques? For an account of the *Agent Orange* litigation by Judge Weinstein himself, see Jack B. Weinstein, *Preliminary Reflections on Administration of Complex Litigations*, 1 Cardozo L. Rev. 1, 6–10 (2009). *See also id.* at 10 (concluding that "[t]he Agent Orange controversy did establish that class actions were useful in very complex cases that often involve political as well as economic and scientific issues").

3. Does the *Manual for Complex Litigation (Fourth)*'s discussion of the role of the judge in complex litigation shed any light on a proper conception of the judge's role in managing a class action? In what ways does the Weinstein model of judging conform to, or depart from, the *Manual*'s description?

2. RULE 23(d)(1)(A)

Rule 23(d) grants courts broad discretion to make appropriate orders in a class action. *See, e.g., Cnty. of Suffolk v. Long Island Lighting Co.*, 710 F. Supp. 1422, 1425 (E.D.N.Y. 1989) (Rule permits court wide latitude in framing orders that facilitate conduct of litigation), aff'd, 907 F.2d 1295 (2d Cir. 1990); *Weight Watchers v. Weight Watchers Int'l*, 53 F.R.D. 647, 650, 652 (E.D.N.Y. 1971) ("The clear intent of [R]ule 23(d) is that the judge assigned to try the class action exercise, in his discretion, power to control the litigation, including the issuance of orders to prevent or remedy abuse."). Under Rule 23(d), the court is not rigidly bound in the types of orders it may issue; nor does the stage of the litigation necessarily restrict when it may issue such orders. The following discussion addresses the court's powers under the former Rule 23(d)(1) [current Rule 23(d)(1)(A)].

CHARLES A. WRIGHT, ARTHUR R. MILLER & MARY K. KANE, FEDERAL PRACTICE AND PROCEDURE
Thomson West (3d ed. 2005), Vol. 7B § 1792, at 6–11.

Due to their multiparty character, class actions often involve significant duplication of effort, which leads to delay and increased expense. In an attempt to reduce these undesirable byproducts to a minimum, Rule 23(d)(1) [current Rule 23(d)(1)(A)] specifically gives the court the power to make appropriate orders "determining the course of proceedings or prescribing measures to prevent undue repetition or complication in the presentation of evidence or argument."† * * *

Many of the powers available to the court to control the course of class actions are specifically delineated in other federal rules. For instance, in combination with its powers under Rule 23(d)(1) the court may order additional parties joined under Rule 19; may order separate trials or make other orders to prevent delay or prejudice under Rule 20(b); and may drop or add parties under Rule 21. In addition, the court may "prevent disruption of the orderly progress of a case involving multiple parties, where some but not all of the parties have disposed of the litigation concerning them and the losing party seeks to appeal therefrom on a piecemeal basis" under Rule 54(b); may issue an order under Rule 26(c) to protect a party or witness from "annoyance, embarrassment or oppression" in discovery; and may consolidate actions under Rule 42(b).

Orders under subdivision (d)(1) may be combined with a pretrial conference order under Rule 16 and all of the powers of a court set out in Rule 16 are available under Rule 23(d)(1). Thus, the court may limit and define the class issues more precisely during a pretrial conference and then prescribe a sequence for the presentation of the issues in order to aid the triers of fact. In addition, the court may place restrictions on the presentation of evidence and the calling of witnesses, especially expert witnesses, in order to minimize duplication at trial. When there are multiple counsel on either side, the court may determine the order in which they will be permitted to present evidence or to examine or cross-examine a witness. In a related vein, the court may decide not to put all of the class action machinery into operation at the outset of the litigation or it may choose to structure the adjudicatory process in the hope of reducing costs and simplifying the trial. * * *

* * *

A number of other types of orders designed to control or expedite the litigation may be issued by the court under Rule 23(d)(1). When similar actions, either class or individual, are proceeding before several courts, one or more of the tribunals may stay the proceeding before it pending the outcome of the other action. The court also may stay an action temporarily. * * * In order to prevent the case from becoming unwieldy, the court, either under Rule 23(d)(1) or Rule 23(d)(3), can direct that the class be closed to future intervenors. * * *

3. OTHER PROVISIONS OF RULE 23(d)(1)

In addition to subsection (d)(1)(A), Rule 23(d)(1) provides several other mechanisms for judicial control and supervision.

a. Rule 23(d)(1)(B)(i) gives courts the power to require that "appropriate notice" be given "to some or all class members" of any step in the action. Does Rule 23(d)(1)(B) also grant substantive rights? For example,

---

† Although subsequent, non-substantive amendments to Rule 23(d) made slight stylistic changes to the language quoted here, the discussion of Rule 23(d) remains up to date. For the current language of Rule 23, see the Preface, following the Table of Secondary Authorities, at the beginning of this casebook. [Ed.]

Rule 23(d)(1)(B)(iii) gives the district court discretion to notify class members of the "opportunity * * * to intervene and present claims or defenses, or to otherwise come into the action * * *." Does this mean that Rule 23(d)(1)(B)(iii) gives class members a substantive right to intervene? *See Baker v. Wade*, 769 F.2d 289 (5th Cir. 1985) (government official "satisfied the requirements of both [former] Fed. R. Civ. P. 23(d)(2) and 24(a)(2) [permissive intervention]").

b. Under Rule 23(d)(1)(C), a court may make appropriate orders that "impose conditions on the representative parties or on intervenors" in a class action suit. According to the Advisory Committee Notes, this subdivision "reflects the possibility of conditioning the maintenance of a class action, *e.g.*, on the strengthening of the representation * * * and recognizes that the imposition of conditions on intervenors may be required for the proper and efficient conduct of the action." [Former] Fed. R. Civ. P. 23(d)(3) Advisory Committee Notes. Some examples of the types of orders often made under subdivision (d)(1)(C) and its functionally equivalent predecessors include the following:

- A court may require the representatives to divide one class action into multiple actions, in order to separate incompatible claims. *See, e.g., Smith v. N. Am. Rockwell Corp.*, 50 F.R.D. 515 (N.D. Okla. 1970) (ordering four plaintiffs with different types of job skills, different jobs, and who were employed by different departments of large company to file four separate class actions).
- When it appears that the attorney chosen by the named plaintiff lacks the resources for the expanded litigation, the court may require, pursuant to Rule 23(d)(3) [current Rule 23(d)(1)(C)], that representative parties appoint additional counsel as a condition of certification. *See, e.g., Cullen v. N.Y. State Civil Serv. Comm'n*, 435 F. Supp. 546, 563–64 (E.D.N.Y. 1977).
- A court has the discretionary power to order class representatives to acquiesce to the intervention of another class member in order to improve representation of the class. *See, e.g., Groves v. Ins. Co. of N. Am.*, 433 F. Supp. 877, 888 (E.D. Pa. 1977).
- A court may impose conditions on intervenors. *See, e.g., Am. Pipe & Constr. Co. v. Utah*, 414 U.S. 538, 555 n.25 (1974). For instance, a court may set a final date for intervention or may limit the intervenors' rights to participate with respect to certain issues. *See, e.g., Shore v. Parklane Hosiery Co.*, 606 F.2d 354, 357 (2d Cir. 1979) (declining to disturb district court's grant of intervention for limited purpose of participation in settlement-approval hearings).
- A court may limit communications between counsel and potential class members. *See, e.g., Weight Watchers v. Weight Watchers Int'l*, 455 F.2d 770, 773 (2d Cir. 1972); *Zarate v. Younglove*, 86 F.R.D. 80, 93 (C.D. Cal. 1980). This issue is discussed in Chapter 5(B)(2).

c. Rule 23(d)(1)(D) authorizes a court to make appropriate orders that "require that the pleadings be amended to eliminate allegations about representation of absent persons and that the action proceed accordingly * * *." The most common order under subdivision (d)(1)(D) is one eliminating all class-action allegations after the denial of a motion for class certification or after the decertification of a class. Other orders issued under (d)(1)(D) include orders limiting or modifying class treatment. For example, the court may require a specific modification of the allegations to reduce the size of the class. *See, e.g., Phila. Elec. Co. v. Anaconda Am. Brass Co.*, 43 F.R.D. 452 (E.D. Pa. 1968) (allowing one of three classes to proceed as originally defined, but narrowing two classes). The court also has the discretion under (d)(1)(D) to direct that a class be divided into subclasses or to order the separate trial of individual issues that cannot be handled on a classwide basis. *See, e.g., Green v. Wolf Corp.*, 406 F.2d 291, 300–01 (2d Cir. 1968).

d. Rule 23(d)(1)(E) authorizes a court hearing a class action to issue orders that "deal with similar procedural matters." Subdivision (d)(1)(E) covers various orders that are not specifically provided for in the other provisions of Rule 23(d)(1). The inclusion of Rule 23(d)(1)(E) "makes it clear that the orders expressly provided for in [current subdivision (d)(1)(A)–(B)] are not exclusive and do not exhaust the court's power to manage a class action." 7B Charles A. Wright, Arthur B. Miller & Mary K. Kane, *Federal Practice and Procedure: Civil 3d* § 1796, at 53 (2005). Although the court has considerable latitude in the management of class actions under subdivision (d)(1)(E), its powers are limited by the words "similar procedural." This makes it clear that a court may not issue orders, "in the guise of managing the action, that actually substantially alter a party's ability to present the merits of his claim or defense." *Id.* at 54.

It is somewhat difficult to determine in court opinions when subdivision (d)(1)(E) is being used, because there is considerable overlap between (d)(1)(E) and (d)(1)(A)–(D). In addition, most courts do not specifically indicate whether their orders are being issued under Rule 23(d)(1)(E). This failure to indicate the source of authority is of little consequence, however, because "as a practical matter it does not make any difference whether the court's order is categorized under [former] clause (d)(5) [current (d)(1)(E)] or another portion of 23(d)." *Id.* at 55.

Rule 23(d)(1)(E) has been used to authorize plaintiffs to opt out of a mandatory class in a Rule 23(b)(1)(B) limited-fund case on the ground that fair and efficient conduct of an action requires allowance of opt-out rights. *See, e.g., Cnty. of Suffolk v. Long Island Lighting Co.*, 907 F.2d 1295, 1304 (2d Cir. 1990) (exercising discretion under [former] (d)(5) [current (d)(1)(E)] to allow class member to opt out); *Eubanks v. Billington*, 110 F.3d 87, 96 (D.C. Cir. 1997) (noting, relying on *Suffolk*, that language of [former] Rule 23(d)(5) [current (d)(1)(E)] is sufficiently flexible to afford district courts discretion to grant opt-out rights in (b)(1) and (b)(2) class actions "when necessary to facilitate the fair and efficient conduct of the litigation"); *In re PaineWebber Ltd. P'ships Litig.*, 147 F.3d 132, 138 (2d Cir. 1998).

F. TRIAL STRUCTURE AND EVIDENTIARY ISSUES

Until the past few years, it was accurate to say that class actions virtually never went to trial and nearly always settled. That trend has changed. In a 2016 article, the author cited numerous class actions that have gone to trial—some resulting in very large plaintiff verdicts and others resulting in defense verdicts. Robert H. Klonoff, *Class Actions in the Year 2026: A Prognosis*, 65 Emory L.J. 1569, 1641–50 (2016). Although it is still true that most class actions settle, numerous cases have raised issues that implicate the trial of class actions. Among those are issues involving jury trials (Seventh Amendment) and issues relating to admissibility of statistical evidence in class actions.

1. SEVENTH AMENDMENT ISSUES

The Seventh Amendment to the United States Constitution reads, in full, "In Suits at common law, where the value of the controversy shall exceed twenty dollars, the right of trial by jury shall be preserved, *and no fact tried by jury, shall be otherwise re-examined in any Court of the United States, than according to the rules of the common law.*" (Emphasis added). The highlighted portion of the Seventh Amendment is known as the Reexamination Clause. That Clause was included out of concern that jury verdicts from local trial courts would be reversed by appellate courts reviewing the facts *de novo*.

The Seventh Amendment was rarely addressed in class action litigation in the early years following the 1966 revision of Rule 23. One important early exception was *Alabama v. Blue Bird Body Co.*, 573 F.2d 309 (5th Cir. 1978). There, the Fifth Circuit suggested in an antitrust case that a trial that bifurcated liability and damages might violate the Reexamination Clause. The court noted that "inherent in the Seventh Amendment guarantee of a trial by jury is the general right of a litigant to have only one jury pass on a common issue of fact." *Id.* at 318. The court added that "[s]uch a rule is dictated for the very practical reason that if separate juries are allowed to pass on issues involving overlapping legal and factual questions the verdicts rendered by each jury could be inconsistent." *Id.*

For almost two decades following *Blue Bird*, the Reexamination Clause was rarely addressed in class action litigation. That changed in 1995, however. In *In re Rhone–Poulenc Rorer, Inc.*, 51 F.3d 1293 (7th Cir. 1995), the Seventh Circuit addressed a nationwide class of hemophiliacs who contracted AIDS from contaminated blood transfusions in the early 1980s. The case is addressed in detail in various parts of this text (*see* Chapters 6(B) and 10(A)(2)(c)). For present purposes, however, the critical point is that one of the grounds upon which the court decertified the class was a Seventh Amendment problem. Under the district court's proposed trial structure, an initial jury would decide various common issues, such as whether defendants were negligent. If defendants were found negligent, individual class members would be allowed to file individual suits throughout the country, with the individual juries being instructed with respect to the first jury's findings. In finding that the district court's approach violated the Seventh Amendment, the Seventh Circuit reasoned:

> The plan of the district judge in this case is inconsistent with the principle that the findings of one jury are not to be reexamined by a second, or third, or nth jury. The first jury will not determine liability. It will determine merely whether one or more of the defendants was negligent under one of the two theories. The first jury may go on to decide the additional issues with regard to the named plaintiffs. But it will not decide them with regard to the other class members. Unless the defendants settle, a second (and third, and fourth, and hundredth, and conceivably thousandth)

jury will have to decide, in individual follow-on litigation by class members not named as plaintiffs in the [present] case, such issues as comparative negligence—did any class members knowingly continue to use unsafe blood solids after they learned or should have learned of the risk of contamination with HIV?—and proximate causation. Both issues overlap the issue of the defendants' negligence. Comparative negligence entails, as the name implies, a comparison of the degree of negligence of plaintiff and defendant. Proximate causation is found by determining whether the harm to the plaintiff followed in some sense naturally, uninterruptedly, and with reasonable probability from the negligent act of the defendant. It overlaps the issue of the defendants' negligence even when * * * the foreseeability of the risk to which the defendant subjected the plaintiff [is] an explicit ingredient of negligence. A second or subsequent jury might find that the defendants' failure to take precautions against infection with Hepatitis B could not be thought the *proximate* cause of the plaintiffs' infection with HIV, a different and unknown virus. How the resulting inconsistency between juries could be prevented escapes us.

Id. at 1303.

Similarly, in *Castano v. American Tobacco Co.*, 84 F.3d 734 (5th Cir. 1996) (*see* Chapters 6(B) and 10(A)(2)(c)), the Fifth Circuit cited the Seventh Amendment as one reason for decertifying a nationwide class action involving smokers who claimed that the tobacco companies negligently failed to inform them of, *inter alia*, the addictive nature of nicotine:

Severing a defendant's conduct from comparative negligence results in the type of risk that our court forbade in [*Blue Bird*]. Comparative negligence, by definition, requires a comparison between the defendant's and the plaintiff's conduct. At a bare minimum, a second jury will rehear evidence of the defendant's conduct. There is a risk that in apportioning fault, the second jury could reevaluate the defendant's fault, determine that the defendant was not at fault, and apportion 100% of the fault to the plaintiff. In such a situation, the second injury would be impermissibly reconsidering the findings of a first jury. The risk of such reevaluation is so great that class treatment can hardly be said to be superior to individual adjudication.

Id. at 747.

Other courts, however, have taken a more restrictive view of the Seventh Amendment. *See, e.g., Valentino v. Carter–Wallace, Inc.*, 97 F.3d 1227, 1232 (9th Cir. 1996) (declining to adopt *Rhone–Poulenc* rationale); *In re Copley Pharm., Inc. "Albuterol: Prods. Liab. Litig."*, 161 F.R.D. 456, 460–61 (D. Wyo. 1995). In *Copley*, the court reasoned that the *Rhone–Poulenc* approach to the Seventh Amendment would "effectively eviscerate[] [former] Fed. R. Civ. P. 23(c)(4)(A)" [current 23(c)(4)] and would conflict with the Advisory Committee Notes' recognition of the appropriateness of certifying a class action on particular issues only. 161 F.R.D. at 460–61.

The following case illustrates the sharp division that remains regarding Seventh Amendment issues in the context of mass tort cases.

MULLEN V. TREASURE CHEST CASINO, LLC
United States Court of Appeals, Fifth Circuit, 1999.
186 F.3d 620.

Before EMILIO M. GARZA, BENAVIDES, and DENNIS, CIRCUIT JUDGES.

BENAVIDES, CIRCUIT JUDGE.

Treasure Chest Casino, LLC ("Treasure Chest") appeals from an interlocutory order of the district court certifying under Federal Rule of Civil Procedure 23(b)(3) a plaintiff class consisting of injured Treasure Chest employees. We affirm the district court's class certification.

I. BACKGROUND

The appellees, Dennis Mullen, Sheila Bachemin, and Margaret Phipps (collectively, the "Named Plaintiffs"), are former employees of the M/V Treasure Chest Casino (the "Casino"), a floating casino owned and operated out of Kenner, Louisiana by appellant Treasure Chest. Mullen was an assistant pit boss, Bachemin was a dealer, and Phipps was employed as a slot-floor person and dealer.

Each Named Plaintiff has suffered respiratory illness allegedly caused by the Casino's defective and/or improperly maintained air-conditioning and ventilating system. Each was diagnosed with asthma and bronchitis while employed aboard the Casino. Mullen and Bachemin, while aboard the Casino, suffered respiratory attacks requiring hospitalization. Kathleen McNamara, the Named Plaintiffs' physician, testified in a deposition that as many as half of the 300 Casino employees that she had treated suffered from similar respiratory problems. She attributed the Named Plaintiffs' and other crew members' maladies to extremely smoky conditions in the Casino.

In January 1996, the Named Plaintiffs filed suit against Treasure Chest, making Jones Act, unseaworthiness, and maintenance and cure claims. They sought Rule 23 certification of a class consisting of

> all members of the crew of the M/V Treasure Chest Casino who have been stricken with occupational respiratory illness caused by or exacerbated by the defective ventilation system in place aboard the vessel.

* * *

On August 29, 1997, the district court certified the proposed class under Rule 23(b)(3). Under the court's plan, the liability issues common to all class members will be tried together in an initial trial phase. Those common issues include whether the employees of the Casino are seamen within the meaning of the Jones Act, whether the Casino is a vessel within the meaning of the Jones Act, whether the Casino was rendered unseaworthy by the air quality aboard, and whether Treasure Chest was negligent in relation to the Casino's ventilation system. If the class prevails on the common liability issues in phase one, the issues affecting only individual class members will be tried in a second phase in waves of approximately five class members at a time. These limited issues include causation, damages, and comparative negligence.

[The Fifth Circuit granted interlocutory review.]

II. DISCUSSION

* * *

[The court upheld the district court's findings that Rule 23(a)'s requirements were satisfied and that Rule 23(b)(3)'s predominance requirement was met. The court further found that various superiority concerns raised by Treasure Chest Casino were without merit.]

In *Castano v. American Tobacco Co.*, 84 F.3d 734 (5th Cir. 1996), this Court expressed a concern that having one jury consider the defendant's conduct and another consider the plaintiffs' comparative negligence could create Seventh Amendment problems. *See Castano*, 84 F.3d at 750–51 (citing *In the Matter of Rhone–Poulenc Rorer Inc.*, 51 F.3d 1293, 1303 (7th Cir. 1995)). This does not change our view of the district court's superiority finding. Treasure Chest did not raise this issue to the district court nor has it been argued on appeal. We are reluctant to find that the district abused its discretion by failing to consider an issue that was not raised by the parties.

In any case, we would not find the risk of infringing upon the parties' Seventh Amendment rights significant in this case. The Seventh Amendment does not prohibit bifurcation of trials as long as the " 'the judge [does] not divide issues between separate trials in such a way that the same issue is reexamined by different juries.' " *Cimino v. Raymark Indus.*, Inc., 151 F.3d 297, 320 n.50 (5th Cir. 1998) (quoting *Rhone–Poulenc*, 51 F.3d at 1303); *see Alabama v. Blue Bird Body Co., Inc.*, 573 F.2d 309, 318 (5th Cir. 1978). In *Castano*, we were concerned that allowing a second jury to consider the plaintiffs' comparative negligence would invite that jury to reconsider the first jury's findings concerning the defendants' conduct. We believe that such a risk has been avoided here by leaving all issues of causation for the phase-two jury. When a jury considers the comparative negligence of a plaintiff, "the focus is upon causation. It is inevitable that a comparison of the conduct of plaintiffs and defendants ultimately be in terms of causation." *Lewis v. Timco, Inc.*, 716 F.2d 1425, 1431 (5th Cir. 1983) (*en banc*); *see id.* (permitting the use of comparative negligence in strict liability claims). Thus, in considering comparative negligence, the phase-two jury would not be reconsidering the first jury's findings of whether Treasure Chest's conduct was negligent or the Casino unseaworthy, but only the degree to which those conditions were the sole or contributing cause of the class member's injury. Because the first jury will not be considering any issues of causation, no Seventh Amendment implications affect our review of the district court's superiority finding.

III. CONCLUSION

For the foregoing reasons, we find that the district court did not abuse its discretion in certifying under Rule 23(b)(3) a class of all Casino employees stricken with occupation-related respiratory illnesses.

EMILIO M. GARZA, dissenting.

[Without addressing the Rule 23(a) requirements or the Rule 23(b)(3) predominance requirement, the dissent focused on Rule 23(b)(3)'s superiority requirement. The dissent first concluded that the district court's bifurcated approach was not superior because the individual class members raised a variety of theories regarding the sources of their injuries (including smoke, temperature, germs, dust, and fumes), and there was nothing to ensure that any hazards found by the phase-one jury to constitute negligence would be the ones upon which the phase-two jury would later base its award of damages.]

* * *

Of course, the risk of unjustified verdicts could be avoided if the individual juries determined for themselves whether a given plaintiffs' injuries were caused by "those risks or hazards whose likelihood made the conduct unreasonably dangerous." To do so, however, the individual juries would be required to make essentially the same inquiry made by the class jury, that is, whether the hazards posed by the Casino's ventilation system unreasonably failed to protect the plaintiffs from harm. This overlap between the issues decided by the class jury and the individual juries impacts a court's superiority inquiry for two reasons. First, it may eviscerate one of the primary rationales for class treatment—judicial efficiency. *See Castano*, 84 F.3d at 749. Where the class jury and the individual juries must consider similar issues, it is likely that evidence presented at the class trial will be repeated during the individual trials. As we have noted, "[t]he net result may be a waste, not a savings, in judicial resources." *Id.*

Second, having separate juries consider essentially the same issue may run afoul of the Seventh Amendment. "[I]nherent in the Seventh Amendment guarantee of a trial by jury is the general right of a litigant to have only one jury pass on a common issue of fact." *Alabama v. Blue Bird Body Co.*, 573 F.2d 309, 318 (5th Cir. 1978); *see* U.S. Const. amend. VII ("no fact tried by a jury shall be otherwise reexamined in any Court of the United States"). Therefore, a court may try a certain issue to a different jury only when that issue is "distinct and separable from the others." *Blue Bird Body*, 573 F.2d at 318. "Such a rule is dictated for the very practical reason that if separate juries are allowed to pass on issues involving overlapping legal and factual questions the verdicts rendered by each jury could be inconsistent." *Id.* When the bifurcation of class and individual issues risks improper reconsideration of issues assigned to the class-wide jury, appellate courts have not hesitated to decertify the class. *See Castano*, 84 F.3d at 751; *In the Matter of Rhone–Poulenc Rorer Inc.*, 51 F.3d 1293, 1302–03 (7th Cir. 1995).

These same concerns—judicial efficiency and the Seventh Amendment—are also implicated by the district court's plan to handle the issue of comparative negligence. Under the trial plan, comparative negligence will be considered by the individual juries, whereas the Casino's negligence will be considered by the class jury. These two issues are too closely related to allow bifurcated treatment. "Comparative negligence, by definition, requires a comparison between the defendant's and the plaintiff's conduct." *Castano*, 84 F.3d at 751; *see also Rhone–Poulenc*, 51 F.3d at 1303. Therefore, to properly try the issue of comparative negligence, the parties may need to repeat evidence concerning the Casino's conduct that was already presented to the class jury. *See Castano*, 84 F.3d at 751. Furthermore, in comparing the negligent conduct of the Casino with the negligent conduct of each plaintiff, the individual juries may "impermissibly reconsider[]" the class jury's determination as to the Casino's negligence, in violation of the Seventh Amendment. *Id.*; *see also Rhone–Poulenc*, 51 F.3d at 1303. Accordingly, "class treatment can hardly be said to be superior to individual adjudication." *Castano*, 84 F.3d at 751 (finding that a bifurcated class action failed Rule 23(b)(3)'s superiority requirement where the district court planned to try the issues of negligence and comparative negligence to separate juries).

IV

* * * [The district court's] failure to adequately examine "how a trial on the alleged causes of action would be tried" constitutes an abuse of discretion and requires that we vacate the class certification order. *Castano*, 84 F.3d at 752. Accordingly, I dissent.

* * *

[End of Excerpt]

The issue of whether bifurcation violates the Seventh Amendment's Reexamination Clause is the subject of intense debate, particularly in the area of employment discrimination class actions. Consider the following:

MELISSA HART, WILL EMPLOYMENT DISCRIMINATION CLASS ACTIONS SURVIVE?
37 Akron L. Rev. 813, 831–34 (2004).

A * * * problem that some have identified with certifying employment discrimination class actions in the wake of the Civil Rights Act of 1991 is the newly established right to a jury trial in cases of intentional discrimination. This argument has two different iterations: first that a class alleging intentional discrimination cannot be divided into a liability phase and a remedial phase, unless the same jury hears both, and second, that disparate impact and disparate treatment claims cannot be brought together in the same case because the judge's findings on the disparate impact claims (for which there is no jury trial right) would inappropriately trample on the jury's authority to find facts in the context of the disparate treatment claim. Neither of these arguments holds the power current detractors of employment discrimination classes have assigned it.

The Reexamination Clause of the Seventh Amendment provides that "no fact tried by a jury, shall be otherwise reexamined in any Court of the United States other than according to the rules of the common law." Because either party in a Title VII suit claiming intentional discrimination may now request a jury, the requirements imposed by this Clause will almost certainly come into play in a disparate treatment class action. The concern that this raises is what impact the Clause may have on bifurcation of the liability and damages phase of the litigation, typical for employment discrimination class litigation. Before 1991, bifurcation of liability and damages did not present any Seventh Amendment difficulties because Title VII suits were tried to the court, not to a jury. With the addition of a jury trial right, bifurcation becomes more complicated.

Some courts and commentators have argued that, in a Title VII case, the issues of liability and damages are not sufficiently "distinct and separable" that they can be tried to separate juries. As one commentator has explained it: "liability and damages issues are only 'distinct and separable' when 'the determination of the amount of damages in phase two becomes little more than an application of the formula found by the jury in phase one.' " In the liability phase of a bifurcated employment class action, the individual claimants may present evidence that goes beyond formulaic application of any findings made by the first jury. Thus, this argument runs, in a bifurcated employment discrimination class action, the same jury would be required to hear not only the broad pattern-and-practice class claim, but also the evidentiary hearings that would resolve the question of each individual plaintiff's entitlement to damages. This is an unworkable solution, as it could require exceptionally lengthy jury service, particularly in a class suit with hundreds, or even thousands, of plaintiffs.

The Reexamination Clause does not, however, require that liability and damages be tried to the same jury. The Seventh Amendment does not prohibit separate juries from considering "overlapping" evidence, and it does not prohibit the same evidence from being presented to two different juries, so long as the two juries do not actually decide the same basic issues. What the Seventh Amendment guarantees is that separate juries will not decide the same issue. In the context of an employment discrimination class action, the question of whether an individual plaintiff has actually been injured does not require a jury to revisit the question of whether the defendant in fact has a discriminatory policy. In fact, several courts have approved the bifurcated approach. If the jury in the liability phase of the proceedings finds no pattern or practice of intentional discrimination, the individual claimants are bound by that ruling and no jury can revisit the question. Of course, the plaintiffs can, as individuals, still bring claims alleging that they were themselves discriminated against, not because of a pattern or practice of discrimination, but through particular behavior with regard to their employment. But they cannot relitigate the question of whether the employer had a pattern of discrimination against the particular class of employees. Similarly, if an employer is found to have a policy or practice of intentional discrimination, that finding is binding on the employer in the subsequent litigation of the individual claims of employees. The employer cannot argue that such a policy does not exist, and therefore the second jury cannot be asked to re-investigate the issue decided by the first jury. Instead, the second jury will be asked to find facts about the individual employment decisions; accepting the pattern of discrimination as a proven fact, the second jury will inquire whether actions taken towards a particular plaintiff were the result of that policy or not. Given this structure for a bifurcated employment class, there is no reason a class suit alleging intentional discrimination should run afoul of the Seventh Amendment.

* * *

[In cases involving both disparate impact and disparate treatment allegations, Seventh Amendment problems could] be eliminated by allowing the jury to consider the disparate treatment claims before a judge considered the allegations of disparate impact discrimination. If the claims are pursued in that order, "a jury will resolve common factual disputes and its resolution will control when the judge takes up" the disparate impact claim. As with the objections to consideration of punitive and compensatory damages in class litigation, the difficulties posed by the 1991 Act's jury trial provision are simply not sufficient to kill the employment discrimination class.

* * *

NOTES AND QUESTIONS

1. Which opinion in *Treasure Chest Casino* is more faithful to the case law discussed—Judge Benavides's or Judge Garza's? How does Professor Hart's excerpt inform the analysis?

2. Professor Patrick Woolley has sharply criticized courts that have struck down bifurcated class actions in mass tort cases on Seventh Amendment grounds:

> [T]he separate trial of overlapping issues does not necessarily violate the Seventh Amendment Reexamination Clause. The Clause requires only that later juries respect the formal findings of the first jury. Within these broad parameters, the Clause does not prohibit later juries from independently evaluating evidence on a previously decided issue in order to decide a related issue. For that reason, the Clause allows a jury charged with deciding the issue of comparative negligence to rehear evidence presented to an earlier jury on the defendant's negligence, provided the later jury understands that the formal findings of the earlier jury are binding.
>
> *Gasoline Products* [*Co. v. Champlin Refining Co.*, 283 U.S. 494 (1931),] imposes an additional requirement under the Trial-by-Jury Clause. The formal findings of the first jury must be in a form that a later jury can easily grasp and apply. It is not enough, for example, for the first jury to return a verdict of negligence. If later juries are to apply the first jury's verdict without perplexity, the verdict must be specific enough to explain, at least in a broad outline, *how* the defendant was negligent. Otherwise, the parties face an unacceptable risk that a later jury will be unable to render a reasoned verdict. Provided the needs of later juries are considered when the court and parties draft the first verdict, however, later juries should be able to render an appropriate verdict.
>
> In short, the mechanical approach championed by the Fifth and Seventh Circuits cannot withstand scrutiny. The separate trial of overlapping issues may not always be desirable. But there is no sound basis for concluding that the convocation of a second jury in such circumstances will necessarily lead to violation of the Seventh Amendment. Reliance on the Seventh Amendment Reexamination Clause thus obscures the real issue: Will certification of an issue class assist in the fair and accurate determination of a particular controversy?

Patrick Woolley, *Mass Tort Litigation and the Seventh Amendment Reexamination Clause*, 83 Iowa L. Rev. 499, 542–43 (1998). It should be noted that Professor Woolley himself acknowledged that "bifurcation violates the Seventh Amendment whenever it leads to 'confusion and uncertainty,' a possibility that should be considered case-by-case before overlapping issues are separated for trial." *Id.* at 502; *see also* Comment, *Bifurcation of Liability and Damages in Rule 23(b) Class Actions; History, Policy, Problems, and a Solution*, 36 Sw. L.J. 743, 750 (1982).

3. Under *Castano* and *Rhone–Poulenc*, what kinds of class actions can still be heard in bifurcated proceedings before more than one jury?

4. For additional discussion of Seventh Amendment issues in the employment context, *see, e.g.*, Daniel F. Piar, *The Uncertain Future of Title VII*

Class Actions After the Civil Rights Act of 1991, 2001 BYU L. Rev. 305, 337–41 (2001); Note, *Evading Friendly Fire: Achieving Class Certification After the Civil Rights Act of 1991*, 100 Colum. L. Rev. 1847, 1875–80 (2000); Suzette M. Malveaux & Christine E. Webber, *Making It Happen: Class Certification in Employment Discrimination Cases*, The Employee Advocate 51, 58–59 (Fall 2002); Meghan E. Changelo, *Reconciling Class Action Certification With the Civil Rights Act of 1991*, 36 Colum. J.L. & Soc. Probs. 133, 153–54 (2003); Comment, *Getting Title VII Back on Track: Leaving* Allison *Behind for the* Robinson *Line*, 17 BYU J. Pub. L. 411, 419, 423–24 (2003).

5. In *Ortiz v. Fibreboard*, 527 U.S. 815 (1999) (*see* Chapter 3(A)(2)), the Supreme Court suggested (but did not resolve) a Seventh Amendment concern that is different from the reexamination issue discussed above—namely, that "the certification of a mandatory class followed by settlement of its action for money damages obviously implicates the Seventh Amendment jury trial rights of absent class members." 527 U.S. at 845–46. What is the Seventh Amendment concern that the Court found to be so "obvious[]"?

6. Although at one time Seventh Amendment arguments in class actions resonated with a number of courts, that trend seems to have subsided. *See* D. McNamara et al., *Reexamining the Seventh Amendment Argument Against Issue Certification*, 34 Pace L. Rev. 1041, 1054 (discussing recent decisions that have "sidestepped (or sideswiped) the Seventh Amendment holding in *Rhone–Poulenc*" but also noting that "defendants facing an issue certification routinely present the Seventh Amendment" argument).

2. DUE PROCESS ISSUES: AGGREGATE PROOF AND TRIAL STRUCTURE

A major issue in litigating class actions is whether damages (or other issues) must be presented on an individual-by-individual basis or can be proven on a classwide basis through statistical or aggregate proof. In some instances, requiring individualized proof is so cumbersome that, as a practical matter, the case could not be adjudicated as a class action. Thus, plaintiffs sometimes contend that classwide forms of proof are necessary to preserve class actions in large, complicated cases. Defendants, on the other hand, contend that such classwide proof violates due process (as well as the Seventh Amendment) and applicable state law.

In *Wal–Mart Stores, Inc. v. Dukes*, 564 U.S. 338 (2011), which has already been discussed at several earlier points in this text (*see* Chapters 2(B)(2), 3(B)(2), and 4(B)(1)(b)(i)–(ii)), the Supreme Court addressed some issues related to aggregate proof of classwide damages. In the decision below, the *en banc* Ninth Circuit had affirmed the district court's "tentative trial plan" for resolving issues such as each class member's entitlement to backpay and how Wal–Mart could contest individual employment decisions to rebut an inference of discrimination. 603 F.3d at 625. While "express[ing] no opinion regarding Wal–Mart's objections to the district court's tentative trial plan (or that trial plan itself)," the court of appeals "simply note[d] that, because there are a range of possibilities—which may or may not include the district court's proposed course of action—that would allow this class action to proceed in a manner that is both manageable and in accordance with due process, manageability concerns present no bar to class certification here." *Id.*

In rejecting Wal–Mart's arguments that the district court's proposed trial plan violated, *inter alia*, the Due Process Clause, § 706(g)(2) of Title VII, and the Rules Enabling Act, the Ninth Circuit relied heavily on one of its previous decisions, *Hilao v. Estate of Marcos*, 103 F.3d 767 (9th Cir. 1996). In *Hilao*, the court had approved the use of statistical sampling of 137 of the 10,059 claims, selected at random, to prove compensatory and punitive damages on a classwide basis. *See* 103 F.3d at 782–87. The Ninth Circuit, in *Dukes*, "s[aw] no reason why a similar procedure to that used in *Hilao* could not be employed in this case," and "conclude[d] that there exists at least one method of managing this large class action that, albeit somewhat imperfect, nonetheless protects the due process rights of all involved parties." 603 F.3d at 627 (footnote omitted). Interestingly, when the case came before the Supreme Court, the plaintiffs (respondents before the Court) did not even cite *Hilao* in their merits brief. Instead, they argued, in part, that "[w]here, as here, the employer's system has been infected with subjective decision-making and lacks records to document the employment decisions at issue, courts have concluded that allocating relief based upon economic models that replicate the decisions at issue 'has more basis in reality . . . than an individual-by-individual approach.'" Respondent's Merits Brief, *Wal–Mart Stores, Inc. v. Dukes*, at 46 (quoting *Pettway v. Am. Cast Iron Pipe Co.*, 494 F.2d 211, 263 (5th Cir. 1974)). The Supreme Court, however, rejected those arguments. In a part of the decision that was unanimous, the Court explained:

> Contrary to the Ninth Circuit's view, Wal–Mart is entitled to individualized determinations of each employee's eligibility for backpay. Title VII includes a detailed remedial scheme. If a plaintiff prevails in showing that an employer has discriminated against him in violation of the statute, the court "may enjoin the respondent from engaging in such unlawful employment practice, and order such affirmative action as may be appropriate, [including] reinstatement or hiring of employees, with or without backpay . . . or any other equitable relief as the court deems appropriate." § 2000e–5(g)(1). But if the employer can show that it took an adverse employment action against an employee for any reason other than discrimination, the court cannot order the "hiring, reinstatement, or promotion of an individual as an employee, or the payment to him of any backpay." § 2000e–5(g)(2)(A).
>
> We have established a procedure for trying pattern-or-practice cases that gives effect to these statutory requirements. When the plaintiff seeks individual relief such as reinstatement or backpay after establishing a pattern or practice of discrimination, "a district court must usually conduct additional proceedings . . . to determine the scope of individual relief." At this phase, the burden of proof will shift to the company, but it will have the right to raise any individual affirmative defenses it may have, and to "demonstrate that the individual applicant was denied an employment opportunity for lawful reasons."
>
> The Court of Appeals believed that it was possible to replace such proceedings with Trial by Formula. A sample set of the class members would be selected, as to whom liability for sex discrimination and the backpay owing as a result would be determined in

depositions supervised by a master. The percentage of claims determined to be valid would then be applied to the entire remaining class, and the number of (presumptively) valid claims thus derived would be multiplied by the average backpay award in the sample set to arrive at the entire class recovery—without further individualized proceedings. We disapprove that novel project. Because the Rules Enabling Act forbids interpreting Rule 23 to "abridge, enlarge or modify any substantive right," a class cannot be certified on the premise that Wal–Mart will not be entitled to litigate its statutory defenses to individual claims. And because the necessity of that litigation will prevent backpay from being "incidental" to the classwide injunction, respondents' class could not be certified even assuming, *arguendo*, that "incidental" monetary relief can be awarded to a 23(b)(2) class.

Id. at 366–67 (some citations omitted). As the Court noted above, Wal–Mart's entitlement to present individualized defenses arose from Title VII's statutory requirements. By basing this part of its decision on the statute, the Court avoided passing on Wal–Mart's argument that "[e]liminating individualized determinations also violates due process." Petitioner's Reply Brief, *Wal–Mart Stores, Inc. v. Dukes*, at 17.

In 2016, the Supreme Court returned to the issue of the admissibility of statistical proof in class actions.

TYSON FOODS, INC. V. BOUAPHAKEO
Supreme Court of the United States, 2016.
136 S. Ct. 1036.

JUSTICE KENNEDY delivered the opinion of the Court.

Following a jury trial, a class of employees recovered $2.9 million in compensatory damages from their employer for a violation of the Fair Labor Standards Act of 1938 (FLSA), 29 U.S.C. § 201 et seq. The employees' primary grievance was that they did not receive statutorily mandated overtime pay for time spent donning and doffing protective equipment.

The employer seeks to reverse the judgment. * * * It argues certification was improper because the damages awarded to the class may be distributed to some persons who did not work any uncompensated overtime.

The Court of Appeals for the Eighth Circuit concluded there was no error in the District Court's decision to certify and maintain the class. This Court granted certiorari.

I

Respondents are employees at petitioner Tyson Foods' pork processing plant in Storm Lake, Iowa. They work in the plant's kill, cut, and retrim departments, where hogs are slaughtered, trimmed, and prepared for shipment. Grueling and dangerous, the work requires employees to wear certain protective gear. The exact composition of the gear depends on the tasks a worker performs on a given day.

Until 1998, employees at the plant were paid under a system called "gang-time." This compensated them only for time spent at their workstations, not for the time required to put on and take off their protective gear. In response to a federal-court injunction, and a Department of Labor suit to enforce that injunction, Tyson in 1998 began to pay all its employees for an additional four minutes a day for what it called "K-code time." The 4-minute period was the amount of time Tyson estimated employees needed to don and doff their gear. In 2007, Tyson stopped paying K-code time uniformly to all employees. Instead, it compensated some employees for between four and eight minutes but paid others nothing beyond their gang-time wages. At no point did Tyson record the time each employee spent donning and doffing.

Unsatisfied by these changes, respondents filed suit in the United States District Court for the Northern District of Iowa, alleging violations of the FLSA. The FLSA requires that a covered employee who works more than 40 hours a week receive compensation for excess time worked "at a rate not less than one and one-half times the regular rate at which he is employed." 29 U.S.C. § 207(a). In 1947, nine years after the FLSA was first enacted, Congress * * * clarified that compensable work does not include time spent walking to and from the employee's workstation or other "preliminary or postliminary activities." § 254(d). The FLSA, however, still requires employers to pay employees for activities "integral and indispensable" to their regular work, even if those activities do not occur at the employee's workstation. The FLSA also requires an employer to "make, keep, and preserve . . . records of the persons employed by him and of the wages, hours, and other conditions and practices of employment." § 211(c).

In their complaint, respondents alleged that donning and doffing protective gear were integral and indispensable to their hazardous work and that petitioner's policy not to pay for those activities denied them overtime compensation required by the FLSA. Respondents also raised a claim under the Iowa Wage Payment Collection Law. This statute provides for recovery under state law when an employer fails to pay its employees "all wages due," which includes FLSA-mandated overtime.

* * *

[After class certification], [t]he case proceeded to trial before a jury. The parties stipulated that the employees were entitled to be paid for donning and doffing of certain equipment worn to protect from knife cuts. The jury was left to determine whether the time spent donning and doffing other protective equipment was compensable; whether Tyson was required to pay for donning and doffing during meal breaks; and the total amount of time spent on work that was not compensated under Tyson's gang-time system.

Since the employees' claims relate only to overtime, each employee had to show he or she worked more than 40 hours a week, inclusive of time spent donning and doffing, in order to recover. As a result of Tyson's failure to keep records of donning and doffing time, however, the employees were forced to rely on what the parties describe as "representative evidence." This evidence included employee testimony, video recordings of donning and doffing at the plant, and, most important, a study performed by an industrial relations expert, Dr. Kenneth Mericle. Mericle conducted 744 videotaped observations and analyzed how long various donning and doffing activities took. He then averaged the time taken in the observations to produce an estimate of 18 minutes a day for the cut and retrim departments and 21.25 minutes for the kill department.

Although it had not kept records for time spent donning and doffing, Tyson had information regarding each employee's gang-time and K-code time. Using this data, the employees' other expert, Dr. Liesl Fox, was able to estimate the amount of uncompensated work each employee did by adding Mericle's estimated average donning and doffing time to the gang-time each employee worked and then subtracting any K-code time. For example, if an employee in the kill department had worked 39.125 hours of gang-time in a 6-day workweek and had been paid an hour of K-code time, the estimated number of compensable hours the employee worked would be: 39.125 (individual number of gang-time hours worked) + 2.125 (the average donning and doffing hours for a 6-day week, based on Mericle's estimated average of 21.25 minutes a day) - 1 (K-code hours) = 40.25. That would mean the employee was being undercompensated by a quarter of an hour of overtime a week, in violation of the FLSA. On the other hand, if the employee's records showed only 38 hours of gang-time and an hour of K-code time, the calculation would be: 38 + 2.125 - 1 = 39.125. Having worked less than 40 hours, that employee would not be entitled to overtime pay and would not have proved an FLSA violation.

Using this methodology, Fox stated that 212 employees did not meet the 40-hour threshold and could not recover. The remaining class members, Fox maintained, had potentially been undercompensated to some degree.

Respondents proposed to bifurcate proceedings. They requested that, first, a trial be conducted on the questions whether time spent in donning and doffing was compensable work under the FLSA and how long those activities took to perform on average; and, second, that Fox's methodology be used to determine which employees suffered an FLSA violation and how much each was entitled to recover. Petitioner insisted upon a single proceeding in which damages would be calculated in the aggregate and by the jury. The District Court submitted both issues of liability and damages to the jury.

Petitioner did not move for a hearing regarding the statistical validity of respondents' studies under *Daubert v. Merrell Dow Pharmaceuticals, Inc.*, 509 U.S. 579, (1993), nor did it attempt to discredit the evidence with testimony from a rebuttal expert. Instead, as it had done in its opposition to class certification, petitioner argued to the jury that the varying amounts of time it took employees to don and doff different protective equipment made the lawsuit too speculative for classwide recovery. Petitioner also argued that Mericle's study overstated the average donning and doffing time. The jury was instructed that nontestifying members of the class could only recover if the evidence established they "suffered the same harm as a result of the same unlawful decision or policy."

Fox's calculations supported an aggregate award of approximately $6.7 million in unpaid wages. The jury returned a special verdict finding that time spent in donning and doffing protective gear at the beginning and end of the day was compensable work but that time during meal breaks was not. The jury more than halved the damages recommended by Fox. It awarded the class about $2.9 million in unpaid wages. That damages award has not yet been disbursed to the individual employees.

Tyson moved to set aside the jury verdict * * *. The District Court denied Tyson's motion, and the Court of Appeals for the Eighth Circuit affirmed the judgment and the award.

* * *

For the reasons that follow, this Court now affirms.

II

* * *

A

Federal Rule of Civil Procedure 23(b)(3) requires that, before a class is certified under that subsection, a district court must find that "questions of law or fact common to class members predominate over any questions affecting only individual members." The "predominance inquiry tests whether proposed classes are sufficiently cohesive to warrant adjudication by representation." This calls upon courts to give careful scrutiny to the relation between common and individual questions in a case. An individual question is one where "members of a proposed class will need to present evidence that varies from member to member," while a common question is one where "the same evidence will suffice for each member to make a prima facie showing [or] the issue is susceptible to generalized, class-wide proof." 2 W. Rubenstein, *Newberg on Class Actions* § 4:50, pp. 196–97 (5th ed. 2012) (internal quotation marks omitted). The predominance inquiry "asks whether the common, aggregation-enabling, issues in the case are more prevalent or important than the non-common, aggregation-defeating, individual issues." *Id.* § 4:49, at 195–96. When "one or more of the central issues in the action are common to the class and can be said to predominate, the action may be considered proper under Rule 23(b)(3) even though other important matters will have to be tried separately, such as damages or some affirmative defenses peculiar to some individual class members." 7AA C. Wright, A. Miller & M. Kane, Federal Practice and Procedure § 1778, pp. 123–24 (3d ed. 2005) (footnotes omitted).

Here, the parties do not dispute that there are important questions common to all class members, the most significant of which is whether time spent donning and doffing the required protective gear is compensable work under the FLSA. To be entitled to recovery, however, each employee must prove that the amount of time spent donning and doffing, when added to his or her regular hours, amounted to more than 40 hours in a given week. Petitioner argues that these necessarily person-specific inquiries into individual work time predominate over the common questions raised by respondents' claims, making class certification improper.

Respondents counter that these individual inquiries are unnecessary because it can be assumed each employee donned and doffed for the same average time observed in Mericle's sample. Whether this inference is permissible becomes the central dispute in this case. Petitioner contends that Mericle's study manufactures predominance by assuming away the very differences that make the case inappropriate for classwide resolution. Reliance on a representative sample, petitioner argues, absolves each employee of the responsibility to prove personal injury, and thus deprives petitioner of any ability to litigate its defenses to individual claims.

Calling this unfair, petitioner and various of its *amici* maintain that the Court should announce a broad rule against the use in class actions of what the parties call representative evidence. A categorical exclusion of that sort, however, would make little sense. A representative or statistical sample, like all evidence, is a means to establish or defend against liability. Its permissibility turns not on the form a proceeding takes—be it a class or individual action—but on the degree to which the evidence is reliable in proving or disproving the elements of the relevant cause of action. *See* Fed. R. Evid. 401, 403, 702.

It follows that the Court would reach too far were it to establish general rules governing the use of statistical evidence, or so-called representative evidence, in all class-action cases. Evidence of this type is used in various substantive realms of the law. Whether and when statistical evidence can be used to establish classwide liability will depend on the purpose for which the evidence is being introduced and on "the elements of the underlying cause of action,"

In many cases, a representative sample is "the only practicable means to collect and present relevant data" establishing a defendant's liability. In a case where representative evidence is relevant in proving a plaintiff's individual claim, that evidence cannot be deemed improper merely because the claim is brought on behalf of a class. To so hold would ignore the Rules Enabling Act's pellucid instruction that use of the class device cannot "abridge . . . any substantive right." 28 U.S.C. § 2072(b).

One way for respondents to show, then, that the sample relied upon here is a permissible method of proving classwide liability is by showing that each class member could have relied on that sample to establish liability if he or she had brought an individual action. If the sample could have sustained a reasonable jury finding as to hours worked in each employee's individual action, that sample is a permissible means of establishing the employees' hours worked in a class action.

This Court's decision in *Anderson v. Mt. Clemens* [*Pottery Co.*, 328 U.S. 680 (1946)] explains why Mericle's sample was permissible in the circumstances of this case. * * *

The Court in *Mt. Clemens* held that when employers violate their statutory duty to keep proper records, and employees thereby have no way to establish the time spent doing uncompensated work, the "remedial nature of [the FLSA] and the great public policy which it embodies . . . militate against making" the burden of proving uncompensated work "an impossible hurdle for the employee." * * *

In this suit, as in *Mt. Clemens,* respondents sought to introduce a representative sample to fill an evidentiary gap created by the employer's failure to keep adequate records. If the employees had proceeded with 3,344 individual lawsuits, each employee likely would have had to introduce Mericle's study to prove the hours he or she worked. Rather than absolving the employees from proving individual injury, the representative evidence here was a permissible means of making that very showing.

Reliance on Mericle's study did not deprive petitioner of its ability to litigate individual defenses. Since there were no alternative means for the employees to establish their hours worked, petitioner's primary defense was to show that Mericle's study was unrepresentative or inaccurate. That defense is itself common to the claims made by all class members. Respondents' "failure of proof on th[is] common question" likely would have ended "the litigation and thus [would not have] cause[d] individual questions . . . to overwhelm questions common to the class." When, as here, "the concern about the proposed class is not that it exhibits some fatal dissimilarity but, rather, a fatal similarity—[an alleged] failure of proof as to an element of the plaintiffs' cause of action—courts should engage that question as a matter of summary judgment, not class certification."

Petitioner's reliance on *Wal–Mart Stores, Inc. v. Dukes*, 564 U.S. 338 (2011), is misplaced. *Wal–Mart* does not stand for the broad proposition that a representative sample is an impermissible means of establishing classwide liability.

Wal–Mart involved a nationwide Title VII class of over 1½ million employees. In reversing class certification, this Court did not reach Rule 23(b)(3)'s predominance prong, holding instead that the class failed to meet even Rule 23(a)'s more basic requirement that class members share a common question of fact or law. The plaintiffs in *Wal–Mart* did not provide significant proof of a common policy of discrimination to which each employee was subject. * * *

The plaintiffs in *Wal–Mart* proposed to use representative evidence as a means of overcoming this absence of a common policy. Under their proposed methodology, a "sample set of the class members would be selected, as to whom liability for sex discrimination and the backpay owing as a result would be determined in depositions supervised by a master." The aggregate damages award was to be derived by taking the "percentage of claims determined to be valid" from this sample and applying it to the rest of the class, and then multiplying the "number of (presumptively) valid claims" by "the average backpay award in the sample set." The Court held that this "Trial By Formula" was contrary to the Rules Enabling Act because it " 'enlarge[d]' " the class members' " 'substantive right[s]' " and deprived defendants of their right to litigate statutory defenses to individual claims.

The Court's holding in the instant case is in accord with *Wal–Mart*. The underlying question in *Wal–Mart,* as here, was whether the sample at issue could have been used to establish liability in an individual action. Since the Court held that the employees were not similarly situated, none of them could have prevailed in an individual suit by relying on depositions detailing the ways in which other employees were discriminated against by their particular store managers. By extension, if the employees had brought 1½ million individual suits, there would be little or no role for representative evidence. Permitting the use of that sample in a class action, therefore, would have violated the Rules Enabling Act by giving plaintiffs and defendants different rights in a class proceeding than they could have asserted in an individual action.

In contrast, the study here could have been sufficient to sustain a jury finding as to hours worked if it were introduced in each employee's individual action. While the experiences of the employees in *Wal–Mart* bore little relationship to one another, in this case each employee worked in the same facility, did similar work, and was paid under the same policy. As *Mt. Clemens* confirms, under these circumstances the experiences of a subset of employees can be probative as to the experiences of all of them.

This is not to say that all inferences drawn from representative evidence in an FLSA case are "just and reasonable." Representative evidence that is statistically inadequate or based on implausible assumptions could not lead to a fair or accurate estimate of the uncompensated hours an employee has worked. Petitioner, however, did not raise a challenge to respondents' experts' methodology under *Daubert*; and, as a result, there is no basis in the record to conclude it was legal error to admit that evidence.

Once a district court finds evidence to be admissible, its persuasiveness is, in general, a matter for the jury. Reasonable minds may differ as to whether the average time Mericle calculated is probative as to the time actually worked by each employee. Resolving that question, however, is the near-exclusive province of the jury. The District Court could have denied class certification on this ground only if it concluded that no reasonable juror could have believed that the employees spent roughly equal time donning and doffing. The District Court made no such finding, and the record here provides no basis for this Court to second-guess that conclusion.

The Court reiterates that, while petitioner, respondents, or their respective *amici* may urge adoption of broad and categorical rules governing the use of representative and statistical evidence in class actions, this case provides no occasion to do so. Whether a representative sample may be used to establish classwide liability will depend on the purpose for which the sample is being introduced and on the underlying cause of action. In FLSA actions, inferring the hours an employee has worked from a study such as Mericle's has been permitted by the Court so long as the study is otherwise admissible. The fairness and utility of statistical methods in contexts other than those presented here will depend on facts and circumstances particular to those cases.

* * *

The judgment of the Court of Appeals for the Eighth Circuit is affirmed, and the case is remanded for further proceedings consistent with this opinion.

It is so ordered.

[Concurring opinion by CHIEF JUSTICE ROBERTS is omitted.]

JUSTICE THOMAS, with whom JUSTICE ALITO joins, dissenting.

* * *

B

The majority * * * errs in concluding that the representative evidence here showed that class members' claims were susceptible to common proof. As the majority observes, representative evidence can be used to prove an individual issue on a classwide basis if each class member, in an individual action, could rely on that evidence to prove his individual claim. But that premise should doom the plaintiffs' case. Even testifying class members would seem unable to use Mericle's averages. For instance, Mericle's study estimated that kill department employees took an average 6.4 minutes to don equipment at their lockers before their shift—but employee Donald

Brown testified that this activity took him around 2 minutes. Others also testified to donning and doffing times that diverged markedly from Mericle's estimates. So Mericle's study could not sustain a jury verdict in favor of these plaintiffs, had they brought individual suits.

[The dissent explained that *Mt. Clemens Pottery* did not support the result reached by the majority.]

* * *

* * * [T]he majority's attempts to distinguish this case from *Wal–Mart* are unavailing. *Wal–Mart* involved a nationwide Title VII class action alleging that Wal–Mart's policy of delegating employment decisions to individual store managers let managers exercise their discretion in a discriminatory manner. We held that discretionary decisionmaking could not be a common policy uniting all class members' claims because managers presumptively exercise their discretion in an individualized manner. Some may rely on performance-based criteria; others may use tests; yet others might intentionally discriminate. Because of this variability, "demonstrating the invalidity of one manager's use of discretion will do nothing to demonstrate the invalidity of another's."

Moreover, the *Wal–Mart* plaintiffs' representative evidence—120 employee anecdotes—did not make this individualized issue susceptible to common proof. Using 120 anecdotes to represent the experiences of 1.5 million class members was too far below the 1:8 ratio of anecdotes to class members that our prior cases accepted. Thus, this representative evidence was "too weak to raise any inference that all the individual, discretionary personnel decisions are discriminatory."

The plaintiffs' reliance on Mericle's study fails for the same reasons. Just as individual managers inherently make discretionary decisions differently, so too do individual employees inherently spend different amounts of time donning and doffing. And, just as 120 employee anecdotes could not establish that all 1.5 million class members faced discrimination, neither can Mericle's study establish that all 3,344 class members spent the same amount of time donning and doffing. Like the 120 Wal–Mart anecdotes, Mericle's study—which used about 57 employees per activity to extrapolate times for 3,344—falls short of the 1:8 ratio this Court deems "significant" to the probative value of representative evidence.

* * *

I respectfully dissent.

NOTES AND QUESTIONS

1. What was the majority's rationale for permitting aggregate statistical proof? Why did the Justice Thomas (joined by Justice Alito) disagree?

2. What is the relevance of the Rules Enabling Act to the majority's analysis?

3. Does the majority opinion open the way to the admissibility of statistical proof in a wide variety of cases? Or is the decision a narrow one? As one way of probing these issues, consider whether *Tyson Foods* would have affected the resolution of *Hilao*. For an argument that *Tyson Foods* will significantly aid plaintiffs' ability to use statistical evidence in class actions, *see* Robert G.

Bone, Tyson Foods *and the Future of Statistical Adjudication*, 95 N.C. L. Rev. ___ (forthcoming 2017), *available at* https://papers.ssrn.com/sol3/papers.cfm?abstract_id=2860332.

4. One commentator has focused on ways that large class actions can be tried, consistent with due process and other constitutional concerns. *See* Laurens Walker, *A Model Plan to Resolve Federal Class Action Cases by Jury Trial*, 88 Va. L. Rev. 405 (2002). Professor Walker explains that a "model" plan for trying a class action has four components: (1) polyfurcation (dividing up the elements of a trial (causes of action, defenses, damages) into multiple phases); (2) sampling (making findings based on representative information from a subset or sample of the class); (3) resolving future claims (those of individuals who have been exposed to a product but do not manifest current injury); and (4) a distribution trust (transfer of property by a civil defendant to a nonparty to make payments to claimants over time). Under this approach, large class actions would be tried by a single jury. As discussed in Chapter 10, however, many of the techniques relied upon by Professor Walker, such as sampling and resolution of future claims, have been the subject of significant controversy and debate. *See* Chapter 10(A)(3)(b). How might the *Tyson Foods* Supreme Court respond to Professor Walker's model?

Chapter 5

Notice of Class Certification, "Opt-Out" Rights, and Communications With Class Members

■ ■ ■

A class action is adjudicated, by definition, on behalf of a large number of persons who are not before the forum court. How are such persons notified of their status as class members? How—and under what circumstances—can they remove themselves from the class? And how are communications with the absent class members regulated? These important issues are addressed in this chapter.

A. NOTICE OF CLASS CERTIFICATION AND "OPT-OUT" RIGHTS

This section discusses whether class members are entitled to notice that a class of which they are members has been certified. It also raises the related question of whether such class members are entitled to "opt out" of the class and pursue individual actions.

This section covers the basic dimensions of those issues as set forth in Rule 23. The issues of notice and opt-out rights, however, are closely related to the concepts of *res judicata* and the due process required to bind absent plaintiffs to a judgment. Indeed, a crucial issue in the context of any adjudication by representatives is whether those who were represented have been accorded due process. Courts have often found that notice that one's claims will be adjudicated, the potential to remove one's self from such adjudication, and assurance that one's interests will be protected during the course of any such adjudication are essential due process elements for binding absent class members to a judgment. These due process issues are addressed in connection with claim and issue preclusion. *See* Chapter 7(C).

The basic requirements of class certification notice and opt-out rights are set forth in Rule 23(c)(2), which states:

(A) *For (b)(1) or (b)(2) Classes*. For any class certified under Rule 23(b)(1) or (b)(2), the court may direct appropriate notice to the class.

(B) *For (b)(3) Classes*. For any class certified under Rule 23(b)(3), the court must direct to class members the best notice that is practicable under the circumstances, including individual notice to all members who can be identified through reasonable effort. The notice must clearly and concisely state in plain, easily understood language:

(i) the nature of the action;

(ii) the definition of the class certified;

(iii) the class claims, issues, or defenses;

(iv) that a class member may enter an appearance through an attorney if the member so desires;

(v) that the court will exclude from the class any member who requests exclusion;

(vi) the time and manner for requesting exclusion; and

(vii) the binding effect of a class judgment on members under Rule 23(c)(3).

According to the *Manual for Complex Litigation (Fourth)* § 21.31 (2004):

> Notice is a critical part of class action practice. It provides the structural assurance of fairness that permits representative parties to bind absent class members. In a Rule 23(b)(3) class, notice conveys the information absent class members need to decide whether to opt out and the opportunity to do so. In all class actions, notice provides an opportunity for class members to participate in the litigation, to monitor the performance of class representatives and class counsel, and to ensure that the predictions of adequate representation made at the time of certification are fulfilled. Proper notice also lessens the vulnerability of the final judgment to collateral attack by class members.
>
> Rule 23(c)(2)(B) specifies information that must be included in a (b)(3) notice, such as the nature of the action, the definition of the class, and the claims, issues, and defenses to be litigated. The rule requires that notices state essential terms "clearly and concisely," "in plain, easily understood language." In addition, the court can require notice to be given when needed for the protection of class members or for the fair conduct of the action. *See* Fed. R. Civ. P. 23(d)(1)(B). Notice generally is given in the name of the court, although one of the parties typically prepares and distributes it.

1. NOTICE AND OPT-OUT RIGHTS IN CLASSES CERTIFIED UNDER RULE 23(b)(3)

a. The Requirement of Notice

The classic discussion of the need for notice in classes certified under Rule 23(b)(3) is *Eisen v. Carlisle & Jacquelin*, 417 U.S. 156 (1974). Although *Eisen* was decided under a prior version of Rule 23(c)(2), that version, in language substantively identical to the current version, required "the best notice practicable [for classes certified under Rule 23(b)(3)] under the circumstances, including individual notice to all members who can be identified through reasonable effort." *See* Fed. R. Civ. P. 23(c)(2)(B).

EISEN V. CARLISLE & JACQUELIN
Supreme Court of the United States, 1974.
417 U.S. 156.

JUSTICE POWELL delivered the opinion of the Court.

[In an antitrust and securities class action involving millions of buyers and sellers of small amounts of securities, the district court ordered that notice of class certification be provided only to all firms that were members of the New York Stock Exchange, approximately 2,000 identifiable class members with numerous trades, and an additional 5,000 class members selected at random, and that prominent publication notice also be placed in the *Wall Street Journal* and other prominent New York and California newspapers. In rejecting the district court's approach, the Supreme Court stated:]

Rule 23(c)(2) provides that, in any class action maintained under subdivision (b)(3), each class member shall be advised that he has the right to exclude himself from the action on request or to enter an appearance through counsel, and further that the judgment, whether favorable or not, will bind all class members not requesting exclusion. To this end, the court is required to direct to class members "the best notice practicable under the circumstances, *including individual notice to all members who can be identified through reasonable effort.*" We think the import of this language is unmistakable. Individual notice must be sent to all class members whose names and addresses may be ascertained through reasonable effort.

The [1966] Advisory Committee's Note to Rule 23 reinforces this conclusion. The Advisory Committee described subdivision (c)(2) as "not merely discretionary" and added that the "mandatory notice pursuant to subdivision (c)(2) . . . is designed to fulfill requirements of due process to which the class action procedure is of course subject." The Committee explicated its incorporation of due process standards by citation to *Mullane v. Central Hanover Bank & Trust Co.*, 339 U.S. 306 (1950), and like cases.

In *Mullane* the Court addressed the constitutional sufficiency of publication notice rather than mailed individual notice to known beneficiaries of a common trust fund as part of a judicial settlement of accounts. The Court observed that notice and an opportunity to be heard were fundamental requisites of the constitutional guarantee of procedural due process. It further stated that notice must be "reasonably calculated, under all the circumstances, to apprise interested parties of the pendency of the action and afford them an opportunity to present their objections." The Court continued:

> But when notice is a person's due, process which is a mere gesture is not due process. The means employed must be such as one desirous of actually informing the absentee might reasonably adopt to accomplish it. The reasonableness and hence the constitutional validity of any chosen method may be defended on the ground that it is in itself reasonably certain to inform those affected.

The Court then held that publication notice could not satisfy due process where the names and addresses of the beneficiaries were known. In such cases, "the reasons disappear for resort to means less likely than the mails to apprise them of [an action's] pendency."

In *Schroeder v. City of New York*, 371 U.S. 208 (1962), decided prior to the promulgation of [the 1966 version of] amended Rule 23, the Court explained that *Mullane* required rejection of notice by publication where the name and address of the affected person were available. The Court stated that the "general rule" is that "notice by publication is not enough with respect to a person whose name and address are known or very easily ascertainable. . . ." The Court also noted that notice by publication had long been recognized as a poor substitute for actual notice and that its justification was " 'difficult at best.' "

Viewed in this context, the express language and intent of Rule 23(c)(2) leave no doubt that individual notice must be provided to those class members who are identifiable through reasonable effort. In the present case, the names and addresses of 2,250,000 class members are easily ascertainable, and there is nothing to show that individual notice cannot be mailed to each. For these class members, individual notice is clearly the "best notice practicable" within the meaning of Rule 23(c)(2) and our prior decisions.

Petitioner contends, however, that we should dispense with the requirement of individual notice in this case, and he advances two reasons for our doing so. First, the prohibitively high cost of providing individual notice to 2,250,000 class members would end this suit as a class action and effectively frustrate petitioner's attempt to vindicate the policies underlying the antitrust and securities laws. Second, petitioner contends that individual notice is unnecessary in this case, because no prospective class member has a large enough stake in the matter to justify separate litigation of his individual claim. Hence, class members lack any incentive to opt out of the class action even if notified.

The short answer to these arguments is that individual notice to identifiable class members is not a discretionary consideration to be waived in a particular case. It is, rather, an unambiguous requirement of Rule 23. As the Advisory Committee's Note explained, the Rule was intended to insure that the judgment, whether favorable or not, would bind all class members who did not request exclusion from the suit. Accordingly, each class member who can be identified through reasonable effort must be notified that he may request exclusion from the action and thereby preserve his opportunity to press his claim separately or that he may remain in the class and perhaps participate in the management of the action. There is nothing in Rule 23 to suggest that the notice requirements can be tailored to fit the pocketbooks of particular plaintiffs.

Petitioner further contends that adequate representation, rather than notice, is the touchstone of due process in a class action and therefore satisfies Rule 23. We think this view has little to commend it. To begin with, Rule 23 speaks to notice as well as to adequacy of representation and requires that both be provided. Moreover, petitioner's argument proves too much, for it quickly leads to the conclusion that no notice at all, published or otherwise, would be required in the present case. This cannot be so, for quite apart from what due process may require, the command of Rule 23 is clearly to the contrary. We therefore conclude that Rule 23(c)(2) requires that individual notice be sent to all class members who can be identified with reasonable effort.[14]

---

[14] We are concerned here only with the notice requirements * * * applicable to class actions maintained under subdivision (b)(3). * * *

* * *

MANUAL FOR COMPLEX LITIGATION (FOURTH)
Federal Judicial Center (2004) § 21.311.

Rule 23(c)(2)(B) requires that individual notice in 23(b)(3) actions be given to class members who can be identified through reasonable effort. Those who cannot be readily identified must be given "the best notice practicable under the circumstances." When the names and addresses of most class members are known, notice by mail usually is preferred.

Posting notices on dedicated Internet sites, likely to be visited by class members and linked to more detailed certification information, is a useful supplement to individual notice, might be provided at a relatively low cost, and will become increasingly useful as the percentage of the population that regularly relies on the Internet for information increases. An advantage of Internet notice is that follow-up information can easily be added, and lists can be created to notify class members of changes that may occur during the litigation. * * * Many courts include the Internet as a component of class certification * * * notice programs.

Publication in magazines, newspapers, or trade journals may be necessary if individual class members are not identifiable after reasonable effort or as a supplement to other notice efforts. For example, if no records were kept of sales of an allegedly defective product from retailers to consumers, publication notice may be necessary. Financial and legal journals or financial sections of broad circulation newspapers, while useful to a degree, might not be read by many members of the general public. Such publications may, however, be useful in certain kinds of cases, such as securities fraud suits. Determination of whether a given notification is reasonable under the circumstances of the case is discretionary. The sufficiency of the effort made might become an issue if the preclusive effect of the class action judgment is later challenged.

NOTES AND QUESTIONS

1. One commentator has expressed frustration with *Eisen*'s analysis of the practicalities of notifying numerous class members without taking cost into account. Kenneth W. Dam, *Class Action Notice: Who Needs It?*, 1974 S. Ct. Rev. 97, 107–09. Dam notes that, despite the district court's finding that postage for classwide notice would cost $225,000, the Supreme Court concluded that notice was "practicable under the circumstances" and that Eisen was required to make a "reasonable effort" under the rule. *Id.* Should an analysis of the "practicability" of notice take cost into account? Would notice accorded a class then depend upon a class representative's wealth, or his or her attorney's wealth?

2. *Eisen* held that the best practicable notice to a class includes individual notice to class members whose identities are known. But what about situations in which all of the class members are not readily identifiable? Courts have used a variety of procedures. *See, e.g., In re Ariz. Dairy Prods. Litig.*, 1975 WL 966, at *1 (D. Ariz. 1975) (notice on side of milk carton). Should notice by publication—standing alone—ever suffice to satisfy the notice requirement of Rule 23(c)(2)(B)? What if a class includes persons who are not yet aware of the fact that they have suffered injury? Or persons who were exposed to a hazardous substance, but have not manifested any readily identifiable symptoms?

3. Does "best practicable notice" mean that each class member must actually receive the notice? What if the notice is sent but contains an error in the class member's address? *See, e.g.*, *Peters v. Nat'l R.R. Passenger Corp.*, 966 F.2d 1483, 1486–87 (D.C. Cir. 1992) (notice sufficient although it omitted class member's apartment number and used an incorrect zip code). Does it matter whether or not the notice is returned as undeliverable? What if the notice is sent to a class member's former address? *See, e.g.*, *In re VMS Ltd. P'ship Sec. Litig.*, 1995 WL 355722 (N.D. Ill. 1995) (notice sufficient when mailed to class member's former address, although class member contended he had previously notified defendant of his new address). What if a designee, such as a securities brokerage firm, is ordered to forward the notices to all of the beneficial stockholders but fails to do so, or delays in doing so such that the deadline for opting out has expired? *See, e.g.*, *Silber v. Mabon*, 18 F.3d 1449 (9th Cir. 1994) (notice sufficient although brokerage firm delayed in mailing notice until after expiration of opt-out deadline).

4. The excerpt from the *Manual for Complex Litigation (Fourth)* states that when "names and addresses of most class members are known, notice by mail is *usually* preferable." (Emphasis added). Does *Eisen* contemplate circumstances in which most class members' names and addresses are known, but some other form of notice alone would suffice?

5. Class actions increasingly involve allegations that would encompass potential class members in other countries. *See, e.g.*, Jonathan E. Richman, *Transnational Class Actions and Judgment Recognition*, 11 Class Action Litig. Report 583 (2010) (surveying U.S. courts' approaches to transnational class actions). What constitutes the "best notice that is practicable under the circumstances" where class members are foreigners? *See, e.g.*, *Vancouver Women's Health Collective Soc. v. A.H. Robins Co.*, 820 F.2d 1359, 1363 (4th Cir. 1987) (justifying different notice programs for U.S. and foreign claimants on grounds that latter are not protected by the United States Constitution). For interesting discussion of notice issues in global class actions, *see* Todd B. Hilsee, *Global Class Actions: Lasting Peace or Ticking Time Bombs?*, 11 Class Action Litig. Report 394 (2010); Jeanne C. Finegan, *Five Key Considerations for a Successful International Notice Program*, 78 Class Action Litig. Report 2611 (2010).

6. A proposed change to Rule 23(c)(2)(B) would provide that notice of certification in a (b)(3) class "may be by United States mail, electronic means, or other appropriate means . . . ." The change would make clear that, contrary to *Eisen* (which long pre-dated the Internet), electronic notice may, in some instances, be the most effective notice. *See* http://www.uscourts.gov/rules-policies/proposed-amendments-published-public-comment (last visited Feb. 6, 2017) (pages 211 & 215, containing proposed amendments to Rule 23).

PROBLEM

Counsel representing a class that has just been certified under Rule 23(b)(3) has prepared and sent notices to the class. Through a computer error, all of the envelopes were printed without states and zip codes noted in the address. Counsel did not discover the problem until months later, after a classwide settlement had been reached in the case. As a result, only about 20 percent of the class members actually received the notice. (a) Should such notice be held to suffice for purposes of binding class members who did not receive the notice? (b) Would the analysis change if 90 percent of the class received the notice? (c) What if plaintiffs' counsel knew of the problem before sending out the notices but sent them out anyway because she did not want to incur the costs of reprinting the envelopes? (d) What if defendants' counsel was aware of the defect, but failed to take action to correct the error?

b. Ability to Opt Out

In addition to requiring notice, Rule 23(c)(2)(B) provides that class members in a Rule 23(b)(3) class must be given the opportunity to exclude themselves from the class. Opt-out rights play two roles:

> In the first role, opt out rights are a method of indicating consent to jurisdiction. By failing to opt out, one can draw the inference that a class member submits to be bound by a judgment of the court. * * * In the second role, opt out rights offer a procedural protection to class members who wish to pursue individual actions. Many commentators have detailed the problems of agency and wholesale justice frequently associated with class litigation. Opt out rights are a procedural device which allows claim holders to escape these dangers and pursue vindication of their rights in another action.

Note, *The Due Process Right to Opt Out of Class Actions*, 73 N.Y.U. L. Rev. 480, 488–89 (1998).

> Compare this discussion by another student commentator:
>
> Plaintiffs' rights to individual claim autonomy can be quite significant in particular cases, and those rights conform to our judicial system's "deep-rooted historic tradition that everyone have his own day in court." There are a number of reasons why the right to assert individual claims may be very important to those opt-out plaintiffs who have disproportionately larger damage claims than most members of the class. First, bargaining within the class-plaintiffs' attorney team tends to disfavor high-stakes plaintiffs. * * * "Plaintiffs whose claimed injuries are near or below the mean may find it expedient to sell out the high stakes plaintiff by negotiating a class settlement with the defendants on a basis that increases the minimum recovery but lowers the maximum recovery per plaintiff." A related problem is that attorneys for the class may find it easier to facilitate a settlement by averaging the damages of all class members rather than by expending the extra time and energy required to differentiate among the respective settlement values of individual claims. These two problems are exacerbated by the typical position of high-stakes plaintiffs as a minority among class members; thus, greater political pressure exists for class attorneys to favor low-stakes plaintiffs. Finally, the predispositions of juries in class cases may work against high-stakes plaintiffs because of some empirical evidence that class action juries award recoveries more on the basis of the defendants' culpability than on the plaintiffs' aggregate injuries. All of these factors imply that high-stakes plaintiffs have better chances for larger recoveries if they opt out and pursue their claims individually. This substantial interest in maintaining individual actions is a legitimate concern, which merits some form of due process protection, and it should be given some weight in a due process balancing analysis. * * *

* * *

Whenever opt-out plaintiffs decide to exclude themselves from a class and to file individual actions, [however,] they reduce the efficiency of the class action and create duplicative litigation. This pursuit of individual suits in turn increases the delays imposed on remainder plaintiffs by further cramping court dockets and decreasing the willingness of defendants to settle. * * *

Note, *Class Actions in the Asbestos Context: Balancing the Due Process Considerations Implicated by the Right to Opt Out*, 70 Tex. L. Rev. 211, 222–25 (1991). Which plaintiffs are most likely to opt out—those with stronger claims or those with weaker ones? Those with high-value claims or those with low-value claims? What impact would opting out have on those who remain in the class? On the defendant? On the efficiencies of the class action device?

In light of these considerations, should absent class members in Rule 23(b)(3) class actions have an unfettered right to opt out? Consider Note, *Constrained Individualism in Group Litigation: Requiring Class Members to Make a Good Cause Showing Before Opting Out of a Federal Class Action*, 100 Yale L.J. 745, 756–57 (1990), which argues that opting out should be limited to a class member who can show "good cause," namely, "that he is alleging some unique substantive legal issue or material fact, or a unique way of presenting a substantive legal issue or material fact, that the class suit will not fully and fairly address." What would be the practical effects of such a rule? Would such an approach raise due process or Rule 23 issues? In *Juris v. Inamed Corp.*, 685 F.3d 1294, 1329–33 (11th Cir. 2012), the Eleventh Circuit rejected the argument of an absent class member—a California resident with "no contacts" in the state where the forum court was located—that the class action court never had personal jurisdiction over her, and that barring her claims against a silicone breast implant manufacturer would therefore violate due process because she did not have an opportunity to opt out of the settlement. "Because established law holds that a court with jurisdiction over a res or fund also has jurisdiction over all claims against that fund, [the absent class member's] personal jurisdiction objection is resolved, and the need for opt-out rights is removed." 685 F.3d at 1333. The court also stated that notice is adequate and due process is satisfied in such cases where "the notice afforded reaches a critical mass of putative class members, such that the facts underlying certification are contested and approached in a sufficiently adversarial manner * * *." *Id.* at 1318.

2. COSTS, TIMING, FORM, AND CONTENT OF NOTICE IN CLASS ACTIONS CERTIFIED UNDER RULE 23(b)(3)

a. The Costs of Notice

Who bears the cost of notifying class members in (b)(3) class actions? The Supreme Court addressed this issue in the following decision.

OPPENHEIMER FUND, INC. V. SANDERS
Supreme Court of the United States, 1978.
437 U.S. 340.

JUSTICE POWELL delivered the opinion of the Court.

[Plaintiffs ("respondents") in a securities fraud case against an investment fund and certain other defendants ("petitioners") moved for class certification. Subsequently, before certification was granted, plaintiffs moved to redefine the class to make it smaller (and thus reduce the cost of providing notice). Defendants opposed the motion. The district court rejected plaintiffs' motion and certified the class as originally defined, but imposed the cost of notice upon the defendants, who eventually sought review by the Supreme Court. The Supreme Court reversed, based largely on its earlier decision in *Eisen v. Carlisle & Jacquelin*, 417 U.S. 156 (1974) (referred to in this opinion as "*Eisen IV*").]

In *Eisen IV*, the Court held that the plain language of [Rule 23(c)(2)] "requires that individual notice be sent to all class members who can be identified with reasonable effort." The Court also found no authority for a district court to hold a preliminary hearing on the merits of a suit in order to decide which party should bear the cost required to prepare and mail the class notice. Instead, it held [that] * * * "[t]he usual rule is that a plaintiff must initially bear the cost of notice to the class. . . . Where, as here, the relationship between the parties is truly adversar[ial], the plaintiff must pay for the cost of notice as part of the ordinary burden of financing his own suit."

In *Eisen IV*, the defendants had offered to provide a list of many of the class members' names and addresses at their own expense in the first instance, if the representative plaintiff would prepare and mail individual notice to these class members. *Eisen IV* therefore did not present issues concerning either the procedure by which a representative plaintiff might require a defendant to help identify class members, or whether costs may be allocated to the defendant in such a case. The specific holding of *Eisen IV* is that where a representative plaintiff prepares and mails the class notice himself, he must bear the cost of doing so.

* * *

* * * [Petitioners] argue that *Eisen IV* always requires a representative plaintiff to pay all costs incident to sending notice, whether he or the defendant performs the required tasks. *Eisen IV* does not compel this * * * conclusion, for it did not involve a situation where a defendant properly was ordered under Rule 23(d) to perform any of the tasks necessary to sending the notice.

The first question that a district court must consider under Rule 23(d) is which party should perform particular tasks necessary to send the class notice. The general rule must be that the representative plaintiff should perform the tasks, for it is he who seeks to maintain the suit as a class action and to represent other members of his class. In *Eisen IV* we noted the general principle that a party must bear the "burden of financing his own suit." Thus ordinarily there is no warrant for shifting the cost of the representative plaintiff's performance of these tasks to the defendant.

In some instances, however, the defendant may be able to perform a necessary task with less difficulty or expense than could the representative plaintiff. In such cases, we think that the district court properly may exercise its discretion under Rule 23(d) to order the defendant to perform the task in question. * * * [I]n identifying the instances in which such an order may be appropriate, a rough analogy might usefully be drawn to practice under Rule 33(c) of the discovery rules. Under that Rule, when one party directs an interrogatory to another party which can be answered by examination of the responding party's business records, "it is a sufficient answer to such interrogatory to specify the records from which the answer may be derived or ascertained and to afford to the party serving the interrogatory reasonable opportunity to" examine and copy the records, if the burden of deriving the answer would be "substantially the same" for either party. Not unlike *Eisen IV*, this provision is intended to place the "burden of discovery upon its potential benefitee." * * *

In those cases where a district court properly decides under Rule 23(d) that a defendant rather than the representative plaintiff should perform a task necessary to send the class notice, the question that then will arise is which party should bear the expense. On one hand, it may be argued that this should be borne by the defendant because a party ordinarily must bear the expense of complying with orders properly issued by the district court; but *Eisen IV* strongly suggests that the representative plaintiff should bear this expense because it is he who seeks to maintain the suit as a class action. In this situation, the district court must exercise its discretion in deciding whether to leave the cost of complying with its order where it falls, on the defendant, or place it on the party that benefits, the representative plaintiff. Once again, a rough analogy might usefully be drawn to practice under the discovery rules. Under those rules, the presumption is that the responding party must bear the expense of complying with discovery requests, but he may invoke the district court's discretion under Rule 26(c) to grant orders protecting him from "undue burden or expense" in doing so, including orders conditioning discovery on the requesting party's payment of the costs of discovery. The analogy necessarily is imperfect, however, because in the Rule 23(d) context, the defendant's own case rarely will be advanced by his having performed the tasks. Thus, one of the reasons for declining to shift costs under Rule 26(c) usually will be absent in the Rule 23(d) context. For this reason, a district court exercising its discretion under Rule 23(d) should be considerably more ready to place the cost of the defendant's performing an ordered task on the representative plaintiff, who derives the benefit, than under Rule 26(c). In the usual case, the test should be whether the expense is substantial, rather than, as under Rule 26(c), whether it is "undue."

Nevertheless, in some instances, the expense involved may be so insubstantial as not to warrant the effort required to calculate it and shift it to the representative plaintiff. * * * In other cases, it may be appropriate to leave the cost where it falls because the task ordered is one that the defendant must perform in any event in the ordinary course of its business. Although we do not attempt to catalogue the instances in which a district court might be justified in placing the expense on the defendant, we caution that courts must not stray too far from the principle underlying *Eisen IV* that the representative plaintiff should bear all costs relating to the sending of notice because it is he who seeks to maintain the suit as a class action.

C.

In this case, we think the District Court abused its discretion in requiring petitioners to bear the expense of identifying class members. The records containing the needed information are kept by the transfer agent, not petitioners. Since petitioners apparently have the right to control these records and since the class members can be identified only by reference to them, the District Court acted within its authority under Rule 23(d) in ordering petitioners to direct the transfer agent to make the records available to respondents. The preparation of the desired list requires * * * the manual sorting out of names and addresses from old records maintained on paper, the keypunching of up to 300,000 computer cards, and the creation of new computer programs for use with extant tapes and tapes that would have to be created from the paper records. It appears that neither petitioners nor respondents can perform these tasks, for both sides assume that the list can be generated only by hiring the services of a third party, the transfer agent, for a sum exceeding $16,000. As the expense of hiring the transfer agent would be no greater for respondents, who seek the information, than for petitioners, respondents should bear the expense.

The District Court offered two reasons why petitioners should pay the transfer agent, but neither is persuasive. First, the court thought that petitioners should bear this cost because it was their opposition to respondents' proposed redefinition of the class and method of sending notice that made it necessary to incur the cost. A district court necessarily has some discretion in deciding the composition of a proper class and how notice should be sent. Nor is it improper for the court to consider the potential impact that rulings on these issues may have on the expense that the representative plaintiff must bear in order to send the notice. But it is neither fair nor good policy to penalize a defendant for prevailing on an argument against a representative plaintiff's proposals. If a defendant's argument has merit, it should be accepted regardless of his willingness to bear the extra expense that its acceptance would require. Otherwise, a defendant may be discouraged from advancing arguments entirely appropriate to the protection of his rights or the rights of absent class members.

* * *

The second reason advanced by the District Court was that $16,000 is a "relatively modest" sum, presumably in comparison to the Fund's total assets, which exceed $500 million. Although in some circumstances the ability of a party to bear a burden may be a consideration, the test in this respect normally should be whether the cost is substantial; not whether it is "modest" in relation to ability to pay. In the context of a lawsuit in which the defendants deny all liability, the imposition on them of a threshold expense of $16,000 to enable the plaintiffs to identify their own class hardly can be viewed as an insubstantial burden. As the expenditure would benefit only respondents, we think that the amount of money involved here would cut strongly against the District Court's holding. * * *

[Judges on the court of appeals] suggested several additional reasons to justify the District Court's order, none of which we find persuasive. [They suggested] that the fact that part of these records are kept on computer tapes justifies imposing a greater burden on petitioners than might be imposed on a party whose records are kept in another form. Thus, the panel dissent warned that potential defendants may be tempted to use computers "irretrievably [to bury] information to immunize business activity from later scrutiny," and the en banc majority argued that even where no bad motive is present, "complex electronic processes may be required to extract information which might have been obtainable through a minimum of effort had different systems been used."

We do not think these reasons justify the order in this case. There is no indication or contention that these petitioners have acted in bad faith to conceal information from respondents. In addition, although it may be expensive to retrieve information stored in computers when no program yet exists for the particular job, there is no reason to think that the same information could be extracted any less expensively if the records were kept in less modern forms. * * * Finally, the suggestion that petitioners should have used "different systems" to keep their records borders on the frivolous. * * * [W]e do not think a defendant should be penalized for not maintaining his records in the form most convenient to some potential future litigants whose identity and perceived needs could not have been anticipated.

Respondents also contend that petitioners should be required to bear the identification expense because they are alleged to have breached a fiduciary duty to respondents and their class. * * * [But a] bare allegation of wrongdoing, whether by breach of fiduciary duty or otherwise, is not a fair reason for requiring a defendant to undertake financial burdens and risks to further a plaintiff's case. Nor would it be in the interests of the class of persons to whom a fiduciary duty is owed to require them, through the fiduciary, to help finance every suit by one of their number that alleges a breach of fiduciary duty, without regard to whether the suit has any merit.

* * *

Given that respondents can obtain the information sought here by paying the transfer agent the same amount that petitioners would have to pay, that the information must be obtained to comply with respondents' obligation to provide notice to their class, and that no special circumstances have been shown to warrant requiring petitioners to bear the expense, we hold that the District Court abused its discretion in not requiring respondents to pay the transfer agent to identify the members of their own class.

* * *

NOTES AND QUESTIONS

1. Under what circumstances does *Oppenheimer* suggest that it would be appropriate to shift the costs of identifying or notifying class members about class certification to the defendants? Under the Court's decision, should a defendant's wealth be taken into account when determining whether that defendant should be forced to pay a portion of the cost of certification notice? What about the relative poverty of a plaintiff? What effect does the *Oppenheimer* rule have on the kinds of cases that may be brought as class actions?

In a denial of a petition for writ of *certiorari* in a much more recent case, Justice Kennedy, joined by Chief Justice Roberts and Justice Sotomayor, wrote separately to note the constitutional implications of considering a defendant's wealth when determining who should pay for class notice:

> * * * The trial court certified the class and ordered [defendant] to bear all the costs of class notification on the sole ground (or so it appears) that petitioner could afford to pay and [plaintiff] could not.
>
> To the extent that [state] law allows a trial court to impose the onerous costs of class notification on a defendant simply because of the relative wealth of the defendant and without any consideration of the underlying merits of the suit, a serious due process question is raised. Where a court has concluded that a plaintiff lacks the means to pay for class certification, the defendant has little hope of recovering its expenditures later if the suit proves meritless; therefore, the court's order requiring the defendant to pay for the notification "finally destroy[s] a property interest."

DTD Enterprises Inc. v. Wells, 130 S. Ct. 7, 7–8 (2009) (Kennedy, J.) (citations omitted). Is Justice Kennedy's *DTD Enterprises* observation consistent with *Oppenheimer*? Should the merits come into play when determining whether a defendant should bear the notice cost? *See Eisen* (Part 1(a) of this chapter).

2. In cases decided after *Oppenheimer*, some courts have imposed on the defendant some notice-related tasks that the defendant performs in the ordinary course of its business. *See, e.g., Sollenbarger v. Mountain States Tel. & Tel. Co.*, 121 F.R.D. 417 (D.N.M. 1988) (in class action against telephone company relating to wire maintenance service contracts, notice would be included in company's monthly billing statements, as alternatives would be unreasonably difficult and expensive). Defendants have also been ordered to bear the costs of notice when they seek certification of the class, *see, e.g., Argo v. Hills*, 425 F. Supp. 151, 159 (E.D.N.Y. 1977), *aff'd*, 578 F.2d 1366 (2d Cir. 1978), or when they have engaged in improper behavior in the litigation, *see, e.g., Nagy v. Jostens, Inc.*, 91 F.R.D. 431, 432–33 (D. Minn. 1981) (defendants required to bear cost of notice as sanction for improper communication with class members).

b. Timing of Class Certification Notice

According to the *Manual for Complex Litigation (Fourth)* § 21.311 (2004):

> Ordinarily, notice to class members should be given promptly after the certification order is issued. When the parties are nearing settlement, however, a reasonable delay in notice might increase incentives to settle and avoid the need for separate class notices of certification and settlement. Delaying notice of certification until after settlement apparently is a common practice in such cases.
>
> Notice to the added class members is required if the certification order is amended to expand the class definition. If the certification order is amended to eliminate previously included class members, consider whether notice is necessary to inform affected individuals who might have relied on the class action to protect their rights. If repetitive notice and frequent orders affect class interests, ordering the parties to use the Internet—especially a specific Web site dedicated to the litigation—may be a particularly

cost-effective means to provide current information in a rapidly evolving situation.

Courts usually refuse to delay notice that a Rule 23(b)(3) class has been certified. *See, e.g., In re Sugar Ind. Antitrust Litig.*, 73 F.R.D. 322, 359 (E.D. Pa. 1976) ("Once a court exercises its power to define a class * * *, it would be derelict in its duties to delay its decision concerning proper identification to the class just defined."); *Beeson v. Med–1 Solutions, L.L.C.*, 2009 WL 3242105 (S.D. Ind. 2009) (despite both parties' stipulated request that class notice be deferred until after court's ruling on defendant's summary judgment motion, court later decertified class because class members' claims were dismissed prior to the class being given notice and a right to opt out). Occasionally, however, courts have been willing to delay notice of Rule 23(b)(3) certification. *See, e.g., R & D Bus. Sys. v. Xerox Corp.*, 150 F.R.D. 87, 91–92 (E.D. Tex. 1993) (delaying notice until three months before trial because defendant claimed that early notice would prejudice it and because delaying notice would not prejudice the class).

c. Form and Content of Class Certification Notice

MANUAL FOR COMPLEX LITIGATION (FOURTH)
Federal Judicial Center (2004) § 21.311.

Rule 23(c)(2)(B) requires that a class certification notice advise class members of the following:

- the nature of the action;
- the definition of the class and any subclasses;
- the claims, issues, and defenses for which the class has been certified;
- the right of a potential class member to be excluded or to opt out from the class;
- the right of a class member to enter an appearance by counsel; and
- the binding effect of a class judgment.

In Rule 23(b)(3) actions, the notice also must describe when and how a class member may opt out of the class.

Sufficient information about the case should be provided to enable class members to make an informed decision about their participation. The notice should:

- describe succinctly the position of the parties;
- identify the opposing parties, class representatives, and counsel;
- describe the relief sought; and
- explain any risks and benefits of retaining class membership and opting out, while emphasizing that the court has not ruled on the merits of any claims or defenses.

A simple and clear form for opting out is often included with the notice.

NOTES AND QUESTIONS

1. What should a class action notice look like? The Federal Judicial Center's website provides examples. *See* http://www.fjc.gov (follow "Class Action

Notices Page" hyperlink) (last visited Feb. 6, 2017). Do these notices adequately inform absent class members about the nature of the action and the steps they need to take to preserve their rights? For an interesting discussion of the notice required to satisfy due process concerns, *see* Todd B. Hilsee, Shannon R. Wheatman & Gina M. Intrepido, *Do You Really Want Me to Know My Rights? The Ethics Behind Due Process in Class Action Notice Is More Than Just Plain Language: A Desire to Actually Inform*, 18 Geo. J. Legal Ethics 1359 (2005).

2. Prior to the 2003 amendments to Rule 23, Rule 23(c)(2) did not provide much detail about the content of notice for classes certified under Rule 23(b)(3). The earlier version stated that "[such] notice shall advise each member that (A) the court will exclude the member from the class if the member so requests by a specified date; (B) the judgment, whether favorable or not, will include all members who do not request exclusion; and (C) any member who does not request exclusion may, if the member desires, enter an appearance through his counsel." Do the subsequently added provisions in Rule 23(c)(2)(B) make notices more informative? Do they make notices easier for a lay person to understand? Should the amendments have included any additional mandatory provisions for a notice? If so, what additional provisions should have been included?

3. One notice expert has noted that "poor notice abounds today," with notice by publication (as opposed to mailed notice) "often the culprit." Todd B. Hilsee, *Nationwide Class Actions: Shine a Light on (Another) Bad Notice*, 9 Class Action Litig. Report 113, 133–34 (2008) (research found that "only 13% of notices were * * * concise, plain language notices which avoided legalese"). What factors work against the provision of the best practicable notice? How can such factors be minimized?

4. Another challenge to providing the best practicable notice is the explosion of new media sources and the American public's changing usage habits. Notice expert Jeanne C. Finegan notes that recent technological advances have changed the legal notice landscape. *See* Jeanne C. Finegan, *On Demand Media Could Change the Future of Best Practicable Notice*, 9 Class Action Litig. Report, 307, 309 (2008) ("Electronic media opens up countless ways in which class members can be reached (e-mail, text messages, mobile media, RSS feeds, etc.), and as a result, what constitutes adequate [n]otice will undoubtedly continue to evolve and expand."); *see also* Robert H. Klonoff, Mark Hermann & Bradley W. Harrison, *Making Class Actions Work: The Untapped Potential of the Internet*, 69 U. Pitt. L. Rev. 727, 734, 748, 762–68 (2008) (describing how increased use of the Internet in class notice programs better informs class members, enhances their direct participation in class litigation, and opens up the possibility of communications among class members, counsel, and the court). Some public interest organizations are posting videos on YouTube to notify class members of settlements. *See, e.g.*, Public Citizen's YouTube notifications of Paxil settlement, at http://youtube.com/ watch?v=ZluS3tutxZU (describing settlement) (last visited Feb. 6, 2017). Should Rule 23(c)(2) be modified to account for changes in communication technologies?

3. THE RIGHT TO MAKE AN APPEARANCE IN RULE 23(b)(3) CLASS ACTIONS

Rule 23(c)(2)(B)(iv) states that "a class member may enter an appearance through an attorney if the member so desires."

There is little authority relating to absent class members' ability to appear in class actions certified under Rule 23(b)(3). In particular, there is a dearth of authority defining the level of participation that Rule 23(c)(2)(B)(iv) allows class members who elect to make an appearance. What rights *should* be provided to those class members who decide to enter an appearance? Should the scope of such rights be constrained by the fact that a court, under Rule 23(d)(1)(B)(iii), may provide "notice" to class members of the "opportunity * * * to intervene and present claims or defenses, or to otherwise come into the action"? *See* Chapter 4(E)(3) (addressing courts' power under Rule 23(d)(1)(B)); *see also* Chapter 7(C)(1)(b)(iii) (discussing possible due process right of class members to participate); Chapter 13(A)(5)(b) (discussing intervention in class action context).

4. NOTICE AND OPT-OUT RIGHTS IN CLASS ACTIONS CERTIFIED UNDER RULES 23(b)(1) OR 23(b)(2)

Prior to 2003, Rule 23(c)(2) by its terms addressed notice of class certification and opt-out rights only for those cases certified under Rule 23(b)(3). Under the 2003 amendments, Rule 23(c)(2)(A) now provides that a court "may" direct "appropriate" notice to members of certified (b)(1) and (b)(2) classes. The Advisory Committee Notes to the amendments state that "there may be less need for notice" for such classes "than in a (b)(3) class action[,]" given that there are no opt-out rights in (b)(1) and (b)(2) actions, and that "[t]he cost of providing notice * * * could easily cripple actions that do not seek damages." Similarly, the *Manual for Complex Litigation (Fourth)* § 21.311 (2004) provides:

> * * * Notice in Rule 23(b)(1) and (b)(2) actions is within the district judge's discretion. Rule 23(c)(2)(A) recognizes the court's authority to direct "appropriate" notice in Rule 23(b)(1) and (b)(2) class actions, but contemplates different and more flexible standards for those cases than for Rule 23(b)(3) actions. Notice to members of classes certified under Rule 23(b)(1) or (b)(2) serves limited but important interests, such as monitoring the conduct of the action. This more flexible role of notice recognizes that in some cases, such as public interest organizations' civil rights class action suits, the costs of a wide-reaching notice might prove crippling and the benefits may be relatively small.
>
> A court must decide whether and how to provide notice in Rule 23(b)(1) and (b)(2) actions. It may be preferable in some cases to forego ordering notice if there is a risk that notice costs could outweigh the benefits of notice, deterring the pursuit of class relief. If notice is appropriate, it need not be individual notice because, unlike a Rule 23(b)(3) class, there is no right to request exclusion from Rule 23(b)(1) and (b)(2) classes.

Like the prior version of Rule 23(c)(2), the current version does not address the issue of opt-out rights for classes certified under (b)(1) and (b)(2). As noted, the Advisory Committee Notes and the *Manual for Complex Litigation (Fourth)* both contemplate that no opt-out rights are required. Under the prior version of Rule 23(c)(2), however, many courts had held that a district court may, in its discretion, afford opt-out rights to members of classes certified under (b)(1) and (b)(2). *See, e.g., Eubanks v. Billington,* 110 F.3d 87 (D.C. Cir. 1997) (discussing case law); *see* Chapter 4(E)(3). Do opt-out rights comport with class certification under Rule 23(b)(1) or 23(b)(2)? In what circumstances should a court grant opt-out rights under (b)(1) or (b)(2) as a matter of discretion? *See also* Robert H. Klonoff, *Class Actions for Monetary Relief Under Rule 23(b)(1)(A) and (b)(1)(B): Does Due Process Require Notice and Opt-Out Rights?*, 82 Geo. Wash. L. Rev. 798 (2014) (discussing Rule 23(b)(1)(A) and (b)(1)(B)).

Because notice and opt-out rights may be related to whether the absent class members will be bound by any resulting judgment, the issue of whether due process requires notice or opt-out rights in some or all (b)(1) and (b)(2) actions is explored in the context of *res judicata*. *See* Chapter 7(C)(1)(b)(ii).

5. NOTICE TO CLASS MEMBERS OF DECERTIFICATION

CULVER V. CITY OF MILWAUKEE
United States Court of Appeals, Seventh Circuit, 2002.
277 F.3d 908.

Before BAUER, POSNER and RIPPLE, CIRCUIT JUDGES.

POSNER, CIRCUIT JUDGE.

A class action suit was brought on behalf of white males who claimed to have been discriminated against in hiring by the Milwaukee police department. The district court granted the defendants' motion to decertify the class and having done so dismissed the suit because the class representative's own claim was conceded to be moot. A properly certified class action survives the mootness of the original representative's claims, but an individual action must be dismissed in identical circumstances, and this suit became an individual action when the class was decertified. The would-be class representative has standing to appeal, however, as otherwise a defendant in a class action could delay appeals indefinitely by buying off successive class representatives.

The suit was filed in 1993. Culver, the plaintiff and class representative, claimed that the previous year he had requested from the Milwaukee police department an application for employment as a police officer and had been told he could not have one because the department would not be accepting applications from white males until 1994. He sought to certify a class consisting not only of other white males whose requests for job applications had been turned down but also white males who had somehow succeeded in applying but had not been hired because the department had changed the scores on the entrances exams to favor women and members of minority groups. The district court certified this broad class in 1995. Six years later, a different district judge, to whom the case had been reassigned, granted the City's motion to decertify the class on the ground that the class was improper and Culver not an adequate representative of any subclass that might be carved out of it. The judge then dismissed the suit, as we said, because Culver's claim was moot.

* * *

Although the class was rightly decertified, and the suit, having thus been demoted to an individual action, therefore rightly dismissed because Culver's claim had become moot, there is a loose end. Rule 23(e) requires that notice of a proposed dismissal "be given to all members of the class." The purpose is to enable the class members to protect their interests in the face of the dismissal of the class action. One thing they may need protection against * * *, and it may be a factor here, is the expiration of the statute of limitations on the class members' claims without their realizing it. The filing of a class action suit tolls the statute of limitations for all the members of the class, but when the suit is dismissed without prejudice or when the class certification is denied the statute resumes running for the class members. Unless they are notified that the suit is dismissed, they may fail to file their own suits and thus fail to "re-arrest" the statute of limitations, and as a result they may find themselves time barred without knowing it.

We are mindful that some cases confine the duty of notice to settlements, on the theory that if a suit is dismissed as the result of an adjudication of the merits, the danger that the class representative or class counsel is selling out the class in exchange for benefits for himself is obviated. But these cases overlook the other danger to the members of the class, the danger that the statute of limitations on their claims will run without their knowing it until it is too late, a danger that is independent of whether the dismissal is voluntary or involuntary.

The district judge failed to notify the class members of the decertification of the class. He thought they probably were unaware of the suit and therefore would not be prejudiced by its demise. "Probably" is not good enough; it implies that some class members may well have been prejudiced.
* * *

Three qualifications or refinements must be noted, however. First, if it is plain that there is no prejudice, violation of the rule is harmless and compliance will not be ordered. A good example of such a case is *Wimber v. Dep't of Soc. & Rehab. Serv.*, 156 F.R.D. 259, 263 (D. Kan. 1994), where the court pointed out that "in light of the small class size, the likelihood of [putative class members] learning of this dismissal through other channels, the early dismissal without prejudice, the lack of possible collusion, and the small danger of the statute of limitations expiring, the court dispenses with the notice and hearing requirements and approves the dismissal without prejudice." But in the present case the danger of prejudice is, so far as we are able to determine, much greater.

Second, the class action was not literally dismissed. First the class was decertified and then the suit, now an individual rather than a class action, was dismissed. But decertification has the same effect on the members of the class, so far as the running of the statute of limitations is concerned, as dismissal of the class action—it is tantamount to dismissal—and so it should be treated the same under Rule 23(e). Another path to this conclusion is Rule 23(c)(1), which provides that an order certifying a class "may be altered . . . before the decision on the merits." It was on the authority of this rule that the district judge decertified the class. Part of any order "altering" the certification in this way should be a provision for notice to the class members.

Third, since it is the class lawyer who is objecting to the district judge's failure to order that notice of decertification be given, and since the cost of the notice will be borne by her or her client, it might seem that if she wants the class members notified she should go ahead and do it, without bothering the district court or us, and will do so whether or not ordered to do so. But of course she may change her mind, or select an inadequate method of notice. Rule 23(e) is for the protection of the class members, not of the class representative or his lawyer—who will usually have no interest in notifying the class members of the failure of the class action—let alone for the protection of the defendant, who will be content to let sleeping dogs lie. Rule 23(e) should therefore be understood as imposing a duty on the district judge that is nondelegable, he being himself a fiduciary of the class. The judge's duty is to order notice unless the risk of prejudice to absent class members is nil and to review for adequacy the form of notice proposed by class counsel in response to the order.

The case is remanded for compliance with Rule 23(e) * * *.

NOTES AND QUESTIONS

1. Did the court in *Culver* reach the right result? Does it matter whether, in another portion of the decision, the *Culver* court stated that "[s]o far as we can tell, no member of the class has any interest beyond that of a curious onlooker in pursuing this litigation." 277 F.3d at 912–13?

2. When a class action has been certified, and subsequently decertified, under Rule 23(b)(1) or 23(b)(2) without notice to the class members, should notice of decertification be provided? *See Clarke v. Ford Motor Co.*, 228 F.R.D. 631, 637 (E.D. Wis. 2005) (not requiring notice of decertification of class certified under 23(b)(2) where there had been no notice at the time of certification and where no publicity of class certification had occurred).

B. COMMUNICATIONS WITH CLASS MEMBERS

The issue of whether—and under what circumstances—litigants and their counsel in a putative class action may contact absent class members depends on the posture of the suit at the time contact is initiated. Those circumstances are discussed in the materials that follow.

1. CONTACTS WITH POTENTIAL CLASS MEMBERS BEFORE A CLASS ACTION IS FILED

A court's authority to regulate communications with members of a potential class does not arise until a class action is filed with the court. Before then, only the relevant rules of professional conduct regulate attorney contacts. State bars generally have adopted versions of either the ABA Model Rules of Professional Conduct ("Model Rules") or the ABA Model Code of Professional Responsibility, and one must always check the relevant rules to establish the pertinent strictures on attorney communications. But using the Model Rules as examples, three are particularly relevant to pre-filing communications—those regulating (i) contacts with unrepresented parties, (ii) solicitation of clients, and (iii) attorney advertising.

Contacts with potential class members of an as-yet unfiled class action by lawyers for plaintiffs or defendants are governed by the rules regulating contacts with unrepresented persons. Model Rule 4.3 states that:

> In dealing on behalf of a client with a person who is not represented by counsel, a lawyer shall not state or imply that the lawyer is disinterested. When the lawyer knows or reasonably should know that the unrepresented person misunderstands the lawyer's role in the matter, the lawyer shall make reasonable efforts to correct the misunderstanding. * * *

Model Rules of Professional Conduct Rule 4.3 (2009).

Potential plaintiffs' attorneys are bound by additional rules. The attorney may advertise his services. *See* Model Rule 7.2. An attorney may even provide mass mailings (or mass recorded communications) directed at potential class members, provided that (i) the prospective client has not made it known that he does not wish to be solicited, (ii) the solicitation does not involve coercion, duress, or harassment, and (iii) such solicitations clearly indicate that they are advertisements. *See* Model Rule 7.3(b), (c). But because of long-standing scruples about the role of lawyers in fostering litigation, potential plaintiffs' counsel are generally prohibited from initiating direct communications with potential class members designed to persuade them to become plaintiffs. For instance, Model Rule 7.3(a)(2) provides:

> A lawyer shall not by in-person, live telephone or real-time electronic contact solicit professional employment from a prospective client when a significant motive for the lawyer's doing so is the lawyer's pecuniary gain, unless the person contacted:
>
> (1) is a lawyer; or
>
> (2) has a family, close personal, or prior professional relationship with the lawyer.

Model Rules of Professional Conduct Rule 7.3(2) (2009).

Notably, the rules of professional conduct apply only to counsel, and do not apply to *parties* to potential litigation. Thus, a defendant is free to contact would-be plaintiffs to a class action for purposes of discovery and settlement. Likewise, a plaintiff contemplating a class action may contact other would-be plaintiffs to attempt to establish interest in a collective action or to investigate potential claims. Under the rules of professional conduct, however, neither side's *counsel* may encourage such contacts, since counsel is prohibited from using a party (or any other non-lawyer) as an agent to accomplish what counsel would be prohibited from doing personally. *See, e.g.*, Model Rule 8.4(a) (2009). Do the ethical rules provide one side or the other with any advantage in the context of potential class actions? Or do they establish a level playing field?

2. COMMUNICATIONS WITH POTENTIAL CLASS MEMBERS BETWEEN FILING AND CLASS CERTIFICATION

Prior to 1981, it was common practice for courts to prohibit all communications by litigants with absent class members prior to class certification. In the following case, however, the Supreme Court changed the rules.

GULF OIL CO. v. BERNARD
Supreme Court of the United States, 1981.
452 U.S. 89.

JUSTICE POWELL delivered the opinion of the Court.

[*Gulf Oil* was a race discrimination case. Before being sued by the proposed class, Gulf Oil had entered into a consent decree with the Equal Employment Opportunity Commission under which Gulf had agreed to cease various allegedly discriminatory practices, undertake an affirmative action program, and offer backpay to alleged prior victims of discrimination. Gulf began providing notices to its employees of the consent decree, including the exact amount of backpay available, and sought agreements and full releases of all claims from those employees who wanted to participate.

After plaintiffs' class action was filed, Gulf asked the trial court to limit communications between the parties and potential class members. Gulf disclosed its prior communications, but stated that it had ceased its communications with potential class members after the lawsuit was filed. Gulf complained that plaintiffs' counsel had since met with absent potential class members and stated that they should not sign the releases and should return any checks they had received, since they could receive double the backpay through the class action.

The trial court issued an order banning all communications by the parties or their counsel and any actual or potential class member without prior court approval, with a few limited exceptions. The order also provided that if a party or counsel asserted a constitutional right to communicate without prior restraint and in fact engaged in such communication, he or she would have five days to file a copy or summary of the communication with the court. Plaintiffs appealed, claiming that the order violated their First Amendment rights.

A divided panel of the United States Court of Appeals for the Fifth Circuit affirmed the trial court, but the full court of appeals, sitting *en banc*, reversed the panel decision and invalidated the trial court order.

When the Supreme Court took up the issue, rather than addressing the question of limitations on communications under the First Amendment, it addressed whether Rule 23(d) permitted a district court to impose such restrictions.]

* * *

Rule 23(d) of the Federal Rules of Civil Procedure provide[d]: "(d) ORDERS IN CONDUCT OF ACTIONS. In the conduct of actions to which this rule applies, the court may make appropriate orders: . . . (3) imposing conditions on the representative parties or on intervenors . . . [and] (5) dealing with similar procedural matters." * * * [P]rior to reaching any constitutional questions, federal courts must consider nonconstitutional grounds for decision. As a result, in this case we first consider the authority of district courts under the Federal Rules to impose sweeping limitations on communications by named plaintiffs and their counsel to prospective class members.

More specifically, the question for decision is whether the limiting order entered in this case is consistent with the general policies embodied in

Rule 23, which governs class actions in federal court. Class actions serve an important function in our system of civil justice. They present, however, opportunities for abuse as well as problems for courts and counsel in the management of cases. Because of the potential for abuse, a district court has both the duty and the broad authority to exercise control over a class action and to enter appropriate orders governing the conduct of counsel and parties. But this discretion is not unlimited, and indeed is bounded by the relevant provisions of the Federal Rules. * * *

In the present case, we are faced with the unquestionable assertion by respondents that the order created at least potential difficulties for them as they sought to vindicate the legal rights of a class of employees. The order interfered with their efforts to inform potential class members of the existence of this lawsuit, and may have been particularly injurious—not only to respondents but to the class as a whole—because the employees at that time were being pressed to decide whether to accept a backpay offer from Gulf that required them to sign a full release of all liability for discriminatory acts. In addition, the order made it more difficult for respondents, as the class representatives, to obtain information about the merits of the case from the persons they sought to represent.

Because of these potential problems, an order limiting communications between parties and potential class members should be based on a clear record and specific findings that reflect a weighing of the need for a limitation and the potential interference with the rights of the parties. Only such a determination can ensure that the court is furthering, rather than hindering, the policies embodied in the Federal Rules of Civil Procedure, especially Rule 23. In addition, such a weighing—identifying the potential abuses being addressed—should result in a carefully drawn order that limits speech as little as possible, consistent with the rights of the parties under the circumstances. * * *

* * *

In the present case, one looks in vain for any indication of a careful weighing of competing factors. Indeed, in this respect, the District Court failed to provide any record useful for appellate review. The court made neither factual findings nor legal arguments supporting the need for this sweeping restraint order. * * *

The result was an order requiring prior judicial approval of all communications, with the exception of cases where respondents chose to assert a constitutional right. Even then, respondents were required to preserve all communications for submission to the court within five days. The scope of this order is perhaps best illustrated by the fact that the court refused to permit mailing of the one notice respondents submitted for approval. This notice was intended to encourage employees to rely on the class action for relief, rather than accepting Gulf's offer. The court identified nothing in this notice that it thought was improper and indeed gave no reasons for its negative ruling.

We conclude that the imposition of the order was an abuse of discretion. * * * Although we do not decide what standards are mandated by the First Amendment in this kind of case, we do observe that the order involved serious restraints on expression. This fact, at minimum, counsels caution on the part of a district court in drafting such an order, and attention to whether the restraint is justified by a likelihood of serious abuses.

We recognize the possibility of abuses in class-action litigation, and agree with petitioners that such abuses may implicate communications with potential class members. But the mere possibility of abuses does not justify routine adoption of a communications ban that interferes with the formation of a class or the prosecution of a class action in accordance with the Rules. * * *

In the present case, for the reasons stated above, we hold that the District Court abused its discretion. Accordingly, the judgment below is affirmed.

NOTES AND QUESTIONS

1. Following *Gulf Oil*, most courts invalidated local rules like the one struck down in that case. *See, e.g., Williams v. U.S. Dist. Court*, 658 F.2d 430 (6th Cir. 1981) (granting writ of mandamus to invalidate local rule restricting communications with unnamed potential class members). Prior to *Gulf Oil*, however, the prevailing attitude among district courts had been that contacts between counsel in litigation and absent class members could be—and often should be—regulated. Thus, in *Waldo v. Lakeshore Estates, Inc.*, 433 F. Supp. 782, 789–91 (E.D. La. 1977), the district court faced a constitutional challenge to a local rule (Rule 2.12e) virtually identical to the rule that had been adopted and applied by the district court in the *Gulf Oil* litigation:

> * * * Considering * * * the possible solicitation of representation and/or funds, we regard regulation aimed at preventing such an abuse as promotive of both the public's and the legal profession's interests. Not only does curbing solicitation by less than scrupulous attorneys serve those laymen liable to be unfairly badgered and/or persuaded by the activity, but it also protects the reputation and professional image of the bar itself. The local rule expressly states that its prohibitions are separate from and in addition to ethical obligations; but furtherance of the same public and professional interests is the aim of those disciplinary rules enacted by the state and national bar associations which prohibit advertising and solicitation. The need to balance regulatory measures in this area against First Amendment guarantees continues to be the subject of judicial scrutiny, as it remains true that the Government cannot invoke its power to regulate the professional conduct of its attorneys at the expense of the individual's free expression or the public's right to fair legal representation. But such traditional self-governance by the bar, both nationally and locally, reflects its own judgment that the service of professional and public interests outweighs the resulting restriction of free expression.

Id. at 789–90. Do the concerns raised by the *Waldo* court about unregulated communications with absent class members have merit? Does the Supreme Court's ruling in *Gulf Oil* adequately address those concerns?

2. *Gulf Oil* addressed communications by *plaintiffs'* counsel with absent class members of an uncertified class. Should the same rules apply to *defense* communications with absent class members prior to class certification? That question is addressed below.

COX NUCLEAR MED., INC. V. GOLD CUP COFFEE SERV., INC.

United States District Court, Southern District of Alabama, 2003.
214 F.R.D. 696.

STEELE, DISTRICT JUDGE.

This case is before the Court on the plaintiff's motion to show cause, in which the plaintiff seeks an order that the defendant be ordered to show cause why sanctions should not be imposed against it in consequence of its contacts with members of the proposed class. The * * * Court concludes that the plaintiff's motion is due to be denied.

"[A]n order limiting communication between parties and potential class members should be based on a clear record and specific findings that reflect a weighing of the need for a limitation and the potential interference with the rights of the parties." *Gulf Oil Co. v. Bernard*, 452 U.S. 89, 101 (1981). *Bernard* involved contact by plaintiff's counsel, but lower courts have applied *Bernard* to contact by defendants and their counsel as well.

* * *

" '[T]o the extent that the district court is empowered . . . to restrict certain communications in order to prevent frustration of the policies of Rule 23, it may not exercise the power without a *specific record showing* by the moving party of the particular abuses by which it is threatened.' " *Bernard*, 452 U.S. at 102 (emphasis added). * * *

There is no question that the defendant has communicated with class members. The plaintiff has submitted a sample letter from the defendant to a class member. The plaintiff asserts that the defendant has sent similar letters to other class members, an assertion the defendant effectively concedes as accurate. The plaintiff has thus satisfied its burden of showing that a particular form of communication has occurred or is threatened to occur.

The letter at issue informs customers that, between January 2000 and June 2001, the defendant delivered to customers boxes labeled as containing 42 packs of Maxwell House Master Blend coffee but in fact containing only 35 packs. The letter encloses a check which the defendant "believes is the value of the difference between 35 and 42 packets of each box of Maxwell House Master Blend coffee that [the customer] purchased, according to Gold Cup's records, between January of 2000 and June of 2001." The letter and the check reflect that cashing or other endorsement of the check releases the defendant from further liability.

The plaintiff complains that the letter "[1] misrepresents material facts of this case, [2] may well be a fraudulent attempt to terminate these proceedings without full or adequate compensation, and [3] intentionally interferes with the proposed class members' ability to make an informed decision as to whether they should remain in the class, if one is certified." As discussed below, none of these allegations satisfies the plaintiff's burden of showing that the defendant's communication with putative class members is "abusive."

The alleged misrepresentation is that the letter describes the defendant's conduct as "inadvertent," while the plaintiff would characterize it as "knowing, willful and intentional." This might be significant had the plaintiff sued for fraud, opening the door to the possibility of extra-contractual damages. The plaintiff, however, explicitly limits this lawsuit to one for breach of contract and seeks only compensatory damages representing "the benefit of the bargain." The plaintiff's pleading thus renders the defendant's mental state irrelevant to the damages sought in this action and equally irrelevant to the instant motion.

The alleged attempt to settle without paying full compensation is based on the letter's provision of "only Defendant's version of the amount of compensation supposedly due, with no verification of that amount." The plaintiff, however, bears the burden of showing that information in the letter is false; simply implying that it *might* be false does not meet that burden.

The alleged interference with class members' ability to make an informed decision as to class participation is based on the letter's "fail[ure] to advise that a putative class action lawsuit has been filed on [the] customers' behalf." The failure to recognize the existence of a putative class action, however, could be abusive only if the class action sought recovery in excess of that proposed by the defendant, because only then could the class action vehicle offer the possibility of a more favorable result than the proposed settlement. As discussed above, the class action seeks only recovery of the benefit of the bargain, the defendant's letter purports to restore the benefit of the bargain, and the plaintiff has offered no evidence that the settlement offer does not in fact restore the benefit of the bargain.

"A defendant . . . has the right to communicate settlement offers directly to putative class member[s]." The discovered cases in which the court conditioned the transmission of settlement offers involved class members in an inherently coercive dependent relationship with the defendant and/or settlement offers for less than that sought in the lawsuit. Here, no inherently coercive relationship is alleged or apparent and, as discussed above, the settlement offer is for the full amount for which suit is brought.

For the reasons set forth above, the plaintiff's motion to show cause is denied. This denial is without prejudice to the plaintiff's right to seek similar relief based on an adequate factual showing.

NOTES AND QUESTIONS

1. Does it make sense for *Gulf Oil* to apply with equal force to communications by plaintiffs' counsel and those by defense counsel? For example, should defense counsel's communications with potential class members after an action is filed but before a class is certified be barred on the theory that the potential class members are represented by plaintiffs' counsel? Rule 4.2 of the Model Rules of Professional Conduct states that, "[i]n representing a client, a lawyer shall not communicate about the subject of the representation with a person the lawyer knows to be represented by another lawyer in the matter, unless the lawyer has the consent of the other lawyer or is authorized by law to do so." Is an absent putative class member "represented" by the named plaintiffs' counsel for purposes of Model Rule 4.2 prior to class certification? Consider the following:

> Much of the prior confusion that existed with respect to how Model Rule 4.2 should be applied to class actions has been dispelled

by case law and by ABA Comm. on Ethics & Prof. Responsibility, Formal Op. 07–445 (2007). It is now the overwhelming majority rule that putative, as distinct from named, class members are not automatically off-limits to opposing counsel prior to certification of the class. Of course, the ability of a defendant or defense counsel to contact putative class members does not justify coercive or misleading communications, and courts may in any event enter specific orders either permitting or prohibiting various kinds of pre- or post-certification communications.

Particularly difficult questions can arise in contexts such as wage and hour class actions in which the class members—pre- or post-certification—are also employees of the defendant employer. Ironically, the employer will need to turn to the very same employees to obtain the technical and statistical information necessary for its defense, and counsel for the employer will in the ordinary course of the litigation be entitled to have conversations with at least some of them that are protected by the *employer's* attorney-client privilege. The best approach in such situations is almost certainly to seek a reasonable compromise with the guidance of the court, if necessary, that allows both sides to prepare and present their cases without invasion of the other side's attorney-client or work product privileged communications and without threats or intimidation by either side.

2 Geoffrey C. Hazard, Jr. & W. William Hodes, *The Law of Lawyering: A Handbook on the Model Rules of Professional Conduct* § 38.4 at 38–8 (2011 Supp.). Should an absent class member be considered a "represented" person for purposes of Rule 4.2 during the pre-certification stage? What are possible counterarguments by Hazard and Hodes?

2. Would *Cox Nuclear Medicine* have come out differently if plaintiff had brought a fraud suit? What if plaintiff had produced evidence showing that the offer of settlement was for less than the full amount of the absent class members' claims?

3. COMMUNICATIONS WITH CLASS MEMBERS AFTER CLASS CERTIFICATION

HAFFER V. TEMPLE UNIV.
United States District Court, Eastern District of Pennsylvania, 1987.
115 F.R.D. 506.

LORD, SENIOR DISTRICT JUDGE.

[The plaintiff class in this sex discrimination suit consisted of female students at Temple University who participated in intercollegiate athletics or had been deterred from such participation because of sex discrimination. In preparation for trial, class counsel began to schedule meetings with class members. Counsel alleged that, in response, the university issued communications that were designed to discourage class members from participating in such meetings. Specifically, Temple distributed a memorandum, entitled "LOYALTY," to all coaches and staff of the women's intercollegiate athletic department, urging them not to "condemn" the university but to "stand by" it. The memorandum also stated, *inter alia*, that, although female student–athletes could meet with plaintiffs' counsel if they chose to, "[a]ny female student–athlete who does not wish to meet with [plaintiffs' counsel] is free not to meet with him." Class counsel testified that he had difficulty convincing student–athletes to meet with him after the memorandum was circulated. Not only did Temple's Associate Director for Women's Intercollegiate Athletics disseminate the memorandum at team meetings, she also spoke to class members directly about the lawsuit. Class members forwarded the memorandum to class counsel and informed him that they interpreted the memorandum and the Associate Director's remarks to discourage class members from meeting with class counsel.]

DISCUSSION

* * *

Disciplinary rule 7–104(A) of the Code of Professional Responsibility (CPR) provides:

During the course of his representation of a client, a lawyer shall not:

> (1) Communicate or cause another to communicate on the subject of the representation with a party he knows to be represented by a lawyer in that matter unless he has the prior consent of the lawyer representing such other party or is authorized by law to do so.

As set forth in Rule 14 of the Local Rules of [this court], the CPR is a part of the standard of conduct required of lawyers practicing before this court. [Defendant's] conduct was a flagrant and inexcusable violation of professional standards.

* * *

It is, of course, correct that each student athlete is free to decide whether to meet with counsel. However, the clear import of the [LOYALTY] memo is that Temple prefers that its student athletes not meet with class counsel. The memo emphasizes the fact that class members are free *"not"* to meet with [class counsel]. * * * I find that this memo was intended to discourage class members from meeting with class counsel.

REMEDIES

Based on the facts outlined above, I find that defendants have improperly communicated with class members, and that Temple has discouraged class members from meeting with class counsel. In light of these findings, I have "both the duty and the broad authority . . . to enter appropriate orders governing the conduct of counsel and parties." *Gulf Oil v. Bernard*, 452 U.S. 89, 100 (1981). I will grant plaintiffs' requests that the court send a corrective notice to all female student-athletes. Plaintiffs' counsel will submit to the court a proposed notice with copy to defendants' counsel. The notice, when approved, shall be distributed at defendants' expense. I will also award plaintiffs the costs and attorneys' fees resulting from defendants' improper communications and thwarting of discovery, the amounts to be determined after a hearing. I will prohibit future improper communications. Finally I will impose a substantial sanction against defendants and their counsel [$7,500].

* * *

An order prohibiting future improper communications is obviously necessary. * * * Neither court orders, the local rules nor the Code of Professional Responsibility have tempered defendants' counsel's enthusiasm for improper communications with class members. Defendants and their counsel are on notice that violation of this order will result in substantial sanctions.

* * *

NOTES AND QUESTIONS

1. Should the university have been prohibited from sending the "LOYALTY" memorandum and having a representative speak directly to students? Were the sanctions imposed by Judge Lord appropriate?

2. Most courts agree that, once a class is certified, class members should be treated as represented by plaintiffs' counsel for purposes of the rules of professional responsibility. This is true even during the opt-out period. *See, e.g., Impervious Paint Indus., Inc. v. Ashland Oil*, 508 F. Supp. 720 (W.D. Ky.) *appeal dismissed*, 659 F.2d 1081 (6th Cir. 1981); *see also* Douglas R. Richmond, *Class Actions and Ex Parte Communications: Can We Talk?*, 68 Mo. L. Rev. 813, 845–49 (2003) (describing same). Some courts, however, have allowed limited communications by the defense, even after certification, such as business-related contacts between the employer and its employees. *See, e.g.*, Michael J. Steiner & Kurt B. Upsahl, *Attorney Communications in Class Litigation*, 115 Banking L.J. 430, 442–45 (1998) (discussing case law). How should a court draw the line between non-litigation, business-related communications and communications designed to impact the litigation? What should defense counsel do if he or she is not clear whether communication would be permissible?

3. Should Rule 23 contain specific provisions addressing communications with absent members of a certified class? If so, what should the rule provide?

CHAPTER 6

MULTI-JURISDICTIONAL CLASS ACTIONS

■ ■ ■

This chapter addresses the potential advantages and special challenges of a nationwide or other multi-jurisdictional class action. Supporters of multi-jurisdictional class actions often contend that such actions are more efficient for the parties and the judicial system than a series of smaller class actions or countless individual suits. A nationwide class suit also provides an opportunity for a uniform national result, as opposed to a series of potentially conflicting rulings. Detractors, however, respond that courts facing such suits must resolve difficult questions involving what law (or laws) to apply, how to deal with pre-existing lawsuits, and how to ensure that any judgment or settlement is binding on the plaintiffs and the defendants.

Although class actions were designed to deal with large numbers of similarly situated claimants, the case law demonstrates that, in some circumstances, a multi-jurisdictional class action can be so massive and unwieldy that it cannot satisfy the prerequisites of Rule 23. How do courts decide whether a multi-jurisdictional class action is manageable? What constitutional constraints are imposed on such suits? What devices are available to a court to make a nationwide or other multi-jurisdictional class action more viable and manageable? This chapter examines these issues.

As a result of the Class Action Fairness Act of 2005 (CAFA), most multi-state class actions are now heard in federal court rather than in state court. This chapter (along with Chapter 7(B)) also discusses the implications of that change.

A. GENERAL CONSIDERATIONS

CALIFANO V. YAMASAKI
Supreme Court of the United States, 1979.
442 U.S. 682.

JUSTICE BLACKMUN delivered the opinion of the Court.

Petitioner, the Secretary of the Department of Health, Education, and Welfare (HEW), has determined that respondents, beneficiaries under the Social Security Act, have been overpaid. He seeks to recoup those overpayments by withholding future benefits to which respondents would otherwise be entitled. Respondents in turn have requested reconsideration or waiver of recoupment under § 204 of the Act, 42 U.S.C. § 404. [A] primary question[] in this case [is] * * * whether jurisdiction under § 205(g) of the Act, 42 U.S.C. § 405(g), permits a federal district court to certify a nationwide class and grant injunctive relief.

I.

* * *

The [HEW] Secretary's practice is to make an *ex parte* determination under § 204(a) that an overpayment [to a Social Security recipient] has been made, to notify the recipient of that determination, and then to shift to the recipient the burden of either (i) seeking reconsideration to contest the accuracy of that determination, or (ii) asking the Secretary to forgive the debt and waive recovery in accordance with § 204(b). If a recipient files a written request for reconsideration or waiver, recoupment is deferred pending action on that request. The papers are sent to one of the seven regional offices where the request is reviewed.

If the regional office decision goes against the recipient, recoupment begins. The recipient's monthly benefits are reduced or terminated until the overpayment has been recouped. Only if the recipient continues to object is he given an opportunity to present his story in person to someone with authority to decide his case. That opportunity takes the form of an on-the-record *de novo* evidential hearing before an independent hearing examiner. The recipient may seek subsequent review by the Appeals Council, and finally by a federal court. If it is decided that the Secretary's initial determination was in error, the amounts wrongfully recouped are repaid.

II.

[The Court described the first of two consolidated cases, which was certified only as a single-state class action. That discussion has been excluded from this excerpt.]

[In the second case,] the Secretary determined that the individual respondents * * * had been overpaid for previous years. After receiving notice, both named respondents sought administrative relief, but were unable to halt recoupment. * * * [Like the class in the first case, they] alleged that the Secretary's recoupment procedures were contrary to both § 204 and the Due Process Clause of the Fifth Amendment. They requested certification of a nationwide class, an injunction ordering repayment of amounts unlawfully withheld, and declaratory and mandamus relief that would require the Secretary to provide notice and an opportunity for a hearing before recoupment began again.

The District Court certified a nationwide class composed of "all individuals eligible for [old-age and survivors' benefits] whose benefits have been or will be reduced or otherwise adjusted without prior notice and opportunity for a hearing." The court, however, excluded from the class residents of Hawaii and the Eastern District of Pennsylvania, where suits raising similar issues were known to have been brought. * * *

The court then granted summary judgment for the class [and] * * * enjoined the Secretary from ordering recoupment without having provided recipients with a prior opportunity for an informal hearing before an independent decisionmaker. * * *

The United States Court of Appeals for the Ninth Circuit consolidated the two cases for disposition on appeal [and] * * * upheld the certification of the classes under Fed. R. Civ. P. 23(b)(2), finding counsel was sufficiently skilled and experienced to represent the class. It rejected the Secretary's contention that a nationwide class should not have been certified. It found nothing in Rule 23 indicating that such a class was improper, and it believed as a practical matter that, because respondents did not seek damages, no manageability problems were present. It indicated that to require recipients to sue individually would result in an unnecessary duplication of actions, the evil that Rule 23 was designed to prevent. On the merits, the Court of Appeals, without directly addressing respondents' statutory claims, affirmed the holdings that the Secretary's recoupment procedures were unconstitutional.

Subsequent to that decision, this Court, in *Mathews v. Eldridge*, 424 U.S. 319 (1976), held that the Due Process Clause does not require an oral hearing prior to termination of Social Security disability insurance benefits. We then granted petitions for writs of *certiorari* filed by the Secretary * * *, vacated the judgments below, and remanded the cases for further consideration in light of *Eldridge*.

On remand, the Court of Appeals adhered to the essential features of its original decision.

* * *

* * * The Secretary filed a petition for a writ of *certiorari* seeking review of both the holding that the Due Process Clause required a prerecoupment oral hearing, and the determination that the class was properly certified.

* * *

IV.

[The Court first concluded that section 205(g) did not preclude relief on a classwide basis and that a class action in this case was consistent with the requirements of Rule 23.]

* * *

B.

The Secretary next argues that, assuming class actions in fact may be maintained under § 205(g), it was error for the courts here to sustain the nationwide class. * * * He argues that a nationwide class is unwise in that it forecloses reasoned consideration of the same issues by other federal courts and artificially increases the pressure on the docket of this Court by endowing with national importance issues that, if adjudicated in a narrower context, might not require our immediate attention * * *.

Nothing in Rule 23, however, limits the geographical scope of a class action that is brought in conformity with that Rule. Since the class here was certified in accordance with Rule 23(b)(2), the limitations on class size associated with Rule 23(b)(3) actions [*i.e.*, manageability] do not apply directly. Nor is a nationwide class inconsistent with principles of equity jurisprudence, since the scope of injunctive relief is dictated by the extent of the violation established, not by the geographical extent of the plaintiff class. If a class action is otherwise proper, and if jurisdiction lies over the claims of the members of the class, the fact that the class is nationwide in scope does not necessarily mean that the relief afforded the plaintiffs will be more burdensome than necessary to redress the complaining parties.

We concede the force of the Secretary's contentions that nationwide class actions may have a detrimental effect by foreclosing adjudication by a number of different courts and judges, and of increasing, in certain cases, the pressures on this Court's docket. It often will be preferable to allow several courts to pass on a given class claim in order to gain the benefit of adjudication by different courts in different factual contexts. For this reason, a federal court when asked to certify a nationwide class should take care to ensure that nationwide relief is indeed appropriate in the case before it, and that certification of such a class would not improperly interfere with the litigation of similar issues in other judicial districts. But we decline to adopt the extreme position that such a class may never be certified. The certification of a nationwide class, like most issues arising under Rule 23, is committed in the first instance to the discretion of the district court. On the facts of this case we cannot conclude that the District Court * * * abused that discretion, especially in light of its sensitivity to ongoing litigation of the same issue in other districts, and the determination that counsel was adequate to represent the class.

[On the merits, the Supreme Court held that recipients who make a written request for waiver under section 204(b) are entitled to a recoupment hearing, but those who merely seek reconsideration under section 204(a) are not. The Court also upheld the award of injunctive relief.]

NOTES AND QUESTIONS

1. Courts have applied varying standards in determining whether a multi-jurisdictional class—as opposed to a more geographically-limited class—should be certified. For example, in *In re American Medical Systems, Inc.*, 75 F.3d 1069, 1088 (6th Cir. 1996), the Sixth Circuit granted mandamus and reversed district court orders certifying a nationwide class in penile implant cases, in part because of the existence of "previously-filed cases at more advanced stages of litigation." According to the court of appeals, the district court orders "threaten[ed] to throw preexisting cases into disarray," and "[t]he waste of judicial resources due to duplicative proceedings [was] plain and [would] not [be] correctable on appeal." *Id.* In *Geraghty v. United States Parole Commission*, 719 F.2d 1199, 1205 (3d Cir. 1983), the Third Circuit upheld the district court's refusal to certify a nationwide class of prisoners challenging federal parole guidelines, reasoning that the litigation "might interfere with the litigation of similar issues in other judicial districts." In so holding, the court of appeals affirmed the district court's ruling that the class should be limited to those prisoners incarcerated in the Middle District of Pennsylvania. Likewise, in *McBride v. Galaxy Carpet Mills, Inc.*, 920 F. Supp. 1278 (N.D. Ga. 1995), the district court refused to certify a nationwide class of persons alleging personal injuries from exposure to carpets manufactured by the defendants. The court rejected the argument that it should certify such a class because of the "substantial hardship" to plaintiffs by not being allowed to pursue a nationwide class. *Id.* at 1286. The court noted that "plaintiffs could possibly file class actions in each of the 50 states, thereby obviating their concern that individual plaintiffs might not have the financial resources to litigate against the defendants." *Id.*; *see also Torres v. Shalala*, 48 F.3d 887, 891 n.7 (5th Cir. 1995) (reading *Yamasaki* as "advis[ing] federal courts to exercise caution before certifying a nationwide class").

By contrast, in *Lynch v. Rank*, 604 F. Supp. 30, 38–39 (N.D. Cal.), *aff'd*, 747 F.2d 528 (9th Cir. 1984), *amended on reh'g on other grounds*, 763 F.2d 1098

(9th Cir. 1985), the district court certified a nationwide class challenging the government's interpretation of an amendment to the Social Security Act. The court noted that it would not be "equitable to pit plaintiffs against * * * the federal government in a state-by-state battle," particularly where the plaintiffs were "poor and disabled." *Id.* at 38. Similarly, in *Perez–Funez v. INS*, 611 F. Supp. 990, 1001 (C.D. Cal. 1984), the district court certified a nationwide class action challenging the manner in which the INS implemented its voluntary departure procedure with respect to unaccompanied minor aliens. The court noted that "there is little need to allow adjudication by different courts in different factual contexts, because the factual context will never change, regardless of the forum in which it is being litigated * * *." *Id.* at 1001.

2. Under *Yamasaki*, what factors should a court utilize in determining whether certification of a nationwide class is appropriate? Should it matter whether there are ongoing cases in other jurisdictions raising the same issues? Should it matter whether federal or state law is at issue? Should the economic circumstances of either the plaintiffs or the defendants be considered? Does Rule 23 itself provide any guidance in resolving these issues?

3. As discussed in Chapter 2(B)(1), geographic distribution of class members is frequently a factor under Rule 23(a)(1) (impracticability of joinder) weighing in favor of class certification. Yet geographic dispersion makes it *more* difficult to manage the class, and thus weighs against certification under Rule 23(b)(3). How should courts balance these competing concerns in multi-jurisdictional contexts?

ALABAMA V. BLUE BIRD BODY CO.
United States Court of Appeals, Fifth Circuit, 1978.
573 F.2d 309.

Before COLEMAN and FAY, CIRCUIT JUDGES, and KING, DISTRICT JUDGE [(S.D. Fla.), by designation].

FAY, CIRCUIT JUDGE.

We are presented today with an interlocutory appeal from a district court order certifying this antitrust case as a class action on behalf of two plaintiff classes. The issue is whether the district court erred when it certified both a "national class" and a "state class" under Fed. R. Civ. P. 23(b)(3). For a number of reasons, we feel that the granting of class action status as to the plaintiff national class was inappropriate, and * * * we reverse the district court's order [with respect to the national class] and remand for further proceedings.

* * *

Plaintiffs brought this lawsuit * * * against the six manufacturers and seven Alabama distributors of school bus bodies and did not join as defendants other distributors throughout the country or the manufacturers of school bus chassis. * * *

* * *

The plaintiffs' claims against the defendants are that the defendants have since 1960 unlawfully engaged in a conspiracy to restrain trade, and have illegally entered into and maintained contracts and agreements in restraint of trade. [In their state claim, plaintiffs "allege a conspiracy to fix prices on the part of these manufacturers and their Alabama distributors through a process of rotation of bids and accommodation bidding." In their national claim, plaintiffs sue only the manufacturers, and allege, "in addition to a price-fixing charge, a conspiracy to monopolize in violation of § 2 of the Sherman Act."] * * *

* * * [R]ather than limiting the scope of the claim to the "State of Alabama and local agencies within said State," [plaintiffs'] national claim alleges violations on behalf of all "similarly situated governmental or public bodies or agencies within the United States except for the State of Georgia, which have been and will continue to be injured in their business and property by the contracts, agreements, conspiracies, and course of conduct herein described."

* * *

III. The National Class Certification
* * *

[The district court] certified the national class for a determination of "liability" after explaining that the question common to the class was the existence of an antitrust violation. * * * [F]or the certification of the national class to be upheld, we must determine whether the existence of the antitrust violation is a question common to all members of the class, and, if so, whether this question predominates over all other issues which affect only individual members of the class. * * *

A. The Antitrust Violation and the Requirement of a Question Common to the Class

The district court's order finds that proof of the national conspiracy is a question common to the class. Unfortunately, we are presently unable to agree with this conclusion because the little evidence that there is in the record as to how the plaintiffs intend to establish the conspiracy seems to indicate that proof of the conspiracy cannot be made in a manner common to all members of the class.

The evidence brought to our attention by the plaintiffs as to how they plan to establish this nationwide conspiracy was set forth in their brief and consists of a deposition of one of the Alabama distributors. According to the plaintiffs, this deposition is "substantial evidence that the manufacturers decide what price their distributor is to bid in any given situation." An examination of this deposition, however, reveals that it is evidence of nothing more than the fact that antitrust violations might have occurred in Alabama and several other southern states. The deposition in no way establishes a nationwide conspiracy. * * *

* * *

The district court's error in certifying this nationwide class for a determination of liability was in failing to take the steps necessary to determine the manner in which the plaintiffs proposed to prove the antitrust violation. No one questions that it is the plaintiffs who have the burden of establishing that all requirements of Rule 23 have been met, and in this case they have failed to prove to us that there are any common issues of law or fact which predominate over individual issues. The excerpts from the deposition of the Alabama distributor are probative only of the possibility of an Alabama conspiracy—they in no way establish that a price fixing scheme was contemplated in California, New York, Idaho, etc. Of greater importance, however, is whether we are supposed to infer from this offer of proof by the plaintiffs that this is the manner in which they plan on establishing the nationwide conspiracy—*i.e.* by an examination through testimony, exhibits, etc. of the various school bus markets on a state by state basis. If this is the situation, then we fail to see how common issues of fact predominate. * * * The plaintiffs' class includes different sizes of governmental buyers, operating under different conditions throughout the United States, and the products involved, while commonly known as school bus bodies, apparently differ in many respects and have been marketed under various arrangements at different times. Because of these factors, the defendants contend that a common scheme to rotate bids, fix prices, etc., cannot be demonstrated as to all defendants. While we do not necessarily agree with this assessment, it does appear from the limited record before us that the plaintiffs plan to proceed state by state and prove by varying evidence fifty different price-fixing conspiracies. Possibly the plaintiffs think if they can prove that a conspiracy existed in every state, they can then term these different violations one nationwide conspiracy. If this is indeed the plaintiffs' plan, then the national class should not have been certified since there would be no evidence linking the different conspiracies to each other in order to establish the one "common" conspiracy. Common issues of fact do not predominate in such a situation even though all the plaintiffs might have separate causes of actions against the same defendants based upon similar theories of recovery.

* * * [A] remand of this case is necessary, and, on remand, the plaintiffs should be afforded the opportunity to attempt to establish through appropriate discovery the proper predicate for class certification.

B.   Proof of Impact and the Rule 23 Requirements

Assuming that at some point the district court finds that the conspiracy issue is a question common to the class, the court must then decide whether this question predominates over all other issues which affect only individual members of the class, and whether the class action is the superior method to deal with this controversy. * * *

* * *

* * * [P]roof of injury in a price-fixing case will generally consist of some showing by the plaintiff that, as a result of this conspiracy, he had to pay supracompetitive prices for school buses. If there was some uniformity in the quality and price of a school bus, then this requirement of "impact" might cause few problems. But, given the diverse nature of the school bus market, we have difficulty envisioning how the plaintiffs can prove in a *manageable manner* that the conspiracy was indeed implemented in a particular geographical area, and that it did in fact cause damage. * * *

We are not attempting, however, to hold as a matter of law that the impact requirement in the case before us defeats any possibility of a class certification. It may be that the defendants' description of the school bus industry is inaccurate or that the plaintiffs can figure out some way to show impact as to each member of the plaintiffs' class without having to resort to lengthy individualized examinations. We have, however, attempted to emphasize the importance of this element of an antitrust cause of action, and to illustrate how this element is closely intertwined with the determinations which must be made before certifying a class under Rule 23.

* * *

IV. The State Class Certification

No useful purpose would be served by setting forth a parallel discussion of Rule 23 and its requirements as to the state class certification. Many of the problems are the same although to a much lesser degree. Drastically reduced numbers are involved and the state distributors are named parties. There is no contemplated distribution of issues or claims—[the same district court] will be dealing with all claims from start to finish. Should multiple individual claims require separate proof of impact or damage, such proof will be presented in the same district court. Nevertheless, the predominance, superiority, and other elements must be dealt with on a continuing basis.

The learned trial judge has demonstrated a keen awareness of both the advantages and difficulties of Rule 23. This judicial tool specifically provides for continuing review with later certification of additional classes, creation of sub-classes, or decertification. We do not feel there has been an abuse of discretion as to the state class certification, and we, therefore, affirm that action.

V. Conclusion

The order of the district court certifying the national class is reversed and the cause remanded for further proceedings consistent with this opinion.

The order of the district court certifying the state class is affirmed.

NOTES AND QUESTIONS

1. The *Blue Bird* case illustrates that the manageability issues in a nationwide class action can be far more difficult than those in a similar case brought only as a statewide class action. What would the district court have to find in certifying a nationwide class on remand in order to avoid being reversed for abusing its discretion?

2. Are there any kinds of nationwide class actions in which the claims are no more complicated than those in a similar statewide class action? Does it matter whether the issues to be resolved are primarily legal or primarily factual in nature?

3. One court noted that "the antitrust principles underpinning the court's reasoning in *Blue Bird* have experienced no significant changes in the 20 years after [its] publication." *In re Polypropylene Carpet Antitrust Litig.*, 178 F.R.D. 603, 616 (N.D. Ga. 1997). Nonetheless, courts have frequently distinguished *Blue Bird* in certifying nationwide classes. *See, e.g., In re Domestic Air Transp. Antitrust Litig.*, 137 F.R.D. 677, 686–88 (N.D. Ga. 1991) ("This is not a case, as is *Blue Bird*, devoid of evidence concerning the structure of the market and the variations in pricing alternatives. * * * [T]he court finds air passenger service a standardized product consisting of the transport of a passenger from an origin to a destination aboard an aircraft."); *In re Catfish Antitrust Litig.*, 826 F. Supp. 1019, 1040 (N.D. Miss. 1993) (unlike *Blue Bird*, "[h]ere, the allegations and proposed proof address one national conspiracy by the [catfish] processors, which are localized in Mississippi and Alabama").

B. PERSONAL JURISDICTION AND CHOICE-OF-LAW ISSUES

PHILLIPS PETROLEUM CO. v. SHUTTS
Supreme Court of the United States, 1985.
472 U.S. 797.

JUSTICE REHNQUIST delivered the opinion of the Court.

Petitioner is a Delaware corporation which has its principal place of business in Oklahoma. During the 1970's it produced or purchased natural gas from leased land located in 11 different States, and sold most of the gas in interstate commerce. Respondents are some 28,000 of the royalty owners possessing rights to the leases from which petitioner produced the gas; they reside in all 50 States, the District of Columbia, and several foreign countries. Respondents brought a class action against petitioner in the Kansas state court seeking to recover interest on royalty payments which had been delayed by petitioner. They recovered judgment in the trial court, and the Supreme Court of Kansas affirmed the judgment over petitioner's contentions that the Due Process Clause of the Fourteenth Amendment prevented Kansas from adjudicating the claims of all the respondents, and that the Due Process Clause and the Full Faith and Credit Clause of Article IV of the Constitution prohibited the application of Kansas law to all of the transactions between petitioner and respondents. * * * We granted *certiorari* to consider these claims. We reject petitioner's jurisdictional claim, but sustain its claim regarding the choice of law.

* * *

Respondents Irl Shutts, Robert Anderson, and Betty Anderson filed suit against petitioner in Kansas state court, seeking interest payments on their suspended royalties which petitioner had possessed pending the Commission's approval of the price increases. Shutts is a resident of Kansas, and the Andersons live in Oklahoma. Shutts and the Andersons own gas leases in Oklahoma and Texas. Over petitioner's objection the Kansas trial court granted respondents' motion to certify the suit as a class action under Kansas law. The class as certified was comprised of 33,000 royalty owners who had royalties suspended by petitioner. The average claim of each royalty owner for interest on the suspended royalties was $100.

After the class was certified, respondents provided each class member with notice through first-class mail. The notice described the action and informed each class member that he could appear in person or by counsel; otherwise each member would be represented by Shutts and the Andersons, the named plaintiffs. The notices also stated that class members would be included in the class and bound by the judgment unless they "opted out" of the lawsuit by executing and returning a "request for exclusion" that was included with the notice. The final class as certified contained 28,100 members; 3,400 had "opted out" of the class by returning the request for exclusion, and notice could not be delivered to another 1,500 members, who were also excluded. Less than 1,000 of the class members resided in Kansas. Only a minuscule amount, approximately one quarter of one percent, of the gas leases involved in the lawsuit were on Kansas land.

After petitioner's mandamus petition to decertify the class was denied, the case was tried to the court. The court found petitioner liable under Kansas law for interest on the suspended royalties to all class members. * * * The trial court did not determine whether any difference existed between the laws of Kansas and other States, or whether another State's laws should be applied to non-Kansas plaintiffs or to royalties from leases in States other than Kansas.

[The Supreme Court of Kansas affirmed.]

* * *

II.

Reduced to its essentials, petitioner's argument is that unless out-of-state plaintiffs affirmatively consent, the Kansas courts may not exert jurisdiction over their claims. Petitioner claims that failure to execute and return the "request for exclusion" provided with the class notice cannot constitute consent of the out-of-state plaintiffs; thus Kansas courts may exercise jurisdiction over these plaintiffs only if the plaintiffs possess the sufficient "minimum contacts" with Kansas as that term is used in cases involving personal jurisdiction over out-of-state defendants. *E.g.*, *Int'l Shoe Co. v. Washington*, 326 U.S. 310 (1945); *Shaffer v. Heitner*, 433 U.S. 186 (1977); *World–Wide Volkswagen Corp. v. Woodson*, 444 U.S. 286 (1980). Since Kansas had no prelitigation contact with many of the plaintiffs and leases involved, petitioner claims that Kansas has exceeded its jurisdictional reach and thereby violated the due process rights of the absent plaintiffs.

* * *

We think petitioner's premise is in error. The burdens placed by a State upon an absent class-action plaintiff are not of the same order or magnitude as those it places upon an absent defendant. An out-of-state defendant summoned by a plaintiff is faced with the full powers of the forum State to render judgment *against* it. The defendant must generally hire counsel and travel to the forum to defend itself from the plaintiff's claim, or suffer a default judgment. The defendant may be forced to participate in extended and often costly discovery, and will be forced to respond in damages or to comply with some other form of remedy imposed by the court should it lose the suit. The defendant may also face liability for court costs and attorney's fees. These burdens are substantial, and the minimum contacts requirement of the Due Process Clause prevents the forum State from unfairly imposing them upon the defendant.

A class-action plaintiff, however, is in quite a different posture. * * *

Modern plaintiff class actions * * * permit[] litigation of a suit involving common questions when there are too many plaintiffs for proper joinder. Class actions also may permit the plaintiffs to pool claims which would be uneconomical to litigate individually. For example, this lawsuit involves claims averaging about $100 per plaintiff; most of the plaintiffs would have no realistic day in court if a class action were not available.

In sharp contrast to the predicament of a defendant haled into an out-of-state forum, the plaintiffs in this suit were not haled anywhere to defend themselves upon pain of a default judgment. * * *

A plaintiff class in Kansas and numerous other jurisdictions cannot first be certified unless the judge, with the aid of the named plaintiffs and defendant, conducts an inquiry [to determine that the requirements for certification have been met]. * * * Unlike a defendant in a civil suit, a class-action plaintiff is not required to fend for himself. The court and named plaintiffs protect his interests. * * *

The concern of the typical class-action rules for the absent plaintiffs is manifested in other ways. Most jurisdictions, including Kansas, require that a class action, once certified, may not be dismissed or compromised without the approval of the court. * * *

Besides this continuing solicitude for their rights, absent plaintiff class members are not subject to other burdens imposed upon defendants. They need not hire counsel or appear. They are almost never subject to counterclaims or cross-claims, or liability for fees or costs. Absent plaintiff class members are not subject to coercive or punitive remedies. Nor will an adverse judgment typically bind an absent plaintiff for any damages, although a valid adverse judgment may extinguish any of the plaintiffs' claims which were litigated.

Unlike a defendant in a normal civil suit, an absent class-action plaintiff is not required to do anything. He may sit back and allow the litigation to run its course, content in knowing that there are safeguards provided for his protection. In most class actions an absent plaintiff is provided at least with an opportunity to "opt out" of the class, and if he takes advantage of that opportunity he is removed from the litigation entirely. This was true of the Kansas proceedings in this case. * * *

Petitioner contends, however, that the "opt out" procedure provided by Kansas is not good enough, and that an "opt in" procedure is required to satisfy the Due Process Clause of the Fourteenth Amendment. Insofar as plaintiffs who have no minimum contacts with the forum State are concerned, an "opt in" provision would require that each class member affirmatively consent to his inclusion within the class.

Because States place fewer burdens upon absent class plaintiffs than they do upon absent defendants in nonclass suits, the Due Process Clause need not and does not afford the former as much protection from state-court jurisdiction as it does the latter. * * * [W]e hold that a forum State may exercise jurisdiction over the claim of an absent class-action plaintiff, even though that plaintiff may not possess the minimum contacts with the forum which would support personal jurisdiction over a defendant. If the forum State wishes to bind an absent plaintiff concerning a claim for money damages or similar relief at law,[3] it must provide minimal procedural due process protection. The plaintiff must receive notice plus an opportunity to be heard and participate in the litigation, whether in person or through counsel. * * * Additionally, we hold that due process requires at a minimum that an absent plaintiff be provided with an opportunity to remove himself

---

[3] Our holding today is limited to those class actions which seek to bind known plaintiffs concerning claims wholly or predominantly for money damages. We intimate no view concerning other types of class actions, such as those seeking equitable relief. Nor, of course, does our discussion of personal jurisdiction address class actions where the jurisdiction is asserted against a *defendant* class.

from the class by executing and returning an "opt out" or "request for exclusion" form to the court. Finally, the Due Process Clause of course requires that the named plaintiff at all times adequately represent the interests of the absent class members.

We reject petitioner's contention that the Due Process Clause of the Fourteenth Amendment requires that absent plaintiffs affirmatively "opt in" to the class, rather than be deemed members of the class if they do not "opt out." * * *

* * * Requiring a plaintiff to affirmatively request inclusion would probably impede the prosecution of those class actions involving an aggregation of small individual claims, where a large number of claims are required to make it economical to bring suit. The plaintiff's claim may be so small, or the plaintiff so unfamiliar with the law, that he would not file suit individually, nor would he affirmatively request inclusion in the class if such a request were required by the Constitution. If, on the other hand, the plaintiff's claim is sufficiently large or important that he wishes to litigate it on his own, he will likely have retained an attorney or have thought about filing suit, and should be fully capable of exercising his right to "opt out."

In this case over 3,400 members of the potential class did "opt out," which belies the contention that "opt out" procedures result in guaranteed jurisdiction by inertia. Another 1,500 were excluded because the notice and "opt out" form was undeliverable. We think that such results show that the "opt out" procedure provided by Kansas is by no means *pro forma* * * *. Petitioner's "opt in" requirement would require the invalidation of scores of state statutes and of the class-action provision of the Federal Rules of Civil Procedure * * *.

We therefore hold that the protection afforded the plaintiff class members by the Kansas statute satisfies the Due Process Clause. * * *

III.

The Kansas courts applied Kansas contract and Kansas equity law to every claim in this case, notwithstanding that over 99% of the gas leases and some 97% of the plaintiffs in the case had no apparent connection to the State of Kansas except for this lawsuit. Petitioner protested that the Kansas courts should apply the laws of the States where the leases were located, or at least apply Texas and Oklahoma law because so many of the leases came from those States. The Kansas courts disregarded this contention. * * *

Petitioner contends that total application of Kansas substantive law violated the constitutional limitations on choice of law mandated by the Due Process Clause of the Fourteenth Amendment and the Full Faith and Credit Clause of Article IV, § 1. We must first determine whether Kansas law conflicts in any material way with any other law which could apply. There can be no injury in applying Kansas law if it is not in conflict with that of any other jurisdiction connected to this suit.

Petitioner claims that Kansas law conflicts with that of a number of States connected to this litigation, especially Texas and Oklahoma [on a range of issues] * * *.

* * *

The conflicts on the applicable interest rates, alone—which we do not think can be labeled "false conflicts" without a more thoroughgoing treatment than was accorded them by the Supreme Court of Kansas—certainly amounted to millions of dollars in liability. We think that the Supreme Court of Kansas erred in deciding on the basis that it did that the application of its laws to all claims would be constitutional.

* * *

Petitioner owns property and conducts substantial business in the State, so Kansas certainly has an interest in regulating petitioner's conduct in Kansas. Moreover, oil and gas extraction is an important business to Kansas, and although only a few leases in issue are located in Kansas, hundreds of Kansas plaintiffs were affected by petitioner's suspension of royalties. * * *

We do not lightly discount * * * [Kansas'] interest in applying its law. There is, however, no "common fund" located in Kansas that would require or support the application of only Kansas law to all these claims * * * There is no specific identifiable *res* in Kansas, nor is there any limited amount which may be depleted before every plaintiff is compensated. * * *

We also give little credence to the idea that Kansas law should apply to all claims because the plaintiffs, by failing to opt out, evinced their desire to be bound by Kansas law. Even if one could say that the plaintiffs "consented" to the application of Kansas law by not opting out, plaintiff's desire for forum law is rarely, if ever controlling * * *. Thus the plaintiffs' desire for Kansas law, manifested by their participation in this Kansas lawsuit, bears little relevance.

The Supreme Court of Kansas in its opinion in this case expressed the view that by reason of the fact that it was adjudicating a nationwide class action, it had much greater latitude in applying its own law to the transactions in question than might otherwise be the case * * *.

We think that this is something of a "bootstrap" argument. The Kansas class-action statute, like those of most other jurisdictions, requires that there be "common issues of law or fact." But while a State may, for the reasons we have previously stated, assume jurisdiction over the claims of plaintiffs whose principal contacts are with other States, it may not use this assumption of jurisdiction as an added weight in the scale when considering the permissible constitutional limits on choice of substantive law. * * *

Kansas must have a "significant contact or significant aggregation of contacts" to the claims asserted by each member of the plaintiff class, contacts "creating state interests," in order to ensure that the choice of Kansas law is not arbitrary or unfair. Given Kansas' lack of "interest" in claims unrelated to that State, and the substantive conflict with jurisdictions such as Texas, we conclude that application of Kansas law to every claim in this case is sufficiently arbitrary and unfair as to exceed constitutional limits.

When considering fairness in this context, an important element is the expectation of the parties. * * * There is no indication that when the leases involving land and royalty owners outside of Kansas were executed, the parties had any idea that Kansas law would control. * * *.

Here the Supreme Court of Kansas took the view that in a nationwide class action where procedural due process guarantees of notice and adequate representation were met, "the law of the forum should be applied unless compelling reasons exist for applying a different law." Whatever practical reasons may have commended this rule to the Supreme Court of Kansas, for the reasons already stated we do not believe that it is consistent with the decisions of this Court. * * * [C]onstitutional limitations * * * must be respected even in a nationwide class action.

We therefore affirm the judgment of the Supreme Court of Kansas insofar as it upheld the jurisdiction of the Kansas courts over the plaintiff class members in this case, and reverse its judgment insofar as it held that Kansas law was applicable to all of the transactions which it sought to adjudicate. We remand the case to that court for further proceedings not inconsistent with this opinion.

NOTES AND QUESTIONS

1. What are the two principal holdings announced by *Shutts*? Consider, with respect to each holding, whether the result makes nationwide class actions more feasible or less feasible.

2. The *Shutts* analysis relating to due process, notice, and opt-out rights is very important in the class action context, but its meaning is obscure. *Shutts* will therefore resurface in a later chapter considering *res judicata* and federal control of state class actions. *See* Chapter 7(C)(1)(b).

3. The argument in *Shutts* that the class members were being denied due process came not from members of the class but from Phillips Petroleum, the party being *sued* by the class. Why was Phillips Petroleum against class certification? Had it prevailed on the merits, it would not have had to worry about any such suits in the future. Did Phillips Petroleum really want to adjudicate each $100 claim separately? How credible is it for a defendant to argue that the plaintiff class members are being denied their constitutional rights? Notably, the Court in *Shutts* specifically held that Phillips Petroleum had standing to object to the class action procedures. *See* 472 U.S. at 805 ("As a class-action defendant petitioner is in a unique predicament. If Kansas does not possess jurisdiction over this plaintiff class, petitioner will be bound to 28,100 judgment holders scattered across the globe, but none of these will be bound by the Kansas decree.").

4. In analyzing the personal jurisdiction issues addressed by *Shutts*, one commentator has noted:

> [A] close reading of *Shutts* demonstrates that the court employed the opt-out right as a form of fictional consent to address a personal jurisdiction issue that might have prevented class certification. * * * Because national class actions are necessary to provide relief where it might otherwise be unattainable, *Shutts* adopted a lower standard of "minimal procedural due process" to replace minimum contacts.

Michael A. Perino, *Class Action Chaos: The Theory of the Core and an Analysis of Opt-Out Rights in Mass Tort Class Actions*, 46 Emory L.J. 85, 95 n.24 (1997). Is *Shutts* faithful to the due process concerns of *International Shoe* and its progeny? Or did the Supreme Court engage in a result-oriented approach to preserve the viability of class actions? Are *International Shoe* and its progeny even applicable?

5. The *Shutts* Court suggests in footnote 3 that its analysis of personal jurisdiction does not necessarily apply to defendant classes. A defendant class involves a suit *against* a class of parties rather than a suit *by* a class. Should the rule in fact be the same? What reasons exist for treating a defendant class differently? *See* Chapter 11(A) (discussing defendant class actions).

6. Although *Shutts* involved a state-court class action, courts have generally recognized that the ruling's due process and choice-of-law requirements apply to federal class actions as well. *See In re Asbestos Litig*, 90 F.3d 963, 1002 n.19 (5th Cir. 1996) (Smith, J., dissenting) (collecting cases), *rev'd on other grounds sub nom., Ortiz v. Fibreboard Corp.* 527 U.S. 815 (1999); *see also* Linda S. Mullenix, *Class Actions, Personal Jurisdiction, and Plaintiffs' Due Process: Implications for Mass Tort Litigation*, 28 U.C. Davis L. Rev. 871, 896 (1995). Are there any reasons why different standards should apply to federal class actions? If so, what standards should apply?

7. Does *Shutts* establish who has the burden of showing whether laws of different jurisdictions conflict? Who *should* have this burden?

8. In *Sun Oil Co. v. Wortman*, 486 U.S. 717 (1988), the Supreme Court addressed the question whether relief is available if a state court, in the context of a multi-state class action, misapplies the law of another jurisdiction:

> To constitute a violation of the Full Faith and Credit Clause or the Due Process Clause, it is not enough that a state court misconstrue the law of another State. Rather, our cases make plain that the misconstruction must contradict law of the other State that is clearly established and that has been brought to the [state] court's attention.

Id. at 730–31. Why is the role of the appellate court so limited in this context? Should the same rule apply if a federal trial court residing in one state misconstrues the law of a different state?

9. *Shutts* was a state-court class action, brought pursuant to a Kansas rule similar to Federal Rule 23. Approximately two thirds of the states have class action rules patterned after Federal Rule 23. *See* H.R. Rep. No. 108–144, 2003 WL 21321526, at *9 (June 9, 2003) ("Thirty-six States have adopted the basic Federal class action rule (amended Federal Rule 23) * * *."). In most of these states, courts view interpretations of Federal Rule 23 as authoritative. *See, e.g., First Ala. Bank v. Martin,* 425 So. 2d 415 (Ala. 1983); *Johnson v. Moore,* 496 P.2d 334 (Wash. 1972). Two states have no class action rule at all. *See* H.R. Rep. No. 108–144, 2003 WL 21321526, at *9 (June 9, 2003) (discussing Virginia and Mississippi). In Virginia, class action suits may be brought only to the extent allowed by judicial decision. *See, e.g., Miller v. Nat'l Wildlife Fed'n.,* 1987 WL 488717 (Va. Cir. Ct. 1987). In Mississippi, class actions do not exist by rule or at common law. *See, e.g., Marx v. Montgomery,* 632 So. 2d 1315, 1322 (Miss. 1994). The remaining states take a variety of approaches. *See generally* H.R. Rep. No. 108–144, 2003 WL 21321526, at *9 (June 9, 2003); Neb. Rev. Stat. § 25–319 (using version from nineteenth century); S.C.R.C.P. 23 (adopting only a portion of Federal Rule 23, with modifications); Pa. R. Civ. P. (adoption only a portion of Federal Rule 23, with modifications different from South Carolina's); *see also, e.g.,* Robert H. Klonoff, *The Adoption of a Class Action Rule: Some Issues for Mississippi to Consider*, 24 Miss. C. L. Rev. 261 (2005) (discussing various state approaches).

10. In *Shutts,* the Court held that Kansas could not constitutionally apply its laws to absent class members under the facts of that case. This constitutional limitation poses challenging problems to courts considering whether to certify multi-jurisdictional class actions involving state-law claims. Several courts have held that, even after *Shutts,* it is proper to apply one state's law in a multi-jurisdictional class action when there are significant contacts with respect to each class member's claim—for example, when the defendant is based in a particular state and the critical acts at issue occurred there. *See, e.g., In re Kirschner Med. Corp. Sec. Litig.,* 139 F.R.D. 74 (D. Md. 1991); *Randle v. Spectran,* 129 F.R.D. 386 (D. Mass. 1988). As one court held in a nationwide securities class action:

> Given that Plaintiffs have alleged that [defendant Worlds of Wonder] has its principal place of business in California, that the corporate officers are all residents of California, and that the alleged misrepresentations emanated from California, there appears to be significant contact between Plaintiffs' claims and California such that application of California law would not be arbitrary or fundamentally unfair.

In re Worlds of Wonder Sec. Litig., 1990 WL 61951, at *17 (N.D. Cal. 1990); *cf. In re Pizza Time Theatre Sec. Litig.,* 112 F.R.D. 15, 20 (N.D. Cal. 1986) (applying California law to class members from 28 states and 15 foreign countries because, *inter alia,* "each of the interested jurisdictions share[d] the goals of deterring fraudulent conduct").

In many circumstances, however, a court cannot conclude, consistent with due process, that the forum's law can be applied on a national basis. *See, e.g., In re St. Jude Med., Inc., Silzone Heart Valve Prods. Liab. Litig.,* 425 F.3d 1116, 1120–21 (8th Cir. 2005) (holding that district court's (b)(3) certification of class of 11,000 Silzone valve recipients "assumedly residing in numerous states" was a violation of Due Process and Full Faith and Credit Clauses because the "district court did not conduct a thorough conflicts-of-law analysis with respect to each plaintiff class member before applying Minnesota law"); *In re Ford Motor Co. Bronco II Prod. Liab. Litig.,* 177 F.R.D. 360 (E.D. La. 1997) (refusing to apply Michigan law to nationwide class of Ford Bronco owners). Unless there is some way to apply federal common law (discussed later in this chapter), courts in those circumstances must then determine whether choice-of-law issues preclude certification of a nationwide class.

The following cases examine various ways in which courts have dealt with choice-of-law issues in the context of class actions.

IN RE RHONE–POULENC RORER, INC.
United States Court of Appeals, Seventh Circuit, 1995.
51 F.3d 1293.

Before POSNER, CHIEF JUDGE, and BAUER and ROVNER, CIRCUIT JUDGES.

POSNER, CHIEF JUDGE.

Drug companies that manufacture blood solids are the defendants in a nationwide class action brought on behalf of hemophiliacs infected by the AIDS virus as a consequence of using the defendants' products. The defendants have filed with us a petition for mandamus, asking us to direct the district judge to rescind his order certifying the case as a class action. * * *

* * *

The suit to which the petition for mandamus relates, *Wadleigh v. Rhone–Poulenc Rorer Inc.*, arises out of the infection of a substantial fraction of the hemophiliac population of this country by the AIDS virus because the blood supply was contaminated by the virus before the nature of the disease was well understood or adequate methods of screening the blood supply existed. The AIDS virus (HIV—human immunodeficiency virus) is transmitted by the exchange of bodily fluids, primarily semen and blood. Hemophiliacs depend on blood solids that contain the clotting factors whose absence defines their disease. These blood solids are concentrated from blood obtained from many donors. If just one of the donors is infected by the AIDS virus, the probability that the blood solids manufactured in part from his blood will be infected is very high unless the blood is treated with heat to kill the virus. * * *

First identified in 1981, AIDS was diagnosed in hemophiliacs beginning in 1982, and by 1984 the medical community agreed that the virus was transmitted by blood as well as by semen. That year it was demonstrated that treatment with heat could kill the virus in the blood supply and in the following year a reliable test for the presence of the virus in blood was developed. By this time, however, a large number of hemophiliacs had become infected. Since 1984 physicians have been advised to place hemophiliacs on heat-treated blood solids, and since 1985 all blood donated for the manufacture of blood solids has been screened and supplies discovered to be HIV-positive have been discarded. Supplies that test negative still are heat-treated, because the test is not infallible and in particular may fail to detect the virus in persons who became infected within six months before taking the test.

The plaintiffs have presented evidence that 2,000 hemophiliacs have died of AIDS and that half or more of the remaining U.S. hemophiliac population of 20,000 may be HIV-positive. Unless there are dramatic breakthroughs in the treatment of HIV or AIDS, all infected persons will die from the disease. The reason so many are infected even though the supply of blood for the manufacture of blood solids (as for transfusions) has been safe since the mid-80s is that the disease has a very long incubation period; the median period for hemophiliacs may be as long as 11 years. Probably most of the hemophiliacs who are now HIV-positive, or have AIDS, or have died of AIDS were infected in the early 1980s, when the blood supply was contaminated.

Some 300 lawsuits, involving some 400 plaintiffs, have been filed, 60 percent of them in state courts, 40 percent in federal district courts under the diversity jurisdiction, seeking to impose tort liability on the defendants for the transmission of HIV to hemophiliacs in blood solids manufactured by the defendants. Obviously these 400 plaintiffs represent only a small fraction of the hemophiliacs (or their next of kin, in cases in which the hemophiliac has died) who are infected by HIV or have died of AIDS. One of the 300 cases is *Wadleigh*, filed in September 1993, the case that the district judge certified as a class action. Thirteen other cases have been tried already in various courts around the country, and the defendants have won twelve of them. All the cases brought in federal court (like *Wadleigh*)—

cases brought under the diversity jurisdiction—have been consolidated for pretrial discovery in the Northern District of Illinois * * *.

The plaintiffs advance two principal theories of liability. The first is that before anyone had heard of AIDS or HIV, it was known that Hepatitis B, a lethal disease though less so than HIV–AIDS, could be transmitted either through blood transfusions or through injection of blood solids. The plaintiffs argue that due care with respect to the risk of infection with Hepatitis B required the defendants to take measures to purge that virus from their blood solids, whether by treating the blood they bought or by screening the donors—perhaps by refusing to deal with *paid* donors, known to be a class at high risk of being infected with Hepatitis B. The defendants' failure to take effective measures was, the plaintiffs claim, negligent. Had the defendants not been negligent, the plaintiffs further argue, hemophiliacs would have been protected not only against Hepatitis B but also, albeit fortuitously or as the plaintiffs put it "serendipitously," against HIV.

The plaintiffs' second theory of liability is more conventional. It is that the defendants, again negligently, dragged their heels in screening donors and taking other measures to prevent contamination of blood solids by HIV when they learned about the disease in the early 1980s. The plaintiffs have other theories of liability as well, including strict products liability, but it is not necessary for us to get into them.

The district judge did not think it feasible to certify *Wadleigh* as a class action for the adjudication of the entire controversy between the plaintiffs and the defendants. Fed. R. Civ. P. 23(b)(3). The differences in the date of infection alone of the thousands of potential class members would make such a procedure infeasible. Hemophiliacs infected before anyone knew about the contamination of blood solids by HIV could not rely on the second theory of liability, while hemophiliacs infected after the blood supply became safe (not perfectly safe, but nearly so) probably were not infected by any of the defendants' products. Instead, the judge certified the suit "as a class action with respect to particular issues" only. Fed. R. Civ. P. 23(c)(4)(A). He explained this decision in an opinion which implied that he did not envisage the entry of a final judgment but rather the rendition by a jury of a special verdict that would answer a number of questions bearing, perhaps decisively, on whether the defendants are negligent under either of the theories sketched above. If the special verdict found no negligence under either theory, that presumably would be the end of all the cases unless other theories of liability proved viable. If the special verdict found negligence, individual members of the class would then file individual tort suits in state and federal district courts around the nation and would use the special verdict, in conjunction with the doctrine of collateral estoppel, to block relitigation of the issue of negligence.

With all due respect for the district judge's commendable desire to experiment with an innovative procedure for streamlining the adjudication of this "mass tort," we believe that his plan so far exceeds the permissible bounds of discretion in the management of federal litigation as to compel us to intervene and order decertification. * * *

* * *

* * * [The district judge] proposes to have a jury determine the negligence of the defendants under a legal standard that does not actually exist

anywhere in the world. One is put in mind of the concept of "general" common law that prevailed in the era of *Swift v. Tyson*, 41 U.S. (16 Pet.) 1 (1842). The assumption is that the common law of the 50 states and the District of Columbia, at least so far as bears on a claim of negligence against drug companies, is basically uniform and can be abstracted in a single instruction. It is no doubt true that at some level of generality the law of negligence is one, not only nationwide but worldwide. Negligence is a failure to take due care, and due care [is] a function of the probability and magnitude of an accident and the costs of avoiding it. A jury can be asked whether the defendants took due care. And in many cases such differences as there are among the tort rules of the different states would not affect the outcome. The Second Circuit was willing to assume *dubitante* that this was true of the issues certified for class determination in the Agent Orange litigation. *In re Diamond Shamrock Chemicals Co.*, 725 F.2d 858, 861 (2d Cir. 1984).

We doubt that it is true in general, and we greatly doubt that it is true in a case such as this in which one of the theories pressed by the plaintiffs, the "serendipity" theory, is novel. If one instruction on negligence will serve to instruct the jury on the legal standard of every state of the United States applicable to a novel claim, implying that the claim despite its controversiality would be decided identically in all 50 states and the District of Columbia, one wonders what the Supreme Court thought it was doing in the *Erie* case when it held that it was *unconstitutional* for federal courts in diversity cases to apply general common law rather than the common law of the state whose law would apply if the case were being tried in state rather than federal court. *Erie R.R. v. Tompkins*, 304 U.S. 64, 78–80 (1938). The law of negligence, including subsidiary concepts such as duty of care, foreseeability, and proximate cause, may as the plaintiffs have argued forcefully to us differ among the states only in nuance, though we think not, for a reason discussed later. But nuance can be important, and its significance is suggested by a comparison of differing state pattern instructions on negligence and differing judicial formulations of the meaning of negligence and the subordinate concepts. * * *

The "serendipity" theory advanced by the plaintiffs in *Wadleigh* is that if the defendants did not do enough to protect hemophiliacs from the risk of Hepatitis B, they are liable to hemophiliacs for any consequences—including infection by the more dangerous and at the time completely unknown AIDS virus—that proper measures against Hepatitis B would, all unexpectedly, have averted. This theory of liability * * * dispenses, rightly or wrongly from the standpoint of the Platonic Form of negligence, with proof of foreseeability, even though a number of states, in formulating their tests for negligence, incorporate the foreseeability of the risk into the test. These states follow Judge Cardozo's famous opinion in *Palsgraf v. Long Island R.R.*, 248 N.Y. 339, 162 N.E. 99 (N.Y. 1928), under which the HIV plaintiffs might (we do not say would—we express no view on the substantive issues in this litigation) be barred from recovery on the ground that they were unforeseeable victims of the alleged failure of the defendants to take adequate precautions against infecting hemophiliacs with Hepatitis B and that therefore the drug companies had not violated any duty of care to them.

The plaintiffs' second theory focuses on the questions when the defendants should have learned about the danger of HIV in the blood supply and when, having learned about it, they should have taken steps to eliminate the danger or at least warn hemophiliacs or their physicians of it. These questions also may be sensitive to the precise way in which a state formulates its standard of negligence. If not, one begins to wonder why this country bothers with different state legal systems.

Both theories, incidentally, may be affected by differing state views on the role of industry practice or custom in determining the existence of negligence. In some states, the standard of care for a physician, hospital, or other provider of medical services, including blood banks, is a professional standard, that is, the standard fixed by the relevant profession. In others, it is the standard of ordinary care, which may, depending on judge or jury, exceed the professional standard. Which approach a state follows, and whether in those states that follow the professional-standard approach manufacturers of blood solids would be assimilated to blood banks as providers of medical services entitled to shelter under the professional standard, could make a big difference in the liability of these manufacturers. We note that persons infected by HIV through blood transfusions appear to have had little better luck suing blood banks than HIV-positive hemophiliacs have had suing the manufacturers of blood solids.

The diversity jurisdiction of the federal courts is, after *Erie*, designed merely to provide an alternative forum for the litigation of state-law claims, not an alternative system of substantive law for diversity cases. But under the district judge's plan the thousands of members of the plaintiff class will have their rights determined, and the four defendant manufacturers will have their duties determined, under a law that is merely an amalgam, an averaging, of the nonidentical negligence laws of 51 jurisdictions. No one doubts that Congress could constitutionally prescribe a uniform standard of liability for manufacturers of blood solids. It might we suppose promulgate pertinent provisions of the Restatement (Second) of Torts. The point of *Erie* is that Article III of the Constitution does not empower the federal courts to create such a regime for diversity cases.

If in the course of individual litigations by HIV-positive hemophiliacs juries render special verdicts that contain findings which do not depend on the differing state standards of negligence—for example a finding concerning the date at which one or more of the defendants learned of the danger of HIV contamination of the blood supply—these findings may be given collateral estoppel effect in other lawsuits, at least in states that allow "offensive" use of collateral estoppel. In that way the essential purpose of the class action crafted by [the court below] will be accomplished. If there are relevant differences in state law, findings in one suit will not be given collateral estoppel effect in others—and that is as it should be.

* * *

* * * The petition for a writ of mandamus is granted, and the district judge is directed to decertify the plaintiff class.

[Dissenting opinion by JUDGE ROVNER is omitted.]

IN RE COPLEY PHARM., INC., "ALBUTEROL" PROD. LIAB. LITIG.

United States District Court, District of Wyoming, 1995.
161 F.R.D. 456.

BRIMMER, DISTRICT JUDGE.

The above-entitled matter comes before the Court on the Defendant's Motion to Decertify the Class and the Plaintiffs' opposition thereto, and the trial plans submitted by the parties, and the Court, having reviewed the relevant materials on file herein, having heard the oral arguments of the parties and being fully informed in the premises, FINDS and ORDERS as follows:

BACKGROUND

This case involves a national class action product liability lawsuit against Defendant Copley Pharmaceutical, Inc. A history of the case can be found in the Court's Order Granting Partial Class Certification. *In re Copley Pharm., Inc.*, 158 F.R.D. 485 (D. Wyo. 1994). Copley manufactures generic drugs including Albuterol, a bronchodilator prescription pharmaceutical. Copley's Albuterol was the subject of a nationwide recall in January 1994 after contamination was discovered in its Albuterol 0.5% solution. The exact nature, cause and extent of this contamination remains the subject of much controversy and is one of the issues pending before this Court.

Following the recall, Copley was named in a large number of lawsuits filed throughout the United States. Ultimately the Judicial Panel on Multidistrict Litigation consolidated all the federal cases brought against Copley in this Court. [*See* Chapter 12 (discussing multidistrict litigation).] * * *

On October 28, 1994, the Court issued its Order Granting Partial Class Certification. In that Order the Court recognized the presence of several common threshold issues affecting the class:

(1) Were the Defendant's manufacturing processes defective?

(2) Was the Defendant negligent in its manufacture and distribution of Albuterol?

(3) Did the Defendant breach any warranties in selling its product? and

(4) Are *pseudomonas fluorescens* or other possible contaminants dangerous to the human body?

The Court also held that individual issues of causation and damages were present and that those issues were not proper for class adjudication. * * *

* * *

[Copley argues that applying multiple jurisdictions' laws] is unmanageable. However, Copley also contends that consideration of different standards of liability violates the Constitution. Despite *Rhone–Poulenc's* holding[,] * * * in many of the cases * * * courts [have] approved nationwide classes and [have not found] that the difference in state laws made such an approach unconstitutional. *E.g., In re Asbestos Sch. Litig.*, 104 F.R.D. 422, 434 (E.D. Pa. 1984), *modified*, 789 F.2d 996 (3d Cir. 1986) (holding that "substantial duplication" of negligence and strict liability laws in fifty-one jurisdictions makes nationwide class manageable). * * * Confident that the

Seventh Circuit may be out of step with its sister circuits, this Court will turn to Copley's primary argument about differing state laws: that they make the class unmanageable.

* * *

Copley raises a very real concern that the laws of the different state jurisdictions make a trial unmanageable. In addition to the *Rhone–Poulenc* decision, Copley contends that states' differing approaches to products liability makes the certification of a nationwide class unmanageable.

For their part, the Plaintiffs give numerous examples of courts who were undeterred by the specter of differing standards of negligence and product liability. Most notable among these was *In re Asbestos School Litigation*, where Judge Kelly observed that "51 jurisdictions are in virtual agreement in that they apply the Restatement (Second) of Torts § 388" and "forty seven jurisdictions have adopted strict liability and all of them start with the concept of a defective product." *See also In re LILCO Sec. Litig.*, 111 F.R.D. 663, 670 (E.D.N.Y. 1986) (application of law of all fifty states does not make class "*per se* unmanageable"); and *In re Cordis Corp. Pacemaker Prod. Liab. Litig.*, MDL No. 850 (S.D. Ohio Dec. 23, 1992) (Slip. Op. at 35) (concluding that even though the source of liability laws may differ, the substance of these laws does not vary greatly).

This differing authority leads the Court to conclude that the decision whether to attempt to manage a class under differing laws is committed to the discretion of the trial court.

Furthermore, several factors make this class an excellent candidate for the application of law to a nationwide class. First, this case involves only one defendant manufacturer, Copley Pharmaceutical, and, at the present time, only one product, Albuterol 0.5%. Second, the product in question is safely manufactured by many other generic drug companies. Third, Copley, through its counsel, has admitted that at least some of its Albuterol was contaminated and that it is liable for any injuries such contamination may have caused.

Because of these facts, many of the "nuances" in state negligence and products liability laws may be irrelevant in this case. For example, comparative negligence, a defense that varies throughout the states, will only be relevant in the rare cases where a plaintiff used Albuterol after the recall. Similarly, the traditional strict liability defenses of risk/utility, state of the art and assumption of the risk are irrelevant because Copley has admitted that it is liable for any injuries caused by its Albuterol. * * * [I]f an individual state's law is at variance with the general law on a relevant point of law, its residents may be removed from the class. Therefore, the Court is not intimidated by the parade of horribles presented by the Defendant.

Finally, Copley's counsel repeatedly argued that there was not a single case where a trial was held in a mass tort case which applied the laws of all fifty states. But the absence of an example does not prove that such classes are *per se* unmanageable. The fact is that most class actions settle and few go to trial whether the class is nationwide or statewide. This Court might indeed be the first to take such a class action to trial, but based on the policy reasons discussed below, the Court is ready to take on that challenge.

* * *

* * * The Court's October 28, 1994 Order Granting Partial Class Certification stands and the Defendant's Motion to Decertify the Class is DENIED.

* * *

CASTANO V. AM. TOBACCO CO.
United States Court of Appeals, Fifth Circuit, 1996.
84 F.3d 734.

Before SMITH, DUHÉ, and DEMOSS, CIRCUIT JUDGES.

SMITH, CIRCUIT JUDGE.

In what may be the largest class action ever attempted in federal court, the district court in this case embarked "on a road certainly less traveled, if ever taken at all," *Castano v. American Tobacco Co.*, 160 F.R.D. 544, 560 (E.D. La. 1995), and entered a class certification order. The court defined the class as:

> (a) All nicotine-dependent persons in the United States * * * who have purchased and smoked cigarettes manufactured by the defendants;
>
> (b) the estates, representatives, and administrators of these nicotine-dependent cigarette smokers; and
>
> (c) the spouses, children, relatives and "significant others" of these nicotine-dependent cigarette smokers as their heirs or survivors.

The plaintiffs limit the claims to years since 1943.

This matter comes before us on interlocutory appeal, under 28 U.S.C. § 1292(b), of the class certification order. Concluding that the district court abused its discretion in certifying the class, we reverse.

I.

A. The Class Complaint

The plaintiffs filed this class complaint against the defendant tobacco companies and the Tobacco Institute, Inc., seeking compensation solely for the injury of nicotine addiction. The gravamen of their complaint is the novel and wholly untested theory that the defendants fraudulently failed to inform consumers that nicotine is addictive and manipulated the level of nicotine in cigarettes to sustain their addictive nature. The class complaint alleges nine causes of action: fraud and deceit, negligent misrepresentation, intentional infliction of emotional distress, negligence and negligent infliction of emotional distress, violation of state consumer protection statutes, breach of express warranty, breach of implied warranty, strict product liability, and redhibition [voidance of a sale because of a product defect] pursuant to the Louisiana Civil Code.

The plaintiffs seek compensatory and punitive damages and attorneys' fees. In addition, the plaintiffs seek equitable relief for fraud and deceit, negligent misrepresentation, violation of consumer protection statutes, and breach of express and implied warranty. The equitable remedies include a declaration that defendants are financially responsible for notifying all class members of nicotine's addictive nature, a declaration that the defendants manipulated nicotine levels with the intent to sustain the addiction of plaintiffs and the class members, an order that the defendants disgorge any profits made from the sale of cigarettes, restitution for sums paid for cigarettes, and the establishment of a medical monitoring fund.

The plaintiffs initially defined the class as "all nicotine dependent persons in the United States," including current, former and deceased smokers since 1943. Plaintiffs conceded that addiction would have to be proven by each class member; the defendants argued that proving class membership will require individual mini-trials to determine whether addiction actually exists.

In response to the district court's inquiry, the plaintiffs proposed a four-phase trial plan. In phase 1, a jury would determine common issues of "core liability." Phase 1 issues would include (1) issues of law and fact relating to defendants' course of conduct, fraud, and negligence liability (including duty, standard of care, misrepresentation and concealment, knowledge, intent); (2) issues of law and fact relating to defendants' alleged conspiracy and concert of action; (3) issues of fact relating to the addictive nature/dependency creating characteristics and properties of nicotine; (4) issues of fact relating to nicotine cigarettes as defective products; (5) issues of fact relating to whether defendants' wrongful conduct was intentional, reckless or negligent; (6) identifying which defendants specifically targeted their advertising and promotional efforts to particular groups (*e.g.*, youths, minorities, etc.); (7) availability of a presumption of reliance; (8) whether defendants' misrepresentations/suppression of fact and/or of addictive properties of nicotine preclude availability of a "personal choice" defense; (9) defendants' liability for actual damages, and the categories of such damages; (10) defendants' liability for emotional distress damages; and (11) defendants' liability for punitive damages.

Phase 1 would be followed by notice of the trial verdict and claim forms to class members. In phase 2, the jury would determine compensatory damages in sample plaintiff cases. The jury then would establish a ratio of punitive damages to compensatory damages, which ratio thereafter would apply to each class member.

Phase 3 would entail a complicated procedure to determine compensatory damages for individual class members. The trial plan envisions determination of absent class members' compensatory economic and emotional distress damages on the basis of claim forms, "subject to verification techniques and assertion of defendants' affirmative defenses under grouping, sampling, or representative procedures to be determined by the Court."

The trial plan left open how jury trials on class members' personal injury/wrongful death claims would be handled, but the trial plan discussed the possibility of bifurcation. In phase 4, the court would apply the punitive damage ratio based on individual damage awards and would conduct a review of the reasonableness of the award.

B. The Class Certification Order

Following extensive briefing, the district court granted, in part, plaintiffs' motion for class certification, concluding that the prerequisites of Fed. R. Civ. P. 23(a) had been met. The court rejected certification, under Fed. R. Civ. P. 23(b)(2), of the plaintiffs' claim for equitable relief, including the claim for medical monitoring. Appellees have not cross-appealed that portion of the order.

The court did grant the plaintiffs' motion to certify the class under Fed. R. Civ. P. 23(b)(3), organizing the class action issues into four categories: (1) core liability; (2) injury-in-fact, proximate cause, reliance and affirmative defenses; (3) compensatory damages; and (4) punitive damages. It then analyzed each category to determine whether it met the predominance and superiority requirements of rule 23(b)(3). Using its power to sever issues for certification under Fed. R. Civ. P. 23(c)(4), the court certified the class on core liability and punitive damages, and certified the class conditionally pursuant to Fed. R. Civ. P. 23(c)(1).

* * *

II.

* * *

The district court erred in its analysis in two different ways. First, it failed to consider how variations in state law affect predominance and superiority. Second, [in a portion of the opinion not reproduced here, the Fifth Circuit held that the lower court erred in failing to articulate how the case would be tried.]

Each of these defects mandates reversal. * * *

A. Variations in State Law

* * *

In a multi-state class action, variations in state law may swamp any common issues and defeat predominance.

Accordingly, a district court must consider how variations in state law affect predominance and superiority. *Walsh v. Ford Motor Co.*, 807 F.2d 1000 (D.C. Cir. 1986) (Ginsburg, J.). The *Walsh* court rejected the notion that a district court may defer considering variations in state law:

> Appellees see the "which law" matter as academic. They say no variations in state warranty laws relevant to this case exist. A court cannot accept such an assertion "on faith." Appellees, as class action proponents, must show that it is accurate. We have made no inquiry of our own on this score and, for the current purpose, simply note the general unstartling statement made in a leading treatise: "The Uniform Commercial Code is not uniform."

Id. at 1016–17.

A district court's duty to determine whether the plaintiff has borne its burden on class certification requires that a court consider variations in state law when a class action involves multiple jurisdictions. * * *

A requirement that a court know which law will apply before making a predominance determination is especially important when there may be differences in state law. Given the plaintiffs' burden, a court cannot rely on assurances of counsel that any problems with predominance or superiority can be overcome.

* * *

A thorough review of the record demonstrates that, in this case, the district court did not properly consider how variations in state law affect predominance. The court acknowledged as much in its order granting class certification, for, in declining to make a choice of law determination, it noted that "[t]he parties have only briefly addressed the conflict of laws issue in this matter." Similarly, the court stated that "there has been no showing that the consumer protection statutes differ so much as to make individual issues predominate."

The district court's review of state law variances can hardly be considered extensive; it conducted a cursory review of state law variations and gave short shrift to the defendants' arguments concerning variations. In response to the defendants' extensive analysis of how state law varied on fraud, products liability, affirmative defenses, negligent infliction of emotional distress, consumer protection statutes, and punitive damages,[15] the court examined a sample phase 1 jury interrogatory and verdict form, a survey of medical monitoring decisions, a survey of consumer fraud class actions, and a survey of punitive damages law in the defendants' home states. The court also relied on two district court opinions granting certification in multi-state class actions.

The district court's consideration of state law variations was inadequate. The surveys provided by the plaintiffs failed to discuss, in any meaningful way, how the court could deal with variations in state law. The consumer fraud survey simply quoted a few state courts that had certified state class actions. The survey of punitive damages was limited to the defendants' home states. Moreover, the two district court opinions on which the court relied did not support the proposition that variations in state law could be ignored. Nothing in the record demonstrates that the court critically analyzed how variations in state law would affect predominance.

The court also failed to perform its duty to determine whether the class action would be manageable in light of state law variations. The court's only discussion of manageability is a citation to *Jenkins v. Raymark Indus.*, 782 F.2d 468 (5th Cir. 1986), and the claim that "[w]hile manageability of the liability issues in this case may well prove to be difficult, the Court

---

[15] We find it difficult to fathom how common issues could predominate in this case when variations in state law are thoroughly considered. * * *

* * * In a fraud claim, some states require justifiable reliance on a misrepresentation. * * * States impose varying standards to determine when there is a duty to disclose facts. * * *

* * * Products liability law also differs among states. Some states do not recognize strict liability. Some have adopted Restatement (Second) of Torts § 402A. Among the states that have adopted the Restatement, there are variations.

Differences in affirmative defenses also exist. Assumption of risk is a complete defense to a products claim in some states. In others, it is a part of comparative fault analysis. Some states utilize "pure" comparative fault; others follow a "greater fault bar," and still others use an "equal fault bar."

Negligent infliction of emotional distress also involves wide variations. Some states do not recognize the cause of action at all. Some require a physical impact.

Despite these overwhelming individual issues, common issues might predominate. We are, however, left to speculate. The point of detailing the alleged differences is to demonstrate the inquiry the district court failed to make.

finds that any such difficulties pale in comparison to the specter of thousands, if not millions, of similar trials of liability proceeding in thousands of courtrooms around the nation."

The problem with this approach is that it substitutes case-specific analysis with a generalized reference to *Jenkins*. The *Jenkins* court, however, was not faced with managing a novel claim involving eight causes of action, multiple jurisdictions, millions of plaintiffs, eight defendants, and over fifty years of alleged wrongful conduct. Instead, *Jenkins* involved only 893 personal injury asbestos cases, the law of only one state, and the prospect of trial occurring in only one district. Accordingly, for purposes of the instant case, *Jenkins* is largely inapposite.

In summary, whether the specter of millions of cases outweighs any manageability problems in this class is uncertain when the scope of any manageability problems is unknown. Absent considered judgment on the manageability of the class, a comparison to millions of individual trials is meaningless.

* * *

III.

In addition to the reasons given above, regarding the district court's procedural errors, this class must be decertified because it independently fails the superiority requirement of rule 23(b)(3). * * *

* * *

We first address the district court's superiority analysis. The court acknowledged the extensive manageability problems with this class. Such problems include difficult choice of law determinations, subclassing of eight claims with variations in state law, *Erie* guesses, notice to millions of class members, further subclassing to take account of transient plaintiffs, and the difficult procedure for determining who is nicotine-dependent. Cases with far fewer manageability problems have given courts pause.

* * *

The complexity of the choice of law inquiry * * * makes individual adjudication superior to class treatment. The plaintiffs have asserted eight theories of liability from every state. Prior to certification, the district court must determine whether variations in state law defeat predominance. While the task *may not* be impossible, its complexity certainly makes individual trials a more attractive alternative and, *ipso facto*, renders class treatment not superior.

Through individual adjudication, the plaintiffs can winnow their claims to the strongest causes of action. The result will be an easier choice of law inquiry and a less complicated predominance inquiry. State courts can address the more novel of the plaintiffs' claims, making the federal court's *Erie* guesses less complicated. * * *

* * *

IV.

The district court abused its discretion by ignoring variations in state law and how a trial on the alleged causes of action would be tried. Those errors cannot be corrected on remand because of the novelty of the plaintiffs' claims. Accordingly, class treatment is not superior to individual adjudication.

* * *

* * * For the foregoing reasons, we REVERSE and REMAND with instructions that the district court dismiss the class complaint.

NOTES AND QUESTIONS

1. In *Johnson v. Nextel Communications Inc.*, 780 F.3d 128 (2d Cir. 2015), the Second Circuit also held (consistent with *Rhone–Poulenc* and *Castano*) that individual issues predominated over common issues because of the application of multiple states' laws. If the approaches set forth in *Rhone–Poulenc*, *Castano*, and *Johnson* are applied expansively, could it be argued that no multi-state class involving numerous state laws could ever be certified? Is there anything in Rule 23 that supports such a result? Are those decisions consistent with *Yamasaki*? As discussed in note 9 below, not all courts are opposed to class certification where multiple states' laws will apply. Courts have been receptive when the various laws are largely the same or where certification is for settlement purposes.

2. Is the rationale of *Castano* and *Rhone–Poulenc* limited to proposed certifications under Rule 23(b)(3)? Should different standards apply in proposed (b)(1) and (b)(2) class actions?

3. Can *Copley Pharmaceutical* be reconciled with *Rhone–Poulenc* and *Castano*? If not, which approach is more consistent with the text and policies of Rule 23?

4. Is there any way that the choice-of-law concerns in *Rhone–Poulenc* and *Castano* could have been avoided, short of decertification? One solution to the problem of differing state laws that some courts have utilized is to propose subclasses. *See, e.g., In re Crazy Eddie Sec. Litig.*, 135 F.R.D. 39, 41 (E.D.N.Y. 1991); *In re LILCO Sec. Litig.*, 111 F.R.D. 663, 670 (E.D.N.Y. 1986); *In re School Asbestos Litig.*, 104 F.R.D. 422, 434 (E.D. Pa. 1984), *aff'd in relevant part*, 789 F.2d 996, 1010–11 (3d Cir. 1986). How could subclasses decrease or eliminate manageability concerns? Does the analysis depend on how many subclasses are needed to account for all of the state-law differences? How would the factfinder adjudicate a class action involving multiple subclasses? *Cf. Central Wesleyan Coll. v. W.R. Grace & Co.*, 6 F.3d 177, 189 (4th Cir. 1993) ("[U]se of subclasses to consider different state laws * * * will pose management difficulties and reduce the judicial efficiency sought to be achieved through certification." (Chapter 4(B)(2)(b))).

5. Other courts have dealt with choice-of-law concerns by "certify[ing] a class subject to decertification if a conflicts problem surfaces later." Larry Kramer, *Class Actions and Jurisdictional Boundaries: Choice of Law in Complex Litigation*, 71 N.Y.U. L. Rev. 547, 564 (1996) (citing authority). This rationale, however, has been sharply criticized:

> The stated premise of provisional certification is that the court can always decertify later if the choice-of-law issues complicate matters too much. But later never comes, and never will, because the cases always settle first—as judges know better than anyone. The provisional certification ploy thus enables the court to create a class with-

out letting any pesky choice-of-law problems get in the way. The applicable law is left undecided—though the fact that a class has been certified, together with the threat that one law may be applied and uncertainty as to what that law will be, undoubtedly plays an important role in settlement.

Id. at 565. Is Professor Kramer's skeptical view warranted? Is it reasonable to believe that courts in fact certify classes in dubious choice-of-law situations, knowing that doing so will coerce defendants to settle? Does the amendment to Rule 23(c)(1) eliminating "conditional" certification (*see* Chapter 4(B)(2)(b)) address Professor Kramer's concern? Does the fact that the Rule had to be amended confirm the reasonableness of Professor Kramer's prior skepticism?

6. The district court opinion in *Castano* illustrates one way in which a court facing a putative class action can attempt to deal with choice-of-law issues. In contrast to the Fifth Circuit, the district court had no difficulty concluding that choice-of-law concerns did not preclude class certification:

> [P]laintiffs argue that the law applicable to each of their causes of action is so generic that individual issues will not predominate. In opposition, defendants posit that the standards for determination of each of plaintiffs' causes of action may vary from state to state and cause mass confusion such that class certification is improper. As a court sitting in diversity, this Court must apply the law of the forum concerning conflict of laws. The Court is persuaded that issues of fraud, breach of warranty, negligence, intentional tort and strict liability do not vary so much from state to state as to cause individual issues to predominate.
>
> Further, there has been no determination at this time of the law to be applied. The parties have only briefly addressed the conflict of laws issues in this matter, and the Court finds a determination of that issue to be premature at present. Finally, Rule 23(c)(4)(B) provides the Court with the option of dividing the class into subclasses if appropriate after the Court resolves the conflict of law issue.
>
> The same reasoning applies to application of the various consumer protection statutes. First, there has been no showing that the consumer protection statutes differ so much as to make individual issues predominate. Indeed, as with the other areas of law, the applicable statute—or statutes—has not yet been determined. The option of subclasses is available as to this issue as well.

Castano v. American Tobacco Co., 160 F.R.D. 544, 554 (E.D. La. 1995), *rev'd*, 84 F.3d 734 (5th Cir. 1996). What arguments can be made in defense of the *Castano* district court's approach?

7. One court has attempted to summarize the various options that a court has in dealing with choice-of-law issues in the class action context:

> (1) find that state law is sufficiently similar that a single class is appropriate, (2) find that the state law varies so much that class certification is inappropriate, or (3) find that state law variations can be categorized and then divided into subclasses.

In re Telectronics Pacing Sys., Inc., 172 F.R.D. 271, 292 (S.D. Ohio 1997), *rev'd on other grounds*, 221 F.3d 870 (6th Cir. 2000). In addressing a nationwide products liability class action involving pacemakers, the *Telectronics* district court found that state law differences were "insignificant" and "irrelevant" or were adequately dealt with through subclasses. *See* 172 F.R.D. at 293–94; *see also* Note, Castano v. American Tobacco Co.: *Class Treatment of Mass Torts is Going Up in Smoke*, 24 N. Ky. L. Rev. 673, 691 (1997) ("Variation in the legal rules is not great, and once a state-by-state survey is completed, judges will find a relatively small number of conflicts and an equally small number of approaches to choice of law."). Can the positions taken by the *Telectronics* court and the Northern Kentucky Law Review Note be reconciled with either *Rhone–Poulenc* or *Castano*?

8. Is one option for choice-of-law problems to apply "federal common law"? In the *Agent Orange* litigation, several classes of armed forces veterans sued numerous chemical manufacturers (under theories of, *inter alia*, strict liability, negligence, and breach of warranty) for injuries allegedly suffered by exposure to herbicides (including Agent Orange) used as defoliants. The Second Circuit rejected the district court's attempt to resolve choice-of-law concerns by applying federal common law:

> Plaintiffs argue that federal common law should be applied to their claims principally because of the unique federal nature of the relationship between the soldier and his government, relying chiefly on *United States v. Standard Oil Co.*, 332 U.S. 301, 305 (1947). They contend that this interest brings the case within the doctrine of *Clearfield Trust Co. v. United States*, 318 U.S. 363, 366 (1943), which held that, in order to ensure uniformity and certainty, "[t]he rights and duties of the United States on commercial paper which it issues are governed by federal rather than local law." * * *
>
> * * *
>
> * * * Since this litigation is between private parties and no substantial rights or duties of the government hinge on its outcome, there is no federal interest in uniformity for its own sake. * * *
>
> * * *
>
> * * * The welfare of veterans and that of military suppliers are clearly federal concerns which Congress should appropriately consider in setting policy for the governance of the nation, and it is properly left to Congress in the first instance to strike the balance between the conflicting interests of the veterans and the contractors, and thereby identify federal policy. Although Congress has turned its attention to the Agent Orange problem, it has not determined what the federal policy is with respect to the reconciliation of these two competing interests. * * *
>
> We conclude that in the present case, while the federal government has obvious interests in the welfare of the parties to the litigation, its interest in the *outcome* of the litigation, *i.e.*, in how the parties' welfare should be balanced, is as yet undetermined * * *. [B]efore federal common law rules should be fashioned, the use of state law must pose a threat to an "identifiable" federal policy. In the present litigation the federal policy is not yet identifiable. We conclude, therefore, that the district court erred in ruling that plaintiffs' claims were governed by federal common law.

In re Agent Orange Prod. Liab. Litig., 635 F.2d 987, 990–95 (2d Cir. 1980). Chief Judge Feinberg, in dissent, disagreed:

Given the "distinctively federal" character of the relationship between the federal government and its soldiers, there is an inherent federal interest in the uniform definition of the aspects of that relationship involved in this case. * * * The application of state law to the present case would severely frustrate this federal interest: If state law is applied in the present litigation, and assuming again that the allegations in the complaint are true, then veterans may well be subjected to sharply differing rules of law in the pursuit of their remedies. For example, the law of the various states is in flux, diverging widely in the definition of what constitutes a "defective" product—especially with respect to defectively designed products—and in the availability of defenses based on the "state of the art" and technological feasibility. * * * In sum, the federal interest here in uniformity would be defeated by the application of discrete and differing state laws.

Id. at 999 (Feinberg, C.J., dissenting).

The Fifth Circuit has dealt with the issue of federal common law in another mass tort context. In *Jackson v. Johns–Manville Sales Corp.*, 750 F.2d 1314, 1327 (5th Cir. 1985) (*en banc*), the court rejected the argument that federal common law should apply to suits alleging injury from asbestos exposure. The *Jackson* court found that there were no uniquely federal interests at stake and that fashioning a federal common law would be difficult (because of the lack of clear standards) and impractical (because the ruling could be applied only within the Fifth Circuit). The dissent asserted that the issue should be certified to the U.S. Supreme Court to determine "whether federal common law must be developed to govern this uniquely interdependent mass of tort litigation." *Id.* at 1329–30 (Clark, C.J., dissenting).

Should "federal common law" be used to provide a viable solution to choice-of-law issues? If so, under what circumstances? What standards should be applied? Can such an approach be reconciled with *Erie*? Even if Judge Feinberg's view had prevailed in *Agent Orange*, could it reasonably be applied in a garden-variety private suit in which the sole ground for subject-matter jurisdiction is diversity?

9. In a case brought by "almost all doctors versus almost all major health maintenance organizations (HMOs)" for conspiring to program their computer systems to systematically underpay physicians for their services, in violation of RICO (the federal racketeering law), the Eleventh Circuit held that the district court abused its discretion in certifying state breach of contract claims for classwide treatment. *Klay v. Humana, Inc.*, 382 F.3d 1241, 1246, 1252 (11th Cir. 2004). Although the court of appeals reversed certification of such claims, its decision was not based on choice-of-law grounds. Instead, the appellate court was satisfied that, even though the laws of all fifty states were implicated, "groupability" suggested that any relevant differences in state law were negligible:

* * * [I]f the applicable state laws can be sorted into a small number of groups, each containing materially identical legal standards, then certification of subclasses embracing each of the dominant legal standards can be appropriate. * * * In such a case, of course, a court must be careful not to certify too many groups. "If more than a few of the laws of the fifty states differ, the district judge would face an impossible task of instructing a jury on the relevant law. . . ." * * *

The burden of showing uniformity or the existence of only a small number of applicable standards (that is, "groupability") among the laws of the fifty states rests squarely with the plaintiffs. * * *

In this case, the plaintiffs allege that the only real legal issue pertinent to their breach of contract claims is the definition of "breach," which does not differ from state to state. We are inclined to agree. A breach is a breach is a breach, whether you are on the sunny shores of California or enjoying a sweet autumn breeze in New Jersey. *See Black's Law Dictionary* 200 (8th ed. 2004) (defining "breach of contract" as a "[v]iolation of a contractual obligation by failing to perform one's own promise"). * * *

Klay, 382 F.3d at 1261–62. Is the Eleventh Circuit's reasoning sound? What are the advantages and risks of the "groupability" approach?

The Second Circuit recently followed the Eleventh Circuit's lead in *Klay*, affirming certification of a litigation class involving RICO and state law breach of contract claims. *In re U.S. Foodservice Inc. Pricing Litig.*, 729 F.3d 108 (2d Cir. 2013), *cert. denied*, 134 S. Ct. 1938 (2014). Noting that state laws relating to breach and fraudulent concealment did not vary materially, the Second Circuit relied in part on the fact that all jurisdictions relevant to the litigation had adopted the Uniform Commercial Code. 729 F.3d at 127. The Second Circuit also emphasized that "the crucial inquiry is not whether the laws of multiple jurisdictions are implicated, but whether those laws differ in a material manner that precludes the predominance of common issues." *Id.*

Similarly, in *Sullivan v. DB Investments*, 667 F.3d 273 (3d Cir. 2011) (en banc), the Third Circuit affirmed class certification for purposes of settlement of nationwide classes of direct and indirect purchasers of gem-quality diamonds. The Third Circuit reasoned that it "had never required the presentation of identical or uniform issues or claims as a prerequisite to certification of a class. Rather, our jurisprudence evinces a pragmatic response to certifications of common claims arising under varying state laws." *Id.* at 301. The Court reasoned, however, that permitting certification notwithstanding variations in state law "is even clearer for certification of a settlement class because the concern for manageability that is a central tenet in the certification of a litigation class is removed from the equation. * * * [S]tate law variations are largely 'irrelevant to certification of a settlement class.'" *Id.* at 301–02 (quoting *In re Warfarin Sodium Antitrust Litig.*, 391 F.3d 516, 529 (3d Cir. 2004)).

10. The ALI, in its *Principles of the Law of Aggregate Litigation* (2010), suggests that a trial court is obligated to undertake a choice-of-law analysis to determine whether a proposed multi-jurisdictional class should be certified. *Id.* § 2.05. Section 2.05 would limit a court's ability to allow a multi-jurisdictional class to situations where a single body of law governs all of the class claims, the claims are governed by different bodies of law that are functionally equivalent, or the claims are governed by different bodies of law that present a limited and manageable number of patterns. *Id.* How does this proposal compare to the rules derived from the cases above?

CHAPTER 7

CIVIL PROCEDURE DOCTRINES WITH SPECIAL CLASS ACTION IMPLICATIONS

■ ■ ■

A number of principles discussed in earlier chapters are unique to class actions. For instance, principles such as typicality, "opt outs," class notice, and predominance find no counterparts in other areas of civil procedure.

At the same time, a number of civil procedure concepts apply equally to class and non-class actions and thus deserve no special attention in a course on aggregate litigation. Examples are contained throughout the Federal Rules of Civil Procedure (such as various rules regarding commencement of actions and motions).

A third category of civil procedure principles (and related substantive doctrines) apply to both class actions and non-class actions, but have special ramifications or complexities in the class action context. For instance, although statutes of limitations apply generally in civil cases, courts have developed special principles involving tolling of limitations periods (that is, suspending the expiration of the period for bringing suit) that apply specifically in class actions. Likewise, although both class and non-class actions can be removed from state to federal court if the requirements for federal question or diversity of citizenship jurisdiction are satisfied, special diversity rules exist for class actions. The same is true for principles of claim and issue preclusion and for related federal and state court proceedings. This chapter addresses these doctrines that have special application in cases brought as class actions.

A. STATUTE OF LIMITATIONS ISSUES IN CLASS ACTIONS

It is fundamental that the filing of a lawsuit "tolls" or suspends the running of the statutes of limitations applicable to the person who files the lawsuit. How does this principle apply to *unnamed* class members when a class action lawsuit is filed? Consider the following case.

ARMSTRONG V. MARTIN MARIETTA CORP.
United States Court of Appeals, Eleventh Circuit, 1998.
138 F.3d 1374.

Before HATCHETT, CHIEF JUDGE, TJOFLAT, ANDERSON, EDMONDSON, COX, BIRCH, DUBINA, BLACK, CARNES, and BARKETT, CIRCUIT JUDGES.

TJOFLAT, CIRCUIT JUDGE.

In *Crown, Cork & Seal Co., Inc. v. Parker*, 462 U.S. 345 (1983), the Supreme Court held that the commencement of a class action suspends the applicable statute of limitations for all asserted members of the putative class "until class certification is denied." The question presented in this case is whether, in the absence of controlling authority, the statute of limitations begins to run again immediately upon the district court's entry of the interlocutory order denying class certification, or whether the statute remains tolled through final judgment in the former class action and completion of an appeal from the order denying class certification. The appellants [plaintiffs below] advocate the latter rule. * * * For the reasons set forth below, we hold that the tolling of the statute of limitations ceases when the district court enters an interlocutory order denying class certification.

I.

This case arises under the Age Discrimination in Employment Act, 29 U.S.C. § 621 *et seq.* (the "ADEA"). The thirty-one appellants in the instant case are former Martin Marietta employees who lost their jobs between 1992 and 1993. * * * Following their terminations, twenty-eight appellants filed timely charges of age discrimination with the Equal Employment Opportunity Commission (the "EEOC"), as is required by statute. Three appellants—Clarke–Iley, Johnson, and Shaw—did not file EEOC charges.

At various times, the EEOC notified each appellant (other than Clarke–Iley, Johnson, and Shaw) that his or her charge of age discrimination was dismissed. Receipt of such notice triggers the statute of limitations for bringing a civil action in court, and the plaintiff must then file suit within ninety days. This ninety-day limitations period is tolled, however, while the plaintiff is a putative member of a class action. *See Crown, Cork,* 462 U.S. at 353–54. Twenty-eight of the thirty-one appellants opted into *Carmichael v. Martin Marietta Corp.*, an age discrimination class action that was already proceeding in the Middle District of Florida, on June 4, 1993.[6] The remaining three appellants—Davis, Havlish, and Hinduja—were named plaintiffs in the *Carmichael* action.

On April 7, 1994, the district court in *Carmichael* determined that the appellants were not "similarly situated" to the other *Carmichael* plaintiffs. The *Carmichael* court therefore certified a plaintiff class that did not include as members the appellants in the instant case. The court then dismissed the claims of appellants Davis, Havlish, and Hinduja without prejudice, and denied the remaining appellants' requests to opt into the *Carmichael* class. * * *

On October 11, 1994, more than ninety days after the *Carmichael* court's partial denial of class certification, the thirty-one appellants and fourteen additional plaintiffs (including former appellants Redding and Tarter) filed the complaint that commenced the instant action in the district court. On October 25, 1994, an amended complaint added a forty-sixth plaintiff, appellant Wallace Black.

On January 17, 1995, Martin Marietta filed a motion for partial summary judgment against the thirty-one appellants, on the ground that they had failed to file their individual lawsuits within ninety days after their dismissal from the *Carmichael* class action. [The district court granted

---

[6] Class actions under the ADEA are authorized by 29 U.S.C. § 626(b), which expressly borrows the opt-in class action mechanism of the Fair Labor Standards Act of 1938, 29 U.S.C. § 216(b) (1994). Section 216(b) provides for a class action where the complaining employees are "similarly situated." * * * [*See* Chapter 10(B)(2).]

summary judgment on the ground that the claims were barred by the statute of limitations.]

* * *

II.

The primary issue on appeal is whether the district court was correct in holding that the statute of limitations, which was tolled while the appellants were putative members of the class action, resumed running when the *Carmichael* court dismissed the appellants' claims in that case. We hold that the limitations period for filing an individual suit (and for intervening in an extant action) did so resume. We therefore affirm the decision of the district court [on the question of when the limitations period resumed.]

* * *

The ADEA's statute of limitations requires the plaintiff to file suit within ninety days after receiving notice that the EEOC has dismissed the plaintiff's age discrimination charge. Membership in a pending action, however, tolls the ninety-day period for filing an individual lawsuit. The purpose of such tolling is to encourage class members reasonably to rely on the class action to protect their rights. Without tolling, class members would have to take action prior to the running of the statute of limitations in order to protect themselves in case class certification is later denied, even when they may reasonably expect to receive relief through the already-filed class action. Once the district court enters the order denying class certification, however, reliance on the named plaintiffs' prosecution of the matter ceases to be reasonable, and, we hold, the excluded putative class members are put on notice that they must act independently to protect their rights.

The appellants, however, argue that statute of limitations should continue to be tolled, even after the district court's denial of class certification, because the denial of certification in an interlocutory order may be reversed by the district court at any time before final judgment, or by the court of appeals after final judgment or, in rare cases, on interlocutory review. We disagree. No reasonable person would rely on the hope that either the district court or this court might someday determine that the suit should have proceeded as a class action.

When the district court denies class certification,[10] the named plaintiffs no longer have a duty to advance the interests of the excluded putative class members. Although it is possible that the district court may reconsider its order denying class certification, or that an appellate court may later reverse it, district courts have broad discretion with respect to such rulings, and denials of class certification usually stand. Indeed, a review of this court's published caselaw reveals that one must go back to 1987—over a decade ago—to find a case in which this court squarely reversed a district court's denial of class certification on grounds that the district court abused its discretion. Thus, reliance on the possibility of a reversal of the court's certification decision is ordinarily not reasonable. We therefore conclude that continued tolling of the statute of limitations after the district court

---

[10] In the instant case, the *Carmichael* court did not deny class certification altogether; rather, it certified a narrow class that did not include the appellants. This of course amounted to a denial of class certification as to the appellants. For simplicity's sake, we refer in the text to the more common situation, where a district court denies class certification altogether.

denies class certification is unnecessary to protect any *reasonable* reliance by putative class members on their former class representatives.

Caselaw from the Supreme Court and several federal appellate courts also indicates that the tolling period should cease upon denial of class certification. The plain language of *Crown, Cork* itself clearly implies that tolling is to end upon the district court's denial of class certification. The *Crown, Cork* Court wrote: "Once the statute of limitations has been tolled, it remains tolled for all members of the putative class until class certification is denied. At that point, class members may choose to file their own suits or to intervene as plaintiffs in the pending action." The dissent [in this case] would have us read the word "denied" in the above passage to mean (among other things) "denied, appealed, denied again, appealed (perhaps) again, and denied again." Even if we were inclined to divine so much from that one word, "denied," we could not do so in light of the fact that in the very next sentence the Court suggests that putative class members who have been denied certification might "intervene as plaintiffs in the pending action." If, as the dissent advocates, we are to read "denied" to mean "finally denied, after all hope for reversal on appeal is gone," then there will rarely be a "pending action" into which the disappointed putative class members might thereafter intervene. We therefore read *Crown, Cork* to imply strongly, if not to hold, that tolling of the statute of limitations ends upon the district court's denial of class certification.

American Pipe & Construction Co. v. Utah, 414 U.S. 538 (1974), provides further guidance from the Court. In *American Pipe*, the State of Utah filed a class action antitrust complaint with just eleven days before the limitations period expired. Several months later, the district court entered an order denying class certification. Eight days after that order was entered, several state and local agencies that had been putative class members moved to intervene in the action and become plaintiffs. The Supreme Court stated

> that the commencement of the class action in this case suspended the running of the limitation period *only during the pendency of the motion to strip the suit of its class action character*. The class suit ... was filed with 11 days yet to run in the [limitations] period ... and the intervenors thus had 11 days after the entry of the order denying them participation in the suit as class members in which to move for permission to intervene. Since their motions were filed only eight days after the entry of [the] order, it follows that the motions were timely.

In *American Pipe,* the parties did not argue that tolling should continue through appeals. It thus might be said that the Court did not squarely reject such an argument. The Court, however, clearly assumed that tolling should end when the district court denies class certification, not after the appeals process has run and some later final order is entered.

[The court discussed additional Supreme Court cases suggesting that tolling ends when the district court denies certification. The court noted that several appellate courts have so held, although it acknowledged that a number of district courts have gone the other way.]

III.

Practical considerations also lead us to conclude that, if class certification is denied in whole or in part, the statute of limitations begins to run again as to excluded putative class members as of the date of the district court's order denying certification.

The district court's class certification decision, which defines which claimants are class members and which are not, is not a "final decision" within the meaning of 28 U.S.C. § 1291, because an excluded putative class member is free to proceed with his individual claim. Class certification decisions are therefore not appealable as a matter of right. * * *

* * *

* * * [C]ontinuing to toll the statute of limitations through trial and through the entire appeals process would seriously contravene the policies underlying statutes of limitations. Statutes of limitations are intended to prevent "the revival of claims that have been allowed to slumber until evidence has been lost, memories have faded, and witnesses have disappeared." If we accept the appellants' argument, the statute of limitations will remain tolled, in many cases, for several years. * * * The potential length of the delay certainly increases the possibility that evidence will be lost, memories will fade, and witnesses will disappear. In short, the dissent's rule * * * would leave cases in limbo for years at a time.

Moreover, the extended tolling period may be expected to prejudice many defendants because plaintiffs will be able to choose when to file their suits.[34] As the Court noted in *American Pipe,* class action procedure prior to the 1966 revision of Rule 23 was criticized for allowing putative class members in some situations to wait until final judgment on the merits of an action before determining whether participation in the action was in their best interests. Putative class members could thereby "benefit from a favorable judgment without subjecting themselves to the binding effect of an unfavorable one." The dissent's preferred rule would make such abuse possible again.

The threat of such delay and such prejudice would cause many defendants not to contest motions for class certification. The costs to a defendant of this unlimited extension of the tolling period—not knowing when its exposure to claims of putative class members will end—may be such that the defendant forgoes a *meritorious* defense to certification and instead agrees to litigate all the putative class claims in the instant case. Thus, the dissent's rule would impose an unnecessary—and perhaps an intolerable—tax on the judiciary, as courts are forced to preside over large class actions as to which a meritorious defense exists but has not been proffered.

Although appeals from denials of class certification can take years, the certification decision itself should come early in the litigation. Rule 23 counsels early determination of motions for class certification. In fact, motions to certify are filed, on average, within three to four months after the filing of an action, and the motions are ruled upon, on average, within three

---

[34] * * * The dissent's rule would * * * encourage plaintiffs and plaintiffs' counsel to file overly broad class complaints; if the limitation period may be tolled indefinitely merely by the filing of a class complaint, there will an incentive to draw the putative class in the broadest terms possible, so as to toll limitations even as regards claimants who cannot reasonably expect to be included in any class.

to eight months. If the district court acts seasonably in deciding the certification issue, the extension of the limitations period under the *Crown, Cork* rule should not be great. Therefore, if the district court's denial of certification triggers the resumption of the limitations period, then the litigants—named plaintiffs, potential class members, and the defendant—should know at an early stage in the litigation how long the statute of limitations will be tolled. In contrast, under the dissent's preferred rule, litigants often would have to wait for years for tolling to end. Waiting until the appellate process has run its course, or until the time for taking an appeal has expired, creates far greater uncertainty as to when the limitations period will resume running than the uncertainty, if any, created by the *Crown, Cork* rule.

D.

* * *

* * * [T]he dissent's analysis fails to delineate how its rule would operate when, as happens in perhaps the greatest number of class actions, the named plaintiffs (along with, perhaps, members of a partially-certified class) settle their claims after denial of certification. When, under the dissent's rule, does the statute of limitations resume running? When the stipulation of dismissal or the final judgment is entered? After appeal by the named plaintiffs (who now have little incentive to pursue years of appeals)? And what if disappointed putative class members seek to intervene * * *? Should they be given the benefit of years of continued tolling, despite the fact that their chances for success on appeal are terribly slim? This is not idle nit-picking. The earlier the event that triggers the resumption of the limitations period—say, the joint stipulation of dismissal—the greater the potential for prejudicial surprise of excluded putative class members. The later that event—say, the final failure of an appeal by intervening putative class members—the greater the potential that cases will grow stale. * * *

We therefore conclude that the pendency of a class action tolls the applicable statute of limitations only until the district court makes a class certification decision. If class certification is denied in whole or in part, the statute of limitations begins to run again as to those putative class members who were excluded from the class. In order to protect their rights, such individuals must seek to intervene in the pending action (like the plaintiffs in *American Pipe*), or file a separate individual action (like the plaintiff in *Crown, Cork*) before the time remaining in the limitations period expires. If the dismissed class member takes no such action within the remainder of the limitations period, then he may neither file a suit in his own name nor intervene in the already-pending action. In such a situation, the dismissed class member's only avenue of relief is to wait until the pending action reaches final judgment, and then * * * file a timely motion to intervene for the limited purpose of appealing the district court's class certification decision.

The appellants argue that the rule we adopt will force disappointed putative class members to choose between 1) filing an individual lawsuit within the statute of limitations period or 2) exercising their right to appeal the denial of class certification. This does not have to be the case. A putative class member who wishes to preserve both rights should file her individual suit and immediately seek a stay of the individual suit pending the outcome of an appeal from the denial of class certification. If, in the judgment of the district (or state) court to whom the application for a stay has been made, the plaintiff's hopes for reversal of the initial denial of class certification are strong, and if the delay caused by the stay will not be too great, the court may, in its discretion, grant the stay; if the court believes that the chances of reversal are slim or the delay caused by waiting for the appellate process to conclude will be too long (as will usually be the case), the stay will properly be denied, and the plaintiff will properly have to proceed individually. This is a just, efficient result.

* * *

CONCLUSION

[W]e hold that, in the absence of controlling authority to the contrary, statutes of limitations resume running immediately upon the district court's entry of an interlocutory order denying class certification. * * *

HATCHETT, CHIEF JUDGE, dissenting in part * * *.

* * *

Crown, Cork & Seal makes it clear that the class action complaint itself eliminates the potential for unfair surprise to defendants—"regardless of the method class members choose to enforce their rights upon denial of class certification." Accordingly, the case for continued tolling when some putative class members have been dismissed from the class turns on whether continued tolling promotes efficiency and economy of litigation without encouraging dismissed class members to sleep on their rights. Continued tolling satisfies these dual objectives in some circumstances.

Consider, for instance, the generic case—not much unlike the case at bar—where a district court makes an arguably erroneous interlocutory decision denying or limiting class certification. The interlocutory decision leaves a large number of putative class members in limbo—unable to obtain an immediate appeal as of right; at least potentially out of the case; and possibly at risk of losing their claims altogether if individual lawsuits are not promptly filed. From a policy standpoint, it is far more preferable for the large number of putative class members to get a prompt appeal and possible reversal of the arguably erroneous class certification decision than it is for them to clog the legal system with a multitude of individual lawsuits filed solely to preserve claims that arguably could and should be dealt with collectively. Without tolling—at least while the putative class members seek permission to pursue an interlocutory or direct appeal—the preferable approach will often not be taken, as the putative class members will have to file individual lawsuits in order to avoid running afoul of the appropriate statute of limitations.

* * * I would grant to plaintiffs who have been dismissed from a class action two options to pursue. First, to avoid the potential problem of litigants "sleeping on their rights," I emphasize that dismissed plaintiffs should act promptly. If dismissed plaintiffs are convinced that the district court's order denying or limiting class certification is legally unassailable, they should promptly file individual actions (or move to intervene in the named plaintiffs' case) within the number of days remaining under the applicable statute of limitations period. If, on the other hand, dismissed plaintiffs are convinced that the district court's class certification order is subject to reversal on appeal as an abuse of discretion, they should promptly [seek interlocutory review] * * *.

* * *

To summarize, the procedure that I would implement would require plaintiffs who have been dismissed from a class action to act promptly to protect their rights to pursue their individual claims. They must file individual lawsuits or intervene in the existing lawsuit within the applicable statute of limitations, or make a prompt effort to obtain appellate review of the denial of class certification. * * * Failure to pursue prompt appellate review, under my approach, would result in a statute of limitations time bar for any individual claims the dismissed plaintiffs may have possessed. Unlike the majority's superficially pleasing bright line, the foregoing options justly provide adequate protection to dismissed class members, discourage the filing of needless lawsuits and provide clear markers for defendants regarding the scope and duration of their potential liability.

* * *

NOTES AND QUESTIONS

1. What are the purposes of the tolling rule of *American Pipe* and *Crown, Cork*? Is the rule sound as a policy matter? For a discussion of the underlying policy rationales for statutes of limitations and their exceptions, *see generally* Suzette M. Malveaux, *Statutes of Limitations: A Policy Analysis in the Context of Reparations Litigation*, 74 Geo. Wash. L. Rev. 68 (2005).

2. The original *American Pipe* rule was a limited one: "[T]he commencement of the original class suit tolls the running of the statute [of limitations] for all purported members of the class who make timely motions to intervene after the court has found the suit inappropriate for class action status." *Am. Pipe & Constr. Co. v. Utah*, 414 U.S. 538, 552–53 (1974). In *Crown, Cork*, the Court ruled that the *American Pipe* rule applied to "all asserted members of the class," not merely those who intervened after the denial of class certification. *Crown, Cork & Seal Co., Inc. v. Parker*, 462 U.S. 345, 350 (1983). The Eleventh Circuit in *Armstrong*, in turn, dealt with the issue of *when* the limitations period begins to run again—after the district court denies certification or after appellate review of that ruling. How does the dissent's view differ from the rule urged by the plaintiffs? Which view has greater merit? Which *Armstrong* opinion—the majority or the dissent—is more consistent with the rules announced in *Crown, Cork* and *American Pipe*?

3. In a portion of the dissent not produced, Chief Judge Hatchett argued that his approach was bolstered by a proposed change to Rule 23 that would make it easier for litigants to seek interlocutory review of orders granting or denying class certification. That proposed rule was subsequently adopted as Rule 23(f). *See* Chapter 9(A). Does the adoption of Rule 23(f) strengthen Chief Judge Hatchett's position? Should application of the *American Pipe* rule depend on the likelihood that litigants can obtain interlocutory review of class certification rulings? Should the adoption of Rule 23(f) change the analysis in *Armstrong*? *See National Asbestos Workers Med. Fund v. Phillip Morris, Inc.*, 86 F. Supp. 2d 137 (E.D.N.Y. 2000) ("The policies undergirding the adoption of Rule 23(f) suggest * * * that the statute of limitations should be tolled where a party files an interlocutory appeal and the district court grants a stay.").

4. *Armstrong* was not a Rule 23 class, but rather an "opt in" class under the Age Discrimination in Employment Act (ADEA). Such classes are discussed in Chapter 10(B)(2). Although *Armstrong* applied *American Pipe*, some courts have held that the tolling rules of *American Pipe* do not apply in ADEA cases. *See, e.g., Basch v. Ground Round, Inc.*, 139 F.3d 6, 10–11 (1st Cir. 1998) (discussing split in authority); *see also Bright v. United States*, 603 F.3d 1273, 1283–86 (Fed. Cir. 2010) (discussing same but concluding that class action tolling is available for opt-in classes).

5. An important issue under *American Pipe* is whether tolling applies when the putative class members file a second suit that is almost identical to the first one. In *Korwek v. Hunt*, 827 F.2d 874 (2d Cir. 1987), plaintiffs filed a class suit similar to an earlier one in which the court had narrowly limited the scope of the class certified because of manageability concerns and conflicts of interest among class members. The second class action was dismissed as time-barred, and the court of appeals affirmed, reasoning that "[p]iggybacking" one class action onto another is "inimical to the purposes behind statutes of limitations and the class action procedure." *Id.* at 879. Is the *Korwek* court's approach correct? Should the answer depend upon *why* the first class suit was dismissed? *See, e.g., Hemenway v. Peabody Coal Co.*, 159 F.3d 255, 265–66 (7th Cir. 1998) (no "piggy-backing" allowed when first class suit dismissed for lack of subject-matter jurisdiction); *Yang v. Odom*, 392 F.3d 97, 99 (3d Cir. 2004) (holding that "*American Pipe* tolling applies to the filing of a new class action where certification was denied in the prior suit based on the lead plaintiffs' deficiencies as class representatives, but that *American Pipe* tolling does not apply where certification was denied based on deficiencies in the purported class itself"); *Catholic Soc. Servs., Inc. v. INS*, 232 F.3d 1139, 1149 (9th Cir. 2000) (*en banc*) (holding that statute of limitations was tolled during pendency of second class action suit, as well as the first, where first case was dismissed after certification because the named plaintiffs did not present cognizable claims; court concluded that plaintiffs in second class action were "not attempting to relitigate an earlier denial of class certification, or to correct a procedural deficiency in an earlier would-be class").

6. To take advantage of tolling, the plaintiff must demonstrate that his or her claim was encompassed within the initial class action upon which the plaintiff relies for tolling. *See, e.g., Smith v. Pennington*, 352 F.3d 884, 891–96 (4th Cir. 2003) (where ministers were not members of a putative class for over a year prior to their seeking intervention, their federal securities claims were not entitled to tolling for that period and were, therefore, time-barred); *Raie v. Cheminova, Inc.*, 336 F.3d 1278, 1282–83 (11th Cir. 2003) (filing of class action complaint alleging primarily products liability claims would not toll statute of limitations for individual wrongful death claims by class members unless class action explicitly included such claims). *See also Phipps v. Wal–Mart Stores, Inc.*, 792 F.3d 637 (6th Cir. 2015) (discussing tolling issues raised by smaller suits filed against Wal–Mart after the Supreme Court's rejection of certification of a nationwide class in *Wal–Mart Stores, Inc. v. Dukes*, 564 U.S. 338 (2011), discussed in Chapters 2(B)(2) and 3(B)(2)). Does this limitation on tolling make sense?

7. *American Pipe* was a Sherman Act antitrust case; *Crown, Cork* was a Title VII discrimination case; and *Armstrong* was an ADEA case. Because these cases all arose under federal law, federal law controlled tolling principles as well. Most courts do not apply the *American Pipe* rule when state-law claims are involved. As the Seventh Circuit noted: "[w]hen state law supplies the period of limitations, it also supplies the tolling rules." *Hemenway v. Peabody*

Coal Co., 159 F.3d 255, 265 (7th Cir. 1998) (looking to Indiana law to determine "whether the filing of a class action satisfies the period of limitations for all class members"); *accord Wade v. Danek Med., Inc.*, 5 F. Supp. 2d 379, 383 (E.D. Va. 1998) (*American Pipe* rule did not apply to "mass tort personal-injury litigation, where [the] court is sitting in diversity"), *aff'd*, 182 F.3d 281 (4th Cir. 1999). *But see Adams Pub. Sch. Dist. v. Asbestos Corp.*, 7 F.3d 717, 719 (8th Cir. 1993) (suggesting that "federal interests" may be sufficiently strong to justify application of *American Pipe* rule even in diversity cases).

8. In *In re American Honda Motor Co. Dealer Relations Litigation*, 979 F. Supp. 365 (D. Md. 1997), the court certified a class limited to certain liability issues presented by plaintiffs' RICO claims. In that context, the court ruled that the statute of limitations would begin running again on the class members' damages claims not included in the class ten days after the court's ruling. The court justified its ruling as follows:

> I recognize that my ruling on the limitations issue may be said to run afoul of the Supreme Court decisions in [*Crown, Cork* and *American Pipe*]. Those cases have come to stand for the black letter rule that the pendency of a class action suspends the tolling of limitations until the termination of the class action proceedings.
>
> What makes the present case different from *Crown, Cork* and *American Pipe* is that in both of the latter cases a class action had been pending during the tolling period as to all aspects of the absent plaintiffs' claims. In contrast, here I am ruling that the tolling period ceases only after I have rendered my decision to certify the class solely as to liability issues and *not* to certify it as to damages issues. In my view this difference is critical. As the Supreme Court recognized in *Crown, Cork*, the rule adopted in *American Pipe* served "[t]he principal purposes of the class action procedure—promotion of efficiency and economy of litigation." If tolling were not permitted "[t]he result would be a needless multiplicity of actions—precisely the situation that Federal Rule of Civil Procedure 23 . . . [was] designed to avoid."
>
> This reasoning is absolutely correct in the context of a proceeding in which all dispositive issues have been certified for class treatment. But it fails where only limited, not fully dispositive, issues have been certified under Rule 23(c)(4). Indeed, rote application of the *Crown, Cork* and *American Pipe* rule in the context of such a case may well frustrate efficiency and economy of litigation by postponing the filing of multiple actions which, instead of being "needless," will be *necessary* to the ultimate resolution of the * * * proceedings.
>
> That certainly is the case here. By virtue of my ruling today, if the plaintiff class succeeds in the liability phase of the litigation, the institution and prosecution of individual lawsuits by the class members (other than the representative plaintiffs, whose damages claims will be submitted to the jury in phase one in order to accomplish an appealable final judgment on all issues resolved in that phase) will be required. If limitations have been tolled in the interim so that these suits have not yet been filed at the completion of the liability phase, valuable time will be unnecessarily lost while the parties and the court wait to see how many new plaintiffs come forward. The pace and momentum of the proceedings will be dissipated, perhaps never

to be recovered. Clearly, this manner of proceeding would promote neither the efficiency nor the economy of the litigation.

Id. at 371. Is this analysis consistent with *Crown, Cork* and *American Pipe*? Does this approach serve the interests of class members? Should courts be permitted to modify class members' rights relating to statutes of limitations?

9. The question sometimes arises whether an otherwise time-barred class action suit will be deemed timely when a plaintiff amends his or her timely individual claim to make class allegations. Rule 15(c)(2) provides, in relevant part, that "an amendment of a pleading relates back to the date of the original pleading when the * * * claim or defense asserted in the amended pleading arose out of the conduct, transaction, or occurrence set forth or attempted to be set forth in the original pleading." The critical issue in applying the "relation back" doctrine is whether "the factual allegations set forth in the original complaint gave the defendants adequate notice of the new claims." *Kim v. Dial Serv. Int'l Inc.*, 1997 WL 5902, at *13 (S.D.N.Y. 1997), *aff'd*, 159 F.3d 1347 (2d Cir. 1998). *Cf. Krupski v. Costa Crociere S.p.A.*, 130 S. Ct. 2485, 2489–90, 2497 n.5 (2010) (holding "that relation back under Rule 15(c)(1)(C) depends on what the party to be added [the proper defendant] knew or should have known[,]" not on what the plaintiff knew when the original complaint mistakenly named the wrong party). In the class action context, the question is whether "the original complaint provided the defendants with adequate notice that a class action was contemplated and would be sought." *Sokolski v. Trans Union Corp.*, 178 F.R.D. 393, 398 (E.D.N.Y. 1998) (finding Rule 15(c) satisfied because original complaint noted that leave would be sought to assert class claims). Thus, filing a class action cannot "save members of the purported class who have slept on their rights," and subsequent efforts to assert classwide claims cannot succeed unless the defendant had notice, "[w]ithin the period set by the statute of limitations," of "the essential information necessary to determine both the subject matter and size of the prospective litigation." *Crown, Cork & Seal Co.*, 462 U.S. at 354–55 (Powell, J., concurring); *see also, e.g., Paskuly v. Marshall Field & Co.*, 646 F.2d 1210, 1211 (7th Cir. 1981) (defendant was on notice of class discrimination claims as a result of individual claim involving same discriminatory practices); *Slack v. Stiner*, 358 F.2d 65, 70 (5th Cir. 1966) (untimely classwide securities suit could not revive time-barred claims even though timely individual claims had been filed); *In re Bausch & Lomb, Inc. Sec. Litig.*, 941 F. Supp. 1352, 1366 (W.D.N.Y. 1996) (amended securities fraud suit did not relate back to earlier suit involving different class period and different purchasers of stock because earlier suit did not put defendant on notice of later claims); *Langley v. Coughlin*, 715 F. Supp. 522, 553–54 & n.31 (S.D.N.Y. 1989) (prisoners' class allegations of Eighth Amendment violations related back to original complaint, which "allege[d] all of the basic facts material to the class claims" and foreshadowed class claims by requesting injunctive relief).

In analyzing "relation back" issues, why should it matter whether the defendant was on notice of the possibility of class claims prior to the expiration of the statute of limitations? How should a court analyze whether an individual claim provides notice of the possibility of classwide claims?

PROBLEM

On May 18, 1971, a class action was filed alleging that members of the Black Panthers were subjected to unconstitutional treatment by various government officials. Class certification was granted on May 24, 1979. On December 1, 1975, more than three years prior to the granting of class certification, Dhoruba Bin Wahad, a member of the putative class, filed an individual action raising similar claims. But for *American Pipe* tolling, Bin Wahad's claims would be time-barred. Should Bin Wahad be entitled to assert tolling protection?

B. ISSUES RELATING TO DIVERSITY JURISDICTION

In many class actions and other forms of party aggregation, parties have waged fierce battles over whether an action should proceed in state court or in federal court. Defendants often want to be in federal court, while plaintiffs have often preferred to be in state court, depending on the type of action. When a case raises federal questions, defendants have a right to remove the case to federal court. See 28 U.S.C. § 1441(b). On the other hand, when plaintiffs bring only *state-law* claims, federal court is normally not a viable option for the defendants unless there is diversity of citizenship. Thus, the issue of diversity jurisdiction has been a major battleground in class actions. Plaintiffs have often drafted their complaints to avoid the possibility of removal based on diversity, and defendants have nevertheless removed such complaints, arguing that the elements of diversity are still satisfied.

This scenario has led to seemingly unusual arguments by defendants and plaintiffs. A defendant might argue that a plaintiff's claim is large enough to meet the jurisdictional-amount requirement for diversity; the plaintiff may respond that he is not seeking sufficient damages to trigger the diversity requirements. The defendant might also remove a case from state to federal court on the ground that one or more defendants were "fraudulently joined" in the action by the plaintiffs in an attempt to defeat diversity jurisdiction. *See, e.g., B., Inc. v. Miller Brewing Co.*, 663 F.2d 545, 549–50 (5th Cir. 1981) (fraudulent joinder requires showing that "there is no possibility of a valid cause of action being set forth against the in-state defendant(s)" or that plaintiffs have fraudulently pleaded jurisdictional facts).

Several important diversity-jurisdiction issues have arisen in the class action context. First, should each class member be required to satisfy the jurisdictional amount? Second, whose citizenship is relevant in determining whether complete diversity exists? Third, is it sound policy to provide broader access to federal courts for class actions? This section addresses these issues.

As detailed later in this chapter, the Class Action Fairness Act of 2005 has fundamentally altered the jurisdictional landscape relating to large class actions. However, it is still important to understand that three Supreme Court cases established the basic ground rules that historically governed diversity-jurisdiction battles in class actions. As one commentator explained in 1998:

> Under *Supreme Tribe of Ben–Hur v. Cauble*, 255 U.S. 356 (1921), it has been the law for almost eighty years that for purposes of complete diversity, the only citizenships of class members

that count are those of the named representatives. The rule is arbitrary and subject to manipulation by choice of the representatives to create or destroy complete diversity, but it has virtues enough to warrant its retention. It provides definiteness and relative ease of administration as opposed to the difficult or impossible job of figuring out the citizenship of each unnamed class member, and the contrary rule would largely eliminate diversity class actions even when federal jurisdiction over a far-flung class in a state law matter might be useful. By contrast to the jurisdiction-widening effect of *Ben–Hur*, *Snyder v. Harris*, 394 U.S. 332 (1969), * * * restricted federal jurisdiction over class actions by forbidding in most cases the aggregation of below-limit claims to satisfy an applicable amount in controversy requirement. Although criticized, *Snyder* keeps out of federal court agglomerations of small state law claims that could not be there individually. With *Ben–Hur* on the books, the opposite outcome in *Snyder* would have let in such cases (for example, a rate overcharge claim against a local utility) even if they were highly localized—as long as an adequate out-of-state member of a dominantly in-state class could be found to serve as the named representative.

The third and most restrictive decision, *Zahn v. International Paper Co.*, 414 U.S. 291 (1973), ha[d] few defenders. *Zahn* held that in a class action involving legally separate claims, even when all the named representatives have claims satisfying the amount requirement, unnamed members with jurisdictionally insufficient claims could not tag along in federal court; only unnamed class members with jurisdictionally sufficient claims could be part of the class. The *Zahn* rule pose[d] the danger of forcing separate litigation in federal and state court if those with large enough claims proceed individually or as part of a heavy-hitters-only class in federal court, and it [could] trigger litigation over the size of unnamed members' claims in a mass tort. * * *

Thomas D. Rowe, Jr., *1367 and All That: Recodifying Federal Supplemental Jurisdiction*, 74 Ind. L.J. 53, 62–63 (1998).

In 1990, Congress enacted the supplemental jurisdiction statute, 28 U.S.C. § 1367, which provides, in pertinent part:

(a) Except as provided in subsections (b) and (c) or as expressly provided otherwise by Federal statute, in any civil action of which the district courts have original jurisdiction, the district courts shall have supplemental jurisdiction over all other claims that are so related to claims in the action within such original jurisdiction that they form part of the same case or controversy under Article III of the United States Constitution. Such supplemental jurisdiction shall include claims that involve the joinder or intervention of additional parties.

(b) In any civil action of which the district courts have original jurisdiction founded solely on section 1332 of this title [diversity jurisdiction], the district courts shall not have supplemental jurisdiction under subsection (a) over claims by plaintiffs against persons made parties under Rule 14, 19, 20, or 24 of the Federal Rules of Civil Procedure, or over claims by persons proposed to be joined as plaintiffs under Rule

19 of such rules, or seeking to intervene as plaintiffs under Rule 24 of such rules, when exercising supplemental jurisdiction over such claims would be inconsistent with the jurisdictional requirements of section 1332.

(c) The district courts may decline to exercise supplemental jurisdiction over a claim under subsection (a) if—

(1) the claim raises a novel or complex issue of State law,

(2) the claim substantially predominates over the claim or claims over which the district court has original jurisdiction,

(3) the district court has dismissed all claims over which it has original jurisdiction, or

(4) in exceptional circumstances, there are other compelling reasons for declining jurisdiction.

For many years, the courts of appeals were sharply divided on the issue of whether section 1367(a) partially overruled *Zahn*. The Supreme Court ultimately resolved the circuit split in *Exxon Mobil Corp. v. Allapattah Services, Inc.*, 545 U.S. 546 (2005), set forth below.

1. AGGREGATION OF CLAIMS FOR PURPOSES OF JURISDICTIONAL AMOUNT

EXXON MOBIL CORP. V. ALLAPATTAH SERVS., INC.
Supreme Court of the United States, 2005.
545 U.S. 546.

JUSTICE KENNEDY delivered the opinion of the Court.

These consolidated cases present the question whether a federal court in a diversity action may exercise supplemental jurisdiction [under 28 U.S.C. § 1367] over additional plaintiffs whose claims do not satisfy the minimum amount-in-controversy requirement, provided the claims are part of the same case or controversy as the claims of plaintiffs who do allege a sufficient amount in controversy. * * *

We hold that [supplemental jurisdiction is authorized in those circumstances]. * * *

I

In 1991, about 10,000 Exxon dealers filed a class-action suit against the Exxon Corporation in the United States District Court for the Northern District of Florida. The dealers alleged an intentional and systematic scheme by Exxon under which they were overcharged for fuel purchased from Exxon. The plaintiffs invoked the District Court's § 1332(a) diversity jurisdiction. After a unanimous jury verdict in favor of the plaintiffs, the District Court certified the case for interlocutory review, asking whether it had properly exercised § 1367 supplemental jurisdiction over the claims of class members who did not meet the jurisdictional minimum amount in controversy.

The Court of Appeals for the Eleventh Circuit upheld the District Court's extension of supplemental jurisdiction to these class members. * * *

In the other case now before us the Court of Appeals for the First Circuit took a different position on the meaning of § 1367(a). In that case, a 9-

year-old girl sued Star–Kist in a diversity action in the United States District Court for the District of Puerto Rico, seeking damages for unusually severe injuries she received when she sliced her finger on a tuna can. Her family joined in the suit, seeking damages for emotional distress and certain medical expenses. The District Court granted summary judgment to Star–Kist, finding that none of the plaintiffs met the minimum amount-in-controversy requirement. The Court of Appeals for the First Circuit, however, ruled that the injured girl, but not her family members, had made allegations of damages in the requisite amount.

The Court of Appeals then addressed whether, in light of the fact that one plaintiff met the requirements for original jurisdiction, supplemental jurisdiction over the remaining plaintiffs' claims was proper under § 1367. The court held that § 1367 authorizes supplemental jurisdiction only when the district court has original jurisdiction over the action, and that in a diversity case original jurisdiction is lacking if one plaintiff fails to satisfy the amount-in-controversy requirement. * * *

II

A

* * * To ensure that diversity jurisdiction does not flood the federal courts with minor disputes, § 1332(a) requires that the matter in controversy in a diversity case exceed a specified amount, currently $75,000. § 1332(a).

* * * [O]nce a court has original jurisdiction over some claims in the action, it may exercise supplemental jurisdiction over additional claims that are part of the same case or controversy. The leading modern case for this principle is *Mine Workers v. Gibbs*, 383 U.S. 715 (1966). * * * [The Court describes the district courts' original jurisdiction over federal claims and supplemental jurisdiction over pendent state law claims.]

As we later noted, the decision allowing jurisdiction over pendent state claims in *Gibbs* did not mention, let alone come to grips with, the text of the jurisdictional statutes and the bedrock principle that federal courts have no jurisdiction without statutory authorization. *Finley v. United States*, 490 U.S. 545, 548 (1989). * * *

We have not, however, applied *Gibbs'* expansive interpretive approach to other aspects of the jurisdictional statutes. For instance, we have consistently interpreted § 1332 as requiring complete diversity: In a case with multiple plaintiffs and multiple defendants, the presence in the action of a single plaintiff from the same State as a single defendant deprives the district court of original diversity jurisdiction over the entire action. *Strawbridge v. Curtiss*, 3 Cranch 267 (1806); *Owen Equipment & Erection Co. v. Kroger*, 437 U.S. 365, 375 (1978). * * * In order for a federal court to invoke supplemental jurisdiction under *Gibbs*, it must first have original jurisdiction over at least one claim in the action. Incomplete diversity destroys original jurisdiction with respect to all claims, so there is nothing to which supplemental jurisdiction can adhere.

In contrast to the diversity requirement, most of the other statutory prerequisites for federal jurisdiction, including the federal-question and amount-in-controversy requirements, can be analyzed claim by claim. * * *

Thus, with respect to plaintiff-specific jurisdictional requirements, the Court held in *Clark v. Paul Gray, Inc.,* 306 U.S. 583 (1939), that every plaintiff must separately satisfy the amount-in-controversy requirement. * * * The Court reaffirmed this rule, in the context of a class action brought invoking § 1332(a) diversity jurisdiction, in *Zahn v. International Paper Co.,* 414 U.S. 291 (1973). It follows "inescapably" from *Clark*, the Court held in *Zahn*, that "any plaintiff without the jurisdictional amount must be dismissed from the case, even though others allege jurisdictionally sufficient claims."

* * *

In *Finley v. United States,* 490 U.S. 545 (1989), we held * * * that "a grant of jurisdiction over claims involving particular parties does not itself confer jurisdiction over additional claims by or against different parties." * * * *Finley* held that in the context of parties, in contrast to claims, "we will not assume that the full constitutional power has been congressionally authorized, and will not read jurisdictional statutes broadly."

* * *

B

* * * In 1990, Congress [passed] § 1367 * * *.

All parties to this litigation and all courts to consider the question agree that § 1367 overturned the result in *Finley*. * * * In order to determine the scope of supplemental jurisdiction authorized by § 1367 * * *, we must examine the statute's text in light of context, structure, and related statutory provisions.

Section 1367(a) is a broad grant of supplemental jurisdiction over other claims within the same case or controversy, as long as the action is one in which the district courts would have original jurisdiction. The last sentence of § 1367(a) makes it clear that the grant of supplemental jurisdiction extends to claims involving joinder or intervention of additional parties. The single question before us, therefore, is whether a diversity case in which the claims of some plaintiffs satisfy the amount-in-controversy requirement, but the claims of other plaintiffs do not, presents a "civil action of which the district courts have original jurisdiction." If the answer is yes, § 1367(a) confers supplemental jurisdiction over all claims, including those that do not independently satisfy the amount-in-controversy requirement, if the claims are part of the same Article III case or controversy. If the answer is no, § 1367(a) is inapplicable and, in light of our holdings in *Clark* and *Zahn*, the district court has no statutory basis for exercising supplemental jurisdiction over the additional claims.

We now conclude the answer must be yes. * * *

Section 1367(a) commences with the direction that §§ 1367(b) and (c), or other relevant statutes, may provide specific exceptions, but otherwise § 1367(a) is a broad jurisdictional grant, with no distinction drawn between pendent-claim and pendent-party cases. * * *

If § 1367(a) were the sum total of the relevant statutory language, our holding would rest on that language alone. The statute, of course, instructs us to examine § 1367(b) to determine if any of its exceptions apply, so we proceed to that section. * * * Section 1367(b), which applies only to diversity cases, withholds supplemental jurisdiction over the claims of plaintiffs proposed to be joined as indispensable parties under Federal Rule of Civil Procedure 19, or who seek to intervene pursuant to Rule 24. Nothing in the text of § 1367(b), however, withholds supplemental jurisdiction over the claims of plaintiffs permissively joined under Rule 20 * * * or certified as class-action members pursuant to Rule 23 * * *. The natural, indeed the necessary, inference is that § 1367 confers supplemental jurisdiction over claims by Rule 20 and Rule 23 plaintiffs. * * *

We cannot accept the view, urged by some of the parties, commentators, and Courts of Appeals, that a district court lacks original jurisdiction over a civil action unless the court has original jurisdiction over every claim in the complaint. As we understand this position, it requires assuming either that all claims in the complaint must stand or fall as a single, indivisible "civil action" as a matter of definitional necessity—what we will refer to as the "indivisibility theory"—or else that the inclusion of a claim or party falling outside the district court's original jurisdiction somehow contaminates every other claim in the complaint, depriving the court of original jurisdiction over any of these claims—what we will refer to as the "contamination theory."

The indivisibility theory is easily dismissed, as it is inconsistent with the whole notion of supplemental jurisdiction. If a district court must have original jurisdiction over every claim in the complaint in order to have "original jurisdiction" over a "civil action," then in *Gibbs* there was no civil action of which the district court could assume original jurisdiction under § 1331, and so no basis for exercising supplemental jurisdiction over any of the claims. * * * The indivisibility theory is further belied by our practice—in both federal-question and diversity cases—of allowing federal courts to cure jurisdictional defects by dismissing the offending parties rather than dismissing the entire action. * * * If the presence of jurisdictionally problematic claims in the complaint meant the district court was without original jurisdiction over the single, indivisible civil action before it, then the district court would have to dismiss the whole action rather than particular parties.

We also find it unconvincing to say that the definitional indivisibility theory applies in the context of diversity cases but not in the context of federal-question cases. The broad and general language of the statute does not permit this result. * * *

The contamination theory * * * makes little sense with respect to the amount-in-controversy requirement, which is meant to ensure that a dispute is sufficiently important to warrant federal-court attention. The presence of a single nondiverse party may eliminate the fear of bias with respect to all claims, but the presence of a claim that falls short of the minimum amount in controversy does nothing to reduce the importance of the claims that do meet this requirement.

* * *

* * * We hold that § 1367 by its plain text overruled *Clark* and *Zahn* and authorized supplemental jurisdiction over all claims by diverse parties arising out of the same Article III case or controversy, subject only to enumerated exceptions not applicable in the cases now before us.

C

The proponents of the alternative view of § 1367 insist that the statute is at least ambiguous and that we should look to other interpretive tools, including the legislative history of § 1367, which supposedly demonstrate Congress did not intend § 1367 to overrule *Zahn*. We can reject this argument at the very outset simply because § 1367 is not ambiguous. * * *

* * *

As we have repeatedly held, the authoritative statement is the statutory text, not the legislative history or any other extrinsic material. * * *

* * *

D

Finally, we note that the Class Action Fairness Act (CAFA), Pub. L. 109–2, 119 Stat. 4, enacted this year, has no bearing on our analysis of these cases. Subject to certain limitations, the CAFA confers federal diversity jurisdiction over class actions where the aggregate amount in controversy exceeds $5 million. It abrogates the rule against aggregating claims, a rule this Court recognized in [*Supreme Tribe of Ben–Hur v. Cauble*, 255 U.S. 356 (1921)] and reaffirmed in *Zahn*. The CAFA, however, is not retroactive, and the views of the 2005 Congress are not relevant to our interpretation of a text enacted by Congress in 1990. The CAFA, moreover, does not moot the significance of our interpretation of § 1367, as many proposed exercises of supplemental jurisdiction, even in the class-action context, might not fall within the CAFA's ambit. The CAFA, then, has no impact, one way or the other, on our interpretation of § 1367.

* * *

[JUSTICE GINSBURG, joined by JUSTICES STEVENS, O'CONNOR and BREYER, dissented. The dissent argued for a more restrained interpretation of Section 1367 that would not overturn *Zahn*. More specifically, the dissent found the statute's language ambiguous and susceptible of a narrower construction that was, in the opinion of the dissenters, more consistent with the legislative history and "less disruptive of our jurisprudence regarding supplemental jurisdiction."]

NOTES AND QUESTIONS

1. What is the rationale of the majority in *Allapattah*? Does that view favor or restrict aggregation?

2. Under the Class Action Fairness Act of 2005 ("CAFA"), enacted four months before the *Allapatttah* decision was issued, members of a class action may aggregate their claims to meet a new $5 million amount in controversy requirement, provided that various other requirements are met (*see* Part (B)(3) of this chapter). CAFA certainly rendered *Allapattah* much less significant, but it did not moot the issue entirely. In *Allapattah*, the court held that § 1367 overruled *Zahn*, and that only one named plaintiff need satisfy the $75,000 amount-in-controversy for the court to exercise diversity jurisdiction over a class action. Nonetheless, *Allapattah* does not permit original diversity jurisdiction or removal in cases in which no plaintiff satisfies the $75,000 requirement.

After CAFA, a federal district court has original jurisdiction over any class action involving more than 100 class members where the amount in controversy exceeds $5 million and any class member is diverse from any defendant. 28 U.S.C. § 1332(d)(2). The putative class members' claims are aggregated to determine whether the $5 million threshold is met. 28 U.S.C. § 1332(d)(6). Therefore, individual plaintiffs (including the named plaintiffs) may have recoveries that fall far below the $75,000 jurisdictional amount under the federal diversity statute, but still have access to federal court so long as they can successfully aggregate their claims to exceed $5 million. By the same token, *Allapattah* permits federal jurisdiction if one plaintiff's claim exceeds $75,000, even if the aggregate amount at issue for the class is less than $5 million. *Allapattah* and CAFA thus provide alternative (and at times overlapping) bases for diversity jurisdiction over class actions.

3. How should the courts determine whether the jurisdictional amount is met in cases seeking injunctive relief? One commentator notes:

> * * * Is it the cost to the defendant or the benefit to the plaintiff that is the appropriate gauge of "value" for jurisdictional purposes? The federal courts have dealt with this issue in the context of the $75,000 amount-in-controversy requirement of § 1332(a). Courts have generally applied one of three approaches: (1) some look at the question from the plaintiff's viewpoint; (2) others hold that the viewpoint of either plaintiff or defendant may be used; and (3) others use the viewpoint of the party invoking federal jurisdiction. The Supreme Court had yet to take a stand on which is the correct viewpoint. The problem is that, in class actions seeking nonmonetary relief, some courts, invoking *Zahn*, measure only the benefit to each plaintiff individually. Applying the defendant's viewpoint in these cases, where the total cost to the defendant would meet the jurisdictional amount, according to some courts, effectively aggregates the claims of all plaintiffs, which is forbidden by *Zahn*.
>
> Section 1332(d)(6) of CAFA arguably overrules *Zahn* to that extent. The new provision expressly contemplates aggregation of the plaintiffs' claim in determining whether the $5 million "value" requirement has been met, and clearly is what Congress intended. However, Congress' failure to add an express provision on how to value claims for injunctive relief means that it is debatable whether § 1332(d)(6) permits aggregation in cases for injunctive relief. In summary, although it is clearly Congress' intent—given its desire to facilitate the assertion of federal jurisdiction over class action cases—to look either at the total benefit to the plaintiff class or the total cost to the defendant to meet the jurisdictional amount, the language of the new provision does not necessarily lead to that conclusion.

Georgene M. Vairo, *Class Action Fairness Act of 2005; With Commentary and Analysis* 1, 24–25 (Matthew Bender 2005).

2. DETERMINING CITIZENSHIP FOR DIVERSITY PURPOSES

As noted above, the Supreme Court's decision in *Supreme Tribe of Ben–Hur v. Cauble*, 255 U.S. 356 (1921), is repeatedly cited for having established that courts only consider the citizenship of the named representatives—not each of the absent class members—in determining whether the requirements of diversity of citizenship have been met. In *Ben–Hur*, several non-residents of Indiana who were policyholders of an Indiana fraternal benefit association had filed suit in Indiana federal court on behalf of all policyholders (including Indiana residents) to enjoin a financial reorganization of the society. A decree was issued in favor of the association. Later, an Indiana policyholder filed suit in Indiana state court to prevent the same proposed reorganization. The association then asked the federal court to issue an injunction to halt the state-court proceeding. The federal trial court dismissed the lawsuit for lack of subject-matter jurisdiction, holding that the earlier federal court decree did not bind Indiana policyholders, who were unnamed class members in the earlier suit, but who could not have been joined without destroying diversity of citizenship. The Supreme Court reversed, holding that the trial court in the earlier lawsuit had properly looked only to the citizenship of the named representatives in determining diversity jurisdiction. 255 U.S. at 364.

Proponents of class action reform long argued that plaintiffs' attorneys deliberately structured their complaints to destroy diversity jurisdiction. Because a plaintiff could defeat diversity under *Supreme Tribe of Ben–Hur* simply by naming one plaintiff in the complaint who shared the same citizenship with one defendant, defendants would argue such complaints were, in effect, unfairly defeating diversity. For instance, in *Triggs v. John Crump Toyota*, 154 F.3d 1284 (11th Cir. 1998), an Alabama resident filed a fraud action in Alabama state court against a Florida financial company and an Alabama Toyota dealership, alleging that defendants conspired to inflate the cost of leasing cars. The class consisted of over 17,000 people, all of whom had dealt with the Florida company but only 2 percent of whom had dealt with the Alabama car dealership. Defendants removed the case to federal court, arguing that the Alabama dealership was fraudulently joined to defeat diversity. In rejecting the argument, the Eleventh Circuit reasoned:

> The contention of defendants in this case focuses upon the claims of the members of the putative plaintiff class, rather than upon the named plaintiff. Defendants argue that [the dealership] must be deemed to have been fraudulently joined merely because 98% of the members of the putative plaintiff class would have no claim against [the dealership]. This focus is inconsistent with the well-settled rule for class actions that a court should consider only the citizenship of the named parties to determine whether there is diversity jurisdiction. *Supreme Tribe of Ben–Hur v. Cauble*, 255 U.S. 356 (1921). Pursuant to this well-settled rule, we look to the citizenship of the named plaintiff * * * and conclude that there is not complete diversity, because, although [the Alabama named plaintiff] is diverse with respect to [the Florida] defendant * * *, he is not diverse with respect to the properly joined defendant, [the Alabama dealership].

154 F.3d at 1288–89. Other courts have agreed with *Triggs* and held that a defendant against whom only a small percentage of putative class plaintiffs have a claim is not fraudulently joined for purposes of establishing diversity. *See, e.g., Gray v. H.A.S.*, 18 F. Supp. 2d 1320, 1322–23 (M.D. Ala. 1998); *Ren–Dan Farms, Inc. v. Monsanto Co.*, 952 F. Supp. 370, 376 (W.D. La. 1997).

As discussed in the following section, the Class Action Fairness Act now makes it unlikely in most class actions that defendants will have to rely on fraudulent-joinder theories.

3. BROADENING THE SCOPE OF FEDERAL DIVERSITY

a. The Origins of the Class Action Fairness Act

The Class Action Fairness Act (CAFA) was enacted in 2005 after years of efforts by proponents to address what some perceived to be abusive class action practices. The Senate Judiciary Committee stated that "[a] mounting stack of evidence reviewed by the Committee demonstrate[d] that abuses [were] undermining the rights of both plaintiffs and defendants." S. Rep. No. 109–14, at 4. One of the primary reasons given for CAFA's enactment was to address forum-shopping by class counsel. *Id.* at 4, 23. As the federal court system became a more difficult forum for plaintiffs to litigate complex cases successfully, class counsel focused increasingly on state courts in hopes of finding a more sympathetic forum. *See* Georgene M. Vairo, *Class Action Fairness Act of 2005; With Commentary and Analysis* 2 (Matthew Bender 2005). Corporate defendants responded by trying to remove class actions to federal court, but strict jurisdictional rules resulted in many remands to state court. *See id.* As class actions migrated from federal to state courts, criticism began to mount that certain state courts were not treating defendants fairly. *See, e.g.*, 151 Cong. Rec. S1225, at S1228 (daily ed. Feb. 10, 2005) (statement of Sen. Hatch); 151 Cong. Rec. H723, at S726 (daily ed. Feb. 17, 2005) (statement of Rep. Sensenbrenner); 151 Cong. Rec. S999–02, at S999 (daily ed. Feb. 7, 2005) (statement of Sen. Specter).

Defense counsel, corporations, politicians, and others began to attack such state fora—characterizing them as "judicial hellholes" that needed to be reined in. *See* Vairo, *supra*, at 3. Proponents of CAFA complained that the "current law enable[d] lawyers to 'game' the procedural rules and keep nationwide or multi-state class actions in state courts whose judges have reputations for readily certifying classes and approving settlements without regard to class member interests." S. Rep. No. 109–14, at 4, 23.

CAFA's detractors, on the other hand, argued that the legislation was an effort to elevate corporate special interests over those of the American consumer. S. Rep. No. 109–14, at 84; 151 Cong. Rec. S999–02, at 1002 (daily ed. Feb.7, 2005) (statement of Sen. Leahy). Detractors contended that the legislation sought to deny citizens access to state courts, where they were better able to protect themselves from violations of civil rights, consumer, environmental, health, and safety laws. S. Rep. No. 109–14, at 83; 151 Cong. Rec. S999–02, at 1002 (daily ed. Feb.7, 2005) (statement of Sen. Leahy). They expressed concern that CAFA would not remove class actions from state to federal court, but would eliminate them altogether, as federal courts would be inhospitable to certifying multi-state class actions. S. Rep. No. 109–14, at 82. Critics also argued that taking cases out of state court deprived citizens of the particular state forum's convenience and expertise, 151 Cong. Rec. S999–02, at S1002 (daily ed. Feb. 7, 2005) (statement of Sen. Leahy)—making it much more expensive, burdensome and time consuming to vindicate rights. S. Rep. No. 109–14, at 83. State and federal judges, as well as the Judicial Conference of the United States and the Conference of Chief Justices, opposed CAFA on the grounds that it violated principles of federalism and threatened to overwhelm an already burdened federal docket. *Id.* at 82–83 & nn.1–2, 92. The National Conference of State Legislatures and several state attorneys general opposed the bill on the grounds that it undermined their ability to bring actions in their own courts and cast doubt on the integrity of the state judiciary. *Id.* S. Rep. No. 109–14, at 82 & n.3, 92.

CAFA dramatically shifted the inquiry relating to diversity jurisdiction in many large class actions. The materials that follow introduce the major areas of reform, as well as some ambiguities and conflicts.

b. CAFA's Expansion of Federal Jurisdiction and Removal

i. Multi-State Class Actions

CAFA greatly expanded the original jurisdiction of federal district courts over multi-state class actions involving state-law claims. CAFA amended 28 U.S.C. § 1332 so that federal courts have jurisdiction over class actions when three criteria are met: (1) there are 100 or more putative class members, 28 U.S.C. § 1332(d)(5)(B); (2) there is "minimal diversity" between the parties, 28 U.S.C. § 1332(d)(2); and (3) the amount in controversy exceeds $5 million, in the aggregate. 28 U.S.C. § 1332(d)(2). This expansion was intended to give the federal courts broad jurisdiction over interstate class actions, while retaining state courts' jurisdiction over class actions that are primarily small and local. S. Rep. No. 109–14, at 27–28.

ii. Mass Actions

CAFA applies not only to cases filed under the state and federal class action rules, but also to "mass actions." "[A] 'mass action' means any civil action * * * in which monetary relief claims of 100 or more persons are proposed to be tried jointly on the ground that the plaintiffs' claims involve common questions of law or fact." 28 U.S.C. § 1332(d)(11)(B). Congress included mass actions under CAFA because of the tendency for some state courts to permit joinder of the claims of large numbers of plaintiffs. The Judiciary Committee concluded that "mass actions are simply class actions in disguise. They involve a lot of people who want their claims adjudicated together and they often result in the same abuses as class actions. In fact, sometimes the abuses are even worse because the lawyers seek to join claims that have little to do with each other and confuse a jury into awarding millions of dollars to individuals who have suffered no real injury." S. Rep. No. 109–14, at 47. For example, in Mississippi, which does not have any class action rule, "litigants ha[d] attempted to squeeze mass actions into the state's joinder rules, particularly Mississippi Rule of Civil Procedure 20." Robert H. Klonoff, *The Adoption of a Class Action Rule: Some Issues For Mississippi to Consider*, 24 Miss. C. L. Rev. 261 (2005).

Although mass actions are considered class actions for jurisdictional purposes to some extent under CAFA, they are not treated precisely the same. Importantly, there is no aggregation available for mass actions under CAFA, so each plaintiff must satisfy the $75,000 amount-in-controversy requirement under 28 U.S.C. § 1332(a) for access to federal court based on diversity. 28 U.S.C. § 1332(d)(11)(B). *See, e.g., Gilmore v. Bayer*

Corp., 2009 WL 4789406, at *3 (S.D. Ill. 2009). Moreover, unlike plaintiffs in class actions, plaintiffs in mass actions do not seek to act on behalf of others similarly situated. *Cf. Cal. Pub. Emps. Ret. Sys. v. Moody's Corp.*, 2009 WL 3809816, at *7 (N.D. Cal. 2009) (holding that although California public pension fund manages pension money for more than 1.6 million people, it was considered one plaintiff under CAFA's "mass action" provision because none of the fund's individual beneficiaries made any direct claims in the action). In a mass action, although plaintiffs elect to try their claims together, each plaintiff acts on his or her own behalf.

iii. Expanded Removal to Federal Court

In addition to liberalizing original jurisdiction in diversity cases, CAFA makes it easier for class actions (and "mass actions") to be removed from state to federal court. CAFA—through new section 28 U.S.C. § 1453—accomplishes this goal, for class actions covered by the Act, in a number of ways:

- Prior to CAFA, complete diversity was required for removal, thus imposing a major barrier to its implementation. 28 U.S.C. 1441(b). After CAFA, only "minimal diversity" is required for covered class actions. 28 U.S.C. § 1453(b).
- Prior to CAFA, under 1446(b) defendants only had one year from the date of filing to remove a class action. 28 U.S.C. 1446(b). For CAFA-covered cases, defendants no longer have a one-year deadline for removal. 28 U.S.C. § 1453(b).
- Prior to CAFA, courts held that under § 1446, a defendant could not remove a diversity class action to federal court without the consent of the other defendants. *See, e.g., Emrich v. Touche Ross & Co.*, 846 F.2d 1190, 1193 n.1 (9th Cir. 1988). For CAFA-covered cases, defendants no longer need such consent. 28 U.S.C. § 1453(b).
- Prior to CAFA, under § 1441(b) a defendant who was a citizen of the state where the class action was originally brought could not seek removal. For CAFA-covered cases, a defendant may remove an otherwise qualifying case to federal court even where a defendant is a citizen of the forum state. 28 U.S.C. § 1453(b).
- Prior to CAFA, under § 1447(d) if a class action was removed to federal court and then remanded to state court, federal appellate interlocutory review of the remand order was generally prohibited. 28 U.S.C. § 1447(d). For CAFA-covered cases, the remand order is subject to immediate review, at the discretion of the federal appellate court. 28 U.S.C. § 1453(c)(1). If the appellate court grants review, it must rule on the order granting or denying a motion to remand within 60 days or the appeal is deemed to be denied. 28 U.S.C. § 1453(c)(2).

c. Exceptions to CAFA's Expanded Jurisdiction

There are a number of exceptions to CAFA's expansion of original diversity jurisdiction. The exceptions are designed to keep those controversies that are truly local in the state courts. S. Rep. No. 109–14, at 39. They include the following.

i. Home State and Local Controversy Exceptions

Even where the "minimal diversity" and the amount-in-controversy criteria have been met, in three circumstances the federal district court is permitted, or even required, to decline jurisdiction. Two options fall under the "Home State" exception, and the third is called the "Local Controversy" exception.

Home State Exception

• The district court *may* decline jurisdiction when: (1) more than one third but fewer than two thirds of the proposed plaintiff class members are citizens of the state where the action was originally filed; and (2) "the primary defendants" are also citizens of the forum state. The court may decline jurisdiction in these circumstances if "in the interests of justice and looking at the totality of the circumstances" abstention seems appropriate. In making this determination, the court must consider six factors relating, among other things, to the nexus between the forum, the claims, and the parties. 28 U.S.C. § 1332(d)(3).

• The district court *must* decline jurisdiction when: (1) two thirds or more of the proposed plaintiff class members are citizens of the state where the action was originally filed; and (2) "the primary defendants" are also citizens of the forum state. 28 U.S.C. § 1332(d)(4)(B).

Local Controversy Exception

• The district court *must* decline jurisdiction when: (1) more than two thirds of the proposed plaintiff class members are citizens of the state where the action was originally filed; (2) at least one defendant is also a citizen of the forum state, "whose alleged conduct forms a significant basis for the claims asserted" and from whom "significant" relief is sought; (3) the principal injuries occurred in the forum state; and (4) a similar class action has not been filed within the preceding three years. 28 U.S.C. § 1332(d)(4)(A).

The home state and local controversy exceptions are not put at issue until the removing party has shown that the case meets CAFA's removal criteria. At that point, the party seeking remand bears the burden of proving an exception applies. *Serrano v. 180 Connect, Inc.*, 478 F.3d 1018, 1023 (9th Cir. 2007) (joining the Fifth, Seventh, and Eleventh Circuits and holding that because the "local controversy" and "home-state controversy" provisions were exceptions under CAFA and not additional *prima facie* elements, party seeking remand must establish those exceptions). *Accord Kaufman v. Allstate New Jersey Ins. Co.*, 561 F.3d 144, 153–54 (3d Cir. 2009) (same); *In re Hannaford Bros. Co. Customer Data Security Breach Litig.*, 564 F.3d 75, 78 (1st Cir. 2009) (same).

The home state and local controversy exceptions require a federal court to make a number of important threshold determinations. These exceptions also require the court to determine the meaning of terms left undefined by CAFA, such as "primary defendants," "significant" relief, and "principal injuries"—determinations that have led to considerable litigation.

Citizenship. As an initial matter, the federal court must determine how many putative class members are citizens of the forum state. Proving citizenship is a very fact-intensive exercise. *Compare Preston v. Tenet Healthsystem Memorial Med. Center*, 485 F.3d 804, 817–18 (5th Cir. 2007) *(Preston I)* (eight affidavits by patients who lived outside Louisiana but expressed intent to return to New Orleans post-Hurricane Katrina, along with billing addresses, emergency contact information, and current addresses were sufficient to meet one-third citizenship requirements for CAFA home state exception), *with Preston v. Tenet Healthsystem Memorial Med. Center*, 485 F.3d 793, 801–04 (5th Cir. 2007) *(Preston II)* (despite allegations similar to *Preston I*, court retained federal jurisdiction where no affidavits were filed indicating class members' intent to return home to Louisiana one year post-Katrina and plaintiffs relied solely on medical records to establish domicile).

Courts are also divided on the impact of a corporate defendant's dual citizenship on federal jurisdiction under CAFA. *See Weaver v. Nestle USA, Inc.*, 2008 WL 5453734, at *1–3 (N.D. Cal. 2008) (discussing split in authority); *Dennison v. Carolina Payday Loans, Inc.*, 2008 WL 5484559, at *3 (D.S.C. 2008) (same). *Compare Johnson v. Advance Am.*, 549 F.3d 932 (4th Cir. 2008) (where class consists solely of South Carolina citizens, and defendant corporation is a citizen of Delaware (its state of incorporation) and South Carolina (its principal place of business), minimal diversity required for CAFA removal does not exist) *and Smalls v. Advance Am.* 2008 WL 4177297, at *2 (D.S.C. 2008) ("dual citizenship of a defendant [with one of the locations being the same as a class member's] does not create minimal diversity under CAFA"), *with Fuller v. Home Depot Servs., L.L.C.*, 2007 WL 2345257, at *3 (N.D. Ga. 2007) (assuming class consists solely of Georgia citizens, and defendant corporation is a citizen of Delaware (its state of incorporation) and Georgia (its principal place of business), minimal diversity required for CAFA removal exists). The Supreme Court has not addressed the impact of a corporation's dual citizenship on jurisdiction under CAFA. The Court, however, has clarified how a corporation's principal place of business should be determined for diversity jurisdiction analysis: namely, the principal place of business is "where a corporation's officers direct, control, and coordinate the corporation's activities[,]" normally its headquarters. *Hertz Corp. v. Friend*, 559 U.S. 77, 81 (2010).

"Primary defendants." Courts have taken varied approaches to interpreting the meaning of "primary defendants" under the home state exception. *See* Beth I.Z. Boland & Melissa G. Liazos, *The Class Action Fairness Act—Three Years Later and Counting*, 9 Class Action Litig. Report 395, at 400–01 (2008) (hereinafter "*CAFA—3 Years Later*") (discussing various approaches). Some courts define primary defendants as those who are *directly* liable to plaintiffs. Defendants who are vicariously liable, sued under aiding and abetting theories, or liable through indemnification or contribution would not be primary defendants. *See, e.g., Anthony v. Small Tube Mfg. Corp.*, 535 F. Supp. 2d 506, 515–16 (E.D. Pa. 2007). Other courts define primary defendants in language similar to the CAFA Senate Report: primary defendants are "the real 'targets of the lawsuit'—*i.e.*, the defendants that would be expected to incur most of the loss if liability is found." *See* S. Rep. No. 109–14, at 43–44 (2005). *See, e.g., Robinson v. Cheetah*

Transp., 2006 WL 3322580, at *2 (W.D. La. 2006), *appeal denied and judgment aff'd*, 2007 WL 28257 (W.D. La. 2007). Still other courts define primary defendants as those who are able to bear the cost of liability. *See, e.g., In re Ingram Barge Co.*, 2007 WL 148647, at *1–2 (E.D. La. 2007) (corporate employer, and not individual defendants, was primary defendant where it was "most able to bear most of the liability if the plaintiffs prevail"). Moreover, a number of courts have interpreted "the primary defendants" to mean that *all* primary defendants must be citizens of the forum state in order for the home state exception to apply. *Kurth v. Arcelormittal USA, Inc.*, 2009 WL 3346588, at * 6–7 (N.D. Ind. 2009); *accord Robinson*, 2006 WL 3322580 at *3 ("[T]he plain language of the statute indicates that remand is only required when *all* of the primary defendants are residents of the state in which the action was originally filed.").

Significant defendants. Similarly, courts have varied in their approach to determining whether a defendant is significant, a requirement under the local controversy exception. More specifically, the courts differ over what constitutes "significant relief" and conduct that forms a "significant basis" for bringing a defendant into the local controversy exception. Courts have used both absolute and comparative approaches when determining the significance of a defendant. *See CAFA—3 Years Later* at 395, 400–01; *Coffey v. Freeport McMoran Copper & Gold*, 581 F.3d 1240, 1244 (10th Cir. 2009) (courts generally use comparative approach). *Compare Kurth v. ArcelorMittal USA Inc.*, 2009 WL 3346588, at *8–13 (N.D. Ind. 2009) (comparing local defendant's conduct to other defendants), *with Anderson v. Hackett*, 646 F. Supp. 2d 1041, 1048–49 (S.D. Ill. 2009) (refusing to compare local defendant's conduct with others and instead looking at complaint as a whole). *See also, e.g., Kaufman v. Allstate N.J. Ins. Co.*, 561 F.3d 144, 155–57 (3d Cir. 2009) ("significant basis" provision does not require that every member of a putative class assert a claim against the local defendant, but instead requires that local defendant's alleged conduct form a significant basis of all the claims asserted; this test requires court to compare local defendant's alleged conduct with alleged conduct of all the defendants); *Coffey v. Freeport McMoran Copper & Gold*, 581 F.3d 1240, 1244–45 (10th Cir. 2009) ("significant relief" provision does not require a district court to assess a defendant's ability to pay a potential judgment; thus, defendant's argument that it lacked assets to satisfy such judgment did not exempt it from the local controversy exception).

"Principal injuries." Another issue is whether the "principal injuries" provision, § 1332(d)(4)(A)(i)(III), requires that the principal injuries resulting from the alleged conduct *and* any related conduct of each defendant must take place in the home state. *See Kaufman*, 561 F.3d at 149–50. In *Kaufman*, the Third Circuit concluded that only one of these is necessary because the plain language of the statute uses "or," not "and." *Id.* at 158. Specifically, the provision requires that "principal injuries resulting from the alleged conduct *or* any related conduct of each defendant were incurred in the State in which the action was originally filed." 28 USC § 1332(d)(4)(A)(i)(III) (emphasis added).

ii. State Action

CAFA excludes actions brought against "primary defendants" who are states, state officials, or other governmental entities. 28 U.S.C.

§ 1332(d)(5)(A). The purpose of this exception is "to prevent [such parties] from dodging legitimate claims by removing class actions to federal court and then arguing that the federal courts are constitutionally prohibited [by sovereign immunity under the Eleventh Amendment] from granting the requested relief." S. Rep. No. 109–14, at 42. The exception "ensure[s] that cases in which such entities are the primary targets will be heard in state courts that do not face the same constitutional impediments to granting relief." *Id.*

But what about a class action filed *by* a state? In *In re Katrina Canal Litigation Breaches*, 524 F.3d 700 (5th Cir. 2008), the Fifth Circuit held that a class action filed by the Louisiana State Attorney General and a class of Louisiana citizens against over two hundred insurance companies was properly removed to federal court. The plaintiffs sued in Louisiana state court, alleging that the defendants failed to pay covered insurance claims post-Hurricanes Katrina and Rita. The defendants removed the case to federal court under CAFA. In response, the Louisiana Attorney General argued that a state is not a "person" whose "citizenship" can be determined for diversity jurisdiction under CAFA and, moreover, a state cannot be party to a suit removed to federal court because of state sovereign immunity. The Fifth Circuit—in a case of first impression—held that the case was removable on two grounds. First, removal was appropriate because Congress "considered and rejected an amendment that would have exempted class actions filed by an attorney general from removal under CAFA." *Id.* at 705. Second, the court concluded that, although a state was not a "person" under CAFA, the state had waived its sovereign immunity by including private citizens as plaintiffs. *Id.* at 711. The Fifth Circuit noted that the federal district court might consider severing and returning the State of Louisiana to state court while retaining the private citizens in federal court. *See id.* at 711–12. Would this resolution adequately address the problem? *See Connecticut v. Moody's Corp.*, 664 F. Supp. 2d 196, 202 (D. Conn. 2009) ("CAFA only applies if one accepts the premise that the State is suing not in its capacity as sovereign but on behalf of a circumscribed group of its citizens[,]" therefore court held CAFA inapplicable where Connecticut brought an enforcement action in its sovereign capacity).

iii. Small Classes

As noted above, CAFA excludes class actions where the proposed plaintiff class has fewer than 100 members. 28 U.S.C. § 1332(d)(5)(B). The purpose of this exception is "to allow class actions with relatively few claimants to remain in state courts." S. Rep. No. 109–14, at 42. This exception is also called the "limited scope" provision.

iv. Securities and Internal Corporate Affairs

CAFA excludes actions relating to:

• a covered security under the federal securities laws (28 U.S.C. § 1332(d)(9)(A));
• "the internal affairs or governance of a corporation" or business enterprise under state law (28 U.S.C. § 1332(d)(9)(B)); or
• the rights, duties, and obligations under the federal securities laws (28 U.S.C. § 1332(d)(9)(C)).

The purpose of excluding the above kinds of claims is "to avoid disturbing the federal versus state court jurisdictional lines already drawn in the securities litigation class action context by the enactment of the Securities Litigation Uniform Standards Act of 1998." S. Rep. No. 109–14, at 45 (2005). *See* Chapter 10(C)(2)(b) (discussing SLUSA).

NOTES AND QUESTIONS

1. The Federal Judicial Center evaluated class actions filed in or removed to 88 federal district courts between July 1, 2001 and June 30, 2007. Its report confirms the prediction that CAFA would increase the number of diversity jurisdiction cases in federal courts. Emery G. Lee III & Thomas E. Willging, Fed. Judicial Ctr., *The Impact of the Class Action Fairness Act of 2005 on the Federal Courts: Fourth Interim Report to the Judicial Conference Advisory Committee on Civil Rules* 1–2 (Apr. 2008). The authors are engaged in phase two of their CAFA analysis, in which they explore CAFA's impact on litigation activity and judicial rulings in class actions in the federal courts two years pre- and post-CAFA. *See* Emery G. Lee III & Thomas E. Willging, Fed. Judicial Ctr., *Impact of the Class Action Fairness Act on the Federal Courts; Preliminary Findings from Phase Two's Pre-CAFA Sample of Diversity Class Actions* 1 (Nov. 2008).

2. In response to CAFA, some plaintiffs have structured their complaints in an attempt to preserve state court jurisdiction. The courts are wrestling with this issue. On the one hand, it is well settled that plaintiffs are the masters of their own complaints and as such may select the forum, the parties, the claims, and the relief sought. On the other hand, some courts have concluded that plaintiffs should not be able to craft their complaints to defeat CAFA removal. *Compare Bell v. Hershey Co.*, 557 F.3d 953, 956 (8th Cir. 2009) ("The enactment of CAFA did not alter the proposition that the plaintiff is the master of the complaint."); *In re Hannaford Bros. Co. Customer Data Sec. Breach Litig.*, 564 F.3d 75 (1st Cir. 2009) (while conceding that court may look beyond the four corners of the complaint when determining whether the home state exception applies, the court held that class consisting entirely of Florida citizens, suing single Florida corporation, in Florida state court, fit squarely into exception, despite defendant's argument that plaintiff crafted complaint to defeat federal jurisdiction); *and Tanoh v. Dow Chem. Co.*, 561 F.3d 945 (9th Cir. 2009) (recognizing that plaintiffs, as masters of their complaint, can choose their forum; and holding that seven individual state court actions, comprised of less than one hundred plaintiffs each and brought against the same local defendant for same alleged misconduct, could not be treated as single "mass action" subject to CAFA removal, where neither parties nor court sought to jointly try the claims), *with Freeman v. Blue Ridge Paper Prods., Inc.*, 551 F.3d 405, 406–09 (6th Cir. 2008) (where five individual state court class actions were filed by plaintiffs from single state against single defendant for same injuries over sequential time period for $4.9 million each, court concluded that there was "no colorable basis" for dividing suit "other than to frustrate CAFA," and found CAFA conferred jurisdiction) *and Bullard v. Burlington N. Santa Fe Ry. Co.*, 535 F.3d 759, 761–62 (7th Cir. 2008) (where complaint filed by 144 residents proposed a trial of 10 exemplary plaintiffs, followed by application of preclusion to 134 additional plaintiffs without another trial, lawsuit qualified as "mass action" because suit involved monetary relief claims of 100 or more persons being tried jointly).

3. In *Standard Fire Insurance Co. v. Knowles*, 133 S. Ct. 1345 (2013), the Supreme Court faced the issue of whether a putative class representative

could, by stipulation, prevent removal of a class action that would otherwise meet jurisdictional requirements under CAFA. The case involved claims filed in Arkansas state court by an Arkansas man against an insurance company. "Knowles claimed that, when the company had made certain homeowner's insurance loss payments, it had unlawfully failed to include a general contractor fee. And Knowles sought to certify a class of 'hundreds, and possibly thousands' of similarly harmed Arkansas policyholders. In describing the relief sought, the complaint says that the 'Plaintiff and Class stipulate they will seek to recover total aggregate damages of less than five million dollars.'" *Id.* at 1348 (citations omitted). After Standard Fire removed the case to federal court under CAFA, the district court remanded, finding that Knowles' stipulation prevented removal. The Eighth Circuit declined to hear the appeal, but the Supreme Court unanimously reversed:

> * * * The District Court in this case found that [the sum potentially at issue in the case, if certified as a class action] would have exceeded $5 million *but for* the stipulation. And we must decide whether the stipulation makes a critical difference.
>
> In our view, it does not. Our reason is a simple one: Stipulations must be binding. The stipulation Knowles proffered to the District Court, however, does not speak for those he purports to represent. That is because a plaintiff who files a proposed class action cannot legally bind members of the proposed class before the class is certified. *See Smith v. Bayer Corp.*, 131 S. Ct. 2368, 2380 (2011).
>
> Because his precertification stipulation does not bind anyone but himself, Knowles has not reduced the value of the putative class members' claims. For jurisdictional purposes, our inquiry is limited to examining the case "as of the time it was filed in state court," *Wisconsin Dept. of Corrections v. Schacht,* 524 U.S. 381, 390 (1998). At that point, Knowles lacked the authority to concede the amount-in-controversy issue for the absent class members. The Federal District Court, therefore, wrongly concluded that Knowles' precertification stipulation could overcome its finding that the CAFA jurisdictional threshold had been met.

133 S. Ct. at 1348–49 (citations and paragraph break omitted); *see also Hammond v. Stamps.com, Inc.*, 844 F.3d 909 (10th Cir. 2016) (holding that jurisdictional amount is satisfied if the amount might be recovered; proponent of jurisdiction did not have to show that the amount would likely be recovered). Do these cases reduce the likelihood that jurisdictional amount will be manipulated? If so, how?

4. In *Dart Cherokee Basin Operating Co., LLC v. Owens*, 135 S. Ct. 547 (2014), the Supreme Court addressed the question whether a removing defendant under CAFA must include *evidence* of the amount in controversy in the removal notice itself. Justice Ginsburg wrote for the Court:

> To remove a case from a state court to a federal court, a defendant must file in the federal forum a notice of removal "containing a short and plain statement of the grounds for removal." 28 U.S.C. § 1446(a). When removal is based on diversity of citizenship, an amount-in-controversy requirement must be met. Ordinarily, "the matter in controversy [must] excee[d] the sum or value of $75,000." § 1332(a). In class actions for which the requirement of diversity of citizenship is relaxed, § 1332(d)(2)(A)–(C), "the matter in controversy [must] excee[d] the sum or value of $5,000,000," § 1332(d)(2). If the

plaintiff's complaint, filed in state court, demands monetary relief of a stated sum, that sum, if asserted in good faith, is "deemed to be the amount in controversy." § 1446(c)(2). When the plaintiff's complaint does not state the amount in controversy, the defendant's notice of removal may do so. § 1446(c)(2)(A).

To assert the amount in controversy adequately in the removal notice, does it suffice to allege the requisite amount plausibly, or must the defendant incorporate into the notice of removal evidence supporting the allegation? * * * The answer, we hold, is supplied by the removal statute itself. A statement "short and plain" need not contain evidentiary submissions.

* * *

In sum, as specified in § 1446(a), a defendant's notice of removal need include only a plausible allegation that the amount in controversy exceeds the jurisdictional threshold. Evidence establishing the amount is required by § 1446(c)(2)(B) only when the plaintiff contests, or the court questions, the defendant's allegation.

135 S. Ct. at 551–54. Justice Scalia wrote a dissenting opinion, but his sole argument was that the Supreme Court lacked jurisdiction over the case and should have dismissed the petition for a writ of certiorari as improvidently granted.

5. Does CAFA have any impact on the holdings in *Phillips Petroleum Co. v. Shutts*, 472 U.S. 797 (1985) (discussed in Chapter 6(B))? *Shutts* held that a Kansas state court was permitted to exercise personal jurisdiction over the claims of non-resident absent class members, even though they did not have the minimum contacts with Kansas that would support personal jurisdiction over a non-resident defendant. *Id.* at 811. *Shutts* thus allowed nationwide class actions in state court where certain minimum due process protections exist, *id.* at 811–14, a ruling that "ultimately encouraged filing of nationwide class actions in state court." Carol Rice Andrews, *The Personal Jurisdiction Problem Overlooked in the National Debate About "Class Action Fairness"*, 58 SMU L. Rev. 1313, 1320 (2005); *see also* Arthur R. Miller & David Crump, *Jurisdiction and Choice of Law in Multistate Class Actions After Phillips Petroleum Co. v. Shutts*, 96 Yale L.J. 1, 32 (1986). One of the primary reasons given for CAFA's enactment was to prevent forum-shopping by plaintiffs' counsel, especially where class counsel filed cases of national scope in "magnet" (pro-plaintiff) state courts to enhance the possibility of class certification and settlement. CAFA sought to curtail this practice by liberalizing the federal courts' diversity jurisdiction. *Id.* Thus, post-CAFA, there are fewer nationwide class actions in state court, despite *Shutts*'s holding.

Shutts also held that the Kansas state court erred by applying its own law to every claim of the case, "notwithstanding that over 99% of the gas leases and some 97% of the plaintiffs in the case had no apparent connection to the State of Kansas except for this lawsuit." 472 U.S. at 814–15. Kansas's application of its own law under these circumstances was "sufficiently arbitrary and unfair as to exceed constitution limits." *Id.* at 821–23. Although CAFA may shift such class actions from state to federal court, the Act does nothing to address choice-of-law problems that may arise. In fact, Senator Dianne Feinstein, on behalf of herself and Senator Bingaman, had introduced an amendment to CAFA that would have made it far more difficult for federal courts to reject class certification on choice-of-law grounds. Specifically, the proposal provided that if the state-law variations could not be addressed through subclassing, the court should not deny certification but should "attempt to ensure that plaintiffs' state laws are applied to the extent practical." 151 Cong. Rec. S1215 (daily ed. Feb. 9, 2005). The amendment was rejected.

6. One premise underlying CAFA was that federal courts are more cautious than state courts in certifying class actions. An empirical study found mixed results. *See* Thomas E. Willging & Shannon R. Wheatman, Fed. Judicial Ctr., *Attorney Reports on the Impact of Amchem and Ortiz on Choice of a Federal or State Forum in Class Action Litigation* (2004). The study examined 621 class action cases filed or removed to federal court from 1994 to 2001 and concluded between 1999 to 2002. *Id.* at 2. The study found that 22% of the federal cases were certified, while 20% of the cases remanded to state court were certified. *Id.* at 8–9, 34. On the other hand, the study found that federal judges denied certification 27% of the time, while state judges denied certification 12% of the time. *Id.* at 34–36. Notably, in most of the cases, the courts did not rule on certification. *Id.* at 34.

7. Appellate review of CAFA remand orders is discretionary. 28 U.S.C. § 1453(c)(1); *Froud v. Anadarko E & P Co. Ltd. P'ship*, 607 F.3d 520, 522 (8th Cir. 2010). The courts have identified a number of factors that judges should consider in determining whether to grant a remand under CAFA. They include: the presence of an important CAFA-related question; uncertainty; an incorrectly decided or debatable opinion; the consequential nature of the question to the case (especially when the outcome is uncertain); likelihood of evading review; likelihood of reoccurrence; finality of opinion; and balance of relevant harms. *See College of Dental Surgeons of Puerto Rico v. Conn. Gen. Life Ins. Co.*, 585 F.3d 33, 36–39 (1st Cir. 2009). For an interesting look at discretionary appeal of a CAFA remand order, including a grammatically close reading of the CAFA "mass action" provision and its interaction with Fed. R. Civ. P. 20, *see Visendi v. Bank of America, N.A.*, 733 F.3d 863 (9th Cir. 2013) (accepting appeal and reversing remand).

8. In 2011, Congress clarified and expanded removal on the basis of diversity jurisdiction. The Federal Courts Jurisdiction and Venue Clarification Act of 2011, Public Law No. 112–63, amends 28 U.S.C. § 1446(c) to create an exception to the one-year limit for removal under 1446(b)(3) based on diversity jurisdiction when the plaintiff acts "in bad faith in order to prevent a defendant from removing the action." 28 U.S.C. § 1446(c)(1). Subsection (c)(3) states that deliberate failure to disclose the actual amount in controversy to prevent removal constitutes bad faith under (c)(1). 28 U.S.C. § 1446(c)(3). Thus, while the CAFA exception to the one-year deadline still applies, the one-year restriction for cases *not* covered by CAFA has been relaxed.

Additionally, subsection (c)(2) provides, *inter alia,* that where a plaintiff seeks nonmonetary relief, the notice of removal may assert the amount in controversy for purposes of diversity removal, and the district court may find that such removal is proper if it finds that the amount in controversy exceeds the required $75,000.

9. Do unnamed real parties in interest count for purposes of establishing whether an action constitutes a "mass action" under § 1332(d)(11)(B)(i)? In *Mississippi ex rel. Hood v. AU Optronics Corp.*, 134 S. Ct. 736 (2014), the Supreme Court provided some guidance. There, the Mississippi Attorney General had sued in state court on behalf of Mississippi, claiming that defendants had formed an international cartel involving liquid crystal display screens. Defendants removed the case under CAFA, alleging, *inter alia,* that the action was a

"mass action" because more than 100 real parties in interest (Mississippi consumers) would benefit from the proposed restitution relief. Justice Sotomayor wrote for a unanimous Court, disagreeing with defendants' theory for removal:

> * * * CAFA defines a "mass action" as "any civil action . . . in which monetary relief claims of 100 or more persons are proposed to be tried jointly on the ground that the plaintiffs' claims involve common questions of law or fact." 28 U.S.C. § 1332(d)(11)(B)(i). The question presented is whether a suit filed by a State as the sole plaintiff constitutes a "mass action" under CAFA where it includes a claim for restitution based on injuries suffered by the State's citizens. We hold that it does not. According to CAFA's plain text, a "mass action" must involve monetary claims brought by 100 or more persons who propose to try those claims jointly as named plaintiffs. Because the State of Mississippi is the only named plaintiff in the instant action, the case must be remanded to state court.
>
> * * * [T]he statute says "100 or more persons," not "100 or more named or unnamed real parties in interest." Had Congress intended the latter, it easily could have drafted language to that effect. Indeed, when Congress wanted a numerosity requirement in CAFA to be satisfied by counting unnamed parties in interest in addition to named plaintiffs, it explicitly said so: CAFA provides that in order for a class action to be removable, "the number of members of all proposed plaintiff classes" must be 100 or greater, § 1332(d)(5)(B), and it defines "class members" to mean "the persons (named or unnamed) who fall within the definition of the proposed or certified class," § 1332(d)(1)(D). Congress chose not to use the phrase "named or unnamed" in CAFA's mass action provision, a decision we understand to be intentional.
>
> More fundamentally, respondents' interpretation cannot be reconciled with the fact that the "100 or more persons" referred to in the statute are not unspecified individuals who have no actual participation in the suit, but instead the very "plaintiffs" referred to later in the sentence—the parties who are proposing to join their claims in a single trial.

134 S. Ct. at 739–42.

10. Another interpretive challenge under CAFA's "mass action" provisions involves the "proposed to be tried jointly" element of 28 U.S.C. § 1332(d)(11)(B)(i). The Ninth Circuit, sitting en banc, ruled on that issue in *Corber v. Xanodyne Pharmaceuticals, Inc.*, 771 F.3d 1218 (9th Cir.) (en banc), *cert. denied*, 134 S. Ct. 2872 (2014). There, plaintiffs in state-court actions filed petitions to consolidate their cases under a California Rule of Civil Procedure that "allows for the coordination of 'all of the actions for all purposes' and presents a factor-based test to determine whether coordination is appropriate." *Id.* at 1223 (quoting Cal. C.C.P. § 404). The en banc court held that, under the circumstances, plaintiffs had indeed proposed a joint trial, thus bringing the case within federal jurisdiction as a mass action. The court's analysis involved "carefully assess[ing] the language of the petitions for coordination to see whether, in language or substance, they proposed a joint trial." *Id.* Although it found that plaintiffs had proposed a joint trial, the court of appeals qualified its ruling, noting that it did not intend "to say that all petitions for coordination under [Cal. C.C.P. § 404] are *per se* proposals to try cases jointly for the purposes of CAFA's mass action provision"; indeed, the court noted that the case

might have come out differently if plaintiffs "had qualified their coordination request by saying that it was intended to be solely for pre-trial purposes." *Id.* at 1224–25. *See generally* Marc S. Werner, Note, *The Viability and Strategic Significance of Class Action Alternatives Under CAFA's Mass Action Provisions*, 103 Geo. L.J. 465, 474–77 (2015) (criticizing the "proposed to be tried jointly element" as poorly drafted, and expressing concern that the mass action provisions therefore do not achieve their purposes).

11. In *Yocupicio v. PAE Group, LLC*, 795 F.3d 1057 (9th Cir. 2015), which involved both class and non-class claims, the court held that where the class claims did not meet the CAFA amount-in-controversy requirement, and the non-class claims did not meet the requirement of complete jurisdiction, jurisdiction could not be cobbled together by picking and choosing from both CAFA and traditional jurisdictional requirements.

C. *RES JUDICATA* AND COLLATERAL ESTOPPEL

The purpose of a class action is to adjudicate the claims of numerous, similarly situated persons in a single action. Thus, one vital objective of a class action judgment is to foreclose further adjudication of claims that were—or could have been—adjudicated in the class action (*res judicata* or claim preclusion), as well as issues that were actually determined in, and were necessary to the adjudication of, the class action (collateral estoppel or issue preclusion).

Res judicata and collateral estoppel are two of the most difficult civil procedure doctrines to understand and apply—even in traditional, one-on-one litigation. In the context of class actions, the rules have additional wrinkles, which are explored in this section.

After setting forth the classic understanding of the claim-preclusive effect of class action judgments, this section illustrates how courts have struggled to reconcile the desire to foreclose future litigation with the potential unfairness that may result. Courts have fashioned exceptions to *res judicata* in the context of certain forms of class actions, but the limits and contours of these exceptions are still being worked out by the courts. The current struggle is not surprising. *See generally* Geoffrey C. Hazard, J. John Gedid & Stephen Sowle, *An Historical Analysis of the Binding Effect of Class Suits*, 146 U. Pa. L. Rev. 1849, 1849 (1998) (case law on the issue of the binding effect of class actions "was from the beginning equivocal and confused, and * * * it remains somewhat so today").

After addressing claim preclusion, this section then addresses issue preclusion, exploring significant collateral estoppel issues that arise in the context of class action litigation.

1. CLAIM PRECLUSION (*RES JUDICATA*) IN THE CLASS ACTION CONTEXT

Recall that the court rendering a class action judgment is required by Rule 23(c)(3) to designate those persons whom the court finds to be members of the class. Some *subsequent* court, however, actually assesses the claim-preclusive effect of the first court's class action judgment. The following materials involve these subsequent-court assessments.

a. The Structural Context of *Res Judicata* in Class Actions Under Rule 23

McDOWELL V. BROWN
United States Court of Veterans Appeals, 1993.
5 Vet. App. 401.

Before FARLEY, HOLDAWAY, and IVERS, JUDGES.

FARLEY, JUDGE.

Appellant appeals from a November 4, 1992, decision of the Board of Veterans' Appeals (BVA) which denied entitlement to the resumption of payment of Department of Veterans Affairs (VA) disability compensation which had been discontinued pursuant to the Omnibus Budget Reconciliation Act of 1990. The BVA determined that appellant had failed to submit a well grounded claim * * * because he met all of the requirements for discontinuance of VA benefits under section 5505: he had been adjudicated incompetent; the value of his estate exceeded $25,000; and he had no spouse, children, or dependent parents.

[The Secretary of Veterans Affairs ("Secretary") moved to dismiss the appeal to the Court of Veterans Appeals, arguing that McDowell was barred, under the doctrine of *res judicata,* from pursuing his claim because (1) he was a member of the plaintiff class in a class action suit in which the constitutionality of 38 U.S.C.A. § 5505 was adjudicated, *Disabled Am. Veterans v. United States Dep't of Veterans Affairs,* 783 F. Supp. 187 (S.D.N.Y. 1992), *vacated and remanded,* 962 F.2d 136 (2d Cir. 1992), and (2) he was a party to a settlement agreement that dismissed with prejudice McDowell's challenges to the constitutionality of the statute. But] appellant contends that the class representatives failed to provide fair and adequate representation to the members of the [*Disabled American Veterans*] class and, therefore, he is not bound by the prior class settlement. * * *

I. Background

[After serving in the Navy from 1963 to 1966, McDowell applied for disability benefits. The VA found him] totally disabled due to a service-connected nervous disability since November 1967. In August 1973, appellant was adjudicated incompetent and the Probate Court of Franklin County, Columbus, Ohio, appointed Joseph J. Murphy, Esq., his representative before this Court, as guardian of his estate.

On November 5, 1990, Congress enacted the Omnibus Budget Reconciliation Act of 1990 which provides in relevant part [OBRA § 8001, 38 U.S.C. § 5505]:

> In any case in which a veteran having neither spouse, child, nor dependent parent is rated by the Secretary in accordance with regulations as being incompetent and the value of the veteran's estate (excluding the value of the veteran's home) exceeds $25,000, further payment of compensation to which the veteran would otherwise be entitled may not be made until the value of such estate is reduced to less than $10,000.

(The provisions of section 5505 expired on September 30, 1992, and have not been reenacted.)

[Appellant unsuccessfully argued in proceedings below before the regional VA office and the BVA that section 5505 was an *ex post facto* law in violation of Article I, Section IX of the United States Constitution, and also violated the Fifth Amendment due process and equal protection guarantees.]

Appellant also was a plaintiff in a class action suit, brought under Rule 23(a) and (b)(1) of the Federal Rules of Civil Procedure, where the constitutionality of section 5505 was at issue. In *Disabled American Veterans, supra,* the certified plaintiff class consisted of all veterans with service-connected disabilities who had been or would be denied disability compensation by the VA because of * * * section [5505]. The suit challenged the constitutionality of the new law on the grounds that it denied the class due process and equal protection of the laws and effected an improper taking of private property without just compensation, in violation of the principles contained in or embodied by the Fifth Amendment. On January 31, 1992, the United States District Court for the Southern District of New York denied the defendant VA's motion to dismiss and granted the plaintiffs' motion for a preliminary injunction which precluded the VA from applying or enforcing the provisions contained in section 5505. On March 19, 1992, the Court of Appeals for the Second Circuit held that the legislation was constitutional and that, as a result, the appellant class was not likely to prevail on the merits; accordingly, the Court of Appeals vacated the District Court's order and remanded the matter back to the District Court for a final ruling on the VA's motion for dismissal. Pursuant to a subsequent agreement between the parties, the District Court, by Order dated March 10, 1993, approved a settlement agreement and dismissed the suit with prejudice. In doing so, the District Court considered each of the objections lodged against the settlement, including that of appellant * * *.

The settlement provided that members of the plaintiff class would be allowed to retain compensation payments, or receive a refund of any repayments, made between January 31 and July 1, 1992, the period in which the District Court's injunction was in force. In return, the stipulation provided that "all claims raised by plaintiffs" and "all claims that could have been raised in [the] action" would be dismissed with prejudice. The only exception was that settling class members would not be precluded from claiming in a separate proceeding that their entitlement to disability compensation did not meet the factual prerequisites of section 5505, *i.e.*, that their estate was below $25,000 or that they had dependents, or from requesting that the Secretary waive recoupment of an overpayment of disability compensation made after June 1992 * * *.

* * * [P]rior to the approval of the settlement agreement but subsequent to the Second Circuit decision, appellant filed with this Court a Notice of Appeal of the BVA's November 1992 decision. * * *

II. Analysis

* * * Under the doctrine of *res judicata*, a judgment entered on the merits by a court of competent jurisdiction in a prior suit involving the same parties or their privies settles that cause of action and precludes further claims by the parties or their privies based on the same cause of action, including the issues actually litigated and determined in that suit, as well

as those which might have been litigated or adjudicated therein. In discussing the *res judicata* doctrine, the United States Supreme Court has stated:

> To preclude parties from contesting matters that they have had a full and fair opportunity to litigate protects their adversaries from the expense and vexation attending multiple lawsuits, conserves judicial resources, and fosters reliance on judicial action by minimizing the possibility of inconsistent decisions.

Montana v. United States, 440 U.S. 147, 153 (1979).

In class actions brought under Rule 23 of the Federal Rules of Civil Procedure, the *res judicata* effect of a final judgment generally extends to the entire certified class. There are two exceptions to this rule which are both grounded in due process requirements. The first exception applies where the court and/or the parties in the class action failed to provide absent class members with requisite notice including, if warranted, an opportunity to opt out of the class prior to certification. The second applies where the class representatives failed to provide fair and adequate representation in the original suit.

Here, appellant does not dispute that his entitlement to disability compensation meets the factual prerequisites for disallowance under section 5505. As the sole basis of his appeal before this Court, appellant reiterates his constitutional challenges previously raised and adjudicated by the Second Circuit in *Disabled American Veterans,* and raises one additional argument that the statute is an *ex post facto* law under Article I, Section IX of the Constitution. Upon review of the record and the filings of the parties, the Court finds that each of appellant's constitutional claims either was raised by the plaintiff class in *Disabled American Veterans* or could have been raised in that action and, therefore, those claims are encompassed by the March 1993 order of the United States District Court of the Southern District of New York approving the proposed stipulation of settlement and dismissing the class action with prejudice. Accordingly, under the doctrine of *res judicata,* the settlement in *Disabled American Veterans* is binding upon appellant, and this Court is precluded from adjudicating the constitutionality of section 5505 unless appellant establishes either that he was not provided with adequate notice in the prior class action or that the class representatives failed to provide the members of the class with fair and adequate representation.

A. Notice

The method of notice required to be afforded to absent class members depends on the type of class action at issue. * * *

The three types of class actions [under Rule 23(b)] differ in terms of the type of notice which must be afforded to potential class members and the ability of class members to elect not to become members of the class. In a class action maintained under Rule 23(b)(3), the court is required to ensure that potential members of the class receive the best notice practicable under the circumstances, including individual notice to those potential class members who can be identified through reasonable efforts. Fed. R. Civ. P. 23(c)(2). * * * The judgment, whether or not it is favorable to the class, must set forth those who have been afforded notice but have not opted out of the class. Fed. R. Civ. P. 23(c)(3).

In a class action maintained under subsections (b)(1) or (b)(2) of Rule 23, however, the representatives are not required to afford potential members with notice of the class action and an opportunity to request exclusion from the class prior to judgment. Instead, the judgment, whether or not it is favorable to the class, must include a designation of those whom the court finds to be members of the class. Fed. R. Civ. P. 23(c)(3). * * * [T]he majority of courts have held that Rule 23 does not require prejudgment notice in class actions maintained under subsections (b)(1) or (b)(2). Rather, due process is gauged by the adequacy of the representation of absent class members' interests by the class representatives. Because absent members of [(b)(1) and (b)(2) classes] are not afforded the notice and opt-out protections granted to Rule 23(b)(3) class members, courts will more carefully scrutinize the adequacy of representation afforded to absent members of such class actions before determining that they are bound, by *res judicata,* by the final judgment or settlement in the prior class action.

Further, irrespective of the type of class action at issue, a class action may be dismissed or settled only with the approval of the court, and notice of the proposed dismissal or settlement must be provided to all members of the class in the manner directed by the court. Fed. R. Civ. P. 23(e). Accordingly, a subsequent suit by an absent class member will not be barred by *res judicata* if the notice of the prior judgment in the class action was inadequate.

Here, appellant was an absent member of a class of plaintiffs certified under Rule 23(b)(1) in *Disabled American Veterans*. As noted above, because the class was certified under Rule 23(b)(1), the class representatives were not required to provide him with prejudgment notice and an opportunity to opt out of the class; rather, the District Court was required to include a designation of the class in the final judgment and to ensure that the class members received notice of the proposed settlement and dismissal. Fed. R. Civ. P. 23(c)(3) and (e). Appellant has not contended that the District Court failed to provide him with this requisite notice. Upon reviewing the District Court's orders certifying the plaintiff class under Rules 23(a) and (b)(1) and approving the settlement and dismissing the class action under Rule 23(e), the Court concludes that due process notice requirements were adequately fulfilled.

B. Adequacy of Representation

* * * [I]n his reply to the Secretary's motion to dismiss, appellant asserts that he should not be bound by the prior judgment in *Disabled American Veterans* because the class representatives failed to provide fair and adequate representation. As the basis for this contention, appellant notes that the class representatives settled the litigation rather than petitioning the Supreme Court for a writ of *certiorari* to review the Second Circuit's decision upholding the constitutionality of section 5505. He notes that by settling the litigation, rather than petitioning for Supreme Court review, the class representatives left the judgment binding on the class in the future. * * *

In determining whether class representatives have fairly and adequately represented the entire class so that a final judgment in the class action will bind absent members of the class, reviewing courts must evaluate the prior class action *as a whole*. In *Gonzales v. Cassidy,* 474 F.2d 67, 74 (5th Cir. 1973), the Court of Appeals for the Fifth Circuit set forth a two-part inquiry. First, the reviewing court must look at whether the trial court, in its original determination, was correct in concluding that the named class representatives would adequately represent the class. Second, the reviewing court must focus on whether it appears, after the termination of the class action, that the class representatives fairly and adequately protected the interests of the absent class members.

In determining whether the trial court correctly determined that the class representatives would protect the interests of the class, the reviewing court must evaluate whether the class representatives had common rather than conflicting interests with the absent class members and whether it appeared that the class representatives would vigorously prosecute the interests of the class through qualified counsel. In *Disabled American Veterans*, Judge Kram entered an order certifying the class after determining that both elements were satisfied * * *. The Court finds no evidence in the record on appeal or the filings of the parties to suggest that Judge Kram erred in her initial certification of the plaintiff class in *Disabled American Veterans*.

In terms of * * * whether, in hindsight, the class representatives failed to represent the class fairly and adequately, courts have focused on whether the class representatives, through qualified counsel, vigorously and tenaciously protected the interests of the class. * * *

In his pleadings, appellant * * * challenges the fairness and adequacy of the class representation based on his bald assertion that class counsel should have sought Supreme Court review of the Second Circuit's decision by filing a petition for a writ of *certiorari*, rather than agreeing to a settlement of the litigation. He opines that " 'FAIR AND ADEQUATE REPRESENTATION' means exhausting every appeal, however arduous and time consuming that may be," noting that "[t]hat is the nature of professional advocacy." The Court finds no authority to support appellant's definition of "fair and adequate representation." * * * [T]he determination of whether a particular litigation strategy, including the decision not to appeal an adverse decision, constitutes inadequate representation is fact-specific and must be evaluated on a case-by-case basis. The fairness and adequacy of class counsel must be measured in terms of the best interests of the class as a whole and not simply in terms of the interests of any individual member of that class. As long as the district court ensures that the interests of all members of the class are properly considered, the class counsel has broad authority in negotiating and proposing a class settlement.

Here, appellant has not established that the failure of the class representatives to seek Supreme Court review of the Second Circuit's decision in *Disabled American Veterans* is indicative of inadequate representation. He has not shown that Supreme Court review was in the best interest of the class as a whole or even, for that matter, that the decision to file a petition for a writ of *certiorari* was supported by a substantial number of the other members of the plaintiff class. On the contrary, in Judge Kram's order approving the settlement and dismissing the class action, she specifically referenced the small number of objections lodged with respect to the proposed settlement and the lack of merit to those objections. Further, the approved settlement treated all class members equally and provided for payment of disability benefits for the five-month period in which the District Court's preliminary injunction was in force. Appellant has not set forth any evidence to establish that the class representatives in *Disabled American Veterans* had conflicting interests with members of the class, failed to pursue the interests of the class through the use of qualified and competent counsel, or otherwise failed to provide fair and adequate representation. Appellant's mere disagreement with class counsel's litigation strategy does not establish inadequate representation on the part of the class representatives so as to preclude the *res judicata* effect of the final judgment in the prior class action.

III. Conclusion

Upon review of the record and the filings of the parties, the Court holds that, under the doctrine of *res judicata,* appellant is precluded from challenging the constitutionality of section 5505 before this Court. Accordingly, * * * the Secretary's motion to dismiss the appeal is GRANTED.

NOTES AND QUESTIONS

1. According to *McDowell*, what prerequisites are required for *res judicata* to bind a class member in a Rule 23(b)(3) class? What about (b)(1) and (b)(2) class members? Why does Rule 23 treat class members differently depending upon the nature of the class action that was brought?

2. Under the facts presented, should the appellant in *McDowell* have been permitted to proceed with his individual action? Should he at least have been provided notice of class certification? Is there anything unsettling about the notion that one could be bound by a judgment adjudicated by strangers, without being told in advance, so that one could at least intervene to ensure that the class representatives and class counsel adequately represent the interests at stake in the litigation? In other words, might notice be important even if one does not have the opportunity to opt out of a class action? Indeed, could one argue that the absence of opt-out rights makes notice *more* important? According to Professor Rutherglen:

> [W]hen exit is not a possibility, the choice between voice and loyalty becomes all the more important. Class members are entitled to notice so that they have an opportunity to object to the class attorney's performance. This form of protest is the only alternative to acquiescence in the decisions of the class attorneys when exit is foreclosed, as it must be in (b)(1) and (b)(2) class actions.
>
> The reason originally given for denying individual notice in these class actions—that the classes are more cohesive than in (b)(3) class actions—simply begs the question at issue. Whether the class is cohesive depends upon the interests of the class members, which can only be ascertained by their response to notice of the class action. Nothing in the present requirements for certification under subdivision (b)(1) or (b)(2) assures any degree of cohesiveness among class members. To the contrary, in one type of class action, for damages against a limited fund under subdivision (b)(1)(B), class members must have antagonistic interests under the terms of the Rule itself. Class actions can be maintained under this subdivision only when the

interests of class members are antagonistic, because recovery by one class member would impede the ability of others to recover.

George Rutherglen, *Better Late Than Never: Notice and Opt-Out Rights at the Settlement Stage of Class Actions*, 71 N.Y.U. L. Rev. 258, 272–73 (1996). How might the drafters of Rule 23 respond to Professor Rutherglen?

3. As noted in Chapter 5(A)(4), the 2003 amendments to Rule 23 now specify that a court "may" direct notice of class certification to members of classes certified under (b)(1) and (b)(2). *See* Fed. R. Civ. P. 23(c)(2)(A). Should this amendment change the *res judicata* analysis articulated in *McDowell*?

4. What if a (b)(3) class is given notice by mail, but a class member does not actually receive that notice? As described in Chapter 5(A)(1)(a), most courts conclude that the class member is bound by the result. Is this fair? Should actual receipt of notice be required to bind a class member?

5. *McDowell* addressed the ordinary case in which a subsequent court finds that the original class representatives were adequate. *Stephenson v. Dow Chemical Co.*, 273 F.3d 249 (2d Cir. 2001), *aff'd in relevant part by equally divided Court,* 539 U.S. 111 (2003), addresses the less frequent case of a judgment not being binding because the original class representatives were inadequate.

Vietnam War veterans Daniel Stephenson and Joe Isaacson alleged that they were injured by exposure to Agent Orange during their military service, and therefore filed lawsuits against Agent Orange manufacturers. Their lawsuits were transferred by the MDL Panel to Judge Jack B. Weinstein, who had presided twelve years earlier over a class settlement involving virtually identical claims. The class action—comprised of military personnel exposed to Agent Orange in Vietnam between 1961 and 1972—settled in 1984. Judge Weinstein dismissed Stephenson's and Isaacson's lawsuits on the grounds that the prior class settlement barred their claims. Plaintiffs appealed, contending that they were inadequately represented in the original Agent Orange settlement, and therefore should not be barred from pursuing their claims. More specifically, plaintiffs argued that they were not adequately represented because they did not learn of their allegedly Agent-Orange-related injuries until 1994, after the 1984 class settlement had expired. The settlement fund, while purporting to cover all future claims, provided funds only for those whose death or disability occurred before 1994. The settlement did not provide for post-1994 claimants, and the settlement fund terminated in 1994. The Second Circuit concluded that the conflict between the future claimants and the class representatives resulted in inadequate representation, in violation of due process required by *Amchem Products, Inc. v. Windsor,* 521 U.S. 591 (1997), and *Ortiz v. Fibreboard Corp.*, 527 U.S. 815 (1999). The court found Stephenson and Isaacson were inadequately represented because of intra-class conflicts and therefore were not proper parties in the Agent Orange settlement. Consequently, the Second Circuit held that plaintiffs' collateral attack on the class settlement was permissible and denied claim-preclusive effect to the settlement.

In 2003, the Supreme Court granted *certiorari* to consider the propriety of the absent class members' collateral attack on the Agent Orange class settlement. The Supreme Court was evenly split on the issue (4–4), leaving open the question of whether a collateral attack on class settlements based on adequacy is permissible. *See Stephenson v. Dow Chem. Co.*, 273 F.3d 249 (2d Cir. 2001), *aff'd in relevant part by equally divided Court,* 539 U.S. 111 (2003). Is the Second Circuit analysis of *res judicata* in *Stephenson* persuasive? *Cf. Wolfert ex rel. Estate of Wolfert v. Transamerica Home First, Inc.,* 439 F.3d 165, 171, 173 (2d Cir. 2006) (distinguishing *Stephenson* on factual grounds).

6. The Third Circuit has taken a markedly different approach from the Second Circuit's *Stephenson* decision on the propriety of collateral attacks based on adequacy. In *In re: Diet Drugs (Phentermine/Fenfluramine/Dexfenfluramine) Products Liability Litigation,* 431 F.3d 141 (3d Cir. 2005), the Third Circuit held that certain class members could not collaterally attack the adequacy of their representation at settlement of a multi-district class action brought against the drug manufacturer Wyeth. A class of former users of Wyeth's diet medications reached a nationwide class action settlement. Three different groups of class members appealed, arguing that they were not bound by the settlement because of inadequate representation. The Third Circuit rejected *Stephenson* and held that collateral review was inappropriate:

> A class member must have certain due process protections in order to be bound by a class settlement agreement. * * * In a class where opt out rights are afforded, these protections are adequate representation by the class representatives, notice of the class proceedings, and the opportunity to be heard and participate in the class proceedings. * * *
>
> There must be a process by which an individual class member or group of class members can challenge whether these due process protections were afforded to them. * * *
>
> Class members are not, however, entitled to unlimited attacks on the class settlement. Once a court has decided that the due process protections did occur for a particular class member or group of class members, the issue may not be relitigated. Appellants understandably rely heavily on *Stephenson v. Dow Chemical Co.*, 273 F.3d 249 (2d Cir.2001), *aff'd by equally divided Court,* 539 U.S. 111 (2003), in support of their insistence that they have a right to collaterally attack the adequacy of representation determination of the class action court. While *Stephenson* supports appellant's position on this issue, it is inconsistent with circuit case law by which this panel is bound. In *Carlough v. Amchem Products, Inc.,* 10 F.3d 189 (3d Cir. 1993), we held that notice and failure to exercise an opportunity to "opt out" constitutes consent to the jurisdiction of the class action court by an absent member of a plaintiff class even when that member lacks minimum contact with the class action forum. * * * [W]e further held that, where the class action court has jurisdiction over an absent member of a plaintiff class and it litigates and determines the adequacy of the representation of that member, the member is foreclosed from later relitigating that issue. Thus, it follows that challenges to the terms of a settlement agreement, itself, are not appropriate for collateral review.

* * *

> Applying due process protections to the facts of each set of Appellants, we find that they have already received adequate procedural protections. No collateral review is available when class members have had a full and fair hearing and have generally had their procedural rights protected during the approval of the Settlement Agreement. Collateral review is only available when class members are raising an issue that was not properly considered by the District Court at an earlier stage in the litigation. Here, the District Court

carefully examined the adequacy of representation and procedural protections at the fairness hearing, and that examination duly covered the variations presented by the appeals before us. Thus, the District Court was correct in rejecting all three challenges.

431 F.3d at 145–47. Which approach is preferable—the Second Circuit's or Third Circuit's?

7. The ALI's *Aggregate Litigation Project* rejects the approach taken by the Second Circuit in *Stephenson*. Instead, the ALI's position on the availability of collateral review of adequacy is more circumscribed. Section 2.07 states:

(a) As necessary conditions to the aggregate treatment of related claims by way of a class action, the court shall

(1) determine that there are no structural conflicts of interest

(A) between the named parties or other claimants and the lawyers who would represent claimants on an aggregate basis, which may include deficiencies specific to the lawyers seeking aggregate treatment or

(B) among the claimants themselves that would present a significant risk that the lawyers for claimants might skew systematically the conduct of the litigation so as to favor some claimants over others on grounds aside from reasoned evaluation of their respective claims or to disfavor claimants generally vis-à-vis the lawyers themselves * * *.

American Law Institute, *Principles of the Law of Aggregate Litigation* § 2.07, at 144 (2010). The ALI emphasizes the importance of judicial scrutiny throughout the aggregate proceedings to ensure that there are no structural conflicts of interest in the representation of claimants on an aggregate basis. *Id.* at 146. Such scrutiny is a precondition to class certification and should have preclusive effect, unless challenged directly on appeal. *Id.* at 149–50. As the ALI *Principles* state: "The treatment of loyalty as a precondition to aggregate treatment in subsection [2.07](a)(1) disapproves of the analysis of adequate class representation in *Stephenson* * * *." *Id.* at 161. According to the ALI, most courts have rejected the *Stephenson* approach. *Id.* ("By and large, *Stephenson* has not garnered much following in subsequent case law. Even courts purporting to follow its reasoning have not sought to permit absent class members such broad escape from the preclusive effects of judgments.").

As the ALI states: "The normal vehicle for challenging a settlement is a direct appeal from the order or judgment approving the settlement. Apart from appeal, a judgment embodying a class action settlement may not be challenged, except" under a few limited circumstances, such as when a court has failed to make the necessary initial adequacy of representation findings. American Law Institute, *Principles of the Law of Aggregate Litigation* § 3.14, at 267–68 (2010). The ALI's *Aggregate Litigation Project* disapproves of post-judgment challenges as a means of relitigating adequacy findings made prior to the judgment by the court approving the settlement. *Id.* at 269. Such limited availability of collateral attack on class settlements stems from the importance of finality, which is central to the settlement process. *Id.* at 268. So long as there are sufficient safeguards and a thorough and careful initial adequacy determination, post-judgment attacks should be minimal. *Id.* at 269. *See also id.* § 3.10, at 240 (addressing issues of adequacy of representation surrounding the settlement of future claims, topics that are also discussed in Chapter 10(A)(3) of this text).

8. Does the ability to collaterally attack adequacy, and therefore avoid preclusion of class judgments, pose practical or fairness problems? Professors Marcel Kahan and Linda Silberman argue that allowing collateral attack on adequacy results creates several problems: (1) disruption of federal and state class settlements; (2) possible multiple and wasteful litigation on the issue of adequacy; and (3) additional forum-shopping. Marcel Kahan & Linda Silberman, *The Inadequate Search for "Adequacy" in Class Actions: A Critique of* Epstein v. MCA, Inc., 73 N.Y.U. L. Rev. 765, 765–66 (1998). Other commentators argue, however, that absent class members' ability to collaterally attack class judgments is a critical aspect of due process. *See, e.g.*, Patrick Woolley, *The Availability of Collateral Attack for Inadequate Representation in Class Suits*, 79 Tex. L. Rev. 383, 388–89, 432 (2000) (arguing that collateral attack on adequacy is essential because "judges presiding over a class may be unduly reluctant to find inadequate representation"); Henry Paul Monaghan, *Antisuit Injunctions and Preclusion Against Absent Nonresident Class Members*, 98 Colum. L. Rev. 1148, 1153–55, 1195, 1197–99 (1998) (collateral attack is important "as a check on collusion" and "is essential if absent class members are to receive adequate representation in fact"). *See also* Susan P. Koniak, *How Like a Winter? The Plight of Absent Class Members Denied Adequate Representation*, 79 Notre Dame L. Rev. 1787 (2004) (arguing that permitting collateral attack on adequacy will not lead to a flood of litigation).

9. What should a court do when a proposed class includes non-U.S. members, but a foreign country is not likely to recognize a U.S. class action judgment? Professor Clopton surveys the case law and commentary on this issue, noting that the prevailing approach has been one that "ask[s] courts to identify relevant foreign plaintiffs"—*i.e.*, those whose home country's law will not give preclusive effect to a U.S. class action judgment—"and exclude them from class actions." Zachary D. Clopton, *Transnational Class Actions in the Shadow of Preclusion*, 90 Ind. L.J. 1387 (2015); *see also* Kevin M. Clermont, *Solving the Puzzle of Transnational Class Actions*, 90 Ind. L.J. Supp. 69, 75–77 (2015). Both Clopton and Clermont criticize the prevailing approach and offer approaches that are more inclusive of foreign class members.

b. Potential Limitations on *Res Judicata*

i. Limitations Upon the Res Judicata Effect of Class Actions Seeking Only Declaratory or Injunctive Relief

Under an orthodox view based upon the structure of Rule 23, Rule 23(b)(1) and 23(b)(2) class actions will bar a class member's later litigation of the same claim against the same defendant under principles of *res judicata* even if class members were not given notice of the action and the right to opt out. Nonetheless, courts have long struggled with whether due process requires something more.

JOHNSON V. GENERAL MOTORS CORP.
United States Court of Appeals, Fifth Circuit, 1979.
598 F.2d 432.

Before THORNBERRY, CLARK, and FAY, CIRCUIT JUDGES.

CLARK, CIRCUIT JUDGE.

[Johnson brought an employment discrimination action for money damages even though he had been a member of a class in a case (the "*Rowe*" action), certified under Rule 23(b)(2), that had successfully sought only injunctive relief. The district court found Johnson's case barred by *res judicata,* but the Fifth Circuit reversed.]

* * *

* * * Although notice is not necessary to bind absent class members in a 23(b)(2) class action seeking only injunctive and declaratory relief, due process does require notice before the individual monetary claims of absent class members may be barred. * * *

* * *

* * * Following *Eisen v. Carlisle & Jacquelin,* 417 U.S. 156 (1974), we have * * * stated that notice is not mandatory in 23(b)(2) type actions. The district court relied on the nonmandatory nature of notice in 23(b)(2) actions in holding that the lack of notice in *Rowe* did not remove the bar of *res judicata* from Johnson's present suit. That reliance was misplaced.

It does not follow that because notice in (b)(2) actions is not made mandatory by Rule 23, every (b)(2) action in which notice is absent will automatically bar all subsequent efforts by members of the class to litigate claims that might have been brought in the original class action. Before the bar of *res judicata* may be applied to the claim of an absent class member, it must be demonstrated that invocation of the bar is consonant with due process. * * * In *Eisen,* the Supreme Court endorsed the Advisory Committee's position that the notice provisions of Rule 23 must be interpreted so as to bring the conduct of class litigation within the minimum requisites of due process.

* * *

Johnson received no notice whatsoever of the class action that would later be invoked to bar his claim. Notice and an opportunity to be heard are "fundamental requisites of the constitutional guarantee of procedural due process." Although under the text of Rule 23 and the cases interpreting it notice is not required in all representative suits in order to bind absent class members, due process requires that it be provided before individual monetary claims may be barred. *Rowe,* therefore, does not preclude the portion of Johnson's present suit which seeks that relief.

Our holding does no violence to the general rule making notice only discretionary in Rule 23(b)(2) cases. The decisions from which that rule derives presuppose that Rule 23(b)(2) class actions will be limited to class suits seeking only equitable relief. Both *Eisen* and *Sosna v. Iowa,* 419 U.S. 393 (1975), explicitly equate actions for equitable relief with subsection (b)(2) of the Rule and actions for monetary relief with subsection (b)(3). The text of the Rule invites this equation by describing 23(b)(2) actions as involving circumstances in which "the party opposing the class has acted or refused to act on grounds generally applicable to the class, thereby making appropriate final injunctive relief or corresponding declaratory relief with respect to the class as a whole." Primarily because of the evolution in the substantive law governing Title VII cases, however, the compartments of Rule 23 have not remained airtight. In *Johnson v. Goodyear Tire and Rubber Co.,* 491 F.2d 1364, 1375 (5th Cir. 1974), we held that class-wide back pay awards were appropriate under Title VII. In *Pettway v. American Cast Iron Pipe Co.,* 494 F.2d 211, 256–57 (5th Cir. 1974), we held that despite the ostensible restriction of Rule 23(b)(2) to injunctive or declaratory relief, individual back pay awards for absent class members can be sought in a (b)(2) class action.

In light of these developments, we have previously suggested that when both monetary and injunctive relief are sought in an action certified under Rule 23(b)(2), notice may be mandatory if absent class members are to be bound. We expressly took note in *Pettway* of "the problem of binding unidentified class members," suggesting that it "may be overcome by particularizing the class members at some point in the litigation or utilizing the notice provision of subdivision (d)(2)." In *United States v. Allegheny–Ludlum Industries, Inc.*, 517 F.2d 826 (5th Cir. 1975), we again commented that some form of notice may be necessary in order to bind absent class members in connection with back pay awards. When only equitable relief is sought in an action involving a cohesive plaintiff group such as a class of black employees at an assembly plant, the due process interests of absent members will usually be safeguarded by adequate representation alone. As the Advisory Committee on Rule 23 stated, "[i]n the degree that there is cohesiveness or unity in the class and the representation is effective, the need for notice to the class will tend toward a minimum." Where, however, individual monetary claims are at stake, the balance swings in favor of the provision of some form of notice. It will not always be necessary for the notice in such cases to be equivalent to that required in (b)(3) actions. In some cases it may be proper to delay notice until a more advanced stage of the litigation; for example, until after class-wide liability is proven. Before an absent class member may be forever barred from pursuing an individual damage claim, however, due process requires that he receive some form of notice that the class action is pending and that his damage claims may be adjudicated as part of it.

* * *

NOTES AND QUESTIONS

1. The Supreme Court has never directly ruled on the issue presented by *Johnson*, but other courts of appeals have agreed with *Johnson*'s analysis. *See, e.g., Hiser v. Franklin*, 94 F.3d 1287, 1291 (9th Cir. 1996) ("the general rule is that a class action suit seeking only declaratory and injunctive relief does not bar subsequent individual damage claims by class members, even if based on the same events"); *Fortner v. Thomas*, 983 F.2d 1024, 1031 (11th Cir. 1993) ("It is clear that a prisoner's claim for monetary damages or other particularized relief is not barred if the class representative sought only declaratory and injunctive relief, even if the prisoner is a member of a pending class action."); *Herron v. Beck*, 693 F.2d 125 (11th Cir. 1982); *Wright v. Collins*, 766 F.2d 841, 848 (4th Cir. 1985) ("Because Wright was not notified that participation in the class action would preclude a subsequent individual damage action, his participation in the * * * class will not bar this individual litigation."); *Crowder v. Lash*, 687 F.2d 996, 1007–09 (7th Cir. 1982); *Bogard v. Cook*, 586 F.2d 399, 406–09 (5th Cir. 1978); *Jones–Bey v. Caso*, 535 F.2d 1360 (2d Cir. 1976); *Robinson v. Lattimore*, 946 F.2d 1566 (D.C. Cir. 1991) ("A suit for damages is not precluded by reason of the plaintiff's membership in a class for which no monetary relief is sought."). *See generally In re Jackson Lockdown/MCO Cases*, 568 F. Supp. 869, 892 (E.D. Mich. 1983) ("Every federal court of appeals that has considered the question has held that a class action

seeking only declaratory and injunctive relief does not bar subsequent individual suits for damages.").

2. The Supreme Court considered preclusion under circumstances similar to *Johnson* in *Wal–Mart Stores, Inc. v. Dukes*, 564 U.S. 338 (2011), discussed in Chapter 3(B)(2). In contrast with *Johnson*, the plaintiffs in *Dukes* sought backpay in addition to injunctive and declaratory relief under Rule 23(b)(2). They did not, however, seek compensatory damages, arguably making it easier for them to meet the Advisory Committee's requirement that money damages not predominate in a (b)(2) class. The Court expressed concern that plaintiffs' decision to forgo compensatory damages in a mandatory class action could preclude absent class members from later seeking such monetary relief in the future. Specifically, the Court stated:

> Respondents' predominance test * * * creates perverse incentives for class representatives to place at risk potentially valid claims for monetary relief. In this case, for example, the named plaintiffs declined to include employees' claims for compensatory damages in their complaint. That strategy of including only backpay claims made it more likely that monetary relief would not "predominate." But it also created the possibility (if the predominance test were correct) that individual class members' compensatory-damages claims would be *precluded* by litigation they had no power to hold themselves apart from. If it were determined, for example, that a particular class member is not entitled to backpay because her denial of increased pay or a promotion was *not* the product of discrimination, that employee might be collaterally estopped from independently seeking compensatory damages based on that same denial. That possibility underscores the need for plaintiffs with individual monetary claims to decide *for themselves* whether to tie their fates to the class representatives' or go it alone—a choice Rule 23(b)(2) does not ensure that they have.

564 U.S. at 364. Should class counsel be allowed to make such strategic choices to enhance the possibility of class certification? Does this discussion undermine *Johnson*?

3. *Dukes* also rejected an underlying premise of *Johnson*, namely, that (b)(2) certification of backpay claims is appropriate. The Fifth Circuit, like the vast majority of federal courts of appeals, had permitted (b)(2) certification of back pay claims because it considered such relief to be equitable. By contrast, the Supreme Court, relying on the rule's language, found the equitable nature of the relief "irrelevant." *Dukes*, 564 U.S. at 365 ("The Rule does not speak of 'equitable' remedies generally but of injunctions and declaratory judgments. As Title VII itself makes pellucidly clear, backpay is neither."). Should monetary relief that is considered equitable in nature weigh against (b)(2) certification? For a discussion of the appellate courts' treatment of this issue, *see* Suzette M. Malveaux, *Class Actions at the Crossroads: An Answer to* Wal–Mart v. Dukes, 5 Harv. L. & Pol'y Rev. 375, 390–400 (2011).

4. Is the reasoning of *Johnson* consistent with principles of *res judicata*? Is there merit in the *Johnson* court's assertion that its reasoning does not "do violence" to the rule that notice is discretionary in cases certified under Rule 23(b)(2)?

5. Would the result in *Johnson* have been different if Johnson had received notice in the *Rowe* action that he would lose his right to bring a later

damages claim? Should absent class members in class actions for declaratory and injunctive relief be forced to bring their damages claims in the class suit?

ii. The Question of Opt-Out Rights—Phillips Petroleum Co. v. Shutts

In *Johnson*, the class claims did not include damages, and the court held that class members were not barred from seeking their damages in separate suits. What happens if a mandatory class action under Rule 23(b)(1) or (b)(2) *includes* a claim for damages? Are the class members bound by the result on damages, even if they received no notice and no opportunity to opt out? Courts and commentators have debated this issue for years.

The Supreme Court's first significant (albeit oblique) reference to the issue was in *Phillips Petroleum Co. v. Shutts*, 472 U.S. 797 (1985) (see Chapter 6(B)). In *Shutts*, one question before the Supreme Court was whether a forum state could bind absent plaintiffs asserting claims "wholly or predominantly for money judgments" who had no contacts with the forum state. The Court observed:

> [A]bsent plaintiffs as well as absent defendants are entitled to some protection from the jurisdiction of a forum State which seeks to adjudicate their claims. In this case we hold that a forum State may exercise jurisdiction over the claim of an absent class-action plaintiff, even though that plaintiff may not possess the minimum contacts with the forum which would support personal jurisdiction over a defendant. If the forum State wishes to bind an absent plaintiff concerning a claim for money damages or similar relief at law, it must provide minimal procedural due process protection. The plaintiff must receive notice plus an opportunity to be heard and participate in the litigation, whether in person or through counsel. The notice must be the best practicable, "reasonably calculated, under all the circumstances, to apprise interested parties of the pendency of the action and afford them an opportunity to present their objections." *Mullane v. Central Hanover Bank & Trust Co.*, 339 U.S. 306, 314–15 (1950); *cf. Eisen v. Carlisle & Jacquelin*, 417 U.S. 156, 174–75 (1974). The notice should describe the action and the plaintiffs' rights in it. Additionally, we hold that due process requires at a minimum that an absent plaintiff be provided with an opportunity to remove himself from the class by executing and returning an "opt out" or "request for exclusion" form to the court. Finally, the Due Process Clause of course requires that the named plaintiff at all times adequately represent the interests of the absent class members. *Hansberry v. Lee*, 311 U.S. 32, 42–43 (1940).

Shutts, 472 U.S. at 811. In an accompanying footnote, the Court stated:

> Our holding today is limited to those class actions which seek to bind known plaintiffs concerning claims wholly or predominately for money judgments. We intimate no view concerning other types of class actions, such as those seeking equitable relief. Nor, of course, does our discussion of personal jurisdiction address class

actions where the jurisdiction is asserted against a *defendant* class.

Id. at 811 n.3.

Courts and commentators have since struggled with what has been termed the "*Shutts* problem"—"the question the Court left open concerning the due process requirements for mandatory classes that include some claims for compensatory relief or for other equitable relief." Linda S. Mullenix, *Getting To* Shutts, 46 U. Kan. L. Rev. 727, 730 (1998).

The Supreme Court has struggled to provide guidance in the face of confusion by the lower courts. In *Brown v. Ticor Title Ins. Co.*, 982 F.2d 386 (9th Cir. 1992), for example, relying upon *Shutts,* the Ninth Circuit ruled that members of an antitrust class action certified under Rules 23(b)(1) and 23(b)(2) who later attempted to bring a damages action based upon the same facts would not be bound by the settlement of the earlier action. Although the earlier suit had sought both injunctive relief and damages, the settlement was limited to injunctive relief. The Ninth Circuit reasoned that, although a subsequent suit for injunctive relief was foreclosed, due process required that class members be allowed to assert claims for damages:

> Brown * * * also argues that minimal procedural due process must be provided in a class action lawsuit in order "to bind known plaintiffs concerning claims wholly or predominately" for monetary damages. *See Phillips Petroleum Co. v. Shutts,* 472 U.S. 797, 811 n.3 (1985). Brown asserts that certifying the [earlier class action] pursuant to Federal Rules of Civil Procedure 23(b)(1) and (b)(2), which do not provide for the right to opt out, would be a violation of minimum due process if the class judgment precluded future recovery of damages, and therefore *res judicata* is not applicable to his case.
>
> * * *
>
> According to *Shutts,* minimal due process requires that "an absent plaintiff be provided with an opportunity to remove himself from the class by executing and returning an 'opt out' or 'request for exclusion' form to the court," if monetary claims are involved. Because Brown had no opportunity to opt out of the [earlier class action] litigation, we hold there would be a violation of minimal due process if Brown's damage claims were held barred by *res judicata.* Brown will be bound by the injunctive relief provided by the settlement in [the earlier class action,] and foreclosed from seeking other or further injunctive relief in this case, but *res judicata* will not bar Brown's claims for monetary damages against Ticor.

982 F.2d at 392. The Supreme Court granted *certiorari* in the *Ticor Title* case, in part to decide the issue of what notice and opt-out rights, if any, due process requires when a mandatory class action is certified. Ultimately, however, the Court dismissed the writ as improvidently granted because of procedural issues. *Ticor Title Ins. Co. v. Brown,* 511 U.S. 117 (1994). The same result occurred in *Adams v. Robertson,* 520 U.S. 83 (1997), in which the Court dismissed a writ of *certiorari* as improvidently

granted, but at the same time noted its "continuing interest" in the *Shutts* issue. 520 U.S. at 92 n.6.

In 1999, the Supreme Court again granted *certiorari* in a case that raised the issue of whether opt-out rights are required in mandatory classes—*Ortiz v. Fibreboard Corp.*, 527 U.S. 815 (1999) (see Chapter 3(A)(2)). In *Ortiz*, the Fifth Circuit had affirmed a district court decision permitting the use of a Rule 23(b)(1)(B) class action to settle numerous current and future claims of existing and potential asbestos plaintiffs. Class members were not provided an opportunity to opt out of the class. In the petition for *certiorari*, objectors to the settlement expressly raised the issue of whether due process permits the federal court to bind absent class members to a class action judgment that resolves their *in personam* claims for money damages without giving them a chance to opt out of the class, and noted the Supreme Court's prior attempts to address the issue in *Ticor Title* and *Adams*.

The Supreme Court, however, decided *Ortiz* on other grounds. With respect to *Shutts*, the *Ortiz* court stated only the following:

> The inherent tension between representative suits and the day-in-court ideal is only magnified if applied to damage claims gathered in a mandatory class. Unlike Rule 23(b)(3) class members, objectors to the collectivism of a mandatory subdivision (b)(1)(B) action have no inherent right to abstain. The legal rights of absent class members (which in a class like this one would include claimants who by definition may be unidentifiable when the class is certified) are resolved regardless either of their consent, or, in a class with objectors, their express wish to the contrary. And in settlement-only class actions the procedural protections built into the Rule to protect the rights of absent class members during litigation are never invoked in an adversarial setting.
>
> In related circumstances, we raised the flag on this issue of due process more-than a decade ago in *Phillips Petroleum Co. v. Shutts*, 472 U.S. 797 (1985). *Shutts* was a state class action for small sums of interest on royalty payments suspended on the authority of a federal regulation. After certification of the class, the named plaintiffs notified each member by first-class mail of the right to opt out of the lawsuit. Out of a class of 33,000, some 3,400 exercised that right, and another 1,500 were excluded because their notices could not be delivered. After losing at trial, the defendant, Phillips Petroleum, argued that the state court had no jurisdiction over claims of out-of-state plaintiffs without their affirmative consent. We said no and held that out-of-state plaintiffs could not invoke the same due process limits on personal jurisdiction that out-of-state defendants had under *International Shoe Co. v. Washington*, 326 U.S. 310 (1945), and its progeny. But we also saw that before an absent class member's right of action was extinguishable due process required that the member "receive notice plus an opportunity to be heard and participate in the litigation," and we said that "at a minimum . . . an absent plaintiff [must] be provided with an opportunity to remove himself from the class."

527 U.S. at 846–48. In an accompanying footnote, the Court stated:

> We also reiterated the constitutional requirement articulated in *Hansberry v. Lee*, 311 U.S. 32 (1940), that "the named plaintiff at all times adequately represent the interests of the absent class members." *Phillips Petroleum Co. v. Shutts*, 472 U.S. at 812. In *Shutts*, as an important caveat to our holding, we made clear that we were only examining the procedural protections attendant on binding out-of-state class members whose claims were "wholly or predominantly for money judgments," 472 U.S. at 812 n.3.

Id. at 848 n.24. What is the implication of the *Ortiz* Court's discussion of notice and opt-out rights? Does the Court provide any indication of how *Shutts* should be applied with respect to mandatory class actions? In *Wal-Mart Stores, Inc. v. Dukes*, 564 U.S. 338 (2011), discussed in Chapters 2(B)(2) and 3(B)(2), the Court reiterated that "[i]n the context of a class action predominantly for money damages we have held that absence of notice and opt-out violates due process[,]" *id.* at 363 (citing *Shutts*), but it declined to address the issue of whether notice and opt-out rights are required as a matter of due process in all mandatory class actions.

iii. The "Other" Shutts *Problem: Does Due Process Require an Opportunity to Participate?*

Although, as discussed in the last subsection, most courts and commentators have focused upon the impact of *Shutts* on mandatory classes (*i.e.*, must there be a way out?), Professor Patrick Woolley, in a provocative 1997 article, examined a different aspect of *Shutts*—whether absent class members have a due process right to be heard and to participate in litigation that would extinguish their individual causes of action.

PATRICK WOOLLEY, RETHINKING THE ADEQUACY OF ADEQUATE REPRESENTATION
75 Tex. L. Rev. 571, 572, 557–77, 580–82, 603–04 (1997).

Although a number of Supreme Court decisions after *Hansberry* cast doubt on the conventional assumption that adequate representation is the touchstone of due process in class suits, the Supreme Court struck the decisive blow in *Phillips Petroleum Co. v. Shutts*, 472 U.S. 797 (1985). *Shutts* leaves no doubt that adequate representation—without more—does not *always* satisfy the requirements of due process. * * * The decision's fundamental importance lies in its affirmation of a core precept of the American constitutional tradition: Individuals have a right "to be heard and participate in [any] litigation" which purports to extinguish their rights.

* * *

* * * [T]he Supreme Court has stated on several occasions that an individual must be given his own opportunity to be heard even when he or she otherwise would be protected by an adequate representative. Of particular interest is the Supreme Court's decision in *Shutts*. There, the Court made clear that even in the context of a class suit "minimal procedural due process" may require an opportunity to be heard. Specifically, the Court held that to bind an absent plaintiff to a judgment in a class suit predominantly for a money judgment,

[T]he forum State . . . must provide *minimal procedural due process protection*. The plaintiff *must receive notice plus an opportunity to be heard and participate in the litigation, whether in person or through counsel*. . . . Additionally, . . . due process requires at a minimum that an absent plaintiff be provided with an opportunity to remove himself from the class by executing and returning an "opt out" or "request for exclusion" form to the court. Finally, the Due Process Clause of course requires that the named plaintiff at all times adequately represent the interests of the absent class members.

On its face, this language indicates (1) that absent class members in a suit "predominately for money judgments" must be afforded an opportunity to be heard, and (2) that the right to opt out and the right to be adequately represented are separate and distinct from the right to be heard. The Court's reference to the right to be heard and participate in the litigation cannot be dismissed as a passing comment. * * * [T]he conclusion that an absent class member has the right to be heard and participate is essential to the Court's holding.

* * *

In some circumstances, a class member may have to choose between [the right to opt out, the right to be heard and participate in the litigation, and the right to be adequately represented]. A plaintiff, for example, is not entitled to participate in the litigation *and* be adequately represented. An absent class member is entitled to adequate representation because he does not exercise control over the class representative or the class counsel who has been appointed to represent him. By contrast, a class member who exercises his right to be heard and participate in the litigation is not bound by the decisions of the class representative or class counsel, and is therefore not entitled to adequate representation.

Similarly, an absent class member is not entitled both to opt out and to participate in the class suit. A decision to opt out indicates that the class member would prefer to conduct the litigation on his own. Because a litigant is entitled to only one opportunity to be heard, it is reasonable to conclude that a class member who opts out of a class has waived his opportunity to be heard and participate in the class litigation.

But a decision to remain in the litigation does not constitute a waiver of the right to be heard and participate in the class suit. That right is valuable only if the class member does not opt out. Because class members generally have not been deemed to have a procedural right to be heard and participate in the litigation under Rule 23, *Shutts* requires a change in class action practice, even if the decision is limited to Rule 23(b)(3) class suits.

* * * [Moreover, *Shutts*] cannot be limited to Rule 23(b)(3) class suits. While the Court specifically stated that it was not deciding what due process requires in other types of class suits, this important caveat cannot possibly limit the fundamental implication of the *Shutts* decision: "Adequate representation" and "the opportunity to be heard" are cumulative requirements, not interchangeable concepts in due process analysis, as they presumably would be if the Court agreed with commentators who believe that adequate representation provides a vicarious day in court. Thus, *Shutts*

presumptively stands for the proposition that all class members—and indeed all litigants whether in a (b)(3) class or otherwise—must be given an opportunity to be heard and participate in the adjudication of their cause of action.

* * *

* * * *Shutts* leaves unclear the extent to which a court may properly regulate the participation of a party in complex, multiparty litigation. Appropriate limitations on participation, however, must be consistent with the rationale for providing a right to participate if the right is not to be rendered meaningless. In my view, the right to be heard and participate in the litigation is properly conceived as the right to present admissible evidence and make nonfrivolous legal arguments that otherwise would not be placed before the Court. * * * [T]he process due litigants cannot include the right to participate when their participation would be merely repetitious.

On the other hand, to construe the right to be heard and participate more narrowly than the right of any party to present admissible evidence and nonfrivolous arguments not otherwise before the court would render illusory the right to participate. * * * [L]imiting the right to participate to those able to persuade the court that they will make an important contribution ignores the foundation of the right to participate. * * * [I]t is the *possibility* that a class member's contributions will decisively affect the adjudication of his rights that warrants an opportunity to be heard.

Thus, the right to participate * * * includes * * * the right to make motions, take discovery, and participate in the actual trial. In short, an intervening class member must be afforded all the rights of a full party.

* * *

NOTES AND QUESTIONS

1. What are the practical implications of Professor Woolley's reading of *Shutts*? Is that reading consistent with the language of Rule 23? Is it consistent with the policies underlying the rule? Is it the only fair reading of *Shutts*? What arguments can be made against Professor Woolley's approach? A number of commentators appear to read *Shutts* more restrictively. *See, e.g.*, Susan P. Koniak, *Feasting While the Widow Weeps:* Georgine v. Amchem Products, Inc., 80 Cornell L. Rev. 1045, 1087–88 (1995) ("In *Phillips Petroleum Co. v. Shutts*, the Supreme Court held that in class actions brought for money damages * * * due process requires that absent class members receive notice and the opportunity to opt-out * * * [as well as] adequate representation."); Note, *Due Process: Accuracy or Opportunity?*, 65 S. Cal. L. Rev. 2705, 2712 (1992) (concluding that "failure to opt out may be characterized as consent to representative procedures"); John E. Kennedy, *The Supreme Court Meets the Bride of Frankenstein:* Phillips Petroleum Co. v. Shutts *and the State Multistate Class Action*, 34 U. Kan. L. Rev. 255, 270 (1985) (interpreting *Shutts* to require only notice, adequate representation, and opt-out rights).

2. In a portion of his article not reproduced, Professor Woolley explains that an absent class member may be bound without the opportunity to be heard in narrow circumstances when that result is "necessary to achieve a 'vital state interest.'" Woolley, *supra*, at 620. This would include, for example, protecting judgments when there is adequate representation but certain class members

cannot be readily identified or located. *Id.* What criteria should be used to determine whether a vital state interest justifies dispensing with the right to be heard?

2. ISSUE PRECLUSION (COLLATERAL ESTOPPEL) IN THE CLASS ACTION CONTEXT

a. General Principles

As students know from their basic civil procedure course, collateral estoppel—or issue preclusion—permits a court to prevent a party who has actually litigated an issue in a prior action from relitigating that issue in a subsequent action. In federal court, collateral estoppel may be applied if (i) the issue in question in the second suit is identical to an issue actually litigated in the prior adjudication; (ii) there was a final judgment on the merits in the prior action; (iii) the party against whom preclusion is asserted was a party or was in privity with a party to the prior adjudication; and (iv) preclusion would not cause unfairness. *See, e.g.,* Jack H. Friedenthal, Mary K. Kane & Arthur R. Miller, *Civil Procedure,* §§ 14.11, 14.13, at 708–13, 718–23 (4th ed. 2005). Collateral estoppel may be applied in situations in which the plaintiff and defendant in the subsequent action are the same as in the initial action—in which case "mutual" collateral estoppel is asserted. Alternatively, it may in some cases be asserted in situations in which one of the parties in the second action was *not* a party to the first action—in which case "non-mutual" collateral estoppel is at stake. *Id.* § 14.14, at 704–10.

Collateral estoppel issues can arise in a variety of class action contexts. Consider what facts would be important to a court in determining whether collateral estoppel should apply in the following scenarios.

Example 1. P1, a member of a plaintiff class that prevailed in a class action against defendant D1, attempts to assert collateral estoppel against defendant D2 concerning issues adjudicated in the first action. Are there situations in which P1 should be able to successfully assert collateral estoppel against D2?

Example 2. P1, a member of a plaintiff class that prevailed in a class action against defendant D1 seeking only declaratory or injunctive relief, attempts to assert collateral estoppel against defendant D1 in a follow-up individual action for damages. *See, e.g., Crowder v. Lash,* 687 F.2d 996, 1011–12 (7th Cir. 1982) (member of class in injunctive class action may use findings underlying grant of class injunctive relief to preclude relitigation of certain issues in subsequent individual damages action). Or, if D1 prevailed in the original class suit, D1 asserts collateral estoppel against P1 in P1's subsequent individual damages suit. *See, e.g., Cooper v. Federal Reserve Bank,* 467 U.S. 867 (1984) (ruling against class plaintiffs in pattern-or-practice trial does not foreclose subsequent individual discrimination suit, but may be used for purposes of collateral estoppel in subsequent trial to preclude relitigation of whether bank engaged in pattern or practice of discrimination against black employees during relevant period) (*see* Chapter 10(B)(1)(ii)).

Example 3. In suit 1 (*PC v. D1*), a plaintiff class loses to D1. In a subsequent individual suit against D2 by P1 (a member of the earlier plaintiff class in *PC v. D1*), D2 asserts collateral estoppel against P1 to bar litigation by P1 of issues litigated in the prior class action against D1.

Example 4. In suit 1, defendant D1 prevails over a class of plaintiffs PC. When a subset of PC brings suit against D1 raising a different claim, D1 asserts collateral estoppel relating to issues decided in suit 1. *See, e.g., Audette v. Sullivan*, 1992 WL 220910 (W.D. Mich. 1992) (plaintiffs in second class action precluded from relitigating issue determined in earlier class action). Would *res judicata* also potentially apply in this example?

Example 5. Interesting issue-preclusion questions arise when addressing suits by plaintiffs who opt out of a Rule 23(b)(3) class action, but later sue the same defendant. Should a defendant who prevails in class action litigation be permitted to preclude opt-out plaintiffs from relitigating issues that were decided against the class in the prior class action? The Fifth Circuit has answered the question in the negative:

> A class action judgment cannot be used to collaterally estop an opt-out plaintiff's action against a defendant in a separate action. An opt-out plaintiff is not a party to the class action and is not bound by the class action judgment. The doctrine of collateral estoppel cannot bind a person who was neither a party nor privy to a prior suit.

In re Corrugated Container Antitrust Litig., 756 F.2d 411, 418–19 (5th Cir. 1985). Should there be circumstances under which collateral estoppel should apply to bar an opt-out plaintiff's litigation of issues that were adjudicated in favor of the defendant in the class action?

Example 6. Consider now the opposite situation, in which the plaintiff class prevails in the initial class action, and an opt-out plaintiff in his subsequent individual suit attempts to assert non-mutual collateral estoppel against the defendant. Should the opt-out plaintiff be entitled to take advantage of issues resolved against the defendant in the earlier litigation? That question, like the questions in the previous example, strikes at the heart of Rule 23's structure, and is addressed in the decision below.

PREMIER ELEC. CONSTR. CO. V. NAT'L ELEC. CONTRACTORS ASS'N, INC.

United States Court of Appeals, Seventh Circuit, 1987.
814 F.2d 358.

Before BAUER, CHIEF JUDGE, and COFFEY and EASTERBROOK, CIRCUIT JUDGES.

EASTERBROOK, CIRCUIT JUDGE.

This antitrust case presents questions concerning issue preclusion [as well as substantive antitrust law]. The questions arise from an agreement in 1976 between the National Electrical Contractors Association, Inc. (the Association), which comprises firms doing 50–60% of the nation's electrical contracting work, and the International Brotherhood of Electrical Workers, AFL–CIO (the Union), which represents employees of these and many other contractors. The agreement established the National Electrical Industry Fund (the Fund), and members of the Association pay 1% of their gross payroll to the Fund to finance its activities. The Fund helps to defray the costs of the Association's bargaining with the Union on behalf of its members and administering their collective bargaining agreements. The Fund also pays for some research and educational programs. The 1976 agreement calls for the Union to obtain, as part of any collective bargaining agreement with a firm that is not a member of the Association, a requirement that the firm contribute 1% of its gross payroll to the Fund.

I.

Firms that were outside the Association objected to the Union's effort to divert 1% of each employer's payroll to the Fund. Characterizing the contribution requirement as a cartel, they filed an antitrust suit in the federal court in Maryland in 1977. Two of the plaintiffs in the Maryland case asked that it be certified as a class action on behalf of all electrical contractors that did not belong to the Association. * * * [T]he district court allowed [the class certification] issue to slide for three years. It then simultaneously decided the merits and the application for certification of the class. The court held the contribution requirement unlawful *per se* under § 1 of the Sherman Act. It also certified a class of electrical contractors that do not belong to the Association and have signed agreements with the Union requiring them to make the 1% contribution to the Fund. The court denominated this as a class under Rule 23(b)(3), which required that each member be given notice and offered an opportunity to opt out. Certification under Rule 23(b)(3) was appropriate, the judge concluded, because all members of the class had identical claims for damages, which could be computed in a mechanical fashion. The district court then deferred the required notice while the Association, Union, and Fund took an appeal under 28 U.S.C. § 1292(a)(1) from the injunction against their demand that firms pay the 1% fee.

On September 16, 1980, seven days after the Maryland court filed its opinion, Premier Electrical Construction Co.—a member of the class that had been certified in Maryland—filed this suit in Chicago. [Premier engaged in extensive procedural maneuvering, including a frustrated attempt to have its case consolidated with the Maryland action using Multi-District Litigation procedures. Meanwhile, the Fourth Circuit affirmed the judgment in the Maryland case.]

[While the Maryland defendants were seeking review before the Supreme Court, they settled with the class, consenting to] entry of an injunction against collecting the 1% contribution from firms that did not belong to the Association. They also offered to create a fund of $6 million, on which class members could draw in proportion to their contributions to the Fund since 1977.

[Premier then attempted to intervene in the Maryland action, but was rebuffed by the Maryland district court, which noted] "that Premier, being a member of the class in this suit, should, if it so desires, object to the settlement, either that or seek to opt out of the settlement and pursue any further claims it may have elsewhere." The notices to the class were issued in April 1983 and told class members that they could accept the benefits of the settlement, object to the settlement, or opt out of the class. Premier opted out. The district court approved the settlement, and in August 1983 the defendants dismissed their petition for *certiorari*.

The Maryland case was over, but the Chicago case had just begun. There had been only limited discovery, and Premier wanted to keep things that way. It asked the Chicago court to hold that the defendants are bound by the Fourth Circuit's decision that they violated the Sherman Act. The defendants opposed this request. * * * Both sides moved for summary judgment.

The district court held that the defendants are bound by the Maryland decision under principles of issue preclusion (collateral estoppel, here the offensive, non-mutual variety). The court concluded that class members should be entitled to the benefit of preclusion even when they opt out, because preclusion will reduce claims on judicial resources.

* * *

II.

We start with the district court's conclusion that Premier is entitled to the benefit of the Maryland court's holding that the defendants violated the Sherman Act. If the question of preclusion had arisen in 1967, there would have been a ready answer. Most federal courts would apply estoppel only among the parties to the original suit. This is the mutuality requirement—the rule that unless a party would have obtained the full benefit of any victory against the person relying on preclusion, it does not bear the risk of loss. Had the settlement broken down and the defendants won this case in the Supreme Court, Premier would not have been bound. Until recently, that would have prevented Premier from taking advantage of a loss by the defendants in the Maryland case.

We choose 1967 as the benchmark because the preceding year the Supreme Court rewrote Fed. R. Civ. P. 23. One of the complaints about the old Rule 23 was that it allowed courts to entertain what were called "spurious class actions"—actions for damages in which a decision for or against one member of the class did not inevitably entail the same result for all. One party could style the case a "class action," but the missing parties would not be bound. A victory by the plaintiff would be followed by an opportunity for other members of the class to intervene and claim the spoils; a loss by the plaintiff would not bind the other members of the class. (It would not be in their interest to intervene in a lost cause, and they could not be bound by a judgment to which they were not parties.) So the defendant could win only against the named plaintiff and might face additional suits by other members of the class, but it could lose against all members of the class. This came to be known as "one-way intervention," which had few supporters. A principal purpose of the 1966 revision of Rule 23 was to end "one-way intervention."

The drafters of new Rule 23 assumed that only parties could take advantage of a favorable judgment. Given that assumption, it was a simple matter to end one-way intervention. First, new Rule 23(b)(3) eliminated the "spurious" class suit and allowed the prosecution of damages actions as class suits with preclusive effects. Second, new Rule 23(c)(3) required the judgment in a Rule 23(b)(3) class action to define all members of the class. These members of the class were to be treated as full-fledged parties to the case, with full advantage of a favorable judgment and the full detriments of an unfavorable judgment. Third, new Rule 23(c)(1) required the district courts to decide whether a case could proceed as a class action "as soon as practicable" after it was filed. The prompt decision on certification would both fix the identities of the parties to the suit and prevent the absent class members from waiting to see how things turned out before deciding what to do. Finally, new Rule 23(c)(2) allowed members of a 23(b)(3) class action to opt out immediately after the certification in accordance with 23(c)(1). So a person's decision whether to be bound by the judgment—like the court's decision whether to certify the class—would come well in advance of the decision on the merits. Under the scheme of the revised Rule 23, a member of the class must cast his lot at the beginning of the suit and all parties are bound, for good or ill, by the results. Someone who opted out could take his chances separately, but the separate suit would proceed as if the class action had never been filed. * * *

The drafters of new Rule 23 did not anticipate that courts would give preclusive effect to judgments in the absence of mutuality. *Blonder–Tongue Laboratories, Inc. v. University of Illinois Foundation*, 402 U.S. 313 (1971), and *Parklane Hosiery Co. v. Shore*, 439 U.S. 322 (1979), which severely curtailed the mutuality doctrine in federal litigation, washed away the foundation on which the edifice of Rule 23 had been built. A rule requiring each person's decision whether to be bound by the judgment to precede the decision on the merits works only when the choice is conclusive. The curtailment of the mutuality requirement meant that a decision to opt out might not be conclusive. The drafters also did not anticipate the degree to which district judges would disregard Rule 23(c)(1). Rules 23(c)(1) and (2) together force class members to choose the binding effect of the judgment in advance of decision on the merits. (If they can choose later, it's one-way intervention all over again.) But district courts frequently postpone deciding whether a case may be maintained as a class action until the case has been settled or a decision has been rendered on the merits. That is what happened in the Maryland litigation. The district judge decided the merits and certified the case as a class action simultaneously, more than three years after it had been filed. The judge then did not give the Rule 23(c)(2) notice for another 2 years, by which time the judgment had been affirmed and the case had been settled. So by the time Premier and the other members of the class were asked to choose, they knew how the case had come out. * * *

The district court in Chicago concluded that these two unanticipated developments make all the difference. * * * It relied principally on *Parklane*, which allowed a private plaintiff in a securities case to obtain the benefit of a judgment against the defendant in an action brought by the Securities and Exchange Commission. The Court criticized the mutuality doctrine for "failing to recognize the obvious difference in position between a party who has never litigated an issue and one who has fully litigated and lost," and for wasting the time of courts (and parties) on the way to a duplication of the initial result. Even if the second case differed from the result of the first, this might mean that the second decision was the error. If the first litigation is complete, and the parties have good reason to present their cases fully, the decision is as likely to be accurate as any later outcome, and there is accordingly no reason to endure a series of similar cases. The application of the first outcome to all parties is as accurate as a sequence of cases with varying outcomes. Still, the Court recognized, the use of non-mutual, offensive issue preclusion might leave the defendant being pecked to death by ducks. One plaintiff could sue and lose; another could sue and lose; and another and another until one finally prevailed; then everyone else would ride on that single success. This sort of sequence, too, would waste resources; it also could make the minority (and therefore presumptively inaccurate) result the binding one. *Parklane* therefore gave the district courts discretion not to use offensive issue preclusion. It stated: "The general rule should be that in cases where a plaintiff could easily have joined in the earlier action or where . . . the application of offensive estoppel would be unfair to a defendant, a trial judge should not allow the use of offensive collateral estoppel."

The parties concentrate their attention on this phrase, from which each draws comfort. Premier points out that both the Panel on Multidistrict Litigation and the Maryland court declined to allow it to press its theory of damages in Maryland. The defendants observe that Premier was a party to the Maryland case for six years before voluntarily opting out, and that it could have raised its damages theory there had it not slept through most of that period. The district judge in Chicago thought Premier closer to the mark. We doubt, however, that *Parklane* contains the answer to our problem. The Supreme Court did not address the extent to which class members may use issue preclusion after opting out of the class; indeed it did not mention Rule 23. The rules that govern the extent to which one judgment in a federal case precludes litigation in a second federal case are part of the federal common law. Issue preclusion is made available when it is sound to do so in light of the effects on the rate of error, the cost of litigation, and other instrumental considerations. When there are good reasons to allow relitigation of a category of disputes, preclusion does not apply. * * *

If the scope of issue preclusion is a matter of federal common law, then *Parklane* is not a sufficient reason to upset the balance struck in Rule 23. Under the Rules Enabling Act, 28 U.S.C. § 2072, the Rules of Civil Procedure have the effect of statutes. A development in the common law of judgments is not a reason to undo a statute, to treat a thorough rethinking of the law as so much fluff. The revision of Rule 23 in 1966 does away with one-way intervention in class actions. It should stay done-away-with until the Supreme Court adopts a new version. Whether class members should get the benefit of a favorable judgment, despite not being bound by an unfavorable judgment, was considered and decided in 1966. That decision binds us still.

* * *

The Supreme Court has not decided when predictions about the effects of a rule should be treated as part of the rule. If suppositions are themselves law, then judges must rummage the minds of the drafters, and what they find there may have more in common with the judges' beliefs than with the authors'. Worse, a transmutation from "intent" to law bypasses the processes that form the heart of the constitutional method of legislation. Yet laws are designed to produce *effects* by the application of prescribed *means*. When the court can both perceive the planned effect and follow the means to the letter, it can fulfill the whole plan, and almost always should. Perhaps it is not possible to reduce to a verbal formula the complex process by which the domain of a rule is fixed. It is unlikely we shall make much headway in this opinion. We need not. Even if a court sometimes may allow the effects of the 1966 revision of Rule 23 to diverge from the course planned by the Advisory Committee, such a modification would not be appropriate when the very problem at hand was anticipated and resolved.

We also lack a sound reason to deviate from the plan of 1966. The district court concluded that application of issue preclusion would produce judicial economy. "Judicial economy" sounds like a sure-fire Good Thing—especially to the ears of judges. Conservation of resources is the principal reason the Supreme Court gave for its decision in *Parklane*. And it has been used as a reason for preclusion when there are two actions, one for injunction and one for damages. For example, we held in *Crowder v. Lash*, 687 F.2d 996, 1011–12 (7th Cir. 1982), that a member of the class in an injunctive case may use the findings underlying the grant of injunctive relief to preclude defendants from relitigating certain issues in a separate suit for damages. *Cf. Cooper v. Federal Reserve Bank of Richmond*, 467 U.S. 867 (1984) (a judgment that an employer did not discriminate against an entire class does not necessarily preclude a member of the class from showing, in a separate action, that the employer discriminated against her, because the issues in the pattern-or-practice class suit may be different from the contentions in the individual action). When there are bound to be two separate actions, as we assumed in *Crowder*, a plaintiff who does not opt out of the injunctive action is entitled to keep his victory, as he will be bound by defeat. (*Crowder* is a case of mutual estoppel.) It serves the interest of economy to have as few issues litigated in the second suit as possible. The district court took our case as a similar situation. Yet this assumes that there will *be* two suits against the Association, Union, and Fund. *Parklane* was a case of this type. The SEC's suit and the private suit were bound to go forward independently; nothing the court could do would reduce the number of cases that had to be litigated. If there are bound to be two suits, why not cut down on the number of issues? The district court treated this case as similar to *Parklane*, but it is not. Here there were not bound to be two suits. There were two suits in fact, but there need not have been.

An approach that asks how to hold down the costs of litigation given the existence of multiple suits is an *ex post* perspective on judicial economy. It is the wrong perspective when inquiring about the consequences of a legal rule. A decision to make preclusion available to those who opt out of a class influences *whether* there will be multiple suits. The more class members who opt out may benefit from preclusion, the more class members will opt out. Preclusion thus may increase the number of suits, undermining the economy the district court hoped to achieve. The effect of the legal rule may be the opposite of the effect of applying preclusion to a given case. To determine whether a rule is beneficial, a court must examine how that rule influences future behavior. The influence of a rule of preclusion cannot be known for sure, but we are not confident that there would be net benefits.

This case makes the point. The class action in Maryland lasted six years. If Premier had known that it must start from scratch in Chicago, it might well have stayed in the Maryland litigation. It had the right under

Rule 23(e) to protest the settlement and obtain a decision about its adequacy. Instead of finishing the litigation in Maryland, Premier walked away to try again, fortified by its belief that it could win in Chicago but not lose. * * * The defendants in Maryland thought that for $6 million and an injunction they would purchase peace. Premier wants to deny defendants that boon, but not to refund any of the $6 million. If enough other class members had opted out, the settlement would have collapsed, and the Maryland litigation would have dragged on. * * * If defendants anticipate significant opting out, they also will reduce the amounts they offer in settlement, which may in turn make it worthwhile for more parties to opt out. The more attractive it is to opt out—and giving the parties who opt out the benefit of preclusion makes it very attractive—the fewer settlements there will be, the less the settlements will produce for the class, and the more cases courts must adjudicate. This is not judicial economy at work!

* * *

[In response to Premier's argument that its damage theory differed from the theory advanced in the Maryland action, the court responded that] this is a reason to establish subclasses (or to appeal the approval of a one-sided settlement) rather than to increase the number of separate suits. If the result of the first class action binds only the parties, then class members who have different theories of damages will be induced to present them as early as possible in order to have a subclass certified. If the differences in the kinds of damages suffered are indeed substantial, perhaps it is mistaken to certify any class. If, as Premier contends, a class member dissatisfied by the measure of damages selected by the representative party may pick up his portfolio and start again, there will be an incentive to stand on the sidelines and see how things turn out. If the first case proceeds well, the bystander will take the benefit, and if not it will try again. The benefits of presenting common claims in a single forum will be lost. Premier should have presented its theory of damages in the Maryland suit as quickly as possible, because it cast doubt on the district court's belief that common questions predominated and that damages could be computed mechanically. It would be an unwelcome development to induce class members to keep to themselves reasons to doubt the propriety of class certifications.

One more consideration. The district court believed that issue preclusion would ensure equal treatment of members of the class. Equality, like judicial economy, is desirable; the judicial system uses a variety of devices, including *stare decisis* and rules of preclusion, to treat likes alike. But the threat to equal treatment of class members came from Premier itself. The class members who stayed in the Maryland litigation were treated equally. Premier wanted to be treated differently; it wanted a unique measure of damages. This measure might well be appropriate * * *; it might even produce "equality" from a different standpoint. "Equality" is an open term. Equal *with respect to what* is the essential question, the answer to which must come from some independent source. Maybe only a unique measure of damages will lead to equal treatment with respect to injury suffered (that is, to recompense for an equal percentage of the damage incurred). Still, Premier's decision to opt out is the best indicator that it wanted special treatment. It wanted a greater recovery without risk. It could have had equal treatment (though not necessarily with identical effect) by staying in the Maryland case.

We conclude that class members who opt out may not claim the benefits of the class's victory. * * *

III.

To say that issue preclusion does not apply is not to say that this case must follow the dreary course of many antitrust matters and bury the court under mountains of documents, to be followed by an interminable trial. Preclusion is not an all-or-nothing matter; there are degrees. The doctrine of *stare decisis* supplies some of the lesser degrees. A decision by the Supreme Court that the Agreement violates the Sherman Act would be authoritative, precluding further contention in Chicago. A decision by the Fourth Circuit is not authoritative in district courts of the Seventh Circuit, but it is entitled to respect, both for its persuasive power and because it involves the same facts. The application of *stare decisis* will produce most of the judicial economy the district court sought to achieve.

The value of the first decision as a prediction of how other courts will act produces part of the savings. If the class wins, the opting-out plaintiff should expect to win for the same reasons that persuaded the first court. If the class loses, the opting-out plaintiff should expect to meet the same fate. He may drop the suit; if he presses the suit, the earlier decision again shortens the path to disposition of the second case. *Stare decisis* should be particularly potent in cases suitable for class treatment. The conclusion of the first court that certification of a class is proper, if correct, means that there will be few significant differences between the class suit and the opt-out suit. The second litigation may safely concentrate on those differences, whether or not issue preclusion comes into play.

When as here the defendant's activities span more than one court of appeals, only the gravest reasons should lead the court in the opt-out suit to come to a conclusion that departs from that in the class suit. This circuit pays respectful attention to the decisions of others, to the point of suppressing doubts in order to prevent the creation of a conflict or overruling existing cases to eliminate a conflict. The benefits of following the decision of another circuit are particularly apparent when the two courts are dealing with the same set of facts. A conflict among the circuits about a single collective bargaining agreement or other common endeavor may compel the Supreme Court to hear the case even though the dispute lacks independent significance. We therefore approach the merits of this case with a strong presumption in favor of the Fourth Circuit's disposition. The presumption does not eliminate the need for independent analysis, but it does mean that doubts should be resolved in favor of the Fourth Circuit's disposition.

[After independent analysis, the Seventh Circuit reached the same conclusion as the Fourth Circuit with respect to whether the defendants' conduct, if proven, would constitute a violation of the Sherman Act. It also found that Premier's damage theory could proceed, and therefore remanded the case for further proceedings consistent with its opinion.]

NOTES AND QUESTIONS

1. What does Judge Easterbrook rely upon as the basis for refusing to permit collateral estoppel? What arguments can be made that an opt-out plaintiff should be entitled to assert collateral estoppel against a defendant who lost an earlier class action? *See, e.g.*, Note, *Offensive Assertion of Collateral Estoppel by Persons Opting Out of a Class*, 31 Hastings L.J. 1189 (1980) (arguing that opt-out plaintiff should be permitted to assert collateral estoppel if he or she presents a "strong individual interest" in pursuing separate suit).

2. To what extent is the result in *Premier* compelled by the history of Rule 23 and the intent of the drafters of the 1966 version to eliminate one-way intervention?

3. As a practical matter, did the Seventh Circuit's resolution of the case end up giving Premier the same benefit as one-way intervention? What is the difference between the analysis adopted by the district court and the analysis adopted by the Seventh Circuit? Do the two approaches normally lead to the same outcome, particularly if, as the Seventh Circuit notes, a federal court of appeals should normally follow a sister court of appeals as a matter of *stare decisis*?

b. Collateral Estoppel Effect of Prior Denial of Class Certification

What, if any, preclusive effect does the denial of class certification have on the putative class? If a court denies class certification, should the same class representatives be able to relitigate that issue? Does it matter whether the attempt is made in the same court or another court? Should *new* class representatives be allowed to relitigate the same class certification issues? Again, does it matter whether the subsequent attempt is before the same court or a different court? Should the answers to these questions depend upon the grounds for denial of certification? Consider the following.

SMITH V. BAYER CORP.
Supreme Court of the United States, 2011.
564 U.S. 299.

JUSTICE KAGAN delivered the opinion of the Court.†

In this case, a Federal District Court enjoined a state court from considering a plaintiff's request to approve a class action. The District Court did so because it had earlier denied a motion to certify a class in a related case, brought by a different plaintiff against the same defendant alleging similar claims. The federal court thought its injunction appropriate to prevent relitigation of the issue it had decided.

We hold to the contrary. In issuing this order to a state court, the federal court exceeded its authority under the "relitigation exception" to the Anti-Injunction Act. That statutory provision permits a federal court to enjoin a state proceeding only in rare cases, when necessary to "protect or effectuate [the federal court's] judgments." 28 U.S.C. § 2283. Here, that standard was not met for two reasons. First, the issue presented in the state court was not identical to the one decided in the federal tribunal. And

---

† JUSTICE THOMAS joins Parts I and II–A of this opinion.

second, the plaintiff in the state court did not have the requisite connection to the federal suit to be bound by the District Court's judgment.

I

Because the question before us involves the effect of a former adjudication on this case, we begin our statement of the facts not with this lawsuit, but with another. In August 2001, George McCollins sued respondent Bayer Corporation in the Circuit Court of Cabell County, West Virginia, asserting various state-law claims arising from Bayer's sale of an allegedly hazardous prescription drug called Baycol (which Bayer withdrew from the market that same month). McCollins contended that Bayer had violated West Virginia's consumer-protection statute and the company's express and implied warranties by selling him a defective product. And pursuant to West Virginia Rule of Civil Procedure 23 (2011), McCollins asked the state court to certify a class of West Virginia residents who had also purchased Baycol, so that the case could proceed as a class action.

Approximately one month later, the suit now before us began in a different part of West Virginia. Petitioners Keith Smith and Shirley Sperlazza (Smith for short) filed state-law claims against Bayer, similar to those raised in McCollins' suit, in the Circuit Court of Brooke County, West Virginia. And like McCollins, Smith asked the court to certify under West Virginia's Rule 23 a class of Baycol purchasers residing in the State. Neither Smith nor McCollins knew about the other's suit.

In January 2002, Bayer removed McCollins' case to the United States District Court for the Southern District of West Virginia on the basis of diversity jurisdiction. *See* 28 U.S.C. §§ 1332, 1441. The case was then transferred to the District of Minnesota pursuant to a preexisting order of the Judicial Panel on Multi-District Litigation, [*see* discussion of multi-district litigation procedure in Chapter 12], which had consolidated all federal suits involving Baycol (numbering in the tens of thousands) before a single District Court Judge. *See* § 1407. Bayer, however, could not remove Smith's case to federal court because Smith had sued several West Virginia defendants in addition to Bayer, and so the suit lacked complete diversity. *See* § 1441(b).[2] Smith's suit thus remained in the state courthouse in Brooke County.

Over the next six years, the two cases proceeded along their separate pretrial paths at roughly the same pace. By 2008, both courts were preparing to turn to their respective plaintiffs' motions for class certification. The Federal District Court was the first to reach a decision.

Applying Federal Rule of Civil Procedure 23, the District Court declined to certify McCollins' proposed class of West Virginia Baycol purchasers. The District Court's reasoning proceeded in two steps. The court first ruled that, under West Virginia law, each plaintiff would have to prove "actual injury" from his use of Baycol to recover. The court then held that because the necessary showing of harm would vary from plaintiff to plaintiff, "individual issues of fact predominate[d]" over issues common to all members of the proposed class, and so the case was not suitable for class

---

[2] The Class Action Fairness Act of 2005, 119 Stat. 4, which postdates and therefore does not govern this lawsuit, now enables a defendant to remove to federal court certain class actions involving nondiverse parties. *See* 28 U.S.C. §§ 1332(d), 1453(b). [*See* discussion in Part (B)(3)(d) of this chapter.]

treatment. In the same order, the District Court also dismissed McCollins' claims on the merits in light of his failure to demonstrate physical injury from his use of Baycol. McCollins chose not to appeal.

Although McCollins' suit was now concluded, Bayer asked the District Court for another order based upon it, this one affecting Smith's case in West Virginia. In a motion—receipt of which first apprised Smith of McCollins' suit—Bayer explained that the proposed class in Smith's case was identical to the one the federal court had just rejected. Bayer therefore requested that the federal court enjoin the West Virginia state court from hearing Smith's motion to certify a class. According to Bayer, that order was appropriate to protect the District Court's judgment in McCollins' suit denying class certification. The District Court agreed and granted the injunction.

The Court of Appeals for the Eighth Circuit affirmed. * * *

We granted *certiorari* because the order issued here implicates two circuit splits arising from application of the Anti-Injunction Act's relitigation exception. The first involves the requirement of preclusion law that a subsequent suit raise the "same issue" as a previous case. The second concerns the scope of the rule that a court's judgment cannot bind nonparties. We think the District Court erred on both grounds when it granted the injunction, and we now reverse.

II

The Anti-Injunction Act, first enacted in 1793, provides that

"A court of the United States may not grant an injunction to stay proceedings in a State court except as expressly authorized by Act of Congress, or where necessary in aid of its jurisdiction, or to protect or effectuate its judgments." 28 U.S.C. § 2283.

The statute, we have recognized, "is a necessary concomitant of the Framers' decision to authorize, and Congress' decision to implement, a dual system of federal and state courts." *Chick Kam Choo v. Exxon Corp.*, 486 U.S. 140, 146 (1988). And the Act's core message is one of respect for state courts. The Act broadly commands that those tribunals "shall remain free from interference by federal courts." That edict is subject to only "three specifically defined exceptions." * * *

This case involves the last of the Act's three exceptions, known as the relitigation exception. That exception is designed to implement "well-recognized concepts" of claim and issue preclusion. *Chick Kam Choo,* 486 U.S. at 147. The provision authorizes an injunction to prevent state litigation of a claim or issue "that previously was presented to and decided by the federal court." *Ibid.* But in applying this exception, we have taken special care to keep it "strict and narrow." After all, a court does not usually "get to dictate to other courts the preclusion consequences of its own judgment." 18 C. Wright, A. Miller, & E. Cooper, Federal Practice and Procedure § 4405, p. 82 (2d ed. 2002). Deciding whether and how prior litigation has preclusive effect is usually the bailiwick of the *second* court (here, the one in West Virginia). So issuing an injunction under the relitigation exception is resorting to heavy artillery. For that reason, every benefit of the doubt goes toward the state court; an injunction can issue only if preclusion is clear beyond peradventure.

The question here is whether the federal court's rejection of McCollins' proposed class precluded a later adjudication in state court of Smith's certification motion. For the federal court's determination of the class issue to have this preclusive effect, at least two conditions must be met. First, the issue the federal court decided must be the same as the one presented in the state tribunal. And second, Smith must have been a party to the federal suit, or else must fall within one of a few discrete exceptions to the general rule against binding nonparties. In fact, as we will explain, the issues before the two courts were not the same, and Smith was neither a party nor the exceptional kind of nonparty who can be bound. So the courts below erred in finding the certification issue precluded, and erred all the more in thinking an injunction appropriate.[7]

A

In our most recent case on the relitigation exception, *Chick Kam Choo v. Exxon,* we applied the "same issue" requirement of preclusion law to invalidate a federal court's injunction. The federal court had dismissed a suit involving Singapore law on grounds of *forum non conveniens.* After the plaintiff brought the same claim in Texas state court, the federal court issued an injunction barring the plaintiff from pursuing relief in that alternate forum. We held that the District Court had gone too far [because federal and Texas *forum non conveniens* law were not the same]. * * *

The question here closely resembles the one in *Chick Kam Choo.* The class Smith proposed in state court mirrored the class McCollins sought to certify in federal court: Both included all Baycol purchasers resident in West Virginia. Moreover, the substantive claims in the two suits broadly overlapped: Both complaints alleged that Bayer had sold a defective product in violation of the State's consumer protection law and the company's warranties. So far, so good for preclusion. But not so fast: a critical question—the question of the applicable legal standard—remains. The District Court ruled that the proposed class did not meet the requirements of Federal Rule 23 (because individualized issues would predominate over common ones). But the state court was poised to consider whether the proposed class satisfied *West Virginia* Rule 23. If those two legal standards differ (as federal and state *forum non conveniens* law differed in *Chick Kam Choo*)— then the federal court resolved an issue not before the state court. In that event, much like in *Chick Kam Choo,* "whether the [West Virginia] state cour[t]" should certify the proposed class action "has not yet been litigated."

The Court of Appeals and Smith offer us two competing ways of deciding whether the West Virginia and Federal Rules differ, but we think the right path lies somewhere in the middle. The Eighth Circuit relied almost exclusively on the near-identity of the two Rules' texts. That was the right place to start, but not to end. Federal and state courts, after all, can and do apply identically worded procedural provisions in widely varying ways. If a State's procedural provision tracks the language of a Federal Rule, but a state court interprets that provision in a manner federal courts have not, then the state court is using a different standard and thus deciding a dif-

---

[7] Because we rest our decision on the Anti–Injunction Act and the principles of issue preclusion that inform it, we do not consider Smith's argument, based on *Phillips Petroleum Co. v. Shutts,* 472 U.S. 797 (1985), that the District Court's action violated the Due Process Clause.

ferent issue. * * * But if state courts have made crystal clear that they follow the same approach as the federal court applied, we see no need to ignore that determination; in that event, the issues in the two cases would indeed be the same. So a federal court considering whether the relitigation exception applies should examine whether state law parallels its federal counterpart. But as suggested earlier, the federal court must resolve any uncertainty on that score by leaving the question of preclusion to the state courts.

Under this approach, the West Virginia Supreme Court has gone some way toward resolving the matter before us by declaring its independence from federal courts' interpretation of the Federal Rules—and particularly of Rule 23. In *In re W. Va. Rezulin Litigation,* 214 W.Va. 52, 585 S.E.2d 52 (2003) *(In re Rezulin),* the West Virginia high court considered a plaintiff's motion to certify a class—coincidentally enough, in a suit about an allegedly defective pharmaceutical product. The court made a point of complaining about the parties' and lower court's near-exclusive reliance on federal cases about Federal Rule 23 to decide the certification question. Such cases, the court cautioned, " 'may be persuasive, but [they are] not binding or controlling.' " And lest anyone mistake the import of this message, the court went on: The aim of "this rule is to avoid having our legal analysis of our Rules 'amount to nothing more than Pavlovian responses to federal decisional law.' " Of course, the state courts might still have adopted an approach to their Rule 23 that tracked the analysis the federal court used in McCollins' case. But absent clear evidence that the state courts had done so, we could not conclude that they would interpret their Rule in the same way. And if that is so, we could not tell whether the certification issues in the state and federal courts were the same. That uncertainty would preclude an injunction.

But here the case against an injunction is even stronger, because the West Virginia Supreme Court has *disapproved* the approach to Rule 23(b)(3)'s predominance requirement that the Federal District Court embraced. Recall that the federal court held that the presence of a single individualized issue—injury from the use of Baycol—prevented class certification. The court did not identify the common issues in the case; nor did it balance these common issues against the need to prove individual injury to determine which predominated. The court instead applied a strict test barring class treatment when proof of each plaintiff's injury is necessary. By contrast, the West Virginia Supreme Court in *In re Rezulin* adopted an all-things-considered, balancing inquiry in interpreting its Rule 23. Rejecting any "rigid test," the state court opined that the predominance requirement "contemplates a review of many factors." Indeed, the court noted, a " 'single common issue' " in a case could outweigh " 'numerous . . . individual questions.' " That meant, the court further explained (quoting what it termed the "leading treatise" on the subject), that even objections to certification " 'based on . . . causation, or reliance' "—which typically involve showings of individual injury—" 'will not bar predominance satisfaction.' " So point for point, the analysis set out in *In re Rezulin* diverged from the District Court's interpretation of Federal Rule 23. A state court using the *In re Rezulin* standard would decide a different question than the one the federal court had earlier resolved.

This case, indeed, is little more than a rerun of *Chick Kam Choo.* A federal court and a state court apply different law. That means they decide distinct questions. The federal court's resolution of one issue does not preclude the state court's determination of another. It then goes without saying that the federal court may not issue an injunction. The *Anti*-Injunction Act's *re*-litigation exception does not extend nearly so far.

B

The injunction issued here runs into another basic premise of preclusion law: A court's judgment binds only the parties to a suit, subject to a handful of discrete and limited exceptions. The importance of this rule and the narrowness of its exceptions go hand in hand. We have repeatedly "emphasize[d] the fundamental nature of the general rule" that only parties can be bound by prior judgments; accordingly, we have taken a "constrained approach to nonparty preclusion." *Taylor v. Sturgell,* 553 U.S. 880, 898 (2008). Against this backdrop, Bayer defends the decision below by arguing that Smith—an unnamed member of a proposed but uncertified class—qualifies as a party to the McCollins litigation. Alternatively, Bayer claims that the District Court's judgment binds Smith under the recognized exception to the rule against nonparty preclusion for members of class actions. We think neither contention has merit.

Bayer's first claim ill-comports with any proper understanding of what a "party" is. In general, "[a] 'party' to litigation is '[o]ne by or against whom a lawsuit is brought,' " *United States ex rel. Eisenstein v. City of New York,* 129 S. Ct. 2230, 2234 (2009), or one who "become[s] a party by intervention, substitution, or third-party practice," *Karcher v. May,* 484 U.S. 72, 77 (1987). And we have further held that an unnamed member of a *certified* class may be "considered a 'party' for the [particular] purpos[e] of appealing" an adverse judgment. *Devlin v. Scardelletti,* 536 U.S. 1, 7 (2002). [*See* Chapter 9(B)(2).] But as the dissent in *Devlin* noted, no one in that case was "willing to advance the novel and surely erroneous argument that a nonnamed class member is a party to the class-action litigation *before the class is certified.*" Still less does that argument make sense *once certification is denied.* The definition of the term "party" can on no account be stretched so far as to cover a person like Smith, whom the plaintiff in a lawsuit was denied leave to represent. If the judgment in the McCollins litigation can indeed bind Smith, it must do so under principles of *non* party preclusion.

As Bayer notes, one such principle allows unnamed members of a class action to be bound, even though they are not parties to the suit. *See Cooper v. Federal Reserve Bank of Richmond,* 467 U.S. 867, 874 (1984) ("[U]nder elementary principles of prior adjudication a judgment in a properly entertained class action is binding on class members in any subsequent litigation"); *see also Taylor,* 553 U.S. at 894 (stating that nonparties can be bound in "properly conducted class actions"). But here Bayer faces a conundrum. If we know one thing about the McCollins suit, we know that it was *not* a class action. Indeed, the very ruling that Bayer argues ought to be given preclusive effect is the District Court's decision that a class could not properly be certified. So Bayer wants to bind Smith as a member of a class action (because it is only as such that a nonparty in Smith's situation can be bound) to a determination that there could not be a class action. And if the logic of that position is not immediately transparent, here is Bayer's attempt to clarify: "[U]ntil the moment when class certification was denied, the *McCollins* case *was* a properly conducted class action." That is true, according to Bayer, because McCollins' interests were aligned with the members of the class he proposed and he "act[ed] in a representative capacity when he sought class certification."

But wishing does not make it so. McCollins sought class certification, but he failed to obtain that result. Because the District Court found that individual issues predominated, it held that the action did not satisfy Federal Rule 23's requirements for class proceedings. In these circumstances, we cannot say that a properly conducted class action existed at any time in the litigation. Federal Rule 23 determines what is and is not a class action in federal court, where McCollins brought his suit. So in the absence of a certification under that Rule, the precondition for binding Smith was not met. Neither a proposed class action nor a rejected class action may bind nonparties. What does have this effect is a class action approved under Rule 23. But McCollins' lawsuit was never that.

We made essentially these same points in *Taylor v. Sturgell* just a few Terms ago. The question there concerned the propriety of binding nonparties under a theory of "virtual representation" based on "identity of interests and some kind of relationship between parties and nonparties." We rejected the theory unanimously, explaining that it "would 'recogniz[e], in effect, a common-law kind of class action.'" Such a device, we objected, would authorize preclusion "shorn of [Rule 23's] procedural protections." Or as otherwise stated in the opinion: We could not allow "circumvent[ion]" of Rule 23's protections through a "virtual representation doctrine that allowed courts to 'create *de facto* class actions at will.'" We could hardly have been more clear that a "properly conducted class action," with binding effect on nonparties, can come about in federal courts in just one way— through the procedure set out in Rule 23. Bayer attempts to distinguish *Taylor* by noting that the party in the prior litigation there did not propose a class action. But we do not see why that difference matters. Yes, McCollins wished to represent a class, and made a motion to that effect. But it did not come to pass. To allow McCollins' suit to bind nonparties would be to adopt the very theory *Taylor* rejected.[11]

Bayer's strongest argument comes not from established principles of preclusion, but instead from policy concerns relating to use of the class action device. Bayer warns that under our approach class counsel can repeatedly try to certify the same class "by the simple expedient of changing the named plaintiff in the caption of the complaint." And in this world of "serial relitigation of class certification," Bayer contends, defendants "would be forced in effect to buy litigation peace by settling."

---

[11] The great weight of scholarly authority—from the Restatement of Judgments to the American Law Institute to Wright and Miller—agrees that an uncertified class action cannot bind proposed class members. *See* Restatement (Second) of Judgments § 41(1), p. 393 (1980) (A nonparty may be bound only when his interests are adequately represented by "[t]he representative of a class of persons similarly situated, designated as such with the approval of the court"); ALI, *Principles of the Law Aggregate Litigation* § 2.11, Reporters' Notes, *cmt. b*, p. 181 (2010) ("[N]one of [the exceptions to the rule against nonparty preclusion] extend generally to the situation of a would-be absent class member with respect to a denial of class certification"); 18A Wright & Miller § 4455, at 457–58 ("[A]bsent certification there is no basis for precluding a nonparty" under the class action exception).

But this form of argument flies in the face of the rule against nonparty preclusion. That rule perforce leads to relitigation of many issues, as plaintiff after plaintiff after plaintiff (none precluded by the last judgment because none a party to the last suit) tries his hand at establishing some legal principle or obtaining some grant of relief. We confronted a similar policy concern in *Taylor,* which involved litigation brought under the Freedom of Information Act (FOIA). The Government there cautioned that unless we bound nonparties a " 'potentially limitless' " number of plaintiffs, perhaps coordinating with each other, could "mount a series of repetitive lawsuits" demanding the selfsame documents. But we rejected this argument, even though the payoff in a single successful FOIA suit—disclosure of documents to the public—could "trum[p]" or "subsum[e]" all prior losses, just as a single successful class certification motion could do. As that response suggests, our legal system generally relies on principles of *stare decisis* and comity among courts to mitigate the sometimes substantial costs of similar litigation brought by different plaintiffs. We have not thought that the right approach (except in the discrete categories of cases we have recognized) lies in binding nonparties to a judgment.

And to the extent class actions raise special problems of relitigation, Congress has provided a remedy that does not involve departing from the usual rules of preclusion. In the Class Action Fairness Act of 2005 (CAFA), 28 U.S.C. §§ 1332(d), 1453 (2006 ed. and Supp. III), Congress enabled defendants to remove to federal court any sizable class action involving minimal diversity of citizenship. Once removal takes place, Federal Rule 23 governs certification. And federal courts may consolidate multiple overlapping suits against a single defendant in one court (as the Judicial Panel on Multi-District Litigation did for the many actions involving Baycol). *See* § 1407. Finally, we would expect federal courts to apply principles of comity to each other's class certification decisions when addressing a common dispute. CAFA may be cold comfort to Bayer with respect to suits like this one beginning before its enactment. But Congress's decision to address the relitigation concerns associated with class actions through the mechanism of removal provides yet another reason for federal courts to adhere in this context to longstanding principles of preclusion.[12] And once again, that is especially so when the federal court is deciding whether to go so far as to enjoin a state proceeding.

The Anti-Injunction Act prohibits the order the District Court entered here. The Act's relitigation exception authorizes injunctions only when a former federal adjudication clearly precludes a state-court decision. As we said more than 40 years ago, and have consistently maintained since that time, "[a]ny doubts . . . should be resolved in favor of permitting the state courts to proceed." *Atlantic Coast Line,* 398 U.S. at 297. Under this approach, close cases have easy answers: The federal court should not issue an injunction, and the state court should decide the preclusion question. But this case does not even strike us as close. The issues in the federal and state lawsuits differed because the relevant legal standards differed. And the mere proposal of a class in the federal action could not bind persons

---

[12] By the same token, nothing in our holding today forecloses legislation to modify established principles of preclusion should Congress decide that CAFA does not sufficiently prevent relitigation of class certification motions. * * *

who were not parties there. For these reasons, the judgment of the Court of Appeals is

Reversed.

NOTES AND QUESTIONS

1. Would the *Smith* court's reasoning have been the same had the subsequent class action suit been filed in (or removed to) federal court? Should that distinction matter?

2. The American Law Institute (ALI) *Principles of the Law of Aggregate Litigation* has taken the following approach:

> A judicial decision to deny aggregate treatment for a common issue or for related claims by way of a class action should raise a rebuttable presumption against the same aggregate treatment in other courts as a matter of comity.

American Law Institute, *Principles of the Law of Aggregate Litigation* § 2.11 at 177 (2010). To what extent did *Smith* adopt the ALI's approach? What does it mean to expect federal courts to apply a "rebuttable presumption" against aggregate treatment? Should courts apply such a presumption?

3. *Smith* describes the use of an injunction under the relitigation exception as "resorting to heavy artillery." Why? Should it be so hard for a court to issue an injunction following a class certification denial?

4. Bayer argues that policy considerations countenance against prohibiting an injunction. What are those considerations? Are they meritorious?

5. *Smith* notes that legislation or a Federal Rules amendment might allay some of Bayer's concerns. How, if at all, could such legislation be drafted to address the issues in *Smith*?

6. In *Duffy v. Si–Sifh Corp.*, 726 So. 2d 438 (La. Ct. App. 1999), the Louisiana Court of Appeal faced the issue of whether *res judicata* bars a class action suit based on the same underlying facts as a previous class action suit filed in the same state. (Although the court spoke in terms of *res judicata*, the only question at issue was whether class action allegations were barred, not whether class members could pursue their individual claims.) Both *Duffy* and the previous case involved classwide allegations of breach of contract, fraud, and other claims in connection with the sale of burial insurance policies in Louisiana. The named plaintiffs in the previous suit (the *Feldheim* case) were different, but the statewide classes sought to be certified in both cases were identical, and the same attorneys represented both sets of plaintiffs. The *Feldheim* trial court held that the case could not proceed as a class action (because individual issues would predominate over common issues) and thus dismissed the class allegations. Although the trial court in *Duffy* held that it was not bound by the dismissal of class claims by the *Feldheim* court, the appellate court in *Duffy* reversed, reasoning as follows:

> The plaintiffs claim * * * that the trial court correctly [rejected the assertion] of *res judicata* because the named plaintiffs are not identically the same in this suit and the *Feldheim* case. * * * Thus, this court must determine whether an identity of parties exists between the two cases.

> "Identity of parties does not mean the parties must be the same physical or material parties, but they must appear in the suit in the

same quality or capacity." The only requirement is that the parties be the same "in the legal sense of the word." Under that definition, an identity of parties exists between the two cases. The named plaintiffs in each case are the proposed class representatives for the exact same class of people, since the definitions of the class as alleged are identical in the two cases. Thus, the parties are the same in the legal sense of the word.

The plaintiffs focus on the fact that the named plaintiffs are different, coupled with the fact that the class was never certified in *Feldheim*. Because the class has never been certified, they argue, the named plaintiffs in the *Feldheim* case cannot be considered to have represented the named plaintiffs in the instant case. However, the plaintiffs fail to acknowledge the reality of the facts of this case. The "party plaintiffs" in the *Feldheim* case are all the members of the defined class; the "party plaintiffs" in the instant case are the very same people. The fact that different proposed representatives filed suit in the instant case does not affect that analysis. Thus, we find that the identity of parties requirement for a class action is present.

Nothing in the *Feldheim* decision or the decision of this court in the instant case affects the rights of the individual plaintiffs who filed the instant suit; those individual plaintiffs still have a right to assert a cause of action for their losses. However, allowing the plaintiffs to relitigate the class action question in the instant case would encourage forum shopping, allowing the plaintiffs numerous "bites" at the class action "apple," and frustrate the purposes of the *res judicata* doctrine.

Id. at 443. Does the *Duffy* court's reasoning conflict with that in *Smith*? If so, which approach is more faithful to the policies underlying collateral estoppel?

7. Would *Duffy* have reached the same result had the second suit involved burial insurance sold throughout the United States? What about a class limited to burial insurance sold within a specific parish (*i.e.*, county) in Louisiana?

8. *Duffy* held that the members of a class could be precluded from relitigating the propriety of a decision dismissing class allegations. In an unusual and unprecedented case, a federal court of appeals went even further, holding that class members could be barred *on the merits* from relitigating issues that class representatives litigated in their *individual* capacities in another court. In *Sondel v. Northwest Airlines, Inc.*, 56 F.3d 934 (8th Cir. 1995), three plaintiffs filed a putative class action against Northwest Airlines in federal court, asserting sex discrimination in violation of Title VII and Minnesota state law. Plaintiffs then dropped the state-law claim from their federal-court suit, and (represented by the same attorneys) filed a proposed class action in Minnesota state court based on the same facts and seeking the same relief under Minnesota law. The federal court certified the federal suit as a class action, but the state court did not. Accordingly, the state suit proceeded in the named plaintiffs' individual capacities, and the defendant prevailed at trial.

Subsequently, the federal district court granted summary judgment in favor of Northwest, holding that the federal class action suit was barred as a result of the state-court verdict. The Eighth Circuit affirmed, reasoning:

When the class action lawsuit was certified by the federal district court, the certified representatives and the class counsel assumed certain fiduciary responsibilities to the Class. Thus, the certified representatives and the class counsel had fiduciary responsibilities to the Class when prosecuting the state court action. For example, the certified representatives may not take any action which will prejudice the Class's interest, or further their personal interests at the expense of the Class. We do not believe that these duties are confined to the four corners of the federal lawsuit. Accordingly, by virtue of their fiduciary duties to refrain from taking any action prejudicial to the Class, the certified representatives were representing the interests of the Class at the state trial.

* * *

* * * [W]e believe it is significant that the same attorneys who represented the state court plaintiffs are the class counsel in the federal class action. At the federal summary judgment motion the class counsel informed the district court that he was not planning to introduce any additional evidence beyond that presented at the state trial. Furthermore, the Class was financially interested in the outcome of the state court suit because its counsel prosecuted the state suit with the intent of using offensive collateral estoppel in the federal suit if successful in the state suit. Thus, we believe that the interests between the certified representatives, the class counsel and the Class are more than coincidental. Accordingly, we hold that the district court properly found that the Class was in privity with the state court plaintiffs.

Id. at 938–40. Is the Eighth Circuit's ruling fair to the unnamed class members? Can it withstand scrutiny in light of *Smith*?

c. Competing and Overlapping Class Actions

A major concern of courts, practitioners, and scholars is the proliferation of competing and overlapping class actions. This issue is closely related to the issue in the prior section—involving the effect on a second court when one court denies class certification in a similar case.

Various procedural mechanisms enable suits pending in different federal courts to be coordinated in the federal court system—such as consolidation of pre-trial proceedings pursuant to the MDL statute, 28 U.S.C. § 1407, and transfers pursuant to 28 U.S.C. § 1404(a). [*See* Chapter 12; Chapter 13(B)(1).] The state court systems, however, operate independently of one another and generally independent of the federal system, resulting in the possibility that identical class actions may exist simultaneously in federal court and state courts all over the country. *See* Note, *Wielding the Sledgehammer: Legislative Solutions for Class Action Jurisdictional Reform*, 75 N.Y.U. L. Rev. 507, 517 (2000) (describing problem). Such duplicative litigation may create several problems:

> Presumably, competing class actions could be resolved only by a race to judgment if no national means for selecting among different courts is developed. Race to judgment would induce several undesirable kinds of behavior. For example, defendants could forum-shop by delaying or accelerating particular actions. Plaintiffs

could collude with similarly aligned parties in 'stalking horse litigation,' diverting their opponents' attention or seeking collateral advantages such as the cumulative benefits of inconsistent discovery rulings. Whatever form it takes, a race is an irrational method of adjudicating controversies of overlapping jurisdiction.

Arthur R. Miller & David Crump, *Jurisdiction and Choice of Law in Multistate Class Actions After* Petroleum Co. v. Shutts, 96 Yale L.J. 1, 24–25 (1986). As another commentator notes:

> In addition to draining systemic resources, competing class actions can potentially harm absent class members because defendants may conduct a "reverse auction" by soliciting the lowest "bids" for settlement of the class. The two (or more) class counsel each have an incentive to settle first, as the first party to settle is likely to receive a much larger share of attorneys' fees.

Note, *Wielding the Sledgehammer*, 75 N.Y.U. L. Rev. at 518. *See also* Richard D. Freer, *Avoiding Duplicative Litigation: Rethinking Plaintiff Autonomy and the Court's Role in Defining the Litigative Unit*, 50 U. Pitt. L. Rev. 809, 832–33 (1989) (because "[c]ourts are a public resource * * * we have a right to insist that their services not be squandered"; "duplication of effort is a major cause of the protraction of time needed to resolve cases and cannot be justified by plaintiffs' selfish strategic desire to sue separately"); Note, *The Path to Preclusion: Federal Injunctive Relief Against Nationwide Classes in State Court*, 54 Duke L.J. 221, 232–33 (2004) ("The problems of competing class actions are well known: they waste judicial resources, confuse class members receiving multiple notices of suit, and may create a 'race to the bottom' favoring settlement.").

Such concerns have prompted the courts to address duplicative litigation in various ways. *Compare Newby v. Enron Corp.*, 338 F.3d 467 (5th Cir. 2003) (MDL court enjoined plaintiffs in related state securities fraud action from conducting discovery and issuing temporary injunction without MDL court's consent), *with Retirement Sys. of Ala. v. J.P. Morgan Chase & Co.*, 386 F.3d 419 (2d Cir. 2004) (MDL court not permitted to enjoin Alabama state court from trying individual case of opt-out plaintiff before federal district court's class action trial). Are competing and overlapping class actions all bad? What are the advantages of duplicative litigation? *See, e.g.*, John C. Coffee, Jr., *The Regulation of Entrepreneurial Litigation: Balancing Fairness and Efficiency in the Large Class Action*, 54 U. Chi. L. Rev. 877, 912 (1987) ("Separate actions do not * * * necessarily disserve clients and benefit only their attorneys. For example, an attorney may wish to pursue a state action in the belief that she can obtain a jury trial more quickly or secure higher damages.").

PROBLEM

Plaintiffs Joe Jones and Mary Collins filed a putative class action in federal district court in Detroit, alleging that their Sporti automobiles had a defective brake system. They sought to represent a nationwide class of all Sporti owners for model years 2006–2010. The court denied class certification. Counsel representing Jones and Collins has decided to use two other class members and give class certification another shot in another lawsuit. Should the new class representatives' attempt to relitigate the same class issue be barred by collateral estoppel? Should it matter whether the case is brought in federal or state court? Should it matter whether the class definition is changed to cover only model years 2006–2007? Should it matter upon what grounds class certification was denied in the first case? Should it matter that the same counsel are bringing the second action? What if, in the second suit, additional lawyers were brought in to assist the attorneys who represented the putative class in the first suit?

D. FEDERAL RELATIONS WITH STATE COURTS IN THE CLASS ACTION CONTEXT

This section addresses in greater depth the important issues implicated when related litigation exists at both the federal and state levels. The Anti-Injunction Act has already been discussed in *Smith*. Two additional doctrines are discussed here: the Full Faith and Credit doctrine, under which federal courts are obligated to give state judgments the same effect in federal courts that the judgments would be given in state court; and the *Rooker–Feldman* doctrine, which limits the jurisdiction of federal district courts to review final adjudications of state courts.

Quite often, when such doctrines are implicated, a state court (or a litigant in a state court) has performed some action that seems inequitable or ill-advised. Another party comes to federal court seeking relief, and the federal court must weigh important—but sometimes abstract—prudential considerations against the desire to take action. While reading the cases below, consider whether our national system of state and federal courts would be better served by a doctrinal scheme in which federal courts would be able to intervene more freely in state-court proceedings. Would the Constitution support greater intervention? What might be the components of such a scheme?

1. OVERVIEW OF THE ISSUES

The following case surveys the various issues discussed in this section. Subsequent cases treat each of these issues in greater detail.

IN RE GEN. MOTORS CORP. PICK-UP TRUCK FUEL TANK PRODS. LIAB. LITIG.
United States Court of Appeals, Third Circuit, 1998.
134 F.3d 133.

Before BECKER and MANSMANN, CIRCUIT JUDGES, and HOEVELER, DISTRICT JUDGE [(S.D. Fla.), by designation].

BECKER, CIRCUIT JUDGE.

This is a sequel to our opinion in *In re General Motors Corp. Pick-Up Truck Fuel Tank Prod. Liab. Litig.*, 55 F.3d 768 (3d Cir. 1995), [hereinafter *GM I*], in which we held that the District Court for the Eastern District of Pennsylvania had erred in certifying a nationwide settlement class of General Motors ("GM") truck owners who sought damages and injunctive relief as the result of the allegedly defective design of the fuel system in certain GM Trucks, which is said to have created a high risk of fire following side collisions. The Eastern District of Pennsylvania litigation was made up of a large number of cases transferred to that court by the Judicial Panel on

Multidistrict Litigation ("JPML") * * * for consolidated pretrial proceedings (the "MDL cases"). In *GM I,* we vacated the class certification order and set aside the settlement but left open the possibility that the defect in the certification procedure might be cured, the class certified, and a revised settlement approved on remand. However, instead of proceeding further in the Eastern District of Pennsylvania, the parties to the settlement repaired to [Louisiana state court], where a similar suit had been pending, restructured their deal, and submitted it to the Louisiana court, which ultimately approved it.

The action before us is an appeal from an order of the district court denying emergency applications by a number of GM truck owners who were members of the Eastern District of Pennsylvania class for an injunction against further class action proceedings in the Louisiana [state court] case. At the time of the district court's order, the Louisiana state court was considering whether to approve a settlement between GM and a certified settlement class of GM pickup truck owners, though it stayed entry of its final order until the district court could rule on the request for injunction.

The Louisiana settlement class is composed of persons who purchased over a fifteen-year period certain mid- and full-size GM pickup trucks * * * with fuel tanks located outside the frame rails. Like the federal plaintiffs, the Louisiana plaintiffs allege that the fuel system design leads to an increased risk of fire following side collisions. Appellants are members of that settlement class, and none of them has chosen to opt out of that class.

Following the conditional certification of the settlement class by the Louisiana court, the present appellants, truck owners who were never parties but were successful objectors to the proposed Eastern District of Pennsylvania settlement, moved to intervene in the on-going proceedings in the MDL cases and requested the court to enjoin the Louisiana state court from considering the settlement agreement before it. The district court * * * denied appellants' motion for intervention as untimely, and also denied the motion for injunctive relief. * * * We denied [requests for emergency relief.] Thereafter, the Louisiana state court entered final judgment approving the settlement. The present appellants also filed notices of appeal from that judgment in the Louisiana appellate system, so that they were proceeding simultaneously with their appeal from the district court's denial of their motion for injunction and their Louisiana appeal.

Appellants' claim centers on their argument that the Louisiana settlement is little changed from the one previously rejected by us in *GM I.* Accordingly, they view the settlement as an "end run" around, and a flagrant violation of, the jurisdiction of the Eastern District of Pennsylvania MDL court to which we had remanded the case for further proceedings. Although the procedure followed by appellees gives us pause, the precedent of this Court and the Supreme Court compels us to disagree with appellants and to affirm the district court's decision on several grounds.

Because the attempt to enjoin the Louisiana court proceedings is functionally an attempt to enjoin the individual plaintiffs and class members from proceeding there, we analyze it in those terms. Viewed from that perspective, neither the district court nor this Court has personal jurisdiction over the almost 5.7 million absentee plaintiffs who are (1) not before the district court, (2) have no minimum contacts with Pennsylvania, and (3) have not consented to personal jurisdiction. Second, now that the Louisiana court has entered a final judgment on the settlement, our review is barred by both the Full Faith and Credit Act and the *Rooker–Feldman* doctrine, which prevents intermediate federal appellate review of state court decisions. * * *

I. FACTS AND PROCEDURAL HISTORY

A. The MDL Proceedings

* * * Between 1973 and 1991, GM sold over 6.3 million pickup trucks with fuel tanks mounted outside of the frame rails. These trucks are allegedly defective because they are subject to an increased risk of fire in the event of a side collision. [Cases filed in numerous federal courts were transferred] to the District Court for the Eastern District of Pennsylvania for coordinated discovery and pre-trial proceedings * * *.

On March 5, 1993, pursuant to an order of the transferee judge, plaintiffs filed a Consolidated Amended Class Action Complaint with 277 named plaintiffs seeking equitable relief and damages. Specifically, the complaint alleged violations of the Magnuson–Moss Warranty Act [and] the Lanham Trademark Act, as well as a variety of state common law claims. * * *

Also on March 5, 1993, plaintiffs filed a consolidated motion for nationwide class certification. * * * [T]he parties [subsequently] agreed to certification of a settlement class of GM pickup truck owners.

[The central feature of the provisional settlement was that] class members would receive a $1,000 coupon, redeemable toward the purchase of any new GMC truck or Chevrolet light duty truck for a fifteen month period. Under its terms, the approved settlement would have had no effect on any accrued or future claims for personal injury or death, and would not have affected the rights of class members to participate in any future remedial action that might be required by the National Traffic and Motor Safety Act of 1966 * * *.

[The district court preliminarily approved the settlement and certified a settlement class under Rule 23(b)(3) consisting of] all persons and entities (except for residents of the State of Texas [where a separate class action was pending relating to the same issues]) who had purchased in the United States and were owners as of July 19, 1993, of (1) a 1973–1986 model year GM full-size pickup truck or chassis cab of the "C" or "K" series; or (2) a 1987–1991 model year GM full-size or chassis cab of the "R" or "V" series.

[After circulation of notice and a hearing, the district court gave final approval to the settlement.]

The objectors appealed, and we reversed [and remanded, holding that the district court erred in approving the settlement without finding that Rule 23 was satisfied].

Following remand, plaintiffs amended their complaint, filed a renewed motion for class certification, and proceeded with discovery pursuant to our opinion. * * * [N]o settlement is pending, and the motion for class certification is not yet ripe.

B. The Louisiana Proceedings

In addition to the [Pennsylvania] litigation[,] plaintiffs had concurrently filed actions in 11 state courts, including Louisiana. * * * On May 18, 1993, a Louisiana trial court granted plaintiffs' motion for class certification of a statewide class as the basis for litigation. This decision was stayed by a Louisiana appellate court on August 8, 1993, based upon the preliminary nationwide settlement reached in the Eastern District of Pennsylvania MDL cases.

After we vacated the order creating the settlement class, a new round of negotiations between Louisiana class counsel and GM began. [The parties reached a settlement in the Louisiana case, which the state court provisionally approved, certifying a nationwide settlement class.] The court ordered individual notices disseminated to the 5.7 million class members, scheduled a formal fairness hearing * * * and requested objections and notices of exclusions. 200 of the 277 plaintiffs in the federal MDL successfully moved to intervene in the Louisiana proceedings.

The new Louisiana settlement, while similar in content to the original settlement provisionally approved by the MDL court in 1993 and later rejected by this Court, differs in several ways, all responsive to our comments in *GM I* about perceived problems with the earlier settlement. First, the Louisiana settlement extends the period during which class members could validly redeem their $1,000 coupons (from 15 to 33 months for consumers and from 15 to 50 months for fleet and government owners). Second, the settlement provides for greater transferability of the coupons. Third, the settlement would allow class members to apply the coupon value toward the purchase of any GM vehicle (except Saturn automobiles), rather than just GM pickup trucks. Fourth, the settlement stipulates that GM and plaintiffs' counsel will fund two new safety programs, researching the safety of general fuel systems and testing proposed retrofits for safety and feasibility, purported to be worth a combined $5.1 million. Fifth, commitments have apparently been made by a major bank to purchase the transferable coupons, thereby creating a secondary market.

Appellants and Appellees strongly dispute the viability and significance of the differences between the two settlements. Appellees contend that these changes satisfy most, if not all, of this Court's problems with the original agreement. They note significantly that all the governmental and fleet entities, as well as the Public Citizen Litigation Group and the Center for Auto Safety, which objected to the original settlement, support the Louisiana settlement. Appellants, conversely, assert that class counsel and GM have essentially repackaged the agreement that had been rejected in Philadelphia, made purely cosmetic changes, and have run off to Louisiana for approval.

* * *

II. PERSONAL JURISDICTION

[The court first found that it did not have personal jurisdiction over the vast majority of class members in the Louisiana nationwide class, because the objectors had not demonstrated that such class members had sufficient minimum contacts with Pennsylvania to permit the exercise of jurisdiction.]

III. FULL FAITH AND CREDIT AND THE *ROOKER–FELDMAN* DOCTRINE

* * * Appellees [also] contend that both the Full Faith and Credit Act * * * and the *Rooker–Feldman* doctrine prevent us from vacating the final judgment of the Louisiana court.

A. The Full Faith and Credit Act

28 U.S.C. § 1738 provides in pertinent part:

> The . . . judicial proceedings of any court of any such State, Territory, or Possession . . . shall have the same full faith and credit in every court within the United States and its Territories and Possessions as they have by law or usage in the courts of such State, Territory, or Possession from which they are taken.

As interpreted by the Supreme Court, § 1738 "directs all courts to treat a state court judgment with the same respect that it would receive in the courts of the rendering state." *Matsushita Elec. Indus. Co. v. Epstein*, 516 U.S. 367, 373 (1996) [see Part (D)(2) of this chapter]. We may not " 'employ [our] own rules . . . in determining the effect of state judgments,' but must 'accept the rules chosen by the State from which the judgment is taken.' " *Id.*

Under Louisiana law, the class action settlement that appellants seek to enjoin here is a final judgment. Facially, therefore, § 1738 leaves us no choice but to decline appellants' request. This conclusion is confirmed by the Supreme Court's recent decision in *Matsushita*.

* * *

* * * [T]he present appellants are members of the Louisiana class who did not exercise their opt out rights. They are active participants in the [state appeal challenging approval of the settlement] * * *. Especially under these circumstances, the Full Faith and Credit Act prevents this Court from vacating the now final judgment of the Louisiana court.

B. The *Rooker–Feldman* Doctrine

Under the *Rooker–Feldman* doctrine, "federal district courts lack subject matter jurisdiction to review final adjudications of a state's highest court or to evaluate constitutional claims that are 'inextricably intertwined with the state court's [decision] in a judicial proceeding.' " *Blake v. Papadakos*, 953 F.2d 68, 71 (3d Cir. 1992) (quoting *District of Columbia Court of Appeals v. Feldman*, 460 U.S. 462, 483 n.16 (1983)); *see also Rooker v. Fidelity Trust Co.*, 263 U.S. 413, 416 (1923). The concerns that underlie the doctrine are respect for the state courts and concerns over finality of judgments. District courts lack subject matter jurisdiction once a state court has adjudicated an issue because Congress has conferred only original jurisdiction, not appellate jurisdiction, on the district courts. We have interpreted the doctrine to encompass final decisions of lower state courts.

As was discussed *supra* * * *, with respect to the Full Faith and Credit Act, the Louisiana court has entered a valid final judgment. The decision by that Court was clearly an adjudicative and not a legislative or ministerial act. Therefore, in order for us to grant appellants' requested relief, we would first have to "determine that the state court judgment was erroneously entered." *Rooker–Feldman* bars exactly this sort of intermediate appellate review of state court judgments and divests this Court of subject matter jurisdiction of this appeal.

* * *

The order of the district court will be affirmed.

* * *

NOTES AND QUESTIONS

1. *GM Truck* provides an introduction to two doctrines that influence the complex relationship between federal and state courts: Full Faith and Credit and the *Rooker–Feldman* doctrine. These doctrines will be more fully fleshed out in the materials that follow, but consider, initially, the purposes and contents of those doctrines as described in *GM Truck*.

2. What is the practical impact of the decision in *GM Truck*? What recourse do the *GM Truck* appellants have?

3. Does the outcome in the case render superfluous the Third Circuit's earlier decision vacating the federal class settlement? Or is the outcome simply a healthy example of federalism at work? Who benefits from the Louisiana state-court settlement? Who, if anyone, is harmed by it?

4. In a portion of the *GM Truck* opinion not excerpted above, the Third Circuit, applying basic personal jurisdiction principles, noted that its ability to grant relief was constrained because it did not have personal jurisdiction over most of the members of the Louisiana class. If the Third Circuit had found that Full Faith and Credit and the *Rooker–Feldman* doctrine did not pose barriers to relief, could the court have done anything to prevent consummation of the settlement, given the Court's limited jurisdiction?

2. FULL FAITH AND CREDIT

The Full Faith and Credit Act requires a federal court to afford the same treatment to a state court judgment that a court in that state would give to the judgment.

MATSUSHITA ELEC. INDUS. CO. V. EPSTEIN
Supreme Court of the United States, 1996.
516 U.S. 367.

JUSTICE THOMAS delivered the opinion of the Court.

This case presents the question whether a federal court may withhold full faith and credit from a state-court judgment approving a class-action settlement simply because the settlement releases claims within the exclusive jurisdiction of the federal courts. The answer is no. Absent a partial repeal of the Full Faith and Credit Act, 28 U.S.C. § 1738, by another federal statute, a federal court must give the judgment the same effect that it would have in the courts of the State in which it was rendered.

I.

In 1990, petitioner Matsushita Electric Industrial Co. made a tender offer for the common stock of MCA, Inc., a Delaware corporation. The tender offer not only resulted in Matsushita's acquisition of MCA, but also precipitated two lawsuits on behalf of the holders of MCA's common stock. First, a class action was filed in the Delaware Court of Chancery against MCA and its directors for breach of fiduciary duty in failing to maximize shareholder value. The complaint was later amended to state additional claims against MCA's directors for, *inter alia*, waste of corporate assets by exposing MCA to liability under the federal securities laws. In addition, Matsushita was added as a defendant and was accused of conspiring with MCA's directors to violate Delaware law. The Delaware suit was based purely on state-law claims.

While the state class action was pending, the instant suit was filed in Federal District Court in California. The complaint named Matsushita as a defendant and alleged that Matsushita's tender offer violated Securities Exchange Commission (SEC) Rules 10b–3 and 14d–10. * * * Section 27 of the [Securities] Exchange Act [of 1934] confers exclusive jurisdiction upon the federal courts for suits brought to enforce the Act or rules and regulations promulgated thereunder. The District Court declined to certify the class, entered summary judgment for Matsushita, and dismissed the case. The plaintiffs appealed to the Court of Appeals for the Ninth Circuit.

After the federal plaintiffs filed their notice of appeal but before the Ninth Circuit handed down a decision, the parties to the Delaware suit negotiated a settlement. In exchange for a global release of all claims arising out of the Matsushita–MCA acquisition, the defendants would deposit $2 million into a settlement fund to be distributed *pro rata* to the members of the class. As required by Delaware Chancery Rule 23, which is modeled on Federal Rule of Civil Procedure 23, the Chancery Court certified the class for purposes of settlement and approved a notice of the proposed settlement. The notice informed the class members of their right to request exclusion from the settlement class and to appear and present argument at a scheduled hearing to determine the fairness of the settlement. * * * The Chancery Court * * * held a hearing [and after considering several objectors' arguments] found the class representation adequate and the settlement fair.

The order and final judgment of the Chancery Court incorporated the terms of the settlement agreement, providing [for the release of all federal and state claims in connection with the tender offer and merger "including without limitation the claims asserted in the California Federal Actions"].

The judgment also stated that the notice met all the requirements of due process. The Delaware Supreme Court affirmed.

Respondents were members of both the state and federal plaintiff classes. Following issuance of the notice of proposed settlement of the Delaware litigation, respondents neither opted out of the settlement class nor appeared at the hearing to contest the settlement or the representation of the class. On appeal in the Ninth Circuit, petitioner Matsushita invoked the Delaware judgment as a bar to further prosecution of that action under the Full Faith and Credit Act.

The Ninth Circuit rejected petitioner's argument, ruling that § 1738 did not apply. Instead, the Court of Appeals fashioned a test under which the preclusive force of a state court settlement judgment is limited to those claims that "could . . . have been extinguished by the issue preclusive effect of an adjudication of the state claims." * * *

II.

The Full Faith and Credit Act * * * directs all courts to treat a state court judgment with the same respect that it would receive in the courts of the rendering state. Federal courts may not "employ their own rules . . . in determining the effect of state judgments," but must "accept the rules chosen by the State from which the judgment is taken." Because the Court of Appeals failed to follow the dictates of the Act, we reverse.

A.

The state court judgment in this case differs in two respects from the judgments that we have previously considered in our cases under the Full Faith and Credit Act. * * * [T]he judgment was the product of a class action and incorporated a settlement agreement releasing claims within the exclusive jurisdiction of the federal courts. Though respondents urge "the irrelevance of section 1738 to this litigation," we do not think that either of these features exempts the judgment from the operation of § 1738.

That the judgment at issue is the result of a class action, rather than a suit brought by an individual, does not undermine the initial applicability of § 1738. The judgment of a state court in a class action is plainly the product of a "judicial proceeding" within the meaning of § 1738. Therefore, a judgment entered in a class action, like any other judgment entered in a state judicial proceeding, is presumptively entitled to full faith and credit under the express terms of the Act.

Further, § 1738 is not irrelevant simply because the judgment in question might work to bar the litigation of exclusively federal claims. Our decision in *Marrese v. American Academy of Orthopaedic Surgeons*, 470 U.S. 373 (1985), made clear that where § 1738 is raised as a defense in a subsequent suit, the fact that an allegedly precluded "claim is within the exclusive jurisdiction of the federal courts *does not necessarily make § 1738 inapplicable.*" * * *

* * *

B.

Marrese provides the analytical framework for deciding whether the Delaware court's judgment precludes this exclusively federal action. When faced with a state court judgment relating to an exclusively federal claim, a federal court must first look to the law of the rendering State to ascertain the effect of the judgment. If state law indicates that the particular claim or issue would be barred from litigation in a court of that state, then the federal court must next decide whether, "as an exception to § 1738," it "should refuse to give preclusive effect to [the] state court judgment."

1.

We observed in *Marrese* that the inquiry into state law would not always yield a direct answer. Usually, "a state court will not have occasion to address the specific question whether a state judgment has issue or claim preclusive effect in a later action that can be brought only in federal court." Where a judicially approved settlement is under consideration, a federal court may consequently find guidance from general state law on the preclusive force of settlement judgments. Here, in addition to providing rules regarding the preclusive force of class-action settlement judgments in subsequent suits in state court, the Delaware courts have also spoken to the particular effect of such judgments in federal court.

[The Court reviewed Delaware law and concluded that the] cases indicate that even if, as here, a claim could not have been raised in the court that rendered the settlement judgment in a class action, a Delaware court would still find that the judgment bars subsequent pursuit of the claim [and that] * * * when the Court of Chancery approves a global release of claims, its settlement judgment should preclude on-going or future federal court litigation of any released claims.

* * *

* * * [Thus] we think that a Delaware court would afford preclusive effect to the settlement judgment in this case, notwithstanding the fact that respondents could not have pressed their Exchange Act claims in the Court of Chancery. The claims are clearly within the scope of the release in the judgment, since the judgment specifically refers to this lawsuit. As required by Delaware Court of Chancery Rule 23, the Court of Chancery found, and the Delaware Supreme Court affirmed, that the settlement was "fair, reasonable and adequate and in the best interests of the . . . Settlement class" and that notice to the class was "in full compliance with . . . the requirements of due process." The Court of Chancery "further determined that the plaintiffs[,] . . . as representatives of the Settlement Class, have fairly and adequately protected the interests of the Settlement Class."[5] Under Delaware Rule 23, as under Federal Rule of Civil Procedure 23, "[a]ll members of the class, whether of a plaintiff or a defendant class, are bound by the judgment entered in the action unless, in a Rule 23(b)(3) action, they make a timely election for exclusion." Respondents do not deny that, as shareholders of MCA's common stock, they were part of the plaintiff class and that they never opted out; they are bound, then, by the judgment.

2.

[Because the Court had found that the settlement judgment would be *res judicata* under Delaware law, it proceeded to analyze whether § 27 of the Exchange Act, which confers exclusive jurisdiction upon the federal courts for suits arising under the Act, partially repealed § 1738. The Court concluded that it did not.]

C.

The Court of Appeals did not engage in any analysis of Delaware law pursuant to § 1738. Rather, the Court of Appeals declined to apply § 1738 on the ground that where the rendering forum lacked jurisdiction over the subject matter or the parties, full faith and credit is not required. The Court of Appeals decided that the subject-matter jurisdiction exception to full

---

[5] Apart from any discussion of Delaware law, respondents contend that the settlement proceedings did not satisfy due process because the class was inadequately represented. Respondents make this claim in spite of the Chancery Court's express ruling, following argument on the issue, that the class representatives fairly and adequately protected the interests of the Class. *Cf. Prezant v. De Angelis*, 636 A.2d 915, 923 (Del. 1994) ("[The] constitutional requirement [of adequacy of representation] is embodied in [Delaware] Rule 23(a)(4), which requires that the named plaintiff 'fairly and adequately protect the interests of the class' "). We need not address the due process claim, however, because it is outside the scope of the question presented in this Court. While it is true that a respondent may defend a judgment on alternative grounds, we generally do not address arguments that were not the basis for the decision below.

faith and credit applies to this case because the Delaware court acted outside the bounds of its own jurisdiction in approving the settlement, since the settlement released exclusively federal claims.

As explained above, the state court in this case clearly possessed jurisdiction over the subject matter of the underlying suit and over the defendants. Only if this were not so—for instance, if the complaint alleged violations of the Exchange Act and the Delaware court rendered a judgment on the merits of those claims—would the exception to § 1738 for lack of subject-matter jurisdiction apply. Where, as here, the rendering court in fact had subject-matter jurisdiction, the subject-matter jurisdiction exception to full faith and credit is simply inapposite. In such a case, the relevance of a federal statute that provides for exclusive federal jurisdiction is not to the state court's possession of jurisdiction *per se,* but to the existence of a partial repeal of § 1738.

The judgment of the Court of Appeals is reversed and remanded for proceedings consistent with this opinion.

* * *

JUSTICE GINSBURG, with whom JUSTICE STEVENS joins, and with whom JUSTICE SOUTER joins [in part], concurring in part and dissenting in part.

I join the Court's judgment to the extent that it remands the case to the Ninth Circuit. I agree that a remand is in order because the Court of Appeals did not attend to this Court's reading of 28 U.S.C. § 1738 in a controlling decision, *Kremer v. Chemical Constr. Corp.,* 456 U.S. 461 (1982). But I would not endeavor, as the Court does, to speak the first word on the content of Delaware preclusion law. Instead, I would follow our standard practice of remitting that issue for decision, in the first instance, by the lower federal courts.

I write separately to emphasize a point key to the application of § 1738: A state-court judgment generally is not entitled to full faith and credit unless it satisfies the requirements of the Fourteenth Amendment's Due Process Clause. *See Kremer,* 456 U.S. at 482–83. In the class action setting, adequate representation is among the due process ingredients that must be supplied if the judgment is to bind absent class members. *See Phillips Petroleum Co. v. Shutts,* 472 U.S. 797, 808, 812 (1985); *Prezant v. De Angelis,* 636 A.2d 915, 923–24 (Del. 1994).

Suitors in this action * * * argued before the Ninth Circuit, and again before this Court, that they cannot be bound by the Delaware settlement because they were not adequately represented by the Delaware class representatives. They contend that the Delaware representatives' willingness to release federal securities claims within the exclusive jurisdiction of the federal courts for a meager return to the class members, but a solid fee to the Delaware class attorneys, disserved the interests of the class, particularly, the absentees. The inadequacy of representation was apparent, the *Epstein* plaintiffs maintained, for at the time of the settlement, the federal claims were *sub judice* in the proper forum for those claims—the federal judiciary. Although the Ninth Circuit decided the case without reaching the due process check on the full faith and credit obligation, that inquiry remains open for consideration on remand.

* * *

Proceedings On Remand

On remand from the Supreme Court, the Ninth Circuit initially issued a split panel decision, referred to as *Epstein II* (Judge Norris writing for the majority, joined by Judge Wiggins, with Judge O'Scannlain dissenting), finding that the *Epstein* appellants were not bound by the Delaware judgment because they had been denied due process in the Delaware proceeding (because of a lack of adequate representation). That decision generated significant academic debate focused upon the issue of due process rights of absent class members. *See, e.g.,* Marcel Kahan & Linda Silberman, *The Inadequate Search for "Adequacy" in Class Actions: A Critique of* Epstein v. MCA, Inc., 73 N.Y.U. L. Rev. 765, 765–66 (1998) (decision was "premised on an expansive, novel—and, in our view, erroneous—reading of the Supreme Court's decision in *Phillips Petroleum Co. v. Shutts*"); William T. Allen, *Finality of Judgments in Class Actions: A Comment on* Epstein v. MCA, Inc., 73 N.Y.U. L. Rev. 1149, 1150 (1998) (result was "novel, and inconsistent with established concepts of finality of judgments, with design of an effective class action mechanism, and with the policies and precedents of full faith and credit"); Geoffrey P. Miller, *Full Faith and Credit to Settlement in Overlapping Class Actions: A Reply to Professors Kahan and Silberman*, 73 N.Y.U. L. Rev. 1167, 1169 (1998) (if interpreted narrowly, decision "might be defensible as a means for policing questionable settlements that present circumstantial evidence of collusion or other undesirable tactics by the settling parties"); Alan B. Morrison, *The Inadequate Search for "Adequacy" in Class Actions: A Brief Rejoinder to Professors Kahan and Silberman*, 73 N.Y.U. L. Rev. 1179, 1186 (1998) (suggesting narrow reading of decision).

Two days after the issuance of the Ninth Circuit's initial decision on remand (*Epstein II*), Judge Norris, who had written *Epstein II,* resigned from the Ninth Circuit. Judge Thomas was drawn to replace Judge Norris, and the reconstituted panel subsequently granted rehearing, withdrew the *Epstein II* decision, and issued the following opinion (*Epstein III*). *Epstein III* analyzes the issue of whether the state court judgment was entitled to full faith and credit if it failed to provide due process to class members because of inadequate representation.

EPSTEIN V. MCA, INC.
United States Court of Appeals, Ninth Circuit, 1999.
179 F.3d 641.

Before WIGGINS, O'SCANNLAIN, and THOMAS, CIRCUIT JUDGES.

O'SCANNLAIN, CIRCUIT JUDGE.

* * *

I.

* * *

[On remand from the Supreme Court,] a divided panel in *Epstein II* held that despite the Court's holding in *Matsushita*, the Delaware judgment was not entitled to full faith and credit because it violated due process based on the inadequacy of the class representation. The panel therefore reversed and remanded for proceedings consistent with those portions of *Epstein I* that were not reversed by the Supreme Court.

* * * Following rehearing, we now withdraw our opinion in *Epstein II* and consider anew whether the *Epstein* appellants are bound by the Delaware judgment.

[The court first concluded that the Supreme Court in *Matsushita* had determined that the Delaware judgment was valid.]

* * *

III.

* * * [T]he *Epstein* appellants assert that *Phillips Petroleum Co. v. Shutts*, 472 U.S. 797 (1985), and *Kremer v. Chemical Constr. Corp.*, 456 U.S. 461 (1982), create a largely unfettered right to challenge collaterally the adequacy of representation in class actions.

A.

Shutts does not support the broad collateral review that the *Epstein* appellants seek. In *Shutts*, the Court identified various procedural safeguards that are necessary to bind absent class members, including notice, the opportunity to be heard, the opportunity to opt out, and adequate representation. However, nowhere in *Shutts* did the Court state or imply that where the certifying court makes a determination of the adequacy of representation in accord with *Shutts*, this determination is subject to collateral review. *Shutts* in fact implies that such review is unwarranted by emphasizing that the certifying court is charged with protecting the interests of the absent class members.

Simply put, the absent class members' due process right to adequate representation is protected not by collateral review, but by the certifying court initially, and thereafter by appeal within the state system and by direct review in the United States Supreme Court.

As the Court stated in *Hansberry v. Lee,* "there has been a failure of due process only in those cases where it cannot be said that *the procedure adopted,* fairly insures the protection of the interests of absent parties who are to be bound by it." 311 U.S. 32, 42 (1940). Due process requires that an absent class member's right to adequate representation be protected by the adoption of the appropriate procedures by the certifying court and by the courts that review its determinations; due process does not require collateral second-guessing of those determinations and that review.

B.

Kremer does not indicate otherwise. * * * *Kremer* held that neither state nor federal courts are required to give full faith and credit to a constitutionally infirm judgment. The extent of collateral review is, however, limited.

Kremer merely recognized that a judgment is not entitled to full faith and credit "if there is reason to doubt the quality, extensiveness, or fairness of procedures followed in prior litigation." Limited collateral review would be appropriate, therefore, to consider whether the procedures in the prior litigation afforded the party against whom the earlier judgment is asserted a "full and fair opportunity" to litigate the claim or issue. This review would not, however, include reconsideration of the merits of the claim or issue, and such a challenge would most likely fail because "state proceedings need do no more than satisfy the minimum procedural requirements of the Fourteenth Amendment's Due Process Clause in order to qualify for the full faith and credit guaranteed by federal law."

C.

Matsushita itself indicates that broad collateral review of the adequacy of representation (or of the other due process requirements for binding absent class members) is not available. *Matsushita* made plain that class action judgments are accorded full faith and credit like other judgments * * *.

The Court did, of course, address the additional due process requirements for binding absent class members, stating, by way of example, that "due process for class action plaintiffs requires notice plus an opportunity to be heard and participate in the litigation," and "that the named plaintiff at all times adequately represent the interests of the absent class members." The Court, however, satisfied itself that these requirements had been met *by referencing the Delaware courts' findings on these matters*, rather than by independently determining whether the requirements were met.

After this analysis, the Court stated the seemingly uncontroversial proposition that:

> Under Delaware Rule 23, as under Federal Rule of Civil Procedure 23, "[a]ll members of the class, whether of a plaintiff or a defendant class, are bound by the judgment entered in the action unless, in a Rule 23(b)(3) action, they make a timely election for exclusion." * * *

The Court's statements in no way imply that a class member who fails to opt out is not bound until collateral review of the adequacy of representation reveals that due process has been satisfied. Nor is there any indication that a "properly entertained" class action is other than one in which a certifying court employs the appropriate procedures to determine that the due process requirements embodied in Rule 23 have been met. Any such implication would be belied by the Court's analysis of the issue because these statements followed on the heels of the Court's review of the Delaware courts' determinations that the Rule 23 requirements were satisfied.

Even footnote five, so heavily relied upon by the *Epstein* appellants, makes the same point. There, the Court specifically noted that the *Epstein* appellants sought to challenge collaterally the adequacy of representation "in spite of the Chancery Court's express ruling, following argument on the issue, that the class representatives fairly and adequately protected the interests of the class." The Court then cited *Prezant v. De Angelis*, 636 A.2d 915 (Del. 1994), for the proposition that the "constitutional requirement [of adequacy of representation] is embodied in [Delaware] Rule 23(a)(4)." These statements indicated that the *Epstein* appellants' challenge to the adequacy of representation in the Delaware proceedings was answered by specific reference to the findings made on the issue in those proceedings.

IV.

For the foregoing reasons, the Delaware judgment was not constitutionally infirm and must be accorded full faith and credit. The district court's decision of April 16, 1992 is

AFFIRMED.

WIGGINS, CIRCUIT JUDGE, concurring.

I concur in the result of Judge O'Scannlain's majority opinion. I write separately to explain why I changed my vote in this appeal.

* * *

I now believe that, while the Supreme Court did not conclusively resolve the due process issue before the remand, it did send unmistakable signals on that very issue. * * *

* * *

Because the adequacy of representation issue was fully and fairly litigated and necessarily decided in the Chancery Court, the Delaware courts would give preclusive effect to that determination. The Full Faith and Credit Act, 28 U.S.C. § 1738, requires that we "treat a state court judgment with the same respect that it would receive in the courts of the rendering state." As such, we are required to give preclusive effect to the Chancery Court's judgment that class representation was adequate irrespective of whether we agree with that determination. I therefore concur.

THOMAS, CIRCUIT JUDGE, dissenting.

* * * The majority opinion [permits] a class settlement obtained without any record evidence that the class representatives were even members of the class. Because the Delaware judgment extinguished the rights of absent class members without affording them due process of law, I respectfully dissent.

[Judge Thomas first concluded that the Supreme Court in *Matsushita* did not conclusively resolve whether absent class members were accorded due process by the Delaware courts.]

II.

Judgments binding absent litigants in class action suits are an exception to the general rule that one is not bound by a judgment in personam in a litigation to which he or she is not a party. *See Hansberry v. Lee*, 311 U.S. 32 (1940). Absent class members may be bound by the judgment if they have, in fact, been adequately represented by parties who are present. Due process requires that the procedure employed to reach a binding judgment "fairly insures the protection of the interests of absent parties who are to be bound by it."

This is, in the words of the *Hansberry* court almost sixty years ago, a "familiar doctrine." Yet its import seems lost in this case. In order for absent class members to have "adequate representation" within the meaning of the Due Process Clause, the class must be free of structural conflict. * * * In a class settlement, there must be "structural assurance of fair and adequate representation for the diverse groups and individuals affected." The class representative "must possess the same interest and suffer the same injury shared by all members of the class he represents."

In the case at hand, there were three different types of shareholders who were part of the class: (a) those who traded on the open market; (b) those who tendered their shares; and (c) those who received spin-off shares. In addition, there were differences among the class members as to the legal theories available. The interests of the *Epstein* plaintiffs in advancing the federal claims were directly antagonistic to those of the Delaware class representatives, who were precluded by federal securities law from asserting those claims in state court. By the time settlement occurred, the statute of limitations prevented the Delaware class from litigating the federal claims in any court. Thus, there were irreconcilable differences in claims and damages among the class members. These structural conflicts should have actuated an inquiry by the Delaware Vice-Chancellor, and should have resulted in the creation of sub-classes to assure the adequate representation of absent class members.

The conflict prior to settlement approval was palpable. Because they could not assert federal causes of action, those claims were of no value to the class representatives and their counsel except as a bargaining chip to enhance the value of their state claims. Indeed, settlement of the federal action was the only method by which the Delaware class could receive any money from the federal claims. Thus, it was plainly in the best interest of class representatives to settle the federal claims at any price. Class representatives had absolutely no incentive to obtain fair valuation of the federal claims, because of their inability to assert the claims.

* * *

"Adequate representation . . . depends on . . . an absence of antagonism." In this case, the antagonistic interests, injury and claims among the class members resulted in significant structural conflicts. Because these conflicts were unresolved, the class representation was constitutionally infirm and cannot bind absent class members. * * *

* * *

The majority decision correctly observes that *Phillips Petroleum Co. v. Shutts*, 472 U.S. 797 (1985), enumerated "various procedural safeguards that are necessary to bind absent class members." In fact, *Shutts* specifically indicates that "the Due Process Clause of course requires that the named plaintiff at all times adequately represent the interests of the absent class members." The litigation leading up to the Delaware settlement thus violated the "minimal procedural due process protection" due to the *Epstein* plaintiffs adequate representation "at all times."

"If the plaintiff was not adequately represented in the prior action, or there was a denial of due process, then the prior decision has no preclusive effect." *Brown v. Ticor Title Ins. Co.*, 982 F.2d 386 (9th Cir. 1992). Thus, the *Epstein* plaintiffs are entitled as a matter of federal law to assert their claims in this action.

III.

* * *

The *Epstein* plaintiffs correctly argue that to be bound by the settlement decision they are entitled under Delaware law to specific findings that they were adequately represented in the Delaware Chancery Court. Such findings are required in order to bind the federal litigants to the settlement terms. In *Prezant,* the Delaware Supreme Court explicitly held that a Court of Chancery is required to "articulate on the record its findings regarding the satisfaction of the Rule 23 criteria and supporting reasoning." Yet the statement offered by the Delaware Chancery Court asserting that the plaintiffs in the action "fairly and adequately protected the interests of the Settlement Class" offers no "supporting reasoning" aside from that offered to address the challenges raised by the four objectors. No findings exist in the Chancery Court's decision that would indicate that the representation of the absent federal plaintiffs was adequate, because the matter was never actually litigated before that court.

Thus, while the Supreme Court decision in *Matsushita* makes it clear that the objectors will be bound by the judgment of the Delaware court with respect to the matters litigated, the Delaware court's decision cannot be read to bind those whose claims were simply never represented before it. The individual objectors who voluntarily appeared at the fairness hearing were not authorized by the absent class members to represent their interests, nor were they certified by the state to do so. Their appearance at the hearing could therefore not bind other parties with respect to the issue of adequacy of representation. Thus, the majority's determination today also runs against the settled law of Delaware.

IV.

Providing the *Epstein* plaintiffs with the opportunity to raise their due process claims does not, as the majority claims, result in the "collateral second guessing" of the determinations and review of the Delaware courts. Those determinations are valid, and, to the extent that they comply with due process protections afforded by the Constitution, they are binding upon this court. Thus, the result originally reached by the panel on remand was not violative of cooperative federalism or comity. The majority today gives license to those who would run to a favorable and remote state court to obtain settlements premised on bargain-basement valuations of federal claims, even when those claims clearly predominate over potential state causes of action. * * *

The *Epstein* plaintiffs seek to raise claims that received neither determination nor review in the Delaware courts. Structural conflicts of interest precluded adequate representation of absent class members. The *Epstein* plaintiffs were not adequately represented in the Delaware state court proceedings by either the class representatives or the objectors, and their claim was never litigated in Delaware state court. In denying them the right to bring their meritorious federal claims before us, we deny them due process of law. We also significantly diminish the proper oversight role of the judiciary over class action settlements.

I respectfully dissent.

* * *

In 2003, the Supreme Court granted review in a Second Circuit case to consider the propriety of a collateral attack made by absent class members on a class settlement that would have extinguished their subsequent claims. The absent class members challenged the preclusive effect of the class settlement based on inadequate representation. The Supreme Court was evenly divided on the issue (4–4), so the question of whether a collateral attack on class settlements based on adequacy is permissible remains unresolved. *See Stephenson v. Dow Chem. Co.*, 273 F.3d 249 (2001), *aff'd in relevant part by equally divided Court*, 539 U.S. 111 (2003). *See* Part C(1)(a) of this chapter.

NOTES AND QUESTIONS

1. The *Matsushita* case and the *Epstein III* majority and dissent raise separate but equally important issues relating to full faith and credit. First, must a federal court accord full faith and credit to a state-court settlement that purports to release claims that the state court would not be competent to hear? The Supreme Court in *Matsushita* answered that question definitively. Second, what is the role of a second court in reviewing issues raised by class members who attempt to collaterally attack an earlier class action judgment? The Supreme Court in *Matsushita* largely ignored this second issue, and the issue sharply divided the Ninth Circuit panels on remand.

2. What is the impact of the Supreme Court's decision in *Matsushita*? Can *any* state court settle claims that could be adjudicated only in federal court? Did the *Matsushita* court reach a just result? *See* Mollie A. Murphy, *The Intersystem Class Settlement: Of Comity, Consent, and Collusion*, 47 U. Kan. L. Rev. 413, 415 (1999) (*Matsushita* "failed to give sufficient consideration and weight to the exclusive federal nature of the subject claim or to the fact that the state action was a class action with the attendant rights and compromises that device entails"). Professors Kahan and Silberman identify drawbacks of the rule announced in *Matsushita*: (1) "[r]educed state class attorney bargaining power"; (2) "[d]efendant's increased ability to engage in plaintiff shopping"; and (3) the "[c]ourt's reduced ability to assess fairness of settlement." Marcel Kahan & Linda Silberman, Matsushita *and Beyond: The Role of State Courts in Class Actions Involving Exclusive Federal Claims*, 1996 Sup. Ct. Rev. 219, 235–46. However, they also identify benefits to having state courts effectuate global settlements, such as: (1) "the state's interest in the matter"; (2) "the efficiency values in a global settlement"; and (3) the fact that "the litigation in the state court may have proceeded much further than the litigation [if any] in the federal courts." *Id.* at 248. Are there other benefits or drawbacks to permitting state courts to effectuate global settlements that include claims that they could not adjudicate?

3. The Ninth Circuit panel in *Epstein III* was sharply divided over the issue of whether the Delaware settlement should bar suit by the *Epstein* plaintiffs. What are the policy implications of each approach?

4. One issue upon which all three Ninth Circuit judges disagreed is whether the Supreme Court in fact decided the issue in *Epstein III* in the course of the *Matsushita* decision: O'Scannlain (yes); Wiggins ("not conclusively" but "it did send unmistakable signals"); Thomas (no). What arguments support each of these judges?

5. The Supreme Court recently addressed another type of clash between state and federal law that, while not sounding in Full Faith and Credit, raises analogous concerns. In *Shady Grove Orthopedic Associates, P.A. v. Allstate Insurance Co.*, 130 S. Ct. 1431 (2010), the Court held that a plaintiff may maintain a class action that satisfies Rule 23 in federal court under diversity jurisdiction, even if the forum state's law would forbid a class action in state court, so long as the state law is not "intimately bound up in the scope of a substantive right or remedy." *Id.* at 1458.

Medical provider Shady Grove Orthopedic Associates brought a putative class action against automobile insurer Allstate Insurance Company for alleged violation of New York's no-fault auto insurance law. Shady Grove sued in federal district court pursuant to CAFA's diversity jurisdiction provision, 28 U.S.C. § 1332(d)(2)(A), seeking statutory interest penalties on overdue payments of insurance benefits owed to plaintiffs. The federal district court dismissed the case on the grounds that Section 901(b) of New York Civil Practice Law and Rules (CPLR 901(b)) prohibits class action suits seeking to recover a statutory penalty or minimum recovery, unless otherwise explicitly authorized by the statute.

On appeal to the Second Circuit, Shady Grove objected that the *Erie* doctrine precluded a federal court from applying a state procedural rule that would limit the use of a procedural device—*i.e.*, the class action—otherwise available under the Federal Rules of Civil Procedure. Shady Grove further argued that, in any event, New York's insurance law fell within 901(b)'s exception, allowing for class actions where a statute explicitly authorizes them. *Shady Grove Orthopedic Associates, P.A. v. Allstate Ins. Co.*, 549 F.3d 137, 141 (2d Cir. 2008), *rev'd*, 559 U.S. 393 (2010). The Second Circuit disagreed and affirmed the district court ruling.

The Supreme Court reversed, holding that Rule 23 governs class actions in federal court and trumps conflicting state laws. The majority opinion was written by Justice Scalia. (Justice Stevens concurred, but with some limiting language.) The majority first concluded that New York's law conflicted with Federal Rule 23:

> Rule 23 unambiguously authorizes *any* plaintiff, in *any* federal civil proceeding, to maintain a class action if the Rule's prerequisites are met. We cannot contort its text, even to avert a collision with state law that might render it invalid.

559 U.S. at 406 (emphases in original).

The majority then concluded that Rule 23 was valid under the Rules Enabling Act (28 U.S.C. § 2072(b)), which prohibits a federal procedural rule from abridging, enlarging, or modifying any rights. This second conclusion, however, was comprised of a plurality and concurrence espousing different rationales.

The dissent, written by Justice Ginsburg, argued that New York's law addressed an "entirely different concern" (*i.e.*, remedies and substance) than Rule 23 (*i.e.*, class action certification and conduct), and rejected the notion of an "inevitable collision" between the statutes. 559 U.S. at 449 (Ginsburg, J., dissenting).

What is the likely impact of *Shady Grove*? The Court itself acknowledged that forum shopping was possible. Where federal rules preempt inhospitable state rules, plaintiffs will gravitate towards federal court. *See id.* at 415–16 ("We must acknowledge the reality that keeping the federal-court door open to class actions that cannot proceed in state court will produce forum shopping.");

id. at 456 (Ginsburg, J., dissenting) ("[F]orum shopping will undoubtedly result if a plaintiff need only file in federal instead of state court to seek a massive monetary award explicitly barred by state law."). *Shady Grove*, in conjunction with CAFA, may contribute to the increase in class actions being filed in federal court based on state-law claims. The confluence of state class action prohibitions and CAFA's expanded federal diversity jurisdiction may transform the federal courts into a "mecca"—as Justice Ginsburg put it—for such class actions. *Id.* at 459 (Ginsburg, J., dissenting). For a discussion of *Shady Grove's* potential impact, *see* Adam N. Steinman, *Our Class Action Federalism:* Erie *and the Rules Enabling Act After* Shady Grove, 86 Notre Dame L. Rev. 1131 (2011).

3. THE "*ROOKER–FELDMAN*" DOCTRINE

KAMILEWICZ V. BANK OF BOS. CORP.
United States Court of Appeals, Seventh Circuit, 1996.
92 F.3d 506.

Before CUMMINGS, RIPPLE, and EVANS, CIRCUIT JUDGES.

EVANS, CIRCUIT JUDGE.

A class action in Alabama cost Dexter Kamilewicz $91.33 in attorney fees to recover $2.19 on the merits. When he learned of this news, he and the other plaintiffs (his wife and Martha Preston) sued the class action attorneys (as well as certain defendants in the Alabama action) in the District Court for the Northern District of Illinois. There, to add to their chagrin, they ran up against another obstacle—the *Rooker–Feldman* doctrine. This is their appeal from an order dismissing their federal case for lack of subject matter jurisdiction.

Kamilewicz and the other plaintiffs have had mortgages serviced by BancBoston Mortgage Corporation, one of the defendants. They were among an estimated 715,000 members of a class in a nationwide class action filed in the circuit court for Mobile County, Alabama. The suit—*Hoffman, et al. v. BancBoston Mortgage Corp.*—challenged the manner in which BancBoston calculated the amount of surplus each member of the class was required to maintain in their escrow accounts. Deposits to the escrow accounts were paid as part of the class members' monthly mortgage payments. There was no question regarding the ultimate ownership of the surplus; it belonged to the mortgagor and was to be returned when the mortgage debt was satisfied. The issue in the lawsuit was the propriety of BancBoston's holding the surplus until the time it would be returned to the mortgagor.

In October 1993, the Alabama court granted partial summary judgment in favor of the plaintiff class. The court found that BancBoston's practice was, in fact, inconsistent with the terms of the mortgages. Then in October 1995, counsel for the class prepared a notice of a proposed settlement of the suit. The notice stated that the settlement was "fair, reasonable, adequate, and in the best interests of the class" and that the attorney fees sought were "reasonable" and would "not exceed one-third of the economic benefit" to the class. Bank of Boston—one of the defendants—objected to the notice because it failed to advise the class that there were "substantial adverse effects" to the proposed settlement.

Those perceived adverse effects were that if BancBoston were ordered to refund the escrow surplus and if the attorneys for the class were to seek attorney fees out of the refund, some class members would suffer an out-of-pocket loss as a result of the lawsuit. It should be noted here that the Bank of Boston and BancBoston had offered, prior to the grant of partial summary judgment in 1993, to settle the litigation. As part of that proposed settlement, the bank and BancBoston would have had to pay $500,000 in attorney fees out of the banks' own funds, and the entire amount of the escrow refund would have gone to the class members.

Nevertheless, the Alabama court approved the proposed notice and held a fairness hearing * * * [and] approved the settlement, under which the class members received one-time interest payments ranging from $0.00 to $8.76. The court also found the attorney fees reasonable. The fee award was a percentage of the escrow accounts, or, the complaint in the present case asserts, in excess of $14 million. * * * Under the settlement, BancBoston deducted attorney fees from the class members' escrow accounts. The deduction was recorded on the 1994 annual tax and interest statements as a "miscellaneous disbursement." In most cases, the "miscellaneous disbursement" was more—far more—than the interest refund. It was this statement that, understandably, caught Mr. Kamilewicz's eye.

Unhappy with the peculiar result of the class action suit in Alabama, Mr. and Mrs. Kamilewicz and Ms. Preston filed the present federal class action against the bank and the mortgage company, and the plaintiffs' attorneys in the Alabama action. The complaint contained allegations of violations of the Racketeer Influenced and Corrupt Organizations Act and of the Civil Rights Act, as well as claims of common law fraud, negligent misrepresentation, attorney malpractice, breach of fiduciary duty, and conversion. In turn, the defendants in the federal case filed a motion with the Alabama court seeking an order directed to the Kamilewicz plaintiffs to show cause why they were not bound by the [settlement] order of that court. A hearing was scheduled in Alabama, to which the Kamilewicz plaintiffs sent an attorney for the purpose of stating that they would not participate in the hearing because they contested whether Alabama had personal jurisdiction over them. * * * [In a 1996 order, t]he Alabama court reaffirmed the order of settlement.

Meanwhile, back in Chicago, * * * Judge Paul Plunkett of the Northern District of Illinois had entered his order dismissing the federal case for lack of subject matter jurisdiction. He found that even though the federal case was "dressed up" as a claim for RICO damages or for attorney malpractice, it was, nevertheless, a collateral attack on a state court judgment which would require that he consider issues "inextricably intertwined" with the state court case. This he was prohibited to do, he concluded, under the doctrine known as *Rooker–Feldman*.

We * * * find ourselves in agreement with the district court.

We first note that the exact ground on which the plaintiffs and, for that matter, the *amici*, who are attorneys general from several states, stand in this appeal is a little like shifting sand. The plaintiffs argue that the judgment of the Alabama court is null and void because the court did not have personal jurisdiction over them and that the special protections required for class actions—notice, adequate representation, etc.—were not complied with. However, they also say that they are not seeking to overturn the Alabama judgment. Then, they state that where the district court went wrong was to use a state court judgment which was "null and void" as the basis for the *Rooker–Feldman* bar. In addition, plaintiffs veer into a claim that the * * * Alabama court order [reaffirming the settlement] cannot be a basis for the *Rooker–Feldman* bar because there was no personal jurisdiction over them, and furthermore that fraud claims are somehow outside the *Rooker–Feldman* bar. The *amici* say that they do not want to establish an exception to the general rule that absent class members may be bound by a nationwide class action settlement, but that on the unusual—and egregious—facts of this case, the Kamilewicz action should be allowed to proceed.

* * * At its core, the [*Rooker–Feldman*] doctrine is a recognition of the principle that the inferior federal courts generally do not have the power to exercise appellate review over state court decisions. In *Rooker,* the Supreme Court stated that because the jurisdiction of the federal district courts was strictly original, those courts cannot reverse or modify a state court judgment—even if that judgment is wrong. Only the Supreme Court has that power. *Feldman* involved proceedings denying him a waiver of a bar admission rule which required that applicants have graduated from an approved law school. The first issue was whether the action constituted a judicial proceeding. The Court determined that it was in fact such a proceeding and that a district court "has no authority to review final judgment of a state court in judicial proceedings."

It becomes necessary to our analysis, then, to determine whether what the federal court was asked to do in this case was, essentially, review a decision of a state court. Our cases offer means by which that determination is made. We ask whether the federal plaintiff seeks to set aside a state court judgment or whether he is, in fact, presenting an independent claim. Put another way, if the injury which the federal plaintiff alleges resulted from the state court judgment itself, then *Rooker–Feldman* controls, and the lower federal courts lack jurisdiction over the claim. It does not matter that the state court judgment might be erroneous or even unconstitutional. Nor does it matter that the time for appeal to the United States Supreme Court may have passed.

In addition, the state and federal cases also do not need to be directly on point. The Court found a lack of jurisdiction in *Feldman* itself when the federal constitutional claims were "inextricably intertwined" with the state court judgment. As we have explained, lower federal courts might be engaging in impermissible appellate review even when asked to entertain a claim that was not argued in the state court but was "inextricably intertwined" with the state court judgment.

* * *

* * * As a preliminary matter, we note that the Alabama court specifically found the settlement to be fair and approved the fees. In [approving the settlement], the state judge found that the notice complied with all requirements of due process, that the consent decree was fair and reasonable, and that the attorney fees were reasonable.

Plaintiffs seem to be urging us to reach the conclusion that we can overturn the decision of the Alabama court insofar as it involved a determination that procedural due process was complied with. As support for this proposition, they rely on decisions which hold that a party can attack a default judgment against him if it is entered by a court without personal jurisdiction over him. We see significant differences between default judgments and the judgment under attack here. We reject the plaintiffs' far-reaching proposed exception to the *Rooker–Feldman* doctrine.

Another argument which seems slightly off-center is that the 1996 order [reaffirming the settlement and] finding the allegations of fraud "baseless," is not subject to a *Rooker–Feldman* bar because it was entered in the absence of personal jurisdiction over the plaintiffs and it was entered after the federal lawsuit was filed. This argument is tied to the claim that the plaintiffs were precluded from litigating their fraud claim in the state court, and thus were required to—or had a right to—litigate it in federal court.

The [second] order itself is not material to the issues before us. It is not necessary to rely on it to determine that the federal lawsuit was properly dismissed. The fact is that the proper court for an assertion of fraud in the procurement of a judgment is the one which rendered the judgment. * * * Alabama has a procedure by which a litigant can assert an independent action for fraud upon the court within three years of the entry of the fraudulently induced judgment. In addition, the Alabama court retained continuing jurisdiction over the class action. It is not for the federal court to decide these issues.

* * *

The Kamilewiczes were class member/plaintiffs in the Alabama suit. The part of the judgment they are unhappy with is the approval of the settlement as to the fees to be paid to their attorneys—fees which were assessed against them. * * * [T]he plaintiffs' injuries are a result of the state court judgment. Their claim in federal court is a multi-pronged attack on the approval of the settlement regarding the attorney fees issue. Regardless of which of the specific federal claims the district court were to consider, it would run directly into the state court finding, entered after a two-day fairness hearing—that the fees were reasonable. The federal claims are "inextricably intertwined" with the state court judgment, whether that judgment is right or wrong.

We won't deny that the Alabama judgment seems questionable on the surface. How can it be right that a plaintiff should recover less than $10 and have to pay nearly $100 in fees? But how can we—or the district court—know that we would have ruled another way? To determine that, we would have to go through the steps already taken in the state court—precisely what lower federal courts are not allowed to do under *Rooker–Feldman*. And perhaps if we undertook that analysis we would find that some less tangible economic benefit to the class justified the settlement.

That the facts seem at least superficially egregious brings us to the arguments of *amici* that on facts such as these an exception of some undefined sort should be carved out, and that if the plaintiff class was actually in the position of defendants on the attorney fees issue, then even under

Phillips Petroleum Co. v. Shutts, 472 U.S. 797 (1985), perhaps personal jurisdiction was lacking in the Alabama court. We decline to take the step urged by the *amici*.

In *Shutts*, the Court loosened somewhat the requirements for assertion of personal jurisdiction over members of a plaintiff class and determined that due process would be satisfied if there was notice, an opportunity to appear in person or by counsel, an opportunity to opt out of the class, and adequate representation. The rationale was, in part, that absent plaintiffs ordinarily do not face the same exposure as defendants. *Amici* argue that if on the attorney fees issue the *Kamilewicz* plaintiffs were actually in the position of defendants, then due process requires that issues of personal jurisdiction be assessed under the traditional minimum contacts analysis of *International Shoe Co. v. Washington*, 326 U.S. 310 (1945).

Even were we to accept the argument, it does not change the fact that lower federal courts cannot review decisions of the state court. Here, the state court approved the settlement, including the fees. The Supreme Court of Alabama or the United States Supreme Court could reverse the decision were either so inclined. The federal district court, on the other hand, cannot review the Alabama decision. We also note the obvious—that the posture of the Alabama case is not unique. In class actions, often the fees are a percentage of the award granted to the plaintiff class. The argument of *amici*, if accepted, could have ramifications far beyond this case.

Because we agree that *Rooker–Feldman* bars this action, the judgment of the district court is AFFIRMED.

NOTES AND QUESTIONS

1. What are the purposes of the *Rooker–Feldman* doctrine? Does the panel decision promote those purposes?

2. Should the *Kamilewicz* plaintiffs be permitted to bring their action in federal court? Were any other options available to the *Kamilewicz* plaintiffs for seeking redress?

3. Since *Kamilewicz*, the Supreme Court has emphasized the narrow scope of the *Rooker–Felman* doctrine:

> Neither *Rooker* nor *Feldman* elaborated a rationale for a wide-reaching bar on the jurisdiction of lower federal courts, and our cases since *Feldman* have tended to emphasize the narrowness of the *Rooker–Feldman* rule. See *Exxon Mobil Corp. v. Saudi Basic Indus. Corp.*, 544 U.S. 280, 292 (2005) (*Rooker–Feldman* does not apply to parallel state and federal litigation); *Verizon Md. Inc. v. Public Serv. Comm'n of Md.*, 535 U.S. 635, 644 n.3 (2002) (*Rooker–Feldman* "has no application to judicial review of executive action, including determinations made by a state administrative agency"); *Johnson v. De Grandy*, 512 U.S. 997, 1005–06 (1994) (*Rooker–Feldman* does not bar actions by a nonparty to the earlier state suit). Indeed, during that period, "this Court has never applied *Rooker–Feldman* to dismiss an action for want of jurisdiction." *Exxon Mobil*, *supra* at 287.
>
> In *Exxon Mobil* * * * we warned that the lower courts have at times extended *Rooker–Feldman* "far beyond the contours of the *Rooker* and *Feldman* cases, overriding Congress' conferral of federal-court jurisdiction concurrent with jurisdiction exercised by state

courts, and superseding the ordinary application of preclusion law pursuant to 28 U.S.C. § 1738." 544 U.S. at 283. *Rooker–Feldman*, we explained, is a narrow doctrine, confined to "cases brought by state-court losers complaining of injuries caused by state-court judgments rendered before the district court proceedings commenced and inviting district court review and rejection of those judgments." 544 U.S. at 284.

Lance v. Dennis, 546 U.S. 459, 464 (2006); *see also id.* at 466 ("*Rooker–Feldman* does not bar actions by nonparties to the earlier state-court judgment simply because, for purposes of preclusion law, they could be considered in privity with a party to the judgment."). Would the *Kamilewicz* plaintiffs still be barred from challenging the Alabama state court action under the doctrine today?

4. The *Kamilewicz* plaintiffs filed a petition for rehearing and suggestion for rehearing *en banc*, which was denied over a strongly-worded dissent by Judge Easterbrook, joined by Chief Judge Posner and Circuit Judges Manion, Rovner, and Wood. *Kamilewicz v. Bank of Boston Corp.*, 100 F.3d 1348 (7th Cir. 1996). Judge Easterbrook argued that the *Rooker–Feldman* doctrine could not apply to bar a subsequent malpractice suit. *Id.* at 1352–53 ("Suing faithless agents [*i.e.*, former class counsel] is far from the core of the *Rooker–Feldman* doctrine, which should not be extended to block suits like this.").

After the Supreme Court denied a petition for a writ of *certiorari* to review the Seventh Circuit decision, Edelman & Combs, the lawyers who had brought and settled the original (*Hoffman*) class action, sued the individuals who had brought the *Kamilewicz* case (Dexter Kamilewicz, his wife, and Martha Preston) and the lawyers who had represented them in that case. The *Edelman* suit—which alleged a variety of claims including malicious prosecution—was brought, predictably, in the same Mobile, Alabama Circuit Court that had approved the *Hoffman* settlement. The individuals and the attorneys moved to dismiss the action, but the state trial court denied that motion. The individuals (but not their attorneys) petitioned the Alabama Supreme Court for a writ of mandamus, and that court issued the writ, finding that the Alabama court lacked personal jurisdiction over the individuals. *Ex Parte Dexter J. Kamilewicz*, 700 So.2d 340, 344–45 (Ala. 1997). The attorney-defendants eventually settled.

But that was not the end of the story. The Vermont Attorney General filed a lawsuit alleging that the Bank of Boston defendants had violated Vermont state law on numerous grounds. The defendants objected that Vermont class members could not collaterally attack the Alabama judgment. The trial court granted summary judgment to defendants, but the Vermont Supreme Court reversed, characterizing the Alabama action as a "drive-by" class action that did not adequately protect or compensate class members. *Vermont v. Homeside Lending, Inc.*, 826 A.2d 997 (Vt. 2003). The Vermont Supreme Court ruled that *Phillips Petroleum Co. v. Shutts*, 472 U.S. 797 (1985), had left open the question of whether an absent plaintiff's failure to opt out after receiving notice suffices to establish jurisdiction over that plaintiff in a multistate class action where the class action would impose particularized burdens on the plaintiff. That question was presented here, since Vermont class members were essentially a "defendant class" concerning the attorneys' claims for fees from class members' escrow accounts. *Homeside Lending*, 826 A.2d at 1008. The Vermont Supreme Court concluded that opt-out notice does not suffice when class members "face personal liability rather than loss of their [cause] of action." *Id.* The

Vermont Supreme Court further found that the notice provided to class members was inadequate because it did not disclose that many class members would end up with fee obligations exceeding the benefit of the settlement. *Id.* at 1011. And the class representatives and class counsel were inadequate representatives: the class representatives' receipt of incentive awards "aligned [them] with the attorneys for the class against the class," *id.* at 1013, and class counsel had economic interests that put them in conflict with class members. *Id.* at 1013–16.

5. As discussed in Chapter 8(A)(7), CAFA's settlement provisions specifically address net-loss settlements. The *Kamilewicz* case was the subject of extensive testimony during the hearings that led to CAFA. *See* S. Rep. No. 109–14, at 14–15 (discussing testimony); Chapter 8(A)(7).

Chapter 8

Resolution and Funding of Class Actions

■ ■ ■

This chapter addresses issues that arise in the course of resolving and funding class actions. First, the chapter discusses a host of issues surrounding the settlement of class actions. Class action settlements are among the most frequently litigated aspects of class action practice, and the United States Supreme Court has weighed in with two major decisions. Second, the chapter addresses the array of remedies—both monetary and nonmonetary—available in class action cases. Third, the chapter discusses awards of attorneys' fees in class actions. The main focus is on the two principal methods for calculating fees: the "lodestar" approach and the "percentage-of-the-fund" method. Fourth, the chapter addresses third-party litigation financing. Fifth, the chapter addresses the use of alternative dispute resolution (or "ADR") in class actions. ADR is an increasingly important, but sometimes controversial, tool for administering and resolving multi-party litigation. A key component of the arbitration topic is the body of case law addressing agreements requiring arbitration and prohibiting class actions.

A. CLASS ACTION SETTLEMENTS

In non-class litigation, court approval of settlements ordinarily is not required. When a class action is settled, however, the rules are different. Rule 23(e)(1) states that "[t]he claims, issues, or defenses of a certified class may be settled, voluntarily dismissed, or compromised only with the court's approval." Rule 23(e) provides relatively little guidance about either the reasons for requiring court approval or the procedural implications. Many of the critical issues, however, are developed in the case law and explored below.

1. INTERESTED PARTICIPANTS

In comparison to traditional one-on-one litigation, settlement negotiations in class actions are necessarily more complex. At the outset, it is important to note some entities with direct stakes in the outcome.

The Defendant. The defendant may want vindication at trial, and it may feel that settlement would set a bad precedent for other, similar suits in the future. Thus, a defendant may want to try the case. Yet:

> [t]he defendant has both direct and indirect financial incentives to settle. Its most direct and immediate financial objectives are to minimize the amount of the damages eventually awarded to the class and to reduce litigation expenses. The indirect costs of full-scale litigation, however, can also be consequential. Consumer

goodwill can be harmed by the adverse publicity that often accompanies class action litigation. Also, the possible disclosure of 'dirty linen' during the trial process can damage the defendant's community standing. In addition, the discovery process can disrupt the day-to-day operations of defendant institutions and corporations. By settling, the defendant can minimize most of these indirect costs and avoid the risk of a large damage award.

Note, *Abuse in Plaintiff Class Action Settlements: The Need for a Guardian During Pretrial Settlement Negotiations*, 84 Mich. L. Rev. 308, 312–13 (1985); *see also* Howard M. Downs, *Federal Class Actions: Diminished Protection for the Class and the Case for Reform*, 73 Neb. L. Rev. 646, 686 (1994). A defendant also may be willing to pay class counsel larger fees to reach a settlement that affords the defendant broad preclusive effects in other litigation. *See* Robert B. Gerard & Scott A. Johnson, *The Role of the Objector in Class Action Settlements: A Case Study of the General Motors Truck "Side Saddle" Fuel Tank Litigation*, 31 Loy. L.A. L. Rev. 409, 415–16 (1998).

Recall that during contested class certification proceedings, the defendant usually vigorously challenges whether the requirements of Rule 23(a) and 23(b) have been satisfied. Defendants in contested certification proceedings thus serve in some ways as a surrogate for the absent class members, who would tend to want a class to proceed only if the class representatives will adequately protect absent class members' interests (tested by the adequacy inquiry) and only if trial of the representatives' claims will in fact adjudicate the claims of the class (tested by the commonality, typicality, and predominance/cohesiveness inquiries). When a class action is settled, however, the defendant has incentives to work closely with class counsel to reach an agreement, even if that agreement shortchanges absent class members.

Defense Counsel. In some ways, the interests of defense counsel and the defendants may be aligned, especially when defense counsel is putting the client's interests first, as required by the canons of ethics. An attorney, however, may instead be motivated by the prospect of handling a high-profile case or the possibility of earning hourly fees for an extended period of time, either of which may conflict with the client's interest in pursuing a prompt and early settlement.

When settlement talks commence, defense counsel's interest in securing a low overall settlement for the client may motivate him or her to reach a settlement that is lucrative for plaintiffs' counsel, but not necessarily for the class. *See, e.g.*, John C. Coffee, Jr., *Class Wars: The Dilemma of the Mass Tort Class Action*, 95 Colum. L. Rev. 1343, 1364 (1995) (excerpted in Part (A)(2)(b) of this chapter).

The Class Representatives. Class representatives have a variety of interests. The plaintiffs may sincerely believe that, as representatives of a class, they have a special responsibility to seek the vindication that comes with a victory at trial. Furthermore, and more pragmatically, a trial victory would presumably bring greater rewards for the class than could be secured by settlement. And "[i]f the requirement of adequate representation, including identity of claims, is satisfied, the named representative[s] will be motivated to seek maximum settlement benefits on all claims." Downs, *supra*, 73 Neb. L. Rev. at 684. But class representatives' significant personal interests often counsel in favor of settlement. If, for example, the "representative[s] [are] offered preferences over the absent class members in the settlement plan," the representatives may have particular interests in settlement. *Id.* Moreover, in some circumstances, the named plaintiffs may be responsible for their own attorneys' fees if they lose at trial (*id.*), although this risk is eliminated if they have a fee arrangement with their attorney under which the attorney is reimbursed for fees only if the plaintiffs prevail. Additionally, the named plaintiffs might put their reputations, personal privacy, and peace of mind at risk by continuing litigation through trial. Discovery may itself be intrusive, but more intrusive still is cross-examination at trial in open court by hostile attorneys. And the representatives may ultimately lose their case.

In addition:

> [E]ven if the named representative[s'] interests are congruent with those of the class, the representative[s] may still be powerless to act on behalf of the class during settlement negotiations and approval. The representative[s'] participation is usually minimal both during litigation and during settlement proceedings. The fact that courts are free to ignore any objections to settlement made by the named representative[s] further encourages passivity; class representatives seldom voice their views during settlement negotiations or appear at settlement hearings.

Id.

Class Counsel. Assuming that class counsel is public-spirited, he or she may have a strong interest in vindicating the rights that are being pursued in the class action. In fact, the "public-spiritedness" of class counsel may create tensions with class representatives if the latter want to settle a potential "high impact" case. But even in cases where such potential conflicts do not arise, class counsel's interests may not be entirely congruent with the interests of the class:

> Even if the prospects for success in the litigation are high, the attorney may nonetheless have a strong incentive to settle. * * * [T]he class attorney's financial interest lies in the amount of her award less the time and effort required to produce it. The attorney may therefore benefit more from a "small settlement . . . bearing a higher ratio to the cost of the work than a much larger recovery obtained only after extensive discovery, a long trial and an appeal." Thus, even the prospect of a large recovery may not be sufficient to cause the class attorney to forgo a settlement that is unfavorable to the members of the absentee class.

Note, *supra*, 84 Mich. L. Rev. at 315; *see also* Downs, *supra*, 73 Neb. L. Rev. at 684–86; Mary Kay Kane, *Of Carrots and Sticks: Evaluating the Role of the Class Action Lawyer*, 66 Tex. L. Rev. 385, 395–96 (1987) (identifying conflicts between counsel and class). Moreover, if numerous class actions are pending around the nation addressing the same issues and the same defendant, a "reverse auction" phenomenon may occur:

> If plaintiffs' counsel in a class action take too strident a position in settlement negotiations, the defendant can seek settlement

in class actions filed in other jurisdictions. If other counsel are willing to accept the defendant's deal, the parties enter a settlement, and if the court approves it, the defendant has a judgment entitled to full faith and credit. The defendant can then move for dismissal of all other class actions, leaving the counsel who objected to the settlement without any ability to recover attorneys' fees.

Gerard & Johnson, *supra*, 31 Loy. L.A. L. Rev. at 416.

Insurers. Although often ignored in the analysis:

> Insurance also plays a dominant role in inducing settlement. Defendants generally want to maximize insurance coverage, and negotiating a settlement to frame the case in terms of claims within the scope of coverage is preferable to taking the case to trial, which could expose defendants to uninsured claims. Typical are settlement agreements that are based on the weaker claim of negligent misrepresentation, instead of intentional misrepresentation which is not covered by insurance. Furthermore, limits on insurance coverage encourage settlements within amounts provided under the policy.

Downs, *supra*, 73 Neb. L. Rev. at 686–87. Indeed, because of their financial interest in the outcome, insurers often get closely involved in the class action settlement process and may actively attempt to shape the ultimate agreement.

Objectors. In some circumstances, one or more class members may come forward as "objectors" to challenge the substantive or procedural fairness of the proposed settlement. In the words of counsel for objectors in one high-profile case:

> The objector's role in preventing collusive settlements is relatively simple. Rule 23(e) requires that parties to a class action settlement obtain court approval of the settlement. The objector must, therefore, attempt to convince the court to reject the settlement by showing that the settlement is not in the class's interests or that it is the product of collusion between class counsel and the defendants. As an outsider—someone without a stake in the attorneys' fee award—the objector provides an unbiased view of the settlement to a court that will otherwise see only a smooth presentation by the defendants' attorneys and class counsel claiming that the settlement is fair and reasonable and the product of hard-fought negotiations.
>
> The objector's role can be very costly and risky. Settlement fairness hearings are often heard in remote areas of the country and involve complexities and procedural requirements that usually necessitate representation by counsel. And the objector can be subject to vigorous attack by the proponents of the settlement, who often have a strong financial interest in seeing the settlement approved.
>
> Certain temptations further complicate the objector's role. A defendant attempting to avoid massive exposure, and class counsel looking to receive a huge award of fees, may try to "buy off" the

objector—in exchange for cash payment to the objector or his counsel, the objector agrees to withdraw his objections, or even voice approval of the settlement. In light of the uncompensated expenses an objector incurs, the buy-off offer is tempting and often significant.

Gerard & Johnson, *supra*, 31 Loy. L.A. L. Rev. at 416–17. Consider as well the views of one student commentator:

> All too often * * * the individual class member has little interest in his potential recovery, and brings an objection only to delay approval of a proposed settlement. With the defendant seeking to extinguish its liability and class counsel seeking approval of its fee award, there is enormous incentive to pay off the objector to facilitate approval of the settlement. These settling objectors are often referred to as "professional objectors."
>
> Professional objectors bring objections solely to extort a side settlement from class counsel. The standard tactic is to file an objection and threaten to pursue it unless a fee is paid in exchange for its withdrawal. Typically, class-action objectors complain that the class recovery is too low or that the attorney's fee award is too high. These objections often have settlement value, not because they truly threaten the class settlement, but because they multiply litigation costs or obstruct the payment of settlement funds to the class and class counsel. * * *
>
> Not surprisingly, professional objectors have become an object of scorn among legal scholars. Their opportunistic and sometimes extortionist behavior has understandably led to increasing skepticism of objector side settlements and widespread condemnation of professional objectors, whom commentators have described as shakedown artists, leeches, and extortionists. The general criticism of these objectors is that they reduce judicial efficiency by tying up litigation in order to profit from the nuisance value of their objection. Further, they are said to violate fairness norms by creating dissimilar treatment for similarly situated class members. Finally, critics argue that settling objectors create incentive for class counsel to violate ethical duties toward the class by buying off class members who would otherwise challenge the settlement.

Mike Absmeier, Note, *The Professional Objector and Revised Rule 23*, 24 Rev. Litig. 609, 610–11 (2005). As discussed in Section 8 below, proposed changes to Rule 23 address problems with serial objectors.

The Court. Courts have an interest in seeing justice done in the individual case, but it is also true that a court may have an interest in clearing its docket—particularly in getting rid of burdensome and intractable cases. *See, e.g.*, Downs, *supra*, 73 Neb. L. Rev. at 687 ("Settlement approval allows the court to quickly resolve hundreds of claims and clear the calendar."). Thus, courts are generally inclined to encourage the parties to settle. Moreover, even if the court intends to perform its tasks with diligence, it may not have sufficient information to assess the fairness of a proposed settlement. Furthermore, courts face substantial practical pressures to approve a proposed settlement, given the parties' expenditures in the settlement process itself. Indeed, Judge Jack B. Weinstein, a prominent district court judge who has adjudicated and resolved numerous class actions (see Chapter 4(E)(1)) made the latter point with his co-author:

> A critical problem is that fairness hearings often come too late to be very useful. By the time the hearings are held, millions of dollars and great effort have already been expended building toward an agreed upon resolution. Aside from the demoralizing effects rejection of the settlement would have on the attorneys and the parties, a late date rejection is wasteful of resources and may introduce unacceptable delays in compensating members of the class.

Jack B. Weinstein & Karin S. Schwartz, *Notes from the Cave: Some Problems of Judges in Dealing With Class Action Settlements*, 163 F.R.D. 369, 375 (1995); *see also* Downs, *supra*, 73 Neb. L. Rev. at 687 ("[C]onstraints on time and resources severely limit the courts' ability to evaluate the scope of class claims, remedies, issues, and the course of settlement negotiations. Courts are generally captive to whatever assertions are made by counsel, and independent investigations by the courts into the fairness of settlements seldom occur.").

Legislative and Executive Entities. Even when a class action settlement does not involve a government actor as a party, legislative and executive entities on the state or federal level may well have a significant interest in how a major class action settlement is negotiated and how proceeds are ultimately divided. *See, e.g.*, Carrie Menkel–Meadow, *Ethics and the Settlement of Mass Torts: When the Rules Meet the Road*, 80 Cornell L. Rev. 1159, 1186 (1995) (discussing potential legislative and administrative interest in settlement of mass torts). They may be considering legislation or administrative action, or they may have constituents who will be directly impacted by any resolution of the dispute. Indeed, administrative agencies (such as the Equal Employment Opportunity Commission) may attempt to intervene—or may even be appointed—to represent the interests of the class. Recognizing the potential interest of state and federal officials in class action settlements, the Class Action Fairness Act requires parties to provide notice of proposed settlements to certain officials (see Part (A)(7) of this chapter).

Absent Class Members. In some respects, although absent class members may benefit from a lucrative settlement, they may have strong interests in continuing the litigation if there is any prospect of prevailing at trial. The class ordinarily consists of persons who did not sue—and would not have sued—on their own because they thought the costs of seeking recovery outweighed the value of their potential recovery. But the institution of a class action on their behalf has reduced those costs significantly, if not practically eliminated them. Moreover, absent class members face neither the potential stress, burden, invasion of privacy, and embarrassment of testimony and cross-examination at trial that their representatives confront, nor the revenue/cost calculus of class counsel. *See* Downs, *supra*, 73 Neb. L. Rev. at 687 ("Absent members of the class face very little risk in going to trial and tend to be more concerned with the merits of the claim and the net recovery. They have little or no burden in terms of discovery, little risk of counterclaims, no need to deal directly with attorneys, and they incur little cost."). Additionally, because they have not been nearly as involved in the litigation as class counsel or even the named representatives, absent class members may have an overly optimistic view of the likelihood of success at trial. Thus, there is a real potential that absent class members may want to proceed with a class action when the class representatives and class counsel do not. Yet, as noted above, unless objectors come forward or some other representative is appointed, absent class members' interests may not be fully represented during settlement negotiations.

In studying the following materials, consider how the interests identified above have influenced both the dynamics of class action settlements and the development of the law. At the end of the settlement discussion (section 8), the text discusses a variety of proposed changes to Rule 23 dealing with settlement.

2. NEGOTIATION OF CLASS ACTION SETTLEMENTS

Class action settlements generally involve more parties—and more competing interests—than settlements in traditional, two-party cases. As a result, a number of complicated issues frequently arise. Below, three different influences on the negotiation process are explored in depth: the issue of intra-class conflicts, the possibility of conflicts between class counsel and their clients, and the possible role of the judge in fostering settlement.

a. Intra-Class Conflicts

NANCY MORAWETZ, BARGAINING, CLASS REPRESENTATION, AND FAIRNESS
54 Ohio St. L.J. 1, 13, 18–21, 23–25 (1993).

* * * [I]t is useful to set out in greater depth some dimensions of divergent interests that are at the heart of the intra-class dilemmas in class action settlements, and the way that these divergent interests are manifested in the choices that class counsel face during a negotiation.

A. Valuation of Forms of Relief

An essential first step in any negotiation is to assess the interests of one's client and the value that the client places on alternative forms of relief. This assessment serves as the crucial backdrop to brain-storming about ways in which the settlement can be structured to best meet the client's interests, and comparing possible settlements with the client's best alternative to a negotiated agreement. Identification of the client's interests is also crucial to the development of non-zero sum solutions to the dispute. * * *

In the class context, ranking possible outcomes is difficult because members of the client group may place very different value on different forms of relief. Even in a situation in which there are only two forms of possible relief, members of the class may disagree as to which they prefer. The problem is made all the more complex when attorneys seek to think creatively about alternative forms of relief. The greater the range of possible relief, the greater the opportunity for divergences in class members' preferences.

* * *

* * * [P]roblems of valuation are not addressed by the traditional procedural mechanisms of class certification, subclassing, and opt out procedures. * * * For example, the definition will not state "all persons affected by XYZ policy who prefer cash relief" or "who place high value on an early settlement." Similarly, the class definition will not reflect class members' concern with the justice of the outcome in terms of punishing the defendant or ensuring that the relief is in some way costly for the defendant. Nor would addressing all of the potential differences in the ways class members value relief be appropriate, given the judicial economy objective underlying the class action rule.

Class definitions also will not address ways in which class members value a form of relief that does not arise from a meritorious legal claim. If the concerns are not cognizable legal claims, a class definition ignores them, even if they might be of greater importance to members of the plaintiff class. In a case concerning procedures regarding a government benefits program, for example, the class may be more concerned with the substantive outcome of applications than with the degree of procedural fairness achieved. * * *

Division of a class into subclasses is also a limited solution. Subclassing has all of the problems of class definitions as a method of circumventing the dilemmas of class counsel. It cannot address any interests that would not form a part of a class definition. * * * Relying on subclassing for all of the myriad ways in which class members' interests could potentially differ could add substantial amounts to the cost of the litigation, and serve to bar relief altogether. Furthermore, while separate counsel for subclasses can protect against the sacrificing of the interests of a subclass, they can also act as an inhibitor to relief simply because of the sheer complexity of negotiations among large numbers of persons.

Opt out procedures are also inadequate to resolve the fairness problems raised by differing valuations. Opting out offers class members an either/or choice—they can participate in the class representation or attempt to vindicate their claims on their own. Because independent representation is costly, many class members do not in fact have a choice. If the claims of the class members are too small to justify separate representation or the class members lack the resources to obtain such representation, opting out only protects the technical right to sue. Relief depends instead on remaining in the class. Thus, while opt out mechanisms may provide a veneer of fairness, because the class member can be seen as having chosen to be represented by class counsel, significant distributional fairness issues remain.
* * *

B. Strength of Claims

In addition to determining what the client values, an essential step in designing a negotiation strategy is to assess the strength of the client's case and the probable outcome of continuing to pursue litigation. The litigation alternatives might include, for example, postponing negotiations pending further factual development or motion practice, or proceeding to a judicial resolution of the case on the merits. The attorney analyzes these options so as to be able to counsel the client about the choice between accepting and rejecting a proposed agreement. The alternatives serve as a standard against which a settlement can be measured.

Because a class action does not involve the interests of a single client, the evaluation of alternatives to settlement is quite complex. Although class certification standards provide some assurance of common claims, there are many ways in which the strength of class members' claims, and their interests in pursuing alternatives to settlement, may differ. * * * Furthermore, the legal context of the case may change during the litigation, revealing differences in the strength of the claims that were not apparent at the start of the litigation. * * *

When there are differences in the strength of claims, some members of the class will be at greater risk in the absence of a settlement than others. If a proposed settlement reflects the relative merits of the claims, it may leave some class members with little to lose by going forward, while others have little to gain. A problem for the class action attorney is how to evaluate the differing interests of class members with respect to both the possible settlement and the alternatives to settlement. * * *

* * *

C. Participation in Relief

In addition to complicating the basic assessment of settlement value and alternatives to settlement, class action negotiations raise some problematic issues that do not arise in bi-polar cases. Two common issues in class action settlements are procedures for alerting class members to the availability of relief and procedures for determining how much relief is accorded to each class member. Both of these issues raise important distributional questions.

All settlements that involve any kind of restitution or money award will include some procedure for members of the class to be notified of their right to come forward for relief. Injunctive settlements may also involve procedures to assure that class members are aware of their rights and able to benefit from the terms of the settlement. Although case law provides some minimum standards for such notices and procedures, their specific content, as negotiated by the parties, can greatly affect the number of class members who actually receive relief. * * *

Procedural provisions raise a particular tension for an attorney balancing responsibilities to an entire class because the cost of the settlement for the party opposing the class will often depend on the number of persons who will be participating in the settlement. In cases in which there is no fixed fund, procedural provisions that result in fewer participants will reduce the overall cost of the agreement to the defendant. Similarly, in cases in which a fixed fund is allocated among members of a class, procedures leading to fewer participants in the settlement will result in greater relief to those class members who respond to those procedures.

Tensions regarding the inclusiveness of a settlement arise even if the procedure for reaching class members is of no extra cost, or is of lower cost. For example, writing a notice in language that is easier to understand may yield a greater response from class members, and add nothing to the notice costs of a settlement. Costly procedures may also operate to make settlements less inclusive, rather than more inclusive. For example, complex procedures for proving class membership can serve to discourage a response from class members, while at the same time being more expensive to administer. * * *

Another issue that arises in class settlements is the choice of mechanism for gearing the relief to the individual circumstances of the member of the class. These mechanisms have been described as "bureaucratic" methods for providing some measure of tailored relief. * * * They do not provide the parties with an opportunity to make the kind of particularized factual showing that they would be able to make if they presented their case in court. On the other hand, they may spare members of the class from the difficult hurdle of meeting judicial evidentiary standards.

The issue facing the attorney is not simply whether to adopt such streamlined proof mechanisms, but which proof mechanisms to choose. * * *

b. Attorney Conflicts of Interest

Writing in 1995, Professor John Coffee identified potential conflicts of interest between plaintiffs' attorneys and their clients in mass tort cases. Consider the following excerpt.

JOHN C. COFFEE, JR., CLASS WARS: THE DILEMMA OF THE MASS TORT CLASS ACTION
95 Colum. L. Rev. 1343, 1367–73, 1375–79, 1381–83 (1995).

* * *

* * * The "*Old*" Collusion

Collusion within the class action context essentially requires an agreement—actual or implicit—by which the defendants receive a "cheaper" than arm's length settlement and the plaintiffs' attorneys receive in some form an above-market attorneys' fee. The mechanics of such an agreement varies with the litigation context. In the corporate and securities litigation settings, the standard means has been the nonpecuniary settlement: the plaintiff sues for money damages, but the final settlement awards only therapeutic relief—new bylaws, additional disclosure to shareholders, and other frequently cosmetic changes. In return for this bloodless settlement, defendants either pay the plaintiffs' attorneys' fees themselves or agree not to contest the plaintiffs' attorneys' application for court-awarded fees from the corporation. In the latter case, the plaintiff shareholder class suffers twice: first, by the abandonment of their claim for money damages, and second, by the payment of a fee by their corporation to a plaintiffs' attorney who has not performed any valuable service.

In the mass tort and antitrust contexts, a variation on the nonpecuniary settlement (known informally as a "scrip settlement") has become popular, involving discount coupons or certificates granting the injured class the right to buy the defendant's product at a discount. Often, the discount is no greater than what an individual plaintiff could receive for a volume purchase, or for a cash sale, or for using a particular credit card, and typically restrictions are placed on its transferability. * * *

Another recent variation, known as a "*cy pres* settlement," involves making a payment in kind of goods or services, not to the plaintiff class but to a third party (often a charity) for the indirect benefit of the class. [*See* Part (B)(2)(b) of this chapter.] A 1994 case, *In re Matzo Food Products Litigation*, 156 F.R.D. 600 (D.N.J. 1994), illustrates this pattern. Convicted under the Sherman Antitrust Act for fixing the prices of matzo and matzo products, B. Manischewitz Co. was sued in a class action brought by several grocery stores on behalf of all retail stores. Under a quickly negotiated settlement agreement, Manischewitz agreed (1) to create a "Food Products Fund," consisting of matzo products that would be distributed to specific charities for a four-year period; and (2) to pay plaintiffs' attorneys between $450,000 and $500,000. The cynically disposed might see this settlement as an excellent way of simultaneously disposing of both stale matzos and a difficult litigation.

Although the *Matzo Food Products* court was unable to swallow this settlement, other courts have regularly accepted similar *cy pres* settlements. It may at first seem puzzling that they do so, but several linked factors probably explain this pattern. First, judicial time is a scarce commodity, which courts struggle to allocate sensibly to high priority matters. "Small claimant" class actions are seldom regarded by courts as among their priorities. Securities class actions, for example, almost never get to trial. One important reason for this phenomenon is that trial judges refuse to give them priority on their trial calendar. Yet, unless the "small claimant" class action can somehow be resolved, it will drag on, consuming scarce judicial time. * * *

Second, most of the cases in which dubious nonpecuniary consideration has been the primary basis for settlement have been "small claimant" class actions. Even if the plaintiffs received a monetary recovery, that recovery would be spread so thinly over a broad plaintiffs' class as to produce little or no meaningful benefit to any individual class member. * * *

Third, the trial court has a limited range of options: basically, it can reject the settlement, or it can approve the settlement but then award only very modest attorneys' fees, thereby signaling its lack of confidence in the outcome. * * *

In any event, the best and bottom line generalization here is not that courts are incapable of detecting the signs of collusion, but that they will not invest scarce judicial time in monitoring "small claimant" class actions; thus they approve some dubious settlements as the lesser evil when dismissal on the merits is not possible.

* * *

* * * The "*New*" Collusion

1. *Inventory Settlements*—At least potentially, courts can respond to signs of collusion (or, more precisely, "non-adversarial" settlements) by reducing the plaintiffs' attorneys' fee award (which in virtually every jurisdiction must be approved by the court in the case of a class action). But in the mass tort context, this may be a particularly ineffective weapon.

To understand its ineffectiveness, one must remember that the mass tort plaintiffs' attorney typically has an inventory of cases that the attorney represents on an individual basis. Often, the inventory may exceed several thousand cases. Normally, the individual cases in this inventory will move slowly through the litigation pipeline and settle only once a trial date has been set. Thus, the plaintiffs' attorney's tactical goal is to expedite cases, pushing them through the pipeline to the eve of trial (and predictable settlement). Conversely, defendants in the mass tort setting are concerned less about existing cases than future claimants, who may dwarf the number of present claimants because of the long latency period associated with mass torts.

Given these different concerns, the possibilities for a deal between the two sides should become evident at this point: both sides have an incentive to trade a settlement of the plaintiffs' attorney's entire inventory (on terms favorable to the attorney) for a global settlement in a class action of all future claims (on terms favorable to the defendants). * * *

* * *

2. *Double-Dipping*—Even in the absence of a separate inventory settlement, a plaintiffs' attorney can favor a mass tort class action for self-interested reasons when the clients' interests would be better served by opting out. This is because one perverse and important characteristic of the mass tort class action is that it permits the attorney to receive two fees: one as class counsel and another as the legal representative of individuals filing claims under it. * * * The initial fee will be the class action fee award, which will be set by the court. It will generally be equal to a percentage of the recovery that is reasonably predictable in advance. * * * However, the second fee, which is paid by the individual client, is not generally controlled by the court and may be grossly disproportionate to the services actually rendered by the attorney at this stage. Individual tort victims tend not to be legally sophisticated and may often sign standard contingency fee contracts that award the attorney as much as forty percent of the recovery received by the victim. Once liability has been established by the class action settlement, the individual attorney often has little more to do than to file a claim establishing the client's eligibility. Typically, this filing can be done by a paralegal in a few hours. * * *

* * *

The mass tort claims resolution facility itself presents still another area where the plaintiffs' attorney may have a sharp conflict of interest. Traditionally, defendants and their counsel have not been involved in the claim allocation process and have been largely indifferent as to how a settlement was distributed so long as they received a release from further liability. For plaintiffs and their attorneys, however, the issues associated with the design of such claims facilities are often fundamental. * * * From a self-interested perspective, plaintiffs' attorneys have little reason to hold back settlement funds for future claimants and considerable reason to prefer a first-come, first-served approach. The latter approach affords them early payment both for existing clients and new clients that they are well positioned to solicit because of their role as class counsel. As a result, this desire for an early payout heightens the possibility that the settlement fund will be exhausted before future claimants are compensated.

3. *Eligibility Restrictions and Illusory Benefits*—Even if a self-interested plaintiffs' attorney is willing to enter into a "cheap" settlement, a problem remains: the court must approve the proposed settlement. In a

mass tort case involving serious physical injuries or illness, this can be a significant hurdle. Few, if any, courts would approve a settlement that accorded desperately ill plaintiffs only nominal consideration. * * *

Accordingly, in order to structure a "cheap" settlement in a mass tort case, the parties must do more than simply agree on compensation levels below the amount that parties at arm's length would negotiate. Various tactics to this end are possible. One is to impose rigorous eligibility criteria that would disqualify many or most within the plaintiff class—but in a manner that is not self-evident to the court or to other third parties. * * *

* * *

4. *Settlement Classes*—Nothing better facilitates collusion than the ability on the part of the defendants to choose the counsel who will represent the plaintiff class. To be sure, even if so chosen, plaintiffs' counsel could behave responsibly. But the dynamics for collusion are set in motion when such a selection process is possible.

Surprisingly, this practice is today not only possible but rapidly becoming common. The new procedure involves negotiations between defendants and plaintiffs' attorneys prior to certification of the class action—and, in some particularly dramatic cases, prior even to the filing of the class action. Obviously, this approach allows the defendants to test out settlement terms (potentially with several teams of plaintiffs' attorneys) before any action is filed. Then, when and if an agreement is reached, the action will be filed as a "settlement class." Originally, the term "settlement class" seems to have meant only that in certifying the class "for settlement purposes," the court would defer any decision as to whether the proposed class actually satisfied Rule 23's certification criteria until after negotiations produced (or failed to produce) a settlement. Under this approach, defendants waived no rights and could still object if the negotiations failed. * * *

From the defendants' perspective, any attempt to reach an agreement by means of a settlement class is a "no lose" proposition: if defendants can obtain agreement from plaintiffs' attorneys and the court to a favorable settlement, the technique advances their interests; if they cannot, they are no worse off and can still object to any attempt by plaintiffs to obtain final class certification. More importantly, at least at the pre-filing stage, the plaintiffs' attorneys with whom the defendants are negotiating are always aware that if they do not reach agreement, the defense attorneys can move on and try their luck with a new team of plaintiffs' attorneys. * * *

* * *

When courts first accepted settlement class actions, the normal pattern was that parties litigated actively for a period of months or longer, sparring over discovery and related motions—until reaching a tentative agreement on a settlement. In contrast, the newer pattern has involved a settlement reached after little or no active litigation (and sometimes before the complaint is filed).

* * *

5. *Restricting Opt Outs*: Mandatory Classes and the Limited Fund Theory—Probably the most aggressive tactic that has been attempted re-

cently in connection with a "friendly" mass tort settlement is the certification of a "mandatory" class action from which class members may not opt out. Normally, a class action seeking money damages must be certified pursuant to Federal Rule of Civil Procedure 23(b)(3), and in such a case, class members have an express right to opt out.

Because "small claimants" have little incentive to opt out and because future claimants have little ability to do so, a "mandatory" class action principally impacts "high stakes" present claimants who would otherwise pursue individual actions. In reality, certification of a Rule 23(b)(1)(B) mandatory class is a protection for defendants against the "danger" that high stakes individual claimants, dissatisfied with the terms of the settlement class, will opt out. * * *

* * *

NOTES AND QUESTIONS

1. Are the conflicts identified by Professor Coffee significant? Which are potentially the most dangerous to a class?

2. Two of the "new collusion" devices identified by Professor Coffee—settlement certification and use of limited-fund class actions—were addressed by the Supreme Court in the years following his article. *See Amchem Prods., Inc. v. Windsor*, 521 U.S. 591 (1997) (*see* Part (A)(3) of this chapter); and *Ortiz v. Fibreboard Corp.*, 527 U.S. 815 (1999) (*see* Chapter 3(A)(2)).

3. Is Professor Coffee correct in arguing that the "new" collusion devices he identifies are uniquely suited to mass tort class actions? If so, what aspects of mass tort class actions make such actions especially amenable to collusion? *See* Chapter 10(A).

4. One approach for addressing potential conflicts of interest between attorneys and their clients is proposed by Professor Klement, who suggests that courts should appoint private individuals who would be paid to monitor the actions of class counsel. Alon Klement, *Who Should Guard the Guardians? A New Approach for Monitoring Class Action Lawyers*, 21 Rev. Litig. 25 (2002). Professor Klement explains:

> **The monitor's fee.** The monitor would be paid a percentage of the total class recovery. That percentage would be the minimum necessary to motivate the monitor to invest the time and costs required for effective supervision of the class attorney. Since that required investment would often be low, the price class members would have to pay by yielding part of their joint fund would be more than outweighed by their gains from adequate supervision of class attorneys' [costs] and opportunistic behavior.
>
> **Selection of the monitor.** The monitor would be selected by an auction in which every candidate would submit the highest price he is willing to pay if he is given the monitor's position. The candidate whose bid is highest would be selected and would then pay his bid, which may be distributed at the court's discretion either to the class or used to finance part of the class's litigation costs. Thus, a large part of the price that the class pays for monitoring would be earned in advance through the winning monitor's bid.
>
> The pool of candidates would not be restricted to class members only. Anyone may bid to monitor, subject to structural restrictions

that are intended to limit possible collusion between monitor and lawyer. The winner of the auction would be the one who would monitor the lawyer most efficiently, as he would be able to earn the highest net [return through] monitoring and thereby being able to bid highest for the job.

The monitor's duties and authority. After being chosen, the monitor would select the class attorney, determine her fee arrangement, and submit it for the court's approval. During litigation the monitor would supervise the class attorney and submit reports to the court when required. Any settlement would have to be approved by the monitor, subject to his absolute discretion.

By awarding the private monitor a percentage of the class's recovery, the proposed scheme would motivate potential candidates to bid for that position and result in the selection of the most efficient monitor from among those candidates. By opening the auction not only to the class members but also to all other potential monitors, the auction process will avoid being restricted to too limited a pool of candidates—among whom the most adequate do not want to monitor and the ones who would want to do so are always inadequate. Private monitors would guard the class attorneys from abusing their rightful beneficiaries, namely, society-at-large and class members in particular. They would succeed where courts and class members have failed because they would be adequately financed, motivated, and informed and would therefore be able to provide a proper check on class attorneys.

Id. at 28–30. Would such monitors decrease conflict-of-interest problems? What new problems might such monitors cause?

The American Law Institute's *Principles of the Law of Aggregate Litigation* (hereinafter "ALI *Principles*") also encourages judges to consider using monitors to facilitate class settlement. American Law Institute, *Principles of the Law of Aggregate Litigation* § 3.09, at 236 (2010) (discussing special officers for the class, neutrals or special masters, and court-appointed experts). What are the potential advantages and disadvantages of monitors?

5. Since 2003, parties seeking approval of a settlement, voluntary dismissal, or compromise under Rule 23(e) have been required to file a statement identifying any agreement made in connection with the proposed settlement, voluntary dismissal, or compromise. Fed. R. Civ. P. 23(e)(3). *See, e.g., In re Initial Pub. Offering Sec. Litig.*, 226 F.R.D. 186, 204–05 (S.D.N.Y. 2005) (finding, after *in camera* review, that disclosed side agreements did not "influence[] the terms of the settlement by trading away possible advantages for the class in return for advantages for others," and denying non-settling parties' requests for discovery of the side agreements). Does this procedure effectively remedy the collusion that Professor Coffee describes? Does such mandatory disclosure address instances of the "new collusion" where, for example, negotiations take place prior to the filing of the class action? Is Rule 23(e) clear in defining what must be disclosed?

It could be argued that requiring disclosure of side agreements is a mistake, since the existence of such agreements could become an excuse for objecting parties to conduct discovery or may cause unnecessary delay in the proceedings. Are such concerns valid? If so, how should they be balanced against the interests of the class in full disclosure? Does the court have other means by which it can become aware of side agreements? Do the parties have any other incentive outside of the rule to disclose these agreements?

Note that the amended rule does not provide what the ramifications are for failure to disclose side agreements that may be related to a settlement. Should the failure to disclose a side agreement constitute a ground for invalidating the settlement after it has been approved and reduced to judgment?

6. One type of intra-class conflict that may arise is between unnamed class members and class representatives who have entered into incentive agreements, promising the representatives—in advance—payment related to a class settlement. For example, in *Rodriguez v. West Publ'g Corp.*, 563 F.3d 948 (9th Cir. 2009), a settlement was reached in an antitrust class action brought against providers of bar review courses. After the district court's approval of the settlement, several class members objected to the settlement upon learning that five of the seven class representatives had incentive agreements in their retainers, requiring class counsel to seek special payments for these representatives in relation to the settlement amount. While recognizing the widespread use of incentive *awards* in class actions, which may be granted by a court upon recognition of a class representative's particular contributions in a case, the Ninth Circuit distinguished such awards from the *ex ante* incentive *agreements* in this case. *Id.* at 958–59. The court disapproved of the incentive agreements because "they created an unacceptable disconnect between the interests of the contracting representatives * * * and members of the class" and "gave rise to a disturbing appearance of impropriety." *Id.* at 960. Moreover, the fact that such agreements were not disclosed during the class certification inquiry compromised the district court's ability to determine adequacy. *Id.*

Despite the Ninth Circuit's disapproval of the incentive agreements, it did not reverse the district court's approval of the settlement. It reasoned that two of the class representatives had no such questionable incentive agreements, received no incentive awards, and were deemed adequate by the district court, and the settlement had been arrived at through arms-length negotiations. *Id.* at 958, 961. Moreover, although neither the settlement agreement nor the settlement notice disclosed the incentive agreements, the Ninth Circuit concluded that the class had received sufficient notice because that notice did specify that incentive *awards* would be sought. *Id.* at 962.

c. The Judge's Role in Fostering Settlement

The judge's supervisory role in the litigation of a class action was previously discussed in Chapter 4(E)(1). That topic is further explored here with regard to settlements. In the first piece below, Judge S. Arthur Spiegel (D. Ohio) provides a thoughtful discussion of various approaches that judges use to foster settlement. In the second piece, Judge Elaine Bucklo (N.D. Ill.) and her co-author provide insights into the types of information judges should have in evaluating settlements.

S. ARTHUR SPIEGEL, SETTLING CLASS ACTIONS
62 U. Cin. L. Rev. 1565, 1567–70 (1994).

* * * [T]here is a legitimate division of opinion as to whether a district judge should be involved in settlement activities if that judge is going to be the one who must pass on the fairness of the settlement. There are those who believe that the district judge should take no part in helping to settle the class action if he or she will ultimately determine whether the proposed

settlement is fair, adequate, and reasonable under Rule 23(e). That opinion favors the view that the judge who chooses to take part in helping to settle a class action should transfer the case to another judge to conduct Rule 23(e) fairness hearings, or should have assigned another judge or magistrate to conduct settlement negotiations, instead of conducting them personally.

Those judges who have had substantial involvement in settling class actions and who have been successful have been subject to some criticism. The argument is that it would be virtually inconceivable that a judge would not find a settlement that he or she crafted or was heavily involved in negotiating to be fair, adequate, and reasonable. In other words, it is hard to believe that the judge could maintain the ability to be the disinterested appraiser envisioned by Rule 23(e).

Other contentions maintain that the judge, in passing on the fairness of the settlement, may overlook the interest of the absent class members. In addition, during the settlement negotiations, if the judge is present, the parties, knowing that the judge will ultimately pass upon the fairness of the settlement, may not be frank about the strengths and weaknesses of their cases. One can agree that if the court makes suggestions to be included in the settlement, it can put itself in the position of having such an investment in the settlement that it will be difficult for the judge to determine objectively whether the settlement is fair.

To remedy these problems, judges have adopted three courses of action. First, the judge may farm out all settlement negotiations to a magistrate judge, a colleague, or a settlement master to help the parties to negotiate. Second, the judge may take on the role of facilitator, to assist the parties in conducting settlement discussions, that role being limited to facilitating the process. In this case, the judge would not be an advocate for any particular settlement and would not mediate between the parties. The judge in such a situation makes available the resources of the court to assist the parties in settlement negotiations, but does not get involved in the substance of the negotiations. Third, the judge may become actively involved as a participant in the settlement negotiations between the parties, to help them craft the proposed settlement; and when it has been tentatively agreed upon, the judge may transfer the case to a colleague to conduct the Rule 23(e) hearings to determine whether it is fair, adequate, and reasonable.

On the other hand, there are those who feel that because a federal district judge does many tasks and must wear many hats, there is no reason why the judge cannot be objective throughout, become involved in the settlement process, and later preside over the fairness hearing. For example, at bench trials, judges pass on the weight of the evidence as well as its competence, many times hearing in proffers testimony that must be excluded under the rules of evidence, yet without being influenced by it.

Likewise, the judge must be objective in ruling on motions for judgment notwithstanding the verdict and other post-trial motions where a jury has decided the case. * * *

Other arguments why a judge should be involved in the settlement of class actions and also the fairness hearing include, for example, the fact that the judge who was involved in the settlement negotiations will be in a better position to consider objections at the fairness hearing, particularly in a complex case. Similarly, a judge who is not involved in the settlement negotiations, but who is substituted at the eleventh hour to ensure objectivity at the fairness hearing, may get hung up on a good faith objection that actually lacks merit, but that seems valid to the substitute judge because of the judge's lack of familiarity with the case and the nuances of the settlement negotiations. This could place in jeopardy the entire settlement agreement or delay approval, adding cost to the litigation. In the same fashion, a seemingly invalid objection that the original judge, who is familiar with the case, would realize had merit and would be worth considering may be overlooked by the substitute judge.

* * *

HON. ELAINE BUCKLO & THOMAS R. MEITES, WHAT EVERY JUDGE SHOULD KNOW ABOUT A RULE 23 SETTLEMENT (BUT PROBABLY ISN'T TOLD)

41 Litig. 18, 18–21 (2015)

* * *

For the past 50 years, Rule 23 of the Federal Rules of Civil Procedure has required district court judges to scrutinize proposed class settlements. * * *

Unfortunately, the dynamics of the Rule 23 settlement process do not favor the judge. While class counsel is generally the movant, plaintiff and defendant share a community of interest in seeing the settlement approved. And in the absence of an objector, the court has no adverse party questioning the settlement. Rather, the burden of ferreting out problems falls wholly on the court.

Yet, too often, the court doesn't get the information the judge needs. Here is what the district court should know but too often isn't told.

Insurance Coverage

The amount of insurance (less amounts expended for costs of defense) is a crucial driver of settlements. If the insurance is meager, a lower settlement may be justified, particularly with a defendant of relatively modest means. Second, even large companies are extremely reluctant to pay their own funds in settlement. Thus, even when there's lots of insurance, it usually marks the outer edge of potential settlement. The real negotiations are often not between class counsel and defendants' attorneys but between class counsel and the insurer.

Because insurance coverage often acts as a *de facto* cap on class recovery, a court should know the amount of insurance available when assessing the fairness of a settlement. However, while Rule 26(a)(1)(A)(iv) requires the parties to exchange copies of all insurance policies, these are not filed with the court or otherwise available. And too often the amount of available coverage is not disclosed to the court in the parties' Rule 23(e) filings.

Thus, except in the rare case of a limited, determinable fund, the court has no reliable measure of the potential recovery against which to evaluate the class settlement. Requiring disclosure of available insurance in the settlement approval filings goes a long way toward providing the needed metric in determining the fairness and adequacy of the settlement.

Discovery

The extent of discovery is a crucial determinant as to how thorough a job class counsel has done. But too often the settlement papers say little more than "x depositions were taken" and "y documents were produced." More disclosure is needed. First, the identity of each person deposed by class counsel should be listed, as well as depositions noticed but not taken. Second, a mere statement that 100,000 pages of documents were produced may not be enough to permit the court to get a handle on what class counsel actually did. What the court needs to know is who produced the documents, what categories of documents were produced, and how many of these documents were actually reviewed. Also helpful—and easily available from the data submitted in support of the fee application—is how many hours were spent by class counsel, contract attorneys, and paralegals in this review.

The court should also be told when the discovery was taken. So-called confirmatory discovery—discovery taken after a settlement in principle is reached—is too often a sham, undertaken to inflate the lodestar rather than assist in the prosecution of the claim. Thus, any discovery taken after the settlement is reached should be identified and treated separately.

Other Pending Actions

Usually, releases in class settlements are all-encompassing and may compromise claims asserted in pending litigation elsewhere. * * * Given the breadth of most settlements, it is incumbent on the parties to disclose this other litigation in their motion for preliminary approval. Obviously, the defendant is fully aware of it. If these other actions are strong, their termination must be taken into account in evaluating the proposed settlement. Under the guise of a general release, the defendant may be buying its peace from litigation that is only tangentially—or not at all—related to the class litigation before the court.

At a minimum, then, the court should be apprised of all actions arguably released by the pending settlement. And because the notice of a settlement usually goes only to the client, his or her lawyer in the other pending actions may not learn of the settlement in a timely fashion. Actual notice must be given to counsel in these other actions, which, of course, the defendant has ready access to.

Claims Rates and *Pro Rata* Share

The settlement papers commonly stress the dollar size of the settlement. After all, a large number is presented as the result of substantial efforts by class counsel capped by a wonderful result. But dollars alone are not the full story. Rather, the expected recovery per dollar loss is what class members—and the court—need to know.

The expected average recovery is a function of the settlement dollars (after deduction of fees and expenses) divided by the estimated claims made. For example, suppose class members are shareholders of a particular company. Then assume (1) the net settlement amount is $1 million, (2) investors purchased 2 million shares of the company's stock during the class period, and (3) the estimated claims rate is only 25 percent. In that case, the expected average recovery per share is $1 million/ (2 million shares x 25 percent), or $2.00 per share. Too often the court is told little or nothing about the second and third elements: class size and expected claims rate.

As part of class discovery or even settlement negotiations, the parties gain a good idea of the size of the class. Though limited, there is also literature on expected claims rates in a number of kinds of actions. *See, e.g.*, Francis E. McGovern, *Distribution of Funds in Class Actions—Claims Administration*, 35 J. Corp. L. 123 (2009). Also, experienced class counsel can advise the court of claims rates in their own experience. To the extent possible, the settlement papers should set out both the per-unit *pro rata* share—net settlement dollars divided by relevant units—and the expected claims rate.

Claims Process

The best settlement is worthless if the claims process is too onerous. Conscientious plaintiffs' counsel should insist on the least difficult claim form that is actually necessary to determine whether a claimant is entitled to recover part of the fund. A form that asks for more than is necessary may well be evidence that the attorneys are not putting the best interests of the class at the forefront of their negotiations. * * *

Some cases do justify a claims process, but it should not be any more difficult than actually necessary to determine eligibility for class participation and the level of recovery, where appropriate. Thus, a court should look very carefully at a process that requires claimants to submit records, especially detailed ones or documents stretching back over time. Similarly, a process that asks claimants to determine particular dates on which, for example, they rented a car or used a credit card will almost surely result in a minuscule number of claims. * * * This sort of burden might be justified if the amount to be recovered is very large and the defendant lacks the information. So too with requirements that claims forms be sworn.

A judge weighing the fairness of a settlement must balance the claim requirements proposed against the value of the benefit to class members. A settlement to which few will make claims, or in which the claims process is unrealistic, is not one with much value for the defined class. * * *

* * *

Reversion of Undistributed Funds to Defendants and *Cy Pres* Awards

A court should look doubly hard at a settlement that allows unclaimed funds to revert to the defendants, rather than being redistributed to the plaintiff class. * * * [T]he combination of a claims process that appeared to be unnecessary (because the defendant had the names, addresses, and other information of the franchisee class) and reversion of unclaimed class funds presented serious questions of potential collusion.

Another red flag is a settlement allowing unclaimed funds to be paid to charities. *Cy pres* awards of residual amounts following distribution to class members are common in consumer class action settlements. But courts need to be wary of settlements that include these awards. First, they need to know that there is a valid reason for the *cy pres* award. Usually, it will be because the real damage that individual claimants have is too small to justify documentation or because the cost of a redistribution after claims are paid would be too high to justify a second payout. Then courts approve a substitute payment to a nonprofit organization so long as the group is really a substitute for the injured plaintiffs. There must be "a driving nexus between the plaintiff class and the *cy pres* beneficiaries." To see if this is true, a court should insist on detailed information about the proposed recipient. The court cannot determine that a settlement is fair and reasonable if part of the proceeds are earmarked for an organization "to be determined at a later time." The nexus must be to the claim made. * * *

The second potential problem with inclusion of *cy pres* awards as part of a class action settlement is that the award may be valued by counsel as part of the total benefit to the class and thus the amount by which counsel's fee is calculated. If that is ever to be justified, there is a particular need for scrutiny of the alleged value of the award both to the class and the defendant, who may be obtaining tax benefits or is already committed to making the same distribution.

Class Notice

Finally, courts must look carefully at the proposed notice to absent class members, both in substance and with an eye toward how it will be disseminated. Notice in federal cases is governed by Federal Rule of Civil Procedure 23(c)(2). That rule requires that class members receive "the best notice that is practicable under the circumstances, including individual notice to all members who can be identified through reasonable effort." In general, if the defendant's records identify class members, they must be sent individual notice. Counsel often propose a "summary notice," which directs class members to a website on which they may obtain more information. But this kind of notification in any case certified under Rule 23(b)(3) must still comply with the requirements of subsection (c)(2), including that it plainly inform the class of the nature of the action, the class definition, and claims and defenses. Class members must also be told that they may file an appearance by an attorney, that they may opt out of the class, and that the action will be binding on them.

Because the adversary element is lacking in the process of preliminarily approving class actions, the court must be alert to what it is not being told as well as to what it is told. Notice, insurance coverage, discovery, claims issues, settlement value, and the defendant's continuing stake are just some of the areas where the court should be on guard. At least that much is owed to absent class members.

* * *

NOTES AND QUESTIONS

1. What should be a judge's role in fostering a class action settlement? How is the judge's role in class action settlement negotiations different from that role in traditional, one-on-one litigation? If trial court judges become intimately involved in the settlement process, are they more or less likely to exercise independent judgment when certifying the settlement class and evaluating the fairness, adequacy, and reasonableness of the settlement? The Third Circuit addressed this issue in *In re Community Bank of Northern Virginia*, 418 F.3d 277 (3d Cir. 2005). There, the Third Circuit expressed concern that

the trial court had failed to exercise its independent judgment when it adopted the proposed findings of the settling parties. The Third Circuit found particularly troubling the district court's "closed door session held *before* the * * * fairness hearing, [at which] the District Court asked the settling parties to submit the proposed findings of fact and conclusions of law, which it 'would adopt basically.' * * * At the actual fairness hearing, class certification itself was never discussed." *Id.* at 301. Does a trial judge's involvement in the settlement process necessarily taint that judge's judgment with respect to a proposed settlement?

2. Can a judge realistically play a central role in settlement talks without developing opinions about the case that could have an impact if the case does not settle?

3. What potential problems may arise if the judge assigns someone else to preside over settlement talks? How can such problems be addressed? *See* ALI *Principles* § 3.09 at 238 (court adjuncts "are not a panacea for ensuring fair settlements") (discussed in Part A(2) of this chapter).

4. As discussed in Section 8 below, one proposed change to Rule 23 would require the parties to provide significant information early in the settlement review process to enable the judge to decide whether to preliminarily approve a settlement and send out notice.

3. SETTLEMENT CERTIFICATION

Before addressing settlements that arise during the course of adversarial litigation, it is important, at the threshold, to separate settlements between litigating adversaries from the different form of class action settlement mentioned earlier in this chapter by Professor Coffee. During the 1980s and 1990s, parties to major class actions increasingly proposed certification of class actions for settlement purposes only. This procedure involved negotiating a settlement of a dispute, then having plaintiffs' counsel file a lawsuit with the proposed settlement and a motion for class certification, to which the defendant would join (or at least acquiesce). Such "settlement certifications" were often approved by courts, and supporters of the practice haled its ability to facilitate efficient, large-scale dispute resolution. As the practice grew, however, courts and commentators became increasingly concerned about whether such settlements were fair, whether they received proper judicial scrutiny, and whether certification for settlement could proceed under a more lenient standard than in circumstances when certification is litigated by adversaries. *See generally Georgine v. Amchem Prods., Inc.*, 83 F.3d 610 (3d Cir. 1996) (describing concerns about and arguments in favor of settlement-only certification), *aff'd*, 521 U.S. 591 (1997). The issue came to a head in the decisions below.

AMCHEM PRODS., INC. V. WINDSOR
Supreme Court of the United States, 1997.
521 U.S. 591.

JUSTICE GINSBURG delivered the opinion of the Court.

This case concerns the legitimacy under Rule 23 of the Federal Rules of Civil Procedure of a class-action certification sought to achieve global settlement of current and future asbestos-related claims. The class proposed for certification potentially encompasses hundreds of thousands, perhaps millions, of individuals tied together by this commonality: Each was, or some day may be, adversely affected by past exposure to asbestos products manufactured by one or more of 20 companies. Those companies, defendants in the lower courts, are petitioners here.

The United States District Court for the Eastern District of Pennsylvania certified the class for settlement only, finding that the proposed settlement was fair and that representation and notice had been adequate. That court enjoined class members from separately pursuing asbestos-related personal-injury suits in any court, federal or state, pending the issuance of a final order. The Court of Appeals for the Third Circuit vacated the District Court's orders, holding that the class certification failed to satisfy Rule 23's requirements in several critical respects. We affirm the Court of Appeals' judgment.

I.

A.

* * *

In the face of legislative inaction, the federal courts—lacking authority to replace state tort systems with a national toxic tort compensation regime—endeavored to work with the procedural tools available to improve management of federal asbestos litigation. Eight federal judges, experienced in the superintendence of asbestos cases, urged the Judicial Panel on Multidistrict Litigation (MDL Panel), to consolidate in a single district all asbestos complaints then pending in federal courts. [The MDL Panel decides whether to transfer federal district court civil cases involving common factual questions for coordinated or consolidated pretrial proceedings. *See* discussion in Chapter 12.] Accepting the recommendation, the MDL Panel transferred all asbestos cases then filed, but not yet on trial in federal courts to a single district, the United States District Court for the Eastern District of Pennsylvania; pursuant to the transfer order, the collected cases were consolidated for pretrial proceedings before Judge Weiner. The order aggregated pending cases only * * *.

B.

After the consolidation, attorneys for plaintiffs and defendants formed separate steering committees and began settlement negotiations. Ronald L. Motley and Gene Locks—later appointed, along with Motley's law partner Joseph F. Rice, to represent the plaintiff class in this action—co-chaired the Plaintiffs' Steering Committee. Counsel for the Center for Claims Resolution (CCR), the consortium of 20 former asbestos manufacturers now before us as petitioners, participated in the Defendants' Steering Committee. Although the MDL order collected, transferred, and consolidated only cases already commenced in federal courts, settlement negotiations included efforts to find a "means of resolving . . . future cases."

* * *

[After initial negotiations failed,] CCR counsel approached the lawyers who had headed the Plaintiffs' Steering Committee in the unsuccessful negotiations, and a new round of negotiations began; that round yielded the mass settlement agreement now in controversy. At the time, the former heads of the Plaintiffs' Steering Committee represented thousands of plaintiffs with then-pending asbestos-related claims—claimants the parties to this suit call "inventory" plaintiffs. CCR indicated in these discussions that it would resist settlement of inventory cases absent "some kind of protection for the future."

Settlement talks thus concentrated on devising an administrative scheme for disposition of asbestos claims not yet in litigation. In these negotiations, counsel for masses of inventory plaintiffs endeavored to represent the interests of the anticipated future claimants, although those lawyers then had no attorney-client relationship with such claimants.

Once negotiations seemed likely to produce an agreement purporting to bind potential plaintiffs, CCR agreed to settle, through separate agreements, the claims of plaintiffs who had already filed asbestos-related lawsuits. In one such agreement, CCR defendants promised to pay more than $200 million to gain release of the claims of numerous inventory plaintiffs. After settling the inventory claims, CCR, together with the plaintiffs' lawyers CCR had approached, launched this case, exclusively involving persons outside the MDL Panel's province—plaintiffs without already pending lawsuits.[3]

C.

The class action thus instituted was not intended to be litigated. Rather, within the space of a single day, January 15, 1993, the settling parties—CCR defendants and the representatives of the plaintiff class described below—presented to the District Court a complaint, an answer, a proposed settlement agreement, and a joint motion for conditional class certification.

The complaint identified nine lead plaintiffs, designating them and members of their families as representatives of a class comprising all persons who had not filed an asbestos-related lawsuit against a CCR defendant as of the date the class action commenced, but who (1) had been exposed—occupationally or through the occupational exposure of a spouse or household member—to asbestos or products containing asbestos attributable to a CCR defendant, or (2) whose spouse or family member had been so exposed. Untold numbers of individuals may fall within this description. All named plaintiffs alleged that they or a member of their family had been exposed to asbestos-containing products of CCR defendants. More than half of the named plaintiffs alleged that they or their family members had already suffered various physical injuries as a result of the exposure. The others alleged that they had not yet manifested any asbestos-related condition. The complaint delineated no subclasses; all named plaintiffs were designated as representatives of the class as a whole.

The complaint invoked the District Court's diversity jurisdiction and asserted various state-law claims for relief * * *. [The] CCR defendants' answer denied the principal allegations of the complaint and asserted 11 affirmative defenses.

---

[3] It is basic to comprehension of this proceeding to notice that no transferred case is included in the settlement at issue, and no case covered by the settlement existed as a civil action at the time of the MDL Panel transfer.

A stipulation of settlement accompanied the pleadings; it proposed to settle, and to preclude nearly all class members from litigating against CCR companies, all claims not filed before January 15, 1993, involving compensation for present and future asbestos-related personal injury or death. An exhaustive document exceeding 100 pages, the stipulation presents in detail an administrative mechanism and a schedule of payments to compensate class members who meet defined asbestos-exposure and medical requirements. * * * The stipulation describes four categories of compensable disease: mesothelioma; lung cancer; certain "other cancers" (colon-rectal, laryngeal, esophageal, and stomach cancer); and "non-malignant conditions" (asbestosis and bi-lateral pleural thickening). Persons with "exceptional" medical claims—claims that do not fall within * * * the four described diagnostic categories—may in some instances qualify for compensation, but the settlement caps the number of "exceptional" claims CCR must cover.

* * *

For each qualifying disease category, the stipulation specifies the range of damages CCR will pay to qualifying claimants. Payments under the settlement are not adjustable for inflation. Mesothelioma claimants—the most highly compensated category—are scheduled to receive between $20,000 and $200,000. The stipulation provides that CCR is to propose the level of compensation within the prescribed ranges; it also establishes procedures to resolve disputes over medical diagnoses and levels of compensation.

Compensation above the fixed ranges may be obtained for "extraordinary" claims. But the settlement places both numerical caps and dollar limits on such claims. The settlement also imposes "case flow maximums," which cap the number of claims payable for each disease in a given year.

Class members are to receive no compensation for certain kinds of claims, even if otherwise applicable state law recognizes such claims. * * * Claims that garner no compensation under the settlement include claims by family members of asbestos-exposed individuals for loss of consortium, and claims by so-called "exposure-only" plaintiffs for increased risk of cancer, fear of future asbestos-related injury, and medical monitoring. "Pleural" claims, which might be asserted by persons with asbestos-related plaques on their lungs but no accompanying physical impairment, are also excluded. Although not entitled to present compensation, exposure-only claimants and pleural claimants may qualify for benefits when and if they develop a compensable disease and meet the relevant exposure and medical criteria. Defendants forgo defenses to liability, including statute of limitations pleas.

Class members, in the main, are bound by the settlement in perpetuity, while CCR defendants may choose to withdraw from the settlement after ten years. A small number of class members—only a few per year—may reject the settlement and pursue their claims in court. Those permitted to exercise this option, however, may not assert any punitive damages claim or any claim for increased risk of cancer. Aspects of the administration of the settlement are to be monitored by the AFL–CIO and class counsel. Class counsel are to receive attorneys' fees in an amount to be approved by the District Court.

D.

On January 29, 1993, as requested by the settling parties, the District Court conditionally certified, under Federal Rule of Civil Procedure 23(b)(3), an encompassing opt-out class. The certified class included persons occupationally exposed to defendants' asbestos products, and members of their families, who had not filed suit as of January 15. * * * At no stage of the proceedings * * * were additional counsel * * * appointed. Nor was the class ever divided into subclasses. In a separate order, Judge Weiner assigned to Judge Reed, also of the Eastern District of Pennsylvania, "the task of conducting fairness proceedings and of determining whether the proposed settlement is fair to the class." Various class members raised objections to the settlement stipulation, and Judge Weiner granted the objectors full rights to participate in the subsequent proceedings.

* * *

Objectors raised numerous challenges to the settlement[, but] Judge Reed concluded that the settlement terms were fair and had been negotiated without collusion. He also found that adequate notice had been given to class members, and that final class certification under Rule 23(b)(3) was appropriate.

As to the specific prerequisites to certification, the District Court observed that the class satisfied Rule 23(a)(1)'s numerosity requirement, a matter no one debates. The Rule 23(a)(2) and (b)(3) requirements of commonality and preponderance were also satisfied, the District Court held, in that

> [t]he members of the class have all been exposed to asbestos products supplied by the defendants and all share an interest in receiving prompt and fair compensation for their claims, while minimizing the risks and transaction costs inherent in the asbestos litigation process as it occurs presently in the tort system. Whether the proposed settlement satisfies this interest and is otherwise a fair, reasonable and adequate compromise of the claims of the class is a predominant issue for purposes of Rule 23(b)(3).

The District Court held next that the claims of the class representatives were "typical" of the class as a whole, a requirement of Rule 23(a)(3), and that, as Rule 23(b)(3) demands, the class settlement was "superior" to other methods of adjudication.

Strenuous objections had been asserted regarding the adequacy of representation, a Rule 23(a)(4) requirement * * * [, but] the District Court rejected these objections. Subclasses were unnecessary, the District Court held, bearing in mind the added cost and confusion they would entail and the ability of class members to exclude themselves from the class during the three-month opt-out period. Reasoning that the representative plaintiffs "have a strong interest that recovery for *all* of the medical categories be maximized because they may have claims in *any*, or several categories," the District Court found "no antagonism of interest between class members with various medical conditions, or between persons with and without currently manifest asbestos impairment." Declaring class certification appropriate and the settlement fair, the District Court preliminarily enjoined all class members from commencing any asbestos-related suit against the CCR defendants in any state or federal court.

The objectors appealed. The United States Court of Appeals for the Third Circuit vacated the certification, holding that the requirements of Rule 23 had not been satisfied.

* * *

IV.

We granted review to decide the role settlement may play, under existing Rule 23, in determining the propriety of class certification. The Third Circuit's opinion stated that each of the requirements of Rule 23(a) and (b)(3) "must be satisfied without taking into account the settlement." That statement, petitioners urge, is incorrect.

We agree with petitioners to this limited extent: Settlement is relevant to a class certification. The Third Circuit's opinion bears modification in that respect. But * * * the Court of Appeals in fact did not ignore the settlement; instead, that court homed in on settlement terms in explaining why it found the absentees' interests inadequately represented. The Third Circuit's close inspection of the settlement in that regard was altogether proper.

Confronted with a request for settlement-only class certification, a district court need not inquire whether the case, if tried, would present intractable management problems, for the proposal is that there be no trial. But other specifications of the Rule—those designed to protect absentees by blocking unwarranted or overbroad class definitions—demand undiluted, even heightened, attention in the settlement context. Such attention is of vital importance, for a court asked to certify a settlement class will lack the opportunity, present when a case is litigated, to adjust the class, informed by the proceedings as they unfold.

* * *

* * * [The approval] prescription [in Rule 23(e)] was designed to function as an additional requirement, not a superseding direction, for the "class action" to which Rule 23(e) refers is one qualified for certification under Rule 23(a) and (b). Subdivisions (a) and (b) focus court attention on whether a proposed class has sufficient unity so that absent members can fairly be bound by decisions of class representatives. That dominant concern persists when settlement, rather than trial, is proposed.

The safeguards provided by the Rule 23(a) and (b) class-qualifying criteria, we emphasize, are not impractical impediments—checks shorn of utility—in the settlement class context. First, the standards set for the protection of absent class members serve to inhibit appraisals of the chancellor's foot kind—class certifications dependent upon the court's gestalt judgment or overarching impression of the settlement's fairness.

Second, if a fairness inquiry under Rule 23(e) controlled certification, eclipsing Rule 23(a) and (b), and permitting class designation despite the impossibility of litigation, both class counsel and court would be disarmed. Class counsel confined to settlement negotiations could not use the threat of litigation to press for a better offer, and the court would face a bargain proffered for its approval without benefit of adversarial investigation.

Federal courts, in any case, lack authority to substitute for Rule 23's certification criteria a standard never adopted—that if a settlement is "fair," then certification is proper. Applying to this case [the] criteria the rulemakers set, we conclude that the Third Circuit's appraisal is essentially correct. Although that court should have acknowledged that settlement is a factor in the calculus, a remand is not warranted on that account. The Court of Appeals' opinion amply demonstrates why—with or without a settlement on the table—the sprawling class the District Court certified does not satisfy Rule 23's requirements.

A.

We address first the requirement of Rule 23(b)(3) that "[common] questions of law or fact . . . predominate over any questions affecting only individual members." The District Court concluded that predominance was satisfied based on two factors: class members' shared experience of asbestos exposure and their common "interest in receiving prompt and fair compensation for their claims, while minimizing the risks and transaction costs inherent in the asbestos litigation process as it occurs presently in the tort system." The settling parties also contend that the settlement's fairness is a common question, predominating over disparate legal issues that might be pivotal in litigation but become irrelevant under the settlement.

* * *

The predominance requirement stated in Rule 23(b)(3), we hold, is not met by the factors on which the District Court relied. The benefits asbestos-exposed persons might gain from the establishment of a grand-scale compensation scheme is a matter fit for legislative consideration, but it is not pertinent to the predominance inquiry. That inquiry trains on the legal or factual questions that qualify each class member's case as a genuine controversy, questions that preexist any settlement.

The Rule 23(b)(3) predominance inquiry tests whether proposed classes are sufficiently cohesive to warrant adjudication by representation. * * * [I]t is not the mission of Rule 23(e) to assure the class cohesion that legitimizes representative action in the first place. If a common interest in a fair compromise could satisfy the predominance requirement of Rule 23(b)(3), that vital prescription would be stripped of any meaning in the settlement context.

The District Court also relied upon this commonality: "The members of the class have all been exposed to asbestos products supplied by the defendants. . . ." Even if Rule 23(a)'s commonality requirement may be satisfied by that shared experience, the predominance criterion is far more demanding. Given the greater number of questions peculiar to the several categories of class members, and to individuals within each category, and the significance of those uncommon questions, any overarching dispute about the health consequences of asbestos exposure cannot satisfy the Rule 23(b)(3) predominance standard.

The Third Circuit highlighted the disparate questions undermining class cohesion in this case:

> Class members were exposed to different asbestos-containing products, for different amounts of time, in different ways, and over different periods. Some class members suffer no physical injury or

have only asymptomatic pleural changes, while others suffer from lung cancer, disabling asbestosis, or from mesothelioma. . . . Each has a different history of cigarette smoking, a factor that complicates the causation inquiry.

The [exposure-only] plaintiffs especially share little in common, either with each other or with the presently injured class members. It is unclear whether they will contract asbestos-related disease and, if so, what disease each will suffer. They will also incur different medical expenses because their monitoring and treatment will depend on singular circumstances and individual medical histories.

Differences in state law, the Court of Appeals observed, compound these disparities.

No settlement class called to our attention is as sprawling as this one. Predominance is a test readily met in certain cases alleging consumer or securities fraud or violations of the antitrust laws. Even mass tort cases arising from a common cause or disaster may, depending upon the circumstances, satisfy the predominance requirement. The Advisory Committee for the 1966 revision of Rule 23, it is true, noted that "mass accident" cases are likely to present "significant questions, not only of damages but of liability and defenses of liability, . . . affecting the individuals in different ways." And the Committee advised that such cases are "ordinarily not appropriate" for class treatment. But the text of the rule does not categorically exclude mass tort cases from class certification, and district courts, since the late 1970s, have been certifying such cases in increasing number. The Committee's warning, however, continues to call for caution when individual stakes are high and disparities among class members great. As the Third Circuit's opinion makes plain, the certification in this case does not follow the counsel of caution. * * *

B.

Nor can the class approved by the District Court satisfy Rule 23(a)(4)'s requirement that the named parties "will fairly and adequately protect the interests of the class." The adequacy inquiry under Rule 23(a)(4) serves to uncover conflicts of interest between named parties and the class they seek to represent. "[A] class representative must be part of the class and 'possess the same interest and suffer the same injury' as the class members."

* * *

As the Third Circuit pointed out, named parties with diverse medical conditions sought to act on behalf of a single giant class rather than on behalf of discrete subclasses. In significant respects, the interests of those within the single class are not aligned. Most saliently, for the currently injured, the critical goal is generous immediate payments. That goal tugs against the interest of exposure-only plaintiffs in ensuring an ample, inflation-protected fund for the future.

The disparity between the currently injured and exposure-only categories of plaintiffs, and the diversity within each category are not made insignificant by the District Court's finding that petitioners' assets suffice to pay claims under the settlement. Although this is not a "limited fund" case certified under Rule 23(b)(1)(B), the terms of the settlement reflect essential allocation decisions designed to confine compensation and to limit defendants' liability. For example, as earlier described, the settlement includes no adjustment for inflation; only a few claimants per year can opt out at the back end; and [certain] claims are extinguished with no compensation.

The settling parties, in sum, achieved a global compromise with no structural assurance of fair and adequate representation for the diverse groups and individuals affected. Although the named parties alleged a range of complaints, each served generally as representative for the whole, not for a separate constituency. * * *

* * *

C.

Impediments to the provision of adequate notice, the Third Circuit emphasized, rendered highly problematic any endeavor to tie to a settlement class persons with no perceptible asbestos-related disease at the time of the settlement. Many persons in the exposure-only category, the Court of Appeals stressed, may not even know of their exposure, or realize the extent of the harm they may incur. Even if they fully appreciate the significance of class notice, those without current afflictions may not have the information or foresight needed to decide, intelligently, whether to stay in or opt out.

Family members of asbestos-exposed individuals may themselves fall prey to disease or may ultimately have ripe claims for loss of consortium. Yet large numbers of people in this category—future spouses and children of asbestos victims—could not be alerted to their class membership. And current spouses and children of the occupationally exposed may know nothing of that exposure.

Because we have concluded that the class in this case cannot satisfy the requirements of common issue predominance and adequacy of representation, we need not rule, definitively, on the notice given here. In accord with the Third Circuit, however, we recognize the gravity of the question whether class action notice sufficient under the Constitution and Rule 23 could ever be given to legions so unselfconscious and amorphous.

V.

* * *

For the reasons stated, the judgment of the Court of Appeals for the Third Circuit is

Affirmed.

JUSTICE BREYER, with whom JUSTICE STEVENS joins, concurring in part and dissenting in part.

Although I agree with the Court's basic holding that "settlement is relevant to a class certification," I find several problems in its approach that lead me to a different conclusion. * * *

* * *

I.

First, I believe the majority understates the importance of settlement in this case. Between 13 and 21 million workers have been exposed to asbestos in the workplace—over the past 40 or 50 years—but the most severe instances of such exposure probably occurred three or four decades ago. This exposure has led to several hundred thousand lawsuits, about 15% of which involved claims for cancer and about 30% for asbestosis. About half of the suits have involved claims for pleural thickening and plaques—the harmfulness of which is apparently controversial. * * * Some of those who suffer from the most serious injuries, however, have received little or no compensation. These lawsuits have taken up more than 6% of all federal civil filings in one recent year, and are subject to a delay that is twice that of other civil suits.

* * *

Although the transfer of the federal asbestos cases [to the Eastern District] did not produce a general settlement, it was intertwined with and led to a lengthy year-long negotiation between the co-chairs of the Plaintiff's Multi-District Litigation Steering Committee (elected by the Plaintiff's Committee Members and approved by the District Court) and the 20 asbestos defendants who are before us here. These "protracted and vigorous" negotiations led to the present partial settlement, which will pay an estimated $1.3 billion and compensate perhaps 100,000 class members in the first 10 years. "The negotiations included a substantial exchange of information" between class counsel and the 20 defendant companies, including "confidential data" showing the defendants' historical settlement averages, numbers of claims filed and settled, and insurance resources. "Virtually no provision" of the settlement "was not the subject of significant negotiation," and the settlement terms "changed substantially" during the negotiations. In the end, the negotiations produced a settlement that, the District Court determined based on its detailed review of the process, was "the result of arms-length adversarial negotiations by extraordinarily competent and experienced attorneys."

The District Court, when approving the settlement, concluded that it improved the plaintiffs' chances of compensation and reduced total legal fees and other transaction costs by a significant amount. Under the previous system, according to the court, "[t]he sickest of victims often go uncompensated for years while valuable funds go to others who remain unimpaired by their mild asbestos disease." The court believed the settlement would create a compensation system that would make more money available for plaintiffs who later develop serious illnesses.

I mention this matter because it suggests that the settlement before us is unusual in terms of its importance, both to many potential plaintiffs and to defendants, and with respect to the time, effort, and expenditure that it reflects. All of which leads me to be reluctant to set aside the District Court's findings without more assurance than I have that they are wrong. I cannot obtain that assurance through comprehensive review of the record because that is properly the job of the Court of Appeals and that court, understandably, but as we now hold, mistakenly, believed that settlement was not a relevant (and, as I would say, important) consideration.

Second, the majority, in reviewing the District Court's determination that common "issues of fact and law predominate," says that the predominance "inquiry trains on the legal or factual questions that qualify each class member's case as a genuine controversy, questions that preexist any settlement." I find it difficult to interpret this sentence in a way that could lead me to the majority's conclusion. If the majority means that these pre-settlement questions are what matters, then how does it reconcile its statement with its basic conclusion that "settlement is relevant" to class certification, or with the numerous lower court authority that says that settlement is not only relevant, but important?

Nor do I understand how one could decide whether common questions "predominate" in the abstract—without looking at what is likely to be at issue in the proceedings that will ensue, namely, the settlement. * * *

* * *

The settlement is relevant because it means that * * * common features and interests are likely to be important in the proceeding that would ensue—a proceeding that would focus primarily upon whether or not the proposed settlement fairly and properly satisfied the interests class members had in common. That is to say, the settlement underscored the importance of (a) the common fact of exposure, (b) the common interest in receiving *some* compensation for certain rather than running a strong risk of *no* compensation, and (c) the common interest in avoiding large legal fees, other transaction costs, and delays.

* * *

Third, the majority concludes that the "representative parties" will not "fairly and adequately protect the interests of the class." It finds a serious conflict between plaintiffs who are now injured and those who may be injured in the future because "for the currently injured, the critical goal is generous immediate payments," a goal that "tugs against the interest of exposure-only plaintiffs in ensuring an ample, inflation-protected fund for the future."

I agree that there is a serious problem, but it is a problem that often exists in toxic tort cases. And it is a problem that potentially exists whenever a single defendant injures several plaintiffs, for a settling plaintiff leaves fewer assets available for the others. * * *

* * * [T]his Court cannot easily safeguard such interests through review of a cold record. "What constitutes adequate representation is a question of fact that depends on the circumstances of each case." * * *

Further, certain details of the settlement that are not discussed in the majority opinion suggest that the settlement may be of greater benefit to future plaintiffs than the majority suggests. The District Court concluded that future plaintiffs receive a "significant value" from the settlement due to a variety of its items that benefit future plaintiffs, such as: (1) tolling the statute of limitations so that class members "will no longer be forced to file premature lawsuits or risk their claims being time-barred"; (2) waiver of defenses to liability; (3) payment of claims, if and when members become sick, pursuant to the settlement's compensation standards, which avoids "the uncertainties, long delays and high transaction costs [including attorney's fees] of the tort system"; (4) "some assurance that there will be funds available if and when they get sick," based on the finding that each defendant "has shown an ability to fund the payment of all qualifying claims" under the settlement; and (5) the right to additional compensation if cancer develops (many settlements for plaintiffs with noncancerous conditions bar such additional claims). For these reasons, and others, the District Court found that the distinction between present and future plaintiffs was "illusory."

* * *

Fourth, I am more agnostic than is the majority about the basic fairness of the settlement. The District Court's conclusions rested upon complicated factual findings that are not easily cast aside. It is helpful to consider some of them, such as its determination that the settlement provided "fair compensation . . . while reducing the delays and transaction costs endemic to the asbestos litigation process" and that "the proposed class action settlement is superior to other available methods for the fair and efficient resolution of the asbestos-related personal injury claims of class members." * * * "The inadequate tort system has demonstrated that the lawyers are well paid for their services but the victims are not receiving speedy and reasonably inexpensive resolution of their claims. Rather, the victims' recoveries are delayed, excessively reduced by transaction costs and relegated to the impersonal group trials and mass consolidations. The sickest of victims often go uncompensated for years while valuable funds go to others who remain unimpaired by their mild asbestos disease. Indeed, these unimpaired victims have, in many states, been forced to assert their claims prematurely or risk giving up all rights to future compensation for any future lung cancer or mesothelioma. The plan which this Court approves today will correct that unfair result for the class members and the . . . defendants." * * * [S]ettlement "will result in less delay for asbestos claimants than that experienced in the present tort system" and will "result in the CCR defendants paying more claims, at a faster rate, than they have ever paid before." Indeed, the settlement has been endorsed as fair and reasonable by the AFL–CIO (and its Building and Construction Trades Department), which represents a " 'substantial percentage' " of class members, and which has a role in monitoring implementation of the settlement.

Finally, I believe it is up to the District Court, rather than this Court, to review the legal sufficiency of notice to members of the class. * * *

II.

The issues in this case are complicated and difficult. The District Court might have been correct. Or not. Subclasses might be appropriate. Or not. I cannot tell. And I do not believe that this Court should be in the business of trying to make these fact-based determinations. That is a job suited to the district courts in the first instance, and the courts of appeal on review. But there is no reason in this case to believe that the Court of Appeals conducted its prior review with an understanding that the settlement could have constituted a reasonably strong factor in favor of class certification. For this reason, I would provide the courts below with an opportunity to analyze the factual questions involved in certification by vacating the judgment, and remanding the case for further proceedings.

NOTES AND QUESTIONS

1. Is Justice Breyer correct to suggest that the Supreme Court second-guessed the fact-finding of the district court? Should *Amchem* be read as holding as a matter of law that a "sprawling" settlement like the one attempted there simply cannot be approved? Or could the settlement have been structured in such a manner so as to secure Supreme Court approval? How could the adequacy issues have been addressed? Predominance? Notice?

2. How is settlement relevant to the majority's class-certification inquiry? Does the relevance of settlement depend upon which requirement of Rule 23(a) and (b) is being considered? How does Justice Breyer's approach differ from the majority's approach?

3. Why, according to the majority (in footnote 3), is it "basic to comprehension of this proceeding to notice that no transferred case is included in the settlement at issue, and no case covered by the settlement existed as a civil action at the time of the MDL Panel transfer"?

4. In portions of *Amchem* not excerpted above, the Court twice noted that its interpretation of Rule 23 was constrained by the Rules Enabling Act (the "REA"), 28 U.S.C. § 2072(b), which states that rules of procedure "shall not abridge, enlarge, or modify any substantive right." *See Amchem*, 521 U.S. at 612–13, 629. How might the district court's certification have violated the REA? Did the *Amchem* majority violate the REA? *See* Note, *The Rules Enabling Act and the Limits of Rule 23*, 111 Harv. L. Rev. 2294, 2294 (1998) (contending that *Amchem*, "which allows certification of a settlement class that could not be certified as a litigation class, alters substantive rights, implicating the REA's limits on Court rulemaking," but that "*Amchem*'s interpretation of Rule 23 is consistent with precedents, which interpret the REA expansively").

5. When reviewing the Third Circuit's decision, the Supreme Court in *Amchem* noted (in a portion of the opinion not excerpted above) that the Advisory Committee on the Federal Rules had proposed an amendment to Rule 23 explicitly permitting settlement-only class certification: "A proposed amendment to Rule 23 would expressly authorize settlement class certification, in conjunction with a motion by the settling parties for Rule 23(b)(3) certification, 'even though the requirements of subdivision (b)(3) might not be met for purposes of trial.'" *Amchem*, 521 U.S. at 619. Similarly, the ALI proposes permitting certification of settlement classes without requiring that all of the requirements for certifying a litigation class be met. In particular, under the ALI approach, the settlement class need not satisfy "predominance." ALI *Principles* § 3.06 at 219. Finally, in connection with the 2016 proposed rule changes, the Advisory Committee again looked at a possible settlement-only class certification but decided not to propose such an amendment to Rule 23. What is the rationale for creating a Rule 23 settlement class that does not have to satisfy all of the requirements for a litigation class? Under the reasoning of *Amchem*, what concerns would be raised by such a class?

6. Can a defendant argue that a class certification should be certified for settlement purposes without having those arguments used against it if the case does not settle? In *Carnegie v. Household Int'l, Inc.*, 376 F.3d 656 (7th Cir. 2004), the Seventh Circuit held that judicial estoppel precluded the defendant in a consumer fraud class action—who initially urged approval of a global class settlement—from later challenging certification of the class for *litigation* purposes after the district court disapproved the settlement. For criticism of *Car-*

negie on the ground that it misapplies judicial estoppel and discourages defendants from reaching class settlements, *see* Note, *Fast and Loose Litigants and Courts:* Carnegie v. Household International, Inc., *and the End of Settlement Classes*, 84 Tex. L. Rev. 541 (2005). Compare *Carnegie*'s approach to the approach advocated by the ALI, which states: "If a proposed settlement class is not approved, no statements, representations, or arguments made by the proponents of the settlement in the settlement context may be used against the proponent making the statement in any subsequent litigation of class-certification or merits issues." ALI *Principles* § 3.06(d) at 219. Which approach is better? Why?

7. Notwithstanding *Amchem*, settlement-only certifications have remained common, at least in cases where some litigation has transpired, so that settlement is not presented at the outset of litigation as a *fait accompli*. *See, e.g.*, *In re Insurance Brokerage Antitrust Litig.*, 579 F.3d 241, 248, 258 (3d Cir. 2009) (affirming settlement-only class certification but requiring "district courts to be even more scrupulous than usual in examining the fairness of the proposed settlement" when such examination is made simultaneously with the certification determination); *In re Warfarin Sodium Antitrust Litig.*, 391 F.3d 516, 529–30 (3d Cir. 2004) (affirming certification of (b)(3) settlement class against pharmaceutical company for anti-competitive conduct and dissemination of false and misleading information, concluding that variations in state law in settlement-only class would not create same manageability problems as would be created in a litigation class).

8. Did the Supreme Court in *Amchem* alleviate all of the potential concerns regarding settlement certifications and inventory settlements identified by Professor Coffee in the article excerpted earlier in this chapter?

9. Some scholars argue that settlement certification is inherently unconstitutional because the settlement class action lacks a live controversy between the parties, as required by Article III. *See* Martin H. Redish & Andrianna D. Kastanek, *Settlement Class Actions, the Case-or-Controversy Requirement, and the Nature of the Adjudicatory Process*, 73 U. Chi. L. Rev. 545, 614–15 (2006) (arguing that federal courts assuming jurisdiction over class settlement suits "have neglected their fundamental Article III obligation to hear only cases or controversies—an obligation rooted in the text, jurisprudence, and values served by the adverseness requirement"). Should courts refrain from exercising jurisdiction over settlement class actions altogether? Would the case or controversy issue depend in part upon whether a settlement class is certified after substantial litigation, as opposed to one, like *Amchem*, in which a lawsuit was filed and settled the same day?

ORTIZ V. FIBREBOARD CORP.
Supreme Court of the United States, 1999.
527 U.S. 815.

[*See* Chapter 3(A)(2).]

NOTES AND QUESTIONS

1. To what extent was the result in *Ortiz* compelled by *Amchem*? Notably, the *Ortiz* case was awaiting review by the Supreme Court when the Court issued *Amchem*, and the Court originally remanded *Ortiz* to the Fifth Circuit after *Amchem* was issued for reconsideration in light of *Amchem*. The Fifth

Circuit found "nothing in the *Amchem* opinion that change[d its] prior decision." *In re Asbestos Litig.*, 134 F.3d 668, 669 (5th Cir. 1998), *rev'd*, *Ortiz v. Fibreboard Corp.*, 527 U.S. 815 (1999). Ultimately, the Supreme Court disagreed.

2. Of the two settlements, *Amchem* and *Ortiz*, which posed more significant problems under Rule 23?

3. Justice Breyer wrote the dissent in both *Amchem* and *Ortiz*, and in both cases was joined only by Justice Stevens. In *Amchem*, Justice Ginsburg wrote the majority opinion, whereas Justice Souter wrote the majority opinion in *Ortiz*. Which majority opinion—Justice Ginsburg's or Justice Souter's—is more convincing?

4. The *Amchem* majority recognized that "legislative inaction" and the federal courts' lack of authority to create a "national toxic tort compensation regime" has resulted in the courts' use of imperfect procedural mechanisms—such as the settlement class—to address the onslaught of asbestos litigation that has overwhelmed the courts for decades. 521 U.S. at 599. The *Amchem* dissent also underscored the importance of the *Amchem* settlement—an agreement that could resolve the claims of potentially millions of persons affected by exposure to asbestos. Likewise, *Ortiz*—while reversing certification of a mandatory settlement class—acknowledged the class action was "prompted by the elephantine mass of asbestos cases." *Ortiz*, 527 U.S. at 821.

For a discussion of how asbestos cases have proceeded in the wake of *Amchem* and *Ortiz*, *see* Deborah R. Hensler, *As Time Goes By: Asbestos Litigation After* Amchem *and* Ortiz, 80 Tex. L. Rev. 1899 (2002). According to Professor Hensler, aggregate settlements have continued at a significant pace post-*Amchem* (in key instances, with settlements involving large numbers of individual claims—thus avoiding class action restrictions—using average amounts instead of case-by-case determinations). Numerous asbestos defendants have declared bankruptcy since *Amchem*, and as a result, plaintiff lawyers have identified new asbestos defendants to sue and have increased the price of settlement for those companies that have avoided bankruptcy. *See also* Samuel Issacharoff, *"Shocked": Mass Torts and Aggregate Asbestos Litigation After* Amchem *and* Ortiz, 80 Tex. L. Rev. 1925, 1925 (2002) (noting that the asbestos judicial crisis shows "no sign of abating any time soon").

In 2005, members of Congress proposed legislation, the Fairness in Asbestos Injury Resolution Act of 2005, that would take asbestos cases out of court and provide a $140 billion fund, financed by asbestos companies and their insurers, from which victims of asbestos exposure could apply for relief. The bill aimed to "create a fair and efficient system to resolve claims of victims for bodily injury caused by asbestos exposure, and for other purposes." S. 852, 109th Cong. (2005). The bill did not pass, and legislative solutions have remained elusive. Given the difficulty of settlement certification of asbestos litigation post-*Amchem*, is a legislative solution preferable?

5. In light of the difficulty plaintiffs have had in obtaining certification of mass tort cases, as illustrated by *Amchem* and *Ortiz*, such litigation is increasingly settled on an aggregate, non-class basis. This issue is explored in Chapter 13(C).

6. In *Juris v. Inamed Corp.*, 685 F.3d 1294 (11th Cir. 2012), an absent class member brought a due process challenge to the res judicata effect of the class action settlement in the limited-fund class settlement in the breast-im-

plant cases that had been consolidated before Judge Sam Pointer in the Northern District of Alabama. The Eleventh Circuit first concluded that there had been no deficiency in the notice campaign that had been utilized as part of the settlement. Turning to plaintiff's attack on Judge Pointer's failure to appoint subclasses for potentially divergent interests within the settlement class, the Eleventh Circuit agreed that "*Amchem* and *Ortiz* appear to hold that Rule 23(a)(4) calls for *some type* of adequate structural protection," but found that the settlement passed muster despite the absence of formal subclasses:

> Judge Pointer and class counsel put in place procedures to protect against antagonistic alignment within the class and avoid the fatal flaw in *Amchem*. Judge Pointer appointed six Inamed breast implant recipients as class representatives, among them, a representative with no manifested injury, one with minor to moderate injuries, and one who was totally disabled. He appointed five attorneys with extensive breast implant trial experience as class counsel. Most significantly, and anticipating an *Amchem* problem, separate counsel, Ernest Hornsby, was specifically brought in for the sole purpose of representing those plaintiffs with only potential, future injuries. Thus, even prior to provisional certification of the class, the interests of those claimants with unmanifested injuries were represented and given a separate seat at the negotiation table through qualified and independent counsel. Hornsby continued his representation of exposure-only plaintiffs throughout the case, including when, at the certification stage, Judge Pointer considered approving the settlement and the settlement fund, and, more significantly, later, when he considered various proposals for allocating the fund. This combination of named plaintiffs representing the full spectrum of breast implant claimants and separate counsel to represent the present injury and future injury claimants addressed the potential and actual divergent interests within the Inamed class.
>
> In contrast with *Amchem* and *Ortiz*, the structure of the negotiations in the case at bar ensured that class representatives operated with a proper understanding of their representative responsibilities. The negotiation process did not resemble that in *Amchem* and *Ortiz* where there were no structural assurances whatsoever and where nobody "exclusively advanced the particular interests of either subgroup." Because of this, we are confident that the class settlement, as well as the plan for distribution, was achieved only by the consent of those who understood that their role was to advocate on behalf of their respective subgroups. We therefore conclude that the structural protections put in place were sufficient to meet the demands of due process.

Id. at 1324–25. Is the court persuasive in distinguishing *Amchem* and *Ortiz*?

4. PROCEDURAL CONSIDERATIONS IN ASSESSING CLASS ACTION SETTLEMENTS

Although courts are charged with approving class action settlements, Rule 23(e) provides little guidance for making such assessments. Procedural aspects of settlement approval are considered in this section; substantive aspects of a court's fairness determination are considered in the next section.

Parties seeking approval of a class action settlement ordinarily follow a well-established path. The parties jointly submit a proposed settlement to the court (and, if a class has not already been certified, a motion for class certification). The court makes a preliminary assessment of the proposed settlement's fairness, sometimes (but not always) holding a hearing at this preliminary stage to assess the negotiations leading up to the settlement. If the court provides preliminary approval (and preliminarily certifies the class for settlement, in a settlement-certification context), the parties prepare and distribute notice of the proposed settlement to the class, explaining the settlement's terms, providing information about class members' options, and explaining how the settlement-approval process will proceed. Discovery relating to the settlement may be propounded. Finally, after holding a fairness hearing at which both proponents and opponents of the settlement may present their positions, the court renders a decision either approving or rejecting the settlement (and, if necessary, making a "final" ruling on class certification).

a. Notice

Rule 23(e)(1), as amended in 2003, states that "[t]he court must direct notice in a reasonable manner to all class members who would be bound by" "a proposed settlement, voluntary dismissal, or compromise." This language invests substantial discretion in the district court when deciding how notice shall be provided. The following case, although decided under the pre-2003 version of Rule 23(e), explores the issue of notice in the interesting context of a lawsuit against the lawyers who represented the class.

ZIMMER PAPER PRODS., INC. V. BERGER & MONTAGUE, P.C.
United States Court of Appeals, Third Circuit, 1985.
758 F.2d 86.

Before ADAMS and WEIS, CIRCUIT JUDGES, and HARRIS, DISTRICT JUDGE [(E. and W.D. Ark.), by designation].

ADAMS, CIRCUIT JUDGE.

The proper elements of notice to class members are a concern in almost every class action; consequently, the interrelated notice requirements of due process and Fed. R. Civ. P. Rule 23 have been frequently litigated. This case, however, raises the question of the adequacy of class notice in a novel context.

Zimmer Paper Products, Incorporated, a member of the plaintiff class in an antitrust action, has sued its own class counsel for a breach of fiduciary duty and negligence in failing to provide to it sufficient notice of the settlement of the action. Zimmer asserts that because it never received notice of the settlement, it failed to file a claim for its share, thereby losing approximately $250,000. * * *

Attorneys for the class provided notice of the settlement and of the necessity to file a claim in a traditional court-approved manner: by both first-class mail and publication in the *Wall Street Journal*. The district court in this action determined that compliance with these approved notice procedures did not constitute a breach of fiduciary duty and further concluded that plaintiff had made no showing of negligence in class counsel's execution of the notice. Consequently, the district court granted defendants summary judgment. * * * [W]e will affirm the judgment of the district court.

I.

Defendants were class counsel in an antitrust class action. Plaintiff, Zimmer Paper Products, was one of more than 1500 plaintiff class members in the litigation. When the lawsuit was settled, Zimmer did not file a claim for its share of the settlement proceeds. It alleges that it failed to assert such a claim because class counsel did not provide adequate notice.

Two separate notices were sent to class members in the course of the antitrust litigation, one in June and the other in November of 1981. Both notices were carried out in the same court-approved manner. On April 10, 1981, after proposed settlements had been reached with three defendants, the court ordered that "Notice of Class Action and Proposed Partial Settlement" be mailed to all plaintiff class members by June 1, 1981, and be published in all regional editions of *The Wall Street Journal*.[3] Zimmer admits to receiving six copies of the June 1 notice.

The second notice, mailed November 10, 1981, and also published in the *Wall Street Journal*, informed class members of proposed additional settlements and, most importantly, of a plan for distribution of the settlement fund. Zimmer asserts that it did not receive any of the November 10th notices mailed to it, and although it did receive the *Wall Street Journal*, the notice that was contained in it apparently did not come to its attention.

Both sets of notices were approved by the court, and were carried out in the same manner—by individual first-class mail and publication. Class counsel retained experienced, professional firms to prepare and mail the notices, as is customarily done. A list of potential class members was supplied to Provcor Services, Inc., a company that regularly engages in class action notice preparation. The list included Zimmer. Provcor placed the class members' names and addresses, and the deviations therefrom,[4] on a computer list. Its list also included Zimmer.

Provcor then verified the accuracy of the list, and printed gum-backed mailing labels. VPI Reproduction Center, Inc., and its subcontractor, Fischler's Printing & Office Products, printed the notices and prepared them for mailing. VPI, Fischler, and Provcor worked together, through Bartholomew Milano, a VPI employee, to ensure that the notices were properly printed, folded, addressed, and mailed. VPI made photocopies of the mailing labels. The photocopies show that seven labels were addressed to Zimmer for each mailing. Provcor then mailed the notices by first-class mail.

Zimmer admits to receiving six of the seven June 1, 1981 notices, which were mailed according to the above-described procedure. When this same procedure was followed on November 10, 1981, Zimmer insists that it received none of the seven notices. Since other plaintiff class members responded by filing claims, it is apparent that at the very least many of the notices were received. Indeed, * * * both Zenith Specialty Bag Co. (whose

---

[3] The June 1st notice was to inform class members of the institution of the antitrust litigation, the partial settlements, their membership in the class, and the procedures to follow if they wished to opt out.

[4] The purpose of multiple mailings to class members is to guard against address errors. Thus, for example, Zimmer was listed seven times; four variations were addressed to its Indianapolis office, and three more to its South San Francisco office.

mailing label appeared on the page preceding Zimmer's), and Zorn Packaging, Inc. (whose mailing label was on the same page as Zimmer's) received the November 10th notice and filed claims.

On August 20, 1982, after the district court had approved the claims filed by class members, the settlement fund was fully distributed, on a *pro rata* basis. Approximately nine months later, in May, 1983, Zimmer filed this action, charging defendants with a breach of their fiduciary duties and with negligence in failing to assure that Zimmer was notified. Zimmer argued before the district court that the notice should have been conducted by certified mail, return receipt requested, rather than first-class mail; that class counsel had a duty to conduct some follow-up procedures upon learning of the 12% response rate to their November 10 notice * * * and that class counsel negligently carried out the mailing.

[Finding that first-class mailing was sufficient and that the mailing procedure was not negligently administered, the district court, after permitting discovery, granted summary judgment to defendants.]

II.

Zimmer advances two principal contentions in this Court. First, it contends that, given the particular circumstances of this case, class counsel breached its fiduciary duty in suggesting and conducting a court-approved notice procedure that utilized only first-class mail and publication. Second, it maintains that even if the court-ordered notice is legally sufficient to meet counsel's fiduciary obligations, there are material issues of fact regarding negligence in the execution of the notice procedure that preclude summary judgment. We address these arguments in order.

A.

It is well settled that in the usual situation first-class mail and publication fully satisfy the notice requirements of both Fed. R. Civ. P. 23 and the due process clause. * * *

First-class mail and publication have consistently been considered sufficient to satisfy the notice requirements of Rule 23(d)(2) and Rule 23(e) for advising class members of a proposed settlement and of their right to file claims.

Indeed, first-class mail and publication regularly have been deemed adequate under the stricter notice requirements, not applicable here, of Rule 23(c)(2).

The two leading Supreme Court cases on notice, *Mullane v. Central Hanover Bank & Trust Co.*, 339 U.S. 306 (1950), and *Eisen v. Carlisle & Jacquelin*, 417 U.S. 156 (1974), both prescribed first-class mail to identifiable individuals together with publication. While the Supreme Court may not have intended this particular procedure to be taken as a hard and fast rule, it has nevertheless become common practice to send notice by first-class mail and publication. * * *

* * *

Zimmer [nonetheless argues that class counsel had a fiduciary duty encompassing] a responsibility to effect notice by certified mail, return receipt requested, and to undertake follow-up procedures after the first notice was sent. It cites no case to support this proposition. Indeed, the only decision we have found that even discusses the relative merits of first-class and certified mail in the notice context expressly reaffirms the adequacy of first-class mail. The bounds of fiduciary duty are undoubtedly not easy to define, but certainly we must be guided by the fact that the practice here alleged to breach such duties is a customary one, and has been approved, after careful judicial scrutiny, not only in this case but in legions of others. If class counsel in this case have breached their fiduciary duties, attorneys throughout the country who have complied with court orders and a Supreme Court-approved notice procedure may well be subject to malpractice lawsuits by anyone who alleges that he or she did not receive notice of the opportunity to file a claim.

These untoward nationwide results need not follow, Zimmer argues, because of the peculiar nature of this case. Specifically, Zimmer points to the large amount of the settlement (over twenty million dollars), the relatively small number of class members (approximately 1550), and what it characterizes as an uncommonly low response rate to the November notices (approximately 12% of the class filed claims to share in the settlement). While each of these factors might be relevant at the time the notice procedure is being considered and implemented in the first instance, we do not believe that they support Zimmer's assertion of malpractice after the notices have been sent out.

First, Zimmer has not offered sufficient evidence to make these figures particularly meaningful. It notes, for example, that the average claim was approximately $12,000, but fails to provide a mean figure. If there were several large claims involved, as is often the situation in such actions, the mean figure might well be considerably lower. The record here shows that several settlement shares in the antitrust litigation were in excess of $1.5 million, while other claims were as low as $21.28. It is certainly reasonable to assume that most of those who did not respond might have been concentrated in the lower rather than the higher end of these figures.

Second, the case law does not make clear what role, if any, the amount of money involved should play in ascertaining whether the notice is reasonably calculated to apprise class members of the action. In *Eisen*, where the cost of individual notice to class members was so considerable with respect to the potential recovery as effectively to end the suit as a class action, the Court nonetheless required individual notice, stating "there is nothing in Rule 23 to suggest that the notice requirements can be tailored to fit the pocketbooks of particular plaintiffs." Yet, Zimmer suggests that we can tailor the notice requirements of fiduciary duty to the pocketbook of a particular plaintiff—itself.

Moreover, the large amount of money involved and the nature of the class in some respects weigh against Zimmer's argument. Zimmer is not an unsophisticated consumer, but a corporation that did considerable business with the defendants named in the antitrust litigation. It received the June 1st notice, and thus was aware that the suit was pending, that half the defendants had already settled, and that Zimmer, which had done a large volume of business with the defendants, probably had a substantial stake in the matter. It would not be unreasonable, in such a situation, for a corporation such as Zimmer to notify its counsel, so that developments in the action might be followed.

These considerations gain significance in light of the fact that the class as a whole consisted primarily of business entities as distinguished from individuals. The presumed expertise of such a class in legal matters suggests that first-class mail would be "reasonably calculated . . . to apprise interested parties" of the action. *Mullane*, 339 U.S. at 314. More elaborate steps, such as certified mail, have been used in situations where class members may be presumed to be less aware of a notice's legal ramifications.

Finally, the 12% response rate does not appear to be determinative. Although at first glance this response rate appears low, there has been considerable debate over whether or not it is in fact low. While the defendants have cited studies by Herbert Newberg, author of a treatise on class actions, to demonstrate that a 12% rate is in line with response rates in similar settlements, Zimmer has come forward with nothing to suggest that the rate is uncharacteristically low. Since it is the plaintiff's burden to establish that a fiduciary duty has been breached, we believe this lack of evidence to be damaging to Zimmer's reliance on the 12% rate.

* * *

We do not hold today that first-class mail and publication will always suffice, either under a due process or a fiduciary duty analysis. Indeed, given the large sums involved and the low response rate, it might have been preferable for the district court in the antitrust litigation to have required certified mail or follow-up procedures. We hold only that in this case, where the procedure employed was customary and court-approved, where there was no suggestion before the district court that a different type of notice be employed, and where the plaintiffs have offered little support for the proposition that more was required, class counsel cannot be said to have breached their duties. * * *

B.

Zimmer also insists that the district court erred in granting summary judgment on its negligence claim. It urges that even if the notice procedure employed does not itself constitute a breach of fiduciary duty, class counsel is liable if it conducted the notice procedure in a negligent manner. The district court concurred in principle with this contention, and therefore allowed Zimmer to conduct substantial discovery to determine whether in fact class counsel had been negligent in preparing and mailing the notifications. Because Zimmer was unable to show any evidence of negligence causing Zimmer to fail to receive notice, the district court awarded defendants summary judgment. We agree [with the district court]. * * *

* * *

Zimmer has not adduced any evidence to suggest that class counsel's hiring of three professional firms to print, prepare and mail the notice was itself below the legal profession's standard of care with regard to class notice. * * * [I]t is undisputed that some verification procedures were followed: a photocopy of the mailing labels was prepared, and the mailing label sheet was checked first for accuracy and later to ascertain whether all mailing labels were peeled off and affixed to envelopes.

III.

For the foregoing reasons, and for the reasons stated by the district court, we will affirm the district court's order for summary judgment against plaintiff Zimmer.

WEIS, CIRCUIT JUDGE, dissenting.

For present purposes, I am willing to accept the majority's position that class counsel followed customary procedures in proposing a first class mailing of the November notice. However, I do not agree that as a matter of law the defendants' fiduciary duties required no further action in the face of an obviously low reply rate. When the initial effort to provide notice elicited a response from only 12% of the class, counsel may have owed their clients the obligation to do more.

* * *

The [district] court cited no authority for its conclusion that counsel did not have a duty to follow-up. Having determined that there had been compliance with the notice requirements of Fed. R. Civ. P. 23(e) and the mailing order, the court apparently concluded that the fiduciary obligation counsel owed to the absentee members of the class had been fulfilled as well.

The inquiry into counsels' duty toward their clients should not have ended at that point. The fiduciary obligation of class counsel may go beyond the notice requirements of Rule 23(e). If the notice procedure is ineffective then there should be an exploration of the availability and feasibility of other steps together with a determination of whether it is reasonable to require counsel to implement them.

To illustrate the point, as an extreme example, one can hypothesize a situation in which none of the absentee class members responds to a settlement notice. In that situation, where adequate funds are available for distribution and reimbursement of expenses, surely counsel is not free to disburse the entire fund to the class representatives and then collect the legal fees without further efforts to contact the absentees. Obviously, the point at which the response level gives reasonable assurance of adequate notice must depend on the circumstances.

* * *

Depriving plaintiff of the opportunity to participate in the distribution is particularly unfortunate here because Zimmer's losses contributed to increasing the amount of the settlement achieved. In arriving at a suitable settlement, counsel no doubt accumulated the losses suffered by each member of the class as a beginning point and then applied the various factors which go into the determination of a fair and reasonable compromise of that total figure.

The settlement amount, therefore, took into account damages sustained by plaintiff, but, in distribution, its share was given *pro rata* to other members of the class. Those parties received not only the amount due them but the plaintiff's portion as well. To that extent, the recipients were overcompensated and plaintiff short changed.

Similarly, the fees which class counsel received were determined by a process in which the size of the settlement was a factor. In this respect, the losses sustained by plaintiff played a part in augmenting counsels' fee. Viewed in this light, it is apparent that counsel were not only fiduciaries, but well compensated ones as well.

In view of these considerations and given the limited response to the November 1981 mailing, I believe that plaintiff has presented sufficient facts to question the reasonableness of the defendants' failure to take follow-up action.

* * *

* * * In view of the large settlement fund and money available for expenses, measures considered unreasonable in other circumstances may have been required here. These and other concerns were for a jury to weigh.

I would vacate the entry of summary judgment and remand for further proceedings.

NOTES AND QUESTIONS

1. Appellate courts have been reluctant to provide detailed guidelines about what information a settlement notice should contain. *See, e.g., DeBoer v. Mellon Mortgage Co.*, 64 F.3d 1171, 1176 (8th Cir. 1995) (settlement notices need not be particularly "extensive or remarkably thorough"). *But see, e.g., White v. Alabama*, 74 F.3d 1058, 1066 n.27 (11th Cir. 1996) (notice describing settlement in small type and "legalese" inappropriate). Moreover, although the 2003 amendments to Rule 23 specified the contents of a notice in the context of the certification of a (b)(3) class, *see* Fed. R. Civ. P. 23(c)(2)(B)), the amendments did not address the contents of notice of a proposed settlement.

2. The Advisory Committee Notes to the 2003 amendments specifically address whether individual notice of a settlement is required:

> Reasonable settlement notice may require individual notice in the manner required by Rule 23(c)(2)(B) for certification notice to a Rule 23(b)(3) class. Individual notice is appropriate, for example, if class members are required to take action—such as filing claims—to participate in the judgment, or if the court orders a settlement opt-out opportunity under Rule 23(e)(3).

Should the question of whether individual notice is required turn on whether the class was certified under (b)(1), (b)(2), or (b)(3)? Should individual notice in a (b)(3) action be required if the settlement involves an automatic payment (without the necessity of submitting a claim form)?

The ALI proposes a flexible and pragmatic approach to what constitutes sufficient notice of a class action settlement. The ALI encourages courts to consider the cost of notice and likelihood of recovery when determining the proper form and content of notice, finding "individual notice * * * presumptively less important when the claims are likely too small to be pursued individually in the absence of a class action." ALI *Principles* § 3.04(b) at 204. Where direct, individual notice does not make economic sense, the ALI would not require it. *Id.* at 205. Is this approach advisable? Does the approach appropriately take into account due process concerns?

Sec. A   RESOLUTION AND FUNDING OF CLASS ACTIONS   573

3. In *Zimmer*, should the issue of the attorneys' negligence have been determined, as the dissent contended, by a jury rather than by a court on summary judgment?

4. There is clear dissatisfaction in academic circles about Rule 23(e) notice as presently administered in class actions. One commentator complains:

> The general rule regarding the content of settlement notices is that the notice must "fairly apprise the prospective members of the class of the terms of the proposed settlement and of the [available] options." Class members should receive enough information in the notice so that they may decide whether to object or, if permitted, to opt out. The usual notices, however, fall substantially short of providing sufficient or accurate information to render rational decisionmaking possible.
>
> a. Adequacy of Representation Is Not Described
>
> Despite the fact that adequate representation is integral to the fairness of a settlement, adequacy of representation is seldom described in notices or even listed as an issue for the settlement hearing. The most fundamental principles underlying class actions limit the powers of the class representatives to the claims they possess in common with other members of the class. Yet the typical settlement notice does not describe the claims and remedies of the named representatives, which means that class members cannot know whether they have been adequately represented in settlement negotiations.
> * * *
>
> Several lower court decisions have justified such deficiencies by holding that notice is only designed to serve as guidance to the major terms of agreement and to enable further inquiry. The flaw in this reasoning, however, is that few if any class members with small or medium-sized claims are willing or able to travel to a distant city to examine the court records in order to obtain necessary information concerning the case. Furthermore, such information is not necessarily available in the court files. * * *
>
> Adequacy of representation in settlement negotiation should be a key issue at the settlement hearing. Courts have the discretionary power to require that class members be notified of an opportunity to state whether they consider the representation to be fair and adequate. Courts should make written determinations concerning adequacy of representation * * *.
>
> b. Objections by Representatives Are Not Disclosed
>
> To avoid dissent, objections, or opt outs, class counsel generally do not include in the notice that some or all of the named representatives oppose the terms of the settlement agreement. Despite the fact that the existence of such opposition is vital to an absent class member's evaluation of her options, this information may not appear in the public file. * * *
>
> c. Plan of Distribution Is Not Revealed
>
> The settlement agreement, notice, and hearing focus on the amount of the settlement fund and related terms. The plan of distribution provides the scheme and details on how and to whom the set-

tlement fund will be paid. Class counsel might not reveal the distribution details until the day of the settlement hearing or even later because such details may disclose preferences or other disparate treatment of class members which could give rise to conflicts of interest and might impede or delay settlement approval. Such distribution information is crucial to class members' decisions whether to object or to opt out, yet various courts have upheld the denial of access to this information.

In summary, the class member who receives the currently accepted form of settlement notice is provided no information in the notice or in the record on the merits as to adequacy of representation, the position of the named representatives, the course of settlement negotiations, the details of attorneys' fees, or the method or amount of settlement distribution. Such notices should be deemed unreasonable and a denial of due process.

Howard M. Downs, *Federal Class Actions: Diminished Protection for the Class and the Case for Reform*, 73 Neb. L. Rev. 646, 693–96 (1994). Should each of the elements identified by Professor Downs be required? How should a court decide? How would a court ensure it had sufficient information to confirm the parties' representations about such information in the notice? What additional guidelines would be appropriate to help courts assess the adequacy of settlement notices?

Another commentator contends that, according to the case law, a class action settlement notice should remain "scrupulously neutral," but at minimum should contain: (i) the terms of the proposed settlement (consideration to be paid, formula for distributing funds, and formula for determining attorneys' fees); (ii) the date and location of the settlement hearing; (iii) a description of the litigation (allegations, relief requested, and proceedings to date); and (iv) procedural details for filing claims and obtaining and inspecting any relevant documents. *See* Note, *Notice and the Protection of Class Members' Interests*, 69 S. Cal. L. Rev. 1121, 1135–37 (1996). That commentator, however, believes that the courts should go further. Drawing on securities law, the commentator proposes that courts provide notice under Rule 23(e) of all "material" information. *Id.* at 1149. In the context of class action settlements, the commentator suggests that the following would surely be material: (i) recovery projections (that is, the percentage of loss suffered that is recovered in the settlement); (ii) opinions of class members with particularly large stakes (*e.g.*, in the securities fraud context, the views of institutional investors); (iii) objections raised by other class members; (iv) the amount of discovery undertaken prior to settlement; (v) information relating to settlement negotiations (including, for example, insurance limits and "factors that suggest the attorney may not be acting in the true interest of the class"); and (vi) an assessment of the strength of the case on the merits. *Id.* at 1151–56. Would such disclosures be useful? Would they be practical? What additional burdens would such standards impose? Would the benefits be worth those costs? *See* Section 8 of this chapter for discussion of a proposed amendment to Rule 23 to provide more information to the district court for its assessment of whether to send notice of the proposed settlement to class members.

5. In what ways can changes in technology enhance class settlement notice programs? Courts, practitioners, and commentators are realizing the potential benefits that technological developments—such as e-mail and Internet sites—can have on class settlement notification, claims administration, and

client communication. For a description of how Internet technology can not only supplement, but supplant, traditional communication in class actions, *see* Robert H. Klonoff, *Class Actions in the Year 2026: A Prognosis*, 65 Emory L.J. 1569, 1650–64 (2016) (discussing how changes in technology have altered the administration of class actions); Robert H. Klonoff, Mark Herrmann & Bradley W. Harrison, *Making Class Actions Work: The Untapped Potential of the Internet*, 69 U. Pitt. L. Rev. 727 (2008). *See also generally* Chapter 5(A).

A number of courts have addressed the proper role that various technologies can play in notifying people of class action settlements. For example, some courts have concluded that electronic notices, such as e-mail, may appropriately be used to notify a class, particularly in cases involving technology companies or online services. E-mail notice can be less expensive, faster, and more convenient than notice by mail. Where e-mails and websites are the standard way in which the parties already communicate, such electronic notification may be reasonable. *See, e.g., Browning v. Yahoo! Inc.*, 2007 WL 4105971, at *4 (N.D. Cal. 2007) (approving notice plan comprised of website, mailings, publication, and emails, and noting "[e]mail notice was particularly suitable in this case, where settlement class members' claims arise from their visits to Defendants' Internet websites."); *Chavez v. Netflix Inc.*, 162 Cal. App. 4th 43, 75 Cal. Rptr. 3d 413, 427 (2008) (under California law, summary notice of class settlement in e-mail that directed class members through hyperlinks to Internet web site with more information was sufficient notice against DVD rental business where plaintiffs regularly conducted business with defendant over the Internet). Electronic notice also enables enhanced tracking and the opportunity for the parties to supplement and update information.

Other courts, however, have held that e-mail notification is inadequate when a defendant has the class members' mailing addresses. *See, e.g., West v. Carfax, Inc.*, 2009 WL 5064143, at *1–6 (Ohio App. 2009) (e-mail and publication settlement notice fell short of *Eisen*'s "reasonable effort" standard where defendant could have retrieved individual addresses of Carfax customers from their vehicle VIN numbers). E-mail notification may be problematic because of consumers' propensity to delete unsolicited e-mails, failure to check their e-mail accounts regularly, or inability to open attachments. *See West*, 2009 WL 5064143 at *6. E-mails can be distorted, bounced back, or sent to spam filters, and there is no system for forwarding e-mails to those who have changed their e-mail accounts, analogous to the U.S. Post Office's forwarding system for paper mail. *Id.; see also, e.g., Reab v. Electronic Arts Inc.*, 214 F.R.D. 623, 630–31 (D. Colo. 2002) (notice of class litigation only through first-class mail approved where there was concern that e-mails could be distorted and forwarded to non-class members); *Karvaly v. eBay Inc.*, 245 F.R.D. 71, 91–93 (E.D.N.Y. 2007) (in class action against online auction company, court rejected e-mail settlement notice as unconstitutional and an inadequate substitute for traditional first-class mail despite fact that parties communicated with each other exclusively online). Notice to mobile devices, such as text messaging, has also proved difficult as a new medium for class notification because of its potential violation of the Telephone Consumer Protection Act of 1991, 47 U.S.C. § 227(b)(1)(A)(iii) (TCPA) (prohibiting a person from making a call to a cell phone number (other than for an emergency or with prior express consent) using an automatic telephone dialing system or artificial or prerecorded voice). Specifically, because unsolicited text messages have been deemed impermissible cell phone calls under the TCPA, text messaging as a form of class notification may be impermissible under certain circumstances. *See Satterfield v. Simon & Schuster Inc.*, 569 F.3d 946 (9th Cir. 2009); *see also Trends: Communication Technology Poses*

Novel Notification Issues, 11 Class Action Litig. Report 183, 184 (2010) (providing tips for effective use of electronic class notice).

Despite new and evolving methods of communication, traditional media are still predominant in class action notice. For an interesting examination of how new and traditional media compare with one another, *see* Katherine Kinsella & Maureen Gorman, *Reality Check: The State of New Media Options for Class Action Notice*, 11 Class Action Litig. Report 187 (Feb. 26, 2010). What are the benefits and risks of relying on new forms of communication when providing class notice?

6. The Federal Judicial Center provides examples of "plain language" notices of class settlements. Those examples are available at www.fjc.gov, under "Class Action Notices Page" (last visited Feb. 6, 2017). *See also* ALI *Principles* § 3.04(c) at 204, 206 (requiring "plain language" and describing minimum contents for class settlement notice).

b. Discovery Relating to Settlement

How do objectors gain access to information necessary to challenge a proposed settlement? It is within the district court's discretion to allow objectors to take discovery, including even depositions of counsel involved in settlement negotiations. *See, e.g., Holden v. Burlington N., Inc.*, 665 F. Supp. 1398, 1425 (D.Minn. 1987). Should discovery occur as a matter of course, given the interests at stake in class action settlement negotiations? Or do other mechanisms adequately protect the varied interests at stake? Consider the following.

MANUAL FOR COMPLEX LITIGATION (FOURTH)
Federal Judicial Center (2004) § 21.643.

Role of Objectors in Settlement

* * * The important role some objectors play might justify additional discovery, access to information obtained by class counsel and class representatives, and the right to participate in the fairness hearing. Parties to the settlement agreement should generally provide access to discovery produced during the litigation phases of the class action (if any) as a means to facilitating appraisal of the strengths of the class position on the merits.

Objectors might seek intervention and discovery to demonstrate the inadequacy of the settlement. Discovery should be minimal and conditioned on a showing of need, because it will delay settlement, introduce uncertainty, and might be undertaken primarily to justify an award of attorney fees to the objector's counsel. A court should monitor post settlement discovery by objectors and limit it to providing objectors with information central to the fairness of the proposed settlement. A court should not allow discovery into the settlement-negotiation process unless the objector makes a preliminary showing of collusion or other improper behavior.

NOTES AND QUESTIONS

1. What showing should be required before an objector may take discovery relating to settlement negotiations? *See Scardelletti v. Debarr*, 265 F.3d 195, 204 n.10 (4th Cir. 2001) (affirming denial of motion to intervene and stating "[w]hile [the court] should extend to any objector to the settlement leave to

be heard, to examine witnesses and to submit evidence on the fairness of the settlement, it is entirely in order for the trial court to limit its proceedings to whatever is necessary to aid it in reaching an informed, just and reasoned decision"), *rev'd on other grounds sub. nom. Devlin v. Scardelletti*, 536 U.S. 1 (2002).

2. If there are no formal objectors to a settlement, how should a court proceed to gather information relating to the settlement's fairness?

3. Are absent class members who timely object to the terms of a class settlement permitted to appeal the settlement without first moving to intervene? The Supreme Court answered in the affirmative in *Devlin v. Scardelletti*, 536 U.S. 1, 10–11 (2002), on the ground that a non-named class member qualifies as a "party" for purposes of lodging an appeal because he or she is bound by the class judgment. *See* Chapter 9(B)(2).

c. Fairness Hearing

Must a district court hold a hearing before approving a proposed settlement? Prior to the 2003 amendments to Rule 23(e), appellate courts had generally ruled that "[t]he district court may not approve a settlement unless it determines after hearings that the settlement is fair, adequate, and reasonable, as well as consistent with the public interest." *Bailey v. Great Lakes Canning, Inc.*, 908 F.2d 38, 42 (6th Cir. 1990). Rule 23(e)(2) now specifies that "[i]f the [proposed settlement, voluntary dismissal, or compromise] would bind class members, the court may approve it only after a hearing and on finding that it is fair, reasonable, and adequate." The Advisory Committee Notes to this provision indicate that the change "confirms and mandates the already common practice of holding hearings as part of the process of approving settlement, voluntary dismissal, or compromise that would bind members of a class."

Must such a hearing include the taking of evidence? One source notes:

> At the fairness hearing, the proponents of the settlement must show that the proposed settlement is "fair, reasonable and adequate." The parties *may* present witnesses, experts, and affidavits or declarations. Objectors and class members *may* also appear and testify. * * * An extended hearing may be necessary.

Manual for Complex Litigation (Fourth) § 21.634 (2004) (emphasis added). *See also* ALI *Principles* § 3.03(b) at 200 (after notice, opt-out period, and receipt of any objections, "court must conduct a full review of the settlement, including an in-court hearing, with an opportunity for the parties and objectors to offer evidence and present arguments" and then "must make on-the-record findings and conclusions in support of its [certification] decision"). The Second Circuit, to the contrary, has held that if the record before the trial court is adequate, "an evidentiary hearing is not required unless the objectors raise 'cogent factual objections to the settlement.'" *Malchman v. Davis*, 706 F.2d 426, 434 (2d Cir. 1983) (citing *City of Detroit v. Grinnell Corp.*, 495 F.2d 448, 464 (2d Cir. 1974)). Should an evidentiary hearing be required even if no one lodges an objection?

d. Second Opt-Out Right

One of the more controversial 2003 revisions to Rule 23 is now set forth as Rule 23(e)(4), which provides: "If the class action was previously certified as a class action under Rule 23(b)(3), the court may refuse to approve a settlement unless it affords a new opportunity to request exclusion to individual class members who had an earlier opportunity to request exclusion but did not do so." According to the Advisory Committee Notes, that provision authorizes the court to refuse to approve a settlement unless there is a new opportunity to opt out, even if the opt-out period set at the time of an earlier class certification order has expired. Why should a court allow for a second opt-out opportunity if the earlier opportunity to elect exclusion has expired? After all, class members are told at the time of certification that they will be bound by the results of the action unless they opt out. If the court allows a member to elect exclusion at the settlement stage, why not also permit class members to opt out after a motion to dismiss or a motion for summary judgment?

The ALI has taken a stronger position than Rule 23(e)(4) on the availability of a second opt out. It proposes that "[i]n any class action in which the terms of a settlement are not revealed until after the initial period for opting out has expired, class members should ordinarily have the right to opt out after the dissemination of notice of the proposed settlement. If the court refuses to grant a second opt-out right, it must make an on-the-record finding that specific reasons exist for its refusal." ALI *Principles* § 3.11 at 253. The ALI *Principles* state that, "as a matter of fairness, a class member should have an opportunity to opt out after learning about the actual terms of a settlement." *Id.* at 254. In addition, the availability of a second opt out would give the parties greater incentive to craft a fair settlement for the class, given the potential threat of massive opt outs and the ultimate unraveling of settlement efforts. *Id.*

According to the ALI *Principles*, Rule 23(e)(4) "has not had a substantial impact" because of the court's broad discretion to deny a second opt out. ALI *Principles* § 3.11 at 254 (noting "paucity" of cases where courts have ordered a second opt out under Rule 23(e)(4)). *See, e.g., Denney v. Deutsche Bank AG*, 443 F.3d 253, 271 (2d Cir. 2006) (despite fact that terms for individuals who had opted out improved, court's denial of second opt out was not abuse of discretion because "[a]n additional opt-out period is not required with every shift in the marginal attractiveness of the settlement"); *In re Nat'l Football League Players' Concussion Injury Litig.*, 307 F.R.D. 351, 423 (E.D. Penn. 2015) (holding due process did not require a second opportunity to opt out when the notice was sufficient and class members had 90 days to opt out or object), *aff'd on other grounds*; 821 F.3d 410 (3d Cir. 2016); *Hicks v. Morgan Stanley & Co.*, 2005 WL 2757792 (S.D.N.Y. 2005) (denying second opt out because not enough at stake for individual action); *In re Visa Check/Mastermoney Antitrust Litig.*, 297 F. Supp. 2d 503, 518 (E.D.N.Y. 2003) (denying second opt out because of small number of objections); *but see Nilsen v. York County*, 382 F. Supp. 2d 206, 210 (D. Me. 2005) (noting in passing that second opt out was granted); *Dare v. Knox County*, 457 F. Supp. 2d 52, 53 (D. Me. 2006) (second opt out granted for class settlement); *Stanley v. United States Steel Co.*, 2008 WL 4225781, at *4 (E.D. Mich. 2008) (noting that "a sub-set of persons identified as having one or more confusing aspects to their status as a class member were given a second opportunity to opt out of the class").

5. SUBSTANTIVE CONSIDERATIONS IN APPROVING CLASS ACTION SETTLEMENTS

a. Fairness Assessment

REYNOLDS V. BENEFICIAL NAT'L BANK
United States Court of Appeals, Seventh Circuit, 2002.
288 F.3d 277.

Before CUDAHY, POSNER, and ROVNER, CIRCUIT JUDGES.

POSNER, CIRCUIT JUDGE.

We have consolidated for decision a number of appeals from orders by the district court approving a settlement of consumer-finance class action litigation, denying petitions to intervene, and awarding attorneys' fees. "Federal Rule of Civil Procedure 23(e) requires court approval of any settlement that effects the dismissal of a class action. Before such a settlement may be approved, the district court must determine that a class action settlement is fair, adequate, and reasonable, and not a product of collusion." The principal issue presented by these appeals is whether the district judge discharged the judicial duty to protect the members of a class in a class action litigation from lawyers for the class who may, in derogation of their professional and fiduciary obligations, place their pecuniary self-interest ahead of that of the class. This problem * * * requires district judges to exercise the highest degree of vigilance in scrutinizing proposed settlements of class actions. We and other courts have gone so far as to term the district judge in the settlement phase of a class action suit a fiduciary of the class, who is subject therefore to the high duty of care that the law requires of fiduciaries.

We do not know whether the $25 million settlement that the district judge approved is a reasonable amount given the risk and likely return to the class of continued litigation; we do not have sufficient information to make a judgment on that question. What we do know is that * * * the judge did not give the issue of the settlement's adequacy the care that it deserved.

This litigation arose out of refund anticipation loans made jointly by the two principal defendants, Beneficial National Bank and H & R Block, the tax preparer. When H & R Block files a refund claim with the Internal Revenue Service on behalf of one of its customers, the customer can expect to receive the refund within a few weeks unless the IRS decides to scrutinize the return for one reason or another. But even a few weeks is too long for the most necessitous taxpayers, and so Beneficial through Block offers to lend the customer the amount of the refund for the period between the filing of the claim and the receipt of the refund. The annual interest rate on such a loan will often exceed 100 percent—easily a quarter of the refund, even though the loan may be outstanding for only a few days. Block arranges the loan but Beneficial puts up the money for it. Not disclosed to the customer is the fact that Beneficial pays Block a fee for arranging the loan and also that Block owns part of the loan.

Beginning in 1990, more than twenty class actions were brought against the defendants on behalf of the refund anticipation borrowers. The suits charged a variety of violations of state and federal consumer-finance laws and also breach of fiduciary duty under state law. Some of the alleged violations appear to be technical. The most damaging charge appears to be that Block's customers are led to believe that Block is acting as their agent or fiduciary, much as if they had hired a lawyer or accountant to prepare their income tax returns, as affluent people do, whereas Block is, without disclosure to them, engaged in self-dealing.

Most of the suits failed on one ground or another; none has resulted in a final judgment against Beneficial or Block. But in the late 1990s several withstood motions to dismiss or motions for summary judgment, and at least one, a Texas suit, was slated for trial.

On September 3, 1997, two lawyers who had prosecuted two of the unsuccessful class actions, Howard Prossnitz and Francine Schwartz, had lunch in Chicago with Burt Rublin, who was and remains Beneficial's lead lawyer in defending against the class-action avalanche. Prossnitz and Schwartz brought with them to the lunch another lawyer, Daniel Harris. Although neither Prossnitz nor Schwartz, nor their friend Harris, had a pending suit against Beneficial (or against Block, which was not represented at the lunch), they discussed "a global RAL [tax refund anticipation] settlement" with Rublin. It is doubtful whether Prossnitz or Schwartz even had a client at this time; and certainly Harris did not. Schwartz later "bought" a client from another lawyer, to whom she promised a $100,000 referral fee. The necessity for such a transaction, when the class contains 17 million members, eludes our understanding.

In hearing before the district judge on the adequacy of the settlement (the "fairness hearing," as it is called), Harris testified that at the lunch Rublin " 'threw out' a number, for purposes of illustration, of $24 or $25 million." The judge described this testimony (which he elsewhere describes as "Harris believes he heard Rublin say the case was worth $23 million or $24 million"), though it is vociferously denied by Rublin, as "credible." There was, however, no actual settlement negotiation at the lunch.

Prossnitz, Schwartz, and Harris, all solo practitioners, brought a substantial law firm, Miller Faucher and Cafferty LLP, into the picture. In April of the following year the foursome filed two class action suits against Beneficial similar to the others that had been filed and that were (those that hadn't flopped) wending their way through the courts of various states. One of the two suits filed also named as defendants H & R Block and three affiliated Block entities, but three of those, including Block itself, were voluntarily dismissed from the suit by the plaintiffs in October 1998 and the fourth was dismissed in February 1999. Shortly after the suits were filed, Harris made a settlement offer to Beneficial that was rejected, but after a hiatus negotiations began. Block was included in the settlement negotiations, despite the fact that there were by then no claims pending against it. It was included because Beneficial was reluctant to settle without Block, having promised to indemnify it for any liability resulting from Block's role in Beneficial's refund anticipation loans.

In October of 1999, a class jointly represented by the three solo practitioners and the Miller firm (we'll call these the "settlement class lawyers"), plus Beneficial and Block, entered into a settlement agreement which they submitted to the district court for its approval. The agreement contemplated the filing of an amended complaint naming H & R Block as a defendant, and by its terms covered claims against five Block entities, of which four were the entities originally named but subsequently dismissed as defendants in one of the two original class action complaints. The agreement defined the class as all persons who had obtained refund anticipation loans from Beneficial between January 1, 1987, and October 26, 1999, and provided for the release of all claims "arising out of or in any way relating to the tax refund anticipation loans ('RALs,' sometimes erroneously referred to as 'Rapid Refunds') obtained by the Class at any time up to and through" that date. The defendants agreed to create a fund of $25 million against which members of the class could file a claim not to exceed $15. Any money left in the fund after the expiration of the period for filing claims was to revert to the defendants, who also agreed to injunctive relief in the form of certain required disclosures to future customers, primarily of the financial arrangements between Beneficial and Block, and to bear the cost of notice to class members and of the class counsel's legal fees out of their own pockets rather than out of the settlement fund. One RAL class action, the *Basile* suit pending in the Pennsylvania courts, was excluded from the agreement, apparently because Block thought it could get the supreme court of that state to reverse a lower court decision that had gone against the company. Beneficial and Block agreed to split the expense of the settlement 50–50.

The district judge approved the settlement except for the reversion and the $15 cap, which at his insistence the parties raised to $30 for those members of the class (apparently the vast majority) who had received two or more tax refund anticipation loans from Block. With these changes the settlement was approved and notices mailed to 17 million persons—most of whom ignored them; several million of the notices, moreover, were undeliverable, presumably because the addressees had moved and left no forwarding address. Only 1 million of the recipients filed claims, which would be enough, however, to exhaust the settlement fund. Only about 6,000 of the recipients opted out of the class action so that they could seek additional relief against the defendants.

* * *

In finding that $25 million was an adequate settlement, the judge relied in part on an unsworn report by James Adler, an accountant who purported to estimate the damages caused by the defendants' alleged violations of law. He was not deposed or subjected to cross-examination and the judge did not discuss the adequacy of his methodology. Adler came up with a figure of $60 million, but it is unclear whether this was intended to be an estimate of the entire damages that the class might hope to recover if the case was tried and went to judgment and what legal assumptions underpinned the estimates.

The various objectors to the settlement, primarily intervening or would-be intervening plaintiffs who have claims that the settlement will release, contend that the settlement agreement is a product of a "reverse auction," the practice whereby the defendant in a series of class actions picks the most ineffectual class lawyers to negotiate a settlement with in the hope that the district court will approve a weak settlement that will preclude other claims against the defendant. The ineffectual lawyers are happy to sell out a class they anyway can't do much for in exchange for generous attorneys' fees, and the defendants are happy to pay generous attorneys' fees since all they care about is the bottom line—the sum of the settlement and the attorneys' fees—and not the allocation of money between the two categories of expense. The defendants agreed to pay attorneys' fees in this case, to the three solo practitioners and the law firm that negotiated the settlement, of up to $4.25 million.

Although there is no proof that the settlement was actually collusive in the reverse-auction sense, the circumstances demanded closer scrutiny than the district judge gave it. He painted with too broad a brush, substituting intuition for the evidence and careful analysis that a case of this magnitude, and a settlement proposal of such questionable antecedents and circumstances, required. The initial agreement submitted for the judge's approval, remember, had provided for a reversion and also capped each class member's recovery at $15. If the parties had an inkling that only 1 million class members would file claims, they were agreeing to a settlement worth only $15 million, and probably less; for if 1 million class members filed claims capped at $30, fewer would have filed claims capped at $15. Yet according to a credibility determination by the district judge that we are not in a position to second guess, two and half years earlier, *before* RAL plaintiffs began having some success in the courts, Beneficials' counsel had indicated that $23 to $25 million were ballpark figures for a settlement with Beneficial alone. Beneficial's share of a $15 million settlement in which Block was a codefendant would be only $7.5 million (remember that Beneficial and Block agreed to split the cost of the settlement 50–50)—yet that is the settlement the lawyers for the settlement class agreed to, plus injunctive relief the value of which no one has attempted to monetize and which is barely discussed in the briefs or by the judge. The injunctive relief signally does not include a requirement that H & R Block disclose its interest in Beneficials' refund anticipation loans.

Moreover, H & R Block appears to have faced substantial exposure in a Texas class action in which it was accused of breach of fiduciary obligations to its customers. The class in that suit was seeking disgorgement of all the fees paid to Block by the banks that made refund anticipation loans through it. The class argued that such a forfeiture was mandatory if Block was found to have violated its fiduciary duties. Disgorgement was also sought of all other fees that Block had received "in connection with each RAL transaction"—that is, the tax-preparation and electronic-filing fees that Block had charged its RAL customers to file their taxes for them—a form of relief that the class claimed was within the trial court's equitable discretion. The total amount sought could have reached $2 billion. The class had been certified, the case was proceeding in the Texas courts, and the theory of liability and damages could not be dismissed as frivolous; indeed, the case had been set for trial. Even if the class had only a 1 percent chance of prevailing, the expected value of its suit might reach $20 million. (This is on the unrealistic assumption that the only possible outcomes were a $2 billion judgment and a zero judgment. Realistic intermediate possibilities would make the $20 million estimate expand.)

Remarkably in view of the progress and promise of the Texas suit relative to the half-hearted efforts of the settlement class counsel, the district judge enjoined the Texas suit on the authority of the All Writs Act, 28 U.S.C. § 1651(a), reasoning that the suit might upend the settlement. The effect of the injunction is that the settlement release, if upheld, would release the claims in the Texas suit. For this release of potentially substantial claims against H & R Block the settlement class received no consideration. In fact the settlement class received no consideration for the release of *any* claims against Block. The only effect of bringing Block into the settlement was to allow Beneficial to cut its own expense of the settlement in half. The lawyers for the settlement class were richly rewarded for negotiations that greatly diminished the cost of settlement to Beneficial from the level that it considered to be in the ballpark years earlier when the cases were running more in its favor than when the settlement agreement was negotiated. In effect, the settlement values the Texas and all other claims against Block at zero.

The district judge enjoined the lawyers for the Texas class from notifying the members of that class of the status of the Texas litigation to assist them in deciding whether to opt out of the settlement that the settlement class counsel had negotiated with Beneficial and Block and continue to litigate in the Texas courts. The judge should not have done this, especially since opting out was likely to be the sensible course of action given the ungenerosity of the settlement to the Texas class. A pattern of withholding information likely to undermine the settlement emerged when, after approving the settlement, the district judge encouraged the solo practitioners to submit their fee applications *in camera*, lest the paucity of the time they had devoted to the case (for which the judge awarded them more than $2 million in attorneys' fees) be used as ammunition by objectors to the adequacy of the representation of the class. There was no sound basis for sealing the fee applications, let alone for sealing the number of hours each of the settlement class counsel had devoted to the case. The applications are not in the appellate record and we do not know what the total number of hours devoted by the class counsel to this litigation was, but apparently it was a small number. This is not surprising, since the lawyers' efforts between the filing of the complaint and the settlement negotiations were singularly feeble, illustrated by their responding to the Block defendants' motion to dismiss for lack of personal jurisdiction with a voluntary dismissal of the claims against those defendants. Their representation of the class was almost certainly inadequate, an independent reason for disapproving a settlement. But in addition it reinforces our concern with the adequacy of the district judge's consideration of the settlement.

The judge approved the settlement primarily because he thought the prospects for the class if the litigation continued were uncertain. They might lose in the end, or win little; and even if they won a lot, the delay in winning would make the relief eventually awarded the class worth much less in present-value terms. To most people, a dollar today is worth a great deal more than a dollar ten years from now. It is especially likely to be worth more to the members of the class in this litigation. Only a person with a very high discount rate (that is, a strong preference for present over future dollars—a preference that may reflect desperation rather than fecklessness or shortsightedness) would borrow at an astronomical interest rate in order to get a sum of money now rather than a few weeks from now.

All this is true, but in the suspicious circumstances that we have recited the judge should have made a greater effort (he made none) to quantify the net expected value of continued litigation to the class, since a settlement for less than that value would not be adequate. Determining that value would require estimating the range of possible outcomes and ascribing a probability to each point on the range, though as just noted those outcomes must be discounted to the present using a reasonable, and in this case perhaps a steep interest rate. We say "perhaps" because even a person with a high discount rate may not care much whether he received $15 to $30 now or in the future, since it is such a trivial amount of money even to a person who is usually strapped for funds. If, moreover, the court would award prejudgment interest in a case litigated to judgment, discounting might wash out of the picture altogether.

A high degree of precision cannot be expected in valuing a litigation, especially regarding the estimation of the probability of particular outcomes. Still, much more could have been done here without (what is obviously to be avoided) turning the fairness hearing into a trial of the merits. For example, the judge could have insisted that the parties present evidence that would enable four possible outcomes to be estimated: call them high, medium, low, and zero. High might be in the billions of dollars, medium in the hundreds of millions, low in the tens of millions. Some approximate range of percentages, reflecting the probability of obtaining each of these outcomes in a trial (more likely a series of trials), might be estimated, and so a ballpark valuation derived.

* * * [O]ur point is only that the judge made no effort to translate his intuitions about the strength of the plaintiffs' case, the range of possible damages, and the likely duration of the litigation if it was not settled now into numbers that would permit a responsible evaluation of the reasonableness of the settlement.

Two classes were absorbed into the settlement even though their claims were sharply different from those of the classes represented by the settlement counsel. * * * [One class action sought damages allegedly arising from Block's "rapid refund" program whereby, for a fee, a customer was promised a rapid tax refund by the IRS although, the plaintiffs alleged, Block knew that would not happen. No loan was involved. That class was inadvertently swept into the settlement class because "rapid refund" was erroneously used to describe refund anticipation loans. The other class action that accidentally was included with the settlement class alleged that Block wrongly intercepted tax refund checks "to offset debts owed by the customer on previous refund anticipation loans." This practice was distinct from Block's alleged nondisclosure and caused separate alleged injuries.]

* * *

All things considered, we conclude that the district judge abused his discretion in approving the settlement. Because of this conclusion, the other issues raised by the appeals need not be decided * * *. [The Seventh Circuit made clear its disapproval of permitting the submission of fee applications *in camera*. Additionally, it made clear that "class counsel's compensation must be proportioned to the *incremental* benefits they confer on the class, not the total benefits." In other words, their compensation would be tied to the effort expended to achieve a higher settlement amount, and not to the amount of the final settlement itself. Finally, assuming that it had jurisdiction to hear the appeals of counsel seeking fees for appearing at the fairness hearing to object (primarily to the reversion plan in the settlement), the Seventh Circuit found it a "compelling ground" to deny their fee application because other lawyers at the hearing raised the same issue—"the objectors added nothing."]

* * *

The judgment approving the class action settlement and awarding attorneys' fees is reversed and the case is remanded to the district court for further proceedings consistent with this opinion. The injunction against the Texas class action must be vacated in light of our disapproval of the settlement. * * *

IN RE NAT'L FOOTBALL LEAGUE PLAYERS CONCUSSION INJURY LITIG.

United States Court of Appeals, Third Circuit, 2016.

821 F.3d 410.

Before AMBRO, HARDIMAN, and NYGAARD, CIRCUIT JUDGES.

AMBRO, CIRCUIT JUDGE.

* * *

I. INTRODUCTION

The National Football League ("NFL") has agreed to resolve lawsuits brought by former players who alleged that the NFL failed to inform them of and protect them from the risks of concussions in football. The District Court approved a class action settlement that covered over 20,000 retired players and released all concussion-related claims against the NFL. Objectors have appealed that decision, arguing that class certification was improper and that the settlement was unfair. * * * [W]e conclude that the District Court was right to certify the class and approve the settlement. Thus we affirm its decision in full.

II. BACKGROUND

A. Concussion Suits Are Brought Against the NFL

In July 2011, 73 former professional football players sued the NFL and Riddell, Inc. in the Superior Court of California. The retired players alleged that the NFL failed to take reasonable actions to protect them from the chronic risks of head injuries in football. The players also claimed that Riddell, a manufacturer of sports equipment, should be liable for the defective design of helmets.

The NFL removed the case to federal court on the ground that the players' claims under state law were preempted by federal labor law. More lawsuits by retired players followed and the NFL moved under 28 U.S.C. §

1407 to consolidate the pending suits before a single judge for pretrial proceedings. In January 2012, the Judicial Panel on Multidistrict Litigation consolidated these cases before Judge Anita B. Brody in the Eastern District of Pennsylvania as a multidistrict litigation ("MDL"). Since consolidation, 5,000 players have filed over 300 similar lawsuits * * *.

To manage the litigation, the District Court appointed co-lead class counsel, a Steering Committee, and an Executive Committee. The Steering Committee was charged with performing or delegating all necessary pretrial tasks and the smaller Executive Committee was responsible for the overall coordination of the proceedings. The Court also ordered plaintiffs to submit a Master Administrative Long-Form Complaint and a Master Administrative Class Action Complaint to supersede the numerous then-pending complaints.

The Master Complaints tracked many of the allegations from the first lawsuits. Football puts players at risk of repetitive brain trauma and injury because they suffer concussive and sub-concussive hits during the game and at practice (sub-concussive hits fall below the threshold for a concussion but are still associated with brain damage). Plaintiffs alleged that the NFL had a duty to provide players with rules and information to protect them from the health risks—both short and long-term—of brain injury, including Alzheimer's disease, dementia, depression, deficits in cognitive functioning, reduced processing speed, loss of memory, sleeplessness, mood swings, personality changes, and a recently identified degenerative disease called chronic traumatic encephalopathy (commonly referred to as "CTE").

Because CTE figures prominently in this appeal, some background on this condition is in order. It was first identified in 2002 based on analysis of the brain tissue of deceased NFL players, including Mike Webster, Terry Long, Andre Waters, and Justin Strzelczyk. CTE involves the build-up of "tau protein" in the brain, a result associated with repetitive head trauma. Medical personnel have examined approximately 200 brains with CTE as of 2015, in large part because it is only diagnosable post-mortem. That diagnosis requires examining sections of a person's brain under a microscope to see if abnormal tau proteins are present and, if so, whether they occur in the unique pattern associated with CTE. Plaintiffs alleged that CTE affects mood and behavior, causing headaches, aggression, depression, and an increased risk of suicide. They also stated that memory loss, dementia, loss of attention and concentration, and impairment of language are associated with CTE.

The theme of the allegations was that, despite the NFL's awareness of the risks of repetitive head trauma, the League ignored, minimized, or outright suppressed information concerning the link between that trauma and cognitive damage. For example, in 1994 the NFL created the Mild Traumatic Brain Injury Committee to study the effects of head injuries. Per the plaintiffs, the Committee was at the forefront of a disinformation campaign that disseminated "junk science" denying the link between head injuries and cognitive disorders. Based on the allegations against the NFL, plaintiffs asserted claims for negligence, medical monitoring, fraudulent concealment, fraud, negligent misrepresentation, negligent hiring, negligent retention, wrongful death and survival, civil conspiracy, and loss of consortium.

After plaintiffs filed the Master Complaints, the NFL moved to dismiss, arguing that federal labor law preempted the state law claims. Indeed, § 301 of the Labor Management Relations Act preempts state law claims that are "substantially dependent" on the terms of a labor agreement. The NFL claimed that resolution of plaintiffs' claims depended upon the interpretation of Collective Bargaining Agreements ("CBAs") in place between the retired players and the NFL. If the CBAs do preempt plaintiffs' claims, they must arbitrate those claims per mandatory arbitration provisions in the CBAs. Plaintiffs responded that their negligence and fraud claims would not require federal courts to interpret the CBAs and in any event the CBAs did not cover all retired players.

B. The Parties Reach a Settlement

On July 8, 2013, while the NFL's motion to dismiss was pending, the District Court ordered the parties to mediate and appointed a mediator. On August 29, 2013, after two months of negotiations and more than twelve full days of formal mediation, the parties agreed to a settlement in principle and signed a term sheet. It provided $765 million to fund medical exams and offer compensation for player injuries. The proposed settlement would resolve the claims of all retired players against the NFL related to head injuries.

In January 2014, after more negotiations, class counsel filed in the District Court a class action complaint and sought preliminary class certification and preliminary approval of the settlement. The Court denied the motion because it had doubts that the capped fund for paying claims would be sufficient. It appointed a Special Master to assist with making financial forecasts and, five months later, the parties reached a revised settlement that uncapped the fund for compensating retired players.

Class counsel filed a second motion for preliminary class certification and preliminary approval in June 2014. The District Court granted the motion, preliminarily approved the settlement, conditionally certified the class, approved classwide notice, and scheduled a final fairness hearing.

* * *

Following preliminary certification, potential class members had 90 days to object or opt out of the settlement. Class counsel then moved for final class certification and settlement approval. On November 19, 2014, the District Court held a day-long fairness hearing and heard argument from class counsel, the NFL, and several objectors who voiced concerns against the settlement. After the hearing, the Court proposed several changes to benefit class members. The parties agreed to the proposed changes and submitted an amended settlement in February 2015. On April 22, 2015, the Court granted the motion for class certification and final approval of the amended settlement, that grant explained in a 123-page opinion. Objectors filed 12 separate appeals that were consolidated into this single appeal before us now.

C. The Proposed Settlement

The settlement has three components: (1) an uncapped Monetary Award Fund that provides compensation for retired players who submit proof of certain diagnoses; (2) a $75 million Baseline Assessment Program that provides eligible retired players with free baseline assessment examinations of their objective neurological functioning; and (3) a $10 million Education Fund to instruct football players about injury prevention.

1. Monetary Award Fund

Under the settlement, retired players or their beneficiaries are compensated for developing one of several neurocognitive and neuromuscular impairments or "Qualifying Diagnoses." By "retired players," we mean players who retired from playing NFL football before the preliminary approval of the class settlement on July 7, 2014. The settlement recognizes six Qualifying Diagnoses: (1) Level 1.5 Neurocognitive Impairment; (2) Level 2 Neurocognitive Impairment; (3) Alzheimer's Disease; (4) Parkinson's Disease; (5) Amyotrophic Lateral Sclerosis ("ALS"); and (6) Death with CTE provided the player died before final approval of the settlement on April 22, 2015. A retired player does not need to show that his time in the NFL caused the onset of the Qualifying Diagnosis.

A Qualifying Diagnosis entitles a retired player to a maximum monetary award:

Qualifying Diagnosis	Maximum Award
Level 1.5 Neurocognitive Impairment	$1.5 Million
Level 2 Neurocognitive Impairment	$3 Million
Parkinson's Disease	$3.5 Million
Alzheimer's Disease	$3.5 Million
Death with CTE	$4 Million
ALS	$5 Million

This award is subject to several offsets, that is, awards decrease: (1) as the age at which a retired player is diagnosed increases; (2) if the retired player played fewer than five eligible seasons; (3) if the player did not have a baseline assessment examination; and (4) if the player suffered a severe traumatic brain injury or stroke unrelated to NFL play.

To collect from the Fund, a class member must register with the claims administrator within 180 days of receiving notice that the settlement has been approved. This deadline can be excused for good cause. The class member then must submit a claims package to the administrator no later than two years after the date of the Qualifying Diagnosis or within two years after the supplemental notice is posted on the settlement website, whichever is later. This deadline can be excused for substantial hardship. The claims package must include a certification by the diagnosing physician and supporting medical records. The claims administrator will notify the class member within 60 days if he is entitled to an award. The class member, class counsel, and the NFL have the right to appeal an award determination. * * *

The Monetary Award Fund is uncapped and will remain in place for 65 years. Every retired player who timely registers and qualifies during the lifespan of the settlement will receive an award. If, after receiving an initial award, a retired player receives a more serious Qualifying Diagnosis, he may receive a supplemental award.

2. Baseline Assessment Program

Any retired player who has played at least half of an eligible season can receive a baseline assessment examination. It consists of a neurological examination performed by credentialed and licensed physicians selected by a court-appointed administrator. Qualified providers may diagnose retired players with Level 1, 1.5, or 2 Neurocognitive Impairment. The results of the examinations can also be compared with any future tests to determine whether a retired player's cognitive abilities have deteriorated.

Baseline Assessment Program funds will also provide Baseline Assessment Program Supplemental Benefits. Retired players diagnosed with Level 1 Neurocognitive Impairment—evidencing some objective decline in cognitive function but not yet early dementia—are eligible to receive medical benefits, including further testing, treatment, counseling, and pharmaceutical coverage.

The Baseline Assessment Program lasts for 10 years. All retired players who seek and are eligible for a baseline assessment examination receive one notwithstanding the $75 million cap. Every eligible retired player age 43 or over must take a baseline assessment examination within two years of the Program's start-up. Every eligible retired player younger than age 43 must do so before the end of the program or by his 45th birthday, whichever comes first.

3. Education Fund

The Education Fund is a $10 million fund to promote safety and injury prevention in football. The purpose is to promote safety-related initiatives in youth football and educate retired players about their medical and disability benefits under the CBA. Class counsel and the NFL, with input from the retired players, will propose specific educational initiatives for the District Court's approval.

4. The Proposed Class

All living NFL football players who retired from playing professional football before July 7, 2014, as well as their representative claimants and derivative claimants, comprise the proposed class. Representative claimants are those duly authorized by law to assert the claims of deceased, legally incapacitated, or incompetent retired players. Derivative claimants are those, such as parents, spouses, or dependent children, who have some legal right to the income of retired players. Even though the proposed class consists of more than just retired players, we use the terms "class members" and "retired players" interchangeably.

The proposed class contains two subclasses based on a retired players' injuries as of the preliminary approval date. Subclass 1 consists of retired players who were not diagnosed with a Qualifying Diagnosis prior to July 7, 2014, and their representative and derivative claimants. Put another way, subclass 1 includes retired players who have no currently known injuries that would be compensated under the settlement. Subclass 2 consists of retired players who were diagnosed with a Qualifying Diagnosis prior to July 7, 2014, and their representative claimants and derivative claimants. Translated, subclass 2 includes retired players who are currently injured and will receive an immediate monetary award under the settlement. The

NFL estimates that the total population of retired players is 21,070. Of this, 28% are expected to be diagnosed with a compensable disease. The remaining 72% are not expected to develop a compensable disease during their lifetime.

Class members release all claims and actions against the NFL "arising out of, or relating to, head, brain and/or cognitive injury, as well as any injuries arising out of, or relating to, concussions and/or sub-concussive events," including claims relating to CTE. The releases do not compromise the benefits that retired players are entitled to receive under the CBAs, nor do they compromise their retirement benefits, disability benefits, and health insurance.

Of the over 20,000 estimated class members (the NFL states that the number exceeds 21,000), 234 initially asked to opt out from the settlement and 205 class members joined 83 written objections submitted to the District Court. Before the fairness hearing, 26 of the 234 opt-outs sought re-admission to the class. After the District Court granted final approval, another 6 opt-outs sought readmission. This leaves 202 current opt-outs, of which class counsel notes only 169 were timely filed.

III. JURISDICTION & STANDARD OF REVIEW

* * *

We review the decision to certify a class and approve a classwide settlement for abuse of discretion. It exists "if the district court's decision rests upon a clearly erroneous finding of fact, an errant conclusion of law or an improper application of law to fact."

This appeal principally presents two questions—whether the District Court abused its discretion (1) in certifying the class of retired NFL players and (2) in concluding that the terms of the settlement were fair, reasonable, and adequate. Objectors (95 in all) have filed 11 separate briefs totaling some 500 pages addressing these questions. We address each of these arguments, but refer to objectors collectively throughout our opinion rather than cross-referencing particular objectors with particular arguments.

IV. CLASS CERTIFICATION

* * *

[The Court found that the requirements for class certification under Rule 23(a) and Rule 23(b)(3) were satisfied.]

V. CLASS NOTICE

[The Court upheld the content and distribution scheme of the notice to class members.]

VI. CLASS SETTLEMENT

A class action cannot be settled without court approval based on a determination that the proposed settlement is fair, reasonable, and adequate. Fed. R. Civ. P. 23(e)(2). The inquiry into the settlement's fairness under Rule 23(e) "protects unnamed class members from unjust or unfair settlements affecting their rights when the representatives become fainthearted before the action is adjudicated or are able to secure satisfaction of their individual claims by a compromise."

"The decision of whether to approve a proposed settlement of a class action is left to the sound discretion of the district court." * * *

A. Presumption of Fairness

We apply an initial presumption of fairness in reviewing a class settlement when: "(1) the negotiations occurred at arms length; (2) there was sufficient discovery; (3) the proponents of the settlement are experienced in similar litigation; and (4) only a small fraction of the class objected." The District Court found each of these elements satisfied and applied the presumption Objectors argue that the presumption should not have applied at all because class counsel did not conduct formal discovery into the fraud and negligence claims against the NFL before reaching the settlement. We conclude that the Court did not abuse its discretion in finding class counsel's informal discovery to be sufficient.

By the time of the settlement, class counsel had undertaken significant informal discovery. For instance, they had obtained a comprehensive database of the claims and symptoms of retired players and had enlisted the assistance of medical experts. They also had a grasp of the legal hurdles that the retired players would need to clear in order to succeed on their fraud and negligence claims, in particular the potentially dispositive issue of federal labor law preemption. Thus, in negotiations with the NFL class counsel "were aware of the strengths and weaknesses of their case." To the extent objectors ask us to require formal discovery before presuming that a settlement is fair, we decline the invitation. In some cases, informal discovery will be enough for class counsel to assess the value of the class' claims and negotiate a settlement that provides fair compensation. * * *

B. *Girsh & Prudential* Factors

In *Girsh v. Jepson,* we noted nine factors to be considered when determining the fairness of a proposed settlement:

> (1) the complexity, expense and likely duration of the litigation; (2) the reaction of the class to the settlement; (3) the stage of the proceedings and the amount of discovery completed; (4) the risks of establishing liability; (5) the risks of establishing damages; (6) the risks of maintaining the class action through the trial; (7) the ability of the defendants to withstand a greater judgment; (8) the range of reasonableness of the settlement fund in light of the best possible recovery; and (9) the range of reasonableness of the settlement fund to a possible recovery in light of all the attendant risks of litigation.

521 F.2d 153, 157 (3d Cir. 1975) (internal quotation marks and ellipses omitted). "The settling parties bear the burden of proving that the *Girsh* factors weigh in favor of approval of the settlement." A district court's findings under the *Girsh* test are those of fact. Unless clearly erroneous, they are upheld.

Later, in *Prudential Insurance* we held that, because of a "sea-change in the nature of class actions," it might be useful to expand the *Girsh* factors to include several permissive and non-exhaustive factors:

> [1] the maturity of the underlying substantive issues, as measured by experience in adjudicating individual actions, the development

of scientific knowledge, the extent of discovery on the merits, and other factors that bear on the ability to assess the probable outcome of a trial on the merits of liability and individual damages; [2] the existence and probable outcome of claims by other classes and subclasses; [3] the comparison between the results achieved by the settlement for individual class or subclass members and the results achieved—or likely to be achieved—for other claimants; [4] whether class or subclass members are accorded the right to opt out of the settlement; [5] whether any provisions for attorneys' fees are reasonable; and [6] whether the procedure for processing individual claims under the settlement is fair and reasonable.

148 F.3d 283, 323 (3d Cir. 1998). "Unlike the *Girsh* factors, each of which the district court must consider before approving a class settlement, the *Prudential* considerations are just that, prudential."

The District Court in our case went through the *Girsh* factors and the relevant *Prudential* factors in great detail before concluding that the terms of the settlement were fair, reasonable, and adequate. Objectors try to challenge the District Court's analysis in several ways, but none convinces us.

1. Complexity, Expense, and Likely Duration of the Litigation

"The first factor 'captures the probable costs, in both time and money, of continued litigation.'" The District Court concluded that the probable costs of continued litigation in the MDL were significant and that this factor weighed in favor of approving the settlement. Some objectors assert that the District Court overestimated the costs of continued litigation because the negligence and fraud claims were "straightforward." This is not the case. Over 5,000 retired NFL players in the MDL alleged a multi-decade fraud by the NFL, and litigating these claims would have been an enormous undertaking. The discovery needed to prove the NFL's fraudulent concealment of the risks of concussions was extensive. The District Court would then resolve many issues of causation and medical science. Finally, if the cases did not settle or were not dismissed, individual suits would be remanded to district courts throughout the country for trial. We agree with the District Court that the expense of this process weighs strongly in the settlement's favor.

2. Reaction of the Class to the Settlement

"The second *Girsh* factor 'attempts to gauge whether members of the class support the settlement.'" As noted, the case began with a class of approximately 20,000 retired players, of which 5,000 are currently represented by counsel in the MDL proceedings. Notice of the settlement reached an estimated 90% of those players through direct mail and secondary publications (in addition to the extensive national media coverage of this case). As of 10 days before the fairness hearing, more than 5,200 class members had signed up to receive additional information about the settlement and the settlement website had more than 64,000 unique visitors. With all this attention, only approximately 1% of class members objected and approximately 1% of class members opted out. We agree with the District Court that these figures weigh in favor of settlement approval.

3. Stage of the Proceedings and Amount of Discovery Completed

"The third *Girsh* factor 'captures the degree of case development that class counsel [had] accomplished prior to settlement. Through this lens, courts can determine whether counsel had an adequate appreciation of the merits of the case negotiating.'"

The District Court concluded that class counsel adequately evaluated the merits of the preemption and causation issues through informal discovery, and, after ten months of settlement negotiations, the stage of the proceedings weighed in favor of settlement approval. Objectors claim that the lack of formal discovery in this matter should have weighed more heavily against settlement. As with the presumption of fairness, formal discovery is not a requirement for the third *Girsh* factor. What matters is not the amount or type of discovery class counsel pursued, but whether they had developed enough information about the case to appreciate sufficiently the value of the claims. Moreover, requiring parties to conduct formal discovery before reaching a proposed class settlement would take a valuable bargaining chip—the costs of formal discovery itself—off the table during negotiations. This could deter the early settlement of disputes.

4. Risks of Establishing Liability and Damages

"The fourth and fifth *Girsh* factors survey the possible risks of litigation in order to balance the likelihood of success and the potential damage award if the case were taken to trial against the benefits of an immediate settlement." We concur with the District Court that this factor weighed in favor of settlement because class members "face[d] stiff challenges surmounting the issues of preemption and causation."

To start, if the NFL were to prevail in its motion to dismiss on the issue of federal labor law preemption, "many, if not all," of the class members' claims would be dismissed. *Id.* Objectors claim the District Court misjudged the risks of establishing liability and damages on this front. They argue that the NFL's preemption defense would not apply to all class members because there were no CBAs in effect before 1968 and between 1987 and 1993. But even if there were a small subset of players unaffected by the preemption defense, the defense still had the capability of denying relief to the majority of class members and this weighs in favor of approving the settlement.

As for causation, the District Court noted that retired players would need to show both general causation (that repetitive head trauma is capable of causing ALS, Alzheimer's, and the like), and specific causation (that the brain trauma suffered by a particular player in fact caused his specific impairments). With general causation, the Court found that even though "[a] consensus is emerging that repetitive mild brain injury is associated with the Qualifying Diagnoses," the "available research is not nearly robust enough to discount the risks" of litigation. And specific causation would be even more troublesome because a player would need to distinguish the effect of hits he took during his NFL career from the effect of those he received in high school football, college football, or other contact sports. Objectors argue that the District Court put too little faith in the ability of the class to show causation because the NFL has admitted that concussions can lead to long-term problems and formal discovery could disclose that it fraudulently concealed the risks of concussions. But neither of these points is particularly helpful for overcoming the general and specific causation hurdles the District Court identified.

5. Risks of Maintaining Class Action Through Trial

The District Court found that the likelihood of obtaining and keeping a class certification if the action were to proceed to trial weighed in favor of approving the settlement, but it deserved only minimal consideration. This was correct. In a settlement class, this factor becomes essentially "toothless" because " 'a district court need not inquire whether the case, if tried, would present intractable management problems[,] . . . for the proposal is that there be no trial.' "

6. Ability of Defendants to Withstand a Greater Judgment

The seventh *Girsh* factor is most relevant when the defendant's professed inability to pay is used to justify the amount of the settlement. In the case of the NFL, the District Court found this factor neutral because the NFL did not cite potential financial instability as justification for the settlement's size. In fact, it agreed to uncap the Monetary Award Fund and is thus duty bound to pay every compensable claim.

Some objectors complain that the settlement, which may cost the NFL $1 billion over its lifetime, represents a "fraction of one year's revenues." Even so, that does not change the analysis of this *Girsh* factor. Indeed, " 'in any class action against a large corporation, the defendant entity is likely to be able to withstand a more substantial judgment, and, against the weight of the remaining factors, this fact alone does not undermine the reasonableness of the . . . settlement.' "

7. Range of Reasonableness of the Settlement in Light of the Best Possible Recovery and All Attendant Risks of Litigation

In evaluating the eighth and ninth *Girsh* factors, we ask "whether the settlement represents a good value for a weak case or a poor value for a strong case." "The factors test two sides of the same coin: reasonableness in light of the best possible recovery and reasonableness in light of the risks the parties would face if the case went to trial." "[T]he present value of the damages plaintiffs would likely recover if successful, appropriately discounted for the risk of not prevailing, should be compared with the amount of the proposed settlement."

If the retired players were successful in their fraud and negligence claims, they would likely be entitled to substantial damages awards. But we must take seriously the litigation risks inherent in pressing forward with the case. The NFL's pending motion to dismiss and other available affirmative defenses could have left retired players to pursue claims in arbitration or with no recovery at all. Hence we agree with the District Court that the settlement represents a fair deal for the class when compared with a risk-adjusted estimate of the value of plaintiffs' claims.

* * *

8. Prudential *Factors*

The District Court found that the relevant *Prudential* factors also weighed in favor of approving the settlement. No objectors engage with the Court's findings on this front. But briefly, we agree that class counsel was able to assess the probable outcome of this case, class members had the opportunity to opt out, and the claims process is reasonable. The provision of attorneys' fees was a neutral factor because class counsel has not yet moved for a fee award.

C. Settlement's Treatment of CTE

Objectors raise other arguments about the fairness of the settlement that do not necessarily fall neatly within one of the *Girsh* factors. The most common of those arguments is that the exclusion of CTE as a Qualifying Diagnosis for future claimants is unfair. Objectors note that CTE, the "industrial disease of football," was at the center of the first concussion lawsuits and argue that claims for CTE compensation are released by the settlement in return for nothing. The District Court carefully considered this argument before deciding that the settlement's treatment of CTE was reasonable. It made detailed factual findings about the state of medical science regarding CTE—findings that we review for clear error—in support of this conclusion.

The Court first determined that "[t]he study of CTE is nascent, and the symptoms of the disease, if any, are unknown." Surveying the available medical literature, it found that researchers have not "reliably determined which events make a person more likely to develop CTE" and "have not determined what symptoms individuals with CTE typically suffer from while they are alive." *Id.* at 398. At the time of the Court's decision, only about 200 brains with CTE had been examined, and the only way currently to diagnose CTE is a post-mortem examination of the subject's brain.

Citing studies by Dr. Ann McKee and Dr. Robert Stern, objectors argued that CTE progresses in four stages. In Stages I and II, the disease affects mood and behavior while leaving a retired player's cognitive functions largely intact. Headaches, aggression, depression, explosive outbursts, and suicidal thoughts are common. Later in life, as a retired player progresses to Stages III and IV, severe memory loss, dementia, loss of attention and concentration, and impairment of language begin to occur. The District Court explained, however, that these studies suffer from several limitations and cannot generate "[p]redictive, generalizable conclusions" about CTE. The studies suffered from a selection bias because they only examined patients with a history of repetitive head injury. They had to rely on reports by family members to reconstruct the symptoms patients showed before death. And they did not take into account other potential risk factors for developing CTE, including a high Body Mass Index ("BMI"), lifestyle change, age, chronic pain, or substance abuse.

With this science in mind, the Court next determined that certain symptoms associated with CTE, such as memory loss, executive dysfunction, and difficulty with concentration, are compensated by the existing Qualifying Diagnoses. *Id.* And many persons diagnosed with CTE after death suffered from conditions in life that are compensated, including ALS, Alzheimer's disease, and Parkinson's disease. Relying on expert evidence, the Court estimated that "at least 89% of the former NFL players" who were examined in CTE studies would have been compensated under the settlement.

To be sure, the mood and behavioral symptoms associated with CTE (aggression, depression, and suicidal thoughts) are not compensated, but this result was reasonable. Mood and behavioral symptoms are common in the general population and have multifactor causation and many other risk factors. Retired players tend to have many of these risk factors, such as sleep apnea, a history of drug and alcohol abuse, a high BMI, chronic pain, and major lifestyle changes. Class members would thus "face more difficulty proving that NFL Football caused these mood and behavioral symptoms than they would proving that it caused other symptoms associated with Qualifying Diagnoses."

The District Court also reviewed the monetary award for post-mortem diagnoses of CTE. It found "[s]ound reasons" for limiting the award to players who died before final approval of the settlement. As we have summarized elsewhere, this compensation for deceased players is a proxy for Qualifying Diagnoses a retired player could have received while living. After final approval, players "should be well aware of the [s]ettlement and the need to obtain Qualifying Diagnoses," and "there no longer is a need for Death with CTE to serve as a proxy for Qualifying Diagnoses."

Finally, the Court addressed the potential development of scientific and medical knowledge of CTE. Objectors argued that the settlement's treatment of CTE was unreasonable in light of the expected developments in CTE research. But even if a diagnosis of CTE during life will be available in the next five or ten years, "the longitudinal epidemiological studies necessary to build a robust clinical profile will still take a considerable amount of time." The Court also noted that the settlement has some mechanism for keeping pace with science, in that the parties must meet and confer every ten years in good faith about possible modifications to the definitions of Qualifying Diagnoses.

Objectors have not shown any of the District Court's findings to be clearly erroneous * * *.

* * *

Finding no clear errors in the District Court's findings on CTE, we are also convinced that the Court was well within its discretion in concluding that the settlement's treatment of this condition was reasonable. Most importantly, objectors are not correct when they assert that CTE claims are released by the settlement in return for "nothing." A primary purpose of the settlement is to provide insurance for living players who develop certain neurocognitive or neuromuscular impairments linked to repetitive head trauma (in addition to the benefits provided by the Baseline Assessment Program). Given what we know about CTE, many of the symptoms associated with the disease will be covered by this insurance. And compensation for players who are coping with these symptoms now is surely preferable to waiting until they die to pay their estates for a CTE diagnosis. Moreover, we agree with the District Court that it would be an uphill battle to compensate for the mood and behavioral symptoms thought to be associated with CTE.

* * *

VII. ATTORNEYS' FEES

[The Court rejected objectors' argument that the settlement should be rejected because the amount of attorneys' fees had not been determined.]

VIII. CONCLUSION

It is the nature of a settlement that some will be dissatisfied with the ultimate result. * * * [Objectors] risk making the perfect the enemy of the good. This settlement will provide nearly $1 billion in value to the class of retired players. It is a testament to the players, researchers, and advocates who have worked to expose the true human costs of a sport so many love. Though not perfect, it is fair.

* * *

NOTES AND QUESTIONS

1. Why did the Seventh Circuit reject the settlement in *Reynolds*? Why did the Third Circuit in *NFL* approve the settlement despite objections of certain class members? Can the Seventh Circuit's analysis in *Reynolds* be squared with the Third Circuit's analysis in *NFL*? Was the Seventh Circuit too rigorous? Can an argument be made that the Third Circuit was not sufficiently rigorous?

2. Could the settlement in *Reynolds* have been salvaged? If so, how?

3. In the *NFL* case, what was the relevance of CTE to objectors' arguments? How did the court resolve the CTE-related issues?

4. What would have been the players' situation (in terms of achieving a recovery) had the Third Circuit agreed with the objectors and struck down the settlement? Would that scenario have been preferable to approval of the settlement?

5. In contrast to the myriad *Girsh* and *Prudential* factors, the ALI has taken a relatively streamlined approach in identifying the relevant criteria for assessing the fairness of a class action settlement. *See* ALI *Principles* § 3.05. Although the ALI would require a fairness hearing and on-the-record findings and conclusions, it explicitly identifies only four criteria that, if met, justify settlement approval:

> (1) the class representatives and class counsel have been and currently are adequately representing the class;
>
> (2) the relief afforded to the class (taking into account any ancillary agreement that may be part of the settlement) is fair and reasonable given the costs, risks, probability of success, and delays of trial and appeal;
>
> (3) class members are treated equitably (relative to each other) based on their facts and circumstances and are not disadvantaged by the settlement considered as a whole; and
>
> (4) the settlement was negotiated at arm's length and was not the product of collusion.

Id. at § 3.05(a) at 208, 210. The absence of any one of these criteria make the settlement unfair. *Id.* Although a court may utilize other criteria such as the duration of the litigation/stage of the proceedings, number of opt outs, and number of objections, the ALI criticizes many of these common factors as of "questionable probative value." *Id.* at 212–14. Is the ALI correct in streamlining the settlement inquiry? Are the ALI's chosen criteria the most important?

In yet another variation, the *Manual for Complex Litigation (Fourth)* § 21.62 (2004), lists a number of factors that may bear on the fairness of a class settlement. They include: the advantages of the proposed settlement versus the probable trial outcome; time, duration, and cost of a potential trial; probability of success on the merits on a classwide basis; maturity of claims; resources of the parties; reasonableness of attorneys' fees; and extent of objections, opt outs, and participation of class members. Do the approaches of the ALI, the *Manual*, and the Third Circuit in *NFL* vary materially?

Also, as discussed in Section (A)(8) below, proposed changes to Rule 23 would emphasize key criteria for courts to consider in reviewing settlements.

6. In scrutinizing the merits of a settlement, should it matter under which subdivision of Rule 23(b) the class was certified? How, if at all, does each subdivision in Rule 23(b) pose different considerations from the perspective of the plaintiffs? From the perspective of plaintiffs' counsel? Defendants? Defense counsel? The court? Potential objectors? Other interested groups?

7. Can a district court impose modifications to a settlement over the objections of the parties? In *Evans v. Jeff D.*, 475 U.S. 717 (1986), the Supreme Court rejected a district court's attempt to award attorneys' fees where the settlement agreement did not provide for fees. In so holding, the Court stated:

> [T]he power to approve or reject a settlement negotiated by the parties before trial does not authorize the court to require the parties to accept a settlement to which they have not agreed. Although changed circumstances may justify a court-ordered modification of a consent decree over the objections of a party after the decree has been entered, and the District Court might have advised petitioners and respondents that it would not approve their proposal unless one or more of its provisions was deleted or modified, Rule 23(e) does not give the court the power, in advance of trial, to modify a proposed consent decree and order its acceptance over either party's objection. The options available to the District Court were essentially the same as those available to respondents: it could have accepted the proposed settlement; it could have rejected the proposal and postponed the trial to see if a different settlement could be achieved; or it could have decided to try the case.

475 U.S. at 726–27. *See also, e.g., In re Domestic Air Transp. Antitrust Litig.*, 148 F.R.D. 297, 305 (N.D. Ga. 1993) ("The Court may only approve or disapprove the settlement as presented. It * * * may not rewrite the settlement as requested by numerous objectors."); ALI *Principles* § 3.05(d) at 209 ("A court may approve or disapprove a class settlement but may not of its own accord amend the settlement to add, delete, or modify any term."). Given the district court's obligation to protect the interests of the class, does this rule make sense? What influence, if any, can a court have on a proposed settlement? *See id.* at 209, 215 (a court may refuse to approve a settlement unless the parties amend it in accordance with the court's specifications, but a court may not "unilaterally modify the settlement or force terms upon the parties").

8. Should the parties who negotiated a settlement agreement be permitted to request modifications while that agreement is before the court? Judge Weinstein and his co-author have observed:

If such changes occur during or after the fairness hearing, there is a problem. Interested parties rely on the information contained in the notice packet to determine if their rights are being adequately protected and if they need to appear at the hearing. Substantial modification of the settlement that affects the rights of the parties may influence their desire to be heard by the court. This issue remains open, with some courts finding broad authority in the district court to approve amendments agreed upon by the parties, and other courts limiting such amendments to those that are 'technical' and 'perfecting' in nature.

Jack B. Weinstein & Karin S. Schwartz, *Notes from the Cave: Some Problems of Judges in Dealing With Class Action Settlements*, 163 F.R.D. 369, 377 (1995). Courts have taken a variety of approaches. *See id.* (citing cases). *Compare White v. National Football League,* 836 F. Supp. 1458, 1488 (D. Minn. 1993), *aff'd,* 41 F.3d 402 (8th Cir. 1994) (court has authority to approve of amended settlement agreement proposed by parties, but not to modify a settlement agreement unilaterally at objector's request), *with Liddell v. Board of Educ.,* 567 F. Supp. 1037, 1047 (E.D. Mo. 1983) (court must approve settlement agreement without alteration save for "technical, perfecting, and non-substantive changes necessary and reasonable"), *rev'd in part on other grounds,* 731 F.2d 1294 (8th Cir. 1984).

The ALI *Principles* propose that if material modifications are made to a class settlement agreement, new notice should be provided to those class members who are substantially adversely affected. *See* ALI *Principles* § 3.05(e) at 209. Does the ALI's approach make sense? What impact would it have on the approval process?

9. Commentators have noted that assessment of a settlement's fairness is especially difficult when the settlement is premised in whole or in on some form of "in-kind" payment:

> * * * Although courts attempt to monetize as in-kind settlement's present value to facilitate comparison to the likely trial outcome, such valuation places a heavy burden on the reviewing court. For example, valuation of scrip settlements requires a court to hear and weigh evidence on the number of coupons that experts predict consumers will redeem, the effect of transferability provisions, and the present value of the certificates. * * * Judges normally base their conclusions on a solid foundation of evidence amassed and tested through adversarial allegation and discovery. When reviewing class settlements, however, a court may have little reliable evidence with which to work * * *. Although this problem is common to all class settlement approval hearings, its effects are exacerbated in the in-kind context because the court must depend upon presented evidence not only for the valuation of the likely trial outcome, but also for the valuation of the settlement package.

Note, *In-Kind Class Action Settlements*, 109 Harv. L. Rev. 810, 816–17 (1996). What should a court do under such circumstances? The author of the Harvard Note suggests three kinds of settlement provisions that may "at least partially alleviate[]" a court's concerns. First, a court may place greater reliance on the value of coupon settlements if the agreement permits the coupons to be freely traded from consumer to consumer, so that the coupons are more likely to be used. Second, courts may view in-kind settlements more favorably if defendant commits to a minimum guaranteed payment to the class. Third, a court may reasonably rely on in-kind settlements that meaningfully tie class counsel's fees to the amount of in-kind relief actually received by class members. *Id.* at 823–26. Do any of these mechanisms alleviate concerns about collusion? Which mechanism best serves the interests of the class? Of defendants? Of class counsel?

10. In 2004, the author expressed concern that "[c]ourts * * * ha[d] almost universally refused to disqualify class counsel [on adequacy of representation grounds] based on misconduct." Robert Klonoff, *The Judiciary's Flawed Application of Rule 23's "Adequacy of Representation" Requirement*, 2004 Mich. St. L. Rev. 671, 692; *see also id.* at 692 & n.134 (noting that research of all class action decisions since the adoption of modern Rule 23 in 1966 revealed only three instances in which courts found class counsel inadequate based on misconduct). This situation has changed dramatically in recent years, however, particularly in the settlement context, as courts have begun focusing greater attention on potential misconduct by class counsel. *See, e.g., Creative Montessori v. Ashford Gear*, 662 F.3d 913, 915 (7th Cir. 2011) (reversing certification where class counsel had obtained information about the case by falsely promising not to turn over the information to third parties, and had falsely implied, in recruiting the class representative, that a certified class already existed; court of appeals criticized the test used by the district court, under which "only the most egregious misconduct" by counsel "could ever arguably justify denial of class status"); *Eubank v. Pella Corp.*, 753 F.3d 718, 723–24 (7th Cir. 2014) (reversing approval of class settlement because of numerous ethical violations by class counsel, including the fact that lead counsel was the lead class representative's son-in-law, creating a conflict of interest); *Redman v. RadioShack Corp.*, 768 F.3d 622, 630–31 (7th Cir. 2014) (reversing class settlement approval where the fee award to counsel was disproportionate to the $10 coupons received by class members for future purchases at RadioShack); *Pearson v. NBTY*, 772 F.3d 778, 781 (7th Cir. 2014) (reversing class settlement approval where attorneys' fees represented "an outlandish 69 percent" of the total settlement value); *Rodriguez v. West Publ'g Corp.*, 563 F.3d 948, 960–61 (9th Cir. 2009) (*Rodriguez I*) (approving class settlement despite the fact that incentive payments to five of seven class representatives (which were based on the amount recovered by the class) created a conflict of interest on the part of those representatives; court of appeals held that only one adequate representative was required, but remanded for the district court to consider whether the ethical violation affected class counsel's fee request), *on remand*, 2010 WL 682096, at *4 (C.D. Cal. 2010) (finding that counsel were not entitled to any attorneys' fees based on the conflict of interest), *aff'd sub nom., Rodriguez v. Disner*, 688 F.3d 645, 653 (9th Cir. 2012) (*Rodriguez II*); *Radcliffe v. Experian Info. Solutions Inc.*, 715 F.3d 1157, 1167 (9th Cir. 2013) (reversing class settlement and fee award where class counsel were inadequate under Rule 23(a)(4) because their agreement with class representatives provided for incentive payments only if the representatives supported the settlement that class counsel entered into with the defendant). *See* Robert H. Klonoff, *Class Actions in the Year 2026: A Prognosis*, 65 Emory L.J. 1569, 1623–35 (2016) (discussing case law addressing adequacy and ethical violations).

b. Resolving Attorney–Client Conflicts

LAZY OIL CO. v. WITCO CORP.
United States Court of Appeals, Third Circuit, 1999.
166 F.3d 581.

Before BECKER, CHIEF JUDGE, STAPLETON, CIRCUIT JUDGE and HARRIS, DISTRICT JUDGE [(D.D.C.), by designation].

BECKER, CHIEF JUDGE.

This is an appeal from an order of the District Court approving a class action settlement of an antitrust case. Ironically, the lead objector, Lazy Oil Co., is also the lead plaintiff, whose principal, Bennie G. Landers, conceived the suit but later became disaffected with its management and direction and ultimately with its fruits—the settlement. All the objectors are producers of Penn Grade Crude Oil, *i.e.*, crude oil drawn from the western side of the Appalachian Basin within the states of New York, Pennsylvania, Ohio, and West Virginia. The objectors contend that the settlement is not fair, at least to the producer plaintiffs in contrast to the investor plaintiffs. The objectors distinguish between these two types of class members in making their objections to the settlement, alleging that producer plaintiffs, as full-time oil-producing enterprises, have distinct interests and, particularly, unique losses, as compared to investor plaintiffs, who simply invest funds in oil-producing businesses.

The objectors maintain that producer plaintiffs lost not only revenues from the lower prices paid for their oil (a loss they share with investor plaintiffs), but also suffered the compounded losses from their inability to invest these lost funds in drilling new oil wells or upgrading their existing ones—losses allegedly not applicable to investor plaintiffs. This alleged distinction is also at the heart of the other two issues raised by objectors in this appeal. They contend that the District Court erred in not certifying a subclass of producer plaintiffs to ensure that their unique interests were adequately represented. Finally, they contend that the Class Counsel—originally hired to bring this suit by the lead plaintiffs, who are now objectors—should have been disqualified from representing the remaining class representatives and the entire class once the objectors chose to attack the settlement.

The District Court conducted three days of hearings regarding, *inter alia*, the objectors' claims * * *. On December 31, 1997, the District Court filed an omnibus order overruling objections to the settlement, approving the terms of the settlement, denying objectors' motion to remove or disqualify Class Counsel, [and] denying objectors' motion for certification of a subclass * * *.

* * * [We] * * * conclud[e] that the * * * District Court did not abuse its discretion in approving the settlement. Neither do we have difficulty with the District Court's order refusing to remove or disqualify Class Counsel, which we also affirm. We do, however, expound on this point to clarify the standard for adjudicating such claims in the class action context. * * *

* * *

I. Background

The subject of this appeal began as two separate class actions, each brought in the District Court for the Western District of Pennsylvania, by sellers of Penn Grade crude against three purchasers and refiners of this crude, Quaker State, Pennzoil, and Witco. The plaintiffs in both actions alleged that the defendants conspired to depress the price of Penn Grade Crude, in violation of the Sherman Antitrust Act. The cases were consolidated and, in June 1995, the District Court certified the consolidated case as a class action under Rule 23(b)(3), with the class comprising all "direct sellers of Penn Grade Crude" who sold oil to the defendants between January 1, 1981, and June 30, 1995. [Plaintiffs settled with one defendant, and that settlement is not at issue.]

In early 1997, after several months of negotiations, plaintiffs reached a settlement with the remaining defendants, under which Pennzoil would pay approximately $9.7 million and Witco would pay approximately $4.8 million, with neither defendant admitting any liability or wrongdoing. Upon presentation of the settlement to the class representatives, two of them, Lazy Oil Co. and Thomas A. Miller Oil Co., objected to the settlement. At least 384 class members joined Lazy Oil *et al.* in objecting to the terms of the settlement after receiving notice of its terms. Class Counsel thereafter moved to withdraw from representing the objectors.

In February 1997, the District Court directed that notice of the proposed settlement be sent to all class members and published in local and national newspapers. The objectors filed motions, *inter alia*, requesting that the Court disapprove the settlement, for establishment of a producer subclass, and for disqualification of Class Counsel. * * * [Based on extensive findings, the district court found the settlement to be fair and thus approved it.] This appeal followed.

* * *

IV. Settlement of the Class Action

[The court summarily affirmed the district court's approval of the settlement and refusal to certify a subclass.]

V. Disqualification of Class Counsel

The objectors contend that Class Counsel should be disqualified because they are now representing a party (*i.e.*, the plaintiffs) adverse to one they previously represented (*i.e.*, the objectors), creating an impermissible conflict of interest. This contention raises an interesting threshold question as to the standard a district court should apply to the conflict determination.

The most extensive discussion of the conflict-of-interest issue within our jurisprudence is found in *In re Corn Derivatives Antitrust Litigation*, 748 F.2d 157 (3d Cir. 1984). In *Corn Derivatives*, we granted a motion to disqualify an attorney who had formerly represented several class representatives; some of the class representatives approved of a proposed settlement and others did not. Unlike the present case, in *Corn Derivatives* counsel had withdrawn from representing the parties approving of the settlement and sought only to represent one objector on appeal. After consulting the relevant portions of the ABA's Model Rules of Professional Conduct and Model Code of Professional Responsibility,[12] we concluded that the prejudice to the former clients would be too great to justify counsel's continued representation of the objector. We focused on the policies underlying the rules against an attorney representing a party in a matter in which a former client is now an adversary, including preventing "even the potential that a former client's confidences and secrets may be used against him"; maintaining "public confidence in the integrity of the bar"; and upholding the duty of loyalty that a client has the right to expect.

Our opinion also discussed countervailing considerations, such as whether the counsel at issue represented the entire class (which was not the case in *Corn Derivatives*, but is true here), and the interest of the party who wishes to retain the counsel in avoiding increased costs and keeping "counsel who has extensive familiarity with the factual and legal issues involved." Overall, however, we analyzed the situation no differently than we would have a non-class action case in which "two clients retained the same law firm to file suit, and where, later, that law firm chose to represent one of those clients against the other in the course of the same litigation."

In his concurring opinion, Judge Adams more explicitly endorsed a balancing approach to attorney-disqualification motions in the class action context. Judge Adams argued that the rules for attorney disqualification could not be "mechanically transpose[d]" to the class action context and that the more appropriate means of addressing such issues was through "a balancing process." After discussing the rationale behind these points, he noted that, "[i]f a class attorney is automatically prevented from continuing to represent the named parties or a majority of a class which supports a settlement, the minority dissenting class members might obtain considerable leverage in the litigation by being able to force the majority to seek new counsel."

We agree with Judge Adams's concerns. In many class actions, one or more class representatives will object to a settlement and become adverse parties to the remaining class representatives (and the rest of the class). If, by applying the usual rules on attorney-client relations, class counsel could easily be disqualified in these cases, not only would the objectors enjoy great "leverage," but many fair and reasonable settlements would be undermined by the need to find substitute counsel after months or even years of fruitful settlement negotiations. "Moreover, the conflict rules do not appear to be drafted with class action procedures in mind and may be at odds with the policies underlying the class action rules." Bruce A. Green, *Conflicts of Interest in Litigation: The Judicial Role*, 65 Fordham L. Rev. 71, 127 (1996).

As the Second Circuit noted, in a case factually similar to *Corn Derivatives*:

---

[12] Currently, the ABA's Model Rules of Professional Conduct provide that "[a] lawyer who has formerly represented a client in a matter shall not thereafter represent another person in the same or a substantially related matter in which that person's interests are materially adverse to the interests of the former client unless the former client consents after consultation." Model Rules of Professional Conduct Rule 1.9(a) (1983); *see also id.* cmt. ("The underlying question is whether the lawyer was so involved in the matter that the subsequent representation can be justly regarded as a changing of sides in the matter in question").

Automatic application of the traditional principles governing disqualification of attorneys on grounds of conflict of interest would seemingly dictate that whenever a rift arises in the class, with one branch favoring a settlement or a course of action that another branch resists, the attorney who has represented the class should withdraw entirely and take no position. Were he to take a position, either favoring or opposing the proposed course of action, he would be opposing the interests of some of his former clients in the very matter in which he has represented them.

. . . . [W]hen an action has continued over the course of many years, the prospect of having those most familiar with its course and status be automatically disqualified whenever class members have conflicting interests would substantially diminish the efficacy of class actions as a method of dispute resolution.

In re "Agent Orange" Prod. Liab. Litig., 800 F.2d 14, 18–19 (2d Cir. 1986). The court then concluded "that the traditional rules that have been developed in the course of attorneys' representation of the interests of clients outside of the class action context should not be mechanically applied to the problems that arise in the settlement of class action litigation." Rather, it held, a balancing approach like that advocated by Judge Adams in *Corn Derivatives* was more appropriate in the class action context.

The *Agent Orange* court listed a number of relevant factors in this balancing inquiry, including some from Judge Adams's opinion: the information in the attorney's possession, the availability of the information elsewhere, the importance of this information to the disputed issues, actual prejudice that could flow from the attorney's possession of the information, the costs to class members of obtaining new counsel and the ease with which they might do so, the complexity of the litigation, and the time needed for new counsel to familiarize himself with the case.

We are persuaded by the well-reasoned opinions in *Agent Orange* and *Corn Derivatives*. We therefore hold that, in the class action context, once some class representatives object to a settlement negotiated on their behalf, class counsel may continue to represent the remaining class representatives and the class, as long as the interest of the class in continued representation by experienced counsel is not outweighed by the actual prejudice to the objectors of being opposed by their former counsel. In making this determination, the district court may consider the factors discussed in *Agent Orange* and in both the majority and concurring opinions in *Corn Derivatives*.

Turning to the present case, we note that the situation here differs from that in *Corn Derivatives* in that counsel there sought to represent only one party, an objector, and not the remaining class members. In a case such as the present one, the balance weighs heavily in favor of denying a motion for disqualification of class counsel that is made on the basis of nothing more than the fact that the objectors include former clients (in the same case) of class counsel, without any showing of impropriety or prejudice.

Objectors contend that Class Counsel in this case did not adequately represent all of the class members because they failed to consider the unique interests and damages of the producer plaintiffs. Given our agreement with the District Court that the objectors' distinction between producer and investor plaintiffs is not supported by the record in this case, we find no clear error in the District Court's finding that Class Counsel adequately represented the interests of all class members, even if some class members and some of the class representatives are unsatisfied with the results of Class Counsel's efforts.

Applying the standard we have outlined above, we are satisfied that the District Court weighed the competing interests appropriately and did not abuse its discretion in denying the motion for disqualification of Class Counsel.

* * *

NOTES AND QUESTIONS

1. Why did the *Lazy Oil* court refuse to disqualify class counsel? Would subclasses have alleviated the objectors' concerns? Should disqualification or mandatory subclassing be used in circumstances like those in *Lazy Oil*? What effects would this have upon the class action settlement process?

2. Were the facts in *Corn Derivatives* sufficiently distinct to warrant disqualification of counsel there, but not in *Lazy Oil*?

3. To what degree should class representatives' objections to a proposed settlement factor into the court's settlement approval decision? In *Olden v. Gardner*, 294 F. App'x 210 (6th Cir. 2008), all three of the original class representatives objected to the initial proposed class settlement. Consequently, class counsel successfully moved to replace them on inadequacy grounds and to have the settlement approved. *Id.* at 215–16. The Sixth Circuit held that the district court did not abuse its discretion by substituting new class representatives and approving the class settlement. Although the court of appeals conceded that the "fairness, reasonableness, and adequacy of the settlement [was] a close call" and that it may have reached a different conclusion as a matter of *de novo* review, it affirmed the district court's ruling because of the "highly deferential standard of review" applicable to review of class settlements. *Id.* at 211. Should appellate review of class settlements be so circumscribed? What factors would justify approving a class settlement when none of the original class representatives support it? In *Olden*, out of roughly 11,000 class members, only 79 objected to the settlement and even fewer participated in the appeal—a factor noted by the Sixth Circuit. *Id.* at 217. Should the class representatives' views be given greater weight than other objectors due to the class representatives' different role in the litigation? How can class representatives effectively protect the interests of the class if class counsel can simply replace them? *See id.* at 219–20. Would it change the analysis if the class representatives at issue were against the settlement because they were holding out for special treatment that favored themselves over the class?

6. DISMISSAL OF CLASS CLAIMS PRIOR TO CLASS CERTIFICATION

Amended Rule 23(e) states that a "certified class" cannot be settled without approval of the court. The Advisory Committee Notes to the 2003 amendments explain that the language was changed to resolve ambiguity suggesting that court approval is required for any settlement or dismissal of any case brought as a putative class action, even if the case is settled or dismissed prior to class certification. Under prior practice, some courts believed that even a precertification settlement by class representatives required notice and/or court approval. *See, e.g., Shelton v. Pargo, Inc.*, 582 F.2d 1298 (4th Cir. 1978); *Roper v. Consurve, Inc.*, 578 F.2d 1106 (5th Cir. 1978); *Magana v. Platzer Shipyard, Inc.*, 74 F.R.D. 61 (S.D. Tex. 1977). The policy justification behind that practice was that if a case could be brought as a class action but settled as an individual action without court approval, class representatives would extort higher-than-justified settlements from defendants in an attempt to eliminate the threat of a class action.

Despite the 2003 clarification, the *Manual for Complex Litigation (Fourth)* notes that "in certain situations in which a voluntary dismissal might represent an abuse of the class action process, the court should inquire into the circumstances behind the dismissal." *Manual for Complex Litigation (Fourth)*, § 21.61 at 309 n.948. The ALI goes even further, proposing that court approval be required for pre-certification settlement of named plaintiffs' claims. ALI *Principles* § 3.02(b) at 193. The ALI's proposed rule is tempered by a presumption in favor of approval when the dismissal "does not involve any payment or other special consideration to class counsel or the named representative." *Id.* Which approach strikes the right balance?

7. THE CLASS ACTION FAIRNESS ACT AND SETTLEMENT ISSUES

In addition to expanding federal court jurisdiction over class actions, the Class Action Fairness Act of 2005 ("CAFA") also sought to address what many perceived to be abusive class action settlement practices. S. Rep. No. 109–14, at 4. The Senate Judiciary Committee concluded that "[i]n too many cases, state court judges are readily approving class action settlements that offer little—if any—meaningful recovery to the class members and simply transfer money from corporations to class counsel." *Id.* Consequently, Congress drafted the "Consumer Bill of Rights," 28 U.S.C. § 1712, a section of CAFA that seeks to address the problem of disproportionately large attorneys' fees and other perceived problems in class action settlements. S. Rep. No. 109–14, at 30.

Government Notification of Class Settlements. A major change in settlement practice resulting from CAFA involves notice. Prior to CAFA, a class action could be settled without any notification to federal and state government officials who have regulatory or supervisory authority over matters in the suit. CAFA, however, requires class action defendants to provide notice to "appropriate" federal and state officials of a proposed settlement ten days after it is filed with the district court. 28 U.S.C. § 1715(b). The required contents of the notice are extensive, and include the following: the complaint (including amendments) and attachments; notice of any class hearings proposed; class notice; any proposed or final settlement; any side agreements; any proposed final judgment or notice of dismissal; certain written judicial opinions; and the names of all proposed class members in each state and their proposed proportionate share of the settlement, or if not feasible, a reasonable estimate of the number of class members in each state and their proportionate shares. 28 U.S.C. § 1715(b).

The court must wait until 90 days after the last service of notice on the appropriate government officials before approving a class settlement. 28 U.S.C. § 1715(d). In the event that a defendant does not comply with the notification requirement, class members "may refuse to comply with [the settlement] and may choose not to be bound" by it. 28 U.S.C. § 1715(e)(1). CAFA does not require notified government officials to do anything once they are informed of the proposed settlement. S. Rep. No. 109–14, at 33.

Coupon Settlements. CAFA also focused on what Congress felt were particularly abusive practices involving settlements in which consumers receive discount coupons instead of cash. CAFA addresses the way class counsel may be compensated in such settlements. Prior to CAFA, class counsel could receive as fees a percentage of the total value of the coupons issued to the class, regardless of whether the class actually redeemed these coupons. Under CAFA, if class counsel is paid on a percentage basis, counsel is paid according to the value of the coupons actually redeemed, rather than on the face value of those distributed. 28 U.S.C. § 1712(a).

Net Loss Settlements. What happens if a class member has to pay class counsel more than what he or she is supposed to receive in monetary recovery from a proposed settlement—thereby incurring a "net loss"? *See, e.g.*, Chapter 7(D)(3). Although CAFA does not prohibit this type of settlement, it explicitly requires the court to scrutinize such agreements more carefully. Specifically, CAFA allows a court to approve of such a settlement only when the court makes written findings that nonmonetary benefits "substantially outweigh" a class member's net loss. 28 U.S.C. § 1713.

Geographic Discrimination. CAFA prohibits class members from receiving greater settlement proceeds "solely on the basis" of "closer geographic proximity to the court." 28 U.S.C. § 1714.

NOTES AND QUESTIONS

1. Commentators have begun to explore the impact of CAFA's provision requiring government notification. *See, e.g.*, Catherine M. Sharkey, *CAFA Settlement Notice Provision: Optimal Regulatory Policy?*, 156 U. Pa. L. Rev. 101, 121–26 (2008) (likely incidental effects of the notice provision include providing attorneys general with greater information that can be used for regulation and facilitating collaboration among attorneys general). What other consequences might flow from the CAFA notice requirement?

2. What constitutes a "coupon" settlement under CAFA? For example, as one commentator asks, "would frequent flyer miles in a settlement with an airline be a 'coupon' settlement?" Georgene M. Vairo, *Class Action Fairness Act of 2005; With Commentary and Analysis*, at 16 (Matthew Bender 2005). How should a court determine "value" based on "coupons that are redeemed"? Can fees be set and paid prior to the redemption period? *See also Redman v. RadioShack Corp.*, 768 F.3d 622, 635–36 (7th Cir. 2014) (rejecting class counsel's attempt to distinguish between a "voucher" and a "coupon" on the basis that a "voucher" can be used to buy entire items (as opposed to simply providing a discounted price); court noted that "from the standpoint of the dominant concerns that animate the provisions of the Class Action Fairness Act regarding coupon settlements it's a matter of indifference whether the coupon is a discount off the full price of an item or is equal to (or for that matter more than) the item's full price"); *In re Online DVD-Rental Antitrust Litig.*, 779 F.3d 934, 950–52 (9th Cir. 2015) (affirming holding that class settlement of $12 Wal-

Mart gift cards did not constitute a "coupon settlement" within the meaning of CAFA where, *inter alia*, class members received "a set amount of money to use on their choice of a large number of products from a large retailer"); *CLRB Hanson Industries, LLC v. Weiss & Associates, PC,* 465 F. App'x 617, 619 (9th Cir. 2012) (affirming the district court's holding that a settlement that gave "every class member the option to receive its share of the settlement proceeds in cash or cash-equivalent forgiveness of indebtedness already incurred" was not a "coupon settlement" triggering CAFA).

3. Is it fair to make attorneys' fees contingent upon consumers' coupon redemption rate? What methods can be used to encourage class members to actually use such coupons—especially when consumers are disinclined to purchase additional products from an alleged wrongdoer?

4. In enacting CAFA, Congress did not address the issue of so-called reversionary settlements, where fees are based on a potential settlement fund but unclaimed funds revert to the defendant. Some courts and commentators favor basing fees on the total potential fund, even if some of that amount is never paid out to the class. *See, e.g., Masters v. Wilhelmina Model Agency, Inc.*, 473 F.3d 423 (2d Cir. 2007) (holding that district court erred in calculating percentage of the fund on the basis of claims made against the fund, rather than on the entire fund, in antitrust class action, and concluding that CAFA's restriction on fees in coupon settlement cases was inapplicable); *Williams v. MGM–Pathe Communications Co.*, 129 F.3d 1026, 1027 (9th Cir. 1997) (holding that district court abused its discretion in awarding fees based on class members' actual claims against the class action settlement fund, rather than on a percentage of the entire fund or on lodestar); Comment, *Attorneys' Fees and Reversionary Fund Settlements in Small Claims Consumer Class Actions*, 50 UCLA L. Rev. 879, 882–83 (2003). The *Manual for Complex Litigation*, by contrast, asserts that fees should be based "on the benefits actually delivered." *Manual for Complex Litigation (Fourth)* § 21.71, at 337; *accord* Robert H. Klonoff & Mark Herrmann, *The Class Action Fairness Act: An Ill-Conceived Approach to Class Settlements*, 80 Tul. L. Rev. 1695, 1713–15 (2006). Which approach is preferable?

5. As noted, CAFA permits net-loss settlements where non-monetary relief "substantially outweighs" the net loss. Under what circumstances might this be true? How should a court determine if this test is met? How prevalent is the problem of net loss settlements? *See* Klonoff & Herrmann, *supra*, 80 Tul. L. Rev. at 1705–06 (concluding that "so-called 'net loss' settlements do not appear to have been a significant problem in the federal courts" and noting that Rule 23(e) was sufficient to address the financial problem, thereby making this CAFA provision unnecessary).

6. As noted, CAFA prohibits class settlements that discriminate among class members solely on their geographic proximity to the courthouse. 28 U.S.C. § 1714. Some have suggested that the provision may be unnecessary. *See* Klonoff & Herrmann, *supra*, 80 Tul. L. Rev. at 1706 (concluding that this CAFA provision was "an unnecessary remedy to cure an essentially nonexistent problem").

8. PROPOSED RULE CHANGES DEALING WITH SETTLEMENT

In August 2016, the Federal Advisory Committee on Civil Rules published, for notice and comment, a series of proposed amendments to Rule 23. Most have to do with settlement-related issues. *See* Committee on Rules of Practice and Procedure of the Judicial Conference of the United States, *Preliminary Draft of Proposed Amendments to the Federal Rules of Appellate, Bankruptcy, Civil and Criminal Procedure* 221–232 (Aug. 2016), available at http://www.uscourts.gov/sites/default/files/2016-08-preliminary_draft_of_rules_forms_published_for_public_comment_0.pdf.

First, new subsection Rule 23(e)(1)(A) would require parties to provide the court with "information sufficient to enable it to determine" whether notice of a proposed settlement should be sent to the class.

Second, Rule 23(e)(2) would be amended to specify the criteria that a court must consider in determining whether a proposed settlement is fair, reasonable, and adequate. These criteria would not replace the specific criteria of individual circuits but would enable the district court to focus on the criteria that are likely to be most important.

Third, two provisions are designed to deter bad faith objectors. A new Rule 23(e)(5)(A) would require objectors to state the grounds for their objections "with specificity" and to identify whether an objection is on behalf of an individual, a subset of the class, or the entire class. Second, to address the problem of objectors seeking payments to dismiss meritless objections, Rule 23(e)(5)(B) would require that the court approve (after a hearing) any request by an objector to withdraw an objection in return for compensation. The proposal is designed to ensure that court approval would be required even after the objector files an appeal. (The proposal invokes Rule 62.1, which allows district courts to render "indicative rulings" while a case is on appeal.)

NOTES AND QUESTIONS

1. What purposes are served by the proposed rule changes discussed above? Would the proposals adequately address the issues of concern?

2. Why did the Federal Civil Rules Advisory Committee focus so heavily on settlement as opposed to other aspects of class action practice?

3. The problem of serial objectors filing baseless objections to extort payments from class counsel has been the subject of several articles and court decisions. *See, e.g.*, Robert H. Klonoff, *Class Actions in the Year 2026: A Prognosis*, 65 Emory L.J. 1569, 1632–35 (2016) (summarizing recent cases challenging the unethical conduct of serial objectors); John E. Lopatka & D. Brooks Smith, *Class Action Professional Objectors: What to Do About Them?*, 39 Fla. St. U. L. Rev. 865 (2012) (noting that professional objectors can hold up class settlements for years by making "insubstantial objections" that are tantamount to "extortion" because the objector "threaten[s] to appeal the judgment approving the settlement unless paid to desist"); *Dennis v. Kellogg Co.*, 2013 WL 6055326, at *4 n.2 (S.D. Cal. 2013) (noting that attorney Darrell Palmer "has been widely and repeatedly criticized as a serial, professional, or otherwise vexatious objector"); *Dennings v. Clearwire Corp.*, 928 F. Supp. 2d 1270 (W.D. Wash. 2013) (imposing an appeal bond after finding that objecting class members had not read the settlement and had prior affiliations with serial objector Christopher Bandas), *settlement aff'd in* No. 13-35038 (9th Cir. Apr. 22, 2013); *In re Cathode Ray Tube (CRT) Antitrust Litig.*, 281 F.R.D. 531, 533 (N.D. Cal. 2012) (compelling discovery of the objectors in another case involving attorney Christopher

Bandas, and noting that "Bandas routinely represents objectors purporting to challenge class action settlements * * * for his own personal financial gain").

9. FINAL THOUGHTS ON SETTLEMENT

What should a court do about the problems inherent in class action settlements? The potential remedies are as diverse as the interests at stake. Professor Susan Koniak, in an article written after the district court had approved the *Amchem* settlement but before the Third Circuit and Supreme Court had weighed in (and long before CAFA), discussed changes in the settlement-approval process that, in her view, would decrease the possibility of collusive settlements. The excerpt below describes two of those suggestions: limiting the ability of plaintiffs' attorneys to represent numerous classes against a single defendant at the same time, and imposing a heightened duty of candor upon attorneys participating in a fairness hearing.

SUSAN P. KONIAK, FEASTING WHILE THE WIDOW WEEPS: *GEORGINE V. AMCHEM PRODUCTS, INC.*
80 Cornell L. Rev. 1045, 1123–27 (1995).

If we abandon the fig leaves that we use to explain how class actions are consistent with individual dignity, we must at least hold on to the notion that due process means conformity to something that can be objectively measured. * * * [B]y definition, due process must mean something other than that the result is just, otherwise some lynchings would be consistent with due process. A "fairness" hearing that appraises a settlement made outside the court's presence only as to the substantive fairness of the terms provides no more process than would be provided by a post-lynching hearing that assessed whether the dead guy really did commit the crime.

If courts are to replace compliments with content, where would the courts look for standards that might fill out the concept of adequate representation and give it meaning? For a start, the courts might * * * limit class counsel to one class action against a defendant at a time. Almost all class actions are settled. Allowing class counsel to have a pocket hidden from the court where money belonging to the class might be put is inappropriate. There is simply no way for the court to monitor attorney's fees or to ensure that the class was not ripped off when class counsel simultaneously negotiates deals on the side that the court can review in only a cursory manner, if at all. * * *

The idea * * * that class counsel should be prohibited from simultaneously representing other classes against a common defendant is similar to the concern expressed in the federal bribery and illegal gratuity statutes, which are designed to ensure the integrity of public officials. Given that a federal court must appoint class counsel and that class counsel have duties to members of the public by virtue of that appointment, it seems sensible to consult the statutes on corruption of federal officials for guidance on the standards a court might apply in assessing the propriety of class counsel receiving money, outside the class action pending before the court, from the defendant in the class action. Not only do these statutes prohibit the receipt of money in exchange for an explicit promise to perform some official duty, they also prohibit the receipt of money from another who hopes for some generalized benefit from the donation or who is expressing gratitude for some past official action.

Class counsel who simultaneously negotiate deals outside of the class action with a common defendant accept payment that might very well be motivated by the donor's generalized hope of benefit. It is almost impossible for a court to determine what the defendant gained or hoped to gain by the side settlements when reviewing a class action settlement for fairness and adequacy of counsel or when appointing class counsel to litigate a class action when those lawyers are simultaneously litigating and potentially settling other cases against the defendant. Therefore, to help ensure the integrity of class counsel and the process, courts should prohibit such simultaneous representation.

But one need not resort to the criminal statutes to find support for a standard that bars class counsel from representing competing groups against a common defendant. Under bankruptcy law, a trustee may avoid any transfer of an interest of a debtor for an antecedent debt made ninety days before bankruptcy, if that transfer leaves the creditor better off. * * * The bankruptcy rule is justified as a prophylactic measure against fraud; I am suggesting a similar prophylactic rule for class actions.

In the same way that transfers of assets soon before bankruptcy make it too easy for potential bankrupts to avoid the protection bankruptcy law affords creditors, side settlements made by class counsel make it too easy for class counsel and the defendants to avoid the protections supposedly afforded class members by Rule 23(e) * * * and the Due Process Clause of the Constitution. Of course, a rule that allowed class counsel to represent competing groups, as long as no settlement was made for the other group in close proximity to the settlement of the class's claim, would be unworkable. Thus, to be effective, any prophylactic rule against fraudulent side deals would have to ban parallel representation against a common defendant completely.

* * *

Although I believe there are times when a court should order the depositions of the lawyers who negotiated the settlement, [here we are] concerned with the duties of the lawyers for settling parties in the vast majority of cases where the courts deny the objectors meaningful discovery. While the presence of objectors makes the proceedings adversarial in fact, the objectors are handicapped by the limits ordinarily placed on their access to relevant evidence. When the opposing party is forced to operate largely in the dark, just as when there is no opposing party, the court must be able to rely on the lawyers who are informed and present to convey to the court "all material facts known to [them]" that are reasonably necessary for the court to reach an informed decision, "whether or not the facts are adverse."

The special nature of the court's responsibility in approving settlements likewise supports imposing a greater duty of candor on lawyers for settling parties in a class action. Normally, the court is expected to be a neutral umpire between the two parties. However, in approving a class settlement, the court sits as a guardian for the absent class members. Class counsel also have fiduciary obligations to the class, but only if the court approves of class counsel assuming that role. Of course, a lawyer owes the guardian for his client more than an advocate's presentation of one side of the story. The guardian, like the client for whom the guardian stands in, is owed all material facts. Class counsel therefore owes the court greater candor in petitioning for approval of a settlement than an ordinary advocate normally owes, whether or not there are objectors and whatever the scope of discovery.

* * *

NOTES AND QUESTIONS

1. Would adoption of Professor Koniak's proposals increase the likelihood that settlements would be fair to all class members? Would it decrease the number of settlements? What effects would such changes have on the dynamics of the settlement-approval process? To what extent, if any, did Congress take any of these steps in CAFA? Should Congress have gone further? Besides the suggestions of Professor Koniak, some commentators suggest using more subclasses with separate counsel, *see, e.g.*, Mary K. Kane, *Of Carrots and Sticks: Evaluating the Role of the Class Action Lawyer*, 66 Tex. L. Rev. 385, 401 (1987); appointing guardians *ad litum* for absent class members during settlement negotiations, *see, e.g.*, Note, *Abuse in Plaintiff Class Action Settlements: The Need for a Guardian During Pretrial Settlement Negotiations*, 84 Mich. L. Rev. 308, 326–29 (1985); or attempting to restructure the class action device, *see, e.g.*, Jonathan R. Macey & Geoffrey P. Miller, *The Plaintiffs' Attorney's Role in Class Action and Derivative Litigation: Economic Analysis and Recommendations for Reform*, 58 U. Chi. L. Rev. 1 (1991) (proposing extensive changes to class action rules in effort to realign interests of attorney and client).

2. Many suggestions concerning class action settlement focus upon increasing the involvement of the district court. For example, Judge Weinstein and his co-author identify a number of "tools" that a court can utilize to address some of the most familiar potential conflicts and to facilitate a just and prompt settlement:

> When potential problems are identified during the settlement negotiations, the judge should be free to comment about them to the parties so that they may be addressed during negotiations. The success of such a practice depends on the judge being apprised of progress directly or through a special master. * * *

* * *

One possible technique [for increasing court participation] is for the judge to schedule preliminary approval conferences. This is, in effect, a common practice in closely monitored major class actions. Such conferences could serve as a kind of miniature preliminary fairness hearing, where the people most interested in the litigation would be given an opportunity to air their concerns about the shape the settlement is taking. Formal notice could be given to anyone who has expressed an interest. * * *

The preliminary approval conference provides the judge with an opportunity to make an initial assessment prior to formal notice being sent to the entire class. The parties can respond to serious concerns of the judge before incurring the expense and publicity of the fairness hearing. Such conferences require a lesser level of notice since only those people most interested need be targeted. Topical reporters, as well as the national media, can provide a useful link to those most interested in a given class action.

* * *

One concern with establishing a pre-fairness hearing conference is that it may create the appearance that the fairness hearing is a sham. If all the substantive issues are sorted out prior to the fairness hearing, the fairness hearing itself might be viewed as a rubber stamp. As it is, fairness hearings are often carefully orchestrated by the parties, who are no longer adversarial but are now joined in support of a proposed settlement, to display the best aspects of their agreement. While the possible denigration of the fairness hearing is troublesome, concern about appearances should not prevent use of devices that may lead to fairer substantive results.

* * *

What if * * * problems with a proposed settlement only come to light late in the process, after notice of the settlement has been distributed and perhaps after the fairness hearing commenced? The discretionary powers of the judge provided in Rule 23(d) suggest a way to provide affected parties with the opportunity to comment on proposed settlement changes while avoiding the costs of full renoticing and a new fairness hearing. Where the parties and the judge can agree on modifications to the settlement, and only a subset of the class's view of the settlement is likely to be affected by the change, the court should adjourn the fairness hearing to provide for new notice to that subset. While Rule 23(e) provides that notice of class action "dismissal or compromise" must be distributed "to all members of the class," Rule 23(1)(B) permits the judge to order notice "to some or all members of the class of any step in the action." * * * To further reduce costs while ensuring that needed views are presented to the court, a judge might consider even narrower targeting of notice to a reasonable sample of those who might be concerned about the change.

If new full notice were to be required in every case, unanimously supported improvements to settlements would sometimes be foregone to avoid additional expense and delay. It should be unnecessary to require the whole negotiation of settlement-notice-hearing process to start over when almost everyone involved would agree on a sensible modification. A judge should not feel pressured to approve a settlement that all agree needs modification in order to avoid the extra costs of disseminating new notice to the entire class and scheduling new hearings.

Jack B. Weinstein & Karin S. Schwartz, *Notes from the Cave: Some Problems of Judges in Dealing With Class Action Settlements*, 163 F.R.D. 369, 379–85 (1995); *see also, e.g.*, Kane, *supra*, 66 Tex. L. Rev. at 402–06 (calling for more court participation in settlement negotiations); Howard M. Downs, *Federal Class Actions: Diminished Protection for the Class and the Case for Reform*, 73 Neb. L. Rev. 646, 696–97 (1994) (same); ALI *Principles* § 3.05(e) at 209 ("If, before or as a result of a fairness hearing, the parties agree to modify the terms of a settlement in any material way, new notice must be provided to any class members who may be substantially adversely affected by the change.").

3. Other commentators have gone further—even advocating lawsuits against lawyers who allegedly collude and defraud those whom they are supposed to protect. Susan P. Koniak & George M. Cohen, *Under Cloak of Settlement*, 82 Va. L. Rev. 1051, 1057 (1996) ("Our answer to class action abuse is 'sue the bastards.'"). Should absent class members have a cause of action against attorneys who enter into settlements that disadvantage either the entire class or certain segments of the class?

B. CLASS ACTION REMEDIES

This section provides a brief overview of various remedies available in class action cases. After providing a brief survey of equitable remedies and damages, it discusses in greater depth one controversial remedy that some courts have used to circumvent manageability problems—the *cy pres* or "fluid" recovery approach.

1. EQUITABLE RELIEF

The district judge's broad discretion in fashioning relief stems from the equitable origins of the class action device. *See* Charles A. Wright, Arthur R. Miller & Mary K. Kane, *Federal Practice & Procedure* § 1784, at 86–87 (2d ed.1986). That discretion permits the judge to shape the remedy according to the exigencies of the case, or to appoint others to help in administering classwide relief. *See id.* Fashioning injunctive or declaratory relief in the class action context often involves the same kind of equitable balancing that courts perform in more traditional, non-class litigation. But the stakes are often greater. Consider the following articles.

JACK GREENBERG, CIVIL RIGHTS CLASS ACTIONS: PROCEDURAL MEANS OF OBTAINING SUBSTANCE
39 Ariz. L. Rev. 575, 577–86 (1997).

I. Introduction

* * *

Civil rights and class actions have an historic partnership. Indeed, those who revised the federal class action rules in 1966 took particularly into account the concerns of civil rights litigants. Professor Albert Sacks, who was Associate Reporter of the revised rules, was intimately familiar with civil rights litigation and had in mind the role of class actions in civil rights litigation in formulating the rule. (For years he was an instructor at legal training sessions of the NAACP Legal Defense and Education Fund and was a consultant to the Fund.) The Advisory Committee specifically noted that Rule 23(b)(2) class certification was designed for class actions in the civil rights field, "where a party is charged with discriminating unlawfully against a class, usually one whose members are incapable of specific enumeration." Most civil rights class actions are certified as 23(b)(2) classes * * * when, "the party opposing the class has acted or refused to act on grounds generally applicable to the class, thereby making appropriate final injunctive relief or corresponding declaratory relief with respect to the class as a whole." The partnership between class actions and civil rights has grown to such an extent that the Advisory Committee revising Rule 23 [in 1966] noted that, "subdivision (b)(2) has cemented the role of class actions in enforcing a wide array of civil rights claims."

*** [I]t is hardly possible to discuss all of the areas of class actions in the civil rights field. I shall limit myself to a few: prisoners' rights, school desegregation, and employment discrimination, and only to some aspects of each. I shall note something about how the rule has functioned in these areas over the years and reactions to that experience.

II. Prisoners' Rights

Class actions have played a major role in securing the rights of prisoners. Since the federal class action rule was revised in 1966, prisoner rights litigation has utilized the mechanism of class action to bring broad relief to inmates and detainees throughout the country. Prisoners' rights litigation has thoroughly reformed entire state prison systems in Texas, Florida and Georgia. In cases which lasted for years, those and other systems have been placed under judicial management for long periods of time. Less far-reaching cases have involved class action relief from double celling, religious discrimination, due process violation in parole standards, restrictions on an inmate's right to marry, solitary confinement, and denial of contact visits.

* * *

*** [T]he broad-based relief ordered as a result of prisoners' rights class actions has resulted in a congressional backlash. The procedural restrictions which Congress has enacted seem to be fueled at least in part by growing hostility to those accused of a crime, typified by the reemergence of chain gangs, the creation of boot camps, proposals to treat juveniles as adults, and three-strikes-and-you're-out legislation. The * * * Prison Litigation Reform Act, 18 U.S.C. §§ 3626, 28 U.S.C. § 1915, 1915f, 42 U.S.C. § 1997e * * * establishes several substantive restraints on court-ordered remedies in all civil litigation, including class actions, involving prison conditions based on federal rights. A court may not grant any relief unless that relief is narrowly drawn, is no further than necessary to correct the violation of a federal right, and is the least intrusive means necessary to correct the violation. The Act precludes a court from issuing a remedy including a prisoner release order unless that court has previously entered less intrusive relief which failed to remedy the violation of rights. Further, the Act prohibits all prisoners from bringing a federal civil action for mental or emotional injury unless accompanied by a prior showing of physical injury. Finally, and perhaps most importantly, the Act applies retroactively, so that any previously entered relief which does not conform to the Act's stringent restrictions may be subject to a motion to terminate that order for failure to comply with the Act. As a consequence, rights once thought settled are already once more in litigation.

* * *

III. School Desegregation

The beginning of school desegregation class actions was *Brown v. Board of Education*, 347 U.S. 483 (1954). *In Brown II*, the "all deliberate speed" implementation decision, the Court, in explaining factors which a court of equity should take into account in fashioning relief, referred to the cases as class actions in explaining why it had prescribed how district courts should proceed in formulating their decrees. 349 U.S. 294, 300 (1955). *Brown* is a curious example of the relationship between substance and class action procedure. At the time *Brown* was decided, it was widely believed that the Constitution would be satisfied by admitting black applicants to white schools. Conforming to this view, most southern states passed laws, known as pupil placement laws, which prescribed procedures for application and transfer by individual black children to white schools. Although these transparently were stratagems for maintaining segregation, and although efforts to transfer routinely were frustrated, the courts, including the Supreme Court, for many years upheld the laws. A class action, therefore, would have involved the right of many black would-be transferees or applicants to move to white schools, but only those who chose to transfer. It would not have involved transfer of white children to black schools. Later, the Court made clear that the constitutional right was [not] the right of a black child to transfer to a white school. *See Swann v. Charlotte–Mecklenburg Bd. of Educ.*, 402 U.S. 1 (1971); *Green v. County Bd.*, 391 U.S. 430 (1968). It was the right to attend school in a desegregated system. Pursuant to this theory a class action, while not inappropriate, presumably would not be necessary. A solitary plaintiff, invoking the right to attend school in a desegregated system, ought to have had the right to desegregate all the schools to vindicate his rights. In fact, however, all school cases have been denominated class actions, a formulation which according to the theory I have described would be surplusage. Such criticism as may be directed at the class action device because courts have come to administer many school systems over many years would more appropriately be directed at the constitutional rule that school segregation is unconstitutional, not so inviting a target.

School desegregation remedies, since the early seventies, have been broad-based. As the Supreme Court noted in 1971 in *Swann v. Charlotte–Mecklenburg Board of Education*, once a violation of *Brown* is found to exist, the breadth and scope of the remedy under a court's broad equitable powers is limited only by the nature of the violation. Thus, the Court declared that district courts overseeing desegregation within a district could (1) order the assignment of teachers to achieve a particular degree of faculty desegregation, (2) oversee the construction of new schools to ensure that segregation was not perpetuated, (3) use mathematical racial ratios as a starting point for racial balancing within a district, (4) gerrymander school districts, including the creation of non-contiguous school zones, as a corrective measure, and (5) order bus transportation to implement desegregation. All of this is quite a large role for judges to carry out.

However, *Swann* contained a note of caution, demonstrating that the Court was clearly worried about the breadth and scope of its remedies and the extent of court oversight required to implement those remedies. The Court first stressed that in the absence of a violation demonstrating that the state had deliberately attempted to fix the racial composition of the schools, a court's equitable powers could not be exercised. Then the Court stated that "at some point, these school authorities and others like them should have achieved full compliance with this Court's decision in *Brown I.*" At that point, a court's oversight would end. While these observations constituted a limitation on the reach of equitable relief, they may also be seen as a hesitation to extend judicial supervision of governmental programs too far and for too long—a caution about the kinds of cases that often invoke class relief.

Milliken v. Bradley, 418 U.S. 717 (1974), began in fact to define some limits of these broad remedies. In that case, parents and students filed a class action seeking to desegregate the Detroit school district. The district court found numerous segregation violations by the Detroit School Board. Reasoning that actions taken by school districts which violated *Brown* were linked to the actions of other non-violating districts, the district court ordered an inter-district remedy to integrate Detroit schools with schools in other school districts. The Supreme Court reversed this remedy, holding that despite the violation within the Detroit school district, the remedy could not be so broad as to include districts in which there was no violation. While the *Milliken* Court placed some limits on a district court's equitable powers, broad relief was still permitted within a school district which violated *Brown*. After the Supreme Court remanded *Milliken* for the formulation of a new remedial order, the district court entered an order requiring not only student reassignments, but also remedial reading and communication skills education programs, training for teachers and administrators, guidance and counseling programs, and revised testing procedures, requiring large expenditures of funds. These remedies were upheld by the Supreme Court as falling within the discretion of the district court in its exercise of its equitable powers.

* * *

[In] *Missouri v. Jenkins*, 495 U.S. 33 (1990), * * * [t]he district court found that the Kansas City, Missouri school district operated a segregated school system and ordered relief which was estimated to cost almost $88 million, and divided the cost between the state and the school district. The district court found, however, that several provisions of Missouri state law prevented the school district from being able to pay its share of the remedy's cost by preventing the raising of local property taxes above a certain level. The district court thus enjoined the enforcement of the state law, and ordered the district court to raise its property taxes to cover the cost of the relief. The Supreme Court reversed. It held that principles of comity which govern the district court's equitable discretion were contravened when the court ordered the district to raise property taxes. Although the broad and expensive relief ordered by the court was within its equitable discretion, the court could not order the district to raise taxes in order to pay for the relief when a less obtrusive method was available. Since the court could have required the school district to formulate its own plan for paying for the relief, the district court erred in not implementing this less obtrusive method.

While the Supreme Court was signaling that the lower court's equitable discretion had clear limits, it was not wholly rejecting broad relief. After all, the $88 million worth of relief ordered by the district court was upheld, as was the court's order enjoining the enforcement of state law that prevented the school district from raising the revenue necessary to pay for the relief. The only part of the order struck down was the order instructing the district to raise property taxes. Nonetheless, *Jenkins* [and other Supreme Court cases] indicate the Supreme Court's willingness to draw clear lines demarcating the boundaries of relief which may be ordered in school desegregation class actions.

In the area of school desegregation, where the substantive right is one to class relief, we see perhaps most clearly the political and social forces which operate on what in other contexts may be called only a procedural issue.

IV. Employment Discrimination

Class actions have played a major role in employment discrimination litigation. While it is impossible for public interest lawyers to calibrate closely the sequence of issues which courts will address in a litigation program such as that undertaken by the NAACP Legal Defense Fund in implementing Title VII of the Civil Rights Act, establishing the propriety of class relief had a high priority. Thus it was no accident that the * * * first [reported] Title VII decision was in a 1966 NAACP Legal Defense Fund case which upheld class relief in Title VII cases. *Hall v. Werthan Bag Corp.*, 251 F. Supp. 184 (M.D.Tenn. 1966), involved a company later made famous in the movie Driving Miss Daisy. In that case, the district court held that Title VII did authorize the filing of a class action. This proposition would later be reaffirmed by the Supreme Court when it stated that "racial discrimination is by definition class discrimination." *General Tel. Co. v. Falcon*, 457 U.S. 147 (1982).

Even more precisely focused on the class action aspect of civil rights lawsuits was the Supreme Court's curtailment of the scope of class relief in *Martin v. Wilks*, 490 U.S. 755 (1989). In that case, a class of black firefighters sued the city alleging that it discriminated in hiring and promoting them. The city and plaintiffs settled the case by a consent decree which provided affirmative action relief for blacks. Blacks would obtain positions in a ratio which meant some whites who might have been appointed would not be. Whites sued, claiming that they were victims of reverse discrimination imposed by a decree in a case in which they had not been parties. The issue was whether such a decree could preclude their rights. The Supreme Court held that it could not, because the white firefighters had not had their day in court.

But Congress overruled that decision in the Civil Rights Act of 1991. That Act, among other things, held that, if persons situated like the *Martin v. Wilks* plaintiffs (a) had notice of the action sufficient to apprise them that it might affect their rights, and (b) a reasonable opportunity to present objections or (c) were adequately represented by another person who had challenged the order on the same legal grounds and with a similar factual situation, then they could be bound by the decree. In essence, the Congress decided that the substantive policies of the Equal Employment Opportunities Act trumped the conventional notice procedure of ordinary litigation.

Class actions make possible monetary relief for many persons in a single case. * * * Without the availability of back pay, an employer who discriminates can continue to do so without cost until an employee wins a case against [it]. If back pay is available, the employer who uses such a tactic will be forced to pay for years of discrimination rather than simply reverse its policy without further costs; in a class action the amounts can be quite large. It is impossible to imagine effective relief in cases of this sort without class actions.

While prisoners' rights and school desegregation have in recent years been curtailed by Congress and the courts, the Supreme Court's effort to limit the effectiveness of employment discrimination class actions provoked a strong negative response from Congress. The Civil Rights Act of 1991 overturned *Martin v. Wilks* and various other decisions which curtailed the scope of Title VII. Moreover, the Act was passed by the largest margin of any civil rights statute in American history, with eighty-nine percent of Congress voting in favor.

While there are many one-on-one employment cases, class actions of considerable scope continue to be filed. * * *

V. Conclusion

In the three areas I have described—prisoners' rights, school desegregation, and employment discrimination—class actions have played a vital role. They have made it possible to afford relief to large numbers of persons who, realistically, could not have been parties to litigation. As a consequence, courts have become involved in administration of complex orders and decrees, sometimes dealing with inevitable clashes of interest in highly politicized, contentious areas. Notwithstanding that such cases have afforded justice to class members whose rights otherwise would have been denied, some kinds of civil rights class actions have engendered legislative and judicial backlash. But, employment discrimination remains a notable exception to this trend, with classes becoming larger, back pay relief increasing dramatically, and the Civil Rights Act of 1991 restoring the gains of previous litigation. It is tempting to speculate about why prisoners and schoolchildren have evoked one reaction and workers another.

Perhaps the simple answer is that prisoners evoke little sympathy. The expense and difficulties of assuring their rights, particularly on a mass scale, offend enough of the public to make possible legislation that curtails those rights or makes it difficult to realize them. Since those rights typically are grounded in the Constitution, there is no realistic chances of repealing them procedurally. Consequently, legislation has been enacted to undo the kinds of relief often awarded in prisoners class action cases, including class relief obtained in the past. It is highly unlikely that the kinds of political reaction we have had towards reformation of entire prison systems or prohibition of certain treatment of prisoners—for example, double or triple celling or improper diets or medical treatment—would have been engendered if a comparable court order had been limited to an individual prisoner.

In the area of school desegregation, even without class action rules, the relief which courts order is, substantively speaking, of a class nature. It is, of course, regulated by the parameters of the class action rules, but the controversies which have arisen in the school desegregation context have stemmed from the mass reassignment of students. Nothing comparable would occur if a court were to order a single child or two to attend a particular school. This has been the driving force behind curtailment of relief in school cases encountered in [various Supreme Court cases].

But employment is different. Whatever residual racial prejudice still afflicts the United States, there is no open support for discrimination in the workplace. The public has shown little sympathy for efforts to make it more difficult to win relief for employment discrimination. On the few recent occasions when courts have curtailed such relief, Congress has reversed those decisions.

LLOYD C. ANDERSON, THE APPROVAL AND INTERPRETATION OF CONSENT DECREES IN CIVIL RIGHTS CLASS ACTION LITIGATION
1983 U. Ill. L. Rev. 579, 583, 585–89, 600–01, 604–05, 615–17, 632 (1983).

Suits seeking structural injunctive relief typically are brought as class actions in federal court. If the parties reach a settlement in the course of the litigation, the parties enter into a consent decree setting forth the terms. * * * [T]his agreement only marks the beginning of a new phase of the case, that of implementation. The proposed decree must be approved by the court before it becomes effective. Even if it is approved, however, neither the case nor judicial involvement necessarily ends. A consent decree setting forth requirements for institutional change over time is likely to be complex and, despite the parties' best efforts, at least partially ambiguous. Undoubtedly, disputes will arise concerning the meaning of various terms. When this occurs, the court must interpret the decree.

* * *

A consent decree is a judicial act, and should be treated as such. First, by its very terms it is the equivalent of a judgment. Since the merger of law and equity, the technical distinctions between a "decree in equity" and a "judgment at law" have been erased and the terms are used interchangeably. Second, consent decrees providing for structural change, unlike money settlements, are a form of equitable relief. Whereas money settlements normally involve one transaction or a series of similar transactions, structural reform requires changes over time in the operations of institutions such as prisons, schools, welfare agencies, and corporations.

* * *

In the context of civil rights class actions the court should pay particular attention to whether a proposed consent decree implements the statutory or constitutional policies that plaintiffs sought to enforce. If a proposed consent decree contains provisions that undermine such policies, the decree should not be approved absent compelling reasons to the contrary. The public interest component in civil rights cases causes the ramifications of a settlement to extend far beyond the interests of individual class members.

* * *

The rights sought to be vindicated by the plaintiff class must be compared to the benefits gained by the settlement, as well as to the likely results of a trial on the merits. Legal benefit to the plaintiff class is more than slight improvement in their circumstances. The extent of the benefit must be measured by the rights the plaintiff class seeks to enforce by litigation. Moreover, in considering the likely results of a trial on the merits, an analysis of the applicable law must be made, even though "unsettled" law is involved.

Therefore the inquiry does not end with a determination that a consent decree does not violate clearly established civil rights. In balancing the benefits of a consent decree against the likely outcome of litigation, the court must make some determination of the rights of the class. It is necessary then to consider how the court can make such a prediction. * * *

* * *

The approval and entry of a consent decree does not terminate the litigation, but rather ushers in a new phase of the case. If a civil rights settlement is to fulfill its bright promise for peaceful redress of social grievances, courts must vigorously enforce the agreement. A mode of interpretation which enhances energetic enforcement is a critical component of the effort to make settlement meaningful.

* * *

A consent decree may be subject to different interpretations by the parties as their competing interests vie for favorable interpretations. Moreover, because the decree is an instrument of compromise, the parties may deliberately include some ambiguous language in anticipation of an impasse in negotiations. Thus, resolution of the controversial matters is deferred to the future. The decree may be framed primarily in general principles, leaving interpretation of those principles to be resolved in the context of future concrete disputes. Even where the parties to a given decree take great care in drafting strict terms, problems of interpretation may arise.

* * *

When post-approval disagreements arise, courts should intervene to decide whether the defendant has violated the consent decree. Therefore, the consent decree ordinarily should contain a provision allowing the court to retain jurisdiction of the case pending full implementation of the required reforms. Retention of jurisdiction allows the court to administer the decree without first reopening the case.

* * *

NOTES AND QUESTIONS

1. What insights relevant to class actions can be gleaned from Professor Greenberg's review of prisoner rights, school desegregation, and employment discrimination cases? What is his view concerning the utility of such cases?

2. Professor Greenberg concludes that civil rights class actions are primarily certified pursuant to Rule 23(b)(2) because of their emphasis on injunctive and declaratory relief. *See also* Thomas E. Willging, Laural L. Hooper & Robert J. Niemic, *Fed. Judicial Ctr., Empirical Study of Class Actions in Four Federal District Courts: Final Report to the Advisory Committee on Civil Rules* (1996) (reporting that civil rights cases accounted for 50% of (b)(2) classes in study of four federal districts). Given the availability of compensatory and punitive damages in Title VII cases following the Civil Rights Act of 1991, however, obtaining certification of a Title VII case for damages under (b)(2)—or even (b)(3)—is now more difficult. *See* Chapter 3(B)(2) and Chapter 10(B)(1)(c) (discussing challenges to certification of employment discrimination cases). Should employment class actions have a favored place in class action law? *See* Melissa Hart, *Will Employment Discrimination Class Actions Survive?*, 37 Akron L. Rev. 813, 844–46 (2004) (suggesting that courts are reticent to certify employment discrimination cases because they believe that the underlying substantive claims lack merit).

3. Professor Greenberg notes that a case seeking to desegregate a school system may achieve its result even if it is not pursued as a class action. He

questions the necessity of the class action designation, calling it "surplusage." Is Professor Greenberg correct? For a fuller discussion of the "necessity doctrine," see Chapter 3(B)(4).

4. Professor Greenberg discusses the broad scope of judicial power in formulating remedies and enforcing them. Is this broad scope appropriate? Assuming courts have the discretion to issue broad relief, are they capable of overseeing the implementation of such relief? Are courts competent to administer large complex cases and monitor consent decrees for years?

5. Professor Anderson's article provides a brief survey of some of the issues involved in crafting and enforcing consent decrees. What is the principal thrust of his analysis?

6. A useful summary of equitable remedies is contained in Gene R. Shreve & Peter Raven–Hansen, *Understanding Civil Procedure* §§ 14.02–14.03 (4th ed. 2009). The basic principles are the same in both class and non-class cases. In brief, as Professor Shreve and Professor Raven–Hansen point out, injunctions differ from damages because, "[w]hile factual elements of damage actions concern the past (what defendant did and what it cost the plaintiff), factual elements in injunction cases concern the future (what the defendant will do to the plaintiff, absent an injunction)." *Id.* § 14.02 at 518. A party seeking a permanent injunction must show that (i) it has succeeded on the merits; (ii) it has no adequate remedy at law; (iii) the balance of equities weighs in its favor; and (iv) issuance of the injunction is in the public interest. *See, e.g., Plummer v. American Inst. of Certified Pub. Accountants*, 97 F.3d 220, 229 (7th Cir. 1996). When an injunction is sought against a state agency or official, the relief ordered must be no broader than necessary to remedy the violation at issue. *See, e.g., Milliken v. Bradley*, 433 U.S. 267, 280 (1977); *Swann v. Charlotte–Mecklenburg Bd. of Educ.*, 402 U.S. 1, 16 (1971).

7. Absent a settlement, "[t]he procedure for obtaining a final (permanent) injunction is a trial on the merits of the case much like that for a damages remedy." Shreve & Raven–Hansen, *supra*, § 14.02. Of course, in the interim, plaintiffs may seek a preliminary injunction or temporary restraining order if they satisfy the strict requirements, including the presence of irreparable injury absent relief and a likelihood of success on the merits. *Id.* Injunctions are enforced by civil or criminal contempt. *Id.*

8. In contrast to injunctive relief and damages, the sole purpose of declaratory relief is to "determine rights and obligations" of the parties. *Id.* § 14.03. Requests for declaratory relief are often made in conjunction with requests for damages or injunctive relief. *Id.* Abstract requests for declaratory relief can raise ripeness issues.

9. Prominent examples of cases seeking broad relief include race discrimination class actions brought against Denny's, Texaco, and Coca-Cola in the 1990s. In 1993, front-page stories in major newspapers brought to light plaintiffs' accusations that waiters at Denny's restaurants had refused to serve African–American Secret Service agents in an Annapolis restaurant, and that African–American customers were being systematically mistreated. This federal case resulted in "the largest and broadest settlement under the Federal public accommodations laws" (over $54 million) at the time, and included an agreement between Denny's and the NAACP that the former would provide $1 billion in jobs and minority contracts. *See Ridgeway v. Flagstar Corp.*, 1994 WL 525553 (N.D. Cal. 1994) (describing settlement provisions).

The Denny's settlement was eclipsed, in 1994, by a $176 million settlement between Texaco and a class of 1,400 African–American current and former employees, alleging discrimination in pay, promotions, and workplace behavior. The consent decree provided broad injunctive relief, including: the formation of a seven-member task force responsible for influencing hiring and promotions policies; adoption of a company-wide diversity and sensitivity program, mentoring program, and ombudsmen program; consideration of changes in job posting requirements; and direct monitoring by the EEOC of defendant's compliance and hiring and promotion practices for five years. *See Roberts v. Texaco, Inc.*, 979 F. Supp. 185, 189–92 (S.D.N.Y. 1997) (describing settlement provisions).

Texaco served as a model for a $192.5 million settlement reached in the fall of 2000 to resolve a class action brought by African–American employees alleging systemic discrimination in promotions, compensation, and performance evaluations against Coca-Cola. The company agreed to make sweeping changes in its employment practices, at a cost of $36 million. The consent decree called for, *inter alia*, the creation of an independent task force responsible for: analyzing company policy and practice; making binding recommendations to the Board of Directors; monitoring company compliance; investigating complaints; and providing written annual reports to the court, counsel, and public over a four year period. Coca–Cola was also required to hire an ombudsman to oversee complaints and investigations of discrimination and retaliation. *See Abdallah v. Coca–Cola Co.*, 133 F. Supp. 2d 1364 (N.D. Ga. 2001) (describing settlement provisions).

10. For those interested in exploring in greater depth the theoretical and practical issues involved in structural reform litigation, a survey of some of the leading works—including writings by Professors Abram Chayes and Owen Fiss—is contained in Margo Schlanger, *The Courts: Beyond the Hero Judge: Institutional Reform Litigation as Litigation*, 97 Mich. L. Rev. 1994, 1994–97 (1999). *See also* Samuel Issacharoff & Robert H. Klonoff, *The Public Value of Settlement*, 78 Fordham L. Rev. 1177 (2009) (arguing that legal system's ability to resolve repetitive harms in mass society through settlement is an important public policy).

2. DAMAGES

a. General Considerations

Various damages issues arise in the class action context.

Class actions for damages pose special problems for judicial administration since conventional mechanisms for calculating and distributing damages may not be practicable in the context of a suit brought on behalf of many small claimants. If all or even a substantial portion of the class members seek individual damage trials, the court may be intolerably burdened. Moreover, class members may not come forward if the burden of proving damages outweighs any potential benefit of doing so. Finally, in some actions, it may be impossible to identify class members so that, if relief is to be distributed at all, it must be through some indirect process.

Developments in the Law: Class Actions, 89 Harv. L. Rev. 1318, 1516 (1976). The Harvard Note groups methods for calculating and distributing damages into four main categories, as described below.

The most individualized method involves the traditional full evidentiary hearing, where each class member claims damages through an individual trial following a common trial on liability. The benefit of this approach is its precision. But it may be very burdensome to engage in such proofs, particularly for those with small claims. *Id.* at 1517.

Alternatively, "innovative summary judgment procedures" and lighter burdens of proof at the individualized damages trials may be used to make it easier for class members to receive compensation "without abandoning the individual trial requirement or significantly increasing the danger that unharmed individuals will recover." *Id.* at 1518–19. These methods maximize compensation, deterrence, and disgorgement, but still may be burdensome for small claimants, and may pose due process risks to defendants. *Id.* at 1519.

Third, individual damages trials may be replaced with classwide calculation of damages. Examples include sampling, averaging, and statistics. The benefit of this approach is that it compensates class members with small claims, promotes deterrence, and disgorges ill-gotten gains. Once damages are calculated on a classwide basis, they can be distributed individually—upon some showing of harm through a type of claims process—or to the class as a whole. *Id.* at 1520–21. The drawback of this approach is the presence of some inaccuracy in individual compensation. *Id.* at 1521. Such procedures again may implicate defendants' due process and may face substantial hurdles in federal courts under the Rules Enabling Act. *See* Chapter 4(F)(2)(a) (discussing due process issues involving aggregated proof).

Fourth, the least individualized method is a *cy pres* procedure, in which all or some portion of unclaimed class damages are distributed to benefit the class as a whole. Unclaimed funds may be distributed in some form as lower prices, or may be paid to an organization sharing plaintiffs' interests. Although such a scheme promotes deterrence and disgorgement, it does not award relief directly to class members based on their individual damages. Consequently, some class members may be overcompensated or undercompensated. Once again, such procedures implicate both due process and the Rules Enabling Act. *Id.* at 1521–23. *Cy pres* is explored next in this chapter.

NOTES AND QUESTIONS

1. The Harvard Note, written relatively soon after modern Rule 23's enactment, discusses a variety of procedures short of individual damage determinations. For a discussion of the use of aggregate statistical proof in class actions see Chapter 4(F)(2)(a) and Chapter 10(A)(3)(b).

2. Damages may, in certain cases, include punitive damages. Such damages can raise a host of issues in class actions, particularly with respect to due process. The Supreme Court has addressed some of these important issues in non-class cases, focusing on both the excessiveness of awards and the procedures for establishing such damages. In 2008, the Supreme Court held that a 1:1 ratio of punitive to compensatory damages was appropriate in the context

of federal maritime law. *See Exxon Shipping Co. v. Baker*, 554 U.S. 471, 512–15 (2008). The Supreme Court reduced a $2.5 billion punitive damages award (already reduced by the Ninth Circuit from $5 billion) to $507.5 million, the same amount as the compensatory damages. *Id.* at 515. *Exxon Shipping*, however, did not address the outer limits of punitive damages under due process (as opposed to federal maritime law). *Id.* at 501–02. In due process challenges, the Supreme Court has embraced a 9:1 punitive-to-compensatory damages ratio. *See State Farm Mut. Automobile Ins. Co. v. Campbell*, 538 U.S. 408, 425 (2003). Although the Court has refused to "impose a bright line ratio" between punitive and compensatory damages, it has noted that "few awards exceeding a single-digit ratio * * * will satisfy due process." *Id.* at 424–25. Beyond this guidance, the Court has indicated that ratios may or may not comport with due process, depending on what is reasonable and proportionate to the harm under the circumstances. *Id.* at 425–26.

b. Cy Pres

IN RE BANKAMERICA CORP. SEC. LITIG.

United States Court of Appeals, Eighth Circuit, 2015.

775 F.3d 1060.

Before: WOLLMAN, LOKEN, and MURPHY, CIRCUIT JUDGES.

LOKEN, CIRCUIT JUDGE.

Following the 1998 merger of NationsBank and BankAmerica to form Bank of America Corporation, shareholders filed multiple class actions around the country alleging violations of federal and state securities laws. The cases were transferred by the Judicial Panel on Multidistrict Litigation to the Eastern District of Missouri. That court certified four plaintiff classes, two classes of NationsBank shareholders and two classes of BankAmerica shareholders. The transferred cases were resolved when the court approved a $490 million global settlement * * *.

After an initial December 2004 distribution, approximately $6.9 million remained in the NationsBank settlement fund. The district court ordered a second distribution of $4.75 million to NationsBank claimants in April 2009. After that distribution, $2,440,108.53 remained. In September 2012, class counsel for the NationsBank Classes, appellee Green Jacobson, P.C., filed a motion to terminate the case with respect to the NationsBank Classes, to award class counsel $98,114.34 in attorneys' fees for work done after the distribution in December 2004, and to distribute *cy pres* the remainder of the "surplus settlement funds" to three St. Louis area charities suggested by class counsel. The district court granted the motion over [class representative David P.] Oetting's objections and ordered "that the balance of the NationsBank Classes settlement fund shall be distributed *cy pres* to the Legal Services of Eastern Missouri, Inc." (LSEM).

Oetting appeals the *cy pres* distribution and the award of attorneys' fees. As to the former, he argues the district court abused its discretion in ordering a *cy pres* distribution because a further distribution to the classes is feasible, and in any event LSEM is unrelated to the classes or the litigation and is therefore an inappropriate "next best" *cy pres* recipient. We agree and therefore reverse. As our disposition results in the case not being terminated, we vacate the award of additional attorneys' fees as premature, leaving that issue to be resolved, consistent with this opinion, when administration of the NationsBank Classes settlement fund can be terminated.

I

In recent years, federal district courts have disposed of unclaimed class action settlement funds after distributions to the class by making "*cy pres* distributions."[5] Such distributions "have been controversial in the courts of appeals." Indeed, many of our sister circuits have criticized and severely restricted the practice. [Court cites numerous circuit cases]. These contrary authorities were not even acknowledged by Green Jacobson in urging a *cy pres* distribution in this case, nor by the district court in ordering the requested distribution. * * *

The American Law Institute addressed the issue of *Cy Pres* Settlements in § 3.07 of its published Principles of the Law of Aggregate Litigation (2010). The ALI recommended:

> A court may approve a settlement that proposes a *cy pres* remedy . . . . The court must apply the following criteria in determining whether a *cy pres* award is appropriate:
>
> (a) If individual class members can be identified through reasonable effort, and the distributions are sufficiently large to make individual distributions economically viable, settlement proceeds should be distributed directly to individual class members.
>
> (b) If the settlement involves individual distributions to class members and funds remain after distributions (because some class members could not be identified or chose not to participate), the settlement should presumptively provide for further distributions to participating class members unless the amounts involved are too small to make individual distributions economically viable or other specific reasons exist that would make such further distributions impossible or unfair.
>
> (c) If the court finds that individual distributions are not viable based upon the criteria set forth in subsections (a) and (b), the settlement may utilize a *cy pres* approach. The court, when feasible, should require the parties to identify a recipient whose interests reasonably approximate those being pursued by the class. If, and only if, no recipient whose interest reasonably approximate those being pursued by the class can be identified after thorough investigation and analysis, a court may approve a recipient that does not reasonably approximate the interests being pursued by the class.

We have approved *cy pres* distribution of unused or unclaimed class action settlement funds in two cases. In both, the distributions met each of the criteria in ALI § 3.07, even though our decisions antedated the ALI's

---

[5] "The term 'cy pres' is derived from the Norman French expression *cy pres comme possible*, which means 'as near as possible.' The *cy pres* doctrine originated as a rule of construction to save a testamentary charitable gift that would otherwise fail, allowing 'the next best use of the funds to satisfy the testator's intent as near as possible.'"

work. * * * By contrast, class counsel and the district court entirely ignored this now-published ALI authority.

Given the substantial history of district courts ignoring and resisting circuit court *cy pres* concerns and rulings in class action cases, we conclude it is time to clarify the [governing] legal principles:

First, we agree with the Fifth Circuit that, "Because the settlement funds are the property of the class, a *cy pres* distribution to a third party of unclaimed settlement funds is permissible '*only* when it is not feasible to make further distributions to class members' . . . except where an additional distribution would provide a windfall to class members with *liquidated*-damages claims that were 100 percent satisfied by the initial distribution." *Klier* [*v. Elf Atochem N. Am., Inc.*, 658 F.3d 468, 475 (5th Cir. 2011)] (quoting ALI § 3.07; emphasis added). Here, from the perspective of administrative cost, a further distribution to the class was clearly feasible. Class counsel advised the district court, "Claims Administrator would distribute, free of charge, the remaining Settlement Fund in the amount of $2,445,248.07, for which the administration fee is estimated to be $27,000."

Class counsel nonetheless contended, and the district court agreed, that "further identification of members for additional distribution would be difficult and costly, considering the time that has passed since the initial distribution." We disagree. As the Claims Administrator's cost estimate confirms, lists of NationsBank class members who received and cashed prior distribution checks exist and would form the basis of a further distribution to the classes. The district court previously ordered that no further search need be made for class members whose checks were returned undelivered, so that potentially burdensome expense need not be incurred. The district court erred in finding that further distributions would be so "costly and difficult" as to preclude a further distribution; that inquiry must be based primarily on whether "the amounts involved are too small to make individual distributions economically viable." ALI § 3.07(a). The court's ultimate conclusion that it was appropriate to order a *cy pres* distribution to unrelated third party charities was therefore an error of law.

Class counsel also argues that a further distribution to the class is inappropriate because it would primarily benefit large institutional investors, who are less worthy than charities such as LSEM. We flatly reject this contention. It endorses judicially impermissible misappropriation of monies gathered to settle complex disputes among private parties, one of the "opportunities for abuse" that make it "inherently dubious" to apply the *cy pres* doctrine from trust law "to the entirely unrelated context of a class action settlement." *Klier*, 658 F.3d at 480 (Jones, C.J., concurring).

The district court also relied on class counsel's contention that "a third distribution simply would not inure to the benefit of those actually harmed; institutional investors would be the primary recipients of the distribution, and beneficial ownership of the [Bank of America] shares has shifted over time." This is simply irrelevant. Though the beneficial ownership of outstanding Bank of America shares changes often, no doubt daily, the identity of the NationsBank *class members* entitled to receive the settlement funds does not change. The possibility that distributing a private settlement to class members long after the events that gave rise to their claims may not "inure to the benefit of those actually harmed" does not give the court presiding over class action litigation power to confiscate the settlement proceeds.

Second, a *cy pres* distribution is not authorized by declaring, as class counsel and the district court did in this case, that "all class members submitting claims have been satisfied in full." It is not true that class members with unliquidated damage claims in the underlying litigation are "fully compensated" by payment of the amounts allocated to their claims in the settlement. *See* ALI § 3.07, cmt. b ("few settlements award 100 percent of a class member's losses, and thus it is unlikely in most cases that further distributions to class members would result in more than 100 percent recovery for those class members").

In this case, the shareholder lawsuits were filed when, after the merger, Bank of America reported that it had written off $372 million of old BankAmerica loans, and its stock closed down $5.87 that day. The district court approved a global settlement in which plaintiffs would recover "only a percentage of the damages that they sought," but which was "neither meager nor inadequate, particularly in light of the many hurdles plaintiffs would face if they chose to proceed to trial." The April 2002 settlement notice to the class stated: "the settling parties disagree as to both liability and damages, and do not agree on the average amount of damages per share that would be recoverable by any of the Classes." Thus, the notion that class members were fully compensated by the settlement is speculative, at best.

Third, we reject Green Jacobson's contention that the *cy pres* distribution must be affirmed because the district court and this court are bound by language in the settlement agreement stating that the balance in the settlement fund "shall be contributed" to non-profit organizations "determined by the court in its sole discretion." * * * "[A] proposed *cy pres* distribution must meet [our standards governing *cy pres* awards] regardless of whether the award was fashioned by the settling parties or the trial court." [*Nachshin v. AOL, LLC*, 663 F.3d 1034, 1040 (9th Cir. 2011)]. * * *

Fourth, Oetting argues that the award must be reversed because Green Jacobson did not notify the class of its motion for a *cy pres* distribution. We agree that, unless the amount of funds to be distributed *cy pres* is *de minimis*, the district court should make a *cy pres* proposal publicly available and allow class members to object or suggest alternative recipients before the court selects a *cy pres* recipient. This gives class members a voice in choosing a "next best" third party and minimizes any appearance of judicial overreaching. As we are vacating the *cy pres* award on other grounds, we need not address whether class members were denied this opportunity and if so, the question of an appropriate remedy.

Fifth, when a district court concludes that a *cy pres* distribution is appropriate after applying the foregoing rigorous standards, such a distribution *must be* "for the next best use . . . for indirect class benefit," and "for uses consistent with the nature of the underlying action and with the judicial function." * * * As we said in [*In re Airline Ticket Commission Antitrust Litigation*, 307 F.3d 679, 682 (8th Cir. 2002)], "the unclaimed funds should be distributed for a purpose as near as possible to the legitimate objectives underlying the lawsuit, the interests of class members, and the interests of those similarly situated."

Applying this standard, it is clear that LSEM, though unquestionably a worthy charity, is not the "next best" recipient of unclaimed settlement funds in this nationwide class action seeking damages for violations of federal and state securities laws. In approving LSEM, the district court found that "there is no immediately apparent organization that will indirectly benefit NationsBank and BankAmerica class members," and that LSEM sufficiently approximated the interests of the class because it serves victims of fraud. But it is not sufficient to find that no "next-best" recipient is "immediately apparent." Rather, a district court must carefully weigh all considerations, including the geographic scope of the underlying litigation, and make a "thorough investigation" to determine whether a recipient can be found that most closely approximates the interests of the class. ALI § 3.07, cmt b. The court must look for a recipient that "relate[s] directly to the [] injury alleged in this lawsuit and settled by the parties." At oral argument, it became apparent there are non-profit organizations devoted to preventing and aiding the victims of securities fraud, such as the SEC Fair Funds. Those alternatives must be thoroughly explored before concluding that a totally unrelated charity such as LSEM is an acceptable "next best" recipient.

On remand, if any settlement funds remain after an additional distribution to the class, and if the district court concludes after proper inquiry that a *cy pres* award is appropriate, it must select next best *cy pres* recipient(s) more closely tailored to the interests of the class and the purposes of the underlying litigation.

II

* * *

* * * [T]he fee award was made in an order that accepted class counsel's suggestion of a *cy pres* distribution, which was contrary to the interests of the NationsBank Classes, and terminated the case with respect to those Classes. "Where a district court has reason to believe that [class] counsel has not met its responsibility to seek an award that adequately prioritizes direct benefit to the class, we therefore think it appropriate for the court to decrease the fee award." * * * [W]e vacate the award of supplemental attorneys' fees, to be redetermined in the exercise of the district court's discretion upon completion of the additional distribution(s) to the NationsBank Classes that result from this decision.

* * *

MURPHY, CIRCUIT JUDGE, dissenting.

I respectfully dissent * * *.

* * *

We have explained that *cy pres* awards are appropriate "where class members 'are difficult to identify or where they change constantly,' or where there are unclaimed funds." * * *

The record in the case now before our court shows that the identification of class members for the two earlier distributions had been difficult, and that a good part of any additional distribution would have to be made to institutional investors holding stock on behalf of clients. Prior distribution efforts had encountered difficulties in locating and correctly processing claims for such class members. Meanwhile, years had passed since the settlement was reached, and $2.4 million remained in the settlement fund because some class members had failed to cash their checks and interest had accumulated on these unclaimed funds. Oetting himself had offered no evidence to show that a further distribution to the class would have been feasible at that time. On this record, the district court did not clearly err in determining that the remaining funds had been unclaimed and that individual members of the class were difficult to identify.

The district court found that additional factors favored a *cy pres* distribution. The parties' settlement agreement, approved by the district court more than ten years earlier, provided that unclaimed funds remaining after one or two distributions "may be contributed as a donation to one or more non-sectarian, not-for-profit 501(c)(3) organizations as determined by the Court in its sole discretion." There was no objection to this provision by any party or counsel at the time of settlement.

Class members who had submitted claims had already received the full compensation due under the settlement agreement * * *. Many of those who were harmed by the underlying fraud had been beneficial owners of stock held by mutual funds and other institutional investors. Given that the beneficial ownership of such shares changes constantly and some 15 years had passed after the securities violations, the district court reasonably concluded that another distribution would not likely reach those who had been actually harmed. All these factors support the district court's determination that the required circumstances for a *cy pres* distribution existed and that such a distribution would not be unwise or unfair to any party.

Counsel were involved in the consideration of an appropriate recipient for a *cy pres* distribution. Class counsel had suggested a distribution among three organizations: Legal Services of Eastern Missouri (LSEM), the Mathews Dickey Boys' and Girls' Club of St. Louis, and The Backstoppers. In his response in the district court, Oetting opposed the suggested distributions to the Boys' and Girls' Club, a youth services organization, and The Backstoppers, a group supporting families of fallen police officers, firefighters, and emergency medical technicians. Oetting argued that the work of these charities was not related to the subject matter of the case before the court. Nothing in the record at that stage, however, reflects any objection by Oetting to LSEM which was the third suggested recipient.

In its *cy pres* order the district court carefully considered Oetting's objections and the circuit precedent requiring it to "consider the full geographic scope of the case" as well as to "tailor[] a *cy pres* distribution to the nature of the underlying lawsuit." Finding that the "multi-district litigation was transferred to this district because much of the harm suffered by the class was felt by individuals in the St. Louis region," the district court found that distribution to an organization serving that area would be proper. Counsel had also pointed out that a St. Louis bank was a major predecessor in interest to NationsBank and that many of the individual stockholders of NationsBank resided in eastern Missouri. The district court found that a final distribution to LSEM would also be consistent with the nature of this securities fraud lawsuit since that organization serves victims of fraud. No party suggested any organization that would benefit class members more directly in these circumstances where the majority of shares were held by large investment firms. The district court found that distributions to the Boys' and Girls' Club or The Backstoppers would not be appropriate because their work did not focus on fraud.

We review the district court's selection of LSEM as the recipient of the *cy pres* distribution for abuse of discretion. The district court's careful application of existing precedent to the facts of this case shows no abuse of its discretion. * * * All parties were given an opportunity for comment and the district court provided adequate reasons for selecting LSEM as the *cy pres* recipient based on the nature of its work as well as its situs in the area where many class members were located when their losses occurred. The district court appropriately "tailor[ed] [the] *cy pres* distribution to the nature of the underlying lawsuit," as our precedent requires.

* * *

The American Law Institute principles support the district court's selection of LSEM as the remainder *cy pres* recipient. The Institute recommends that *cy pres* distributions be awarded to a recipient "whose interests reasonably approximate those being pursued by the class." * * *

In the case now before our court, the district court similarly selected a recipient whose geographic location related to the underlying securities fraud and whose mission included combating fraud. LSEM related "as nearly as possible, to the original purposes of the class action and its settlement," taking into account "the amount of the remaining unclaimed funds and the costs of searching for another qualified recipient."

On this record the district court did not abuse its discretion by applying such criteria and selecting LSEM as a *cy pres* recipient.

* * *

For all these reasons, I respectfully dissent. * * *

* * *

NOTES AND QUESTIONS

1. The majority and Judge Murphy disagreed on whether the *cy pres* award was proper. Which analysis is more persuasive and why?

2. Chief Justice Roberts authored a statement regarding the Supreme Court's denial of certiorari in a case involving a *cy pres* remedy. In that statement, he noted the existence of "fundamental concerns surrounding the use of [*cy pres*] in class action litigation," suggesting that the "Court may need to clarify the limits on the use of such remedies" in a future case. *Marek v. Lane*, 134 S. Ct. 8, 9 (2013) (statement by Chief Justice Roberts respecting denial of certiorari). The Chief Justice added that the *cy pres*-related issues that the Court has yet to address include "when, if ever, such relief should be considered; how to assess its fairness as a general matter; whether new entities may be established as part of such relief; if not, how existing entities should be selected; what the respective roles of the judge and parties are in shaping a *cy pres* remedy; how closely the goals of any enlisted organization must correspond to the interests of the class; and so on." *Id.* Based on his statement, does it appear that Chief Justice Roberts is a fan of *cy pres* settlements?

3. As the *In re Bank America Corp.* case reveals, a *cy pres* remedy is not governed by Rule 23. Rather, courts have looked elsewhere for guidance, including the American Law Institute's *Principles of the Law of Aggregate Litigation*. Does the American Law Institute's approach, (as described by the *BankAmerica Corp.* court) make sense? What arguments can be made against it?

4. *Cy pres* awards in class actions have also been the subject of academic criticism. As one article argued:

> * * * Use of *cy pres* simultaneously violates the constitutional dictates of separation of powers by employing a Federal Rule of Civil Procedure to alter the compensatory enforcement mechanism dictated by the applicable substantive law being enforced in the class action proceeding. * * * *Cy pres* creates the illusion of class compensation. It is employed when—and only when—absent its use, the class proceeding would be little more than a mockery. To be sure, the defendants would still gain the protections of *res judicata* and collateral estoppel, and the class attorneys would most assuredly still get at least some fees. But in cases in which *cy pres* is deemed necessary it is very likely that the bulk of the class of victims will go uncompensated. This is due to the simple fact that, purely as a practical matter, in at least certain situations there simply exists no way that a class proceeding can effectively aggregate and satisfy the small claims of individual right holders. Yet when the class action court introduces a wholly extraneous but sympathetic charitable actor into the suit, purportedly on the basis of its authority under a procedural rule, the redistributive goals of the substantive law are somehow assumed to be satisfied. But the substantive law authorizes no such relief; no legislative body has expressly chosen to abandon its compensatory enforcement mode in favor of some directive of a charitable contribution as punishment for a defendant's unlawful behavior. *Cy pres*, then, is far more than the neutral disposition of unclaimed property that it is thought to be.

Martin H. Redish, Peter Julian & Samantha Zyontz, *Cy Pres Relief and the Pathologies of the Modern Class Action: A Normative and Empirical Analysis*, 62 Fla. L. Rev. 617, 623 (2010). Are the concerns about *cy pres* awards raised by Professor Redish and his co-authors justified?

C. ATTORNEYS' FEES IN CLASS ACTIONS

Attorneys' fees play a fundamental role in shaping the dynamics of class action litigation. The following materials explore some of the most important issues—including the methodology to be used in calculating fees, the district court's discretion in applying a given methodology, and the occasionally bitter disputes that arise in the division of attorneys' fees in class actions involving multiple groups of attorneys.

MANUAL FOR COMPLEX LITIGATION (FOURTH)
Federal Judicial Center (2004) § 21.7.

Attorney fee applications may arise as part of the settlement of a class award or after litigation of the class proceedings. The request may be based on a percentage of a common fund that the class action has produced or may be based on a statutory fee award. Statutory awards are generally calculated using the lodestar method (number of hours reasonably spent on the litigation multiplied by the hourly rate, enhanced in some circumstances by a multiplier), subject to any applicable statutory ceiling on the hourly rate. Some courts use a lodestar method as a crosscheck to ensure that the percentage method does not result in an excessive award.

The court's settlement review should include provisions for the payment of class counsel. In class actions whose primary objective is to recover money damages, settlements may be negotiated on the basis of a lump sum that covers both class claims and attorney fees. Although there is no bar to such arrangements, the simultaneous negotiation of class relief and attorney fees creates a potential conflict. Separate negotiation of the class settlement before an agreement on fees is generally preferable. This procedure does not entirely eliminate the risk of conflict, and, if negotiations are to be conducted in stages, counsel must scrupulously avoid making concessions affecting the class for personal advantage. If an agreement is reached on the amount of a settlement fund and a separate amount for attorney fees and expenses, both amounts must be disclosed to the class. Moreover, the sum of the two amounts ordinarily should be treated as a settlement fund for the benefit of the class, with the agreed-on fee amount constituting the upper limit on the fees that can be awarded to counsel. The total fund could be used to measure whether the portion allocated to the class and to attorney fees is reasonable. Although the court may not rewrite the parties' agreement, it can find the proposed funds for the class inadequate and the proposed attorney fees excessive, and can allow the parties to renegotiate their agreement. The judge can condition approval of the settlement on a separate review of the proposed attorneys' compensation.

§ 21.71 Criteria for Approval

Compensating counsel for the actual benefits conferred on the class members is the basis for awarding attorney fees. The "fundamental focus is the result actually achieved for class members." That approach is premised on finding a tangible benefit actually obtained by the class members. In comparing the fees sought by the lawyers to the benefits conferred on the class, the court's task is easiest when class members are all provided cash benefits that are distributed. It is more complicated when class members receive nonmonetary or delayed benefits. In such cases, the judge must determine the value of those benefits.

Nonmonetary benefits can take a number of forms. In a Rule 23(b)(3) case, nonmonetary benefits can include coupons, discounts, or securities, or other forms. In a Rule 23(b)(2) case, the benefits may include different forms of injunctive relief, or relief that may mix injunctive and damages elements. A court may need to determine the dollar value of medical monitoring programs or warranty programs. A civil rights case may require evaluating an injunction redressing employment or other forms of discrimination. The court's evaluation and review of such benefits as part of the settlement review process is important for its review of fee applications. If a settlement provides only speculative, uncertain, or amorphous benefits to the class, that resists valuation in dollar terms.

The court should carefully scrutinize any agreement providing that attorneys for the class receive a noncontingent cash award. The court should refuse to allow attorneys to receive fees based on an inflated or arbitrary evaluation of the benefits to be delivered to class members. It might be appropriate to require attorneys to share in the risk of fluctuations in the value of an in-kind settlement, either by taking all or part of its counsel fees in in-kind benefits or by deferring collection of fees and making them contingent on the value of in-kind benefits that are actually delivered to the class members.

In some instances, the court might find the benefit to the class so speculative that it will use the lodestar method rather than the common-fund method to determine the amount of fees to which the attorneys are entitled. In other instances, the court may greatly reduce the parties' estimates of the dollar value of the benefits delivered to the class members and base the attorney fee award on the reduced amount. In cases involving a claims procedure or a distribution of benefits over time, the court should not base the attorney fee award on the amount of money set aside to satisfy potential claims. Rather, the fee awards should be based only on the benefits actually delivered. It is common to delay a final assessment of the fee award and to withhold all or a substantial part of the fee until the distribution process is complete.

If a case is primarily concerned with injunctive or declaratory relief, exclusive concern with monetary benefits may not be appropriate. If the value of such relief cannot be reliably determined or estimated, consider using the lodestar method, including any appropriate multiplier, to calculate fee awards.

The common-fund theory may call for awarding attorney fees to counsel other than class counsel. If the court has appointed as class counsel attorneys who did not file one of the original complaints, attorneys who investigated and filed the case might be entitled to a fee award. Attorneys for objectors to the settlement or to class counsel's fee application might also have provided sufficient benefits to a class to justify an award.

Rule 23(h) also authorizes the award of nontaxable costs in class action litigation and settlements.

§ 21.72 Procedure for Reviewing Fee Requests

§ 21.721 Motions

Rule 23(h)(1) calls for the court to fix a time for submission of motions for attorney fees in class actions. * * * Rule 23(h) does not contemplate application of the fourteen-day rule specified in Rule 54(d)(2)(B) unless the court chooses to set that time. In general, parties should be prepared to submit such motions as soon as possible after announcing a settlement so that the required Rule 23(h)(1) notice of the fee request can be combined with the required Rule 23(e) notice of settlement and sent to the class at the same time.

§ 21.722 Notice

Rule 23(h)(1) requires that notice of fee requests be "directed to class members in a reasonable manner." The rule contemplates that, in cases involving settlement review under Rule 23(e), "notice of class counsel's fees motion should be combined with notice of the proposed settlement" and afforded the same notice as Rule 23(e) requires. In adjudicated class actions, "the court can calibrate the notice to avoid undue expense."

§ 21.723 Objections

Rule 23(h)(2) limits the right to object to class members or parties from whom payment is sought. Specifically, nonsettling defendants who will not be contributing to the fee payment sought may not object to the motion for a fee award.

§ 21.724 Information Supporting Request and Discovery for Fee Requests

The party seeking fees has the burden of submitting sufficient information to justify the requested fees and taxable costs. Even in common fund cases, judges frequently call for an estimate of the number of hours spent on the litigation and a statement of the hourly rates for all attorneys and paralegals who worked on the litigation. Such information can serve as a "cross-check" on the determination of the percentage of the common fund that should be awarded to counsel. In lodestar or statutory fee award cases, applicants must provide full documentation of hours and rates. To facilitate meaningful review of fee petitions, the court may specify the categories that attorneys should use to group their fee requests (*e.g.*, by motion, brief, or other product) and establish other guidelines for any requests.

If there is a request for discovery to support an objection to a motion for attorney fees, the court should consider "the completeness of the material submitted in support of the fee motion, which depends in part on the fee measurement standard." If "the motion provides thorough information, the burden should be on the objector to justify discovery to obtain further information." As provided in Rule 23(e)(2), objectors should usually have access to the parties' statement about "any agreement made in connection with the proposed settlement." Whether the actual agreement will be discoverable depends on the extent to which the parties demonstrate a legitimate interest in confidentiality.

§ 21.725 Required Disclosures

Side agreements provide information relevant to the allocation of fees among counsel for various parties and interests. Any concurrent settlements of individual plaintiffs' cases by class counsel may be of particular interest. The court should examine the fee arrangements and the terms of individual settlements to avoid some plaintiffs' being favored over similarly situated class members.

§ 21.726 Hearing and Findings

Rule 23(h)(3) permits the court to hold a hearing on a fee motion and directs the court to find the facts and state its conclusions of law. The circumstances and needs of the case will dictate the form of any hearing. For example, where the fee request depends on an evaluation of the relief earned for the class, a hearing may be necessary to provide evidence of such an appraisal. Usually, evidence of the value of the settlement will have been presented at the hearing on settlement review. In many instances, hearings on settlement review and fees can be conducted at the same time.

§ 21.727 Use of Special Masters or Magistrate Judges

Rule 23(h)(4) provides broad authority to refer issues related to the amount of a request for fees to a special master or magistrate judge. In this

IN RE THIRTEEN APPEALS ARISING OUT OF THE SAN JUAN DUPONT PLAZA HOTEL FIRE LITIG.

United States Court of Appeals, First Circuit, 1995.
56 F.3d 295.

Before SELYA, CIRCUIT JUDGE, BOWNES, SENIOR CIRCUIT JUDGE, and CYR, CIRCUIT JUDGE.

SELYA, CIRCUIT JUDGE.

These appeals require us to revisit the war zone where two groups of plaintiffs' lawyers have struggled over the proposed allocation of roughly $68,000,000 in attorneys' fees. One camp, dissatisfied with the district court's latest formula for distributing the fees, attacks the court's order on three fronts. The disgruntled lawyers contend that the district court (1) violated their due process rights, (2) used an improper method to determine the awards, and (3) divided the available monies in an arbitrary and unreasonable manner. We find appellants' first two plaints to be without merit, but we agree with them that allocating 70% of the fees to the appellees constituted an abuse of the trial court's discretion. And, because we are reluctant to prolong a matter that, like the proverbial cat, seems to have nine lives, we take matters into our own hands and reconfigure the fee awards.

I. BACKGROUND

* * * We explored much the same terrain in an earlier encounter, *see In re Nineteen Appeals Arising Out of San Juan Dupont Plaza Hotel Fire Litig.*, 982 F.2d 603 (1st Cir. 1992), and a plethora of opinions describing the details of the underlying litigation pockmark the pages of the Federal Reports. Thus, a brief overview of the litigation will suffice.

In 1987, the Judicial Panel on Multidistrict Litigation consolidated over 270 cases arising out of the calamitous conflagration that had ravaged the San Juan Dupont Plaza Hotel on the evening of December 31, 1986. The designated trial judge, Hon. Raymond L. Acosta, hand-picked certain attorneys, denominated collectively as the Plaintiffs' Steering Committee (PSC), to act as lead and liaison counsel for the plaintiffs. In *Nineteen Appeals*, we summarized the roles played by the PSC and the individually retained plaintiffs' attorneys (IRPAs), respectively:

> The PSC members looked after the big picture: mapping the overarching discovery, trial, and settlement strategies and coordinating the implementation of those strategies. The IRPAs handled individual client communication and other case-specific tasks such as answering interrogatories addressed to particular plaintiffs, preparing and attending the depositions of their clients, and taking depositions which bore on damages. The IRPAs also worked with Judge Bechtle [the "settlement judge"] on a case-by-case basis in his efforts to identify and/or negotiate appropriate

settlement values for individual claims. When Judge Acosta determined that the plaintiffs should try twelve representative claims as a means of facilitating settlement, a collaborative composed of three PSC members and four IRPAs bent their backs to the task.

The combined efforts of all concerned generated a settlement fund approximating $220,000,000. The district court computed the payments due under the various contingent fee agreements, deducted the total (roughly $68,000,000) from the overall settlement proceeds, and placed that sum in an attorneys' fee fund (the Fund). In his initial attempt to disburse the Fund, Judge Acosta used an enhanced lodestar [defined below] to compute the PSC's fees, and awarded some $36,000,000 (52% of the Fund) to PSC members in their capacity as such, leaving the balance to be distributed among the IRPAs. A group of lawyers (mostly, but not exclusively, "non-PSC" IRPAs) succeeded in vacating this award on the ground that the proceedings were procedurally flawed.

The victory proved to be illusory. On remand, the district court abandoned the lodestar approach, adopted the percentage of the fund (POF) method [defined below], and recalculated the fees based on what it termed "the relative significance of the labor expended by the IRPAs and PSC members in instituting, advancing, or augmenting the plaintiffs' settlement fund." Using this methodology, the court awarded 70% of the Fund to PSC members in their capacity as such, thereby *increasing* their share of the fees by some $11,000,000, while simultaneously *reducing* the IRPAs' share of the Fund by the same amount. These appeals ensued.

II. ADEQUACY OF THE PROCEEDINGS

In a virtual echo of the claims advanced in *Nineteen Appeals*, appellants (all of whom are IRPAs) characterize the proceedings by which the district court determined the allocation of the Fund as unfair. Specifically, appellants assert that the revamped procedural framework violated their rights to due process, and that, in all events, the court abused its discretion in erecting the framework. We consider these assertions in sequence.

A. Due Process

[The court concluded that the district court provided the IRPAs due process in presenting their position.]

B. Abuse of Discretion

Appellants strive to convince us that Judge Acosta abused his discretion in authoring three procedural rulings, namely, (1) denying appellants' entreaty that an evidentiary hearing be held; (2) denying the bulk of their discovery requests; and (3) denying them the privilege of cross-examination. We are not persuaded.

1. *Lack of an Evidentiary Hearing.* We need not tarry over the supposed error in refusing to hold an evidentiary hearing. A district court is not obliged to convene an evidentiary hearing as a means of resolving every attorneys' fee dispute. * * *

* * * Even in situations far more inviting than fee disputes, we have been chary about mandating such hearings. We favor a "pragmatic approach" to the question of whether, in a given situation, an evidentiary

hearing is required. The key determinant is whether, "given the nature and circumstances of the case . . . the parties [had] a fair opportunity to present relevant facts and arguments to the court, and to counter the opponents' submissions." * * *

* * * Judge Acosta knew the case inside and out. He gave the protagonists ample opportunity to present both factual data and legal arguments. He set no page restrictions on written submissions, permitting the IRPAs to proffer thousands of pages of documents both in opposition to the PSC's requisitions and in support of their own fee requests. These filings allowed the IRPAs to go into painstaking detail both as to their own contribution to the litigation and as to the reasons why the PSC members deserved a relatively modest slice of the pie for their services in that capacity.

To be sure, this is a high-stakes dispute, but that fact, in and of itself, does not warrant handcuffing the trial court. Matters of great consequence are often decided without live testimony. In the last analysis, what counts is not the prize at stake, but whether particular parties received "a fundamentally fair chance to present [their] side of the story."

* * * Here, it is pellucid that the litigants' extensive written submissions comprised an effective substitute for * * * a hearing—particularly since the judge had lived with the litigation from the start and had an encyclopedic knowledge of it. Under these circumstances, the court did not err in refusing to hold yet another hearing.

2. *Restrictions on Discovery*. Apart from the refusal to convene a full-scale hearing, appellants also complain that the court demonstrated too great an aversion to discovery initiatives. But unlimited adversarial discovery is not a necessary—or even a usual—concomitant of fee disputes, and, in the circumstances of this case, we think that the court acted well within the province of its discretion in refusing to allow more elaborate discovery.

* * *

Furthermore, the court below also had a right to consider the extent to which appellants' request for discovery threatened to multiply the proceedings and turn the fee dispute into a litigation of mammoth proportions. Judge Acosta characterized the IRPAs' discovery foray—which encompassed, *inter alia*, production of tax returns for employees of all PSC members' firms and details anent fringe benefits (including vacations, maternity leaves, and the provision of training programs)—as "a discovery scheme of needless and unreasonable proportions." It is surpassingly difficult to fault this characterization.

* * *

3. *Lack of Cross-Examination*. As a subset of their claims regarding the supposed necessity for both an evidentiary hearing and additional discovery, appellants contend that the district court should have allowed them to cross-examine the PSC members concerning the hours that they logged and their contribution to the creation of the Fund. This is merely a backdoor attempt to rekindle an extinguished flame and satisfy appellants' thwarted desire for either an evidentiary hearing or extensive depositions.

* * *

The bottom line is that the district court did not err in refusing to convene an evidentiary hearing, declining to permit more wide-ranging discovery, and barring cross-examination. Thus, whether the issue is cast in a constitutional mold or considered under an abuse-of-discretion rubric, appellants' challenge fails. Either way, the adjudicative process employed on remand passes muster.

III. APPROPRIATENESS OF THE METHODOLOGY

Appellants claim that the district court erred as a matter of law in embracing the POF method, rather than the lodestar method, during the fee-setting pavane. The issue of whether a district court may use a given methodology in structuring an award of attorneys' fees is one of law, and, thus, is subject to *de novo* review.

A. Historical Perspective

A few introductory comments may lend a sense of perspective. Traditionally, under what has come to be known as the "American Rule," litigants bear their own counsel fees. This rule is not without exceptions. Fee-shifting statutes comprise one category of exceptions. *See, e.g.*, 42 U.S.C. §§ 1988, 2000e–5(k). So, too, certain equitable doctrines furnish a basis for departing from the American Rule.

When statutory exceptions pertain, we have directed district courts, for the most part, to compute fees by using the time-and-rate-based lodestar method. A court arrives at the lodestar by determining the number of hours productively spent on the litigation and multiplying those hours by reasonable hourly rates. *See Blum v. Stenson*, 465 U.S. 886, 896–902 (1984); *Hensley v. Eckerhart*, 461 U.S. 424, 433 (1983).

Although the lodestar method is entrenched in the statutory fee-shifting context, a growing number of courts have looked elsewhere in "common fund" cases—a category that encompasses cases in which "a litigant or lawyer who recovers a common fund for the benefit of persons other than himself or his client is entitled to a reasonable attorney's fee from the fund as a whole." *Boeing Co. v. Van Gemert*, 444 U.S. 472, 478 (1980). The POF method represents one such alternative approach to fee-setting. This method functions exactly as the name implies: the court shapes the counsel fee based on what it determines is a reasonable percentage of the fund recovered for those benefitted by the litigation.

Contrary to popular belief, it is the lodestar method, not the POF method, that breaks from precedent. Traditionally, counsel fees in common fund cases were computed as a percentage of the fund, subject, of course, to considerations of reasonableness. It was not until the mid-1970s that judicial infatuation with the lodestar method started to spread. Many courts embraced the new approach, and a wall of cases soon arose.

A crack in the wall appeared in 1984 when the Supreme Court took pains to distinguish the calculation of counsel fees under fee-shifting statutes from the calculation of counsel fees under the common fund doctrine. The court described the latter group as comprising cases in which "a reasonable fee is based on a percentage of the fund bestowed on the class." *Blum*, 465 U.S. at 900 n.16. Since *Blum* involved the application of the lodestar under a fee-shifting statute, footnote 16 is *dictum*. Yet, it can hardly be dismissed as a slip of the pen, and considered *dictum* emanating from the High Court carries great persuasive force.

Hard on the heels of footnote 16, the Third Circuit, which had been in the forefront of the movement toward the lodestar method, sounded a note of caution. Its blue-ribbon task force, although recommending continued use of the lodestar technique in statutory fee-shifting cases, concluded that all fee awards in common fund cases should be structured as a percentage of the fund. *See Report of the Third Circuit Task Force, Court Awarded Attorney Fees*, 108 F.R.D. 237, 255 (1985) (hereinafter "*Third Circuit Report*").

Together, footnote 16 and the *Third Circuit Report* led to a thoroughgoing reexamination of the suitability of using the lodestar method in common fund cases. This reexamination, in turn, led to more frequent application of the POF method in such cases. Today, the D.C. Circuit and the Eleventh Circuit require the use of the POF method in common fund cases, and four other circuits confer discretion upon the district court to choose between the lodestar and POF methods in common fund cases. We have yet to pass upon the legitimacy of the POF method in common fund cases.

B. Computing Fees in Common Fund Cases

We have previously classified this as a common fund case.[9] Appellants do not dispute this taxonomy, but, rather, they insist that Judge Acosta erred in using the POF method because the lodestar technique should hold sway in *all* attorneys' fee determinations. Though appellants concede that this court has not yet decided what method(s) of fee allocation appropriately may be invoked in common fund cases, they assert that the lodestar is a far better alternative and that its use should be mandated in this circuit.

We think that a more malleable approach is indicated. Thus, we hold that in a common fund case the district court, in the exercise of its informed discretion, may calculate counsel fees either on a percentage of the fund basis or by fashioning a lodestar. Our decision is driven both by our recognition that use of the POF method in common fund cases is the prevailing praxis and by the distinct advantages that the POF method can bring to bear in such cases.

In complex litigation—and common fund cases, by and large, tend to be complex—the POF approach is often less burdensome to administer than the lodestar method. Rather than forcing the judge to review the time records of a multitude of attorneys in order to determine the necessity and reasonableness of every hour expended, the POF method permits the judge

---

[9] We reached this conclusion because the Fund emanates from "the disproportionate strivings of a few (the PSC members) to the benefit of a much larger number (the plaintiffs and, derivatively, the IRPAs)," and possesses each of the three distinguishing characteristics identified by the *Boeing* Court:

> First, the . . . beneficiaries can be determined with complete assurance. Second, while the extent to which each individual plaintiff and each IRPA benefited from the PSC's efforts cannot be quantified with mathematical precision, it is possible to study the PSC's contribution to the overall success of the litigation and approximate the incremental benefits with some accuracy. Finally, the district court controls [the Fund], and, therefore, possesses the ready ability to prorate the cost of achieving the incremental benefits in an equitable manner.

to focus on "a showing that the fund conferring a benefit on the class resulted from" the lawyers' efforts. While the time logged is still relevant to the court's inquiry—even under the POF method, time records tend to illuminate the attorneys' role in the creation of the fund, and, thus, inform the court's inquiry into the reasonableness of a particular percentage—the shift in focus lessens the possibility of collateral disputes that might transform the fee proceeding into a second major litigation.

For another thing, using the POF method in a common fund case enhances efficiency, or, put in the reverse, using the lodestar method in such a case encourages inefficiency. Under the latter approach, attorneys not only have a monetary incentive to spend as many hours as possible (and bill for them) but also face a strong disincentive to early settlement. If the POF method is utilized, a lawyer is still free to be inefficient or to drag her feet in pursuing settlement options—but, rather than being rewarded for this unproductive behavior, she will likely reduce her own return on hours expended.

Another point is worth making: because the POF technique is result-oriented rather than process-oriented, it better approximates the workings of the marketplace. We think that Judge Posner captured the essence of this point when he wrote that "the market in fact pays not for the individual hours but for the ensemble of services rendered in a case of this character." *In re Continental Ill. Sec. Litig.*, 962 F.2d 566, 572 (7th Cir. 1992). In fine, the market pays for the result achieved.

Let us be perfectly clear. We do not pretend that the POF approach is foolproof, or that it suffers from no disadvantages. For example, it may result in the overcompensation of lawyers in situations where actions are resolved before counsel has invested significant time or resources. The converse is also true; law firms may be less willing to commit needed resources to common fund cases, even those for the public benefit, if the likely recovery is relatively small. It can also be argued that the percentage method may lend itself to arbitrary fee awards by some courts. Given the peculiarities of common fund cases and the fact that each method, in its own way, offers particular advantages, we believe the approach of choice is to accord the district court discretion to use whichever method, POF or lodestar, best fits the individual case. We so hold, recognizing that the discretion we have described may, at times, involve using a combination of both methods when appropriate.

* * *

C. Applying the Rule

Having placed our imprimatur on a decisional model that maximizes flexibility, we move from the general to the specific and turn next to the order under review. In this connection, we rule that the court below did not err in purposing to allocate fees based on the POF method, emphasizing the attorneys' "relative contribution" to the creation of the Fund. In the first place, Judge Acosta had originally stated an intent to compensate the PSC members under a percentage approach. In "justifiable reliance" on this statement, the majority of the IRPAs did not maintain time records. The difficulties inherent in implementing the lodestar under these circumstances militate in favor of sticking to the POF method. In the second place, as we have explained above, the POF approach offers significant structural

IV. APPROPRIATENESS OF THE ALLOCATION

In allocating counsel fees, the district court assigned 70% of the Fund to the PSC, leaving 30% to be split among the IRPAs. Appellants object. We review this allocation for abuse of discretion, mindful that, in respect to fee awards, the trial court's latitude is "extremely broad[.]" After scrutinizing the Brobdingnagian record in this case, we are convinced that the court below erred in weighing and synthesizing the factors relevant to a division of the fees, and in settling upon so lopsided a split.

A. Cutting the Pie

In the proceedings on remand, Judge Acosta lavished praise on all the plaintiffs' lawyers, lauding the "high caliber legal representation" provided by both the PSC and the IRPAs. He then summarized the tasks undertaken by the two sets of attorneys in the course of the litigation. In the judge's view, the PSC's most significant accomplishments included (1) performing a comprehensive on-site investigation of the accident scene, (2) "identif[ying] the manufacturers and suppliers of many . . . products and services . . . and develop[ing] theories of liability against each opponent," (3) drafting plethoric pleadings, including the master complaint, weekly agendas, and several pretrial memoranda, (4) filing "literally hundreds of motions . . . on numerous topics, including many novel and creative issues," (5) orchestrating extensive pretrial discovery, (6) conducting the nine-week Phase I trial and the fifteen-month Phase II trial (in the course of which the PSC called 313 witnesses and offered 1,455 exhibits), and (7) "aggressively pursu[ing] settlement negotiations." The court visualized the IRPAs' main accomplishments as comprising (1) maintaining direct client communication, counselling [sic] clients, and keeping them abreast of developments in the litigation, (2) carrying out the factual investigation incident to individual cases, with especial emphasis on issues pertaining to damages, (3) retaining experts, including physicians, economists, and actuaries, and, once the experts had been located, collaborating with them to establish damages, (4) researching client-specific legal issues (*e.g.*, standing, assumption of risk), (5) representing individual plaintiffs in connection with ancillary matters, including probate, inheritance, insurance, and domestic relations matters, (6) meeting with Judge Bechtle "as part of the settlement scheme to negotiate settlement values for [individual] cases," and (7) assisting clients in reaching informed decisions (including decisions about whether to accept or reject proffered settlements). Moreover, certain selected plaintiffs were used as exemplars for purposes of the Phase II trial, and the IRPAs who represented those plaintiffs actually presented the evidence pertaining to their clients' damages.

Having made these ledger entries, the district court then tabulated the columns. It concluded that "reasonable compensation for the work undertaken requires recognition of the massive undertaking of the PSC in terms of the organizational and financial requirements, the overwhelming amount of work performed, the significant time constraints, and the numerous complex and novel issues addressed during the proceedings. . . ." Contrasting this workload "with the IRPAs' efforts in client communication and counseling, client preparation for settlement, and handling of the damages issues," the court awarded the PSC 70% of the fee due under each individual contingency agreement, thus permitting each IRPA to retain only 30% of the fee promised by the client.

B. Evaluating the Court's Handiwork

We are uneasy with the way in which the lower court cut the fee pie, and with the size and shape of the resultant wedges, for several reasons.

First, we are troubled by the implications of a scheme in which the trial judge selects a chosen few from many lawyers who volunteer, assigns legal tasks to those few (thereby dictating, albeit indirectly, the scope of the work remaining to be done by the many), and then, in awarding fees, heavily penalizes the very lawyers to whom he has relegated the "lesser" duties. Courts must recognize that while such an arrangement may be a necessary concomitant to skillful case management of mass tort suits, it nevertheless significantly interferes with an attorney's expectations regarding the fees that his or her client has agreed to pay. Conversely, lead counsel are typically volunteers, as in this case, and, as such, they have no right to harbor any expectation beyond a fair day's pay for a fair day's work if a fee fund develops. *Cf.* Matthew 20:1–16 (recounting parable of the laborers in the vineyard). We believe that trial courts should take these differing expectations into account in allocating fees. Here, the judge's rescript does not suggest that he factored these expectations into the decisional calculus.

Courts must also be sensitive to a second facet of economic reality: the power to appoint lead counsel gives the trial judge an unusual degree of control over the livelihood of the lawyers who practice before the court. Though such appointments are often an administrative necessity in complex litigation, and disproportionate fees are at times an unavoidable consequence of the classic common fund "free rider" problem, the judge must attempt to avoid any perception of favoritism. This need is especially acute in mass tort litigation where, as this case illustrates, free rider concerns are minimized by the important nature of the work to be done by claimants' individually retained attorneys. In this case, moreover, free rider concerns are also lessened by the fact that [40 of the 56] IRPAs applied for appointment to the PSC, thus signifying their willingness to pay full fare. The record does not contain any clue intimating that Judge Acosta considered these factors in ordering that 70% of the fees be paid to the PSC.

Third, and relatedly, this case required the IRPAs not merely to go along for a free ride but to earn their keep. They exhibited great versatility, [in performing all of the tasks described in Section IVA]. This is a far cry from the paradigmatic common fund case—say, a securities class action—in which class counsel do virtually all the work, and other counsel piggyback on their efforts. We see no sign that the district court gave significant weight to this reality.

This leads directly to a fourth point. We have carefully considered the IRPAs' compendious submissions and are of the view that Judge Acosta undervalued the worth of the client contact/counseling aspect of this litigation. Such services are labor-intensive and frequently low in visibility—at least in visibility from the bench. Thus, they are susceptible to being overlooked, leading to an overemphasis on the relative value of the court-related work. Despite their lack of visibility, however, the mundane chores incident to client representation are particularly critical in a mass tort common fund case. * * *

* * *

Fifth, although we do not dispute the district court's assessment of the quality of the PSC's work, this factor cancels itself out to some extent. After all, the district court repeatedly commented upon "the excellence of the work performed by *all* attorneys" (emphasis supplied), and left no doubt but that both sets of plaintiffs' lawyers had rendered exemplary service. Given these widespread plaudits, it seems manifestly unfair to reward excellence on the part of one group and not the other.

Sixth, the district court failed to advance any reasoned explanation as to why it boosted the PSC's share of the Fund from 52% in the initial go-round to 70% on remand. * * * [H]is silence on this subject leaves the award open to a perception that appellants have been penalized for successfully prosecuting their previous appeals.

Seventh, the district court erred in failing to compensate the representative trial counsel—those IRPAs who, though not members of the PSC, prepared and/or tried the so-called "representative" cases—for their work in that capacity. Just as the PSC members deserved compensation for their endeavors on behalf of the whole, the IRPAs who labored as representative counsel conferred a common benefit, and must be compensated accordingly.

Last—but far from least—we are persuaded, on whole-record review, that it is simply unreasonable to award 70% of the aggregate fees to the attorneys who managed the litigation, leaving only 30% of the Fund to those who brought in the clients and worked hand-in-hand with them throughout the pendency of this long safari of a case. * * *

Concluding, as we do, that the fee allocation reflects a serious error of judgment, and therefore an abuse of discretion, we vacate the award.

V. REMEDY

[Instead of remanding the case, the court itself allocated 50 percent of the attorneys' fees fund to the PSC and 50 percent to the IRPAs as a "fair and reasonable allocation."]

NOTES AND QUESTIONS

1. The *Manual for Complex Litigation (Fourth)* states that an award of attorneys' fees should be linked to tangible benefits actually conferred on the class. As discussed above in Part (A)(7)(a) of this chapter, in coupon settlements where class counsel is paid on percentage basis, the Class Action Fairness Act (CAFA) links attorneys' fees to the value of the coupons actually redeemed, rather than to the face value of those distributed. *See also* ALI *Principles* § 3.13(a) at 261 (fees should be based on actual value to class and value of properly awarded *cy pres* remedy). But how are tangible benefits to be determined? What if the class did not actually benefit, but class counsel exerted tremendous effort on the class's behalf?

2. Although objectors may petition for fees if they have improved a settlement, should they be rewarded for persuading a court to reject a class settlement in its entirety? The ALI has attempted to address what it perceives to be "a serious gap under existing law: the absence of any mechanism for compensating objectors who succeed in convincing the court to reject a settlement altogether." ALI *Principles* § 3.08(b) at 231–33. As it stands, objectors' counsel who successfully challenge a class settlement in its entirety are not awarded fees for a later settlement or judgment that results from such efforts. *Id.* The ALI proposes to reward legitimate efforts by objectors' counsel that materially improve an outcome (even if this means that the settlement is rejected). Payments would come from a future trial verdict or settlement. At the same time, the ALI *Principles* would punish illegitimate conduct by counsel and parties. *See* ALI *Principles* § 3.08(a) at 231. The ALI proposal provides: "If the court concludes that objectors have lodged objections that are insubstantial and not reasonably advanced for the purpose of rejecting or improving the settlement, the court should consider imposing sanctions against objectors or their counsel under applicable law." ALI *Principles* § 3.08(d) at 231. Does the ALI strike the right balance?

3. Rule 23(h) establishes a procedure for dealing with attorneys' fee requests. In contrast to the text of the rule, the Advisory Committee Notes to the 2003 amendments to Rule 23 provide extensive comments on criteria for determining attorneys' fees. For instance, the Notes point out that the court should look closely to determine the value of results achieved for the class; that the court may wish to defer a fee determination until the actual payout is known; that courts should scrutinize non-monetary settlements particularly closely to ensure that the provisions give actual value to the class; and that the court needs to scrutinize fees with care even if there are no objections to a requested fee. Should these criteria be included in the actual text of the rule?

4. As the law had developed prior to the addition of Rule 23(h) in 2003, courts considered a variety of factors when analyzing whether a fee request is appropriate. These included "the size of the fund and the number of persons who actually receive monetary benefits"; "the skill and efficiency of the attorneys"; "the complexity and duration of the litigation"; "any substantial objections to the settlement terms or fees requested by counsel for the class by class members"; "any understandings reached with counsel at the time of appointment concerning the amount or rate for calculating fees"; and several other factors. *Manual for Complex Litigation (Fourth)* § 14.121, at 192 (citing case law).

5. What methods of awarding attorneys' fees are mentioned in *Thirteen Appeals*? According to the First Circuit, how are fees awarded under each method? What factors should bear on a court's selection of one method over another?

6. Rule 23(h) takes no position on whether the lodestar approach or percentage approach is preferable. Should the drafters have attempted to resolve this issue? Or is it better left to case-by-case adjudication? The American Law Institute has proposed guidelines, for the use of each, preferring the percentage approach for common fund cases, with lodestar possibly being used as a cross check. ALI *Principles* § 3.13(b) at 261. Apart from use as a cross check, the ALI would limit the use of lodestar to: "(1) situations in which fees will be awarded under a fee-shifting statute that requires the lodestar method, or (2) cases in which the court makes a specific finding that the percentage method would be unfair or inapplicable based on the specific facts of the case." *Id.* at § 3.13(c)(1)

& (2) at 261–62. What are some of the advantages and disadvantages of the lodestar method? What kinds of incentives does it create? Are those incentives desirable? *See* Charles Silver, *Due Process and the Lodestar Method: You Can't Get There From Here*, 74 Tul. L. Rev. 1809 (2000).

7. In *Thirteen Appeals*, the First Circuit noted that using the lodestar method in a common fund case may discourage early settlement because of the incentive to pad attorneys' fees. Would the percentage method, by contrast, encourage counsel to settle too quickly?

8. The First Circuit in *Thirteen Appeals* did not require the district court to hold an evidentiary hearing to determine attorneys' fees. Moreover, the drafters of Rule 23(h)(3) also chose to keep this decision discretionary. Should an evidentiary hearing be mandatory? Rule 23(h)(3) does require the court to make findings of fact and conclusions of law. Why is this important? *See Burke v. Ruttenberg*, 317 F.3d 1261, 1263 (11th Cir. 2003) (fee allocation order remanded where district court failed to make factual findings or provide rationale for fee award).

9. In *Thirteen Appeals*, the challenge to the fees came from a subset of plaintiffs' counsel, who were unhappy with the allocation among the plaintiffs' lawyers as a whole. Challenges to attorneys' fees can also come from named plaintiffs, defendants, or objecting class members. Sometimes the court raises concerns *sua sponte*, even when plaintiffs and defendants agree on the reasonableness of proposed fees. Should the nature and scope of review depend upon who is challenging the fees? Should the courts give more weight to objections to fee requests made by the named or lead plaintiffs? *See In re Cendant Corp. Sec. Litig.*, 404 F.3d 173, 199–200 (3d Cir. 2005) (holding that when district court evaluates whether non-lead class counsel is entitled to fee award under the Private Securities Litigation Reform Act, lead plaintiff's refusal to compensate non-lead counsel is entitled to presumption of correctness).

10. In *Goldberger v. Integrated Resources, Inc.*, 209 F.3d 43 (2d Cir. 2000), the district court, using the lodestar method, had awarded plaintiffs' counsel fees of approximately four percent of a $54 million securities fraud settlement. Plaintiffs' counsel appealed, challenging the district court's failure to use the percentage-of-fund method and failing to award counsel 25 percent of the settlement, which counsel argued was the "benchmark" for attorneys' fees. The Second Circuit ruled that either the lodestar method or the percentage method could be used by courts in calculating fees. With respect to counsel's arguments about their entitlement to 25 percent of the settlement, the Second Circuit responded:

> We are not unaware of the assumption that "[t]wenty-five percent is the 'benchmark' that district courts should award in common fund cases." Indeed, the Ninth Circuit has cautioned that district courts must justify departure from the 25% benchmark by pointing to unusual circumstances. * * * And we concede that district courts across the nation have apparently eased into a practice of "systematically" awarding fees in the 25% range, "regardless of the type of case, benefits to the class, numbers of hours billed, size of fund, size of plaintiff class, or any other relevant factor."
>
> This routine largesse has been justified on the theory that a reasonable fee should reflect prevailing rates in the relevant market, and that 25%—as a "formula born from judicial practice and experience"—reflects the best estimate of what the market practice would

be in a typical common fund case. There is also commendable sentiment in favor of providing lawyers with sufficient incentive to bring common fund cases that serve the public interest.

We are nonetheless disturbed by the essential notion of a benchmark. We agree that many class actions serve a useful purpose, that lawyers who successfully prosecute them deserve reasonable compensation, and that market rates, where available, are the ideal proxy for their compensation. The problem is that we cannot know precisely what fees common fund plaintiffs in an efficient market for legal services would agree to, given an understanding of the particular case and the ability to engage in collective arm's-length negotiation with counsel. And "hard data" on analogous situations—such as the fees sophisticated corporate plaintiffs typically agree to pay their attorneys—are "sketchy."

Moreover, even a theoretical construct as flexible as a "benchmark" seems to offer an all too tempting substitute for the searching assessment that should properly be performed in each case.

Goldberger, 209 F.3d at 51–52. Applying "principles of moderation" to the assessment of reasonable attorneys' fees in the case before it, the Second Circuit concluded that the district court did not abuse its discretion simply because the court awarded less than the 25% benchmark, or even less than the 11% to 19% "usually awarded in similar cases." Instead, the court "adhere[d] to [its] prior practice that a fee award should be assessed based on scrutiny of the unique circumstances of each case, and 'a jealous regard to the rights of those who are interested in the fund.'" *Id.* at 53. Should courts utilize benchmarks in awarding attorneys' fees in common fund cases? Or was the Second Circuit correct in expressing concerns about such benchmarks?

11. Should market forces directly influence how the court sets attorneys' fees? Consider an approach, called the "Lead Counsel Auction," where judges accept bids by plaintiffs attorneys to represent a particular class. *Developments in the Law—The Paths of Civil Litigation*, 113 Harv. L. Rev. 1827, 1837–45 (2000). The Lead Counsel Auction has gained acceptance in only a few federal district courts (and generally only in securities and antitrust class actions). *Id.* at 1842. *See* Chapter 10(C)(2)(a)(ii) (discussing auctions). What role should risk play in the determination of fees? Does the auction approach make sense?

12. Should the court take into account the "value" of injunctive relief when determining the value of a common fund from which attorneys' fees are calculated? The Ninth Circuit concluded that this should be done only rarely, given the ease with which this "value" can be manipulated by class counsel. *Staton v. Boeing Co.*, 327 F.3d 938 (9th Cir. 2003). In *Staton*, a case alleging race discrimination, a class settlement decree required payment to the class of $7.3 million (less certain reversions and opt-out credits), provided certain injunctive relief (*e.g.*, hiring a consultant for human resource, improving the flow of information to employees), and awarded class counsel $4.05 million in attorneys' fees. On appeal by certain objectors, the Ninth Circuit invalidated the settlement. The Ninth Circuit held, *inter alia*, that the district court erred in placing a precise monetary value on the injunctive relief based on the amount that Boeing was required to spend to implement the relief. The appellate court noted that Boeing had planned to implement some of the relief even before the settlement. *Id.* at 973. According to the Ninth Circuit, "only in the unusual instance where the value to individual class members of benefits deriving from injunctive relief can be accurately ascertained may courts include such relief

as part of the value of a common fund for purposes of applying the percentage method of determining fees." *Id.* at 974. Does the Ninth Circuit take too narrow a view of when the value of injunctive relief may be considered in calculating attorneys' fees?

13. Significant criticism has been leveled against class counsel for allegedly exorbitant fee awards in comparison to the relief received by the class. Is such criticism warranted? In an analysis covering the period 1993–2008, Professors Eisenberg and Miller found that the most important factor in the determination of fees was the amount recovered by the class. *See* Theodore Eisenberg & Geoffrey P. Miller, *Attorneys' Fees in Class Action Settlements: 1993–2008*, Oct. 30, 2009, at 1, *available at* http://ssrn.com/abstract=1497224 (last visited Feb. 6, 2017) ("the overwhelmingly important determinant of the fee was simply the size of the recovery obtained by the class."). The study also found that attorneys' fees are generally higher in high-risk cases, *id.* at 18, and are higher on a percentage basis in federal court than in state court. *Id.* at 14. Another evaluation of 621 federal class actions by the Federal Judicial Center found that fees as a percentage of class recoveries had not increased significantly since an earlier analysis by the FJC in 1996, with fees averaging roughly 29% of total recovery. *See* Thomas E. Willging & Shannon R. Wheatman, Fed. Judicial Ctr., *Attorney Reports on the Impact of Amchem and Ortiz on Choice of a Federal or State Forum in Class Action Litigation* (2004), *available at* http://www.fjc.gov/public/pdf.nsf/lookup/amort02.pdf/$file/amort02.pdf (last visited Feb. 6, 2017). Professor Brian Fitzpatrick argues that in class actions involving "small stakes," class action lawyers are making too little. *See* Brian Fitzpatrick, *Do Class Action Lawyers Make Too Little?*, 158 U. Pa. L. Rev. 2043, 2044–47 (2010) (finding "in the aggregate, class action lawyers appear to be taking only 15% of all of the money they recover for class members in federal court" and suggesting that for "small stakes" claims, they should be able to take 100% to ensure deterrence objectives).

14. Should the analysis of attorneys' fees differ if the settlement fund is unusually large (*e.g.*, in the billions of dollars)? The Third Circuit contemplated that question in *In re Diet Drugs Prod. Liability Litig.*, 582 F.3d 524 (3d Cir. 2009), a nationwide products liability class action brought against prescription diet drug manufacturer Wyeth that resulted in a $6.4 billion settlement and $567 million fee award. Using the percentage of recovery method, class counsel sought approval of this fee award for litigation that, *inter alia*, benefited over 800,000 class members; was complex, innovative, and took "an extraordinary amount of time"; "endured significantly longer than did other super-mega-fund cases"; and served as a model for other large settlements. *Id.* at 545. The fee amount did not exceed market value and was, "in percentage terms, slightly below the average award granted in the super-mega-fund cases." *Id.* A cross check with the lodestar indicated that the multiplier was in fact low for these sorts of cases. *Id.* at 545 n. 42. For all of these reasons, the Third Circuit affirmed the fee award. *Id.* at 529, 553. Is there a point at which fees should be capped, no matter what benefit was achieved for the class?

15. Should lawyers be rewarded for extraordinary performance? The Supreme Court recently addressed this issue in a case where, pursuant to 42 U.S.C. § 1988, the class counsel were awarded a lodestar amount of $6.1 million and an additional $4.5 million (a 75% enhancement) for their "extraordinary" performance in representing thousands of children in Georgia's foster-care system, which resulted in sweeping, systemic reforms. *Perdue v. Kenny A.*, 130 S. Ct. 1662, 1670 (2010). The Court held that an attorney's fee, calcu-

lated under a fee-shifting provision based on the lodestar method, can be enhanced for "superior performance and results" under "extraordinary circumstances." *Id.* at 1669. The Court, however, held that this rule was subject to certain qualifiers:

- "[T]here is a strong presumption that the lodestar is sufficient;"

- "[F]actors subsumed in the lodestar calculation cannot be used as a ground for increasing an award above the lodestar; and"

- "[A] party seeking fees has the burden of identifying a factor that the lodestar does not adequately take into account and proving with specificity that an enhanced fee is justified."

Id. at 1669. The Court noted that performance enhancements should be "rare" and awarded only under "exceptional" circumstances. *Id.* at 1673. The Court reversed and remanded for proceedings consistent with the Court's opinion. How, if at all, should this analysis apply in common fund cases?

D. THIRD-PARTY LITIGATION FINANCING

The topic of third-party litigation financing is new in this edition of the casebook. In the past five years, it has been the subject of extensive analysis (and concern) by many scholars. The focus here is on third-party financing in the aggregate litigation context. The first section discusses class actions; the second section discusses non-class aggregate litigation. Finally, the third section discusses efforts by defendants to obtain discovery regarding funders.

1. CLASS ACTION CONTEXT

DEBORAH R. HENSLER, THIRD-PARTY FINANCING OF CLASS ACTION LITIGATION IN THE UNITED STATES: WILL THE SKY FALL?
63 DePaul L. Rev. 499, 499–505, 507–18, 525 (2014).

I. Introduction

The advent of third-party litigation financing—the funding of lawsuits by entities other than parties or their legal representatives—in the United States has stimulated legal scholarship, policy debate, and interest group advocacy. * * * No group has been as strident or as active in opposition to third-party litigation financing as the U.S. Chamber of Commerce's Institute for Legal Reform, and no area of legal practice has been more clearly targeted for prohibition of such financing than class action litigation.

In its advocacy materials, the Chamber focuses attention on Australia, where third-party litigation financing has shaped class action litigation over the past two decades. In the Chamber's telling, the Australian experience should warn the other animals in the barnyard that the sky is falling. * * *

This Article discusses the possible consequences of third-party litigation financing for class action litigation in the United States. * * *

II. Background

Roughly speaking, there are two claim markets that third-party litigation financers in the United States have targeted: (1) ordinary tort claims, typically for modest amounts, brought by individuals of limited means; and (2) commercial claims for damages, typically for quite large amounts, brought or defended by corporations. Virtually everything about these markets is different, save for the fact that in each market the financers' interest in the lawsuits is solely monetary.

A. The Potential for Third-Party Litigation Financing of Class Actions in the United States

Some have likened the tort claims market to the payday loan market: the financers provide funds to relatively unsophisticated people who have colorable personal injury claims, but whose personal circumstances are so straitened that they find it attractive to promise a large portion of the recovery they may ultimately receive in court in exchange for immediate help in covering current expenses. The funder provides money directly to the claimant, usually in the form of a nonrecourse loan, in order to skirt usury law restrictions on the share of the recovery the funder can obtain. The loans are usually for a few thousand dollars, and sometimes tens of thousands of dollars, but rarely larger. The typical claims arise out of automobile accidents and slip-and-falls for which there is a high likelihood of recovery, and thus some return on the loan is almost certain. The funder has no formal relationship with the claimant's lawyer, thereby forestalling charges that lawyers and nonlawyers are splitting fees. The law firms representing claimants who obtain loans are typically small, although a single firm may handle a large volume of small-to-moderate-value claims. The funders minimally screen claims to determine whether to offer funding; like many of the lawyers in this claim market, their approach is routinized and their business model relies on handling a high volume of similar cases without much, if any, individualized treatment. * * * Lenders are attracted to the market by its potential to earn high rates of return per claim on a large volume of loans. The high rate of return is likely the result of the circumstances of the borrower-victims, rather than the riskiness of the loan. Because of its characteristics, some have described this market as the litigation lending market.

The second market is akin to an equity market: in exchange for a share of the damages recovered, the financers fund either a business with a colorable legal claim or the lawyers representing the business (or both) to pursue litigation that would otherwise be too risky or too expensive to pursue with the intensity that would maximize net benefit. The claimants in this market are sophisticated business decision makers who are represented by corporate law firms. The funders are institutional investors—including banks, insurance companies, and hedge funds—whose investments are managed by specialized litigation financing firms. These entities focus on high-value claims, which they investigate carefully in order to estimate accurately the expected payoff. The financers rarely consider funding claims worth less than several millions of dollars, and some operate at a much higher dollar threshold. These claims are typically much more expensive to litigate than an automobile accident claim and also more risky. In contrast to the litigation lending market, this might be described as the "litigation investment" market, although the financial instruments, as in the first market, are loans.

Although not treated as third-party funders by most litigation financing scholars, law firms that invest time and expense in litigation with the expectation of sharing their clients' recoveries form another segment of the litigation financing market. However, in contrast to the funders and investors who are conventionally considered litigation financers, plaintiff-side law firms have a fiduciary duty to their clients. Law firms representing plaintiffs may receive funding from other law firms whose role is more similar to that of litigation investors. The relationships between the law firm representing the plaintiffs and the law firms helping fund the litigation may not be known to all involved in the litigation. The role and characteristics of these investor law firms have yet to be systematically described.

Although class actions are sometimes brought on behalf of large numbers of individuals of modest means who resemble claimants in the litigation lending market, a damages class action most closely resembles a single large commercial claim, both procedurally and financially. Whether the class members receive damages depends on the outcome of a single lawsuit. In the U.S. class action regime, a law firm is appointed as class counsel by the judge assigned to the case. Class counsel must invest resources up front to develop the facts and law relevant to the litigation and represent the class in court proceedings and settlement discussions. If the class prevails, the judge awards legal fees that usually are proportionate to the size of recovery; if the class action fails, class counsel does not recoup its expenses. As a consequence of the procedural and financing rules, only firms with access to substantial financial resources can participate in this sector of the legal services market.

Traditionally, plaintiff-side class action firms have financed their activities by lines of credit that are secured ultimately by their personal assets. As is the case with commercial litigation investors, plaintiff-side class action firms have good reason to carefully select cases that will permit them to maximize return on investment. Because litigating a class action is expensive and time consuming, class action firms are unlikely to represent a class unless there is a potential for large damages. If class actions were to attract litigation financing, the funding would come from the litigation investors, not the litigation lenders who target individual plaintiffs.

To date, it appears that only one class action initiative in the United States has secured third-party litigation financing: the Ecuadorian environmental damages litigation against Chevron. [The author describes how the lawsuit generated charges of fraud by Chevron against plaintiffs' counsel, and the funder ultimately cut off its investment after investing millions of dollars, claiming that it had been misled about the case.]

* * *

The history of the Chevron-Ecuador litigation seems unlikely to persuade third-party litigation investors to flock to high-profile, high-value mass litigation against multinational corporations.

* * *

Putting aside * * * the Chevron-Ecuador experience[,] * * * how likely is it that third-party litigation financers will find success in the U.S. class action litigation market? In return for providing funding and absorbing a significant fraction of the risk associated with commercial claims, third-party litigation investors expect a large share of any monetary recovery. Today in the United States, the most successful plaintiff class action firms are unlikely to find these terms attractive in comparison to their return on investment that relies on conventional financing. Commercial litigation financing might be attractive to new entrants to the market or as a means of allowing an established firm to penetrate or develop a new segment of the class action market while limiting its risk. Experienced federal judges who appoint class counsel in Rule 23 class actions might balk at appointing inexperienced litigators to the position, but a firm with adequate financial resources might succeed in persuading a less experienced state court judge that it could satisfy the core class action requirement of "adequacy of representation." However, one third-party litigation financer has speculated that a law firm that disclosed its need for third-party financing to support its representation would impair its chances of being selected as lead counsel in a class action.

III. Unpacking the Critique of Third-Party Financing of Class Action Litigation

What concerns would third-party litigation financing raise in the U.S. class action domain? Traditionally, common law jurisdictions forbade third parties from taking a financial interest in someone else's lawsuit—a practice that lawmakers feared would encourage "frivolous" or "vexatious" litigation. Rules against champerty and maintenance are still on the books in many states and have acted as brakes on third-party litigation financing in those jurisdictions. In the United States, contingency fee agreements between lawyers and clients do not violate these traditional rules, but such agreements are prohibited or restricted in many non-U.S. jurisdictions.

The critique of third-party litigation financing in class actions echoes both the traditional normative concerns about champerty and maintenance and the political attack on contingency fee litigation. However, critics of third-party litigation financing of class actions also have concerns that are specific to class actions. The first set of concerns focuses on the effect of third-party litigation investment on the number of class actions, while the second set focuses on the potential of third-party investment to exacerbate conflicts of interest and representational issues inherent in class action litigation.

A. The Effect of Third-Party Litigation Investment on the Number of Class Actions

No one knows the total number of class actions that are filed annually in U.S. federal or state courts (or in most jurisdictions outside the United States), but it likely ranges in the thousands, constituting a small fraction of the total U.S. civil litigation caseload. If there are many instances that could lead to class actions but do not because law firms lack the financial resources to pursue these cases, then the introduction of additional financing into the legal market could logically lead to an increase in litigation. There are no data that allow us to determine the number of potentially viable class actions, but available data on individual litigation rates suggest that a sizeable fraction of individual justiciable injurious incidents do not result in litigation, and there is reason to think that this is also true with regard to mass injuries.

However, in attacking the third-party litigation financing of class actions, the corporate community does not assert that there are proper class actions that are currently barred from the courts because of insufficient funding, but rather that third-party litigation financing will produce a flood of frivolous class actions. This assertion is based on three assumptions about U.S. class actions: first, that the current class action regime produces a host of frivolous class actions that defendants are forced to settle because of their in terrorem effect; second, that class action jurisprudence enables easy access to courts for frivolous class claims; and third, that litigation investors' business models will favor frivolous claims. The available empirical data do not support the first assumption about the current regime, and recent U.S. Supreme Court jurisprudence as well as the economics of third-party litigation financing militate against a flood of frivolous class actions going forward.

1. Assumption 1: The In Terrorem Effect of Class Actions Currently Forces Defendants to Settle Frivolous Class Claims

The claim of in terrorem effects of class filings leading to settlement of frivolous complaints is so ingrained in public policy rhetoric that it has been echoed by the U.S. Supreme Court. The claim may have gained credence as a result of an apparent increase in consumer class actions against insurers and other financial institutions during the 1990s, but there is little empirical evidence of in terrorem effects. The two best sources of empirical information on the outcomes of class action complaints are a 2007 RAND Institute for Civil Justice study of class actions against insurers brought in state and federal courts and a 2008 Federal Judicial Center study of diversity class action complaints filed in federal court prior to the effective date of the Class Action Fairness Act of 2005 (CAFA). Only 14% of the state and federal class actions that RAND studied were certified; of these, most settled. As a result, 12% of all class complaints resulted in class-wide remedies. In contrast, 37% resulted in a ruling on a dispositive motion in favor of defendants; 20% resulted in a settlement with an individual class representative; and 27% of the cases were voluntarily dismissed by the plaintiffs. The Federal Judicial Center reports that of the class action lawsuits that were filed in federal court pre-CAFA and not remanded to state courts, more than half (55%) were dismissed without class certification or class settlement, 29% were resolved by a ruling in favor of the defendant on a dispositive motion, and 13% resulted in a class certification and settlement.

* * * If there is an in terrorem effect of class action filings, its magnitude is likely modest.

2. Assumption 2: Class Action Jurisprudence in the United States Enables Easy Access to the Courts for Class Actions

If a marked increase in damages class actions in state and federal courts during the 1990s really did provoke an in terrorem effect among corporate defendants, by now that effect should be significantly diminished. Over the past two decades, the Supreme Court, aided on occasion by the U.S. Congress, has steadily raised the bar for plaintiff success in damages class actions. Mass tort class actions, which never had much of a run in the United States, have virtually disappeared[,] * * * replaced by aggregated lawsuits resolved in multidistrict litigation. The Private Securities Litigation Reform Act of 1995 (PSLRA) raised the standards for selecting class representatives, and the Securities Litigation Uniform Standards Act of 1998 (SLUSA) prevented plaintiff class counsel from turning to state courts to evade these restrictions. CAFA shifted formerly state court class actions to federal court in an effort to subject them to more conservative judicial rulings. The Supreme Court * * * restrict[ed] federal court jurisdiction over securities class actions[,] * * * narrow[ed] the substantive definitions of Rule 23(a)'s core requirements for certification and increas[ed] plaintiffs' evidentiary burden of proving that the certification requirements are met, and endors[ed] defendants' strategy of precluding any kind of collective proceeding by imposing mandatory pre-dispute arbitration clauses.

3. Assumption 3: The Third-Party Litigation Investment Model Will Favor Frivolous Class Claims

The U.S. class action fee regime is unlikely to enable a plaintiff-side firm to long sustain itself on frivolous claims, which available data suggest would result, at best, in a small settlement with a putative class representative—with proportionately small fees for the putative class counsel. At worst, bringing a frivolous claim would result in an expensive pretrial battle and a defense victory, with a financial loss for class counsel, who will neither recover expenses nor win fees for time spent on the case. Whether because of this financial regime or because of class action jurisprudence, there are no objective data to support the proposition that the U.S. class action system is overrun with frivolous suits. * * * [T]he frequent corporate community charge that plaintiff-side class action lawyers are "entrepreneurs" is intended to convey that they are market-driven, rather than driven by non-monetary professional or ideological ideals.

The financial incentives inherent in class actions (and other civil litigation where fee amounts depend on damages obtained) are more likely to pervert lawyers' settlement behavior than filing behavior. A class counsel whose fees and recovery of expenses depend on obtaining a settlement from the defendant may well agree too easily to suboptimal (from the class members' perspective) settlement offers so as to ensure some payment. As the value of the class injuries increases, the divergence between class counsel's interests and the interests of individual class members may grow. Defendants' ability to achieve res judicata "on the cheap" in return for an overly generous class counsel fee is central to the scholarly critique of class actions. Requiring judges to approve class action settlements and to award class counsel fees—neither of which judges have authority to do in ordinary individual litigation—and encouraging judges to require detailed notices that specify settlement provisions and the amount of fees that has been requested are all intended to mitigate the agency costs of class actions. However, anecdotal evidence suggests that these restraints are not always effective, with the result that defendants are at least sometimes able to obtain settlements favorable to themselves and to plaintiff class counsel, but less so to class members. There are no systematic data indicating how frequently this occurs.

From a defendant's perspective, providing class counsel with access to resources by introducing a new funding model that incentivizes the latter to pursue class complaints more doggedly poses a more realistic threat than the possibility of an avalanche of new class actions. Third-party litigation investors who have carefully screened claims to determine where to place their funds have a strong interest in ensuring that the plaintiffs' lawyers maximize the value of the claims in which the financers invest. There is no reason to expect that third-party litigation investors' screening processes, which are emphasized in their individual commercial claims' policies and practices, would not apply similarly to class actions if and when investors decided to enter the class action market.

Moreover, an investor managing a portfolio of class action claims might have a different risk calculus with regard to a single class action lawsuit than a plaintiff-side law firm whose resources are concentrated in that same class action. Like third-party investors, successful plaintiff-side class action firms invest in a portfolio of cases. Rather than changing these successful firms' risk calculus (and settlement behavior), the entrance of third-party litigation investors into the class action market might produce more competition for such firms by providing access to resources for smaller, and perhaps new, plaintiffs' law firms.

Third-party investment might also incentivize corporate law firms to agree to represent business entities that step forward as class representatives in securities or antitrust litigation, as seems to be occurring in Europe and is already happening in individual business-to-business patent litigation in the United States. How third-party litigation investment would affect settlement values for different types of class actions if and when third-party investors enter the market is unclear, but corporate defendants might have a rational basis for fearing these outcomes. However, it is difficult to discern the public policy argument against increased settlement values in meritorious cases if such values are currently suboptimal as a result of the agency costs of class action litigation, as some scholars have argued.

B. The Effect of Third-Party Litigation Financing on Conflicts of Interest and Representational Challenges in Class Actions

Scholars have long treated "low ball" settlements as the primary indicator of conflicts of interest between class counsel and class members. * * * [T]here is reason to believe that such settlements would be less attractive to third-party litigation investors than to underfinanced plaintiff-side class action law firms, and that plaintiff-side class action firms that secure third-party funding would be enabled as well as incentivized to pursue litigation and obtain better settlements for class members.

Some observers are concerned that the terms of third-party litigation contracts with plaintiff class counsel might be contrary to class members' interests, albeit attractive to class counsel. Even if the class representative were privy to the contract terms, there is a reasonable concern that absent class members would be unaware of the terms, and, indeed, unaware of third-party involvement in the case. Some have suggested that this is a reason to prohibit third-party litigation financing of class actions. However, federal judges (and judges in states with class action rules that mimic the Federal Rules) have tools for confronting this challenge: Under Rule

23(e)(3), "[t]he parties seeking approval must file a statement identifying any agreement made in connection with the [settlement] proposal," which should include an agreement between class counsel and third-party litigation financers. In reviewing and approving a proposed settlement, the judge could decide that such an agreement is not fair to class members and decline to approve the settlement. Under Rule 23(e)(1), the judge could direct that the notice to class members of a pending settlement include the terms of the litigation financing agreement, so that class members would understand how their share of the settlement would be affected by these terms, and either have the chance to object to the terms or opt out. Given the tradition of public interest organizations and others coming forward to object to proposed settlement terms and proposed class counsel fees, it seems likely that litigation financing agreements would attract attention. The potential for such attention would likely constrain class counsel and third-party litigation investors from agreeing to terms that were clearly against class members' interest.

However, federal judges need not rely on the interest of public or private intervenors to inquire into the terms of third-party litigation financing contracts with class counsel because the judges control the appointment of counsel. Under Rule 23(g)(1)(A)(iv), in appointing class counsel, the judge must consider "the resources that counsel will commit to representing the class." Under Rule 23(g)(1)(B), the judge "may consider any other matter pertinent to counsel's ability to fairly and adequately represent the interests of the class," and under Rule 23(g)(1)(C), the judge "may order potential class counsel to provide information on any subject pertinent to the appointment." Together these provisions give the judge broad authority to inquire into the terms of any litigation financing agreement the proposed class counsel has entered into and to decline such an appointment if she believes the terms do not serve the class well.

When considering how third-party litigation financing might evolve in the class action context, it is useful to recall that the much criticized third-party litigation investment contract in the Chevron-Ecuador case related to proceedings in Ecuador, which has no procedural rules governing collective actions. It is also notable that aggregated nonclass proceedings in the United States do not authorize judges presiding over such litigation to inquire into attorneys' fee agreements with their clients nor, perhaps by extension, their agreements with third-party investors. In this regard, as in many others, the U.S. class action regime provides greater due process protections for claimants than nonclass aggregated litigation—protections that could be deployed to protect class members against third-party litigation financing agreements that are inimical to their interests.

IV. Lessons from Australia

In its advocacy materials, the U.S. Chamber of Commerce draws attention to the experience of third-party litigation financing in Australia, where it claims the advent of litigation investment has increased the amount of civil litigation generally and the number of class actions in particular.

* * *

Class actions were introduced by statute in Australia's federal courts effective 1992, and in the states of Victoria, effective 2000, and New South Wales, effective 2011. The federal rule was modeled after Rule 23(b)(3) by plaintiffs attorneys who had represented Australian plaintiffs in mass litigation in the United States and concluded that their clients' interests would be better protected in their home jurisdiction. Third-party litigation financing emerged in Australia to address the barriers the traditional Australian fee regime imposed on class action litigation and has succeeded in enabling class lawsuits. However, contrary to the suggestion of the U.S. Chamber of Commerce, the empirical data show that the actual number of class lawsuits has been small. Moreover, the outcomes of financed cases suggest that third-party litigation financers have adopted quite conservative strategies in deciding whether to invest in class litigation.

* * *

V. Conclusion: Will the Sky Fall If Third-Party Litigation Funders Invest in U.S. Class Actions?

* * *

Neither anecdotal evidence of third-party litigation investors' strategies in the United States, nor contemporary U.S. class action jurisprudence, nor empirical data on trends in Australian class actions, suggest that the sky will fall any time soon should third-party litigation financing migrate to the class action domain in the United States.

* * *

2. THE NON-CLASS AGGREGATION CONTEXT

ELIZABETH CHAMBLEE BURCH, FINANCIERS AS MONITORS IN AGGREGATE LITIGATION
48 Georgia Law Advocate 1, 8–13 (2014) (excerpted from 87 N.Y.U. L. Rev. 1273 (2012)).

The class action isn't quite dead, though efforts aimed at extinguishing it have metastasized [in recent years]. Without class certification, aggregate litigation offers all of the perils and few of the promises of a class action. Granted, class actions posed problems too, but without the closure they generate and the judge ensuring a fair settlement, lawyers have dreamed up new means for achieving finality that evoke class-action nostalgia. To name but a few, they have exploited the attorney-client relationship to coerce clients into accepting a settlement, threatened to withdraw from representing nonconsenting clients, paid off holdouts to fulfill defendants' demands for complete resolution, forged ongoing "sweetheart" business relationships with settling defendants and overcompensated weak but prevalent claims to attract more clients.

The problem, in part, is that plaintiffs' attorneys are both financiers and agents, and those dual roles sometimes pull them in divergent directions. Just as they did in class actions, lawyers front the costs of litigating massive nonclass cases. But these cases are even more expensive than class actions; attorneys must spend time advertising and recruiting clients. Then they must track each case, hire paralegals to handle the added paperwork, establish specific causation, and spend time persuading each client to settle. Add to that the cost of expert witnesses, investigation, document review and coordinating with other multidistrict litigation attorneys and the expenses could easily bankrupt a small firm. So, when a defendant puts money on the table—even money with many strings attached, like withdrawing the settlement offer if too few plaintiffs accept it—it tempts plaintiffs' attorneys to strong arm their clients to settle so they can recoup and profit from their financial investment. Because the plaintiff's and the lawyer's interests never overlap perfectly, the lawyer's monetary self-interest and duty of loyalty may be at odds with one another.

Yet, nonclass aggregation lacks a monitor to police these settlements the way a judge polices class actions. Although some judges have likened large multidistrict litigations to class actions and tried to oversee them accordingly, the existence of a legal basis for policing a "voluntary" settlement between private parties is uncertain at best. The clients themselves are unlikely to monitor their attorneys because the very aggregation that increases the economic viability of their claims fosters collective-action problems and makes meaningful information from their attorney difficult to attain. When cases are interdependent, learning the progress of one's own case may yield little information about the overall litigation and vice versa. Plus, individual plaintiffs tend to be unsophisticated about legal matters and trust their attorney's advice—that is, after all, why they hired her.

But the potential for a private monitor does exist in the unlikely guise of third-party financiers—hedge funds, private investors and venture capitalists. Alternative litigation financing has gradually made its way from Australia and the United Kingdom into the United States, causing substantial controversy in the process.

Despite the controversy, allowing third parties to fund nonclass aggregation helps to manage principal-agent problems by freeing attorneys from their financial self-interest and encouraging them to act as more faithful agents. It does so by (1) unbundling the attorney's competing roles as investor and adviser, (2) shifting financial risk to a third party who pays the attorneys on a billable-hour basis (plus, perhaps some small percentage of the recovery as a bonus) and (3) putting in place a sizeable stakeholder with the sophistication and incentive to monitor the agents. If plaintiffs assign a financier a portion of the litigation's proceeds (as the contingent fee does now) in exchange for financing the lawsuit on a nonrecourse basis, the financier would become a super stakeholder.

Third-party financiers have already started funding aggregate litigation: Napoli Bern made headlines when it borrowed some $35 million from Counsel Financial to fund the Ground Zero workers' personal-injury cases against the City of New York and tried to pass $6.1 million in interest costs onto the workers. Burford Capital funded thousands of Ecuadorian plaintiffs in their controversial personal-injury battle against Chevron. Likewise, in a toxic-tort case against BNSF Railway, attorney Jared Woodfill borrowed more than $3.5 million from a hedge fund to help finance litigation on behalf of some 400 plaintiffs with skin and gastrointestinal cancers allegedly caused by chemicals used to make railroad ties. These financing arrangements, however, do not follow this article's blueprint. Lending money to plaintiffs' law firms on a recourse basis (where the firm must repay the loan regardless of whether it wins or loses the lawsuit), as was the case for Napoli Bern and Jared Woodfill, may either intensify the pressure on plaintiffs to settle or present them with unexpected interest charges. As this suggests, the way in which financiers bankroll aggregate litigation is critical; this new relationship raises a panoply of questions about maintenance, champerty, barratry, confidentiality, privileges, consent, decisionmaking authority and incentives.

Taxonomy of Third-Party Financing

Presently, there are three main types of third-party financing—consumer legal funding, loans to plaintiffs' law firms and commercial dispute funding—each of which raise distinct legal and ethical concerns. Third-party funding took root in the United States when companies started loaning money to cash-strapped plaintiffs who could not use their lawsuit as bank collateral but needed money for day-to-day expenses. This so-called "consumer legal funding" is a nonrecourse loan where a litigant would not need to pay any more than what she receives from the lawsuit; there is no personal liability—if she loses the suit, the lender loses the money. The way in which financiers bankroll aggregate litigation is critical; this new relationship raises a panoply of questions about maintenance, champerty, barratry, confidentiality, privileges, consent, decisionmaking authority and incentives. Given the risk involved, however, interest rates can be quite high—between 36 and 150 percent per year—but the nonrecourse basis enables funders to avoid state usury laws. Consumer legal funders making cash advances to plaintiffs traditionally run up against historical maintenance doctrines, which prohibit third parties from assisting a litigant in pursing a lawsuit.

Over time, a second type of financing emerged: loaning money to plaintiffs' law firms, as opposed to cash-advance loans to plaintiffs themselves. As of early 2010, only around nine companies provided loans to law firms; but as of late 2011, that number had grown to around 12. When financiers lend money to law firms, they secure those debts not by a single case, but by all of the firm's assets, including future fee awards from other cases. Occasionally, funders will lend lawyers money based on a trial verdict on appeal. Unlike a nonrecourse loan, plaintiffs' firms must repay the money regardless of whether they win or lose a particular case. Such was the case in financing the Ground Zero workers' litigation; Napoli Bern would have to reimburse Counsel Financial regardless of the litigation's outcome. Interest rates are significantly higher than what a bank might charge for a loan based on traditional assets—rates tend to be "north of 20 percent"—which makes the loans unattractive to well-financed firms. Still, lenders in this area can do what banks cannot; banks loan money based on traditional assets and collateral, not on potential winnings.

Finally, a burgeoning market of around seven lenders provide money directly to businesses to finance commercial, business-versus-business disputes in exchange for either a percentage of the plaintiff's eventual recovery or a multiple of the supplied capital. Those percentages range from 35 to 67 percent of the lawsuit's recovery. This kind of lending may run into historical prohibitions on champerty, a form of maintenance where the lender receives an interest in the suit's outcome. Two of the lenders in this area, Juridica Investments and Burford Capital, are publicly traded companies in the Alternative Investment Market on the London Stock Exchange and principally bankroll international arbitrations, as well as intellectual property, breach of contract and antitrust disputes. Most commercial dispute lenders currently steer clear of funding aggregate litigation and leave those investments to funders who loan money to plaintiffs' law firms. But this model of contracting with the plaintiffs for a portion of their proceeds has the most potential for creating a workable monitor. And for those investors seeking a longer-term investment with a potentially exponential payoff, funding aggregate litigation is a logical next step.

Financiers as Intermediaries in Aggregate Litigation

Layering a financier's incentives atop an already complex principal-agent relationship can fundamentally alter litigation and settlement dynamics. An investor who bankrolls a plaintiffs' law firm on a recourse basis and accrues monthly interest may care less about speedy settlements so long as the law firm's financial solvency is not in doubt. If the loan is non-recourse in the same scenario, then both the funder and the lawyer have powerful incentives to settle quickly, perhaps at their clients' expense. But it is also possible to overlay the financier's incentives with the plaintiffs' incentives such that the financier, who has litigation expertise, sophistication, and substantial capital involved, will monitor the attorney and thwart at least some of the agency problems that tend to arise between contingent-fee attorneys and their clients.

Allowing third parties like commercial-claims lenders to invest in the dispute's outcome by contracting directly with plaintiffs generates two principally positive effects. First, it disentangles—at least in part—the lawyer's role as investor from her role as a fiduciary and adviser. When litigating no longer threatens the law firm's solvency or ability to take on other matters, the attorney's loyalty no longer divides between self-preservation and the clients' best interest; she can afford to be a faithful representative. Second, assigning a financier a percentage of the plaintiffs' winnings converts that financier into a sizeable stakeholder and incentivizes it to monitor the attorney's and the litigation's costs. Because aggregate litigation is capital intensive, the investor can act as an advocate for the plaintiff by keeping costs reasonable. If the attorney wants to borrow money for travel and experts at a high interest rate, the investor has the incentive to prevent that transaction and finance those expenses at a much lower cost. And unlike geographically dispersed plaintiffs who face collective-action problems, a single, experienced financier can, for instance, require attorneys to keep their travel budgets reasonable.

But the need for monitoring and the degree to which agency is disentangled from risk depends chiefly on how the third-party financier compensates the lawyer for her services.

Third-Party Compensation Options

Consider three options for compensating attorneys and third-party financiers: (1) financiers pay the attorneys an hourly rate on the billable-hour system, (2) attorneys receive a discounted contingent fee that accounts for the lack of financial risk, or (3) financiers pay attorneys on a billable-hour rate plus some small percentage of the proceeds as a bonus.

1. Paying plaintiffs' attorneys on a billable-hour system

Paying attorneys a billable-hour rate cleanly cleaves a lawyer's role as a risk-taking investor from her role as a client adviser and fiduciary, which means that she may be more loyal to her clients and have less incentive to arrange a quick settlement or collude with the defendant to settle on suboptimal terms. Moreover, a litigation-savvy financier could negotiate a better hourly rate and thereby prevent astronomical fees while ensuring that the case is adequately funded. Were a quick settlement offer generous enough to cover the financier's expenses and provide it with some return on the risk, the financier might push plaintiffs to accept the settlement, but here the billable-hour attorney's self-interest checks the financier's. If anything, a billable-hour attorney would prefer to prolong the litigation, would advise plaintiffs to wait for a better deal, and would thus counterbalance the investor.

Billing hours also encourages lawyers to spend time counseling their clients about the alternative options available and explain the risks of litigating versus settling, which curtails the effect of contrast biases and uninformed risk preferences. This arrangement may likewise negate some of the pressure attorneys feel to cram the settlement down on their clients and misallocate settlement funds to payoff holdouts. When an attorney's payday isn't inherently tied to settling the lawsuit (as is the case when she works on a contingent fee), it alleviates her pressing financial concerns. So, though the attorney's ability to tender finality to the defendant is still vital for achieving a satisfactory settlement, she no longer feels the accompanying financial urgency and self-interest tugs that the current system engenders. There are hazards involved with this billable-hour option, too.

There is some risk that the billable-hour attorney would encourage her clients to accept a settlement that was not in their best interests if it furthers her prospects of doing repeat business with the financier. Thus, the collusion occurs not between plaintiffs' attorneys and defense attorneys, but between plaintiffs' attorneys and funders. But perhaps the most worrisome aspect of this compensation scheme is whether it would still attract the best and brightest plaintiffs' attorneys. Although defense attorneys on the billable-hour system make a very nice income, one rarely sees them with their own private planes and yachts, trappings common for successful mass-tort plaintiffs' attorneys. While third-party financing would increase competition among the plaintiffs' bar and may thus foster innovation and loyalty, the question remains whether plaintiffs would still receive advocacy of the same quality and creativity and whether trading some ingenuity for greater loyalty is worth the cost.

2. Financiers and plaintiffs' attorneys split a contingent fee

This second option allows attorneys and financiers to split the attorneys' standard contingent fee. The lawyers would receive a reduced award since they are shouldering less financial risk, but the payoff is still potentially momentous. This option recognizes that contingent fees and their attendant rewards encourage entrepreneurial attorneys to accept monolith cases and thus promote ex post law enforcement. It likewise accounts for the lingering reputational risks that attorneys must shoulder despite taking on less financial risk.

As noted, most claimants agree to a 33–40 percent contingent fee, though some judges have reduced that fee to between 25–28 percent. Assuming the initial agreement's range provides ample incentive to accept the litigation's risks, the total percentage allocated to parties other than the plaintiffs should not exceed those parameters. Attorneys and financiers might divide the total by splitting the percentage in some agreed upon fashion.

The trouble is, if both funders and attorneys operated purely on a percentage-of-the-proceeds payment plan, their incentives would overlap with one another, but not necessarily with plaintiffs. Like the contingent-fee attorney today, both would have some motivation to achieve a higher settlement since it means a greater profit, but the attendant risks of that fee arrangement would plague plaintiffs to an even greater degree. Both financiers and attorneys may prefer to settle quickly (provided the offer exceeds costs and fees), collude with the defendant if the deal benefits them financially, pressure plaintiffs to accept an offer through questionable means and misallocate settlement funds if it is necessary for achieving the deal's required consensus. So, while a third-party funder could ensure that litigation is not underfunded and might negotiate a reduced attorneys' fee, the savings would benefit the investor, not the plaintiffs. ... the question remains whether plaintiffs would still receive advocacy of the same quality and creativity and whether trading some ingenuity for greater loyalty is worth the cost.

3. Billable hours plus a small percentage of the proceeds

While awarding attorneys a pure percentage of the proceeds would attract creative, entrepreneurial attorneys, the better approach is for the funder to negotiate a billable-hour rate plus a small percentage of the proceeds as a successful litigation bonus. Providing a bonus and having a sophisticated financier oversee the billable hours allays at least some of the traditional objections to having a billable-hour system. These objections include that billable hours encourage lawyers to duplicate their efforts and not communicate effectively with their clients, fail to provide predictable client costs and penalize efficient and productive lawyers. Having a financier foot the bill actually encourages attorneys to spend time communicating with their clients. And bonuses reward efficiency and productivity while helping to counteract any tendency to unduly prolong the litigation or duplicate effort. Granted, there is still some risk that attorneys might cherry pick certain cases for continued litigation (and the billable hours that accompany them). Yet, the attorney's reputation among the financiers might serve as a failsafe. If the attorney hopes to gain repeat business from financiers while maintaining her reputation as a faithful agent to her clients, then she may continue to litigate only where it best serves her client's interests.

By injecting a sophisticated financier into the lawsuit and making it the largest stakeholder, this arrangement improves the status quo. First, financiers enable plaintiffs' law firms with less monetary capital to litigate high stakes, resource intensive cases, which increases competition within the private bar. Once a market for funding aggregate litigation emerges, it is also likely to spur competition among financiers, which could, in turn, mean that they would accept a lower percentage of the proceeds for stronger cases. Second, this proposal incentivizes financiers to monitor the attorneys, while reducing the need for monitoring in the first place. The demand for oversight swelled from bundling financial risk with the attorney's duty of loyalty to clients: self-interest in avoiding financial strain tempted attorneys to engage in self-dealing, overbearing—if not unethical—settlement practices. But uncoupling these divergent interests permits the financier to negotiate a competitively priced fee and to monitor the monthly costs. With the lawyer's financial wellbeing secured by the financier's nonrecourse investment in the litigation's proceeds, she can faithfully and loyally represent her clients' best interests as well as counterbalance any undue settlement pressure the financier exerts.

Making Third-Party Financing Work

As one might imagine, shifting the status quo from contingent-fee arrangements to litigation-funding agreements necessitates reexamining historical bans on maintenance and champerty as well as contemplating how a financier may affect the attorney-client privilege, work-product doctrine and attorney confidentiality.

First, if financiers take a more active role in funding aggregate litigation, they need to be able to independently evaluate the claim's merits and communicate with both the plaintiffs and the attorneys without waiving plaintiffs' attorney-client privilege or losing objections based on the work-product doctrine. Although some financiers rely principally on publicly filed pleadings and memoranda and thus do not need privileged information, it seems that a financier considering whether to invest millions of dollars into funding aggregate litigation would need more information. Sharing privileged information requires plaintiffs' informed consent to satisfy attorneys' ethical duties of confidentiality, but it also entails considering the attorney-client privilege and the work-product doctrine. Because lawyers generally waive the work-product doctrine only when they make disclosures that substantially increase the likelihood of putting documents in their adversary's hands, it raises fewer concerns than the attorney-client privilege.

One possibility for addressing the attorney-client privilege is to extend the common-interest doctrine to include financiers who invest in the lawsuit as well as those who considered investing. Covering the latter category of investors encourages price competition among financiers without jeopardizing plaintiffs' confidential information. The common-interest doctrine evolved from situations where two clients retained the same attorney to pursue their common interest and has long been used by insurance companies, in joint defense strategies (such as by asbestos and tobacco defendants), and by plaintiffs involved in group litigation. In these contexts, the doctrine extends to "two or more clients with a common interest in a litigated or nonlitigated matter" who are represented by the same or separate lawyers to encourage full and efficient case preparation.[6] Although the third-party financier seems to fit neatly under this common-interest umbrella, there is one critical matter worth clarifying: the financier and the plaintiff cannot be considered joint clients of the plaintiff's attorney. Having a financier foot the bill actually encourages attorneys to spend time

---

[6] Restatement (Third) of the Law Governing Lawyers § 75 (2000).

communicating with their clients. If that were the case, the lawyers would have duties of loyalty to the financier, not just her client. That would undermine the disaggregated incentive structure that promotes loyalty to plaintiffs.

Second, states should continue to lift the historical prohibition on champerty such that the enforceability of a financing agreement does not hinge on a particular state's laws or an ad-hoc balancing approach to conflict of laws, both of which provide further impetus for forum shopping. One recent survey showed that 26 of 51 jurisdictions (including the District of Columbia) permit champerty to some degree so long as the financier does not promote clearly frivolous litigation, participate in "malice champerty" ("meritorious litigation employed for an improper end") or "intermeddling" (controlling trial strategy or settlement). Further, * * * the arguments against assignment and maintenance are "not currently persuasive from either a historical or jurisprudential perspective." And most studies about champerty predict that lifting this ban will be beneficial by increasing access to justice and improving the likelihood that settlements will reflect the claim's merit as opposed to economic pressures. The trouble is that attorneys are likely the ones referring clients to a financier. And attorneys' preferred financiers may depend more on the hourly rate and percentage of the proceeds the financier will pay them than the clients' best interests. This brings us back to the potential for collusion between the financier and attorney.

Unlike clients, who are typically oneshot players, financiers and lawyers are both repeat players; their relationship is more enduring. This potentially powerful bond between financiers and attorneys suggests that judges must play a mitigating role. But two things must happen before they can do so. First, they must know that an alternative-financing arrangement exists. Accordingly, in multidistrict litigation, there should be mandatory, in camera disclosure of financing agreements. Currently, financing agreements contain confidentiality provisions and financiers regularly require plaintiffs to sign additional non-disclosure agreements. Although these measures keep the defendant from exploiting this information, submitting the funding agreement to the judge in camera allows the judge not only to learn of its existence and ensure its terms are not unconscionable, but to recuse herself if she has a disqualifying relationship with the financier. Moreover, should it become necessary, this enables the judge to report unethical behavior between attorneys and financiers to the relevant bar authorities. Second, as Congress has done in similar areas of consumer concern, it, or perhaps the newly minted Bureau for Consumer Financial Protection, should prohibit arbitration in consumer-financing agreements. This would ensure some transparency in the funding process through enforcement challenges, allow consumers to vindicate their contractual rights in a convenient forum and, through judicial adjudication, outline the permissible bounds of litigation-funding agreements. Potential judicial enforcement also deters collusive behavior between the financier and the plaintiffs' attorneys; when the two know that the agreement is not shrouded in arbitration's confidentiality and could land before a judge (and in publicly filed documents), they are far less likely to engage in clandestine behavior.

Conclusion

Alternative litigation financing, if properly engineered, could help alleviate the financial pressure on the attorney-client relationship and thereby encourage ethical behavior in litigating and settling aggregate litigation. Presently, attorneys who specialize in large-scale litigation bear the crushing burden of funding it, a practice that prevents lawyers with less capital from entering the field and tempts those who do to prefer their own financial self-interest over their clients' best interests. If financial risk is no longer an integral part of an attorney's relationship with her clients, it opens the door to several new possibilities. First, financiers might bankroll talented attorneys who could not otherwise afford to initiate aggregate litigation. Second, new entrants could intensify competition among the plaintiffs' bar that could encourage innovation and drive down fees. Finally, given the increased costs and risks associated with multidistrict litigation as opposed to class actions, allowing financiers to enter the picture ensures that meritorious suits will not wither alongside the class action. To be sure, adding an intermediary can introduce competing incentives and is thus not a cure-all for principal-agent problems. Rather, third-party financiers offer one means for managing some of these problems in aggregate litigation.

3. DISCLOSURE OF FUNDERS

The following case addresses disclosure of funders in class actions. In reading the case, however, consider whether the reasoning also applies to non-class aggregate cases.

NATTO IYELA GBARABE V. CHEVRON CORP.
United States District Court, Northern District of California, 2016.

2016 WL 4154849.

ILLSTON, DISTRICT JUDGE.

* * *

BACKGROUND

On January 16, 2012, an explosion occurred on the KS Endeavor (Panama) drilling rig, which was drilling for natural gas in the North Apoi Field off of the coast of Nigeria. The explosion caused a fire that burned for forty-six days. Plaintiff alleges that the KS Endeavor was operated by KS Drilling under the management of Chevron Nigeria Limited, which in turn acted at defendant Chevron Corporation's direction.

Plaintiff Natta Iyela Gbarabe is a fisherman who lives in a coastal community of Bayelsa State in Nigeria who depends on fishing for his primary method of earning a living. The [complaint] alleges that plaintiff suffered "personal loss by way of an almost total loss of yield in the waters customarily fished by plaintiff after the KS Endeavor rig explosion and 46-day fire, as well as damage to fishing equipment." The [complaint] also alleges that "Plaintiff further suffered health issues from the effects of the polluted air and water caused by the gas rig explosion of the KS Endeavour, which included diarrhea and vomiting." Plaintiff seeks to represent "a prospective class comprising individuals who live and work in communities and co-operatives located in the Niger Delta region of southern Nigeria and identifies presently as comprising some 12,600 individuals spread across communities at or near the coastal waters of Bayelsa State, Nigeria." The [complaint] seeks compensation and punitive damages arising out of Chevron's alleged gross negligence, willful misconduct, negligence per se, acts of nuisance, and breaches of Nigerian law.

This lawsuit was filed on January 13, 2014. * * * The class certification motion is scheduled for a hearing on December 9, 2016.

DISCUSSION

I. Defendant's motion to compel

Chevron requests that plaintiff be ordered to produce "documents reflecting or relating to the actual or potential financing or funding of the prosecution of this litigation[.]"

* * * Chevron contends that plaintiff's funding agreement and related documents are relevant to determining adequacy of representation in this putative class action. Chevron argues that when the Court rules on the upcoming class certification motion, the Court must examine "the resources that counsel will commit to representing the class," Fed. R. Civ. P. 23(g)(1)(A)(iv), and Chevron argues that "this requirement is especially important in a case like this, involving claims that are likely to be expensive to investigate, prepare for trial, and try." Chevron notes that plaintiff does not dispute that his counsel, who appear to be solo practitioners, are dependent on outside funding to prosecute this case. Chevron states that after initially refusing to produce the requested documents, plaintiff produced a heavily redacted copy of a litigation funding agreement, and that the redactions make it impossible for Chevron to assess whether counsel can commit adequate resources to the class.

Plaintiff's opposition concedes the relevance of the funding agreement to the class certification adequacy determination, and plaintiff does not assert that the agreement is privileged. Plaintiff states, "Plaintiff and his counsel have no personal objection to providing the requested information, contrary to defendant's assertions. However, plaintiff and his counsel are under a contractual obligation to preserve the confidentiality of the funder's identity, as well as the terms of the agreement, absent a Court order or a determination that it would be prudent to do so." Plaintiff proposes submitting an unredacted copy of the litigation funding agreement to the Court for in camera review, along with "an executed declaration by the funder's Chief Investment Officer which addresses each item identified by defendant in their motion. In this manner, plaintiff can meet the funder's confidentiality desire while satisfying the Court and defendant as to the adequacy of funding for this litigation." Plaintiff's opposition only addresses the litigation funding agreement and does not address Chevron's request for other documents regarding plaintiff's funding.

The Court concludes that under the circumstances of this case, the litigation funding agreement is relevant to the adequacy determination and should be produced to defendant. The confidentiality provision of the funding agreement does not prohibit plaintiff from producing the agreement, and instead simply states that "if at any time such a requirement [to produce the agreement] arises or to do so would be prudent . . . the lawyers will promptly take all such steps as reasonably practicable to make such disclosure . . . ." Plaintiff's proposal for in camera review of the agreement by the Court is inadequate because it would deprive Chevron of the ability to make its own assessment and arguments regarding the funding agreement and its impact, if any, on plaintiff's ability to adequately represent the class.

Accordingly, the Court GRANTS Chevron's motion to compel and orders plaintiff to produce the litigation funding agreement to Chevron.

* * *

CONCLUSION

For the foregoing reasons, the Court GRANTS in part Chevron's motion to compel[.]

* * *

NOTES AND QUESTIONS

1. What arguments can be made in favor of the rise of third-party financing? What arguments can be made against this phenomenon?

2. Should third-party funders be regulated? If so, by what body and in what fashion? What restrictions on third-party funding would make the practice less concerning?

3. What arguments did the defendants advance in the *Chevron* case in favor of disclosure of funders? Do those arguments dovetail with any points raised by Professor Hensler or Professor Burch? What are plaintiffs' arguments against disclosure? Are those arguments persuasive?

4. Is the *Chevron* court correct in holding that the litigation funding agreement is relevant to adequacy of representation? Does the reasoning apply in non-class cases? Why or why not?

5. The *Chevron* court refused to grant the plaintiffs' request for in camera review. Is that aspect of the court's ruling persuasive?

6. In January 2017, the Northern District of California became the first federal court to announce a rule mandating disclosure of third-party funding in class action cases. *See* Ben Hancock, *Calif. Court Mandates Disclosure of Third-Party Funding in Class Actions*, LAW.COM (Jan. 24, 2017), http://www.law.com/sites/almstaff/2017/01/24/calif-court-mandates-disclosure-of-third-party-funding-in-class-actions/ (local civil rules amended to require automatic disclosure, as part of joint case management statement, of all funding agreements "in any proposed class, collective or representative action").

7. For useful commentary (in addition to the articles by Professors Hensler and Burch), *see, e.g.*, Joanna M. Shepherd, *Ideal Versus Reality in Third-Party Litigation Financing*, 8 J.L. Econ. & Pol'y 593 (2012) (arguing that "rather than improving access to justice, third-party financing is increasing inefficiency and threatening both the compensatory and deterrent functions of the legal system"); Joshua G. Richey, *Tilted Scales of Justice? The Consequences of Third-Party Financing of American Litigation*, 63 Emory L.J. 489 (2013) (noting that "third-party litigation financing has * * * created risk imbalances that favor plaintiffs").

E. ALTERNATIVE DISPUTE RESOLUTION

Because of the complexity of class action ligation, courts and litigants have frequently turned to alternative dispute resolution (ADR) for the management and resolution of class actions. ADR includes many different possibilities:

> The ADR roster includes such well-known processes as arbitration, mediation, conciliation, and, perhaps, negotiation. * * * There are also new hybrid devices that borrow from courtroom procedure—including, most prominently, the mini-trial. The roster may also be expanded to include the roles played by certain officials and quasi-officials (such as court-appointed masters, special masters, and neutral experts), by private persons retained as neutrals, by ombudsmen, and by private judges. Changes in procedural rules to provide incentives to the parties to settle * * * and the greater use of partial summary judgment might also be viewed as ADR techniques.
>
> * * * ADR * * * [has] a fundamental premise: it is worthwhile both to reduce the costs of resolving disputes * * * and to improve the quality of the final outcome. * * *

Jethro K. Lieberman & James F. Henry, *Lessons From the Alternative Dispute Resolution Movement*, 53 U. Chi. L. Rev. 424, 424–26 (1986). This section surveys some of the pertinent issues raised by ADR.

1. THE PROMISE OF ADR IN CLASS ACTIONS

Carrie Menkel–Meadow, When Dispute Resolution Begets Disputes of Its Own: Conflicts Among Dispute Professionals
44 UCLA L. Rev. 1871, 1900–01 (1997).

Whatever the merits of the use of ADR in individual disputes * * *, the use of some ADR-like settlement devices in several recent class actions provoked a sharp debate about the tensions between individual and aggregate justice. The uses of ADR in class actions have been varied, including: a choice of ADR in the form of arbitration in Dalkon Shield;[†] appeals for mediation or arbitration after "grid" assessments of compensation in asbestos and breast implant cases; and now similar uses of mediation or other forms of ADR following grid-like claims assessments in the class action settlements of major insurance fraud cases. In contrast to consumer or securities class actions settlements in which claimants receive either nominal amounts of money or simple discounts on future purchases of goods, some of the recent uses of ADR in the mass tort or insurance context permit a hearing to contest or present evidence on amounts to be received. * * * [I]n my view, applications of ADR processes to class actions offer the promise of process integrity and catharsis for individual disputants while preserving some of the efficiencies and benefits of mass litigation. To the extent

---

[†] Arbitration was used to resolve the products liability claims of thousands of women brought against the A.H. Robins Company, the manufacturer of Dalkon Shield, an intrauterine birth control device. For a history of the litigation, *see* Deborah R. Hensler & Mark A. Peterson, *Understanding Mass Personal Injury Litigation: A Socio–Legal Analysis*, 59 Brook. L. Rev. 961, 983–86 (1993). [Ed.]

that federal judges cannot hear all the claims in a class action, it may still be important for claimants to have a hearing, "vent" their anger, concerns, emotions, and harms experienced, and to tell their story, as well as to explore a more individualized assessment of their claims. * * *

What is required, in my view, is a more sophisticated understanding of the different processes and forms of ADR, and the situations in which they are best applied. In cases involving strictly monetary value, arbitration following some claim assessment may be appropriate because of its "decisional" quality; but in cases in which the parties want to participate in more open-ended narrative about what happened to them or seek some negotiation over some nonmonetary claims (such as in some of the mass tort cases), then mediation or other ADR forms may be more appropriate (when more variable and flexible solutions are possible). It is important that particular forms of ADR not become inflexibly and rigidly adopted in repetitive form in these cases. * * * [W]e may need to adapt the "forum to the fuss" and consider what kinds of ADR processes are appropriate in different kinds of mass cases to maximize the individualized treatment that is most appropriate for each particular claim. In my own experience, some claimants desire an in-person "confrontation" with some representative of the wrongdoer, while others are quite content to accept a more anonymous payment. Different litigants may desire different processes and/or remedies, and offering an adaptive menu of process choices could respond to these different requirements within mass litigation settings.

The author of the following article, Kenneth R. Feinberg, served as the Special Master of the September 11th Victim Compensation Fund, established by the federal government to provide compensation for the victims' families of the 9/11 terrorist attack. He also served President Obama's Administration as the independent administrator of a $20 billion fund to compensate victims of BP's Deepwater Horizon oil spill and as the special master for executive compensation for large financial firms receiving federal bailout funds. In addition, he has functioned as special master and mediator in a variety of other important matters (including several cases discussed in the article).

KENNETH R. FEINBERG, CREATIVE USE OF ADR: THE COURT-APPOINTED SPECIAL SETTLEMENT MASTER
59 Alb. L. Rev. 881, 881–93 (1996).

Increased access to both federal and state courts in an effort to resolve controversies pertaining to mass torts, environmental disputes, employment discrimination claims, and other burgeoning litigation has resulted in a new effort by the judiciary to achieve settlement through the innovative use of court-appointed Special Settlement Masters. Docket control and shrinking judicial resources require new creative case management techniques aimed at the comprehensive resolution of such complex litigation. The use of Special Masters to expedite settlement by means of a structured settlement process under the auspices of the court is one striking example of how to accomplish this goal.

Special Masters are usually experienced private attorneys or law Professors authorized by the court to conduct settlement negotiations. * * * [C]ourts have recognized the utility of designating an individual with quasi-judicial authority to act as a buffer between the court and the parties in effectuating a settlement. The court-appointed Special Settlement Master coordinates settlement discussions, while, on a parallel track, the court prepares for trial.

The use of such Settlement Masters has proven particularly beneficial in complex cases involving numerous plaintiffs and multiple defendants, especially when the disputes have "matured" and have become both repetitive and time-consuming. In disputes involving protracted mass torts, such as asbestos, DES, and the Dalkon Shield, as well as in many environmental insurance coverage disputes, Special Masters can enter the fray and efficiently resolve trial-ready disputes by coordinating settlement negotiations using case values long recognized by the parties themselves.

Increased use of such Special Masters has given rise to provocative ethical questions concerning the relationship of the Master to both the parties and the appointing court. The most common issue surrounds the use of *ex parte* communications between the Special Master, the litigants, and the court. For example, in conducting settlement negotiations, the Special Master may obtain information which, if conveyed to the court, might prejudice any subsequent trial. Ethical limitations concerning the authority and wisdom of conveying such information to the court, in whole or in part, continues to bedevil experts on judicial ethics, as well as the courts themselves.

Nevertheless, the use of court-appointed Special Settlement Masters will likely increase. The sheer magnitude of the modern trial docket and the proliferation of creative litigation in such areas as mass torts place unprecedented burdens on the court system. * * * The court-appointed Special Settlement Master is one of the bolder initiatives implemented by the judiciary (along with complementary devices such as consolidated trials, common issues trials, and bifurcated or even trifurcated trials).

What types of disputes are most amenable to the appointment of a Special Settlement Master? One expert commentator has identified four types of cases: (1) cases requiring a protracted bench trial; (2) cases requiring protracted negotiations; (3) cases requiring travel outside the jurisdiction; and (4) cases involving complex, technical data.

Timing is also a critical factor in securing a comprehensive settlement with the assistance of a Special Master. Again, there appears to be a series of "optimum times" within which a facilitated settlement can best be accomplished, including: (1) "shortly after the complaint has been filed and the case has been identified by the judge as a likely candidate for mediation;" (2) "immediately prior to the lawyer's arduous task of preparing the proposed joint pretrial order for submission at a pretrial conference;" or (3) "immediately prior to a firm trial date."

What are the devices and techniques used by the court-appointed Special Settlement Master to encourage the parties to reach a comprehensive settlement? * * * First, it must be recognized that any settlement blueprint will vary from case to case, depending upon the type of case, the stage of the litigation, and the personalities and qualities of the litigating counsel, as well as the Special Master himself or herself. Second, it is necessary for the Special Master to educate himself or herself in the underlying facts of the dispute; it is critically important to any settlement negotiation that the

Master have a thorough knowledge of the legal and factual issues in dispute. And third, the Special Master must develop a methodology for resolving the dispute—exchanging demands and offers by the parties (the Special Master as passive facilitator); developing an independent recommendation and evaluation (the Special Master as active participant); or a hybrid of both passive and active characteristics. How "activist" the Special Master may be in attempting to promote settlement negotiations will depend not only on the style and personality of the Master, but also on the requirements of the parties and the nature of the court's appointive authority.

Specific illustrations demonstrate the different techniques and creative methodologies used by Special Masters to achieve a comprehensive settlement. For example, in the *Agent Orange Products Liability Litigation*, the Special Master acted as a "go between" among the parties themselves and the court, engaging in a type of "shuttle diplomacy" in an effort to bridge differences and forge an agreement. Acting as a mediator, the Special Master facilitated a settlement by suggesting alternative terms and conditions to the parties themselves without expressing a view as to what type of settlement would be deemed "most reasonable." After each of the co-defendant companies and plaintiff class counsel argued their cases separately to the Special Master, all parties agreed to ask the court for its view concerning final settlement terms. Eventually, all parties accepted settlement terms proposed by the court and the Special Master.

In the *Brooklyn Naval Shipyard* asbestos litigation, the Special Master implemented a different technique. First, he met with various plaintiffs' counsel to establish an aggregate settlement figure for thousands of cases based upon prior settlement history. Next, by weighing a number of factors, including the years of asbestos exposure alleged by various plaintiffs, identification of particular co-defendant asbestos companies at the Navy Yard site during the relevant years, and the seriousness of asbestos related diseases, the Special Master performed the "activist" role of fashioning a proposed settlement figure for each co-defendant company, in order to achieve the aggregate sum reached in negotiations with plaintiffs' counsel. This settlement plan called for a "blind contribution" in that plaintiffs were not advised of the amount requested from each defendant and defendants were not aware of the aggregate amounts requested from other co-defendant companies. When the individual defendant companies did not contribute the amounts sought from each of them by the Special Master, face-to-face negotiations between plaintiffs' counsel and individual co-defendant companies were successfully implemented. The plaintiffs achieved early resolution of their asbestos claims and the co-defendant companies settled thousands of asbestos cases with minimal transaction costs and avoidance of the spectre of huge jury verdicts.

In analyzing the role of court-appointed Special Settlement Masters, it is useful to highlight other functions which are often overlooked once settlement is achieved. First, in cases involving more than one defendant, an issue often arises of how to allocate the aggregate settlement amount reached with plaintiffs' counsel among the various co-defendants. This issue of how the co-defendant companies will allocate financial responsibility among themselves in funding the aggregate settlement amount reached with plaintiff counsel may be more provocative and emotional than the primary negotiations themselves. Thus, in addition to coordinating settlement discussions between plaintiff counsel and the co-defendants, the Special Master also frequently conducts what may be termed a second "mini-mediation" among the co-defendants.

Second, the Special Settlement Master may often be called upon by the court, after a settlement is reached, to develop the framework for the distribution of settlement proceeds to various plaintiff claimants. In mass tort litigation such as the *"Agent Orange"* and *Dalkon Shield* cases, resolution between plaintiffs and defendants is only the first step, and the serious obstacle of determining eligibility criteria for payment of limited amounts to a wide variety of plaintiffs claiming a wide ranging series of illnesses and adverse medical conditions remains to be dealt with. In *"Agent Orange,"* for example, various options were considered by the Special Master, including: traditional tort compensation tied to a list of priority diseases and conditions (rejected primarily because of the difficulties associated with proving causation in individual cases); funding of a classwide benefit program, including research into medical causation, lobbying and special services for Vietnam veterans (accepted in part but rejected as a sole remedy); and payments based upon a worker's compensation model (lower levels of proof as to causation and a cap based upon lower payment levels). The Special Master concluded—and the court ultimately concurred—that this latter plan would be the most equitable and efficient.

As already indicated, the evolving role of the court-appointed Special Settlement Master has given rise to a series of provocative ethical questions. It would appear that, as a court-appointed officer with quasi-judicial functions, the Special Master is governed by the Code of Judicial Conduct for United States Judges, but this is unclear. Special Masters are not judges, and traditional rules surrounding judicial conduct may not fit with their new, evolving extrajudicial role. The Code seems to apply to Special Masters, particularly in areas such as the prohibition of *ex parte* contacts and conflicts of interest. But it is obvious that a restrictive interpretation of the Code would completely gut the ability of a Special Settlement Master to coordinate and effectuate settlement discussions. It is one thing to argue that *ex parte* contacts between the Special Master and the appointing court should be limited in scope and detail; it is quite another matter to maintain that *all* such contacts should be deemed inappropriate. In occupying the role of being both a buffer between the court and the parties, as well as being a conduit for settlement communications the Special Master must maintain the confidence of all parties. The Special Master seeks candor if settlement negotiations are to be successful. At the same time, the parties might be reluctant to offer their candid assessment of settlement terms if there is concern that settlement negotiations will be relayed by the Special Master to the court. What formal rules should apply concerning the relationship of the Special Master to the court and the parties has not yet been developed in all respects.

* * *

Finally, there is the issue of conflict of interest. A Special Master is often appointed by a court because of his or her special expertise in the subject-matter of the dispute. It is of critical importance that the court-appointed Special Master be unbiased and impartial. Previous representation of any of the parties should be prohibited, at least absent a clear and unambiguous waiver. More important than substantive expertise concerning the matter in dispute are other characteristics of an effective Master: negotiation skills, mediation techniques, and litigation experience. Specialized expertise is a much less important factor to consider when appointing a Special Settlement Master.

It is apparent that, in light of mushrooming caseloads and shrinking judicial budgets, courts will continue to expand the role of Special Masters. The functions and duties of such court appointed officials appear to be limited only by the creativity and imagination of litigating lawyers themselves. Docket control requires innovative case management techniques and the court-appointed Special Settlement Master is one example of innovative use of limited judicial resources. During the next few years, consumers of justice can anticipate the increased use of Special Masters. Their evolving role, and limitations concerning their various functions, should be carefully scrutinized and monitored. But it is difficult to argue with the bottom line conclusion that court-appointed Special Settlement Masters are here to stay.

NOTES AND QUESTIONS

1. How does a class action ADR differ from an ADR in an individual-plaintiff lawsuit?

2. Should the availability of ADR be a factor in determining whether a class action is manageable?

3. What are the constitutional implications of ADR? Consider a class action settlement that instituted a dispute-resolution process as the sole means by which class members could bring claims of sexual harassment, discrimination, or retaliation against the defendant corporation. *See USA Today*, Feb. 12, 1999, at 7B (containing settlement notice from *Martens v. Smith Barney, Inc.*, 181 F.R.D. 243 (S.D.N.Y. 1998)). What potential constitutional issues might arise in *Martens*? Does the fact that a settlement is involved eliminate any constitutional concerns? Should the constitutional analysis depend upon whether class members have opt-out rights?

4. When, if ever, should courts have the authority to *require* parties to engage in ADR against their will? Should courts at least make it widely available? The Federal Alternative Dispute Resolution Act of 1998 went into effect on October 3, 1998. *See* 28 U.S.C. §§ 651–58. This act requires federal district courts to authorize the use of ADR in civil proceedings, although it allows each court to determine what types of cases will be covered and what categories will be excluded. *See* 28 U.S.C. § 652(b). It allows courts to order parties to enter mediation or early neutral evaluation, but requires the parties' consent for arbitration or summary jury trial. *See* 28 U.S.C. §§ 652(a), 654(a).

5. To what extent does ADR signify the failure of the judicial system to deal efficiently and effectively with its case load? Should reform focus primarily on making ADR more widely available? Or should it instead focus upon expanding the availability of judicial resources (such as filling judicial vacancies more promptly or establishing more judgeships)?

6. One of the most important roles that special master Kenneth Feinberg has played was his job as the Special Master of the September 11th Victim Compensation Fund, where he was tasked with deciding how to distribute

monetary compensation to the victims' families. For a detailed look at this complicated task, *see* Kenneth R. Feinberg, Lecture, 56 Ala. L. Rev. 543 (2004) (describing role of Special Master and problems that arose under the federal statute). Despite initial criticism, the overwhelming majority of the victims' families decided to participate in the Fund.

7. As the foregoing excerpts suggest, ADR has strong support among judges, practitioners, and scholars. The ADR movement is not without detractors, however. Owen M. Fiss, in *Against Settlement*, 93 Yale L.J. 1073 (1984), calls into question the legitimacy and desirability of settlement. He criticizes ADR advocates who exalt settlement because they perceive it to be preferable to a lengthy and costly trial. The crux of Professor Fiss's article is that adjudication should be understood more broadly. Adjudication is a public process, utilizing public resources and public officials who exercise power conferred by public law. "Their job is not to maximize the ends of private parties, nor simply to secure the peace, but to explicate and give force to the values embodied in authoritative texts such as the Constitution and statutes; to interpret those values and to bring reality into accord with them." Fiss warns:

> * * * To be against settlement is only to suggest that when the parties settle, society gets less than what appears, and for a price it does not know it is paying. Parties might settle while leaving justice undone. The settlement of a school suit might secure the peace, but not racial equality. Although the parties are prepared to live under the terms they bargained for, and although such peaceful coexistence may be a necessary precondition of justice, and itself a state of affairs to be valued, it is not justice itself. To settle for something means to accept less than some ideal.

Id. at 1085–86. Are Professor Fiss's criticisms valid? For a response to some of Professor Fiss's positions, *see* Samuel Issacharoff & Robert H. Klonoff, *The Public Value of Settlement*, 78 Fordham L. Rev. 1177, 1200–02 (2009).

8. Other critics of ADR have cited other alleged shortcomings. For example, Professor Kim Dayton concludes that ADR does not reduce backlogs, result in speedier trials, or confer other advantages justifying broad-scale adoption in federal courts. *See* Kim Dayton, *The Myth of Alternative Dispute Resolution in the Federal Courts*, 76 Iowa L. Rev. 889, 896 (1991). Professor Richard Delgado and his co-authors contend that ADR poses an unacceptable risk that racial and ethnic prejudice will infect settlements resulting from ADR because of the informal nature of the process. Relying on social science data, they argue that minorities may be placed at a disadvantage by resolving problems through ADR, because those with prejudicial attitudes are more likely to act on them in informal environments. *See* Richard Delgado et al., *Fairness and Formality: Minimizing the Risk of Prejudice in Alternative Dispute Resolution*, 1985 Wis. L. Rev. 1359 (1985); *see also* Trina Grillo, *The Mediation Alternative: Process Dangers for Women*, 100 Yale L.J. 1545 (1991) (arguing that ADR disadvantages women). Others are critical of a specific type of ADR—arbitration—discussed in the section below. *See, e.g.*, Christopher R. Drahozal, *Arbitration Costs and Forum Accessibility: Empirical Evidence*, 41 U. Mich. J.L. Reform 813, 815 (2007–2008) ("[T]he available evidence suggests * * * the upfront costs of arbitration will in many cases be higher than, and at best be the same as, the upfront costs in litigation."); David S. Schwartz, *Mandatory Arbitration and Fairness*, 84 Notre Dame L. Rev. 1247, 1252 (2008–2009) ("[E]ach assertion in the argument for the fairness of mandatory arbitration is

based on a combination of false premises, faulty empirical research, unproven assumptions or mere debators' tricks."). Are these criticisms of ADR justified?

9. Apart from the debate over whether it is good policy to avoid trials, there is also a debate about whether claimants fare better under litigation than under ADR. For example, do plaintiffs do better in arbitration than litigation? Empirical studies comparing outcomes between them are mixed. *Compare* Lewis Maltby, *Employment Arbitration and Workplace Justice*, 38 U.S.F. L. Rev. 105, 114 (2003) (suggesting that employees may fare better in arbitration than in litigation) *and* Michael Delikat & Morris M. Kleiner, *Comparing Litigation and Arbitration of Employment Disputes: Do Claimants Better Vindicate Their Rights in Litigation?*, 6 A.B.A. Litig. Sec. Conflict Mgmt. 1, 10 (2003) (claimants in employment disputes in securities industry recovered slightly more money in arbitration than litigation), *with* Theodore Eisenberg & Elizabeth Hill, *Arbitration & Litigation of Employment Claims: An Empirical Comparison*, 58 Disp. Res. J. 44, 45, 48, 50–51 (Nov. 2003–Jan. 2004) (study of employment cases in arbitration and litigation revealed less favorable outcomes in arbitration for employees earning less than $60,000, but not less favorable outcomes in arbitration for higher earners) *and* William M. Howard, *Arbitrating Claims of Employment Discrimination, What Really Does Happen?, What Really Should Happen?*, Disp. Res. J. 40, 45 (Oct.–Dec. 1995) (mean and median jury verdicts in litigation exceeded arbitration awards in employment disputes). *See also* Peter B. Rutledge, *Whither Arbitration?*, 6 Geo. J.L. & Pub. Pol'y 549, 560 (2008) (surveying empirical studies comparing arbitration and litigation outcomes and concluding that "most measures * * * do not support the claims that consumers and employees achieve inferior results in arbitration compared to litigation").

For discussion of another alternative to mandatory, pre-dispute arbitration—namely, one-way binding arbitration—*see* Suzette M. Malveaux, *Is It the "Real Thing"? How Coke's One-Way Binding Arbitration May Bridge the Divide Between Litigation and Arbitration*, 2009 J. Disp. Resol. 77. That alternative gives the employee, but not the employer, the option of rejecting the arbitrator's decision and pursuing litigation in court. What are the pros and cons of such an approach?

2. INDIVIDUAL ARBITRATION IN LIEU OF CLASS ACTIONS

One ADR issue that has received substantial attention in recent decades is the attempt by defendants to impose arbitration on potential plaintiffs, including claimants in potential class actions. In an arbitration, a neutral or panel of neutrals resolves a dispute between parties based on the contractual terms set forth in an arbitration agreement. The decision is generally binding and subject to appeal only on limited contractual grounds, such as fraud, duress, bias, or unconscionability. Mandatory pre-dispute arbitration agreements require signatories to agree in advance that if they have a dispute in the future, they will resolve it in an arbitral forum rather than a judicial forum.

Arbitration differs from adjudication in significant ways. On the one hand, arbitration may offer benefits such as greater flexibility, lower costs, and more expedient resolution of claims. On the other hand, arbitration may dispense with many rights ordinarily available in court, including a jury trial, a public and subsidized forum, a written record, robust discovery, and binding legal precedents.

For decades, the Supreme Court has promoted a federal policy favoring the enforcement of arbitration agreements. Consequently, there has been a proliferation of arbitration clauses in employment and consumer contracts, requiring the parties to agree in advance to use arbitration if a dispute arises in the future. Such mandatory pre-dispute arbitration clauses have come under fire as companies increasingly inserted provisions prohibiting class or aggregate arbitration procedures in their agreements.

Courts' reactions to such class arbitration waivers have been mixed. Some courts have enforced such contracts, in deference to parties' freedom to contract and the Federal Arbitration Act's requirement that arbitration agreements be put on equal footing with other contracts. Other courts found certain class arbitration waivers unenforceable—particularly those in consumer agreements involving small-value claims—based on various rationales, such as state law unconscionability principles and public policy grounds. The Supreme Court addresses class arbitration waivers in the case below.

AT&T MOBILITY LLC V. CONCEPCION
Supreme Court of the United States, 2011.
563 U.S. 333.

JUSTICE SCALIA delivered the opinion of the Court.

Section 2 of the Federal Arbitration Act (FAA) makes agreements to arbitrate "valid, irrevocable, and enforceable, save upon such grounds as exist at law or in equity for the revocation of any contract." 9 U.S.C. § 2. We consider whether the FAA prohibits States from conditioning the enforceability of certain arbitration agreements on the availability of classwide arbitration procedures.

I

In February 2002, Vincent and Liza Concepcion entered into an agreement for the sale and servicing of cellular telephones with AT&T Mobility LCC (AT&T). The contract provided for arbitration of all disputes between the parties, but required that claims be brought in the parties' "individual capacity, and not as a plaintiff or class member in any purported class or representative proceeding." * * * The version at issue in this case reflects revisions made in December 2006, which the parties agree are controlling.

The revised agreement provides that customers may initiate dispute proceedings by completing a one-page Notice of Dispute form available on AT&T's Web site. AT&T may then offer to settle the claim; if it does not, or if the dispute is not resolved within 30 days, the customer may invoke arbitration by filing a separate Demand for Arbitration, also available on AT&T's Web site. In the event the parties proceed to arbitration, the agreement specifies that AT&T must pay all costs for nonfrivolous claims; that arbitration must take place in the county in which the customer is billed; that, for claims of $10,000 or less, the customer may choose whether the arbitration proceeds in person, by telephone, or based only on submissions; that either party may bring a claim in small claims court in lieu of arbitration; and that the arbitrator may award any form of individual relief, including injunctions and presumably punitive damages. The agreement, moreover, denies AT&T any ability to seek reimbursement of its attorney's fees, and, in the event that a customer receives an arbitration award greater than AT&T's last written settlement offer, requires AT&T to pay a $7,500 minimum recovery and twice the amount of the claimant's attorney's fees.

The Concepcions purchased AT&T service, which was advertised as including the provision of free phones; they were not charged for the phones, but they were charged $30.22 in sales tax based on the phones' retail value. In March 2006, the Concepcions filed a complaint against AT&T in the United States District Court for the Southern District of California. The complaint was later consolidated with a putative class action alleging, among other things, that AT&T had engaged in false advertising and fraud by charging sales tax on phones it advertised as free.

In March 2008, AT&T moved to compel arbitration under the terms of its contract with the Concepcions. The Concepcions opposed the motion, contending that the arbitration agreement was unconscionable and unlawfully exculpatory under California law because it disallowed classwide procedures. The District Court denied AT&T's motion. It described AT&T's arbitration agreement favorably noting, for example, that the informal dispute-resolution process was "quick, easy to use" and likely to "promp[t] full or . . . even excess payment to the customer *without* the need to arbitrate or litigate"; that the $7,500 premium functioned as "a substantial inducement for the consumer to pursue the claim in arbitration" if a dispute was not resolved informally; and that consumers who were members of a class would likely be worse off. Nevertheless, relying on the California Supreme Court's decision in *Discover Bank v. Superior Court,* 36 Cal.4th 148, 30 Cal.Rptr.3d 76, 113 P.3d 1100 (2005), the court found that the arbitration provision was unconscionable because AT&T had not shown that bilateral arbitration adequately substituted for the deterrent effects of class actions.

The Ninth Circuit affirmed, also finding the provision unconscionable under California law as announced in *Discover Bank*. It also held that the *Discover Bank* rule was not preempted by the FAA because that rule was simply "a refinement of the unconscionability analysis applicable to contracts generally in California." In response to AT&T's argument that the Concepcions' interpretation of California law discriminated against arbitration, the Ninth Circuit rejected the contention that "'class proceedings will reduce the efficiency and expeditiousness of arbitration'" and noted that "'*Discover Bank* placed arbitration agreements with class action waivers on the *exact same footing* as contracts that bar class action litigation outside the context of arbitration.'" We granted *certiorari*.

II

The FAA was enacted in 1925 in response to widespread judicial hostility to arbitration agreements. Section 2, the "primary substantive provision of the Act," reflect[s] both a "liberal federal policy favoring arbitration," and the "fundamental principle that arbitration is a matter of contract." In line with these principles, courts must place arbitration agreements on an equal footing with other contracts, and enforce them according to their terms.

The final phrase of § 2, however, permits arbitration agreements to be declared unenforceable "upon such grounds as exist at law or in equity for the revocation of any contract." This saving clause permits agreements to arbitrate to be invalidated by "generally applicable contract defenses, such as fraud, duress, or unconscionability," but not by defenses that apply only to arbitration or that derive their meaning from the fact that an agreement to arbitrate is at issue. The question in this case is whether § 2 preempts California's rule classifying most collective-arbitration waivers in consumer contracts as unconscionable. We refer to this rule as the *Discover Bank* rule.

Under California law, courts may refuse to enforce any contract found "to have been unconscionable at the time it was made," or may "limit the application of any unconscionable clause." A finding of unconscionability requires "a 'procedural' and a 'substantive' element, the former focusing on 'oppression' or 'surprise' due to unequal bargaining power, the latter on 'overly harsh' or 'one-sided' results."

In *Discover Bank,* the California Supreme Court applied this framework to class action waivers in arbitration agreements and held as follows:

> "[W]hen the waiver is found in a consumer contract of adhesion in a setting in which disputes between the contracting parties predictably involve small amounts of damages, and when it is alleged that the party with the superior bargaining power has carried out a scheme to deliberately cheat large numbers of consumers out of individually small sums of money, then . . . the waiver becomes in practice the exemption of the party 'from responsibility for [its] own fraud, or willful injury to the person or property of another.' Under these circumstances, such waivers are unconscionable under California law and should not be enforced."

California courts have frequently applied this rule to find arbitration agreements unconscionable.

III

A

The Concepcions argue that the *Discover Bank* rule, given its origins in California's unconscionability doctrine and California's policy against exculpation, is a ground that "exist[s] at law or in equity for the revocation of any contract" under FAA § 2. Moreover, they argue that even if we construe the *Discover Bank* rule as a prohibition on collective-action waivers rather than simply an application of unconscionability, the rule would still be applicable to all dispute-resolution contracts, since California prohibits waivers of class litigation as well.

When state law prohibits outright the arbitration of a particular type of claim, the analysis is straightforward: The conflicting rule is displaced by the FAA. But the inquiry becomes more complex when a doctrine normally thought to be generally applicable, such as duress or, as relevant here, unconscionability, is alleged to have been applied in a fashion that disfavors arbitration. * * *

An obvious illustration of this point would be a case finding unconscionable or unenforceable as against public policy consumer arbitration agreements that fail to provide for judicially monitored discovery. The rationalizations for such a holding are neither difficult to imagine nor different in kind from those articulated in *Discover Bank*. A court might reason that no consumer would knowingly waive his right to full discovery, as this would enable companies to hide their wrongdoing. Or the court might simply say that such agreements are exculpatory—restricting discovery would be of greater benefit to the company than the consumer, since the former is more likely to be sued than to sue. And, the reasoning would continue, because such a rule applies the general principle of unconscionability or public-policy disapproval of exculpatory agreements, it is applicable to "any" contract and thus preserved by § 2 of the FAA. In practice, of course, the rule would have a disproportionate impact on arbitration agreements; but it would presumably apply to contracts purporting to restrict discovery in litigation as well.

Other examples are easy to imagine. [The Court describes rules requiring adherence to the Federal Rules of Evidence or jury-like dispositions as examples of rules that would have a disproportionate impact on arbitration agreements, but presumably apply to litigation and arbitration alike.]

The Concepcions suggest that all this is just a parade of horribles, and no genuine worry. "Rules aimed at destroying arbitration" or "demanding procedures incompatible with arbitration," they concede, "would be preempted by the FAA because they cannot sensibly be reconciled with Section 2." The "grounds" available under § 2's saving clause, they admit, "should not be construed to include a State's mere preference for procedures that are incompatible with arbitration and 'would wholly eviscerate arbitration agreements.'"

* * *

We largely agree. Although § 2's saving clause preserves generally applicable contract defenses, nothing in it suggests an intent to preserve state-law rules that stand as an obstacle to the accomplishment of the FAA's objectives. * * *

We differ with the Concepcions only in the application of this analysis to the matter before us. We do not agree that rules requiring judicially monitored discovery or adherence to the Federal Rules of Evidence are "a far cry from this case." The overarching purpose of the FAA * * * is to ensure the enforcement of arbitration agreements according to their terms so as to facilitate streamlined proceedings. Requiring the availability of classwide arbitration interferes with fundamental attributes of arbitration and thus creates a scheme inconsistent with the FAA.

B

The "principal purpose" of the FAA is to "ensur[e] that private arbitration agreements are enforced according to their terms." This purpose is readily apparent from the FAA's text. * * * In light of these provisions, we have held that parties may agree to limit the issues subject to arbitration, to arbitrate according to specific rules, and to limit *with whom* a party will arbitrate its disputes.

The point of affording parties discretion in designing arbitration processes is to allow for efficient, streamlined procedures tailored to the type of dispute. * * * And the informality of arbitral proceedings is itself desirable, reducing the cost and increasing the speed of dispute resolution.

* * *

Contrary to the dissent's view, our cases place it beyond dispute that the FAA was designed to promote arbitration. They have repeatedly described the Act as "embod[ying] [a] national policy favoring arbitration," and "a liberal federal policy favoring arbitration agreements, notwithstanding any state substantive or procedural policies to the contrary." Thus, in *Preston v. Ferrer*, 552 U.S. 346 (2008), holding preempted a state-law rule requiring exhaustion of administrative remedies before arbitration, we said: "A prime objective of an agreement to arbitrate is to achieve 'streamlined proceedings and expeditious results,' " which objective would be "frustrated" by requiring a dispute to be heard by an agency first. That rule, we said, would "at the least, hinder speedy resolution of the controversy."

California's *Discover Bank* rule similarly interferes with arbitration. Although the rule does not *require* classwide arbitration, it allows any party to a consumer contract to demand it *ex post*. The [*Discover Bank*] rule is limited to adhesion contracts, but the times in which consumer contracts were anything other than adhesive are long past. The rule also requires that damages be predictably small, and that the consumer allege a scheme to cheat consumers. The former requirement, however, is toothless and malleable * * *, and the latter has no limiting effect, as all that is required is an allegation. Consumers remain free to bring and resolve their disputes on a bilateral basis under *Discover Bank*, and some may well do so; but there is little incentive for lawyers to arbitrate on behalf of individuals when they may do so for a class and reap far higher fees in the process. And faced with inevitable class arbitration, companies would have less incentive to continue resolving potentially duplicative claims on an individual basis.

Although we have had little occasion to examine classwide arbitration, our decision in *Stolt–Nielsen S.A. v. AnimalFeeds Int'l Corp.*, [559 U.S. 662] (2010), is instructive. In that case we held * * * that the [arbitration] agreement at issue, which was silent on the question of class procedures, could not be interpreted to allow them because the "changes brought about by the shift from bilateral arbitration to class-action arbitration" are "fundamental." This is obvious as a structural matter: Classwide arbitration includes absent parties, necessitating additional and different procedures and involving higher stakes. Confidentiality becomes more difficult. And while it is theoretically possible to select an arbitrator with some expertise relevant to the class-certification question, arbitrators are not generally knowledgeable in the often-dominant procedural aspects of certification, such as the protection of absent parties. The conclusion follows that class arbitration, to the extent it is manufactured by *Discover Bank* rather than consensual, is inconsistent with the FAA.

First, the switch from bilateral to class arbitration sacrifices the principal advantage of arbitration—its informality—and makes the process slower, more costly, and more likely to generate procedural morass than final judgment. "In bilateral arbitration, parties forgo the procedural rigor and appellate review of the courts in order to realize the benefits of private dispute resolution: lower costs, greater efficiency and speed, and the ability to choose expert adjudicators to resolve specialized disputes." But before an arbitrator may decide the merits of a claim in classwide procedures, he must first decide, for example, whether the class itself may be certified, whether the named parties are sufficiently representative and typical, and how discovery for the class should be conducted. * * *

Second, class arbitration *requires* procedural formality. The AAA's rules governing class arbitrations mimic the Federal Rules of Civil Procedure for class litigation. And while parties can alter those procedures by contract, an alternative is not obvious. If procedures are too informal, absent class members would not be bound by the arbitration. For a class-action money judgment to bind absentees in litigation, class representatives must at all times adequately represent absent class members, and absent members must be afforded notice, an opportunity to be heard, and a right to opt out of the class. *Phillips Petroleum Co. v. Shutts*, 472 U.S. 797, 811–12 (1985). At least this amount of process would presumably be required for absent parties to be bound by the results of arbitration.

We find it unlikely that in passing the FAA Congress meant to leave the disposition of these procedural requirements to an arbitrator. Indeed, class arbitration was not even envisioned by Congress when it passed the FAA in 1925; as the California Supreme Court admitted in *Discover Bank,* class arbitration is a "relatively recent development." And it is at the very least odd to think that an arbitrator would be entrusted with ensuring that third parties' due process rights are satisfied.

Third, class arbitration greatly increases risks to defendants. Informal procedures do of course have a cost: The absence of multilayered review makes it more likely that errors will go uncorrected. Defendants are willing to accept the costs of these errors in arbitration, since their impact is limited to the size of individual disputes, and presumably outweighed by savings from avoiding the courts. But when damages allegedly owed to tens of thousands of potential claimants are aggregated and decided at once, the risk of an error will often become unacceptable. Faced with even a small chance of a devastating loss, defendants will be pressured into settling questionable claims. Other courts have noted the risk of "in terrorem" settlements that class actions entail, and class arbitration would be no different.

Arbitration is poorly suited to the higher stakes of class litigation. In litigation, a defendant may appeal a certification decision on an interlocutory basis and, if unsuccessful, may appeal from a final judgment as well. Questions of law are reviewed *de novo* and questions of fact for clear error. In contrast, 9 U.S.C. § 10 allows a court to vacate an arbitral award *only* where the award "was procured by corruption, fraud, or undue means"; "there was evident partiality or corruption in the arbitrators"; "the arbitrators were guilty of misconduct in refusing to postpone the hearing . . . or in refusing to hear evidence pertinent and material to the controversy[,] or of any other misbehavior by which the rights of any party have been prejudiced"; or if the "arbitrators exceeded their powers, or so imperfectly executed them that a mutual, final, and definite award . . . was not made." The AAA rules do authorize judicial review of certification decisions, but this review is unlikely to have much effect given these limitations; review under § 10 focuses on misconduct rather than mistake. And parties may not contractually expand the grounds or nature of judicial review. We find it hard to believe that defendants would bet the company with no effective means of review, and even harder to believe that Congress would have intended to allow state courts to force such a decision.

The Concepcions contend that because parties may and sometimes do agree to aggregation, class procedures are not necessarily incompatible with arbitration. But the same could be said about procedures that the Concepcions admit States may not superimpose on arbitration: Parties *could* agree to arbitrate pursuant to the Federal Rules of Civil Procedure, or pursuant to a discovery process rivaling that in litigation. Arbitration is a matter of contract, and the FAA requires courts to honor parties' expectations. But what the parties in the aforementioned examples would have agreed to is not arbitration as envisioned by the FAA, lacks its benefits, and therefore may not be required by state law.

The dissent claims that class proceedings are necessary to prosecute small-dollar claims that might otherwise slip through the legal system. But States cannot require a procedure that is inconsistent with the FAA, even if it is desirable for unrelated reasons. Moreover, the claim here was most unlikely to go unresolved. As noted earlier, the arbitration agreement provides that AT&T will pay claimants a minimum of $7,500 and twice their attorney's fees if they obtain an arbitration award greater than AT&T's last settlement offer. The District Court found this scheme sufficient to provide incentive for the individual prosecution of meritorious claims that are not immediately settled, and the Ninth Circuit admitted that aggrieved customers who filed claims would be "essentially guarantee[d]" to be made whole. Indeed, the District Court concluded that the Concepcions were *better off* under their arbitration agreement with AT&T than they would have been as participants in a class action * * *.

Because it "stands as an obstacle to the accomplishment and execution of the full purposes and objectives of Congress," California's *Discover Bank* rule is preempted by the FAA. The judgment of the Ninth Circuit is reversed, and the case is remanded for further proceedings consistent with this opinion.

It is so ordered.

* * *

JUSTICE THOMAS, concurring.

* * *

* * * As I would read it, the FAA requires that an agreement to arbitrate be enforced unless a party successfully challenges the formation of the arbitration agreement, such as by proving fraud or duress. 9 U.S.C. §§ 2, 4. Under this reading, I would reverse the Court of Appeals because a district court cannot follow both the FAA and the *Discover Bank* rule, which does not relate to defects in the making of an agreement.

This reading of the text, however, has not been fully developed by any party and could benefit from briefing and argument in an appropriate case. Moreover, I think that the Court's test will often lead to the same outcome as my textual interpretation and that, when possible, it is important in interpreting statutes to give lower courts guidance from a majority of the

Court. *See U.S. Airways, Inc. v. Barnett*, 535 U.S. 391, 411 (2002) (O'Connor, J., concurring). Therefore, although I adhere to my views on purposes-and-objectives pre-emption, *see Wyeth v. Levine*, 129 S. Ct. 1187 (2009) (opinion concurring in judgment), I reluctantly join the Court's opinion.

* * *

Under [Justice Thomas's] reading, the question here would be whether California's *Discover Bank* rule relates to the making of an agreement. I think it does not.

* * *

The court's analysis and conclusion that the arbitration agreement was exculpatory reveals that the *Discover Bank* rule does not concern the making of the arbitration agreement. Exculpatory contracts are a paradigmatic example of contracts that will not be enforced because of public policy. Refusal to enforce a contract for public-policy reasons does not concern whether the contract was properly made.

Accordingly, the *Discover Bank* rule is not a "groun[d] ... for the revocation of any contract" as I would read § 2 of the FAA in light of § 4. Under this reading, the FAA dictates that the arbitration agreement here be enforced and the *Discover Bank* rule is pre-empted.

JUSTICE BREYER, with whom JUSTICE GINSBURG, JUSTICE SOTOMAYOR, and JUSTICE KAGAN join, dissenting.

The Federal Arbitration Act says that an arbitration agreement "shall be valid, irrevocable, and enforceable, *save upon such grounds as exist at law or in equity for the revocation of any contract*." 9 U.S.C. § 2 (emphasis added). California law sets forth certain circumstances in which "class action waivers" in *any* contract are unenforceable. In my view, this rule of state law is consistent with the federal Act's language and primary objective. It does not "stan[d] as an obstacle" to the Act's "accomplishment and execution." And the Court is wrong to hold that the federal Act pre-empts the rule of state law.

I.

The California law in question consists of an authoritative state-court interpretation of two provisions of the California Civil Code. The first provision makes unlawful all contracts "which have for their object, directly or indirectly, to exempt anyone from responsibility for his own ... violation of law." The second provision authorizes courts to "limit the application of any unconscionable clause" in a contract so "as to avoid any unconscionable result."

The specific rule of state law in question consists of the California Supreme Court's application of these principles to hold that "some" (but not "all") "class action waivers" in consumer contracts are exculpatory and unconscionable under California "law." In particular, in *Discover Bank* the California Supreme Court stated that, when a class-action waiver

> "is found in a consumer contract of adhesion in a setting in which disputes between the contracting parties predictably involve small amounts of damages, and when it is alleged that the party with the superior bargaining power has carried out a scheme to deliberately cheat large numbers of consumers out of individually

small sums of money, then . . . the waiver becomes in practice the exemption of the party 'from responsibility for [its] own fraud, or willful injury to the person or property of another.'"

In such a circumstance, the "waivers are unconscionable under California law and should not be enforced."

The *Discover Bank* rule does not create a "blanket policy in California against class action waivers in the consumer context." Instead, it represents the "application of a more general [unconscionability] principle." Courts applying California law have enforced class action waivers where they satisfy general unconscionability standards. And even when they fail, the parties remain free to devise other dispute mechanisms, including informal mechanisms, that, in context, will not prove unconscionable.

II

A

The *Discover Bank* rule is consistent with the federal Act's language. It "applies equally to class action litigation waivers in contracts without arbitration agreements as it does to class arbitration waivers in contracts with such agreements." Linguistically speaking, it falls directly within the scope of the Act's exception permitting courts to refuse to enforce arbitration agreements on grounds that exist "for the revocation of *any* contract." 9 U.S.C. § 2 (emphasis added). The majority agrees.

B

The *Discover Bank* rule is also consistent with the basic "purpose behind" the Act. We have described that purpose as one of "ensur[ing] judicial enforcement" of arbitration agreements. As is well known, prior to the federal Act, many courts expressed hostility to arbitration, for example by refusing to order specific performance of agreements to arbitrate. The Act sought to eliminate that hostility by placing agreements to arbitrate "'*upon the same footing as other contracts.*'"

Congress was fully aware that arbitration could provide procedural and cost advantages. The House Report emphasized the "appropriate[ness]" of making arbitration agreements enforceable "at this time when there is so much agitation against the costliness and delays of litigation." And this Court has acknowledged that parties may enter into arbitration agreements in order to expedite the resolution of disputes.

But we have also cautioned against thinking that Congress' primary objective was to guarantee these particular procedural advantages. Rather, that primary objective was to secure the "enforcement" of agreements to arbitrate. The relevant Senate Report points to the Act's basic purpose when it says "[t]he purpose of the [Act] is *clearly set forth in section 2,*" namely, the section that says that an arbitration agreement "shall be valid, irrevocable, and enforceable, save upon such grounds as exist at law or in equity for the revocation of any contract," 9 U.S.C. § 2.

Thus, insofar as we seek to implement Congress' intent, we should think more than twice before invalidating a state law that does just what § 2 requires, namely, puts agreements to arbitrate and agreements to litigate "upon the same footing."

III

The majority's contrary view (that *Discover Bank* stands as an "obstacle" to the accomplishment of the federal law's objective) rests primarily upon its claims that the *Discover Bank* rule increases the complexity of arbitration procedures, thereby discouraging parties from entering into arbitration agreements, and to that extent discriminating in practice against arbitration. These claims are not well founded.

For one thing, a state rule of law that would sometimes set aside as unconscionable a contract term that forbids class arbitration is not (as the majority claims) like a rule that would require "ultimate disposition by a jury" or "judicially monitored discovery" or use of "the Federal Rules of Evidence." Unlike the majority's examples, class arbitration is consistent with the use of arbitration. It is a form of arbitration that is well known in California and followed elsewhere. Indeed, the AAA has told us [in its amicus brief] that it has found class arbitration to be "a fair, balanced, and efficient means of resolving class disputes." And unlike the majority's examples, the *Discover Bank* rule imposes equivalent limitations on litigation; hence it cannot fairly be characterized as a targeted attack on arbitration.

Where does the majority get its contrary idea—that individual, rather than class, arbitration is a "fundamental attribut[e]" of arbitration? The majority does not explain. And it is unlikely to be able to trace its present view to the history of the arbitration statute itself.

When Congress enacted the Act, arbitration procedures had not yet been fully developed. Insofar as Congress considered detailed forms of arbitration at all, it may well have thought that arbitration would be used primarily where merchants sought to resolve disputes of fact, not law, under the customs of their industries, where the parties possessed roughly equivalent bargaining power. This last mentioned feature of the history—roughly equivalent bargaining power—suggests, if anything, that California's statute is consistent with, and indeed may help to further, the objectives that Congress had in mind.

Regardless, if neither the history nor present practice suggests that class arbitration is fundamentally incompatible with arbitration itself, then on what basis can the majority hold California's law pre-empted?

For another thing, the majority's argument that the *Discover Bank* rule will discourage arbitration rests critically upon the wrong comparison. The majority compares the complexity of class arbitration with that of bilateral arbitration. And it finds the former more complex. But, if incentives are at issue, the *relevant* comparison is not "arbitration with arbitration" but a comparison between class arbitration and judicial class actions. After all, in respect to the relevant set of contracts, the *Discover Bank* rule similarly and equally sets aside clauses that forbid class procedures—whether arbitration procedures or ordinary judicial procedures are at issue.

Why would a typical defendant (say, a business) prefer a judicial class action to class arbitration? AAA statistics "suggest that class arbitration proceedings take more time than the average commercial arbitration, but may take *less time* than the average class action in court." Data from California courts confirm that class arbitrations can take considerably less time than in-court proceedings in which class certification is sought. And a single class proceeding is surely more efficient than thousands of separate proceedings for identical claims. Thus, if speedy resolution of disputes were all that mattered, then the *Discover Bank* rule would reinforce not obstruct, that objective of the Act.

The majority's related claim that the *Discover Bank* rule will discourage the use of arbitration because "[a]rbitration is poorly suited to . . . higher stakes" lacks empirical support. Indeed, the majority provides no convincing reason to believe that parties are unwilling to submit high-stake disputes to arbitration. And there are numerous counterexamples.

Further, even though contract defenses, *e.g.*, duress and unconscionability, slow down the dispute resolution process, federal arbitration law normally leaves such matters to the States. * * * California is free to define unconscionability as it sees fit, and its common law is of no federal concern so long as the State does not adopt a special rule that disfavors arbitration.

Because California applies the same legal principles to address the unconscionability of class arbitration waivers as it does to address the unconscionability of any other contractual provision, the merits of class proceedings should not factor into our decision. If California had applied its law of duress to void an arbitration agreement, would it matter if the procedures in the coerced agreement were efficient?

Regardless, the majority highlights the disadvantages of class arbitrations, as it sees them. But class proceedings have countervailing advantages. In general, agreements that forbid the consolidation of claims can lead small-dollar claimants to abandon their claims rather than to litigate. I suspect that it is true even here, for as the Court of Appeals recognized, AT&T can avoid the $7,500 payout (the payout that supposedly makes the Concepcions' arbitration worthwhile) simply by paying the claim's face value, such that "the maximum gain to a customer for the hassle of arbitrating a $30.22 dispute is still just $30.22."

What rational lawyer would have signed on to represent the Concepcions in litigation for the possibility of fees stemming from a $30.22 claim? In California's perfectly rational view, nonclass arbitration over such sums will also sometimes have the effect of depriving claimants of their claims (say, for example, where claiming the $30.22 were to involve filling out many forms that require technical legal knowledge or waiting at great length while a call is placed on hold). *Discover Bank* sets forth circumstances in which the California courts believe that the terms of consumer contracts can be manipulated to insulate an agreement's author from liability for its own frauds by "deliberately cheat[ing] large numbers of consumers out of individually small sums of money." Why is this kind of decision—weighing the pros and cons of all class proceedings alike—not California's to make?

Finally, the majority can find no meaningful support for its views in this Court's precedent. * * * But we have not, to my knowledge, applied the Act to strike down a state statute that treats arbitrations on par with judicial and administrative proceedings.

At the same time, we have repeatedly referred to the Act's basic objective as assuring that courts treat arbitration agreements "like all other contracts."

* * *

IV

By using the words "save upon such grounds as exist at law or in equity for the revocation of any contract," Congress retained for the States an important role incident to agreements to arbitrate. 9 U.S.C. § 2. * * * But federalism is as much a question of deeds as words. It often takes the form of a concrete decision by this Court that respects the legitimacy of a State's action in an individual case. Here, recognition of that federalist ideal, embodied in specific language in this particular statute, should lead us to uphold California's law, not to strike it down. We do not honor federalist principles in their breach.

With respect, I dissent.

NOTES AND QUESTIONS

1. Which opinion in *Concepcion* is more persuasive: the majority, concurrence, or dissent?

2. Following *Concepcion*, numerous members of Congress co-sponsored the Arbitration Fairness Act of 2011, H.R. 1873, 112th Cong. (2011); S. 987, 112th Cong. (2011), which was reintroduced in 2015, H.R. 2087, 114th Cong. (2015); S. 1133, 114th Cong. (2015). The proposed legislation would amend the FAA to make any pre-dispute arbitration agreement invalid or unenforceable if it requires arbitration of an employment, consumer, or civil rights dispute. What are the pros and cons of this proposal?

3. *Concepcion* followed several other Supreme Court cases involving class actions and arbitration. *See, e.g., Stolt-Nielsen S.A. v. AnimalFeeds Int'l Corp.*, 559 U.S. 662, 684–85 (2010) (holding that a party may not be compelled under the FAA to submit to class arbitration absent contractual evidence that the party had agreed to do so); *Green Tree Financial Corp. v. Bazzle*, 539 U.S. 444 (2003) (plurality concluded that arbitrator and not court should decide on whether contracts were silent on issue of class arbitration); *cf. Buckeye Check Cashing, Inc. v. Cardegna*, 546 U.S. 440 (2006) (holding that arbitrator, not state court, was to decide whether contract containing arbitration provision was illegal).

4. Class arbitration procedures are still available through organizations like the AAA, *see* AAA Supplementary Rules for Class Arbitrations (Oct. 8, 2003), https://www.adr.org/aaa/ShowPDF?url=/cs/groups/commercial/documents/document/dgdf/mda0/~edisp/adrstg_004129.pdf (last visited Feb. 6, 2017), but it remains to be seen whether these procedures will be used with any frequency in light of *Concepcion*. In what contexts might class arbitrations still arise?

5. In *American Express Co. v. Italian Colors Restaurant*, 133 S. Ct. 2304 (2013), set out below, the Supreme Court addressed whether a class action waiver provision in a mandatory arbitration agreement was unenforceable where it would render the plaintiff unable to vindicate federal antitrust rights.

AM. EXPRESS CO. V. ITALIAN COLORS REST.
Supreme Court of the United States, 2013.
133 S. Ct. 2304.

JUSTICE SCALIA delivered the opinion of the Court.

* * *

I

Respondents are merchants who accept American Express cards. Their agreement with petitioners—American Express and a wholly owned subsidiary—contains a clause that requires all disputes between the parties to be resolved by arbitration. The agreement also provides that "[t]here shall be no right or authority for any Claims to be arbitrated on a class action basis."

Respondents brought a class action against petitioners for violations of the federal antitrust laws. According to respondents, American Express used its monopoly power in the market for charge cards to force merchants to accept credit cards at rates approximately 30% higher than the fees for competing credit cards. This tying arrangement, respondents said, violated § 1 of the Sherman Act. They sought treble damages for the class under § 4 of the Clayton Act.

Petitioners moved to compel individual arbitration under the Federal Arbitration Act (FAA), 9 U.S.C. § 1 *et seq.* In resisting the motion, respondents submitted a declaration from an economist who estimated that the cost of an expert analysis necessary to prove the antitrust claims would be "at least several hundred thousand dollars, and might exceed $1 million," while the maximum recovery for an individual plaintiff would be $12,850, or $38,549 when trebled. The District Court granted the motion and dismissed the lawsuits. The Court of Appeals reversed and remanded for further proceedings. It held that because respondents had established that "they would incur prohibitive costs if compelled to arbitrate under the class action waiver," the waiver was unenforceable and the arbitration could not proceed.

We granted certiorari, vacated the judgment, and remanded for further consideration in light of *Stolt–Nielsen S.A. v. AnimalFeeds Int'l Corp.*, 559 U.S. 662 (2010), which held that a party may not be compelled to submit to class arbitration absent an agreement to do so. The Court of Appeals stood by its reversal, stating that its earlier ruling did not compel class arbitration. It then *sua sponte* reconsidered its ruling in light of *AT&T Mobility LLC v. Concepcion,* 131 S. Ct. 1740 (2011), which held that the FAA pre-empted a state law barring enforcement of a class-arbitration waiver. Finding *AT&T Mobility* inapplicable because it addressed pre-emption, the Court of Appeals reversed for the third time. It then denied rehearing en banc with five judges dissenting. We granted certiorari to consider the question "[w]hether the Federal Arbitration Act permits courts . . . to invalidate arbitration agreements on the ground that they do not permit class arbitration of a federal-law claim[.]"

II

* * *

Th[e] text [of the FAA] reflects the overarching principle that arbitration is a matter of contract. And consistent with that text, courts must "rigorously enforce" arbitration agreements according to their terms, including terms that "specify *with whom* [the parties] choose to arbitrate their disputes," *Stolt–Nielsen, supra*, at 683, and "the rules under which that arbitration will be conducted," *Volt Information Sciences, Inc. v. Board of Trustees of Leland Stanford Junior Univ.*, 489 U.S. 468, 479 (1989). That holds true for claims that allege a violation of a federal statute, unless the FAA's mandate has been "'overridden by a contrary congressional command.'" *CompuCredit Corp. v. Greenwood*, 132 S. Ct. 665, 668–69 (2012).

III

No contrary congressional command requires us to reject the waiver of class arbitration here. Respondents argue that requiring them to litigate their claims individually—as they contracted to do—would contravene the policies of the antitrust laws. But the antitrust laws do not guarantee an affordable procedural path to the vindication of every claim. Congress has taken some measures to facilitate the litigation of antitrust claims—for example, it enacted a multiplied-damages remedy. *See* 15 U.S.C. § 15 (treble damages). In enacting such measures, Congress has told us that it is willing to go, in certain respects, beyond the normal limits of law in advancing its goals of deterring and remedying unlawful trade practice. But to say that Congress must have intended whatever departures from those normal limits advance antitrust goals is simply irrational. * * *

The antitrust laws do not "evinc[e] an intention to preclude a waiver" of class-action procedure. The Sherman and Clayton Acts make no mention of class actions. In fact, they were enacted decades before the advent of Federal Rule of Civil Procedure 23, which was "designed to allow an exception to the usual rule that litigation is conducted by and on behalf of the individual named parties only." The parties here agreed to arbitrate pursuant to that "usual rule," and it would be remarkable for a court to erase that expectation.

Nor does congressional approval of Rule 23 establish an entitlement to class proceedings for the vindication of statutory rights. To begin with, it is likely that such an entitlement, invalidating private arbitration agreements denying class adjudication, would be an "abridg[ment]" or "modif[ication]" of a "substantive right" forbidden to the Rules, *see* 28 U.S.C. § 2072(b). But there is no evidence of such an entitlement in any event. The Rule imposes stringent requirements for certification that in practice exclude most claims. And we have specifically rejected the assertion that one of those requirements (the class-notice requirement) must be dispensed with because the "prohibitively high cost" of compliance would "frustrate [plaintiff's] attempt to vindicate the policies underlying the antitrust" laws. *Eisen v. Carlisle & Jacquelin,* 417 U.S. 156, 166–68, 175–76 (1974). One might respond, perhaps, that federal law secures a nonwaivable *opportunity* to vindicate federal policies by satisfying the procedural strictures of Rule 23 or invoking some other informal class mechanism in arbitration. But we have already rejected that proposition in *AT&T Mobility*.

IV

Our finding of no "contrary congressional command" does not end the case. Respondents invoke a judge-made exception to the FAA which, they say, serves to harmonize competing federal policies by allowing courts to invalidate agreements that prevent the "effective vindication" of a federal statutory right. Enforcing the waiver of class arbitration bars effective vindication, respondents contend, because they have no economic incentive to pursue their antitrust claims individually in arbitration.

The "effective vindication" exception to which respondents allude originated as dictum [in *Mitsubishi Motors Corp. v. Soler Chrysler–Plymouth, Inc.*, 473 U.S. 614 (1985),] where we expressed a willingness to invalidate, on "public policy" grounds, arbitration agreements that "operat[e] . . . as a prospective waiver of a party's *right to pursue* statutory remedies." Dismissing concerns that the arbitral forum was inadequate, we said that "so long as the prospective litigant effectively may vindicate its statutory cause of action in the arbitral forum, the statute will continue to serve both its remedial and deterrent function." Subsequent cases have similarly asserted the existence of an "effective vindication" exception, but have similarly declined to apply it to invalidate the arbitration agreement at issue.

And we do so again here. As we have described, the exception finds its origin in the desire to prevent "prospective waiver of a party's *right to pursue* statutory remedies." That would certainly cover a provision in an arbitration agreement forbidding the assertion of certain statutory rights. And it would perhaps cover filing and administrative fees attached to arbitration that are so high as to make access to the forum impracticable. But the fact that it is not worth the expense involved in *proving* a statutory remedy does not constitute the elimination of the *right to pursue* that remedy. The class-action waiver merely limits arbitration to the two contracting parties. It no more eliminates those parties' right to pursue their statutory remedy than did federal law before its adoption of the class action for legal relief in 1938. Or, to put it differently, the individual suit that was considered adequate to assure "effective vindication" of a federal right before adoption of class-action procedures did not suddenly become "ineffective vindication" upon their adoption.

* * *

The regime established by the Court of Appeals' decision would require—before a plaintiff can be held to contractually agreed bilateral arbitration—that a federal court determine (and the parties litigate) the legal requirements for success on the merits claim-by-claim and theory-by-theory, the evidence necessary to meet those requirements, the cost of developing that evidence, and the damages that would be recovered in the event of success. Such a preliminary litigating hurdle would undoubtedly destroy the prospect of speedy resolution that arbitration in general and bilateral arbitration in particular was meant to secure. The FAA does not sanction such a judicially created superstructure.

The judgment of the Court of Appeals is reversed.

[Concurring opinion by JUSTICE THOMAS omitted. JUSTICE SOTOMAYOR took no part in the consideration or determination of the case.]

JUSTICE KAGAN, with whom JUSTICE GINSBURG and JUSTICE BREYER join, dissenting.

Here is the nutshell version of this case, unfortunately obscured in the Court's decision. The owner of a small restaurant (Italian Colors) thinks that American Express (Amex) has used its monopoly power to force merchants to accept a form contract violating the antitrust laws. The restaurateur wants to challenge the allegedly unlawful provision (imposing a tying arrangement), but the same contract's arbitration clause prevents him from doing so. That term imposes a variety of procedural bars that would make pursuit of the antitrust claim a fool's errand. So if the arbitration clause is enforceable, Amex has insulated itself from antitrust liability—even if it has in fact violated the law. The monopolist gets to use its monopoly power to insist on a contract effectively depriving its victims of all legal recourse.

And here is the nutshell version of today's opinion, admirably flaunted rather than camouflaged: Too darn bad. * * *

* * *

I

Start with an uncontroversial proposition: We would refuse to enforce an exculpatory clause insulating a company from antitrust liability—say, "Merchants may bring no Sherman Act claims"—even if that clause were contained in an arbitration agreement. Congress created the Sherman Act's private cause of action not solely to compensate individuals, but to promote "the public interest in vigilant enforcement of the antitrust laws." *Lawlor v. National Screen Service Corp.,* 349 U.S. 322, 329 (1955). Accordingly, courts will not enforce a prospective waiver of the right to gain redress for an antitrust injury, whether in an arbitration agreement or any other contract. *See Mitsubishi Motors Corp.* The same rule applies to other important federal statutory rights. But its necessity is nowhere more evident than in the antitrust context. Without the rule, a company could use its monopoly power to protect its monopoly power, by coercing agreement to contractual terms eliminating its antitrust liability.

If the rule were limited to baldly exculpatory provisions, however, a monopolist could devise numerous ways around it. Consider several alternatives that a party drafting an arbitration agreement could adopt to avoid antitrust liability, each of which would have the identical effect. On the front end: The agreement might set outlandish filing fees or establish an absurd (*e.g.*, one-day) statute of limitations, thus preventing a claimant from gaining access to the arbitral forum. On the back end: The agreement might remove the arbitrator's authority to grant meaningful relief, so that a judgment gets the claimant nothing worthwhile. And in the middle: The agreement might block the claimant from presenting the kind of proof that is necessary to establish the defendant's liability—say, by prohibiting any economic testimony (good luck proving an antitrust claim without that!). Or else the agreement might appoint as an arbitrator an obviously biased person—say, the CEO of Amex. The possibilities are endless—all less direct than an express exculpatory clause, but no less fatal. So the rule against prospective waivers of federal rights can work only if it applies not just to a contract clause explicitly barring a claim, but to others that operate to do so.

And sure enough, our cases establish this proposition: An arbitration clause will not be enforced if it prevents the effective vindication of federal statutory rights, however it achieves that result. The rule originated in *Mitsubishi,* where we held that claims brought under the Sherman Act and other federal laws are generally subject to arbitration. By agreeing to arbitrate such a claim, we explained, "a party does not forgo the substantive rights afforded by the statute; it only submits to their resolution in an arbitral, rather than a judicial, forum." But crucial to our decision was a limiting principle, designed to safeguard federal rights: An arbitration clause will be enforced only "so long as the prospective litigant effectively may vindicate its statutory cause of action in the arbitral forum." If an arbitration provision "operated . . . as a prospective waiver of a party's right to pursue statutory remedies," we emphasized, we would "condemn[]" it. Similarly, we stated that such a clause should be "set [] aside" if "proceedings in the contractual forum will be so gravely difficult" that the claimant "will for all practical purposes be deprived of his day in court." And in the decades since *Mitsubishi,* we have repeated its admonition time and again, instructing courts not to enforce an arbitration agreement that effectively (even if not explicitly) forecloses a plaintiff from remedying the violation of a federal statutory right.

Our decision in *Green Tree Financial Corp.–Ala. v. Randolph,* 531 U.S. 79 (2000), confirmed that this principle applies when an agreement thwarts federal law by making arbitration prohibitively expensive. The plaintiff there (seeking relief under the Truth in Lending Act) argued that an arbitration agreement was unenforceable because it "create[d] a risk" that she would have to "bear prohibitive arbitration costs" in the form of high filing and administrative fees. We rejected that contention, but not because we doubted that such fees could prevent the effective vindication of statutory rights. To the contrary, we invoked our rule from *Mitsubishi,* making clear that it applied to the case before us. Indeed, we added a burden of proof: "[W]here, as here," we held, a party asserting a federal right "seeks to invalidate an arbitration agreement on the ground that arbitration would be prohibitively expensive, that party bears the burden of showing the likelihood of incurring such costs." Randolph, we found, had failed to meet that burden: The evidence she offered was "too speculative." But even as we dismissed Randolph's suit, we reminded courts to protect against arbitration agreements that make federal claims too costly to bring.

Applied as our precedents direct, the effective-vindication rule furthers the purposes not just of laws like the Sherman Act, but of the FAA itself. That statute reflects a federal policy favoring actual arbitration—that is, arbitration as a streamlined "method of resolving disputes," not as a foolproof way of killing off valid claims. * * *

The [value of the rule] becomes all the more obvious given the limits we have placed on the rule, which ensure that it does not diminish arbitration's benefits. The rule comes into play only when an agreement "operate[s] . . . as a prospective waiver"—that is, forecloses (not diminishes) a plaintiff's opportunity to gain relief for a statutory violation. So, for example, *Randolph* assessed whether fees in arbitration would be "prohibitive" (not high, excessive, or extravagant). Moreover, the plaintiff must make that showing through concrete proof: "[S]peculative" risks, "unfounded assumptions," and "unsupported statements" will not suffice. With the inquiry that confined and the evidentiary requirements that high, courts have had no trouble assessing the matters the rule makes relevant. [Lower] courts have followed our edict that arbitration clauses must usually prevail, declining to enforce them in only rare cases. * * *

And this is just the kind of case the rule was meant to address. Italian Colors, as I have noted, alleges that Amex used its market power to impose a tying arrangement in violation of the Sherman Act. The antitrust laws, all parties agree, provide the restaurant with a cause of action and give it the chance to recover treble damages. Here, that would mean Italian Colors could take home up to $38,549. But a problem looms. As this case comes to us, the evidence shows that Italian Colors cannot prevail in arbitration without an economic analysis defining the relevant markets, establishing Amex's monopoly power, showing anticompetitive effects, and measuring damages. And that expert report would cost between several hundred thousand and one million dollars. So the expense involved in proving the claim in arbitration is ten times what Italian Colors could hope to gain, even in a best-case scenario. That counts as a "prohibitive" cost, in *Randolph*'s terminology, if anything does. No rational actor would bring a claim worth tens of thousands of dollars if doing so meant incurring costs in the hundreds of thousands.

An arbitration agreement could manage such a mismatch in many ways, but Amex's disdains them all. As the Court makes clear, the contract expressly prohibits class arbitration. But that is only part of the problem. The agreement also disallows any kind of joinder or consolidation of claims or parties. And more: Its confidentiality provision prevents Italian Colors from informally arranging with other merchants to produce a common expert report. And still more: The agreement precludes any shifting of costs to Amex, even if Italian Colors prevails. And beyond all that: Amex refused to enter into any stipulations that would obviate or mitigate the need for the economic analysis. In short, the agreement as applied in this case cuts off not just class arbitration, but any avenue for sharing, shifting, or shrinking necessary costs. Amex has put Italian Colors to this choice: Spend way, way, way more money than your claim is worth, or relinquish your Sherman Act rights.

So contra the majority, the court below got this case right. Italian Colors proved what the plaintiff in *Randolph* could not—that a standard-form agreement, taken as a whole, renders arbitration of a claim "prohibitively expensive." * * *

II

The majority is quite sure that the effective-vindication rule does not apply here, but has precious little to say about why. It starts by disparaging the rule as having "originated as dictum." But it does not rest on that swipe, and for good reason. As I have explained, the rule began as a core part of *Mitsubishi*: We held there that federal statutory claims are subject to arbitration "*so long as*" the claimant "effectively may vindicate its [rights] in the arbitral forum." * * *

The next paragraph of the Court's decision (the third of Part IV) is the key: It contains almost the whole of the majority's effort to explain why the effective-vindication rule does not stop Amex from compelling arbitration. The majority's first move is to describe *Mitsubishi* and *Randolph* as covering only discrete situations: The rule, the majority asserts, applies to arbitration agreements that eliminate the "right to pursue statutory remedies" by "forbidding the assertion" of the right (as addressed in *Mitsubishi*) or imposing filing and administrative fees "so high as to make access to the forum impracticable" (as addressed in *Randolph*). Those cases are not this case, the majority says: Here, the agreement's provisions went to the possibility of "*proving* a statutory remedy."

But the distinction the majority proffers, which excludes problems of proof, is one *Mitsubishi* and *Randolph* (and our decisions reaffirming them) foreclose. Those decisions establish what in some quarters is known as a principle: When an arbitration agreement prevents the effective vindication of federal rights, a party may go to court. That principle, by its nature, operates in diverse circumstances—not just the ones that happened to come before the Court. * * *

Nor can the majority escape the principle we have established by observing, as it does at one point, that Amex's agreement merely made arbitration "not worth the expense." That suggestion, after all, runs smack into *Randolph*, which likewise involved an allegation that arbitration, as specified in a contract, "would be prohibitively expensive." * * * The expense at issue in *Randolph* came from a filing fee combined with a per-diem payment for the arbitrator. But nothing about those particular costs is distinctive; and indeed, a rule confined to them would be weirdly idiosyncratic. * * *

That leaves the three last sentences in the majority's core paragraph. Here, the majority conjures a special reason to exclude "class-action waiver[s]" from the effective-vindication rule's compass. Rule 23, the majority notes, became law only in 1938—decades after the Sherman Act. The majority's conclusion: If federal law in the interim decades did not eliminate a plaintiff's rights under that Act, then neither does this agreement.

But that notion, first of all, rests on a false premise: that this case is only about a class-action waiver. It is not, and indeed could not sensibly be. The effective-vindication rule asks whether an arbitration agreement *as a whole* precludes a claimant from enforcing federal statutory rights. No single provision is properly viewed in isolation, because an agreement can close off one avenue to pursue a claim while leaving others open. In this case, for example, the agreement could have prohibited class arbitration without offending the effective-vindication rule *if* it had provided an alternative mechanism to share, shift, or reduce the necessary costs. The agreement's problem is that it bars not just class actions, but also all mechanisms—many existing long before the Sherman Act, if that matters—for joinder or consolidation of claims, informal coordination among individual claimants, or amelioration of arbitral expenses. * * *

In any event, the age of the relevant procedural mechanisms (whether class actions or any other) does not matter, because the effective-vindication rule asks about the world today, not the world as it might have looked when Congress passed a given statute. * * * [W]hat has stayed the same is this: Congress's intent that antitrust plaintiffs should be able to enforce their rights free of any prior waiver. The effective-vindication rule carries out that purpose by ensuring that any arbitration agreement operating as such a waiver is unenforceable. And that requires courts to determine in the here and now—rather than in ye olde glory days—whether an agreement's provisions foreclose even meritorious antitrust claims.

* * *

The Court today mistakes what this case is about. To a hammer, everything looks like a nail. And to a Court bent on diminishing the usefulness of Rule 23, everything looks like a class action, ready to be dismantled. So the Court does not consider that Amex's agreement bars not just class actions, but "other forms of cost-sharing . . . that could provide effective vindication." In short, the Court does not consider—and does not decide—Italian Colors's (and similarly situated litigants') actual argument about why the effective-vindication rule precludes this agreement's enforcement.

As a result, Amex's contract will succeed in depriving Italian Colors of any effective opportunity to challenge monopolistic conduct allegedly in violation of the Sherman Act. The FAA, the majority says, so requires. Do not be fooled. Only the Court so requires; the FAA was never meant to produce this outcome. * * * I respectfully dissent.

* * *

NOTES AND QUESTIONS

1. Under the majority's approach, what must a plaintiff show in order to establish that an arbitration provision prevents effective vindication of federal rights? How does the dissent's approach differ from the majority's?

2. In *DIRECTV, Inc. v. Imburgia*, 136 S. Ct. 463 (2015), the Supreme Court addressed a challenge to the refusal of California's state appellate courts to enforce an arbitration clause with a class action waiver. The state intermediate court had refused to require enforcement of the clause in the context of two class actions filed in state court, and the California Supreme Court denied review. The intermediate court found that the issue was governed entirely by state law, and thus it did not address preemption under the FAA. Under the arbitration agreement at issue, the clause was unenforceable if the "law of your state" made the waiver of class arbitration unenforceable. *Id.* at 466.

In an opinion by Justice Breyer, the U.S. Supreme Court reversed. According to the Court, the kind of clause at issue was held to be unenforceable in a 2005 California Supreme Court decision, but that decision was no longer good law in light of *Concepcion*. Justice Breyer's opinion emphasized that *Concepcion* was binding on all courts even though "it was a closely divided case, resulting in a decision from which four Justices dissented." *Id.* at 468. In her dissent, Justice Ginsburg opined that the phrase "law of your state" could reasonably be read *not* to include the preemptive effect of federal law and thus DIRECTV was bound by the terms of its contract—which gave consumers a defense for state law rendering the clause unenforceable. *Id.* at 473-75. She noted that *Concepcion* and its progeny (including DIRECTV) had "resulted in the deprivation of consumers' rights to seek redress for losses, and, turning the coin, . . . insulated powerful economic interests from liability for violations of consumer-protection laws." *Id.* at 477. Justice Ginsburg's dissent attracted only one other vote (Justice Sotomayor). Is it surprising that Justices Breyer and Kagan joined the majority in *DIRECTV*?

3. Notwithstanding *Concepcion*, *American Express*, and *DIRECTV*, some circuits have refused to enforce arbitration clauses and class action bans in the labor context, relying on the National Labor Relations Act (NLRA), 29 U.S.C. § 157. *See, e.g., Lewis v. Epic Systems Corp.* 823 F.3d. 1147 (7th Cir. 2016). Other circuits, however, have found *Concepcion* controlling despite the NLRA. *See, e.g., D.R. Horton, Inc. v. NLRB*, 737 F.3d 344 (5th Cir. (2013). The Supreme Court has granted certiorari to resolve this conflict. *Epic Systems Corp. v. Lewis*, 2017 WL 125664 (U.S. Jan. 13, 2017) (No. 16-285); *Morris v. Ernst & Young, LLP*, 834 F.3d 975 (9th Cir. 2016), *cert. granted*, 2017 WL 125665 (U.S. Jan. 13, 2017) (No. 16-300).

4. Numerous commentators have expressed concern that the Supreme Court's arbitration opinions will decimate the class action device, as companies increasingly rely on class action waivers in a host of circumstances. One of the most pessimistic scholars is Professor Brian Fitzpatrick. *See* Brian T. Fitzpatrick, *The End of Class Actions?*, 57 Ariz. L. Rev. 161, 163 (2015). *See also, e.g.*, Einer Elhauge, *How* Italian Colors *Guts Private Antitrust Enforcement by Replacing It with Ineffective Forms of Arbitration*, 38 Fordham Int'l L.J. 771, 775 (2015). Are these concerns justified?

CHAPTER 9

APPELLATE REVIEW

■ ■ ■

This chapter addresses three topics: interlocutory review of class certification decisions; review of class action issues on appeal from a final judgment; and standards of review.

A. INTERLOCUTORY APPELLATE REVIEW OF CLASS CERTIFICATION DECISIONS

1. BACKGROUND TO RULE 23(f)

Rule 23(f) provides that "[a] court of appeals may permit an appeal from an order granting or denying class-action certification under this rule if a petition for permission to appeal is filed with the circuit clerk within 14 days after the order is entered. An appeal does not stay proceedings in the district court unless the district judge or the court of appeals so orders."

Rule 23(f) was a sea change for class action practice. Before its adoption, appellate courts provided only sporadic guidance about Rule 23. The reason is plain: litigants who lost the class certification ruling rarely had the resources or will to proceed to final judgment in order to appeal that crucial decision. As a result of Rule 23(f), the federal appellate courts have issued hundreds of opinions involving Rule 23 certification.

This section provides background to Rule 23(f).

a. Introduction

After modern Rule 23 was adopted in 1966, challenging issues arose when parties sought interlocutory review of decisions relating to class certification. Litigants attempted to use a variety of mechanisms, including the judicially created (but now judicially discredited) "death knell" doctrine; the "collateral order" exception to 28 U.S.C. § 1291 articulated by the Supreme Court in *Cohen v. Beneficial Industrial Loan Corp.*, 337 U.S. 541 (1949); interlocutory review under 28 U.S.C. § 1291(a)(1) (permitting appeal of the granting or denial of an injunction); interlocutory review under 28 U.S.C. § 1292(b) (permitting appeal of an issue certified by the district court for immediate appeal); and mandamus.

Rule 23(f), which is discussed in detail below, permits appellate courts to grant discretionary review of decisions granting or denying class certification, even if the district court has not certified the ruling for interlocutory review under 28 U.S.C. § 1292(b).

Rule 23(f) applies, however, only to decisions granting or denying class certification, not to other issues that may arise in a class action, such as notice, discovery, or trial structure. Although Rule 23(f) has simplified the appellate calculus, at least as to class certification, it is useful background to understand the various ways—apart from Rule 23(f)—in which litigants have sought to gain immediate review of decisions relating to class actions.

b. The "Death Knell" Doctrine and "*Cohen*" Review

To be appealable as a matter of right under 28 U.S.C. § 1291, a district court's decision must be final and effectively end the litigation on the merits. To obtain appellate review under § 1291 of a district court's class certification decision, litigants argued that the denial of class certification signaled the "death knell" of the action, effectively ending the litigation. Litigants also argued that the "collateral order" exception to the final judgment rule, which the Supreme Court had articulated in *Cohen v. Beneficial Industrial Loan Corp.*, 337 U.S. 541 (1949), permitted appeals from class certification decisions. Under *Cohen*, appealable collateral orders include decisions that:

> finally determine claims of right separable from, and collateral to, rights asserted in the action, too important to be denied review and too independent of the cause itself to require that appellate consideration be deferred until the whole case is adjudicated.

337 U.S. at 546.

In *Coopers & Lybrand v. Livesay*, 437 U.S. 463 (1978), however, the Supreme Court made clear that the collateral order exception to the final judgment rule does not apply to an order ruling on class certification:

> First, such an order is subject to revision in the District Court. Second, the class determination generally involves considerations that are "enmeshed in the factual and legal issues comprising the plaintiff's cause of action." Finally, an order denying class certification is subject to effective review after final judgment at the behest of the named plaintiff or intervening class members. For these reasons, as the Courts of Appeals have consistently recognized, the collateral-order doctrine is not applicable to the [class decertification] order involved in this case.

437 U.S. at 469.

The Supreme Court in *Coopers & Lybrand* also put to rest the "death knell" doctrine as a ground for appeal from rulings on class certification:

> * * * Under the "death knell" doctrine, appealability turns on the court's perception of that impact in the individual case. Thus, if the court believes that the plaintiff has adequate incentive to continue, the order is considered interlocutory; but if the court concludes that the ruling, as a practical matter, makes further litigation improbable, it is considered an appealable final decision.
>
> * * *
>
> Perhaps the principal vice of the "death knell" doctrine is that it authorizes *indiscriminate* interlocutory review of decisions made by the trial judge. * * *
>
> Additional considerations reinforce our conclusion that the "death knell" doctrine does not support appellate jurisdiction of prejudgment orders denying class certification. First, the doctrine operates only in favor of plaintiffs even though the class issue—

whether to certify, and if so, how large the class should be—will often be of critical importance to defendants as well. Certification of a large class may so increase the defendant's potential damages liability and litigation costs that he may find it economically prudent to settle and to abandon a meritorious defense. Yet the Courts of Appeals have correctly concluded that orders granting class certification are interlocutory. * * * Moreover, allowing appeals of right from nonfinal orders that turn on the facts of a particular case thrusts appellate courts indiscriminately into the trial process and thus defeats one vital purpose of the final-judgment rule—"that of maintaining the appropriate relationship between the respective courts. . . . This goal, in the absence of most compelling reasons to the contrary, is very much worth preserving."

437 U.S. at 470–71, 474–76.

c. Interlocutory Appeal Under 28 U.S.C. § 1292(a)(1)

Under 28 U.S.C. § 1292(a)(1), the courts of appeals have jurisdiction over appeals from "[i]nterlocutory orders of the district courts of the United States * * * granting, continuing, modifying, refusing or dissolving injunctions, or refusing to dissolve or modify injunctions, except where a direct review may be had in the Supreme Court * * *." In *Gardner v. Westinghouse Broad. Co.*, 437 U.S. 478 (1978), the plaintiff sought injunctive relief for herself and other females adversely affected by the defendant's alleged gender-based employment discrimination. The district court denied plaintiff's request for class certification, and she appealed under § 1292(a)(1), arguing that the denial of class certification was appealable because it effectively denied a substantial portion of the injunctive relief sought in the complaint. 437 U.S. at 478–79. The Third Circuit dismissed her appeal, and the Supreme Court affirmed, finding:

> * * * [Section 1292(a)(1)'s] * * * exception is a narrow one and is keyed to the "need to permit litigants to effectually challenge interlocutory orders of serious, perhaps irreparable, consequence."
>
> The order denying class certification in this case did not have any such "irreparable" effect. It could be reviewed both prior to and after final judgment; it did not affect the merits of petitioner's own claim; and it did not pass on the legal sufficiency of any claims for injunctive relief. * * *

437 U.S. at 480–81.

Notwithstanding *Gardner*'s cautionary language about the narrowness of review under 28 U.S.C. § 1292(a)(1), courts of appeals have occasionally applied the doctrine of "pendent appellate jurisdiction" to review, on an interlocutory basis, class certification decisions when a party has properly appealed other issues under § 1292(a)(1). *See, e.g., Paige v. California*, 102 F.3d 1035 (9th Cir. 1996).

d. Interlocutory Review Under 28 U.S.C. § 1292(b)

28 U.S.C. § 1292(b) states, in pertinent part:

When a district judge, in making in a civil action an order not otherwise appealable under this section, shall be of the opinion that such order involves a controlling question of law as to which there is substantial ground for difference of opinion and that an immediate appeal from the order may materially advance the ultimate termination of the litigation, he shall so state in writing in such order. The Court of Appeals which would have jurisdiction of an appeal of such action may thereupon, and in its discretion, permit an appeal to be taken from such order, if application is made to it within ten days after the entry of the order; *Provided, however,* That application for an appeal hereunder shall not stay proceedings in the district court unless the district judge or the Court of Appeals or a judge thereof shall so order.

Prior to the adoption of Rule 23(f) parties often asked district courts to certify—and courts of appeals to accept—decisions relating to class certification for interlocutory review under section 1292(b). On rare occasions, that tactic worked. For example, in *Castano v. American Tobacco Co.*, 162 F.R.D. 112 (E.D. La. 1995), the district court agreed to certify its class certification decision for interlocutory appeal under section 1292(b). *See id.* at 115–17. The district court's decision to certify its interlocutory ruling for review facilitated the Fifth Circuit's landmark tobacco ruling, *Castano v. American Tobacco Co.*, 84 F.3d 734 (5th Cir. 1996). On the whole, however, § 1292(b) was an unsatisfactory avenue for appellate review of a class certification decision, because the district court had to agree that such review was appropriate.

e. **Mandamus**

One of the most potent weapons in the arsenal of appellate courts is the power, under the All Writs Act, 28 U.S.C. § 1651, to issue a writ of mandamus. Under the mandamus power, the courts of appeals can take jurisdiction and intervene to prevent or correct fundamental injustices by a district court. Because appellate action of this sort is so drastic and intrusive, however, the Supreme Court has instructed that courts must use this power sparingly: "[o]nly exceptional circumstances amounting to a judicial 'usurpation of power' will justify the invocation of this extraordinary remedy." *Will v. United States*, 389 U.S. 90, 95 (1967).

Parties occasionally petitioned appellate courts to exercise this extraordinary power to intervene when district courts had granted or refused to grant class certification. Indeed, during the mid-1990s, courts of appeals occasionally granted writs of mandamus to review and reverse class certification decisions. *See, e.g., Jackson v. Motel 6 Multipurpose, Inc.*, 130 F.3d 999 (11th Cir. 1997); *In re Am. Med. Sys., Inc.*, 75 F.3d 1069 (6th Cir. 1996); *In re Rhone–Poulenc Rorer, Inc.*, 51 F.3d 1293 (7th Cir. 1995); *see* Chapter 6(B) & Chapter 10(A)(2)(c). But the use of such extraordinary powers of mandamus in the class certification context clearly troubled many judges and commentators. *See, e.g., Philip Morris Inc. v. Nat'l Asbestos Workers Med. Fund*, 214 F.3d 132 (2d Cir. 2000) (denying petition for writ of mandamus); *Armstrong v. Martin Marietta Corp.*, 138 F.3d 1374 (11th Cir. 1998) (same); *Demasi v. Weiss*, 669 F.2d 114 (3d Cir. 1982) (same). Rule

23(f), which would permit courts of appeals to review class certification decisions without undermining traditional principles of appellate review, was therefore widely viewed as a salutary development in the law.

2. RULE 23(f)

ADVISORY COMMITTEE NOTES TO 1998 AMENDMENT TO FEDERAL RULE OF CIVIL PROCEDURE 23

This permissive interlocutory appeal provision is adopted under the power conferred by 28 U.S.C. § 1292(e) [power of the Supreme Court to adopt rules providing for interlocutory appeals to the circuit courts]. Appeal from an order granting or denying class certification is permitted in the sole discretion of the court of appeals. No other type of Rule 23 order is covered by this provision. The court of appeals is given unfettered discretion whether to permit the appeal, akin to the discretion exercised by the Supreme Court in acting on a petition for *certiorari*. This discretion suggests an analogy to the provision in 28 U.S.C. § 1292(b) for permissive appeal on certification by a district court. Subdivision (f), however, departs from the § 1292(b) model in two significant ways. It does not require that the district court certify the certification ruling for appeal, although the district court often can assist the parties and court of appeals by offering advice on the desirability of appeal. And it does not include the potentially limiting requirements of § 1292(b) that the district court order "involve[] a controlling question of law as to which there is substantial ground for difference of opinion and that an immediate appeal from the order may materially advance the ultimate termination of the litigation."

The courts of appeals will develop standards for granting review that reflect the changing areas of uncertainty in class litigation. [A contemporaneous] Federal Judicial Center study support[ed] the view that many suits with class-action allegations present familiar and almost routine issues that are no more worthy of immediate appeal than many other interlocutory rulings. Yet several concerns justify expansion of present opportunities to appeal. An order denying certification may confront the plaintiff with a situation in which the only sure path to appellate review is by proceeding to final judgment on the merits of an individual claim that, standing alone, is far smaller than the costs of litigation. An order granting certification, on the other hand, may force a defendant to settle rather than incur the costs of defending a class action and run the risk of potentially ruinous liability. These concerns can be met at low cost by establishing in the court of appeals a discretionary power to grant interlocutory review in cases that show appeal-worthy certification issues.

Permission to appeal may be granted or denied on the basis of any consideration that the court of appeals finds persuasive. Permission is most likely to be granted when the certification decision turns on a novel or unsettled question of law, or when, as a practical matter, the decision on certification is likely dispositive of the litigation.

* * *

The 10-day [now 14-day] period for seeking permission to appeal is designed to reduce the risk that attempted appeals will disrupt continuing proceedings. It is expected that the courts of appeals will act quickly in making the preliminary determination whether to permit appeal. Permission to appeal does not stay trial court proceedings. A stay should be sought first from the trial court. If the trial court refuses a stay, its action and any explanation of its views should weigh heavily with the court of appeals.

Appellate Rule 5 [governing appeal by permission] has been modified to establish the procedure for petitioning for leave to appeal under subdivision (f).

CHAMBERLAN V. FORD MOTOR CO.
United States Court of Appeals, Ninth Circuit, 2005.
402 F.3d 952.

Before LEAVY, MCKEOWN, and BERZON, CIRCUIT JUDGES.

PER CURIAM.

Federal Rule of Civil Procedure 23(f) permits discretionary interlocutory appeal from a district court order denying or granting a class action certification. * * * We take this opportunity to identify for the first time the criteria we will consider in evaluating whether to permit an interlocutory appeal under Rule 23(f).

We begin with the premise that Rule 23(f) review should be a rare occurrence. We adopt the principles justifying review that are set out in the Advisory Committee Notes—the presence of a death knell situation for either party absent review and the presence of an unsettled and fundamental issue of law related to class actions—along with an additional criterion, manifest error in the district court's certification decision. Employing these guidelines in the present case, we conclude that the application for permission to appeal should be denied.

BACKGROUND

Plaintiffs Susan Chamberlan and Henry Fok ("Class Plaintiffs") filed a class action lawsuit in state court against Ford Motor Company ("Ford") and several John Does, alleging that Ford knowingly manufactured, sold, and distributed automobiles containing a defective engine part, in violation of the California Consumers Legal Remedies Act ("CLRA"), California Civil Code § 1750, *et seq.* [which makes illegal various specified "unfair methods of competition and unfair or deceptive acts or practices undertaken by any person in a transaction intended to result or which results in the sale or lease of goods or services to any consumer." Cal. Civ. Code § 1770(a)]. The action was removed to federal court and the district court certified a plaintiff class of Ford automobile owners.

The engine parts at issue are plastic intake manifolds that Ford used in some, but not all, of its automobiles. The manifold distributes air to the engine's cylinders, where the air mixes with fuel and ignites to power the engine. The manifold includes water crossover tubes that distribute coolant from one side of the engine to the other, and then to the radiator. Plastic manifolds, particularly the plastic water crossover component, are allegedly more likely to crack and cause coolant leaks than the aluminum intake manifolds Ford used in some of its cars.

* * *

After the case was removed to federal court, Class Plaintiffs moved for class certification. Ford opposed certification on the grounds that the facts pertaining to the causes of action differ depending on which vehicle the claimant owns, when that vehicle was produced, and what each individual buyer's expectations were regarding the durability of the intake manifold on the vehicle. Ford argued that these claimant-specific issues predominate over whatever common issues might exist. Ford also sought to defeat certification on the ground that certain potential defenses—such as the CLRA's three-year statute of limitations period—might apply only to some individuals within the proposed class. Finally, Ford argued that Class Plaintiffs had not shown how the class trial would be managed to account for these potential distinctions.

The district court granted the certification motion and certified a class consisting of:

> All consumers residing in California who currently own, or paid to repair or replace the plastic intake manifold in any of [certain specified cars and model years, and subject to certain exceptions].

* * *

Ford filed a timely petition asking this court to allow an immediate, interlocutory appeal from the district court's certification order under Rule 23(f). Ford challenges the rigor of the district court's analysis, particularly with respect to whether common issues predominate over individual ones. Ford additionally faults the district court for neglecting to address CLRA's elements and affirmative defenses and for failing to establish a trial plan. In its supplemental brief, Ford complains that the certification creates tremendous pressure to settle, even though it believes the district court order is manifestly incorrect and likely to be reversed or vacated.

DISCUSSION

* * *

When, as here, an appeal falls within the court of appeals' discretion, a party must file a petition for permission to appeal. Fed. R. App. P. 5(a)(1).

The Advisory Committee's Notes provide a good starting point for exploring the contours of Rule 23(f). The drafters intended the court of appeals to enjoy "unfettered discretion" to grant or deny permission to appeal based on "any consideration that the court of appeals finds persuasive." Fed. R. Civ. P. 23, Advisory Committee Notes to 1998 Amendments, Subdivision (f). The Committee contemplated that "[t]he courts of appeals will develop standards for granting review that reflect the changing areas of uncertainty in class litigation."

Despite the wide open grant of discretion, and the absence of any articulated standards in the rule itself, the drafters identified three situations in which an appeal under Rule 23(f) would most likely be appropriate. The first occurs when a denial of certification effectively ends the litigation for the plaintiff. A plaintiff who is denied certification might be left with only one path to appellate review: proceeding to a final judgment on the merits of an individual claim that, without the class, is worth far less than the cost of litigation. The second situation arises when a grant of certification may "force a defendant to settle rather than incur the costs of defending a class action and run the risk of potentially ruinous liability." In both situations, the certification "sounds the death knell of the litigation." *Blair v. Equifax Check Servs., Inc.*, 181 F.3d 832, 834 (7th Cir. 1999). The drafters identified as a third circumstance one in which the certification decision turns on a novel or unsettled question of law.

These criteria reflect the dual purposes of Rule 23(f), which the First Circuit aptly summarized. First, the rule provides a "mechanism through which appellate courts, in the interests of fairness, can restore equilibrium when a doubtful class certification ruling would virtually compel a party to abandon a potentially meritorious claim or defense before trial." *Waste Mgmt. Holdings, Inc. v. Mowbray*, 208 F.3d 288, 293 (1st Cir. 2000). And second, "the rule furnishes an avenue, if the need is sufficiently acute, whereby the court of appeals can take earlier-than-usual cognizance of important, unsettled legal questions, thus contributing to both the orderly progress of complex litigation and the orderly development of law."

Relying on the purposes of the rule and the guidance provided by the Advisory Committee's Notes, several of our sister circuits have examined the appropriate scope of Rule 23(f). In the first decision to thoroughly consider Rule 23(f), the Seventh Circuit articulated fundamental principles that have been echoed by other circuits. *Blair*, 181 F.3d at 834–35.

In *Blair*, the Seventh Circuit rejected the adoption of a bright-line rule for granting review and instead identified three general categories of cases in which appellate review under Rule 23(f) would be appropriate. These categories essentially mirror the three situations identified in the Committee Notes. First are those cases where "denial of class status sounds the death knell of the litigation, because the representative plaintiff's claim is too small to justify the expense of litigation." Second are cases where a grant of certification sounds the death knell of the litigation for the defendant because the grant "can put considerable pressure on the defendant to settle" independent of the merits of the plaintiffs' claims. Third are cases in which an interlocutory appeal "may facilitate the development of the law" of class actions because such actions often settle or are resolved without clear resolution of procedural matters. Although some circuits have elaborated on the three categories listed in *Blair*, each of the circuits that has considered Rule 23(f) agrees that *Blair* identifies the core situations when interlocutory review is most appropriate. *See, e.g., In re Delta Air Lines*, 310 F.3d 953, 960 (6th Cir. 2002); *In re Lorazepam & Chlorazepate Antitrust Litig.*, 289 F.3d 98, 105 (D.C. Cir. 2002); *Newton v. Merrill Lynch, Pierce, Fenner & Smith*, 259 F.3d 154, 165 (3d Cir. 2001); *Sumitomo Copper Litig. v. Credit Lyonnais Rouse, Ltd.*, 262 F.3d 134, 139 (2d Cir. 2001); *Lienhart v. Dryvit Sys., Inc.*, 255 F.3d 138, 145–46 (4th Cir. 2001); *Prado-Steiman ex rel. Prado v. Bush*, 221 F.3d 1266, 1273 (11th Cir. 2000); *Mowbray*, 208 F.3d at 293.

The most notable modification of the *Blair* trilogy has been the development of a fourth category of cases in which review is warranted: when the district court's decision is manifestly erroneous. The Eleventh Circuit initiated the evolution of the manifest error factor by noting that when the certification decision is obviously wrong, Rule 23(f) review "may be warranted even if none of the other factors supports granting the Rule 23(f) petition." *Prado–Steiman*, 221 F.3d at 1275. Other circuits have subsequently announced that interlocutory review of a certification decision is appropriate based solely on a manifest error. *In re Lorazepam*, 289 F.3d at 105; *Newton*, 259 F.3d at 164; *Lienhart*, 255 F.3d at 145.

Some circuits also have modified the third *Blair* category—unsettled questions of law—in order to limit the filing of meritless Rule 23(f) petitions. The First Circuit was concerned that the unsettled law situation would foster too many fruitless Rule 23(f) applications because "a creative lawyer almost always will be able to argue that deciding her case would clarify some 'fundamental' issue." *Mowbray*, 208 F.3d at 294. To limit review of cases in which a novel legal issue is claimed, *Mowbray* restricted review to issues that are both important to particular litigation and likely to escape effective review after the conclusion of the trial. Other circuits have followed suit by confining the third category to novel legal questions that are important to class action law and likely to evade effective review after the completion of the case.

The Committee Notes provide the essential guidelines for determining when interlocutory appellate review is appropriate under Rule 23(f). Although Rule 23(f) expands opportunities to appeal certification decisions, the drafters intended interlocutory appeal to be the exception rather than the rule. "The note reflects, on balance, a reluctance to depart from the traditional procedure in which claimed errors" are reviewed only after a final judgment. Interlocutory appeals are generally disfavored because they are "disruptive, time-consuming, and expensive." These appeals add to the heavy work-load of the appellate courts, require consideration of issues that may become moot, and undermine the district court's ability to manage the class action.

Like other circuits that have considered the issue, we are of the view that petitions for Rule 23(f) review should be granted sparingly. We nonetheless recognize that there are rare cases in which interlocutory review is preferable to end-of-the-case review.

Bearing in mind that many class certification decisions "present familiar and almost routine issues that are no more worthy of immediate appeal than many other interlocutory rulings," Fed. R. Civ. P. 23(f), Advisory Committee Notes to 1998 Amendments, we adopt the following guidelines for consideration of Rule 23(f) petitions. Review of class certification decisions will be most appropriate when: (1) there is a death-knell situation for either the plaintiff or defendant that is independent of the merits of the underlying claims, coupled with a class certification decision by the district court that is questionable; (2) the certification decision presents an unsettled and fundamental issue of law relating to class actions, important to both the specific litigation and generally, that is likely to evade end-of-the-case review; or (3) the district court's class certification decision is manifestly erroneous. * * *

Unlike the courts in *Mowbray* and *Blair*, we view interlocutory review as warranted when the district court's decision is manifestly erroneous—even absent a showing of another factor. We see no reason for a party to endure the costs of litigation when a certification is erroneous and inevitably will be overturned. The error in the district court's decision must be significant; bare assertions of error will not suffice. Any error must be truly "manifest," meaning easily ascertainable from the petition itself. If it is not, then consideration of the petition will devolve into a time consuming consideration of the merits, and that delay could detract from planning for the trial in the district court.

The kind of error most likely to warrant interlocutory review will be one of law, as opposed to an incorrect application of law to facts. A manifest error of law will be more obvious and susceptible to review at an early stage than an error that must be evaluated based on a well developed factual record.

The parties have urged us to adopt a "sliding scale" approach to reviewing Rule 23(f) petitions, in which a particularly weak district court decision would reduce the showing required for other factors. We decline to adopt such an approach. Instead we simply set forth factors for consideration and do not circumscribe the court's evaluation of the strength of showing required for any individual factor.

The three categories we outline do not constitute an exhaustive list of factors and are not intended to circumscribe the broad discretion granted the courts of appeal by Rule 23(f). These factors are merely guidelines, not a rigid test. When considering whether to allow interlocutory appeals, we will avoid "both micromanagement of complex class actions as they evolve in the district court and inhibition of the district court's willingness to revise the class certification for fear of triggering another round of appellate review." We underscore that the decision to permit interlocutory appeal is, at bottom, a discretionary one. We acknowledge the possibility that a petition that does not fit within any of the foregoing situations may be worthy of interlocutory appeal. Ordinarily, however, a case warranting review pursuant to Rule 23(f) must come within one or more of the specified categories.

* * *

[Applying the standards just articulated, the court denied Ford's petition for interlocutory review. Among other things, the court rejected Ford's death knell argument, because Ford failed to submit any evidence supporting its conclusory claims that the alleged damages would force it to settle without regard to the merits of the case. Nor was the court persuaded by Ford's argument that its petition raised an issue of unsettled law within the Ninth Circuit. Ford argued that Ninth Circuit cases were in conflict with respect to the depth with which a trial court must analyze the issues before certifying a class. The Ninth Circuit rejected Ford's contention that a split existed within the circuit, concluding that the degree of analysis required in each case is fact-specific—in some cases the issues will be plain, while in others the trial court may need to undertake a more detailed analysis.]

NOTES AND QUESTIONS

1. After the adoption of Rule 23(f), what role, if any, should pendent appellate jurisdiction under 28 U.S.C. § 1292(a)(1), review under 28 U.S.C.

§ 1292(b), or mandamus review play with respect to class certification decisions?

2. As described in *Chamberlan*, how do the various courts of appeals differ in their articulation of the Rule 23(f) standards? What standards should be utilized? Does the *Chamberlan* court strike the right balance?

3. Does Rule 23(f) lead to additional litigation delay and cost? What steps can appellate courts—and district courts—take in order to minimize any additional burdens?

4. How does the increased availability of an appeal from the denial of class certification affect the *American Pipe* doctrine (*see* Chapter 7(A)) regarding the tolling of statutes of limitations for absent class members? As noted in Chapter 7(A), in *Armstrong v. Martin Marietta Corp.*, 138 F.3d 1374 (11th Cir. 1998), a divided en banc court held that the tolling of statutes of limitations under *American Pipe* ended when class certification was denied. The majority's reasoning was based, in part, on the fact that appeals from orders denying class certification were "relatively uncommon and * * * very rarely successful." *Id.* at 1389. In response to the *Armstrong* dissent's concern that (then-proposed) Rule 23(f) might change that calculus, the *Armstrong* majority responded:

> If the rule passes, and if it significantly increases the frequency of interlocutory appeals of class certification orders—a development which would depend in large part upon how this court chooses to exercise the discretion granted to it by the proposed rule—then we may revisit the decision taken today, and might for instance allow continued tolling of statutes of limitations during the pendency of an appeal under the new rule. We decline, however, to speculate regarding how we might exercise our discretion under the proposed rule and to decide the instant case in reliance upon an as-yet un-enacted rule.

Id. at 1390 n.35. Now that Rule 23(f) has been adopted, should the Eleventh Circuit reconsider its ruling in *Armstrong*? Should tolling of the statutes of limitations for absent class members' claims extend at least through the pendency of any appeal under Rule 23(f)? *See Nat'l Asbestos Workers Med. Fund v. Philip Morris, Inc.*, 2000 WL 1424931 (E.D.N.Y. 2000) (staying proceedings and tolling statute of limitations pending appeal under Rule 23(f)).

5. Rule 23(f) provides that a petition for review of a grant or denial of class certification must be filed with the court of appeals within 14 days "after the order is entered." In *Blair v. Equifax Check Services, Inc.*, 181 F.3d 832 (7th Cir. 1999), the Seventh Circuit determined that the filing of a motion for reconsideration with the district court within the specific period tolled the period until the district court ruled on that motion. *Id.* at 837. In *Shin v. Cobb County Board of Education*, 248 F.3d 1061 (11th Cir. 2001), the Eleventh Circuit agreed. With respect to reconsideration, the Eleventh Circuit found that a rule tolling the petition period was particularly suited to class action litigation: "Because the district court retains the ability, and perhaps even a duty, to alter or amend a certification decision, a motion for reconsideration is a better way to correct any errors in the certification order or to recognize the importance of new facts." *Id.* at 1064. (Both the *Blair* and *Shin* opinions had also addressed whether the petitioning period included weekends or holidays, but those rulings were obviated by amendments to the Federal Rules of Civil Procedure in 2009, under which weekend days *do* count.)

Courts have issued rulings policing the outer boundaries of the Rule 23(f) petitioning period. In *Gutierrez v. Johnson & Johnson*, 523 F.3d 187 (3d Cir. 2008) (decided back when the petitioning period was ten days), the Third Circuit held that even though the district court had granted the plaintiff class an extension on filing a motion for reconsideration, the resulting motion was not "timely and proper" so as to toll the statutory period. The *Gutierrez* court concluded that, "regardless of any conflicting local rules, a motion to reconsider a class certification decision that is filed more than ten days [now 14 days] after the order granting or denying class certification is 'untimely' with respect to Rule 23(f)." *Id.* at 193.

Similarly, the Eleventh Circuit addressed another circumstance in which a potential appellant sought to enlist the district court in an attempt to toll the petitioning period. In *Jenkins v. BellSouth Corp.*, 491 F.3d 1288 (11th Cir. 2007), the Eleventh Circuit held that, unlike in the context of interlocutory appeals, *see* 28 U.S.C. § 1292(b), "the district court was without the authority to circumvent the * * * deadline for obtaining interlocutory review of its order denying class certification by vacating and reentering that order after the original deadline for seeking interlocutory relief under Rule 23(f) had expired." *Id.* at 1292.

In *Gutierrez* and *Jenkins*, the courts were concerned with limiting the district court's ability to evade the filing deadline in Rule 23(f). What advantages or disadvantages flow from strict construction of the window for potential appeal?

6. In *Tilley v. TJX Companies, Inc.*, 345 F.3d 34 (1st Cir. 2003), the First Circuit addressed the Rule 23(f) criteria for a defendant class action. *See* Chapter 11(A) (discussing defendant class actions). The court held that Rule 23(f) review is warranted in defendant class actions "when one of three circumstances exists: (i) denial of certification effectively disposes of the litigation because the plaintiff's claim would only be worth pursuing as against a full class of defendants; or (ii) an interlocutory appeal would clarify an important and unsettled legal issue that would likely escape effective end-of-case review; or (iii) an interlocutory appeal is a desirable vehicle either for addressing special circumstances or avoiding manifest injustice." *Id.* at 39. What differences, if any, arise under Rule 23(f) when a proposed class is comprised of defendants instead of plaintiffs?

7. In *In re National Football League Players Concussion Injury Litigation*, 775 F.3d 570 (3d Cir. 2014), the Third Circuit faced the question of whether appellate jurisdiction under Rule 23(f) extended to a district court's order that "preliminarily approved" a proposed class settlement and "conditionally certified" the class "for settlement purposes only." *Id.* at 571. A group of objectors sought immediate review under Rule 23(f), but the Third Circuit dismissed the appeal, concluding that "Rule 23(f) permits the court of appeals to review only an 'order granting or denying class certification' issued pursuant to Rule 23(c)(1)." *Id.* at 584 (quoting Rule 23(f)). By contrast, "[a]n order issued under some other subdivision of Rule 23, such as a case management order issued pursuant to Rule 23(e) that 'preliminarily' or 'conditionally' addresses class certification but reserves the class certification determination for a later time, does not qualify as an 'order granting or denying class-action certification' that is subject to interlocutory review under Rule 23(f)." *Id.* In short, the Third Circuit held, the objectors needed to wait until the district court definitively ruled on class certification and settlement fairness to seek appellate re-

view. A proposed rule change would make clear that Rule 23(f) does not authorize appeals from orders that preliminarily approve class certification pending a fairness hearing. Committee on Rules of Practice and Procedure of the Judicial Conference of the United States, *Preliminary Draft of Proposed Amendments to the Federal Rules of Appellate, Bankruptcy, Civil and Criminal Procedure* 217 (August 2016), http://www.uscourts.gov/rules-policies/proposed-amendments-published-public-comment.

8. In *Baldridge v. SBC Communications, Inc.*, 404 F.3d 930 (5th Cir. 2005), the Fifth Circuit addressed the applicability of Rule 23(f) to a collective action brought under § 216(b) of the Fair Labor Standards Act (FLSA). One of the primary distinctions between a § 216(b) collective action and a Rule 23 class action is that for the former, each absent class member must affirmatively opt into the class as a party plaintiff. *Id.* at 933 n.6; *see* Chapter 10(B)(2). The Fifth Circuit held that in FLSA collective actions, the final judgment rule of 28 U.S.C. § 1291 applied rather than Rule 23(f). *Baldridge*, 404 F.3d at 932–33.

9. Who benefits most from Rule 23(f)—plaintiffs or defendants? *See* Richard D. Freer, *Interlocutory Review of Class Action Certification Decisions: A Preliminary Empirical Study of Federal and State Experience*, 35 W. St. U. L. Rev. 13 (2007) (finding courts more likely to review orders certifying class actions than orders denying certification); Robert H. Klonoff, *The Decline of Class Actions*, 90 Wash U. L. Rev. 729, 741–42, 832–38 (2013) (concluding, based on statistical analysis of Rule 23(f) appeals from November 30, 1988, to May 31, 2012, that Rule 23(f) has primarily benefited defendants). Are these conclusions surprising?

B. APPEAL FROM FINAL JUDGMENT

Parties can, of course, appeal from final judgments involving class actions. Moreover, decisions relating to class certification merge into the final judgment for purposes of appeal. *Coopers & Lybrand v. Livesay*, 437 U.S. 463 (1978). Yet important issues regarding appealability still arise.

1. INTERVENTION FOR PURPOSES OF APPEAL

UNITED AIRLINES, INC. V. MCDONALD
Supreme Court of the United States, 1977.
432 U.S. 385.

JUSTICE STEWART delivered the opinion of the Court.

Fed. Rule Civ. Proc. 24 requires that an application to intervene in federal litigation must be "timely." In this case a motion to intervene was filed promptly after the final judgment of a District Court, for the purpose of appealing the court's earlier denial of class action certification. The question presented is whether this motion was "timely" under Rule 24.

Until November 7, 1968, United Airlines required its female stewardesses to remain unmarried as a condition of employment; no parallel restriction was imposed on any male employees, including male stewards and cabin flight attendants. This "no-marriage rule" resulted in the termination of the employment of a large number of stewardesses, and in turn spawned a good deal of litigation.

[An initial plaintiff, Mary Sprogis, brought administrative charges in 1966, then filed suit. When the district court found that United's no-marriage rule violated Title VII, United filed an interlocutory appeal, and the court of appeals affirmed. While the *Sprogis* appeal was pending, the present action was filed by Carole Romasanta, who brought the action as a class action "on behalf of herself and all other United stewardesses discharged because of the no-marriage rule." The district court later struck the class allegations in *Romasanta*, ruling that "the class could properly consist of only those stewardesses who, upon the loss of their employment because of marriage, had filed charges under either a fair employment statute or United's collective-bargaining agreement." As defined, the class did not satisfy numerosity. As part of that order, 12 more stewardesses were permitted to intervene in the action. The district court certified its order for interlocutory review, but the court of appeals declined to take the appeal. The action then proceeded in district court, and that court eventually ruled that the plaintiffs were entitled to a remedy. The parties agreed on remedial amounts, and the district court entered a judgment of dismissal on October 3, 1975.]

The specific controversy before us arose only after the entry of the *Romasanta* judgment. The respondent, a former United stewardess, had been discharged in 1968 on account of the no-marriage rule. She was thus a putative member of the class as defined in the original *Romasanta* complaint. Knowing that other stewardesses had challenged United's no-marriage rule, she had not filed charges with the EEOC or a grievance under the collective-bargaining agreement.

After learning that a final judgment had been entered in the *Romasanta* suit, and that despite their earlier attempt to do so the plaintiffs did not now intend to file an appeal challenging the District Court's denial of class certification, she filed a motion to intervene for the purpose of appealing the District Court's adverse class determination order. Her motion was filed 18 days after the District Court's final judgment, and thus was well within the 30-day period for an appeal to be taken. The District Judge denied the motion. * * *

The respondent promptly appealed the denial of intervention as well as the denial of class certification to the Court of Appeals for the Seventh Circuit. The appellate court reversed, holding that the District Court had been wrong in believing that the motion to intervene was untimely under Rule 24(b), and had also erred in refusing to certify the class as described in the *Romasanta* complaint—a class consisting of all United stewardesses discharged because of the no-marriage rule, whether or not they had formally protested the termination of their employment.

United's petition for *certiorari* did not seek review of the determination that its no-marriage rule violated Title VII, nor did it contest the merits of the Court of Appeals' decision on the class certification issue. Instead, it challenged only the Court of Appeals' ruling that the respondent's post-judgment application for intervention was timely. We granted the petition to consider that single issue.

In urging reversal, United relies primarily upon *American Pipe & Construction Co. v. Utah*, 414 U.S. 538 (1974). [*See* Chapter 7(A).] That case involved a private antitrust class action that had been filed 11 days short of the expiration of the statutory limitations period. The trial court later denied class certification because the purported class did not satisfy the numerosity requirement of Rule 23(a)(1). Neither the named plaintiffs nor any unnamed member of the class appealed that order, either then or at any later time. Eight days after entry of the order, a number of the putative class members moved to intervene as plaintiffs, but the trial court denied the motions as untimely. This Court ultimately reversed that decision, ruling that in those circumstances "the commencement of the original class suit tolls the running of the statute for all purported members of the class who make timely motions to intervene after the court has found the suit inappropriate for class action status." Since 11 days remained when the statute of limitations again began to run after denial of class certification, and the motions to intervene as plaintiffs were filed only eight days after that denial, they were timely.

It is United's position that, under *American Pipe*, the relevant statute of limitations began to run after the denial of class certification in the *Romasanta* action. United thus reasons that the respondent's motion to intervene was time barred, and in support of this position makes alternative arguments based on two different statutory periods of limitations prescribed by Title VII.

This argument might be persuasive if the respondent had sought to intervene in order to join the named plaintiffs in litigating her individual claim based on the illegality of United's no-marriage rule, for she then would have occupied the same position as the intervenors in *American Pipe*. But the later motion to intervene in this case was for a wholly different purpose. That purpose was to obtain appellate review of the District Court's order denying class action status in the *Romasanta* lawsuit, and the motion complied with, as it was required to, the time limitation for lodging an appeal prescribed by Fed.Rule App.Proc. 4(a). Success in that review would result in the certification of a class, the named members of which had complied with the statute of limitations; the respondent is a member of that class against whom the statute had not run at the time the class action was commenced.

The lawsuit had been commenced by the timely filing of a complaint for classwide relief, providing United with "the essential information necessary to determine both the subject matter and size of the prospective litigation. . . ." To be sure, the case was "stripped of its character as a class action" upon denial of certification by the District Court. But "it does not . . . follow that the case must be treated as if there never was an action brought on behalf of absent class members." The District Court's refusal to certify was subject to appellate review after final judgment at the behest of the named plaintiffs, as United concedes. And since the named plaintiffs had attempted to take an interlocutory appeal from the order of denial at the time the order was entered, there was no reason for the respondent to suppose that they would not later take an appeal until she was advised to the contrary after the trial court had entered its final judgment.

The critical fact here is that once the entry of final judgment made the adverse class determination appealable, the respondent quickly sought to enter the litigation. In short, as soon as it became clear to the respondent that the interests of the unnamed class members would no longer be protected by the named class representatives, she promptly moved to intervene to protect those interests.

United can hardly contend that its ability to litigate the issue was unfairly prejudiced simply because an appeal on behalf of putative class members was brought by one of their own, rather than by one of the original named plaintiffs. And it would be circular to argue that unnamed member of the putative class was not a proper party to appeal, on the ground that her interests had been adversely determined in the trial court. United was put on notice by the filing of the *Romasanta* complaint of the possibility of classwide liability, and there is no reason why Mrs. McDonald's pursuit of that claim should not be considered timely under the circumstances here presented.

* * *

The judgment is

Affirmed.

NOTES AND QUESTIONS

1. The *United Airlines* Court ruled that putative class members in a proposed class action that was denied certification can intervene for purposes of appealing the denial of certification. On what ground does the Court distinguish *American Pipe*? Is that distinction valid? What policy reasons support the Court's approach? In dissent, Justice Powell contended that "[c]onsiderations of policy militate strongly against the result reached by the Court." 432 U.S. at 400 (Powell, J., dissenting). He relied on two policy grounds that he felt the majority had undermined. First, he argued that the Court's ruling denigrated statutes of limitations, which serve important interests in promoting repose, stimulating timely activity, and protecting courts against having to adjudicate stale claims. Second, he argued that the Court's ruling ignored the important "principle that settlement agreements are highly favored in the law and will be upheld whenever possible because they are a means of amicably resolving doubts . . . and preventing lawsuits." *Id.* at 401. Justice Powell believed that the majority's ruling would deter settlements by injecting "additional uncertainty as to whether the agreements will be nullified by the action of persons who enter the litigation only after final judgment." *Id.* How would the majority respond? In light of Rule 23(f)'s adoption, should the rule in *United Airlines* be reconsidered?

2. When a case presents multiple claims or parties, a district court may enter judgment on fewer than all the claims or parties and certify such a judgment, under Fed. R. Civ. P. 54(b), as final for purposes of appeal. The Seventh Circuit in *In re Brand Name Prescription Drugs Antitrust Litigation*, 115 F.3d 456 (7th Cir. 1997), faced appeals by opt-outs and unnamed class members of partial summary judgment in favor of certain defendants in an antitrust action. Because the named plaintiffs did not appeal, however, the Seventh Circuit dismissed the opt-outs' and unnamed class members' appeals, reasoning as follows:

> Pending in the district court is an antitrust class action on behalf of pharmacies all over the United States against twenty-four manufacturers, and seven wholesalers, of pharmaceuticals. The class was certified under Fed. R. Civ. P. 23(b)(3). A number of class members

opted out of the class action and brought their own suits against the manufacturers, but did not name the wholesalers as defendants. The district judge granted summary judgment for the wholesaler defendants in the class action and entered a final, appealable judgment in their favor under Fed. R. Civ. P. 54(b), precipitating appeals by some of the opt-out plaintiffs and also by some of the class members who are not named plaintiffs in the class action. The wholesalers ask us to dismiss these appeals on the ground that the appellants, not being parties to the class action, have no right to appeal from a judgment entered in it.

We begin with the opt-outs. Having opted out of the class action, they were no longer members of the class and so in no sense were parties. A nonparty has no right to appeal. If he wants to have that right, he should intervene in the district court, since an intervenor has the rights of a party (*is* a party), including the right to appeal. If the district court denies the motion to intervene, the disappointed movant can appeal that denial.

Now it is true that the opt-outs were permitted to participate in the pretrial proceedings in the class action by attending depositions, responding to requests for discovery, and answering the wholesalers' motion for summary judgment. But their participation was authorized in a pretrial order that expressly denied that these participants were to be deemed parties; the purpose of allowing their participation was merely to facilitate the coordination of the opt-outs' parallel suits with the class action. * * * The opt-outs argue that the judgment in favor of the wholesalers will affect them even though they have not sued the wholesalers. It will not have a preclusive effect on them, because they are neither parties, nor in privity with any parties, to the class action. Maybe it will affect their interests enough in some other way to permit them to intervene in the class action—we cannot tell on the record before us. Although it would be peculiar for an opt-out to seek to opt back in, this is occasionally sought and allowed.

But a request for intervention must be addressed to the district court. Although some cases have allowed nonparties to appeal without first intervening in the district court, this bypass is no longer permissible after *Marino v. Ortiz*; 484 U.S. 301 (1988). The present case shows the wisdom of this approach. Here we have some 163 claimants who having exercised their right to exit from the case in the district court now wish to come charging back in on appeal. We would be facing a veritable avalanche of appeals if all opt-outs could appeal from any appealable judgment in the action.

So much for the opt-outs; as for the class members (some 90 in number) who want to appeal even though they are not named plaintiffs, to allow them to appeal would be an even worse affront to intelligent judicial administration because it would fragment the control of the class action. Such economies of litigation as the class action confers are due in large part to its enabling a large number of individual claims to be treated, at least for liability purposes, as if they were a single claim. If the certified class representative does not adequately represent the interests of some of the class members, those class members can opt out of the class action, can seek the creation of a separately represented subclass, can ask for the replacement of the class representative, or can intervene of right and become named plaintiffs themselves, or even class representatives, represented by their own lawyer. Any such adjustment is made by the district court, and the structure of the action remains clear. If class members can file their own appeals, the coherence of the class is destroyed, the scope of the class action becomes unclear, and the control over the action becomes divided and confused. So they may not appeal. * * * Class members who don't want to opt out or create a subclass can move to intervene (if they want, for the limited purpose of being able to appeal) and if their motion is denied they can appeal from that denial just like the opt-outs.

Id. at 457–58. What arguments can be made in favor of allowing appeal by the opt-outs? What about by the unnamed class members who had not intervened for purposes of appeal? What policy concerns were most critical to the Seventh Circuit in denying the attempted appeals?

2. APPEAL BY UNNAMED CLASS MEMBERS AFTER SETTLEMENT

DEVLIN V. SCARDELLETTI
Supreme Court of the United States, 2002.
536 U.S. 1.

JUSTICE O'CONNOR delivered the opinion of the Court.

Petitioner, a nonnamed member of a class certified under Federal Rule of Civil Procedure 23(b)(1), sought to appeal the approval of a settlement over objections he stated at the fairness hearing. The Court of Appeals for the Fourth Circuit held that he lacked the power to bring such an appeal because he was not a named class representative and because he had not successfully moved to intervene in the litigation. We now reverse.

* * *

[The Court first concluded that, as a member of the class, petitioner had an interest in the settlement and thus had standing to appeal.]

What is at issue, instead, is [not standing but] whether petitioner should be considered a "party" for the purposes of appealing the approval of the settlement. We have held that "only parties to a lawsuit, or those that properly become parties, may appeal an adverse judgment." *Marino v. Ortiz*, 484 U.S. 301, 304 (1988) (*per curiam*). Respondents argue that, because petitioner is not a named class representative and did not successfully move to intervene [despite appealing the denial of intervention], he is not a party for the purposes of taking an appeal.

We have never, however, restricted the right to appeal to named parties to the litigation. In *Blossom v. Milwaukee & Chicago R. Co.*, 1 Wall. 655 (1864), for instance, we allowed a bidder for property at a foreclosure sale, who was not a named party in the foreclosure action, to appeal the refusal of a request he made during that action to compel the sale. In *Hinckley v. Gilman, C. & S.R. Co.*, 94 U.S. 467 (1877), we allowed a receiver, who was an officer of the court rather than a named party to the case, to appeal from an order "relat[ing] to the settlement of his accounts," reasoning that "[f]or this purpose he occupies the position of a party to the suit." More recently, we have affirmed that "[t]he right of a nonparty to appeal an adjudication of contempt cannot be questioned," *United States Catholic Conference v. Abortion Rights Mobilization, Inc.*, 487 U.S. 72, 76 (1988), given the binding nature of that adjudication upon the interested nonparty.

JUSTICE SCALIA attempts to distinguish these cases by characterizing them as appeals from collateral orders to which the appellants "*were* parties." But it is difficult to see how they were parties in the sense in which JUSTICE SCALIA uses the term—those "named as a party to an action," usually "in the caption of the summons or complaint." Because they were not named in the action, the appellants in these cases were parties only in the sense that they were bound by the order from which they were seeking to appeal.

Petitioner's interest in the District Court's approval of the settlement is similar. Petitioner objected to the settlement at the District Court's fairness hearing, as nonnamed parties have been consistently allowed to do under the Federal Rules of Civil Procedure. *See* Fed. Rule Civ. Proc. 23(e) ("A class action shall not be dismissed or compromised without the approval of the court, and notice of the proposed dismissal or compromise shall be given to all members of the class in such manner as the court directs"); *see also* 2 H. Newberg & A. Conte, Class Actions § 11.55, p. 11–132 (3d ed. 1992) (explaining that Rule 23(e) entitles all class members to an opportunity to object). The District Court's approval of the settlement—which binds petitioner as a member of the class—amounted to a "final decision of [petitioner's] right or claim" sufficient to trigger his right to appeal. *See Williams v. Morgan*, 111 U.S. 684, 699 (1884) (describing the cases discussed above). And like the appellants in the prior cases, petitioner will only be allowed to appeal that aspect of the District Court's order that affects him—the District Court's decision to disregard his objections. Petitioner's right to appeal this aspect of the District Court's decision cannot be effectively accomplished through the named class representative—once the named parties reach a settlement that is approved over petitioner's objections, petitioner's interests by definition diverge from those of the class representative.

Marino v. Ortiz, supra, is not to the contrary. In that case, we refused to allow an appeal of a settlement by a group of white police officers who were not members of the class of minority officers that had brought a racial discrimination claim against the New York Police Department. Although the settlement affected them, the District Court's decision did not finally dispose of any right or claim they might have had because they were not members of the class.

Nor does considering nonnamed class members parties for the purposes of bringing an appeal conflict with any other aspect of class action procedure. In a related case, the Seventh Circuit has argued that nonnamed class members cannot be considered parties for the purposes of bringing an appeal because they are not considered parties for the purposes of the complete diversity requirement in suits under 28 U.S.C. § 1332. *See* [*Navigant Consulting, Inc. Sec. Litig.*, 275 F.3d 616, 619 (7th Cir. 2001)]. According to the Seventh Circuit, "[c]lass members cannot have it both ways, being non-parties (so that more cases can come to federal court) but still having a party's ability to litigate independently." Nonnamed class members, however, may be parties for some purposes and not for others. The label "party" does not indicate an absolute characteristic, but rather a conclusion about the applicability of various procedural rules that may differ based on context.

Nonnamed class members are, for instance, parties in the sense that the filing of an action on behalf of the class tolls a statute of limitations against them. *See American Pipe & Constr. Co. v. Utah*, 414 U.S. 538 (1974). Otherwise, all class members would be forced to intervene to preserve their claims, and one of the major goals of class action litigation—to simplify litigation involving a large number of class members with similar claims—would be defeated. The rule that nonnamed class members cannot defeat complete diversity is likewise justified by the goals of class action litigation. Ease of administration of class actions would be compromised by having to consider the citizenship of all class members, many of whom may even be unknown, in determining jurisdiction. Perhaps more importantly, considering all class members for these purposes would destroy diversity in almost all class actions. Nonnamed class members are, therefore, not parties in that respect.

What is most important to this case is that nonnamed class members are parties to the proceedings in the sense of being bound by the settlement. It is this feature of class action litigation that requires that class members be allowed to appeal the approval of a settlement when they have objected at the fairness hearing. To hold otherwise would deprive nonnamed class members of the power to preserve their own interests in a settlement that will ultimately bind them, despite their expressed objections before the trial court. Particularly in light of the fact that petitioner had no ability to opt out of the settlement, *see* Fed. Rule Civ. Proc. 23(b)(1), appealing the approval of the settlement is petitioner's only means of protecting himself from being bound by a disposition of his rights he finds unacceptable and that a reviewing court might find legally inadequate.

JUSTICE SCALIA rightly notes that other nonnamed parties may be bound by a court's decision, in particular, those in privity with the named party. True enough. It is not at all clear, however, that such parties may not themselves appeal. Although this Court has never addressed the issue, nonnamed parties in privity with a named party are often allowed by other courts to appeal from the order that affects them.

Respondents argue that, nonetheless, appeals from nonnamed parties should not be allowed because they would undermine one of the goals of class action litigation, namely, preventing multiple suits. Allowing such appeals, however, will not be as problematic as respondents claim. For one thing, the power to appeal is limited to those nonnamed class members who have objected during the fairness hearing. This limits the class of potential appellants considerably. As the longstanding practice of allowing nonnamed class members to object at the fairness hearing demonstrates, the burden of considering the claims of this subset of class members is not onerous.

* * *

We hold that nonnamed class members like petitioner who have objected in a timely manner to approval of the settlement at the fairness hearing have the power to bring an appeal without first intervening.

* * *

JUSTICE SCALIA, with whom JUSTICE KENNEDY and JUSTICE THOMAS join, dissenting.

* * *

Petitioner was offered the opportunity to be named the class representative, but he declined; nor did he successfully intervene. Accordingly, he is not a party to the class judgment.

* * *

The Court does not deny that, at least as a general matter, only those persons named as such are the "parties." Rather, it contends that persons "may be parties for some purposes and not for others," and that petitioner is a party to the class judgment at least for the "purposes of appealing." The Court bases these contentions on three of our precedents, which it says stand for the proposition that "[w]e have never . . . restricted the right to appeal to named parties to the litigation." These precedents stand for nothing of the sort.

All of these precedents are perfectly consistent with the rule that only named parties to a judgment can appeal the judgment because they involved appeals not from judgments but from collateral orders. The appellants were allowed to appeal from the collateral orders to which they *were* parties, even though they were *not* named parties to (and hence would not have been able to appeal from) the underlying judgments. We made this distinction between appealing the judgment and appealing a collateral order quite explicit in *Blossom v. Milwaukee & Chicago R. Co.*, 1 Wall. 655 (1864). In that case, the appellant was not a named party to the underlying foreclosure decree, from which it was therefore "certainly true that he [could not] appeal," yet he was a party (obviously, as the movant) to the motion he filed asking the court to complete the foreclosure sale, and therefore could appeal from *the order denying that motion*. Our decisions in *Hinckley v. Gilman, C. & S.R. Co.*, 94 U.S. 467 (1877), and *United States Catholic Conference v. Abortion Rights Mobilization, Inc.*, 487 U.S. 72 (1988), are to the same effect. In the former, the appellant was not a named party to the underlying foreclosure decree, from which we said he "cannot and does not attempt to appeal," but he was obviously a party to the collateral order directing him by name to transfer funds to the court, from which we said he could appeal. In the latter, witnesses who had been dismissed as named parties to the underlying litigation, were allowed to appeal from a collateral order holding them in contempt for their failure to comply with a subpoena addressed to them (and to which they were therefore obviously parties). These cases demonstrate why, even though petitioner should not be able to appeal the District Court's judgment approving the class settlement, there is no dispute that petitioner could (and did) appeal the District Court's collateral order denying his motion to intervene; as the movant, he was a party to the latter. See *Marino*, 484 U.S. at 304 ("[S]uch motions are, of course, appealable").

* * *

The Court's other grounds for holding that petitioner is a party to the class judgment are equally weak. First, it contends that petitioner should be considered a party to the judgment because, as a member of the class, he is bound by it. This will come as news to law students everywhere. There are any number of persons who are not parties to a judgment yet are nonetheless bound by it. *See* Restatement [(Second) of Judgments] § 41(1), at 393 (listing examples); *id.*, § 75, Comment *a*, at 210 ("A person is bound by a judgment in an action to which he is not a party if he is in 'privity' with a party"). Perhaps the most prominent example is precisely the one we have here. Nonnamed members of a class are bound by the class judgment, even though they are not parties to the judgment, because they are represented by class members who are parties:

> "A person who is not a party to an action but who is represented by a party is bound by and entitled to the benefits of a judgment as though he were a party. A person is represented by a party who is . . . [t]he representative of a class of persons similarly situated, designated as such with the approval of the court, of which the person is a member." *Id.*, § 41(1)(e), at 393.

Petitioner here, in the words of the Restatement, "is not a party" but "is bound by [the] judgment as though he were a party." Because our "well-settled" rule allows only "parties" to appeal from a judgment, petitioner may not appeal the class settlement.

* * *

NOTES AND QUESTIONS

1. Which side has the better of the argument in *Devlin*—the majority or the dissent? What are the implications of permitting class members like Devlin to appeal?

2. In establishing its rule, the *Devlin* Court imposed a restriction on which unnamed class members can appeal without intervening. What is that restriction? Does it make sense?

3. Does it make a difference to the *Devlin* analysis that the class at issue in that case was a mandatory (*i.e.*, non-opt-out) class? Some courts have restricted *Devlin* to mandatory class actions. *See, e.g.*, *Ballard v. Advance Am.*, 79 S.W.3d 835, 837 (Ark. 2002) ("[A]ppellants had the ability to opt out [but] instead elected to object to the settlement and risk being bound by it, if approved by the court over their objections * * *. Appellants' strategic election not to opt out of the settlement has left them without standing to pursue this appeal."); *Barnhill v. Fla. Microsoft Antitrust Litig.*, 905 So. 2d 195, 198–99 (Fla. Dist. Ct. App. 2005) (distinguishing *Devlin* and holding that unnamed class members who had the opportunity to opt-out, but failed to move to intervene, did not have standing to appeal order approving settlement and attorneys' fees, although they timely objected to settlement and participated in fairness hearing); *see also In re Gen. Am. Life Ins. Co. Sales Practices Litig.*, 302 F.3d 799, 800 (8th Cir. 2002) (in *dicta*, questioning whether *Devlin* applies to opt-out class actions certified under Rule 23(b)(3), and expressing tentative approval of *Ballard*). The Ninth Circuit, however, has refused to construe *Devlin* so narrowly, finding that, for all practical purposes, the right to opt out of a class action can be illusory where "each objector's claim is too small to justify

individual litigation." *Churchill Vill., L.L.C. v. Gen. Elec.*, 361 F.3d 566, 572 (9th Cir. 2004).

4. Should *Devlin* be read to overrule *In re Brand Name Prescription Drugs Antitrust Litigation*, 115 F.3d 456 (7th Cir. 1997) (*see* Chapter 8(A)(5)(a) & Part (B)(1) of this chapter), at least with respect to unnamed class members? Or do different considerations come into play with respect to appeals by unnamed class members during the pendency of litigation, as opposed to at the time of settlement?

3. MOOTNESS OF CLASS REPRESENTATIVE'S CLAIM

In addressing the threshold requirements for class certification in Chapter 2(A), this text touched on the issue of mootness. Many mootness issues involve attempted appeals by class representatives whose claims have become moot. Thus, the mootness materials in Chapter 2 should be reexamined in connection with this chapter.

C. STANDARDS OF REVIEW ON APPEAL FROM CLASS CERTIFICATION

This section provides materials relating to the standard of review applicable to class certification decisions.

YOKOYAMA V. MIDLAND NAT'L LIFE INS. CO.
United States Court of Appeals, Ninth Circuit, 2010.
594 F.3d 1087.

Before SCHROEDER, PAEZ, and N. RANDY SMITH, CIRCUIT JUDGES.

SCHROEDER, CIRCUIT JUDGE.

Defendant Midland National Life Insurance Company marketed annuities to senior citizens in Hawaii. At issue in this case are Midland annuities that were sold by independent brokers between 2001 and 2005. Plaintiff Gary Yokoyama purchased one of those annuities through an independent broker and filed this class action claiming that Midland marketed the annuities through deceptive practices, in violation of Hawaii's Deceptive Practices Act. *See* Haw. Rev. Stat. § 480–2. The complaint specifically targets representations made in Midland's brochures, which promoted the annuities as appropriate for seniors. * * *

The district court denied class certification, holding that in order to succeed under the Hawaii Act, each plaintiff would have to show subjective, individualized reliance on deceptive practices within the circumstances of each plaintiff's purchase of the annuity. Principally for that reason, the district court held that the plaintiffs could not satisfy Federal Rule of Civil Procedure 23(b)(3)'s requirements that common issues predominate over individual issues and that a class action is a superior method of adjudication. The dispositive issue is thus an issue of Hawaii state law, namely whether Hawaii's Deceptive Practices Act requires a showing of individualized reliance.

The Hawaii Supreme Court has considered the issue of whether the statute requires actual, *i.e.*, subjective reliance. It has said that the dispositive issue is whether the allegedly deceptive practice is "likely to mislead consumers acting reasonably under the circumstances." *Courbat v. Dahana Ranch, Inc.*, 111 Hawaii 254, 141 P.3d 427, 435 (2006). "[A]ctual deception need not be shown[;] the capacity to deceive is sufficient." *State of Bronster v. U.S. Steel Corp.*, 82 Hawaii 32, 919 P.2d 294, 313 (1996) (citation omitted). This is an objective test, and therefore actual reliance need not be established. Accordingly, there is no reason to look at the circumstances of each individual purchase in this case, because the allegations of the complaint are narrowly focused on allegedly deceptive provisions of Midland's own marketing brochures, and the fact-finder need only determine whether those brochures were capable of misleading a reasonable consumer.

* * *

The prerequisites for maintaining a class action pursuant to Rule 23(a), and the findings necessary under Rule 23(b)(3) to certify the type of class sought in this case, include some determinations that may, depending on the nature of the case, present questions of law, or of fact, or involve issues requiring a discretionary determination. Rule 23(a)'s prerequisite that there must be questions of law or fact common to the class, for example, is obviously one where the trial court must look to both the legal and factual contexts of the litigation before it. Fed. R. Civ. P. 23(a)(2). The same is true for Rule 23(b)(3)'s stricture that the court find that "the questions of law or fact common to class members predominate" over individualized issues. Fed. R. Civ. P. 23(b)(3). Such a determination also generally contains an element of discretion, as do most of the Rule's requirements, particularly the prerequisites of numerosity, typicality, and adequacy of representation. The most important determination, *i.e.*, the ultimate decision as to whether or not to certify the class, must, at least in any non-frivolous putative class action, involve a significant element of discretion.

It is, therefore, unsurprising that when a district court's class action certification is on appeal, we say that the overall standard of review is for abuse of discretion. In addition, when any particular underlying Rule 23 determination involving a discretionary determination is appealed, our standard of review must be for abuse of discretion.

While our review of discretionary class certification decisions is deferential, it is also true that we accord the decisions of district courts no deference when reviewing their determinations of questions of law. Further, this court has oft repeated that an error of law *is* an abuse of discretion. Indeed, since *Salve Regina Coll. v. Russell*, 499 U.S. 225, 231 (1991), no federal court has ever held that a district court's error as to a matter of law is not an abuse of discretion, in the class action context, or in any other.

Thus, when an appellant raises the argument that the district court premised a class certification determination on an error of law, our first task is to evaluate whether such legal error occurred. *See, e.g., Zinser v. Accufix Research Inst.*, 253 F.3d 1180, 1186–88 (9th Cir. 2001) (reviewing a district court's choice of law determination de novo, and its factual findings for clear error); *Knight v. Kenai Peninsula Borough Sch. Dist.*, 131

F.3d 807, 811–12 (9th Cir. 1997) (finding an issue of law, regarding a mootness determination, is reviewed without deference to the district court and that an error of law is a per se abuse of discretion).

As *Zinser* and *Knight* illustrate, once we have determined the threshold question of whether an error of law has occurred, we review the class certification determination for abuse of discretion. If the district court's determination was premised on a legal error, we will find a per se abuse of discretion. If no legal error occurred, we will proceed to review the district court's class certification decision for abuse of discretion as we always have done.

The Supreme Court has addressed this same dichotomy in the sanctions context of Rule 11 of the Federal Rules of Civil Procedure. The Court resolved it by holding that when a district court errs as a matter of law in imposing sanctions, the legal error automatically becomes an abuse of discretion. *Cooter & Gell v. Hartmarx Corp.*, 496 U.S. 384, 405 (1990) ("A district court would necessarily abuse its discretion if it based its ruling on an erroneous view of the law. . . .").

Our court's method in *Zinser* and *Knight* is also consistent with the practices of other circuits. For example, in *Miles v. Merrill Lynch & Co.*, the Second Circuit held that the standard for appellate review of the Rule 23 requirements "is whether discretion has been exceeded (or abused). . . . Of course, this leeway, with all matters of discretion, is not boundless. To the extent that the ruling on a Rule 23 requirement . . . involves an issue of law, review is de novo." 471 F.3d 24, 40–41 (2d Cir. 2006). *See also Andrews v. Chevy Chase Bank*, 545 F.3d 570, 573 (7th Cir. 2008) ("We generally review a grant of class certification for abuse of discretion, but 'purely legal' determinations made in support of that decision are reviewed de novo."); *In re Hydrogen Peroxide Antitrust Litig.*, 552 F.3d 305, 312 (3d Cir. 2008) ("We review a class certification order for abuse of discretion. . . . Whether an incorrect legal standard has been used in an issue of law to be reviewed de novo.") (internal quotations omitted).

In light of the above, in reviewing this case, we must first determine whether the law of Hawaii requires a finding of individual reliance in the application of its consumer protection statutes. As a federal court sitting in diversity, we answer this question of state law de novo. *Salve Regina*, 499 U.S. at 231. Our conclusion of whether or not the district court erred in interpreting Hawaii law will then inform our abuse of discretion review of the district court's denial of class certification.

* * *

The district court refused to certify a class in this case because it determined that Hawaii's consumer protection laws require individualized reliance showings. Believing that the plaintiffs' claims would "require inspection of whether the class members individually relied on Midland's misstatements," the district court concluded that class issues do not predominate over issues affecting individual members.

The district court's premise was contrary to the Hawaii Supreme Court's interpretation of Hawaii state law, because the Hawaii Supreme Court has made it clear that reliance is judged by an "objective 'reasonable person' standard." Hawaii's Supreme Court has said as much: "[A]ctual deception need not be shown; the capacity to deceive is sufficient." Because Hawaii uses an objective test to effectuate its remedial consumer protection statute, the district court erred in holding that individual reliance issues make this case inappropriate for class certification.

These plaintiffs base their lawsuit only on what Midland did not disclose to them in its forms. The jury will not have to determine whether each plaintiff subjectively relied on the omissions, but will instead have to determine only whether those omissions were likely to deceive a reasonable person. This does not involve an individualized inquiry.

The district court also determined that the plaintiffs' claims "involve separate questions of fact as to what information the independent brokers selling the [annuities] conveyed." The plaintiffs' allegations, however, are that the deceptive acts or practices are omissions or misstatements in Midland's own brochures. More specifically, their Fourth Amended Complaint alleges that the deception was perpetrated by Midland through its "fail[ure] to disclose to Plaintiffs and Class Members material information concerning the benefits/detriments from, and suitability and impact of" the annuities. The plaintiffs have thus crafted their lawsuit so as to avoid individual variance among the class members. Plaintiffs' case will not require the fact-finder to parse what oral representations each broker made to each plaintiff. Instead, the fact-finder will focus on the standardized written materials given to all plaintiffs and determine whether those materials are "likely to mislead consumers acting reasonably under the circumstances."

* * *

CONCLUSION

Because the proper inquiry under Hawaii law considers the effect upon a reasonable consumer, not a particular consumer, there are no individualized issues of reliance under Rule 23. Moreover, Hawaii's state courts have made clear that Hawaii's consumer protection laws are flexible and may be enforced through the class action mechanism. We express no opinion on the merits of the claims.

REVERSED and REMANDED for FURTHER PROCEEDINGS.

NOTES AND QUESTIONS

1. Did the Ninth Circuit reach the correct result in *Yokoyama*?

2. Are the standards of review set forth in *Yokoyama* sufficiently flexible so that, in effect, an appellate court can review virtually any class certification ruling *de novo*? Or are appellate courts truly constrained by the applicable standards of review?

Chapter 10

Special Focus on Mass Tort, Employment Discrimination, and Securities Fraud Class Actions

■ ■ ■

This chapter focuses in detail on three important types of class actions: mass torts, employment discrimination, and securities fraud. In each substantive area, courts have faced a variety of interesting and important issues. Indeed, mass tort, employment discrimination, and securities fraud cases and commentary have appeared repeatedly throughout the previous chapters. By concentrating in depth on these three areas, however, the chapter illustrates how the substantive law may influence—or be influenced by—Rule 23.

At the outset, recall from basic civil procedure that the Federal Rules of Civil Procedure were designed to be "trans-substantive" rules—that is, neutral rules that applied the same regardless of the underlying substance of a dispute. *See generally* Robert M. Cover, *For James Wm. Moore: Some Reflections on a Reading of the Rules*, 84 Yale L.J. 718 (1975). Consider, while reviewing the material below, the extent to which modern Rule 23, as adopted in 1966, was trans-substantive in its original application, and the extent to which it has remained so through the present day.

John Leubsdorf, Class Actions at the Cloverleaf
39 Ariz. L. Rev. 453, 453–57 (1997).

I. Substance Drives Procedure?

* * * [I]nnovations changing class actions in specific substantive fields of law have proliferated. One of the clearest examples is found in the Private Securities Litigation Reform Act of 1995 * * *. In addition to modifying securities litigation in other ways, the Act contains detailed class action provisions concerning the selection of class representatives and counsel, attorney fees, security for costs, and settlement procedures.

There are many other instances. In the civil rights area, * * * legislation [enacted in 1991 increased] the preclusive effect of employment discrimination class actions and slash[ed] the relief available in prison reform suits. * * * Congress has authorized states to bring *parens patriae* antitrust actions on behalf of their citizens, and the FTC to bring somewhat similar actions. In 1974, Congress amended the Truth in Lending Act to limit the recovery of liquidated damages in class actions. In 1996, it prohibited Legal Services Corporation lawyers from bringing class actions for their clients—a provision not explicitly directed at any substantive area, but obviously limiting certain kinds of class actions, such as those concerning AFDC and disability benefits.

We are witnessing the decline of a single, trans-substantive system of civil procedure where class actions are concerned. Legislators have, in effect, amended Rule 23, not across the board, but in specified substantive areas, and for substantive reasons. While scholars were debating the merits of trans-substantive procedure, Congress acted. The resulting fragmentation parallels the increasing geographic fragmentation of federal civil procedure.

The breach in trans-substantive procedure concerned class actions because class actions involve an unusual interplay of substance and procedure. They provide an unusually powerful way of enforcing substantive law, and hence draw the attention of those who want to promote or discourage enforcement. Their mass production procedures modify the law being enforced, and those who shape that law have now turned their attention to class action procedure.

Although class action law is moving in substantive directions, procedure may still have a hand on the wheel. Often, indeed, it is hard to separate changes in substantive law from class action changes, particularly in areas where class actions have become the predominant remedy. Professor Greenberg persuasively treats as class action changes modifications in the remedial law of school desegregation and prisoner rights, even though these modifications make no explicit reference to class actions, because in practice they are applied in class actions. [*See* Chapter 10(B)(1)]. The "safe harbor" provisions of the Private Securities Litigation Reform Act of 1995 contain no procedural or remedial clauses, but would they have been enacted without the growth in securities class action that made securities litigation important to corporate management?

The congressional origin of most class action changes links with their substantive impetus. Procedural rulemakers have continued to write general, trans-substantive rules. Because so many groups have conflicting interests in class action rules, no consensus supporting significant class action changes of trans-substantive impact has arisen. Interest groups seeking narrower changes have found Congress a more receptive audience whether the changes they sought were substantive, procedural, or both.

Because most of the recent changes originated with interest groups working through Congress, they have usually aided defendants. It was defendants who felt the impact of class actions, and who enjoyed access to recent conservative Congresses. Potential class members are usually unorganized—that is one justification for class actions—and even the plaintiffs' bar has had more success in resisting some legislative proposals it opposes than in promoting those it favors. The Civil Rights Act of 1991 is a rare example of an organized group obtaining a pro-plaintiff change in class action law.

* * *

II. CURVES OF DISTRUST

Although substantive discontent provides the impetus that propels innovation, procedural theories steer the innovators toward particular class action changes. Recently, these have been theories of distrust: distrust of plaintiffs' lawyers and distrust of judges.

Distrust of plaintiffs' lawyers has many sources. Academics have developed a series of critiques of class action lawyers, focusing on conflicts within classes, on the lack of effective client monitoring of most class lawyers, and on lawyers' temptation to place their own ideological or economic interests ahead of those of class members. Defendants complain of lawyers who bring groundless suits, and feel no fondness for those who bring grounded suits yielding large recoveries. Some politicians gladly direct an ancient tradition of anti-lawyer feeling against the plaintiffs' bar.

This distrust marks some recent class action legislation. The Private Securities Litigation Reform Act of 1995 seeks to control baseless allegations and excessive attorney fees, as well as to promote designation of lead plaintiffs whose large stakes will spur them to control class lawyers. Prohibiting Legal Services Corporation lawyers from bringing class actions rests in part on portrayals of them as leftist zealots. Authorizing state attorneys general to bring *parens patriae* antitrust actions for state citizens reflects a desire to limit the role of the private bar.

Civil rights litigators are one group of lawyers that has so far managed to escape distrust leading to legislation. Apparently its members are too poor to be considered greedy. * * * The Civil Rights Act of 1991, by allowing damage recovery in employment discrimination actions, has given rise to a resurgence of class actions that may in turn make it possible for some to apply the greedy lawyer stereotype to some of the civil rights bar.

Distrust for judges has also inspired class action changes. The Prison Litigation Reform Act and the Supreme Court's recent school desegregation decisions both limit the powers of judges to grant broad, class-wide relief in institutional reform litigation. Restrictions on Legal Services Corporations lawyers indicate not only distrust for the lawyers themselves, but distrust of what they may persuade judges to decree. Of course, this distrust of judges shades into distrust of the law that they enforce, and that class actions enable them to enforce more effectively. But it also builds on criticism of judicial activism in class actions.

We might have expected that the growth of class actions would lead to distrust of participating lawyers and judges. Distrust of the government led many in the 1960s and 1970s to welcome the class action brought by the "private attorney general" as an alternative. Now, the conflicting values and the disbelief in a common good that fostered distrust of the government have infected trust in class actions. Those who want to cut back government also want to cut back class actions.

* * *

A. MASS TORT CLASS ACTIONS

1. OVERVIEW

No area of class action law has generated more analysis and controversy by both courts and commentators during the past four decades than mass tort class actions. A key element of that controversy stems from the Advisory Committee's Note to the 1966 revisions to Rule 23, which states:

> A "mass accident" resulting in injuries to numerous persons is ordinarily not appropriate for a class action because of the likelihood

that significant questions, not only of damages but of liability and defenses of liability, would be present, affecting the individuals in different ways. In these circumstances an action conducted nominally as a class action would degenerate in practice into multiple lawsuits separately tried.

This comment caused a number of early courts to refuse to certify mass tort cases. Later, several courts sought ways to distinguish or limit the Advisory Committee's Note. In fact, Federal District Court Judge Jack B. Weinstein, who wrote the article that was cited by the Advisory Committee in support of its comment on mass torts, *see* Jack B. Weinstein, *Revision of Procedure: Some Problems in Class Actions*, 9 Buff. L. Rev. 433, 469 (1960), later took a different position:

> I wrote * * * the article that the Federal Advisory Committee—Judge Kaplan's committee—used in concluding that they should not use this rule for torts. But I was wrong because society is completely different from the society I saw while I was up in my tower at Columbia. I did not know about all the people who were out there on the streets of our nation hurting, and I did not fully understand that our technology and our science are organized on a national and international scale. The people are hurt on an individual scale. The whole technology and the whole society that we face call out for a way of dealing with these problems.
>
> Our Federal Civil Rules are based on the old Rules of Equity. The rules of equity won in the fight over the adoption of the Federal Rules of Civil Procedure in 1938. The rules of Equity provide a very loose and effective way of meeting new situations, as they have for the last six hundred years in English and American practice.
>
> You can do anything with the Rules—or almost anything—by interpreting them in the light of history and the current needs of society.

The Future of Class Actions in Mass Tort Cases: A Roundtable Discussion, 66 Fordham L. Rev. 1657, 1670 (1998).

In recent years, however, many courts have been skeptical of efforts to bring mass tort class actions. This skepticism has led some courts of appeals to invalidate class certifications in major mass tort cases.

During all of these phases, commentators have inundated scholarly journals with articles on mass tort class actions, agreeing with—or attacking—the various approaches of the courts and proposing their own solutions. This section provides a historical overview of mass tort class actions and focuses on some of the key issues facing courts today.

Preliminarily, it is important to define the term "mass tort." That term has "become a catch-all phrase encompassing almost any multiparty litigation based on tort theories." Anne Cohen, *Mass Tort Litigation After Amchem*, ALI–ABA Course on Civil Practice and Litigation Techniques in the Federal Courts 269, 273 (1998). But as Professor Cohen further notes, "such claims tend to break into four general areas":

Mass accidents * * * are single catastrophic events in which a number of people are injured. This is the sort of circumstance that the drafters of revised Rule 23 of the Federal Rules of Civil Procedure had in mind in 1966 when they suggested that "mass accidents" were "ordinarily not appropriate" for class action treatment.

Personal injury mass torts involve injuries allegedly developed in connection with widely available or mass marketed products and their manufacture, design, use, implantation, ingestion, exposure, etc. * * *

(Somewhere between mass accident and personal injury cases are "mass exposure" cases, where a group of claimants alleges the same type of exposure from the same source, often over an extended period of time.)

Property damage mass torts are generally claims for replacement or repair of allegedly defective products. Plaintiffs in such cases seek compensation for the failure of the product to perform as intended, with resulting damage to the product itself or other property, often with personal injury overtones.

Economic loss cases make defect claims similar to those in property damage situations but are really more in the nature of consumer fraud or warranty actions on a grand scale. In contrast to property damage claims, economic loss cases usually involve allegations of the existence of a defect without actual product failure or injury.

Id. at 275–76. In this section, "mass torts" will be used broadly to refer to all of these categories of cases, although distinctions will be noted when relevant. In reviewing the following materials, consider whether the viability of a class action should depend upon which type of mass tort is involved.

DEBORAH R. HENSLER & MARK A. PETERSON, UNDERSTANDING MASS PERSONAL INJURY LITIGATION: A SOCIO–LEGAL ANALYSIS
59 Brook. L. Rev. 961, 965–69, 1030, 1033, 1034–45 (1993).

I. WHAT DISTINGUISHES MASS TORTS FROM ORDINARY HIGH VOLUME LITIGATION?

Three factors distinguish mass torts from ordinary personal injury litigation: the large number of claims associated with a single "litigation;" the commonality of issues and actors among claims within a litigation; and the interdependence of claim values. Numerosity is the primary defining characteristic of a mass tort litigation. The best known examples of mass litigation, such as asbestos workers' personal injury suits and the Dalkon Shield bankruptcy litigation, have involved hundreds of thousands of cases; the most recent examples of mass torts involve at least a thousand individual claims. The high visibility of mass torts and the burdens they impose on courts and parties are direct consequences of the large numbers of claims in each litigation.

But numerosity, by itself, is not sufficient to distinguish mass tort litigation from ordinary tort litigation. The court system routinely disposes of half a million or so automobile accident cases per year, far more than the number involved in any single mass tort. Mass torts are distinguished from automobile accident litigation and other ordinary, high-volume litigation by the commonality of issues and actors among individual mass tort claims. Mass torts involve a common set of injuries which are incurred in the same or similar circumstances. Most plaintiffs are represented by a relatively small number of law firms, each of which may represent hundreds or thousands of claimants. Claims are brought against one or a few defendants, and a relatively small number of law firms defend or at least control the defense of thousands of claims. In addition, mass tort litigation is usually concentrated in a few jurisdictions, either as a result of the circumstances of injury or as a result of court action.

For example, almost all asbestos personal injury cases involve claims of either respiratory or gastro-intestinal cancers or other respiratory injuries incurred in the course of handling asbestos in shipyards or maritime industries, petrochemical factories or other workplaces. Each asbestos case typically names about twenty of the same thirty to forty asbestos manufacturers and distributors as defendants. Most of the hundreds of thousands of claimants are represented by fewer than fifty plaintiffs' law firms that specialize in this litigation, and their law suits are concentrated in a dozen courts. Similarly, most Dalkon Shield claimants alleged a few types of gynecological injuries due to pelvic inflammatory disease * * *, all attributed to a particular intrauterine device, which was manufactured by a single company, A.H. Robins Co. The majority of Dalkon Shield claimants were represented by thirty firms, and suits were concentrated in a few states, notably Minnesota, Maryland and California.

Because of their high degree of commonality, similar factual issues and legal questions will arise in all claims in a mass tort litigation, or at least in significant subsets of claims. The same injuries will involve similar causation issues. Liability issues will be similar among claims alleging similar exposures to a particular defendant's products. Because of the common legal representation within each side, even the litigation strategies will be similar among large groups of claims.

The contrast with ordinary tort litigation is sharp. In ordinary automobile accident litigation, claimants allege a vast array of disparate injuries to different parts of the body—ranging from soft tissue injuries to fractures to paraplegia—incurred under diverse circumstances. Causation, liability and damages issues differ from case to case. Most cases have one or, perhaps, two defendants, and there are as many or more different defendants involved in automobile litigation as there are cases. Tens of thousands of law firms represent automobile injury victims, whose claims are spread among every state court in the country.

Courts' attempts to manage mass torts efficiently often further increase the commonality among mass tort claims. Courts typically assign mass torts to one or a few judges for pretrial purposes, either through formal mechanisms, such as the federal multi-district litigation procedure [see Chapter 12], or through informal court assignment practices. As a result, a small number of judges may be responsible for critical decisions which affect hundreds or thousands of cases, adding another common factor to the litigation.

This commonality produces the third defining characteristic of mass tort litigation: the monetary values of mass tort claims are highly interdependent. In mass litigation, the likely amount that one plaintiff will receive for a claim depends upon the values of other claims. Indeed, the claims are so similar that the prospective value of many claims will rise or fall sharply with a large plaintiff award, a defense verdict or even a signal discovery event or evidentiary decision in a single case that is part of the mass of pending claims.

Of course, the values of all tort claims are interdependent to some extent. In many large metropolitan trial court jurisdictions, personal injury attorneys regularly consult reports of recently tried cases to determine the "going rate" for particular types of injuries. But the determination of causation and liability in an ordinary tort claim is not dependent on outcomes of other claims: whether a particular driver was liable for a particular accident usually has nothing to do with the liability of another driver in a different accident. Although trends in average jury awards do influence settlement values of ordinary claims over time, the prospective value of ordinary claims does not rise or fall dramatically as the result of a single verdict on a similar claim.

The interdependence of values in mass tort claims is far more striking. No claim in a mass tort litigation will have value until plaintiffs are able to establish causation, liability and damages for at least a few representative claims. For example, asbestos claims became viable only after the United States Court of Appeals for the Fifth Circuit in *Borel v. Fibreboard Paper Products*, 493 F.2d 1076 (5th Cir. 1973), held that asbestos manufacturers could be held strictly liable for workers' injuries. Moreover, a large award in one case increases the value of other, similar mass tort claims. * * * Conversely the adverse disposition of some mass tort claims can sharply reduce the values of all other claims. * * *

Critical events other than trial outcomes also can greatly change the value of all other claims in the same mass tort. For example, the discovery of the "Sumner–Simpson" papers, indicating knowledge among major defendants of asbestos' injurious effects, exposed these defendants to significant punitive damages. This increased the value of all asbestos claims against those defendants, not simply those claims directly involved in the relevant discovery. Similarly, the Food and Drug Administration's ("FDA") decision to prohibit silicone breast implantation under most circumstances likely increased the value of pending and future breast implantation claims and encouraged a large number of new claims.

The enormous social and financial consequences of mass torts derive from the combination of large numbers of claims and interdependency of case values. In ordinary litigation a major adverse outcome—a multimillion dollar plaintiff award or a defendant victory in a high stakes case—may be a significant blow to the parties. But such outcomes take on far greater significance when they are multiplied many times over through their impact on other mass claims. Numerosity and interdependency create incentives for plaintiffs' attorneys to seek out potential mass tort claims, for defendants to invest enormous sums in defending against these claims, and for judges to devise strategies to arrive at global resolution of mass claims. * * *

IV. WHY ARE MASS TORTS SO DIFFICULT TO RESOLVE?

* * *

A. Factual and Legal Issues

* * *

1. Causation

All successful tort litigation requires that the plaintiff establish (or persuade the defendant that she could establish), to the satisfaction of the factfinder, that an action or omission on the part of the defendant was the cause-in-fact of the claimant's injuries. Whether incurred in a single accident or as a result of a mass catastrophe, such as a building collapse, linking traumatic injuries, such as fractures, to an event is usually relatively easy. But for latent injuries, establishing causation is far more difficult. The plaintiff first must establish that the type of product use or exposure that she alleges is capable of causing her alleged injuries (general causation), and then establish that this use or exposure was the cause-in-fact of injury in this case (specific causation).

Mass toxic tort litigation will not move forward unless plaintiffs' attorneys can persuade themselves and defendants that they can establish general causation. Usually this will require winning at least a few jury trials, which in turn will require that judges permit plaintiffs to introduce the scientific evidence on which their causation claims rest, and that juries accept that evidence as proof of causation. As they contemplate initiating or defending toxic tort litigation, both plaintiff attorneys and defendants have a number of reasons to be uncertain about plaintiffs' ability to prevail on the causation issue.

First, at the early stages of litigation the scientific evidence of a causal link between product use or exposure and the damages claimed, in truth, may be uncertain. Science evolves over time: Evidence that first appears to support a causal link, later may be controverted. Conversely, evidence of causation that first appears shaky, over time, may be bolstered by new studies. Moreover, there are a variety of scientific approaches for investigating causal links between substance exposure and disease, including epidemiology (the study of the spread of disease in human populations) and laboratory experimentation with tissue cultures (*i.e.*, *in vitro*) and live animals (*i.e.*, *in vivo*). Each of these has its strengths and weaknesses. * * *

* * *

In addition to the uncertainties attendant upon science itself, there are uncertainties about how courts will respond to whatever scientific evidence is available. There has been considerable variation in judges' willingness to permit plaintiffs to present key causation evidence to juries. * * * Appellate courts have generally (although not always) upheld trial courts' evidentiary decisions.

* * *

Finally, there has been considerable variation in juries' evaluation of evidence of causation, even within the same litigation. For example, although the jury that heard the consolidated trial of Bendectin cases in the middle district of Ohio delivered a defense verdict on causation, at least two juries prior to that trial and four juries subsequently found for the plaintiff in individual Bendectin cases. Over the long course of asbestos worker injury litigation, some juries have delivered defense verdicts on general causation, notwithstanding substantial scientific evidence that asbestos exposure causes various injuries.

2. Liability

In addition to persuading themselves and defendants that they can prove general causation, plaintiffs' attorneys need to convince themselves and the defendants that the fact finders will hold the defendants legally responsible for plaintiffs' injuries. For a number of reasons, this may be less difficult than it is to demonstrate their ability to prevail on the causation issue.

First, in the face of the expansion of product liability doctrine and the evidence in the late 1970s and early 1980s of rising product liability caseloads, increasing rates of plaintiff success at trial and increasing jury awards, manufacturers have apparently become convinced that the civil justice system has tilted against them. In particular, many corporate defendants believe that juries tend to sympathize with injured individuals and, therefore, consistently deliver verdicts against so-called "deep pocket" defendants, without regard to the evidence and legal rules that should govern their decision. Thus, defendants may be inclined to believe that if plaintiffs' attorneys can get their liability case before juries, the plaintiffs will prevail.

In addition, experienced defense counsel for mass toxic tort defendants fear that in many instances, the extensive discovery permitted under contemporary rules of civil procedure will uncover documents related to corporate review of the risks and benefits associated with their products that plaintiffs may be able to use to persuade juries that defendants inappropriately discounted potential harms to product users. For their part, plaintiffs' attorneys may well expect that if they invest sufficient time and effort in the discovery process they will be able to locate such "smoking guns." In a unitary trial (where causation, liability, and damages are tried together and the jury deliberates after it has heard evidence on all matters of fact), such documents may loom larger in jurors' minds than the likely more ambiguous scientific evidence on general causation. * * * The potential for exposing "bad documents" also poses broader risks to corporate defendants with an interest in protecting brand names and corporate image.

* * *

Mass toxic tort litigation poses other challenges to plaintiffs' attorneys' ability to demonstrate liability * * *. These challenges derive from the long period between initial exposure to the injurious product or substance and the filing of the lawsuit. To establish liability of any particular defendant, the plaintiff generally must be able to link that defendant's product to the alleged injury. But in cases where injuries occurred some years ago and

where different manufacturers' products were used interchangeably, it may be difficult—if not impossible—to establish this product-injury nexus.
* * *

Demonstrating a product-injury nexus poses even larger problems when neither plaintiff nor defendant [has] any way of establishing what specific product was associated with the plaintiff's injury. For example, in DES cases, the injured party is the daughter or grandchild of a woman who took DES while pregnant. Usually, the DES user does not recall the specific brand of the drug that was prescribed, nor is there any documentary record. In [one case], the court responded to this problem by recognizing a "market share" theory of liability, which held all DES manufacturers liable for the injury and apportioned damages among them in proportion to their individual shares of the market. * * *

As a practical matter, most mass tort litigation to date has not posed this problem: the Dalkon Shield was manufactured only by A.H. Robins, Bendectin only by Merrell–Dow and the Shiley Heart Valve by Shiley, Inc., which was later purchased by Pfizer. * * * Asbestos was manufactured by many corporations, but litigators have been able to develop evidence indicating what specific products were actually used at different work sites.
* * *

3. Damages

Finally, to succeed, plaintiffs must demonstrate that their claims have real monetary value. Although the total monetary value of mass litigation is the sum of damages for all individuals in the injury pool who can establish causation and liability, it usually requires some number of jury trials to establish that these individuals' cases, in fact, do have substantial monetary value. Thus, the nationwide surge of silicone breast implant litigation occurred after an award of $7.3 million by a San Francisco jury, and gained further impetus when a Texas jury awarded $28 million in a similar trial the following year. A large damage award to users of the Copper–7 intrauterine device led many to believe that litigation over that product ultimately might assume the dimensions of the Dalkon Shield litigation. Sizeable awards to asbestos cancer victims appear to have increased the value of all asbestos claims, even for those victims who do not allege any current impairment.

Conversely, if plaintiffs' attorneys fail to establish that individual claims have significant value, the value of the entire litigation will be called into question. * * * [And if punitive damage claims fail, the value of mass litigation may likewise fall dramatically.]

* * *

B. The Special Risk Profile of Mass Litigation

Although uncertainty about the plaintiffs' ability to establish causation and liability and win large damages colors the early stages of mass personal injury litigation, the risks that plaintiff attorneys and defendants face at the litigation's inception are not symmetric. For plaintiffs' attorney firms, the cost of losing is determined by the size of the firm's investment in the litigation, including the cost to cover expenses associated with identifying clients (*e.g.*, advertising, referral fees, medical screening exams);

developing the facts of individual plaintiffs' cases (*e.g.*, discovery of documents and medical exams); preparing cases for trial (*e.g.*, deposing expert witnesses); and, perhaps, aiding in developing scientific evidence of general causation. There is wide variation in how much plaintiffs' law firms invest to obtain and prepare their cases. * * *

Experienced firms, however, can balance the size of their caseload and their expenses to limit their risk to an amount they deem acceptable. Much of the financial risk of acquiring cases is mitigated by fee arrangements with lawyers who refer cases: Referring lawyers continue to represent a client as co-counsel and are paid a share of the contingency fee only if and when defendants settle. By joining forces either through court-appointed plaintiffs' steering committees or informal litigation groups, plaintiffs' law firms can limit the risk to each firm by sharing costs of discovery and scientific investigation. * * *

Balanced against the costs for a plaintiffs' firm is the huge potential recovery if the firm successfully represents scores, hundreds or even thousands of claims. Several implications follow from this balance. First, a plaintiffs' law firm may be willing to invest substantial sums in developing scientific information and otherwise preparing and trying one or a few cases. Investments that could not be justified for a single case are, in contrast, sound when the firm knows that its entire portfolio of cases will gain value if lead cases succeed. Second, as a result of the special cost-benefit relationship for mass torts, the firm can justify additional expenses simply by acquiring a larger portfolio of claims. With a sufficient number of claims, the potential returns will exceed any costs. Third, plaintiffs' firms may pursue potential mass tort cases even where liability and causation are highly uncertain. Because potential returns are so great, plaintiffs' firms can accept high risks that they would not bear in ordinary litigation where returns are limited to one or a few cases.

For defendants, the cost of losing early in the litigation is determined not just by the cost of defending the early cases and indemnifying claimants who prevail, but also by the increase in value of other pending claims that will then ensue, and by the fact that each plaintiff verdict will encourage new case filings. When the pool of potential claimants (all those who used the product or were exposed to the substance) numbers in the hundreds of thousands or millions, when there is a finite possibility that each exposed individual might be deemed to have a viable claim, if only for emotional damages, and when punitive damages of large and unpredictable amounts can be awarded over and over, the defendant's exposure may appear well-nigh unlimited—in the common parlance, a "bet the company" proposition.

In deciding what strategy they should adopt, defendants must consider the possibility that one or more judges or juries will decide against them, even if they have been advised that their scientific case is strong. Indeed, plaintiffs won the first Bendectin trial and several subsequent trials. Litigation is uncertain even with strong cases and fair judges and juries, and defendants should expect a few anomalous verdicts among the universe of trial dispositions. If such verdicts occur randomly, there is a finite chance that they will occur during the initial phase of litigation. Thus, while the special characteristics of mass torts spur plaintiffs' attorneys to invest heavily in preparing for trial, they may lead defendants to shy away from trial. This extreme risk aversion is becoming more apparent as defendants (and their insurers) better understand mass torts. * * *

Moreover, some judges are not adverse to using the potential for such jury outcomes as levers to achieve settlement even when the scientific evidence is thin. * * *

Because the risks facing the corporate defendant are larger than the risks facing any one plaintiffs' law firm, and because plaintiffs' firms have discovered the value of joining forces and pursuing cooperative strategies against defendants, defendants in mass tort litigation may not hold the same advantages over the plaintiff that they have in ordinary tort litigation. As a result, they may be more willing to settle questionable claims than would ordinarily be the case. But this in turn further strengthens the plaintiffs' attorney's hand, and may provide incentives for plaintiffs' attorneys to take on more questionable litigation and to dip even deeper into the potential claimant pool once litigation is well underway. * * * Thus, the economics of mass tort litigation, and the asymmetric risks facing plaintiff attorneys and defendants have the potential to drive the litigation forward, ever broadening its scope, until it reaches either the limits of the exposed population or the limits of the available defendant assets.

* * *

NOTES AND QUESTIONS

1. As the Hensler and Peterson article reveals, the successful prosecution of a mass tort case involves numerous strategic, financial, and legal considerations. Under what circumstances should a plaintiffs' attorney bring a class action suit in a mass tort case? Under what circumstances should defense counsel choose to settle rather than try a mass torts class action? What relevance does the outcome of prior individual cases have in these assessments?

2. One recent student note observes certain common patterns among mass tort class actions certified under Rule 23(b)(3). Note, *Locating Investment Asymmetries and Optimal Deterrence in the Mass Tort Class Action*, 117 Harv. L. Rev. 2665 (2004). On the one hand, they are difficult to manage, "can create the potential for intra-class conflicts and self-interested or deceitful behavior by attorneys," and can "allow plaintiffs to 'blackmail' relatively powerless defendants into settlement and to cash in on 'frivolous' lawsuits." *Id.* at 2665–66. On the other hand, mass tort actions foster "administrative efficiency, meaning relatively quick and inexpensive resolution of similar claims[,]" and may foster "optimal deterrence, as promoted through the alleviation of systemic investment asymmetries that tend to exist in mass tort cases litigated in the conventional separate action litigation process." *Id.* at 2666–67. More specifically, a defendant that harms many people in a similar way has more incentive in developing its case than an individual plaintiff, because the defendant can spread the cost of developing its defense over many claims. *Id.* at 2667. An individual plaintiff proceeding alone, however, will invest only in his claim. *Id.* at 2667–68. Class certification gives individual plaintiffs the ability to "exploit investment scale advantages[,]" thereby "alleviat[ing] this systemic investment asymmetry and the resulting effect on deterrence." *Id.* at 2668. Does this Note suggest that courts should generally be receptive to certification of mass tort class actions? Are the points raised in the Note unique to mass torts?

3. In addition to the Hensler and Peterson article and the Harvard Note, numerous other articles provide an overview of procedural, ethical, and practical problems stemming from mass tort class actions. Some of the leading articles are excerpted in the subsections below.

2. A HISTORICAL REVIEW: THE COURTS' TREATMENT OF MASS TORT CLASS ACTIONS

This subsection discusses the various approaches that courts have adopted over the years concerning whether mass tort cases should be certified as class actions under modern Rule 23.

a. Late 1960s Through Early 1980s

As noted, many courts in the 1960s and 1970s relied on the Advisory Committee Notes in rejecting efforts to certify mass tort cases. In the late 1970s, a number of federal trial courts began permitting plaintiffs to bring mass tort class actions. One case that played a role in stimulating other courts to certify mass tort class actions was Judge Rubin's decision to certify a class of more than 100 injured victims (or estates of deceased victims) of a fire at the Beverly Hills Supper Club in Kentucky. *See Coburn v. 4-R Corp.*, 77 F.R.D. 43 (E.D. Ky. 1977). That case, one of the first mass tort cases ever certified, ultimately settled, although certain common questions were tried to a jury before all defendants had settled. The certification order was never reviewed on appeal. In contrast with the Beverly Hills Supper Club litigation, however, most of the early publicized orders granting class certification in mass tort cases were reversed on appeal. The following are prominent examples.

Hyatt Regency Hotel, Kansas City, Missouri: Collapse Of Two Skywalks

In 1981, two skywalks collapsed at the Kansas City Hyatt Regency, killing 114 persons and injuring hundreds of others. Several plaintiffs filed suit, seeking class certification under Rules 23(b)(1) and (b)(3). The district court certified a Rule 23(b)(1)(A) class on the issues of liability for compensatory and punitive damages and a Rule 23(b)(1)(B) class on the issues of liability for punitive damages and amount of punitive damages. The Eighth Circuit reversed. *In re Federal Skywalk Cases*, 93 F.R.D. 415 (W.D. Mo. 1982), *vacated*, 680 F.2d 1175 (8th Cir. 1982).

Although "[s]everal commentators [at the time] suggested that the appellate court decision in the *Skywalk* mass tort case * * * struck the death knell for the use of the class action procedure in the management of mass tort litigation," in fact, "[a]fter the mandatory class action was vacated by the appellate court, two nearly identical voluntary class actions were certified and settled in the federal and state trial courts." Scott O. Wright & Joseph Colussi, *The Successful Use of the Class Action Device in the Management of the Skywalks Mass Tort Litigation*, 52 UMKC L. Rev. 141, 141–42 (1984).

Dalkon Shield IUD Litigation

In 1981, in the context of a putative class action claiming injuries and deaths as a result of the use of the Dalkon Shield intrauterine device, a federal district court in California certified a nationwide class under Rule

23(b)(1)(B) on the issue of punitive damages and a California statewide class on liability issues under Rule 23(b)(3). *See In re N. Dist. of Cal. "Dalkon Shield" IUD Prods. Liab. Litig.*, 521 F. Supp. 1188 (N.D. Cal. 1981), *vacated*, 693 F.2d 847 (9th Cir. 1982). The alleged injuries included, among others, infections, uterine pregnancies, spontaneous abortions, fetal injuries, and sterility. The Ninth Circuit, however, reversed the district court, finding problems under Rule 23(a) involving commonality, typicality, and adequacy. The Ninth Circuit also found that the requirements of Rule 23(b)(1)(B) and Rule 23(b)(3) were not satisfied. In its decision, the Ninth Circuit explained why, in its view, a "product liability" suit was more difficult to certify than "a typical mass tort":

> In the typical mass tort situation, such as an airplane crash or a cruise ship poisoning, proximate cause can be determined on a class-wide basis because the cause of the common disaster is the same for each of the plaintiffs.
>
> In products liability actions, however, individual issues may outnumber common issues. No single happening or accident occurs to cause similar types of physical harm or property damage. No one set of operative facts establishes liability. No single proximate cause applies equally to each potential class member and each defendant. Furthermore, the alleged tortfeasor's affirmative defenses (such as failure to follow directions, assumption of the risk, contributory negligence, and the statute of limitations) may depend on facts peculiar to each plaintiff's case.

693 F.2d at 853.

b. Mid-1980s

The mid-1980s witnessed a growing acceptance of mass tort class actions among some federal courts. Some commentators attributed this shift in attitude to a growth in massive complex litigation, including the explosion of asbestos suits and the highly publicized *Agent Orange* litigation.

Significant appellate court rulings upholding class certification during the mid-1980s included the *School Asbestos* and *Agent Orange* cases. *See In re "Agent Orange" Prods. Liab. Litig.*, 818 F.2d 145 (2d Cir. 1987); *In re Sch. Asbestos Litig.*, 789 F.2d 996 (3d Cir. 1986). In *School Asbestos*, the Third Circuit upheld the certification under Rule 23(b)(3) of a class action by school districts in several states seeking recovery of the costs of testing and removing asbestos from school buildings. In so doing, the court noted that "the trend has been for courts to be more receptive to use of the class action in mass tort litigation." 789 F.2d at 1009. In *Agent Orange*, the Second Circuit upheld the certification of a class of former military personnel and their families seeking damages for injuries caused by exposure to the herbicide Agent Orange during the Vietnam War. While noting agreement with the "prevalent skepticism" about certifying mass tort class actions, the court found that, because the defendants were private manufacturers producing a product for use by the United States Government, class certification was justified under Rule 23(b)(3) "in light of the centrality of the military contractor defense." *Agent Orange*, 818 F.2d at 166. This appellate green light led plaintiffs' lawyers throughout the country to bring a variety of mass tort class actions: toxic spills, pharmaceutical products, medical devices, and other kinds of cases. In 1989, certification of a class action in the Dalkon Shield litigation by a different trial court was given the imprimatur of a federal appellate court (albeit in the settlement context). *In re A.H. Robins Co.*, 880 F.2d 709 (4th Cir. 1989).

A 1986 asbestos opinion by the Fifth Circuit, *Jenkins v. Raymark Indus., Inc.*, 782 F.2d 468 (5th Cir. 1986), reflected the prevailing judicial attitude during this period. There, the court upheld the certification of a class action alleging personal injuries from asbestos in order to determine one overarching issue—the "state-of-the-art defense," *i.e.*, whether the dangerous nature of asbestos could reasonably have been known at the time the substance was placed on the market. *Id.* at 470, 475. The court found that a class action was "clearly superior to the alternative of repeating, hundreds of times over, the litigation of the state of the art issues with, as [the] experienced [trial] judge says, 'days of the same witnesses, exhibits and issues from trial to trial.'" *Id.* at 472. The court found that "the defendants enjoy all the advantages, the plaintiffs incur the disadvantages, of the class action—with one exception: the cases are to be brought to trial." *Id.* at 473. For a discussion of later proceedings in *Jenkins*, see Part (A)(3)(b) of this chapter.

As part of a shift in favor of certifying mass tort cases in the 1980s (and into the 1990s), certain federal district court judges took leading roles in aggregating claims. For example, Judge Jack Weinstein of the Eastern District of New York presided over the resolution of more than 240,000 Agent Orange claims; Judge Robert Parker of the Eastern District of Texas presided over thousands of asbestos claims; Judge Robert Merhige of the Eastern District of Virginia certified the pollution class action involving the Chesapeake Bay in *Pruitt v. Allied Chemical Corp.*, 85 F.R.D. 100 (E.D. Va. 1980) (*see* Chapter 4(B)(2)(d)), and administered the settlement of 195,000 Dalkon Shield cases; and Judge Sam Pointer of the Northern District of Alabama presided over various aspects of Dow Corning's Breast Implant litigation.

c. Subsequent Appellate Court Skepticism

Champions of the shift toward more liberal class certification of mass tort cases claimed that a liberal approach leveled the playing field between large companies and underfunded victims. Yet some responded that courts had adopted a posture in which the mere threat of class certification was so devastating that defendants routinely chose to settle rather than risk bankruptcy on the results of a single trial. This skepticism about certifying mass tort class actions became prominent in the mid-1990s, when certain federal appellate courts issued a series of rulings viewed by some commentators as fundamentally undermining the use of Rule 23 to adjudicate mass torts. Indeed, in the *Rhone–Poulenc* case set forth below, the Seventh Circuit went so far as to issue a writ of mandamus decertifying the class.

IN RE RHONE–POULENC RORER, INC.
United States Court of Appeals, Seventh Circuit, 1995.
51 F.3d 1293.

Before POSNER, CHIEF JUDGE, and BAUER and ROVNER, CIRCUIT JUDGES.

POSNER, CHIEF JUDGE.

[Portions of this case, including the facts, are set forth in Chapter 6(B). In brief, hemophiliacs infected by the AIDS virus brought suit in various courts around the nation against drug companies that manufactured blood solids. After the actions were consolidated under multidistrict litigation procedures in the Northern District of Illinois, that district court certified a nationwide class action, on limited issues, with the proviso that if plaintiffs prevailed on those issues, the class members could return to their respective jurisdictions and would not need to relitigate the common issues.]

Drug companies that manufacture blood solids are the defendants in a nationwide class action brought on behalf of hemophiliacs infected by the AIDS virus as a consequence of using the defendants' products. The defendants have filed with us a petition for mandamus, asking us to direct the district judge to rescind his order certifying the case as a class action. We have no *appellate* jurisdiction over that order.† * * * For obvious reasons, however, mandamus is issued only in extraordinary cases. Otherwise, interlocutory orders would be appealable routinely, but with "appeal" renamed "mandamus."

[The court concluded that the case satisfied the exacting requirements for mandamus: 1) that the conduct at issue cannot be effectively reviewed after final judgment, and 2) that the order at issue is "patently erroneous" or "usurpative."]

* * *

With all due respect for the district judge's commendable desire to experiment with an innovative procedure for streamlining the adjudication of this "mass tort," we believe that his plan so far exceeds the permissible bounds of discretion in the management of federal litigation as to compel us to intervene and order decertification. The plaintiffs' able counsel argues that we need not intervene now, that it will be time enough to intervene if and when a special verdict adverse to the defendants is entered and an appeal taken to us. But of course a verdict as such is not an appealable order. Only when a final judgment is entered, determining liability and assessing damages, will the case, including interim rulings such as the certification of certain issues in the case for determination in a class action, be appealable to us. Since without a final judgment the special verdict would not (with an exception noted later in this opinion) even have collateral estoppel effect, the district judge may have intended that the special verdict would be followed by a trial on any remaining liability issues, and on damages, limited to * * * [the] named plaintiffs. * * * That trial would culminate in a final judgment, which would both be appealable to us and impart collateral estoppel effect to the special verdict. The members of the class, other than the named plaintiffs, would take the special verdict back to their home districts and use it to limit the scope of the individual trials that would be necessary—for remember that the district judge has refused to certify the case as a class action for a final adjudication of the controversy between the class and the defendants—to determine each class member's actual entitlement to damages and in what amount.

---

† This decision was issued prior to the adoption of Rule 23(f) in 1998. *See* Chapter 9(A). [Ed.]

* * *

[W]e shall assume in accordance with [information elicited from the district court] that eventually there will be a final judgment to review. Only it will come too late to provide effective relief to the defendants; and this is an important consideration in relation to the first condition for mandamus, that the challenged ruling of the district court have inflicted irreparable harm, which is to say harm that cannot be rectified by an appeal from the final judgment in the lawsuit. The reason that an appeal will come too late to provide effective relief for these defendants is the sheer *magnitude* of the risk to which the class action, in contrast to the individual actions pending or likely, exposes them. Consider the situation that would obtain if the class had not been certified. The defendants would be facing 300 suits. More might be filed, but probably only a few more, because the statutes of limitations in the various states are rapidly expiring for potential plaintiffs. The blood supply has been safe since 1985. That is ten years ago. The risk to hemophiliacs of having become infected with HIV has been widely publicized; it is unlikely that many hemophiliacs are unaware of it. Under the usual discovery statute of limitations, they would have to have taken steps years ago to determine their infection status, and having found out file suit within the limitations period running from the date of discovery, in order to preserve their rights.

Three hundred is not a trivial number of lawsuits. The potential damages in each one are great. But the defendants have won twelve of the first thirteen, and, if this is a representative sample, they are likely to win most of the remaining ones as well. Perhaps in the end, if class action treatment is denied (it has been denied in all the other hemophiliac HIV suits in which class certification has been sought), they will be compelled to pay damages in only 25 cases, involving a potential liability of perhaps no more than $125 million altogether. These are guesses, of course, but they are at once conservative and usable for the limited purpose of comparing the situation that will face the defendants if the class certification stands. All of a sudden they will face thousands of plaintiffs. * * *

Suppose that 5,000 of the potential class members are not yet barred by the statute of limitations. And suppose the named plaintiffs in [the case below] win the class portion of this case to the extent of establishing the defendants' liability. * * * It is true that this would only be *prima facie* liability, that the defendants would have various defenses. But they could not be confident that the defenses would prevail. They might, therefore, easily be facing $25 billion in potential liability (conceivably more), and with it bankruptcy. They may not wish to roll these dice. That is putting it mildly. They will be under intense pressure to settle. * * *

* * *

We do not want to be misunderstood as saying that class actions are bad because they place pressure on defendants to settle. That pressure is a reality, but it must be balanced against the undoubted benefits of the class action that have made it an authorized procedure for employment by federal courts. We have yet to consider the balance. All that our discussion to this point has shown is that the first condition for the grant of mandamus—that the challenged ruling not be effectively reviewable at the end of the case—is fulfilled. The ruling will inflict irreparable harm; the next question is whether the ruling can fairly be described as usurpative. We have formulated this second condition as narrowly, as stringently, as can be, but even so formulated we think it is fulfilled. We do not mean to suggest that the district judge is engaged in a deliberate power-grab. We have no reason to suppose that he *wants* to preside over an unwieldy class action. We believe that he was responding imaginatively and in the best of faith to the challenge that mass torts, graphically illustrated by the avalanche of asbestos litigation, pose for the federal courts. But the plan that he has devised for the HIV-hemophilia litigation exceeds the bounds of allowable judicial discretion. Three concerns, none of them necessarily sufficient in itself but cumulatively compelling, persuade us to this conclusion.

The first is a concern with forcing these defendants to stake their companies on the outcome of a single jury trial, or be forced by fear of the risk of bankruptcy to settle even if they have no legal liability, when it is entirely feasible to allow a final, authoritative determination of their liability for the colossal misfortune that has befallen the hemophiliac population to emerge from a decentralized process of multiple trials, involving different juries, and different standards of liability, in different jurisdictions; and when, in addition, the preliminary indications are that the defendants are not liable for the grievous harm that has befallen the members of the class. These qualifications are important. In most class actions—and those the ones in which the rationale for the procedure is most compelling—individual suits are infeasible because the claim of each class member is tiny relative to the expense of litigation. That plainly is not the situation here. A notable feature of this case, and one that has not been remarked upon or encountered, so far as we are aware, in previous cases, is the demonstrated great likelihood that the plaintiffs' claims, despite their human appeal, lack legal merit. This is the inference from the defendants' having won 92.3 percent (12/13) of the cases to have gone to judgment. Granted, thirteen is a small sample and further trials, if they are held, may alter the pattern that the sample reveals. But whether they do or not, the result will be robust if these further trials are permitted to go forward, because the pattern that results will reflect a consensus, or at least a pooling of judgment, of many different tribunals.

For this consensus or maturing of judgment the district judge proposes to substitute a single trial before a single jury. * * * One jury, consisting of six persons (the standard federal civil jury nowadays consists of six regular jurors and two alternates), will hold the fate of an industry in the palm of its hand. This jury, jury number fourteen, may disagree with twelve of the previous thirteen juries—and hurl the industry into bankruptcy. That kind of thing can happen in our system of civil justice (it is not likely to happen, because the industry is likely to settle—whether or not it really is liable) without violating anyone's legal rights. But it need not be tolerated when the alternative exists of submitting an issue to multiple juries constituting in the aggregate a much larger and more diverse sample of decision-makers. That would not be a feasible option if the stakes to each class member were too slight to repay the cost of suit, even though the aggregate stakes are very large and would repay the costs of a consolidated proceeding. But this is not the case with regard to the HIV-hemophilia litigation. Each plaintiff if successful is apt to receive a judgment in the millions. With the aggregate stakes in the tens or hundreds of millions of dollars, or even in the billions, it is not a waste of judicial resources to conduct more than one trial, before more than six jurors, to determine whether a major segment of the international pharmaceutical industry is to follow the asbestos manufacturers into Chapter 11.

[The court's discussion of the second reason for concern, involving the need to instruct the jury on the laws of 50 states, is excerpted in Chapter 6(B).]

[The court's discussion of the third reason for concern, that a bifurcated classwide trial would violate defendants' Seventh Amendment right to a jury trial, is excerpted in Chapter 4(F)(1).]

* * *

We know that an approach similar to that proposed by [the court below] has been approved for asbestos litigation. *See in particular Jenkins v. Raymark Industries, Inc.*, 782 F.2d 468 (5th Cir. 1986); *In re School Asbestos Litigation*, 789 F.2d 996 (3d Cir. 1986). Most federal courts, however, refuse to permit the use of the class-action device in mass-tort cases, even asbestos cases. Those courts that have permitted it have been criticized, and alternatives have been suggested which recognize that a sample of trials makes more sense than entrusting the fate of an industry to a single jury. The number of asbestos cases was so great as to exert a well-nigh irresistible pressure to bend the normal rules. No comparable pressure is exerted by the HIV-hemophilia litigation. That litigation can be handled in the normal way without undue inconvenience to the parties or to the state or federal courts.

* * * The petition for a writ of mandamus is granted, and the district judge is directed to decertify the plaintiff class.

ROVNER, CIRCUIT JUDGE, dissenting.

* * *

I find the majority's reasoning troubling in several respects. First, it means that the preliminary requirement for mandamus—the lack of an alternative means of obtaining relief—will be satisfied by virtually every class certification order, which then authorizes the court to assess the relative merits of the order to determine whether it is "usurpative." The majority's complaint about [the district court's] order—that it will make a settlement more likely than if defendants' negligence were to be determined by separate juries in individual trials—is true of most every order certifying a large plaintiff class. Certification orders almost always increase the likelihood of settlement by expanding the scope of defendants' exposure. Yet that does not make the order any less reviewable if defendants resist the temptation to settle and litigate to final judgment. * * *

* * *

Furthermore, * * * [I] cannot agree with the majority's premise that [the district court's] order in fact will prompt a settlement. Contrary to the clear implication of the majority's opinion, the class portion of the anticipated trial in this case would not go so far as to establish defendants' *liability* to a class of plaintiffs; it would instead resolve *only* the question of whether defendants were negligent in distributing tainted [blood] at any particular point in time. Even if defendants were faced with an adverse class verdict, then, a plaintiff still would be required to clear a number of hurdles before he would be entitled to a judgment. For example, defendants no doubt would contest at that stage whether a particular plaintiff could establish proximate causation or whether his or her claim is in any event barred by the statute of limitations. Thus, contrary to the majority's implication, a class verdict in favor of plaintiffs would not automatically entitle each member of the class to a seven figure judgment. The defendants will thus have ample opportunity to settle should they lose the class trial. And that would seem to me an advisable strategy in light of the success they have had in earlier cases. That factor distinguishes this case from a more standard class action, where a non-bifurcated trial would resolve all relevant issues and conclusively establish liability to the class. * * *

Finally, although the availability of review on direct appeal after final judgment makes it unnecessary for me to discuss the merits of the certification order, the majority's arguments addressed to the propriety of forcing "defendants to stake their companies on the outcome of a single jury trial" or of allowing a single jury to "hold the fate of an industry in the palm of its hand" seem to me at odds with Fed. R. Civ. P. 23 itself. That rule expressly permits class treatment of such claims when its requirements are met, regardless of the magnitude of potential liability. And I see nothing in Rule 23, or in any of the relevant cases, that would make likelihood of success on the merits a prerequisite for class certification. The majority's preference for avoiding a class trial and for submitting the negligence issue "to multiple juries constituting in the aggregate a much larger and more diverse sample of decision-makers" is a rationale for amending the rule, not for avoiding its application in a specific case. * * *

* * *

CASTANO V. AM. TOBACCO CO.
United States Court of Appeals, Fifth Circuit, 1996.
84 F.3d 734.

Before SMITH, DUHE, and DEMOSS, CIRCUIT JUDGES.

SMITH, CIRCUIT JUDGE.

[Portions of this case, including the facts, are excerpted in Chapter 6(B). In brief, the district court certified a class under Rule 23(b)(3) of all nicotine-dependent persons in the United States who had purchased and smoked cigarettes manufactured by defendants since 1943 (along with the estates, spouses, children, relatives, and "significant others" of those nicotine-dependent smokers).]

* * *

The district court erred in its analysis in two distinct ways. First, it failed to consider how variations in state law affect predominance and superiority. [*See* Chapter 6(B)]. Second, its predominance inquiry did not include consideration of how a trial on the merits would be conducted.

Each of these defects mandates reversal. Moreover, at this time, while the tort is immature, the class complaint must be dismissed, as class certification cannot be found to be a superior method of adjudication.

B. Predominance

The district court [erred in failing] to consider how the plaintiffs' addiction claims would be tried, individually or on a class basis. The district court * * * believed that it could not go past the pleadings for the certification decision. The result was an incomplete and inadequate predominance inquiry.

* * *

A district court certainly may look past the pleadings to determine whether the requirements of rule 23 have been met. Going beyond the pleadings is necessary, as a court must understand the claims, defenses, relevant facts, and applicable substantive law in order to make a meaningful determination of the certification issues.

The district court's predominance inquiry demonstrates why such an understanding is necessary. The premise of the court's opinion is a citation to *Jenkins* and a conclusion that class treatment of common issues would significantly advance the individual trials. Absent knowledge of how addiction-as-injury cases would actually be tried, however, it was impossible for the court to know whether the common issues would be a "significant" portion of the individual trials. The court just assumed that because the common issues would play a part in every trial, they must be significant.[18] [Such an approach] would write the predominance requirement out of the rule, and any common issue would predominate if it were common to all the individual trials.[19]

The court's treatment of the fraud claim also demonstrates the error inherent in its approach. According to both the advisory committee's notes to Rule 23(b)(3) and this court's decision in *Simon v. Merrill Lynch, Pierce, Fenner & Smith, Inc.*, 482 F.2d 880 (5th Cir. 1973), a fraud class action cannot be certified when individual reliance will be an issue. The district court * * * refused to consider whether reliance would be an issue in individual trials.

The problem with the district court's approach is that after the class trial, it might have decided that reliance must be proven in individual trials. The court then would have been faced with the difficult choice of decertifying the class after phase 1 and wasting judicial resources, or continuing with a class action that would have failed the predominance requirement of rule 23(b)(3).

III.

In addition to the reasons given above, regarding the district court's procedural errors, this class must be decertified because it independently

---

[18] The district court's approach to predominance stands in stark contrast to the methodology the district court used in *Jenkins*. There, the district judge had a vast amount of experience with asbestos cases. He certified the state of the art defense because it was the most significant contested issue in each case. To the contrary, however, the district court in the instant case did not, and could not, have determined that the common issues would be a significant part of each case. Unlike the judge in *Jenkins*, the district judge *a quo* had no experience with this type of case and did not even inquire into how a case would be tried to determine whether the defendants' conduct would be a significant portion of each case.

[19] An incorrect predominance finding also implicates the court's superiority analysis: The greater the number of individual issues, the less likely superiority can be established. * * *

fails the superiority requirement of rule 23(b)(3). In the context of mass tort class actions, certification dramatically affects the stakes for defendants. Class certification magnifies and strengthens the number of unmeritorious claims. Aggregation of claims also makes it more likely that a defendant will be found liable and results in significantly higher damage awards.

In addition to skewing trial outcomes, class certification creates insurmountable pressure on defendants to settle, whereas individual trials would not. The risk of facing an all-or-nothing verdict presents too high a risk, even when the probability of an adverse judgment is low. *In the Matter of Rhone–Poulenc Rorer Inc.*, 51 F.3d 1293, 1298 (7th Cir. 1995). These settlements have been referred to as judicial blackmail.

It is no surprise then, that historically, certification of mass tort litigation classes has been disfavored. The traditional concern over the rights of defendants in mass tort class actions is magnified in the instant case. Our specific concern is that a mass tort cannot be properly certified without a prior track record of trials from which the district court can draw the information necessary to make the predominance and superiority requirements required by rule 23. This is because certification of an immature tort results in a higher than normal risk that the class action may not be superior to individual adjudication.

We first address the district court's superiority analysis. The court acknowledged the extensive manageability problems with this class. Such problems include difficult choice of law determinations, subclassing of eight claims with variations in state law, *Erie* guesses, notice to millions of class members, further subclassing to take account of transient plaintiffs, and the difficult procedure for determining who is nicotine-dependent. Cases with far fewer manageability problems have given courts pause.

The district court's rationale for certification in spite of such problems—*i.e.*, that a class trial would preserve judicial resources in the millions of inevitable individual trials—is based on pure speculation. Not every mass tort is asbestos, and not every mass tort will result in the same judicial crises. The judicial crisis to which the district court referred is only theoretical.

What the district court failed to consider, and what no court can determine at this time, is the very real possibility that the judicial crisis may fail to materialize.[25] The plaintiffs' claims are based on a new theory of liability and the existence of new evidence. Until plaintiffs decide to file individual claims, a court cannot, from the existence of injury, presume

---

[25] The plaintiffs, in seemingly inconsistent positions, argue that the lack of a judicial crisis justifies certification; they assert that the reason why individual plaintiffs have not filed claims is that the tobacco industry makes individual trials far too expensive and plaintiffs are rarely successful. The fact that a party continuously loses at trial does not justify class certification, however. The plaintiffs' argument, if accepted, would justify class treatment whenever a defendant has better attorneys and resources at its disposal.

The plaintiffs' claim also overstates the defendants' ability to outspend plaintiffs. Assuming *arguendo* that the defendants pool resources and outspend plaintiffs in individual trials, there is no reason why plaintiffs still cannot prevail. The class is represented by a consortium of well-financed plaintiffs' lawyers who, over time, can develop the expertise and specialized knowledge sufficient to beat the tobacco companies at their own game. Courts can also overcome the defendant's alleged advantages through coordination or consolidation of cases for discovery and other pretrial matters.

that all or even any plaintiffs will pursue legal remedies. Nor can a court make a superiority determination based on such speculation.

Severe manageability problems and the lack of a judicial crisis are not the only reasons why superiority is lacking. The most compelling rationale for finding superiority in a class action—the existence of a negative value suit—is missing in this case.

As he stated in the record, plaintiffs' counsel in this case has promised to inundate the courts with individual claims if class certification is denied. Independently of the reliability of this self-serving promise, there is reason to believe that individual suits are feasible. First, individual damage claims are high, and punitive damages are available in most states. The expense of litigation does not necessarily turn this case into a negative value suit, in part because the prevailing party may recover attorneys' fees under many consumer protection statutes.

In a case such as this one, where each plaintiff may receive a large award, and fee shifting often is available, we find Chief Judge Posner's analysis of superiority in *Rhone–Poulenc* to be persuasive. * * * So too here, we cannot say that it would be a waste to allow individual trials to proceed, before a district court engages in the complicated predominance and superiority analysis necessary to certify a class.

* * *

The remaining rationale for superiority—judicial efficiency—is also lacking. In the context of an immature tort, any savings in judicial resources is speculative, and any imagined savings would be overwhelmed by the procedural problems that certification of a *sui generis* cause of action brings with it.

Even assuming *arguendo* that the tort system will see many more addiction-as-injury claims, a conclusion that certification will save judicial resources is premature at this stage of the litigation. Take for example the district court's plan to divide core liability from other issues such as comparative negligence and reliance. The assumption is that after a class verdict, the common issues will not be a part of follow-up trials. The court has no basis for that assumption.

It may be that comparative negligence will be raised in the individual trials, and the evidence presented at the class trial will have to be repeated. The same may be true for reliance. The net result may be a waste, not a savings, in judicial resources. Only after the courts have more experience with this type of case can a court certify issues in a way that preserves judicial resources.

Even assuming that certification at this time would result in judicial efficiencies in individual trials, certification of an immature tort brings with it unique problems that may consume more judicial resources than certification will save. These problems are not speculative; the district court faced, and ignored, many of the problems that immature torts can cause.

The primary procedural difficulty created by immature torts is the inherent difficulty a district court will have in determining whether the requirements of rule 23 have been met. We have already identified a number of defects with the district court's predominance and manageability inquiries, defects that will continue to exist on remand because of the unique nature of the plaintiffs' claim.

The district court's predominance inquiry, or lack of it, squarely presents the problems associated with certification of immature torts. Determining whether the common issues are a "significant" part of each individual case has an abstract quality to it when no court in this country has ever tried an injury-as-addiction [sic—addiction-as-injury] claim. * * *

Yet, an accurate finding on predominance is necessary before the court can certify a class. It may turn out that the defendant's conduct, while common, is a minor part of each trial. Premature certification deprives the defendant of the opportunity to present that argument to any court and risks decertification after considerable resources have been expended.

The court's analysis of reliance also demonstrates the potential judicial inefficiencies in immature tort class actions. Individual trials will determine whether individual reliance will be an issue. Rather than guess that reliance may be inferred, a district court should base its determination that individual reliance does not predominate on the wisdom of such individual trials. The risk that a district court will make the wrong guess, that the parties will engage in years of litigation, and that the class ultimately will be decertified (because reliance predominates over common issues) prevents this class action from being a superior method of adjudication.

[The court's discussion of choice-of-law problems is excerpted in Chapter 6(B). Its discussion of Seventh Amendment jury trial concerns is excerpted in Chapter 4(F)(1)].

* * *

The plaintiffs' final retort is that individual trials are inadequate because time is running out for many of the plaintiffs. They point out that prior litigation against the tobacco companies has taken up to ten years to wind through the legal system. While a compelling rhetorical argument, it is ultimately inconsistent with the plaintiffs' own arguments and ignores the realities of the legal system. First, the plaintiffs' reliance on prior personal injury cases is unpersuasive, as they admit that they have new evidence and are pursuing a claim entirely different from that of past plaintiffs.

Second, the plaintiffs' claim that time is running out ignores the reality of the class action device. In a complicated case involving multiple jurisdictions, the conflict of law question itself could take decades to work its way through the courts. Once that issue has been resolved, discovery, subclassing, and ultimately the class trial would take place. Next would come the appellate process. After the class trial, the individual trials and appeals on comparative negligence and damages would have to take place. The net result could be that the class action device would lengthen, not shorten, the time it takes for the plaintiffs to reach final judgment.

* * *

The district court abused its discretion by ignoring variations in state law and how a trial on the alleged causes of action would be tried. Those errors cannot be corrected on remand because of the novelty of the plaintiffs' claims. Accordingly, class treatment is not superior to individual adjudication. * * *

* * *

AMCHEM PRODS., INC. V. WINDSOR
Supreme Court of the United States, 1997.
521 U.S. 591.

[*See* Chapter 8(A)(3).]

ORTIZ V. FIBREBOARD CORP.
Supreme Court of the United States, 1999.
527 U.S. 815.

[*See* Chapter 3(A)(2).]

MANUAL FOR COMPLEX LITIGATION (FOURTH)
Federal Judicial Center (2004) § 22.7.

* * * Mass tort personal injury cases are rarely appropriate for class certification for trial. In a settlement context, the proposed class must meet Rule 23 requirements, with the exception of trial manageability, and the court must carefully review the proposed settlement terms to ensure that they are fair, reasonable, and adequate. The trend appears to be that cases involving significant personal injuries should not be certified for trial, particularly on a nationwide or multistate basis, because individual issues of causation and individual damages often predominate and state law often varies. Property damage claims may be different—if the amounts at issue in each individual claim are too small, individual litigation may not be a superior, or even feasible, alternative for resolution, especially when the proposed mass tort rests on a novel or untested scientific or legal claim. Some courts have addressed these difficulties by certifying some, but not all, issues for class treatment, and by structuring subclasses under Federal Rule of Civil Procedure 23(c)(4) to reflect state law differences. * * *

22.72   Post-*Amchem* Class Certification

* * *

After *Amchem*, judges asked to certify mass tort class actions for settlement purposes only must scrutinize the cohesiveness, adequacy of representation, and predominance of common issues presented in the proposed class. In *Amchem* itself, indications of the lack of cohesiveness included the nationwide dispersal of cases and the wide range of differences in the asbestos products, claimants' exposures to varied asbestos products, medical histories, severity of injuries, and the presence of alternative causal agents, particularly smoking history. Judges have also applied *Amchem*'s teachings to mass tort litigation outside of the asbestos context, finding deficiencies under Rule 23 that preclude certification.

Courts have created subclasses to respond to concerns about adequacy of representation, providing separate representation for each. Each subclass, however, must also meet all the applicable certification criteria of Rule 23. The individual nature of many exposure, causation, and damages issues may predominate even within a proposed subclass. Such differences can extend far beyond conflicts between present and future claimants and can defeat certification even if there are no future claimants involved.

Two post-*Amchem* mass tort exposure cases illustrate the importance of subclassing. Both involve claims related to defective pacemaker leads. In the first case, a district judge certified subclasses for medical monitoring, negligence, and strict liability claims, but rejected a subclass for punitive damages. Where the laws of various states differed, the judge created subclasses for each of the major groups of state laws, and later approved a settlement of an opt-out class based on the subclasses previously created.[1325] The other case [*Zinser v. Accufix Research Inst., Inc.*, 253 F.3d 1180, 1198 (9th Cir. 2001)] involved a similar product manufactured by the same defendant. The district judge denied plaintiffs' motion to certify a class to litigate claims for negligence, products liability, and medical monitoring. The court of appeals affirmed, holding that the common issues did not predominate, in part because plaintiffs had not submitted a plan for designating subclasses that would satisfy Rule 23.

Amchem does not categorically preclude certification of a mass tort personal injury or property damage settlement class action. Since *Amchem*, however, a number of district courts have refused to certify dispersed personal injury or property damage mass tort class actions for the purpose of trial, or have decertified them, finding that varying state laws and individual issues of exposure, causation, and damages defeat the predominance requirement of Rule 23(b)(3), making trial unmanageable. Another basis for rejecting certification is that such variations make class representatives inadequate or atypical of the interests of the absent class members.

Since *Amchem*, a number of district courts have also refused to certify, or have decertified, mass tort class actions proposed for settlements, or have refused to approve the settlement terms. For example, in a case [*Levell v. Monsanto Research Corp.*, 191 F.R.D. 543, 548–49 (S.D. Ohio 2000)] dealing with a proposed settlement arising out of alleged intentional exposure of workers to radioactive isotopes, the judge rejected a proposed settlement in part because it favored the interests of current employees over the interests of past employees and retirees. In a case dealing with the alleged exposure of cancer patients to high doses of radiation without their consent, the judge declined to review a proposed settlement because the proposed class did not satisfy the requirements of either Rule 23(a) or (b).[1331] In the [*Levell*] case, the judge reviewed and rejected the entire settlement before ruling on the certification motion. In the [*Cincinnati Radiation*] case, the judge denied certification at the preliminary approval stage

---

[1325] *In re Telectronics Pacing Sys., Inc., Accufix Atrial "J" Leads Prods. Liab. Litig.*, 172 F.R.D. 271 (S.D. Ohio 1997) (certifying a mandatory class pursuant to Rule 23(b)(1)(B) and approving a settlement creating a "limited fund" and releasing the parent corporations as well as the subsidiary from further liability). The court of appeals rejected the settlement and the certification of a Rule 23(b)(1)(B) class and held that "bootstrapping of a Rule 23(b)(3) class into a Rule 23(b)(1)(B) class is impermissible and highlights the problem with defining and certifying class actions by reference to a proposed settlement." *In re Telectronics Pacing Sys., Inc., Accufix Atrial "J" Leads Prods. Liab. Litig.*, 221 F.3d 870, 880 (6th Cir. 2000). After remand, the district court approved a revised settlement providing opt-out rights. *In re Telectronics Pacing Sys., Inc., Accufix Atrial "J" Leads Prods. Liab. Litig.*, 137 F. Supp. 2d 985 (S.D. Ohio 2001).

[1331] *In re Cincinnati Radiation Litig.*, 1997 WL 1433832 (S.D. Ohio 1997). Two years later, the same judge reviewed and approved a revised settlement and certified a hybrid opt-out class under Rules 23(b)(2) and (d)(2). *In re Cincinnati Radiation Litig.*, 187 F.R.D. 549 (S.D. Ohio 1999).

[before sending out notice] and thereby avoided the need to conduct a full review of the settlement. The better practice is to determine class certification at the preliminary approval stage, thus resolving the central issue of class certification before investing the significant resources required in reviewing what is often a complex settlement agreement and the considerable costs of providing notice to the class.

In a number of cases, however, judges have continued to certify settlement class actions in the mass tort context, particularly when there are no unknown future claimants and the absent class members are readily identifiable and can be given notice and an opportunity to opt out.[1333] Those judges have emphasized that because the case will be settled rather than tried, differing state laws that might make a class-wide trial unmanageable do not defeat certification for settlement purposes only. The judges address the differences among state laws by certifying subclasses and appointing separate class representatives and counsel for each subclass. In evaluating the proposed settlements, judges have taken differing state laws into account to ensure that similarly situated claimants do not receive disparate treatment. In other settlements dealing with the laws of more than one state, parties and judges have avoided choice-of-law and adequacy-of-representation problems by framing settlement allocations in terms of matrices of benefits based on differences in the severity and impact of various injuries.

22.73   Post-*Ortiz* Mandatory Limited Fund Class Settlements

* * *

Based on *Ortiz*, several judges have invalidated limited fund settlements approved before the Court's decision. Some commentators have expressed doubts as to whether a limited-fund class action is ever appropriate in a mass tort and whether a class action provides structural fairness equivalent to the Bankruptcy Code. Others have declared that bankruptcy is the only recourse for companies facing tort claims exposure that may last for years and ultimately prove overwhelming. The *Ortiz* decision itself did not go this far, and the Court expressly recognized that an undetermined portion of a company's limited funds may go back into the business.

NOTES AND QUESTIONS

1. Another important appellate decision decertifying a mass tort class is *In re American Medical Systems, Inc.*, 75 F.3d 1069 (6th Cir. 1996). There, the Sixth Circuit granted a writ of mandamus, holding that class certification was not appropriate for people claiming assorted injuries as a result of penile implants manufactured by the defendants. In reaching its decision, the court stated:

> Unlike a mass tort action arising out of a single accident or single course of conduct, in medical device products liability litigation of the

---

[1333] *See, e.g., In re Sulzer Hip Prosthesis & Knee Prosthesis Liab. Litig.*, 2001 WL 1842315, at *7 n.9, *14 (N.D. Ohio 2001) (conditionally certifying settlement class and noting that a " 'single set of operative facts establishes liability' " and a "single proximate cause applies to each potential class member"); *In re Diet Drugs Prods. Liab. Litig.*, 2000 WL 1222042, at *41, *69 (E.D. Pa. 2000) (certifying settlement class and finding claimants shared single product and common injury).

sort involved here the factual and legal issues often *do* differ dramatically from individual to individual because there is no common cause of injury. * * *

As this case illustrates, the products are different, each plaintiff has a unique complaint, and each receives different information and assurances from his treating physician. Given the absence of evidence that common issues predominate, certification was improper. In this situation, the economies of scale achieved by class treatment are more than offset by the individualization of numerous issues relevant only to a particular plaintiff.

Thus, even assuming common questions of law or fact, it cannot be said that these issues predominate, and that class treatment would be superior to other methods of litigation. In fact, a number of other courts have denied class certifications in drug or medical product liability actions for these reasons.

The superiority aspect of Rule 23(b)(3) also has not been established. A single litigation addressing every complication in every model of prosthesis, including changes in design, manufacturing, and representation over the course of twenty-two years, as well as the unique problems of each plaintiff, would present a nearly insurmountable burden on the district court. By contrast, an individual case of this type is relatively simple to litigate if narrowly focused on a claim regarding a specific model, a specific component, or specific statements made to a particular urologist during a particular period of time.

Id. at 1084–85.

2. In *Rhone–Poulenc*, *Castano*, and *American Medical Systems*, appellate courts intervened and decertified the classes *before* trial. Why did those courts believe that prompt intervention was necessary? Could they simply have waited until the cases had reached final judgments after trial?

3. The majority and dissent in *Rhone–Poulenc* disagreed sharply over whether the pressure on the defendants to settle after class certification warranted emergency appellate review. Should that concern be a factor in deciding whether to grant pretrial review of the class certification decision? Should that concern be a factor in deciding whether to certify a class in the first instance? Is Judge Rovner correct that the concern about pressure to settle is true in virtually every class action and did not justify emergency review? Is she correct that the majority overstated the pressure on the defendants in *Rhone–Poulenc* to settle? Recall that Rule 23(f), as implemented effective December 1, 1998, permits discretionary appellate review in part because of the pressure on defendants to settle after a ruling granting class certification. *See* Chapter 9(A).

4. Can *Rhone–Poulenc* be squared with case law (discussed in Chapter 4(B)(1)(b)(i)) establishing that a court should not decide the merits (unless there is overlap with class certification requirements) in analyzing whether a class should be certified? Should Rule 23 be amended to permit courts to assess the merits in ruling on class certification?

5. Would the result in *Rhone–Poulenc* have been different if the amount sought by each putative class member had been relatively small? Is Judge Posner's analysis limited, either explicitly or implicitly, to mass tort or other high-value cases?

6. Did the *Castano* court credibly distinguish *Jenkins*? Did the court in effect overrule *Jenkins*, notwithstanding its effort to distinguish the case?

7. Was the *Castano* court persuasive in stating that courts should be particularly reluctant to certify class actions involving "immature torts"? One leading commentator describes a "mature" tort as one "where there has been full and complete discovery, multiple jury verdicts, and a persistent vitality in the plaintiffs' contentions." Francis E. McGovern, *Resolving Mature Mass Tort Litigation*, 69 B.U. L. Rev. 659, 659 (1989). How, in each particular case, should a court distinguish between mature and immature torts?

8. *Castano* raises a number of other interesting issues.

   a. The court stated that, even absent class certification, the defendant's alleged advantage in being able to pool resources can be overcome by specialization and experience of plaintiff's counsel, consolidation, and coordination of pretrial matters (*see* footnote 25 of excerpt). Is the court's solution realistic?

   b. In *Castano*, plaintiffs' counsel threatened that they would inundate the courts with individual lawsuits if the Fifth Circuit decertified the class. Are defendants always better off when certification is denied?

   c. *Castano* also discussed the propriety of certifying a fraud class action. For additional discussion of that issue, see Chapter 3(C)(1)(b)(i).

9. Are *Amchem* and *Ortiz* necessary outgrowths of *Rhone–Poulenc*, *Castano*, and *American Medical Systems*? Or are the Supreme Court decisions significantly broader in scope?

10. As suggested by the *Manual for Complex Litigation (Fourth)*, federal courts have become increasingly inhospitable to mass torts. *See* Emery G. Lee III & Thomas E. Willging, Fed. Judicial Ctr., *The Impact of the Class Action Fairness Act of 2005 on the Federal Courts: Fourth Interim Report to the Judicial Conference Advisory Committee on Civil Rules*, at 5 (Apr. 2008) ("[T]orts-personal injury class actions declined from 52 in July–December 2001 to 35 in January–June 2007, a decrease of 33 percent. Personal injury class actions constituted 1.5 percent of class action activity in January–June 2007, down from 3.8 percent in July–December 2001.").

d. Responses to Judicial Skepticism

It would be premature to view decisions such as *Rhone–Poulenc*, *Castano*, *American Medical Systems*, *Amchem*, and *Ortiz* as the end of mass tort actions. Mass tort actions will not go away any time soon, in part for the reasons stated by Professors Hensler and Peterson, who, writing in 1993, did not have the benefit of those relatively recent decisions:

> * * * The specialized mass tort plaintiffs' bar that emerged during the 1980s has accumulated capital as a result of its success in litigating earlier mass claims, and is skillful and aggressive in identifying new investment opportunities. A mass tort defense bar has developed to counter these plaintiffs' attorney efforts. An elite of trial judges has come forward, ready to set aside traditional case-at-a-time disposition procedures in favor of aggregative procedures for disposing of hundreds or even thousands of cases. A

cottage industry of experts and special masters supports their efforts by designing complex procedures and crafting complex settlements. Appellate courts wrestle with collective disposition of mass claims. Lawyers, judges, and business executives no longer wonder whether or not there will be another mass tort, but rather what the next mass tort will be.

Deborah R. Hensler & Mark A. Peterson, *Understanding Mass Personal Injury Litigation: A Socio–Legal Analysis*, 59 Brook. L. Rev. 961, 964 (1993). Not surprisingly, plaintiffs' lawyers have continued to pursue classwide mass tort actions or surrogates for class treatment.

Continued Certifications. Federal courts have not abandoned class treatment of mass torts in all circumstances. The Sixth Circuit, in *Olden v. LaFarge Corp.*, 383 F.3d 495 (6th Cir. 2004), held that class certification under Rule 23(b)(3) (and (b)(2)) was proper where a class of 3,600 homeowners sued the owner of a cement manufacturing plant for alleged real and personal property damage caused by hazardous toxic pollutants originating from the plant. Plaintiffs alleged that the air contaminants interfered with the use and enjoyment of their property and diminished their property values. Plaintiffs additionally alleged that the defendant exposed them to toxins, increasing the risk of cancer and other life-threatening health problems that would require medical monitoring. *Id.* at 497. Rejecting the defendant's arguments that common issues did not predominate under (b)(3), the Sixth Circuit concluded, *inter alia*, that while defendant raised issues that "may suggest that individual damage determinations might be necessary," the plaintiffs still "raised common allegations which likely allow the court to determine liability (including causation) for the class as a whole." *Id.* at 508–09. The Sixth Circuit also noted the district court could bifurcate the issue of liability from the issue of damages, rejecting defendant's argument that its Seventh Amendment jury trial right might be violated.

The First Circuit, in *Gintis v. Bouchard Transportation Co., Inc.*, 596 F.3d 64 (1st Cir. 2010), noted the division among courts over class certification of cases involving a single tortfeasor and multiple victims, and cited *Amchem* for proposition that "even mass tort cases arising from a common cause or disaster may, depending on the circumstances, satisfy the predominance requirement." *Id.* at 67. In *Gintis*, a class of homeowners of waterfront property sued the owners and operators of a fuel barge that spilled thousands of barrels of fuel oil into Buzzards Bay, contaminating 90 miles of the shoreline. *Id.* at 65. Plaintiffs asserted strict liability, negligence, and common law nuisance claims and sought Rule 23(b)(3) certification. The district court denied certification on the ground that common issues did not predominate over individual ones. In light of the sparse factual record, the First Circuit concluded that it could not reverse the denial of certification, but remanded the case because of the "substantial evidence of predominating common issues." *Id.* at 66. More specifically, the First Circuit noted that defendant's own arguments seemed to show "substantial and serious common issues would arise over and over in potential individual cases" and that a class action would be superior because individuals would be unlikely to pursue their own cases given that potential individual recoveries were small. *Id.* at 67–68. *See also Mejdrech v. Met–Coil Systems Corp.*, 319 F.3d 910, 911–12 (7th Cir. 2003) (holding class certification appropriate where homeowners sued factory for allegedly leaking noxious solvent that contaminated area).

The mass tort case law suggests that a pattern has emerged:

> Although courts will often certify classes involving claims arising out of a mass accident (such as a plane crash or a building collapse) in which causation may be proven on a class-wide basis, they typically will not certify a class involving claims that arise out of mass exposure to a toxic product or chemical because causation must be proven on a case-by-case basis. * * *
>
> * * *
>
> Courts have repeatedly drawn distinctions between proposed classes involving a single incident or single source of harm and proposed classes involving multiple sources of harm occurring over time. The former warrant certification, while the latter do not.

In re Methyl Tertiary Butyl Ether (MTBE) Prods. Liab. Litig., 241 F.R.D. 435, 442, 447 (S.D.N.Y. 2007); *see id.* at 447 & nn. 98–104 (collecting cases where courts granted certification of cases involving single mass tort incident).

Federal courts have also been receptive to certifying mass torts in the settlement context. One prominent example involves the National Football League Concussion Litigation. *See* Chapter 8(A)(5)(a). In that case, the district court certified a settlement class of retired players alleging injuries as a result of playing professional football. In affirming class certification, the Third Circuit noted that "this class of retired NFL players does not present the same obstacles for predominance as the *Amechem* class of hundreds of thousands (maybe millions) of persons exposed to asbestos." *In re Natl. Football League Players Concussion Injury Litig.*, 821 F.3d 410, 434 (3d Cir.), *cert. denied sub nom. Gilchrist v. natl. Football League* (U.S. Dec. 12, 2016), and *cert. denied sub nom. Armstrong v. Natl. Football League* (U.S. Dec. 12, 2016). Does it make sense to apply more liberal criteria in certifying mass tort cases for settlement purposes?

Another prominent example of mass tort cases that settled on a class-wide basis is the *Deepwater Horizon* oil spill litigation. Hundreds of lawsuits were brought against Transocean, Ltd. and BP, Plc., following an April 20, 2010 explosion of the Deepwater Horizon drilling rig and subsequent oil spill in the Gulf of Mexico. *See* John Schwartz, *First the Spill Then the Lawsuits*, N.Y. Times, June 10, 2010, *available at* http://www.nytimes.com/2010/06/11/us/11liability.html (last visited Feb. 6, 2017). The Judicial Panel on Multidistrict Litigation transferred those claims—including personal injury, wrongful death, economic loss, and environmental harm—to the Eastern District of Louisiana for consolidated pretrial proceedings. Ultimately, the district court approved two class settlements—one for economic and property injuries and one for personal injuries. *In re Oil Spill by Oil Rig Deepwater Horizon in Gulf of Mexico, on Apr. 20, 2010*, 910 F. Supp. 2d 891, 900, 966 (E.D. La. 2012), *aff'd sub nom, In re Deepwater Horizon*, 739 F.3d 790 (5th Cir. 2014) (economic and property); *In re Oil Spill by Oil Rig Deepwater Horizon*, 295 F.R.D. 112 (E.D. La. 2013) (medical benefits).

Objectors failed in their effort to challenge the economic/property settlement, and no appeal was filed challenging the medical benefits settlement.

It should also be noted that mass tort cases have been frequently subject to consolidation under the multidistrict litigation statute. *See* Chapter 12(A). Although the claims generally remain as individual actions, the consolidation of potentially thousands of mass torts for pretrial purposes has enabled judges to achieve broad settlements.

State courts have also occasionally certified mass tort actions. For example, in 1996 a state trial court certified a class action involving tobacco (*R.J. Reynolds Tobacco Co. v. Engle*, 672 So.2d 39 (Fla. Dist. Ct. App. 1996), *rev. denied*, 682 So.2d 1100 (Fla. 1996), *subsequently decertified*, 853 So.2d 434 (Fla. Dist. Ct. App. 2003), *rev. granted*, 873 So.2d 1222 (Fla. 2004), 2004 Fla. LEXIS 807 (Fla. 2004), *approved in part and quashed in part*, 945 So.2d 1246 (Fla. 2006)); and courts have upheld certification of mass tort cases involving explosions (*Clement v. Occidental Chem. Corp.*, 699 So.2d 1110 (La. App. Ct. 1997); *Daniels v. Witco Corp.*, 877 So.2d 1011 (La. App. Ct. 2004)).

Expanded Targets and Creative Theories. Plaintiffs have widened the net of target industries for mass tort lawsuits and have targeted traditional industries in creative ways. Such litigation has been highly controversial, and not always successful. *See* Andrew M. Dansider, *The Next Big Thing for Litigators*, 37 Md. B.J. 12, 13–16 (July/Aug. 2004) (describing tobacco class actions as the "mother lode" because it was "an amalgamation of unimaginably deep pockets, smoking gun documents, undeniably deadly products, startling insider testimony, and a bottomless pool of potential clients," and speculating as to the "next perfect litigation storm"); *Lawyers Look to the Future of Toxic Torts, See New Claims, New Plaintiffs, New Defendants*, 24 Toxics L. Reporter 1331 (2009) (identifying emerging issues for toxic tort practitioners, such as climate change, Chinese drywall, water pollution, food quality and marketing, nanotechnology, animal feeding operations, mining waste, and diesel exposure).

Although some commentators and litigators thought that class actions against the gun industry would become the new wave of mass torts litigation, Congress acted to prevent that outcome. In October 2005, it enacted the Protection of Lawful Commerce in Arms Act, Pub. L. 109–92, 119 Stat. 2095, which prohibits any person from bringing a civil action against a firearms or ammunition product manufacturer or seller resulting from the criminal or unlawful misuse of such product.

Surrogates For Class Treatment. One important development is the assertion by plaintiffs of various surrogates for class treatment. One highly publicized example involved cost-recoupment suits filed against the tobacco industry. Beginning in 1994, attorneys general in numerous states brought suits against the major U.S. tobacco companies and other defendants to recover costs incurred in providing medical care to their residents, including Medicaid-related costs, as a result of the use of cigarettes and smokeless tobacco. Several courts upheld these suits in whole or in part, and the tobacco companies eventually settled with all 50 states and the District of Columbia for hundreds of billions of dollars. *See, e.g., Int'l Bhd. of Teamsters, Local 734 Health & Welfare Trust Fund v. Philip Morris, Inc.*,

196 F.3d 818, 820 (7th Cir. 1999) (private lawsuit discussing attorney general settlements).

Recoupment suits against tobacco companies have also been brought by non-government entities, but such suits have not been successful. For example, numerous cases have been filed by union trust funds seeking recovery of costs to treat smoking-related illnesses of union members. A vast majority of courts have dismissed those cases in whole or in part on the ground that the trust funds were too far removed to bring such a claim. *See Or. Laborers–Employers Health & Welfare Trust Fund v. Philip Morris, Inc.*, 185 F.3d 957, 964 (9th Cir. 1999) (so holding and citing cases); *accord, e.g., Laborers Local 17 Health & Benefit Fund v. Philip Morris, Inc.*, 191 F.3d 229 (2d Cir. 1999).

* * *

In short, plaintiffs' counsel will continue to pursue mass tort litigation aggressively, even though the traditional class action model has become more difficult to invoke. *See also* Chapter 13 (discussing non-class party aggregation of mass tort claims).

3. OTHER ISSUES IN MASS TORT CLASS ACTIONS

In addition to the topics addressed above, several other topics arise frequently in mass tort litigation and thus are worthy of consideration.

a. Exposure-Only Claimants

In a number of mass tort cases, the class is defined as encompassing all individuals who were exposed to a toxic substance during a specified period of time. Some substances, however, have long latency periods, so in some instances someone who has not manifested any injury will still be part of the class. Assume that (1) a mass tort settlement requires that all claims for injuries be submitted by a certain date, and (2) at least some class members have no injuries as of that date. Are such class members bound by such a settlement? This issue arises in a number of contexts, including (1) whether the uncompensated future claimants can collaterally attack the adequacy of the class representatives and/or counsel, and (2) whether such claimants can avoid a binding judgment by contending that future claimants lack standing to sue because they have no injury in fact. These issues are addressed below.

i. *Adequacy of Representation*

What happens if a victim of exposure to a toxic substance does not manifest injury during the period for submitting claims in a classwide settlement? Is the class representative and/or class counsel inadequate in permitting such a settlement? If an earlier court already found the representative and counsel adequate, should the class member who was denied a remedy be allowed to mount a collateral attack on the adequacy of the representative or counsel?

In *Stephenson v. Dow Chemical Co.*, 273 F.3d 249, *aff'd in part and vacated in part*, 539 U.S. 111 (2003) [also discussed in Chapter 7(D)(2)], the Second Circuit faced a collateral attack on the Agent Orange settlement by two Vietnam veterans—Joe Isaacson and Daniel Stephenson—who, according to the district court, were barred by the 1984 Agent Orange settlement even though injuries did not manifest until *after* the settlement's cut-off period for submitting claims. The veterans argued that they were not adequately represented because the settlement purported to resolve the future claims of individuals, such as Isaacson and Stephenson, who would be unable to recover. The Second Circuit, after finding that a collateral attack was permissible, agreed that the plaintiffs had not been adequately represented in the earlier litigation. The court also found that notice could not properly be given to exposure-only plaintiffs. Thus, the court held that Isaacson and Stephenson could assert claims alleging injury from Agent Orange. The Supreme Court granted Dow Chemical's petition for a writ of *certiorari*, but ultimately did not reach the collateral attack issue. *See* 539 U.S. 111 (2003). As to Stephenson (who filed originally in federal court), the Court affirmed by an equally divided court, a ruling that has no precedential effect. The Court vacated the decision as to the other plaintiff Isaacson, in light of an intervening decision, *Syngenta Crop Protection, Inc. v. Henson*, 537 U.S. 28 (2002), which raised issues about the propriety of the defendants' removal of the case to federal court. On remand, the Second Circuit held that the removal had indeed been improper. *Stephenson v. Dow Chem. Co.*, 346 F.3d 19 (2d Cir. 2003).

Is the Second Circuit's decision allowing a collateral attack on adequacy the proper way to address the problem of future claimants? What arguments can be made in favor of the ruling? What arguments can be made against it? What other approaches exist for ensuring that the rights of future claimants are protected?

ii. Standing

Does someone who has been exposed to a hazardous substance, but has suffered no physical injury, have a sufficient legal basis to file suit? This important issue was raised, but not decided, by *Amchem* and *Ortiz*. An earlier decision in the *Amchem* litigation addressed the issue in detail.

CARLOUGH V. AMCHEM PRODS., INC.
United States District Court, Eastern District of Pennsylvania, 1993.
834 F. Supp. 1437.

REED, DISTRICT JUDGE.

This lawsuit is a class action for asbestos-related personal injuries. This memorandum opinion addresses whether this Court has subject matter jurisdiction over this case.

I. BACKGROUND

On January 15, 1993, counsel for the plaintiff class (or the "*Carlough* class") filed the complaint in this action along with motions for class certification and for approval of a proposed settlement agreement ("proposed settlement" or "settlement") between the plaintiff class and the defendants. The complaint alleges that the defendants, members of the Center for Claims Resolution ("the CCR defendants"), are liable to the plaintiff class under the legal theories of (1) negligent failure to warn, (2) strict liability,

(3) breach of express and implied warranty, (4) negligent infliction of emotional distress, (5) enhanced risk of disease, (6) medical monitoring, and (7) civil conspiracy. In their complaint, the named plaintiffs allege that jurisdiction is based upon diversity of citizenship * * *.

On the same day as the complaint was filed, the CCR defendants answered the complaint and joined in plaintiffs' request that the class be certified and the settlement agreement approved.

On January 29, 1993, the Honorable Charles R. Weiner of this Court conditionally certified an opt-out class consisting of:

> 1. All persons (or their legal representatives) who have been exposed in the United States or its territories (or while working aboard U.S. military, merchant or passenger ships), either occupationally or through occupational exposure of a spouse or household member, to asbestos or to asbestos containing products for which one or more of the defendants may bear legal liability and who, as of January 15, 1993, reside in the United States or its territories, and who have not, as of January 15, 1993, filed a lawsuit for asbestos-related personal injury or damage, or death in any state or federal court against the defendant(s) (or against entities for whose actions or omissions the defendant(s) bear legal liability).
>
> 2. All spouses, parents, children, and other relatives (or their legal representatives) of the class members described in paragraph 1 above who have not, as of January 15, 1993, filed a lawsuit for the asbestos-related personal injury, or damage, or death of a class member described in paragraph 1 above in any state or federal court against the defendant(s) (or against entities for whose actions or omissions the defendant(s) bear legal liability).

* * *

This memorandum addresses [among other things, plaintiffs' standing to sue, an issue raised by various unnamed class members who objected to the settlement].

II. DISCUSSION

A. Standing

It is fundamental that a federal court lacks jurisdiction to hear any matter that is not a justiciable case or controversy under Article III of the U.S. Constitution, and that an action is not justiciable if the plaintiff does not have standing to sue. "In essence the question of standing is whether the litigant is entitled to have the court decide the merits of the dispute or of particular issues." This question is answered by determining whether the plaintiff has a "personal stake in the outcome of the controversy." Such a personal stake assures "concrete adverseness which sharpens the presentation of the issues." * * *

* * *

In this lawsuit, the objectors claim that many of the members of the *Carlough* class do not have Article III standing because they have not sustained an "injury in fact." The objectors note that the *Carlough* class includes those who have been occupationally exposed to asbestos but who do not manifest any asbestos-related condition (hereinafter "the exposure-only plaintiffs"). And, in their memoranda of law, the objectors point to several state and federal cases which have held that "subclinical injury resulting from exposure to asbestos is insufficient to constitute actual loss or damage to a plaintiff's interest required to sustain a cause of action under generally applicable principles of tort law." The objectors argue that the lack of a cause of action under applicable state tort law mandates a finding that the exposure-only plaintiffs have alleged no injury in fact for purposes of Article III standing.[3]

* * *

* * * I must * * * determine whether, pursuant to federal precedent, the harm alleged by the exposure-only plaintiffs, namely exposure to asbestos, constitutes injury in fact which is fairly traceable to the defendants' conduct and is likely to be redressed by a favorable decision.

1. Injury in Fact

To satisfy the first requirement of standing, the exposure-only plaintiffs must demonstrate that they have suffered an injury in fact which is concrete and particularized, and actual or imminent rather than merely conjectural or hypothetical. * * *

The severity of the injury is immaterial. The Supreme Court and the Court of Appeals for the Third Circuit have explained that "[t]hese injuries need not be large, an 'identifiable trifle' will suffice." * * *

* * *

* * * [T]he Second Circuit's recent decision in the Agent Orange Litigation [*In re "Agent Orange" Prod. Liab. Litig. (Ivy v. Diamond Shamrock Chemicals Co.)*, 996 F.2d 1425 (2d Cir. 1993),] is directly on point here. *Ivy* turned on the effect of the settlement of a prior Agent Orange class action lawsuit in which the class had included "future claimants," that is, persons who had been exposed to Agent Orange but did not yet manifest any disease. Subsequently, several individuals whose disease manifested itself after the settlement filed new lawsuits. In seeking to avoid the binding effect of the class action settlement, they argued that, at the time of the class action, they lacked injury in fact for purposes of Article III standing because they manifested no disease as a result of their exposure to Agent Orange. They argued that, because of their lack of standing, their claims were not within the Article III jurisdiction of the court that approved the class action settlement and, therefore, could not have been settled.

The Second Circuit rejected that argument. It held that " 'some types of injury to the body occur prior to the appearance of any symptoms; thus, the manifestation of the injury may well occur after the injury itself,' " and rejected the argument that " 'injury in fact' means injury that is manifest, diagnosable or compensable." Instead, the Second Circuit agreed that the plaintiffs' injury in fact occurred at the time of exposure.

In another case involving a settlement in an asbestos class action, objectors argued that those members of the class who had not yet manifested an asbestos-related illness did not allege Article III injury in fact. *In re*

---

[3] The objectors concede, and I agree, that those members of the plaintiff class who already manifest an asbestos-related condition have Article III standing to bring this lawsuit.

Joint Eastern & Southern Dist. Asbestos Litig. (*In re Johns–Manville Corp.*), 129 B. R. 710, 834 (E. & S.D.N.Y. 1991). In response to these objections, the Honorable Jack B. Weinstein held:

> Since asbestos-related illnesses progress over time, the injury can be presumed to have occurred though the victim may not be aware of it. * * *

* * *

Finally, in *Ashton v. Pierce*, 541 F. Supp. 635 (D.D.C. 1982), *aff'd*, 716 F.2d 56, *modified on other grounds*, 723 F.2d 70 (D.C. Cir. 1983), the district court held that persons exposed to lead-based paint, but who did not yet manifest disease, had standing because their "alleged exposure to the risk of lead poisoning as a result of the continued presence of lead-based paint in [Washington,] D.C. public housing clearly constitutes a sufficient claim of injury in fact." In fact, many federal class action cases have involved a class that included persons who had been exposed to a toxin but manifested no disease. Although in many of those cases there is no express finding as to Article III standing, it is clear to me that the courts were satisfied as to their Article III jurisdiction because a finding of such jurisdiction is a necessary predicate to taking action on the merits.

Based upon the foregoing analysis, I conclude that exposure to a toxic substance constitutes sufficient injury in fact to give a plaintiff standing to sue in federal court. The objectors do not dispute, nor could they, that asbestos is a toxin. In this case, the class consists of persons who have been exposed to asbestos either occupationally or through the occupational exposure of a spouse or household member. Accordingly, by definition, each class member sues on the basis of *actual* exposure and not future exposure to asbestos. Without more, the exposure-only plaintiffs have alleged sufficient injury in fact.

Apart from the authority dealing with exposure to a toxin as Article III injury in fact, I conclude that the available medical data on the health consequences of exposure to asbestos also require a conclusion that the exposure-only plaintiffs have alleged a demonstrable physical injury which satisfies the Article III injury in fact requirement.

The Pennsylvania Supreme Court recently characterized the immediate consequences of exposure to asbestos as a "direct injury." *J.H. France Refractories Co. v. Allstate Ins. Co.*, 626 A.2d 502, 505–06 (Pa. 1993). The court summarized current medical evidence which shows that:

> asbestos fibers in the respiratory tract interact with the membranes of the cells lining the trachea and cause the release of enzymes and superoxides which either damage or kill individual cells. If sufficient cells are damaged, tissue (an accumulation of cells) is damaged or destroyed. This injury occurs within minutes after asbestos fibers enter the cells.

The court went on to hold that, for purposes of triggering an insurer's duty to indemnify, "the medical evidence of discrete cellular injuries occurring upon exposure to asbestos justifies the conclusion that exposure to asbestos causes immediate 'bodily injury' * * *," even if disease is not manifested until much later * * *. Thus, to show injury in fact, the exposure-only plaintiffs are not relying on speculative future harm, but on their *present* injuries resulting from exposure to asbestos.

In sum, the weight of recognized medical research on asbestos-related diseases shows that exposure to asbestos causes immediate cellular changes. And, only those who have been exposed to asbestos are members of the plaintiff class. They have been personally affected by defendants' conduct in a concrete and particular way whether or not they ever develop a serious medical condition. This is exactly the type of personal stake the Article III injury-in-fact requirement demands. Therefore, I conclude that the exposure-only plaintiffs have alleged Article III injury in fact.

* * *

JOHN C. COFFEE, JR., CLASS WARS: THE DILEMMA OF THE MASS TORT CLASS ACTION
95 Colum. L. Rev. 1343, 1422–29 (1995).

The utility of the mass tort class action to the defendant today probably hinges on its ability to resolve future claims. * * *

Understandable as it is that defendants want litigation closure from the typically spiraling costs of future claims, constitutional limits may constrain the ability of a federal court to provide it. The primary doctrinal obstacle is Article III, Section 2 of the U.S. Constitution, which permits federal courts to exercise jurisdiction only over "cases" and "controversies." Traditionally, this constitutional barrier has been employed to deny subject matter jurisdiction in two quite distinct contexts, both of which have applicability to the mass tort class action. First, numerous cases have held that federal courts may not hear "friendly," "feigned," or collusive lawsuits, in which there is no legitimate dispute between the parties. Such actions both misuse judicial authority (because the court's perception of the facts and legal arguments is distorted by the absence of true adversaries), and confuse judicial decisionmaking. * * *

Second, the deeper policy rationale for the "case or controversy" requirement is to preserve the separation of powers by limiting the matters that the judicial branch may address. The traditional rhetoric of the case law says that federal courts may not decide "abstract or hypothetical questions." At bottom, this limitation prevents activist judges from making essentially legislative policy judgments as to which they typically have neither expertise nor legitimacy. Accordingly, a plaintiff must have more than an ideological interest in a dispute to have standing, but rather must have a " 'personal stake in the outcome of the controversy.' " The Supreme Court has framed a tripartite test for determining when this requisite personal stake exists, which requires that (1) the plaintiff have suffered a concrete injury in fact; (2) the injury is fairly traceable to the challenged conduct; and (3) the injury is likely to be redressed by a favorable decision.

Do future claimants have the requisite "injury-in-fact" to give them standing? * * * Obviously, one can assert that highly contingent and delayed future claims in mass tort cases are not sufficiently "actual or imminent" * * *. Here, however, it is necessary to refine and break down the somewhat overbroad concept of future claims. In overview, future claimants can be subdivided into three distinct subcategories: (1) persons who have suffered a legally cognizable injury but (for whatever reason) have not yet filed suit; (2) persons who have been exposed to the toxic or defective substance, drug, or product but have not yet manifested injury; and (3) persons who have not yet been exposed or injured but who will be in the future as a result of conduct by the defendants that has already occurred. This last category arises typically when the product or substance remains in use (contrary to the fact patterns in the asbestos or silicone gel breast implants cases where the product had been withdrawn from the market) * * *. [T]his third category is the one that can be most clearly excluded under a constitutional analysis.

As a practical matter, however, the critical category is the second one: the "exposure only" victims who lack symptoms at the time of the settlement. Defendants have zealously sought to cover such "exposure only" plaintiffs in recent settlement class actions, and indeed probably would not have settled had this category been excluded. For example, in *Carlough*, the complaint expressly asserted that the "exposure only" plaintiffs had sustained no physical harm as a result of their exposure to asbestos, but sought relief instead for (1) their increased risk of developing asbestos-related disease; (2) their fear and mental anguish at the prospect of developing asbestos-related disease; and (3) their need for medical monitoring and surveillance to detect asbestos-related illness at an early stage. If intangible and contingent injuries such as these, which essentially spring from an increased base expectancy rate of future illness, amount to a concrete injury-in-fact sufficient to confer standing, then it would seem that few meaningful barriers remain. Indeed, on this basis, a settlement class action today might also resolve, consistent with Article III, the future claims of all citizens in the United States who have been exposed to secondary tobacco smoke.

But what practical lines can be drawn that would find such claims to be non-justiciable? Probably the simplest "bright line" standard would be to look to state law and assert that if a claim, as pleaded, was not cognizable under state law, then it also should not be a sufficient "injury-in-fact" for purposes of Article III. Today, in most state jurisdictions, exposure alone to toxic substances does not give rise to a legally cognizable injury for fear or emotional distress. These decisions have generally held that increased risk of future injury, or fear of such injury, does not constitute an independent ground for the recovery of damages, absent some "direct physical injury or impact." Some cases have said that even a "subclinical injury resulting from exposure to asbestos is insufficient to constitute the actual loss or damage to a plaintiff's interest required to sustain a cause of action."

Ironically, the same district court that decided [*Carlough*] had earlier found that "exposure only" plaintiffs lacked Article III standing in the absence of an actual asbestos-related injury. Yet, when faced with the * * * settlement class, the court reversed its prior position. * * *

* * * [C]ases that have found mere exposure sufficient to confer Article III standing have largely arisen in two very different contexts: injunctive actions and bankruptcy proceedings.* * * [I]njunctive actions stand apart from actions for money judgments because most injunctive actions will unavoidably affect unrepresented future claimants. * * * [S]chool boundaries in a desegregation case necessarily and inevitably affect future claimants,

many of whom have not yet even been exposed to the unlawful condition or danger. Given that such future claimants will inevitably be affected, it may be appropriate to recognize their standing and unnecessary to provide them a right to opt out. Precisely for this reason, Rule 23 permits non-opt out class actions when the plaintiff seeks relief that will necessarily affect absent parties.

The bankruptcy context is even more distinguishable. * * * [T]he irony is that future claimants currently receive more protection in bankruptcy than in a class action. Today, in bankruptcy, the majority of recent cases have found that a legally cognizable claim in bankruptcy does not arise simply because negligent or reckless conduct by the defendant occurred prior to the time of the filing of the bankruptcy petition. Rather, these decisions have held that there must be some pre-petition relationship between the future claimants and the bankrupt entity in order for the future claimants to have standing. Some of these decisions also require that the claim was within the "fair contemplation of the parties" at the time of the bankruptcy filing. When the claim was not within the parties' "fair contemplation," they have said, the bankruptcy reorganization will not act as a bar and the future claimant can still sue the reorganized entity years later when the claimant's injury first manifests itself.

* * * [T]his intermediate standard, which requires both the existence of a pre-petition relationship and that the claim be within the parties' "fair contemplation," makes good sense and could easily be applied to govern justiciability in the class action context as well. From a policy perspective, the mass tort class action and the mass tort bankruptcy contexts are functional substitutes, and the same limitations should apply in both contexts.

* * *

NOTES AND QUESTIONS

1. The *Carlough* case was a preliminary ruling on subject-matter jurisdiction. Judge Reed later ruled that the proposed settlement satisfied a sufficient threshold standard of fairness so that notice could be sent to the class. *Carlough v. Amchem Prods., Inc.*, 158 F.R.D. 314 (E.D. Pa. 1993). He subsequently certified a settlement class, *Georgine v. Amchem Prods., Inc.*, 157 F.R.D. 246 (E.D. Pa. 1994), and enjoined class members from initiating claims against the defendants pending a final judgment, *Georgine v. Amchem Prods.*, 878 F. Supp. 716 (E.D. Pa. 1994). These rulings resulted in review by the Third Circuit in *Georgine*, 83 F.3d 610 (3d Cir. 1996), and ultimately the Supreme Court in *Amchem Prods., Inc. v. Windsor*, 521 U.S. 591 (1997) (*see* Chapter 8(A)(3)). Both the Third Circuit and the Supreme Court declined to resolve the question of whether exposure-only victims have standing to bring a cause of action, concluding that the class did not meet the certification requirements of Rule 23(a)(4) and Rule 23(b)(3). The Supreme Court reasoned that " '[t]he class certification issues [were] dispositive,' because their resolution here is logically antecedent to the existence of any Article III issues * * *." 521 U.S. at 612. Likewise, in *Ortiz v. Fibreboard Corp.*, 527 U.S. 815, 831 (1999) (*see* Chapter 3(A)(2)), the Court addressed the Rule 23 issues without deciding the Article III issue. Is it logical to decide the Rule 23 issues before deciding whether plaintiffs have standing to assert their claims? *Cf. Easter v. Am. W. Fin.*, 381 F.3d 948, 962 (9th Cir. 2004) (noting that "[t]he district court correctly addressed the issue of standing before it addressed the issue of class certification"). For a

detailed discussion of this issue, *see* Linda S. Mullenix, *Standing and Other Dispositive Motions After* Amchem *and* Ortiz: *The Problem of "Logically Antecedent" Inquiries*, 2004 Mich. St. L. Rev. 703 (2004).

2. Is the *Carlough* court persuasive in finding that exposure to asbestos is sufficient to establish injury-in-fact? If so, is the court persuasive in finding that the exposure-only plaintiffs alleged a demonstrable *physical* injury? Should the court instead have concluded that plaintiffs who claim mere exposure to a harmful substance but manifest no physical symptoms lack Article III standing?

3. Professor Coffee notes that in most states, exposure alone does not justify a cognizable lawsuit. Should the *Carlough* court have looked to state law for guidance?

4. Does Professor Coffee's critique of *Carlough* withstand scrutiny? Should the court have applied a more rigorous standard, such as that used in the bankruptcy context? How would the "pre-petition relationship" standard discussed by Professor Coffee work outside of the bankruptcy context? *See, e.g.,* Coffee, *supra*, 95 Colum. L. Rev. at 1429 (asserting that someone who received breast implants through surgical procedure would satisfy pre-petition relationship and "fair contemplation" standards, while individuals exposed to secondhand tobacco smoke would not). Where would asbestos exposure fall on this continuum? Would such a determination depend upon the specific facts involved? Bankruptcy issues are explored in Chapter 13(B)(2).

5. Numerous commentators have proposed ways to deal with the problem of future claimants. *See, e.g.,* David Rosenberg, *The Causal Connection in Mass Exposure Cases: A "Public Law" Vision of the Tort System*, 97 Harv. L. Rev. 849, 919–20 (1984) (proposing awarding insurance policies to exposure-only plaintiffs); Linda S. Mullenix, *Back to the Futures: Privatizing Future Claims Resolution*, 148 U. Pa. L. Rev. 1919, 1925, 1928–31 (2000) (proposing "privatiz[ing] the resolution of future claims through a vendor bidding process whereby vendors would submit bids to administer future claims"); Geoffrey C. Hazard, Jr., *The Futures Problem*, 148 U. Pa. L. Rev. 1901, 1915–18 (2000) (proposing a statutory approach—based on a "workers' compensation model"—for dealing with mass torts, including future claimants); Note, *Settlement Class Actions and "Mere-Exposure" Future Claimants: Problems in Mass Toxic Tort Liability*, 47 Drake L. Rev. 113, 136 (1998) (proposing opt-out opportunity be delayed in a class action suit or settlement until plaintiff's disease becomes manifest); Note, *Standing on Its Head: The Problem of Future Claimants in Mass Tort Class Actions*, 77 Tex. L. Rev. 215, 258 (1998) (proposing "a bright line denial of standing to future claimants in mass tort class actions"); Note, *When Futures Fight Back: For Long-Latency Injury Claimants in Mass Tort Class Actions, Are Asymptomatic Subclasses the Cure to the Disease*? 72 Fordham L. Rev. 1219, 1278–80 (2004) (proposing an "opt in futures subclass" for class actions involving "exposure aware" future claimants so that "future injury plaintiffs [could] receive funds" and "current injury plaintiffs would not suffer from the inclusion of the futures subclasses"; individuals who are not aware that they were exposed to an allegedly toxic substance cannot be part of such a subclass but instead "should enter the traditional tort system when they do manifest injuries").

6. The ALI's *Principles of Aggregate Litigation* addresses issues of adequacy of representation surrounding the settlement of future claims. Section 3.10 provides:

(a) "Future claims" are those claims of class members that might be brought against the respondent, depending on potential future events that are contingent at the time of the class settlement.

(b) A class settlement may not resolve future claims unless the court determines that persons with such claims are represented in a manner that avoids structural conflicts of interest * * * .

(c) When the parties simultaneously seek class certification and approval of a class settlement that would resolve future claims, structural conflicts of interest under subsection (b) may be avoided insofar as the class settlement:

> (1) does not make tradeoffs with respect to class members with future claims vis-à-vis other class members; or
>
> (2) provides additional structural assurances of protection for persons with future claims, such as deferred opt-out rights or delayed determination of the fee award for class counsel pending experience with the operation of the settlement as to future claims.

American Law Institute, *Principles of the Law of Aggregate Litigation* § 3.10, at 240 (2010). Does this approach to settlement of future claims make sense?

b. Problems of Classwide Proof in Mass Tort Cases

This section examines an important and controversial issue: whether plaintiffs in a mass tort class action can establish elements of their claims for the entire class by extrapolation—that is, by offering evidence relating to only a sample group of class members. This issue is addressed in the two cases below, which involve asbestos claims.

IN RE FIBREBOARD CORP.
United States Court of Appeals, Fifth Circuit, 1990.
893 F.2d 706.

Before HIGGINBOTHAM, DAVIS, and DUHE, CIRCUIT JUDGES.

HIGGINBOTHAM, CIRCUIT JUDGE.

[After *Jenkins* (*see* Part (A)(2) of this chapter), the district court devised a comprehensive plan for trying asbestos claims in the Eastern District of Texas. This decision reviewed that trial plan.]

Defendants Fibreboard Corporation and Pittsburgh Corning Corporation * * * petition for writ of mandamus, asking that we vacate pretrial orders consolidating 3,031 asbestos cases for trial entered by Judge Robert Parker, Eastern District of Texas.

In 1986 there were at least 5,000 asbestos-related cases pending in this circuit. We then observed that "because asbestos-related diseases will continue to manifest themselves for the next fifteen years, filings will continue at a steady rate until the year 2000." That observation is proving to be accurate. In *Jenkins v. Raymark,* 782 F.2d 468 (5th Cir. 1986), we affirmed Judge Parker's certification of a class of some 900 asbestos claimants, persuaded that the requirements of Rule 23(b)(3) were met for the trial of certain common questions including the "state of the art" defense. After that order and certain settlements, approximately 3,031 asbestos personal injury cases accumulated in the Eastern District of Texas.

The petitions for mandamus attack the district court's effort to try these cases in a common trial. In summary, * * * the district court has set these 3,031 cases for trial commencing February 5, 1990. The trial will proceed in three phases. Phase I is similar to the procedure approved in *Raymark* in which common defenses and punitive damages will be tried. In Phase II, and before the same jury, certain representative cases will be fully tried and the jury will decide the total, or "omnibus" liability to the class. In Phase III, any awarded damages will be distributed utilizing various techniques. Petitioners grumble over Phase I, conceding that it is no more than we have approved in *Raymark,* and focus their fire upon Phase II. * * *

* * *

I.

[In September of] 1989, Professor Jack Ratliff of the University of Texas Law School filed his special master's report in *Cimino v. Raymark* [Special Master's Report, *Cimino v. Raymark,* 1989 WL 253889 (E.D. Tex. 1989)]. The special master concluded that it was "self-evident that the use of one-by-one individual trials is not an option in the asbestos cases." The master recommended four trial phases: I (classwide liability, class representatives' cases), II (classwide damages), III (apportionment) and IV (distribution). On October 26, the district court entered the first of the orders now at issue. The district court concluded that the trial of these cases in groups of 10 would take all of the Eastern District's trial time for the next three years, explaining that it was persuaded that "to apply traditional methodology to these cases is to admit failure of the federal court system to perform one of its vital roles in our society . . . an efficient, cost-effective dispute resolution process that is fair to the parties." The district court then consolidated 3,031 cases under Fed. R. Civ. P. 42(a) "for a single trial on the issues of state of the art and punitive damages and certified a class action under rule 23(b)(3) for the remaining issues of exposure and actual damages." The consolidation and certification included all pending suits in the Beaumont Division of the Eastern District of Texas filed as of February 1, 1989, by insulation workers and construction workers, survivors of deceased workers, and household members of asbestos workers who were seeking money damages for asbestos-related injury, disease, or death.

Phase I is to be a single consolidated trial proceeding under Rule 42(a). It will decide the state of the art and punitive damages issues. The district court explained that:

> the jury will be asked to decide issues such as (a) which products, if any, were asbestos-containing insulation products capable of producing dust that contained asbestos fibers sufficient to cause harm in its application, use, or removal; (b) which of the Defendants' products, if any, were defective as marketed and unreasonably dangerous; (c) when each Defendant knew or should have known that insulators or construction workers and their household members were at risk of contracting an asbestos-related injury or disease from the application, use, or removal of asbestos-

containing insulation products; and (d) whether each Defendant's marketing of a defective and unreasonably dangerous product constituted gross negligence. In answering issue (d), the Jury will hear evidence of punitive conduct including any conspiracy among the Defendants to conceal the dangers (if any) of asbestos. * * *

* * *

The district court also described the proceedings for Phase II in its October 26 order. In Phase II the jury is to decide the percentage of plaintiffs exposed to each defendant's products, the percentage of claims barred by statutes of limitation, adequate warnings, and other affirmative defenses. The jury is to determine actual damages in a lump sum for each disease category for all plaintiffs in the class. Phase II will include a full trial of liability and damages for 11 class representatives and such evidence as the parties wish to offer from 30 illustrative plaintiffs. Defendants will choose 15 and plaintiffs will choose 15 illustrative plaintiffs, for a total of 41 plaintiffs. The jury will hear opinions of experts from plaintiffs and defendants regarding the total damage award. The basis for the jury's judgment is said to be the 41 cases plus the data supporting the calculation of the experts regarding total damages suffered by the remaining 2,990 class members.

Class members have answered questionnaires and are testifying in scheduled oral depositions now in progress. * * * [D]efendants are allowed a total of 45 minutes to interrogate each class member in an oral deposition. These depositions will not be directly used at the trial in Phase II. Rather, the oral depositions, with the other discovery from class members, provide information for experts engaged to measure the damages suffered by the class.

II.

Defendants find numerous flaws in the procedures set for Phase II of the trial. They argue with considerable force that such a trial would effectively deny defendants' rights to a jury under the seventh amendment, would work an impermissible change in the controlling substantive law of Texas, would deny procedural due process under the fifth amendment of the United States Constitution, and would effectively amend the rules of civil procedure contrary to the strictures of the enabling acts.

Plaintiffs deny that Phase II would deny defendants any right. Plaintiffs argue that every plaintiff is effectively before the court; that the evidence to be offered by their experts is more the use of summary evidence under Rule 1006 of the Federal Rules of Evidence than the use of math models to extrapolate total damages from sample plaintiffs. Plaintiffs concede that the contemplated trial is extraordinary, but argue that extraordinary measures are necessary if these cases are to be tried at all. While extraordinary, the measures are no more than a change in the mode of proof, plaintiffs say. The argument continues that Rule 23 is not the necessary vehicle for the ordered trial, but will sustain it, if the "consolidation" is viewed as a class. We turn to these arguments.

A.

The contentions that due process would be denied, the purposes of *Erie* would be frustrated, and the seventh amendment circumvented are variations of a common concern of defendants. Defendants insist that one-to-one adversarial engagement or its proximate, the traditional trial, is secured by the seventh amendment and certainly contemplated by Article III of the Constitution itself. Defendants point out, and plaintiffs quickly concede, that under Phase II there will inevitably be individual class members whose recovery will be greater or lesser than it would have been if tried alone. Indeed, with the focus in Phase II upon the "total picture," with arrays of data that will attend the statistical presentation, persons who would have had their claims rejected may recover. Plaintiffs say that "such discontinuities" would be reflected in the overall omnibus figure. Stated another way, plaintiffs say that so long as their mode of proof enables the jury to decide the total liability of defendants with reasonable accuracy, the loss of one-to-one engagement infringes no right of defendants. Such unevenness, plaintiffs say, will be visited upon them, not the defendants.

With the procedures described at such a level of abstraction, it is difficult to describe concretely any deprivation of defendants' rights. Of course, there will be a jury, and each plaintiff will be present in a theoretical, if not practical, sense. Having said this, however, we are left with a profound disquiet. First, the *assumption* of plaintiffs' argument is that its proof of omnibus damages is in fact achievable; that statistical measures of representativeness and commonality will be sufficient for the jury to make informed judgments concerning damages. We are pointed to our experience in the trial of Title VII cases and securities cases involving use of fraud on the market concepts and mathematical constructs for examples of workable trials of large numbers of claims. We find little comfort in such cases. It is true that there is considerable judicial experience with such techniques, but it is also true we have remained cautious in their use. * * *

The plaintiffs' answers to interrogatories and the depositions already conducted have provided enough information to show that if, as plaintiffs contend, the representative plaintiffs accurately reflect the class, it is a diverse group. The plaintiffs' "class" consists of persons claiming different diseases, different exposure periods, and different occupations. The depositions of ten tentative class representatives indicate that their diseases break down into three categories: asbestosis (plural and pulmonary)—eight representatives; lung cancer—three representatives; and mesothelioma—one representative. * * * The class breaks down [into pleural cases, asbestosis cases, lung cancer cases, other cancer cases, and mesothelioma cases]. In addition, plaintiffs' admissions of fact show [various disparities among the class members, summarized by the court, including different injuries and damages, different exposure dates, and exposure to different products.]

We are also uncomfortable with the suggestion that a move from one-on-one "traditional" modes is little more than a move to modernity. Such traditional ways of proceeding reflect far more than habit. They reflect the very culture of the jury trial and the case and controversy requirement of Article III. It is suggested that the litigating unit is the class and, hence, we have the adversarial engagement or that all are present in a "consolidated" proceeding. But, this begs the very question of whether these 3,031 claimants are sufficiently situated for class treatment; it equally begs the question of whether they are actually before the court under Fed.R.Civ.Proc. Rules 23 and 42(b) in any more than a fictional sense. Ultimately, these concerns find expression in defendants' right to due process.

B.

These concerns are little more than different ways of looking at a core problem. The core problem is that Phase II, while offering an innovative answer to an admitted crisis in the judicial system, is unfortunately beyond the scope of federal judicial authority. It infringes upon the dictates of *Erie* that we remain faithful to the law of Texas, and upon the separation of powers between the judicial and legislative branches.

Texas has made its policy choices in defining the duty owed by manufacturers and suppliers of products to consumers. These choices are reflected in the requirement that a plaintiff prove both causation and damage. In Texas, it is a "fundamental principle of traditional products liability law . . . that the plaintiffs must prove that the defendant supplied the product which caused the injury." These elements focus upon individuals, not groups. The same may be said, and with even greater confidence, of wage losses, pain and suffering, and other elements of compensation. These requirements of proof define the duty of the manufacturers.

Plaintiffs say, of course, that these requirements will be met by the proposed procedures. This proof for 2,990 class members will be supplied by expert opinion regarding their similarity to 41 representative plaintiffs. Plaintiffs deny that they will be extrapolating a total universe from a sample. While we are skeptical of this assertion, plaintiffs' characterization is of little moment. The inescapable fact is that the individual claims of 2,990 persons will not be presented. Rather, the claim of a unit of 2,990 persons will be presented. Given the unevenness of the individual claims, this Phase II process inevitably restates the dimensions of tort liability. Under the proposed procedure, manufacturers and suppliers are exposed to liability not only in 41 cases actually tried with success to the jury, but in 2,990 additional cases whose claims are indexed to those tried.

Texas has made its policy choices in its substantive tort rules against the backdrop of a trial. Trials can vary greatly in their procedures, such as numbers of jurors, the method of jury instruction, and a large number of other ways. There is a point, however, where cumulative changes in procedure work a change in the very character of a trial. Significantly, changes in "procedure" involving the mode of proof may alter the liability of the defendants in fundamental ways. We do not suggest that procedure becomes substance whenever outcomes are changed. Rather, we suggest that changes in substantive duty can come dressed as a change in procedure. We are persuaded that Phase II would work such a change.

The basic changes in the dynamics of trial caused by the rules of evidence and procedure have been particularly noted with respect to the use of expert testimony. A contemplated "trial" of the 2,990 class members without discrete focus can be no more than the testimony of experts regarding their claims, as a group, compared to the claims actually tried to the jury. That procedure cannot focus upon such issues as individual causation, but ultimately must accept general causation as sufficient, contrary to Texas law. It is evident that these statistical estimates deal only with general causation, for "population-based probability estimates do *not* speak to a probability of causation in any one case; the estimate of relative risk is a property of the studied population, not of an individual's case." This type of procedure does not allow proof that a particular defendant's asbestos "really" caused a particular plaintiff's disease; the only "fact" that can be proved is that *in most cases* the defendant's asbestos *would have been* the cause. This is the inevitable consequence of treating discrete claims as fungible claims. Commonality among class members on issues of causation and damages can be achieved only by lifting the description of the claims to a level of generality that tears them from their substantively required moorings to actual causation and discrete injury. Procedures can be devised to implement such generalizations, but not without alteration of substantive principle.

We are told that Phase II is the only realistic way of trying these cases; that the difficulties faced by the courts as well as the rights of the class members to have their cases tried cry powerfully for innovation and judicial creativity. The arguments are compelling, but they are better addressed to the representative branches—Congress and the State Legislature. The Judicial Branch can offer the trial of lawsuits. It has no power or competence to do more. We are persuaded on reflection that the procedures here called for comprise something other than a trial within our authority. It is called a trial, but it is not.

The * * * class members cannot be certified for trial as proposed under Rule 23(b)(3). Rule 23(b)(3) requires that "the questions of law or fact common to the members of the class predominate over any questions affecting individual members." There are too many disparities among the various plaintiffs for their common concerns to predominate. The plaintiffs suffer from different diseases, some of which are more likely to have been caused by asbestos than others. The plaintiffs were exposed to asbestos in various manners and to varying degrees. The plaintiffs' life-styles differed in material respects. To create the requisite commonality for trial, the discrete components of the class members' claims and the asbestos manufacturers' defenses must be submerged. The procedures for Phase II do precisely that, but, as we have explained, do so only by reworking the substantive duty owed by the manufacturers. * * *

* * *

III.

We admire the work of our colleague, Judge Robert Parker, and are sympathetic with the difficulties he faces. This grant of the petition for writ of mandamus should not be taken as a rebuke of an able judge, but rather as another chapter in an ongoing struggle with the problems presented by the phenomenon of mass torts. The petitions for writ of mandamus are granted. The order for Phase II trial is vacated and the cases are remanded to the district court for further proceedings. We find no impediment to the trial of Phase I should the district court wish to proceed with that trial. We encourage the district court to continue its imaginative and innovative efforts to confront these cases. We also caution that defendants are obligated to cooperate in the common enterprise of obtaining a fair trial.

CIMINO V. RAYMARK INDUS., INC.
United States Court of Appeals, Fifth Circuit, 1998.
151 F.3d 297.

Before REYNALDO GARZA, GARWOOD, and DAVIS, CIRCUIT JUDGES.

GARWOOD, CIRCUIT JUDGE.

[This case is part of the same litigation as *Jenkins* and *Fibreboard*. After remand by the Fifth Circuit in *Fibreboard*, this case went to trial in a multi-phase proceeding before Judge Robert Parker. Phase I involved a jury trial of the ten class representatives' claims and a classwide determination of issues of product defectiveness, warning, and punitive damages, including a multiplier for each defendant. This phase was similar to the approach approved in *Jenkins* for the trial of common issues (*see* Part (A)(2) of this chapter). Phase II, which was to determine which asbestos-containing products were used at particular sites, was avoided pursuant to a stipulation of the parties. Under the stipulation, the parties agreed that the jury would have apportioned causation among each non-settling defendant at ten percent. The phase III trial involved 160 sample cases, randomly selected by the court, with some from each of five different diseases allegedly caused by asbestos (mesothelioma, lung cancer, other cancer, asbestosis, and pleural disease). The phase III cases were divided up (after certain general medical testimony was presented) and tried to two juries to determine each sample plaintiff's actual damages from his or her asbestos-related disease. The court then determined, after a one-day bench trial involving expert testimony, that there was a reliable basis to extend the results to the class as a whole. Accordingly, the court determined the damage awards for the remaining 2,128 cases by extrapolation (using average damages and disease categories for the 160 sample cases). Specifically, after utilizing the 160 sample cases to determine an average damages award for each of the five categories, each of the remaining 2,128 class members was placed in one of the five categories and received the average damages for that category. (The averages were reduced in some instances because the district court ordered remittiturs in 35 of the 160 cases.)]

Defendants had attempted, prior to trial, to obtain mandamus review, but the Fifth Circuit refused to grant relief. The phase I trial started in February 1990, and the last phase III verdict for the 160 individual plaintiffs was received in October 1990. The one-day bench trial occurred a month later. At trial, there was testimony by 271 expert witnesses and 292 fact witnesses, and the parties introduced 6,176 exhibits totaling 577,000 pages. A total of 58 lawyers participated in the trial, and several district judges and magistrate judges assisted Judge Parker. *See* 751 F. Supp. 649, 653 (E.D. Tex. 1990) (district court opinion). By the time the trial was over, most of the defendants had settled or declared bankruptcy. Only two defendants remained, Pittsburgh Corning and Asbestos Corporation, Limited (ACL). Only Pittsburgh Corning raised the broad Seventh Amendment and due process issues addressed below. ACL's appeal was limited to two narrow issues not discussed in the following excerpts.]

* * *

We begin by stating some very basic propositions. These personal injury tort actions for monetary damages are "a prototypical example of an action at law, to which the Seventh Amendment applies." The Seventh Amendment applies notwithstanding that these are diversity cases. But because these are diversity cases, the Rules of Decision Act, 28 U.S.C. § 1652, and *Erie R. Co. v. Tompkins*, 304 U.S. 64 (1938), with its seeming constitutional underpinning, mandate that the substantive law applied be that of the relevant state, here Texas. Substantive law includes not only the factual elements which must be found to impose liability and fix damages, but also the burdens of going forward with evidence and of persuasion thereon.

None of the foregoing is or can be altered by the utilization of Fed. R. Civ. P. 23(b)(3) or Fed. R. Civ. P. 42(a) [consolidation, *see* Chapter 13(A)(6)].

* * *

Similarly, use of Rule 23(b)(3) or 42(a) does not alter the required elements which must be found to impose liability and fix damages (or the burden of proof thereon) or the identity of the substantive law—here that of Texas—which determines such elements. We squarely so held in *Fibreboard*. And the Rules Enabling Act, 28 U.S.C. § 2072, likewise mandates that conclusion.

* * *

Nor is deviation from these settled principles authorized because these are asbestos cases whose vast numbers swamp the courts. *Fibreboard* clearly so holds. * * *

* * *

When, after *Fibreboard*, the district court adopted the present trial plan, it initially justified doing so on the basis of its conclusion that "the Texas Supreme Court, if faced with the facts of this case, would apply a collective liability theory, such as the Court's plan, to an asbestos consolidated action." * * * We are compelled to reject the district court's conclusion for each of several independently sufficient reasons. To begin with, it is contrary to *Fibreboard*, which plainly holds that under Texas substantive law causation of plaintiff's injury by defendant's product and plaintiff's resultant damages must be determined as to "individuals, not groups." *Fibreboard's* determination of Texas law is precedent which binds this panel. * * * No Texas appellate decision or statute subsequent to *Fibreboard* casts doubt on the correctness of its reading of Texas law. In the second place, even were we not bound by *Fibreboard* we would reach the same conclusion it did, namely that under Texas personal injury products liability law causation and damages are determined respecting plaintiffs as "individuals, not groups." * * *

* * *

Thus, the question becomes: did the implemented trial plan include a litigated determination, consistent with the Seventh Amendment, of the Texas-law mandated issues of whether, as to each individual plaintiff, Pittsburgh Corning's product was a cause of his complained-of condition and, if so, the damages that plaintiff suffered as a result.

We turn first to the phase III plaintiffs. In these cases, the trial plan was adequately individualized and preserved Seventh Amendment rights with respect to each individual's actual damages from an asbestos-related disease. However, it was not designed or intended to, and did not, provide any trial or any determination of whether a Pittsburgh Corning product was a cause of that disease. It was strictly a damages trial as to those individual plaintiffs. * * * Phase III did not litigate or determine whether or to what extent any of the one hundred sixty individual plaintiffs was exposed to Pittsburgh Corning's—or any other defendant's—asbestos, or was exposed to asbestos at any of the twenty-two worksites, or whether any such exposure was in fact a cause of that plaintiff's illness or disease. Nor did phase III litigate or determine either any individual plaintiff's past connection with any particular worksite or craft, or whether or to what extent such individual was exposed to asbestos otherwise than at any of the specified worksites. Indeed, for the most part exposure evidence was not allowed and the jury was instructed to assume sufficient exposure. Nor did phase III either litigate or determine whether or to what extent asbestos exposure, either generally or to the product of any particular defendant, was uniform or similar for members of any given craft at any one or more of the specified worksites.

* * *

With one exception, noted below, we are aware of no appellate decision approving such a group, rather than individual, determination of cause in a damage suit for personal injuries to individuals at widely different times and places. * * *

In *Hilao v. Estate of Marcos*, 103 F.3d 767 (9th Cir. 1996), [*see* Chapter 4(F)(2)(a)], a divided panel of the Ninth Circuit in a rule 23(b)(3) class action permitted recoverable tort damages to be determined in a lump sum for the entire class. *Hilao* was a suit under the Alien Tort Claims Act, and the Court essentially applied substantive principles of federal or international "common law." The majority distinguished *Fibreboard* on the basis that there "the proposed procedure worked a change in the parties' substantive rights under Texas law that was barred by the *Erie* doctrine." *Id.* at 785. By the same token, *Hilao* is distinguishable here; it did not operate under the constraints of the Rules of Decision Act or *Erie*; the present case, by contrast, does operate under those constraints. If *Hilao* is not thus distinguishable it is simply contrary to *Fibreboard*, which binds us and which in our opinion is in any event correct. Further, *Hilao* did not address—and there was apparently not presented to it any contention concerning—the Seventh Amendment. Finally, we find ourselves in agreement with the thrust of the dissenting opinion there. * * *

In sum, as *Fibreboard* held, under Texas law causation must be determined as to "individuals, not groups." And, the Seventh Amendment gives the right to a jury trial to make that determination. There was no such trial determination made, and no jury determined, that exposure to Pittsburgh Corning's products was a cause of the asbestos disease of any of the one hundred sixty phase III plaintiffs. Nor does the stipulation determine or establish that. Accordingly, the judgments in all the * * * phase III cases before us must be reversed and remanded.

We turn now to the extrapolation cases. As to the matter of individual causation, it is obvious that the conclusion we have reached in respect to the phase III cases applies *a fortiori* to the extrapolation cases. In the extrapolation cases there was no trial and no jury determination that any individual plaintiff suffered an asbestos-related disease. Indeed, in the extrapolation cases there was no trial at all—by jury or otherwise—and there was no evidence presented. So, our holding as to the phase III cases necessarily requires reversal of the judgments in the * * * extrapolation cases before us.

As to the matter of actual damages, the extrapolation cases are likewise fatally defective. Unlike the phase III cases, in the extrapolation cases there was neither any sort of trial determination, let alone a jury determination, nor even any evidence, of damages. The district court considered that these deficiencies were adequately compensated for by awarding each extrapolation case plaintiff who alleged an asbestos-related disease an amount of actual damages equal to the average of the awards made in the phase III cases for plaintiffs claiming the same category of disease. This plainly contravenes *Fibreboard*'s holding that under the substantive law of Texas recoverable damages are the "wage losses, pain and suffering, and other elements of compensation" suffered by each of the several particular plaintiffs as "individuals, not groups." We also observe in this connection that none of the experts at the extrapolation hearing purported to say that the damages suffered by the phase III plaintiffs in a given disease category (whether as disclosed by the phase III evidence or as found by the jury) were to any extent representative of the damages suffered by the extrapolation plaintiffs in the same disease category. The procedure also violates Pittsburgh Corning's Seventh Amendment right to have the amount of the legally recoverable damages fixed and determined by a jury. The only juries that spoke to actual damages, the phase I and III juries, received evidence *only* of the damages to the particular plaintiffs before them, were called on to determine *only*, and *only* determined, each of those some one hundred seventy particular plaintiffs' actual damages individually and severally (not on any kind of a group basis), and were *not* called on to determine, and did *not* determine or purport to determine, the damages of any other plaintiffs or group of plaintiffs. We have held that "inherent in the Seventh Amendment guarantee of a trial by jury is the general right of a litigant to have only one jury pass on a common issue of fact." This requires that if separate trials are ordered, the separately tried issues must be "distinct and separable from the others." By the same token, where the issues to be separately tried *are* separable and distinct, the Seventh Amendment rights of the parties are preserved as to *both* sets of issues. * * * [T]hese principles are fully applicable in class actions for damages. It necessarily follows from these principles that the jury's phase III findings of the actual damages of each of the individual phase III plaintiffs cannot control the determination of, or afford any basis for denial of Pittsburgh–Corning's Seventh Amendment rights to have a jury determine, the distinct and separable issues of the actual damages of each of the extrapolation plaintiffs.

We conclude that the extrapolation case judgments, as well as the phase III judgments, are fatally flawed, are contrary to the dictates of *Fibreboard*, and contravene Pittsburgh–Corning's Seventh Amendment rights. We do not act in ignorance or disregard of the asbestos crises. * * * [But as] we said in *Fibreboard*, federal courts must remain faithful to *Erie* and must maintain "the separation of powers between the judicial and legislative branches." "The Judicial Branch can offer the trial of lawsuits. It has no power or competence to do more."

* * *

LAURENS WALKER & JOHN MONAHAN, SAMPLING DAMAGES
83 Iowa L. Rev. 545, 545–46, 559, 561, 563–68 (1998).

The astonishing number of claimants in mass tort litigation overwhelms traditional commitment to individual, case by case, adjudication of compensatory damage claims. Some cases have involved millions of claimants and many cases have involved thousands of injured persons seeking compensation. Numbers such as these rule out any serious consideration of individual trials and have prompted controversial experimentation by courts with various forms of aggregation. * * *

* * * [Prior mass tort cases such as *Hilao*] incorporate cautious, tentative measures that fail to realize the full potential of statistical sampling to solve many of the problems posed by throngs of claimants. The difficulty * * * is that the pretense of individual adjudication is maintained. * * * [T]ime and money were wasted in an effort to provide a few claimants "individual" adjudication, while using a survey to resolve other claims. Our thesis is that a complete solution of the numbers problem in mass torts can only be achieved by abandoning any pretense of individual adjudication and randomly sampling damages without apology. Our proposal draws on areas of the law, such as trademarks, that have long accepted the use of a strong form of survey methodology.

If our proposal were adopted, mass torts would be adjudicated with less cost and more efficiency than with any existing model. Regardless of the number of claimants, cases would be resolved by one judge, one jury and, typically, the testimony of one or two expert witnesses per side. The parties would be left largely in control of the management of this process, which may increase their acceptance of the ultimate results. Defendants might pay somewhat less in total damages than under conventional practices, but plaintiffs would gain enhanced access to class adjudication and hence either to a speedy verdict and possible compensation or to the choice of an individual—though problematic—trial. Thus, under our proposal neither plaintiffs nor defendants would be systematically prejudiced.

* * *

As late as 1960, it could be said that "[t]he law with respect to survey evidence is still far from settled doctrine." In recent decades, however, the appearance of surveys in adjudication has become ubiquitous. Evidence in the form of surveys has been introduced in areas as diverse as obscenity, employment discrimination, antitrust, false advertising, and change of venue. * * * To more fully describe the use of survey methods as a form of proof, we use the illustration of "consumer confusion" in trademark litigation under the Lanham Act, a topic which "has relied . . . on the institutionalized use of statistical evidence" more than any other area of the law.

The Federal Patent and Trademark Office will refuse to register a new trademark if it so resembles a trademark already registered to another person "as to be likely, when used on or in connection with the goods of the applicant, to cause confusion or to cause mistake, or to deceive." A person who sells a product that is likely to cause confusion with an already trademarked product is liable for trademark infringement. If the plaintiff—the party with the existing trademark—can prove by a preponderance of the evidence that the defendant has caused consumers to be confused, an injunction can be issued ordering the defendant to cease using the product designation in question, and civil damages can be awarded.

When empirical data in the form of surveys first began to be introduced as evidence of consumer confusion in trademark cases, courts often rejected it as violating the hearsay rule: the respondents in the surveys were seen as offering statements in evidence, despite the fact that they were not present at trial to testify and be cross-examined on the truth of those statements. * * *

All hearsay objections to the use of surveys in trademark litigation ceased in 1963 with the landmark case of *Zippo Manufacturing Co. v. Rogers Imports, Inc.*, 216 F. Supp. 670 (S.D.N.Y. 1963). Responding to the defendant's objection to the admissibility of survey evidence of consumer confusion, Judge Feinberg wrote:

> The weight of case authority, the consensus of legal writers, and reasoned policy considerations all indicate that the hearsay rule should not bar the admission of properly conducted public surveys. Although courts were at first reluctant to accept survey evidence or to give it weight, the more recent trend is clearly contrary.

The court gave two alternate grounds for admitting surveys as evidence. One was that surveys are not hearsay because they are not "offered in evidence to prove the truth of the matter asserted." That is, the fact that survey respondents confused Rogers lighters with Zippo lighters was not being offered to prove that Rogers, Inc., actually manufactured Zippos. The other ground for admitting surveys was that, even if they are hearsay, one of the exceptions to the hearsay rule is the "present sense impression," which allows the introduction of a statement "describing or explaining an event or condition made while the declarant was perceiving the event or condition, or immediately thereafter." On either ground, surveys were admissible as evidence.

Since *Zippo*, surveys have routinely been admitted in trademark disputes. * * *

* * *

Application of the trademark example to mass torts would yield an alternative different from [prior mass tort] models. As in the trademark cases, the pretense of individualized treatment would be abandoned, and the survey data themselves would become the only mechanism of proof.

* * *

* * * The first step would be certification of a class of plaintiffs co-extensive with the population to be surveyed. This step would provide plaintiffs a class representative who could, with expert assistance, produce a survey and present it at a class trial. The motion to certify should include a description of the plan to conduct a survey, which would be important in

assessing the superiority requirement according to the manageability criteria for certification. A plan to conduct a survey would provide in most cases a solution to the manageability and superiority problems which today often block certification of mass tort claims. After certification, the class representative, charged with the burden of proof on damages, would employ an expert to conduct the damage survey. This choice would not need to be approved by the court or by the opposing party because the class representative would only be engaging in the traditional collection of evidence for use at trial. The damage survey of plaintiffs could be carried out without using coercive discovery procedures because the class representative's expert would be collecting information from friendly parties. * * *

In our proposal, the trial judge would not take a role in planning or carrying out the survey. Instead, the class representative would ask the court to approve the admission at trial of the survey results. At that time, opposing parties would be invited to examine the survey and make any objections. Both the court and opposing parties would be presented a comprehensive report of the survey. * * *

The defendant would also have access to survey methodology to collect evidence regarding damages. In cases involving large stakes, the defendant might well choose to employ an expert and survey the opposing class members about their damages. Because the defendant would be collecting information from opposing parties, use of discovery procedures would be required. * * * If the defense replication were valid and yet produced substantially different results from the prior study, the argument against admission would surely be strong. If the class representative's survey were nevertheless admitted, the defense replication should also be heard by the jury as relevant to the weight accorded the class representative's research.

Alternatively, both sides might choose to employ an expert and conduct a joint survey of damages, though apparently few joint surveys have been carried out. The cost savings of joint research would be considerable, and the results would likely prove decisive, which would all but eliminate the opportunity for advocacy and may be a reason the practice is not popular.

Finally, * * * under our proposal the results of the survey or surveys, if permitted by the court * * *, would be presented by expert testimony to the jury with the data aggregated to suggest a total amount of compensation to be divided among the class or among subclasses. No individual data would be presented to the jury and no individual damage verdicts would be required or permitted.

* * *

In doctrinal terms, our model poses few if any due process questions. * * * [T]he survey method of proof has not generated complaints by defendants that the technique is fundamentally unfair, and no decision has barred a survey on due process grounds. * * *

Plaintiffs have not objected to the use of surveys in prior cases, but might in the event of predicted general underpayment. Fortunately, our model brings compensating benefits to plaintiffs which offset lower damage awards. The availability of highly efficient survey techniques for proving damages would open the door to certification of many proposed mass tort class actions, because the use of surveys would often render a class action "superior to other available methods for the fair and efficient adjudication of the controversy," and would virtually eliminate "the difficulties likely to be encountered in the management of a class."

Increased availability of the class format offers the benefit of much earlier receipt of compensation because a class trial can be conducted. Also, increased access to the damage class action means increased access to a choice between a class trial and individual adjudication. * * * [T]he class format provides members with a technique for either accepting a speedy class verdict based on a survey or continuing toward an individual adjudication accepting the risk that adjudication may never take place.

A doctrinal analysis also leads to the conclusion that our proposal is fundamentally fair to plaintiffs and the use of surveys to establish damages in mass tort cases should also not compromise the plaintiff's due process rights. * * *

* * *

NOTES AND QUESTIONS

1. Given the asbestos crisis facing Judge Parker (the district judge in *Jenkins* and later a circuit judge on the Fifth Circuit), should the *Fibreboard* appellate court have been more deferential in reviewing his trial plan? Can *Fibreboard* be reconciled with the Fifth Circuit's *Jenkins* opinion?

2. What is the legal rationale underlying the *Fibreboard* ruling? Is it a violation of Texas law? Is it a violation of federal law? If it is the latter, what violation did the court find? *Fibreboard* highlights the distinction between procedure and substance. How can they be distinguished?

3. In *Fibreboard*, the trial court proposed to try 41 sample plaintiffs (the 11 class representatives and 15 class members selected by each side). Based on that evidence and an expert opinion, the jury would award damages for the entire class. By contrast, in *Cimino*, the phase III trial involved five disease categories, 160 randomly selected trial plaintiffs (some from each category), and an award to the remaining class members (who were assigned to one of the five categories) of the average damages for the particular category. Did Judge Parker respond to the *Fibreboard* court's concerns in a meaningful way in the *Cimino* trial? Are the differences between the two plans mere form, or are they substantive? Should the Fifth Circuit have been more deferential in reviewing the *Cimino* trial, particularly since (i) the Fifth Circuit had refused to grant mandamus prior to trial; and (ii) the district court spent the better part of a year actually trying the case? Or did the Fifth Circuit in *Cimino* act properly in holding that Judge Parker's approach was contrary to *Fibreboard*? Note that the Fifth Circuit's *Cimino* decision was rendered almost eight years after the trial was completed. *See generally* Linda S. Mullenix, *Class Actions in the Gulf South Symposium: Abandoning the Federal Class Action Ship: Is There Smoother Sailing for Class Actions in Gulf Waters?*, 74 Tul. L. Rev. 1709, 1738–44 (2000) (discussing *Cimino* in detail).

4. Does the proposal by Professors Walker and Monahan address the legal concerns raised in *Fibreboard* and *Cimino*? Is the proposal one that defense counsel in mass tort cases should embrace? What about plaintiffs' counsel? Is the analogy to "consumer confusion" trademark cases compelling? How does the proposal deal with the situation in which some class members suffer

severe injuries and others suffer only minor injuries? Could the proposal be modified to deal more effectively with that situation?

5. A variant of the Walker and Monahan approach is the "damage scheduling" approach urged by Professor Rosenberg. *See* David Rosenberg, *The Causal Connection in Mass Exposure Cases: A "Public Law" Vision of the Tort System*, 97 Harv. L. Rev. 849, 917 (1984). "Damage scheduling would award compensation to claimants not on the basis of their personal characteristics, but rather on the basis of characteristics of a class of which the individual was a member." *Id.* According to Professor Rosenberg, "[a]t its most general, the schedule might simply compensate all class members at a level equal to the average loss." *Id.* Professor Rosenberg's "public law" approach to mass torts has received criticism by some scholars. *See, e.g.*, Linda S. Mullenix, *Mass Tort as Public Law Litigation: Paradigm Misplaced*, 88 Nw. U. L. Rev. 579, 580–83 (1994).

6. Does *Tyson Foods, Inc. v. Bouaphakeo*, 136 S. Ct. 1036 (2016), have any implications for mass tort cases? *See* Chapter 3(C)(1)(b).

7. For additional scholarly discussion of sampling and aggregation, *see* Michael J. Saks & Peter D. Blanck, *Justice Improved: The Unrecognized Benefits of Aggregation and Sampling in the Trial of Mass Torts*, 44 Stan. L. Rev. 815 (1992). For a skeptical perspective on whether juries are capable of correctly evaluating statistical proof, *see* Laurence H. Tribe, *Trial By Mathematics: Precision and Ritual in the Legal Process*, 84 Harv. L. Rev. 1329 (1971).

PROBLEM

Plaintiff Bill Jones has filed suit on behalf of a class, claiming that the ABC Brewing Company failed to disclose the serious health effects of consuming its beer. According to the complaint, ABC's beer causes severe liver damage far greater than that caused by other national brands. Plaintiff seeks recovery of, among other things, the medical costs incurred by the class in treating liver damage related to ABC beer. The putative class consists of all present and former ABC beer drinkers who have suffered liver problems. To eliminate individual causation and damage questions, plaintiffs' counsel plans to hire statisticians and medical experts to estimate how much the class as a whole spent for such medical treatment stemming from liver damage linked to ABC beer. For example, the experts would estimate how much non-ABC alcohol the class members consumed in order to assess what percentage of alcohol-related illnesses were caused by other products (a process that would require the experts to take into account the fact that non-ABC alcohol has a less serious impact than the ABC alcohol). To control for non-alcohol related causes, experts estimate the percentage of non-consumers of alcohol in the general population who have suffered similar liver damage. The experts would also estimate, through sampling and public records, the total amount of medical expenses that the class incurred for liver damage caused by ABC beer. ABC would be allowed to depose 100 class members and offer the results of that testimony at trial. In the face of Seventh Amendment and due process objections by ABC, should such evidence be allowed in lieu of individual-by-individual proof? What are the advantages of such an approach?

4. MASS TORT REFORM

a. Legislative Inertia

Congress has not passed any significant legislation specifically addressing mass torts litigation. This is in marked contrast, for example, to securities litigation (discussed in Part C of this chapter) in which Congress has passed important legislation addressing securities fraud class actions. Why the inaction in the mass torts area? Consider the following.

PETER H. SCHUCK, MASS TORTS: AN INSTITUTIONAL EVOLUTIONIST PERSPECTIVE
80 Cornell L. Rev. 941, 969–73 (1995).

Like the discovery by the Molière character that he had been speaking prose all his life, the fact that virtually all mass tort law is judge-made seems embarrassingly obvious—once attention is called to it. Even so, it is a striking fact, one that cries out for explanation. The public and private interests involved in mass tort litigation are enormous. Moreover, almost all commentators view the current litigation approach as a costly, tragic, social policy failure. Why, then, have politicians allowed judges to fashion this high visibility, high stakes legal regime without any meaningful political direction, let alone a comprehensive statutory or regulatory framework? * * *

* * *

In seeking to account for this legislative inaction, we can quickly dispose of two relatively straightforward explanations. The first possible explanation is that cautious politicians simply refuse to confront so controversial an issue as mass torts policy, involving as it does powerful political interests, enormous sums of money, serious human suffering, conflicting values, and so forth * * *. But this ignores the fact that, like it or not, politicians simply cannot avoid addressing controversial issues indefinitely: Given sufficient public outcry, they *must* respond one way or another. Mass tort law, moreover, evokes far less controversy and political division than such explosive issues as abortion, taxation, affirmative action, gun control, and health care reform—issues on which legislators routinely must take public positions, even at their political peril. Finally, this argument fails to recognize the *eagerness* with which many politicians position themselves on some of the most controversial issues, including those just mentioned and indeed on tort reform itself. A second explanation—that legislative inaction bespeaks satisfaction with the mass tort system—seems clearly false. Virtually all politicians (and judges) who comment on the mass torts system perceive a crisis and assert that there are better ways to handle mass tort claims * * *.

Public choice theory suggests a somewhat more plausible explanation. Perhaps legislators cannot, or do not wish to, assemble a successful coalition in favor of any statutory change. Several factors might support legislative inaction. First, expanding mass tort liability may be highly advantageous to a forum state's citizens (and politicians and judges) in that the plaintiffs tend to be state residents while the defendants tend to be foreign corporations; hence, the benefits of broad liability will inure to the forum state while the costs will largely be borne by out-of-staters. Second, powerful interest groups may prefer the *status quo*. This would be true, for example, if the beneficiaries of the current system were highly organized, with few conflicting interests and large per capita stakes in the outcome. These conditions might, in fact, seem to hold, because plaintiffs' natural allies—the plaintiffs' bar, some "public interest" groups, and many labor unions—which ardently oppose any systemic change in mass tort law, are highly effective lobbyists and shapers of public opinion. Potential mass tort claimants, on the other hand, are difficult to organize politically because they may be unaware that they have been exposed or that they may have valuable tort claims now or in the future. Even claimants with existing claims will experience such difficulties because they constitute a large and diverse group. Their conflicting interests (they differ, for example, in the nature of their exposures, in the strength of their claims, and the quality of their lawyers), and their incentives to free ride on others' organizational efforts would also impede their ability to form a broad reform coalition.

It is true, of course, that mass tort defendants and their insurers strongly advocate some changes. Indeed, they have succeeded in securing state-level tort reform legislation reducing their liability risks, and although they have failed for almost two decades to win broad protection at the federal level, they might finally succeed. Not all mass tort defendants, however, support the same changes. * * *

A convincing public choice analysis would, of course, require a more refined distinction among and consideration of particular group interests. Moreover, such an analysis would also have to consider the role of groups such as judges and investors and the political force of ideology as well as that of economic interests. But enough has already been said to suggest that public choice analysis is complex and * * * yields no unambiguous explanation of why politicians have allowed the judiciary to initiate, develop, and refine its own mass torts jurisprudence despite widespread public and professional condemnation of the results.

Finally, a legal process or "public interest" explanation is also worth considering. Perhaps legislators have left mass tort lawmaking to the courts because they believe that, all things considered, the courts can do it better. Although many politicians perceive a mass tort "crisis," they might nevertheless conclude that the scientific, legal, economic, political, and social conditions relevant to mass injuries are too complex and fluid to permit an adequate legislative response * * *. In this view, legislators might leave resolution of systemic problems to the courts, the plaintiffs' bar, and corporate defendants, with the expectation that these powerful, well-informed, roughly balanced interests will develop workable solutions on their own as needed—always subject, of course, to the possibility of legislative fine-tuning. * * *

* * *

NOTES AND QUESTIONS

1. Congress has generally failed to take the initiative in the mass torts area. Indeed, in June 1999, four years after Professor Schuck wrote his article, members of the Supreme Court were still urging Congress to address the crisis in asbestos litigation. *See Ortiz v. Fibreboard Corp.*, 527 U.S. 815, 865 (1999)

(Rehnquist, C.J., concurring, joined by Scalia and Kennedy, JJ.) ("[t]he 'elephantine mass of asbestos case' cries out for a legislative solution").

2. Does Professor Schuck correctly explain why Congress has failed to act? Are there other possible reasons not mentioned by Professor Schuck?

b. Reform Proposals

Congressional inertia certainly does not stem from a lack of creative proposals by judges, scholars, and practitioners. Although some commentators question whether any "crisis" exists, scores of others have offered potential solutions for managing mass torts in a fair and efficient manner. What follows is a brief sampling of the spectrum of proposals—in addition to those discussed in other parts of this text—that have been offered.

Make Greater Use of Rule 23(b)(3) In Mass Tort Cases

* * *

It does not make sense to reject the class action in mass torts because the number of victims is so large and the harm so great. This is precisely why the class action is appropriate—one culpability determination would greatly increase the efficiency of the court system while recognizing the reality of the product marketplace. Why should a defendant or group of defendants be entitled to thousands of chances to convince thousands of jurors that one identical set of facts does not give rise to liability? That is what happened in the asbestos litigation that consensus says has been a dismal failure of judicial efficiency and fairness to litigants. Even though our judicial system is built on individualized adjudication, it does not also have to stand for the proposition that the greater the harm, the more difficult it is to obtain redress. By failing to recognize the value of class actions for mass torts, we are letting the judicial system destroy the chance of many victims of mass harms to obtain redress in a meaningful fashion. Judicial integrity is a valuable asset only if it is achieved not for the sake exclusively of the judiciary as an institution, but also, and most importantly, for the sake of the timely and meaningful vindication of rights and the enforcement of responsibilities. The fact that the class action procedure requires compromises is an insufficient reason to fear and thus reject it.

Mary J. Davis, *Toward the Proper Role for Mass Tort Class Actions*, 77 Or. L. Rev. 157, 229, 232 (1998).

Rely More on Administrative Agencies

The enterprise of scholarship in the aftermath of the mass tort class action should be to consider how the administrative state may assist in the resolution of mass tort claims by drawing upon features of the tort system. * * *

* * * [S]uch a coordinated system should exhibit two major features. First, Congress should explore the prospect of enacting a statutory framework—initially, on an experimental basis confined to a single agency—that would create an avenue for the initiation of agency action with regard to mass torts. Second, upon the creation of this statutory framework, courts should * * * defer their disposition of individual claims pending agency action.

* * *

* * * The statutory framework envisioned here would require agency consideration of mass tort disputes upon the presence of two conditions: consolidation of mass tort litigation by the Panel on Multidistrict Litigation [*see* Chapter 12] plus either the agency's own initiative or the filing of a petition for agency action. * * * In essence, consolidation pursuant to the current multidistrict litigation statute would serve as a signal that a particular area of mass tort litigation warrants the attention of a federal administrative agency. Indeed, in practice, it could become the norm for a petition to follow immediately upon such consolidation.

* * *

By positing a role for the administrative state with regard to mass torts, Congress need not afford agencies a free-floating delegation of authority in the area. Instead, Congress should seek to link the matters amenable to agency consideration under the statute to the issues and modes of action already familiar to agencies in the course of their regulatory responsibilities. Specifically, petitioners might request an agency determination of a particular disputed issue, such as general causation, that implicates the agency's ongoing statutory responsibilities with respect to the product or substance in question. In this manner, petitioners simply would call upon the agency to consider the sort of issue likely to arise, in any event, with respect to prospective regulation in the area.

* * *

Under [this proposed] regime, the tort system would not serve as the one and only backstop to prospective regulation. Instead, the law of mass torts would use the distinctive features of both the tort system and the administrative state to forge solutions worthy of political legitimacy.

Richard Nagareda, *In the Aftermath of the Mass Tort Class Action*, 85 Geo. L.J. 295, 352, 353, 367–68 (1996).

Ensure More Effective Judicial Oversight

* * * [W]hatever criticisms can be levelled at the use of Rule 23—and there are many—can be addressed by the diligent, sure, and certain power of district court oversight. A hands-on federal judge making effective use of Rule 23 subclasses and ever vigilant to the ethical problems of conflict of interest and dual allegiances, can assure that due process considerations are not ignored. The alternatives—distorted, inefficient, and ideological battles in the bankruptcy court or piecemeal settlements in various regions of the nation which do not provide total peace and promote inconsistency of awards and accompanying unhappiness and mistrust among litigants—have proven to be unsatisfactory.

Kenneth R. Feinberg, *Reporting from the Front Line—One Mediator's Experience With Mass Torts*, 31 Loy. L.A. L. Rev. 359, 365 (1998).

Make Greater Use of Alternative Dispute Resolution

[A] proposed solution to the mass tort dilemma is alternative dispute resolution (ADR). * * * Appointing a special master may help in delineating important issues so as to avoid duplication of efforts. ADR techniques also can assist in resolving causation issues by bringing in a neutral third party with scientific knowledge to issue non-binding decisions, which can facilitate settlement discussions. Additionally, neutral intermediaries may be helpful in resolving issues of latency of disease, where negotiations may present ethical problems for attorneys.

Genine C. Swanzey, *Using Class Actions to Litigate Mass Torts: Is There Justice for the Individual?*, 11 Geo. J.Legal Ethics 421, 433 (1998).

Enact Legislation to Create Specific Compensation Funds

In several instances, Congress has enacted legislation to address specific mass tort issues. For instance, after the September 11, 2001 terrorist attacks, Congress passed (and the President signed) the September 11 Victim Compensation Fund of 2001. The September 11 Fund provided compensation to individuals (or relatives) who were injured or killed as a result of the terrorist attacks of September 11, 2001. The claimants (as defined in the statute) were able to obtain compensation under the Fund by agreeing to waive their right to pursue traditional tort remedies (such as lawsuits against the airlines involved). Although the events of September 11 were unique, the concept of a legislatively created fund could conceivably be used in a variety of other mass torts. For a discussion of the September 11 Fund and other funds addressed to particular mass torts, see Linda S. Mullenix & Kristen B. Stewart, *The September 11th Victim Compensation Fund: Fund Approaches to Resolving Mass Tort Litigation*, 9 Conn. Ins. L.J. 121 (2002/2003); Note, *The September 11 Victim Compensation Fund: Legislative Justice Sui Generis*, 59 N.Y.U. Ann. Surv. Am. L. 513 (2004).

NOTES AND QUESTIONS

1. Would any of these proposals effectively address the mass tort issues facing the courts?

2. What other possible solutions exist for ensuring fair, efficient, and constitutional adjudication of mass tort claims on an aggregated basis?

B. EMPLOYMENT DISCRIMINATION CLASS ACTIONS

Employment discrimination suits may be brought under a variety of statutes, including (among others) Title VII, 42 U.S.C. §§ 2000e to 2000e–17; 42 U.S.C. § 1981; the Americans With Disabilities Act of 1990 (ADA), 42 U.S.C. §§ 12101–12213; the Fair Labor Standards Act (FLSA), 29 U.S.C. §§ 201–19; and the Age Discrimination in Employment Act of 1967 (ADEA), 29 U.S.C. §§ 621–34. The first three may be brought as class actions if the requirements of Rule 23 are met. The FLSA and ADEA, by contrast, are not governed by Rule 23, but instead by Section 16(b) of the FLSA, 29

U.S.C. § 216(b). As set forth below, most courts have concluded that the standards governing Title VII class actions differ in significant ways from those governing representative actions under the FLSA and ADEA. There are, however, themes common to both types of employment discrimination suits. This section explores these various issues.

At the outset, it is useful to provide a brief overview of these key employment discrimination statutes. (This section focuses mainly on Title VII and the ADEA, but all five statutes cited above are mentioned.)

- **Title VII**: This statute, enacted as part of the Civil Rights Act of 1964, and amended by the Civil Rights Act of 1991, prohibits employment discrimination based on "race, color, religion, sex, or national origin." 42 U.S.C. §§ 2000e to 2000e–17. Prohibited practices include termination, refusal to hire, or other adverse actions for discriminatory reasons. *Id.* Persons who establish a claim under Title VII may be entitled to backpay and, in some instances, equitable relief, such as reinstatement, hiring, or promotion. 42 U.S.C. §§ 2000e–5 to 2000e–16. Relief is available for both intentional discrimination and discriminatory effect ("disparate impact"). *Id.* Under the Civil Rights Act of 1991, compensatory damages are available for intentional discrimination, including damages for pain and suffering and mental anguish. 42 U.S.C. § 1981a(a)(1). In addition, the 1991 Act authorizes punitive damages if the discrimination was the result of "malice" or "reckless indifference." *Id.*

- **42 U.S.C. § 1981**: Section 1981, enacted as part of the Civil Rights Act of 1866, gives to "all persons" the right "to make and enforce contracts" to the same extent "as enjoyed by white citizens." 42 U.S.C. § 1981(a); *see also McDonald v. Santa Fe Trail Transp. Co.*, 427 U.S. 273, 295 (1976) (applying to all races). Although the Supreme Court had applied section 1981 only to the initial formation of employment contracts, the Civil Rights Act of 1991 amended section 1981 to cover "the making, performance, modification, and termination of contracts, and the enjoyment of all benefits, privileges, terms, and conditions of the contract." 42 U.S.C. § 1981(b), *overruling Patterson v. McLean Credit Union*, 491 U.S. 164 (1989). Section 1981 addresses race discrimination, not discrimination based upon gender, national origin, or religion. The courts, however, have permitted Section 1981 claims based on color. Compensatory and punitive damages are available under section 1981. 42 U.S.C. § 1981a(b). Unlike Title VII, section 1981 requires proof of intentional discrimination (as opposed to disparate impact). 42 U.S.C. § 1981a(a).

- **ADA**: Enacted in 1990, Title I of the ADA prohibits discrimination in employment on the basis of disability, including discrimination in hiring, advancement, and discharge. 42 U.S.C. § 12112(a). To be covered under the ADA, a person must have a physical or mental impairment that substantially limits a major life activity, have a record of such an impairment, or be regarded as having such an impairment. 42 U.S.C. § 12102(1). The ADA Amendment Act—effective January 2009—amended the ADA, *inter alia*, to broaden the scope of those covered by the statute. *See* Pub. L. No. 110–325, 122 Stat. 3553 (Sept. 25, 2008). Remedies include backpay, reinstatement, and compensatory and punitive damages. 42 U.S.C. § 12117(a).

• **FLSA**: Enacted in 1938, the FLSA, 29 U.S.C. § 201–19, as amended, regulates minimum wages, overtime compensation, gender-based wage discrimination (Equal Pay Act of 1963, 29 U.S.C. § 206(d)), and child labor. The statute applies generally to interstate commerce and industry, and covers most employers. Section 216(b) of the FLSA permits an employee to bring a claim on behalf of other similarly situated employees, but they must consent in writing ("opt in") to participate in any such "collective action." Class members must affirmatively "opt in" to be bound or benefit from a judgment in the collective action.

• **ADEA**: Enacted in 1967, and amended by the Civil Rights Act of 1991, the ADEA prohibits employment discrimination on the basis of age and applies to individuals 40 years of age and older. 29 U.S.C. § 623(a). Proof of intentional discrimination under the ADEA is required. *See Gross v. FBL Fin. Servs., Inc.*, 129 S. Ct. 2343, 2348–52 (2009). Remedies include reinstatement, backpay, damages (not including mental anguish), and double damages for willful violations. 29 U.S.C. § 626. As noted, ADEA suits may not be brought as Rule 23 class actions, but only as "opt in" similarly-situated "collective" actions. 29 U.S.C. § 626(b).

1. APPLICABILITY OF RULE 23 TO TITLE VII SUITS

a. General Principles

For many years, courts applied a permissive approach in addressing class certification in employment discrimination cases, reasoning that the requirements of Rule 23 did not need to be rigidly enforced. In 1977, the Supreme Court considered the validity of that approach.

E. TEX. MOTOR FREIGHT SYS., INC. V. RODRIGUEZ
Supreme Court of the United States, 1977.
431 U.S. 395.

JUSTICE STEWART delivered the opinion of the Court.

These cases * * * involve alleged employment discrimination on the part of an employer and unions in the trucking industry. The employer, East Texas Motor Freight System, Inc., is a common carrier that employs city and over-the-road, or "line," truck drivers.[7] The company has a "no-transfer" policy, prohibiting drivers from transferring between terminals or from city-driver to line-driver jobs. In addition, under the applicable collective-bargaining agreements between the company and the unions, competitive seniority runs only from the date an employee enters a particular bargaining unit, so that a line driver's competitive seniority does not take into account any time he may have spent in other jobs with the company.

The respondents brought this suit against the company and the unions in a Federal District Court, challenging the above practices. Although their complaint denominated the cause as a class action, they did not move for

---

[7] Under this policy a city driver must resign his job and forfeit all seniority in order to be eligible for a line-driver job. He gets no priority over other line-driver applicants by virtue of formerly having been with the company, and if he fails to become a line driver he is not automatically entitled to be restored to his city job.

class certification in the trial court. After a two-day hearing the court dismissed the class allegations of the complaint and decided against the individual respondents on the merits. The Court of Appeals for the Fifth Circuit reversed, after itself certifying what it considered an appropriate class and holding that the no transfer rule and the seniority system violated the statutory rights of that class under 42 U.S.C. § 1981 and Title VII of the Civil Rights Act of 1964. This court granted *certiorari* to review the judgment of the Court of Appeals.

I.

The respondents are three Mexican–Americans who initiated this litigation as the named plaintiffs, Jesse Rodriguez, Sadrach Perez, and Modesto Herrera. They were employed as city drivers at the company's San Antonio terminal, and were members of Teamsters Local Union 657 and of the Southern Conference of Teamsters. There was no line-driver operation at the San Antonio terminal, and the respondents stipulated that they had not been discriminated against when they were first hired. In August 1970, some years after they were hired, each of them applied in writing for a line-driver job. In accord with its no-transfer policy, the company declined to consider these applications on their individual merits. The respondents then filed complaints with the Equal Employment Opportunity Commission, and after receiving "right to sue" letters from the Commission, they brought this lawsuit.

According to the complaint, the suit was brought on behalf of the named plaintiffs and all Negroes and Mexican–Americans who had been denied equal employment opportunities with the company because of their race or national origin. The complaint specifically alleged that the appropriate class should consist of all "East Texas Motor Freight's Mexican–American and Black in-city drivers included in the collective bargaining agreement entered into between East Texas Motor Freight and the Southern Conference of Teamsters covering the State of Texas. Additionally that such class should properly be composed of all Mexican–American and Black applicants for line driver positions with East Texas Motor Freight . . . from July 2, 1965 [the effective date of Title VII] to present."[3]

Despite the class allegations in their complaint, the plaintiffs did not move prior to trial to have the action certified as a class action pursuant to Fed. Rule Civ. Proc. 23, and no such certification was made by the District Judge. Indeed, the plaintiffs had stipulated before trial that " 'the only issue presently before the Court pertaining to the company is whether the failure of the Defendant East Texas Motor Freight to consider Plaintiffs' line driver applications constituted a violation of Title VII and 42 U.S.C. § 1981.' " And the plaintiffs confined their evidence and arguments at trial to their individual claims. The defendants responded accordingly, with

---

[3] In addition to attacking the legality of the company's no-transfer and seniority policies, the complaint charged that the company excluded Negroes and Mexican–Americans from line-driver jobs, and that it had discharged plaintiff Perez and harassed plaintiff Rodriguez in retaliation for their having filed charges with the EEOC. The Southern Conference of Teamsters and Teamsters Local 657 were charged with participating in the exclusion of minority persons from line-driver jobs, acquiescing in the company's other discriminatory practices, and entering into collective-bargaining agreements that perpetuated the discrimination against Mexican–Americans and Negroes and erected "dual lines of seniority." In addition to other relief, the plaintiffs demanded that the company "merge its line-driver and city-driver seniority lists so as to provide for a singular seniority system based solely on an employee's anniversary date with the company."

much of their proof devoted to showing that Rodriguez, Perez, and Herrera were not qualified to be line drivers.

Following trial, the District Court dismissed the class-action allegations. It stressed the plaintiffs' failure to move for a prompt determination of the propriety of class certification, their failure to offer evidence on that question, their concentration at the trial on their individual claims, their stipulation that the only issue to be determined concerned the company's failure to act on their applications, and the fact that, contrary to the relief the plaintiffs sought, a large majority of the membership of Local 657 had recently rejected a proposal calling for the merger of city-driver and line-driver seniority lists with free transfer between jobs.[4]

The District Court also held against the named plaintiffs on their individual claims. It ruled that the no-transfer policy and the seniority system were proper business practices, neutrally applied, and that the company had not discriminated against the plaintiffs or retaliated against them for filing charges with the EEOC. The court further found: "None of the plaintiff employees could satisfy all of the qualifications for a road driver position according to the company manual due to age or weight or driving record.... The driving, work, and/or physical records of the plaintiffs are of such nature that only casual consideration need be given to determine that the plaintiffs cannot qualify to become road drivers."

The Court of Appeals for the Fifth Circuit reversed. With respect to the propriety of the class action, the appellate court discounted entirely the plaintiffs' failure to move for certification. Determination of the class nature of a suit, the court ruled, is a "responsibility [that] falls to the court." Although the plaintiffs had acknowledged on appeal that only their individual claims had been tried, and had requested no more than that the case be remanded to the trial court for consideration of the class-action allegations, the Court of Appeals itself certified a class consisting of all of the company's Negro and Mexican–American city drivers covered by the applicable collective-bargaining agreements for the State of Texas. Stating that "the requirements of Rule 23(a) must be read liberally in the context of suits brought under Title VII and Section 1981," the court found that the named plaintiffs could " 'fairly and adequately protect the interests of the class.' " The court minimized the antagonism between the plaintiffs and other city drivers with respect to the complaint's demand that seniority lists be merged, since "[t]he disagreement . . . concerned only the proper remedy; there was no antagonism with regard to the contention that the defendants practiced discrimination against the plaintiff class."

After certifying the class, the Court of Appeals went on to find class-wide liability against the company and the union on the basis of the proof adduced at the trial of the individual claims. Contrary to the understanding of the judge who had tried the case, the appellate court determined that the trial had proceeded "as in a class action," with the acquiescence of the judge and the defendants. The parties' stipulation that the only issue before the trial court concerned the company's failure to consider the named plaintiffs' applications for line-driver jobs was discounted as no more than

---

[4] The large majority of the members of Local 657 at the meeting that rejected the proposal were Mexican–American or Negro city drivers, negating any possibility that the vote was controlled by white persons or by line drivers.

"an attempt to eliminate some confusion in the exposition of evidence at trial."

Accordingly, the Court of Appeals concluded, upon the trial record, that the company had discriminated against Negroes and Mexican–Americans in hiring line drivers, that the company's no-transfer rule and seniority system perpetuated the past discrimination and were not justified by business necessity, that the company's requirement of three years of immediately prior line-haul experience was an illegal employment qualification, and that the unions had violated Title VII and 42 U.S.C. § 1981 by "their role in establishing separate seniority rosters that failed to make allowance for minority city drivers who had been discriminatorily relegated to city driver jobs." The Court of Appeals did not disturb the trial court's finding that none of the named plaintiffs was qualified to be a line driver; rather, it held only that that finding had been "premature," because each plaintiff, as a member of the class, would be entitled to have his application considered on the merits when future line-driver vacancies arose.

II.

It is our conclusion that on the record before it the Court of Appeals plainly erred in declaring a class action and in imposing upon the petitioners classwide liability. In arriving at this conclusion we do not reach the question whether a court of appeals should ever certify a class in the first instance. For it is inescapably clear that the Court of Appeals in any event erred in certifying a class in this case, for the simple reason that it was evident by the time the case reached that court that the named plaintiffs were not proper class representatives under Fed.Rule Civ.Proc. 23(a).

* * * [T]he trial court proceedings made clear that Rodriguez, Perez, and Herrera were not members of the class of discriminatees they purported to represent. As this Court has repeatedly held, a class representative must be part of the class and "possess the same interest and suffer the same injury" as the class members. *Schlesinger v. Reservists Comm. to Stop the War,* 418 U.S. 208, 216 (1974). The District Court found upon abundant evidence that these plaintiffs lacked the qualifications to be hired as line drivers [because of lack of experience, poor driving record, poor on-the-job performance and other reasons]. Thus, they could have suffered no injury as a result of the alleged discriminatory practices, and they were, therefore, simply not eligible to represent a class of persons who did allegedly suffer injury. Furthermore, each named plaintiff stipulated that he had not been discriminated against with respect to his initial hire. In the light of that stipulation they were hardly in a position to mount a classwide attack on the no-transfer rule and seniority system on the ground that these practices perpetuated past discrimination and locked minorities into the less desirable jobs to which they had been discriminatorily assigned.

Apart from the named plaintiffs' evident lack of class membership, the record before the Court of Appeals disclosed at least two other strong indications that they would not "fairly and adequately protect the interests of the class." One was their failure to move for class certification prior to trial. Even assuming, as a number of courts have held, that a district judge has an obligation on his own motion to determine whether an action shall proceed as a class action, the named plaintiffs' failure to protect the interests of class members by moving for certification surely bears strongly on the adequacy of the representation that those class members might expect to receive. Another factor, apparent on the record, suggesting that the named plaintiffs were not appropriate class representatives was the conflict between the vote by members of the class rejecting a merger of the city- and line-driver collective-bargaining units, and the demand in the plaintiffs' complaint for just such a merger.

We are not unaware that suits alleging racial or ethnic discrimination are often by their very nature class suits, involving classwide wrongs. Common questions of law or fact are typically present. But careful attention to the requirements of Fed.Rule Civ.Proc. 23 remains nonetheless indispensable. The mere fact that a complaint alleges racial or ethnic discrimination does not in itself ensure that the party who has brought the lawsuit will be an adequate representative of those who may have been the real victims of that discrimination.

For the reasons we have discussed, the District Court did not err in denying individual relief or in dismissing the class allegations of the respondents' complaint.[12] The judgment of the Court of Appeals is, accordingly, vacated, and the cases are remanded to that court for further proceedings consistent with this opinion.

NOTES AND QUESTIONS

1. The Supreme Court held in *Rodriguez* that Title VII cases brought by private plaintiffs are subject to the requirements of Rule 23, and that the court of appeals erred in construing those requirements permissively simply because Title VII claims were involved. Is there any justification for the Fifth Circuit's markedly different approach in the case?

2. Five years after *Rodriguez*, in *General Telephone Co. of Southwest v. Falcon*, 457 U.S. 147 (1982), the Supreme Court reiterated the principle that Title VII cases were fully subject to Rule 23's requirements. At issue was whether Falcon, who alleged that he was not *promoted* at General Telephone's Irving, Texas facility because he was Mexican–American, could bring a class action on behalf of Mexican–American applicants for employment whom General Telephone did not *hire*. The Court held that the court of appeals erred in affirming the district court's order certifying a class:

> Our holding in [*Rodriguez*] was limited; we noted that "a different case would be presented if the District Court had certified a class and only later had it appeared that the named plaintiffs were not class members or were otherwise inappropriate class representatives." We also recognized the theory behind the Fifth Circuit's across-the-board rule, noting our awareness "that suits alleging racial or ethnic discrimination are often by their very nature class suits, involving classwide wrongs," and that "[c]ommon questions of law or

---

[12] Obviously, a different case would be presented if the District Court had certified a class and only later had it appeared that the named plaintiffs were not class members or were otherwise inappropriate class representatives. In such a case, the class claims would have already been tried, and, provided the initial certification was proper and decertification not appropriate, the claims of the class members would not need to be mooted or destroyed because subsequent events or the proof at trial had undermined the named plaintiffs' individual claims. Where no class has been certified, however, and the class claims remain to be tried, the decision whether the named plaintiffs should represent a class is appropriately made on the full record, including the facts developed at the trial of the plaintiffs' individual claims. At that point, as the Court of Appeals recognized in this case, "there [are] involved none of the imponderables that make the [class action] decision so difficult early in litigation."

fact are typically present." In the same breath, however, we reiterated that "careful attention to the requirements of Fed. Rule Civ. Proc. 23 remains nonetheless indispensable" and that the "mere fact that a complaint alleges racial or ethnic discrimination does not in itself ensure that the party who has brought the lawsuit will be an adequate representative of those who may have been the real victims of that discrimination."

We cannot disagree with the proposition underlying the across-the-board rule—that racial discrimination is by definition class discrimination. But the allegation that such discrimination has occurred neither determines whether a class action may be maintained in accordance with Rule 23 nor defines the class that may be certified. Conceptually, there is a wide gap between (a) an individual's claim that he has been denied a promotion on discriminatory grounds, and his otherwise unsupported allegation that the company has a policy of discrimination, and (b) the existence of a class of persons who have suffered the same injury as that individual, such that the individual's claim and the class claims will share common questions of law or fact and that the individual's claim will be typical of the class claims. For respondent to bridge that gap, he must prove much more than the validity of his own claim. Even though evidence that he was passed over for promotion when several less deserving whites were advanced may support the conclusion that respondent was denied the promotion because of his national origin, such evidence would not necessarily justify the additional inferences (1) that this discriminatory treatment is typical of petitioner's promotion practices, (2) that petitioner's promotion practices are motivated by a policy of ethnic discrimination that pervades petitioner's Irving division, or (3) that this policy of ethnic discrimination is reflected in petitioner's other employment practices, such as hiring, in the same way it is manifested in the promotion practices. These additional inferences demonstrate the tenuous character of any presumption that the class claims are "fairly encompassed" within respondent's claim.

Respondent's complaint provided an insufficient basis for concluding that the adjudication of his claim of discrimination in promotion would require the decision of any common question concerning the failure of petitioner to hire more Mexican–Americans. Without any specific presentation identifying the questions of law or fact that were common to the claims of respondent and of the members of the class he sought to represent, it was error for the District Court to presume that respondent's claim was typical of other claims against petitioner by Mexican–American employees and applicants. If one allegation of specific discriminatory treatment were sufficient to support an across-the-board attack, every Title VII case would be a potential companywide class action. We find nothing in the statute to indicate that Congress intended to authorize such a wholesale expansion of class-action litigation.

The trial of this class action followed a predictable course. Instead of raising common questions of law or fact, respondent's evidentiary approaches to the individual and class claims were entirely different. He attempted to sustain his individual claim by proving intentional discrimination. He tried to prove the class claims through statistical evidence of disparate impact. Ironically, the District Court rejected the class claim of promotion discrimination, which conceptually might have borne a closer typicality and commonality relationship with respondent's individual claim, but sustained the class claim of hiring discrimination. * * *

We do not, of course, judge the propriety of a class certification by hindsight. The District Court's error in this case, and the error inherent in the across-the-board rule, is the failure to evaluate carefully the legitimacy of the named plaintiff's plea that he is a proper class representative under Rule 23(a).

* * *

* * * [W]e reiterate today that a Title VII class action, like any other class action, may only be certified if the trial court is satisfied, after a rigorous analysis, that the prerequisites of Rule 23(a) have been satisfied.

457 U.S. at 156–61. In footnote 15 of the *Falcon* decision, the Court stated:

If petitioner used a biased testing procedure to evaluate both applicants for employment and incumbent employees, a class action on behalf of every applicant or employee who might have been prejudiced by the test clearly would satisfy the commonality and typicality requirements of Rule 23(a). Significant proof that an employer operated under a general policy of discrimination conceivably could justify a class of both applicants and employees if the discrimination manifested itself in hiring and promotion practices in the same general fashion, such as through entirely subjective decisionmaking processes. In this regard it is noteworthy that Title VII prohibits discriminatory employment *practices*, not an abstract policy of discrimination. The mere fact that an aggrieved private plaintiff is a member of an identifiable class of persons of the same race or national origin is insufficient to establish his standing to litigate on their behalf all possible claims of discrimination against a common employer.

457 U.S. at 159 n.15.

3. What is the significance of footnote 15 of *Falcon*? Consider the following decisions.

JOHNSON V. MONTGOMERY CNTY. SHERIFF'S DEP'T
United States District Court, Middle District of Alabama, 1983.
99 F.R.D. 562.

THOMPSON, DISTRICT JUDGE.

The plaintiff Lois Johnson has brought this cause of action charging the defendants Montgomery County Sheriff's Department and its officials with sex discrimination in employment, in violation of Title VII of the Civil Rights Act of 1964. This cause is now before the court on Johnson's request that it be maintained as a class action. Upon consideration of the allegations of the complaint, as amended, the facts provisionally found at this time, and the law, the court is of the opinion that the requirements of Fed. R. Civ. P. 23(a) and (b)(2) are satisfied and that this cause should be certified as a class.

I.

Lois Johnson, a woman, has been employed by the Montgomery County Sheriff's Department since September 17, 1979. Although she has requested to be transferred or promoted to another position, she still works as a deputy sheriff in the Department's jail division.

Johnson has brought this lawsuit charging the Department and its officials with discrimination against women in hiring, promotions, and transfers. She is suing on behalf of herself and a putative class composed of all past, present and future female employees of the Department and all present and future female applicants. She is seeking declaratory and injunctive relief, including back pay and front pay, for herself and the putative class. The putative class consists of approximately 12 past female employees, 14 present female employees, 33 female applicants presently on the register of the Montgomery City–County Personnel Board, and unidentifiable future female employees and applicants.

The three primary divisions in the Sheriff's Department are jail, civil and criminal which employ approximately 100 deputy sheriffs and ranking officers. Present job assignments of male and female deputies by divisions are as follows:

	Deputy Sheriffs				Ranking Officers			
	Male	Female	Total	% Female	Male	Female	Total	% Female
Jail	19	6	25	24	9	1	10	10
Crimnal	38	1	39	2.6	14	0	14	0
Civil	4	6	10	60	2	0	2	0
Total	61	13	74	17.5	25	1	26	3.8

The sheriff has a general policy * * * of assigning all new female deputies to the jail, of limiting the number of female deputies in the jail to six, and of promoting and transferring female deputies from the jail only when a female applicant is hired. Furthermore, the evidence now before the court reflects that while the criteria for hiring, transfers and promotions include ability, attitude toward job, experience and seniority, there is a high degree of subjectivity in the application of the criteria [and] * * * that the application of the criteria varies depending on whether the employee or applicant is male or female. Johnson alleges * * * that under this policy women have been passed over while less well-qualified men have been hired, promoted or transferred to other divisions.

II.

The question of class certification is a procedural one distinct from the merits of the action. Nevertheless, the court must "evaluate carefully the legitimacy of the named plaintiff's plea that he is a proper class representative under Rule 23(a)." *General Tel. Co. of Southwest v. Falcon,* 457 U.S. 147, 160 (1982). * * *

* * *

* * * The requirements of commonality and typicality tend to merge. To satisfy them, there must be common elements of law or fact in the class and individual claims such that the class action would be an economical way of prosecuting and defending these claims, and the named plaintiff's claim and the class claims must be "so interrelated that the interests of the class members will be fairly and adequately protected in their absence."

The requirements for typicality and commonality were considered in some detail * * * by the Supreme Court in *General Telephone Co. of Southwest v. Falcon, supra*. While agreeing with the proposition "that racial discrimination is by definition class discrimination," the Court disapproved the wholesale use of "across the board" attacks on both hiring and promotion when the plaintiff has been the victim of discrimination in only one. * * * The Court, however, noted that where there is significant proof that the employer operated under a general policy of discrimination which manifested itself in the same general fashion both in hiring and promotion, an across the board attack on both may be appropriate. Examples given by the court were a biased testing procedure used to evaluate both applicants and employees, and an entirely subjective decisionmaking process affecting both applicants and employees. The centerpiece of the Court's opinion was that in order to sustain an across the board attack on both hiring and promotion there must be significant proof of "discriminatory employment *practices*" common to both.

The evidence in the present case substantiates the inclusion of both applicants and employees in the class Johnson seeks to represent. First of all, the evidence reflects a reciprocal relationship between hiring and transfer and promotion opportunities. Female applicants cannot be hired into jail positions unless vacancies occur in jobs now held by women; and female deputies cannot move up and out of jail jobs unless new female applicants are hired. Also, if the evidence is approached from a slightly different angle, the following language from *Richardson v. Byrd*, 709 F.2d 1016, 1020 (5th Cir. 1983), addressing a similar fact situation, is applicable and dispositive:

> Unlike the disapproved class representative in *Falcon*, we find that Richardson demonstrated a sufficient Rule 23(a) nexus to enable her to represent a class consisting of both employees and applicants. One of the Sheriff's practices that Richardson attacked involved the assignment of all new female deputies to the jail and a restriction on their transfer to more desirable sections. Because the section of the jail available for females was smaller than the male section, the Sheriff's policy by necessity limited the number of female deputies that could be employed by the Sheriff's Office. As such, both applicants and employees were adversely affected by the same practice.

Finally, the evidence reflects an overarching subjective decisionmaking process affecting both applicants and employees and thus warranting inclusion of both in the same class.

Admittedly, there may be distinct issues related to the merits of the claims of individuals or the type of relief to be afforded them, as the Sheriff's Department has claimed in its brief. Such issues of proof and remedy are not due to be resolved at the present time. It is sufficient that the claims, the injuries alleged and remedies sought weave together issues of fact and law common to all putative class members.

* * *

In conclusion and for the above reasons a class is due to be certified consisting of all past, present, and future female employees of the Montgomery County Sheriff's Department and all present and future female applicants for positions in the Department. * * *

WAL–MART STORES, INC. v. DUKES
Supreme Court of the United States, 2011.
564 U.S. 338.

[*See* Chapter 2(B)(2).]

NOTES AND QUESTIONS

1. Can the result in *Johnson* be reconciled with *Rodriguez*? With *Falcon*? Is the Supreme Court's approach in *Rodriguez* and *Falcon* persuasive? Or should courts be allowed to certify employment class actions without rigorously analyzing whether the requirements of Rule 23 have been met in a particular instance? Has *Dukes* answered this question?

2. Prior to *Dukes*, one leading employment discrimination treatise had described a trend among lower courts in across-the-board class actions in light of *Falcon*:

> The typical case now brought under [*Falcon*'s footnote 15] involves allegations that all of the challenged decisions (only some of which affected the named plaintiffs) are made through a subjective process, in which a group of white and/or male supervisors exercised total or near-total discretion and did so in a discriminatory fashion. * * * Like all other employment class actions, cases falling under *Falcon*'s general policy of discrimination exception must still satisfy the rigorous analysis of Rule 23 requirements mandated by *Falcon*.

II Barbara Lindemann & Paul Grossman, *Employment Discrimination Law* 2115–16, 2135–38 (4th ed. 2007, Supp. 2009). Is this theory of discrimination viable for employment discrimination class actions post-*Dukes*? As the opinion makes clear, the *Dukes* plaintiffs also relied on a theory of excessive subjective decision-making. The majority concluded that the *only* evidence of a general policy of discrimination was the expert sociologist's testimony that Wal–Mart's "undisciplined system of subjective decisionmaking" resulted in gender-biased personnel decisionmaking. *Dukes*, 564 U.S. at 355 (citation and internal quotation marks omitted). The Court, however, discounted this testimony because the expert could not discern to what extent gender bias permeated supervisors' decisionmaking nationwide. More specifically, the expert could not answer "whether 0.5 percent or 95 percent of the employment decisions at Wal–Mart might be determined by stereotyped thinking." *Id.* at 354 (citation and internal quotation marks omitted). Since the Court concluded that the answer to this question—rather than the question itself—was the only legitimate basis for commonality, the Court found his testimony useless. What evidence would suffice to provide the "significant proof" of a general policy of discrimination in light of *Dukes*?

Even if Wal–Mart operated under an "undisciplined system of subjective decisionmaking" potentially actionable under Title VII, the *Dukes* majority found that such a system did not satisfy commonality. The majority stated: "* * * [L]eft to their own devices most managers in any corporation—and surely most managers in a corporation that forbids sex discrimination—would select sex-neutral, performance-based criteria for hiring and promotion that produce no actionable disparity at all." 564 U.S. at 355. The dissent, by contrast, citing the district court's findings of fact, observed:

> The practice of delegating to supervisors large discretion to make personnel decisions, uncontrolled by formal standards, has long been known to have the potential to produce disparate effects. Managers, like all humankind, may be prey to biases of which they are unaware. The risk of discrimination is heightened when those managers are predominantly of one sex, and are steeped in a corporate culture that perpetuates gender stereotypes.

Id. at 372–73 (Ginsburg, J., concurring in part and dissenting in part). Does the determination of whether there is "significant proof" of a general policy of discrimination depend upon one's view of how managers in fact make decisions about performance? Which view—the majority or dissent—is more persuasive?

3. In *Dukes*, the Court observed—as had the Court in *Falcon*—that there may be a wide "conceptual gap" between an individual case and a class action. Has the Court arguably widened the gap, in reliance on *dicta* in *Falcon*'s footnote 15, by concluding that plaintiffs must provide "significant proof" that an employer "operated under a general policy of discrimination" in order to demonstrate commonality? 564 U.S. at 353.

4. Will *Dukes* have a significant impact on employment discrimination class actions? On the one hand, there are very few employment cases of *Dukes*'s size and scope, thereby limiting the case's impact. On the other hand, because plaintiffs' underlying theory of liability—*i.e.*, an undisciplined system of discretionary decisionmaking that results in disparate impact and disparate treatment—has been a standard contention in employment cases, the opinion may have a far-reaching impact.

Professor John C. Coffee, Jr., contends that *Dukes*'s requirement that plaintiffs identify "a common mode of exercising discretion that pervades the entire company" will "probably force plaintiffs to reduce the size of proposed classes, limiting them to single plants or job classifications—or at the least to a common supervisor who arguably exercised discretion in a discriminatory fashion." John C. Coffee, Jr., *A Primer on* Wal–Mart v. Dukes, 80 Law Week Legal News 95 (2011). He surmises that commonality will remain easy to satisfy for certain cases, like securities class actions, but will be harder to satisfy for cases with "disfavored classes that encompass both workers and supervisors or production line workers in different plants with different production capabilities." *Id.*; *see also* Robert H. Klonoff, *Class Actions Part II: A Respite from the Decline*, 92 N.Y.U. L. Rev. ___ (forthcoming October 2017) (arguing that "*Dukes* has by no means meant the end of employment discrimination class actions" and citing cases and commentary).

5. *Dukes* addressed several other important class certification issues, discussed in Chapter 4(B)(1)(b)(i) and Chapter 4(F)(2)(a).

b. Administrative Enforcement

i. *The Equal Employment Opportunity Commission and Rule 23*

The Equal Employment Opportunity Commission (EEOC), the federal agency principally charged with enforcement of Title VII, can sue in its own right under Title VII. If it does so, it need not comply with the requirements of Rule 23 to seek classwide relief. *General Tel. Co. of the Nw., Inc. v. EEOC*, 446 U.S. 318 (1980). In *General Telephone*, the Supreme Court first found that the language and legislative history of Title VII supported this conclusion. It then found that applying Rule 23 to the EEOC would not be desirable, reasoning:

> It is apparent that forcing EEOC civil actions into the Rule 23 model would in many cases distort the Rule as it is commonly interpreted and in others foreclose enforcement actions not satisfying prevailing Rule 23 standards * * * . The undesirability of doing either supports our conclusion that the procedural requirements of the Rule do not apply.
>
> Rule 23(a) * * * imposes the prerequisites of numerosity, commonality, typicality, and adequacy of representation. When considered in the light of these requirements, it is clear that the Rule was not designed to apply to EEOC actions brought in its own name for the enforcement of federal law. Some of the obvious and more severe problems are worth noting.
>
> The numerosity requirement requires examination of the specific facts of each case and imposes no absolute limitations. Title VII, however, applies to employers with as few as 15 employees. When judged by the size of the putative class in various cases in which certification has been denied, this minimum would be too small to meet the numerosity requirement. In such cases, applying Rule 23 would require the EEOC to join all aggrieved parties despite its statutory authority to proceed solely in its own name.
>
> The typicality requirement is said to limit the class claims to those fairly encompassed by the named plaintiff's claims. If Rule 23 were applicable to EEOC enforcement actions, it would seem that the Title VII counterpart to the Rule 23 named plaintiff would be the charging party, with the EEOC serving in the charging party's stead as the representative of the class. Yet the Courts of Appeals have held that EEOC enforcement actions are not limited to the claims presented by the charging parties. Any violations that the EEOC ascertains in the course of a reasonable investigation of the charging party's complaint are actionable. The latter approach is far more consistent with the EEOC's role in the enforcement of Title VII than is imposing the strictures of Rule 23, which would limit the EEOC action to claims typified by those of the charging party.
>
> We note finally that the adequate-representation requirement is typically construed to foreclose the class action where there is a conflict of interest between the named plaintiff and the

members of the putative class. In employment discrimination litigation, conflicts might arise, for example, between employees and applicants who were denied employment and who will, if granted relief, compete with employees for fringe benefits or seniority. Under Rule 23, the same plaintiff could not represent these classes. But unlike the Rule 23 class representative, the EEOC is authorized to proceed in a unified action and to obtain the most satisfactory overall relief even though competing interests are involved and particular groups may appear to be disadvantaged. The individual victim is given his right to intervene for this very reason. The EEOC exists to advance the public interest in preventing and remedying employment discrimination, and it does so in part by making the hard choices where conflicts of interest exist. We are reluctant, absent clear congressional guidance, to subject [EEOC] actions to requirements that might disable the enforcement agency from advancing the public interest in the manner and to the extent contemplated by the statute.

General Tel., 446 U.S. at 329–31. Should the Court instead have found that EEOC actions must satisfy Rule 23? Four justices dissented, citing a Fifth Circuit case as providing their rationale. *Id.* at 334 (*citing EEOC v. D.H. Holmes Co., Ltd.*, 556 F.2d 787 (5th Cir. 1977)). In *D.H. Holmes*, the court reasoned that nothing in Title VII or in Rule 23 exempted the EEOC from Rule 23's requirements. It further noted that "chaos" could result by exempting the EEOC, since "[s]uch matters as notice, exclusion, intervention, dismissal or compromise, and statute of limitations treatment would be in question." 556 F.2d at 796. Do the concerns raised in *D.H. Holmes* have merit?

The Seventh Circuit has held that although *General Telephone* involved only injunctive relief and backpay, *General Telephone*'s conclusion that the EEOC is exempt from Rule 23 also applies to EEOC actions seeking compensatory and punitive damages. *In re Bemis Co., Inc.*, 279 F.3d 419 (7th Cir. 2002). *See also EEOC v. Pemco Aeroplex, Inc.*, 383 F.3d 1280 (11th Cir. 2004) (noting EEOC's enforcement role and exemption from Rule 23 requirements, and holding that EEOC was not bound by judgment in private suit); *cf. EEOC v. Waffle House, Inc.*, 534 U.S. 279 (2002) (holding that charging party's agreement to arbitrate dispute did not foreclose EEOC from bringing suit seeking backpay, reinstatement, and damages on behalf of charging party).

ii. *Exhaustion of Administrative Remedies*

One important aspect of an employment discrimination case is the requirement—under Title VII, ADA, and ADEA (but not under the FLSA or 42 U.S.C. § 1981)—that the employee file a timely charge with the proper administrative agency before seeking relief in court. This requirement that the plaintiff exhaust administrative remedies finds no counterpart, for example, in tort, consumer fraud, or securities fraud cases. As one treatise explains in the context of Title VII:

> Title VII sets out federal and state agency prerequisites to suit. In general, the private sector applicant or employee need only comply with two such prerequisites: (1) timely filing of a charge with

the U.S. Equal Employment Opportunity Commission ("EEOC"), either in the first instance or, in the majority of states that have parallel state or local antidiscrimination legislation and agencies, after filing with those agencies; and (2) timely filing of a federal or state court action within 90 days after receipt from EEOC of a "notice of right to sue." Failure to follow the specified procedures and meet the charge-filing and suit-commencement deadlines usually results in dismissal of the administrative charge or ensuing judicial action.

1 Harold S. Lewis & Elizabeth J. Norman, *Litigating Employment Discrimination and Civil Rights Cases* § 6.1, at 572 (2005). One purpose of such a requirement is "to give state or local and discrimination agencies and EEOC opportunities to obtain voluntary resolution of discrimination disputes * * *." *Id.*

In a class action, it is not necessary for all class members to file a charge in order to be part of a class. Under certain circumstances, class members may "piggyback" on a timely-filed charge by the class representative (*i.e.*, the "single filing rule"). For example, in *Oatis v. Crown Zellerbach Corp.*, 398 F.2d 496 (5th Cir. 1968), the Fifth Circuit held that members of a class action brought under Title VII need not each individually file a timely administrative charge as a prerequisite to being part of the suit. So long as one named plaintiff timely exhausted his administrative remedies in a lawsuit alleging class claims, the class members are accorded the benefit of that filing. As the following case reveals, however, a court must carefully scrutinize the scope of the administrative charge to determine if piggybacking is permissible.

HOFFMAN V. R.I. ENTERS., INC.
United States District Court, Middle District of Pennsylvania, 1999.
50 F. Supp. 2d 393.

VANASKIE, DISTRICT JUDGE.

I. BACKGROUND

On November 1, 1996, plaintiff Jessica Hoffman (Hoffman) filed this Title VII action against defendant R.I. Enterprises, Inc. d/b/a Ramada Inn d/b/a Cristallo Steak House (Ramada), contending, *inter alia*, that she had been subject to a sexually hostile work environment during her employment as a waitress for Ramada. Hoffman's complaint sought class certification to allow her to proceed as a class representative on behalf of other women employed by Ramada who had allegedly been subject to the same hostile environment. * * * [In her administrative charge, Hoffman had alleged that she was the victim of sex discrimination and also mentioned one other person by name who was allegedly a victim of sex discrimination as well. There were, however, no allegations going beyond Hoffman and this one other person.] After considering the evidence presented by Hoffman as well as the legal arguments of the parties, I denied Hoffman's request for class certification, finding that Hoffman's EEOC charge had failed to provide adequate notice to Ramada of potential class claims. Hoffman moved for reconsideration of this determination. Hoffman also filed a notice of appeal to the Third Circuit, and the Third Circuit stayed that appeal pending resolution of her motion for reconsideration.

II. DISCUSSION

* * *

In my oral ruling on February 1, 1999, I relied upon Third Circuit cases which have held that a plaintiff may not assert class claims of discrimination unless the plaintiff has placed the defendant on notice of class-based discrimination in his or her EEOC charge. * * * I determined that Hoffman's EEOC charge provided Ramada with notice of Hoffman's individual claims of discriminatory treatment, not that she intended to file a class claim for such discriminatory treatment.

* * *

* * * Hoffman's charge was not filed *pro se*, but had been filed by an attorney acting on her behalf. Although there were allegations concerning a hostile work environment, Hoffman's counsel conceded during oral argument that a hostile work environment claim is not by definition a class-based allegation. Furthermore, the mere fact that Hoffman indicated that another employee had been discriminated against is insufficient to place Ramada on notice of class-based discrimination. Hoffman argues that a reasonable EEOC investigation would have uncovered the class-based discrimination. * * * [But] "it is primarily the charge" that must provide the notice to the employer of the scope of its potential liability, not the results of a hypothetical investigation. Ramada was clearly on notice that Hoffman believed that she had been discriminated against in her employment. Ramada would be provided with the opportunity at conciliation on *Hoffman's* claims disclosed by a reasonable investigation through the EEOC administrative proceedings.

Ramada's notice of Hoffman's individual claims, however, fails to rise to the level of notice of a class-based discrimination claim. Hoffman's EEOC charge, drafted and submitted by counsel, contains no reference to a class-based discrimination claim. To premise notice of a class-based discrimination claim upon the facts that may have been revealed in a hypothetical EEOC investigation * * * abrogates [case law] which emphasized the importance of fairly appraising the employer of the extent of potential liability. * * *

* * * Therefore, Hoffman's motion for reconsideration will be denied.

* * *

NOTES AND QUESTIONS

1. Why did the *Hoffman* court hold that the plaintiff could not bring a classwide claim? How, if at all, would the defendant have been prejudiced by allowing a class action to go forward? Was the plaintiff in *Hoffman* correct in arguing that a reasonable EEOC investigation would have uncovered class-wide discrimination? If that argument was correct, should the plaintiff have been permitted to bring a class action?

2. As *Hoffman* illustrates, a plaintiff must give sufficient notice in his EEOC charge of class claims for such claims to be covered by the administrative exhaustion requirement and for others to benefit from the single-filing rule. Exhaustion is required to promote the dual goals of giving notice to the

defendant and allowing for conciliation. The courts, however, are in disagreement over the proper approach. As recognized by a leading employment discrimination treatise:

> The claims of the class must be "like or related to" the claims of its representatives. Moreover, the scope of the class action generally is limited by the scope of the EEOC charge. A class action thus normally may be brought only when the representative's charge put the employer on notice of the class-based nature of the allegations. But some courts have allowed class treatment where the class issues "could reasonably be expected to grow out of" the EEOC charge. Similarly, subsequent allegations in a class action complaint may require no further exhaustion of administrative remedies where those allegations reasonably could be expected to grow from the original charge.

II Barbara Lindemann & Paul Grossman, *Employment Discrimination Law*, 2170–71 (4th ed. 2007, Supp. 2009).

3. In deciding whether a class action should be allowed, should it be relevant whether the named plaintiff was represented by counsel at the administrative level? Would *Hoffman* have come out the other way had plaintiff proceeded *pro se*? *See, e.g., Fellows v. Universal Rest.*, 701 F.2d 447, 451 (5th Cir. 1983) ("Given the liberal construction accorded EEOC charges, especially those by unlawyered complainants, we are inclined to believe that the wordings of her actual and of our hypothetical charges could equally be understood to complain of discriminatory employment treatment of all women applicants and employees, as well as of [plaintiff] herself."); *see also Federal Express Corp. v. Holowecki*, 552 U.S. 389, 406 (2008) (holding that intake questionnaire and affidavit constituted a "charge" where it complied with implementing regulations and was reasonably construed by EEOC as a request to take remedial action to protect employee's right to resolve employment dispute under the ADEA).

c. Issues Under Rule 23(b)(2)

One of the most important developments in employment discrimination law involves efforts to curtail use of Rule 23(b)(2) when damages—and most recently backpay—are sought in addition to injunctive relief. Because a major purpose of Rule 23(b)(2) was to facilitate the use of class actions in discrimination cases, such efforts have generated considerable debate. This debate is discussed fully in Chapter 3(B)(2). That section should be reviewed prior to the material below.

Given *Dukes*'s holding that plaintiffs' claims for backpay were inappropriate for Rule 23(b)(2) certification (*see Dukes* case excerpted in Chapter 3(B)(2)), what is the potential impact of *Dukes* on employment cases? One commentator has noted:

> * * * [T]he Court's ruling on back pay will make it more difficult for employees alleging systemic misconduct under Title VII to seek monetary relief. This is because it is now harder for plaintiffs to use the Rule 23 provision designed for such cases—(b)(2). First, the Court makes no distinction between equitable and non-equitable monetary relief as a basis for Rule 23(b)(2) certification. This means that back pay—normally favored because of its equitable nature—enjoys no preference over compensatory and punitive damages sought under this class action provision. Second, any monetary relief that is not

incidental to the injunctive or declaratory relief cannot survive Rule 23(b)(2) certification. For those cases brought in the Second and Ninth Circuits, or in circuits that have not ruled on the matter, a court must use the harshest standard established for evaluating the availability of relief that is neither injunctive nor declaratory. Third, courts are more likely to conclude that back pay must be determined on an individual, rather than aggregate, basis. The individualized nature of the relief, in turn, makes it non-incidental, and thus unavailable under the Rule 23(b)(2) provision.

Suzette M. Malveaux, *How Goliath Won: The Future Implications of* Dukes v. Wal–Mart, 106 NW. U. L. Rev. Colloquy 34, 51 (2011). In light of *Dukes*, what options do employees seeking monetary relief have when pursuing class certification for employment discrimination? Can employees bringing a pattern-or-practice Title VII class action still seek backpay under Rule 23(b)(3) or a hybrid Rule 23(b)(2)/Rule 23(b)(3) class? How realistic are these alternatives? Professor John C. Coffee, Jr. offers a bleak outlook:

> The problem is not the U.S. Supreme Court's 5–4 decision that Fed. R. Civ. P. 23(a)(2)'s "commonality" requirement was not satisfied (that outcome was widely expected), but rather the court's unanimous decision that back pay (and other forms of money damages) could not be awarded in a Rule 23(b)(2) class action.
>
> Most commentary has focused on the issue on which the court split and ignored the greater significance of the issue on which they agreed. That the court's liberals went docilely along with the conservative majority on the Rule 23(b)(2) money damages issue seems surprising and raises a question: Did they really understand the impact of what they were doing?
>
> The simple truth is that employment discrimination litigation cannot normally be certified under Rule 23(b)(3) because of the "predominance" requirement of that rule, which requires that the common questions of law and fact "predominate" over the individual ones. Even in a far simpler, more streamlined case than [*Dukes*], there will still typically be a host of individual issues that will make it difficult (and usually impossible) to satisfy that predominance standard.
>
> * * *
>
> This suggests that the liberal wing of the court may not have recognized how procedurally cut off and trapped employment discrimination victims are if back pay cannot be obtained as a form of "incidental" relief under Rule 23(b)(2). Reinforcing this sense is the casual assertion by Justice Ruth Bader Ginsburg in her [*Dukes*] dissent that the case should be remanded to the district court for a determination as to whether it could be certified under Rule 23(b)(3). That idea is a non-starter. In all circuits, the predominance standard has long been the Grim Reaper of putative class actions, and the sprawling character of the *Wal-Mart* class (with 1.5 million or more class members working in 3,500 stores in 50 states at a broad assortment of jobs) doomed it from the start—if the predominance standard applied.

John C. Coffee, Jr., *A Primer on* Wal–Mart v. Dukes, 80 Law Week Legal News 93–94 (2011). Is it reasonable to believe the dissenting Justices misunderstood the impact of their ruling?

NOTES AND QUESTIONS

1. The Advisory Committee Notes to the 1966 version of Rule 23(b)(2) state: "The subdivision [(b)(2)] does not extend to cases in which the appropriate final relief relates exclusively or predominantly to money damages." Despite the appellate courts' reliance on the Advisory Committee's predominance formulation, the Supreme Court rejected the Committee's guidance in *Dukes*, stating: "Of course it is the Rule itself, not the Advisory Committee's description of it, that governs." 564 U.S. at 363. Should the Advisory Committee's statement on Rule 23(b)(2) have been given more weight in *Dukes*? Consider the following argument:

> * * * Legislative history comes under fire as an interpretive tool because it is arguably "murky, ambiguous, and contradictory;" unreliable and subject to manipulation; and exempt from the formal legislative process.
>
> The Advisory Committee notes, however, are not susceptible to the same criticisms as traditional legislative history. Significant distinctions between the Advisory Committee notes and congressional legislative history justify the Court's reliance on the former when discerning the drafters' intent. The unique process involved in creating the Federal Rules and the distinct nature of the notes themselves make reliance on them a more productive enterprise. More specifically, unlike other extrinsic sources that accompany federal statutes, the Advisory Committee notes are a single source, designed to provide official guidance for rule interpretation, drafted by the same authors of the rule, subject to review from inception to final enactment, and formally approved of by the United States Judicial Conference and the Supreme Court itself before transmission to Congress. Moreover, given the active role that judges play in drafting and commenting on the rules and accompanying notes, the review by the Judicial Conference, and the ultimate promulgation by the Supreme Court (subject only to congressional override), there is not the same concern over the balance of power between the judicial and legislative branches when courts interpret the Advisory Committee notes as there is when they interpret traditional legislative history. In sum, these safeguards make the Advisory Committee notes a reliable and authoritative source for discerning the rule makers' intent.

Suzette M. Malveaux, *Class Actions at the Crossroads: An Answer to* Wal–Mart v. Dukes, 5 Harv. L. & Pol'y Rev. 375, 386 (2011). Should the distinction between the legislative and rulemaking process matter?

2. The Fifth Circuit had concluded that monetary relief predominates under Rule 23(b)(2) unless it is "incidental" to the injunctive or declaratory relief sought. *See Allison v. Citgo Petroleum, Corp.*, 151 F.3d 402, 415 (5th Cir. 1998) (discussed in Chapter 3(B)(2)). According to the *Allison* formulation, "incidental" damages flow directly from liability to the class *as a whole* on the claims forming the basis of the injunctive or declaratory relief." 151 F.3d at 415. When discussing (b)(2) certification in *Dukes*, the Supreme Court used the Fifth Circuit's "incidental" language without endorsing its underlying premise—that incidental monetary relief is permissible in a class action under (b)(2). *Dukes*, 564 U.S. at 366 (noting that it did not have to decide whether "there are any forms of 'incidental' monetary relief that are consistent with the interpretation of Rule 23(b)(2) we have announced and that comply with the

Due Process Clause"). The Court also refrained from comparing the three different damage predominance tests used by the courts of appeals. For a comparative analysis of the three different predominance approaches, *see* Suzette M. Malveaux, *Class Actions at the Crossroads: An Answer to* Wal–Mart v. Dukes, 5 Harv. L. & Policy Rev. 375, 400–14 (2011).

3. Should claims for backpay relief be treated differently than claims for other forms of monetary relief for purposes of Rule 23(b)(2) certification? What policy arguments would favor or disfavor such an approach?

d. Allegations of a "Pattern or Practice"

i. *General Principles*

Disparate treatment is shown when a member of a protected group was intentionally afforded less favorable employment-related treatment than those similarly situated outside the protected group. The Supreme Court has instructed that, in the ordinary employment discrimination case, a plaintiff may present a *prima facie* case of disparate treatment either by providing "direct" evidence that discriminatory animus motivated the employment decision or, if such direct evidence is unavailable, by utilizing what has become known as a "shifting burdens" approach. "Direct" evidence, according to one source, is "evidence of oral or written statements by those persons who decided [to discharge/not to hire/etc. the plaintiff] that, if believed, directly prove that the plaintiff's [membership in a protected class] was a motivating factor in the defendant's decision [to discharge/not to hire/etc.] the plaintiff." American Bar Association, *Model Jury Instructions: Employment Litigation* § 1.02[2] (2d ed. 2005). Under the "shifting burdens" approach articulated in such cases as *McDonnell Douglas Corp. v. Green*, 411 U.S. 792, 802 (1973), a plaintiff makes a *prima facie* showing of disparate treatment by submitting evidence that (i) he or she is a member of a protected class, (ii) he or she applied for a vacant position for which he or she was qualified, (iii) he or she was rejected, despite his or her qualifications, and (iv) the position remained open and the employer continued to seek similarly situated applicants outside the protected class. *See also Tex. Dept. of Comm. Affairs v. Burdine*, 450 U.S. 248, 253–54, n.6 (1981) (noting flexible standard based on circumstances). "If the plaintiff establishes the *prima facie* case, a judicially created presumption declares the resulting inference of discrimination conclusive unless the defendant offers evidence that it had one or more 'legitimate, nondiscriminatory reasons' for an employment decision." 1 Harold S. Lewis & Elizabeth J. Norman, *Litigating Employment Discrimination and Civil Rights Cases* § 5.10, at 494 (2005).

In pattern or practice cases, a different approach has been used. The following discussion reflects the approach taken by one court:

> Plaintiffs have alleged, *inter alia*, that defendant engaged in a "pattern and practice" of discrimination against its employees * * *. Although originally pattern and practice cases were brought only by the government, the Supreme Court has expanded the pattern and practice claim to include private litigants. *See Bazemore v. Friday,* 478 U.S. 385 (1986). [When] a claim is based on an allegation of a pattern and practice of discrimination, the typical burden-shifting analysis of *McDonnell Douglas Corp. v. Green,*

411 U.S. 792 (1973), is altered. *International Bhd. of Teamsters v. United States*, 431 U.S. 324 (1977). Unlike typical disparate treatment cases, pattern and practice cases are divided into two phases: liability and remedy. *Teamsters*, [*Id.*] at 357–62.

In the liability phase, plaintiffs carry the burden to demonstrate the existence of a pattern and practice of discrimination. In particular, plaintiffs "must establish by a preponderance of the evidence that * * * discrimination was the company's standard operating procedure—the regular rather than the unusual practice." [*Id.*] at 336. Plaintiffs must establish a *prima facie* case supporting the inference that the defendant engaged in a pattern and practice of discrimination. "The burden then shifts to the employer to defeat the *prima facie* showing of a pattern and practice by demonstrating that the [plaintiffs'] proof is either inaccurate or insignificant." [*Id.*] at 360. The plaintiffs may then offer evidence of pretext.

If plaintiffs prove a pattern and practice of discrimination, the court may fashion an award of class-wide prospective relief without further evidence. If, however, individual relief is also sought, the court must conduct a second, "remedial" phase. The term "remedial" is somewhat of a misnomer because the defendant's liability to any individual class member must still be determined. However, for purposes of that remedial phase:

> The proof of the pattern or practice supports an inference that any particular employment decision, during the period in which the discriminatory policy was in force, was made in pursuit of that policy. The [plaintiff] need only show that an alleged individual discriminatee [suffered an adverse employment decision] and therefore was a potential victim of the proved discrimination. . . . The burden then rests on the employer to demonstrate that the individual [suffered the adverse employment decision] for lawful reasons.

[*Id.*] at 362. It is unclear from the opinion whether the burden of persuasion or merely the burden of going forward with the evidence is shifted to the defendant in the remedial phase.

* * * [Here, p]laintiffs have provided significant evidence to support their claim that defendant engaged in a pattern and practice of discrimination. More importantly, whether plaintiffs can meet their burden in the liability phase of the *Teamsters* procedure is irrelevant to the question of * * * certification. I am not deciding a dispositive motion by defendant. Rather, it is critical here that the liability phase of a pattern and practice action is unaffected by the number of plaintiffs asserting the claim.

The sole issue in the liability phase is whether defendant engaged in a pattern and practice of discrimination. At that stage, plaintiffs are not required to provide specific evidence that they were individually discriminated against. [*Id.*] at 361. Therefore, phase one of the trial will not be affected by the expansion of this claim from [a small number of] named plaintiffs to the hundreds who might be encompassed by the proposed class. Any disparities among the employment situations of the individual plaintiffs are irrelevant during the liability phase, judicial economies are clearly served by proceeding collectively, and the defendant is not prejudiced.

Vaszlavik v. Storage Tech. Corp., 175 F.R.D. 672, 679–80 (D. Colo. 1997). Although *Vaszlavik* discusses the approach in the context of an age discrimination collective action (*see* discussion in Part (B)(2) of this chapter), courts have used a similar approach in pattern or practice cases brought under Rule 23. *See also Dukes*, 564 U.S. at 352 n.7 (2011) (describing *Teamsters* approach in pattern-or-practice cases).

Prior to *Dukes*, a number of courts relied on pattern-or-practice allegations to certify cases under Rule 23(b)(2) and, occasionally, (b)(3). For example, in *Warnell v. Ford Motor Co.*, 189 F.R.D. 383 (N.D. Ill. 1999), the court certified a class action under (b)(3) (as well as (b)(2)). *Id.* at 388. The plaintiffs alleged a pattern of pervasive sexual harassment by over 850 females who worked at an automobile plant. *Id.* at 385. They cited "generalized groping and other offensive physical contact" as well as derogatory sexual terms, suggestive remarks, and use of pornography. *Id.* The district court concluded that individual variances did not overcome a finding of predominance. *Id.* at 387. The district court concluded that " 'the landscape of the total work environment, rather than the subjective experiences of each individual claimant, is the focus for establishing a pattern or practice of unwelcome sexual harassment which is severe and pervasive.' 'The existence of a company's policy of tolerating sexual harassment is the basis for pattern or practice liability.' " *Id.* (citation omitted). Thus, the district court held that "plaintiff's sexual harassment claims here predominate[d] over any individual issues" and certified the class under Rule 23(b)(3). *Id.* Moreover, because the plaintiffs challenged defendant's policy of failing to enforce sexual harassment rules within the context of a centralized personnel system, the district court concluded that there was a pattern of conduct generally applicable to the class that justified Rule 23(b)(2) certification. *Id.* at 388–90. Similarly, in *Carter v. West Publishing Co.*, 1999 WL 376502 at * 7–8 (M.D. Fla. 1999), *rev'd on other grounds*, 225 F.3d 1258 (11th Cir. 2000), the court granted certification under (b)(3) in a case involving a class of female employees alleging a pattern or practice of discrimination in the company's stock ownership program, finding that common issues predominated over individual ones.

Some pre-*Dukes* courts refused to certify employment discrimination cases, notwithstanding an allegation of a pattern or practice. Those courts indicated that the individual circumstances of each plaintiff are *highly* relevant even in a *Teamsters*-model trial, because a defendant may defeat a Phase I pattern or practice claim by "articulat[ing] a non-discriminatory, nonpretextual reason for *every* discharge." *Ardrey v. United Parcel Serv.*, 798 F.2d 679, 683–84 (4th Cir. 1986) (holding that district court did not abuse its discretion by foreclosing discovery on plaintiffs' pattern or practice claims where broad discovery was allowed for individual plaintiffs' claims); *see also Coates v. Johnson & Johnson*, 756 F.2d 524, 548 (7th Cir. 1985).

In *Dukes*, the Supreme Court repeatedly noted—and did not purport to reject—the *Teamsters* approach to litigating Title VII cases. It did not, however, attempt to describe how a *Teamsters*-style case could be litigated as a class action by private litigants in light of its (a)(2) and (b)(2) holdings.

NOTES AND QUESTIONS

1. What evidence should be sufficient in a pattern or practice case to obtain class certification under Rule 23(b)(2) or Rule 23(b)(3)?

2. Would subclasses, bifurcation, or limited issue certification make a class action alleging a pattern or practice more feasible? Could any of those tools address the commonality problem identified in *Dukes*?

3. Do the concerns that courts have identified in trying classwide pattern or practice cases raise difficulties in achieving settlements? What are the implications in the employment context of *Amchem*'s heightened scrutiny of class action settlements? *See* Chapter 8(A)(3).

4. The plaintiffs in *Dukes* alleged both disparate treatment and disparate impact theories of discrimination. As noted, there is an important distinction between "disparate treatment" claims and "disparate impact" claims. In a disparate treatment claim, "the plaintiff is required to prove that the defendant had a discriminatory intent or motive." *Watson v. Fort Worth Bank & Trust*, 487 U.S. 977, 986 (1988). In a disparate impact claim, by contrast, there is no need to prove discriminatory motive. "[T]he necessary premise of the disparate impact approach is that some employment practices, adopted without a deliberately discriminatory motive, may in operation be functionally equivalent to intentional discrimination." *Id.* at 987. In other words, disparate impact can be shown if a facially neutral policy has a discriminatory impact. Courts have been more lenient in certifying disparate impact cases than they have been in certifying disparate treatment cases. As one court explained:

> As is now well recognized, the class action commonality criteria are, in general, more easily met when a disparate impact rather than a disparate treatment theory underlies a class claim. The disparate impact "pattern or practice" is typically based upon an objective standard, applied evenly and automatically to affected employees: an intelligence or aptitude test, *e.g., Griggs v. Duke Power Co.*, 401 U.S. 424 (1971); an educational requirement, *id.*; a physical requirement, *e.g., Weeks v. Southern Bell Tel. & Tel. Co.*, 408 F.2d 228 (5th Cir. 1969). Both the existence and the "common reach" of such objectively applied patterns or practices are likely to be indisputable from the outset, so that no real commonality problems for class action maintenance ever arise in this regard. On the other hand, the disparate treatment pattern or practice must be one based upon a specific intent to discriminate against an entire group, to treat it as a group less favorably simply because of its sex (or other impermissible reason). The greater intrinsic difficulty in establishing the existence and common reach of such a subjectively based practice is obvious.

Stastny v. S. Bell Tel. & Tel. Co., 628 F.2d 267, 274 n.10 (4th Cir. 1980). In *Watson*, however, the Supreme Court recognized that the disparate impact theory may also apply to subjective employment criteria, thereby calling into question a clear dichotomy between the disparate treatment and disparate impact theories. *See Watson*, 487 U.S. at 990–91. And in *Dukes*, the Court reversed certification involving both disparate impact and disparate treatment theories. *See* 564 U.S. at 354–59. The future of disparate impact class actions is therefore also clouded.

5. The Supreme Court and Congress have made important determinations about statutes of limitations that may impact how cases (including class actions) alleging systemic discrimination will fare in the future. In *Lewis v. City of Chicago*, 560 U.S. 205 (2010), African–American applicants brought a class action under Title VII because of an alleged adverse impact a written test had on their selection for firefighter jobs. The Court held that so long as all the necessary elements of a disparate-impact Title VII claim are properly alleged, a plaintiff who does not timely file an EEOC charge following the *adoption* of a policy that violates Title VII's disparate impact provision may still challenge the policy by timely filing an EEOC charge following the *application* of the policy. *Id.* at 209–17.

Consider also *Ledbetter v. Goodyear Tire & Rubber Co., Inc.*, 550 U.S. 618 (2007) (holding that an employer's discriminatory pay decision—rather than each subsequent discriminatory paycheck—was the discriminatory act that triggered Title VII's 180 day statute of limitations to start running), *abrogated by* the Lilly Ledbetter Fair Pay Act of 2009, Pub. L. No. 111–2, 123 Stat. 5 (EEOC charge of discrimination is timely if it was filed within the limitations period following receipt of a discriminatory paycheck).

What impact, if any, might these developments have on employees' ability to challenge systemic discriminatory employment practices?

ii. Res Judicata Effect of a Finding of No Pattern or Practice

If the plaintiffs in a class action fail to demonstrate a pattern or practice of discrimination, can individual class members nonetheless pursue separate claims that *they* were victims of discrimination? In other words, if the defendant proves that discrimination was not the standard operating procedure, are individual class members foreclosed from bringing their own discrimination claims? The Supreme Court addressed that issue in the following case.

COOPER V. FEDERAL RESERVE BANK
Supreme Court of the United States, 1984.
467 U.S. 867.

JUSTICE STEVENS delivered the opinion of the Court.

The question to be decided is whether a judgment in a class action determining that an employer did not engage in a general pattern or practice of racial discrimination against the certified class of employees precludes a class member from maintaining a subsequent civil action alleging an individual claim of racial discrimination against the employer.

I.

On March 22, 1977, the Equal Employment Opportunity Commission commenced a civil action against respondent, the Federal Reserve Bank of Richmond. Respondent operates a branch in Charlotte, N.C. (the Bank), where during the years 1974–1978 it employed about 350–450 employees in several departments. The EEOC complaint alleged that the Bank was violating § 703(a) of Title VII of the Civil Rights Act of 1964 by engaging in "policies and practices" that included "failing and refusing to promote *blacks* because of race."

Six months after the EEOC filed its complaint, four individual employees were allowed to intervene as plaintiffs. In their "complaint in intervention," these plaintiffs alleged that the Bank's employment practices violated 42 U.S.C. § 1981, as well as Title VII; that each of them was the victim of employment discrimination based on race; and that they could adequately represent a class of black employees against whom the Bank had discriminated because of their race. In due course, the District Court entered an order conditionally certifying the following class pursuant to Federal Rules of Civil Procedure 23(b)(2) and (3):

> All black persons who have been employed by the defendant at its Charlotte Branch Office at any time since January 3, 1974 [6 months prior to the first charge filed by the intervenors with EEOC], who have been discriminated against in promotion, wages, job assignments and terms and conditions of employment because of their race.

After certifying the class, the District Court ordered that notice be published in the Charlotte newspapers and mailed to each individual member of the class. The notice described the status of the litigation, and plainly stated that members of the class "will be bound by the judgment or other determination" if they did not exclude themselves by sending a written notice to the Clerk. Among the recipients of the notice were Phyllis Baxter and five other individuals employed by the Bank. It is undisputed that these individuals—the *Baxter* petitioners—are members of the class represented by the intervening plaintiffs and that they made no attempt to exclude themselves from the class.

At the trial the intervening plaintiffs, as well as the *Baxter* petitioners, testified. The District Court found that the Bank had engaged in a pattern and practice of discrimination from 1974 through 1978 by failing to afford black employees opportunities for advancement and assignment equal to opportunities afforded white employees in pay grades 4 and 5. Except as so specified, however, the District Court found that "there does not appear to be a pattern and practice of discrimination pervasive enough for the court to order relief." With respect to the claims of the four intervening plaintiffs, the court found that the Bank had discriminated against Cooper and Russell, but not against Moore and Hannah. Finally, the court somewhat cryptically stated that although it had an opinion about "the entitlement to relief of some of the class members who testified at trial," it would defer decision of such matters to a further proceeding.

Thereafter, on March 24, 1981, the *Baxter* petitioners moved to intervene, alleging that each had been denied a promotion for discriminatory reasons. With respect to Emma Ruffin, the court denied the motion because she was a member of the class for which relief had been ordered and therefore her rights would be protected in the Stage II proceedings to be held on the question of relief. With respect to the other five *Baxter* petitioners, the court also denied the motion, but for a different reason. It held that because all of them were employed in jobs above the grade 5 category, they were not entitled to any benefit from the court's ruling with respect to discrimination in grades 4 and 5. The District Court stated: "The court has found no proof of any classwide discrimination above grade 5 and, therefore, they are not entitled to participate in any Stage II proceedings in this case." The court added that it could "see no reason why, if any of the would be intervenors are actively interested in pursuing their claims, they cannot file a Section 1981 suit next week...."

A few days later the *Baxter* petitioners filed a separate action against the Bank alleging that each of them had been denied a promotion because of their race in violation of 42 U.S.C. § 1981. The Bank moved to dismiss the complaint on the ground that each of them was a member of the class that had been certified in the *Cooper* litigation, that each was employed in a grade other than 4 or 5, and that they were bound by the determination that there was no proof of any classwide discrimination above grade 5. The District Court denied the motion to dismiss, but certified its order for interlocutory appeal under 28 U.S.C. § 1292(b). The Bank's interlocutory appeal from the order was then consolidated with the Bank's pending appeal in the *Cooper* litigation.

The United States Court of Appeals for the Fourth Circuit reversed the District Court's judgment on the merits in the *Cooper* litigation, concluding that (1) there was insufficient evidence to establish a pattern or practice of racial discrimination in grades 4 and 5, and (2) two of the intervening plaintiffs had not been discriminated against on account of race. The court further held that under the doctrine of *res judicata*, the judgment in the *Cooper* class action precluded the *Baxter* petitioners from maintaining their individual race discrimination claims against the Bank. The court thus reversed the order denying the Bank's motion to dismiss in the *Baxter* action, and remanded for dismissal of the *Baxter* complaint. We granted *certiorari* to review that judgment, and we now reverse.

II.

Claims of two types were adjudicated in the *Cooper* litigation. First, the individual claims of each of the four intervening plaintiffs have been finally decided in the Bank's favor. Those individual decisions do not, of course, foreclose any other individual claims. Second, the class claim that the Bank followed "policies and practices" of discriminating against its employees has also been decided. It is that decision on which the Court of Appeals based its *res judicata* analysis.

* * *

III.

A plaintiff bringing a civil action for a violation of § 703(a) of Title VII has the initial burden of establishing a *prima facie* case that his employer discriminated against him on account of his race, color, religion, sex, or national origin. A plaintiff meets this initial burden by offering evidence adequate to create an inference that he was denied an employment opportunity on the basis of a discriminatory criterion enumerated in Title VII.

A plaintiff alleging one instance of discrimination establishes a *prima facie* case justifying an inference of individual racial discrimination by showing that he (1) belongs to a racial minority, (2) applied and was qualified for a vacant position the employer was attempting to fill, (3) was rejected for the position, and (4) after his rejection, the position remained open and the employer continued to seek applicants of the plaintiff's qualifications. *McDonnell Douglas Corp. v. Green,* 411 U.S. 792, 802 (1973). Once these facts are established, the employer must produce "evidence that the plaintiff was rejected, or someone else was preferred, for a legitimate, nondiscriminatory reason." *Texas Dept. of Community Affairs v. Burdine,* 450 U.S. 248, 254 (1981). At that point, the presumption of discrimination "drops from the case," [*Id.*] at 255, n.10, and the district court is in a position to decide the ultimate question in such a suit: whether the particular employment decision at issue was made on the basis of race. The ultimate burden of persuading the trier of fact that the defendant intentionally discriminated against the plaintiff regarding the particular employment decision "remains at all times with the plaintiff," and in the final analysis the trier of fact "must decide which party's explanation of the employer's motivation it believes." *United States Postal Service Bd. of Governors v. Aikens,* 460 U.S. 711, 716 (1983).

In *Franks v. Bowman Transp. Co.,* 424 U.S. 747 (1976), the plaintiff, on behalf of himself and all others similarly situated, alleged that the employer had engaged in a pervasive pattern of racial discrimination in various company policies, including the hiring, transfer, and discharge of employees. In that class action we held that demonstrating the existence of a discriminatory pattern or practice established a presumption that the individual class members had been discriminated against on account of race. Proving isolated or sporadic discriminatory acts by the employer is insufficient to establish a *prima facie* case of a pattern or practice of discrimination; rather it must be established by a preponderance of the evidence that "racial discrimination was the company's standard operating procedure— the regular rather than the unusual practice." *Teamsters v. United States,* 431 U.S. 324, 336 (1977).[9] While a finding of a pattern or practice of discrimination itself justifies an award of prospective relief to the class, additional proceedings are ordinarily required to determine the scope of individual relief for the members of the class.

The crucial difference between an individual's claim of discrimination and a class action alleging a general pattern or practice of discrimination is manifest. The inquiry regarding an individual's claim is the reason for a particular employment decision, while "at the liability stage of a pattern-or-practice trial the focus often will not be on individual hiring decisions, but on a pattern of discriminatory decision making."

This distinction was critical to our holding in *General Tel. Co. v. Falcon,* 457 U.S. 147 (1982), that an individual employee's claim that he was denied a promotion on racial grounds did not necessarily make him an adequate representative of a class composed of persons who had allegedly been refused employment for discriminatory reasons. * * * After analyzing the particulars of the plaintiff's claim in that case, we pointed out that if "one allegation of specific discriminatory treatment were sufficient to support an across-the-board attack, every Title VII case would be a potential companywide class action." * * *

Falcon thus holds that the existence of a valid individual claim does not necessarily warrant the conclusion that the individual plaintiff may successfully maintain a class action. It is equally clear that a class plain-

---

[9] Although *Teamsters* involved an action litigated on the merits by the Government as plaintiff under § 707(a) of the Act, it is plain that the elements of a *prima facie* pattern-or-practice case are the same in a private class action.

tiff's attempt to prove the existence of a companywide policy, or even a consistent practice within a given department, may fail even though discrimination against one or two individuals has been proved. The facts of this case illustrate the point.

The District Court found that two of the intervening plaintiffs, Cooper and Russell, had both established that they were the victims of racial discrimination but, as the Court of Appeals noted, they were employed in grades higher than grade 5 and therefore their testimony provided no support for the conclusion that there was a practice of discrimination in grades 4 and 5. Given the burden of establishing a *prima facie* case of a pattern or practice of discrimination, it was entirely consistent for the District Court simultaneously to conclude that Cooper and Russell had valid individual claims even though it had expressly found no proof of any classwide discrimination above grade 5. It could not be more plain that the rejection of a claim of classwide discrimination does not warrant the conclusion that no member of the class could have a valid individual claim. * * *

The analysis of the merits of the *Cooper* litigation by the Court of Appeals is entirely consistent with this conclusion. In essence, the Court of Appeals held that the statistical evidence, buttressed by expert testimony and anecdotal evidence by three individual employees in grades 4 and 5, was not sufficient to support the finding of a pattern of bankwide discrimination within those grades. It is true that the Court of Appeals was unpersuaded by the anecdotal evidence; it is equally clear, however, that it did not regard two or three instances of discrimination as sufficient to establish a general policy. It quite properly recognized that a "court must be wary of a claim that the true color of a forest is better revealed by reptiles hidden in the weeds than by the foliage of countless freestanding trees." *NAACP v. Claiborne Hardware Co.*, 458 U.S. 886, 934 (1982). Conversely, a piece of fruit may well be bruised without being rotten to the core.

The Court of Appeals was correct in generally concluding that the *Baxter* petitioners, as members of the class represented by the intervening plaintiffs in the *Cooper* litigation, are bound by the adverse judgment in that case. The court erred, however, in the preclusive effect it attached to that prior adjudication. That judgment (1) bars the class members from bringing another class action against the Bank alleging a pattern or practice of discrimination for the relevant time period and (2) precludes the class members in any other litigation with the Bank from relitigating the question whether the Bank engaged in a pattern and practice of discrimination against black employees during the relevant time period. The judgment is not, however, dispositive of the individual claims the *Baxter* petitioners have alleged in their separate action. Assuming they establish a *prima facie* case of discrimination under *McDonnell Douglas*, the Bank will be required to articulate a legitimate reason for each of the challenged decisions, and if it meets that burden, the ultimate questions regarding motivation in their individual cases will be resolved by the District Court. Moreover, the prior adjudication may well prove beneficial to the Bank in the *Baxter* action: the determination in the *Cooper* action that the Bank had not engaged in a general pattern or practice of discrimination would be relevant on the issue of pretext.

The Bank argues that permitting the *Baxter* petitioners to bring separate actions would frustrate the purposes of Rule 23. We think the converse is true. The class-action device was intended to establish a procedure for the adjudication of common questions of law or fact. If the Bank's theory were adopted, it would be tantamount to requiring that every member of the class be permitted to intervene to litigate the merits of his individual claim.

It is also suggested that the District Court had a duty to decide the merits of the individual claims of class members, at least insofar as the individual claimants became witnesses in the joint proceeding and subjected their individual employment histories to scrutiny at trial. Unless these claims are decided in the main proceeding, the Bank argues that the duplicative litigation that Rule 23 was designed to avoid will be encouraged, and that defendants will be subjected to the risks of liability without the offsetting benefit of a favorable termination of exposure through a final judgment.

This argument fails to differentiate between what the District Court might have done and what it actually did. The District Court did actually adjudicate the individual claims of *Cooper* and the other intervening plaintiffs, as well as the class claims, but it pointedly refused to decide the individual claims of the *Baxter* petitioners. Whether the issues framed by the named parties before the court should be expanded to encompass the individual claims of additional class members is a matter of judicial administration that should be decided in the first instance by the District Court. Nothing in Rule 23 requires as a matter of law that the District Court make a finding with respect to each and every matter on which there is testimony in the class action. Indeed, Rule 23 is carefully drafted to provide a mechanism for the expeditious decision of *common* questions. Its purposes might well be defeated by an attempt to decide a host of individual claims before any common question relating to liability has been resolved adversely to the defendant. We do not find the District Court's denial of the *Baxter* petitioners' motion for leave to intervene in the *Cooper* litigation, or its decision not to make findings regarding the *Baxter* petitioners' testimony in the *Cooper* litigation, to be inconsistent with Rule 23.

The judgment of the Court of Appeals is reversed, and the case is remanded for further proceedings consistent with this opinion.

NOTES AND QUESTIONS

1. The Supreme Court's opinion in *Cooper* was without dissent (Justice Marshall concurred in the judgment and Justice Powell did not participate). How does the Supreme Court's approach differ from that of the court of appeals? Which approach is more persuasive?

2. One commentator criticizes *Cooper* for giving employees an unfair advantage over employers, essentially allowing employees to have two bites at the apple:

> * * * [T]his risk is one-sided: should the phase-one jury rule against the plaintiffs, that decision has no *res judicata* effect as to the class members' individual claims of discrimination because all that the decision means is that the employer does not discriminate against em-

ployees as a matter of standard practice. *See Cooper v. Federal Reserve Bank*, 467 U.S. 867, 877–80 (1984). Each class member remains free to file his own lawsuit (if timely), and the employer may gain little peace of mind by prevailing in this phase of the class action. In essence, the plaintiffs have two chances instead of one to press their claims, and they and their lawyers have little incentive not to "shoot the moon" in seeking class certification.

Daniel F. Piar, *The Uncertain Future of Title VII Class Actions After the Civil Rights Act of 1991*, 2001 BYU L. Rev. 305, n.123 (2001). Are these critiques of *Cooper* valid?

Another commentator argues that the courts have not adequately considered the potential preclusive effects of class judgments, and that the Supreme Court's *Cooper* decision failed to provide a serious analysis of the role of preclusion in class action litigation. *See* Tobias Barrington Wolff, *Preclusion in Class Action Litigation*, 105 Colum. L. Rev. 717, 724–31 (2005). Has this concern been rectified by *Smith v. Bayer Corp.*, 131 S. Ct. 2368 (2011)? *See* Chapter 7(C)(2)(b).

2. EMPLOYMENT DISCRIMINATION SUITS NOT SUBJECT TO RULE 23

As noted, cases brought under § 216(b) of the FLSA, including those asserting age discrimination in violation of the ADEA, are not subject to Rule 23. Individual class members must opt into the case in order to participate in the "collective" action, as it is called. Once they opt in, they have the status of parties. A number of interesting questions have arisen in the context of ADEA collective actions, including the permissibility of notice to potential opt-in class members and the requirements for certifying a collective action.

a. Notice in an Age Discrimination Collective Action

In an ADEA action or other actions under § 216(b) of the FLSA, the function of notice is different from that in a Rule 23 class action. Notice is designed to allow individuals the chance to opt into the class, not to opt out. In 1989, the Supreme Court addressed whether ADEA notice was authorized (and whether such authorization could be derived by analogy to Rule 23).

HOFFMANN–LA ROCHE INC. V. SPERLING
Supreme Court of the United States, 1989.
493 U.S. 165.

JUSTICE KENNEDY delivered the opinion of the Court.

The Age Discrimination in Employment Act of 1967 (ADEA), 29 U.S.C. § 621 *et seq.*, provides that an employee may bring an action on behalf of himself and other employees similarly situated. To resolve disagreement among the Courts of Appeals, we granted *certiorari* on the question whether a district court conducting a suit of this type may authorize and facilitate notice of the pending action.

I.

Age discrimination in employment is forbidden by § 4 of the ADEA. 29 U.S.C. § 623. Section 7(b) of the ADEA incorporates enforcement provisions of the Fair Labor Standards Act of 1938 (FLSA), as amended, 29 U.S.C. § 201 *et seq.*, and provides that the ADEA shall be enforced using certain of the powers, remedies, and procedures of the FLSA. This controversy centers around one of the provisions the ADEA incorporates, which states, in pertinent part, that an action

> may be maintained against any employer ... in any Federal or State court of competent jurisdiction by any one or more employees for and in behalf of himself or themselves and other employees similarly situated. No employee shall be a party plaintiff to any such action unless he gives his consent in writing to become such a party and such consent is filed in the court in which such action is brought.

In 1985, petitioner Hoffmann–La Roche Inc. ordered a reduction in work force and discharged or demoted some 1,200 workers. Richard Sperling, a discharged employee and one of the respondents, filed an age discrimination charge with the Equal Employment Opportunity Commission for himself and all employees similarly situated. With the assistance of counsel, Sperling and some other employees formed a group known as Roche Age Discriminatees Asking Redress (R.A.D.A.R.). The group mailed a letter, on R.A.D.A.R. letterhead, to some 600 employees whom it had identified as potential members of the protected class. The letter advised that an action would be brought against petitioner under the ADEA and invited the addressees to join the suit by filling out and returning an enclosed consent form, thus fulfilling the statutory requirement of joinder by "consent in writing."

Respondents filed this ADEA action in Federal District Court and, through R.A.D.A.R.'s letters and informal contacts, received and filed with the court over 400 consents. To ensure that all potential plaintiffs would receive notice of the suit, respondents moved for discovery of the names and addresses of all similarly situated employees. They also requested that the court send notice to all potential plaintiffs who had not yet filed consents. Petitioner opposed both motions and filed a cross-motion asking the court to invalidate the consents already filed on the ground that the solicitation had been misleading. In addition, petitioner requested that the court send out a "corrective notice" to the individuals who had filed consents.

To resolve these matters the District Court ordered petitioner to produce the names and addresses of the discharged employees. The District Court held that it was "permissible for a court to facilitate notice of an ADEA suit to absent class members in appropriate cases, so long as the court avoids communicating to absent class members any encouragement to join the suit or any approval of the suit on its merits." The court also authorized respondents to send to all employees who had not yet joined the suit a notice and a consent document, with a text and form approved by the court. The court attached the authorized notice to its interlocutory order. At the end of the approved notice was a statement that the notice had been authorized by the District Court, but that the court had taken no position on the merits of the case. Finally, the District Court refused to invalidate the consents already filed.

The District Court found that its orders regarding discovery and further notice met the requirements for immediate appeal, 28 U.S.C. § 1292(b), and the Court of Appeals permitted an appeal from that portion of the ruling. The Court of Appeals affirmed the discovery order and the order for further notice, ruling that "there is no legal impediment to court-authorized notice in an appropriate case." The Court of Appeals declined to review the form and contents of the notice to potential plaintiffs and, in particular, it declined to pass upon the concluding statement of the notice stating that it had been authorized by the District Court.

II.

As it comes before us, this case presents the narrow question whether, in an ADEA action, district courts may play any role in prescribing the terms and conditions of communication from the named plaintiffs to the potential members of the class on whose behalf the collective action has been brought. We hold that district courts have discretion, in appropriate cases, to implement 29 U.S.C. § 216(b), as incorporated by 29 U.S.C. § 626(b), in ADEA actions by facilitating notice to potential plaintiffs. The facts and circumstances of this case illustrate the propriety, if not the necessity, for court intervention in the notice process. As did the Court of Appeals, we decline to examine the terms of the notice used here, or its concluding statement indicating court authorization. We confirm the existence of the trial court's discretion, not the details of its exercise.

The District Court was correct to permit discovery of the names and addresses of the discharged employees. Without pausing to explore alternative bases for the discovery, for instance that the employees might have knowledge of other discoverable matter, we find it suffices to say that the discovery was relevant to the subject matter of the action and that there were no grounds to limit the discovery under the facts and circumstances of this case.

The ADEA, through incorporation of § 216(b), expressly authorizes employees to bring collective age discrimination actions "in behalf of . . . themselves and other employees similarly situated." Congress has stated its policy that ADEA plaintiffs should have the opportunity to proceed collectively. A collective action allows age discrimination plaintiffs the advantage of lower individual costs to vindicate rights by the pooling of resources. The judicial system benefits by efficient resolution in one proceeding of common issues of law and fact arising from the same alleged discriminatory activity.

These benefits, however, depend on employees receiving accurate and timely notice concerning the pendency of the collective action, so that they can make informed decisions about whether to participate. Section 216(b)'s affirmative permission for employees to proceed on behalf of those similarly situated must grant the court the requisite procedural authority to manage the process of joining multiple parties in a manner that is orderly, sensible, and not otherwise contrary to statutory commands or the provisions of the Federal Rules of Civil Procedure. *See* Fed.Rule Civ.Proc. 83. It follows that, once an ADEA action is filed, the court has a managerial responsibility to oversee the joinder of additional parties to assure that the task is accomplished in an efficient and proper way.

We have recognized that a trial court has a substantial interest in communications that are mailed for single actions involving multiple parties. In *Gulf Oil Co. v. Bernard*, 452 U.S. 89, 101 (1981), we held that a District Court erred by entering an order that in effect prohibited communications between the named plaintiffs and others in a Rule 23 class action. Observing that class actions serve important goals but also present opportunities for abuse, we noted that "[b]ecause of the potential for abuse, a district court has both the duty and the broad authority to exercise control over a class action and to enter appropriate orders governing the conduct of counsel and the parties." The same justifications apply in the context of an ADEA action. Although the collective form of action is designed to serve the important function of preventing age discrimination, the potential for misuse of the class device, as by misleading communications, may be countered by court-authorized notice.

Because trial court involvement in the notice process is inevitable in cases with numerous plaintiffs where written consent is required by statute, it lies within the discretion of a district court to begin its involvement early, at the point of the initial notice, rather than at some later time. One of the most significant insights that skilled trial judges have gained in recent years is the wisdom and necessity for early judicial intervention in the management of litigation. A trial court can better manage a major ADEA action if it ascertains the contours of the action at the outset. The court is not limited to waiting passively for objections about the manner in which the consents were obtained. By monitoring preparation and distribution of the notice, a court can ensure that it is timely, accurate, and informative. Both the parties and the court benefit from settling disputes about the content of the notice before it is distributed. This procedure may avoid the need to cancel consents obtained in an improper manner.

The instant case is illustrative. Petitioner objected to the form of the notice first sent by respondents' counsel, alleging that it was so inaccurate that any consents based on it should be found invalid by the court, and at the same time petitioner resisted discovery of the names and addresses of the discharged employees. Questions of notice, proper discovery, and the validity of consents were intertwined.

Court authorization of notice serves the legitimate goal of avoiding a multiplicity of duplicative suits and setting cutoff dates to expedite disposition of the action. In this case, the trial court, as part of its order, set a cutoff date for the filing of consents, as it was bound to do if the action was to proceed in diligent fashion. By approving the form of notice sent, the trial court could be assured that its cutoff date was reasonable, rather than having to set a cutoff date based on a series of unauthorized communications or even gossip that might have been misleading.

In the context of the explicit statutory direction of a single ADEA action for multiple ADEA plaintiffs, the Federal Rules of Civil Procedure provide further support for the trial court's authority to facilitate notice. Under the terms of Rule 83, courts, in any case "not provided for by rule," may "regulate their practice in any manner not inconsistent with" federal or local rules. Rule 83 endorses measures to regulate the actions of the parties to a multiparty suit. * * * The interest of courts in managing collective actions in an orderly fashion is reinforced by Rule 16(b), requiring entry of a scheduling order limiting time for various pretrial steps such as joinder of additional parties. At pretrial conferences, courts are encouraged to address "the need for adopting special procedures for managing potentially difficult or protracted actions that may involve complex issues, [or] multiple parties . . ." Fed.Rule Civ. Proc. 16(c)(10).

* * *

Our decision does not imply that trial courts have unbridled discretion in managing ADEA actions. Court intervention in the notice process for case management purposes is distinguishable in form and function from the solicitation of claims. In exercising the discretionary authority to oversee the notice-giving process, courts must be scrupulous to respect judicial neutrality. To that end, trial courts must take care to avoid even the appearance of judicial endorsement of the merits of the action.

The judgment of the Third Circuit is affirmed, and the case remanded for proceedings consistent with this opinion.

JUSTICE SCALIA, with whom CHIEF JUSTICE REHNQUIST joins, dissenting.

The Court holds that in a § 216(b) action the district court can use its compulsory process to assist counsel for the plaintiff in locating nonparties to the litigation who may have similar claims, and in obtaining their consent to his prosecution of those claims. Because I know of no source of authority for such an extraordinary exercise of the federal judicial power, I dissent.

To read the Court's opinion, one would think that what is at issue here is nothing but a routine exercise in case management. We are told that the district court has a "managerial responsibility to oversee the joinder of additional parties" in § 216(b) actions, in order to protect potential plaintiffs and avoid duplicative litigation. We are told that all concerned—plaintiffs, defendants, and the judicial system itself—benefit when the district courts abandon their "passive" stance and instead undertake "early judicial intervention" in the process of identifying people who have a cause of action and securing their consent to join the litigation. And we are told that by doing good in this fashion the district courts merely avail themselves of their "considerable authority to manage their own affairs so as to achieve the orderly and expeditious disposition of cases."

The difficulty with sweeping these orders under the rug of "case management" is that they were *not at all* designed to facilitate the adjudication of any claim before the court. The individuals whom the court helped notify were not, at the time of the orders, part of the case. Section 216(b) provides that "no employee shall be a party plaintiff . . . unless he gives his consent in writing to become such a party and such consent is filed in the court in which such action is brought." 29 U.S.C.§ 216(b). It is true, of course, that the orders can be regarded as managing *future* cases—assuring, to the extent the plaintiffs are willing, that such cases will not be filed in different courts and at different times. But that does not make *this* court's handling of *the case before it* any simpler or more efficient. Surely the judge's authority to "manage" cases has never before been thought to be more expansive than his authority to adjudicate them—*i.e.*, to extend to cases that have not actually been filed in his court.

The activity approved today is an extraordinary application of the federal judicial power, which is limited by Article III of the Constitution to the adjudication of cases and controversies. * * *

First, nothing in § 216(b) itself confers this power. The portion of the statute dealing with collective employee actions provides that employees may sue in a representative capacity for other similarly situated employees who have consented to the representation. The Court characterizes this as an "affirmative permission" for representative actions, from which it derives a "grant [of] the requisite procedural authority to *manage the process of joining multiple parties*. . . ." Of course the reality of the matter is that it is not an "affirmative permission" for representative actions at all, but rather *a limitation* upon the affirmative permission for representative actions that already exists in Rule 23 of the Federal Rules of Civil Procedure. (That is to say, were it not for this provision of § 216(b) the representative action could be brought even *without* the prior consent of similarly situated employees.) But accepting the notion that it is an "affirmative permission" for representative actions, I do not see how that converts into an implied authorization for courts to undertake the unheard-of role of midwifing those actions. I have no doubt that courts possess certain powers over the § 216(b) joinder process, most prominently the power to satisfy themselves that the employees who purportedly become parties are *in fact* similarly situated to the representative, and have *in fact* given valid consents to the litigation. That is simply part of the courts' ever-present duty to inquire into their jurisdiction over claims brought before them. But to reason from that to the existence of a more general "procedural authority to manage the process of joining multiple parties" seems to me fallacious. Nothing in § 216 remotely confers the extraordinary authority for a court—either directly or by lending its judicial power to the efforts of a party's counsel—*to search* out potential claimants, ensure that they are accurately informed of the litigation, and inquire whether they would like to bring their claims before the court.

The Court seeks to minimize the novelty of the authority it confers by analogizing it to the authority we have earlier acknowledged for district courts to regulate communications between class members and their representatives in Rule 23 class actions, in order to ensure that the former are kept accurately informed of the litigation. There is no comparison. In Rule 23 class actions, the members of a class which qualifies for certification are parties to the action and will be bound by the judgment (except for those members of a (b)(3) class who elect to opt out). *See* Fed.Rule Civ.Proc. 23(c)(3). It is not at all extraordinary for courts to supervise and regulate the participation of *existing* parties *in actions that are pending*. The Rules specifically provide, for example, that courts may, and in some instances must, notify absent class members of the pendency of the litigation. *See* Fed.Rule Civ.Proc. 23(c)(2) (requiring court in 23(b)(3) action to notify absent class members that they will be bound by judgment unless they opt out by a certain date); Fed.Rule Civ.Proc. 23(d) (authorizing court in 23(b)(1) or (b)(2) actions to notify class members of pendency of litigation). But what courts may do with respect to absent parties says nothing about what they may do with respect to members of the public at large.

Nor do I agree with the Court that the Federal Rules of Civil Procedure themselves provide the authority claimed by the District Court. To begin with, authorization from that source may be expressly foreclosed by Rule 82, which provides that the Rules "shall not be construed to extend or limit the jurisdiction of the United States district courts or the venue of actions therein." Authority for the courts to use their power for a purpose that neither achieves nor assists the resolution of claims before them appears to violate that prohibition—and the urgings of judicial efficiency are no justification for ignoring it. But even if the Federal Rules could expand judicial power in this fashion, nothing in their language suggests that they have done so. The Court relies upon Rule 16, which, in authorizing pretrial conferences to facilitate the disposition of cases, admonishes the court to address "the need for adopting special procedures for managing potentially difficult or protracted actions that may involve complex issues, multiple parties, difficult legal questions, or unusual proof problems." Fed.Rule Civ.Proc. 16(c)(10). It would certainly be strange to confer an unusual new power by simply mentioning that power (as one of the subjects that can be considered) in a provision designed to authorize pretrial conferences. But in any case, the authority to "manage actions" cannot reasonably be read to refer to the management of claims and parties not before the court. This is made entirely clear by the Rule's catch-all provision, which admonishes the court to address "such *other* matters as may aid in the disposition *of the action.*" Fed.Rule Civ.Proc. 16(c)(11).

The Court's repeated reliance upon Rule 83 is so strained that it snaps. Rule 83 states: "In all cases not provided for by rule, the district judges ... may regulate their practice in any manner not inconsistent with these rules or those of the district in which they act." The contention here is that this is not a "regulation of practice" *pertinent to resolution of the controversy before the court.* To respond to that contention by pointing out that the court has been given authority to "regulate practice" is not to respond at all—unless the Court means that "regulating practice" includes impositions upon the parties and their counsel for any purpose whatever.

* * *

In the end, the only serious justification for today's decision is that it makes for more efficient and economical adjudication of cases—not more efficient and economical adjudication of the *pending* case, but of *other* cases that might later be filed separately on behalf of plaintiffs who would have been perfectly willing to join the present suit instead. I concede that this justification, at least, is entirely valid. The problem is that it is a justification in policy but not in law.

If the benefits of judicial efficiency and economy constitute sufficient warrant for the District Court's action, then one can imagine numerous areas in which district courts should similarly take on the function of litigation touts—*whenever*, in fact, they have before them a claim that is similar to claims which other identifiable individuals might possess. The Court's suggestion that ADEA suits are rendered distinctive by § 216(b)'s "explicit statutory direction of a single ADEA action for multiple ADEA plaintiffs," is entirely unpersuasive. Section 216 no more *directs* a single action in ADEA litigation than Rule 20 (permissive joinder) *directs* a single action in all other litigation. Both provisions *permit* (in the words of Rule

20) that persons may "join in one action as plaintiffs [who] assert [a] right to relief * * * in respect of or arising out of the same transaction, occurrence, or series of transactions or occurrences and if any question of law or fact common to all these persons will arise in the action." Fed.Rule Civ.Proc. 20(a).

There is more than a little historical irony in the Court's decision today. "Stirring up litigation" was once exclusively the occupation of disreputable lawyers, roundly condemned by this and all American courts. But in the age of the "case managing" judicial bureaucracy, our perceptions have changed. Seeking out and notifying sleeping potential plaintiffs yields such economies of scale that what was once demeaned as a drain on judicial resources is now praised as a cutting-edge tool of efficient judicial administration. Perhaps it is. But that does not justify our taking it in hand when Congress has not authorized it. Even less does it justify our rush to abandon (not only without compulsion but without invitation) what the Court deprecatingly calls the courts' "passive" role in determining which claims come before them, but which I regard as one of the natural components of a system in which courts are not inquisitors of justice but arbiters of adversarial claims.

NOTES AND QUESTIONS

1. Which *Sperling* opinion, the majority or dissent, is more faithful to the text of the Fair Labor Standards Act and the Federal Rules of Civil Procedure? Which is more consistent with the policies of the ADEA?

2. Courts since *Sperling* have disagreed over the factual showing required to warrant sending notice. Some courts hold that a plaintiff can show that potential class members are "similarly situated" for purposes of allowing the issuance of notice based solely on the allegations in the complaint. *See, e.g., Allen v. Marshall Field & Co.*, 93 F.R.D. 438, 442–45 (N.D. Ill. 1982). Other courts hold that a plaintiff must offer factual support for the allegations before notice may be sent. *See, e.g., Jackson v. N.Y. Tel. Co.*, 163 F.R.D. 429, 431 (S.D.N.Y. 1995). Which approach makes more sense? Which is more consistent with *Sperling*? *See generally Belcher v. Shoney's, Inc.*, 927 F. Supp. 249, 251 (M.D. Tenn. 1996) (discussing conflicting approaches).

3. An interesting issue regarding the opt-in requirement for FLSA collective actions arises in the class arbitration context. The American Arbitration Association (AAA)—whose rules permit class actions in arbitration—follows the Rule 23 opt-out model for its class arbitrations, even though claims brought under the FLSA and similar statutes require an opt-in approach. *See* 29 U.S.C. § 216(b) ("No employee shall be a party plaintiff to any * * * action [under the FLSA] unless he gives his consent in writing to become such a party and such consent is filed in the court in which such action is brought"). Are employers who have arbitration agreements governed by the AAA rules required to utilize an opt-in model in FLSA and similar cases? In *Long John Silver's Restaurants, Inc. v. Cole*, 514 F.3d 345, 351 (4th Cir. 2008), the Fourth Circuit said no, concluding that Congress did not intend to forbid employees from waiving the opt-in procedure for FLSA claims subject to an arbitration agreement.

4. Opt-out procedures have also been permitted in FLSA cases that include class claims where plaintiffs are intimidated from participating in a collective action for fear of retaliation by their defendant employer. For example,

in *Guzman v. VLM Inc.*, 2008 WL 597186 (E.D.N.Y. 2008), immigrant workers primarily from Pakistan, South America, and Central America filed a class action in federal district court against their employer under a state wage and hour law and under the FLSA for similar conduct. *See id.* at *1–4. The district court certified the class under the state law, using the Rule 23 opt-out approach, and conditionally certified the class under the FLSA, using the opt-in approach. The district court rejected the argument that certifying the class under Rule 23 opt-out procedures for conduct covered by the FLSA undermined the FLSA opt-in procedures. *Id.* at *9–10. Recognizing the immigrant workers' legitimate fear of retaliation, the district court noted that "the opt-out nature of a class action is a valuable feature lacking in an FLSA collective action." *Id.* at *8. Is such reasoning persuasive?

5. One interesting trend in federal courts is the increase in FLSA collective actions. A recent study conducted by the Federal Judicial Center notes their dominance among labor class actions filed in or removed to federal court from July 1, 2001, through June 30, 2007. Emery G. Lee III & Thomas E. Willging, Fed. Judicial Ctr., *The Impact of the Class Action Fairness Act of 2005 on the Federal Courts; Fourth Interim Report to the Judicial Conference Advisory Committee on Civil Rules*, at 3 (Apr. 2008) ("Much of the increase in total class action activity in the federal courts is driven by increases in filings of class actions based on federal question jurisdiction * * *. The most notable increase of this kind * * * is in labor class actions. Most of the class actions in this category are opt-in collective actions brought under the * * * FLSA * * *.").

6. Are opt-in classes permitted under Rule 23? In *Kern v. Siemens Corp.*, 393 F.3d 120 (2d Cir. 2004), a ski train in Austria caught on fire and killed more than 150 people. The surviving family members of those killed brought separate wrongful death actions against the manufacturer and operator of the train. The cases were consolidated and transferred by the MDL Panel to the Southern District of New York. The district court granted the plaintiffs' motion for class certification solely for liability purposes under Rule 23(b)(3), and created an opt-in class, whereby putative class members had to affirmatively consent to inclusion. The Second Circuit reversed, concluding that an opt-in class was contrary to Rule 23. In so holding, the Second Circuit reasoned: "[R]equiring the individuals affirmatively to request inclusion in the lawsuit would result in freezing out the claims of people—especially small claims held by small people—who for one reason or another, ignorance, timidity, unfamiliarity with business or legal matters, will simply not take the affirmative step." 393 F.3d at 124–25. *Kern* was not an employment case. Do the same concerns apply to discrimination cases? If so, is there any valid basis for the current treatment of ADEA cases as opt-in cases?

b. Requirements for Certifying an Age Discrimination Collective Action

What are the requirements for certifying a collective action under the ADEA? Should they parallel those for obtaining certification under Rule 23? Consider the following decision.

SHUSHAN V. UNIV. OF COLO.
United States District Court, District of Colorado, 1990.
132 F.R.D. 263.

NOTTINGHAM, DISTRICT JUDGE.

According to their Complaint, Dr. Sam Shushan and Dr. Erik Bonde, the two named plaintiffs, are full-time, tenured professors of biology in the University of Colorado at Boulder's College of Arts and Sciences. Professor Shushan is 67 years old, has been employed by the University for approximately 40 years, and is paid an annual salary of $26,118.00. Professor Bonde is 66 years old, has been employed by the University for approximately 35 years, and is paid an annual salary of $32,889.00.

In November of 1988, according to plaintiffs, the dean of the College of Arts and Sciences and the chairman of the Biology Department "urged" them to accept early retirement. (Defendant denies that plaintiffs were "urged" to take early retirement; they were merely informed of their retirement "options.") In December of 1988, the professors say, they declined to accept early retirement.

This lawsuit asserts that the University retaliated against the professors when they refused to take early retirement and thus violated the Age Discrimination in Employment Act (ADEA). * * * The alleged retaliation included acts such as moving the professors from private offices equipped with laboratory space to "designated storerooms" without such space, denying them earned sabbatical leave, taking away their laboratory assistants, and depriving them of certain teaching responsibilities. Plaintiffs also assert that the University generally has discriminated against them and other "older faculty members similarly situated" by paying them salaries lower than salaries paid younger faculty members and by awarding them lesser annual increases in salary.

The matter before me is plaintiffs' motion for "conditional certification" of a class. Plaintiffs argue that, because their lawsuit is a "statutory" class action pursuant to the Fair Labor Standards Act of 1938, 29 U.S.C.A. § 216(b), incorporated by reference into the ADEA in 29 U.S.C. § 626(b), they may proceed unencumbered by the procedural restraints which Fed. R. Civ. P. 23 usually imposes on class actions. Citing a recent Supreme Court decision, *Hoffmann–La Roche, Inc. v. Sperling,* 493 U.S. 165 (1989), for the proposition that the court has the power to authorize notice to potential class members, their motion asks the court to (1) make a preliminary determination concerning the scope of the potential class, (2) grant them the right to discover the identity of potential class members, and (3) approve a form of notice to potential class members. Under 29 U.S.C.A. § 216(b), the "final class" would then consist of those people who file with the court a written consent to become plaintiffs.

To evaluate plaintiffs' contention that no part of Fed. R. Civ. P. 23 applies to an action under the ADEA, I must first discuss the peculiar form of proceeding established by the ADEA. As I noted earlier, section 7(b) of the ADEA, 29 U.S.C. § 626(b), states that the ADEA's "provisions . . . shall be enforced in accordance with the powers, remedies, and procedures provided in" 29 U.S.C.A. § 216(b)—a part of the Fair Labor Standards Act of 1938, as amended by the Portal-to-Portal Act of 1947. The pertinent part of section 216(b) provides:

> Action[s] . . . may be maintained . . . by any one or more employees for and in behalf of himself or themselves and other employees similarly situated. No employee shall be a party plaintiff to any such action unless he gives his consent in writing to become such

a party and such consent is filed in the court in which such action is brought.

The form of action contemplated by section 216 is a hybrid, sharing characteristics of both Fed. R. Civ. P. 20 (permissive joinder of parties) and Fed. R. Civ. P. 23. Like a person who would join as a plaintiff under rule 20 (and in contrast to a member of a plaintiff class under rule 23), the person who would be a plaintiff under section 216 must affirmatively act, by filing "his consent in writing," in order to be associated with the lawsuit; if he does nothing, he will not be bound by the outcome, whether it is favorable or unfavorable. Like a member of a plaintiff class under rule 23, however (and in contrast to a plaintiff who joins as a plaintiff under rule 20), the section 216 plaintiff does not formally appear before the court or file a pleading; he simply files his written consent. He is therefore not named in the caption, Fed. R. Civ. P. 10(a), and he would not ordinarily be served with papers filed after he files the written consent. Fed. R. Civ. P. 5(a). Once the consent is filed, the section 216 action is maintained by the named plaintiffs "for and in behalf of" the person who has consented.

The peculiar nature of a section 216 action has led courts to different conclusions on the question of the extent to which rule 23 applies in such an action. A few district courts have held that rule 23 applies *in toto* and that the "class" represented in a section 216 action may even include persons who have not filed the written consent mentioned in section 216. Most courts, however, have suggested, by way of holdings or broad *dicta*, that rule 23 simply does not apply to section 216 actions. I am not completely persuaded by either line of authority, and I believe that the Supreme Court's decision in *Hoffmann–La Roche, Inc. v. Sperling* undermines the rationale of many cases in the latter line of authority. Consequently, I hold that the named representative plaintiffs in an ADEA class action must satisfy all of the requirements of rule 23, *insofar as those requirements are consistent with* 29 U.S.C.A. § 216(b).

The reasons for applying rule 23 to an ADEA class action have been articulated in *Blankenship v. Ralston Purina Co.*, 62 F.R.D. 35 (N.D. Ga. 1973). In holding that rule 23 applies *in toto* to an ADEA class action, *Blankenship* noted the "broad, remedial purposes of the ADEA," and analogized the ADEA's prohibitions against age discrimination to the prohibitions against other forms of discrimination contained in the Civil Rights Act of 1964. It suggested that a "literal application" of the section 216 procedures adopted by reference in the ADEA (including a refusal to apply rule 23) would frustrate these broad purposes and draw an unwarranted distinction between age discrimination and other prohibited forms of discrimination. Directly addressing the section 216 requirement that each "party plaintiff" must file a written consent with the court, *Blankenship* suggested that this requirement "is met when the representatives of the class file their consents."

Blankenship is ultimately unpersuasive because it does not provide a sensible way of reading section 216's requirement that each person who would be a "party plaintiff" file a written consent with the court. Each person seeking to represent the class in a section 216 action is—and has surely consented to be—a "party plaintiff" by virtue of having been named in the complaint. *See* Fed. R. Civ. P. 7(a), 10(a). To suggest that section 216's requirement of written consent is satisfied if the named representative merely files his own written consent is to deprive the requirement of any real meaning or significance. I therefore conclude that Congress meant what it said and said what it meant by incorporating section 216 into ADEA: ADEA may be enforced by way of class actions; but no person may be a "party plaintiff," represented by the named plaintiff(s), unless he files with the court his written consent to be one.

As numerous courts have observed, the section 216 action may thus be characterized as an "opt-in" class action—one in which the class of persons bound by the result consists *only* of those who have taken the affirmative step of filing their written consents. This "opt-in" feature of a section 216 action is obviously inconsistent with certain aspects of rule 23. In a class action maintained under rule 23(b)(3), the court is required to give notice to the members of the class, advising them that "the judgment, whether favorable or not, will include all members *who do not request exclusion.*" In a class action under rule 23(b)(1) or (b)(2), the judgment, whether favorable or not, binds all persons whom the court finds to be members; they do not have the option of requesting exclusion. The rule 23 class action, then, is an "opt-out" or "no option" class action—one in which the class of persons bound by the result consists of persons whom the court determines to be members of the class, regardless of their desires, or (in the case of (b)(3) actions) persons who fail to take the affirmative step of excluding themselves.

While the "opt-in" feature of section 216 is manifestly "irreconcilable" with the "opt-out" feature of rule 23, it does not necessarily follow that every other feature of rule 23 is similarly irreconcilable with section 216. Cases holding that rule 23 is wholly inapplicable in ADEA actions are premised partly on this *non sequitur*, and that is part of the reason they do not seem entirely persuasive. If rule 23 were wholly inapplicable, then an ADEA class under section 216 would be practically formless: the only requirement in the statute itself is embodied in the vague provision that the representatives and the class members must be "similarly situated." The legislative history of the two relevant statutes—the ADEA and the Portal-to-Portal Act of 1947—is equally unilluminating, because the procedural aspects of the class action codified in section 216 are simply not mentioned. The most definite conclusion which can be drawn from this history is that the Portal-to-Portal Act, which added the requirement that each party plaintiff in a section 216 action file a written consent, was part of a broad Congressional response to court decisions imposing unwanted liabilities and burdens on employers under the Fair Labor Standards Act of 1938. In light of this deafening silence, it does not seem sensible to reason that, because Congress has effectively directed the courts to alter their usual course and not be guided by rule 23's "opt-out" feature in ADEA class actions, it has also directed them to discard the compass of rule 23 entirely and navigate the murky waters of such actions by the stars or whatever other instruments they may fashion.

Two other reasons are sometimes advanced for holding rule 23 inapplicable in ADEA class actions. The first has been stated as follows:

The legislative history of the Age Discrimination Act clearly establishes that the Act is to be enforced in accordance with the procedures of the Fair Labor Standards Act. Congress at the time the Act was adopted was well aware of Rule 23 of the Federal Rules. If Congress had wished to adopt the Rule 23 enforcement technique for the Age Discrimination Act, it would not have explicitly stated that the Act was to be enforced in accordance with the Fair Labor Standards Act.

This argument would have considerable force if it could be demonstrated that Congress, when it enacted the ADEA in 1967, legislated against a background of established case authority holding that rule 23 did not apply to the section 216 action which it was adopting by reference in the ADEA. This, however, is not the case; in fact, it appears that most of the authority refusing to apply rule 23 in section 216 actions is really post-1967 authority involving the ADEA itself. The pre-1967 cases involving section 216, decided before rule 23 was extensively restructured in 1966, applied rule 23 and treated section 216 cases as "spurious" (rather than "true") class actions under the then-existing version of the rule. [*See* Chapter 1(C)(3) (discussing the pre-1966 version of Rule 23).] It therefore seems plausible to suppose that Congress, when it adopted section 216 into the ADEA in 1967, thought that rule 23 would apply, except that the section 216 class would consist only of persons who affirmatively "opted in" to the action—which was exactly how the old "spurious" class action operated.

The second argument sometimes advanced for refusing to apply rule 23 in ADEA class actions is that rule 23's procedural requirements are designed primarily to protect the rights of class members who are not before the court as named parties but will nonetheless be bound by the judgment. Since a judgment in a section 216 class action binds only those who have filed their written consents to be parties, the argument goes, the protections afforded by rule 23 are unnecessary. The argument overlooks two considerations. *First*, the procedures embodied in rule 23 are designed not only to protect the rights of class members, but also to allow effective disposition and management of the litigation. For example, the requirement that the class be "numerous," the requirement that there be "questions of law or fact common to the class," or the requirement that, in one type of action, common questions of law or fact "predominate over any questions affecting only individual members" have little to do with protection of class rights and much to do with handling the lawsuit effectively. *Second*, the fact that a person must file his written consent before he is bound by any judgment should not significantly lessen the court's responsibility to protect his rights by employing the procedures provided in rule 23. For example, in contrast to a person who actually intervenes in the action, either in person or through counsel, the person who merely files his written consent should not be expected fully to appreciate actual or potential conflicts between himself and the class representatives or counsel for the class representatives. The court should protect him by insuring that the representative will fully and adequately protect his interest. Fed. R. Civ. P. 23(a)(4).

The two considerations discussed in the previous paragraph take on added significance in light of the Supreme Court's decision in *Hoffmann–LaRoche, Inc. v. Sperling*. Before *Sperling*, the nature of an ADEA class action and the role of the district courts in managing such actions was unclear. In some circuits, both the court and counsel for the class representatives were prohibited from notifying potential class members that an action was pending. Other circuits, including the Tenth, permitted plaintiffs' counsel to communicate with potential class members but held that the district court had no discretion to issue any notice to potential plaintiffs or to facilitate such notice. Discovery designed solely to identify potential class members was not permitted. Elsewhere, district courts were permitted to (1) supervise the process of giving notice to potential class members and (2) allow discovery designed solely to identify potential members and facilitate notice.

Sperling resolved this conflict and adopted the view that the district courts have discretion—indeed, a "managerial responsibility"—to facilitate notice to potential class members and to order discovery of their identity. Stressing the benefits of collective action to both ADEA plaintiffs and the judicial system, the Court observed that district courts have "the requisite procedural authority to manage the process of joining multiple parties in a manner that is orderly, sensible, and *not otherwise contrary to statutory commands or the provisions of the Federal Rules of Civil Procedure.*" Citing *Gulf Oil Co. v. Bernard*, 452 U.S. 89, 99 n.10 (1981) (a case interpreting rule 23), the Court also confirmed that district courts have broad authority to control class actions and to prevent potential misuse of such actions.

Sperling both facilitates ADEA class actions and suggests that the district courts take a greater role in managing them. The ADEA class action after *Sperling* is more like the familiar class action under rule 23 than a permissive joinder device in which the passive role of the court is "to administer and monitor the litigation process." A predictable practical effect of *Sperling* is that district courts will be confronted with more motions, such as the one before me, which seek to define a potential class in broad terms, to obtain discovery identifying all members of the class, and to notify all such persons so that they can decide whether to "opt-in" to the action. In dealing with such motions, I cannot see why the district courts should fail to utilize existing procedures, embodied in rule 23, which are designed to promote effective management, prevent potential abuse, and protect the rights of all parties.

In the complaint and motion now before me, there is no assertion or discussion of any of the normal class action requirements—numerosity, typicality, adequacy, etc. *See* Fed. R. Civ. P. 23(a). The motion for "conditional certification," rather, suggests the following:

> The appropriate procedure would seem to be that when the Plaintiff files a Complaint in Federal Court alleging the Statutory Class Action, the Plaintiff may properly request certification upon discovery from the employer of the putative members of the class. The Court may wish to approve the form of the notice to the putative class members.

I cannot accept the extraordinary assertion that an aggrieved party can file a complaint, claiming to represent a class whose preliminary scope is defined by him, and by that act alone obtain a court order which conditionally determines the parameters of the potential class and requires discovery concerning the members of that class. Before I conditionally determine the scope of the class, plaintiffs will need to satisfy me that there exists a definable, manageable class and that they are proper representatives of the class. They will, in other words, need to show that they satisfy the requirements of rule 23 or convince me that a particular requirement is inconsistent with 29 U.S.C.A. § 216(b). When that showing is made, I will consider the question of notice under the guidelines set forth in rules 23(c) and 23(d) and in *Hoffmann–LaRoche, Inc. v. Sperling.*

* * *

For the reasons recited herein, it is

ORDERED that plaintiffs' motion for conditional certification of a class * * * [is] DENIED.

NOTES AND QUESTIONS

1. Few courts have followed the reasoning of *Shushan*, and many have rejected it. *See, e.g., Jackson v. N.Y. Tel. Co.*, 163 F.R.D. 429, 432 (S.D.N.Y. 1995) (subjecting ADEA plaintiffs to requirements of Rule 23 is at odds with "the remedial purposes of ADEA, and the prompt and efficient resolution of similar claims"); *Church v. Consol. Freightways, Inc.*, 137 F.R.D. 294, 306 (N.D. Cal. 1991) ("[R]equiring ADEA plaintiffs to show that common questions of law or fact predominate over questions affecting only individual members under rule 23(b)(3) is far more stringent a test than the similarly situated requirement under section 216(b).").

2. Is the *Shushan* court persuasive in holding that the requirements of Rule 23 apply to ADEA claims unless inconsistent with 29 U.S.C. § 216(b)? What about the approach of the *Blankenship* case (discussed in *Shushan*), which holds that the requirements of Rule 23 should apply in their entirety to classwide age discrimination claims under section 216(b)? For further discussion of these issues, *see* Note, *Opt-In Class Action Under the FLSA, EPA, and ADEA: What Does It Mean to Be "Similarly Situated"?*, 38 Suffolk U. L. Rev. 95 (2004) (arguing that Rule 23 is the preferable rule for governing class certification in all employment discrimination suits, not just those brought under Title VII).

THIESSEN V. GEN. ELEC. CAPITAL CORP.
United States Court of Appeals, Tenth Circuit, 2001.
267 F.3d 1095.

Before BRISCOE, REAVLEY [SENIOR CIRCUIT JUDGE (5th Cir.), by designation], and MURPHY, CIRCUIT JUDGES.

BRISCOE, CIRCUIT JUDGE.

Plaintiff Gary Thiessen, an employee of defendants General Electric Capital Corporation (GE) and Montgomery Ward Credit Services, Inc., filed this putative class action under the Age Discrimination in Employment Act (ADEA) alleging that he and other similarly situated employees had been adversely affected by a pattern or practice of age discrimination on the part of defendants. Although the district court initially certified a class of twenty-three plaintiffs, it ultimately decertified the class, dismissed the opt-in plaintiffs, and granted summary judgment in favor of defendants with respect to Thiessen's individual claims. Thiessen now appeals claiming the district court erred in [among other things] decertifying the class and dismissing the opt-in plaintiffs * * *. We * * * reverse and remand for further proceedings.

I.

GE is the parent company of General Electric Capital Services (GECS), which in turn owns General Electric Capital Credit (GECC). Within GECC is the Retail Financial Services unit (RFS). In 1989, GECC purchased Monogram Retail Credit Services, Inc. (MRCSI), which had been the credit division of retailer Montgomery Ward. MRCSI became a subsidiary of the RFS unit after the acquisition, and in 1997, it was renamed Montgomery Ward Credit Services, Inc.

Thiessen, who was born on March 7, 1947, began working as a credit manager trainee for MRCSI in 1968. From 1972 to mid-1994, he held various management positions within MRCSI and progressed to Band 4 on the company's five-band pay-grade scale. Between May 1994 and August 1996, Thiessen was placed on "special assignments" and assisted in the construction of MRCSI facilities in Kansas, Illinois, and Georgia. At the completion of those projects, Thiessen transferred to MRCSI's Las Vegas facility and assumed his current position as Band 4 collection manager. According to statements in the record, Thiessen's position at the Las Vegas facility was to "be eliminated as of May 30, 1998," and Thiessen allegedly was not "allowed to post for any other positions within GE."

On February 5, 1996, Thiessen filed a charge of discrimination with the Kansas Human Rights Commission and the Equal Employment Opportunity Commission (EEOC). He alleged that defendants had "an express but covert 'White Blockers' or 'Blockers' policy of discriminating against older white employees . . . by forcing [them] into early retirement or by eliminating [their] . . . position[s] through restructuring." He further alleged that defendants exercised this "pattern and practice of employment decisions motivated by age and/or race and related factors" against him. Specifically, Thiessen alleged he was repeatedly denied promotions because of his age and race. He subsequently filed this action alleging, in pertinent part, that defendants committed willful violations of the ADEA by denying him various promotions and placing him on "special assignments." Thiessen further alleged in his complaint that defendants undertook a pattern or practice of systematically discriminating against older employees.

The centerpiece of both Thiessen's individual claims of age discrimination and his claims of class-wide discrimination was a "blocker policy" allegedly adopted and implemented by defendants in the early 1990s. According to Thiessen, in 1991, "GECC management began referring to the older [executive] employees as 'blockers,' because in their view these employees were 'blocking' the advancement of younger, newly recruited employees," in particular those younger employees who were participants in defendants' Management Development Program (MDP). On March 2, 1992, Dave Ekedahl, a vice-president at RFS, and David Ferreira, vice-president of human resources for GECC, sent a memorandum to Steve Joyce, the then president and CEO of MRCSI, and Jeff Faucette, vice-president of human resources for MRCSI, asking, "What are plans to upgrade executive talent

... [and] remove blockers[?]" In response to this memo, Faucette directed his subordinates to prepare severance worksheets and retirement packages for various MRCSI employees over the age of forty, including Thiessen and several of the opt-in plaintiffs[,] * * * none of whom had requested such packages. On March 1, 1993, Ferreira circulated a memo to Faucette and others again discussing the subject of "blockers." Joyce and Faucette allegedly gave a presentation discussing Band 4 Blockers at a 1993 leadership review meeting attended by Ferreira. At a May 1993 meeting of MRCSI human resource managers, the concept of "blockers" was again discussed and outlined by Faucette. At a June 18, 1993, meeting at MRCSI's Merriam, Kansas facility, Faucette distributed a list of possible blockers to the human resource managers. The managers were effectively instructed to discuss the blocker policy with their respective operational managers, and assist the operational managers in identifying blockers and carrying out the policy. Ultimately, Thiessen alleges, the operational managers implemented the "blocker policy" by taking various negative employment actions (*e.g.*, negative performance evaluations, demotions, terminations, reductions in force, placement on "special projects," etc.) toward older employees identified as blockers.

Thiessen alleged defendants' "blocker policy" impacted all of the opt-in plaintiffs, each of whom allegedly suffered some type of adverse employment action. On an individual level, Thiessen alleged he was identified by defendants as a blocker, and he was (1) denied a business center manager position in Las Vegas in 1993, (2) phased out of his position as National Attorney–Agency manager in 1994 and placed on "special assignment," (3) downgraded on his 1993 and 1994 performance reviews, and (4) denied two remittance processing manager positions in 1995.

Defendants denied having any pattern or practice of discrimination. Although they acknowledged there had been some discussion among certain employees of blockers, they denied that any type of "blocker policy" was implemented anywhere in the organization. Further, defendants alleged that in the fall of 1994, Gail Lanik, the CEO of MRCSI and successor to Steve Joyce expressly repudiated the notion that employment decisions were based on any "blocker policy." In response to defendants' denials, Thiessen alleged that, notwithstanding Lanik's purported repudiation, the "blocker policy" continued to be used on a covert basis. In support of his allegation, Thiessen pointed to alleged acts of employment discrimination against him and the other proposed plaintiffs after the fall of 1994. Thiessen also pointed to statistical evidence that allegedly demonstrated older workers were treated less favorably than younger employees.

During the course of discovery, the district court conditionally certified a class of twenty-three plaintiffs * * *.

* * *

The court cautioned Thiessen that, "[i]n order to survive a motion to decertify," he would "need to set forth what he deem[ed] to be the specific link between the blocker policy and what occurred with each opt-in plaintiff." Further, the court noted that if, in a subsequent motion to decertify, defendants could "truly convince the court that individual [defense] issues would predominate at trial, the contention that the opt-in plaintiffs [we]re similarly situated would likely be largely eviscerated." Finally, the court noted it would make a final determination regarding whether the trial of all the opt-in plaintiffs' claims could be coherently managed and presented "in a manner that w[ould] not confuse the jury or unduly prejudice any party."

At the conclusion of discovery, defendants moved to decertify the class. * * * The district court [granted the motion].

II.

Decertification of plaintiff class and dismissal of opt-in plaintiffs

Thiessen contends the district court erred in decertifying the plaintiff class and dismissing the opt-in plaintiffs' claims without prejudice. * * *

Class actions under the ADEA are authorized by 29 U.S.C. § 626(b), which expressly borrows the opt-in class action mechanism of the Fair Labor Standards Act of 1938, 29 U.S.C. § 216(b) (1994). Section 216(b) provides for a class action where the complaining employees are "similarly situated." Unlike class actions under Rule 23, "[n]o employee shall be a party plaintiff to any such action unless he gives his consent in writing to become such a party and such consent is filed in the court in which such action is brought." *Id.*

The overriding question here is whether Thiessen and the twenty-two opt-in plaintiffs are "similarly situated" for purposes of § 216(b). Unfortunately, § 216(b) does not define the term "similarly situated," and there is little circuit law on the subject. Federal district courts have adopted or discussed at least three approaches to determining whether plaintiffs are "similarly situated" for purposes of § 216(b). Under the first approach, a court determines, on an *ad hoc* case-by-case basis, whether plaintiffs are "similarly situated." In utilizing this approach, a court typically makes an initial "notice stage" determination of whether plaintiffs are "similarly situated." In doing so, a court " 'require[s] nothing more than substantial allegations that the putative class members were together the victims of a single decision, policy, or plan.' " At the conclusion of discovery (often prompted by a motion to decertify), the court then makes a second determination, utilizing a stricter standard of "similarly situated." During this "second stage" analysis, a court reviews several factors, including "(1) disparate factual and employment settings of the individual plaintiffs; (2) the various defenses available to defendant which appear to be individual to each plaintiff; (3) fairness and procedural considerations; and (4) whether plaintiffs made the filings required by the ADEA before instituting suit."

Under the second approach, district courts have incorporated into § 216(b) the requirements of current Federal Rule of Civil Procedure 23. [Court cited *Shushan*.] * * *

In a third approach, district courts have suggested incorporating into § 216(b) the requirements of the pre-1966 version of Rule 23, which allowed for "spurious" class actions. [*See* Chapter 1(C)(3) (discussing the pre-1966 version of Rule 23).] Under the pre-1966 version of Rule 23, the "character of the right sought to be enforced for" the class of plaintiffs must be "several," there must be "a common question of law or fact affecting the several rights," and "a common relief" must be sought. *Id.* Further, under the old

Rule 23, district courts "had inherent authority to refuse to proceed collectively where it would waste judicial resources or unfairly prejudice the party opposing the proposed class."

In the present case, the district court adopted the *ad hoc* approach to determining whether the plaintiffs were "similarly situated" for purposes of § 216(b). It first conditionally certified the class during the course of discovery, applying a fairly lenient standard for what constituted "similarly situated." During its second-stage analysis (prompted by the defendants' motion to decertify), the court applied a stricter standard, focusing on three factors: "(1) whether a sufficient link existed between the alleged blocker policy and the challenged employment decisions; (2) whether individual issues would predominate at trial; and (3) whether a trial of the action could be coherently managed and evidence presented in a manner that would not confuse the jury or unduly prejudice any party." Ultimately, the district court concluded that all three factors warranted decertifying the class.

With respect to the first factor, the district court concluded "the mere fact that plaintiffs suffered adverse employment actions after having been designated as 'blockers,' standing alone, [wa]s insufficient to support an inference that a causal connection exist[ed] between the blocker policy and the adverse actions, particularly in light of the significant time lag and critical intervening events." The "significant time lag" was the time period between the plaintiffs' alleged designations as "blockers" in 1993 and the filing of Thiessen's EEOC charge in February 1996, which the district court concluded allowed Thiessen and the other opt-in plaintiffs to reach back 300 days from the charge, or until approximately April 11, 1995. The "critical intervening events" included the express repudiation of the "blocker policy" by MRCSI CEO Gail Lanik in the fall of 1994. Because there was insufficient evidence of a "causal link between the blocker policy or plaintiffs' purported blocker status and the challenged employment actions," the district court stated it could not "conclude that the plaintiffs [we]re similarly situated for purposes of proceeding as a collective action."

In conducting its analysis of the first factor, the district court also rejected the suggestion forwarded by Thiessen that it should apply a summary judgment-type standard in determining whether, for purposes of the "similarly situated" analysis, there was a sufficient link between the blocker policy and the adverse employment actions taken against plaintiffs. Instead, the court concluded that whether plaintiffs were "similarly situated" was a factual determination it was entitled to make based on the evidence presented by the parties.

With respect to the second factor, the district court noted that defendants had come forward with "highly individualized" defenses with regard to each of the various adverse employment actions alleged by plaintiffs. Allowing defendants to assert these defenses during a collective trial, the court concluded, would effectively result in "23 individual jury trials to determine defendants' liability to each plaintiff." Although the court acknowledged the "common thread" of the blocker policy, it nevertheless concluded that "the judicial inefficiencies" associated with resolving "what appear[ed] to be 23 distinct cases" clearly outweighed "any potential benefits in proceeding as a collective action."

With respect to the third factor, the district court noted that plaintiffs had proposed separating the trial into two phases. Plaintiffs proposed that during the first phase of the trial the court "would submit the pattern and practice allegations as well as the individual claims and damages of nine plaintiffs [seven of whom appeared on various lists of proposed blockers, and two of whom were told they were blockers]." According to plaintiffs, this initial phase would "involve a determination of common class issues relating to the existence, implementation, and discriminatory nature of the Blocker Policy as well as class issues regarding wilfulness under the ADEA." "If the jury determined that the blocker policy existed and that defendants had engaged in a pattern and practice of age discrimination, according to plaintiffs' proposed plan, then the same jury would . . . hear Phase Two of the trial, which would involve the remaining 14 plaintiffs."

The district court concluded that plaintiffs' proposed trial plan had "numerous, serious deficiencies." In particular, the court concluded that plaintiffs' plan "render[ed] individualized consideration of the claims impossible and impose[d] extraordinary burdens on the jury, both in terms of the quantity of evidence and the length of trial." Thus, the court stated that "the absence of any workable trial management plan . . . reinforce[d]" its decision to decertify the class.

The initial question, which we address de novo, is whether it was proper for the district court to adopt the *ad hoc* approach in determining whether plaintiffs were "similarly situated" for purposes of § 216(b). Arguably, the *ad hoc* approach is the best of the three approaches outlined because it is not tied to the Rule 23 standards. Congress clearly chose not to have the Rule 23 standards apply to class actions under the ADEA, and instead adopted the "similarly situated" standard. To now interpret this "similarly situated" standard by simply incorporating the requirements of Rule 23 (either the current version or the pre 1966 version) would effectively ignore Congress' directive. That said, however, there is little difference in the various approaches. All approaches allow for consideration of the same or similar factors, and generally provide a district court with discretion to deny certification for trial management reasons. We find no error on the part of the district court in adopting the *ad hoc* approach.

Turning to the merits of Thiessen's arguments, the question is whether the district court abused its discretion in applying the *ad hoc* approach and decertifying the class. If plaintiffs were simply attempting to collectively assert their individual claims of discrimination, the decision to decertify would appear to be entirely proper. The problem, however, is that plaintiffs were asserting a pattern-or-practice claim modeled on *International Brotherhood of Teamsters v. United States*, 431 U.S. 324 (1977). In particular, plaintiffs alleged that defendants, by way of the MDP and the blocker policy, had a company-wide policy of age discrimination. Stated differently, plaintiffs alleged that it was defendants' standard operating procedure, implemented through the MDP and the blocker policy, to discriminate against employees (particularly executive employees) on the basis of age. Although the district court acknowledged that all of the plaintiffs relied on the existence of the "blocker policy" to support their claims, it failed to recognize the pattern-or-practice nature of the class claim. For the reasons discussed below, we conclude the district court's failure in this regard adversely impacted its "similarly situated" analysis and resulted in an abuse of discretion.

Pattern-or-practice cases differ significantly from the far more common cases involving one or more claims of individualized discrimination. In a case involving individual claims of discrimination, the focus is on the reason(s) for the particular employment decisions at issue. *Cooper v. Fed. Reserve Bank of Richmond*, 467 U.S. 867, 876 (1984). In contrast, the initial focus in a pattern-or-practice case is not on individual employment decisions, "but on a pattern of discriminatory decisionmaking." *Id.* Thus, the order and allocation of proof, as well as the overall nature of the trial proceedings, in a pattern-or-practice case differ dramatically from a case involving only individual claims of discrimination. *Teamsters*, 431 U.S. at 357–62.

Pattern-or-practice cases are typically tried in two or more stages. During the first stage of trial, the plaintiffs' "burden is to demonstrate that unlawful discrimination has been a regular procedure or policy followed by an employer or group of employers." *Id.* at 360. Thus, "[a]t the initial, 'liability' stage of a pattern-or-practice suit the [plaintiffs are] not required to offer evidence that each person for whom [they] will ultimately seek relief was a victim of the employer's discriminatory policy." *Id.* Instead, plaintiffs' "burden is to establish that such a policy existed." *Id.* "The burden then shifts to the employer to defeat the prima facie showing of a pattern or practice by demonstrating that the [plaintiffs'] proof is either inaccurate or insignificant." *Id.* "If an employer fails to rebut the inference that arises from the [plaintiffs'] prima facie case," the finder of fact can conclude "that a violation has occurred" and the trial court can award prospective equitable relief. *Id.* at 361. If the plaintiffs also seek "individual relief for the victims of the discriminatory practice," the case moves into the second or subsequent stages. *Id.* In these additional proceedings,[7] it must be determined whether each individual plaintiff was a victim of the discriminatory practice. Importantly, by having prevailed in the first stage of trial, the individual plaintiffs reap a significant advantage for purposes of the second stage: they are entitled to a presumption that the employer had discriminated against them. *See Cooper*, 467 U.S. at 875.[8]

Returning to the district court's decision to decertify, we conclude the district court erred in its determination of "whether a sufficient link existed between the alleged blocker policy and the challenged employment decisions." Given the pattern-or-practice nature of plaintiffs' claim, this factor necessarily encompasses factual issues relevant to both the first and second stages of trial, *e.g.*, whether the blocker policy continued after Lanik's alleged repudiation and, if it did, whether a link existed between that policy and the individual employment decisions affecting the named plaintiffs. The problem is that the district court effectively made findings regarding these issues in the guise of determining whether plaintiffs were "similarly situated." By doing so, the district court essentially deprived plaintiffs of

---

[7] "The second stage of a pattern and practice claim is essentially a series of individual lawsuits, except that there is a shift of the burden of proof in the plaintiffs' favor." Newberg on Class Actions, § 4.17 (3d ed. 1992).

[8] If the plaintiffs do not prevail during the first stage of a pattern-or-practice trial, they are nevertheless entitled to proceed on their individual claims of discrimination. *See Cooper*, 467 U.S. at 878[.] Naturally, however, they [do not benefit] from a presumption of discrimination. *Id.* at 880.

their right to have the issues decided by a jury, or to at least have the court determine, under summary judgment standards, whether there was sufficient evidence to send the issue to the jury. Further, the district court failed to take into account the fact that, if plaintiffs were able to establish a pattern or practice of discrimination, they would be entitled to a presumption that the individual employment actions taken against them were the result of such discrimination. Indeed, the district court effectively deprived plaintiffs of this procedural advantage as well.

The district court's consideration of the second factor (whether individual issues would predominate at trial), was likewise adversely affected by its failure to recognize that plaintiffs were proceeding under a pattern-or-practice theory. Although it is true that defendants asserted "highly individualized" defenses to each of the instances of individual discrimination asserted by plaintiffs, those defenses would not become the focal point until the second stage of trial and could be dealt with in a series of individual trials, if necessary. With respect to the first stage of trial and the initial issues of whether they had in place a pattern or practice of discrimination and whether it continued after the fall of 1994, defendants had only a few common defenses. Specifically, defendants alleged that the blocker policy, though perhaps mentioned by Faucette at various times, was never implemented anywhere in the organization and was expressly repudiated by Lanik. Further, with respect to the discriminatory nature of the MDP program, defendants claimed it was open to all employees, including those over age forty. Thus, the presence of the "highly individualized" defenses clearly did not, as the district court concluded, outweigh "any potential benefits in proceeding as a collective action." As previously noted, there was a significant procedural advantage for plaintiffs to proceed in a collective action: if they prevailed in the first stage of trial, they would be entitled to a presumption of discrimination in subsequent proceedings to decide the merits of their individual claims. By bowing to the individualized defenses relevant only to the second stage of trial, the district court deprived plaintiffs of this opportunity.

The district court's consideration of the third factor (trial management concerns) was also adversely affected by its failure to recognize the pattern-or-practice nature of plaintiffs' claim. Most notably, the district court failed to acknowledge that plaintiffs' proposed trial plan, though perhaps deficient in some respects, was consistent with the framework outlined in *Teamsters* for pattern-or-practice claims. The court also failed to make any effort to modify the plaintiffs' proposed trial plan. Finally, the district court was wrong in concluding that trying the case in two phases, as suggested by plaintiffs, "render[ed] individualized consideration of the claims impossible."

We conclude the district court abused its discretion in decertifying the class. Taking into consideration the "pattern or practice" nature of plaintiffs' lawsuit, as discussed above, plaintiffs were, in fact, "similarly situated" for purposes of § 216(b). In particular, many of the plaintiffs were specifically listed or classified by defendants as "blockers" and suffered adverse employment consequences during the relevant time period. The remainder of the plaintiffs, though never specifically classified by defendants as "blockers," fell within the alleged definition of "blockers" and were likewise subjected to adverse employment consequences during the relevant time period.

A district court considering a motion to certify [or decertify] is entitled to look past the pleadings and examine the evidence produced during discovery, but when an ADEA plaintiff relies upon a "pattern or practice" theory and comes forward with legitimate evidence to support that theory, the district court must take into account the framework for pattern-or-practice cases outlined by the Supreme Court in *International Brotherhood of Teamsters v. United States*, 431 U.S. 324 (1977). That did not occur in this case, and hence our application of those factors using the correct legal framework. We do not hold that whenever there is evidence of a pattern-or-practice, a class must be certified. Whether certification or decertification is appropriate depends upon application of the factors we have identified in the ad hoc approach.

* * *

III.

The decision of the district court decertifying the class of opt-in plaintiffs is REVERSED * * *.

NOTES AND QUESTIONS

1. The Tenth Circuit and the district court in *Thiessen* (as summarized by the Tenth Circuit) approach the "similarly situated" issue very differently. How do the approaches differ? Which approach makes more sense? Are there any similarities between the two?

2. Prior to the Tenth Circuit's decision, a Fifth Circuit decision had articulated a two-stage process for determining whether to certify ADEA collective actions. *Mooney v. Aramco Servs. Co.*, 54 F.3d 1207 (5th Cir. 1995). The court noted that at the first stage, a court should apply a "fairly lenient" standard. *Id.* at 1214. At the first stage, the court determines whether notice of the case should be given to potential class members. At this stage, the court usually has only pleadings and affidavits as evidence, so the standard is not rigorous and will normally result in conditional certification. Notice and the opportunity to opt in are given to the class, followed by discovery. *Id.* Noting the difficulty in stage two, however, the *Aramco* court observed that "[b]ased on our review of the case law, no representative class has ever survived the second stage of review." *Id.* At the second stage, the court determines whether the claimants are "similarly situated," based on evidence gathered through discovery. If they pass this test, the case proceeds to trial as a representative action. But if they fail, the case is decertified. The opt-in class members are dismissed without prejudice and the original plaintiffs proceed to trial on their individual cases. *Id.* How does the approach of the Tenth Circuit in *Thiessen* differ from that of the Fifth Circuit in *Aramco*?

3. How, if at all, does the *Aramco* court's analytical approach differ from that applied in Rule 23? How, if at all, does the approach of the Tenth Circuit in *Thiessen* differ from that under Rule 23? Which approach—*Aramco*, *Thiessen*, or Rule 23—makes the most sense? Why?

4. Under the standards applied in *Aramco*, is it easier to certify an ADEA case or a Rule 23 case? What about the *Thiessen* test—is that test more or less exacting than the test under Rule 23?

5. What is the basis for the *Thiessen* court's criticism that the district court improperly made factual findings in the course of applying the "similarly situated" standard? Is that criticism valid? *See* Chapter 4(B)(1)(b)(i).

PROBLEM

The president of Redmark, Inc. was secretly recorded by her secretary. The recording captured the president remarking that she wanted to rid her company of older workers and minority workers, and that she would make sure their "days were numbered" and that such people would not be hired in the future "as long as I'm running the company." When the secretary leaked the tape to the media, several class action lawsuits were immediately filed. Plaintiffs sought compensatory damages and injunctive relief, and alleged discrimination on the basis of age, race, and national origin for a variety of practices. There was enormous pressure on Redmark to settle the cases promptly. What issues would the company need to address in any settlement?

C. SECURITIES FRAUD CLASS ACTIONS

Professor Louis Loss once noted with respect to federal securities laws that "[t]he ultimate effectiveness of the federal remedies, when the defendants are not prone to settle, may depend in large measure on the applicability of the class action device." 3 Louis Loss, *Securities Regulation* 1819 (2d ed. 1961). As illustrated by the securities cases already cited and discussed in earlier portions of this casebook, Rule 23 and securities fraud law have developed—and been tested—together over the years since 1966. Moreover, in no other area of the law has Congress taken a more hands-on interest in the asserted abuses of class actions.

This section will focus on class actions proceeding under § 10(b) of the Securities Exchange Act of 1934 (the 1934 Act), 15 U.S.C. § 78j ("Section 10(b)"), and Securities Exchange Commission Rule 10b–5, 17 CFR § 240.10b–5 ("Rule 10b–5"),† since most securities fraud suits proceed under these provisions.†† Chapter 11 addresses shareholder derivative actions under Rule 23.1.

---

† Section 10(b) of the Securities Exchange Act provides that "It shall be unlawful for any person, directly or indirectly * * * [t]o use or employ, in connection with the purchase or sale of any security * * *, any manipulative or deceptive device or contrivance in contravention of such rules and regulations as the Commission may prescribe * * *." 15 U.S.C. § 78j. SEC Rule 10b–5 provides that "it shall be unlawful for any person, directly or indirectly, by the use of any means or instrumentality * * *

    (a) To employ any device, scheme, or artifice to defraud,

    (b) To make any untrue statement of a material fact or * * * [omission of a material fact], or

    (c) To engage in any act, practice, or course of business which operates or would operate as a fraud or deceit upon any person, in connection with the purchase or sale of any security."

17 C.F.R. § 240.10b–5.

†† Other federal statutory provisions often at issue in securities fraud class actions include Sections 14(a), 18(a) and 20(a) of the 1934 Act, and Sections 11, 12(a)(2), and 17(a)(1), (2) & (3) of the 1933 Act.

1. MATERIALITY AND RELIANCE IN 10b–5 CLASS ACTIONS

In order to establish a claim under Rule 10b–5, a plaintiff must prove that, in connection with the purchase or sale of a security covered by Section 10(b), a defendant made a misrepresentation or omission of material fact, with scienter, upon which the plaintiff justifiably relied, and which caused the plaintiff damages. *See, e.g., Bruschi v. Brown*, 876 F.2d 1526, 1528 (11th Cir. 1989). In *Basic, Inc. v. Levinson*, 485 U.S. 224 (1988), however, which is set forth below, the Supreme Court approved a theory under which analysis of certain of those elements may be truncated in appropriate cases.

BASIC, INC. V. LEVINSON
Supreme Court of the United States, 1988.
485 U.S. 224.

JUSTICE BLACKMUN delivered the opinion of the Court.

This case requires us to apply the materiality requirement of § 10(b) of the Securities Exchange Act of 1934, 15 U.S.C. § 78a *et seq.* (1934 Act), and the Securities and Exchange Commission's Rule 10b–5, promulgated thereunder, 17 CFR § 240.10b–5 (1987), in the context of preliminary corporate merger discussions. We must also determine whether a person who traded a corporation's shares on a securities exchange after the issuance of a materially misleading statement by the corporation may invoke a rebuttable presumption that, in trading, he relied on the integrity of the price set by the market.

I.

Prior to December 20, 1978, Basic Incorporated was a publicly traded company primarily engaged in the business of manufacturing chemical refractories for the steel industry. As early as 1965 or 1966, Combustion Engineering, Inc., a company producing mostly alumina-based refractories, expressed some interest in acquiring Basic, but was deterred from pursuing this inclination seriously because of antitrust concerns it then entertained. In 1976, however, regulatory action opened the way to a renewal of Combustion's interest. The "Strategic Plan," dated October 25, 1976, for Combustion's Industrial Products Group included the objective: "Acquire Basic Inc. $30 million."

Beginning in September 1976, Combustion representatives had meetings and telephone conversations with Basic officers and directors, including petitioners here, concerning the possibility of a merger. During 1977 and 1978, Basic made three public statements denying that it was engaged in merger negotiations [including one on October 21, 1977]. On December 18, 1978, Basic asked the New York Stock Exchange to suspend trading in its shares and issued a release stating that it had been "approached" by another company concerning a merger. On December 19, Basic's board endorsed Combustion's offer of $46 per share for its common stock, and on the following day publicly announced its approval of Combustion's tender offer for all outstanding shares.

Respondents are former Basic shareholders who sold their stock after Basic's first public statement of October 21, 1977, and before the suspension of trading in December 1978. Respondents brought a class action against Basic and its directors, asserting that the defendants issued three false or misleading public statements and thereby were in violation of § 10(b) of the 1934 Act and of Rule 10b–5. Respondents alleged that they were injured by selling Basic shares at artificially depressed prices in a market affected by petitioners' misleading statements and in reliance thereon.

[The district court certified the class, adopting a presumption of reliance, but granted summary judgment to the defendant on the ground that any misstatements were not material. The Court of Appeals affirmed the class certification but reversed the summary judgment ruling. In its decision, the] Court of Appeals joined a number of other circuits in accepting the "fraud-on-the-market theory" to create a rebuttable presumption that respondents relied on petitioners' material misrepresentations, noting that without the presumption it would be impractical to certify a class under Federal Rule of Civil Procedure 23(b)(3).

We granted *certiorari* to resolve [a] split * * * among the Courts of Appeals as to the standard of materiality applicable to preliminary merger discussions, and to determine whether the courts below properly applied a presumption of reliance in certifying the class, rather than requiring each class member to show direct reliance on Basic's statements.

II.

The 1934 Act was designed to protect investors against manipulation of stock prices. Underlying the adoption of extensive disclosure requirements was a legislative philosophy: "There cannot be honest markets without honest publicity. Manipulation and dishonest practices of the market place thrive upon mystery and secrecy." This Court "repeatedly has described the 'fundamental purpose' of the Act as implementing a 'philosophy of full disclosure.'"

Pursuant to its authority under § 10(b) of the 1934 Act, the Securities and Exchange Commission promulgated Rule 10b–5. Judicial interpretation and application, legislative acquiescence, and the passage of time have removed any doubt that a private cause of action exists for a violation of § 10(b) and Rule 10b–5, and constitutes an essential tool for enforcement of the 1934 Act's requirements.

The Court previously has addressed various positive and common-law requirements for a violation of § 10(b) or of Rule 10b–5. The Court also explicitly has defined a standard of materiality under the securities laws, *see TSC Industries, Inc. v. Northway, Inc.*, 426 U.S. 438 (1976), concluding in the proxy-solicitation context [§ 14(a) of the 1934 Act] that "[a]n omitted fact is material if there is a substantial likelihood that a reasonable shareholder would consider it important in deciding how to vote." Acknowledging that certain information concerning corporate developments could well be of "dubious significance," the Court was careful not to set too low a standard of materiality; it was concerned that a minimal standard might bring an overabundance of information within its reach, and lead management "simply to bury the shareholders in an avalanche of trivial information—a result that is hardly conducive to informed decision-making." It further explained that to fulfill the materiality requirement "there must be a substantial likelihood that the disclosure of the omitted fact would have been viewed by the reasonable investor as having significantly altered the 'total mix' of information made available." We now expressly adopt the *TSC Industries* standard of materiality for the § 10(b) and Rule 10b–5 context.

III.

The application of this materiality standard to preliminary merger discussions is not self-evident. Where the impact of the corporate development on the target's fortune is certain and clear, the *TSC Industries* materiality definition admits straightforward application. Where, on the other hand, the event is contingent or speculative in nature, it is difficult to ascertain whether the "reasonable investor" would have considered the omitted information significant at the time. Merger negotiations, because of the ever-present possibility that the contemplated transaction will not be effectuated, fall into the latter category.

* * *

Whether merger discussions in any particular case are material therefore depends on the facts. Generally, in order to assess the probability that the event will occur, a factfinder will need to look to indicia of interest in the transaction at the highest corporate levels. Without attempting to catalog all such possible factors, we note by way of example that board resolutions, instructions to investment bankers, and actual negotiations between principals or their intermediaries may serve as indicia of interest. To assess the magnitude of the transaction to the issuer of the securities allegedly manipulated, a factfinder will need to consider such facts as the size of the two corporate entities and of the potential premiums over market value. No particular event or factor short of closing the transaction need be either necessary or sufficient by itself to render merger discussions material.

It has been suggested that given current market practices, a "no comment" statement is tantamount to an admission that merger discussions are underway. That may well hold true to the extent that issuers adopt a policy of truthfully denying merger rumors when no discussions are underway, and of issuing "no comment" statements when they are in the midst of negotiations. There are, of course, other statement policies firms could adopt; we need not now advise issuers as to what kind of practice to follow, within the range permitted by law. Perhaps more importantly, we think that creating an exception to a regulatory scheme founded on a prodisclosure legislative philosophy, because complying with the regulation might be "bad for business," is a role for Congress, not this Court.

As we clarify today, materiality depends on the significance the reasonable investor would place on the withheld or misrepresented information. The fact-specific inquiry we endorse here is consistent with the approach a number of courts have taken in assessing the materiality of merger negotiations. Because the standard of materiality we have adopted differs from that used by both courts below, we remand the case for reconsideration of the question whether a grant of summary judgment is appropriate on this record.

IV.

A.

We turn to the question of reliance and the fraud-on-the-market theory. Succinctly put:

> The fraud on the market theory is based on the hypothesis that, in an open and developed securities market, the price of a company's stock is determined by the available material information regarding the company and its business.... Misleading statements will therefore defraud purchasers of stock even if the purchasers do not directly rely on the misstatements.... The causal connection between the defendants' fraud and the plaintiffs' purchase of stock in such a case is no less significant than in a case of direct reliance on misrepresentations.

Peil v. Speiser, 806 F.2d 1154, 1160–61 (3d Cir. 1986). Our task, of course, is not to assess the general validity of the theory, but to consider whether it was proper for the courts below to apply a rebuttable presumption of reliance, supported in part by the fraud-on-the-market theory. * * *

This case required resolution of several common questions of law and fact concerning the falsity or misleading nature of the three public statements made by Basic, the presence or absence of scienter, and the materiality of the misrepresentations, if any. In their amended complaint, the named plaintiffs alleged that in reliance on Basic's statements they sold their shares of Basic stock in the depressed market created by petitioners. Requiring proof of individualized reliance from each member of the proposed plaintiff class effectively would have prevented respondents from proceeding with a class action, since individual issues then would have overwhelmed the common ones. The District Court found that the presumption of reliance created by the fraud-on-the-market theory provided "a practical resolution to the problem of balancing the substantive requirement of proof of reliance in securities cases against the procedural requisites of [Fed. R. Civ. P. 23]." The District Court thus concluded that with reference to each public statement and its impact upon the open market for Basic shares, common questions predominated over individual questions, as required by Federal Rule of Civil Procedure 23(a)(2) and (b)(3).

Petitioners and their *amici* complain that the fraud-on-the-market theory effectively eliminates the requirement that a plaintiff asserting a claim under Rule 10b–5 prove reliance. They note that reliance is and long has been an element of common-law fraud, and argue that because the analogous express right of action includes a reliance requirement, *see, e.g.*, § 18(a) of the 1934 Act, as amended, 15 U.S.C. § 78r(a), so too must an action implied under § 10(b).

We agree that reliance is an element of a Rule 10b–5 cause of action. Reliance provides the requisite causal connection between a defendant's misrepresentation and a plaintiff's injury. There is, however, more than one way to demonstrate the causal connection. Indeed, we previously have dispensed with a requirement of positive proof of reliance, where a duty to disclose material information had been breached, concluding that the necessary nexus between the plaintiffs' injury and the defendant's wrongful conduct had been established. *See Affiliated Ute Citizens v. United States*, 406 U.S. 128, 153–54 (1972). * * *

The modern securities markets, literally involving millions of shares changing hands daily, differ from the face-to-face transactions contemplated by early fraud cases, and our understanding of Rule 10b–5's reliance requirement must encompass these differences.

> In face-to-face transactions, the inquiry into an investor's reliance upon information is into the subjective pricing of that information by that investor. With the presence of a market, the market is interposed between seller and buyer and, ideally, transmits information to the investor in the processed form of a market price. Thus the market is performing a substantial part of the valuation process performed by the investor in a face-to-face transaction. The market is acting as the unpaid agent of the investor, informing him that given all the information available to it, the value of the stock is worth the market price.

In re LTV Sec. Litig., 88 F.R.D. 134, 143 (N.D. Tex. 1980).

* * *

B.

Presumptions typically serve to assist courts in managing circumstances in which direct proof, for one reason or another, is rendered difficult. The courts below accepted a presumption, created by the fraud-on-the-market theory and subject to rebuttal by petitioners, that persons who had traded Basic shares had done so in reliance on the integrity of the price set by the market, but because of petitioners' material misrepresentations that price had been fraudulently depressed. Requiring a plaintiff to show a speculative state of facts, *i.e.*, how he would have acted if omitted material information had been disclosed, or if the misrepresentation had not been made, would place an unnecessarily unrealistic evidentiary burden on the Rule 10b–5 plaintiff who has traded on an impersonal market.

Arising out of considerations of fairness, public policy, and probability, as well as judicial economy, presumptions are also useful devices for allocating the burdens of proof between parties. The presumption of reliance employed in this case is consistent with, and, by facilitating Rule 10b–5 litigation, supports, the congressional policy embodied in the 1934 Act. In drafting that Act, Congress expressly relied on the premise that securities markets are affected by information, and enacted legislation to facilitate an investor's reliance on the integrity of those markets * * *.

The presumption is also supported by common sense and probability. Recent empirical studies have tended to confirm Congress' premise that the market price of shares traded on well-developed markets reflects all publicly available information, and, hence, any material misrepresentations. It has been noted that "it is hard to imagine that there ever is a buyer or seller who does not rely on market integrity. Who would knowingly roll the dice in a crooked crap game?" Indeed, nearly every court that has considered the proposition has concluded that where materially misleading statements have been disseminated into an impersonal, well-developed market for securities, the reliance of individual plaintiffs on the integrity of the market price may be presumed. Commentators generally have applauded the adoption of one variation or another of the fraud-on-the-market theory. An investor who buys or sells stock at the price set by the market does so in reliance on the integrity of that price. Because most publicly available information is reflected in market price, an investor's reliance on any public material misrepresentations, therefore, may be presumed for purposes of a Rule 10b–5 action.

C.

The Court of Appeals found that petitioners "made public material misrepresentations and [respondents] sold Basic stock in an impersonal, efficient market. Thus the class, as defined by the district court, has established the threshold facts for proving their loss." The court acknowledged that petitioners may rebut proof of the elements giving rise to the presumption, or show that the misrepresentation in fact did not lead to a distortion of price or that an individual plaintiff traded or would have traded despite his knowing the statement was false.

Any showing that severs the link between the alleged misrepresentation and either the price received (or paid) by the plaintiff, or his decision to trade at a fair market price, will be sufficient to rebut the presumption of reliance. For example, if petitioners could show that the "market makers" were privy to the truth about the merger discussions here with Combustion, and thus that the market price would not have been affected by their misrepresentations, the causal connection could be broken: the basis for finding that the fraud had been transmitted through market price would be gone. Similarly, if, despite petitioners' allegedly fraudulent attempt to manipulate market price, news of the merger discussions credibly entered the market and dissipated the effects of the misstatements, those who traded Basic shares after the corrective statements would have no direct or indirect connection with the fraud. Petitioners also could rebut the presumption of reliance as to plaintiffs who would have divested themselves of their Basic shares without relying on the integrity of the market. For example, a plaintiff who believed that Basic's statements were false and that Basic was indeed engaged in merger discussions, and who consequently believed that Basic stock was artificially underpriced, but sold his shares nevertheless because of other unrelated concerns, *e.g.*, potential antitrust problems, or political pressures to divest from shares of certain businesses, could not be said to have relied on the integrity of a price he knew had been manipulated.

* * *

JUSTICE WHITE, with whom JUSTICE O'CONNOR joins, * * * dissenting in part.

I * * * dissent [in part] from * * * the Court's holding because I do not agree that the "fraud-on-the-market" theory should be applied in this case.

I.

* * *

B.

* * *

* * * [W]hile the economists' theories which underpin the fraud-on-the-market presumption may have the appeal of mathematical exactitude and scientific certainty, they are—in the end—nothing more than theories which may or may not prove accurate upon further consideration. Even the most earnest advocates of economic analysis of the law recognize this. Thus, while the majority states that, for purposes of reaching its result it need only make modest assumptions about the way in which "market professionals generally" do their jobs, and how the conduct of market professionals affects stock prices, I doubt that we are in much of a position to assess which theories aptly describe the functioning of the securities industry.

* * *

C.

At the bottom of the Court's conclusion that the fraud-on-the-market theory sustains a presumption of reliance is the assumption that individuals rely "on the integrity of the market price" when buying or selling stock in "impersonal, well-developed market[s] for securities." Even if I was prepared to accept (as a matter of common sense or general understanding) the assumption that most persons buying or selling stock do so in response to the market price, the fraud-on-the-market theory goes further. For in adopting a "presumption of reliance," the Court *also* assumes that buyers and sellers rely—not just on the market price—but on the "*integrity*" of that price. It is this aspect of the fraud-on-the-market hypothesis which most mystifies me.

To define the term "integrity of the market price," the majority quotes approvingly from cases which suggest that investors are entitled to " 'rely on the price of a stock as a reflection of its value.' " But the meaning of this phrase eludes me, for it implicitly suggests that stocks have some "true value" that is measurable by a standard other than their market price. While the scholastics of medieval times professed a means to make such a valuation of a commodity's "worth," I doubt that the federal courts of our day are similarly equipped.

Even if securities had some "value"—knowable and distinct from the market price of a stock—investors do not always share the Court's presumption that a stock's price is a "reflection of [this] value." Indeed, "many investors purchase or sell stock because they believe the price *inaccurately* reflects the corporation's worth." If investors really believed that stock prices reflected a stock's "value," many sellers would never sell, and many buyers never buy (given the time and cost associated with executing a stock transaction). * * *

***

II.

[The dissent argued that the legislative history was contrary to the majority's fraud-on-the-market approach.]

III.

***

*** [T]he facts of this case lead a casual observer to the almost inescapable conclusion that many of those who bought or sold Basic stock during the period in question flatly disbelieved the statements which are alleged to have been "materially misleading." Despite three statements denying that merger negotiations were underway, Basic stock hit record-high after record-high during the 14–month class period. It seems quite possible that, like Casca's knowing disbelief of Caesar's "thrice refusal" of the Crown, clever investors were skeptical of petitioners' three denials that merger talks were going on. Yet such investors, the savviest of the savvy, will be able to recover under the Court's opinion, as long as they now claim that they believed in the "integrity of the market price" when they sold their stock (between September and December, 1978). Thus, persons who bought after hearing and relying on the *falsity* of petitioner's statements may be able to prevail and recover money damages on remand.

And who will pay the judgments won in such actions? I suspect that all too often the majority's rule will "lead to large judgments, payable in the last analysis by innocent investors, for the benefit of speculators and their lawyers." This Court and others have previously recognized that "inexorably broadening . . . the class of plaintiff[s] who may sue in this area of the law will ultimately result in more harm than good." Yet such a bitter harvest is likely to be the reaped from the seeds sewn by the Court's decision today.

***

AMGEN INC. V. CONN. RET. PLANS & TRUST FUNDS
Supreme Court of the United States, 2013.
133 S. Ct. 1184.

[*See* Chapter 4(B)(1)(b)(i)]

***

NOTES AND QUESTIONS

1. In the term following *Amgen*, the Supreme Court confronted the question whether *Basic* should be overruled. In *Halliburton Co. v. Erica P. John Fund, Inc.*, 134 S. Ct. 2398 (2014), it declined to do so. Chief Justice Roberts wrote for the Court:

> Halliburton urges us to overrule *Basic*'s presumption of reliance and to instead require every securities fraud plaintiff to prove that he actually relied on the defendant's misrepresentation in deciding to buy or sell a company's stock. Before overturning a long-settled precedent, however, we require "special justification," not just an argument that the precedent was wrongly decided. *Dickerson v. United*

States, 530 U.S. 428, 443 (2000). Halliburton has failed to make that showing. * * *

* * *

Halliburton's primary argument for overruling *Basic* is that the decision rested on two premises that can no longer withstand scrutiny. The first premise concerns what is known as the "efficient capital markets hypothesis." *Basic* stated that "the market price of shares traded on well-developed markets reflects all publicly available information, and, hence, any material misrepresentations." From that statement, Halliburton concludes that the *Basic* Court espoused "a robust view of market efficiency" that is no longer tenable, for " 'overwhelming empirical evidence' now 'suggests that capital markets are not fundamentally efficient.' " * * *

Halliburton does not, of course, maintain that capital markets are *always* inefficient. Rather, in its view, *Basic*'s fundamental error was to ignore the fact that " 'efficiency is not a binary, yes or no question.' " The markets for some securities are more efficient than the markets for others, and even a single market can process different kinds of information more or less efficiently, depending on how widely the information is disseminated and how easily it is understood. Yet *Basic*, Halliburton asserts, glossed over these nuances, assuming a false dichotomy that renders the presumption of reliance both underinclusive and overinclusive: A misrepresentation can distort a stock's market price even in a generally inefficient market, and a misrepresentation can leave a stock's market price unaffected even in a generally efficient one.

Halliburton's criticisms fail to take *Basic* on its own terms. * * * Indeed, in making the presumption rebuttable, *Basic* recognized that market efficiency is a matter of degree and accordingly made it a matter of proof. * * * Even though the efficient capital markets hypothesis may have "garnered substantial criticism since *Basic*," (Thomas, J., concurring in judgment), Halliburton has not identified the kind of fundamental shift in economic theory that could justify overruling a precedent on the ground that it misunderstood, or has since been overtaken by, economic realities.

Halliburton also contests a second premise underlying the *Basic* presumption: the notion that investors "invest 'in reliance on the integrity of [the market] price.' " Halliburton identifies a number of classes of investors for whom "price integrity" is supposedly "marginal or irrelevant." * * * But *Basic* never denied the existence of such investors. As we recently explained, *Basic* concluded only that "it is reasonable to presume that *most* investors—knowing that they have little hope of outperforming the market in the long run based solely on their analysis of publicly available information—will rely on the security's market price as an unbiased assessment of the security's value in light of all public information." *Amgen, Inc. v. Conn. Ret. Plans & Trust Funds,* 133 S. Ct. 1184, 1192 (2013) (emphasis added).

* * *

* * * Although the presumption is a judicially created doctrine designed to implement a judicially created cause of action, we have

described the presumption as "a substantive doctrine of federal securities-fraud law." That is because it provides a way of satisfying the reliance element of the Rule 10b–5 cause of action. As with any other element of that cause of action, Congress may overturn or modify any aspect of our interpretations of the reliance requirement, including the *Basic* presumption itself. Given that possibility, we see no reason to exempt the *Basic* presumption from ordinary principles of *stare decisis*. * * *

* * *

Halliburton also argues that the *Basic* presumption cannot be reconciled with our recent decisions governing class action certification under Federal Rule of Civil Procedure 23. *See Wal-Mart Stores, Inc. v. Dukes*, 564 U.S. 338, 351 (2011); *Comcast Corp. v. Behrend*, 133 S. Ct. 1426, 1432 (2013). Those decisions have made clear that plaintiffs wishing to proceed through a class action must actually *prove*—not simply plead—that their proposed class satisfies each requirement of Rule 23, including (if applicable) the predominance requirement of Rule 23(b)(3). According to Halliburton, *Basic* relieves Rule 10b–5 plaintiffs of that burden, allowing courts to presume that common issues of reliance predominate over individual ones.

That is not the effect of the *Basic* presumption. In securities class action cases, the crucial requirement for class certification will usually be the predominance requirement of Rule 23(b)(3). The *Basic* presumption does not relieve plaintiffs of the burden of proving—before class certification—that this requirement is met. *Basic* instead establishes that a plaintiff satisfies that burden by proving the prerequisites for invoking the presumption—namely, publicity, materiality, market efficiency, and market timing. The burden of proving those prerequisites still rests with plaintiffs and (with the exception of materiality) must be satisfied before class certification. *Basic* does not, in other words, allow plaintiffs simply to plead that common questions of reliance predominate over individual ones, but rather sets forth what they must prove to demonstrate such predominance. * * *

Id. at 2407–12. Having thus resolved the most significant issue (*i.e.*, whether *Basic* should be overruled) in plaintiffs' favor, the Court further rejected Halliburton's first fallback position, which would have "require[d] plaintiffs to prove that a defendant's misrepresentation actually affected the stock price—so-called 'price impact'—in order to invoke the *Basic* presumption." *Id.* at 2413. The Court explained:

Far from a modest refinement of the *Basic* presumption, this proposal would radically alter the required showing for the reliance element of the Rule 10b–5 cause of action. What is called the *Basic* presumption actually incorporates two constituent presumptions: First, if a plaintiff shows that the defendant's misrepresentation was public and material and that the stock traded in a generally efficient market, he is entitled to a presumption that the misrepresentation affected the stock price. Second, if the plaintiff also shows that he purchased the stock at the market price during the relevant period, he is entitled to a further presumption that he purchased the stock in reliance on the defendant's misrepresentation.

By requiring plaintiffs to prove price impact directly, Halliburton's proposal would take away the first constituent presumption.

Halliburton's argument for doing so is the same as its primary argument for overruling the *Basic* presumption altogether: Because market efficiency is not a yes-or-no proposition, a public, material misrepresentation might not affect a stock's price even in a generally efficient market. But as explained, *Basic* never suggested otherwise; that is why it affords defendants an opportunity to rebut the presumption by showing, among other things, that the particular misrepresentation at issue did not affect the stock's market price. For the same reasons we declined to completely jettison the *Basic* presumption, we decline to effectively jettison half of it by revising the prerequisites for invoking it.

Id. at 2414. In taking up Halliburton's second alternative argument, however, the Court gave some ammunition to defendants in securities fraud cases:

Even if plaintiffs need not directly prove price impact to invoke the *Basic* presumption, Halliburton contends that defendants should at least be allowed to defeat the presumption at the class certification stage through evidence that the misrepresentation did not in fact affect the stock price. We agree. * * *

Our choice in this case * * * is not between allowing price impact evidence at the class certification stage or relegating it to the merits. Evidence of price impact will be before the court at the certification stage in any event. The choice, rather, is between limiting the price impact inquiry before class certification to indirect evidence, or allowing consideration of direct evidence as well. * * * We adhere to [*Basic*] and decline to modify the prerequisites for invoking the presumption of reliance. But to maintain the consistency of the presumption with the class certification requirements of Federal Rule of Civil Procedure 23, defendants must be afforded an opportunity before class certification to defeat the presumption through evidence that an alleged misrepresentation did not actually affect the market price of the stock. * * *

Id. at 2414–17.

Justice Ginsburg, in a concurring opinion joined by Justices Breyer and Sotomayor, suggested that the Court's decision did not significantly change the state of class action securities law:

Advancing price impact consideration from the merits stage to the certification stage may broaden the scope of discovery available at certification. But the Court recognizes that it is incumbent upon the defendant to show the absence of price impact. The Court's judgment, therefore, should impose no heavy toll on securities-fraud plaintiffs with tenable claims. * * *

134 S. Ct. at 2417 (Ginsburg, J., concurring).

Justice Thomas disagreed with the Court's upholding of the *Basic* presumption in *Halliburton*, writing that "[l]ogic, economic realities, and [the Court's] subsequent jurisprudence have undermined the foundations of the *Basic* presumption, and *stare decisis* cannot prop up the façade that remains." 134 S. Ct. at 2417 (Thomas, J., concurring in judgment). Joined by Justices Scalia and Alito, Justice Thomas argued that *Basic* should be overturned on multiple grounds:

> First, the [*Basic*] Court based both parts of the presumption of reliance on a questionable understanding of disputed economic theory and flawed intuitions about investor behavior. Second, *Basic*'s rebuttable presumption is at odds with our subsequent Rule 23 cases, which require plaintiffs seeking class certification to " 'affirmatively demonstrate' " certification requirements like the predominance of common questions. *Comcast Corp. v. Behrend*, 133 S. Ct. 1426, 1432 (2013) (quoting *Wal–Mart Stores, Inc. v. Dukes*, 564 U.S. 338, 350–51 (2011)). Finally, *Basic*'s presumption that investors rely on the integrity of the market price is virtually irrebuttable in practice, which means that the "essential" reliance element effectively exists in name only.

Id. at 2419.

2. Thus far, defendants have not benefited widely by the *Halliburton* Court's recognition that defendants should be allowed to defeat the *Basic* presumption at the class certification stage. *See, e.g.*, Robert H. Klonoff, *Class Actions in the Year 2026: A Prognosis*, 65 EMORY L.J. 1569, 1588–89 (2016) (discussing post-*Halliburton* cases).

3. The *Basic* opinion addressed both materiality and reliance in securities fraud suits. Both aspects of the opinion are important. Notes 4–7 address materiality; notes 8–15 address reliance. And note 16 addresses an interesting conflict-of-interest issue.

4. The Court in *Basic* adopts a standard by which "materiality" can be assessed on a classwide basis. What is that standard? What other standard could have prevailed? Would any alternative approach better serve the objectives of Section 10(b) and Rule 10b–5? Would any other alternative have permitted class actions to proceed in securities fraud cases?

5. From whose perspective should materiality and misrepresentation be viewed? John M. Newman, Jr., Mark Herrmann, & Geoffrey J. Ritts argue in Basic *Truths: The Implications of the Fraud-on-the-Market Theory for Evaluating the "Misleading" and "Materiality" Elements of Securities Fraud Claims*, 20 J.Corp.L. 571 (1995), that only the views of professional investors—such as analysts, investment managers, market managers, investment banking firms, and other institutional investors—are important, because it is *their* views that move the markets. What would be the practical implications of focusing upon highly sophisticated stock traders instead of average investors? Would that mean that an unsophisticated investor would not be able to recover if he were misled unless a group of other, differently-situated, *sophisticated* investors were also misled?

6. Just as *Basic* permits "materiality" to be objectively determined, courts have adopted other doctrines that permit them to determine, on a classwide basis, whether defendants' statements were *immaterial* as a matter of law.

   a. *Puffery*. One doctrine involves "puffery"—statements that no reasonable investor would rely upon. The Eighth Circuit, in *Parnes v. Gateway 2000, Inc.*, 122 F.3d 539 (8th Cir. 1997), described both generally immaterial statements and puffery:

   > * * * Where a reasonable investor could not have been swayed by an alleged misrepresentation, * * * a court may determine, as a matter of law, that the alleged misrepresentation is immaterial.

There are a variety of reasons why an alleged misrepresentation or omission may, as a matter of law, be immaterial. Some matters are such common knowledge that a reasonable investor can be presumed to understand them. For example, "[a]s a general matter, investors know of the risk of obsolescence posed by older products forced to compete with more advanced rivals. '[T]echnical obsolescence of computer equipment in a field marked by rapid technological advances is information within the public domain.'"

Alleged misrepresentations may also present or conceal such insignificant data that, in the total mix of information, it simply would not matter to a reasonable investor. * * *

Furthermore, some statements are so vague and such obvious hyperbole that no reasonable investor would rely upon them. "The role of the materiality requirement is not to attribute to investors a childlike simplicity but rather to determine whether a reasonable investor would have considered the omitted information significant at the time." [*Hillson Partners Ltd. P'ship v. Adage, Inc.*, 42 F.3d 204, 213 (4th Cir. 1994).] The *Hillson* court explained that "soft, puffing statements ... generally lack materiality because the market price of a share is not inflated by vague statements predicting growth. No reasonable investor would rely on these statements, and they are certainly not specific enough to perpetrate a fraud on the market." *Id.* at 211.

Parnes, 122 F.3d at 546–47. For more analysis of the puffery doctrine, *see, e.g.*, Stephen M. Bainbridge & G. Mitu Gulati, *How Do Judges Maximize? (The Same Way Everyone Else Does—Boundedly): Rules of Thumb in Securities Fraud Opinions*, 51 Emory L.J. 83, 119–22 (2002); Note, *Securities Fraud or Mere Puffery: Refinement of the Corporate Puffery Defense*, 51 Vand. L. Rev. 1049 (1998).

b. *Bespeaks Caution.* According to the Third Circuit in *In re Donald J. Trump Casino Securities Litigation*, 7 F.3d 357, 364 (3d Cir. 1993), under the "bespeaks caution" doctrine, "a court may determine that the inclusion of sufficient cautionary statements in a prospectus renders misrepresentations and omissions contained therein nonactionable." The court explained, however, that in its view, "'bespeaks caution' is essentially shorthand for the well-established principle that a statement or omission must be considered in context, so that accompanying statements may render it immaterial as a matter of law." *Id.* The court explained the basis of the "bespeaks caution" doctrine as follows:

The application of bespeaks caution depends on the specific text of the offering document or other communication at issue, *i.e.*, courts must assess the communication on a case-by-case basis. Nevertheless, we can state as a general matter that, when an offering document's forecasts, opinions or projections are accompanied by meaningful cautionary statements, the forward-looking statements will not form the basis for a securities fraud claim if those statements did not affect the "total mix" of information the document provided investors. In other words, cautionary language, if sufficient, renders the alleged omissions or misrepresentations immaterial as a matter of law.

Id. at 371.

c. *Truth on the Market.* A related doctrine, often called "truth on the market," provides that alleged misrepresentations and omissions cannot serve as a basis of liability if the allegedly misstated or withheld information has already credibly entered the market. As the Ninth Circuit explained in *Provenz v. Miller*, 102 F.3d 1478, 1492 (9th Cir. 1996):

> In a "fraud on the market" case "an omission is materially misleading only if the information has not already entered the market." As we have explained, "[i]f the market has become aware of the allegedly concealed information, 'the facts allegedly omitted by the defendant would already be reflected in the stock's price' and the market 'will not be misled.' " This principle has been termed by some courts as the "truth-on-the-market" doctrine or corollary.
>
> However, before the "truth-on-the-market" doctrine can be applied, the defendants must prove that the information that was withheld or misrepresented was "transmitted to the public with a degree of intensity and credibility sufficient to effectively counter-balance any misleading impression created by insider's one-sided representations."

Given the weight that the market assigns to statements of corporate officers and directors, could anything short of a recantation ever establish that an insider's misrepresentation has been so effectively countered that the statement is rendered unactionable? Should a defendant escape liability because someone else has corrected the misinformation?

d. *Zero Price Change.* When there has been no change in the price of a stock upon the disclosure of the fraud, some courts have determined that defendants' statements were immaterial as a matter of law. The Third Circuit, in *Oran v. Stafford*, 226 F.3d 275 (3d Cir. 2000), described the zero price change approach as a way of determining materiality in an efficient market:

> * * * [W]hen a stock is traded in an efficient market, the materiality of disclosed information may be measured *post hoc* by looking to the movement, in the period immediately following disclosure, of the price of the firm's stock. Because in an efficient market "the concept of materiality translates into information that alters the price of the firm's stock," if a company's disclosure of information has no effect on stock prices, "it follows that the information disclosed * * * was immaterial as a matter of law."

Id. at 282. *But see, e.g., No. 84 Employer–Teamster Joint Council Pension Trust Fund v. America W. Holding Corp.*, 320 F.3d 920, 924 (9th Cir. 2003) (criticizing *Oran* for following "bright line rule" that determines immateriality based on whether market immediately reacts to disclosure of information); *see also* Note, *The Plight of the Private Securities Litigation Reform Act in the Post-Enron Era: The Ninth Circuit's Interpretation of Materiality in* Employer–Teamster v. America West, 2004 BYU L. Rev. 863, 892 (2004) (arguing that *Oran*'s bright line test "strips the jury of its role as factfinder [and] also insulates fraudulent corporate officials, accountants, and attorneys from liability").

e. *Trivial Matters.* Misstatements or omissions regarding unimportant matters are viewed by courts as immaterial as a matter of law. But this is so only if "the alleged misstatements or omissions * * * are so obviously unimportant to a reasonable investor that reasonable minds could not differ on the question of their importance." *Goldman v. Belden*, 754 F.2d 1059, 1067 (2d Cir. 1985).

7. Should materiality be determined on a case-by-case basis? Or should the courts be permitted to find lack of materiality as a matter of law based upon bright-line rules? *Compare, e.g., In re PetsMart, Inc. Sec. Litig.*, 61 F. Supp. 2d 982, 994 (D. Ariz. 1999) ("Although materiality is generally a question for the jury, under Ninth Circuit precedent, revenue shortfalls of 10% or less may be immaterial as a matter of law."), *with In re Unisys Corp. Sec. Litig.*, 2000 WL 1367951, at *5–6 (E.D. Pa. 2000) (rejecting conclusion that misrepresentations were immaterial as a matter of law and cautioning against a 5–10% of net income or loss as rule-of-thumb for determining immateriality).

Relying on *Basic*, the Supreme Court recently rejected the use of a bright-line test for determining the materiality of adverse event reports in *Matrixx Initiatives, Inc. v. Siracusano*, 563 U.S. 27 (2011). *Matrixx* involved whether a plaintiff in a securities fraud class action could state a claim under Section 10(b) and Rule 10b–5 based on a pharmaceutical company's failure to disclose reports of adverse events associated with its product that did not disclose a statistically significant number of adverse events. Plaintiffs contended that Matrixx failed to disclose reports of a possible link between its cold medicine and loss of smell, thereby misleading consumers. Matrixx countered that plaintiffs failed to allege a material misrepresentation because the reports did not disclose a statistically significant number of adverse events. The Court held that a lack of statistically significant data showing that a drug company's cold medicine caused adverse health effects did not necessarily preclude the data from being material to a class of investors:

> Like the defendant in *Basic,* Matrixx urges us to adopt a bright-line rule that reports of adverse events associated with a pharmaceutical company's products cannot be material absent a sufficient number of such reports to establish a statistically significant risk that the product is in fact causing the events. Absent statistical significance, Matrixx argues, adverse event reports provide only "anecdotal" evidence that "the user of a drug experienced an adverse event at some point during or following the use of that drug." Accordingly, it contends, reasonable investors would not consider such reports relevant unless they are statistically significant because only then do they "reflect a scientifically reliable basis for inferring a potential causal link between product use and the adverse event."
>
> As in *Basic,* Matrixx's categorical rule would "artificially exclud[e]" information that "would otherwise be considered significant to the trading decision of a reasonable investor." Matrixx's argument rests on the premise that statistical significance is the only reliable indication of causation. This premise is flawed: As the SEC points out [in its brief], "medical researchers . . . consider multiple factors in assessing causation." Statistically significant data are not always available. * * * Moreover, ethical considerations may prohibit researchers from conducting randomized clinical trials to confirm a suspected causal link for the purpose of obtaining statistically significant data.
>
> A lack of statistically significant data does not mean that medical experts have no reliable basis for inferring a causal link between a drug and adverse events. As Matrixx itself concedes, medical experts rely on other evidence to establish an inference of causation. * * * We note that courts frequently permit expert testimony on causation based on evidence other than statistical significance. * * * We

need not consider whether the expert testimony was properly admitted in those cases, and we do not attempt to define here what constitutes reliable evidence of causation. It suffices to note that, as these courts have recognized, "medical professionals and researchers do not limit the data they consider to the results of randomized clinical trials or to statistically significant evidence."

The FDA similarly does not limit the evidence it considers for purposes of assessing causation and taking regulatory action to statistically significant data. * * *

Not only does the FDA rely on a wide range of evidence of causation, it sometimes acts on the basis of evidence that suggests, but does not prove, causation. * * *

* * *

Given that medical professionals and regulators act on the basis of evidence of causation that is not statistically significant, it stands to reason that in certain cases reasonable investors would as well. As Matrixx acknowledges, adverse event reports "appear in many forms, including direct complaints by users to manufacturers, reports by doctors about reported or observed patient reactions, more detailed case reports published by doctors in medical journals, or larger scale published clinical studies." As a result, assessing the materiality of adverse event reports is a "fact-specific" inquiry that requires consideration of the source, content, and context of the reports. This is not to say that statistical significance (or the lack thereof) is irrelevant—only that it is not dispositive of every case.

Application of *Basic*'s "total mix" standard does not mean that pharmaceutical manufacturers must disclose all reports of adverse events. Adverse event reports are daily events in the pharmaceutical industry * * *. The fact that a user of a drug has suffered an adverse event, standing alone, does not mean that the drug caused that event. * * * The question remains whether a *reasonable* investor would have viewed the nondisclosed information " 'as having *significantly* altered the "total mix" of information made available.' " For the reasons just stated, the mere existence of reports of adverse events—which says nothing in and of itself about whether the drug is causing the adverse events—will not satisfy this standard. Something more is needed, but that something more is not limited to statistical significance and can come from "the source, content, and context of the reports." This contextual inquiry may reveal in some cases that reasonable investors would have viewed reports of adverse events as material even though the reports did not provide statistically significant evidence of a causal link.

* * *

Applying *Basic*'s "total mix" standard in this case, we conclude that respondents have adequately pleaded materiality. * * *

Id. at 39–45 (emphasis added). Is the Court's flexible approach to materiality appropriate? What impact might this approach have on the future of securities fraud class actions?

8. Which side has the better argument concerning the fraud-on-the-market theory—the *Basic* majority or Justice White's dissent?

9. How can a defendant rebut the presumption of reliance? Is Justice White correct in contending that the presumption is effectively unrebuttable? *See* Comment, *Rebutting the* Levinson *Presumption of Reliance: The Consistency and Relevancy of Enquiring Into a Plaintiff's Conduct in Certain Rule 10b–5 Fraud on the Market Cases*, 61 U. Colo. L. Rev. 625 (1990) (arguing that plaintiffs' conduct remains relevant in 10b–5 cases).

10. As noted in *Basic* itself, in *Affiliated Ute Citizens v. United States*, 406 U.S. 128 (1972), the Supreme Court addressed a situation in which omissions, rather than misrepresentations, were at issue. The facts were unusual. A federal statute (the Ute Partition Act) was enacted to divide certain assets of the Ute Indian tribe between mixed-blood and full-blood members and to provide for the gradual termination of federal supervision over the tribe. Members representing both "full-bloods" and "mixed-bloods" divided the assets, based upon the relative numbers of persons in each group, but certain other, non-divisible assets (oil, gas, and mineral rights, as well as claims against the United States) remained. Under the Act, these other non-divisible assets were to be jointly managed by representatives of both groups.

The "mixed-bloods" organized the Affiliated Ute Citizens ("AUC"), an unincorporated association, which created the Ute Distribution Corporation ("UDC") to manage the remaining claims with the "full-bloods." UDC issued ten shares of stock in the name of each mixed-blood and entered into an agreement with First Security Bank of Utah under which the bank became UDC's stock transfer agent, holding the stock certificates and issuing receipts to shareholders. Under the UDC's articles, any mixed-blood wanting to sell shares in UDC before August 27, 1964, had to give right of first refusal to tribe members. UDC shares could be sold to nonmembers only if no member accepted the price, and the price at which the stock was sold to nonmembers could be no lower than the price offered to members.

In February 1965, mixed-bloods sued the bank, two bank employees (Gale and Haslem), and the United States, charging violations of the Securities Exchange Act of 1934 and Rule 10b–5, claiming, *inter alia*, that Gale and Haslem had devised a scheme, perpetuated through a series of misrepresentations and omissions, to acquire UDC shares for themselves and others at less than the shares' fair value. The district court, trying 12 mixed-bloods' claims as "bellwether[s]," found in favor of Gale, Haslem, the bank, and the United States. The court of appeals reversed most of the district court's decision, but found, in pertinent part, that Gale and Haslem were liable only for *misrepresentations*. The Supreme Court, however, found this interpretation of Rule 10b–5 too restrictive:

> Clearly, the Court of Appeals was right to the extent that it held that the two employees had violated Rule 10b–5; in the instances specified in that holding the record reveals a misstatement of a material fact, within the proscription of Rule 10b–5(2), namely, that the prevailing market price of the UDC shares was the figure at which their purchases were made.

> We conclude, however, that the Court of Appeals erred when it held that there was no violation of the Rule unless the record disclosed evidence of reliance on material fact misrepresentations by Gale and Haslem. We do not read Rule 10b–5 so restrictively. To be sure, the second subparagraph of the rule specifies the making of an untrue statement of a material fact and the omission to state a material fact. The first and third subparagraphs are not so restricted.

These defendants' activities * * * disclose, within the very language of one or the other of those subparagraphs, a "course of business" or a "device, scheme, or artifice" that operated as a fraud upon the Indian sellers. This is so because the defendants devised a plan and induced the mixed-blood holders of UDC stock to dispose of their shares without disclosing to them material facts that reasonably could have been expected to influence their decisions to sell. The individual defendants, in a distinct sense, were market makers, not only for their personal purchases * * *, but for the other sales their activities produced. This being so, they possessed the affirmative duty under the Rule to disclose this fact to the mixed-blood sellers. It is no answer to urge that, as to some of the petitioners, these defendants may have made no positive representation or recommendation. The defendants may not stand mute while they facilitate the mixed-bloods' sales to those seeking to profit in the non-Indian market the defendants had developed and encouraged and with which they were fully familiar. The sellers had the right to know that the defendants were in a position to gain financially from their sales and that their shares were selling for a higher price in that market.

* * * [Because of] the circumstances of this case, involving primarily a failure to disclose, positive proof of reliance is not a prerequisite to recovery. All that is necessary is that the facts with-held be material in the sense that a reasonable investor might have considered them important in the making of this decision. This obligation to disclose and this withholding of a material fact establish the requisite element of causation in fact.

406 U.S. at 152–54. The *Affiliated Ute* presumption, as it has become known, is frequently used by securities fraud plaintiffs seeking class certification. Given *Affiliated Ute's* unusual facts, should it apply to securities fraud cases involving a large, impersonal market?

11. More generally, how much emphasis should the courts place upon economic theory in developing rules of law? *See, e.g.*, Donald C. Langevoort, *Theories, Assumptions, and Securities Regulation: Market Efficiency Revisited*, 140 U. Pa. L. Rev. 851, 853 (1992) (noting ascendancy of efficient capital market hypothesis); Lynn A. Stout, *Are Stock Markets Costly Casinos? Disagreement, Market Failure, and Securities Regulation*, 81 Va. L. Rev. 611, 648–50 (1995) (noting skepticism over efficient capital market hypothesis).

12. As discussed in *Gruber v. Price Waterhouse*, 776 F. Supp. 1044, 1050–51 (E.D. Pa. 1991), courts are divided over whether *Affiliated Ute* applies solely when the allegations involve *only* omissions, or also when both misrepresentations and omissions are involved. In *Gruber* itself, the court found that *Affiliated Ute* did not apply because, although several counts in the complaint referred to the failure of the defendant, an accounting firm, to disclose certain facts, the "crux of plaintiffs' allegations" was that the accounting firm's "materials did not accurately portray * * * [the] financial health" of the company being audited. *Id.* at 1051. Should the *Affiliated Ute* presumption apply when both omissions and misrepresentations are involved? Or should it apply only in cases involving purely omissions?

13. Does the Court in *Basic* provide sufficient guidance about the circumstances under which the fraud-on-the-market theory applies? In other words, what market must be efficient, and how should a court determine whether the

market is efficient? Courts and commentators have wrestled with these difficult questions, which are more difficult because they are premised upon economic theory rather than legal doctrine. Consider *Cammer v. Bloom*, 711 F. Supp. 1264, 1285–87 (D.N.J. 1989), a case involving a defendant accounting firm accused of publishing false financial reports relating to a company:

> There are several types of facts which, if alleged, might give rise to an inference that [a company's stock] traded in an efficient market. * * *
>
> First, plaintiffs could have alleged there existed an average weekly trading volume during the class period in excess of a certain number of shares. * * * The reason the existence of an actively traded market, as evidenced by a large weekly volume of stock trades, suggests there is an efficient market is because it implies significant investor interest in the company. Such interest, in turn, implies a likelihood that many investors are executing trades on the basis of newly available or disseminated corporate information.
>
> Second, it would be persuasive to allege a significant number of securities analysts followed and reported on a company's stock during the class period. The existence of such analysts would imply, for example, the [defendant's] reports were closely reviewed by investment professionals, who would in turn make buy/sell recommendations to client investors. In this way the market price of the stock would be bid up or down to reflect the financial information contained in the [defendant's] reports, as interpreted by the securities analysts.
>
> Third, it could be alleged the stock had numerous market makers. The existence of market makers and arbitrageurs would ensure completion of the market mechanism; these individuals would react swiftly to company news and reported financial results by buying or selling stock and driving it to a changed price level.
>
> Fourth, * * * it would be helpful to allege the Company was [subject to certain SEC filing requirements usable by widely-traded companies]. * * *
>
> Finally, it would be helpful to a plaintiff seeking to allege an efficient market to allege empirical facts showing a cause and effect relationship between unexpected corporate events or financial releases and an immediate response in the stock price. This, after all, is the essence of an efficient market and the foundation for the fraud on the market theory.

Is each of these factors necessary for proof that a market for a stock is sufficiently "open and developed" to permit plaintiffs to benefit from the fraud-on-the-market presumption? Is any of these factors sufficient by itself? How should a court decide? *See generally* Comment, *Fraud-on-the-Market Theory and Thinly-Traded Securities Under Rule 10b–5: How Does A Court Decide If a Stock Market Is Efficient?*, 25 Wake Forest L. Rev. 223 (1990) (suggesting factors relevant to court's determination); *see also Unger v. Amedisys Inc.*, 401 F.3d 316, 323 (5th Cir. 2005) (listing the *Cammer* factors and three additional ones: the company's market capitalization; the bid-ask spread for stock sales; and float—the stock's trading volume excluding insider-owned stock); *In re Initial Public Offerings Sec. Litig.*, 471 F.3d 24 (2d Cir. 2006) (concluding that plaintiffs alleging fraud in connection with an IPO could not invoke the *Basic* presumption of reliance because the market for IPO shares is not efficient, and consequently finding individual questions of reliance predominated over common ones).

14. Should the *Basic* and *Ute* presumptions apply in non-10b–5 contexts? *See* Chapter 3(C)(1)(b)(i) (discussing attempts to use presumptions to overcome individual issues in other cases involving Rule 23(b)(3)); *cf. In re Constar Int'l Inc. Securities Litig.*, 585 F.3d 774, 783–86 (3d Cir. 2009) (court need not determine whether market is efficient under § 11 of the Securities Exchange Act of 1934, in contrast to § 10(b), because reliance and loss causation are not required for securities fraud claim based on false registration statement).

15. In addition to the *Basic* and *Affiliated Ute* presumptions, federal courts have grappled with another theory, popularly known as the "fraud-created-the-market" theory. Unlike the fraud-on-the-market theory, there is no pre-existing, established market in such cases. The Fifth Circuit was the first to articulate this theory. In *Shores v. Sklar*, 647 F.2d 462 (5th Cir. 1981) (*en banc*), a case involving the fraudulent issuance of tax-exempt revenue bonds, the Fifth Circuit ruled that in a new, undeveloped, or inefficient market, plaintiffs may be presumed to have relied upon the integrity of the market to ensure that "unmarketable" securities are not proposed for sale. The Fifth Circuit, however, subsequently cut back significantly on the fraud-created-the-market theory in *Abell v. Potomac Ins. Co.*, 858 F.2d 1104 (5th Cir. 1988), *vacated and remanded on other grounds*, 492 U.S. 914 (1989), ruling that plaintiffs could not prevail unless they demonstrated that "the promoters knew the enterprise itself was patently worthless." 858 F.2d at 1122. Other courts have adopted similar (or competing) formulations of the doctrine. *See, e.g., Joseph v. Wiles*, 223 F.3d 1155, 1163 (10th Cir. 2000); *contra Malack v. BDO Seidman LLP*, 617 F.3d 743, 745 (3d Cir. 2010) (holding that reasonable reliance could not be presumed on basis of fraud-created-the-market theory and concluding that the theory "lacks a basis in common sense, probability, or any of the other reasons commonly provided for the creation of a presumption").

For interesting discussions of the fraud-created-the-market theory, *see, e.g.*, Note, *Which Came First, the Fraud or the Market: Is the Fraud-Created-the-Market Theory Valid Under Rule 10b–5?*, 69 Fordham L. Rev. 2611 (2001) (describing case law and arguing that fraud-created-the-market theory is a valid application of the presumption of reliance and a necessary tool for combating securities fraud); Julie A. Herzog, *Fraud Created the Market: An Unwise and Unwarranted Extension of Section 10(b) and Rule 10b–5*, 63 Geo. Wash. L. Rev. 359, 359 (1995) (contending that "the theory stretches private causes of action under section 10(b) and Rule 10b–5 beyond their intended purpose"); Comment, *The Fraud-Created-The-Market Theory: The Presumption of Reliance in the Primary Issue Context*, 60 U. Cin. L. Rev. 495, 498 (1991) (fraud-created-the-market theory is "a valuable tool which, properly applied, will further the goals of the securities laws").

16. The materials described above illustrate economic or financial theories that plaintiffs have developed to facilitate class certification. Defendants have occasionally tried to rely on sophisticated economic or financial theories to *defeat* class certification. One notable example involves a series of cases in which defendants argued, usually without success, that conflicts existed among class members who bought and sold stock at different points during the class period, because some class members would want to maximize the materiality of corporate disclosures or omissions at particular points in time, while others would want to minimize the materiality of such disclosures or omissions. *See, e.g., In re Seagate Tech. II Sec. Litig.*, 843 F. Supp. 1341 (N.D. Cal.

1994) (accepting theory); *In re Seagate Tech. II Sec. Litig.*, 156 F.R.D. 229 (N.D. Cal. 1994) (refusing to dismiss class claims after plaintiffs narrowed class period); *but see, e.g., Freeland v. Iridium World Communications, Ltd.*, 233 F.R.D. 40, 48 (D.D.C. 2006) (noting that *Seagate* has been "almost universally attacked" by other courts); *see generally* David J. Ross, *Do Conflicts Between Class Members Vitiate Class Action Securities Fraud Suits?*, 70 St. John's L. Rev. 209 (1996) (discussing *Seagate II* rationale).

2. LOSS CAUSATION AND CLASS CERTIFICATION

The Supreme Court held that an investor who alleges securities fraud must provide allegations that the purported fraud actually *caused* the loss at issue. *See Dura Pharm., Inc. v. Broudo*, 544 U.S. 336 (2005). It is generally not enough to allege simply that the price of the stock was inflated. As the Court explained:

> [A]s a matter of pure logic, at the moment the transaction takes place, the plaintiff has suffered no loss; the inflated purchase payment is offset by ownership of a share that *at that instant possesses* equivalent value. Moreover, the logical link between the inflated share purchase price and any later economic loss is not invariably strong. Shares are normally purchased with an eye toward a later sale. But if, say, the purchaser sells the shares quickly before the relevant truth begins to leak out, the misrepresentation will not have led to any loss. If the purchaser sells later after the truth makes its way into the market place, an initially inflated purchase price *might* mean a later loss. But that is far from inevitably so. When the purchaser subsequently resells such shares, even at a lower price, that lower price may reflect, not the earlier misrepresentation, but changed economic circumstances, changed investor expectations, new industry-specific or firm-specific facts, conditions, or other events, which taken separately or together account for some or all of that lower price. * * * Other things being equal, the longer the time between purchase and sale, the more likely that this is so, *i.e.*, the more likely that other factors caused the loss.

Id., 125 S. Ct. at 1631–32. Will this decision make it more difficult for plaintiffs to bring securities fraud claims? If so, how? *See, e.g., McAdams v. McCord*, 584 F.3d 1111, 1114–15 (8th Cir. 2009) (affirming dismissal of case where complaint failed to allege sufficient facts showing causal connection between shareholders' losses and auditor's alleged misstatements under § 10(b) and Rule 10b–5).

Does an investor need to *prove* loss causation in a private securities fraud case as a condition of class certification? The Supreme Court answered this question in the case below.

ERICA P. JOHN FUND, INC. v. HALLIBURTON CO.
Supreme Court of the United States, 2011.
131 S. Ct. 2179.

CHIEF JUSTICE ROBERTS delivered the opinion of the Court.

To prevail on the merits in a private securities fraud action, investors must demonstrate that the defendant's deceptive conduct caused their claimed economic loss. This requirement is commonly referred to as "loss causation." The question presented in this case is whether securities fraud plaintiffs must also prove loss causation in order to obtain class certification. We hold that they need not.

I

Petitioner Erica P. John Fund, Inc. (EPJ Fund), is the lead plaintiff in a putative securities fraud class action filed against Halliburton Co. and one of its executives (collectively Halliburton). The suit was brought on behalf of all investors who purchased Halliburton common stock between June 3, 1999, and December 7, 2001.

EPJ Fund alleges that Halliburton made various misrepresentations designed to inflate its stock price, in violation of § 10(b) of the Securities Exchange Act of 1934 and Securities and Exchange Commission Rule 10b–5. The complaint asserts that Halliburton deliberately made false statements about (1) the scope of its potential liability in asbestos litigation, (2) its expected revenue from certain construction contracts, and (3) the benefits of its merger with another company. EPJ Fund contends that Halliburton later made a number of corrective disclosures that caused its stock price to drop and, consequently, investors to lose money.

After defeating a motion to dismiss, EPJ Fund sought to have its proposed class certified pursuant to Federal Rule of Civil Procedure 23. The parties agreed, and the District Court held, that EPJ Fund satisfied the general requirements for class actions set out in Rule 23(a): The class was sufficiently numerous, there were common questions of law or fact, the claims of the representative parties were typical, and the representative parties would fairly and adequately protect the interests of the class.

The District Court also found that the action could proceed as a class action under Rule 23(b)(3), but for one problem: Circuit precedent required securities fraud plaintiffs to prove "loss causation" in order to obtain class certification. As the District Court explained, loss causation is the " 'causal connection between the material misrepresentation and the [economic] loss' " suffered by investors. After reviewing the alleged misrepresentations and corrective disclosures, the District Court concluded that it could not certify the class in this case because EPJ Fund had "failed to establish loss causation with respect to any" of its claims. The court made clear, however, that absent "this stringent loss causation requirement," it would have granted the Fund's certification request.

The Court of Appeals affirmed the denial of class certification. It confirmed that, "[i]n order to obtain class certification on its claims, [EPJ Fund] was required to prove loss causation, *i.e.*, that the corrected truth of the former falsehoods actually caused the stock price to fall and resulted in the losses." Like the District Court, the Court of Appeals concluded that EPJ Fund had failed to meet the "requirements for proving loss causation at the class certification stage."

We granted the Fund's petition for *certiorari* to resolve a conflict among the Circuits as to whether securities fraud plaintiffs must prove loss causation in order to obtain class certification.

II

EPJ Fund contends that the Court of Appeals erred by requiring proof of loss causation for class certification. We agree.

A

As noted, the sole dispute here is whether EPJ Fund satisfied the prerequisites of Rule 23(b)(3). In order to certify a class under that Rule, a court must find "that the questions of law or fact common to class members predominate over any questions affecting only individual members, and that a class action is superior to other available methods for fairly and efficiently adjudicating the controversy." Fed. Rule Civ. Proc. 23(b)(3). Considering whether "questions of law or fact common to class members predominate" begins, of course, with the elements of the underlying cause of action. The elements of a private securities fraud claim based on violations of § 10(b) and Rule 10b–5 are: " '(1) a material misrepresentation or omission by the defendant; (2) scienter; (3) a connection between the misrepresentation or omission and the purchase or sale of a security; (4) reliance upon the misrepresentation or omission; (5) economic loss; and (6) loss causation.' " *Matrixx Initiatives, Inc. v. Siracusano*, 563 U.S. 27, 37–38 (2011) (quoting *Stoneridge Investment Partners, LLC v. Scientific–Atlanta, Inc.*, 552 U.S. 148, 157 (2008)).

Whether common questions of law or fact predominate in a securities fraud action often turns on the element of reliance. The courts below determined that EPJ Fund had to prove the separate element of loss causation in order to establish that reliance was capable of resolution on a common, classwide basis.

"Reliance by the plaintiff upon the defendant's deceptive acts is an essential element of the § 10(b) private cause of action." *Stoneridge, supra,* at 159. This is because proof of reliance ensures that there is a proper "connection between a defendant's misrepresentation and a plaintiff's injury." *Basic Inc. v. Levinson,* 485 U.S. 224, 243 (1988). The traditional (and most direct) way a plaintiff can demonstrate reliance is by showing that he was aware of a company's statement and engaged in a relevant transaction— *e.g.,* purchasing common stock—based on that specific misrepresentation. In that situation, the plaintiff plainly would have relied on the company's deceptive conduct. A plaintiff unaware of the relevant statement, on the other hand, could not establish reliance on that basis.

We recognized in *Basic,* however, that limiting proof of reliance in such a way "would place an unnecessarily unrealistic evidentiary burden on the Rule 10b–5 plaintiff who has traded on an impersonal market." We also observed that "[r]equiring proof of individualized reliance from each member of the proposed plaintiff class effectively would" prevent such plaintiffs "from proceeding with a class action, since individual issues" would "overwhelm[] the common ones."

The Court in *Basic* sought to alleviate those related concerns by permitting plaintiffs to invoke a rebuttable presumption of reliance based on what is known as the "fraud-on-the-market" theory. According to that theory, "the market price of shares traded on well-developed markets reflects all publicly available information, and, hence, any material misrepresentations." Because the market "transmits information to the investor in the processed form of a market price," we can assume, the Court explained, that an investor relies on public misstatements whenever he "buys or sells stock at the price set by the market." The Court also made clear that the presumption was just that, and could be rebutted by appropriate evidence.

B

It is undisputed that securities fraud plaintiffs must prove certain things in order to invoke *Basic*'s rebuttable presumption of reliance. It is common ground, for example, that plaintiffs must demonstrate that the alleged misrepresentations were publicly known (else how would the market take them into account?), that the stock traded in an efficient market, and that the relevant transaction took place "between the time the misrepresentations were made and the time the truth was revealed."

According to the Court of Appeals, EPJ Fund also had to establish loss causation at the certification stage to "trigger the fraud-on-the-market presumption." The court determined that, in order to invoke a rebuttable presumption of reliance, EPJ Fund needed to prove that the decline in Halliburton's stock was "because of the correction to a prior misleading statement" and "that the subsequent loss could not otherwise be explained by some additional factors revealed then to the market." This is the loss causation requirement as we have described it.

The Court of Appeals' requirement is not justified by *Basic* or its logic. To begin, we have never before mentioned loss causation as a precondition for invoking *Basic*'s rebuttable presumption of reliance. The term "loss causation" does not even appear in our *Basic* opinion. And for good reason: Loss causation addresses a matter different from whether an investor relied on a misrepresentation, presumptively or otherwise, when buying or selling a stock.

We have referred to the element of reliance in a private Rule 10b–5 action as "transaction causation," not loss causation. *Dura Pharmaceuticals, Inc. v. Broudo*, 544 U.S. 336, 341–42 (2005) (citing *Basic, supra*, at 248–49). Consistent with that description, when considering whether a plaintiff has relied on a misrepresentation, we have typically focused on facts surrounding the investor's decision to engage in the transaction. Under *Basic*'s fraud-on-the-market doctrine, an investor presumptively relies on a defendant's misrepresentation if that "information is reflected in [the] market price" of the stock at the time of the relevant transaction.

Loss causation, by contrast, requires a plaintiff to show that a misrepresentation that affected the integrity of the market price *also* caused a subsequent economic loss. As we made clear in *Dura Pharmaceuticals,* the fact that a stock's "price on the date of purchase was inflated because of [a] misrepresentation" does not necessarily mean that the misstatement is the cause of a later decline in value. We observed that the drop could instead be the result of other intervening causes, such as "changed economic circumstances, changed investor expectations, new industry-specific or firm-specific facts, conditions, or other events." If one of those factors were responsible for the loss or part of it, a plaintiff would not be able to prove loss causation to that extent. This is true even if the investor purchased the stock at a distorted price, and thereby presumptively relied on the misrepresentation reflected in that price.

According to the Court of Appeals, however, an inability to prove loss causation would prevent a plaintiff from invoking the rebuttable presumption of reliance. Such a rule contravenes *Basic*'s fundamental premise—that an investor presumptively relies on a misrepresentation so long as it was reflected in the market price at the time of his transaction. The fact that a subsequent loss may have been caused by factors other than the revelation of a misrepresentation has nothing to do with whether an investor relied on the misrepresentation in the first place, either directly or presumptively through the fraud-on-the-market theory. Loss causation has no logical connection to the facts necessary to establish the efficient market predicate to the fraud-on-the-market theory.

The Court of Appeals erred by requiring EPJ Fund to show loss causation as a condition of obtaining class certification.

* * *

NOTES AND QUESTIONS

1. Did the Court in *Halliburton* correctly apply *Basic*?

2. Is there any argument to support requiring proof of loss causation at the class certification stage?

3. The Supreme Court has held that a "scheme liability" theory—enabling investors to sue for fraud against third parties—is not available under the 1934 Securities Exchange Act. *See Stoneridge Investment Partners LLC v. Scientific–Atlanta Inc.*, 552 U.S. 148 (2008). In *Stoneridge*, investors brought a class action under 10(b) of the Securities Exchange Act of 1934 and SEC Rule 10b–5 against vendors and customers for allegedly helping a cable television operator inflate its earnings in financial statements that they knew investors would rely upon. The Supreme Court held that the vendors and customers did not have a duty to disclose; and moreover, did not make their deceptive acts public, thereby rendering it impossible for the investors to have relied upon the third parties' deception. Even in the absence of a public statement, the investors contended that the conduct of the vendors and customers was to further a *scheme* to misrepresent investors which should, therefore, trigger the *Basic* presumption of reliance. In other words, where the vendors and customers "engaged in conduct with the purpose and effect of creating a false appearance of material fact to further a scheme to misrepresent" the company's revenue, this should provide a sufficient causal link between the third parties and the securities market to invoke the rebuttable presumption of reliance. *Id.* at 770. The Court rejected this approach. This limitation on the scope of relief available to investors may impact future class actions. *See* John C. Coffee & Max Heur, *Class Certification: Developments Over the Last Five Years 2005–2010*, 11 Class Action Litig. Report; Special Report S–3, S–34 (2010) ("[R]eliance on a course of conduct may be harder to establish in the future after *Stoneridge*."); Mark Klock, *What Will It Take to Label Participation in a Deceptive Scheme to Defraud Buyers of Securities a Violation of Section 10(b)? The Disastrous Result and Reasoning of* Stoneridge, 58 U. Kan. L. Rev. 309, 310, 336–37 (2010) (arguing that *Stoneridge* promotes forum shopping by driving securities fraud controversies into state courts where they can be litigated as aiding and abetting a breach of fiduciary duty, and "creates moral hazard, whereby economic incentives to behave ethically are removed and positive economic incentives to engage in unethical conduct are created").

4. In *Morrison v. National Australia Bank Ltd.*, 561 U.S. 247 (2010) the Supreme Court addressed the extent to which the Securities Exchange Act of 1934 (the "Exchange Act") applies to transnational securities transactions. In *Morrison*, private foreign investors brought a putative class action against the National Australia Bank, alleging securities fraud related to foreign transactions. In the absence of clear congressional intent, in either the statute's text or legislative history, the Second Circuit had formulated a "conduct-and-effects" test to determine the statute's extraterritorial reach for "F-cubed" cases (*i.e.*, lawsuits filed in U.S. courts under U.S. securities laws by *foreign* plaintiffs against *foreign* issuers based on securities purchased on *foreign* exchanges). This test, in various forms, has been adopted and used by other circuit courts for almost four decades and was applied by the Second Circuit to permit plaintiffs' F-cubed case in *Morrison*. The Supreme Court, however, reversed, favoring a presumption against extraterritorial application of the Exchange Act. In a unanimous opinion written by Justice Scalia, the Court held that the antifraud provision of the Exchange Act did not provide a private right of action to foreign plaintiffs suing a foreign defendant for misconduct connected to securities traded on foreign exchanges. *Id.* Why would foreign plaintiffs have filed F-cubed cases in the U.S. courts?

What is the potential impact of *Morrison*? Professor Rhonda Wasserman contends that the immediate impact will be a drastic reduction in the number of F-cubed securities fraud class actions filed in the U.S. courts. *See* Rhonda Wasserman, *Transnational Class Actions and Interjurisdictional Preclusion*, 86 Notre Dame L. Rev. 313, 313–14 n.3 (2011). In response to *Morrison*, Congress has directed the Securities and Exchange Commission to study whether private rights of action under Section 10(b) should be extended to encompass conduct previously covered pre-*Morrison*. *See* Dodd–Frank Wall Street Reform and Consumer Protection Act, Pub. L. No. 111–203, § 929Y, 124 Stat. 1376, 1871 (2010).

3. SECURITIES CLASS ACTION REFORM

In contrast to other substantive areas of class litigation, such as mass torts, securities class actions have been subjected to Congressional action aimed directly at remedying perceived abuses of the class action device.

a. The Private Securities Litigation Reform Act of 1995

i. Overview

In 1995, Congress overhauled many rules governing private securities fraud suits. Against a background of hearings contending that such suits were stifling legitimate business ventures, Congress enacted the Private Securities Litigation Reform Act of 1995 ("PSLRA" or "Reform Act"). The major goals of the Reform Act were "(1) to encourage the voluntary disclosure of information by corporate issuers; (2) to empower investors so that they—not their lawyers—exercise primary control over private securities litigation; and (3) to encourage plaintiffs' lawyers to pursue valid claims and defendants to fight abusive claims." S. Rep. No. 104–98 at 4 (1995). Although many of the Reform Act's provisions—affecting such issues as damages, stays of discovery when defendants file a motion to dismiss, and pleading standards—are applicable whether or not a suit is brought as a class action (and hence are beyond the scope of this casebook), many of the Reform Act's provisions directly addressed securities fraud class actions and sought to impose rules that would reduce or eliminate perceived problems. Thus, the Reform Act requires, *inter alia,* the following:

- Each plaintiff named in a class action complaint who wishes to become a class representative must file a sworn certification that (i) states that the plaintiff has read the complaint and authorized its filing, that the plaintiff did not purchase the security at issue at the direction of counsel or for purposes of participating in a securities fraud action, and that the plaintiff is willing to serve as a representative, including providing deposition and trial testimony; (ii) describes all transactions in the security made by the plaintiff during the class period; (iii) discloses any other federal securities fraud action the plaintiff has been involved in during the preceding three years; and (iv) confirms that the plaintiff will not accept any payment beyond his or her *pro rata* share of the recovery except as authorized by the court (for such things as wage losses directly attributable to service as class representative). *See* 15 U.S.C. § 78u–4(a)(2)(4).

- Within 20 days of the filing of a securities fraud class action, the attorneys must publish, in "a widely circulated national business-oriented publication or wire service," a notice advising potential class members of the suit, its claims, and the potential class period, and stating that within 60 days of the notice, any plaintiff may move the court to serve as lead plaintiff. The court is then required, within 90 days after that notice, to determine any motion made pursuant to the notice, and "shall appoint as lead plaintiff the member or members of the purported plaintiff class that the court determines to be most capable of adequately representing the interests of class members * * *." In making this determination from among the persons who have submitted motions, the court must apply a rebuttable presumption that the person or group of persons with the "largest financial interest in the relief sought by the class" should be chosen "most adequate plaintiff." Any person who has served as a lead plaintiff in a class action in five actions in the preceding three years shall be presumptively disqualified. The most adequate plaintiff then shall select and retain counsel, subject to court approval. *See* 15 U.S.C. § 78u–4(a)(3).

- Courts are required to award attorneys fees of no more than a "reasonable percentage of the amount of any damages and prejudgment interest actually paid to the class." 15 U.S.C. § 78u–4(a)(6).

- Securities fraud class action settlements generally cannot be placed under seal except for good cause shown, with good cause defined as "direct and substantial harm to any party." 15 U.S.C. § 78u–4(a)(5). Furthermore, any proposed settlement disseminated to a class must include, in addition to any other information required by the court, a statement of the amount of the settlement proposed to be distributed to the class (both in the aggregate and on a per share basis); a statement of the potential outcome of the case (if the parties agree on the damages that would be recoverable, then a statement of that amount; otherwise, a statement from each party concerning the issue(s) with respect to which there is disagreement); a statement of the attorneys' fees sought and an explanation in support of the request; the name and contact information of a representative of plaintiffs' counsel who is available to answer questions; and a brief statement of the reasons for proposing settlement. See 15 U.S.C. § 78u–4(a)(7).

NOTES AND QUESTIONS

1. Notwithstanding the Reform Act, the number of federal securities class actions has grown. *See, e.g.*, Warren R. Stern & Sarah E. McCallum, *The Private Securities Litigation Reform Act: Ten Years After*, 38 Rev.Sec. & Commodities Reg. 789 (2005) (noting, *inter alia*, in the context of post-Enron and public corporate misconduct scandals, the increase in securities class actions, settlements, and disposition time for cases brought pursuant to the PSLRA). In the past decade, federal securities class actions have surged as a result of various conditions, including: problems in the subprime mortgage industry; the depressed state of the economy; the collapse of Ponzi schemes, particularly that of Bernard Madoff; the high costs of settlements; and the expanded role of major institutions as lead plaintiffs. *See* David Daly & Patricia Etzold, *2015 Securities Litigation Study*, at iii (PricewaterhouseCoopers LLP 2016), *available at* http://www.pwc.com/us/en/forensic-services/publications/assets/pwc-securities-litigation-study.pdf ("For the third straight year, we saw an annual increase in the number of federal securities class action lawsuits filed[.]"); Svetlana Starykh & Stefan Boettrich, *Recent Trends in Securities Class Action Litigation: 2015 Full-Year Review* (NERA Economic Consulting 2016), *available at* http://www.nera.com/content/dam/nera/publications/2016/2015_Securities_Trends_Report_NERA.pdf ("2015 saw federal securities class action filings reach levels not seen since 2008.").

2. Is there any reason to believe that the perceived problems addressed by the PLSRA described above occur with any less frequency in other areas, such as antitrust, civil rights, consumer actions, employment law, environmental law, or mass torts? For example, is there any reason to believe that securities class action plaintiffs are particularly susceptible to manipulation by plaintiffs' attorneys? In short, is there any reason to believe that plaintiffs file more meritless securities class actions than other types of class actions?

ii. Litigation Under the Reform Act

Most of the litigation under the Reform Act following its enactment focused on the technical requirements of pleading securities fraud—stating claims with sufficient particularity, and providing allegations of "scienter" (wrongful state of mind) consistent with the somewhat ambiguous terms of the Act. *See* 15 U.S.C. § 78u–4(b)(1) (complaint must provide "each statement alleged to have been misleading, the reason or reasons why the statement is misleading, and, if an allegation regarding the statement or omission is made on information and belief, the complaint shall state with particularity all facts on which that belief is formed"); 15 U.S.C. § 78u–4(b)(2) ("the complaint shall, with respect to each act or omission alleged to violate this chapter, state with particularity facts giving rise to a strong inference that the defendant acted with the required state of mind").

In *Tellabs, Inc. v. Makor Issues & Rights, Ltd.*, 551 U.S. 308 (2007), the Supreme Court provided guidance concerning the pleading required to state a "strong inference" of fraud sufficient to withstand a motion to dismiss under the PSLRA:

> [I]n determining whether the pleaded facts give rise to a "strong" inference of scienter, the court must take into account plausible

opposing inferences. * * * In § 21D(b)(2), Congress did not merely require plaintiffs to "provide a factual basis for [their] scienter allegations," *i.e.*, to allege facts from which an inference of scienter rationally *could* be drawn. Instead, Congress required plaintiffs to plead with particularity facts that give rise to a "strong"—*i.e.*, a powerful or cogent—inference.

The strength of an inference cannot be decided in a vacuum. The inquiry is inherently comparative: How likely is it that one conclusion, as compared to others, follows from the underlying facts? To determine whether the plaintiff has alleged facts that give rise to the requisite "strong inference" of scienter, a court must consider plausible nonculpable explanations for the defendant's conduct, as well as inferences favoring the plaintiff. The inference that the defendant acted with scienter need not be irrefutable, *i.e.*, of the "smoking-gun" genre, or even the "most plausible of competing inferences[.]" Recall in this regard that § 21D(b)'s pleading requirements are but one constraint among many the PSLRA installed to screen out frivolous suits, while allowing meritorious actions to move forward. Yet the inference of scienter must be more than merely "reasonable" or "permissible"—it must be cogent and compelling, thus strong in light of other explanations. A complaint will survive, we hold, only if a reasonable person would deem the inference of scienter cogent and at least as compelling as any opposing inference one could draw from the facts alleged.

551 U.S. at 323–24 (citations omitted). In resolving the question of what it means for a plaintiff to plead a "strong inference" of scienter, the *Tellabs* Court chose a rigorous approach. Is such rigor warranted? What potential impact might this have on plaintiffs' ability to recover damages for securities fraud?

Applying *Tellabs*, the Supreme Court in *Matrixx Initiatives, Inc. v. Siracusano*, 563 U.S. 27 (2011), held that investors successfully pled scienter under this rigorous standard. (*See* Section (C)(1) of this chapter for a discussion of the facts of *Matrixx*.) The Court rejected a "bright-line rule" that would have required allegations of statistically significant causation evidence to establish a "strong inference of scienter"—and assumed, without deciding, that plaintiffs could adequately plead scienter by a showing of reckless indifference. *Id.* at 48–50.

Some Reform Act litigation has focused upon the automatic discovery stay that is triggered when a defendant files a motion to dismiss. *See, e.g., SG Cowen Sec. Corp. v. U.S. Dist. Court*, 189 F.3d 909, 912 (9th Cir. 1999) (automatic stay barred plaintiffs' discovery relating to motion to dismiss); *Swartz v. Deutsche Bank AG*, 2008 WL 534535, at *1–2 (W.D. Wash. 2008) (automatic stay barred plaintiff's discovery relating to motion to dismiss despite fact that relevant information had been produced to defendant through government investigations); *In re Spectrum Brands, Inc. Sec. Litig.*, 2007 WL 1483633, at *5 (N.D. Ga. 2007) (automatic stay barred plaintiffs' discovery seeking information necessary to state a claim that would overcome motion to dismiss); *but cf. Latham v. Stein*, 2010 WL 3294722, at *1–3 (D.S.C. 2010) (allowing discovery against six defendants whose motions to dismiss had been denied, even though motion to dismiss by one other defendant was still pending).

The pleading requirements and discovery stay are applicable whether or not a securities fraud action is filed as a class action. Other cases, however, have focused upon the peculiarities of bringing a class action in the Reform Act era. Such cases address the process for choosing "lead plaintiffs" and "lead counsel," and provide important insights into the structure of contemporary securities fraud class actions. Examples are set forth below.

a) Lead Plaintiff—Notice and Standing to Object

GREEBEL V. FTP SOFTWARE, INC.
United States District Court, District of Massachusetts, 1996.
939 F. Supp. 57.

TAURO, CHIEF JUDGE.

Presently before the court is the motion of Lawrence Greebel, Brian Robinson, and Richard Crane (collectively, "Movants") to be appointed Lead Plaintiff and for Milberg, Weiss, Bershad, Hynes & Lerach to be appointed Lead Counsel, pursuant to the Private Securities Litigation Reform Act of 1995 (the "PSLRA"). Resolution of this motion involves questions of first impression regarding interpretation of the procedural reforms effectuated by the PSLRA.

I.
BACKGROUND

A. The Private Securities Litigation Reform Act of 1995

In enacting the PSLRA, Congress altered the procedures for bringing class actions under the federal securities laws. The principal impetus underlying this congressional initiative was the belief that the plaintiff's bar had seized control of class action suits, bringing frivolous suits on behalf of only nominally interested plaintiffs in the hope of obtaining a quick settlement. To ameliorate these perceived abuses of the class action device in actions brought under the federal securities laws, section 21D [of the PSLRA] imposes disclosure requirements on the plaintiff filing the lawsuit and mechanisms for the appointment of a lead plaintiff.

Section 21D(a)(2) requires plaintiffs to file with their complaint sworn certifications describing, among other things, their transaction in the security and their prior appearances as a plaintiff in a securities class action lawsuit. 15 U.S.C.A. § 78u–4(a)(2). Section 21D(a)(3) sets forth procedures for early notice to purported class members of the filing of the action. 15 U.S.C.A. § 78u–4(a)(3). Under that section, the named plaintiff in the action must file notice to potential class members within 20 days of filing the suit to inform them of their right to move to be appointed lead plaintiff. Such notice must be published "in a widely circulated national business-oriented publication or wire service."

Section 21D(a)(3) also alters the procedure for appointment of lead plaintiff for the purported class. Section 21D(a)(3)(B)(i) provides that:

> Not later than 90 days after the date on which a notice is published . . . the court shall consider any motion made by a purported class member in response to the notice, including any motion by a class member who is not individually named as a plaintiff in the complaint or complaints, and shall appoint as lead plaintiff the member or members of the purported plaintiff class that the court determines to be most capable of adequately representing the interests of class members. . . .

15 U.S.C.A. § 78u–4(a)(3)(B)(i). In making this determination, the statute erects a rebuttable presumption that the most capable plaintiff is the person with the largest financial interest in the relief sought by the class, and "otherwise satisfies the requirements of Rule 23 of the Federal Rules of Civil Procedure." 15 U.S.C.A. § 78u–4(a)(3)(B)(iii)(I). The presumption may be rebutted only "upon proof by a member of the purported plaintiff class" that the presumptively most capable plaintiff "will not fairly and adequately protect the interests of the class" or is "subject to unique defenses." 15 U.S.C.A. § 78u–4(a)(3)(B)(iii)(II). A purported class member may undertake discovery to mount such a challenge only if he or she "first demonstrates a reasonable basis for finding that the presumptively most adequate plaintiff is incapable of adequately representing the class." 15 U.S.C.A. § 78u–4(a)(3)(B)(iv).

Finally, under section 21D(a)(3)(B)(v), the lead plaintiff "shall, subject to the approval of the court, select and retain lead counsel." 15 U.S.C.A. § 78u–4(a)(3)(B)(v).

B. Procedural History

On March 14, 1996, Lawrence Greebel, on behalf of himself and all other similarly situated persons, filed this action against FTP Software, Inc. and various officers of FTP (collectively, "FTP"). * * * Greebel alleges that, between July 14, 1995 and January 3, 1996, FTP made materially false representations and omissions regarding FTP, in violation of sections 10(b) and 20(a) of the Securities Exchange Act. With his complaint, Greebel filed a certification pursuant to section 21D(a)(2).

On March 18, 1996, Greebel supplied a press release to *Business Wire* for transmission over its computer database. *Business Wire* "electronically disseminate[s] full-text news releases for public and investor relations professionals simultaneously to the news media, on-line services and databases, the Internet and the investment community worldwide." The press release contained the information required by section 21D(a)(3)(A).

The full text of the press release was picked up by the Bloomberg *Business News Wire, The Wall Street Journal, Boston Globe,* and *Dow Jones Wire Service,* among others, picked up the story of the filing of the lawsuit, but did not run the paragraphs of the press release relating to a purported class members' right to move to be lead plaintiff.

On May 15, 1996, Movants filed the instant motion to be appointed Lead Plaintiff and for [Milberg Weiss] to be appointed Lead Counsel. Crane and Robinson did not file certifications pursuant to section 21D(a)(2), though they did represent through counsel that they met the criteria set forth in that section. FTP opposes the motion.

II.
DISCUSSION

FTP articulates three objections to Movants' motion to be appointed lead plaintiff: (1) that Robinson and Crane have failed to comply with the PSLRA's certification requirement, (2) that Greebel's notice failed to satisfy the PSLRA's publication requirement, and (3) that it is premature to determine whether Movants meet the criteria for a lead plaintiff set forth in section 21D(a)(3)(B)(iii). As well as responding to the merits of these objections, Movants contend that FTP lacks standing to oppose their motion.

A. Standing

Movants maintain that the PSLRA's lead plaintiff provisions were enacted for the benefit of investors, *i.e.*, members of the putative class, and, therefore, Congress did not intend to give defendants in securities class actions standing to oppose a motion for appointment of a lead plaintiff. FTP disagrees.

Neither of the parties' positions accurately capture the procedural scheme created by Congress. Rather, the standing of a defendant to challenge a motion to be appointed lead plaintiff depends on the basis of that challenge.

The structure of the new procedural provisions demarcates the line at which defendants have an interest in challenging the adequacy of a person seeking to become a lead plaintiff. Section 21D(a)(2) and section 21D(a)(3)(A) set forth prerequisites for bringing a class action. Failure of the named plaintiff to file a certification with the complaint and to serve notice to class members are fatal to maintenance of the putative class action.

And so, defendants have the same interest in demanding compliance with these provisions as they have with other requirements relating to certification of a class. Further, permitting a defendant to object on these grounds enhances effective judicial administration of the case. Where, for example, questions arise regarding the adequacy of the notice, it is doubtful that a court could make an informed analysis without the input of a defendant. If notice is indeed inadequate, the court cannot rely on other putative class members to proffer opposition because, *a fortiori*, they are unaware of the lawsuit.

By the same token, however, the provisions in section 21D(a)(3)(B) relate to who will stand as the lead plaintiff, subject to reconsideration at the time of class certification. The text of that subsection clearly indicates that this issue is one over which only potential plaintiffs may be heard. For example, Congress provided that rebuttal of the lead plaintiff presumption shall be limited to "proof by a member of the purported plaintiff class." 15 U.S.C.A. § 78u–4(a)(3)(B)(iii)(II). Similarly, the right to conduct discovery is explicitly restricted to purported class members. 15 U.S.C.A. § 78u–4(a)(3)(B)(iv).

FTP maintains that, because they have a due process right to challenge certification of a class, they have a similar concern with respect to who is appointed lead plaintiff. They point out that, in applying the standards of section 21D(a)(3)(B)(iii)(I), a court should presume that the most adequate plaintiff is the person or group of persons that:

> (aa) has either filed the complaint or made a motion in response to a notice . . .;
>
> (bb) in the determination of the court has the largest financial interest in the relief sought by the class; and
>
> (cc) *otherwise satisfies the requirements of Rule 23 of the Federal Rules of Civil Procedure.*

15 U.S.C.A. § 78u–4(a)(3)(B)(iii)(I). FTP argues that appointment by the court of a lead plaintiff would prejudice FTP's ability to later challenge the lead plaintiff as an inadequate class representative in light of the court's finding of "satisfaction," pursuant to subsection (cc).

Congress intended that the lead plaintiff be determined at an early stage of the litigation. Though neither the text of the PSLRA nor its legislative history explicitly describe the relationship between motions for lead plaintiff and motions for class certification, it seems clear that Congress recognized that these motions involved distinct inquiries. Section 21D(a)(3)(B) refers throughout its text to "purported class members." Congress implicitly understood, therefore, that lead plaintiff motions would be decided prior to consideration of certification issues.

This court concludes, therefore, that FTP lacks standing to challenge whether Movants satisfy the criteria set forth in section 21D(a)(3)(B)(iii). But, this court also concludes that its determination to appoint a person or persons as lead plaintiff must be without prejudice to the possibility of revisiting that issue in considering a motion for class certification. Any other view would frustrate the congressional purpose underlying the lead plaintiff provisions, which is to allow early intervention and control of the lawsuit by the most adequate plaintiff—presumably, the investor with the largest stake.

In sum, the court concludes that FTP may object to the adequacy of certification and notice, insofar as they are procedural prerequisites for consideration of a motion for lead plaintiff. But FTP may not oppose the motion on grounds relating to the moving parties' satisfaction of the criteria enumerated in section 21D(a)(3)(B)(iii)(I).

[The court also held, *inter alia*, that Greebel's press release, published in *Business Wire*, satisfied the requirements of "a widely circulated national business-oriented publication or wire service" pursuant to Section 21D(a)(3)(A). The court noted that the full text of the press release was picked up by *Bloomberg Wire Service* and could also be accessed directly by consumers.]

NOTES AND QUESTIONS

1. Should a defendant in a securities fraud class action have standing to weigh in on which plaintiff should be the "lead" plaintiff? Should the answer depend on the substance of the challenge, as *Greebel* held? The courts are split on this issue. *Blake Partners, Inc. v. Orbcomm, Inc.*, 2008 WL 2277117, at *3–4 (D.N.J. 2008) (discussing split among district courts). *Compare, e.g., Prissert*

v. Emcore Corp., 2010 U.S. Dist. LEXIS 86598, at *7–8 (D.N.M. 2010) (defendants have no standing to object to adequacy or typicality of lead plaintiff); *In re Universal Access, Inc., Sec. Litig.*, 209 F.R.D. 379, 383 (E.D. Tex. 2002) (same), *with King v. Livent, Inc.*, 36 F. Supp. 2d 187, 190 (S.D.N.Y. 1999) (explaining why lead plaintiff process "will work better with more information [including from defendant] rather than less"); *In re Flight Safety Techs., Inc. Sec. Litig.*, 231 F.R.D. 124, 129 n.3 (D. Conn. 2005) (to the same effect). Which approach makes more sense?

2. What purposes are served by the Reform Act's notice requirement? Was the *Greebel* court correct in concluding that the notice published on the *Business Wire* sufficed to notify prospective lead plaintiffs of the pendency of the suit and their ability to participate in it? What notice suffices? *See generally Lane v. Page*, 250 F.R.D. 634, 641, 643–45 (D.N.M. 2007) (characterizing notice drafting as an "art" that requires balancing and describing various court rulings on adequacy of PSLRA notice). *Compare, e.g., Poptech, L.P. v. Stewardship Inv. Advisors, L.L.C.*, 2010 WL 4365669, at *1–5 (D. Conn. 2010) (upholding sufficiency of PSLRA notice even where it does not detail all claims in the complaint, including state law claims), *with Cal. Public Emps. Ret. Sys. v. The Chubb Corp.*, 127 F. Supp. 2d 572, 579, 580–82 (D.N.J. 2001) (holding PSLRA notice inadequate where "the information provided lacks sufficient detail and depth to permit an interested class member to make an informed decision as to whether he, she or it should seek appointment as lead plaintiff").

3. The *Greebel* court (in its discussion of standing) noted that a plaintiff's failure to satisfy the Reform Act's certification or notice provisions would be "fatal" to maintenance of a class action. *Compare Carson v. Merrill Lynch, Pierce, Fenner & Smith Inc.*, 1998 WL 34076402 (W.D. Ark. 1998). In *Carson*, plaintiff had indisputably failed to satisfy the notice requirement, but moved to amend his complaint to add other class representatives, and represented that the new representatives would timely comply with the notice provision after the filing of the amended complaint. The court held that dismissal of the complaint was not required:

> The PSLRA does not direct a court to dismiss a complaint when a plaintiff fails to comply with either the certification requirement or the notice provisions. The PSLRA does require, however, that a court dismiss a complaint when a plaintiff fails to properly plead the requirements of a § 10(b) securities fraud action. 15 U.S.C. § 78u–4(b)(3)(A) (1997). Thus, if Congress had wanted the courts to dismiss a complaint when a plaintiff failed to file a sworn certification or publish timely notice, then Congress could have included such language in the PSLRA.
>
> * * * The court in *Greebel* [in its use of "fatal"] was simply stating in *dicta* that if a plaintiff never complies with the provisions of the PSLRA, then the class action cannot go forward. The court did not state that a named plaintiff could not correct such a failure to comply by filing a certification with an amended complaint and serving such notice within 20 days of the amended complaint. Therefore, we conclude that nothing under the PSLRA prohibits the court from allowing a plaintiff to file a sworn certification with an amended complaint and to publish belated notice to the other purported class members.

Carson, 1998 WL 34076402 at *16. Should a plaintiff, consistent with the Reform Act, be permitted to add additional plaintiffs and have those plaintiffs comply with the certification and notice provisions?

4. In *Police & Fire Retirement Systems of Detroit v. IndyMac MBS, Inc.*, 721 F.3d 95 (2d Cir. 2013), the Second Circuit held that the tolling rule set forth by the Supreme Court in *American Pipe* (discussed in Chapter 7(A)) does not apply to the three-year statute of repose in section 13 of the PSLRA. The court reasoned that section 13 "creates a *substantive* right" and that "[p]ermitting a plaintiff to file a complaint or intervene after the repose period * * * would therefore necessarily enlarge or modify a substantive right and violate the Rules Enabling Act". *Id.* at 109. Does the *IndyMac* ruling undermine the purpose of *American Pipe* by forcing plaintiffs to file individual actions to prevent their claims from being time barred?

b) Lead Plaintiff—Selection

IN RE OXFORD HEALTH PLANS, INC., SEC. LITIG.
United States District Court, Southern District of New York, 1998.
182 F.R.D. 42.

BRIEANT, DISTRICT JUDGE.

Presently before the Court in these cases alleging securities fraud, which have been consolidated for pre-trial purposes, are a number of motions relating to the designation of lead plaintiff and approval of lead counsel under the provisions of section 21D(a)(3)(B) of the Securities and Exchange Act of 1934 ("Exchange Act"), as amended by the Private Securities Litigation Reform Act of 1995 (the "PSLRA" or "the Act"), 15 U.S.C. § 78u–4. A hearing was held on June 11, 1998 and decision reserved.

On April 28, 1998 the Judicial Panel on Multidistrict Litigation filed an order consolidating the 52 separate actions in this litigation * * * and transferring them to this Court for pretrial purposes pursuant to 28 U.S.C. § 1407 [discussed in Chapter 12(F)]. Two additional cases have since been filed in this District. For the reasons discussed below, this Court now grants the motions of the Public Employee's Retirement Association of Colorado, the Vogel Group (as defined below) and PBHG to be appointed co-lead plaintiffs for the securities fraud cases. The Court also approves the plaintiffs' respective choices—Grant & Eisenhofer, P.A., Milberg Weiss Bershad Hynes & Lerach, L.L.P., and Chitwood & Harley—to act as co-lead counsel. Such counsel shall assemble and consult with an Executive Committee as set forth below.

I. The Private Securities Litigation Reform Act of 1995

* * *

The PSLRA directs the Court to "appoint as lead plaintiff the *member or members* of the purported plaintiff class that the court determines to be most capable of adequately representing the interests of the class." 15 U.S.C. § 78u–4(a)(3)(B)(i). The Act creates a "rebuttable presumption . . . that the most adequate plaintiff . . . is the person or group of persons that (aa) has either filed the complaint or made a motion in response to a notice . . .; (bb) in the determination of the court, has the largest financial interest in the relief sought by the class; and (cc) otherwise satisfies the requirements of Rule 23 of the Federal Rules of Civil Procedure." 15 U.S.C. § 78u–4(a)(3)(B)(iii)(I).

The presumption may be rebutted "only upon proof by a member of the purported plaintiff class that the presumptively most adequate plaintiff— (aa) will not fairly and adequately represent the interests of the class; or (bb) is subject to unique defenses that render such plaintiff incapable of adequately representing the class." 15 U.S.C. § 78u–4(a)(3)(B)(iii)(II). Before obtaining discovery in this regard, the objecting plaintiff must demonstrate a reasonable basis for a finding "that the presumptively most adequate plaintiff is incapable of representing the class." 15 U.S.C. § 78u–4(a)(3)(B)(iv).

Finally, the PSLRA states that "[t]he most adequate plaintiff shall, subject to the approval of the court, select and retain counsel to represent the class." 15 U.S.C. § 78u–4(a)(3)(B)(v).

II. Background

Oxford Health Plans, Inc. ("Oxford") is a Delaware corporation engaged in the managed health care business, providing health benefit plans in New York, New Jersey, Pennsylvania, Connecticut and New Hampshire. The individual defendants named in the complaints were the principal executive officers and directors of Oxford.

The securities fraud actions which have been consolidated in this Court were brought on behalf of persons and entities who purchased Oxford common stock during varying alleged class periods ranging from November 1996 through December 1997. The complaints generally claim violations of §§ 10(b) and 20(a) of the Securities and Exchange Act and Rule 10b–5 promulgated thereunder by the SEC. Specifically the plaintiffs allege that Oxford failed to disclose ongoing problems with its computer system and its resulting financial deterioration, while substantial insider trading occurred.

III. The Movants for Appointment as Lead Counsel

Numerous motions seeking lead plaintiff status in this action have been filed, some of which were withdrawn after the cases were consolidated. The Public Employee's Retirement Association of Colorado ("ColPERA") appears to have suffered the largest financial loss, followed by the Vogel plaintiffs and the PBHG Funds. This was conceded at the June 11, 1998 hearing.

A. ColPERA

ColPERA is a pension fund for state of Colorado employees which moved to be appointed lead counsel on December 22, 1997 alleging losses in excess of $25 million. On January 28, 1998 ColPERA moved for leave to supplement its motion revising its loss, after offsetting for certain gains, to $19,435,749.25 (using the class period of November 11, 1996–December 12, 1997). On June 4, 1998 ColPERA submitted a proposed order appointing ColPERA as lead plaintiff, Grant & Eisenhofer, P.A. as lead counsel and an executive committee composed of Grant & Eisenhofer as Chair and four other law firms which also made lead plaintiff motions as members * * *.

B. Vogel

On December 23, 1997 the Vogel plaintiffs ("Vogel"), consisting of approximately 35 individual plaintiffs and entities, filed a motion for appointment as lead plaintiff and appointment of Milberg Weiss Bershad Hynes &

Lerach, L.L.P., as lead counsel. On May 14, 1998 Vogel submitted a motion to supplement its original lead plaintiff motion, estimating its collective losses at $10,072,120.63 for the November 6, 1996–December 9, 1997 class period. The majority of Vogel's losses were sustained by three individuals: Daniel Hurley ($3,409,423.11); Gary Weber ($3,104,594.57); and Michael Sabbia ($2,014,520.50) (hereinafter "the Vogel Group").

C. The PBHG Funds

The PBHG Funds, Inc. is a Maryland corporation registered under the Investment Company Act of 1940, as amended, as a diversified open-end management company. It consists of 14 series or funds including the 5 funds that purchased Oxford common stock and sustained significant losses * * *. The five funds which sustained the losses (hereinafter "PBHG") moved on December 30, 1997 to be appointed lead plaintiff and for Chitwood & Harley to be appointed lead counsel. PBHG originally alleged losses in excess of $4.3 million, but in a May 27, 1998 motion to supplement its original motion, PBHG revised its estimate to $2.756 million using the November 6, 1996–December 9, 1997 class period.

IV. The PSLRA Determinations

A. Most Adequate Plaintiff Presumption

The PSLRA calls for greater supervision by the Court in the selection of which plaintiffs will control the litigation. Since the Act was passed courts interpreting the lead plaintiff provisions have taken different views, some allowing only a single lead plaintiff, others allowing groups of more than one plaintiff. I find and conclude that in the circumstances of this particular case, the interests of the proposed class will be best served by a group of three co-lead plaintiffs consisting of (1) ColPERA; (2) the Vogel Group (limited to Mr. Hurley, Mr. Weber and Mr. Sabbia); and (3) PBHG, with each exercising a single equal vote. This structure provides the proposed class with the substantial benefits of joint decision-making and joint funding and is consistent with the language of the PSLRA and the purpose of Congress in enacting it.

The House Conference Report on the PSLRA stated that the lead plaintiff provisions were "intended to encourage the most capable *representatives* of the plaintiff class to participate in class action litigation and to exercise supervision and control of the lawyers for the class." The House Report also stated that:

> Throughout the process, it is clear that the plaintiff class has difficulty exercising any meaningful direction over the case brought on its behalf . . . Because class counsels' fees and expenses sometimes amount to one-third or more of recovery, class counsel frequently has a significantly greater interest in the litigation than any individual member of the class.

In this case ColPERA, the Vogel Group and PBHG have all suffered significant losses. Two of the plaintiffs are institutional investors, as specifically encouraged by the PSLRA. The third plaintiff, the Vogel Group, while not an institutional investor, has been limited by the Court to three individuals, each of whom has suffered from two to three million dollars in losses. The Court is convinced that the limited size of the Vogel Group coupled with the scope of each individuals' loss will make the Vogel Group, as reduced by the Court, an effective monitor of its counsels' performance, thereby fulfilling the purpose of the PSLRA.

The Court is also concerned with the potential costs and expenses of this litigation. * * * The use of multiple lead plaintiffs will best serve the interests of the proposed class in this case because such a structure will allow for pooling, not only of the knowledge and experience, but also of the resources of the plaintiffs' counsel in order to support what could prove to be a costly and time-consuming litigation.

While the legislative history of the PSLRA suggests a desire that institutional investors be preferred as class representatives, not all institutional investors are similarly situated. A class representative, once designated by the Court, is a fiduciary for the absent class members. ColPERA enters the litigation already burdened by a primary fiduciary obligation to the present and future government pensioners of the state of Colorado. Private claimants such as the Vogel Group may incur deposition costs and other disbursements in pursuit of their own claims and that of the class, without limitation. ColPERA, on the other hand, cannot pursue litigation with trust funds for the benefit of class members who are not beneficially interested in the trust. If the reasonable prospects of recovery do not exceed the costs accrued, such a fiduciary becomes conflicted and may have to drop out. Such a potential conflict has a serious adverse bearing on settlement dynamics.

In addition the plain language of the PSLRA expressly contemplates the appointment of more than one lead plaintiff, *see* 15 U.S.C. §§ 78u–4(a)(3)(B)(i) (court "should appoint as lead plaintiff *the member or members* of the purported plaintiff class that the court determines to be the most capable of adequately representing the interests of the class members . . ."); 78u–4(a)(3)(B)(iii)(I) ("the court shall adopt a presumption that the most adequate plaintiff in any private action arising under this chapter is *the person or group of persons* that . . ."); 78u–4(a)(3)(B)(iv) ("discovery relating to whether *a member or members* of the purported plaintiff class is the most adequate plaintiff may be conducted by a plaintiff only if . . ."). Finally the use of a tripartite lead plaintiff structure with each of the three lead plaintiffs exercising one equal vote will prevent any possibility of deadlock over an issue.

* * *

* * * Allowing for diverse representation, including in this case a state pension fund, significant individual investors and a large institutional investor, ensures that the interests of all class members will be adequately represented in the prosecution of the action and in the negotiation and approval of a fair settlement, and that the settlement process will not be distorted by the differing aims of differently situated claimants.

* * *

C. Rule 23 Requirements

The final requirement of the PSLRA for appointment of lead plaintiff is that a lead plaintiff must "otherwise satisf[y] the requirements of Rule 23 of the Federal Rules of Civil Procedure." 15 U.S.C. § 78u–4(a)(3)(B)(iii)(1)(cc). * * *

Typicality and adequacy of representation are the only provisions relevant to a determination of lead plaintiff under the PSLRA. The claims of ColPERA, the Vogel Group and PBHG are typical of the class because their claims and injuries arise from the same conduct from which the other class members' claims and injuries arise. At the present time it is unclear what defenses, if any, will be raised against particular class members, but it is far less likely that any potential defenses would successfully rebut a finding of typicality where more than one investor or group of investors who made the decision to purchase the security is appointed as class representative.

All three plaintiffs also satisfy the adequacy requirement because there is no conflict of interest between any of the three lead plaintiffs and the members of the class and because each lead plaintiff has obtained qualified, experienced counsel.

* * *

NOTES AND QUESTIONS

1. Why would the Reform Act have a "presumption" that the plaintiff (or plaintiffs) with the largest claimed losses is the "most adequate" plaintiff, and should presumptively be the "lead" plaintiff? How does that presumption compare with traditional analysis under Rule 23(a)(4)? One well-accepted proposition is that the Reform Act "reflect[s] a congressional intent to transfer power from counsel who win the race to the courthouse to those shareholders who possess a sufficient financial interest in the outcome to maintain some supervisory responsibility over both the litigation and their counsel." *In re Horizon/CMS Healthcare Corp. Sec. Litig.*, 3 F. Supp. 2d 1208, 1212 (D.N.M. 1998). In an influential article credited with persuading Congress to enact the lead plaintiff provisions—and to adopt a presumption that the plaintiff with the greatest financial stake is the "most adequate plaintiff"—Professors Weiss and Beckerman argued that "constructive institutional participation * * * has the potential to alleviate many current concerns about the legitimacy of class action litigation, and thus might increase significantly the extent to which such litigation advances the disclosure policies of the federal securities laws." Elliott J. Weiss & John S. Beckerman, *Let The Money Do The Monitoring: How Institutional Investors Can Reduce Agency Costs in Securities Class Actions*, 104 Yale L.J. 2053, 2058 (1995). They continued:

> Institutions with the largest stakes in class actions are better situated than plaintiffs' attorneys or courts to protect class members' interests. Those institutions' interests parallel the interests of the plaintiff class much more closely than do the interests of plaintiffs' attorneys or district judges, the parties now responsible for protecting the class. Moreover, the size of those institutions' stakes suggests they are likely to be reasonably diligent in seeking to ensure that plaintiffs' counsel represent effectively their interests and the interests of the plaintiff class.
>
> The largest benefit of institutional supervision of class actions is likely to be settlement terms that are more favorable to the plaintiff class, on average, than those now negotiated by essentially unsupervised plaintiffs' attorneys. * * *

Id. at 2121.

Another commentator, Professor Jill Fisch, challenges the Weiss and Beckerman thesis that institutional investors should be preferred over other securities-fraud plaintiffs:

> Participation by institutions as lead plaintiffs must be consistent with the protection that Rule 23 and due process provide for absent class members through the use of the class representative. To insure that the interests of class members are treated fairly, Rule 23 requires the court to identify a class representative. The court must determine that the class representative fairly and adequately represents the interests of the class, that the class representative's claims are typical of those of the class, and that the class representative is not subject to unique or personal defenses. Institutional investors may not meet these criteria.
>
> * * * [Because of their] larger stake, greater sophistication and better access to information[,] * * * defendants [may] challenge [institutional investors'] reliance on public disclosures or assert a failure to exercise due diligence. Moreover some [institutional investors] enjoy a degree of informal access to corporate management not shared by individual investors. Some courts have found that these qualities may subject a sophisticated investor to unique defenses in securities fraud litigation. * * *
>
> The litigation objectives of institutional investors may also differ from those of the individual investors in the class. Obviously an institution that continues to own stock is poorly suited to represent investors who are no longer invested in the company. * * * Similarly, an institution may have diversified away the risks associated with being on the losing end of a securities fraud, and recognizing that over time, it is likely to gain an equal amount from being an innocent beneficiary of improper disclosure, it may be unwilling to incur the costs associated with litigating the redistribution of damage claims within its own pocket. * * *
>
> * * *
>
> A still darker side of institutional participation in securities litigation is the potential for collusion. To the extent that institutions exercise control of litigation decisions, their control need not be exercised for the general benefit of the shareholder class but could instead be used for the creation and appropriation of private gains. * * * Institutions may seek to obtain favorable investment opportunities, better access to corporate information, or influence over corporate governance decisions, in exchange for cooperation in addressing the concerns of securities fraud defendants. These exchanges can result in institutions exercising their decision making authority in ways that are inconsistent with the needs of the shareholder class.
>
> The risk of collusion is enhanced by the fact that institutions have traditionally maintained the ability to act through informal contacts with issuers in ways not subject to public view. The Reform Act operates to reduce this prospect by mandating increased disclosure of settlement terms. * * * The extent to which this disclosure will limit collusive settlement is unclear, however. * * * [C]ourts have evidenced limited ability to scrutinize inadequate or collusive settlements, and there is little reason to believe that disclosure under the

Reform Act will substantially increase judicial monitoring of settlements. * * * Moreover, litigants retain ample opportunities through the discovery process to control the record upon which settlement review is based. This enables litigants to convince a reviewing court that the settlement terms are reasonable.

The lead plaintiff's control over the selection of class counsel may also create an opportunity for collusion. * * *

Jill E. Fisch, *Class Action Reform: Lessons From Securities Litigation*, 39 Ariz. L. Rev. 533, 545–50 (1997). Who is correct: Professor Fisch or Professors Weiss and Beckerman? Can their positions be harmonized?

2. The Eleventh Circuit has rejected the argument that a representative's sophistication, by use of investment advisors, can render it atypical for class representation. *See Loc. 703, I.B. of T. Grocery & Food Emps. Welfare Fund v. Regions Fin. Corp.*, 762 F.3d 1248 (11th Cir. 2014). Looking to 15 U.S.C. § 77z–1(a)(3)(B)(iii)(I), the court reasoned that "both Congress and the courts have recognized that [large institutional investors who rely on investment advisors] are generally preferred as class representatives in securities litigation." 762 F.3d at 1260.

3. In *Oxford Health Plans*, the court decided not to appoint ColPERA as sole lead plaintiff despite its status as an institutional investor and the moving plaintiff with the greatest alleged losses. Instead, the court appointed multiple lead plaintiffs. The courts are divided over the propriety of grouping unrelated persons and entities for appointment as lead plaintiff. *See Friedman v. Quest Energy Partners L.P.*, 261 F.R.D. 607, 613–14 (W.D. Okla. 2009) (describing courts' various approaches); *Rozenboom v. Van Der Moolen Holding, N.V.*, 2004 WL 816440, at *3–4 (S.D.N.Y. 2004) (same).

Specifically, like *Oxford Health Plans*, many courts have permitted aggregation of unrelated class members for appointment as lead plaintiff. *See, e.g., Weltz v. Lee*, 199 F.R.D. 129, 132 (S.D.N.Y. 2001). The fundamental question, however, is how many can be grouped together. The courts have generally made this determination on a case-by-case basis but have typically narrowed the groups proposed by plaintiffs. *See, e.g., In re Star Gas Sec. Litig.*, 2005 WL 818617, at *5 (D. Conn. 2005) ("The majority of courts * * *, allow[] a group of unrelated investors to serve as lead plaintiffs when it would be most beneficial to the class under the circumstances of a given case, but selecting only a few lead plaintiffs from within a larger group proposed by counsel.").

Other courts, however, have rejected the aggregation of unrelated investors. *See, e.g., City of Roseville Emps. Ret. Sys.*, 2009 WL 4545161, at *3 (D.R.I. 2009) (rejecting combination of unrelated Pension Trust Fund and Employees' Retirement Systems because "[a]llowing these plaintiffs to aggregate into an artificial group would frustrate the PSLRA's goal of restoring plaintiffs' control over lawsuits"); *In re Razorfish, Inc. Sec. Litig.*, 143 F. Supp. 2d 304, 308–09 (S.D.N.Y. 2001) (rejecting combination of large financial institution, two smaller companies, and individual investor as "an artifice cobbled together by cooperating counsel"); *Aronson v. McKesson HBOC, Inc.*, 79 F. Supp. 2d 1146, 1152–53 (N.D. Cal. 1999) (rejecting aggregation of unrelated plaintiffs, concluding that "one client will provide more control than a disjointed group concocted by plaintiffs' counsel—even if the group consists of institutional investors"). Which approach makes the most sense?

Does it make sense to limit the number of lead plaintiffs—related or not? *See, e.g., D'Hondt v. Digi Int'l*, 1997 WL 405668, at *3 (D. Minn. 1997) (noting that "when more greatly numbered, the Lead Plaintiffs can more effectively withstand any supposed effort by the class counsel to seize control of the class claims" and concluding where class may comprise thousands, if not millions, of persons "an arbitrary limit" is counterproductive).

c) Lead Counsel Disputes

Courts in Reform Act cases have often accepted the lead plaintiff's proposal for lead counsel without rigorous analysis. But what happens when there is a dispute?

IN RE MILESTONE SCIENTIFIC SEC. LITIG.
United States District Court, District of New Jersey, 1999.
187 F.R.D. 165.

LECHNER, DISTRICT JUDGE.

This is an action for securities fraud brought on behalf of shareholders of Milestone Scientific, Inc. ("Milestone"), seeking damages for violations of Section 10(b) and Section 20(a) of the Securities Exchange Act of 1934 (the "Exchange Act"), as amended, and Rule 10b–5 promulgated thereunder. * * *

Plaintiffs Robert M. Gintel [and others] (collectively, the "Gintel Group"), moved to be appointed lead plaintiff (the "Lead Plaintiff Motion") and for the approval of lead counsel (the "Lead Counsel Motion") (collectively, the "Motions"). In *In re Milestone Scientific Securities Litigation* ("*Milestone I*"), 183 F.R.D. 404 (D.N.J. 1998), the Lead Plaintiff Motion was granted; the Gintel Group was appointed Lead Plaintiff.

Decision on the Lead Counsel Motion was reserved, however, pending re-briefing on the issue of the propriety of multiple lead counsel. The Gintel Group was directed to proffer sufficient justification, if any, for the approval of a "Plaintiffs' Executive Committee" and "Liaison Counsel" to represent the class of plaintiffs (the "Plaintiff Class"). * * *

Additional submissions on the issue were received from three of the four firms originally retained by the Gintel Group and counsel for Milestone. An *amicus* brief from the SEC (the "SEC *Amicus* Brief") also was received.

Presently pending is the application of Abbey, Gardy [one of the firms retained by the Gintel Group] seeking the appointment as sole lead counsel for the Plaintiff Class (the "Abbey, Gardy Lead Counsel Application"), pursuant to § 21D(a)(3) of the Exchange Act, as amended, 15 U.S.C. § 78u–4(a)(3). For the reasons set forth below, the Abbey, Gardy Lead Counsel Application is granted.

Background

A. Facts

1. The Wand

[Milestone develops and markets products primarily for use by dental practitioners. Milestone began marketing "The Wand," "a computer-controlled device used to anaesthetize dental patients," in 1997. Plaintiffs contend that Milestone artificially inflated the price of its stock by making false and misleading statements about The Wand and by compensating apparently independent sources who, in exchange, made positive statements about The Wand's effectiveness. After Milestone's payments to these sources was reported in newspapers, the price of Milestone's stock plummeted.]

* * *

3. The Gintel Group

As indicated in *Milestone I,* it appeared the Gintel Group had the largest financial stake in the litigation, having collectively purchased during the Class Period more than 1,400,000 shares of Milestone common stock and suffered losses exceeding $11,700,000.

B. Procedural History

The initial Complaint in the instant securities class action was filed by [a single plaintiff named] Wanda on 17 June 1998. On the same date, as previously discussed, the Notice of Pendency of the class action was published over the *Business Wire* by Cohen, Milstein, counsel for Wanda.

Following the publication of the Notice of Pendency, other plaintiffs filed related securities class action complaints alleging similar facts. Sixteen complaints were filed against Milestone, and certain of its officers and/or directors * * *. By order, dated 17 August 1998, ("Pre–Trial Order No. 1") the actions were consolidated. These plaintiffs were represented by approximately twenty-seven law firms and individual practitioners.

The Gintel Group subsequently proposed the entry of a second pretrial order (the "Proposed Pre–Trial Order No. 2"). Proposed Pre–Trial Order No. 2 outlined, *inter alia,* [a three-tiered counsel approach assigning Abbey, Gardy as "chair" of a proposed "Plaintiffs' Executive Committee" and Goldstein, Lite & DePalma as proposed "Liaison Counsel."]

Milestone I reserved decision on the Lead Counsel Motion pending rebriefing of the issue of the suitability of multiple lead counsel. Abbey, Gardy then submitted the Revised Lead Counsel Order, requesting the appointment of Abbey, Gardy as sole lead counsel. * * *

* * *

Schoengold and Cohen, Milstein, who, along with Abbey, Gardy were originally suggested by the Gintel Group to comprise the Plaintiffs' Executive Committee, [proposed the creation of an Executive Committee comprised of the Abbey firm as chair and the Schoengold and Cohen firms as the other members]. * * *

Discussion

* * *

* * * Appointment of Lead Counsel

The approval of lead counsel pursuant to Section 21D(a)(3)(B)(v) is not governed by the same statutory guidelines which control the lead plaintiff determination. The decision to approve counsel selected by the lead plaintiff is a matter within the discretion of the district court. The legislative history of the PSLRA reveals that Congress wished to encourage the exercise of discretion in approving the selection of lead counsel. * * * The exercise of such discretion necessitates an inquiry into the appropriateness of the appointment of several lead counsel; the nature and extent of such inquiry may vary from case to case.

The judgment of a lead plaintiff or proposed lead counsel is not dispositive in the appointment of lead counsel. Approval of lead counsel necessarily requires an independent evaluation of, among other considerations, the effectiveness of proposed class counsel to ensure the protection of the class. As well, a court must be mindful that the lead plaintiff has significant responsibilities and duties, including the management of the direction of the case. Disputes concerning the direction of the case should be resolved by the lead plaintiff. This task can be complicated, or even thwarted, by pressure or impute from several lead counsel.

The PSLRA does not expressly prohibit the lead plaintiff from selecting more than one law firm to represent the class. In certain situations, the appointment of multiple lead counsel may better protect the interests of the plaintiff class. Where a single firm lacks the resources or expertise to prosecute an action, for example, the approval of multiple lead counsel may expedite litigation. However, as discussed below, the appointment of several firms as lead counsel can raise a number of concerns, including the hindrance of the ability of lead plaintiff to manage the case and supervise counsel, duplication of efforts, absence of coordination, delay and increased fees and costs.

As the SEC observes, the approval of multiple lead counsel may engender inefficiency in class action litigation. The potential for duplicative services and the concomitant increase in attorneys' fees works against the approval of multiple lead counsel.

* * *

It is impossible, during the preliminary stages of litigation, to evaluate the potential of, much more guarantee, the non-duplication of services or the reasonableness of attorneys' fees during the course of the prosecution of the action. It is, however, possible at the outset of the litigation, to structure lead counsel so as to avoid the inevitable inefficiency and expense resulting from an inappropriate multiple lead counsel arrangement.

Additionally, where several lead counsel are appointed, there is the potential they may ultimately seize control of the litigation, an occurrence the PSLRA intended to foreclose. As discussed, the PSLRA was designed, in part, to effectuate the transfer of control of securities class actions from the lawyers to the investors. Accordingly, those seeking the appointment of several lead counsel must demonstrate the lead plaintiff will be able to withstand any limitation on, or usurpation of, control, and effectively supervise the several law firms acting as lead counsel.

* * *

The selection of counsel by a lead plaintiff also must be the product of independent, arms length negotiations. This Circuit has observed: "[T]he lead attorney position is coveted as it is likely to bring its occupant the largest share of the fees generated by the litigation." *Garr v. U.S. Healthcare, Inc.*, 22 F.3d 1274, 1277 (3d Cir. 1994). Consequently, there arises the possibility that several law firms may exert pressure on the lead plaintiff. * * *

Not only should the proposed counsel fees be the result of hard-bargaining, but the initial selection of counsel should also be the result of independent decision-making by the lead plaintiff. The SEC argues that "unless there has been active, effective client participation in the [selection] process, it is possible that the counsel arrangement may simply reflect bargaining among lawyers for their own stake in the case, and not serve the best interests of the class." It appears this may be the situation in the instant case.

The potential for interference with the independent judgment of a lead plaintiff may be amplified when several law firms are vying for the appointment of lead counsel. Where the proposed organizational structure for lead counsel markedly increases the likelihood of interference with the decision-making process of the lead plaintiff, the selection of counsel by the lead plaintiff should not automatically be accorded deference. Simply stated: class actions are not to be used as a vehicle to promote attorney employment.

* * *

Applying these principles to the instant case, it appears the appointment of several lead counsel will not promote the efficient prosecution of this case, and is not warranted. * * *

In challenging the Abbey, Gardy Revised Lead Counsel Order, Schoengold and Cohen, Milstein argued, *inter alia*, the Plaintiffs' Executive Committee will not foster duplication of attorney services. They attempted to isolate three issues they suggest predominate the instant litigation, proposing these issues be divided among the three-member Plaintiffs' Executive Committee: "Each firm on the committee would be responsible for its issue throughout the course of the litigation, and would thereby develop expertise on that issue."

It appears, however, the issues described by Schoengold and Cohen, Milstein are general in nature and overlap to a significant degree. The three issues all concern alleged misrepresentations made by representatives of Milestone in conjunction with the marketing and sale of The Wand, and the resulting consequences. As such, these issues will likely permeate the litigation, and may not be so easily isolated and divided. Even if each member of the proposed Plaintiffs' Executive Committee is able to focus on one issue, this suggestion nevertheless does not protect against, much more ensure, the non-duplication of efforts. Rather, it appears this proposal will increase costs and decrease efficiency. * * *

* * *

Schoengold and Cohen, Milstein also have not addressed the danger the proposed Plaintiffs' Executive Committee may usurp control of the litigation. Schoengold and Cohen, Milstein failed to demonstrate the lead plaintiff would be able to effectively supervise and control the direction of the litigation if the firms comprising the proposed Plaintiffs' Executive Committee were appointed co-lead counsel. * * *

It further appears the objectives of the law firms proposed as the Plaintiffs' Executive Committee already conflict. As indicated, Abbey, Gardy submitted a Revised Lead Counsel Order proposing itself as sole lead counsel. Schoengold and Cohen, Milstein, by contrast, opposed the Abbey, Gardy Lead Counsel Application and the proposed Revised Lead Counsel Order. Schoengold and Cohen, Milstein instead submitted [a proposed order] advocating the appointment of a three firm Plaintiffs' Executive Committee. Such conflicts have the potential to undermine future coordination among counsel.

* * *

Other policy considerations also weigh in favor of appointing a single law firm as lead counsel in this case. In support of the approval of the proposed Plaintiffs' Executive Committee, Schoengold and Cohen, Milstein argued:

> Certainly, the 16 law firms who chose not to file motions for lead plaintiff and lead counsel in this action did so with the assumption that the executive committee structure would be in effect. . . . If such consensual motions are not recognized by the courts, it may engender competing motions for lead plaintiff, causing a significant delay in the progress of the litigation and further congestion in court dockets.

This so-called "policy" argument, or threat, ignores the rationale behind the lead plaintiff provisions of the PSLRA. As discussed in *Milestone I,* the PSLRA was implemented to replace the outdated practice of selecting representative plaintiffs by a "race to the courthouse," with a selection system which focuses on the adequacy of the representative. Indeed, the selection system embodied in the PSLRA provisions is governed by a presumption which is rebuttable. Contrary to the argument of Schoengold and Cohen, Milstein, the identification of the most adequate plaintiff may necessitate, and the PSLRA provisions encourage, competing motions for lead plaintiff and counsel. Accordingly, granting the consensual motion of the lead plaintiff for co-lead counsel simply to deter competing motions in the future would be antithetical to the express policies of the PSLRA.

Abbey, Gardy appears able to singly undertake the responsibilities of lead counsel in this action. Schoengold and Cohen, Milstein, by contrast, rigidly advocate an inefficient litigation by committee approach, similar to that originally proposed by the lead plaintiff. Neither Schoengold nor Cohen, Milstein has demonstrated a willingness to individually assume all of the responsibilities associated with the sole lead counsel position. Consequently, in this case it appears Abbey, Gardy is a more suitable lead counsel selection.

It further appears Abbey, Gardy has sufficient resources and flexibility to effectively manage the litigation for the entire Plaintiff Class. * * *

While appointment of several firms as lead counsel may at times promote effective management of a class action, this is not such a case. * * *

Conclusion

For the foregoing reasons, the Abbey, Gardy Lead Counsel Application is granted.

NOTES AND QUESTIONS

1. What purpose would be served by appointing multiple lead counsel? Should the *Milestone* court have appointed multiple counsel in that case?

2. Consider *Raftery v. Mercury Finance Co.*, 1997 WL 529553, at *1–3 (N.D. Ill. 1997), in which the court appointed the Minnesota State Board of Investment ("MSBI") as lead plaintiff, but was concerned about MSBI's 33 1/3 percent contingency agreement with its lawyers:

> [T]he court suspects that the cap of 33 1/3 percent on MSBI's retainer agreement is not the result of hard bargaining. In any event, here, as elsewhere, the reasonable fee is the lowest fee that would be paid by a discerning client in an arms length negotiation with well-qualified counsel. And it is a familiar phenomenon in today's legal world that discerning clients make use of free market competitive principles (as in the familiar "beauty contest" among highly qualified law firms interested in the representation).
>
> * * *
>
> [One plaintiff's group opposed to competitive bidding] boldly assert[s] that competitive bidding to select lead counsel would "clearly be detrimental to the interests of the class." They argue that the best counsel are not likely the lowest paid counsel, a valid proposition, just as the best handbag is not the lowest priced one in the store. The list of lawyers who have filed appearances in these cases, however, leave the court little concern that an ample number of very able counsel are available and interested in the representation. Next the [same] group argues that the proposal would put undue pressure on counsel to "low ball" their bids in order to capture the appointment but to cut corners in ways that would adversely affect the result achieved. Although this argument has superficial appeal, illustrated by occasional newspaper stories on public works projects, both the lead plaintiff and the court are in a position to monitor the performance of counsel. Certainly attorneys who over the years have earned a reputation for excellence in this field are not likely to squander it in this situation. Counsel simply should not submit a proposal that is economically undesirable or unrealistic. The [same] group finally argue[s] that capping fees and expenses based on aggressive bids would give the defendants an unfair advantage, spurring them to engage in an expensive strategy that would overtax class counsel and burden the court with unnecessary motion practice. Again, this confuses the question of what is a reasonable fee with what is the best prediction of the most adequate plaintiff (and counsel). The court is in a position to adjust the fee at the end of the case should it appear that the agreed fee is no longer reasonable.
>
> * * *
>
> * * * [Accordingly, t]he court authorizes any plaintiff or group of plaintiffs who appeared on a single complaint that has been consolidated in this action, in conjunction with their counsel who filed that complaint on their behalf, to submit a proposal [to serve as lead counsel]. The proposal may be submitted under seal and must be prepared without consultation with other bidding counsel. The proposal must

contain a presentation of counsel's experience, knowledge, reputation, and ability to finance the litigation, as well as a proposal for fees and expenses. * * *

Id. at *1–3.

By contrast, in *In re Cendant Corp. Litig.*, 264 F.3d 201 (3d Cir. 2001), the Third Circuit concluded that plaintiff-counsel auctions are inconsistent with the language of the PSLRA under most circumstances:

> The statutory section most directly on point provides that "[t]he most adequate plaintiff shall, subject to the approval of the court, select and retain counsel to represent the class." 15 U.S.C. § 78u–4(a)(3)(B)(v). This language makes two things clear. First, the lead plaintiffs right to select and retain counsel is not absolute—the court retains the power and the duty to supervise counsel selection and counsel retention. But second, and just as importantly, the power to "select and retain" lead counsel belongs, at least in the first instance, to the lead plaintiff, and the court's role is confined to deciding whether to "approv[e]" that choice. Because a court-ordered auction involves the court rather than the lead plaintiff choosing lead counsel and determining the financial terms of its retention, this latter determination strongly implies that an auction is not generally permissible in a Reform Act case, at least as a matter of first resort.
>
> This conclusion gains support when we examine the overall structure of the PSLRA's lead plaintiff section. The Reform Act contains detailed procedures for choosing the lead plaintiff, indicating that congress attached great importance to ensuring that the right person or group is selected. * * *
>
> Adding support to our view that auctions are not generally permitted is the fact that the Reform Act's lead plaintiff provisions were clearly modeled after the Weiss and Beckerman proposal [Elliott J. Weiss and John S. Beckerman, *Let the Money Do the Monitoring: How Institutional Investors Can Reduce Agency Costs in Securities Class Actions*, 104 Yale L.J. 2053 (1995)]. * * * The entire thrust of Weiss and Beckerman's argument was that large investors would do a better job at counsel selection, retention, and monitoring than judges have traditionally done * * * This goal would be significantly undermined were we to interpret the Reform Act as permitting courts to take decisions involving counsel selection and retention away from the lead plaintiff by ordering an auction.
>
> Lastly, our belief that the PSLRA does not allow an auction in the ordinary case is well supported in the Reform Act's legislative history. Both the Conference Committee Report and the Senate Report state that the purpose of the legislation was to encourage institutional investors to serve as lead plaintiff, predicting that their involvement would significantly benefit absent class members. Both Reports * * * confirm[] that the court's role is generally limited to "approv[ing] or disapprov[ing] lead plaintiffs choice of counsel"; and that it is not the court's responsibility to make that choice itself. [In addition, both reports] indicate[] that the court should generally employ a deferential standard in reviewing the lead plaintiffs' choices.

Id. at 273–77. *See also In re Cavanaugh*, 306 F.3d 726, 734 n.14 (9th Cir. 2002) (rejecting auction approach and adopting *In re Cendant* analysis). Should courts adopt auction procedures, like those utilized in the *Raftery* case, in securities fraud class actions? Or is *In re Cendant* correct that such a procedure would be inconsistent with the Reform Act?

3. Consider the language in Rule 23(g)(1): "Unless a statute provides otherwise, a court that certifies a class must appoint class counsel." The Committee Notes explicitly recognize the Reform Act as the primary statute contemplated by this prefatory language in 23(g)(1), pointing out that the Reform Act "contain[s] directives that bear on selection of a lead plaintiff and the retention of counsel." What is the relationship between 23(g)(1) and the Reform Act?

b. Removal of Securities Fraud Cases to Federal Court

In late 1998, Congress passed the Securities Litigation Uniform Standards Act of 1998, Pub. L. No. 105–353, 112 Stat. 3227 ("SLUSA"). That law is designed to prevent plaintiffs from avoiding the rigors of the Reform Act by bringing securities fraud suits in state court. As with the Reform Act, the merits of SLUSA were subject to debate. *Compare, e.g.*, Kenneth J. Blackwell, *Securities Loophole in Need of Repair*, Wash.Times, Aug. 25, 1997, at A13, *with* Richard W. Painter, *Responding to a False Alarm: Federal Preemption of State Securities Fraud Causes of Action*, 84 Cornell L. Rev. 1 (1998).

SLUSA amended the 1933 Act to provide as follows:

(b) Class action limitations

No covered class action based upon the statutory or common law of any State or subdivision thereof may be maintained in any State or Federal court by any private party alleging—

(1) an untrue statement or omission of a material fact in connection with the purchase or sale of a covered security; or

(2) that the defendant used or employed any manipulative or deceptive device or contrivance in connection with the purchase or sale of a covered security.

(c) Removal of covered class actions

Any covered class action brought in any State court involving a covered security, as set forth in subsection (b), shall be removable to the Federal district court for the district in which the action is pending, and shall be subject to subsection (b).

15 U.S.C. § 77p(b)–(c). Congress passed an identical amendment to the 1934 Act. *See id.* § 78bb(f)(1)–(2).

SLUSA defines a "covered class action" as

any single lawsuit in which * * * damages are sought on behalf of more than 50 persons or prospective class members, and questions of law or fact common to those persons or members of the prospective class, without reference to issues of individualized reliance on an alleged misstatement or omission, predominate over any questions affecting only individual persons or members.

15 U.S.C. §§ 77p(f)(2)(A)(i)(I), 78bb(f)(5)(B)(i)(I).

The Supreme Court, in *Merrill Lynch, Pierce, Fenner & Smith, Inc., v. Dabit*, 547 U.S. 71 (2006), resolved a split among the circuits over the scope of SLUSA. In *Blue Chip Stamps v. Manor Drug Stores*, 421 U.S. 723, 731–36 (1975), the Supreme Court had held that only those who purchased or sold securities had standing to bring a private cause of action for damages under section 10(b) and Rule 10b–5. Consequently, the appellate courts were divided over whether a class action involving solely the retention, as opposed to the sale or purchase, of securities was cognizable under 10(b), and therefore, preempted by SLUSA. *Dabit* resolved this dispute, concluding:

> * * * For purposes of SLUSA preemption, * * * the identity of the plaintiffs does not determine whether the complaint alleges fraud "in connection with the purchase or sale" of securities. The misconduct of which respondent complains here—fraudulent manipulation of stock prices—unquestionably qualifies as fraud "in connection with the purchase or sale" of securities * * *.

547 U.S. at 89. Based on SLUSA's background, text, and purpose, the Court concluded that SLUSA's preemptive scope was sufficiently broad to encompass Dabit's state-law class claims that Merrill Lynch used "misrepresentations and manipulative tactics," *id.* at 76, to cause him and other brokers and clients to hold onto their overvalued securities. Among other grounds, the Court reasoned:

> The presumption that Congress envisioned a broad construction follows not only from ordinary principles of statutory construction but also from the particular concerns that culminated in SLUSA's enactment. A narrow reading of the statute would undercut the effectiveness of the 1995 Reform Act and thus run contrary to SLUSA's stated purpose, *viz.*, "to prevent certain State private securities class action lawsuits alleging fraud from being used to frustrate the objectives" of the 1995 Act. * * *

Id. at 72.

NOTES AND QUESTIONS

1. The issue raised in *Dabit* was not the only divisive one under SLUSA. In *Kircher v. Putnam Funds Trust*, 547 U.S. 633 (2006), mutual fund investors had brought separate putative class actions against several defendants in state court—alleging that defendants caused them injury by devaluing their holdings, in violation of state law. 547 U.S. at 637. The defendants removed the actions to federal court under SLUSA. *Id.* The district court remanded the actions to state court on the grounds that the federal court lacked subject matter jurisdiction—concluding that SLUSA did not preclude the investors' claims because they were injured as "holders" and not purchasers or sellers of mutual fund shares. *Id.* at 637–38. The Seventh Circuit held that the district court's remand order was substantive and therefore, reviewable, despite Section 1447(d)'s language. *Id.* at 637–39. The Supreme Court disagreed on the issue of reviewability. *Id.* at 639. Although the *Kircher* Court did not rule that a court of appeals could never look past the label placed on a ruling by the district court, where, as in *Kircher*, the ruling was based on a district court finding that it lacked jurisdiction, the remand order was unreviewable. *Id.* at 640–43.

2. Should actions like *Dabit* be subject to removal to federal court and dismissal? Why or why not?

3. As noted above, SLUSA permits removal of state securities-related actions to federal court and preemption of state law claims where certain criteria are met. 15 U.S.C. § 77p(b)–(c); 15 U.S.C. § 78bb(f)(1)–(2). SLUSA was enacted to prohibit plaintiffs from escaping the Reform Act's more demanding criteria by litigating in state court. *See Anderson v. Merrill Lynch Pierce Fenner & Smith*, 521 F.3d 1278, 1285–88 (10th Cir. 2008) (discussing SLUSA preemption standard and holding state-law class action claims do not have to be virtually identical to those made under Rule 10b–5 to be precluded by SLUSA); *Segal v. Fifth Third Bank, N.A.*, 581 F.3d 305, 310–11 (6th Cir. 2009) (explaining that substance of complaint's allegations determines application of SLUSA, rather than absence of "magic words" or presence of disclaimer).

In 2014, the Supreme Court decided another case involving the scope of SLUSA's preclusion of state law. At issue in *Chadbourne & Parke LLP v. Troice*, 134 S. Ct. 1058 (2014), was § 78bb(f)(1)(A) of SLUSA, which provides that "[n]o covered class action based upon the statutory or common law of any State or subdivision thereof may be maintained in any State or Federal court by any private party alleging a misrepresentation or omission of a material fact in connection with the purchase or sale of a covered security." In the consolidated cases before the Court, plaintiffs alleged "(1) that they 'purchase[d]' *uncovered* securities (certificates of deposit that are *not* traded on any national exchange), but (2) that the defendants falsely told the victims that the *uncovered* securities were backed by *covered* securities." 134 S. Ct. at 1062. "Under these circumstances," the Court concluded that SLUSA did not preclude the state law actions from going forward. *Id.* The Court focused on the statutory phrase "in connection with the purchase or sale of a covered security," finding that the statute applied only to "misrepresentations that are material to the purchase or sale of a covered security." *Id.* at 1066. The Court explained: "A fraudulent misrepresentation or omission is not made 'in connection with' such a 'purchase or sale of a covered security' unless it is material to a decision by one or more individuals (other than the fraudster) to buy or to sell a 'covered security.'" *Id.*

Later in 2014, the First Circuit explored the contours of *Troice*. In *Hidalgo-Velez v. San Juan Asset Management*, 758 F.3d 98 (1st Cir. 2014), the controversy centered around a fund that promised (in its prospectus) to invest assets according to the following allocation: 75% of assets in "investment grade corporate bond indices" with "no more than 25% of its assets in securities issued by a single issuer." *Id.* at 102. The investment plan included both *covered* and *uncovered* securities (the latter consisting of certificates of deposit that were *not* traded on any national exchange). Subsequently, the fund invested more than 75% of its assets in *uncovered* securities sold by a single issuer. After the subprime mortgage collapse in 2008, investors filed a putative class action in Puerto Rico state court alleging noncompliance with promised investment policies, in violation of Puerto Rican law. The defendants removed the action to federal court under SLUSA and then moved to dismiss the claim based on SLUSA preclusion. The court held that "*Troice* teaches that a misrepresentation in connection with the purchase of an uncovered security, by itself, is insufficient to bring a claim within the SLUSA's grasp," and therefore "the link between the alleged misrepresentations and the covered securities [was] * * * too attenuated to bring the complaint within the maw of the SLUSA." *Id.* at 107–08. Here, the particular shares held by plaintiffs were not covered securities, and thus the investment at issue was not "in connection with" covered securities as was required to invoke SLUSA. The court stated, however, that SLUSA *could* preclude a claim involving the purchase of *uncovered* securities if there was "an intent [by the plaintiff] to take an ownership interest in covered securities." *Id.* at 108. Under *Hidalgo-Velez*, are courts now charged with the difficult task of interpreting the ownership intentions of *plaintiffs* rather than the misrepresentations of the defendant? *See* Holly Ovington, *IV, SLUSA Preclusion of State Law Investor Class Actions*, 34 Rev. Banking & Fin. L. 36 (2014) (discussing the future implications of *Troice* on SLUSA's preclusion provisions in light of *Hidalgo-Velez*).

4. A circuit split has arisen over the interplay of Section 22(a) of the 1933 Act and the Class Action Fairness Act ("CAFA"). *See generally* Chapter 7(B)(3)(d). On the one hand, Section 22(a) restricts the removal of securities cases. In particular, Section 22(a) provides, "Except as provided in section 77p(c) of this title, no case arising under this subchapter and brought in any State court of competent jurisdiction shall be removed to any court of the United States." 15 U.S.C. § 77v(a). Section 77p(c) was added by SLUSA, and describes those exceptions where securities class actions may be removed (*i.e.*, those "covered class actions"). 15 U.S.C. § 77p(c). On the other hand, CAFA permits removal for all civil actions that satisfy 28 U.S.C. § 1453(b) (*i.e.*, at least 100 class members, over $5 million in controversy, minimal diversity), subject to the exceptions set forth in 28 U.S.C. § 1339(d) & § 1453(d), for certain securities class actions. *See* Chapter 7(B)(3)(b). The question that has arisen is whether a securities action involving a non-SLUSA "covered class action" may nevertheless be removed if it meets the requirements for CAFA removal.

The Seventh Circuit, in *Katz v. Gerardi*, 552 F.3d 558 (7th Cir. 2009), concluded that Section 22(a), as the older statute, must yield and held that securities class actions covered by CAFA are removable, subject to CAFA's exceptions. *Id.* at 561–62. To read Section 22(a) otherwise would make most of CAFA's Section 1453(d) "pointless." *Id.* at 562. By contrast, the Ninth Circuit, in *Luther v. Countrywide Home Loans Servicing L.P.*, 533 F.3d 1031 (9th Cir. 2008), held that although Section 22(a) is older, it should control because it is more specific (*i.e.*, it covers securities cases only, rather than all civil actions). *Id.* at 1032, 1034 (holding that CAFA "does not supersede Section 22(a)'s *specific* bar against removal of cases arising the under § 33 Act"). Which construction of the removal statutes should be adopted—the Seventh Circuit's or the Ninth Circuit's?

PROBLEM

Using the Reform Act as a model, draft criteria for "lead plaintiffs" that could be used in mass tort class actions. Perform a similar task for employment discrimination cases.

Chapter 11

Defendant Class Actions, Derivative Suits, and Suits Involving Unincorporated Associations

■ ■ ■

The traditional model of a class action is a suit by a class of plaintiffs against one or more individual defendants. This chapter discusses three types of class suits that do not fit strictly within the traditional model: defendant class actions, shareholder derivative suits, and suits involving unincorporated associations. These topics are not only important in their own right, but also yield important insights into traditional class actions and other forms of aggregate litigation.

A. DEFENDANT CLASS ACTIONS

Rule 23, by its terms, permits suits *against* a class as well as *by* a class. *See* Fed. R. Civ. P. 23(a) ("One or more members of a class may sue *or be sued* as representative parties * * *." (emphasis added)). In fact, the concept of a defendant class long pre-dates modern Rule 23. Even a century and a half ago, the Supreme Court acknowledged the defendant class action's settled place in class action jurisprudence:

> The rule is *well established*, that where the parties interested are numerous, and the suit is for an object common to them all, some of the body may maintain a bill on behalf of themselves and of the others; and *a bill may also be maintained against a portion of a numerous body of defendants, representing a common interest.*

Smith v. Swormstedt, 57 U.S. (16 How.) 288, 302 (1853) (emphasis added).

Rule 23, however, provides no specific guidance concerning the application of class action procedures to defendant classes. This has caused some commentators to complain that, "because the prerequisites and requirements of [R]ule 23 do not always apply to defendant class actions, courts are forced to fit potential defendant class actions into an inappropriate and awkward framework." Comment, *Defendant Class Actions: The Failure of Rule 23 and a Proposed Solution*, 38 UCLA L. Rev. 223, 224 (1990).

This section examines how courts have applied class action concepts to defendant classes. As discussed below, the problems are difficult, and courts and commentators have not been consistent in how they have approached the issues.

1. OVERVIEW OF RULE 23 CONSIDERATIONS

THILLENS, INC. v. CMTY. CURRENCY EXCH. ASS'N
United States District Court, Northern District of Illinois, 1983.
97 F.R.D. 668.

HART, DISTRICT JUDGE.

Plaintiff Thillens, Inc. ("Thillens") filed this action in 1981 against the Community Currency Exchange Association of Illinois ("Association"), former and current members of the Association ("individual defendants") and the community currency exchanges owned by those members ("exchange defendants"). Also named are three former Illinois officials ("public defendants"). Thillens alleges that over the past twenty-three years the Association and the individual defendants conspired with the public defendants to restrain Thillens' trade as an ambulatory currency exchange, in violation of federal and state antitrust laws, 42 U.S.C. § 1983, and 18 U.S.C. § 1961 ("RICO"). Also included are various pendent claims. Thillens seeks compensatory and punitive damages, injunctive relief and attorneys' fees.

Thillens is an Illinois corporation, licensed as an "ambulatory currency exchange" providing "mobile check cashing services" within the greater Chicago metropolitan area. ["Currency exchanges" are entities that perform check-cashing and other services for a fee. An "ambulatory currency exchange" is mobile, and therefore can, for example, operate at a factory gate on payday. "Community currency exchanges" (*see* below), by contrast, operate from a single fixed location (*e.g.*, a building).] Thillens claims to be the only ambulatory currency exchange operating in the Chicago area and perhaps in all of Illinois. Thillens has never belonged to the Association. The Association is an Illinois not-for-profit corporation serving as the trade association for approximately 300 persons who own or control at least 500 "community currency exchanges" in Illinois. Most Chicago area community currency exchanges allegedly belong to the Association. All currency exchanges are required to be licensed by the Illinois Department of Financial Institutions ("DFI").

The gist of Thillens' complaint is that the alleged conspiracy caused the DFI since 1958 to (1) deny Thillens 400 license applications to operate ambulatory currency exchanges in the relevant markets; (2) deprive Thillens of fair hearings to protest the denial of the licenses sought by Thillens; and (3) promulgate unreasonable rules and regulations substantially to Thillens' detriment.

* * * This Opinion and Order considers only Thillens' motion for certification of a defendant class. The proposed class includes 17 named individual defendants, approximately 350 unnamed individual past and current members of the Association and the more than 500 community currency exchanges owned by those members and represented by the Association. Neither the Association nor the public defendants is named as a class member. Thillens, however, nominates the Association as class representative.

Thillens argues that the class proposed is highly cohesive. In its view, the Association is the logical choice for class representative, precisely because it is the self-selected industry representative of the individual and exchange defendants. Thillens also claims that the Association is financially able to perform representational duties. Finally, Thillens notes that at least 95 individual defendants are represented by the law firm which represents the Association and 16 named defendants.

Thillens also supports its motion for certification of a defendant class by arguing that no unfairness would result: Supposedly each proposed defendant member paid dues to the Association during the relevant period. All of the defendants in the proposed class are alleged to have knowingly participated or acquiesced in the conspiracy and political bribery fund. In light of what Thillens characterizes as virtually identical behaviors, giving rise to identical defenses, Thillens claims that certification will result in substantial savings of judicial and personal resources, without significant sacrifice by class members.

The Association and various individual defendants oppose the motion for certification of a defendant class. They argue that defendant classes are uncommon, especially in antitrust actions. Their primary objection is that certification would be inconsistent with each defendant's due process rights. The defendants also claim that the Association would be an inadequate representative of the class' interests because it formerly pled guilty to mail fraud and acknowledged the existence of a political bribery fund, acts which Thillens seeks to prove in this action. According to the Association, it would be collaterally estopped from denying those acts, to the detriment of the class members.

For the reasons stated below, Thillens' motion for certification of a defendant class is granted. The class is certified under Fed. R. Civ. P. 23(b)(3). Each member of the class must be notified personally of its status as a class member consistent with the requirements of Fed. R. Civ. P. 23(c)(2). In the event that liability is determined in Thillens' favor, each member of the class who has not opted out may attempt to prove its nonparticipation in any conspiracy or nonperformance of any unlawful act. Furthermore, each member of the class may be represented by the counsel of its choice.

DISCUSSION

A. A Defendant Class May Be Certified if Due Process is Satisfied

As a preliminary matter, the Court considers whether and under what conditions a defendant class may be certified. Rule 23 of the Federal Rules of Civil Procedure clearly contemplates both plaintiff *and* defendant class actions. For example, its very first clause provides "[o]ne or more members of a class may sue *or be sued* as representative parties on behalf of all." That Rule 23 was designed to permit both plaintiff classes and defendant classes is underscored by the appearance in the Rule of phrases such as "the claims *or defenses* of the representative parties," Fed. R. Civ. P. 23(a)(3), and "the prosecution of separate action by *or against* individual members of the class." Fed. R. Civ. P. 23(b)(1). Unquestionably, a defendant class *may* be certified.

The analysis of *when* a defendant class will be certified is more complicated than the consideration of *if* such certification is ever possible. Regardless of whether a plaintiff or defendant class is certified, the class action device yields substantial economic and practical savings. Many parties may be brought before the court in a single suit. Each class member will be bound by the ultimate decision. Furthermore, a class action expands, by collateral estoppel effect, the scope of the decision by binding parties not before the court in the class action. Thus, the need to relitigate the same questions in multiple suits, at the risk of inconsistent judgments, is avoided.

Simultaneously, the binding nature of the class action poses a dilemma. Fundamental fairness to absentee members must be balanced against judicial savings. Where representative adjudication occurs pursuant to a defendant class, due process concerns not inherent in plaintiff class actions arise. The crux of the distinction is: the unnamed plaintiff stands to gain while the unnamed defendant stands to lose.

It is the hallmark of our system of justice that personal rights cannot be compromised without due process. If, however, a binding judgment depended on the assertion of *in personam* jurisdiction over each member of a class, the action's economies would be dissipated. The Supreme Court has resolved the apparent tension by holding that due process is satisfied and absent members of a class are bound so long as the interests of the absentees are adequately represented. *Hansberry v. Lee*, 311 U.S. 32, 42 (1940) (plaintiff class); *Sam Fox Publ'g Co. v. United States*, 366 U.S. 683, 691 (1961) (defendant class).

Arguably, therefore, a finding that a defendant class is adequately represented should resolve the due process dilemma which attaches to certification of a defendant class. Nonetheless the concern lingers. Defendant classes seldom are certified. If at all, such certification most commonly occurs (1) in patent infringement cases; (2) in suits against local public officials challenging the validity of state laws; or (3) in securities litigation. Attempts to certify defendant classes in antitrust actions generally are unsuccessful.

* * *

Several rules * * * emerge from * * * [the] cases: (1) A defendant class will not be certified unless each named plaintiff has a colorable claim against each defendant class member; (2) A defendant class will not be certified under Fed. R. Civ. P. 23(b)(3) without a clear showing that common questions do *in fact* predominate over individual issues; (3) The requirement that each named plaintiff must have a claim against each defendant may be waived where the defendant members are related by a conspiracy or "juridical link."

A "juridical link" is some legal relationship which relates all defendants in a way such that single resolution of the dispute is preferred to a multiplicity of similar actions. * * *

* * * [T]his action is not a bilateral class action. Rather, a single plaintiff, Thillens, alleges that it has been injured by each member of the proposed defendant class. Instead of being an amorphous entity, the proposed defendant class of currency exchanges and their individual owners is highly cohesive and self-organized. It is juridically linked at least by allegations that each defendant class member voluntarily joined a conspiracy to harm Thillens. Additionally, this Court has subject matter jurisdiction over the claims made.

There are no theoretical roadblocks to certification of this defendant class antitrust action so long as due process safeguards are imposed. However, the proposed class still must be tested by the provisions of Fed. R. Civ. P. 23(a) and (b).

B. The Defendant Class Proposed Meets the Requirements of Fed. R. Civ. P. 23(a)

* * *

[The court found that numerosity, commonality, and typicality were satisfied.]

4. The Association is an Adequate Representative

Because of the serious due process problems which attend the certification of a defendant class, the 23(a)(4) mandate for an adequate representative must be strictly observed. The test of adequacy of representation * * * is two-pronged: (1) the representative must be able to conduct the litigation and (2) the representative's interests must not be antagonistic to those of the class members. * * * [T]here is the further requirement that the class representative must have injured the plaintiff in the same way as other defendants have injured him.

The Association allegedly has injured Thillens in precisely the same way as did every individual defendant, exchange defendant, and public defendant. All defendants allegedly conspired to ruin Thillens' ambulatory currency exchange business, maintained a secret bribery fund for that purpose and engaged in antitrust and common law violations to Thillens' detriment.

Nonetheless, the Association is an unwilling class representative. That fact alone should not deter a court from naming it as representative, however. * * * If the sheer volume of the briefs which have been filed by the Association (and Thillens) in this case are any indication, adversary presentation of all issues by the Association is guaranteed.

The real concern with a reluctant representative should be for his ability to carry the expense and other practical burdens of a class defense. * * *

Here, no serious suggestion can be raised that the Association either is financially unable or without requisite skills to act as the class representative. In fact, the Association does not argue the point. Presumably, the Association is fiscally sound. It owns a bank and at least one currency exchange. No individual defendant could better afford the role of class representative. Furthermore, the Association through its attorneys, has considerable litigation experience. It has sued to protect the rights of the Association in matters of common interest to its members. The lawyers currently representing the Association represented the Association and certain individual defendants in the criminal action which prompted Thillens to bring this suit.

Moreover, the Association's directors coincidentally are defendant class members. They have a clear channel of communication from the defendant class to the proposed representative. No doubt the director/defendants will consult on trial strategy and concerns of class members with the Association. Furthermore, the defendant class members fund the Association and, therefore, to some extent control it.

Finally, the Association is the self-selected representative of the member defendants. Each named and unnamed class member allegedly has voluntarily joined the Association seeking to have its business interests represented by the Association. The defendant members pay dues for the very purpose of having the Association represent their interests.

* * *

The second prong of 23(a)(4) also is met. The Association's interests are not antagonistic to the interests of the members of the class. Certification of a class on the grounds of antagonism should be denied only if that antagonism goes to the subject matter of the litigation.

The main subject matter in this case is antitrust. All parties, the representative, defendant class members and public defendants are expected to try to avoid liability by disclaiming an antitrust conspiracy. Arguably, the Association will not passively raise that defense. In defending itself vigorously, the Association necessarily will raise all defenses of the class members except for individual members' claims of nonparticipation in the conspiracy. In fact, this Association has an added incentive to vigorously defend the interests of the members. The Association's by-laws provide that it will indemnify, on request, Association members who are found liable for actions arising out of membership in the Association. Clearly, the interests of the Association are not antagonistic to the interests of the class members.

Nonetheless, the Association raises a troublesome point in opposition to its adequacy. The Association claims that it cannot adequately represent the members of the class since it has pled guilty to several counts of mail fraud and has admitted the existence of a political bribery fund. The argument runs that defendant class members would be prejudiced because the Association will be collaterally estopped from denying those actions.

In the offensive use of collateral estoppel, a plaintiff seeks to prevent a defendant from relitigating an issue which the defendant unsuccessfully litigated in an action with another party. In order to give collateral estoppel effect in a civil proceeding to matters decided in a criminal adjudication, the matter must have actually been decided or have been necessary to the resolution of the matter decided in the prior proceedings. * * *

Unlike *res judicata*, collateral estoppel does not apply to matters which *could have been* litigated. If there is a reasonable doubt as to what was decided in a prior judgment, that doubt should be resolved against using collateral estoppel unless the issue clearly appears on the face of the former complaint.

The Association entered a guilty plea on May 20, 1980 in which it admitted keeping and using a secret cash fund for making political contributions to Illinois public officials. The purpose of the "bribes" was to influence actions affecting the currency exchange industry and its members. The Association also pled guilty to five counts of mail fraud in furtherance of that scheme. The Court supposes, without deciding, that the Association will be collaterally estopped from denying the existence of the fund. * * *

The Association's forced admission in this action of political bribery and mail fraud, however, would not result in an automatic finding of a conspiracy in violation of the antitrust laws. Nor would such admissions necessarily indicate that Thillens was the target of the conspiracy. At a minimum, Thillens still must prove the existence of a conspiracy, its focus on Thillens and an anticompetitive effect of the conspiracy in the relevant markets. Undoubtedly the Association intends to vehemently oppose Thillens' effort to establish the antitrust claims or any of the other claims it raises in this case. Based on the history of the relationship between the parties thus far, the Court is sure that the Association's defense will be rigorous and spirited. All members of the defendant class proposed will be adequately represented by the Association regardless of any collateral estoppel effect which might be imposed to coerce admissions against the Association's interest. The due process rights of the defendant class members will not be offended by naming the Association as class representative. All the requirements of 23(a), therefore, are satisfied.

C. The Defendant Class Proposed Meets the Requirements of Fed. R. Civ. P. 23(b)(3)

A class action which meets the terms of 23(a) also must qualify under any *one* of the subsections of Rule 23(b). This proposed defendant class will be certified under Rule 23(b)(3). * * *

Most antitrust class actions are certified under 23(b)(3). However, the Court must not perfunctorily find predominance, for only where predominance exists will the economic utility of the class action device be realized. * * *

As noted throughout, the primary common issue is to prove the existence of a conspiracy against Thillens in violation of antitrust laws. Clearly that issue will predominate the litigation. In fact, all the issues common to establishing antitrust violations are overriding. The only noncommon issue will be the individual members' defenses of non-participation. Given the complexity of the antitrust matters, the individual defenses will occupy only a minor portion of the trial time.

Rule 23(b)(3) also requires a finding that a class action is superior to other available methods of adjudication. For Thillens, a class action is [the] superior [way], if not the only way, by which all its claims can be litigated. The cost of individual service and suits would be high if not prohibitive. If forced to separately litigate, Thillens likely would forego actions against numerous defendant class members.

From the defendants' perspective, the class action also is superior to other forms of dispute resolution. No individual defendant will have to carry the whole cost of this litigation. Although dues to the Association might increase as the suit progresses, any one defendant's proportionate share would be far smaller than his cost for a separate action. Individual class members would not be expected to take time from their business or personal pursuits to continuously appear at what no doubt will be a lengthy trial.

Furthermore, because their Association is the representative, class members will not relinquish total control over the management of the case. Since some class members serve as Association directors they undoubtedly will advise the Association in this matter. Presumably, even nondirector class members are in contact with the Association and can assist with and be apprised of the Association's defense through membership meetings, elections and newsletters. In the event that some members desire additional counsel, they will be permitted to seek such assistance.

Finally, this class action is especially superior from a judicial standpoint [because numerous individual actions might otherwise be filed in this court]. Precisely because most defendants are local, this Court does not contemplate any serious problems in the management of the action. In sum, absent voluntary agreement to arbitrate their differences or to settle, the class action is the superior method by which to adjudicate Thillens' claims.

Although this defendant class meets all the relevant requirements of 23(b)(3) and most defendant classes are certified under 23(b)(3), certification of a defendant class thereunder is questionable. Sometimes called the "exclusionary section," Fed. R. Civ. P. 23(c)(2)(A) [now 23(c)(2)(B)] expressly permits any defendant in a class certified under 23(b)(3) to opt-out of the class if he does so by a specific date. Thus, the risk in certifying a defendant class under 23(b)(3) is that all or many class members will "jump ship." The risk is minimized, however, because opting-out defendants are at risk of "losing" the effect of a favorable decision in the event that this action is determined against Thillens. Opting-out defendants also may have to underwrite much of the cost of a separate litigation should Thillens decide to sue them individually. Those risks may be sufficient incentive to cause most defendants to stay in the class action.

Despite the exclusionary limitation, 23(b)(3) certification is the best way to address the serious due process concerns which pervade the prosecution of a defendant class. All class members will be given notice of Thillens' intent to include them in the class and of their right to opt-out. Each defendant who elects to remain may seek individual counsel. Any defendant class member who does not timely quit the class cannot, therefore, argue in good faith that certification of the class was a violation of its due process rights.

* * *

IT IS THEREFORE ORDERED that

* * * A defendant class will be certified under Fed. R. Civ. P. 23(b)(3) to consist of: 17 named individual defendants, approximately 350 unnamed individual past and current members of the Community Currency Exchange Association of Illinois, Inc., and the more than 500 community currency exchanges owned by those members and represented by the Association.

* * *

NOTES AND QUESTIONS

1. The *Thillens* court noted that defendant classes have been most commonly certified in patent infringement cases, suits against local government officials challenging the validity of state laws, and securities suits. *Accord, e.g.*, *In re Gap Stores Sec. Litig.*, 79 F.R.D. 283, 292–93 (N.D. Cal. 1978) (collecting examples of certified defendant classes). One commentator explained why patent suits have been particularly suited for defendant class actions:

> The holder of patent rights may learn that a number of manufacturers are employing a production device like the one he has patented. Absent the availability of a defendant class action, he would, under current principles of collateral estoppel, have to establish his claims against each manufacturer individually. Given the considerable expense entailed by an action alleging patent infringement, a suit against the class of infringers will save significant resources and assure consistent determinations of the patent's validity and scope by allowing those issues to be decided in a single proceeding. Further, vindication of the patentee's rights will be even more complete, as the class action allows him to include any infringers whose liability is too small to merit an individual suit.

Note, *Defendant Class Actions*, 91 Harv. L. Rev. 630, 631–32 (1978). Can analogous reasons be identified that explain why suits against local officials and suits involving securities may be well-suited for treatment as defendant classes? As this edition went to print, new legislation was enacted that aims to limit joinder of defendants in actions involving patent infringement. *See* Leahy–Smith America Invents Act, H.R. 1249, 112th Cong., 1st Sess., § 19.

2. The *Thillens* court also noted that antitrust suits generally have not been found suitable for certification as defendant class actions. Does the *Thillens* court's analysis of Rule 23 shed any light on why this may be so? In addition to the examples cited in *Thillens*, do any other kinds of cases come to mind that are either particularly well-suited or particularly ill-suited for defendant class actions?

3. The *Thillens* court noted that defendant classes are "seldom" certified. Other courts have noted that "a heightened burden" is imposed on parties seeking certification of a defendant class. *See Columbia Health Serv., Inc. v. Columbia/HCA Healthcare Corp.*, 1996 WL 812934, at *5 (W.D. Tex. 1996). Should courts be reluctant to certify defendant classes?

4. The *Thillens* court noted that the Community Currency Exchange Association (the "Association") was "an unwilling class representative," but concluded that "[t]hat fact alone should not deter a court from naming [the Association] as a representative." *See Thillens* excerpt, *supra*. Is that reasoning correct? Does the same reasoning apply to class representatives of plaintiff classes? If not, why are defendant-class representatives different?

5. In reviewing the adequacy of the Association as a representative, the *Thillens* court explained that the Association had previously "pled guilty to several counts of mail fraud and ha[d] admitted the existence of a political bribery fund." *See Thillens* excerpt, *supra*. Given the issues involved in the case, was the court correct in finding that the Association could still be a proper class representative?

6. Was the *Thillens* court correct that the risk of opt-outs was not serious? Would that be true of Rule 23(b)(3) defendant classes generally, or only under the particular circumstances in *Thillens*?

7. *Thillens* indicates that a plaintiff need not allege injury by every defendant in the class, provided that there is a "juridical link" or "conspiracy" alleged between the defendants. Although the concept of a conspiracy is well known, the notion of a "juridical link" is more obscure. One court has explained that "a 'juridical link' refers to some type of legal relationship which relates all defendants in a way that would make a single resolution of a dispute preferable to a multiplicity of similar actions." *In re Itel Sec. Litig.*, 89 F.R.D. 104, 121

(N.D. Cal. 1981). Another court has stated that a "juridical link" exists when the "plaintiff class as a whole has been [the] victim of a unified governmental policy carried out by the individual defendants." *Akerman v. Oryx Commc'ns, Inc.*, 609 F. Supp. 363, 376 (S.D.N.Y. 1984), *aff'd in part and appeal dismissed in part*, 810 F.2d 336 (2d Cir. 1987). The notion of a juridical link "frequently arises in civil rights suits, in which the plaintiff alleges that a category of defendants, such as all sheriffs, have violated some constitutional right." Comment, *Mandatory Notice and Defendant Class Actions: Resolving the Paradox of Identity Between Plaintiffs and Defendants*, 40 Emory L.J. 611, 656 n.190 (1991) ("Emory Comment"). It also arises in securities defendant class actions involving an alleged common course of conduct by underwriters. *See id.* at 656 n.191. *See generally* William D. Henderson, *Reconciling the Juridical Links Doctrine with the Federal Rules of Civil Procedure and Article III*, 67 U. Chi. L. Rev. 1347 (2000) (in-depth analysis of the "juridical link" doctrine in defendant class actions).

8. One commentator has described the benefits of a defendant class action as follows:

> The main impetus behind defendant class certification is the extremely attractive notion of expanded preclusion, which is magnified in these cases. * * * The benefits of *res judicata* and collateral estoppel occur in two key forms in the defendant class action context. First, an aggrieved plaintiff who has been harmed by numerous defendants may achieve "complete relief" by suing the defendants as a class, rather than by suing them individually.
>
> * * *
>
> Another important benefit to the plaintiff inherent in defendant class actions is litigative economy and efficiency. * * * By effecting certification of a defendant class, the plaintiff saves the time and cost of drafting and filing separate complaints, pleadings, and motions, and of trying separate cases, perhaps in different fora. Furthermore, the court is relieved from committing the time necessary to process and hear each of the cases individually.
>
> [Another] advantage gained in a defendant class action is that it circumvents many requirements of traditional litigation. First, it is generally accepted that a court does not need personal jurisdiction over each class member to certify a defendant class and bind absent members to the class judgment. Rather, only the named representative must possess sufficient minimum contacts with the chosen forum for the suit to proceed in that forum. Second, the plaintiff must only establish that the court possesses subject matter jurisdiction over the named representative. Third, the venue statutes need only be satisfied with respect to the named representative because the harm against which the venue rules purport to guard, namely, unfairness in travelling to a particular forum to defend a claim *pro se*, does not exist for the individual class members who need not attend the adjudication. Finally, a plaintiff choosing to bring a defendant class action does not have to worry about the joinder rules and any problems resulting from improper joinder of parties. These four exemptions are necessary because, absent each exemption, the underlying requirement has the potential to defeat the use of defendant classes. The benefits these exemptions yield, however, favor only the plaintiff.

Emory Comment, *supra*, 40 Emory L.J. at 616, 618–20.

The benefits identified in the Emory Comment can be considerable from the standpoint of plaintiffs. What about from the perspective of defendants? Do any of these asserted benefits raise fairness or due process concerns from the standpoint of the defendant class? The *Thillens* court indicated that personal jurisdiction need not be obtained over individual defendant class members. *See Thillens* excerpt, *supra*. Consider the view of one commentator that the circumvention of personal jurisdiction requirements is unfair to defendant class members:

> On the surface, the commonly stated policies of personal jurisdiction appear to be served if a court in a defendant class action obtains jurisdiction over only the named defendants. Since only the named parties are actually required to appear and defend, no due process burden is placed on the absent parties. Thus, arguably, the plaintiff's interest in effective relief and the judicial system's interest in efficient resolution of controversy should prevail and personal jurisdiction and venue should be required only for the named defendants.
>
> Closer analysis indicates the fallacies of this reasoning. The absent defendant may eventually be subjected to the remedial power of the court if judgment is entered against the class. That judgment could consist of onerous injunctive relief or monetary relief in the form of damages or restitution. Although the class representative may litigate the substantive issues for the absent parties, the class representative cannot respond to the judgment on behalf of those parties. Even before judgment, an absent defendant could be forced to respond to discovery in the distant forum. The only ways for defendants to protect themselves against such actions are by either opting out of the class (which is not available in (b)(1) and (2) actions) or intervening. The price of intervention, when permitted, is the waiver of lack of personal jurisdiction. Such hapless defendants must travel to a distant forum, where they did not either reasonably anticipate litigating or purposefully avail themselves of privileges. * * *

Elizabeth B. Brandt, *Fairness to the Absent Members of a Defendant Class: A Proposed Revision of Rule 23*, 1990 BYU L. Rev. 909, 935–36 (1990). Are the concerns raised by Professor Brandt significant? If so, are defendant classes unconstitutional when personal jurisdiction cannot be established over each class member?

9. Courts and commentators are split over whether notice to all class members should be mandatory in all defendant class actions. *Compare, e.g., Nw. Nat'l. Bank v. Fox & Co.*, 102 F.R.D. 507, 516 (S.D.N.Y. 1984) (notice to each class member of right to opt out is required), *and In re Gap Stores Sec. Litig.*, 79 F.R.D. 283, 292 (N.D. Cal. 1978) ("Notice to each class member guarantees [that] no absent defendant will be held liable for a money judgment without knowing of the pendency of the proceedings."), *with Leist v. Shawano*, 91 F.R.D. 64, 69 (E.D. Wis. 1981) (not requiring individualized notice to all class members "because they are just too numerous"). What are the advantages and disadvantages of a mandatory notice requirement? *See* Emory Comment, *supra*, 40 Emory L.J. at 617–20.

10. The Supreme Court has held that the relevant statute of limitations is tolled for all members of a potential plaintiff's class by the filing of a proposed class action (*see* Chapter 7(A)), but has not addressed whether the same rationale applies in defendant class actions. The lower courts are split over

whether statutes of limitations should be tolled in putative defendant class actions. *Compare Robinson v. Fountainhead Title Grp. Corp.*, 447 F. Supp. 2d 478, 484 (D. Md. 2006) (statute runs as to unnamed members), *and Meadows v. Pac. Inland Sec. Corp.*, 36 F. Supp. 2d 1240, 1248–49 (S.D. Cal. 1999) (statute runs as to unnamed members unless they have actual notice of the existence of the action), *with Appleton Elec. Co. v. Graves Truck Line, Inc.*, 635 F.2d 603, 609–10 (7th Cir. 1980) (filing of defendant class action tolls statute with respect to all members of defendant class), *and In re Activision Sec. Litig.*, 1986 WL 15339, at *2–3 (N.D. Cal. 1986) (same). Does tolling of statutes of limitations make sense in the defendant-class context? One commentator has argued that tolling the statute of limitations in defendant-class cases is fundamentally unfair:

> The unfairness resulting from the subordination of the statute of limitations is unique to defendant class actions. Regardless of whether the class is certified, if a defendant absentee is denied notice before the expiration of the original statutory period of the nature of the claim and identities of the plaintiffs who may partake in the judgment, then it is likely that, based on a belief that the period of repose has arrived, evidence will not be preserved relating to the claim or any defenses. Therefore, when faced with a subsequent suit by the plaintiff, the absentee may be denied his constitutional opportunity to be heard, thereby violating due process.

Emory Comment, *supra*, 40 Emory L.J. at 635–36. Is this a legitimate concern? If so, how should it be addressed?

11. Defendant class actions remain relatively uncommon. *See* Graham L. Lilly, *Modeling Class Action: The Representative Suit as an Analytic Tool*, 81 Neb. L. Rev. 1008, 1040 (2003) ("[V]ery few defendant class actions are filed under any category [of Rule 23(b)], and even fewer are certified.").

2. ADDITIONAL ISSUES INVOLVING ADEQUACY OF DEFENDANT CLASS REPRESENTATIVES

a. Intra-Class Conflicts

COAL. FOR ECON. EQUITY V. WILSON
United States District Court, Northern District of California, 1996.
1996 WL 788376.

HENDERSON, CHIEF JUDGE.

[Proposition 209 added Section 31 to Article 1 of the California Constitution. The most significant language is the first clause, which provides:

> The state shall not discriminate against, *or grant preferential treatment to*, any individual or group on the basis of race, sex, color, ethnicity, or national origin in the operation of public employment, public education, or public contracting.

(Emphasis added). Opponents of Proposition 209 contended that the measure was an unlawful effort to eliminate affirmative action programs.]

Plaintiffs in this suit mount a facial challenge to Proposition 209, codified as Article 1, Section 31, of the California Constitution, arguing that the enactment violates the Equal Protection and Supremacy Clauses of the

United States Constitution. Plaintiffs in the instant motion seek to certify a defendant class composed of:

> All state officials, local government entities or other governmental instrumentalities bound by Proposition 209.

The plaintiffs also name Governor Pete Wilson, Attorney General Daniel Lungren, and Richard Atkinson, in his official capacity as President of the University of California, as representatives of the class. This Court [previously] certified a plaintiff class in this matter; the instant motion seeks to make this suit a "bilateral" class action.

* * *

The chief dispute in connection with this motion arises from Rule 23(a)(4)'s requirement that the class representative "fairly and adequately protect the interests of the class." This dispute, however, is not between the plaintiffs and the defendants, but is instead between two groups of defendants. On one side are those defendants, exemplified by Governor Pete Wilson, Attorney General Daniel Lungren, State and Consumer Services Agency Secretary Joanne Corday Kozberg, and James H. Gomez, Director of the California Department of Corrections (hereafter "State Defendants"), who vigorously defend the constitutionality of Proposition 209. On the other side are those defendants, exemplified by the City and County of San Francisco (hereafter "San Francisco"), who agree with the plaintiffs that Proposition 209 is unconstitutional.

Because the members of a defendant class must rely on the class representative to defend their interests, a court must carefully evaluate any intra-class conflicts to ensure such conflicts do not make the representative an unfit commander for the common defense of the class. At the same time, it is unrealistic to require a total lack of antagonism between members of the defendant class. The central question is whether the appointment of the proposed representatives compromises the due process rights of any dissident faction.

In the instant case, the Court concludes that Governor Pete Wilson and Attorney General Daniel Lungren will adequately represent the defendant class. * * * None of the parties disputes that counsel for the Governor and Attorney General are eminently qualified and that these representatives have the resources to litigate this case fully. With respect to dissident class members such as San Francisco, the Court cannot at this time perceive any likely prejudice to their due process rights. To the extent they believe Proposition 209 to be unconstitutional, their position will be vigorously represented by the plaintiffs in this case. The dissident members of the class, of course, might well prefer a less ardent champion in this case. The purposes of Rule 23(a)(4), however, are best served by representatives that will vigorously litigate on behalf of the defendant class. San Francisco, and any members of the defendant class similarly situated, are free to petition this Court at a later date for the creation of subclasses should circumstances change.

Plaintiffs also seek to name Richard Atkinson, in his official capacity as the President of the University of California, as a representative of the defendant class. Because the Court is satisfied that Governor Wilson and Attorney General Lungren will adequately represent the class, it does not appear that additional representatives are necessary. The Court also notes that Mr. Atkinson has indicated in his papers that the University, because it is in the process of dismantling affirmative action programs independent of the requirements of Proposition 209, does not share the same interests in this litigation as do most other members of the class. Accordingly, the Court finds that Governor Wilson and Attorney General Lungren are better situated to represent the interests of the defendant class.

[The court certified a class action under Rule 23(b)(2).]

* * *

NOTES AND QUESTIONS

1. Could Governor Wilson and Attorney General Lungren adequately represent those defendant class members who *opposed* Proposition 209? Does the court's opinion jeopardize the rights of such class members? Is the proper solution simply to note that dissident defendant class members can seek the creation of subclasses?

2. Setting aside the problems of dissident class members, is it realistic to believe that a governor and an attorney general will devote the attention necessary to be adequate class representatives? Or was the court assuming that the defendants' *lawyers* are the real representatives?

3. Did the court err in rejecting plaintiffs' designation of University of California President Atkinson as a class representative? If this issue were on appeal, how much discretion should the appellate court give to Chief Judge Henderson's decision to reject Atkinson?

4. According to one leading treatise, "some courts have noted that closer scrutiny is necessary in determining the adequacy of the representative of a defendant class because of the risk that plaintiff will seek out weak adversaries to represent the class." Charles A. Wright, Arthur R. Miller & Mary Kay Kane, 7A *Federal Practice and Procedure* § 1770, at 476–77 (3d ed. 2005). Is this a valid concern? *See id.* at 477 (noting that "[t]he reported decisions reveal little evidence of abuse" because, in many cases "the defendant class has an obvious representative" and because courts "have demonstrated a willingness * * * to consider the adequacy of representation carefully"). Should courts give greater scrutiny to adequacy issues in defendant class actions than in plaintiff class actions?

5. As *Thillens* and *Coalition for Economic Equity* illustrate, adequacy can be a complex issue in defendant class actions. The Rule 23(a) elements of numerosity and commonality, however, generally have not raised unique issues in the defendant class action context. *See* Robert R. Simpson & Craig L. Perra, *Defendant Class Actions*, 32 Conn. L. Rev. 1319, 1324–29 (2000) (discussing application of Rule 23(a) criteria to defendant class actions). Typicality could conceivably raise issues similar to adequacy, given the fact that the plaintiff, not the defendants, selects the class representative. But most of the concerns under Rule 23(a) arise in the context of adequacy, not typicality. *See id.* at 1328–29 (noting "[s]trong due process considerations surround[ing] the selection of adequate class representatives since adequate representation is the key to constitutionality of defendant class actions").

b. Bilateral Classes

LA MAR v. H & B NOVELTY & LOAN CO.
United States Court of Appeals, Ninth Circuit, 1973.
489 F.2d 461.

Before ELY and SNEED, CIRCUIT JUDGES, and SWEIGERT, DISTRICT JUDGE [(N.D. Cal.), by designation].

SNEED, CIRCUIT JUDGE.

The common issue of these [two] cases [*La Mar* and *Kinsling*] is whether a plaintiff having a cause of action against a single defendant can institute a class action against the single defendant *and* an unrelated group of defendants who have engaged in conduct closely similar to that of the single defendant on behalf of all those injured by all the defendants sought to be included in the defendant class. We hold that he cannot. Under proper circumstances, the plaintiff may represent all those suffering an injury similar to his own inflicted by the defendant responsible for the plaintiff's injury, but in our view he cannot represent those having causes of action against other defendants against whom the plaintiff has no cause of action and from whose hands he suffered no injury.

In a condensed form the facts of these cases are as follows. In *La Mar* the plaintiff initiated an action against all the pawn brokers licensed to conduct business under the laws of Oregon on behalf of all customers of such pawn brokers to recover either $100 or double the finance charges for alleged violations by the defendant pawn brokers of the Truth-in-Lending Act, 15 U.S.C. §§ 1601–77. In his complaint La Mar estimated that there were 33,000 such customers and that the recovery should approximate three million dollars. In fact La Mar did business with only one such pawn broker, the H & B Novelty and Loan Company. The district court determined that La Mar's action was a proper class action on behalf of all those who borrowed from the H & B Novelty and Loan Company as well as on behalf of those who borrowed from all other defendants. Rule 23(b)(3) of the Federal Rules of Civil Procedure was the basis for the court's action. Subsequent to this determination, an interlocutory appeal therefrom was authorized. Thereafter, a settlement between H & B Novelty and Loan Company and La Mar on behalf of himself and all those who did business with H & B, save those who requested exclusion, was approved by the district court. No settlement has been reached with the other named defendants. The appeal before us, therefore, concerns the appropriateness of the court's determination that La Mar's action was a proper class action with respect to those pawn brokers with whom he had no dealings.

In *Kinsling* [the second case], the plaintiff purchased a round trip ticket between Kansas City, Missouri and Augusta, Georgia from Trans World Airlines and Piedmont Aviation Corp. Because there was no published joint fare for the route, a fare construction was required under the applicable tariff rules. The plaintiff alleged that he was overcharged in the amount of $10 in violation of certain provisions of the Federal Aviation Act. This suit was brought against Trans World Airlines and Piedmont Aviation Corp. and the six appellee air carriers on behalf of Kinsling and all others who had suffered a similar overcharge in dealings with these carriers. The aggregate amount of such overcharges in the four years prior to filing the suit was alleged to be approximately eighty million dollars. In due course, the district court dismissed the complaint as to the six appellee carriers on the ground that the plaintiff had no dealings with, nor suffered any injury at the hands of, these carriers. This appeal was taken from that dismissal.

* * *

III.

* * *

Subsection (a) of Rule 23 sets forth four conditions that must be met to justify a class action. We need not dwell on the first two, although it should be noted that the prerequisite that the class be so numerous as to make joinder impracticable strongly suggests that the draftsmen did not have in mind classes so numerous as to present severe issues of manageability.

The third prerequisite is that the claims of the representative parties be typical of the class. Obviously this requirement is not met when the "representative" plaintiff never had a claim of *any* type against *any* defendant. There is nothing in the rule to suggest that the zeal or talent of the "representative" plaintiff's attorney can supply this omission. * * * In brief, typicality is lacking when the representative plaintiff's cause of action is against a defendant unrelated to the defendants against whom the cause of action of the members of the class lies.

The fourth prerequisite is that "the representative parties will fairly and adequately protect the interest of the class." This is particularly troublesome in class actions, such as these, in which the injury to any possible representative party is quite small. Either no one of the injured class is a suitable representative or anyone is. From this it may be said to follow that each possible representative party could "fairly and adequately protect the interests of the class."

The difficulty with this position is that compliance with the prerequisite must necessarily be determined more by examination of the fitness of the counsel of the candidate for representative party status than by the attributes of the candidate. Once the ability of counsel becomes the measure by which compliance with the fourth prerequisite is determined, there remains only a formal and technical reason for insisting that there be a representative party at all.

Assuming * * * that in this type of class action the role of the representative party is largely formal, it is reasonable in our view to design its formal characteristics in a manner that is consistent with what we perceive to be the tone of the Advisory Committee's Note. In keeping with that tone and to reduce the incidence of proceedings in which the trial judge and the representative plaintiff's counsel become a part-time regulatory agency, we assert that a plaintiff who has no cause of action against the defendant cannot "fairly and adequately protect the interests" of those who do have such causes of action. This is true even though the plaintiff may have suffered an identical injury at the hands of a party other than the defendant and even though his attorney is excellent in every material respect. Obviously this position does not embrace situations in which all injuries are the result of a conspiracy or concerted schemes between the defendants at whose hands the class suffered injury. Nor is it intended to apply in instances in which all defendants are juridically related in a manner that suggests a single resolution of the dispute would be expeditious.

* * *

Because reason and authority so indicate, *La Mar* is reversed, and *Kinsling* is affirmed.

NOTES AND QUESTIONS

1. Assuming vigorous counsel for plaintiffs, are the unnamed plaintiffs in *La Mar* really disadvantaged if the representative plaintiff has a claim against only certain defendants?

2. What potential problems could arise if the court had decided that the *La Mar* and *Kinsling* cases could both proceed as bilateral class actions? What are the potential ways to avoid or mitigate such problems?

3. SPECIAL PROBLEMS UNDER RULE 23(b)(2)

HENSON V. E. LINCOLN TOWNSHIP
United States Court of Appeals, Seventh Circuit, 1987.
814 F.2d 410.

Before POSNER and RIPPLE, CIRCUIT JUDGES, and CAMPBELL, SENIOR DISTRICT JUDGE [(N.D.Ill.), by designation].

POSNER, CIRCUIT JUDGE.

The question for decision is whether classes of defendants are permissible in actions governed by Rule 23(b)(2). * * * The district judge said "no," and we must decide whether he was right.

Following *Goldberg v. Kelly*, 397 U.S. 254 (1970), this court, in *White v. Roughton*, 530 F.2d 750 (7th Cir. 1976), held that the due process clause of the Fourteenth Amendment requires local welfare departments in Illinois to establish written standards for welfare ("general assistance") eligibility, and notice-and-hearing procedures for the grant or denial of applications for welfare. The *White* case involved the welfare department of the township of Champaign, and the consent decree that was entered in the wake of our decision * * * provided no state-wide relief. A downstate legal-aid bureau, the Land of Lincoln Legal Assistance Foundation, filed the present suit in 1980. The purpose of the suit is to make other welfare departments in Illinois comply with the principles laid down in our 1976 decision. The suit is on behalf of one named plaintiff, Henson, a resident of East Lincoln Township, and every other person in 65 downstate Illinois counties (the counties served by the Foundation) who has been denied due process of law in connection with an application for welfare. The suit is against East Lincoln Township and its welfare supervisor—they are the named defendants—plus every other local welfare department (and its supervisor) in the 65 counties that does not receive any state aid. The defendant departments are all what are called "non-receiving" departments; welfare departments that receive state aid are bound by state procedural regulations that comply with the principles of *White v. Roughton*. Henson believes there are 770 "non-receiving" departments in the 65 counties, and they and their supervisors are the members of the defendant class. The suit seeks only injunctive relief, and the Foundation asked for certification of the defendant class only under subsection (b)(2) of Rule 23.

The Foundation notified each of the 770 departments of the suit, and the district judge allowed it to serve each of them with a deposition on written questions (Fed. R. Civ. P. 30). Most of the 525 departments that answered at least some of the Foundation's questions acknowledged that they were not complying with one or more of the principles announced in *White v. Roughton*—at least that is the construction that the Foundation places on their answers and for purposes of this appeal we shall assume it is correct.

* * *

It is apparent from the words of Rule 23(a) ("sue or be sued as representative parties") that suits against a defendant class are permitted. But it does not follow that they are permitted under all three subsections of Rule 23(b). They plainly are permitted under (b)(1), which speaks of "separate actions by or against individual members of the class." Nor is there anything to preclude them under (b)(3). Henson (realistically, the Foundation) cannot fit his case under (b)(1), however, because that subsection contemplates a joint right or obligation. An example would be a suit against members of an unincorporated association naming the officers of the association as the representatives of the defendant class. *See* Advisory Committee's Notes to 1966 Amendment of Rule 23. And Henson is not interested in bringing the action under (b)(3). Any member of a defendant (as of a plaintiff) class in a (b)(3) suit can "opt out" and thus not be bound by the judgment. Henson fears that every member of the defendant class would do just that. It is (b)(2) or nothing.

The question whether there can be a defendant class in a Rule 23(b)(2) suit cannot be answered by reference to authority. Although the question was declared "settled" in favor of permitting a defendant class in *Marcera v. Chinlund*, 595 F.2d 1231, 1238 (2d Cir.), *vacated on other grounds* [*sub nom.*] *Lombard v. Marcera*, 442 U.S. 915 (1979), in neither of the cases that the court in *Marcera* cited for this proposition—*Washington v. Lee*, 263 F. Supp. 327 (M.D. Ala. 1966) (3-judge court), *aff'd without opinion*, 390 U.S. 333 (1968), and *Lynch v. Household Finance Corp.*, 360 F. Supp. 720, 722 n.3 (D. Conn. 1973) (3-judge court)—had the issue been discussed. *Lee* had been filed before the 1966 amendments to Rule 23 that added (b)(2) (though it was decided after); the opinion does not even mention (b)(2). According to a count by the defendants in this case that Henson does not suggest is inaccurate, district courts have certified a defendant class in 45 cases under (b)(2) since 1966. * * * But the only courts of appeals to discuss the permissibility of such actions (there is decision but no discussion in *Marcera*) have held that they are not permissible. *See Thompson v. Board of Educ.*, 709 F.2d 1200, 1203–04 (6th Cir. 1983); *Paxman v. Campbell*, 612 F.2d 848, 854 (4th Cir. 1980) (*per curiam*). We expressed skepticism about the permissibility of such actions in *Adashunas v. Negley*, 626 F.2d 600, 604–05 (7th Cir. 1980), but did not have occasion to resolve the issue then. Similar skepticism is evident in *Greenhouse v. Greco*, 617 F.2d 408, 413 n.6 (5th Cir. 1980).

*** [T]here are those 45 district court cases in which a defendant class was certified under (b)(2)—but their aggregate precedential significance is small. In most there is no discussion of the lawfulness of the certification; the court just does it. In some the issue is discussed but the discussion is perfunctory; the best explanation for these cases is that "the courts are simply unwilling to deprive the plaintiff of this useful measure." ***

Henson appeals to the language of Rule 23, which begins, "One or more members of a class may sue or be sued as representative parties on behalf of all. . . ." But the next word is "only," and is followed by a list of prerequisites to maintaining a suit as a class action. The first sentence does not authorize defendant classes but merely states limitations common to all class action[s]. Nowhere does it imply that defendant class actions are possible under every subsection of Rule 23(b).

Henson points out that (b)(2) speaks of "the party opposing the class" and that the draftsmen could easily have said "the defendant" instead if they had meant to limit (b)(2) to plaintiff classes. But (b)(2) speaks of declaratory as well as injunctive relief, and in a declaratory judgment action the parties frequently get reversed. A debtor for example might bring a suit against a class of creditors, seeking a declaration of nonliability. In such a case it could be argued that the "real" plaintiffs were the creditors and the "real" defendant the debtor—that it was the debtor who had "acted or refused to act on grounds generally applicable to the class." In such a case a (b)(2) "defendant" class might conceivably be permissible, though that is not an issue we need resolve today. ***

Actually the language of (b)(2) is against Henson. Always it is the alleged wrongdoer, the defendant—never the plaintiff (except perhaps in the reverse declaratory suit)—who will have "acted or refused to act on grounds generally applicable to the class." In this case, for example, the plaintiff class is complaining about the conduct of the named defendants and of the unnamed defendant class members in not promulgating written standards for welfare eligibility and in otherwise not complying with the requirements of due process of law spelled out in *White v. Roughton*. No one is complaining about any act or refusal to act by Henson or by any member of the plaintiff class.

The drafting history is also against Henson. The Advisory Committee's Notes make no reference to defendant class actions in connection with (b)(2). They describe the (b)(2) class action as an action by a plaintiff class against a defendant who has done something injurious to the class as a whole. "Illustrative are various actions in the civil-rights field where a party is charged with discriminating against a class, usually one whose members are incapable of specific enumeration." Henson's counsel acknowledged at oral argument that the draftsmen of (b)(2) did not contemplate defendant classes, but he argued that nevertheless the language they used brought such actions (perhaps inadvertently) under the rule. It does not, as we have shown; so we need not decide whether draftsmen of rules or statutes should ever be held to meanings that are inadvertent—the product of the ambiguities inherent in language.

Henson's main argument is that to interpret Rule 23(b)(2) as excluding defendant class actions would create a remedial gap so large that the draftsmen's failure to provide for such actions must be ascribed to oversight. The premise of this argument is not persuasive. The ease and speed with which the Federal Rules of Civil Procedure can be amended by those whom Congress entrusted with the responsibility for doing so should make federal judges hesitate to create new forms of judicial proceeding in the teeth of the existing rules. Neither the rules committee nor any of its advisors has ever considered whether actions such as the present should be maintainable and if so under what conditions and with what limitations; and the fact that in 45 out of almost two million civil lawsuits filed in federal district courts since 1966 a defendant class has been certified under (b)(2) does not prove that the (b)(2) defendant class action fills an essential need. Such an action creates as we shall see severe problems of manageability and due process, and if the need for such actions is nonetheless an urgent one, the problems they create should be addressed by the persons charged with primary responsibility for formulating the rules of procedure for the federal courts.

The Foundation points out that if this suit cannot be maintained against a class of defendants, the plaintiff class will shrink to welfare applicants in East Lincoln Township—for they alone have a quarrel with the named defendants. To get all the relief this suit seeks the Foundation will have to find a plaintiff in each of the other 770 townships (or in however many actually are violating the Fourteenth Amendment)—and one suit will become several hundred and clog the over-crowded dockets of the federal district courts in central and southern Illinois. The Foundation paints with too vivid a palette. Any township that is violating the principles of *White v. Roughton* has strong incentives to bring itself voluntarily into prompt and full compliance (and all or most of them may, for all we know, have done so during the five-year course of this litigation). By virtue of 42 U.S.C. § 1988, the plaintiff in a federal civil rights suit is normally entitled to the award of a reasonable attorney's fees if he prevails, so townships that prove obdurate in defending the indefensible will pay not only their own legal expenses but those of their adversaries. Furthermore, it may be that in many of these townships either there are no denials of due process or the denials aren't hurting anyone who cares to step forward and be a class representative, in which event the number of separate suits that would replace this two-sided class action might be many fewer than the Foundation predicts. (Indeed, it acknowledged at argument that the difficulty of lining up plaintiffs in the other townships was one of its motivations for seeking to certify a defendant class.) Even if several hundred cases are filed, they can be consolidated for pretrial discovery and for trial in one court, before one judge, and all but the lead case stayed until that case is resolved, and then the others resolved summarily. *See* 28 U.S.C. § 1407 [*see* Chapter 12(F)]. The practical difference between class treatment and individual-case treatment, so far as securing the constitutional rights of welfare recipients in Illinois is concerned, could turn out to be small.

It is relevant to our consideration to note that a double class action would be unwieldy, or worse, in the circumstances disclosed by this case, and probably generally. The law firm retained by one Illinois township of modest size is being asked to shoulder responsibility for defending the interests of hundreds of others, which by the same token are being asked to place the responsibility for a litigation vital to the discharge of their essential and financially burdensome public functions in lawyers they may never have heard of. Indeed, "told" rather than "asked"; for not only is there no provision in (b)(2) for a class member to opt out of the suit, but there is no requirement of notifying the members of the class, though such notice was provided here. It would be odd if the rule permitted a defendant class without requiring notice; this is one more bit of evidence against Henson's reading of the statute.

And because the defendant class consists of local governments and their officials, in effect the federal district court is being asked to override the state's allocation of powers among local governmental bodies and treat the welfare system as if it were a state system rather than a local system—though it really is local, except for those townships that receive state aid, and they are not involved in this case. It is only an accident, moreover, that this litigation is limited to 65 counties in Illinois. On the Foundation's reading of (b)(2), as it acknowledged at argument, this suit could have been brought as a nationwide class action pitting all welfare applicants in the United States who are being denied due process of law against all the welfare departments in the United States that are thought to be denying those benefits. The welfare department of Eugene, Oregon might find itself an unnamed defendant in the Central District of Illinois, represented by the law firm retained by the township of East Lincoln, Illinois. True, it might be able to interpose objections based on lack of personal jurisdiction. But this would not solve the deeper problems of such a suit. By the very definition of a double class action there is no controversy between most plaintiffs and most defendants. Residents of East Lincoln have no quarrel with any defendant except East Lincoln; East Lincoln has no quarrel with any plaintiff except Henson. And so it goes for all the members of the plaintiff and defendant classes. The double class action is a legislative or regulatory device for bringing about general compliance with law (the injunction issued at the end of the action corresponding to a statute or regulation that binds all persons within its scope, whether or not they have been guilty of any wrongdoing in the past), rather than an adjudicative device for resolving a dispute. Indeed, as we have said, the Foundation's fear of not being able to enlist a plaintiff against each and every one of the allegedly noncomplying townships was one of the motivations behind seeking the certification of a defendant class. It is possible that in a double class action with thousands of parties only two would have a dispute—Hensen and East Lincoln Township. Without having to decide whether Article III permits a federal court to assert jurisdiction over a mass of parties that may not be engaged in an actual controversy with anyone, we believe that a federal court should not claim such jurisdiction on the basis of a rule of procedure not intended by its draftsmen to confer it.

* * *

One might argue that concerns about a nationwide (b)(2) defendant class action or about the use of the (b)(2) defendant class action to get around an absence of willing plaintiffs should be addressed on a case-by-case basis rather than used to create an absolute rule against such an action. We disagree. Our job is to interpret the existing rule, and the fact that the rule does not set forth the explicit limitations that would be necessary and appropriate to prevent such a class action from becoming a monstrous perversion of the principles of civil procedure is evidence that the rule does not authorize such actions. Nothing in the structure or history of the rule suggests that it was intended as a broad delegation to the courts of a power that judges would domesticate by bringing to bear limiting principles found elsewhere in Rule 23, or in the Constitution, or in the Judicial Code.

Granted, such limiting principles abound. We have mentioned one already—the limitations on a court's personal jurisdiction. There are others, so that even if (b)(2) double class actions were possible in principle, the present class action or our hypothetical nationwide class action might be precluded—whether by Rule 11, which requires that counsel inquire before rather than after bringing suit whether his client has a claim against the defendant (including we suppose members of a defendant class), or by Rule 23(a)(4), which requires that "the representative parties will fairly and adequately protect the interests of the class." At the very least, such actions might be trimmed down to manageability by orders issued under Rule 23(d), such as an order permitting the district court to allow each member of the defendant class to intervene in the suit with the full rights of a named party. But the managerial burdens placed on the district court would be great, and the potential for litigation over rulings under these provisions considerable. We are loath to embark on these uncharted and, as it seems to us, perilous seas without some indication that the framers of Rule 23 would have wanted us to do so; there is no such indication. Previous judicial experience with such class actions is too limited to persuade us that our fears are chimerical or our interpretation of the rule unsound. If as we doubt there is a great need for defendant classes in Rule 23(b)(2) suits, we do not doubt that the Advisory Committee on the Federal Rules of Civil Procedure will repair the gap left by our interpretation by the present rule. It is more likely that the Committee can come up with a rule that will solve (if they are soluble) the notice and management problems that suits such as this pose than that *ad hoc* decisions by federal district judges around the country will produce a satisfactory standard.

Our conclusion is supported not only by the cases cited earlier but by the Wright and Miller treatise, *see* 7A Charles A. Wright, Arthur R. Miller & Mary K. Kane, *Federal Practice and Procedure* § 1775, at p. 461–62 (2d ed. 1986), and by the thorough discussion in Comment, *Defendant Class Actions and Federal Civil Rights Litigation*, 33 UCLA L. Rev. 283, 316–25 (1985). Professor Moore, though sympathetic to allowing (b)(2) suits against classes, admits that it would require stretching the language of the rule and would create a variety of problems; why he nevertheless favors the device is unclear. *See* 3B James W. Moore, Moore's Federal Practice, ¶ 23.40[6] (2d ed. 1985). The case for the (b)(2) defendant class is well argued in Note, *Certification of Defendant Classes Under Rule 23(b)(2)*, 84 Colum. L. Rev. 1371 (1984), stressing the utility of the device in a case such as the present where local officials are alleged to be unwilling to comply with decisional law; but for reasons explained earlier we are less impressed than the note's author is by the practical arguments for the device. We note, finally, that double class actions remain possible under (b)(3), as in *Appleton Electric Co. v. Advance–United Expressways*, 494 F.2d 126, 137 and n.22 (7th Cir. 1974).

The district court's order declining to certify a defendant class is

AFFIRMED.

CAMPBELL, SENIOR DISTRICT JUDGE, concurring in part and dissenting in part.

I concur in the result reached in this case by the majority, however I have no desire to join in the majority's issuance of an absolute prohibition against Rule 23(b)(2) defendant class actions. There are respected authorities on both sides of this difficult issue and both schools of thought, in my opinion, do a sufficient job of advocating their beliefs. I believe 23(b)(2) defendant class actions should be reserved for rare sets of circumstances. Yet they are viable for stubborn or neglectful groups of defendants who refuse to make honest attempts to comply with settled substantive law. Let me say at the outset that the Supreme Court had its chance to condemn and prohibit 23(b)(2) defendant class actions on the appeal of *Marcera v. Chinlund*, 595 F.2d 1231 (2d Cir. 1979). It didn't. While I realize a lack of comment by the Court on an issue does not necessarily mean approval, it seems to me inescapable that the practical effect of the Court's inaction here was to allow such a class action under such circumstances; that is, when attempting to effectuate general compliance with statutory law or uniform, well-recognized administrative policies. I believe under circumstances constituting an "enforcement" setting, certifying defendant classes under 23(b)(2) can, on occasion, pose remarkably few constitutional problems (which could probably be avoided subsequently in the litigation through the wise use of Rule 23(c)(4) and (d)). In their best light, 23(b)(2) defendant class actions can eliminate the perpetuation of substantial injustices.

* * *

When to certify a defendant class under 23(b)(2) is admittedly a very difficult question to answer. Maybe when in doubt, a court shouldn't. However, I do not believe this problem, as perplexing as it can be, should lead to an absolute prohibition of 23(b)(2) class actions. A systematic analysis employing rigid criteria would obviously not be desirable. Inherent in the process is a flexible approach focusing on various factors including the degree of complexity (constitutionally, administratively and financially) that would be created by a 23(b)(2) defendant class certification. In *Certification of Defendant Classes Under Rule 23(b)(2)*, 84 Colum. L. Rev. 1371 (1984), a helpful article mentioned by the majority, several guideposts are listed. First, the less heterogeneity in a defendant class, the better. Also, it is preferable that the defendants be "judicially linked"—the members of the proposed class should share some type of a relationship which predates the litigation. * * * The majority raises a good point when it asks what would stop the instant suit from becoming a nationwide class action on behalf of all welfare applicants in the United States (although there is the personal jurisdiction issue). Further, why should one medium sized law firm in Illinois have to defend the interests of hundreds of others? And should the hundreds of others have to depend on that Illinois law firm? These are good points, yet as a longtime district judge I'm more willing to trust the district courts and give them the responsibility and discretion to create and certify defendant classes that will not become constitutional or administrative monsters. A district judge can also use Rule 23(d) to alleviate headaches as the litigation progresses.

In the instant case, I concur in the result because I view the suit as too unmanageable and the remedies too unfocused. * * * In the action at bar there are 770 defendants. All 770 defendants presumably would have to formulate notice and hearing procedures subject to court approval. Various defendants undoubtedly represent populations of various sizes in locales with varied resources. * * *

A constant undercurrent throughout the majority's argument is that allowing 23(b)(2) defendant class actions would result in large numbers of uncontrollable lawsuits with managerial burdens galore. The majority hesitates "to embark on these uncharted and . . . perilous seas." Yet these uncharted seas have been visible since 1966 and there have been few casualties since. Indeed, there is a bit of a contradiction in the majority's thought process here. On the one hand, it is worried 23(b)(2) defendant class actions would create unwieldy scenarios and great constitutional wrongs, yet on the other hand it admits there have been few 23(b)(2) defendant class actions (45 or so) since 1966 and it uses this low number to conclude their precedential value is insignificant. Hence the majority uses the small number of past 23(b)(2) defendant class actions to doubt their legitimacy, while at the same time saying that if they were condoned the floodgates to constitutional deprivation and administrative chaos would be opened. The reality appears to be that district courts have used the 23(b)(2) defendant class action tool scarcely and responsibly since the 23(b)(2) defendant class action outlet has been available to them. Looking at the problem from this angle, I must conclude that allowing such defendant class actions would not necessarily subject the federal bench to constitutional chaos or judicial disorder.

I see no need to indulge in a detailed word by word analysis of Rule 23(b)(2). As stated earlier, there are respected schools of thought on both sides of this issue and both sides have repeatedly done a remarkable job of proving why the Advisory Committee meant whatever each side wants it to say. There is also the double-edged argument as to why the Advisory Committee hasn't more definitely stated what it means. The majority would have it that if the Advisory Committee really approved of 23(b)(2) defendant class actions it would have amended the rule by now. I say if the Advisory Committee saw such class actions as a threat, it (or the Supreme Court) could have just as easily ended the debate by now, some 20 years after the creation of Rule 23(b)(2). The arguments in this area on both sides are, at this point, stale and inconclusive.

In summation, I see little reason to dig a hole and bury a potentially helpful tool for litigants as well as the federal bench until directed to do so by higher authorities. I believe the approach taken by the majority today borders on the simplistic in view of past cases like *Marcera*. Further, the majority's worries about constitutional (mainly due process) and managerial concerns are less based on history and more on an unsubstantiated view of the future. The majority is short on constitutional horror stories from cases where courts certified 23(b)(2) defendant class actions. The majority refuses to reflect upon future possibilities, in view of cases like *Marcera*, to envision cases where 23(b)(2) defendant class actions are constitutionally and managerially plausible and just. Because I prefer to look at this question in a different light, I am forced to separate myself from the broad scope of the opinion. Therefore, I respectfully dissent from the part of this opinion that expands itself from the denying of the 23(b)(2) defendant class certification as it relates to this case.

NOTES AND QUESTIONS

1. Judge Posner's decision touches upon numerous concepts that appear throughout this book, including the use of other aggregation devices in lieu of class actions (Chapter 13(A) & (B)); the problems stemming from the lack of notice or opt-out rights under Rule 23(b)(2) (Chapter 5(A)(4)); the use of class actions when "case or controversy" problems may exist (Chapter 10(A)(3)(a)(ii)); the ways in which nationwide classes can magnify administrative and fairness issues (Chapter 6(A)); the distinction between a class action and an administrative proceeding (Chapter 4(E)(1)); adequacy issues raised when someone with a narrow claim seeks relief that will affect hundreds or thousands of others (Chapter 2(B)(4)(b)); and the basic differences between (b)(1), (b)(2), and (b)(3) classes (Chapter 3(B)(4)). How does each of these elements support Judge Posner's analysis? Is each element persuasive?

2. Review Rule 23(b)(2) and the relevant Advisory Committee Notes. Did Henson's counsel err in conceding that the draftsmen of (b)(2) did not contemplate defendant class actions? Was such a concession necessary? Or could counsel have legitimately argued that the intent of the draftsmen was at least unclear?

3. Is Judge Posner convincing in stating that the Foundation does not, as a practical matter, need a class action in order to get the relief it seeks? *See also* Chapter 3(B)(4) (discussing the "necessity doctrine"). Does that rationale support the conclusion that a defendant class action is *never* appropriate under Rule 23(b)(2)?

4. Are Judge Posner's concerns about an unwieldy nationwide class action legitimate in interpreting Rule 23(b)(2)? Is it relevant that Rule 23(b)(2), unlike Rule 23(b)(3), does not, by its terms, require any inquiry into manageability? *But see* Chapter 3(B).

5. Does the dissent make a compelling case for refusing to decide whether defendant classes are barred under Rule 23(b)(2)? Does the majority go beyond what is necessary to resolve the case? In a subsequent case, the Seventh Circuit stated that *Henson* "[left] open the possibility of a debtor's bringing a class action [under (b)(2)] against a class of creditors seeking a declaration of nonliability." *Ameritech Benefit Plan Comm. v. Communications Workers of Am.*, 220 F.3d 814, 820 (7th Cir. 2000). *See Henson* excerpt, *supra*. Does this language in *Ameritech* undercut the *Henson* court's rationale? How could such a case be certified under (b)(2) if, as *Henson* concluded, the text and drafting history suggest that the drafters did not intend to permit defendant classes under (b)(2)?

6. As *Henson* notes, courts are divided concerning whether defendant class actions are allowed under Rule 23(b)(2). Although the Supreme Court granted *certiorari* in *Henson* to resolve this issue, it later dismissed the case by joint request of the parties without ruling on the issue. The First Circuit sided with *Henson* in 2003. *See Tilley v. TJX Cos., Inc.*, 345 F.3d 34, 39–40 (1st Cir.2003) (relying on text and drafting history of (b)(2), commentary, and federal appellate court case law). *See also Clark v. McDonald's Corp.*, 213 F.R.D. 198, 217 (D.N.J. 2003) (noting, with supporting citations, "significant split of opinion as to whether Rule 23 (b)(2) ever permits injunctive relief against a

defendant class"). The issue has generated considerable academic commentary. *See, e.g.*, David H. Taylor, *Defendant Class Actions Under Rule 23(b)(2): Resolving the Language Dilemma*, 40 U.Kan. L. Rev. 77 (1991); Note, *Certification of Defendant Classes Under Rule 23(b)(2)*, 84 Colum. L. Rev. 1371 (1984); Comment, *Defendant Class Actions: The Failure of Rule 23 and a Proposed Solution*, 38 UCLA L. Rev. 223 (1990) ("UCLA Comment"); Comment, *Defendant Class Certification: The Difficulties Under Rule 23(b)(2) and the Rule 65(d) Solution*, 8 N.Ill.U. L. Rev. 143 (1987).

7. Rule 23(b)(2) is not the only subdivision of 23(b) that has raised concerns for courts when applied to defendant classes.

a. "Courts have generally refused Rule 23(b)(1)(A) certification because no incompatible standards of conduct are created [for the party opposing the class, *i.e.*, the plaintiff] by refusal to certify the class." UCLA Comment, *supra*, 38 UCLA L. Rev. at 237 (citing *In re Seagate Techs. Sec. Litig.*, 115 F.R.D. 264, 273–74 (N.D. Cal. 1987), and *Webcraft Techs., Inc. v. Alden Press, Inc.*, 228 U.S.P.Q. 182, 185–86 (N.D. Ill. 1985)).

b. With respect to Rule 23(b)(1)(B), "a defendant class should be certified pursuant to this subsection when a victory for a plaintiff in a suit against one defendant would be dispositive of the interest of other defendants or would seriously impair the ability of the other defendants to defend themselves in subsequent suits." UCLA Comment, *supra*, 38 UCLA L. Rev. at 237. Few cases have addressed the applicability of this subsection to defendant classes. Those that have are "divided over whether the effect of *stare decisis* may so impair the absentees' abilities to protect their interests as to justify certification under (b)(1)(B)." *Id.* (citing cases). *Compare Tilley v. TJX Cos., Inc.*, 345 F.3d 34, 40–43 (1st Cir. 2003) (noting conflict and holding that "the possibility of *stare decisis*" does not justify certification under Rule 23 (b)(1)(B)), *with In re Integra Realty Res., Inc.*, 354 F.3d 1246, 1264 (10th Cir. 2004) (upholding certification of a (b)(1)(B) defendant class because adjudication of the issue "would present more than the 'mere possibility' of a *stare decisis* effect on future defendants" and "would almost inevitably prove dispositive in those cases").

c. Rule 23(b)(3) has been a common basis for certifying defendant class actions. One potential problem with applying this rule, however, is that, under Rule 23(b)(3), a class action must be a superior vehicle for adjudicating the case. Since that subdivision allows opt-outs, and since a defendant class member has at least some incentive to opt out, the risk of large numbers of opt-outs may suggest that a Rule 23(b)(3) class action is not the superior device. Nonetheless, as in *Thillens*, "most courts have held that the actual risk of all defendants opting out is sufficiently small that superiority is not destroyed." UCLA Comment, *supra*, 38 UCLA L. Rev. at 241 (citing cases).

d. In defendant class actions seeking injunctive relief, courts have sometimes denied certification on the ground (similar to the "necessity doctrine" (*see* Chapter 3(B)(4))) that "a permanent injunction * * *, if issued, would provide equally-effective protection, not only to plaintiffs but to all others similarly situated, with no residual risk of inconsistent or arbitrary prosecution." *N.C. Right to Life, Inc. v. Bartlett*, 1998 U.S. Dist. LEXIS 6443, at *5 (E.D.N.C. 1998), *rev'd in part* *on other grounds,* 168 F.3d 705 (4th Cir. 1999). Does this rationale apply only if every putative class member is subject to the injunction?

8. The criteria for determining the appropriateness of interlocutory review of a defendant class action under Rule 23(f) are discussed in Chapter 9(A).

B. SHAREHOLDER DERIVATIVE SUITS

The derivative action permits shareholders to bring an action on behalf of a corporation when the corporation itself has failed to redress a corporate injury. The derivative action serves two purposes. "First, it is the equivalent of a suit by the shareholders to compel the corporation to sue. Second, it is a suit by the corporation, asserted by the shareholders on its behalf, against those liable to it." *Aronson v. Lewis,* 473 A.2d 805, 811 (Del. 1984). Because the derivative action is brought to redress a corporate injury, any recovery is paid to the corporation.

Devised as a suit in equity, the derivative action is now governed by Rule 23.1 of the Federal Rules of Civil Procedure, which was adopted in 1966.

FED. R. CIV. P. 23.1: DERIVATIVE ACTIONS

(a) Prerequisites. This rule applies when one or more shareholders or members of a corporation or an unincorporated association bring a derivative action to enforce a right that the corporation or association may properly assert but has failed to enforce. The derivative action may not be maintained if it appears that the plaintiff does not fairly and adequately represent the interests of shareholders or members who are similarly situated in enforcing the right of the corporation or association.

(b) Pleading Requirements. The complaint must be verified and must:

> (1) allege that the plaintiff was a shareholder or member at the time of the transaction complained of, or that the plaintiff's share or membership later devolved on it by operation of law;
>
> (2) allege that the action is not a collusive one to confer jurisdiction that the court would otherwise lack; and
>
> (3) state with particularity:
>
>> (A) any effort by the plaintiff to obtain the desired action from the directors or comparable authority and, if necessary, from the shareholders or members; and
>>
>> (B) the reasons for not obtaining the action or not making the effort.

(c) Settlement, Dismissal, and Compromise. A derivative action may be settled, voluntarily dismissed, or compromised only with the court's approval. Notice of a proposed settlement, voluntary dismissal, or compromise must be given to shareholders or members in the manner that the court orders.

1966 ADVISORY COMMITTEE NOTES TO RULE 23.1

A derivative action by a shareholder of a corporation or by a member of an unincorporated association has distinctive aspects which require the special provisions set forth in the new rule. The next-to-the-last sentence [now second sentence of subsection 23.1(a)] recognizes that the question of adequacy of representation may arise when the plaintiff is one of a group of shareholders or members. *Cf.* 3 Moore's *Federal Practice*, par. 23.08 (2d ed. 1963).

The court has inherent power to provide for the conduct of the proceedings in a derivative action, including the power to determine the course of the proceedings and require that any appropriate notice be given to the shareholders or members.

This section examines some of the principal issues implicated in derivative actions. First, it considers the nature of the injury required for a derivative suit and how such injury differs from that required for a direct suit. Second, it addresses two important requirements of Rule 23.1: the "contemporaneous ownership rule," which requires a shareholder to own the stock of the corporation on whose behalf suit is brought; and the "demand requirement," which specifies that, in most circumstances, the corporation's board of directors must be given the chance to address the shareholder's concerns prior to the filing of the derivative suit. Finally, this section addresses various requirements (adequacy of representation, notice of proposed settlement, and court approval of settlement) that are similar to those under Rule 23, as well as some (numerosity, typicality, and commonality) that are pertinent to Rule 23, but not necessarily to shareholder derivative suits.

1. NATURE OF INJURY REQUIRED

BAGDON V. BRIDGESTONE/FIRESTONE, INC.
United States Court of Appeals, Seventh Circuit, 1990.
916 F.2d 379.

Before WOOD, JR., and EASTERBROOK, CIRCUIT JUDGES, and GRANT, SENIOR DISTRICT JUDGE [(N.D.Ind.), by designation].

EASTERBROOK, CIRCUIT JUDGE.

[Bridgestone/Firestone ("Firestone") acquired 300 auto centers from J.C. Penney Co. and operated some in competition with its already-existing auto centers, some of which had been separately incorporated. One of the newly-acquired J.C. Penney auto centers ("Ford City East") was located in the same shopping center as a separately-incorporated, already-existing Firestone auto center ("Ford City West") managed by plaintiff. Plaintiff, Bagdon, owned 49% of the stock of Ford City West, and Firestone owned the remaining 51%.]

* * *

Bagdon filed this suit in 1987, invoking the diversity jurisdiction of 28 U.S.C. § 1332(a). He is a citizen of Illinois; in 1987 Firestone was incorporated in Ohio and has its principal place of business there. Bagdon contends that had Firestone sold the former Penney store to a third party rather than operating it as an auto center, Ford City West would have picked up a substantial fraction of Penney's sales, greatly increasing Ford City West's profits—and his 49% share of them, not to mention his bonus from Firestone. Firestone moved to dismiss, contending that the store-corporation is an indispensable party because Bagdon's loss derives from injury to the corporation. Ford City West is incorporated in Delaware and has its principal place of business in Illinois. *Smith v. Sperling*, 354 U.S. 91 (1957), requires the corporation to be aligned as a defendant in shareholders' derivative litigation if it opposes the suit (as the store-corporation does). Its presence as a defendant would destroy the complete diversity of citizenship that since *Strawbridge v. Curtiss*, 7 U.S. (3 Cranch) 267 (1806), has been essential to jurisdiction under § 1332. * * *

Count I of Bagdon's complaint alleges that by establishing Ford City East in competition with Ford City West, Firestone violated the duty a controlling shareholder owes to the corporation, and derivatively to the minority investors. Diverting business from Ford City West to Ford City East reduced the store's sales, and thus its profits. This looks like a standard derivative suit, for any injury to Bagdon is mediated through the corporation: Bagdon does not lose unless Ford City West loses. Firestone's duty as a majority shareholder ran to the corporation, not directly to the minority investor. As the American Law Institute puts it, summarizing the theme of the cases, "An action in which the holder can prevail only by showing an injury or breach of duty to the corporation should be treated as a derivative action." *Principles of Corporate Governance: Analysis and Recommendations*, § 7.01(a) (Tent. Draft No. 8, 1988). * * *

Other counts in the complaint did not depend on injury to Ford City West. Count II alleges that Firestone defrauded Bagdon personally, telling him that he would be appointed to manage Ford City East or that Ford City East would be added to his store-corporation. Assurances of this kind led him to remain with Firestone, to his detriment, although he would have left had he known the truth. Count III states a claim under the Illinois Consumer Fraud and Deceptive Business Practices Act, on the theory that Ford City East engendered confusion in consumers' minds. In denying Firestone's motion to dismiss the case, the district judge observed that Counts II and III are claims personal to Bagdon, which he is entitled to pursue without involving the store-corporation. Even Count I involves some injury external to the store-corporation: Bagdon seeks to recover the diminution in the value of his bonuses, paid directly by Firestone. The district judge concluded that this suit therefore may proceed without the store-corporation, a jurisdictional spoiler.

Bagdon had claims that he could pursue without adding the corporation. Often a single series of events gives rise to both direct and derivative litigation. The plaintiff as master of the complaint may choose which claims to present. Had Bagdon argued only that Firestone defrauded him personally, he would have been free to proceed. His claims were not so limited but included a demand for damages on account of the reduction in corporate profits. * * *

Bagdon insisted on recovering profits the corporation lost. If that claim is derivative, then the corporation had to be joined. * * *

* * *

Smith v. Sperling adopts a mechanical rule: the unwilling corporation is aligned as a defendant. Sometimes this creates diversity (as in *Sperling*), sometimes it defeats diversity. *Sperling* is not a one way street, with the corporation participating only when its presence creates federal jurisdiction. If Count I of Bagdon's complaint states a derivative claim, then the complaint must be dismissed [for lack of diversity jurisdiction]. * * *

Thus we arrive at the question whether a claim that the majority stockholder wrongly competed with the corporation is derivative. Bagdon and Firestone agree that this is a question of state law—for the identity of the real party in interest depends on the law creating the claim.

* * *

* * * Delaware [the jurisdiction whose law applied] follows the venerable rule that a claim is derivative if injury is mediated through the corporation. It also follows the "special injury" exception to this rule, allowing a shareholder to litigate independently if the wrong to the corporation inflicts a distinct and disproportionate injury on the investor. The "special injury" rule allows Bagdon to pursue his claim that Firestone defrauded him by promising him suzerainty over Ford City East. Bagdon's claim for lost bonus comes within the same shelter. Although the bonus varies with Ford City West's profits, the injury to Bagdon is nonetheless "special" because Firestone pays Bagdon directly.

* * *

Ohio, like a few other states, has expanded the "special injury" doctrine into a general exception for closely held corporations, treating them as if they were partnerships. The American Law Institute recommends that other states do the same. *Principles of Corporate Governance* § 7.01(d) and pp. 22–25 (comment), 30–36 (reporter's note). The premise of this extension may be questioned. Corporations are *not* partnerships. Whether to incorporate entails a choice of many formalities. Commercial rules should be predictable; this objective is best served by treating corporations as what they are, allowing the investors and other participants to vary the rules by contract if they think deviations are warranted. So it is understandable that not all states have joined the parade.

* * * When the controlling stockholder of a family corporation transferred its assets for inadequate consideration, Delaware required the minority investors to pursue derivative litigation, observing that the value of the minority shares went down only to the extent the corporation as an entity was worth less. When the owner of 95% of a closely held firm's stock proposed to liquidate the corporation at what the minority thought was an inadequate price, Delaware again required the minority to bring the objection derivatively. In neither case did the [Delaware court] think it important that the wrong alleged involved the controlling stockholder enriching itself at corporate expense, or that the corporation was closely held. * * *

Jurisdictional rules should be simple. Why spend years litigating the right court in which to litigate? Certainty is elusive in a case such as this, in which jurisdiction depends on a question of characterization that different states would resolve differently. Lest the details of the "special injury" doctrine, and its implementation in Delaware, obscure the fundamentals, we repeat the theme. Bagdon believes that Firestone wrongly competed with Ford City West. Firestone owed that duty to the store-corporation, not to its employee Bagdon—an employee Firestone was free to dismiss for any or no reason. Violation of the duty injured the store-corporation, and Bagdon's loss was derivative (he could not receive dividends out of profits the corporation did not make). Bagdon alleged some direct injuries, which he was free to litigate, but he could not recover on account of the store-corporation's diminished profits without making the corporation a party. The district court therefore should have granted Firestone's motion to dismiss the case for want of diversity jurisdiction.

* * *

NOTES AND QUESTIONS

1. The last claim considered by the court in *Bagdon*—diminished corporate profits—is a classic example of a derivative claim. *See, e.g., Stevens v. Lowder*, 643 F.2d 1078, 1079 (5th Cir. 1981); *Burghart v. Landau*, 821 F. Supp. 173, 176–77 (S.D.N.Y.), *aff'd*, 9 F.3d 1538 (2d Cir. 1993). Consider how the issue of direct versus derivative claim has been resolved in other contexts:

   a. Breach of contract, fraud, interference with contract rights, and other tort or contract claims alleging injury to the corporation. *See, e.g., Labovitz v. Wash. Times Corp.*, 172 F.3d 897, 900–04 (D.C. Cir. 1999) (derivative); *Stewart Coach Indus., Inc. v. Moore*, 512 F. Supp. 879, 888 (S.D.Ohio 1981) ("Shareholders have no personal interest in the property of the corporation * * * [and] are not normally proper parties-plaintiff in an action to redress injury to the corporation's property, including actions for fraud, breach of contract, or interference with contract rights."). *But see Grogan v. Garner*, 806 F.2d 829, 835–36 (8th Cir. 1986) (shareholder claims for fraud and breach of fiduciary duty are direct where shareholders suffer distinct injury, such as agreeing to sell their stock at artificially low price because of fraudulent misrepresentations concerning terms of sale of corporate assets).

   b. Wrongful withholding of dividends. *See, e.g., U.S. Indus., Inc. v. Anderson*, 579 F.2d 1227, 1230 (10th Cir. 1978) (wrongful withholding of dividends is type of harm that may be remedied on individual basis because it is wrongfully inflicted on stockholder alone, rather than on corporation); *Mann–Paller Found., Inc. v. Econometric Research, Inc.*, 644 F. Supp. 92, 95–96 (D.D.C. 1986) (same).

   c. Antitrust claims and claims under the Racketeer Influenced and Corrupt Organization Act ("RICO"). *See, e.g., Bivens Gardens Office Bldg., Inc. v. Barnett Banks, Inc.*, 140 F.3d 898, 907–08 (11th Cir. 1998) (racketeering activity resulting in skimming of corporate profits constitutes injury to corporation); *Sears v. Likens*, 912 F.2d 889, 892 (7th Cir. 1990) (racketeering activity resulting in diminution in stock value constitutes injury to corporation); *Peck v. General Motors Corp.*, 894 F.2d 844, 847–48 (6th Cir. 1990) (antitrust activities inflict corporate, not individual, injury); *Moran v. Household Int'l, Inc.*, 490 A.2d 1059, 1070 (Del.Ch.), *aff'd*, 577 A.2d 753 (Del. 1990) (claim that corporation failed to pursue antitrust claim is derivative).

d. Self-dealing by officers or directors. *See, e.g., Joy v. North*, 692 F.2d 880 (2d Cir. 1982) (derivative); *Lewis v. Anselmi*, 564 F. Supp. 768 (S.D. N.Y. 1983) (same).

2. How does a shareholder derivative claim differ from a direct securities fraud claim? What is the "special injury" exception to the derivative claim rule, as described by *Bagdon*?

2. RECURRING THEMES IN RULE 23.1 LITIGATION

a. Contemporaneous Ownership Rule

BLASBAND V. RALES
United States Court of Appeals, Third Circuit, 1992.
971 F.2d 1034.

Before GREENBERG and SCIRICA, CIRCUIT JUDGES, and DEBEVOISE, DISTRICT JUDGE [(D.N.J.), by designation].

GREENBERG, CIRCUIT JUDGE.

I. FACTUAL AND PROCEDURAL HISTORY

Alfred Blasband appeals from a district court order * * * dismissing his complaint pursuant to Fed. R. Civ. P. 12(b)(6) and Fed. R. Civ. P. 23.1 in this shareholder derivative suit. This appeal raises difficult issues regarding shareholder standing and demand futility in derivative actions brought under Delaware law. * * *

Blasband is a former shareholder of Easco Hand Tools, Inc. On September 1, 1988, while Blasband was an Easco shareholder, Easco initiated a public offering of $100 million of 12.875% Senior Subordinated Notes (the "Note Offering"). In the prospectus for the Note Offering, Easco disclosed that the proceeds would be used for repayment of outstanding indebtedness, general corporate purposes, and expansion of Easco's business through internal growth and acquisitions. The prospectus further stated that "pending such uses, the Company will invest the balance of the net proceeds from this offering in government and other marketable securities which are expected to yield a lower rate of return than the rate of interest borne by the Notes."

After the Note Offering was completed, Easco invested at least $61.9 million of the proceeds in high-yield, highly speculative debt securities, commonly known as junk bonds. In its Form 10–K filed with the Securities and Exchange Commission for the year ended December 31, 1988, Easco disclosed these investments as "temporary investments in marketable securities and cash equivalents." One year later, in its 1989 Annual Report and 10–K, Easco disclosed that it still held these investments but that "during 1989, the market for these securities became volatile and some market values declined significantly." Explaining that "[g]reater risk is generally associated with these high-yield securities, for which a thinly traded market exists and for which market quotations are not always available[,]" Easco stated that it had reduced the carrying value of its portfolio by $14 million and that it would probably suffer further losses if the remaining issues were sold. Easco disclosed an additional $1 million loss in its March 31, 1990 Form 10–Q filed with the SEC.

In February 1990, Easco entered into a merger agreement with the nominal defendant Danaher Corporation and Combo Acquisition Corporation, a wholly owned subsidiary of Danaher, providing for Easco shareholders to receive .4175 shares of Danaher common stock for each of their shares of Easco common stock. The merger was consummated in June 1990 with Easco surviving as a wholly owned subsidiary of Danaher. Consequently, Blasband's 1,100 shares of Easco were converted into 458 shares of Danaher.

Prior to the merger, Mitchell P. Rales was Chairman of Easco's board of directors and owned approximately 25% of Easco's common stock. His brother, Steven M. Rales, was a director of Easco and owned 27% of its stock. Mitchell Rales is also President and a director of Danaher, and Steven Rales is Chairman of the board of directors of Danaher. Together the brothers own 44% of Danaher's common stock. Beginning sometime in the mid-1980's, the Rales brothers retained Drexel Burnham Lambert Incorporated to assist in the Rales' corporate acquisition strategy. Through junk bond financing arranged by Drexel, the Rales brothers expanded Danaher by acquiring Western Pacific Corporation and Chicago Pneumatic Corporation. In 1988 the Rales brothers hired Drexel in connection with an ultimately unsuccessful $2.5 billion bid to acquire another company. In addition, Drexel assisted the Rales brothers in acquiring an interest in Easco in 1986 by partially providing the financing. Furthermore, Drexel was selected as the sole underwriter for the Note Offering.

The junk bond investment of the proceeds of the Note Offering did not go unnoticed for, on October 25, 1990, Blasband's counsel sent a letter to the boards of directors of Easco and Danaher setting forth the discrepancy between the proposed use of the proceeds in the prospectus for the Note Offering and Easco's financial statements disclosing the actual investments in junk bonds. The letter requested additional information to explain, *inter alia*: (1) why the junk bond portfolio had lost $14 million in one year; (2) what securities Easco had purchased and sold between September 1, 1988, and December 31, 1989, and at what prices and through which brokerage house; (3) which Easco officers and directors approved or selected the purchases and sales; and (4) why Easco used the proceeds of the Note Offering in a manner contrary to that described in the prospectus. Counsel for Blasband stated that, although much of this information "could be obtained through a formal demand for inspection of the Company's books and records, we believe that it is in our mutual interest to proceed on a less formal basis."

Counsel for Danaher and Easco responded in a letter dated December 17, 1990, that "it would be inappropriate at this time to provide" the requested information. Further, counsel stated that "Easco fully and fairly complied with the requirements of the federal securities laws and regulations in disclosing all material information concerning the Note Offering and the subsequent use of the proceeds of that offering to its shareholders in its public financing." Additionally, counsel stated that compliance with the request "would impose a substantial burden on our clients . . . [and] would be time consuming and highly disruptive of the day-to-day management of the business. . . ."

Unsatisfied with this response, Blasband filed this derivative action in the United States District Court for the District of Delaware on behalf of Danaher on March 25, 1991. The essence of Blasband's claim is that the Rales brothers violated their fiduciary duties owed to Easco by investing proceeds of the Note Offering in highly speculative junk bonds as consideration for their business dealings with Drexel and not for a legitimate corporate purpose. * * *

Prior to discovery, the appellees moved to dismiss the complaint pursuant to Rules 12(b)(6) and 23.1 [contending, *inter alia*,] that Blasband lacked standing to bring this action.

* * *

We * * * believe, contrary to the district court, that Blasband [has] standing to maintain this derivative action * * *.

* * *

III. STANDING

* * * The appellees argue that as a result of the merger Blasband lacks standing to bring this derivative action. Blasband counters that he meets the statutory standing requirements and further that he has "successor derivative standing" by virtue of his status as a former Easco shareholder and his current status as a Danaher shareholder.

In general under Delaware law which the parties agree is applicable a plaintiff must have been a shareholder at the time of the challenged transaction to have standing to maintain a shareholder derivative suit. Delaware General Corporation Law § 327, Del. Code Ann. tit. 8, § 327 (1983). The sole purpose of section 327, as stated by Chancellor Seitz, is "to prevent what has been considered an evil, namely, the purchasing of shares in order to maintain a derivative action designed to attack a transaction which occurred prior to the purchase of the stock." *Rosenthal v. Burry Biscuit Corp.*, 30 Del. Ch. 299, 60 A.2d 106, 111 (Del.Ch. 1948). In addition to section 327's requirement, the Delaware courts require that the plaintiff remain a shareholder at the time of the filing of the suit and throughout the litigation. This requirement ensures that the plaintiff has sufficient incentive to represent adequately the corporation's interests during litigation. Additionally, as with section 327, the continuing ownership requirement is intended to prevent abuses associated with derivative actions.

Where there has been a cash-out merger, it is clear that a former shareholder may not maintain a derivative action, for he or she would no longer have an interest in a subsequent corporate recovery. However, where, as here, the plaintiff receives shares of a new corporate entity, the standing issue is less clear, as the plaintiff will have a financial interest in the derivative action. * * *

* * *

* * * [T]he Delaware courts regularly indicate that there are two exceptions to the general rule that a plaintiff loses standing where he or she loses stock as a result of a merger. These exceptions apply (1) where the merger itself is the subject of a claim of fraud; or (2) where the merger is in

reality a reorganization not affecting the plaintiff's ownership in the business enterprise. In this case, however, Blasband does not contend that either of these exceptions applies to him.

* * *

[Nevertheless], we believe that the Delaware Supreme Court *sub silentio* recognized an indirect financial interest as a basis for standing in 1988 when in *Sternberg v. O'Neil*, 550 A.2d 1105 (Del. 1988), apparently for the first time, it permitted a plaintiff to pursue a double derivative suit. A double derivative action is identical in form to a traditional derivative action, except that in a double derivative the suit is brought on behalf of one corporation (*e.g.* a parent) to enforce a cause of action in favor of a related corporation (*e.g.* its subsidiary). As explained by one leading authority:

> The holding company owes a duty to use its control of the subsidiary to sue to right wrongs to it, and the shareholder may in effect compel specific performance of these connected duties in a double representative action. . . .
>
> In a 'double derivative' action, the shareholder is effectively maintaining the derivative action on behalf of the subsidiary, based upon the fact that the parent or holding company has derivative rights to the cause of action possessed by the subsidiary. The wrong sought to be remedied by the complaining shareholder is not only that done directly to the parent corporation in which he or she owns stock, but also the wrong done to the corporation's subsidiaries which indirectly, but actually, affects the parent corporation and its shareholders. *Notwithstanding that the recognition of double derivative suits relaxes the plaintiff's contemporaneous ownership requirement, the acceptance of the action acknowledges the realities of the changing techniques and structures of the modern corporation. The ultimate beneficiary of a double derivative action is the corporation that possesses the primary right to sue.*

13 Charles R.P. Keating, Gail A. O'Gradney, *Fletcher Cyclopedia of Corporations* § 5977, at 240 (rev. ed. 1991) (emphasis added).

We believe that this logic applies equally in the context at hand. The plaintiff's personal stake in the litigation in *Sternberg*—which was sufficient to confer standing—was no greater than Blasband's stake in this action. Blasband continues to own shares in Danaher, the parent of the corporation, Easco, that has the primary right to sue to redress the wrongs asserted in his complaint and thus he has an indirect financial interest in the litigation. Therefore, Blasband meets the continuing ownership requirement to the same extent that a plaintiff in a double derivative action satisfies this requirement. Additionally, it is undisputed that Blasband was a shareholder at the time of the challenged transaction as required by 8 Del.C. § 327 and thus could not have purchased his shares to institute a strike suit challenging the investment of the proceeds of the Note Offering.

* * *

We acknowledge that this case may not fit neatly into existing Delaware corporation law. However, we are guided by the recognition of the

Delaware courts that "[a] shareholder derivative suit is a uniquely equitable remedy. . . ." Thus, the Delaware courts have consistently refused to apply its corporate law rigidly where to do so would be inequitable. Further, the Delaware courts have observed in shareholder actions that "equity will not suffer a wrong without a remedy. . . ."

Hence, our conclusion that Blasband has standing is bolstered by the fact that a dismissal of Blasband's complaint may well leave a wrong unremedied. * * * [H]ere Blasband alleges that the successor company has a cause of action that it refuses to pursue. This is precisely where Delaware courts permit shareholders to step in and sue derivatively.

* * *

* * * Had Blasband been given shares of the post-merger Easco, there would be no doubt that he could now maintain a derivative action on its behalf. Inasmuch as Delaware recognizes double derivative actions, the fact that Blasband has been given shares of Easco's parent rather than the new subsidiary should be of little consequence. Accordingly, we hold that * * * Blasband has satisfied Delaware's statutory and common law standing requirements to maintain this derivative action.

* * *

NOTES AND QUESTIONS

1. Three justifications have been offered for imposing a contemporaneous-ownership requirement: (i) to prevent collusive jurisdiction; (ii) to prevent strike suits; and (iii) to ensure that plaintiff adequately represents the corporation's best interests. *See generally* Jonathan R. Macey & Geoffrey P. Miller, *The Plaintiffs' Attorney's Role in Class Action and Derivative Litigation: Economic Analysis and Recommendations for Reform*, 58 U. Chi. L. Rev. 1, 76–78 (1991). Does the contemporaneous ownership rule effectively serve those purposes? Note that North Carolina, for example, has chosen to strengthen its standing requirement to include that a shareholder hold his or her shares for one year prior to commencing suit on behalf of a public company. N.C. Gen. Stat. § 55-7-48. Does the North Carolina approach have merit? What are the competing considerations?

2. How, if at all, should a merger affect a plaintiff's standing to sue derivatively? Should it matter whether the merger was a "cash-out" merger or an exchange of shares?

3. Was the Third Circuit justified in holding that Blasband satisfied the policies behind the contemporaneous ownership rule? What are the purposes of that rule? At what point does a plaintiff's indirect financial interest become sufficiently attenuated that the contemporaneous ownership rule no longer has any teeth?

4. Note that the Third Circuit relies on state law to determine the standing issue in this case. In 1993, the Supreme Court in *Kamen v. Kemper Financial Services*, 500 U.S. 90 (1991), ruled that the *demand* provision of Rule 23.1 (*see* the following section of this chapter) was substantive and therefore, under *Erie R.R. Co. v. Tompkins*, 304 U.S. 64 (1938), was to be determined by state law. In so ruling, the Court reasoned that, "although Rule 23.1 clearly *contemplates* both the demand requirement and the possibility that the demand may be excused, it does not *create* a demand requirement of any particular dimen-

sion. On its face, Rule 23.1 speaks only to the adequacy of the shareholder representative's pleadings." *Kamen*, 500 U.S. at 96. Should analysis of the contemporaneous ownership rule similarly be determined by reference to state law?

5. Despite the Third Circuit's conclusion that the Delaware courts would permit standing under the facts of the case, the Delaware courts later rejected *Blasband. See Lewis v. Ward*, 2003 WL 22461894, at *3 n.15 (Del. Ch. 2003) (citing Delaware cases rejecting *Blasband*). As a matter of policy, is the Blasband court's analysis correct? *See, e.g., Prof'l Mgmt. Assocs. Inc. v. Coss*, 598 N.W.2d 406, 413 (Minn. App. 1999) (agreeing with reasoning in *Blasband*).

6. Which, if any, class action principle is similar in purpose to the contemporaneous ownership requirement?

7. Should the contemporaneous ownership rule permit a plaintiff to sue when he or she acquired stock *during* the period of alleged wrongdoing? Some courts have held the contemporaneous ownership rule should not bar a claim as long as the plaintiffs owned the stock while the alleged wrongdoing was underway, even if plaintiffs did not own stock at the time the wrongdoing commenced. *See, e.g., Bateson v. Magna Oil Corp.*, 414 F.2d 128, 130 (5th Cir. 1969) ("[W]here the complaint charged continuing wrongs, occurring at the time plaintiff owned stock, the complaint should not be dismissed on defendant's contention that the claims actually arose prior to the time plaintiff acquired his stock."). Other courts, however, have not embraced this approach, at least if significant misconduct was alleged to have occurred prior to the acquisition of the stock. *See, e.g., In re Bank of N.Y. Derivative Litig.*, 320 F.3d 291, 290 (2d Cir. 2003) ("[W]e decline to adopt the expansive definition of the term 'transaction' that is inherent in the continuing wrong doctrine. * * * [A] proper plaintiff must have acquired his or her stock in the corporation before the core of the allegedly wrongful conduct transpired.") For a critical analysis of cases refusing to endorse the "continuing wrong" approach, see Comment, *Maintaining Standing in a Shareholder Derivative Action*, 38 U.C. Davis. L. Rev. 343 (2004).

b. Demand Requirement

GARBER V. LEGO
United States Court of Appeals, Third Circuit, 1993.
11 F.3d 1197.

Before BECKER, HUTCHINSON, and ROTH, CIRCUIT JUDGES.

ROTH, CIRCUIT JUDGE.

This case arises from a dispute over monetary awards from corporate incentive funds to officers and employees of Westinghouse Electric Corporation ("Westinghouse"). Alexander Garber, a holder of Westinghouse common stock, brought a shareholder derivative suit against the individual members of Westinghouse's board of directors in response to the incentive awards. The derivative suit sought damages on behalf of Westinghouse, jointly and severally against the individual directors, for their actions relating to the incentive awards.

* * * Defendants filed a motion to dismiss, contending that Garber failed to sufficiently establish the reasons for not making a pre-complaint demand on Westinghouse to secure the corporation's enforcement of the

actions Garber sought. The district court dismissed Garber's amended complaint without prejudice for failure to comply with the pre-complaint demand requirement of Federal Rule of Civil Procedure 23.1 and Pennsylvania Rule of Civil Procedure 1506. We agree with the district court and will affirm its decision.

I.

[Garber's] * * * amended complaint acknowledges that no demand was made on Westinghouse's board of directors. Instead, his amended complaint sets forth the reasons why such a demand would have been futile. This appeal is concerned solely with the question of whether Garber set forth sufficient pleadings to excuse demand pursuant to Federal Rule 23.1 and Pennsylvania Rule 1506.

The genesis of this suit was action taken by Westinghouse to reward its top employees. Specifically, Garber objected to awards provided by Westinghouse pursuant to its Annual Performance Plan for "key" employees ("Key Plan") and at least one other incentive plan for other employees. The shareholder-approved Key Plan is designed to provide payments to Westinghouse's key employees as an incentive to enhance efficiency and profitability. The Key Plan is administered by the five members of the Management Compensation Policy Committee ("Compensation Committee") of the board of directors. At the time of the awards which are the subject of Garber's suit, the Compensation Committee was comprised of * * * five members [who] were non-employee, non-management directors. Garber does not allege that any of these individuals received incentive awards.

Under the Key Plan, the Compensation Committee is authorized to determine when, to whom, in what form, in what amount, over what period of time and under what terms, conditions, and limitations awards will be made. The Compensation Committee's determinations are conclusive, except that the Key Plan may be amended or terminated at any time by the board of directors. Participation is limited to "key" employees, defined as employees selected by the Compensation Committee who are in a position to influence the results of Westinghouse's operations. Under the Key Plan, total annual awards can not exceed five percent of the consolidated net income of the corporation and its subsidiaries during such year, before deducting income taxes and any provision for such additional compensation, plus any unused incentive fund amounts carried forward from the previous year. If the full amount available under the Key Plan is not allocated in a given year, such portion of the balance as determined by the Compensation Committee may be carried forward and be available for incentive awards in any subsequent year or years.

In his amended complaint, Garber avers that in or about January 1991 the Compensation Committee made awards under the Key Plan and other incentive plans totaling $168,490,050 for the three year period ending December 31, 1990. * * * While the amended complaint is ambiguous, it is apparent from proxy statements filed with the Securities and Exchange Commission by Westinghouse that the amount pleaded by Garber represents annual awards made over the three year period between 1988 and 1990. The district court found that the Compensation Committee awarded $28 million in Key Plan awards to 292 Westinghouse employees on January 29, 1991. This total included compensation awards to board members

Paul Lego and Theodore Stern, the only board members employed as officers of the corporation.

Prior to the time the awards were approved by the Compensation Committee, Westinghouse reported consolidated net income of $1,403 million for 1990. On February 27, 1991, Westinghouse restated its consolidated net income before taxes for 1990 to reflect a re-valuation of certain Westinghouse Credit Corporation assets, the effect of which was to reduce Westinghouse's consolidated net income by $975 million, from $1,403 million to $428 million before taxes.

Garber contends that prior to the incentive awards, defendant Lego was advised that the assets held by Westinghouse Credit had substantially deteriorated. He further contends that individual members of the Compensation Committee and the board of directors "knew or were told that a major write-down could be pending which would eliminate or substantially reduce Westinghouse's reported net income for 1990." Garber alleges that, despite this knowledge, the Compensation Committee and board "intentionally or recklessly" proceeded to make or approve the incentive awards and that, after the write-down was announced, the individual defendants "intentionally or recklessly" approved or acquiesced in the awards and did nothing to cancel or recover them.

Garber asserts that the incentive awards "constituted such a gross misuse and abuse of the Key Plan and the other plans as to amount to waste" and that because the Compensation Committee knew of the write-down, the incentive awards exceeded the limits imposed under the Key Plan.

Garber also avers that he made no pre-complaint demand on Westinghouse's board of directors because doing so would have been futile. In support of this assertion, Garber contends that such action would have been futile because Westinghouse's directors would not sue themselves, having acted intentionally or recklessly in making, approving, or acquiescing in the incentive awards despite their knowledge of the impending write-down. Garber's brief to this court asserts that this pleading complied with Federal Rule 23.1 and Pennsylvania Rule 1506 governing shareholder derivative suits.

* * * [T]he district court * * * grant[ed] defendant's motion to dismiss Garber's amended complaint for failure to comply with the pre-litigation demand requirement of Federal Rule 23.1 and Pennsylvania Rule 1506. * * *

* * *

III.

A shareholder derivative suit "permits an individual shareholder to bring suit to enforce a corporate cause of action against officers, directors, and third parties." *Kamen v. Kemper Financial Services, Inc.*, 500 U.S. 90, 95 (1991) (*quoting Ross v. Bernhard*, 396 U.S. 531, 534 (1970)). Both the federal and the Pennsylvania Rules of Civil Procedure require that, prior to filing a derivative suit, a shareholder must either make a demand on the corporation to obtain the desired action or allege in the complaint the reasons for not making the effort. These rules are predicated on the notion that "[t]he decision to bring a lawsuit or to refrain from litigating a claim on behalf of the corporation is a decision concerning the management of the corporation and consequently is the responsibility of the directors."

In discussing the origins of the derivative suit, the Supreme Court in *Kamen* noted:

> Devised as a suit in equity, the purpose of the derivative action was to place in the hands of the individual shareholder a means to protect the interests of the corporation from the misfeasance and malfeasance of "faithless directors and managers." To prevent abuse of this remedy, however, equity courts established as a "precondition for the suit" that the shareholder demonstrate "that the corporation itself had refused to proceed after suitable demand, unless excused by extraordinary conditions."

This precondition requirement established by courts of equity has been incorporated in Federal Rule of Civil Procedure 23.1 * * *.

[Following *Kamen*, the Third Circuit determined that it should look to Pennsylvania law to determine the substance of the "demand" requirement.]

In Pennsylvania, the filing of a shareholder derivative suit is governed by Pennsylvania Rule of Civil Procedure 1506. Prior to the adoption of Rule 1506 by the state legislature in 1952, the state Supreme Court considered on a number of occasions the ability of a shareholder to bring a derivative suit on behalf of a corporation. In doing so, the state Supreme Court has thoroughly developed the scope of its futility exception. In addition, the state Supreme Court had adopted Equity Rule 37. This precursor to Rule 1506 is virtually identical in the procedural requirements it established before a shareholder derivative suit could be maintained. Because Rule 1506 is based on this earlier jurisprudence, it is helpful to consider the state Supreme Court's decisions in this area of the law.

[Under Pennsylvania law,] "[t]he right of an individual shareholder to act for the corporation is exceptional, and only arises on a clear showing of special circumstances, among which inability or unwillingness of the corporation itself, demand upon the regular corporate management, and refusal to act, are imperative requisites." The Pennsylvania Supreme Court recognized that in some instances demand would be "useless" and thus would be excused. In such instances, the "charge should rest on some act, affirmative or permissive, manifestly, in violation of duty [to act], and *manifestly the result of fraud, and not erroneous judgment*."

* * *

In sum, in order to excuse demand under Pennsylvania law, the plaintiff must allege that a majority of the board of directors engaged in acts that are fraudulent; not that they merely exercised erroneous business judgment. * * *

A.

* * *

Garber acknowledges that he has not made a demand on Westinghouse or the individual defendants. * * * The relevant portion of his amended complaint states that no demand has been made because each defendant is liable for their alleged misconduct.

Each individual defendant acted intentionally or recklessly, in making or approving the aforesaid improper incentive compensation awards, after being told that a major write-down could be pending. Each individual defendant acted intentionally or recklessly in approving or acquiescing in the improper aforesaid awards, after the write-down of $975 million was announced about a month later, and did nothing to cancel or recover the awards which were improper and which, further, were in violation of the [Key] Plan's provisions. The individual defendants could not and would not diligently prosecute this action because by doing so the individual defendants would be suing themselves for their own intentional or reckless misconduct in respect of the awards for which each is liable in this action to Westinghouse.

Our task is to determine whether this averment is sufficient to excuse demand as formulated by Pennsylvania law. On its face, the amended complaint does not allege that the individual defendants engaged in fraud or fraudulent acts. However, because Garber intimates that Westinghouse's directors have engaged in misconduct, we will look behind the form of the complaint to determine whether the averment is sufficient to excuse demand. * * *

Garber maintains that each individual defendant was aware of the $975 million write-down at the time of the incentive awards and that they proceeded with the awards despite this knowledge. There are two major facets to Garber's assertion that the individual defendants acted intentionally and recklessly. First, that the members of the Compensation Committee granted the incentive awards in violation of the Key Plan's limits. Second, that the awards were granted at a time when the members of the Compensation Committee knew that Westinghouse was about to reduce its 1990 net income by more than sixty percent. We must decide whether, assuming the facts alleged in the complaint as true, it alleges specific acts of fraud enough for us to determine that proper demand should have been excused.

Even if the individual members of the Compensation Committee knew that Westinghouse's consolidated net income before taxes and the awards would be sixty percent lower in 1990 as a result of the write-down, nothing specific in the complaint alleges that the Key Plan awards for 1990 violated the conditions of the Plan. Garber acknowledges that, if the full amount available under the Key Plan is not allocated in a given year, such portion of the balance as determined by the Compensation Committee may be carried forward and be available for incentive awards in any subsequent year. The amended complaint fails to specify the amount of awards provided in each individual year. Without more, it is impossible to determine whether the Compensation Committee carried forward surplus amounts from years prior to 1990. The amended complaint fails to specify how the conditions of the Key Plan were violated in the approval of incentive awards for 1990. It simply asserts that it was violated. Without more, Garber has failed to state with specificity any acts amounting to fraudulent activity by members of the Compensation Committee.

Garber's second major contention is that the individual defendants acted intentionally and recklessly in granting these awards in the context of the $975 million write-down by Westinghouse. Compensation awards are a matter of business judgment. While Westinghouse Credit Corporation suffered a huge loss in 1990, other divisions of Westinghouse Corporation may have been successful. Westinghouse argued on appeal that, even if a division is performing poorly, the Compensation Committee may believe that individual officers within that division should be rewarded, or that incentive awards are necessary to retain a high achiever. These are matters of business judgment and, without specific allegations of fraudulent acts, we are compelled to find under Pennsylvania law that demand should not be excused.

Searching throughout Garber's amended complaint, we fail to find any such specific allegations. Moreover, cases in which the Pennsylvania Supreme Court has held that demand on the corporation was not necessary have generally involved situations in which individual defendants personally profited from their own actions. * * *

[Here, however], the shareholder in the present dispute fails to allege any acts of self-dealing by members of the Compensation Committee. Garber's amended complaint does not allege that the members of the Compensation Committee personally profited from any of the actions at issue in his complaint.

Nor does Garber allege any collusion between the two members of the board who did receive incentive awards and the five members of the Compensation Committee who approved of the awards. * * *

* * *

Garber also contends that demand was futile because the defendants would not pursue this cause of action because to do so "would be suing themselves." But merely charging that demand was futile because board members would not approve of litigation to repeal actions which they had approved, without more, does not amount to an allegation of fraud and thus does not excuse Garber from the substantive requirements necessary to comply with Pennsylvania Rule 1506.

Lastly, Garber asserts that the awards constituted such an abuse of the Key Plan and the other plans as to amount to corporate waste. However, a charge of corporate waste which does not include allegations of fraud or self-dealing does not meet the degree of specificity required under Pennsylvania law to excuse demand. What a corporation decides to do with its assets is primarily a matter of business judgment. The demand futility exception under Pennsylvania Rule 1506 does not provide the authority for shareholders to bring suit simply because they disagree with the board of directors' business judgment. Without specific allegations of fraudulent activity engaged in by a majority of the board of directors, Garber's amended complaint fails to set forth sufficient reasons to excuse demand.

* * *

IV.

For the foregoing reasons, we hold that Garber failed to set forth sufficient pleadings to excuse demand pursuant to Federal Rule 23.1 and Pennsylvania Rule 1506. We will affirm the order of the district court dismissing the amended complaint.

NOTES AND QUESTIONS

1. *Garber* held that demand was not excused because no specific allegations of fraud were made. What if the five members of the Compensation Committee were officers of the corporation and had received large compensation awards? What if all of the members of the Compensation Committee were appointed by the two board members who had received the large awards? What if the only officers of the corporation who had received large compensation awards were board members Lego and Stern? As a practical matter, was demand futile in *Garber*?

2. Three rationales for the demand requirement have been offered. First, derivative actions necessarily impinge upon the directors' prerogative of managing the corporation. According to this point of view, demand is seen as a corporate governance issue. Second, demand can be understood as a means of promoting intra-corporate dispute resolution and thereby conserving resources. Third, it is thought to discourage strike (*i.e.*, meritless) suits. *See, e.g.*, Carol B. Swanson, *Juggling Shareholder Rights and Strike Suits in Derivative Litigation: The ALI Drops the Ball*, 77 Minn. L. Rev. 1339, 1350–51 (1993). Which of these rationales does Pennsylvania law adopt? What is the proper rationale (or rationales) for the demand requirement? Note that the underlying rationale for the demand that one adopts may influence one's view about what substantive requirements must be met to satisfy (or excuse) demand.

3. Pennsylvania courts excuse demand only when the shareholder plaintiff alleges acts of fraud. Other jurisdictions use different formulations. In Delaware, for example, the test for excusing demand is "whether, under the particularized facts alleged, a reasonable doubt is created that: (1) the directors are disinterested and independent [or] (2) the challenged transaction was otherwise the product of a valid exercise of business judgment." *Aronson v. Lewis*, 473 A.2d 805, 814 (Del. 1984). Is this difference in formulation merely a matter of terminology? Or does the difference appear to be substantive?

4. Demand futility has been extensively litigated in the courts because of its central role in the derivative action. If demand is not excused, a shareholder may continue to pursue a derivative action only if the denial of the demand was wrongful. Understandably, many shareholders tend to claim that demand is futile. As a result of the extensive litigation on this issue, the legislatures of some states have adopted a universal demand requirement, meaning that demand must be made regardless of its perceived futility. *See, e.g.*, Fla. Stat. Ann. § 607.07401(2); Ga. Code Ann. § 14–2–742; Mich. Comp. Laws § 450.1493a. In addition, the American Bar Association's *Revised Model Business Corporation Act* and the American Law Institute's *Principles of Corporate Governance* have advocated a universal demand requirement. Should demand always be required? What are the counter arguments?

5. In *Kanter v. Barella*, 388 F. Supp. 2d 474 (D.N.J. 2005), the court, in finding that the demand requirement was not satisfied, noted that although "the Complaint allege[d] reckless oversight by all Defendants during the relevant period," it "acknowledge[d] that at least three of the director defendants were not even directors during part of that period." *Id.* at 480. According to the court, "[s]uch conclusory allegations do not satisfy the heightened pleading requirements of Rule 23.1." *Id.* The court also cited to plaintiff's "fail[ure] to point to any 'red flags' that may have put the Directors on notice of any wrongdoing * * *." *Id.* Is such a stringent approach warranted?

6. Corporate boards have attempted to reassert control over derivative litigation by creating special litigation committees. "A special litigation committee is a committee of one or more independent directors who are appointed by a majority of the board to review and make a binding determination with respect to whether the corporation should seek dismissal of a pending derivative action against or involving a majority of the board of directors." Ralph C. Ferrara, Kevin T. Abikoff, and Laura L. Gansler, *Shareholder Derivative Litigation* § 8.01 (1995). A number of the states have passed legislation expressly authorizing the use of special litigation committees. *See, e.g.,* Ga. Code Ann. § 14–2–744(b)(2); Ind. Code Ann. § 23–1–32–4; Minn. Stat. Ann. § 302A.241; N.D. Cent. Code § 10–19.1–48.

An important issue regarding the special litigation committee is the degree of deference that should be paid to the decisions of the committee. In one of the first cases to consider the issue, the New York Court of Appeals held in *Auerbach v. Bennett*, 393 N.E.2d 994 (N.Y. 1979), that the merits of the decision to terminate derivative litigation, if made in good faith and after sufficient investigation by a committee of disinterested directors, fell under the business judgment doctrine. Some commentators have criticized the *Auerbach* approach as being too deferential to management. *See, e.g.,* Charles W. Murdock, *Corporate Governance—The Role of Special Litigation Committees*, 68 Wash.L. Rev. 79 (1993); Carol B. Swanson, *Juggling Shareholder Rights and Strike Suits in Derivative Litigation: The ALI Drops the Ball*, 77 Minn. L. Rev. 1339 (1993).

Although most courts have concluded that special litigation committees deserve some degree of deference, the Iowa Supreme Court has held that directors who are defendants and who constitute a majority of the corporation's board may not delegate to a committee the power to bind the corporation as to the conduct of the litigation. *See Miller v. Register & Tribune Syndicate, Inc.*, 336 N.W.2d 709 (Iowa 1983). The *Miller* court did not believe that the special litigation committee could be "disinterested" when it was appointed by an "interested" board. What arguments can be made in response to the *Miller* court?

3. SIMILARITIES TO RULE 23

a. Adequacy of Representation

General Considerations. Rule 23.1 provides that a shareholder derivative action "may not be maintained" if the plaintiff "does not fairly and adequately represent the interests of shareholders or members who are similarly situated in enforcing the right of the corporation * * *." Although the "fair and adequate" representation component of Rule 23.1 is virtually identical to the adequacy requirement of Rule 23(a)(4) (*see* Chapter 2(B)(4)), cases construing this portion of Rule 23.1 often do not mention traditional class action case law or Rule 23. *See, e.g., Larson v. Dumke*, 900 F.2d 1363, 1367 (9th Cir. 1990); *Rothenberg v. Security Mgmt. Co.*, 667 F.2d 958, 961 (11th Cir. 1982). One leading case on the issue of adequacy in shareholder derivative actions is *Davis v. Comed, Inc.*, 619 F.2d 588 (6th Cir. 1980). In *Davis*, a shareholder brought suit to set aside the sale of corporate real estate. Although the *Davis* court did not specifically mention the adequacy standard under Rule 23, it listed elements commonly examined in traditional class actions:

> Among the elements * * * [to consider in determining] whether the derivative plaintiff meets Rule 23.1's requirements are: economic antagonisms between representative and class; the remedy

sought by plaintiff in the derivative action; indications that the named plaintiff was not the driving force behind the litigation; plaintiff's unfamiliarity with the litigation; other litigation pending between the plaintiff and defendants; the relative magnitude of plaintiff's personal interests as compared to his interest in the derivative action itself; plaintiff's vindictiveness toward the defendants; and, finally, the degree of support plaintiff was receiving from the shareholders he purported to represent.

Id. at 593–94. The court compared the plaintiff's interests (he wanted to acquire the property for himself) with those of the rest of the shareholders, and concluded that plaintiff was an inadequate representative because of this economic antagonism.

A few courts have held, without detailed analysis, that the adequacy standards of Rule 23 and Rule 23.1 are the same. *See, e.g., Guenther v. Pacific Telecom., Inc.*, 123 F.R.D. 341, 344 n.5 (D. Or. 1987) ("[B]oth rules use identical language as to the requirement of adequate representation. Consequently, it is well established that the analysis applied in class actions is equally applicable to derivative cases."); *Fradkin v. Ernst*, 98 F.R.D. 478, 484 (N.D. Ohio 1983) (adequacy requirements are "virtually identical linguistically," and precedent developed in class actions is applicable to adequacy issues raised under Rule 23.1); *see also Lewis v. Curtis*, 671 F.2d 779, 788–89 (3d Cir. 1982) (Rule 23.1 adequacy standard is "similar" to that used under Rule 23(a)(4), and "cases decided under Rule 23(a)(4) may be used in analyzing the requirements of Rule 23.1").

Even many of these courts, however, have noted that differences in the purposes of class actions and shareholder derivative suits may require distinctions in the adequacy analysis. For example, in a class action, the class representative has a direct stake in the outcome. In derivative suits, however, only the corporation benefits directly from a successful result. Accordingly, courts have indicated that the dollar value of a derivative plaintiff's stock holdings is not relevant in assessing his or her adequacy. *See, e.g., Lewis*, 671 F.2d at 788. Does that reasoning make sense?

Some courts have gone even further—concluding that the standards for adequacy under Rule 23.1 are significantly different. As one court reasoned:

> The contrasting difference between a stockholder's suit for his corporation and a suit by him against it is crucial. In the former, he has no claim of his own; he merely has a personal controversy with his corporation regarding the business wisdom or legal basis for the latter's assertion of a claim against third parties. Whatever money or property is to be recovered would go to the corporation, not a fraction of it to the stockholder. When such a suit is entertained, the stockholder is in effect allowed to conscript the corporation as a complainant on a claim that the corporation, in the exercise for what it asserts to be its uncoerced discretion, is unwilling to initiate. This is a wholly different situation from that which arises when the corporation is charged with invasion of the stockholder's independent right. * * *

Thus, given the distinct nature of a derivative claim and the special role which the shareholder plaintiff plays in its prosecution, it is apparent * * * that many of the factors looked to in the class action context become irrelevant in derivative suits and questions going to the fairness and adequacy of a derivative plaintiff's representation must be viewed through a somewhat different looking glass. * * *

If, from the foregoing, a rule might be synthesized it is: when a derivative plaintiff demonstrates to the court an intent and desire to vigorously prosecute the underlying corporate claim and when he has engaged competent counsel to assist in the endeavor then, absent either a conflict of interest which goes to the forcefulness of the prosecution or the existence of antagonism between the plaintiff and other shareholders arising from differences of opinion concerning the best method of vindicating the corporate claim, the representation requirement of Rule 23.1 is met.

Sweet v. Bermingham, 65 F.R.D. 551, 554 (S.D.N.Y. 1975); *see also, e.g., Kirkpatrick v. J. C. Bradford & Co.*, 827 F.2d 718, 728 n.7 (11th Cir. 1987) ("A derivative suit poses inherent conflicts between those minority shareholders who are bringing the suit and the majority shareholders whose administration is being challenged either directly or indirectly. In contrast, a class suit by definition serves to benefit the members of the class.").

Conflicts. Regardless of whether the analysis is tied to that under Rule 23(a)(4), the adequacy factor that has generated the most controversy in shareholder derivative suits is whether a conflict of interest exists between the representative and other class members. Courts disagree over which other shareholders, if any, must be compared with the named plaintiff. For example, in *Kuzmickey v. Dunmore Corp.*, 420 F. Supp. 226 (E.D. Pa. 1976), and *Rathborne v. Rathborne*, 508 F. Supp. 515 (E.D. La. 1980), *aff'd on other grounds*, 683 F.2d 914 (5th Cir. 1982), the courts compared the interests of the named plaintiff to those of all the other shareholders and found the named plaintiffs inadequate because they did not represent the interests of the majority of the other shareholders. Other courts have taken the position that refusing to allow any shareholder to maintain a derivative suit would sometimes leave both the plaintiff and the corporation "without a remedy for defendants' alleged misconduct." *See, e.g., Halsted Video, Inc. v. Guttillo*, 115 F.R.D. 177 (N.D. Ill. 1987).

One commentator argues that the approach in such cases as *Kuzmickey* and *Rathborne* is erroneous in light of the purposes of Rule 23.1:

> * * * [F]ederal courts considering potential conflicts are arguably comparing the interests of the wrong parties. The federal courts in a derivative suit currently compare the interests of the derivative plaintiff to those of the remaining shareholders. * * *
>
> This method, comparing the interests of the plaintiff to the similarly situated shareholders, is apparently carried over from the class action cases. * * * In a class action, it may be appropriate to compare the interests of the representative to those of the class whose individual rights the plaintiff is asserting. In a derivative suit, however, the plaintiff occupies a different position which the

class action test for adequacy of representation arguably fails to recognize.

In a derivative suit, three parties with potentially conflicting interests can be identified—the plaintiff, the remaining shareholders, and the corporation itself. In determining whose interests should be compared for the purposes of ascertaining conflicts, the language of Rule 23.1 should be examined. The Rule states that the plaintiff need only represent the interests of shareholders similarly situated in enforcing the right of the corporation. The heart of the cause of action is the interest being asserted by the corporation. Therefore, it seems appropriate to ascertain conflicts by comparing the interests of both the plaintiff and the other shareholders with the best interests of the corporation itself. If the economic or personal agenda of the remaining shareholders conflicts with that of the corporation, the plaintiff should not be required to represent them in enforcing the corporate cause. If the plaintiff's own economic or personal interests conflict with those of the corporation, then he or she should be disqualified as an adequate champion of that corporate right.

Mary M. Matthews, *Derivative Suits and the Similarly Situated Shareholder Requirement*, 8 DePaul Bus. L.J. 1, 25–28 (1995).

Standing to Raise Adequacy. Can a director or officer who is sued in a derivative action raise an issue regarding the adequacy of the shareholder representative and counsel? Consider the following case.

DELEO V. SWIRSKY

United States District Court, Northern District of Illinois, 2002.
2002 WL 989526.

MARTIN C. ASHMAN, UNITED STATES MAGISTRATE JUDGE.

Report and Recommendation†

Defendant Benjamin Swirsky seeks to disqualify named plaintiff Neal DeLeo and his attorney Bruce Golden from representing the interests of the shareholders of Easy Access International, Inc. ("EAI") in this derivative suit. Swirsky contends that DeLeo and Golden have an irreconcilable conflict of interest with the shareholders of EAI that cannot be waived. DeLeo and Golden question Swirsky's standing to raise the issue of disqualification * * *. For the following reasons, we recommend that Swirsky's Motion to Disqualify be denied due to lack of standing. On our own motion, however, we find that DeLeo [and Golden] should be disqualified [on adequacy grounds] * * *.

I.

The instant motion to disqualify concerns DeLeo's position as a plaintiff in two pending lawsuits against Swirsky relating to Zconnexx Corporation, which prior to May 1999 was a wholly owned subsidiary of EAI. One of the lawsuits is pending in New York, the other, this derivative suit, in Illinois.

---

† The Report and Recommendation was approved in its entirety by the district court. 2002 WL 1447855 (N.D. Ill. July 2, 2002). [Ed.]

DeLeo and Internet Yellow Pages Network, Inc., a corporation half-owned by DeLeo, filed the lawsuit in New York on April 18, 2000, against Zconnexx, Swirsky, and six other defendants for breach of fiduciary duty, trademark infringement, domain name theft, misappropriation of trade secrets, unfair competition, and fraud. The gravamen of DeLeo and Internet Yellow's complaint is that Zconnexx stole www.yellowpage.net and other property from DeLeo and Internet Yellow in March 1999. DeLeo and Internet Yellow seek to hold Swirsky, a director of Zconnexx at the time, and some of the other defendants individually liable because they allegedly acted in concert to deprive DeLeo and Internet Yellow of their property. * * * As of December 17, 2001, the New York lawsuit has been stayed, apparently because Zconnexx and one of the other defendants are in bankruptcy. * * *

DeLeo filed this derivative suit on behalf of EAI shareholders in Illinois on November 3, 2000, against Zconnexx, Swirsky, and two other defendants for breach of fiduciary duty, fraudulent concealment, conversion, and fraud under § 10(b) of the Securities Act of 1934 and Rule 10b–5 of the Securities and Exchange Commission. This derivative suit involves an allegedly fraudulent transaction of securities between EAI and Swirsky in April 1999. According to DeLeo, EAI, a corporation controlled by Swirsky, pledged all of the issued and outstanding shares of Zconnexx to Beswir Properties, Inc., another corporation controlled by Swirsky, for no consideration. Shortly thereafter, Beswir informed EAI that Beswir was foreclosing on the pledge and that it would assume full rights, title, and interest to the pledged shares of Zconnexx. EAI and Zconnexx, both under the control of Swirsky, acceded to Beswir's demand, and on April 27, 1999, the three-member board of Zconnexx, which consisted of Swirsky, Swirsky's son-in-law, and Swirsky's attorney, adopted a resolution approving the transfer of the pledged shares from EAI to Beswir. Accordingly, EAI lost ownership of Zconnexx, and Zconnexx became a wholly owned subsidiary of Beswir.

In this derivative suit, DeLeo, on behalf of EAI shareholders, alleges that the pledge, the foreclosure of the pledge, and the board resolution were intentionally concealed from EAI shareholders in violation of the law. As a matter of fact, DeLeo alleges that Swirsky never informed anyone, including the SEC, that EAI had lost its entire interest in Zconnexx, although trading in EAI's stock continued. It was not until October 2000 that DeLeo uncovered Swirsky's purported intentional concealment of this information upon receiving Swirsky's response to a discovery request in the course of the litigation in New York.

For relief in this derivative suit, DeLeo seeks money damages against Swirsky * * *. DeLeo also seeks an accounting of Swirsky and punitive damages against him. Zconnexx *was* a defendant [but a default judgment was entered against it.] * * *

Golden, who represents DeLeo and other EAI shareholders in this derivative suit against Swirsky in Illinois, also represents DeLeo and Internet Yellow against Zconnexx, Swirsky, and the other defendants in New York.

* * *

II.

* * *

A.

DeLeo and Golden first challenge Swirsky's standing to bring the instant motion to disqualify. DeLeo and Golden assert that only EAI, which * * * is not a party to this derivative suit, has standing to contest the adequacy of DeLeo's and Golden's representation of EAI shareholders.

To bring a motion before the court, the moving party must establish an " 'injury in fact resulting from the action which [he] seek[s] to have the court adjudicate.' " An injury in fact generally must be sustained by the moving party himself. An injury in fact exists not only if the moving party shows that he is suffering harm, but also if he shows that there is a reasonable probability that he will suffer harm. In addition, the moving party must show that his injury in fact is capable of being redressed by the relief that he asks the court to provide.

* * *

The importance of having a fair and adequate named plaintiff and attorney in a derivative suit cannot be overstated. In a derivative suit, the named plaintiff assumes a position of fiduciary character, taking into his hands not his claims alone, but also those of a class of individuals who are similarly situated. All of the shareholders depend on the named plaintiff's and his attorney's diligence, wisdom, and integrity. Though shareholders can elect a director or manager, they have no such election with regard to who represents them in a derivative suit. And unlike a class suit, shareholders have no ability to opt out of a derivative suit. Thus, all shareholders are bound by the outcome of the derivative suit regardless of their objections.

Against this backdrop, we turn to the issue presented—whether Swirsky, in his role as an individual defendant in this derivative action, has standing to bring a motion to disqualify DeLeo, a named plaintiff, and his attorney, Golden. The parties agree that a defendant corporation may raise the issue of disqualification. The corporation, although ordinarily positioned as a nominal defendant in a derivative suit, is realistically the true plaintiff, as any avails realized from the derivative suit belong to it and it alone. In terms of the shareholders' having fair and adequate representation, the benefit of this condition runs directly to the corporation; fair and adequate representation of the shareholders in the prosecution of a corporate claim places the corporation in a better position to recover against the alleged wrongdoer. It only makes sense, then, that the corporation has standing to challenge the adequacy of the named plaintiff and his attorney in a derivative suit. It suffers the injury caused by unfair and inadequate representation.[3]

The interests that serve as the basis for allowing the defendant corporation to challenge the fairness and adequacy of the representation provided by the named plaintiff and his attorney in a derivative suit, however,

---

[3] EAI * * *, has presented no motion to disqualify in this case as it has not been a participant in this case in any way.

do not provide a basis for allowing a defendant director charged with fraud to make the same challenge. Any avails realized from such a derivative suit would not belong to the director. In terms of the shareholders' having fair and adequate representation, the benefit of this condition would not run to the director, it would offer him no protection and would not increase his chances of successfully defending the derivative suit. Actually, the benefit of the shareholders' having fair and adequate representation would place the director in a worse position, so to speak. The better the representation of the shareholders, the more difficult it should be for the director to obtain a decision in his favor.

This lack of any injury caused by unfair and inadequate shareholder representation establishes that defendant directors charged with fraud, like Swirsky, are unable to object to the fairness and adequacy of the named plaintiff and his attorney in a derivative suit. Therefore, Swirsky's Motion to Disqualify should be denied.

It would be perverse indeed to allow a defendant director charged with fraud, like Swirsky, to assume the contorted position of defending his actions against charges brought by a group of shareholders while simultaneously discommending their representation and requesting the court to pave the way for a more suitable foe. The fairness and adequacy requirement would be misplaced as another weapon in the director's arsenal to eliminate the derivative suit, rather than serve its true purpose as a safeguard of the interests of the shareholders. This reality militates against allowing Swirsky to challenge the fairness and adequacy of DeLeo and Golden.

* * *

[The Magistrate nonetheless examined the adequacy of Deleo and Golden *sua sponte* and recommended that the court disqualify both of them for lack of adequacy.]

NOTES AND QUESTIONS

1. Should the adequacy requirement under Rule 23.1 differ from the inquiry under Rule 23(a)(4)? Why have courts taken such diverse approaches to adequacy under Rule 23.1? Is the rule itself ambiguous? Does the approach suggested by Professor Matthews have merit?

2. In finding no standing, can the court's analysis in *Deleo* be reconciled with the analysis applied in the class action context, in which the defendants in a case are allowed to raise the adequacy of plaintiffs and plaintiffs' counsel (*see* Chapter 2(B)(4)(c))? Under the approach taken in *Deleo*, how would issues of adequacy of representation ever be raised?

3. An interesting issue arises when the same plaintiff seeks to bring both a derivative action on behalf of the corporation and a class action naming the corporation as a defendant. Few courts have directly commented on the issue, and cases are often brought simultaneously as direct and derivative suits, with the same named plaintiffs bringing both claims. Some courts, however, have noted that there is an irreconcilable conflict in that situation—one cannot simultaneously attempt to take money away from the corporation (in a class action when the corporation is a defendant) and recover money for the corporation (in a derivative action when plaintiff is suing on behalf of the corporation). *See, e.g., Ruggiero v. Am. Bioculture, Inc.*, 56 F.R.D. 93 (S.D.N.Y.

1972) (named plaintiffs in derivative action against former directors for mismanagement of corporate funds could not simultaneously serve as class representatives in suit against corporation for securities fraud arising from same transaction). *See also In re Analytical Surveys, Inc. Securitites Litig.*, 2001 WL 406332, at *4 (S.D. Ind. 2001) (citing cases). Should courts find an irreconcilable conflict in this situation?

b. Notification and Court Approval of Settlement

In 1966, when Rule 23.1 was created specifically for derivative suits, the original Rule 23 language concerning court approval and notice was carried forward without change in Rule 23.1. Rule 23.1 currently provides that a derivative action "may be settled, voluntarily dismissed, or compromised only with the court's approval. Notice of a proposed settlement, voluntary dismissal, or compromise must be given to shareholders or members in the manner that the court orders." Because of the common pedigree and closely parallel wording of Rule 23(e) and Rule 23.1, most courts facing derivative suits apply the same notice and settlement approval standards used in class actions.

The essential purpose of notice of settlement or dismissal under Rule 23.1 is to protect the shareholders' due process rights: "to fairly apprise the prospective [shareholders] of the terms of the proposed settlement and of the options that are open to them * * * [and to provide] sufficient information for them to make a rational decision whether they should intervene in the settlement approval procedure." *Maher v. Zapata Corp.*, 714 F.2d 436, 451 (5th Cir. 1983). Notice also inhibits collusive or fraudulent settlements (*see Rogosin v. Steadman*, 71 F.R.D. 514, 520 (S.D.N.Y. 1976)), and encourages those with differing views to come forth, thereby allowing the court to identify possible inadequacies in the proposed settlement (*see Cohen v. Young*, 127 F.2d 721, 725 (6th Cir. 1942)).

Courts generally require that the notice contain a description of the derivative suit's claims and defenses, the terms of the proposed settlement, and the time and place for shareholders to appear to show cause why the settlement should not be adopted. *See, e.g., Maher*, 714 F.2d at 451; *Susquehanna Corp. v. Korholz*, 84 F.R.D. 316, 324–25 (N.D. Ill. 1979). Although some courts have permitted notice by publication, the difficulty in ascertaining who should be personally notified in a derivative suit is not as complicated as in some class actions (in which the identity of many class members is unknown or unascertainable), because corporations are required to keep information concerning their current shareholders of record. *See, e.g., Boggess v. Hogan*, 410 F. Supp. 433 (N.D. Ill. 1975); William E. Haudek, *The Settlement and Dismissal of Stockholder's Actions—Part II: The Settlement*, 23 S.W.L.J. 765, 788 (1969).

Rule 23.1 also requires courts to approve settlement agreements, but gives no guidance on how such agreements should be evaluated. Courts generally employ the same analysis that is applied in class actions— whether the settlement is "fair, adequate, and reasonable." *Maher*, 714 F.2d at 454. Additionally, courts consider whether the agreement was reached through fraud or collusion (*id.*), and the objections lodged by shareholders (*see, e.g., Bell Atl. Corp. v. Bolger*, 2 F.3d 1304 (3d Cir. 1993)). In assessing fairness and reasonableness, most courts also consider:

the extent of the benefit to be derived from the proposed settlement by the corporation, the real party in interest * * *. The adequacy of the recovery must be considered in the light of the best possible recovery, of the risks of establishing liability and proving damages in the event the case is not settled, and of the cost of prolonging the litigation.

Id. at 1310.

c. Other Rule 23 Issues

Application of Rule 23(a) Requirements. Numerosity is not an issue in a derivative action, since the shareholders are bringing suit on behalf of the corporation, not on behalf of other shareholders. Indeed, as one treatise has noted, "a derivative action may be brought even when the number of shareholders is too small to justify a class suit." 7C Charles A. Wright, Arthur R. Miller & Mary K. Kane, *Federal Practice and Procedure* § 1821, at 17 (3d ed. 2007). Issues of typicality and commonality likewise do not generally arise in shareholder derivative suits. As one court summarized:

> [Defendants claim that plaintiffs'] inadequacy to serve as named parties if this were a Rule 23 class action necessarily renders them inadequate to sue on behalf of the [corporation] under Rule 23.1.
>
> The defendants' analogy to class actions is untenable. The named plaintiffs in a Rule 23 class action must themselves have suffered the kind of injury common to the class. But the plaintiffs in a Rule 23.1 derivative action must simply be capable of presenting the issues fairly in court; how the events in question affected them personally never enters the picture. The Rule 23.1 derivative action is based on the right of the [corporation], and hence, only the injury to the [corporation] is at issue. Shareholders qualify to bring suit on behalf of the [corporation] based on their stock ownership, through which they suffer an indirect injury.

Bolton v. Gramlich, 540 F. Supp. 822, 835 (S.D.N.Y. 1982). Are there circumstances in which commonality and typicality concepts should come into play in a derivative suit? *See generally* Angel R. Oquendo, *Six Degrees of Separation: From Derivative Suits to Shareholder Class Actions*, 48 Wake Forest L. Rev. 643 (2013) (discussing differences between shareholder class actions under Rule 23 and derivative suits under Rule 23.1).

Application of *Devlin v. Scardelletti.* The application of *Devlin v. Scardelletti*, 536 U.S. 1 (2002) (discussed in Chapter 9(B)(2)) to derivative suits remains uncertain. In *Robert F. Booth Trust v. Crowley*, 687 F.3d 314 (7th Cir. 2012), the Seventh Circuit stated:

> * * * In *Crawford v. Equifax Payment Services, Inc.*, 201 F.3d 877, 881 (7th Cir. 2000), we told district judges to grant intervention freely to persons who want to contest settlements in class actions under Fed. R. Civ. P. 23; that is no less true of derivative actions under Rule 23.1.
>
> Our conclusion that Frank is entitled to intervene makes it unnecessary to decide whether *Felzen* [*v. Andreas,* 134 F.3d 873 (7th Cir. 1998), *aff'd by an equally divided Court,* 525 U.S. 315

(1999)] survives *Devlin*. *Devlin* holds that a member of a class certified under Rule 23, who asks the district court not to approve a settlement, need not intervene in order to appeal an adverse decision. Our opinion in *Felzen* gives several reasons why investors in a derivative suit differ from members of a certified class. For example: a class member holds a personal claim for relief, which could be extinguished or cashed out by a settlement; but an investor does not hold any kind of personal stake in a derivative suit. The chose in action belongs to the corporation. Intervention separates an objecting investor from the thousands or even millions of shareholders, bondholders, employees, suppliers, and customers who could be affected, more or less directly, by the resolution of a derivative action.

The Supreme Court affirmed *Felzen* without opinion by a vote of 4–4. *Devlin* was decided by a vote of 6–3. This suggests that one or two Justices see a difference between the Rule 23 situation and the Rule 23.1 situation. It is thus hard for a court of appeals to be confident that the Supreme Court as a whole would conclude that *Devlin* controls derivative actions as well as class actions. We think it best to leave the status of *Felzen* to another day—a day that, if district judges grant party status to serious objectors as they should, need never arrive.

Id. at 318–19. Based on the court's discussion in *Crowley,* what is the correct answer to the question of whether *Felzen* survives *Devlin*?

C. SUITS INVOLVING UNINCORPORATED ASSOCIATIONS

The Federal Rules of Civil Procedure provide a special rule, Rule 23.2, for class actions involving unincorporated associations, such as unions, certain trade associations, and the like.

FED. R. CIV. P. 23.2 ACTIONS RELATING TO UNINCORPORATED ASSOCIATIONS

This rule applies to an action brought by or against the members of an unincorporated association as a class by naming certain members as representative parties. The action may be maintained only if it appears that those parties will fairly and adequately protect the interests of the association and its members. In conducting the action, the court may issue any appropriate orders corresponding with those in Rule 23(d), and the procedure for settlement, voluntary dismissal, or compromise must correspond with the procedure in Rule 23(e).

1966 ADVISORY COMMITTEE NOTES TO RULE 23.2

Although an action by or against representatives of the membership of an unincorporated association has often been viewed as a class action, the real or main purpose of this characterization has been to give "entity treatment" to the association when for formal reasons it cannot sue or be sued as a jural person under Rule 17(b). *See* Louisell & Hazard, *Pleading and Procedure: State and Federal* 718 (1962); 3 Moore's *Federal Practice*, par. 23.08 (2d ed. 1963); Story, J. in *West v. Randall*, 29 Fed.Cas. 718, 722–23,

No. 17,424 (C.C.D.R.I. 1820); and, for examples, *Gibbs v. Buck*, 307 U.S. 66 (1939); *Tunstall v. Brotherhood of Locomotive F. & E.*, 148 F.2d 403 (4th Cir. 1945); *Oskoian v. Canuel*, 269 F.2d 311 (1st Cir. 1959). Rule 23.2 deals separately with these actions, referring where appropriate to Rule 23.

At first blush, it may seem peculiar that a separate rule was enacted to provide for class actions involving unincorporated associations. In *Sembach v. McMahon College, Inc.*, 86 F.R.D. 188 (S.D.Tex. 1980), the court provided an explanation:

> In order to properly interpret Rule 23.2, it is necessary to understand its historical background. At common law, an unincorporated association was not a legal entity. It could not be a formal party to a lawsuit and could only sue or be sued through joinder of all of its members. [The court noted that this distinction could be important for two reasons: "First, damages in a suit through joinder would not be recoverable from the association's funds. It would only be recoverable from the funds of the individual association members, if the members were not judgment-proof. Second, as the development of class action proceedings indicate, joinder was often, as a practical matter, impossible."] In 1922, however, the United States Supreme Court held in *United Mineworkers of America v. Coronado Coal Co.*, 259 U.S. 344 (1922), that an unincorporated association could *be sued*, even if state and common law said otherwise, if the purpose of the suit was to enforce a substantive federal right against it. In 1938, the holding of that case was extended by the passage of the original Rule 17(b), Fed. R. Civ. P. That rule, which for our purposes has not changed, said that an unincorporated association could *sue*, as well as *be sued*, when the purpose of the suit was to enforce a substantive federal right. Rule 17(b) also said that, when no federal right was involved in the suit, the federal court should look to the law of the state in which it was sitting to determine the capacity of the unincorporated association to sue or be sued.
>
> This solved the problem of unincorporated associations' access to federal courts where jurisdiction was based on the presence of a federal question, 28 U.S.C. § 1331, but left two problems where jurisdiction was based on diversity of citizenship. 28 U.S.C. § 1332. First, some federal courts were still sitting in states which followed the common law rule. In diversity actions brought in these courts, unincorporated associations could still not be treated as legal entities and could neither sue nor be sued in their own names. Second, unincorporated associations, for diversity purposes, have no citizenship of their own. The courts look to the citizenship of each of the unincorporated association's members to determine whether diversity jurisdiction exists. Since diversity jurisdiction does not exist unless there is complete diversity of citizenship, *Strawbridge v. Curtiss*, 7 U.S. (3 Cranch) 267 (1806), many unincorporated associations still could not sue or be sued in federal courts, even when they could sue and be sued in state courts.

The federal courts soon came upon a solution to these problems: the class action device. One or two members of the unincorporated association were named as representatives of a class consisting of all of the association's members and the class was certified as a "true class" under the original Fed. R. Civ. P. 23(a)(1). [*See* Chapter 1(C)(3).] Through this device, the unincorporated association could essentially be treated as a jural entity, although it still could not be an official party to the suit. Furthermore, as the citizenship of a class is determined for diversity purposes by the citizenship of the class representatives, an unincorporated association could get into federal court so long as any of its members had citizenship diverse from that of the opposing party.

In 1966, the Federal Rules of Civil Procedure were revised. Rule 23 was completely rewritten and Rule 23.2 was added. The latter's purpose was a simple one: to allow the practice followed prior to 1966 under the original Rule 23 to be conducted without change. Rule 23.2 was promulgated to permit unincorporated associations to continue to utilize the class action procedure to get into federal court in diversity cases. As the Advisory Committee Note to Rule 23.2 states:

> Although an action by or against representatives of the membership of an unincorporated association has often been viewed as a class action, the real or main purpose of this characterization has been to give "entity treatment" to the association when for formal reasons it cannot sue or be sued as a jural person under Rule 17(b).

86 F.R.D. at 191–92.

The federal courts rarely use—or even mention—Rule 23.2. Indeed, an electronic search of Westlaw and LEXIS during the preparation of the current edition of this casebook found fewer than 100 cases mentioning Rule 23.2 and unincorporated associations (compared to thousands of cases mentioning Rule 23).

Three important issues that have arisen under Rule 23.2 are discussed below. The first issue is whether the rule is available only in circumstances in which an unincorporated association is not permitted to sue as a "jural entity" in state court. The second issue is whether an association must exist prior to the litigation or may be formed solely for litigation purposes. The third issue is whether the requirements of Rule 23 are applicable to suits under Rule 23.2.

1. APPLICABILITY OF RULE 23.2 WHEN AN UNINCORPORATED ASSOCIATION CAN SUE AS A "JURAL ENTITY" IN STATE COURT

NORTHBROOK EXCESS AND SURPLUS INS. CO. V. MED. MALPRACTICE JOINT UNDERWRITING ASS'N
United States Court of Appeals, First Circuit, 1990.
900 F.2d 476.

Before TORRUELLA and SELYA, CIRCUIT JUDGES, and BOWNES, SENIOR CIRCUIT JUDGE.

BOWNES, SENIOR CIRCUIT JUDGE.

Northbrook Excess and Surplus Insurance Company, plaintiff-appellant, is an Illinois corporation. Defendant-appellee, the Medical Malpractice Joint Underwriting Association (JUA), is an unincorporated association created by the Massachusetts Legislature.[8] Northbrook prevailed in a suit for declaratory judgment it had brought in federal district court. The court found that two doctors against whom malpractice actions had been brought were covered under their prior JUA insurance policies and not their present Northbrook policies. Having won a judgment on the merits, Northbrook now finds itself the appellant in a late-blooming jurisdictional dispute turning on the interpretation of Rule 23.2 * * *.

Jurisdiction over Northbrook's declaratory judgment action was premised upon diversity of citizenship. After the United States District Court for the District of Massachusetts entered a judgment on the merits for Northbrook, and while appeal to this court was pending, the JUA challenged the district court's jurisdiction for lack of complete diversity. The JUA correctly pointed out that the citizenship of each of the members of an unincorporated association must be considered for diversity purposes in federal court and that at least one member of the JUA is a citizen of Illinois, as is Northbrook.

In order to surmount this hurdle, Northbrook sought leave to amend its complaint by naming one of the members of the JUA, a non-Illinois citizen, as representative of the association's members as a class pursuant to Rule 23.2. We remanded to the district court for consideration of the jurisdictional question. The district court held that (1) a representative suit under Rule 23.2 cannot be brought against an entity that has jural status under state law, and (2) the JUA is a jural entity under Massachusetts law. The court therefore denied Northbrook's motion to amend its complaint and dismissed the suit for want of subject matter jurisdiction. Northbrook appealed.

I. DISCUSSION

* * * The purpose of [Rule 23.2] is explained by the Advisory Committee Note immediately following it:

---

[8] The JUA was established to provide malpractice insurance to health care professionals unable to obtain coverage in the private market. It comprises all insurers writing personal injury liability insurance in Massachusetts. Continued membership is a condition of transacting such business within the Commonwealth.

Although an action by or against representatives of the membership of an unincorporated association has often been viewed as a class action, the real or main purpose of this characterization has been to give "entity treatment" to the association when for formal reasons it cannot sue or be sued as a jural person under Rule 17(b).

Under Rule 17(b), the capacity of an unincorporated association to sue or be sued is determined by the law of the state in which the district court is held.³ "Although the Advisory Committee's comments do not foreclose judicial consideration of the Rule's validity and meaning, the construction given by the Committee is 'of weight.'" *Schiavone v. Fortune*, 477 U.S. 21, 31 (1986). Thus, Rule 23.2 provides a mechanism by which an association may sue or be sued through a representative where state law prevents the association from doing so in its own name.

Northbrook argues that in addition to providing "entity treatment," Rule 23.2 permits a representative suit to be maintained in order to achieve diversity for the purpose of establishing federal subject matter jurisdiction. It asserts that under Rule 23.2's plain language, the only limitation on its availability is that the representative fairly and adequately protect the interests of the association and its members. Therefore, even where state law allows an association to be sued in its own name, a representative suit is a permissible alternative. Northbrook further contends that the district court erred in holding that the JUA is a jural entity under Massachusetts law. Thus, regardless of whether Rule 23.2 is applicable to associations with state recognized jural status, Northbrook maintains that the rule may be applied to the JUA.

For the reasons discussed below, we reject both of these contentions.

A. Availability of Rule 23.2

We think a restrictive application of Rule 23.2 is necessary for three reasons. First, the logical implication of the Advisory Committee Note is that the rule may not be used merely to create diversity jurisdiction. As the district court reasoned, the note states in plain English that the rule's purpose is to give entity treatment to unincorporated associations where state law does not permit them to sue or be sued. It follows that where an association does have the capacity under state law to sue or be sued as an entity, Rule 23.2 is unnecessary and may not be invoked.

Second, federal court jurisdiction is strictly limited by statute to cases meeting specific criteria. 28 U.S.C. §§ 1330–1366. A party that does not meet those criteria cannot manufacture diversity in order to gain access to the federal courts. "Pleas for extension of the diversity jurisdiction to hitherto uncovered broad categories of litigants ought to be made to Congress and not to the courts." *United Steelworkers of America, AFL–CIO v. R.H. Bouligny, Inc.*, 382 U.S. 145 (1965).

Third, most courts that have examined the scope of Rule 23.2's availability have concluded that where an association has jural status under

---

³ Rule 17(b) reads in pertinent part:

... In all other cases capacity to sue or be sued shall be determined by the law of the state in which the district court is held, except (1) that a partnership or other unincorporated association, which has no such capacity by the law of such state, may sue or be sued in its common name for the purpose of enforcing against it a substantive right existing under the Constitution or laws of the United States. ...

state law, the rule does not come into play. *See Suchem, Inc. v. Central Aguirre Sugar Co.*, 52 F.R.D. 348 (D.P.R.1971).

In *Suchem*, as here, the plaintiff sought to convert its action against an unincorporated association into one under Rule 23.2 when it became apparent that diversity jurisdiction against the association was lacking. The court denied the plaintiff's motion to amend its complaint, holding that

> [when] the law of the state in a particular case does not provide an unincorporated association with capacity as a jural person to sue or be sued, then and *only* then does the mechanism of Rule 23.2 come into operation. . . .

Id. at 355.

We have considered the cases cited by Northbrook and are not persuaded by them to adopt a broader reading of the rule. In *Kerney v. Fort Griffin Fandangle Ass'n, Inc.*, 624 F.2d 717 (5th Cir. 1980), the court permitted a Rule 23.2 representative suit even though the association had jural status under state law. It did so because under state law inclusion of individual members as defendants increased the assets available to satisfy a judgment. There were no allegations that the plaintiff was seeking to employ Rule 23.2 merely to manufacture diversity jurisdiction. The court expressly declined to decide whether the rule is available when the plaintiff has "elected to bring a class action rather than an entity suit only in order to select diverse parties as named class representatives and thereby create jurisdiction and not in order to obtain different relief."

In *Lumbermen's Underwriting Alliance v. Mobil Oil Corp.*, 612 F. Supp. 1166 (D. Idaho 1985), the court denied a motion for class certification by the individual members of an unincorporated association because under state statute the association could only sue and be sued in its own name. The court held, however, that Rule 23.2 permitted individual members of an unincorporated association to maintain suit as a class where state law did not prevent them from doing so. Although the *Lumbermen's Underwriting* court carefully traced the development of class actions involving unincorporated associations, we think its conclusion as to Rule 23.2's availability was in error. It reasoned that because the Advisory Committee Note's reference to entity treatment did not specifically refer to an unincorporated association's capacity to sue or be sued, "entity treatment" can be achieved either "by suing the entity in its common name *or* by suing the members of the association individually as a class." 612 F. Supp. at 1170. We think this conclusion was flawed for the same reason articulated by Judge Young in denying Northbrook's motion to amend:

> [S]uch a reading ignores the purpose of the Rule, expressly stated, which is merely to confer upon an unincorporated association entity treatment "when for formal reasons it cannot sue or be sued as a jural person under Rule 17(b)." Fed. R. Civ. P. 23.2, Advisory Committee Note. Significantly, the Note does not add to this stated purpose, "[or] to avoid the practical difficulties of joining all members of the association."

***

We hold that the availability of Rule 23.2 turns, *inter alia*, on the unincorporated association's capacity to sue and be sued as a jural entity under state law. If the JUA can institute or defend a suit in its common name under Massachusetts law, Northbrook may not use Rule 23.2 to bring a class action against its members in federal court.

[The court then reviewed Massachusetts law and affirmed the district court's conclusion that the JUA had the capacity to sue or be sued as a jural entity.]

NOTES AND QUESTIONS

1. As the *Northbrook* court noted, courts are split over how to address the inconsistency between Rule 23.2's language and the accompanying Advisory Committee Notes. The result will frequently determine whether the requirements for federal diversity jurisdiction have been satisfied. In *Curley v. Brignoli, Curley & Roberts Associates*, 915 F.2d 81 (2d Cir. 1990), the Second Circuit rejected the restrictive interpretation of Rule 23.2 espoused in cases like *Northbrook*, noting:

> * * * It must be remembered that the class action mechanism provides litigants with important procedural advantages. For example, class status may expand the number of districts where venue is proper; may permit a party to litigate the rights of class members not within the court's personal jurisdiction, or may allow a plaintiff to name as representatives only those association members whose citizenship will not disturb diversity jurisdiction. If the drafters of rule 23.2 intended to provide only a vehicle for capacity, it seems that they would have simply extended to the diversity realm rule 17(b)'s grant of association capacity in federal question cases.
>
> Further, even if the drafters felt compelled to grant capacity in an indirect manner, perhaps to avoid *Erie* problems in circumventing state capacity limitations, a restrictive interpretation of rule 23.2 does not follow. The more reasonable interpretation is that the drafters, having found it necessary to grant advantageous procedures in states which restrict association capacity, would make those procedures available in all district courts. If they intended the anomaly that the availability of class actions would turn on state capacity laws, the drafters could have so provided in the text of rule 23.2. Accordingly, we agree with those courts that have refused to impose such an interpretation upon the advisory committee note.

Id. at 87. Does this view have merit? Or is *Northbrook* better reasoned?

2. Is *Northbrook* correct that, in construing Rule 23.2, courts should proceed from the premise that federal jurisdiction should be "strictly limited"? Did the *Curley* case analyze the issue from that vantage point?

3. A threshold issue under Rule 23.2 is whether an entity or group has "'characteristics which justify its recognition as an entity or a distinct group of individuals.'" *Murray v. Sevier*, 50 F. Supp. 2d 1257, 1274 (M.D. Ala. 1999) (citation omitted), *vacated and remanded on other grounds*, 253 F.3d 1308 (11th Cir. 2001). "'[I]ndividuals who form an unincorporated association certainly should know what sort of an organization it is, how it happened to be formed, who influenced its formation, and who controls it.'" 50 F. Supp. 2d at

1276; *see also id.* at 1275 (citing case finding group of hunters failed to qualify as an unincorporated association because, although they "each contributed money to cover the annual rental for the property, as well as divided the cost of groceries and other supplied equally," they "never agreed or consented to form an unincorporated association"). Why is it relevant whether the parties specifically "agreed or consented to form an unincorporated association"? What concerns would be raised by giving a group the status of an unincorporated association in the absence of such agreement or consent?

2. PRIOR EXISTENCE OF ASSOCIATION

Another issue under Rule 23.2 is whether the unincorporated entity that litigants seek to certify as a Rule 23.2 class must exist *prior* to the litigation in which certification is sought. Although rarely addressed, this issue was discussed in *Sembach v. McMahon Coll., Inc.*, 86 F.R.D. 188, 192 (S.D. Tex. 1980), in which the court stated:

> In the present case, [the plaintiff organization] did not exist at the time the events which created the cause of action occurred. It was formed after those events took place, for the express purpose of instituting this suit. The problem with permitting such organizations to proceed under Rule 23.2 is an obvious one. Assume thirty individuals, twenty-nine of whom reside in Texas, have a cause of action against a Texas defendant under Texas state law. By forming an unincorporated association and naming the sole non-Texan as the class representative in an action under Rule 23.2, those individuals could successfully bring a diversity action in federal court, in spite of the complete diversity requirement of *Strawbridge v. Curtiss*, [7 U.S. (3 Cranch) 267 (1806)]. To prevent wholesale evasion of the diversity requirement, the application of Rule 23.2 must be limited to unincorporated associations which exist when the events which form the basis of the cause of action occur. As [the plaintiff organization] is not such an association, the proposed class cannot be certified under Rule 23.2.

Is there any valid argument that parties should be able to form an unincorporated association solely for purposes of litigation?

3. APPLICABILITY OF RULE 23(a) AND RULE 23(b) TO ANALYSIS OF CERTIFICATION UNDER RULE 23.2

Courts and commentators have disagreed over whether the prerequisites of Rule 23(a) and 23(b) have any place in Rule 23.2 cases. For example, in *Curley v. Brignoli, Curley & Roberts Assocs.*, 915 F.2d 81 (2d Cir. 1990), the Second Circuit found that Rule 23 was inapposite:

> We consider the prerequisites to class certification contained in Fed. R. Civ. P. 23(a), such as the requirement that the class be "so numerous that joinder of all members is impracticable," to be inapplicable to a [R]ule 23.2 class action. While there is some disagreement on this point, the more persuasive reasoning supports this interpretation. Rule 23.2 expressly refers to subdivisions (d) and (e) of Rule 23 when incorporating the provisions of [R]ule 23

with respect to orders regarding the conduct of class actions, subdivision (d), and dismissal or compromise, subdivision (e). It would therefore seem that if the drafters sought to incorporate the requirements of subdivision (a) of Rule 23, as well, they would have done so expressly. Indeed, the advisory committee note specifies that Rule 23.2 deals "separately" with actions under its purview, "referring *where appropriate* to Rule 23." Fed. R. Civ. P. 23.2 Advisory Committee's Note.

915 F.2d at 86. *See also, e.g.*, 7C Charles A. Wright, Arthur R. Miller, & Mary K. Kane, *Federal Practice & Procedure* § 1861, at 249–51 (3d ed. 2007) (finding no reason to read Rule 23(a) requirements, other than fair and adequate representation, into Rule 23.2); 5 James Moore, *Moore's Federal Practice* § 23.2.06[2][c] (3d ed. 2009) ("[T]he omission in Rule 23.2 of references to Rules 23(a), (b), or (c) implies it would be inappropriate to incorporate those provisions into Rule 23.2.").

Although *Curley* articulates the majority rule, the courts are not uniform. For example, in *Stolz v. United Bhd. of Carpenters & Joiners of America, Local Union No. 971*, 620 F. Supp. 396, 403 (D.Nev. 1985), the court reached the opposite conclusion in a case brought by a group of union members:

> There is substantial dispute in the cases as to whether this rule supplants entirely the normal class action provisions of Rule 23 as far as unincorporated associations are concerned. Some courts have argued that a class action by such an association need satisfy only the provisions of Rule 23.2. These courts argue, in essence, that the language of Rule 23.2 and the fact that it refers to some, but not all of Rule 23's provisions indicate that 23.2 was intended to govern completely class actions by unincorporated associations.
>
> Other courts, however, contend that Rule 23's requirements of numerosity, commonality, typicality, and adequacy of representation apply to class actions of unincorporated associations, in spite of Rule 23.2. Essentially, these courts argue persuasively that Rule 23.2 was enacted to grant unincorporated associations "entity status," thereby allowing them to sue and be sued as a body. At common law the unincorporated association was simply the sum of its members, and not a legal entity such as a person or a corporation. In order for the association to sue or be sued, all of its members had to be named parties to the action. The common law rule had to be abrogated, therefore, to give the unincorporated association status as a jural person.
>
> This is, therefore, the essential purpose of Rule 23.2. In this sense, Rule 23.2 supplements Rule 17, by allowing unincorporated associations the same legal status as a person or corporation. Rule 23 therefore remains unsullied by Rule 23.2, and a labor union, or those representing the union's membership, must comply with its provisions when bringing a class action suit.

Similarly, in *Management Television Sys., Inc. v. National Football League*, 52 F.R.D. 162, 164 (E.D.Pa. 1971), the court concluded that, in some form, commonality and typicality must be present for a case to proceed on a class basis under Rule 23.2: "[T]he conduct alleged must be conduct taken by the association and at least acquiesced in by its members. In this sense, questions common to all class members must be presented. Also, to be a proper representative, a party must occupy a position similar to other members of the class."

The author of a note on Rule 23.2 agrees:

> Rule 23.2 * * * can fairly be read as including the other Rule 23 prerequisites. Two of the prerequisites—common questions of law and fact and typical claims and defenses—are inherent in a class action by or against the members of an unincorporated association. Members impliedly acquiesce in the activities of their association; therefore, when associational activities give rise to a suit, there will necessarily be questions of law and fact common to the class. Also, the class representatives will have typical claims or defenses by virtue of their membership in the association. Moreover, commonality and typicality are often viewed as part of the broader concept of adequacy of representation that the rule explicitly requires.
>
> The final requirement of numerosity is not something an unincorporated association inherently possesses, but it too ought to apply. Without the numerosity requirement, a small association could be certified as a class under Rule 23.2. For example, a two-person partnership—treated as an unincorporated association under the Federal Rules—could use a class action to create diversity if the citizenship of one partner differed from that of the opposing party. This result could not have been achieved under former rule 23 and there is no evidence that the Supreme Court could have intended rule 23.2 to effect such a change. Rather, the term "association" in Rule 23.2 should be read as incorporating a numerosity requirement.
>
> Rule 23.2 should be read as incorporating all four requirements from subdivision (a) of Rule 23. After all, despite their placement in Rule 23.2, these actions are still *class* actions and Rule 23.2 denominates them as such. The inclusion of the requirement that the representatives protect the interests of the association and the members is best seen as adding an additional requirement—protecting the association's interest—rather than raising the inference that none of the general requirements apply. Moreover, this interpretation comports with practice under the former rule and with the idea that Rule 23.2 was not intended to alter that practice.

Note, *Capacity and Class Actions Under Federal Rule 23.2*, 61 B.U. L. Rev. 713, 731–33 (1981). In a footnote, the author further suggested that the requirements of Rule 23(b)(3) should apply to an analysis of certification under Rule 23.2:

> Class actions by or against the members of an unincorporated association fit best into the Rule 23(b)(3) category * * *. Application of the (b)(3) [predominance and superiority] requirements to actions under Rule 23.2 would allow courts to dismiss actions which,

although technically within the language of Rule 23.2, are unfair to one or the other of the parties.

Id. at 733 n.113. Should the elements of Rule 23 apply to cases brought under Rule 23.2? If the drafters of Rule 23.2 had intended to have all of Rule 23's criteria apply to certifications under Rule 23.2, wouldn't they have provided that explicitly? On the other hand, could it be argued that at least typicality and commonality are inherent in the notion of the fair representation required under Rule 23.2? And might one argue that if joinder is practicable, class treatment under Rule 23.2 is unnecessary?

CHAPTER 12

MULTIDISTRICT LITIGATION

■ ■ ■

This chapter addresses multidistrict litigation (MDL) under the Multidistrict Litigation statute, 28 U.S.C. § 1407 ("MDL statute"). MDL has become one of the most important aggregation devices in the federal system. In some circumstances, MDL involves class action cases, but in others it involves the consolidation of individual lawsuits (or lawsuits joined under a non-class procedure, such as Federal Rule of Civil Procedure 20).

Aggregate litigation cannot be understood without detailed knowledge of the MDL process. Virtually every recent, high-profile aggregate settlement has involved the MDL process—including the British Petroleum oil spill litigation, the National Football League concussion litigation, and the Volkswagen Clean Diesel litigation, as well as numerous pharmaceutical cases, such as the *Vioxx* and *Zyprexa* litigation.

MDL cases constitute more than a third of the entire federal civil docket. *See* Elizabeth Chamblee Burch & Margaret S. Williams, *Repeat Players in Multidistrict Litigation: The Social Network*, ___ Cornell L. Rev. ___ (forthcoming 2017), *available at* https://papers.ssrn.com/sol3/papers.cfm?abstract_id=2724637. In the past few years, numerous commentators have focused on the MDL process, addressing statistics, mechanics, and potential concerns (such as arguments that lawyers appointed for key posts in MDLs tend to be repeat players). *See, e.g., id.*

This chapter surveys the MDL process. After providing an overview and statistical information, it focuses on the mechanics of the process (including the role of the Judicial Panel on Multidistrict Litigation ("JPML" or the "MDL Panel"), the standards for transfer, and the selection of the transferee judge); the resolution of MDLs (settlement, remand, and trial (including bellwether trials)); policy issues; and a special focus on the *VW Clean Diesel* litigation, with a description of this high-profile MDL and links to key documents in the case. Because MDL applies only in federal court, the final section of the chapter addresses the issue of federal/state coordination.

A. OVERVIEW AND STATISTICS

The MDL statute was enacted in 1968 to address close to 2,000 antitrust actions that had been filed against the electrical equipment industry in the early 1960s. *See, e.g.*, Earle F. Kyle, IV, *The Mechanics of Motion Practice Before the Judicial Panel on Multidistrict Litigation*, 175 F.R.D. 589 (1997); Comment, *The Judicial Panel on Multidistrict Litigation: Time for Rethinking*, 140 U. Pa. L. Rev. 711 (1991) ("Penn. Comment"). That statute established the JPML. The principal function of the Panel is to "decide[]—either on motion or *sua sponte*—whether to transfer federal district court civil cases involving common questions of fact for coordinated or consolidated pretrial proceedings." Kyle, *supra*, 175 F.R.D. at 589–90. "[T]ransfer orders * * * are meant to achieve efficiency and judicial economy by providing convenience to the parties and witnesses, and promoting the efficient conduct of 'complex litigation.'" *Id.* at 590; *see* David F. Herr, *Multidistrict Litigation* § 2.3, at 9–14 (1986) (describing legislative history of MDL statute).

Between 1968 and September 30, 2016, the MDL Panel centralized 593,711 civil actions for pretrial proceedings. More than 132,000 individual actions subject to Section 1407 proceedings were pending as of December 15, 2016, and more than 4,000 had been transferred by the Panel during the preceding twelve months. *See* Statistical Year Summary of Transfer Cases under 28 U.S.C. § 1407, *available at* http://www.jpml.uscourts.gov/sites/jpml/files/JPML_Statistical_Analysis_of_Multidistrict_Litigation-FY-2016_1.pdf (last visited Feb. 6, 2017); *see also* Distribution of Pending MDL Dockets by District, *available at* http://www.jpml.uscourts.gov/sites/jpml/files/Pending_MDL_Dockets_By_District-December-15-2016.pdf (last visited Feb. 6, 2017). Coordinated proceedings have been ordered in a variety of cases, including mass torts, antitrust, securities, product liability, patent litigation, and employment litigation. Penn. Comment, *supra*, 140 U. Pa. L. Rev. at 723.

MULTIDISTRICT LITIGATION ACT
28 U.S.C. § 1407.

(a) When civil actions involving one or more common questions of fact are pending in different districts, such actions may be transferred to any district for coordinated or consolidated pretrial proceedings. Such transfers shall be made by the judicial panel on multidistrict litigation authorized by this section upon its determination that transfers for such proceedings will be for the convenience of parties and witnesses and will promote the just and efficient conduct of such actions. Each action so transferred shall be remanded by the panel at or before the conclusion of such pretrial proceedings to the district from which it was transferred unless it shall have been previously terminated: *Provided, however*, That the panel may separate any claim, cross-claim, counter-claim, or third-party claim and remand any of such claims before the remainder of the action is remanded.

(b) Such coordinated or consolidated pretrial proceedings shall be conducted by a judge or judges to whom such actions are assigned by the judicial panel on multidistrict litigation. For this purpose, upon request of the panel, a circuit judge or a district judge may be designated and assigned temporarily for service in the transferee district by the Chief Justice of the United States or the chief judge of the circuit, as may be required * * *. With the consent of the transferee district court, such actions may be assigned by the panel to a judge or judges of such district. The judge or judges to whom such actions are assigned, the members of the judicial panel on multidistrict litigation, and other circuit and district judges designated when needed by the panel may exercise the powers of a district judge in any district for the purpose of conducting pretrial depositions in such coordinated or consolidated pretrial proceedings.

(c) Proceedings for the transfer of an action under this section may be initiated by—

(i) the judicial panel on multidistrict litigation upon its own initiative, or

(ii) motion filed with the panel by a party in any action in which transfer for coordinated or consolidated pretrial proceedings under this section may be appropriate. A copy of such motion shall be filed in the district court in which the moving party's action is pending.

The panel shall give notice to the parties in all actions in which transfers for coordinated or consolidated pretrial proceedings are contemplated, and such notice shall specify the time and place of any hearing to determine whether such transfer shall be made. * * * The panel's order of transfer shall be based upon a record of such hearing at which material evidence may be offered by any party to an action pending in any district that would be affected by the proceedings under this section, and shall be supported by findings of fact and conclusions of law based upon such record. * * *

(d) The judicial panel on multidistrict litigation shall consist of seven circuit and district judges designated from time to time by the Chief Justice of the United States, no two of whom shall be from the same circuit. The concurrence of four members shall be necessary to any action by the panel.

(e) No proceedings for review of any order of the panel may be permitted except by extraordinary writ pursuant to the provisions of title 28, section 1651, United States Code. Petitions for an extraordinary writ to review an order of the panel to set a transfer hearing and other orders of the panel issued prior to the order either directing or denying transfer shall be filed only in the court of appeals having jurisdiction over the district in which a hearing is to be or has been held. Petitions for an extraordinary writ to review an order to transfer or orders subsequent to transfer shall be filed only in the court of appeals having jurisdiction over the transferee district. There shall be no appeal or review of an order of the panel denying a motion to transfer for consolidated or coordinated proceedings.

(f) The panel may prescribe rules for the conduct of its business not inconsistent with Acts of Congress and the Federal Rules of Civil Procedure.

(g) Nothing in this section shall apply to any action in which the United States is a complainant arising under the antitrust laws. * * *

(h) Notwithstanding the provisions of [28 U.S.C. § 1404] or subsection (f) of this section, the judicial panel on multidistrict litigation may consolidate and transfer with or without the consent of the parties, for both pretrial purposes and for trial, any action brought under section 4C of the Clayton Act.

RICHARD D. FREER, EXODUS FROM AND TRANSFORMATION OF AMERICAN CIVIL LITIGATION
65 Emory L.J. 1491, 1492, 1511–12 (2016).

* * * [F]ew cases go to trial: in federal court, fewer than 2%. The judge is in chambers, more often than not managing the case toward a non-merits-based conclusion. Two decades ago, one judge famously said, "Members of the bench should keep in mind that the word 'judge' is a verb as well as a noun." The focus on conciliation and consensus is so dominant that, stunningly, going to trial is seen as pathological—as a "failure" of the system.

The settlement culture is especially prevalent in mass tort litigation, which today is dominated by consolidation under the multidistrict (MDL) litigation procedure. A * * * stunning 96% of * * * cases pending in MDL proceedings are mass-tort cases. Thus, very few federal-court mass-tort plaintiffs have their claims to themselves; they must share the stage with suits filed by other plaintiffs. Lawyers lose control, as the aggregated mass starts to look like a class action, with the MDL judge appointing lead counsel and overseeing the management of the aggregate proceedings. Increasingly, the prevalent goal of these consolidated proceedings is to buy "global peace" for the defendants. MDL judges have invented the "quasi-class action" to justify a great many practices, including the ability to foster (some would say coerce) settlement.

* * *

EDWARD F. SHERMAN, THE MDL MODEL FOR RESOLVING COMPLEX LITIGATION IF A CLASS ACTION IS NOT POSSIBLE
82 Tul. L. Rev. 2205, 2205–09 (2008).

The [MDL] device, created in the 1960s * * *, was a modest procedural development. A panel of federal judges could transfer cases with "common questions of fact" to a single federal judge "for coordinated or consolidated pretrial proceedings." Coordinated discovery was the principal benefit, insuring that all the cases could share discovery that would be rationally scheduled and avoid wasteful repetition. Over the years the "transferee judge" to whom the cases were transferred came to assert a more prominent managerial role over the litigation, making dispositive pretrial rulings on motions and encouraging settlement. * * *

* * * [T]he MDL model [has become] attractive as a central device for resolving complex litigation. A number of federal courts have applied increasingly stringent requirements for class certification, particularly for cases arising in multiple states. Thus, federal MDL litigation like *In re Vioxx Products Liability Litigation* * * * against a single pharmaceutical company on behalf of some 20,000 persons in all fifty states who alleged heart attacks and strokes from taking the medication, could likely not have been certified as a nationwide class action. Differences in state law standards, as well as individualized issues as to such matters as prior medical condition, length of time taking the drug, and injuries alleged, would demonstrate a lack of predominance of common issues, as well as problems with typicality and manageability.

The Class Action Fairness Act of 2005 (CAFA) was another blow to the centrality of the class action for resolving mass complex litigation. CAFA allows defendants to remove to federal court most multistate class actions. Given the aversion of many federal courts to class certification of multistate class actions, CAFA removal could often mean that a case would not be certified as a class action in the federal court. In order to avoid this, plaintiffs lawyers might file state-only class actions in state courts under the limited exceptions to CAFA or avoid class actions entirely by filing individual suits (usually in state courts that have been perceived in recent years as more sympathetic to plaintiffs than federal courts). However, this increases the likelihood of disparate litigation in multiple courts and overlapping class actions, making global settlement more difficult.

MDL transfer and consolidation can be an attractive procedural mechanism for dealing with this problem. An MDL transferee judge need not rely on the class action, with its demanding requirements, to achieve the benefits of aggregation and promote a global settlement. In fact, in most mass tort cases today (like *Vioxx*), class certification is unlikely. Furthermore, although a federal transferee judge does not have jurisdiction over related state cases, settlement negotiations as to the federal cases can be coordinated with the attorneys in the state cases, and the federal MDL can serve as a catalyst for a global settlement. As demonstrated in *Vioxx*, joint negotiations between lawyers in the state and federal actions, and the collaboration of state judges with the federal MDL judge, can bridge the jurisdictional divide to accomplish an aggregate settlement without resort to class actions.

* * *

B. HOW MDL WORKS

1. THE ROLE OF THE MDL PANEL

Stanley A. Weigel, The Judicial Panel on Multidistrict Litigation, Transferor Courts and Transferee Courts
78 F.R.D. 575, 575–77, 579–84 (1977).

[28 U.S.C. § 1407] eliminates the need to rely on cooperation as the means of coordinating or consolidating pretrial proceedings when "civil actions involving one or more common questions of fact are pending in different districts." The statute, providing for a Judicial Panel on Multidistrict Litigation, empowers that body to order transfer "to any district for coordinated or consolidated pretrial proceedings" upon the Panel's "determination that transfers for such proceedings will be for the convenience of parties and witnesses and will promote the just and efficient conduct of such actions."

Under the statute, transfer proceedings can be initiated by motion filed with the Panel or by the Panel itself. Parties in all actions for which such proceedings are contemplated are given notice of a hearing to determine whether transfer should be ordered. The Panel's order of transfer is reviewable only by extraordinary writ, issued by a court of appeals pursuant to 28 U.S.C. §§ 1407(e) and 1651. Under authority granted by Section 1407, the Panel has prescribed rules of procedure which set forth the mechanics of transfer.

A case can be transferred under Section 1407 only if the prospective transferor court has subject matter jurisdiction. Lack of personal jurisdiction, however, is not grounds for opposing transfer because any party contesting personal jurisdiction can make the appropriate motion before the transferee court.

A transfer under Section 1407 becomes effective upon the filing of the Panel's order of transfer with the clerk in the transferee district. Thereafter it is generally accepted that the jurisdiction of the transferor court ceases and the transferee court assumes complete pretrial jurisdiction. The mere pendency of a motion or of an order to show cause before the Panel in no way limits the jurisdiction of the court in which the action is pending. Nor does such pendency before the Panel "affect or suspend orders and pretrial proceedings" in that court. All discovery in progress and all orders of the transferor court remain in effect after transfer unless and until modified by the transferee judge who may modify, expand, or vacate prior orders of the transferor court.

* * *

The transferee judge assigned to multidistrict litigation possesses all pretrial powers over the transferred actions exercisable by a district court under the Federal Rules of Civil Procedure. In other words, the transferee judge may make any pretrial order that the transferor court might have made in the absence of transfer.

It is the province of the transferee judge to determine the degree and manner in which pretrial proceedings are coordinated or consolidated. The Panel has neither the power nor the inclination to make any determinations regarding the actual conduct of the coordinated or consolidated pretrial proceedings.

The transferee judge has control over all aspects of discovery. The unique discovery interests of any party can be accommodated by him in a schedule providing for discovery on non-common issues to proceed concurrently with those which are common. Or the transferee judge may leave discovery on any unique issue for the supervision of the transferor court upon remand. The transferee judge can make results of completed discovery available to parties in related actions, and to parties in actions that are later filed in the transferee district or in "tag-along" actions, *i.e.*, those transferred by the Panel to be joined with cases previously ordered to be transferred.

* * *

The transferee court is free to rule on the sufficiency of any pleadings filed in transferred actions and to allow amendments. It is not bound by the complaints or other pleadings filed in the transferor districts. An amended complaint filed after transfer must be filed in the transferee court.

* * *

It is generally accepted that a transferee judge has authority to decide all pretrial motions, including motions that may be dispositive, such as motions for judgment approving a settlement, for dismissal, for judgment on the pleadings, for summary judgment, for involuntary dismissal under Rule 41(b), for striking an affirmative defense, for voluntary dismissal under Rule 41(a) and to quash service of process. In several instances, there has been appellate review of the rulings of a transferee court on such motions. In each instance, the authority of the transferee court has either been taken for granted, or expressly affirmed.

* * *

The Panel alone has the power to remand an action or claim. In the exercise of that power, the Panel defers to the views of the transferee judge. Absent a recommendation of remand from the transferee judge, any party advocating remand bears an especially heavy burden.

The transferee judge may, at the conclusion of the common pretrial proceedings, recommend that an action or claim be remanded for local discovery or further proceedings. The transferee judge may also, at any time, recommend remand of an action or claim deemed no longer appropriate for inclusion in the coordinated or consolidated pretrial proceedings.

While the powers of the transferee judge are extremely broad, they are not unlimited. For one example, although the transferor court no longer has jurisdiction over the case, it is inappropriate for a transferee judge to permit parties to ignore prior unmodified orders of the transferor judge. * * * And the transferee court must apply the substantive law of the transferor forum, including that forum's choice of law rules.

* * *

NOTES AND QUESTIONS

1. For a description of the MDL process and some of its limitations, *see* Yvette Ostolaza & Michelle Hartmann, *The Judicial Panel on Multidistrict Litigation and Coordinating Multijurisdictional Disputes*, 16 No. 4 Prac. Litigator 23 (2005). Another useful article on the MDL process, written by retired judge Louis Bechtle, provides an overview of how an MDL judge actually manages an MDL proceeding—including the formation of lead counsel committees, development of a case management plan, appointment of special masters, discovery, and consideration of class action issues. Louis C. Bechtle, *Administration in the MDL Transferee Court*, 10 No. 2 Andrews Class Actions Litig. Rep. 26 (2003); *see also* Louis C. Bechtle, *Multidistrict Litigation: A Judicial Perspective*, 45 For the Def. 8 (2003) (describing MDL process).

2. How is a multidistrict litigation transfer under section 1407 initiated? Can a district judge before whom litigation is pending initiate transfer? If not, how could a trial court initiate such a process informally?

3. Based on its text, does section 1407 favor either plaintiffs or defendants?

4. How has the MDL process facilitated the settlement of cases that cannot be certified as class actions?

2. STANDARDS FOR TRANSFER

In re Multi-Piece Rim Prods. Liab. Litig.
Judicial Panel on Multidistrict Litigation, 1979.
464 F. Supp. 969.

Before WISDOM, CHAIRMAN, and WEINFELD, ROBSON, WEIGEL, CAFFREY, HARPER, and WEINER, JUDGES of the Panel.

PER CURIAM.

I. BACKGROUND

This litigation consists of nineteen actions pending in fourteen federal districts. * * *

These actions have all been brought to recover compensation for personal injuries or wrongful death allegedly resulting from, among other causes, the failure and separation of a multi-piece truck wheel (rim and tire assembly). The complaints in eighteen of these actions allege that a multi-piece rim assembly separated under pressure and flew apart with explosive force during tire inflation, mounting of an inflated wheel on a vehicle, or removal of an inflated wheel from a vehicle. Plaintiffs or plaintiffs' decedents in these eighteen actions were individuals who were in the proximity of the wheel when it separated, either as service persons or bystanders. The complaint in the nineteenth action (the Oregon action) alleges that a multi-piece rim assembly separated during operation of the vehicle on which the rim was being used, causing the vehicle to go out of control and strike an oncoming vehicle containing plaintiff and plaintiff's decedent. In each action, one or more of the following four manufacturers of multi-piece rim components are named as defendants: Firestone Tire and Rubber Co. (fourteen actions), Goodyear Tire and Rubber Co. (eight actions), Kelsey–Hayes Co. (three actions) and Redco Corp. (one action). Either Firestone or Goodyear is a defendant in every action. Besides the four manufacturers of multi-piece rim components, 21 other defendants are named in these actions, nineteen of which are named in only one action and two of which are named in two actions. These additional defendants include, in specific actions, the manufacturer of the tire which was included in the wheel assembly; the employers of plaintiff or plaintiff's decedent; and the manufacturers and/or owners of the vehicle on which the wheel was located.

Plaintiffs allege a number of theories of relief against the various defendants in these actions. The allegations against the manufacturers of multi-piece rim components generally concern defects in the design and manufacture of multi-piece rim components and failure to warn adequately of the risks involved with multi-piece rim assemblies. All parties agree that in some instances multi-piece rim components manufactured by different defendants can be used interchangeably.

In addition, the complaints in three of the Missouri actions allege that Firestone and/or Goodyear 1) failed to advise the United States Department of Transportation of the hazards associated with use of multi-piece rims and intentionally minimized the frequency and severity of personal injuries caused by multi-piece rims in testimony before the Department of

Transportation; 2) withheld information from and gave misinformation to the Department of Transportation concerning the feasibility of a recall and retrofit of multi-piece rims; 3) maintained a political slush fund to make illegal payments for the purpose of avoiding a recall of multi-piece rims; and 4) conspired with other manufacturers to withhold the dissemination of adequate safety warnings concerning multi-piece rims.

II. PROCEEDINGS BEFORE THE PANEL

The Panel, pursuant to 28 U.S.C. § 1407(c)(i) and Rule 8 [Rules of Procedure, Judicial Panel on Multidistrict Litigation], ordered the parties to show cause why eighteen of these nineteen actions should not be transferred to a single district for coordinated or consolidated pretrial proceedings. Plaintiffs in eleven actions (including plaintiffs in the three Missouri actions containing the additional allegations against Firestone and/or Goodyear) favor transfer. Plaintiffs in ten of these actions favor selection of the Western District of Missouri as the transferee forum. Plaintiff in the eleventh action has expressed no view on that issue. Plaintiffs in five actions and all defendants except one (which has not responded) oppose transfer. Plaintiffs in the other three actions have not responded. In the event transfer is ordered, Goodyear favors selection of the Northern District of Ohio as the transferee forum. In the event transfer is ordered, several opponents also request either that actions in which they are involved be excluded from transfer because pretrial proceedings in these actions are well advanced or that the claims against them be excluded from transfer because those claims are unrelated to the common factual issues involved in this litigation.

III. DECISION OF THE PANEL

We find that these actions involve common questions of fact and that, with the exception of the Oregon and Mississippi actions, their transfer to the Western District of Missouri under section 1407 for coordinated or consolidated pretrial proceedings will serve the convenience of the parties and witnesses and promote the just and efficient conduct of the litigation.

Opponents present the following primary arguments in opposition to transfer in this litigation:

1) The questions of fact involved in each action are primarily individual.

    a) A diversity of multi-piece rim components produced by a diversity of manufacturers is involved. * * *

    b) A diversity of parties is involved as plaintiffs and defendants. The factual situation with respect to most parties is individual to a single action.

    c) The circumstances surrounding each accident primarily involve factual variables unique to that accident.

2) The factual aspects that may be shared by these actions with respect to the design and manufacture of multi-piece rim components are minimal in comparison to the unique issues involved in each action.

3) Discovery is progressing well in most of these actions, some of which have been pending for a long time, are well advanced in discovery, and are nearing readiness for trial. Transfer would merely delay pretrial and trial proceedings in these well advanced actions.

* * * [P]roponents of transfer maintain that all multi-piece rims are essentially the same * * * because they all operate on the same engineering principle of maintaining a delicate equilibrium among the multi-piece rim components in order to keep the rim components from separating and flying apart under inflation pressure. Proponents assert that the sources of discovery common to all actions include engineers familiar with multi-piece rim design, as well as documents and witnesses from the national trade association of tire and rim manufacturers. Several plaintiffs also contend that Firestone and Goodyear exchanged information concerning whether to distribute certain warning labels for use with multi-piece rims. In addition, several plaintiffs argue that defendants have concertedly suppressed evidence concerning the risks associated with the use of multi-piece rims.

We are persuaded that centralized pretrial proceedings under Section 1407 are appropriate in this litigation. We recognize that certain individual factual issues will be present in each action. Nevertheless, we are convinced that substantial common factual issues are present concerning the overall design of multi-piece rims, the state of knowledge within the industry of the risks involved with use of multi-piece rims, and the alleged failure of defendants to warn adequately of those risks. Centralization pursuant to Section 1407 is necessary in order to prevent duplication of discovery and eliminate the possibility of conflicting pretrial rulings * * *.

The transferee judge, of course, has the authority to group the pretrial proceedings on different discovery tracks according to the common factual issues or according to each defendant if necessary for the just and efficient conduct of the litigation, and to schedule any discovery unique to particular parties, actions or claims to proceed in separate discovery tracks concurrently with the common discovery, thus enhancing the efficient processing of all aspects of the litigation. Moreover, no party need participate in pretrial proceedings unrelated to that party's interests.

On the basis of the record before us, it appears that discovery has been completed in the Mississippi action and that discovery on all common factual issues in this docket has been completed in the Oregon action. Accordingly, transfer of these actions would not now be appropriate and they will therefore be excluded from our transfer order. Some parties have argued that additional actions are also sufficiently advanced to warrant their exclusion from transfer. We recognize that all actions are not at the same stage of discovery, but based on the information before us, we conclude that the remaining actions in this litigation will all benefit from transfer under Section 1407. We further decline all requests for the separation and remand of the claims against specific parties because we are unable to determine from the record presently before us whether any of those claims are sufficiently distinct to warrant their exclusion from the coordinated or consolidated pretrial proceedings. Although we are sensitive to the requests of these individual parties, we believe these requests should be addressed to the transferee judge following transfer. The transferee judge will be in the best position, in connection with the organization of the pretrial program in this litigation, to determine which, if any, actions or claims are susceptible to immediate separation and remand. If and when the transferee judge determines that any action or claim is, in fact, ready for trial, or otherwise ready for remand because the common pretrial proceedings pertaining to that action or claim have been completed and the action or claim would no longer benefit from inclusion in the coordinated or consolidated pretrial proceedings, the transferee judge may suggest to the Panel that the Panel remand the action or claim to its transferor district. * * *

* * *

MARGARET S. WILLIAMS & TRACEY E. GEORGE, WHO WILL MANAGE COMPLEX CIVIL LITIGATION?
10 J. Empirical Legal Stud. 424, 425–27, 436–42 (2013).

I. INTRODUCTION

Parties usually control where they litigate their disputes. The U.S. Constitution and federal and state statutes constrain the available options. However, in large-scale and/or high-stakes cases, a plaintiff typically may choose among multiple locations and between state and federal court. Indeed, the preliminary fight in modern litigation is over where a lawsuit will be litigated. The parties have meaningful control over this fight as well. They set the range of possibilities through motions to challenge personal jurisdiction, to change venue, or to remove to federal court (or remand to state court). The motions are resolved either by the judge before whom the suit is pending or the by court to which the case would be assigned. The plaintiff's choice of forum is usually strongly favored.

The Multidistrict Litigation Act of 1968 takes a significantly different approach. The U.S. Judicial Panel on Multidistrict Litigation (MDL Panel), a court of seven federal circuit and district judges, may transfer factually related actions filed in different federal districts to a single judge in any federal district for consolidated pretrial litigation. The consolidated [MDL] may involve only a few cases with a small number of parties or include hundreds (or even thousands) of cases and parties. The transferee judge has significant discretion over the management of the litigation prior to trial. Questions of federal law are controlled by the law of the transferee, not the transferor, court. While a case theoretically returns to the transferor judge for trial, nearly all cases are resolved in the transferee court. Thus, as a practical matter, the MDL Panel controls where these disputes will be resolved.

The MDL Panel has substantial discretion in making the centralization decision. The Panel rules on parties' motions for consolidation but also may act on its own initiative, issuing a show cause order to parties in cases that seem appropriate for centralization. The Panel may designate a court or judge recommended by a party, or one of its own choosing. The transferee district court need not have personal jurisdiction over the parties or satisfy the venue requirements. The transferee judge can be an active or senior judge in the selected district or can sit in a different district and be designated to sit in that district solely for purposes of the MDL. Members of the

MDL Panel as well as chief judges are eligible to serve as an MDL transferee judge. Actions that are filed later and are factually related (even if legally distinct) may be transferred subsequently as "tag-along" matters. The Panel's decision on whether, where, and to whom to transfer these actions is effectively unreviewable and has never been overturned.

In its nearly 50 years of existence, the MDL Panel has consolidated nearly 400,000 lawsuits for pretrial proceedings. The cases are torn from the headlines, including high-profile securities and derivative lawsuits related to the collapse of financial services firm Lehman Brothers and to the Ponzi scheme of Bernie Madoff; consumer protection claims involving thousands of plaintiffs and millions of dollars, including those arising from the subprime mortgage crisis of 2006; products liability actions, including more than 40,000 asbestos cases and thousands of silicone gel breast implant suits; as well as common disasters like the Union Carbide chemical plant disaster in Bhopal, India and the bombing of Pan Am Flight 103 over Lockerbie, Scotland, the Soviet's downing of a Korean Air Lines flight over the Sea of Japan, and nearly every other air crash claim filed in federal court. These MDLs are simply illustrative of the scope and scale of multidistrict litigation in federal courts.

The importance of the transfer and consolidation decision can be seen by focusing on litigation resulting from the 2010 Deep Water Horizon oil spill disaster. Hundreds of tort suits were filed against BP seeking compensation for economic loss, property damage, and personal injuries. Tort victims filed suit in every district along the Gulf Coast as well as in districts scattered across the country. BP quickly moved to consolidate and transfer all suits to Judge Lynn Hughes in the Southern District of Texas. Judge Hughes sits in Houston where BP has its North American headquarters and where it bases its Gulf-drilling operations. BP's motion drew strong opposition from most plaintiffs as well as from the U.S. Department of Justice, which asked for assignment in New Orleans in the Eastern District of Louisiana (with some plaintiffs asking the Panel to assign Southern District of New York Judge Shira Scheindlin, who has extensive MDL experience). The Panel ultimately assigned the matter to Judge Carl Barbier in New Orleans. While the Panel did not side with BP on the location for pretrial litigation in the tort suits, the judges unanimously granted BP's contested motion to transfer securities and shareholder derivative suits, also related to the oil spill, to District Judge Keith Ellison in Houston. BP later agreed to pay $7.8 billion to settle the tort suits consolidated in Louisiana. BP won the dismissal of nearly all shareholder derivative, securities, and ERISA claims transferred to Texas.

The current article seeks to understand the MDL Panel's decisions to transfer and consolidate pending federal civil lawsuits through an empirical analysis of its rulings on transfer motions.

* * *

III. HYPOTHESES ABOUT THE DECISION TO CONSOLIDATE MULTIDISTRICT LITIGATION

To construct a model of MDL Panel rulings, it is helpful to break its decisions into three aspects or stages: (1) the decision on whether to consolidate, (2) if consolidation is granted, the designation of a transferee district court, and (3) if consolidation is granted, the designation of a transferee judge. These determinations are related. The decision to consolidate turns in part on the availability of an appropriate forum and judge, for example. However, the consolidation decision can be modeled independently given both the high rate of consolidation and the expert consensus, supported by our own analysis, that centralization will not be prevented by the lack of a suitable transferee court.

Modeling the choice of court and judge is more challenging, however. The order of decision may vary from case to case. In some cases, the Panel focuses first on an appropriate district and then appears to select a judge from within that district. In other cases, the Panel appears to identify a judge and then chooses the district where that judge is located. Finally, in a small number of cases, the Panel views the two decisions as independent, using intercircuit assignment to select a judge outside the chosen physical location. We explain in our methodological section how we handle these interactions.

A. The Decision to Transfer

The decision to grant a transfer motion should be explained, in part, by the law. The [MDL] Act sets forth one formal requirement for transfer: at least one common question of fact in cases in more than one district, but it also lays out three goals or criteria relevant to granting a motion for transfer: the parties' convenience and the just and efficient conduct of the action. The statutory language leaves a great deal of discretion to the MDL Panel for defining and weighing those considerations. We also hypothesize that the Panel will be predisposed to consolidation given its mandate from Congress and the Judicial Conference of the United States and the panelists' experience as MDL judges.

The language of the statute does not contain any qualitative or quantitative standard or test that must be met to determine how many common issues must be present to merit consolidation. It "does not require that there be strict identity of issues, a predominance of common questions, or that any common questions be central to or determinative of the controversy in order to justify transfer under Section 1407, and the Panel's decisions reflect this." The Panel has suggested, however, that common questions justifying consolidated pretrial proceedings should be complex, numerous, unresolved, and unique.

The cases do not need to share common questions of law. While the Panel has ordered transfer and consolidation of actions with common questions of fact and questions of law, it has explicitly rejected the argument that it should deny transfer where common facts are controlled by different states' laws. The availability of the MDL process where claims are subject to different state liability rules is one reason it is well suited for products liability cases that are not appropriate for class action certification. Nevertheless, we would expect that cases with common questions of law or common mixed questions of fact and law would be more likely to be consolidated. One way to detect such common legal questions is to look for "the existence of conflicting or overlapping class action claims."

The statute also states that transfer and consolidation should be convenient for the parties. The Panel may make transfers if it determines that it "will be for the convenience of parties and witnesses and will promote the just and efficient conduct of such actions." However, objections due to inconvenience of transfer are typically overruled because the efficient management of consolidated pretrial proceedings will result in overall savings in time and cost. Moreover, the parties' agreement to voluntarily coordinate discovery will not prevent the Panel from ordering transfer and consolidation.

The stated goal of the statute is the just and efficient conduct of litigation. That goal has informed the Panel's reasoning in its decisions. Whether evaluating the sufficiency of the common question of fact or considering the costs imposed on scattered parties by litigation in a single forum, the Panel has explained how those considerations compare to potential benefits to the judicial process itself, including the avoidance of duplicative discovery, the conservation of judicial resources, and the prevention of inconsistent judicial decisions.

Parties cannot avoid transfer and consolidation through efforts to achieve efficiency and consistency by voluntarily approximating the MDL process. The MDL Panel has granted MDL motions notwithstanding the parties' existing voluntary agreements to coordinate discovery. Multiple lawsuits against a single defendant represented by one national law firm have been consolidated, as have suits by dispersed plaintiffs represented by common counsel. The Panel has concluded that "[w]hile informal coordination . . . is commendable, Section 1407 transfer will ensure overall economies."

B. The Choice of Transferee Court and Judge

Having consolidated the litigation, the MDL Panel must decide where to send the cases and to whom to assign the MDL. No rule limits the Panel's options. Any district and any trial judge may be chosen. The transferee judge may be a judge to whom one of the cases is currently assigned or a judge who is not handling any related matter. The judge may be active or senior, a chief judge, or a new appointee. The transferee judge's workload may be heavy and may include another active MDL, and current and former members of the MDL Panel are eligible to serve as MDL transferee judges.

* * *

Although the choice of a transferee court can affect the law governing a dispute, the MDL Panel has rejected parties' arguments that it consider whether one district may be more favorable than another for the litigants. This extends to any consideration of a possible negative effect on plaintiffs who chose to file based in part on circuit law. Appeals of transferee court decisions go to the court of appeals for that circuit and any remand by the circuit court goes to the transferee court rather than the court in which the action was initiated.

The MDL Panel may send consolidated litigation to any federal district court in the country (with the consent of the district's chief judge), but seems likely to select a district from those recommended by the parties.

The greater the consensus in support of a district, the more likely the Panel will choose that court. * * *

Not only the parties have an interest in where a matter is assigned: district judges also have a stake in the decision. The appointment is seen as recognition of a judge's skill and acumen and a sign of his or her status. * * *

The MDL Panel will look for district judges who are best able to manage aggregate litigation with the complexity and challenges posed by MDLs. Familiarity with the MDL process would be an important factor, as would experience with other types of complex litigation. Current and former chief judges also are likely to have greater managerial experience. Judges who have a heavy workload would seem to be weaker candidates. Finally, the Panel will be attentive to party recommendations.

* * *

NOTES AND QUESTIONS

1. How rigorous was the JPML's analysis of whether the *Multi-Piece Rim* cases should be transferred? Should transfer be ordered simply because there are common factual issues? Should the prevalence of individual fact issues defeat transfer?

2. As the *Multi-Piece Rim* decision reveals, identifying common questions of fact has not been difficult. *See* Stanley J. Levy, *Complex Multidistrict Litigation and the Federal Courts*, 40 Fordham L. Rev. 41, 48 (1971). How does the court's analysis compare and contrast with the decision to certify a Rule 23(b)(3) class? How, if at all, should the analysis of commonality under Rule 23(a)(2) in *Wal–Mart Stores, Inc. v. Dukes*, 564 U.S. 338 (2011), impact the availability of MDL consolidation on the basis of common questions? For example, if Wal–Mart were sued for sex discrimination in many different federal jurisdictions, should those cases be consolidated under the MDL statute?

3. Strategically, how can plaintiffs in class action litigation argue that related cases should not be transferred under section 1407, but that class certification is warranted? How can defendants in class actions who seek transfer of related cases simultaneously argue that there are no common issues justifying class treatment?

4. Why did the *Multi-Piece Rim* court believe that transfer would prevent duplication of discovery? What other efficiencies did the court envision would result from the transfer?

5. The *Multi-Piece Rim* court noted that transfer would eliminate the possibility of conflicting pretrial rulings. What sorts of conflicting rulings would be eliminated?

6. Why did the *Multi-Piece Rim* court view transfer as inappropriate in cases in which discovery had been completed? Can an argument be made that transfer would still have been appropriate?

7. In addition to the existence of common factual questions, other factors assessed by the MDL Panel in determining whether to transfer cases include considerations of justice, efficiency, and convenience of the parties and witnesses. With respect to justice and efficiency, what standards should be applied by the MDL Panel? Should justice and efficiency be assessed in terms of

each individual plaintiff and defendant, or in terms of broader societal and judicial objectives? With respect to the last factor (convenience), one commentator has noted that "the weight accorded the convenience factor has been minuscule." Penn. Comment, *supra*, 140 U. Pa. L. Rev. at 720. In fact, "the Panel may consolidate even if all parties in the matter object." *Id.* In explaining the convenience factor, this commentator observed:

> Despite inconveniences to individual litigants, benefits may accrue to the parties collectively as a result of consolidation. In litigation where documents abound, central depositories can greatly reduce the overall cost duplication, and common depositions may save hundreds of hours of the attorneys' and deponents' time. If "convenience" is viewed from a group perspective, the Panel may be satisfying § 1407's command that transfers be "for the convenience of parties and witnesses" more often than some commentators imply.

Id.

8. As the *Multi-Piece Rim* case illustrates, a request to coordinate multidistrict litigation often leads to vigorous opposition. *See also In re Asbestos Prod. Liab. Litig.*, 771 F. Supp. 415, 415 (J.P.M.L. 1991) (ordering transfer over opposition by plaintiffs in 5,200 actions and by 454 defendants; transfer supported by plaintiffs in 17,000 actions and by 30 defendants). One or more plaintiffs may object to losing control over the litigation, and plaintiffs' counsel may be concerned about having to share fees with attorneys handling similar cases. In addition, plaintiffs may believe that their particular judge and jurisdiction give them the greatest likelihood of success, and they may not want to risk moving their suit to a less friendly forum, even for purely pretrial purposes.

Defendants likewise do not always favor coordination of multidistrict litigation. In some cases, they and their attorneys may believe that separate lawsuits—and the expense and inefficiencies resulting therefrom—provide the best way of discouraging further litigation, whereas coordinated treatment could give increased legitimacy to the lawsuits and thereby raise the pressure to agree to an expensive settlement. For an insightful analysis of the pros and cons of MDL from the defendant's perspective, *see* Mark Herrmann, *To MDL or Not to MDL? A Defense Perspective*, 24 Litig. 43, 44–45, 47 (1998).

9. Should the MDL Panel give any significant weight to the self-interested views of parties favoring or opposing consolidation? Should the Panel be concerned that judges originally assigned to cases may, in some instances, be unhappy about having those cases transferred?

10. One article focuses on the strategic issues, from plaintiffs' perspective, of joining an ongoing MDL as opposed to pursuing a separate state-court suit. Mark P. Robinson, Jr. & Kevin F. Calcagnie, *To Join an MDL . . . Or Not*, 37 Trial 7 (2001). Among the advantages listed are opportunities to work with experienced plaintiffs' counsel and access to a better-qualified and better-prepared pool of experts. Among the disadvantages are potentially more rigorous federal standards for discovery, dispositive motions, and admissibility of evidence (particularly scientific evidence and expert testimony), and longer waiting time for a trial date. If there is a basis for removal (for example, on diversity grounds), defendants may be able to frustrate a decision by plaintiffs to remain in state court and not become part of a federal MDL proceeding.

11. The Williams & George excerpt notes that, unlike Rule 23(b)(3), the MDL statute does not require a showing that common issues predominate. In that sense, the requirement is more akin to the commonality requirement of

Rule 23(a)(2). Yet, unlike (a)(2), the MDL statute focuses solely on common questions of fact. Why does the statute not focus, in addition, on common questions of law? Are questions of law irrelevant to the MDL Panel's decision whether to consolidate cases for pretrial purposes?

12. Williams & George note that the MDL Panel has a wide range of options in selecting the MDL judge. Should the statute have more restrictions? For instance, should the statute limit candidates to judges who have a pending case in the litigation at issue?

3. SELECTION OF TRANSFEREE JUDGE

IN RE SILICONE GEL BREAST IMPLANTS PRODS. LIAB. LITIG.

Judicial Panel on Multidistrict Litigation, 1992.
793 F. Supp. 1098.

Before NANGLE, CHAIRMAN, DILLIN, MILTON POLLACK, LOUIS H. POLLAK, MERHIGE, JR., and ENRIGHT, JUDGES of the Panel.

NANGLE, PANEL JUDGE.

* * *

The record before us suggests that more than a million women have received silicone gel breast implants. Since the Food and Drug Administration held highly publicized hearings a few months ago about the safety of this product, a rush to the courthouse has ensued, although some litigation concerning the product has periodically been filed in the federal courts in the last several years.

This litigation presently consists of * * * 78 actions * * * pending in 33 federal districts. * * * Before the Panel are four separate motions pursuant to 28 U.S.C. § 1407: 1) motion of plaintiffs in three Northern District of California actions to centralize all actions in the Northern District of California or any other appropriate transferee forum (these plaintiffs now favor centralization in the Southern District of Ohio); 2) motion of plaintiffs in one Northern District of California action to centralize all actions in that district; 3) motion of plaintiffs in seven actions to centralize all actions in either the Northern District of California or the District of Kansas; and 4) motion of plaintiffs in the Eastern District of Virginia action * * * to centralize in that district the medical monitoring claims that are presented in seven purported class actions.

The overwhelming majority of the more than 200 responses received by the Panel supports transfer. The major issue presented in the responses is selection of the transferee forum, with two large groups of parties aligned in favor of opposing views. The first large group of parties favors selection of either the Northern District of California (Judge Thelton E. Henderson or Judge Marilyn H. Patel) or the District of Kansas (Judge Patrick F. Kelly). This group includes 1) plaintiffs in at least 65 of the 78 actions before the Panel; 2) plaintiffs in at least 69 potential tag-along actions; and 3) approximately 250 attorneys who are purportedly investigating claims of more than 2,000 potential plaintiffs. The second large group of parties favors selection of the Southern District of Ohio (Judge Carl B. Rubin). This group includes 1) plaintiffs in nine of the 78 actions before the Panel; 2) plaintiffs in at least nine potential tag-along actions; 3) approximately 75 law firms that purport to represent approximately 4,000 actual and potential plaintiffs; and 4) sixteen defendants, including major silicone gel breast implant manufacturers Dow Corning Corporation (Dow Corning), Baxter Healthcare Corporation, McGhan Medical Corporation (McGhan), Bristol–Meyers Squibb Company and Mentor Corporation (Mentor).

* * *

Selection of the transferee court and judge for this litigation has been a challenging task. The parties' arguments in their briefs and at the Panel hearing in this matter have focused primarily on the relative merits of the suggested California and Ohio forums. Proponents of the California forum stress that i) both Judge Henderson and Judge Patel have tried breast implant actions and are thus very familiar with the issues raised in this docket, ii) several implant manufacturers, including McGhan and Mentor, have their principal places of business in California, and iii) California is presumptively the state with the largest number of actual and potential claimants in the breast implant litigation. Meanwhile, proponents of the Ohio forum emphasize Judge Rubin's familiarity with the litigation, gained by presiding over the consolidated breast implant action * * * in his district since January 1992. During that time, Judge Rubin has conditionally certified a nationwide, opt-out class of breast implant recipients; established a document depository; appointed a Plaintiffs' Lead Counsel Committee consisting of seven members; scheduled trial on common issues for June 1993; and initiated the dissemination of notice to class members.

We observe that either the Northern District of California or the Southern District of Ohio could be an appropriate forum for this docket and certainly the judges referred to are experienced and well-qualified to handle this litigation. We are troubled, however, by the volume and tone of the negative arguments with which opposing counsel have sought to denigrate each other's forum choices, litigation strategies and underlying motives. A brief recitation of a few of these arguments sufficiently conveys the flavor. For example, various parties argue that 1) parties in the Ohio forum have engendered a flurry of pretrial activity in an effort to dictate our decision on selection of the transferee court; 2) the class in the Southern District of Ohio was certified in a precipitous fashion, without according adequate notice or opportunity to be heard to interested parties nationwide; 3) defendants oppose the California forum only because the two trials there resulted in substantial verdicts against one of them; and 4) the plaintiffs who favor the California forum are forum shopping for a judge who has tried a breast implant action in which plaintiffs prevailed.

Essentially, these arguments are fueled by an acrimonious dispute among counsel, relating to control of the litigation as well as to how it should proceed (class versus individual treatment). It is neither our function nor our inclination to take sides in this dispute. But we are indeed persuaded that the level of acrimony has caused the parties and counsel on each side to harbor a perception that they would be unfairly affected by selection of any of the suggested forums. This perception of "unfairness" is unwarranted, because this Panel believes that all of the federal judges involved in these 78 actions would conduct these proceedings in a fair and impartial manner. Nevertheless, we recognize that in a mega-tort docket of this nature, involving claimants who may be experiencing litigation for the first time, such a perception could become a dark cloud over these proceedings and threaten their just and efficient conduct.

In light of these considerations, we have determined to look beyond the preferences of the parties in our search for a transferee judge with the ability and temperament to steer this complex litigation on a steady course that will be sensitive to the concerns of all parties. Because no single location stands out as the geographic focal point for this nationwide docket, the scope of our search embraced the universe of federal district judges. By selecting Chief Judge Pointer [of the Northern District of Alabama], a former member of our Panel, Chairman of the Board of Editors of the Manual for Complex Litigation, Chairman of the Judicial Conference's Advisory Committee on Civil Rules, and an experienced multidistrict transferee judge, we are confident that we are entrusting this important and challenging assignment to a distinguished jurist. We urge all parties and counsel to work cooperatively with one another and with Judge Pointer toward the goal of a just, efficient and expeditious resolution of the litigation.

* * *

JAIME DODGE, FACILITATIVE JUDGING: ORGANIZATIONAL DESIGN IN MASS-MULTIDISTRICT LITIGATION
64 Emory L.J. 329, 337–42 (2014).

Our early conception of the judicial role focused upon an external, objective judge simply balancing the parties' arguments and rendering an adjudicative decision on the merits. Thirty years ago, the managerial model took hold. MDL judges of the era were leaders in shaping this mode * * *. No longer were judges "disinterested" parties; instead, they became managers, supervising case preparation and actively meeting with litigants in chambers to encourage resolution of the case.

Today, transferee judges have embraced a new role, ushering in a new generation of judges. Modern MDL judges no longer press settlement at all costs but instead embrace a wider variety of outcomes as successful resolutions. If settlement is to occur, the judge often utilizes private neutrals or special masters to negotiate settlements, preserving his or her neutrality as the litigation moves forward and motion practice continues. Sophisticated transferee judges also increasingly recognize the benefit of retaining distance from the settlement process, particularly in highly complex cases in which motions may be heard while settlement talks are ongoing or challenges may be made to the settlement's terms or its implementation. Indeed, this new breed of settlement is highly technical, often requiring the assistance of a mass tort neutral (whether a private mediator or appointed special master), a claims administrator, and supporting professional teams——even after the parties have reached an agreement in principle——to ensure the creation of a functioning and effective claims facility. But, today's judges are recognizing that resolving cases through motion practice and remand are equally valid resolution mechanisms; the parties must settle when the litigation has matured, not simply because of overbearing judicial pressure.

* * *

NOTES AND QUESTIONS

1. The MDL Panel in *Breast Implant* selected an experienced MDL judge. Is there any argument that judges who are *not* experienced in multi-party litigation could provide a "fresh" approach, even if their lack of experience might result in some inefficiencies? Should judges from whom cases would be transferred have a voice in the decision?

2. In arguing for its choice of transferee judge, each side in *Breast Implant* seemed to be urging selection of the court most likely to favor its interests in the case—an approach that backfired. Would any group have increased its chances of having its choice selected had it relied on more objective criteria? What criteria would be most persuasive?

3. Given the reasoning in the *Breast Implant* order, is it tactically helpful to attack the fairness or competence of an opponent's proposed choice of transferee judge? Does zealous advocacy require counsel to engage in such an attack?

4. In addition to seeking an experienced transferee judge, the MDL Panel also considers numerous other factors. "The more influential include the parties' principal place of business, the number of cases pending in a given district, the location of documents and witnesses, whether discovery is at an advanced stage in one of the districts, and the convenience of the parties." Penn. Comment, *supra*, 140 U. Pa. L Rev. at 722 (citing examples); *see also Manual for Complex Litigation (Fourth)* § 20.131 at 221 (describing factors used in selecting transferee judge).

5. Subsequent history of the *Breast Implant* MDL is discussed in *In re Dow Corning Corp.*, 211 B.R. 545 (Bankr. E.D. Mich. 1997). As the *Dow Corning* court noted, efforts by Judge Pointer to fashion a lasting global settlement ultimately failed. Faced with a crushing number of pending trials, as well as lawsuits involving other silicone-containing medical products, Dow Corning filed for bankruptcy relief under Chapter 11. *See* John C. Coffee, Jr., *Class Wars: The Dilemma of the Mass Tort Class Action*, 95 Colum. L. Rev. 1343, 1409–10 (1995); *see also* discussion of the Dow Corning bankruptcy in Chapter 13(B)(2)(e).

6. According to Dodge, the role of the MDL judge has changed over time. What, according to Dodge, is the MDL judge's current role? How does that role differ from prior roles? What are the pros and cons of each approach?

C. THE ADMINISTRATION AND RESOLUTION OF MDL CASES

1. SETTLEMENTS

HOWARD M. ERICHSON & BENJAMIN C. ZIPURSKY, CONSENT VERSUS CLOSURE
96 Cornell L. Rev. 265, 270–81 (2011).

I. Seeking Closure in Mass Tort Settlements

* * *

In what has become a predictable pattern, defendants fighting mass litigation reach a point when they seek to settle claims en masse. * * * The timing of this settlement moment varies. In some cases, * * * the settlement moment occurs after defendants suffer numerous defeats at trial. In others, * * * it occurs after defendants have had notable trial success. Still in others, * * * it occurs before any actions have reached verdicts. In each case, however, the defendant sees a risk of liability and faces the burden of lengthy and widespread litigation.

When defendants settle mass litigation, they prefer to settle wholesale. Not only do individual negotiations require greater resource expenditures, but piecemeal settlements simply do not provide sufficient peace to allow a defendant to put a dispute behind it. Worse, piecemeal settlements may draw more claimants into the litigation, as prospective plaintiffs and attorneys smell blood in the water. From the defendant's perspective, the more comprehensive the deal, the better.

During the 1990s, the preferred device for global peace in mass litigation was the settlement class action. * * * However, the Supreme Court dealt a blow to the use of settlement class actions in mass tort litigation * * * in *Amchem* and *Ortiz*.

* * *

Amchem imposed constraints that made it impossible for parties to settle mass torts on a classwide basis unless they bent over backward to ensure that all claimants were treated fairly in light of intraclass conflicts. * * *

This background explains the state of affairs as lawyers considered ways to resolve the burgeoning *Vioxx* litigation * * *.

II. The *Vioxx* Settlement

For the past twenty years, mass tort defendants have searched doggedly for ways to obtain closure. Outside of bankruptcy, most of these attempts failed in one way or another—until *Vioxx*.

* * *

The lawyers in *Vioxx* understood that once the identity of the claimants was known, a nonclass aggregate settlement could provide as comprehensive a resolution as a class action, but only if those claimants consented to be bound by the settlement. In the absence of *Vioxx*-like terms, however, most nonclass aggregate settlements have not accomplished truly comprehensive resolutions. In the *OxyContin* litigation, despite a wholesale settlement of tort claims and a plea deal with federal prosecutors, Purdue Pharma continued to face individual plaintiffs' claims. In the *Zyprexa* litigation, Eli Lilly reached a deal in 2006 to pay hundreds of millions of dollars to settle about 8,000 claims in the federal multidistrict litigation and several months later paid hundreds of millions more to settle 18,000 claims that were not included in the first deal. Johnson & Johnson settled Ortho Evra claims on a piecemeal basis. By striking a deal for a nonclass settlement but including clauses for mandatory recommendation and mandatory withdrawal, Merck avoided class certification hurdles while achieving a high degree of finality.

* * *

Unlike many mass tort settlement agreements, the *Vioxx* agreement was made public, so the full details of its terms are available. Merck agreed to put $4.85 billion into a compensation fund—$4 billion for heart attack victims and $850 million for stroke victims. The deal included a walkaway clause that conditioned the settlement on the participation of 85% of the eligible claimants in each of several categories. To be eligible for the fund, *Vioxx* plaintiffs had to enroll in the program, which required putting a release in escrow. Each claimant had to demonstrate that he or she (or the victim in a wrongful-death suit) had a heart attack or an ischemic stroke and ingested a certain amount of Vioxx over a certain period. Additionally, a claimant had to establish a temporal nexus between ingestion and injury. A "gate committee" composed of three Merck representatives and three plaintiff representatives determined eligibility.

Once claimants were eligible, a claims administrator would score them. The more serious the heart attack or stroke was, the more points the claimant received. The longer the claimants or victims took Vioxx, the more points they received. Finally, claimants or victims who were older and had greater risk factors, such as weight, family history, and diabetes, received fewer points. The total points of all claimants for heart disease and stroke, divided into the total settlement pot, would determine the dollar value per point. Each eligible claimant would receive an award equal to the number of the claimant's points multiplied by the value of each point. This calculation structure meant that claimants had to decide whether to enroll before knowing what their payments would be. Thus, the settlement payments were doubly contingent: they were contingent on how many points the claims administrator granted and on how many dollars each point was worth.

The indeterminacy that each plaintiff faced was exacerbated (or made easier, depending on one's view) by the role that each lawyer would play. All lawyers who signed the agreement or who enrolled anyone in the program were obligated to recommend enrollment to each and every client. Moreover, if the client did not find the recommendation persuasive, the lawyer had something else to make the decision easier: if the client did not accept the offer, the lawyer would no longer represent the client. The option of not settling was remarkably unattractive.

These provisions—the mandatory-recommendation provision and the mandatory-withdrawal provision—were the two most controversial aspects of the *Vioxx* settlement. The mandatory-recommendation provision took the form of an affirmation by participating lawyers:

> By submitting an Enrollment Form, the Enrolling Counsel affirms that he has recommended, or . . . will recommend by no later than [the deadline], to 100% of the Eligible Claimants represented by such Enrolling Counsel that such Eligible Claimants enroll in the Program.

The mandatory-withdrawal provision, notwithstanding several ethical caveats, clearly indicated that Merck expected participating lawyers to cease representing any nonsettling clients. More importantly, when deciding whether to take part in the settlement, clients would be aware that saying "no" meant losing their lawyer:

> If any such Eligible Claimant disregards such recommendation, or for any other reason fails (or has failed) to submit a non-deficient and non-defective Enrollment Form on or before [the deadline], such Enrolling Counsel shall . . . [by the required date], to the extent permitted by the equivalents to Rules 1.16 and 5.6 of the ABA Model Rules of Professional Conduct in the relevant jurisdiction(s), (i) take (or have taken, as the case may be) all necessary steps to disengage and withdraw from the representation of such Eligible Claimant and to forego any Interest in such Eligible Claimant and (ii) cause (or have caused, as the case may be) each other Enrolling Counsel, and each other counsel with an Interest in any Enrolled Program Claimant, which has an Interest in such Eligible Claimant to do the same.

Other language reinforced the expectation that all of each participating law firm's eligible *Vioxx* clients would take part in the settlement: "The parties agree that a key objective of the Program is that, with respect to any counsel with an Interest in the claims of any Enrolled Program Claimant, all other Eligible Claimants in which such counsel has an Interest shall be enrolled in the Program."

Some *Vioxx* plaintiffs' lawyers, troubled by the mandatory-recommendation and mandatory-withdrawal provisions, sought a declaratory judgment that these terms were unenforceable. In response, Merck and the negotiating plaintiffs' lawyers added explanatory language to the agreement: "Each Enrolling Counsel is expected to exercise his or her independent judgment in the best interest of each client individually before determining whether to recommend enrollment in the Program." Although this amendment apparently satisfied the objecting lawyers, it was put forth as a "clarification" rather than as a substantive change; neither of the controversial provisions was removed.

* * *

NOTES AND QUESTIONS

1. What, if any, ethical issues are raised by the *Vioxx* settlement?

2. Erichson and Zipursky note that "a nonclass aggregate settlement [can] provide as comprehensive a resolution as a class action, but only if those claimants consent[] to be bound by the settlement." Why is this so? Using the *Vioxx* case as an example, what problems arise in attempting to settle mass tort cases without the vehicle of a class action? How can an MDL proceeding facilitate such a settlement?

3. Should the protections of Rule 23 be adopted in the context of non-class MDL proceedings? How would such protections avoid the problems faced by the parties in *Vioxx*?

2. REMAND AND TRIAL ISSUES

CATHERINE R. BORDEN, EMERY G. LEE III & MARGARET S. WILLIAMS, CENTRIPETAL FORCES: MULTIDISTRICT LITIGATION AND ITS PARTS
75 La. L. Rev. 425, 430–31, 452–53 (2014).

* * *

Simply put, there are a lot of MDL cases. The Panel Cases Database contains information on 463,795 cases that have appeared on the Panel's docket. Products liability cases heavily dominate this database, accounting for 93% of the cases. Securities is the next largest case category, making up just 1.4% of the database. Only 20% of all MDL proceedings involve products liability claims, but the overwhelming majority of cases that are considered by the Panel involve such claims. The Panel Cases Database is, in fact, dominated by a few mammoth products liability proceedings. The largest, not surprisingly, is MDL No. 875, *In re Asbestos Products Liability Litigation* (No. VI), which accounts for 200,265 cases, or 43% of the database. MDL No. 875 and the ten next largest products liability proceedings account for 71% of the database. All the non-products liability cases account for just 7%. There are almost as many cases in MDL No. 926 (*In re Silicone Gel Breast Implant Products Liability Litigation*) in the database as there are cases from all other non-product liability types of proceedings (air disaster, antitrust, and so on) combined.

* * *

The Panel has in recent years made clear that remand is not a failed outcome in MDL proceedings. Once efficiencies in pretrial proceedings have been exploited, it is appropriate to return the cases to their transferor districts. By statute, one of the goals of the MDL process is to create efficiencies in the judicial system. By having one judge working through several similar cases in a single proceeding, instead of multiple judges working on individual cases across the country, judicial time and resources are saved. The Panel frequently cites efficiency as a reason for centralizing cases in a proceeding. Commentators have expressed concern about remand because transferor judges may lack the expertise in the subject matter of the litigation that transferee judges have accumulated during the proceedings. Nonetheless * * * these cases [are] similar to all other civil litigation in how they terminate: relatively few go to trial. Given a goal of efficiency, it is hardly surprising that centralization is so often the Panel's decision, and that substantially many more cases are centralized than denied. * * * Moreover, if efficiency is a goal—and it seems fair to say that it is—the rarity of remanding cases should not be surprising either. Remand is a tool transferee judges can use to manage litigation, but it is rarely necessary, even in the most complex of MDLs * * *. In a world of aggregate litigation, there is relatively little disaggregation once constituent cases are combined through centralization.

* * *

NOTES AND QUESTIONS

1. In the view of Borden and her co-authors, why are more cases centralized than denied centralization? Is the MDL Panel correct that remand should not be viewed as a failure?

2. Why do product liability cases so overwhelmingly dominate the MDL database?

LEXECON, INC. v. MILBERG WEISS BERSHAD HYNES & LERACH

Supreme Court of the United States, 1998.
523 U.S. 26.

JUSTICE SOUTER delivered the opinion of the Court.

Title 28 U.S.C. § 1407(a) authorizes the Judicial Panel on Multidistrict Litigation to transfer civil actions with common issues of fact "to any district for coordinated or consolidated pretrial proceedings," but imposes a duty on the Panel to remand any such action to the original district "at or before the conclusion of such pretrial proceedings." The issue here is whether a district court conducting such "pretrial proceedings" may invoke § 1404(a) to assign a transferred case to itself for trial. We hold it has no such authority.

I.

In 1992, petitioners, Lexecon Inc., a law and economics consulting firm, and one of its principals (collectively, Lexecon), brought this diversity action in the Northern District of Illinois against respondents, the law firms of Milberg Weiss Bershad Hynes & Lerach (Milberg) and Cotchett, Illston & Pitre (Cotchett), claiming malicious prosecution, abuse of process, tortious interference, commercial disparagement, and defamation. The suit arose out of the firms' conduct as counsel in a prior class action brought against Charles Keating and the American Continental Corporation for violations of the securities and racketeering laws. Lexecon also was a defendant, charged with giving federal and state banking regulators inaccurate and misleading reports about the financial condition of the American Continental Corporation and its subsidiary Lincoln Savings and Loan. Along with other actions arising out of the failure of Lincoln Savings, the case against Lexecon was transferred under § 1407(a) for pretrial proceedings before Judge Bilby in the District of Arizona, where the matters so consolidated were known as the Lincoln Savings litigation. Before those proceedings were over, the class action plaintiffs and Lexecon reached what they termed a "resolution," under which the claims against Lexecon were dismissed in August 1992.

Lexecon then filed this case in the Northern District of Illinois charging that the prior class action terminated in its favor when the respondent law firms' clients voluntarily dismissed their claims against Lexecon as meritless, amounting to nothing more, according to Lexecon, than a vendetta. When these allegations came to the attention of Judge Bilby, he issued an order stating his understanding of the terms of the resolution agreement between Lexecon and the class action plaintiffs. Judge Bilby's characterization of the agreement being markedly at odds with the allegations in the instant action, Lexecon appealed his order to the Ninth Circuit.

Milberg, joined by Cotchett, then filed a motion under § 1407(a) with the Judicial Panel on Multidistrict Litigation seeking transfer of this case to Judge Bilby for consolidation with the Lincoln Savings litigation. Although the judge entered a recusal because of the order he had taken it upon himself to issue, the law firms nonetheless renewed their motion for a § 1407(a) transfer.

The Panel ordered a transfer in early June 1993 and assigned the case to Judge Roll, noting that Lexecon's claims "share questions of fact with an as yet unapproved settlement involving Touche Ross, Lexecon, Inc. and the investor plaintiffs in the Lincoln Savings investor class actions in MDL–834." The Panel observed that "i) a massive document depository is located in the District of Arizona and ii) the Ninth Circuit has before it an appeal of an order [describing the terms of Lexecon's dismissal from the Lincoln Savings litigation] in MDL–834 which may be relevant to the *Lexecon* claims." Prior to any dispositive action on Lexecon's instant claims in the District of Arizona, the Ninth Circuit appeal mentioned by the Panel was dismissed, and the document depository was closed down.

In November 1993, Judge Roll dismissed Lexecon's state-law malicious prosecution and abuse of process claims. * * * Although the law firms then moved for summary judgment on the claims remaining, the judge deferred action pending completion of discovery, during which time the remaining parties to the Lincoln Savings litigation reached a final settlement, on which judgment was entered in March 1994.

In August 1994, Lexecon moved that the District Court refer the case back to the Panel for remand to the Northern District of Illinois, thus heeding the point of Multidistrict Litigation Rule 14(d), which provides that "the Panel is reluctant to order remand absent a suggestion of remand from the transferee district court." The law firms opposed a remand because discovery was still incomplete and filed a countermotion under § 1404(a) requesting the District of Arizona to "transfer" the case to itself for trial. Judge Roll deferred decision on these motions as well.

In November 1994, Lexecon again asked the District Court to request the Panel to remand the case to the Northern District of Illinois. Again the law firms objected and requested a § 1404 transfer, and Judge Roll deferred ruling once more. On April 24, 1995, however, he granted summary judgment in favor of the law firms on all remaining claims except one in defamation brought against Milberg, and at the same time he dismissed the [law firms'] counterclaims. Cotchett then made a request for judgment under Federal Rule of Civil Procedure 54(b). Lexecon objected to the exercise of Rule 54(b) discretion, but did not contest the authority of the District Court in Arizona to enter a final judgment in Cotchett's favor. On June 7, 1995, the court granted respondent Cotchett's Rule 54(b) request.

In the meantime, the Arizona court had granted the law firms' § 1404(a) motions to assign the case to itself for trial, and simultaneously had denied Lexecon's motions to request the Panel to remand under § 1407(a). Lexecon sought immediate review of these last two rulings by filing a petition for mandamus in the Ninth Circuit. After argument, a majority of the Circuit panel, over the dissent of Judge Kozinski, denied Lexecon's requests to vacate the self-assignment order and require remand to the Northern District of Illinois. The Circuit so ruled even though the majority was "not prepared to say that [Lexecon's] contentions lack merit" and went so far as to note the conflict between "what appears to be a clear statutory mandate [of § 1407 and § 1404]" and Multidistrict Litigation Rule 14(b), which explicitly authorizes a transferee court to assign an action to itself for trial. The majority simply left that issue for another day, relying on its assumption that Lexecon would have an opportunity to obtain relief from the transfer order on direct appeal: "[t]he transfer order can be appealed immediately along with other issues in the event the petitioners lose on the merits [at trial]."

Trial on the surviving defamation claim then went forward in the District of Arizona, ending in judgment for Milberg, from which Lexecon appealed to the Ninth Circuit. It again appealed the denial of its motion for a suggestion that the Panel remand the matter to the Northern District of Illinois, and it challenged the dismissal of its claims for malicious prosecution and abuse of process, and the entry of final judgment in favor of Cotchett. Lexecon took no exception to the Arizona court's jurisdiction (as distinct from venue) and pursued no claim of error in the conduct of the trial.

A divided panel of the Ninth Circuit affirmed, relying on the Panel's Rule 14 and appellate and District Court decisions in support of the District Court's refusal to support remand under § 1407(a) and its decision to assign the case to itself under § 1404(a). While the majority indicated that permitting the transferee court to assign a case to itself upon completion of its pretrial work was not only consistent with the statutory language but conducive to efficiency, Judge Kozinski again dissented, relying on the texts of §§ 1407(a) and 1404(a) and a presumption in favor of a plaintiff's choice of forum. We granted *certiorari* to decide whether § 1407(a) does permit a transferee court to entertain a § 1404(a) transfer motion to keep the case for trial.

II.

A.

In defending the Ninth Circuit majority, Milberg may claim ostensible support from two quarters. First, the Panel has itself sanctioned such assignments in a rule issued in reliance on its rulemaking authority under 28 U.S.C. § 1407(f). The Panel's Rule 14(b) provides that "[e]ach transferred action that has not been terminated in the transferee district court shall be remanded by the Panel to the transferor district for trial, unless ordered transferred by the transferee judge to the transferee or other district under 28 U.S.C. § 1404(a) or 28 U.S.C. § 1406." Thus, out of the 39,228 cases transferred under § 1407 and terminated as of September 30, 1995, 279 of the 3,787 ultimately requiring trial were retained by the courts to which the Panel had transferred them. Although the Panel's rule and the practice of self-assignment have not gone without challenge, * * * federal courts have treated such transfers with approval. * * *

The second source of ostensible authority for Milberg's espousal of the self-assignment power here is a portion of text of the multidistrict litigation statute itself:

> "When civil actions involving one or more common questions of fact are pending in different districts, such actions may be transferred to any district for coordinated or consolidated pretrial proceedings."

28 U.S.C. § 1407(a).

Although the statute limits a transferee court's authority to the conduct of "coordinated or consolidated" proceedings and to those that are "pretrial," these limitations alone raise no obvious bar to a transferee's retention of a case under § 1404. If "consolidated" proceedings alone were authorized, there would be an argument that self-assignment of one or some cases out of many was not contemplated, but because the proceedings need only be "coordinated," no such narrow limitation is apparent. While it is certainly true that the instant case was not "consolidated" with any other for the purpose literally of litigating identical issues on common evidence, it is fair to say that proceedings to resolve pretrial matters were "coordinated" with the conduct of earlier cases sharing the common core of the Lincoln Savings debacle, if only by being brought before judges in a district where much of the evidence was to be found and overlapping issues had been considered. Judge Bilby's recusal following his decision to respond to Lexecon's Illinois pleadings may have limited the prospects for coordination, but it surely did not eliminate them. Hence, the requirement that a transferee court conduct "coordinated or consolidated" proceedings did not preclude the transferee Arizona court from ruling on a motion (like the § 1404 request) that affects only one of the cases before it.

Likewise, at first blush, the statutory limitation to "pretrial" proceedings suggests no reason that a § 1407 transferor court could not entertain a § 1404(a) motion. Section 1404(a) authorizes a district court to transfer a case in the interest of justice and for the convenience of the parties and witnesses. *See* § 1404(a) [*see infra* Part (B)(2) of this chapter]. Such transfer requests are typically resolved prior to discovery, and thus are classic "pretrial" motions.

Beyond this point, however, the textual pointers reverse direction, for § 1407 not only authorizes the Panel to transfer for coordinated or consolidated pretrial proceedings, but obligates the Panel to remand any pending case to its originating court when, at the latest, those pretrial proceedings have run their course.

> "Each action so transferred shall be remanded by the panel at or before the conclusion of such pretrial proceedings to the district

from which it was transferred unless it shall have been previously terminated."

§ 1407(a) * * *.

The Panel's instruction comes in terms of the mandatory "shall," which normally creates an obligation impervious to judicial discretion. In the absence of any indication that there might be circumstances in which a transferred case would be neither "terminated" nor subject to the remand obligation, then, the statutory instruction stands flatly at odds with reading the phrase "coordinated or consolidated pretrial proceedings" so broadly as to reach its literal limits, allowing a transferee court's self-assignment to trump the provision imposing the Panel's remand duty. If we do our job of reading the statute whole, we have to give effect to this plain command, even if doing that will reverse the longstanding practice under the statute and the rule.

As the Ninth Circuit panel majority saw it, however, the inconsistency between an expansive view of "coordinated or consolidated pretrial" proceedings and the uncompromising terms of the Panel's remand obligation disappeared as merely an apparent conflict, not a real one. The "focus" of § 1407 was said to be constituting the Panel and defining its authority, not circumscribing the powers of district courts under § 1404(a). Milberg presses this point in observing that § 1407(a) does not, indeed, even apply to transferee courts, being concerned solely with the Panel's duties, whereas § 1407(b), addressed to the transferee courts, says nothing about the Panel's obligation to remand. But this analysis fails to persuade, for the very reason that it rejects that central tenet of interpretation, that a statute is to be considered in all its parts when construing any one of them. To emphasize that § 1407(b) says nothing about the Panel's obligation when addressing a transferee court's powers is simply to ignore the necessary consequence of self-assignment by a transferee court: it conclusively thwarts the Panel's capacity to obey the unconditional command of § 1407(a).

A like use of blinders underlies the Circuit majority's conclusion that the Panel was not even authorized to remand the case under its Rule 14(c), the terms of which condition the remand responsibility on a suggestion of the transferee court, a motion filed directly with the Panel, or the Panel's *sua sponte* decision to remand. None of these conditions was fulfilled, according to the Court of Appeals, which particularly faulted Lexecon for failing to file a remand motion directly with the Panel, as distinct from the transferee court. This analysis, too, is unpersuasive; it just ignores the fact that the statute places an obligation on the Panel to remand no later than the conclusion of pretrial proceedings in the transferee court, and no exercise in rulemaking can read that obligation out of the statute. *See* 28 U.S.C. § 1407(f) (express requirement that rules be consistent with statute).

B.

Milberg proffers two further arguments for overlooking the tension between a broad reading of a court's pretrial authority and the Panel's remand obligation. First, it relies on a subtle reading of the provision of § 1407(a) limiting the Panel's remand obligation to cases not "previously terminated" during the pretrial period. To be sure, this exception to the Panel's remand obligation indicates that the Panel is not meant to issue ceremonial remand orders in cases already concluded by summary judgment, say, or dismissal. But according to Milberg, the imperative to remand is also inapplicable to cases self-assigned under § 1404, because the self-assignment "terminates" the case insofar as its venue depends on § 1407. When the § 1407 character of the action disappears, Milberg argues, the strictures of § 1407 fall away as well, relieving the Panel of any further duty in the case. The trouble with this creative argument, though, is that the statute manifests no such subtlety. Section 1407(a) speaks not in terms of imbuing transferred actions with some new and distinctive venue character, but simply in terms of "civil actions" or "actions." It says that such an action, not its acquired personality, must be terminated before the Panel is excused from ordering remand. The language is straightforward, and with a straightforward application ready to hand, statutory interpretation has no business getting metaphysical.

Second, Milberg tries to draw an inference in its favor from the one subsection of § 1407 that does authorize the Panel to transfer a case for trial as well as pretrial proceedings. Subsection (h) provides that,

> "[n]otwithstanding the provisions of section 1404 or subsection (f) of this section, the judicial panel on multidistrict litigation may consolidate and transfer with or without the consent of the parties, for both pretrial purposes and for trial, any action brought under section 4C of the Clayton Act."

Milberg fastens on the introductory language explicitly overriding the "provisions of section 1404 or subsection (f)," which would otherwise, respectively, limit a district court to transferring a case "to any other district or division where it might have been brought," § 1404(a), and limit the Panel to prescribing rules "not inconsistent with Acts of Congress," § 1407(f). On Milberg's reasoning, these overrides are required because the cited provisions would otherwise conflict with the remainder of subsection (h) authorizing the Panel to order trial of certain Clayton Act cases in the transferee court. The argument then runs that since there is no override of subsection (a) of § 1407, subsection (a) must be consistent with a transfer for trial as well as pretrial matters. This reasoning is fallacious, however. Subsections (a) and (h) are independent sources of transfer authority in the Panel; each is apparently written to stand on its own feet. Subsection (h) need not exclude the application of subsection (a), because nothing in (a) would by its terms limit any provision of (h).

Subsection (h) is not merely valueless to Milberg, however; it is ammunition for Lexecon. For the one point that subsection (h) does demonstrate is that Congress knew how to distinguish between trial assignments and pretrial proceedings in cases subject to § 1407. Although the enactment of subsection (a) preceded the enactment of subsection (h), the fact that the later section distinguishes trial assignments from pretrial proceedings generally is certainly some confirmation for our conclusion, on independent grounds, that the subjects of pretrial proceedings in subsections (a) and (b) do not include self-assignment orders.

* * *

[The Court found nothing in the legislative history to support Milberg's position.]

* * *

D.

In sum, none of the arguments raised can unsettle the straightforward language imposing the Panel's responsibility to remand, which bars recognizing any self-assignment power in a transferee court and consequently entails the invalidity of the Panel's Rule 14(b). *See* 28 U.S.C. § 1407(f). Milberg may or may not be correct that permitting transferee courts to make self-assignments would be more desirable than preserving a plaintiff's choice of venue (to the degree that § 1407(a) does so), but the proper venue for resolving that issue remains the floor of Congress.

[The Court also rejected Milberg's argument that, under the harmless error doctrine, no remedy was available to Lexecon.]

Accordingly, the judgment of the Court of Appeals is reversed, and the case is remanded for further proceedings consistent with this opinion.

* * *

NOTES AND QUESTIONS

1. Was the *Lexecon* Court correct in finding that the language of the MDL statute was so clear that policy arguments were legally irrelevant? Or should the Court have devoted more attention to the wisdom of self-assignment?

2. Does it make sense from an efficiency standpoint to prohibit a court from transferring a case to itself for trial? Consider the following discussion:

> [A] decision by an MDL court to self-transfer for trial purposes will often mean that the parties and the witnesses must travel to a distant city for the trial. * * * Beyond such inconvenience, the consolidation that results from a self-transfer often undermines the integrity of the trial process in at least four concrete ways.
>
> First, such consolidation of trial-related issues frequently causes litigants to lose control of individual cases. Thus, consolidation often deprives an individual litigant of the ability to craft and present its own case to the jury in the most effective manner. Instead, differences in individual cases tend to be ignored. * * *
>
> Second, consolidated trials often result in prejudice to those defendants (or plaintiffs, for that matter) whose cases are stronger than those of the other parties aligned on the same side of the case. For example, a defendant with a particularly strong defense may suffer from having its case tried with those of other defendants with weaker defenses. The jury may be confused by the multiple defenses and may be prejudiced against the former defendant by virtue of its apparent association with the latter defendants.
>
> Third, regardless of such differences among the cases, consolidated trials often require a jury to sift through and understand far

more evidence than they would if the cases were tried one-by-one. The problem of "jury overload"—particularly in complex financial or antitrust cases—has been frequently noted by courts and commentators. Consolidating numerous cases for trial exacerbates the risk that a jury will not be able to understand and digest the evidence and will instead reach a decision based on secondary, or even improper, factors. This overload will inevitably create unfair prejudice to some parties and give an unfair advantage to others. * * *

Fourth, even if a jury is able to understand all the evidence, the sheer length of a consolidated MDL trial creates its own problems. Better-educated jurors, whose jobs might allow them to sit on a one- or two-week trial, will often be excused from service if it appears that the trial is likely to drag on for months. This will have an obvious, and often dispositive, effect on the make-up of the jury. Moreover, the remaining jurors may become angry at having to devote a large amount of time to a trial—anger that rarely falls evenly on all the parties.

In short, the consolidated trials that generally result from self-transfer raise a host of concerns about the integrity of the trial process. * * *

* * *

Proponents of self-transfer will undoubtedly contend that any anomalies created by the procedure are justified on efficiency grounds. However, it is not at all evident that consolidating cases for trial will achieve the putative benefits claimed by the proponents of self-transfer.

Trials are much less amenable to consolidation than are most pretrial proceedings. For example, both motions to dismiss and motions for summary judgment are decided as a matter of law, and "Congress may have felt that federal judges are fungible for purposes of resolving legal questions." The reasoning underlying the decisions on such motions should therefore apply to any case with analogous facts. Also, consolidating discovery proceedings makes sense: separate discovery proceedings can often result in unnecessary duplication of effort because each proceeding seeks disclosure of the same materials. The same cannot be said of trial matters, which vary from trial to trial depending on factual differences and varying litigation strategies.

Indeed, in trial proceedings, factual differences between cases can often be the basis for reaching opposite results in otherwise similar cases. Such differences, however, are generally exposed through careful examination and cross-examination of witnesses and other trial procedures. Development and presentation of such case-specific facts, moreover, can generally be accomplished no more efficiently in a single, omnibus trial than in individual trials.

For similar reasons, there are few, if any, benefits to be gained from consolidating rulings on evidentiary issues. Evidentiary issues are often fact-bound, and a full airing of the relevant facts is often necessary to achieve sensible rulings on such matters. This process is generally not amenable to consolidation, but rather demands individualized attention.

Moreover, it is no simple matter even to administer a consolidated trial for cases brought from all over the country. * * *

Carter G. Phillips, Gene C. Schaerr & Anil K. Abraham, *Rescuing Multidistrict Litigation From the Altar of Expediency,* 1997 BYU L. Rev. 821, 833–37, 841–42 (1997). Are these authors correct? What arguments can be made in *favor* of self-transfer for trial? *See, e.g.,* Comment, *A Catalyst for Reforming Self-Transfer in Multidistrict Litigation:* Lexecon, Inc. v. Milberg Weiss, 72 St. John's L. Rev. 623, 633–35 (1998) (collecting authorities favoring self-transfer); *see also* Blake M. Rhodes, *The Judicial Panel on Multidistrict Litigation: Time for Rethinking,* 140 U. Pa. L. Rev. 711, 731–33 (1991) (pre-*Lexecon* article describing advantages of trial in transferee court); *Manual for Complex Litigation (Fourth)* § 20.132 at 223 (2004) (describing policy reasons for self-transfer).

3. One commentator summarizes other tools for transfer in light of *Lexecon*:

> First, in many situations, the plaintiff and defendant will agree that it would be better if the MDL transferee court could try a case sent to it for coordinated pretrial proceedings. When the parties agree on this issue, they can secure a trial by the MDL transferee court through mechanisms other than self-transfer under § 1404(a).
>
> The plaintiff could, for example, dismiss the action the MDL Panel had transferred home for trial and re-file the case in the transferee district, with the defendant waiving any statute of limitations, venue or personal jurisdiction objections to the re-filing. After the case has been dismissed and refiled in the transferee court, that court indisputably would have the power to try the case.
>
> As a second alternative, the MDL Panel could transfer a case in which pretrial proceedings had been concluded back to its home court for trial. The plaintiff and defendant then could file a joint motion in the home court for re-transfer back to the MDL transferee court for trial.
>
> If the MDL transferee court was one in which venue originally would have been proper, this re-transfer under § 1404(a) would be entirely permissible. *Lexecon* does not prohibit the remand court from transferring the case back to the MDL transferee court for trial. Presumably, given that all parties would be stipulating to this relief, most courts would grant it.
>
> * * *
>
> Finally, the Chief Justice is statutorily authorized to designate a trial judge in one district to act as a judge in a different district "upon presentation of a certificate of necessity by the chief judge or circuit justice of the circuit wherein the need arises." [28 U.S.C. § 292(d).] This statute has been used to designate that an MDL transferee judge be deemed a judge of a different court to permit that judge to try a case, and could be put to that use again.
>
> This last self-transfer vehicle may pose a practical difficulty. If, for example, the MDL transferee court is in Chicago and a particular case must be transferred to Dallas for trial, the transferee judge may be required to conduct the trial in Dallas to ensure that a jury is drawn from the proper pool. Inconveniences such as this are a small

price to pay, however, if trial by the transferee court is the prod needed to resolve complex multidistrict litigation.

Mark Herrmann, *Self-Transfers Gone After* "*Lexecon*"?, N.Y.L.J., Nov. 23, 1998, at 58.

4. Some courts have used creative approaches post-*Lexecon*. *See Manual for Complex Litigation (Fourth)* § 20.132, at 224–25 (2004). For example, in *Kenwin Shops, Inc. v. Bank of La.*, 1999 WL 294800 (S.D.N.Y. 1999), two actions were originally brought in the Southern District of New York. *Id.* at *1. The MDL Panel transferred the actions to the Eastern District of Louisiana for consolidated pre-trial proceedings, where other actions were pending. At the request of the defendant, the Bank of Louisiana ("BOL"), the MDL Panel remanded the cases to the Southern District of New York, with the approval of the transferee judge. BOL then moved to transfer the cases from the Southern District of New York back to the Eastern District of Louisiana pursuant to Section 1404(a). Despite arguments to the contrary, the Southern District of New York concluded that 1404(a) transfer was appropriate for the convenience of the parties and witnesses, and in the interest of justice. Thus, the transferee court was ultimately able to retain jurisdiction.

5. The *Manual for Complex Litigation (Fourth)* notes that when MDL treatment is unavailable, courts can nonetheless take various steps to coordinate related cases. These include (i) specially assigning all cases to a single judge under 28 U.S.C. §§ 292–94, whereby the judge would "sit temporarily in the district where the cases are pending"; (ii) obtaining agreement of the parties to "treat one case as the 'lead case'" and either "staying proceedings in the other cases pending resolution of the lead case" or allowing rulings in the lead case to have "presumptive" effect in other cases; (iii) conducting "joint conferences or hearings" and issuing "joint or parallel orders"; (iv) having experts or special masters appointed jointly for multiple cases; (v) coordinating discovery to avoid duplication; (vi) coordinating class definitions where applicable; and (vii) staying actions pending the resolution of related cases. *Manual for Complex Litigation (Fourth)* § 20.14 (2004). What disadvantages do these approaches have compared with MDL?

6. The American Law Institute (ALI) has noted some deficiencies with the MDL process under section 1407, stating:

> Section 1407 centralization does not work as well in practice as it theoretically might. * * * For example, because the initial transfer ostensibly is limited to the pretrial phase, the parties cannot determine at an early stage where their claims ultimately will be tried. Problems also are created by the fact that related cases come to the Multidistrict Litigation Panel in very different stages of development, yet have to be administered jointly. New cases are often filed after the initial group is well into pretrial, or even has been resolved, in the transferee court. This timing problem causes unnecessary litigation, slows the movement of the proceeding, and consumes judicial resources.

American Law Institute, *Complex Litigation: Statutory Recommendations and Analysis* 22–23 (1994). Are the ALI's concerns about the usefulness of section 1407 as an aggregation device justified?

7. Choice of law is sometimes an issue in MDL cases. For example, the district court in *In re Toyota Motor Corp. Unintended Acceleration Marketing, Sales Practices, & Products Liability Litigation*, 785 F. Supp. 2d 925 (C.D. Cal.

2011), issued a ruling denying plaintiffs' motion for application of California law. The moving plaintiffs resided in various states, but had all filed suit in California (the MDL transferee court). The district court acknowledged that it might appear, under the general rule, that California's choice-of-law analysis applied. *See id.* at 928. The court held, however, that "other considerations, some unique to multidistrict litigation, convince the Court that a fuller analysis compels a different result":

> There are three independent but related reasons why the Court should not undertake the analysis suggested by Plaintiffs. First, Supreme Court authority strongly suggests that a plaintiff's strategic decisions should not be permitted to dictate the applicable substantive law. Second, granting the relief sought by Plaintiffs here would undermine the purposes of the present MDL because it fails to take into account the requirement that the cases retain their separate and distinct identities in a manner that facilitates their statutorily mandated return to their home states for trial. Finally, granting the relief sought here would elevate the status of the Master Consolidated Complaint beyond that of a mere procedural device and would instead have the impermissible effect of altering the parties' substantive rights.

785 F. Supp. 2d at 928.

3. BELLWETHER TRIALS IN MDL PROCEEDINGS

ELDON E. FALLON, JEREMY T. GRAYBILL & ROBERT PITARD WYNNE, BELLWETHER TRIALS IN MULTIDISTRICT LITIGATION
82 Tul L. Rev. 2323, 2324, 2330–31, 2337–47, 2365–67 (2008).

I. Introduction

* * *

[This article discusses] the primary practical consideration for courts and counsel in employing bellwether trials, namely the method of selecting bellwether cases from a wider group of related lawsuits. * * *

II. Overview of the Multidistrict Litigation Process

* * *

* * * [T]he strongest criticism of the traditional MDL process is that the centralized forum can resemble a "black hole," into which cases are transferred never to be heard from again. The fact that MDL practice is relatively slow is to be expected, however, when one court is burdened with thousands of claims that would otherwise be spread throughout courts across the country. Despite criticisms of inefficiency, judicial economy is undoubtedly well-served by MDL consolidation when scores of similar cases are pending in the courts. The relevant comparison is not between a massive MDL and an "average case," but rather between a massive MDL and the alternative of thousands of similar cases clogging the courts with duplicative discovery and the potential for unnecessary conflict. Nevertheless, the excessive delay and "marginalization of juror fact finding" (*i.e.*, dearth of jury trials) sometimes associated with traditional MDL practice are developments that cannot be defended. The use of bellwether trials can temper both of these negative tendencies.

III. The Rise of Bellwether Trials

* * *

C. Benefits of the Modern Approach

In the MDL setting, bellwether trials can be effectively employed for nonbinding informational purposes and for testing various theories and defenses in a trial setting. Although the results of such "nonbinding" bellwether trials are obviously binding upon the parties to the specific cases that are tried, the results need not be binding on consolidated claimants in order to be beneficial to the MDL process. The Fifth Circuit has recognized the potential value of employing bellwether trials in this manner:

> * * * If a representative group of claimants are tried to verdict, the results of such trials can be beneficial for litigants who desire to settle such claims by providing information on the value of the cases as reflected by the jury verdicts.[72]

Another significant benefit of bellwether trials is that they provide a vehicle for putting litigation theories into practice. As most experienced litigators know, trials rarely proceed exactly as planned. In addition to the unexpected logistical problems that may arise, one can never be sure how certain arguments and evidence will "play" before a trier of fact. In multidistrict litigation, these uncertainties are often exacerbated by variations that exist among the circumstances of consolidated claimants and by the sheer volume of relevant material produced during discovery.

Bellwether trials thus assist in the maturation of any given dispute by providing an opportunity for coordinating counsel to organize the products of pretrial common discovery, evaluate the strengths and weaknesses of their arguments and evidence, and understand the risks and costs associated with the litigation. Indeed, the utilization of bellwether jury trials can enhance and accelerate the MDL process in two key respects. First, bellwether trials allow coordinating counsel to hone their presentation for subsequent trials and can lead to the development of "trial packages" for use by local counsel upon the dissolution of MDLs. Second, and perhaps more importantly, bellwether trials can precipitate and inform settlement negotiations by indicating future trends, that is, by providing guidance on how similar claims may fare before subsequent juries.

1. Trial Packages

The bellwether process can benefit all consolidated litigants in an MDL by providing the impetus for coordinating attorneys to assemble "trial packages." As noted above, bellwether trials force litigants to organize and streamline the massive wealth of material that is often produced during pretrial discovery in multidistrict litigation. Trial packages are a valuable by-product of this forced organization, and can be distributed to litigants and local counsel when an MDL is dissolved and individual cases are remanded to transferor courts for trial.

---

[72] *In re Chevron U.S.A., Inc.*, 109 F.3d 1016, 1019 (5th Cir. 1997) * * *.

Trial packages come in different shapes and sizes, but typically will include various databases of material such as the relevant documents acquired in discovery, other valuable background information, expert reports, deposition and trial testimony (both transcripts and video, if available), biographies of potential witnesses, transferee court rulings and transcripts, and the coordinating attorneys' work product and strategies with respect to all of this material. Ideally, these materials will be well-organized, indexed, and electronically searchable.

To the extent that trial lawyers can be analogized to actors in a play, it is helpful to think of coordinating counsel as playwrights in this aspect of the bellwether process. A bellwether trial forces these playwrights to draft their manuscripts in a relatively short period of time—that is, to develop fully the presentation of their clients' cases within the MDL. Multiple bellwether trials allow counsel to hone their presentations, making minor adjustments based on previous performances and the realities of litigation * * *.

Ultimately, the availability of a trial package ensures that the knowledge acquired by coordinating counsel is not lost if a global resolution cannot be achieved in the transferee court. Trial packages also ensure that the products of pretrial common discovery do not overwhelm local counsel in the event that cases are remanded for trial. In this way, the bellwether process guarantees that, at a minimum, the transferee court is effective at its intended goal of streamlining pretrial discovery and preparing cases for trial in their local districts. Indeed, the creation of a complete trial package is tangible evidence that the transferee court's statutory role in overseeing pretrial discovery is nearing an end and that the dissolution of the MDL is a real possibility. By ushering in these realities, the bellwether process can also precipitate global settlement negotiations.

2. Enhancing Global Settlements

* * * By virtue of the temporary national jurisdiction conferred upon it by the MDL Panel, the transferee court is uniquely situated to preside over global settlement negotiations. Indeed, the centralized forum created by the MDL Panel truly provides a "once-in-a-lifetime" opportunity for the resolution of mass disputes by bringing similarly situated litigants from around the country, and their lawyers, before one judge in one place at one time. Transferee courts can contribute to the fulfillment of this important role through the initiation and management of the bellwether trial process.

"[M]ass tort litigation frequently proceeds from an immature stage to a mature stage and, thereafter, to what one might call a peacemaking stage, where efforts focus on the crafting of a comprehensive settlement." When the MDL Panel first centralizes related cases in a transferee court, chances are that the litigation is still in its "immature" stage * * *.

Over time, as the litigation matures, both litigants and counsel begin to shift their focus to the potential for global resolution. By bringing fact-finding to the forefront of multidistrict litigation, bellwether trials can make a significant contribution to the maturation of disputes and, thus, can naturally precipitate settlement discussions.

In addition to this valuable contribution, bellwether trials also allow MDL litigants and their lawyers to gain an understanding of the litigation that is exponentially more grounded in reality than that which has traditionally persisted in the absence of jury trials. * * *

IV. The Selection Process

After the threshold determination to utilize bellwether trials, the transferee court and coordinating counsel should focus on the mechanics of the trial-selection process. If bellwether trials are to serve their twin goals as informative indicators of future trends and catalysts for an ultimate resolution, the transferee court and the attorneys must carefully construct the trial-selection process. Ideally, the trial-selection process should accurately reflect the individual categories of cases that comprise the MDL in toto, illustrate the likelihood of success and measure of damages within each respective category, and illuminate the forensic and practical challenges of presenting certain types of cases to a jury. Any trial-selection process that strays from this path will likely resolve only a few independent cases and have a limited global impact.

At the very outset, it must be noted that the sheer number and type of feasible trial-selection processes are limited only by the ingenuity of each transferee court and the coordinating attorneys. * * * [E]ach transferee court that chooses to conduct its own bellwether trials must consider all the unique factual and legal aspects specific to its litigation and then fashion an appropriate, custom-made trial-selection formula.

There are three separate but equally important sequential steps that will streamline any trial-selection process and allow that process to achieve its full potential, regardless of the type of MDL. The first step requires the transferee court and the attorneys to catalogue the entire universe of cases that comprise the MDL and then to divide the cases into several distinct, easily ascertainable categories of cases. The second step necessitates that the transferee court and the attorneys select a manageable pool of cases, which reflects the various categories and contains cases that are both amenable to trial in the MDL and close to being trial-ready. Once the pool has been constructed, all the cases comprising the pool should be set on a fast track for case-specific discovery. Third, near the conclusion of the case-specific discovery, the transferee court and the attorneys should select a predetermined number of individual cases within the sample and set these cases for trial. * * *

A. Cataloguing the Entire Universe of Cases

Before the transferee court and the attorneys can determine which cases to set for trial, they should first ascertain the makeup of the MDL. The rationale behind cataloguing and dividing the entire universe of cases within the MDL is simple. A bellwether trial is most effective when it can accurately inform future trends and effectuate an ultimate culmination to the litigation * * *.

To discharge this task effectively, the transferee court and the attorneys should each conduct a census of the entire litigation and identify all the major variables. * * *

In any given MDL, there will be innumerable variables differentiating each case from the others. Rather than attempt to delineate every identifiable variable, the transferee court and the attorneys should focus on those variables that can be easily identified, are substantively important, and provide clear lines of demarcation—*i.e.*, the major variables. By identifying the major variables, the transferee court and the attorneys can create sensible and easily ascertainable groupings by which to categorize the entire MDL, providing manageability and order to what may otherwise appear to be a massive, chaotic conglomeration of loosely analogous cases. * * *

After the transferee court and the attorneys have each separately evaluated the composition of the MDL and considered all the major variables, the transferee court should hold a status conference at which time it and the attorneys should discuss all of the relevant variables in an attempt to reach a consensus on which variables are the most predominant and important. By the conclusion of this status conference, the court should determine how the MDL will be divided and, more importantly, the attorneys should know why the groupings have been chosen.

* * *

B. Creating a Pool of Potential Bellwether Cases

After determining the composition of the MDL and creating groupings by which to divide the MDL, the transferee court and coordinating counsel should begin the process of creating a pool of cases that accurately represents the different divisions within the MDL from which the bellwether cases will be selected. This step requires the transferee court and the attorneys to (1) determine the size of the pool, (2) determine who will select the cases to fill the pool and how they will do so, and (3) fill the pool with cases that are both amenable to trial within the MDL and close to being trial-ready.

* * *

C. Case-Specific Discovery

Once the trial-selection pool has been assembled, each of the cases within the pool must undergo case-specific discovery. This discovery process will typically be no different from that which occurs in an ordinary case, and thus requires no additional explanation here.

D. Selecting Individual Cases from the Pool for Trial

Near the conclusion of case-specific discovery in the cases comprising the trial-selection pool, the transferee court and coordinating counsel can begin the final step of selecting the actual cases to serve as bellwether trials. In anticipation of the exercise of trial-selection picks, the transferee court, with the input of the attorneys, should have set forth the method by which the final selections will be made. As can be imagined, there are multiple methods, or any combination of methods, that can be used, such as (1) random selection, (2) selection by the transferee court, and (3) selection by the attorneys. * * *

* * *

V. Conclusion

*** [T]he injection of juries and fact-finding into multidistrict litigation through the use of bellwether trials can greatly assist in the maturation of disputes. ***

*** [But] there are some potential disadvantages associated with the practice. First, bellwether trials are often exponentially more expensive for the litigants and attorneys than a normal trial. *** Second, tactical opportunities can arise for trial counsel to become familiar with the rulings, expectations, customs, and practices of one transferee judge. Astute trial lawyers will learn the tendencies or preferences of any judge with repeated exposure, and given the realities of representation, such opportunities may be subject to exploitation. Finally, because bellwether trials are typically held in the transferee court's judicial district, the informational output is generally limited to the views of one local jury pool. *** But even recognizing these disadvantages, the use of bellwether trials proves on balance an effective tool in resolving complex multidistrict litigation.

NOTES AND QUESTIONS

1. Judge Fallon and his co-authors characterize the primary purposes of bellwether trials as providing non-binding information and testing theories and defenses in a trial setting. How do bellwether trials accomplish these ends? Do bellwether trials thereby enhance the utility of MDL proceedings? If so, how?

2. One of the benefits of bellwether trials is the creation of "trial packages," which provide individual attorneys with databases of material, background information, and expert reports that can be used if the cases get remanded. Given the relatively few cases get remanded, is this justification a legitimate basis for conducting bellwether trials?

3. What are the potential disadvantages of having bellwether trials? Which are the most concerning and why? Do these disadvantages suggest that courts should generally resist the idea of conducting bellwether trials?

D. POLICY AND REFORM ISSUES

1. OVERVIEW OF POLICY CONCERNS

ELIZABETH CHAMBLEE BURCH, JUDGING MULTIDISTRICT LITIGATION
90 N.Y.U. L. Rev. 71, 72–75, 78–81, 84–87, 101–12, 115, 118–19 (2015).

Introduction

Multidistrict litigation often involves billion-dollar lawsuits steeped in media attention ***. Yet, the transferee judges who use innovative procedures to usher these cases toward settlement are rarely subject to appellate scrutiny or legislative oversight. And while multidistrict litigation is ostensibly for pretrial purposes only, in practice, *** transferee judges have remanded a scant 2.9% of cases to their original districts.

Three practices in particular raise concerns about how judicial power affects adequate representation, doctrinal consistency, predictability, public perception, and plaintiffs' attorneys' incentives to shoulder expensive and time-consuming litigation. First, transferee judges create hierarchies of influence. To streamline cases and avoid having to communicate with hundreds of attorneys, judges appoint steering committees and other lead lawyers to conduct discovery, disseminate information, draft motions, negotiate settlements, and try bellwether cases. Yet, they rarely explain why they choose particular attorneys and may even handpick counsel with few or no involved clients. Although lead attorneys control the litigation and wrest decision-making power away from plaintiffs' individually retained counsel, judges focus on lead lawyers' financing abilities, cooperative tendencies, and expertise—not adequate representation. These criteria further entrench repeat players, who are often settlement artists and may be more concerned about pleasing judges, fostering reciprocity among fellow attorneys, and positioning themselves for future appointments than advancing plaintiffs' heterogeneous interests.

Second, judges compensate lead lawyers. When lead attorneys assume work that goes well beyond what they would do for their own clients, they should be paid accordingly. But judges lack a unified doctrinal basis for doing so. They have borrowed piecemeal from class actions' common-fund doctrine, contract principles, ethics, and equity while ignoring the corresponding constraints of each. This mishmash has resulted in unpredictable outcomes, disgruntled attorneys, and a reduced incentive for "non-elite" lawyers to shoulder expensive, time-consuming litigation. Those costs are further exacerbated in cases where judges have cut individually retained counsel's contingent fees even after deducting lead-lawyer fees.

Third, judges have presided over private settlements without a legal basis. They cite public-policy concerns or analogize multidistrict litigation to class actions, but most multidistrict cases are not certified as classes. Unlike class actions, in which Rule 23(e) demands a searching judicial inquiry into whether the settlement is fair, reasonable, and adequate, nonclass settlements are private contracts. Thus, by one view, unless the settlement itself authorizes the court to act, these judges overstepped their power and paternalistically meddled with plaintiffs' ability to contract with defendants. Others advocate extending the dubious "quasi-class action" moniker to allow judges to monitor nonclass settlements as they do class actions. But both views miss the mark. The first ignores attorneys' temptation to cross ethical boundaries to achieve finality and pretends that plaintiffs have conventional, one-on-one attorney-client relationships that allow them to monitor their own suits. This is plainly not the case when lawyers represent thousands of clients in the same litigation. Yet, the second view allows litigants and the judiciary to end-run Rule 23, strip away its due-process protections, and use it as a grab bag from which they can select helpful provisions while ignoring those that impede finality.

As class certification dwindles and courts rely increasingly on multidistrict litigation to resolve aggregate litigation, much work remains to be done on how we understand and theorize these practices. * * *

* * *

I. Multidistrict Litigation Minus Class Certification

* * *

A. Transferee Judges' Evolving Role

Transferee judges' experiences and preferences are increasingly constrained by changing procedural options, chiefly the gradual decline of class certification. Since the mid-1990s, Congress and the appellate courts have made it harder to certify a class by requiring plaintiffs to prove Rule 23's prerequisites by a preponderance of the evidence, instructing judges to delve into a case's merits when the merits overlap with class-certification requirements, and complicating choice-of-law questions and manageability by providing federal courts with jurisdiction. As researchers at the Federal Judicial Center found, the number of personal-injury and product-liability cases consolidated through multidistrict litigation has increased, while the number of class-certification motions has decreased, which "suggest[s] a declining rate of class certification." Yet, certification offered transferee judges a dizzying array of judicial powers to appoint class counsel, ensure a fair settlement, and award fees, all of which helped prevent counsel from exploiting absent class members.

Waning class certification contributed to two developments. First, it forced multidistrict litigation to become the primary means for resolving aggregate litigation. Yet, Congress never envisioned transferee judges concluding multidistrict cases; the plan was simply to streamline the discovery and pretrial process and then return cases to their home districts for trial. Thus, nothing in § 1407 confers any additional authority beyond what is available through the ordinary Federal Rules. This leads to the second development: Transferee judges have had to adapt to ambiguous authority despite lingering concerns over collusion, contingent fees, and attorney overreaching. So, as experienced transferee judges struggle to police the same self-interested behavior they witnessed in class-action practice, they find themselves without the tools that Rule 23 provided.

B. Judicial Misgivings over Attorney Conduct

Collusive circumstances in class actions initially forced judges into uncharted territory: No longer were they acting as neutral arbiters, but as inquisitors. When both parties become "friends" of the deal and ask the court to approve and enforce a settlement class, judges can no longer depend on the adversarial system. * * *

* * * [E]ven though class certification has decreased, experiments with ethically questionable means for achieving finality have not. Conflicts between attorneys and their clients and among the clients themselves continue to materialize. Plaintiffs' firms might have tacit agreements or fee-sharing arrangements with one another that further their collective self-interest and tether their financial interests to each other instead of to each client's outcome. Competing interests, attorney funding, and contingent fees can lead to quick or collusive settlements, underfunded litigation, exorbitant attorneys' fees, coercive settlement terms, and misallocated settlement proceeds. * * *

Repeat players influence on this trend * * *.

* * *

* * * [T]he Panel views quickly settling a complex case as a hallmark of success that disposes it to reward that judge with new litigation. Multidistrict litigations are plum judicial assignments; they involve interesting facts, media attention, and some of the nation's most talented attorneys. So, even though conflicting interests, misaligned incentives, and attorney overreaching crop up most prominently during settlement, judges have their own incentives to broker deals.

II. The Limits of Judicial Power and Inherent Authority

Despite facing a task of mythic proportions, transferee judges possess no more power than their mortal counterparts. Yet, the need for settlement, judicial misgivings about attorney misconduct and free riding, and the lack of Rule 23's explicit policing power persist—so judges innovate. * * *

Three practices, in particular, warrant scrutiny. First, in appointing attorneys to leadership positions, judges focus on experience, cooperative tendencies, and an ability to finance the litigation—factors that favor repeat players, as evidenced by their filling over 63% of all leadership positions. Emphasizing these traits can have detrimental effects like group decision-making biases and fear of dissenting. Second, when judges invoke a variety of legal doctrines, analogies, and their inherent judicial authority to compensate lead lawyers, their decisions can be unpredictable and difficult to challenge. Finally, judges who publicly approve or disapprove private settlements have not identified explicit authority that allows private parties to predict when judicial interference will occur or the boundaries for such conduct.

Despite attorney dissatisfaction with these decisions, several factors inoculate them from thorough appellate review. First, because most multidistrict litigations result in private settlements, they are not reviewable on appeal, even when subject to public judicial commentary. Second, because most interim rulings are not dispositive orders, they are reviewable only through an extraordinary writ of mandamus or subsequent dismissal. Motions to disqualify a lead attorney, for example, are not immediately appealable as a matter of right even though an attorney could theoretically petition for mandamus. Third, even if the appellate court grants mandamus or reviews a dismissed case, it tends to do so using the highly deferential abuse-of-discretion standard. Vague initial standards, subjective decisions about which attorney would best serve the plaintiffs, and the lack of precedent make this standard a formidable hurdle. Fourth, practical incentives counsel against objecting, at least with regard to lead-lawyer selections. An objecting attorney faces the risk that her peers will dub her non-cooperative and thus "ineligible" for future leadership roles. Plus, early objections could alienate dissenters from both the chosen leaders and the transferee judge, making them less effective advocates. Consequently, if change is to be had, transferee judges must initiate it.

A. Appointing Lead Lawyers

Current judicial practice in selecting attorney leadership, where courts stress expertise, cooperative abilities, and financial means, can raise several concerns. First, valuing cooperation may encourage attorneys to be more concerned with impressing judges or their peers than vigorously representing clients whose interests differ from the majority's. Second, cooperation fosters a need for attorneys to curry favor with one another, which, when combined with the prevalence of repeat players, can infect leadership committees with well-documented group decision-making biases, like conformity. Third, appointing only repeat players may create groups of homogeneous thinkers who are less innovative. * * *

* * *

B. Awarding and Cutting Attorneys' Fees

As the push to become a lead lawyer suggests, attorneys' fees in multidistrict litigation are big business. * * * While defense fees are typically paid through billable hours, plaintiffs' attorneys often have their clients sign contingent-fee contracts, which entitle counsel to some percentage of her client's settlement or judgment—typically in the neighborhood of 33%. When collected from thousands of clients, attorneys' fees can be staggering—one of the many reasons that judges feel compelled to intervene. Compared to class-action awards, which average around 20%, these fees may seem excessive. Consequently, judges have grappled with two critical questions: (1) how to compensate lead attorneys using a coherent rationale, and (2) how lead lawyers' compensation should affect the fees of non-lead attorneys who no longer have to bear the lion's share of the work or the financing risk.

1. Compensating Common-Benefit Work

To justify awarding fees to lead lawyers, judges have borrowed ad hoc from class-action law's common-fund doctrine, contract principles, ethics, and equity. * * * [T]hese theories appear to create a seamless facade. Yet, this doctrinal patchwork lacks predictable limits, prompts unexpected awards, and can undermine attorneys' incentives to shoulder complex, time-consuming cases.

First, even though judges often deny class certification, they nevertheless tend to invoke the class action's common-fund doctrine to compensate lead lawyers. The common-fund doctrine rests on restitution principles: A self-appointed, non-contractually-retained attorney litigates on behalf of absent class members and benefits them when she settles (the "common fund"). If the settlement compensated class members without paying counsel, it would unjustly enrich them at counsel's expense. Yet, this doctrine assumes that claimants implicitly consent to fee awards and count as passive beneficiaries, which is not the case in multidistrict litigation where active plaintiffs retain their own attorneys and have no ability to exit the multidistrict litigation. * * *

Still, the common-fund doctrine's underlying rationale is attractive: When lead lawyers perform the work for individually retained attorneys, they benefit them. Failing to pay lead lawyers could thus unjustly enrich non-lead attorneys, particularly free riders who simply wait for lead lawyers to negotiate a proposed settlement. Moreover, a non-lead attorney's retainer agreement assumes that she will complete the work and thus pays her a contingent fee. But she's no longer doing most of the work. Of course, this isn't due to neglect on her part; it's the result of a changed procedural environment. The question is whether that change creates compensable fees on a restitutionary basis, or noncompensable spillover effects.

Thus enters the second but related doctrine: contract law. The *Restatement (Second) of Contracts* suggests that a contract such as a retainer agreement can be discharged if "a party's principal purpose is substantially frustrated without his fault by the occurrence of an event the non-occurrence of which was a basic assumption on which the contract was made." Like the common fund, this doctrine's initial attractiveness is apparent, but ultimately translates poorly into multidistrict litigation. First, the client's principal purpose in hiring her attorney is for the attorney to satisfactorily resolve her case. Yet, appointing lead lawyers frustrates the retainer agreement's purpose by putting the client's case into the lead lawyers' hands. Second, the client, having little legal knowledge, may not contemplate the possibility that someone other than her attorney would litigate her case without her consent. So, "without the default of either party, [the] contractual obligation becomes incapable of performance because the circumstances . . . render it a thing radically different from the undertaking contemplated by the contract." But the remedy is to discharge the contractual duty to pay. And transferee judges do not discharge contingent fees; they essentially reform the contract and institute the bargain they think the parties would have reached. While judges can reform agreements if they fail to reflect the parties' true agreement, or if there has been a mutual or unilateral mistake, multidistrict litigation fits neither category.

Finally, transferee judges have cited their "inherent managerial authority" or "inherent equitable authority" as authorizing them to compensate lead attorneys. * * * This power, they claim, somehow derives from Federal Rule of Civil Procedure 42, which allows courts to consolidate actions and "issue any other orders to avoid unnecessary cost or delay." But * * * inherent authority appears to have no limits: It is guided by neither consent nor contract principles and swells to fill whatever role it must, sacrificing transparency, predictability, and restraint in its wake.

Adding to this doctrinal patchwork, judges invoke these rationales at different litigation stages and depend on various means for implementing them. They have asked special masters and committees of attorneys to recommend fees, but the recent trend has been to require attorneys to sign fee-transfer agreements at the beginning of litigation. Fee-transfer agreements (and most allocation systems) depend on the court creating a fund, which taxes plaintiffs' gross monetary recovery—usually between 2% and 6%—and places the money in an interest-bearing account to be divvied up among the lead lawyers. Like the nebulous rationales supporting them, the percentages are arbitrary. Most judges do not explain their chosen percentages, and when they do, they cite the piecemeal theories just mentioned, previous multidistrict litigation assessments, or proposals from the steering committee—none of which have a dependable theoretical mooring.

In theory, fee-transfer agreements and fee provisions in settlements buttress tenuous doctrinal rationales by lending a veneer of coherence and consent to an unruly legal minefield. Fee-transfer agreements often contain recitals that mimic consideration, such as "Participating Attorneys are desirous of acquiring the PSC Work Product and establishing an amicable, working relationship with the PSC for the mutual benefit of their clients," so they intend "to be legally bound hereby" and "agree" to certain assessments. Similarly, when lead lawyers embed fee provisions within settlements, they impart a consensual pretense even though the "settlement" may actually be a contract between plaintiffs' attorneys and the defendant that requires attorneys to recommend the deal to their clients or withdraw from representing them. Consenting attorneys receive their contingent fee, minus lead lawyers' fees, only after enough clients agree. Instead of chastising attorneys for self-dealing or holding them in contempt of court for undermining previous common-fund orders, judges appear to embrace these "consensual" settlement measures by increasing lead lawyers' fees in accordance with the settlement.

Of course, as in many contracts of adhesion, there is little genuine consent involved in accepting either fee-transfer agreements or settlements with embedded fees. Fee-transfer agreements are standardized forms, presented by those with superior bargaining power (the court and the steering committee) to attorneys with pending cases in the multidistrict litigation who effectively have no choice but to accept them. Attorneys cannot conduct discovery on their own, so they have few options but to use the common work product unless they remain solely in state courts.

* * *

Similarly, there is little true consent when lead lawyers negotiate settlement offers that require plaintiffs' law firms to tender their entire client inventory or continue litigating in front of a judge who promoted and then publicly blessed the deal. Were those circumstances not cause enough for concern, some judges have even allowed lead lawyers to increase the fees set forth in initial fee-transfer agreements by upping the percentage through a later settlement.

* * *

2. Capping Contingent Fees

Capping private contingent-fee contracts is perhaps the most controversial emerging judicial practice in multidistrict litigation. * * * [S]ome judges have taken fee awards into their own hands without sound justification. Specifically, some judges have awarded lead lawyers a percentage of the total settlement amount, capped non-lead attorneys' contingent fees, and based those capped percentages on the already reduced settlement amount. So, depending on the calculation method, a non-lead attorney initially entitled to 33% of a $1 million award, who must allocate 8% of that total award to lead lawyers * * * and whose fee is then capped at 20% of the remaining settlement * * *, might receive $184,000 as opposed to $330,000—a significant reduction.

* * *

* * * Reducing contingent fees should be the exception, not the rule. If such a cap is warranted, then it should be justified on an individual basis.

C. Approving Aggregate Settlements

Given their concern over attorneys' fees and analogies to class actions, judges' interest in ostensibly private settlements is not surprising. After all, settlement and fees go hand in hand, with some lead lawyers negotiating their fee and the settlement in one fell swoop. Plus, the controversy over what many commentators view as meddling in fee awards extends to settlement review, in part because judges cite similar authority for both. Unlike class actions, in which Rule 23(e) requires judges to thoroughly assess whether the settlement is fair, reasonable, and adequate, nonclass settlements * * * are private agreements that parties presumably enter voluntarily. Thus, the existence of a legal basis for policing a "voluntary" settlement between private parties is uncertain at best.

* * *

III. Rethinking Best Practices in Multidistrict Litigation

As evidenced thus far, multidistrict litigation places transferee judges in uncharted territory, yet burdens them with enormous responsibility. * * * Accordingly, this Part suggests some substantive and procedural improvements for the three principal areas [previously] critiqued: appointing lead lawyers, awarding those lawyers fees, and reviewing nonclass settlements.

First, because dissent promotes adequate representation, thwarts detrimental group decision-making biases, and encourages innovation, judges should embrace avenues for changing the current norms that silence objectors and pressure attorneys toward cooperation and consensus. This can be achieved by designating lead lawyers to represent plaintiffs' various interests, inviting objections, and conducting evidentiary hearings before choosing leaders. Second, compensating lead counsel on a quantum-meruit basis could clarify the muddled doctrinal lineage that judges have previously cited and would reflect the true nature of appointing lead lawyers, which is more akin to a forced client referral than a common fund. Finally, if judges embrace the quantum-meruit proposal, it would give them a legitimate basis to assess how much lead lawyers benefitted the plaintiffs through the results they achieved. Although this settlement review would be limited as compared with judicial review under Rule 23(e), conducting that review in the context of awarding fees supplies a powerful incentive against collusion.

* * *

NOTES AND QUESTIONS

1. How has the difficulty in obtaining class certification in certain types of cases (especially mass torts) led to MDL becoming the primary means of resolving aggregate litigation? What sorts of procedural safeguards are lost by not utilizing the class action device? What is gained, if anything, when Rule 23 is not applied? How does Rule 23 safeguard against the occurrence of potentially collusive settlements?

2. Professor Burch notes three practices that, in her view, are concerning. What are those three practices, and what concerns are raised by each of them?

3. What solutions does Professor Burch propose to address her concerns? What are the benefits of each solution? What are the potential downsides?

Should the solutions she proposes be embodied in a statute? Or should judges simply utilize them as a matter of discretion?

4. What advantages does an MDL judge obtain by selecting repeat players? Is there an explanation for the practice that is not nefarious?

5. Numerous states have MDL statutes analogous to 28 U.S.C. § 1407. *See generally* Mark Herrmann, Geoffrey J. Ritts & Katherine Larson, *Statewide Coordinated Proceedings*: *State Court Analogues to the Federal MDL Process* (Thomson/West 2d ed. 2004); Yvette Ostolaza & Michelle Hartmann, *The Judicial Panel on Multidistrict Litigation and Coordinating Multijurisdictional Disputes*, 16 Prac. Litigator 23, 30–32 (2005). These state analogues provide a means for consolidating related cases within a single state. As discussed in Part (B)(4) of this chapter, there is no formal mechanism for aggregating related cases pending in multiple state courts.

2. BEST PRACTICES

The Standards and Best Practices ("MDL Standards") excerpted below were drafted by the Duke Law Center for Judicial Studies. The MDL Standards were drafted by 22 defense and plaintiffs' attorneys with significant MDL experience. Numerous federal and state judges also provided input. Jaime Dodge of the University of Georgia School of Law served as editor-in-chief.

STANDARDS AND BEST PRACTICES FOR LARGE AND MASS-TORT MDLS

Duke Law Center for Judicial Studies (2014) http://law.duke.edu/sites/default/files/centers/judicialstudies/MDL_Standards_and_Best_Practices_2014-REVISED.pdf

MDL STANDARD 1: The transferee court, in consultation with the parties, should articulate clear objectives for the MDL proceeding and a plan for pursuing them. The objectives of an MDL proceeding should usually include: (1) the elimination of duplicative discovery; (2) avoiding conflicting rulings and schedules among courts; (3) reducing litigation costs; (4) saving the time and effort of the parties, attorneys, witnesses, and courts; (5) streamlining key issues; and (6) moving cases toward resolution (by trial, motion practice, or settlement).

* * *

MDL STANDARD 2: In an MDL action with many parties with separate counsel, the transferee judge should establish a leadership structure for the plaintiffs, and sometimes for the defendants, to promote the effective management of the litigation.

* * *

MDL STANDARD 3: The transferee judge should select lead counsel, liaison counsel, and committee members as soon as practicable after the JPML transfers the litigation.

* * *

MDL STANDARD 4: As a general rule, the transferee judge should ensure that the lawyers appointed to the leadership team are effective managers in addition to being conscientious advocates.

* * *

MDL STANDARD 5: The transferee judge should consider setting aside a portion of the anticipated monetary proceeds from a settlement to establish a common benefit fund (CBF) for the purpose of paying reasonable attorneys' fees, costs, and expenses from that fund.

* * *

MDL STANDARD 6: Effective coordination between the federal and state courts in an MDL action promotes cooperation in scheduling hearings, conducting and completing discovery, facilitates efficient distribution of and access to discovery work product, avoids inconsistent federal and state rulings on discovery and privilege issues, if possible, and fosters communication and cooperation among litigants and courts that may facilitate just and inexpensive determination.

* * *

MDL STANDARD 7: The transferee judge should endeavor to use the MDL forum to resolve or streamline the litigation before remand to the district courts.

* * *

NOTES AND QUESTIONS

1. Explain the rationale for each of the seven MDL Standards identified by the Duke Law Center. Of the seven standards, which are the most important and why?

2. Should any of the MDL Standards be embodied as amendments to the MDL statute? If so, which one(s)? Or are the standards best used merely at the discretion of the particular MDL Judge?

3. To what extent do the MDL standards address various concerns discussed in prior sections of this chapter?

E. MDL CASE STUDY: THE *VW CLEAN DIESEL* LITIGATION

One MDL case that has achieved wide publicity among the general public is the *Volkswagen Clean Diesel* litigation. This litigation started with hundreds of lawsuits against Volkswagen throughout the United States for the fraudulent sale and marketing of more than 500,000 diesel vehicles (years 2009–2015). VW (as well as Porsche and Audi) allegedly installed defeat devices in those vehicles, which enabled the vehicles to pass emissions tests, even though the vehicles were polluting at up to 40 times the legal limit. The cases were transferred by the MDL Panel to Judge Charles Breyer in the Northern District of California. Ultimately, the parties reached classwide settlements that were approved by Judge Breyer. Numerous orders were issued during the course of the MDL, first by the MDL panel (consolidating the cases for pretrial purposes before Judge Breyer), and then by Judge Breyer as MDL judge. The following is a list of the key orders from the docket, the issues that they address, and where to find them online.

Selection of the Transferee Court. In the *VW* case, the MDL Panel determined that consolidation for pre-trial purposes was appropriate and selected Judge Breyer as the MDL judge. *In re Volkswagen "Clean Diesel" Mktg., Sales Practices, and Prods. Liab. Litig.*, 148 F. Supp. 3d 1367 (J.P.M.L. 2015).

Appointment of Lead Counsel and Steering Committees. A major task for the MDL judge is the appointment of lead counsel and members of the plaintiffs' steering committee ("PSC"). Those attorneys have primary responsibility for representing plaintiffs' interests in the MDL. In the *VW* case, the court selected Elizabeth J. Cabraser as lead counsel, and the court appointed 21 lawyers from firms across the country to serve on the PSC. *See Pretrial Order No. 2: Applications for Appointment of Plaintiffs' Lead Counsel and Steering Committee Members, In re Volkswagen "Clean Diesel" MDL*, No. 15-MD-2672-CRB (JSC) (N.D. Cal. Dec. 22, 2015), Docket No. 336, *available at* http://www.cand.uscourts.gov/crb/nwmdl; *Pretrial Order No. 7: Order Appointing Plaintiffs' Lead Counsel, Plaintiffs' Steering Committee, and Government Coordinating Counsel, In re Volkswagen "Clean Diesel" MDL*, No. 15-MD-2672-CRB (JSC) (N.D. Cal. Jan. 21, 2016), Docket No. 1084, *available at* http://www.cand.uscourts.gov/crb/vwmdl.

Common Benefit Work. In MDL proceedings, payment for the plaintiffs' lead counsel and steering committee comes out of a "common benefit fund." Judge Breyer issued an order establishing a protocol for common benefit work and expenses. *See Pretrial Order No. 11: Protocol for Common Benefit Work and Expenses, In re Volkswagen "Clean Diesel" MDL*, No. 15-MD-2672-CRB (JSC) (N.D. Cal. Feb. 25, 2016), Docket No. 1254, *available at* http://www.cand.uscourts.gov/crb/vwmdl.

Initial Case Management. Initial case management orders provide the groundwork for various stages of an MDL. Judge Breyer issued an initial case management order in the *VW* case. *See Pretrial Order No. 8: Initial Case Management, In re Volkswagen "Clean Diesel" MDL*, No. 15-MD-2672-CRB (JSC) (N.D. Cal. Jan. 22, 2016), Docket No. 1087, *available at* http://www.cand.uscourts.gov/crb/vwmdl.

Discovery Orders. Discovery orders set out the protocol for both plaintiffs' and defense counsel, such as the requirement that defense counsel serve all discovery requests on plaintiffs' lead counsel. For the *VW* discovery order, *see Pretrial Order No. 9: Discovery Schedule, In re Volkswagen "Clean Diesel" MDL*, No. 15-MD-2672-CRB (JSC) (N.D. Cal. Feb. 25, 2016), Docket No. 1252, *available at* http://www.cand.uscourts.gov/crb/vwmdl.

Preservation of Documents. It is frequently necessary to ensure that key documents, particularly electronically stored information ("ESI"), are preserved. For the *VW* preservation order, *see Pretrial Order No. 15: Order Regarding the Preservation of Documents and Electronically stored Information, In re Volkswagen "Clean Diesel" MDL*, No. 15-MD-2672-CRB (JSC) (N.D. Cal. Mar. 24, 2016), Docket No. 1379, *available at* http://www.cand.uscourts.gov/crb/vwmdl.

Appointment of Special Settlement Master. In some MDL proceedings, the judge may decide to appoint a "Special Settlement Master" to facilitate settlement discussions. In the *VW* MDL, Judge Breyer appointed

Robert Muller, former director of the FBI, as settlement counsel. *See Pretrial Order No. 6: Order Appointing Robert S. Mueller III as Settlement Master, In re Volkswagen "Clean Diesel" MDL*, No. 15-MD-2672-CRB (JSC) (N.D. Cal. Jan. 19, 2016), Docket No. 973, *available at* http://www.cand.uscourts.gov/crb/nwmdl.

Granting Approval of the Settlement. Settling an MDL is often a lengthy, multi-step process. In the *VW* litigation, a proposed settlement was preliminarily approved in July of 2016. It applied to the 2.0-liter class of plaintiffs (*i.e.*, those plaintiffs who purchased 2.0 liter vehicles from VW). *See Amended Order Granting Preliminary Approval of Settlement, In re Volkswagen "Clean Diesel" MDL*, No. 15-MD-2672-CRB (JSC) (N.D. Cal. July 29, 2016), Docket No. 1698, *available at* http://www.cand.uscourts.gov/crb/vwmdl; *see also* Alan Katz & John Lippert, *Volkswagen to Face $15 Billion Tab in U.S. Settlement*, BLOOMBERG (June 28, 2016), www.bloomberg.com/news/articles/2016-06-27/volkswagen-said-to-face-15-billion-tab-in-u-s-settlement. In October 2016, after full briefing, consideration of objections, and a fairness hearing, Judge Breyer entered an order granting final approval of the settlement. *See Order Granting Final Approval of the 2.0-Liter TDI Consumer and Reseller Dealership Class Action Settlement, In re Volkswagen "Clean Diesel" MDL*, No. 15-MD-2672-CRB (JSC) (N.D. Cal. Oct. 25, 2016), Docket No. 2102, *available at* http://www.cand.uscourts.gov/crb/vwmdl. A separate settlement for 3.0-liter vehicles was preliminarily approved in January 2017, but at the time this text went to press, the final approval hearing had not yet occurred.

PROBLEM

Attorney Teresa Rodriguez has filed nine suits in six different federal courts (mostly in the western states) alleging that cellular phones manufactured by GMAX cause brain cancer. Currently, 250 other suits have been filed, mainly in Florida and New York. Of those, 200 are in federal courts and 50 are in state courts. Rodriguez has learned that a prominent Texas lawyer plans to file a nationwide class action suit against GMAX in federal court in Texas within the next 30 days, raising similar claims. That same lawyer also plans to file 200 individual suits in Mississippi, Alabama, and Arkansas, probably within 60 days.

Five of Rodriguez's suits are in front of judges whom she views as very pro-plaintiff. Two other judges each have two of Rodriguez's cases. These latter judges are, in Rodriguez's view, pro-defense and very reluctant to allow claims such as hers in the absence of compelling scientific evidence of a cause-and-effect relationship. Should Rodriguez seek to have all of her federal cases transferred to a single judge under 28 U.S.C. § 1407? Should she file a transfer motion now or wait until the Texas class action is filed? Which judge and location should she request?

F. COORDINATION OF FEDERAL AND STATE CLAIMS

MDL treatment under 28 U.S.C. § 1407 is available only to coordinate *federal* cases, not to coordinate federal and *state* cases. Additional creativity is therefore necessary when related cases exist in both federal and state courts.

1. INFORMAL COORDINATION

MANUAL FOR COMPLEX LITIGATION (FOURTH)
Federal Judicial Center (2004) § 20.31–20.313.

Increasingly, complex litigation involves related cases brought in both federal and state courts. Such litigation often involves mass torts. Some sets of cases may involve numerous claims arising from a single event, confined to a single locale (such as a plane crash or a hotel fire). Other more-complicated litigations may arise from widespread exposure to harmful products or substances dispersed over time and place.

No single forum has jurisdiction over these groups of cases. Unless the defendant files for bankruptcy, no legal basis exists for exercising exclusive federal control over state litigation. Interdistrict, intradistrict, and multidistrict transfer statutes and rules apply only to cases filed in, or removable to, federal court.

State and federal judges, faced with the lack of a comprehensive statutory scheme, have undertaken innovative efforts to coordinate parallel or related litigation so as to reduce the costs, delays, and duplication of effort that often stem from such dispersed litigation. State judges, for example, can bring additional resources that might enable an MDL transferee court to implement a nationwide discovery plan or a coordinated national calendar. * * *

State and federal judges also have initiated state-federal cooperation between jurisdictions to minimize conflicts that distract from the primary goal of resolving the parties' disputes.

Identifying the Need and Opportunity

Coordination approaches differ depending on the nature of the litigation. Coordination is relatively easy if all of the cases are pending in a single state. States increasingly have adopted procedures for assigning complex multiparty litigation to a single judge or judicial panel or have created courts to deal with complex business cases, facilitating coordination between state and federal courts. Federal judges should learn about their own state or local courts' practices and procedures for consolidating cases.

The Judicial Panel on Multidistrict Litigation has no power over cases pending in state courts, but has facilitated coordination by transferring federal cases to a district where related cases are pending in the state courts.

Coordination is easier when counsel for some or all of the parties in the related actions have the same counsel. In appointing lead or liaison counsel or otherwise organizing counsel, consider including attorneys from jurisdictions with cases that may need to be coordinated with either class action or multidistrict litigation.

The need to coordinate is especially acute where overlapping or multiple identical class actions are filed in more than one court. It is best to communicate with state and federal judicial counterparts at an early stage to begin coordinating such cases. Unilateral action by any judge to certify a class or assert nationwide jurisdiction can fatally undermine future coordination efforts.

Coordination becomes much more complex when cases are dispersed across a number of states, even where the federal cases are all centered in a single MDL transferee court. Electronic media—*e.g.*, Internet Web sites and list-servs—can improve communication in such circumstances.

Reciprocity and cooperation create trust and mutual respect so that attempts to coordinate are not perceived as attempts to dominate. The special master who facilitated state-federal coordination in the silicone gel breast implant litigation observed that the more transparent, formal, evenhanded, and administrative the proposed cooperative venture is, the more acceptable it will be to other judges.

Threshold Steps

The nature and extent of multiple filings related to the same subject matter in different courts should be clarified, so as to minimize conflicts. The court should direct counsel to identify the names of all similar cases in other courts, their state of pretrial preparation, and the assigned judges. Such a direction should be part of the initial case-management order in any case with related litigation pending in other courts, and many courts have local rules requiring disclosure of similar information.

Dispersed litigation makes essential an information network, perhaps formalized as a judicial advisory committee, which can serve as a catalyst for some degree of state-federal coordination. If the litigation warrants it, a meeting of a judicial advisory committee can help to develop relationships among the judges and ease coordination efforts. An Internet list-serv is another economical way to foster communications among geographically dispersed attorneys and judges. In some mass torts litigation, the National Conference of State Chief Justices, the National Center for State Courts, and the State Justice Institute have helped create and fund coordinating committees of state court judges with significant mass tort assignments. Federal judges with mass tort responsibilities have sometimes participated in person or by presenting written or telephonic reports and updates of federal activities. Such committees help identify specific types of coordination that can be recommended to other state and federal judges assigned to the same type of litigation. It may also be helpful to organize attorneys from states with significant numbers of cases into an advisory committee, to be a channel of communication between the judges and other attorneys.

Federal judges should communicate personally with state court judges who have a significant number of cases in order to discuss mutual concerns and suggestions, such as designating a liaison attorney and judge to communicate with federal counterparts. These communications provide an opportunity to exchange pretrial orders and proposed schedules that help avoid potential conflicts. One special master has concluded that "[t]he earlier and more comprehensive the cooperative intervention occurs in the litigation cycle, the greater the benefits and the less the resistance."

* * *

* * * Lawyers should be encouraged to resolve fee disputes among themselves and to seek judicial intervention only if necessary. It may be helpful to appoint a special master to coordinate proceedings among the state and federal courts, reducing to manageable proportions the challenge of communicating and coordinating with dozens of judges.

In the silicone gel breast implant and diet drug litigations, state and federal judges created working relationships that came close to achieving a comprehensive approach to state-federal cooperation. Extending that approach to other mass torts "could build upon generally accepted models for resolving local mass torts, such as the use of test plaintiffs for discovery, with settlement discussions based upon the results of the test cases." In the diet drug and silicone gel breast implant litigations, the federal MDL transferee judge took the lead in implementing a comprehensive state-federal discovery plan while state judges presided over individual trials and settlements. The parties achieved the economies of consolidated discovery and developed information about the value of individual cases, providing a basis for aggregated settlements and judgments.

Specific Forms of Coordination

Aggregation and consolidation decisions. Discussions between state and federal judges about the timing of class certification hearings and decisions have a beneficial effect on other aspects of cooperation. The prospect that one judge might unilaterally certify a nationwide class and enter a binding national judgment has a chilling effect on cooperative relationships. Joint deferral of decisions on certification and perhaps joint hearings on motions to certify a class enhance the chances that both sets of courts will find appropriate roles in managing the litigation. Judges might agree that the court with most of the cases or the strongest interest should take the lead in certain proceedings, such as class certification.

The court should also consider staying cases until actions in the other tribunal have been tried. * * *

Pretrial motions and hearings. State and federal judges have often worked together during the pretrial process. They have jointly presided over hearings on pretrial motions, based on a joint motions schedule, sometimes alternating between state and federal courthouses. Joint hearings have used coordinated briefs so that one set of briefs can be used in both state and federal courts, with supplements for variations in the applicable laws and choice-of-law questions.

Cooperative approaches might also include jointly appointing a special master, court-appointed expert, or other adjunct to assist the courts with some aspect of the litigation. * * *

At a minimum, judges should exchange case-management orders, master pleadings, questionnaires, and discovery protocols. This simple step can encourage judges to adopt the same or similar approaches to discovery and pretrial management.

Also, consider joint appointments of lead counsel, committees of counsel, or liaison counsel to coordinate activities between the courts. * * *

Pretrial discovery. State and federal judges have considerable experience coordinating and managing nationwide discovery. * * *

Coordination could involve inviting state judges to participate in a coordinated national discovery program while retaining control of local discovery. Depending on the progress of the state litigation, some aspects of discovery in state cases may in some instances serve as the basis for national discovery. For example, in the silicone gel breast implant litigation, state judges in Texas had progressed further in discovery than had federal courts at the time the MDL cases were assigned to Judge Pointer. Recognizing the state court's advantage, Judge Pointer "agreed to designate certain Texas depositions as official ones for the entire multidistrict litigation (MDL)." Procedures to minimize duplicative discovery activity include consolidating depositions of experts who will testify in numerous cases and maintaining document depositories. It is important to remember that the rulings of a single court can become preemptive; for example, the first court to reject a particular privilege claim likely will cause the material sought to be protected to become discoverable for the entire litigation.

Specific elements of discovery coordination have included

• creating joint federal-state, plaintiff-defendant document depositories, accessible to attorneys in all states;

• ordering coordinated document production and arrangements for electronic discovery;

• ordering discovery materials from prior state and federal cases to be included in the document depository;

• scheduling and cross-noticing joint federal-state depositions;

• designating state-conducted depositions as official MDL depositions;

• enjoining attorneys conduction federal discovery from objecting to use of that discovery in state courts on the grounds that it originated in federal court;

• adopting standard interrogatories developed by state judges for litigation in their cases; and

• coordinating rulings on discovery disputes, such as the assertion of privilege, and using parallel orders to promote uniformity to the extent possible.

Settlement. State and federal judges should consider conducting joint comprehensive settlement negotiations, hearings, and alternative dispute resolution procedures to establish case values. Insurance coverage disputes may require special attention and coordination because resolution of the primary litigation may depend on resolution of the coverage dispute.

Trial. State and federal judges have developed coordinated management plans for an entire litigation. Joint trials, where separate state and federal juries sit in the same courtroom and hear common evidence, present substantial procedural and practical difficulties, but differences in state and federal procedures have not been insurmountable barriers to useful coordination. Any coordination must be flexible because cases in some state courts will reach trial sooner than those in others. State and federal courts should establish a mechanism to coordinate trial dates so that they do not unduly burden parties or their attorneys with multiple conflicting trial settings. Judges may also set the order and location of trials cooperatively to provide better information as to the diverse range of value of the cases included in the mass tort.

NOTES AND QUESTIONS

1. Does the excerpt from the *Manual* suggest that informal coordination has adequately addressed inefficiencies and other problems arising from related cases in federal and state court? What shortcomings stem from an entirely voluntary approach?

2. What are the disadvantages of federal/state coordination? For a useful discussion of the pros and cons of cooperation among judges (including federal/state cooperation), *see* Francis E. McGovern, *Rethinking Cooperation Among Judges in Mass Tort Litigation*, 44 UCLA L. Rev. 1851 (1997).

3. One commentator has noted that there has been a substantial increase in informal coordination by plaintiffs' lawyers and a similar increase in informal coordination by defense lawyers. *See* Howard M. Erichson, *Informal Aggregation: Procedural and Ethical Implications of Coordination Among Counsel in Related Lawsuits*, 50 Duke L.J. 381 (2000). The author attributes this trend to "the failure of formal aggregation mechanisms to achieve a unified handling of controversies involving large numbers of claimants." *Id.* at 408. He notes that "the existence of parallel federal and state court systems [offers] little opportunity for formal intersystem coordination * * *." *Id.* The author explores a variety of ethical issues raised by informal aggregation, including confidentiality, loyalty, and conflicts of interest, and urges the adoption of more formalized aggregation mechanisms to address those ethical concerns.

4. A number of proposals have been offered for formalizing coordination of related federal and state cases. The following subsection addresses two of the most prominent proposals.

2. PROPOSED FORMAL FEDERAL-STATE COORDINATION

Some commentators believe that a more formal approach would vastly improve the coordination of federal and state cases. The following two excerpts provide possible approaches.

COMPLEX LITIGATION: STATUTORY RECOMMENDATIONS AND ANALYSIS
American Law Institute, 1994.

§ 3.01. Standard for Consolidation

(a) Actions commenced in two or more United States District Courts may be transferred and consolidated if

(1) they involve one or more common questions of fact, and

(2) transfer and consolidation will promote the just, efficient, and fair conduct of the actions.

(b) Factors to be considered in deciding whether the standard set forth in subsection (a) is met include

(1) the extent to which transfer and consolidation will reduce duplicative litigation, the relative costs of individual and consolidated litigation, the likelihood of inconsistent adjudications, and the comparative burdens on the judiciary, and

(2) whether transfer and consolidation can be accomplished in a way that is fair to the parties and does not result in undue inconvenience to them and the witnesses. In considering those factors, account may be taken of matters such as [the number of parties and actions involved, geographic dispersion, local concerns, subject matter, amount in controversy, common issues and applicable law, likelihood of related actions being filed, parties' preferences, and status pending actions.]

* * *

§ 3.02. The Complex Litigation Panel

A special Complex Litigation Panel of federal judges shall be established and have responsibility for deciding whether separate actions should be transferred for consolidation under the criteria set forth in § 3.01 and, if so, determining to what district court they should be transferred for consolidation in accordance with the standard set forth in § 3.04. * * *

§ 3.04. Standard For Determining Whether To Transfer Consolidated Actions

(a) Cases may be transferred to and consolidated in any district court in which the just and efficient resolution of the actions will be promoted and fairness to the individual litigants can be facilitated.

(b) When the just, efficient, and fair resolution of the actions will be promoted, the Complex Litigation Panel may designate more than one transferee court. The Panel should give great weight to the convenience to the litigants in assigning individual actions among multiple transferee courts.

* * *

§ 3.06. Powers of the Transferee Court

(a) Unless the Complex Litigation Panel otherwise provides, transfer and consolidation shall be for all purposes, and the transferee judge shall have the full power to manage and organize the consolidated proceeding so as to promote its just, efficient, and fair resolution. * * *

* * *

§ 5.01 Removal Jurisdiction

(a) Except as otherwise provided by Act of Congress, the Complex Litigation Panel may order the removal to federal court and consolidation of one or more civil actions pending in one or more state courts, if the removed actions arise from the same transaction, occurrence, or series of transactions or occurrences as an action pending in the federal court, and share a common question of fact with that action. The Complex Litigation Panel shall evaluate whether to order removal and consolidation by reference to

(1) the criteria set forth in § 3.01 to determine whether the transfer and consolidation of the cases is warranted and

(2) consideration of whether removal will unduly disrupt or impinge upon state court or regulatory proceedings or impose an undue burden on the federal courts. * * *

[End of Excerpt.]

Consider an alternative proposal by Judge Schwarzer and his co-authors.

WILLIAM W. SCHWARZER, ALAN HIRSCH & EDWARD SUSSMAN, A PROPOSAL TO AMEND THE MULTIDISTRICT LITIGATION STATUTE TO PERMIT DISCOVERY COORDINATION OF LARGE-SCALE LITIGATION PENDING IN STATE AND FEDERAL COURT

73 Tex. L. Rev. 1529, 1552–64 (1995).

The following sections describe the operation of [the authors' multidistrict litigation] proposal.

A. Initiation of Proceedings

* * *

This proposal goes beyond the present [Multidistrict Litigation] statute by allowing any party to a state court action to initiate removal by filing a motion to consolidate. Furthermore, borrowing from the ALI proposal, it authorizes any court in which an action is pending to move the [Multidistrict Litigation] Panel for consolidation. The timely identification of related actions is critical to the efficacy of the statute. Allowing both federal and state courts, as well as parties, to suggest pretrial coordination of cases will help the Panel become aware of litigation that may be appropriate for consolidation.

* * *

B. Subject-Matter Jurisdiction

Under the proposal, removal would not be self-executing; the Panel would have to make the requisite findings, including a finding that jurisdiction exists. Subject-matter jurisdiction under this proposal is based principally on minimal diversity, the constitutional validity of which has been upheld. Minimal diversity requires that any two adverse parties must be citizens of different states. Few cases will fail to qualify under minimal diversity because claims against a single non-diverse defendant will be rare in large-scale litigation.

In addition, the proposal authorizes the Panel to remove claims on the basis of supplemental jurisdiction. * * *

***

C. Notice and Hearing

The proposal requires that notice be served on parties that may be affected by a Panel decision to consolidate, and it gives the parties an opportunity to participate in a hearing on the merits of consolidating or coordinating cases. * * *

***

D. Criteria for Consolidation

The criteria for pretrial consolidation of related state actions under the proposal would build upon the existing multidistrict litigation statute.

First, removal of state actions would be authorized only when the multidistrict litigation process has been previously or simultaneously invoked to consolidate related federal litigation. Thus, the federal courts will coordinate pretrial activity only in litigation that would be before them even without the intersystem procedure.

Second, the Panel may remove only state court actions involving questions of fact common to federal cases. The consolidation mechanism primarily attempts to avoid duplication in common factual investigations—depositions, interrogatories, and document discovery. It is not designed to resolve common questions of law (although they may be resolved in the federal actions).

In addition to the presence of a common question of fact in already (or simultaneously) consolidated federal litigation, three other conditions must be met before the Panel can order removal and consolidation of state cases. The following paragraphs describe these conditions.

1. Subject-Matter Jurisdiction—The Panel must find the existence of subject-matter jurisdiction in the cases proposed to be removed. * * *

2. Convenient, Just, and Efficient—The * * * Panel must find that removal is "for the convenience of parties and witnesses and will promote the just and efficient conduct of such actions." * * *

* * * The Panel needs to take [geographic inconvenience] into account, but measures are available to minimize its impact—the transferee judge may hold hearings at different locations, and the appointment of lead counsel may reduce the number of persons that need to travel.

3. No Undue Disruption of State Court Proceedings—Removal may be ordered only upon a finding that it will not unduly disrupt pending state court proceedings. * * * Consolidation would not be appropriate when state court proceedings are close to trial or when existing state consolidation or coordination arrangements adequately meet the needs of the litigation.

***

F. Conduct of the Multidistrict Litigation Proceedings

The transferee court will conduct the consolidated pretrial proceedings in the same general manner as other multidistrict litigation proceedings with one major difference: the court will not be authorized to make dispositive rulings terminating or disposing of claims or defenses. Following the limited pretrial proceedings, the state cases would be remanded to the originating state courts for any remaining proceedings, including resolution of the merits by motion or trial.

* * *

Management of discovery will often require the transferee judge to rule on the scope of discovery. Such rulings will, under the proposal, control in all subsequent proceedings. * * *

The process of managing consolidated discovery would not differ from current practice under Section 1407. Representation of the parties in the consolidated proceedings would be principally by lead counsel * * *.

* * *

G. Settlement

One objective of the proposal is to facilitate the settlement of the entire litigation by consolidating all the cases before a single judge, albeit for limited purposes. * * *

H. Tag-Along Actions

The proposal would authorize the Panel to remove later-in-time (or "tag-along") state cases for consolidation, using the same criteria as the initial consolidation. * * *

* * *

J. Remand to State Court

The state cases would be remanded to state court for trial upon conclusion of the consolidated discovery, or earlier by order of the transferee judge. Any case could be remanded upon a showing of good cause, such as a state court judge's suggestion or a party's motion that the case was ready to go to trial. * * *

* * *

* * * Conclusion
* * *

The proposed amendment of the multidistrict litigation statute has sufficient coercive force to achieve meaningful coordination. * * * At the same time, because the proposal is limited to non-merits pretrial activity, it does not significantly compromise federalism or litigant autonomy. * * *

NOTES AND QUESTIONS

1. What are the major differences between the ALI proposal and the one advanced by Judge Schwarzer and his co-authors? With respect to each proposal, what are its merits? What are its negative aspects? Which of the two is more compelling?

2. As noted above, the ALI proposal addresses federal coordination, state coordination, and federal/state coordination. In addition, it contains numerous sections addressing choice-of-law issues (§§ 6.01 *et seq.*). The proposal

generated extensive debate and controversy when it was released, but Congress has not implemented it. For a sample of the debate, *see* Symeon C. Symeonides, *Introduction: The ALI's Complex Litigation Project: Commencing the National Debate*, 54 La. L. Rev. 843 (1994); Russell J. Wood, *Redrafting Reverse Removal: Four Recommendations to Improve the American Law Institute's Complex Litigation Project*, 44 Case W. Res. L. Rev. 1129 (1995). For a useful overview of the issue of federal/state coordination, *see* William W. Schwarzer, Nancy E. Weiss & Alan Hirsch, *Judicial Federalism in Action: Coordination of Litigation in State and Federal Courts*, 78 Va. L. Rev. 1689 (1992).

Chapter 13

Miscellaneous Aggregation Devices

■ ■ ■

Although class actions are the main focus of this casebook, Rule 23 does not define the boundaries of party aggregation. Chapter 12 focused on MDL, which is by no means limited to class actions. Moreover, there are numerous other aggregation devices apart from Rule 23 and MDL.

This chapter first discusses various aggregation devices under the Federal Rules of Civil Procedure in addition to Rule 23: permissive joinder (Rule 20), compulsory joinder (Rule 19), impleader (Rule 14), interpleader (Rule 22, along with interpleader by statute), intervention (Rule 24), and consolidation (Rule 42). It then discusses transfer under 28 U.S.C. § 1404 and aggregation under the federal bankruptcy code. Finally, the chapter discusses settlement constraints imposed by the aggregate settlement rule.

A. AGGREGATION DEVICES UNDER THE FEDERAL RULES OF CIVIL PROCEDURE

As noted, many federal rules other than Rule 23 permit party aggregation in federal court. The permissive and compulsory joinder rules (Rule 20 and Rule 19) provide for joinder of persons whose claims are either sufficiently similar to other persons' claims or whose presence in the litigation is necessary in order to achieve justice. The "impleader" rule (Rule 14) permits a party defending an action to bring others into the litigation who may be liable to the defendant for some or all of the original plaintiff's claim. The "interpleader" rule (Rule 22) and its statutory counterpart (28 U.S.C. § 1335) permit a party who holds some contested "stake," and who may be exposed to double or multiple liability from numerous claimants of the stake, to bring an action in federal court naming the potential claimants as defendants. The intervention rule (Rule 24) permits a person who is not a party to a case to enter the lawsuit and become a party if he or she has a sufficient interest or stake in the controversy. Finally, the consolidation rule (Rule 42(a)) provides that a district court may consolidate for purposes of trial or pre-trial proceedings two or more actions involving a common question of law or fact. These rules are explored in the first section of this chapter.

1. PERMISSIVE JOINDER

Permissive joinder is the classic alternative to a class action for litigating multi-party cases. Indeed, the very first requirement of Rule 23(a) is that "joinder of all members" of a putative class must be "impracticable." In contrast to a class action, in which only the named plaintiffs are parties, in a case involving joinder under Rule 20 all parties joined are actually before the court. As will be seen, the requirements for joinder are less rigorous than those for a class action. Yet even joinder is not allowed when different transactions or occurrences are involved or when the matters do not share any common legal or factual issues.

FED. R. CIV. P. 20: PERMISSIVE JOINDER OF PARTIES

(a) Persons Who May Join or Be Joined.

(1) Plaintiffs. Persons may join in one action as plaintiffs if:

(A) they assert any right to relief jointly, severally, or in the alternative with respect to or arising out of the same transaction, occurrences, or series of transactions or occurrences; and

(B) any question of law or fact common to all plaintiffs will arise in the action.

(2) Defendants. Persons—as well as a vessel, cargo, or other property subject to admiralty process in rem—may be joined in one action as defendants if:

(A) any right to relief is asserted against them jointly, severally, or in the alternative with respect to or arising out of the same transaction, occurrence, or series of transactions or occurrences; and

(B) any question of law or fact common to all defendants will arise in the action.

(3) Extent of Relief. Neither a plaintiff nor a defendant need be interested in obtaining or defending against all the relief demanded. The court may grant judgment to one or more plaintiffs according to their rights, and against one or more defendants according to their liabilities.

(b) Protective Measures. The court may issue orders—including an order for separate trials—to protect a party against embarrassment, delay, expense, or other prejudice that arises from including a person against whom the party asserts no claim and who asserts no claim against the party.

GUEDRY V. MARINO

United States District Court, Eastern District of Louisiana, 1995.
164 F.R.D. 181.

JONES, DISTRICT JUDGE.

Pending before the Court is a "Motion to Sever/Separate Trials" by defendant, Johnny Marino. * * * Having reviewed the memoranda of the parties, the record and the applicable law, the Court DENIES the motion.

BACKGROUND

Defendant, Johnny Marino, individually and in his official capacity as sheriff of St. Charles Parish, has been sued by seven plaintiffs * * * under 42 U.S.C. §§ 1981 and 1983 for alleged violations of the First and Fourteenth Amendments. Plaintiffs also allege state-law violations. Plaintiffs have brought suit against Marino because their commissions as deputies were not renewed as of July 1, 1992, the date that the sheriff assumed office after his re-election.

* * *

George Guedry, Jr. alleges that his commission was terminated by defendant in violation of his First and Fourteenth Amendment rights because of (1) his decision to speak out at a parish council meeting; (2) his membership in and association with members of the New Sarpy Civic Association; and (3) his refusal to participate in the defendant's re-election efforts.

Robert Lewis alleges First and Fourteenth Amendment violations as a result of defendant's harassment and retaliation, because of (1) defendant's belief that plaintiff supported defendant's opponent in the election; (2) defendant's belief that plaintiff influenced his neighbor to support defendant's opponent; (3) plaintiff's decision to speak out on a matter of public concern; and (4) plaintiff's race.

Nicholas Vitrano also claims violations of his First and Fourteenth Amendment rights as a result of defendant's harassment and retaliation, because of defendant's belief that plaintiff had supported the defendant's opposing candidate.

Claudette Wilson asserts that her First and Fourteenth Amendment rights were violated due to defendant's harassment and retaliation efforts against her because she filed a worker's compensation complaint alleging that defendant refused to pay her medical bills for a job related injury. Further, plaintiff maintains that her Constitutional rights were violated because defendant terminated her commission because of her race and/or sex.

David Zeringue declares that he has been deprived of his right to equal employment opportunities as a result of defendant's harassment of him solely because of (1) defendant's belief that he had not actively supported defendant's re-election bid; and (2) defendant's belief that plaintiff sought to enforce the law against individuals who were political allies of the defendant.

Brent Mashia proclaims that his First and Fourteenth Amendment rights were violated by defendant's harassment of plaintiff solely because of (1) defendant's belief that plaintiff did not actively support the defendant's re-election bid; (2) plaintiff's decision to speak out against defendant's policies of racial discrimination, and (3) plaintiff's race.

Orvett Smith charges that defendant harassed and retaliated against plaintiff solely because of (1) defendant's belief that plaintiff supported his opponent's bid for election; (2) defendant's belief that plaintiff was closely associated with defendant's opponent; and (3) plaintiff's race in violation of plaintiff's First and Fourteenth Amendment rights.

The defendant has filed a "Motion to Sever/Separate Trials" claiming that the plaintiffs' cases are improperly joined, entitling him to have the claims severed under Fed. R. Civ. P. 20 and 21. [Rule 21 permits a court, *inter alia*, to dismiss or sever parties who have been misjoined.] In the alternative, the defendant claims that sufficient reasons exist to sever each plaintiff's case pursuant to Fed. R. Civ. P. 42(b). The defendant postulates that severance is proper because separate trials will promote judicial economy and will prevent jury confusion.

In their opposition, plaintiffs contend that the claims have been properly joined because each plaintiff was terminated for refusing to support defendant's election bid or for supporting defendant's re-election bid but being accused of not doing so. Further, four plaintiffs also allege that they were discharged because of their race. Thus, plaintiffs argue that there is a common question of law or fact with respect to these claims. In the alternative, plaintiffs argue that severing these claims would result in unnecessary delay and prejudice to the litigants. In addition, plaintiffs argue that any possible confusion to the jury can be handled by the Court through its jury instructions.

Law and Application

I. Misjoinder

* * *

The purpose of Rule 20(a) is to promote trial convenience and expedite the final determination of disputes, thereby preventing multiple lawsuits. Moreover, under the Federal Rules of Civil Procedure, "joinder of claims, parties and remedies is strongly encouraged." *Mosley v. General Motors Corp.*, 497 F.2d 1330, 1332 (8th Cir. 1974) (citing *United Mine Workers v. Gibbs*, 383 U.S. 715, 724 (1966)).

The court in *Mosley* noted that

> [p]ermissive joinder is not * * * applicable in all cases. The rule imposes two specific requisites to the joinder of parties: (1) a right to relief must be asserted by, or against, each plaintiff or defendant relating to or arising out of the same transaction or occurrence, or series of transactions or occurrences; and (2) some question of law or fact common to all the parties must arise in the action.

There is no strict rule for determining what constitutes the same occurrence or series of transactions or occurrences for purposes of Rule 20(a). Furthermore, Rule 20(a) does not require that every question of law or fact in the action be common among the parties; rather, the rule permits party joinder whenever there will be at least one common question of law or fact.

Applying these principles to the present case, the Court rejects defendant's argument that plaintiffs' complaint does not satisfy the tests for joinder because they involve different transactions or occurrences and they do not raise common factual or legal issues[,] except as to plaintiff Claudette Wilson. All of the plaintiffs' claims arise out of separate factual circumstances, but all of plaintiffs' allegations revolve around claims of termination after alleged violations of First Amendment rights except Claudette Wilson. This includes enforcement of the law as to defendant's supporters and/or failure to support defendant (or allegations thereto) in his re-election bid and/or speaking at a public meeting. Such conduct may constitute a single transaction or occurrence for purposes of Rule 20(a). The alleged discriminatory activity directly affecting each of them, includes common legal and factual questions.

As to plaintiff Claudette Wilson, however, review of the Complaint clearly seems to indicate that, although she was terminated on the same day as the other plaintiffs, there is no other relevant similarity between her claim and the other plaintiffs' claims. Wilson alleges that she was forced to file a Worker's Compensation complaint for defendant's refusal to reimburse her for medical payments related to an on-the-job injury. As noted, Wilson claims that her commission was not renewed in retaliation for filing such a claim and also because of her race and/or sex. Although Wilson makes a claim for violation of First Amendment rights as the other plaintiffs do, it is clear that her claims do not arise out of the same transaction or occurrence as the other plaintiffs, insofar as they make a claim for First Amendment violations as to speaking at civic forums and/or not supporting (or allegedly refusing to support) defendant in his re-election campaign.

However, plaintiff Wilson also makes a claim for racial discrimination, as do [other] plaintiffs * * *. Thus, Wilson's claims arise out of similar transactions or occurrences and involve similar questions of fact and law such that joinder of her claims with the other plaintiffs' claims under Rule 20(a) is proper.

* * *

Defendant argues that the evidence used to prove any one plaintiff's claims would not be admissible in a trial of any of the other plaintiffs based on relevancy. In addition to the fact that defendant cites no law in support of this contention, the foregoing discussion belies the fallacy of this contention.

Defendant also argues that exposure to irrelevant evidence would "taint and confuse the jury." [But] * * * any potential confusion to the jury can surely be remedied at trial through a limiting instruction by the Court. Moreover, courts have broad discretion in interpreting the requirements of Rule 20 in an effort to reduce inconvenience, delay and added expense to the parties and to the court, and to promote judicial economy. The time, expense and inconvenience to the parties associated with seven separate trials is readily apparent in this case. Severance of the plaintiffs' claims at this juncture would be imprudent, as it may result in a waste of judicial time and resources. Moreover, the Court does not agree that joinder of plaintiffs' claims will result in prejudice to the defendant or that his right to a fair trial will be compromised.

* * *

[The court thus denied defendant's motion.]

DIRECTV, INC. v. ADRIAN

United States District Court, Northern District of Illinois, 2004.
2004 WL 1146122.

PLUNKETT, SENIOR JUDGE.

Plaintiff DIRECTV, Inc. ("Directv") has sued a number of individual defendants under federal and state law for possession and use of illegal devices and equipment designed to intercept Directv's encrypted satellite communications. Defendants Ozie Lewis ("Lewis") and Ken Vanderploeg ("Vanderploeg") have filed motions to dismiss or sever for improper joinder. They have also filed motions to dismiss two of the claims against them.

[Robert Adrian is the first named defendant in the lawsuit and one of a group of individuals accused of purchasing one or more Pirate Access Devices from Whiteviper Technologies during a certain period of time, in violation of various federal and state laws. Although the court's opinion is not clear, it appears that Adrian did not join in Lewis' and Vanderploeg's motions.] For the reasons stated below, the motions are granted in part and denied in part.

Background

We accept the allegations in the complaint as true for purposes of this motion. The following recitation is taken from the complaint. Directv, a California-based company, is in the business of distributing satellite television broadcasts throughout the United States. It does this by relaying digital signals from within the United States up to satellites hovering thousands of miles above earth. Those signals are then broadcast back to earth, where they are captured by a fixed outdoor satellite dish that is connected by cable to an indoor satellite receiver. The satellite receiver is in turn connected by cable to a television monitor.

Directv's signals are encrypted to prevent unauthorized reception and use of Directv's broadcasts. A programmable "access card" contained within the satellite receiver is used to unscramble the signals. The access card is about the size of a credit card. Directv programs the access card electronically to unscramble portions of the satellite signal so that a subscriber can view the specific television channels (or listen to audio programs) to which he has subscribed. When a subscriber wants to view programming on a limited basis (such as a pay-per-view movie or a special sporting event), he can do so by ordering the program through the remote control or through a phone call. The access card records these purchases and communicates the information to Directv.

Despite the encryption technology used to protect Directv's signal, there are many individuals in the United States and other countries involved in the development of devices and equipment (including the illegal programming of valid access cards) used to pirate Directv's signals ("Pirate Access Devices"). In general, the Pirate Access Devices provide the user with access to all of Directv's satellite programming with no payment to Directv. Directv's main revenue source is from subscriptions paid by authorized users of its signals. It has a significant interest in preventing the unauthorized receipt and use of its satellite programming.

During the past few years, Directv has conducted several raids on businesses that market and sell Pirate Access Devices. The information from these raids has led Directv to the individuals purchasing and using the devices. On or about May 25, 2001, with the cooperation of local law enforcement, Directv obtained shipping records and other documents from a mail shipping facility used by major distributors of Pirate Access Devices. On or about September 2001, Directv obtained shipping records, e-mail communications and other records from one Pirate Access Device distributor in particular, operating under the name of "Whiteviper" and/or "Whiteviper Technologies" ("Whiteviper"). The records indicate that each of the defendants purchased one or more Pirate Access Devices from

Whiteviper at different times. The defendants' activities violate federal telecommunication and wiretapping laws and state law.

Directv has brought a five-count complaint against these defendants. Defendants Lewis and Vanderploeg have each filed a motion to dismiss or sever for improper joinder under Federal Rule of Civil Procedure ("Rule") 21. * * *

Discussion

We address first the motions to dismiss of Lewis and Vanderploeg, or alternatively, to sever under Rule 21. They argue that Directv has not met the requirements set forth in Rule 20(a) for permissive joinder. Under Rule 20(a) [as of 2004], joinder of defendants in one action is permitted if: (1) the plaintiff asserts "any right to relief [jointly, severally, or in the alternative] arising out of the same transaction [or occurrence]"; and (2) "if any question of law or fact common to all defendants will arise in the action." Misjoinder occurs when a plaintiff fails to satisfy either requirement. The district court has wide discretion to decide whether joinder in any given situation is proper.

In their motions, Lewis and Vanderploeg focus on plaintiff's failure to satisfy the first prong of Rule 20(a), the "same transaction" requirement. According to Lewis, the complaint alleges only similar wrongs by a group of separate and unrelated defendants. It does not suggest a particular reason why these defendants have been grouped together in this action. Each defendant's actions, says Lewis, were independent, discrete acts. He continues, saying "[t]here is no allegation of any conspiracy, joint action, or other facts to tie the conduct of all [d]efendants together transactionally, as required by Rule 20(a)." Vanderploeg makes a similar argument, saying that the "alleged wrongful actions were taken by different people on separate occasions under different circumstances" and that Directv does not allege that Vanderploeg has acted in concert with the other defendants.

Directv responds that it has satisfied the requirements of Rule 20(a). As for the first prong, Directv links the defendants through the following: (1) they all purchased Pirate Access Devices through the same distribution center in California; (2) the purpose of the Pirate Access Devices they purchased was the same; and (3) they all purchased Pirate Access Devices during the same time period. Directv also argues that it will present similar evidence against each defendant, including similar testimony about the purchasing and operation of the Pirate Access Devices. It argues that permissive joinder rules should be interpreted broadly in the interest of judicial economy.

Directv says that it has also satisfied the second prong of Rule 20(a). It has asserted the same legal claims against each defendant, alleging that they each purchased multiple Pirate Access Devices through the same distribution center for the same purpose. According to Directv, it has established that common questions of law or fact exist.

Even keeping in mind that the purpose of permissive joinder under Rule 20(a) is judicial economy, we do not agree that Directv has satisfied Rule 20(a)'s requirements. Directv alleges that each defendant bought one or more Pirate Access Devices from Whiteviper through the same distribution center and that they each violated the same laws, but there the similarities end. There is no allegation that defendants acted in concert with each other or that they even knew each other before being named in this suit. Allegations of similar statutory violations do not satisfy the "same transaction" requirement.

Defendants, each apparently acting on his own and at different times, purchased various types of devices which were used in different ways. The facts that relate to Lewis's alleged violations of law with respect to Pirate Access Devices will be different from those that relate to Vanderploeg (and, for that matter, the other defendants). With respect to each defendant, a jury will be deciding whether he "actually ordered, possessed, manufactured, assembled, modified, and/or used each device in dispute, or converted Directv's satellite communications, and whether each such device or behavior violates" the law. The claims against each defendant therefore do not arise from the same transaction or occurrence. Directv has not satisfied the "same transaction" requirement of Rule 20(a). Accordingly, joinder of these defendants is improper.

Finding that the requirements of Rule 20(a) have not been met, we must decide a proper remedy. Under Rule 21, we may either dismiss defendants without prejudice or sever them from this action. *See* Fed. R. Civ. P. 21. Directv says that a possible statute of limitations problem may ensue if Lewis and Vanderploeg are dismissed without prejudice. It argues that in such a case, the misjoined defendants should be severed. * * *

We are duty-bound to sever claims rather than dismiss defendants if a dismissal would bring statute of limitations consequences. * * * [*See*] Fed. R. Civ. P. 21.

Conclusion

For the reasons state above, we deny Lewis and Vanderploeg's motions to dismiss under Rule 21 but grant their motions to sever. * * *

NOTES AND QUESTIONS

1. Can *Guedry* be reconciled with *DIRECTV*? Which case is more suitable for joinder?

2. The *Guedry* court contends that jury instructions could ameliorate any potential jury confusion that joinder of the parties might create. How persuasive is this argument?

3. The *Guedry* court stated that no hard and fast rules determine whether events are part of the same transaction or occurrence. In *Moore v. N.Y. Cotton Exch.*, 270 U.S. 593 (1926), the Supreme Court construed the meaning of "transaction" to determine when a counterclaim is compulsory under Rule 13: "Transaction is a word of flexible meaning. It may comprehend a series of many occurrences, depending not so much upon the immediateness of their connection as upon their logical relationship." 270 U.S. at 610. This construction of "transaction" has been utilized by courts when interpreting Rule 20. *See, e.g., A.M. Alexander v. Fulton Cnty., Ga.*, 207 F.3d 1303, 1323 (11th Cir. 2000); *Mosley v. Gen. Motors Corp.*, 497 F.2d 1330, 1333 (8th Cir. 1974). What is the logical relationship among the plaintiffs' encounters with Sheriff Marino in *Guedry*? Are they part of the same transaction? What about plaintiff Wilson?

4. Was *DIRECTV* correctly decided? What arguments can be made in favor of joinder? Although some other courts in similar cases have agreed that joinder of defendants is not appropriate, *e.g., DIRECTV, Inc. v. Patel*, 2003 WL 22669031, at *1 (N.D. Ill. 2003), other courts have found joinder to be proper. *E.g., DIRECTV, Inc. v. Essex*, 2002 U.S. Dist. LEXIS 26923, at *3–4 (W.D. Wash. 2002) (relying on allegation that 18 defendants all "purchased and used Pirate Access Devices * * * from the same distribution center * * * within a twelve month time frame" in finding joinder requirements satisfied).

5. The requirement that there be a common question of law or fact for permissive joinder resembles the preliminary requirement of common questions of law or fact for class certification under Rule 23(a)(2). In both contexts, the requirement of common questions promotes judicial efficiency. In the context of permissive joinder, common questions of law or fact need not *predominate* over other individual claims, a point made in *Guedry*. By contrast, in certain types of class actions (under Rule 23(b)(3)), a showing of predominance is required. *See* Chapter 3(C)(1)(a). Should a person seeking joinder under Rule 20(a) be required to show that common questions predominate? In light of the Supreme Court's interpretation of commonality in *Wal–Mart Stores, Inc. v. Dukes*, 564 U.S. 338 (2011), should "common questions" under Rule 20(a)(1)(B) be strictly interpreted to require substantial evidence?

6. *DIRECTV* is not the only example of a case applying Rule 20 strictly. Another such case is *Insolia v. Philip Morris Inc.*, 186 F.R.D. 547 (W.D. Wis. 1999). Plaintiffs were three former smokers and their spouses who sued various tobacco companies, alleging that the defendants conspired to deceive them about the harmful effects of smoking. The court had previously denied a motion for class certification, and defendants subsequently argued that the three suits were misjoined under Rule 21 and should be severed. While recognizing that joinder under Rule 20 was easier to satisfy than class certification under Rule 23, the court held that joinder was improper:

> I conclude that plaintiffs' claims do not arise from the same transaction or series of transactions, as they must in order to satisfy Rule 20. On an abstract level, dissimilarities in the claims brought by plaintiffs suggest that these claims are not related logically to one another. Plaintiffs began smoking at different ages; they bought different brands throughout their years as smokers; and they quit for different reasons and under different circumstances. * * * [T]he only thread holding these disparate factual scenarios together is the allegation of an industry-wide conspiracy, but this theory does not hold up on its terms, much less under the weight of the individual issues associated with each plaintiff. In [an earlier] opinion on class certification, I discussed at length why these claims did not arise from one another for the purpose of the typicality requirement of Rule 23(a). Among other observations, I noted that plaintiffs' depositions revealed that tobacco industry propaganda regarding the health effects of smoking reached them, if at all, through a variety of different channels and with varying degrees of success. Complicating matters further, defendants allegedly unleashed the stream of misrepresentations in furtherance of the conspiracy over the course of a 30-year period. As emphasized by defendants, plaintiff Vincent Insolia began smoking almost two decades before the industry hatched its scheme and has not smoked for more than a quarter of a century. By contrast,

plaintiffs Billy Mays and Maureen Lovejoy took up the habit in the early '50s and continued to smoke well into [the] '90s. Even if the conspiracy charged held together, serious questions exist regarding medical causation. * * * For example, medical evidence suggests that the cancer contracted by Mays may be attributable to a work-related accident, not smoking, and that Insolia's risk of developing lung cancer returned to that of a nonsmoker ten years after he quit. With this motion, defendants have submitted the report of a pathologist that casts into doubt whether plaintiff Maureen Lovejoy ever had cancer.

In the face of this evidence, plaintiffs' argument that causation and other medical issues can be resolved without engaging in highly individualized inquiries is even less persuasive here than it was in their briefs in support of class certification.

Id. at 550. Does the *Insolia* court's analysis comport with Rule 20? What arguments can be made in favor of Rule 20 joinder? Could the court have reasonably justified denying class certification but permitting joinder? *See generally* Elizabeth J. Cabraser, *The Class Action Counterreformation*, 57 Stan. L. Rev. 1475, 1486–87 (2005) (noting divergent approaches of courts on joinder issues).

7. Courts have identified important differences between a Rule 20 joinder and a Rule 23 class action. As one court explained:

A class representative in a Rule 23 circumstance with a single voice represents the entire class. * * * The Rule 23 class plaintiff is the only party entitled to control that civil action through the Rule 23 class action mechanism. The safeguards are extensive and the court's control over the certification of the class and any sub-classes, the designation of the class representative and counsel, as well as the control over the entire course of litigation, including settlement, provides the protection that the hundreds or thousands of unidentified class members are entitled to when a single class or sub-class representative speaks, and thereby acts to bind everyone.

Consolidation through joinder under Rule 20 presents an entirely different landscape to a certain extent, but * * * similarities as well. Here, each of the individual plaintiffs is entitled to be a named party in the civil action in which the joinder occurs. The voice of one of the joined plaintiffs does not speak for all plaintiffs, nor does the voice of one counsel speak for all plaintiffs' counsel. While the practical realities in the assembling and marketing of consolidated cases under a Rule 20 joinder often result in a number of plaintiffs being represented by the same counsel or a small group of lead counsel, there is nothing in the joinder rule that either requires or prohibits that phenomena. * * *

In re: Orthopedic Bone Screw Prods. Liab. Litig., 1995 WL 428683, at *3 (E.D. Pa. 1995).

8. When plaintiffs' rights to relief arise from the same alleged course of behavior by the same defendant during the same time period, many courts hold that the events creating a right to relief are transactionally related, and thus joinder of plaintiffs is proper. *See, e.g., Anderson Poleon v. Gen. Motors Corp.*, 1999 WL 1289473, at *1–2 (D.V.I. 1999) (joinder proper where complaint against GM alleged that vehicles were all manufactured by the same defendant in the same year and were of the same make and model—thereby resulting in products liability charges sharing common questions of law and fact, despite

differences among plaintiffs' accidents and injuries); *Hanley v. First Investors Corp.*, 151 F.R.D. 76, 78–80 (E.D. Tex. 1993) (joinder of plaintiffs was proper because common pattern of oral misrepresentations committed by same stockbroker during roughly same period of time constituted same series of transactions or occurrences). That approach, however, is not universal. *See, e.g., Coughlin v. Rogers*, 130 F.3d 1348, 1350–51 (9th Cir. 1997) (joinder improper although plaintiffs made common allegation of delay by the INS and each plaintiff claimed a violation under the Constitution and Administrative Procedure Act).

9. Even when the moving party meets the requirements of Rule 20(a), the court has discretion to deny Rule 20 joinder or to order separate trials. *See* Fed. R. Civ. P. 20(b). Joinder is encouraged, however, when it would not prejudice the parties. *See, e.g., Hill v. BASF Wyandotte Corp.*, 782 F.2d 1212, 1213–14 (4th Cir. 1986). Should a court be *required* to permit joinder when the requirements of Rule 20(a) are met?

10. A series of transactions or occurrences satisfying Rule 20(a) may occur over an extended period of time. In *Kedra v. City of Philadelphia*, 454 F. Supp. 652 (E.D. Pa.1978), for example, plaintiffs complained of a series of unlawful detentions, searches, beatings, and similar occurrences representing a systematic pattern of harassment, threats, and coercion with the intention of depriving the plaintiffs of their rights. The court found that joinder of the various members of the Philadelphia police force as defendants was proper even though the events occurred over a period of one and one-half years. "There is no logical reason why the systematic conduct alleged could not extend over a lengthy time period and, on the face of these allegations, there is nothing about the extended time span that attenuates the factual relationship among all of these events." *Id.* at 662. The court noted that, pursuant to the provisions of Rule 20(b), the court would retain flexibility in order to make such orders as necessary to prevent prejudice to the defendants from a single trial of all the claims pending against them. *Id.*

11. When a plaintiff seeks to join other plaintiffs or multiple defendants, the complaint must state facts sufficient to show that joinder is proper. For instance, in *Abdullah v. Acands, Inc.*, 30 F.3d 264, 266 (1st Cir. 1994), plaintiffs sued the defendant for designing, manufacturing, or supplying asbestos and asbestos-containing products or machinery for vessels on which plaintiffs had served as crew members. The complaint supplied only the names and social security numbers of the plaintiffs, and alleged that plaintiffs had suffered asbestos-related diseases as a result of exposure to the defendants' asbestos products. The district court rejected the plaintiffs' attempt to join 1,000 plaintiffs and 93 defendants in their action. On appeal, the First Circuit agreed that the complaint as it stood failed to state factual allegations that would support joinder. The First Circuit noted that the complaint should state whether plaintiffs had served on the same vessels during the same periods, and whether they were injured by exposure to the same asbestos-containing products or equipment. What other factual allegations would have supported joinder of all of the parties?

12. The issue of supplemental jurisdiction arises not only in class actions (*see* Chapter 7(B)), but also under non-class aggregation devices. Although the technicalities of invoking supplemental jurisdiction under Rule 20 are beyond the scope of this text, the reader should be aware that these technicalities have confounded the courts in the context of suits involving diversity jurisdiction.

The wording of section 1367(b) differentiates between Rule 20 (permissive joinder) and Rule 19 (compulsory joinder) with respect to whether supplemental jurisdiction may be exercised in a diversity case over claims by persons proposed to be joined as plaintiffs. (The statute explicitly precludes supplemental jurisdiction in this circumstance only under Rule 19.) *See* 28 U.S.C. § 1367(b); Chapter 7(B). Thus, courts were divided on how to apply section 1367 in the Rule 20 context. In *Exxon Mobil Corp. v. Allapattah Servs., Inc.*, 545 U.S. 546 (2005), the Supreme Court resolved this split, holding that a federal court that has diversity jurisdiction over the claim of one plaintiff (whose claim satisfies the amount-in-controversy requirement) may exercise supplemental jurisdiction over claims brought by additional plaintiffs who fail to satisfy the amount-in-controversy requirement. The Court concluded that, because one plaintiff met the amount-in-controversy requirement and the additional plaintiffs' claim arose out of the same case or controversy, supplemental jurisdiction was proper.

13. Rule 21, cited in *Guedry* and *DIRECTV*, provides that "[m]isjoinder of parties is not a ground for dismissing an action," and provides that "[o]n motion or on its own, the court may at any time, on just terms, add or drop a party." Applying Rule 21, the court may drop parties from the action even if all the claims and parties are properly before it, subject only to review for abuse of discretion. *See, e.g.*, *Lenon v. St. Paul Mercury Ins. Co.*, 136 F.3d 1365, 1372–73 (10th Cir. 1998). Does this rule make sense? Was it properly applied in *DIRECTV*?

14. In *Acevedo v. Allsup's Convenience Stores, Inc.*, 600 F.3d 516 (5th Cir. 2010), the Fifth Circuit held that the district court did not abuse its discretion in denying joinder of approximately 800 current or former employees of the defendants, all of whom were seeking unpaid wages and overtime under the Fair Labor Standards Act, 29 U.S.C. §§ 201–19. The court reasoned that "certain plaintiffs stated in their depositions that they were told by their managers that working off the clock was forbidden, while others indicated that they were only asked to work off the clock by certain managers and not others." *Id.* at 522. Thus, even assuming there was a company-wide policy of encouraging working off the clock, there was no abuse of discretion in denying joinder. What arguments can be made that the refusal to join was an abuse of discretion?

15. As the materials in this section show, permissive joinder may be limited with respect to its ability to serve as an aggregation device for a large number of claims. The American Law Institute (ALI) has observed that:

> joinder generally is sought only in relatively small-scale suits because each new party must be joined separately and is expected to appear personally in the action. In cases involving large numbers of parties, the utility of Rule 20 joinder ordinarily is superseded by the class action device. The utility of permissive joinder also is limited by the fact that each party must satisfy jurisdiction and venue requirements. * * * Finally, because permissive joinder is left to the parties' initiative, the presence of all persons necessary to a unitary adjudication cannot be ensured because there often are tactical reasons to omit certain potential parties.

American Law Institute, *Complex Litigation: Statutory Recommendations and Analysis* 25 (1994). Is the ALI unduly pessimistic about the usefulness of joinder as an aggregation device?

PROBLEM

Attorney Elizabeth Hanson is approached by a group of 40 people who reside in a low-income area of Philadelphia where the Newsome Company has just located a factory. They wish to bring a claim premised on a theory of "environmental racism"—that the company deliberately sought out a location in a predominantly African–American neighborhood, knowing that the factory would be discharging noxious fumes. (The neighborhood has 650 residents, about 600 of whom are African–American.) The potential clients wish to seek all damages that they can recover, and they want to request a medical monitoring program, because they are concerned that the fumes may cause cancer. Hanson has agreed to take the case and must decide whether to join her 40 clients as plaintiffs under Rule 20 or file the suit as a class action. What should she do? Are there any viable alternatives to either a class action or joinder of all 40 clients? What are the pros and cons of each approach?

2. COMPULSORY JOINDER

a. General Principles

The focus of compulsory joinder under Rule 19 is whether an absent party is essential to the case. As the following materials reveal, when an important absent party cannot be joined (for example, because personal jurisdiction is lacking), courts face the difficult issue of whether the absent party is so critical that the case must be dismissed.

FED. R. CIV. P. 19: REQUIRED JOINDER OF PERSONS

(a) Persons Required to Be Joined if Feasible.

(1) Required Party. A person who is subject to service of process and whose joinder will not deprive the court of subject-matter jurisdiction must be joined as a party if:

(A) in that person's absence, the court cannot accord complete relief among existing parties; or

(B) that person claims an interest relating to the subject of the action and is so situated that disposing of the action in the person's absence may:

(i) as a practical matter impair or impede the person's ability to protect the interest; or

(ii) leave an existing party subject to a substantial risk of incurring double, multiple, or otherwise inconsistent obligations because of the interest.

(2) Joinder by Court Order. If a person has not been joined as required, the court must order that the person be made a party. A person who refuses to join as a plaintiff may be made either a defendant or, in a proper case, an involuntary plaintiff.

(3) Venue. If a joined party objects to venue and the joinder would make venue improper, the court must dismiss that party.

(b) When Joinder Is Not Feasible. If a person who is required to be joined if feasible cannot be joined, the court must determine whether, in equity and good conscience, the action should proceed among the existing parties or should be dismissed. The factors for the court to consider include:

> (1) the extent to which a judgment rendered in the person's absence might prejudice that person or the existing parties;
>
> (2) the extent to which any prejudice could be lessened or avoided by:
>
>> (A) protective provisions in the judgment;
>>
>> (B) shaping the relief; or
>>
>> (C) other measures;
>
> (3) whether a judgment rendered in the person's absence would be adequate; and
>
> (4) whether the plaintiff would have an adequate remedy if the action were dismissed for nonjoinder.

(c) Pleading the Reasons for Nonjoinder. When asserting a claim for relief, a party must state:

> (1) the name, if known, of any person who is required to be joined if feasible but is not joined; and
>
> (2) the reasons for not joining that person.

(d) Exception for Class Actions. This rule is subject to Rule 23.

As the Supreme Court explained in *Republic of the Philippines v. Pimentel*, 553 U.S. 851 (2008):

> Subdivision (a) of Rule 19 states the principles that determine when persons or entities must be joined in a suit. The Rule instructs that nonjoinder even of a required person does not always result in dismissal. Subdivision (a) opens by noting that it addresses joinder "if feasible." Where joinder is not feasible, the question whether the action should proceed turns on the factors outlined in subdivision (b). The considerations set forth in subdivision (b) are nonexclusive, as made clear by introductory statement that "[t]he factors for the court to consider include." Fed. Rule Civ. Proc. 19(b). The general direction is whether "in equity and good conscience, the action should be dismissed." The design of the Rule, then, indicates that the determination whether to proceed will turn upon factors that are case specific, which is consistent with a Rule based on equitable considerations. This is also consistent with the fact that the determination of who may, or must, be parties to a suit has consequences for the persons and entities affected by the judgment; for the judicial system and its interest in the integrity of its processes and the respect accorded to its decrees; and for society and its concern for the fair and prompt resolution of disputes. For these reasons, the issue of joinder can be complex, and determinations are case specific.

* * *

* * * [I]t is clear that multiple factors must bear on the decision whether to proceed without a required person. This decision "must be based on factors varying with the different cases, some such factors being substantive, some procedural, some compelling by themselves, and some subject to balancing against opposing interests."

Id., 553 U.S. at 862–63.

IRON WORKERS LOCAL UNION NO. 17 INS. FUND V. PHILIP MORRIS, INC.†

United States District Court, Northern District of Ohio, 1998.
182 F.R.D. 512.

GWIN, DISTRICT JUDGE.

[Union trust funds that provide medical benefits to union members brought suit against the major tobacco companies seeking reimbursement for payments to treat smoking-related illnesses. The funds did not join as plaintiffs the union members' employers, the individual union members (the beneficiaries), or the insurers who provided medical payments.]

On January 8, 1998, the defendants filed a motion to dismiss this cause for plaintiffs' failure to join necessary parties pursuant to Fed. R. Civ. P. 12(b)(7) and Rule 19. In this motion, defendants argue that plaintiffs must join others who may have claim against defendants. * * *

* * *

For the reasons that follow, * * * the Court denies the defendants' motion to dismiss this cause for failure to join necessary or indispensable parties.

I. Procedural History of Case

Plaintiffs are certain trusts organized to provide health-related benefits to workers and their families. The plaintiffs are nonprofit, union-sponsored tax-exempt trusts organized under the Employee Retirement Income Security Act ("ERISA"), 29 U.S.C. §§ 1001, *et seq.* The trusts provide medical or hospital care benefits to [individual trust fund] participants and their beneficiaries as an employee retirement income security program.

On May 20, 1997, Plaintiff Funds brought this action against [the major U.S. cigarette manufacturers and other] tobacco-related entities. Plaintiffs allege that, since about 1953, the defendants have shifted the large health care costs of smoking onto plaintiffs, proposed class members, and other health care payers. Plaintiffs say defendants expected, foresaw, and planned this shift of expenses. Plaintiffs allege that as the direct result of the defendants' wrongdoing, plaintiffs and other similar trust funds had to make substantial expenditures to pay for [participants'] treatment of smoking-related illnesses and addiction.

---

† [For purposes of clarity, we have conformed the citations in this opinion to the 2007 version of Rule 19. Eds.]

[The plaintiff trust funds brought claims under RICO and Ohio's equivalent to RICO; federal and state antitrust laws; and common law civil conspiracy.]

* * *

II. Standard of Review

Fed. R. Civ. P. 12(b)(7) provides that a complaint may be dismissed for "failure to join a party under Rule 19." Questions concerning joinder of indispensable parties require courts to consider the policy considerations underlying the * * * federal rules. Resolving the question of joinder under Rule 19, and thus of dismissal for failure to join an indispensable party under Rule 12(b)(7), involves a three-step process. This analysis begins by determining whether a person is necessary to the action and should be joined if possible.

To decide whether a party is "necessary," courts need to review Fed. R. Civ. P. 19(a). * * *

If the person or entity sought to be joined does not fall within one of the [Rule 19(a)] provisions, joinder is not "necessary" and the court's analysis need go no further. However, "if the court finds that one of the criteria is satisfied, the person is one to be joined if 'feasible' and the court must then consider issues of personal jurisdiction and indispensability under Rule 19(b)."[7]

Should the Court need to consider related issues of personal jurisdiction and venue under Rule 19(b), it will also be necessary to decide whether the case may proceed without the absent party or whether that party is so "indispensable" [as] to require the case to be dismissed.

To determine whether a party is "indispensable," courts consider the four factors set forth in Rule 19(b). The four factors are: (1) to what extent a judgment rendered in the person's absence might be prejudicial to [the person] or to those already parties; (2) the extent to which, by protective provisions in the judgment, by the shaping of relief, or other measures, the prejudice can be lessened or avoided; (3) whether a judgment rendered in the person's absence will be adequate; (4) whether the plaintiff will have an adequate remedy if the action is dismissed for nonjoinder. In making this review, courts are not to evaluate the factors above in a "rigid manner" but should instead be governed by the practicalities of the individual case.

Applying the standards above, the Court first turns to whether the parties sought to be joined in the instant case are "necessary" to this litigation.

III. Discussion

In this case, the defendants argue that fund participants, employers, and insurers are necessary parties under Fed. R. Civ. P. 19(a). In making this argument, defendants generally say that joinder is required because Rule [19(a)(1)(B)] mandates joinder of all parties who claim an "interest relating to the subject of the action" and whose absence would "impair or

---

[7] If personal jurisdiction is present, the party shall be joined. However, if personal jurisdiction is not present or if venue for the persons or entities to be joined is improper, the party cannot properly be brought before the court.

impede the person's ability to protect [the] interest," or would expose persons already parties to "substantial risk of incurring double, multiple, or otherwise inconsistent obligations [because] of the claimed interest." Defendants say that not joining the individual participants, employers, and insurers to this action would potentially give these absent persons opportunity to file similar claims against the defendants to recover other independent tobacco-related illness costs. Defendants say this could subject them to multiple or potentially inconsistent obligations.

* * *

The Court first considers whether individual Fund participants are to be joined, then considers whether insurers or employers are to be joined. The Court then considers defendants' arguments regarding claims splitting. After making this review, the Court finds that neither the participants, insurers, or employers are so necessary or indispensable to this litigation such to warrant dismissal of this case.

A. Necessary Parties under Rule 19(a)(1)[(A)]

* * *

Under Rule 19(a), a court must first consider whether, in the absence of the party sought to be joined, complete relief cannot be accorded among those already parties to the case. Rule 19(a)(1)[(A)] "commands that a party be joined if in his absence complete relief cannot be accorded among those already parties." In deciding this factor, courts should focus " 'on relief between the parties and not on the speculative possibility of further litigation between a party and an absent person.' " The requirement under Rule 19(a)(1)[(A)] that complete relief be available does not mean that "every type of relief sought must be available, only that meaningful relief be available."

In the instant case, the relief sought by Plaintiff Funds is to recover economic losses incurred as a result of the defendants' alleged wrongful conduct. Because the plaintiffs classify their damages as economic loss resulting from the "improper diminishment and expenditure of the Funds' assets," plaintiffs contend the relief they seek is unique to the institutional interests of the Funds and not the type of relief otherwise recoverable by Fund participants, employers, or insurers. The Court agrees.

First, the record is clear that the Plaintiff Funds seek specific relief for the economic losses the Funds allegedly incurred as a result of having to pay health care costs for tobacco-related illnesses. The plaintiffs' claims are not for personal injury nor are they subrogation claims.

Second, the Plaintiff Funds' claims are not dependant upon whether Fund participants are or were smokers. This is not a "smoker-personal injury case." Although some Fund participants may be smokers, and although some of these participants may have independent personal injury claims against the defendants, the Funds' claims do not incorporate elements of potential individual participant claims.

Third, the Plaintiff Funds sue the defendants "directly" and not on behalf of individual participants, employers, or insurers. To this extent, the

Plaintiff Funds do not make subrogation or indemnity claims. Rather, the Funds base their claims for relief on independent, economic losses. These claims seek to recover "institutional" losses that were suffered or realized only by the Funds. Individual participants, employers, or insurers would not be able to recover damages allegedly suffered by the Funds.

Considering these factors, the Court finds that resolution of the plaintiffs' claims against the defendants in this case would, if the Funds were to prevail, give the plaintiffs the relief they seek. Because the Plaintiff Funds do not seek to recover damages for or on behalf of individual participants, employers, or insurers, this Court's decision not to join the absent parties would not impair the plaintiffs' ability to obtain "meaningful relief." Accordingly, the Court concludes that under Rule 19(a)(1), complete relief can be accorded among those already parties to this action.

Having decided this, the Court turns to the defendants' arguments for joinder under Rule 19(a)[(1)(B)].

B. Necessary Parties under Rule [19(a)(1)(B)]

Rule [19(a)(1)(B)] requires that a person be joined as a party in an action if "[that person] claims an interest relating to the subject of the action and is so situated that the disposition of the action in his absence" may prejudice his rights or those of the persons already parties. Fed. R. Civ. P. [19(a)(1)(B)]. By its terms, Rule [19(a)(1)(B)] is limited to an absent person "who claims an interest" relating to the subject of the action. Courts have generally construed "claims an interest" to mean "having an interest" in the case. Because an absent party will not have stated an interest in the case, this language infers that the absent party's interest will be "potential claims" that such a party might later bring.

In this case, the defendants first argue under Rule [19(a)(1)(B)] that individual Fund participants, employers, or insurers must be joined to avoid putting the defendants at risk of "double, multiple, or otherwise inconsistent obligations." Here, the defendants argue that if this Court allows these plaintiffs to bring a "direct action" against the defendants to recover health care costs, that others with similar claims will follow suit. Defendants argue the possibility of future litigation brought against them by these absent parties is sufficient to require joinder. The Court disagrees.

The Court finds defendants' argument regarding the risk of facing future lawsuits to be speculative. First, the defendants give no compelling evidence showing that any of the absent parties either intend to file such suits or have at all an interest in pursuing similar claims against the defendants. Second, even if such a showing were made, the defendants would need to establish that any future suits by participants, employers, or insurers, were brought to recover the same damages that the Plaintiff Funds presently seek. As discussed, the damages at issue here are unique to the Funds. The present lawsuit does not seek to recover for or on behalf of participants, employers, or insurers.

The defendants also argue that not joining the parties sought to be joined will require them to defend against duplicative suits or potentially face "multiple or inconsistent obligations" from individual Fund participants, employers, or insurers. Again, the Court disagrees.

1. Individual Fund Participants

The defendants first argue that failing to join individual Fund participants would subject the defendants to multiple suits or double recovery for the same injury.

In making this argument, defendants construe Plaintiff Funds' claims as being analogous to other tobacco-related lawsuits that involve either personal injury or subrogation claims. However, these are not the type of claims brought by Plaintiff Funds in this case. As discussed, the Funds do not seek damages for tobacco-related personal injuries suffered by individual participants, nor do the Funds assert claims for subrogation. Rather, the Funds assert claims for damages directly related to a depletion of trust funds assets as a result of the defendants' alleged wrongful conduct. Plaintiff Funds allege the defendants purposefully shifted the expenses and costs for health care to avoid having to absorb these expenditures themselves.

* * *

Defendants suggest that they would be exposed to double recovery should this Court permit plaintiffs to bring this action. Specifically, defendants say that both Fund beneficiaries and the plaintiffs would seek, and might recover for, the same damages.

The Court finds little potential for double recovery. First, an injured beneficiary could not recover under antitrust or RICO for the medical costs paid by any of plaintiffs' trust funds. Both antitrust law and RICO require a showing of injury to a plaintiff's business or property. Medical expenses paid on behalf of an injured smoker's beneficiary could not make up a monetary loss or other injury to a smoker's "business or property."

* * * [T]he Court concludes that individual participants are not parties with a[n] "interest relating to the subject" of this action, that being the depletion of Fund assets. The Court also finds insufficient evidence showing that such individual participants are "so situated that the disposition" of this action in their absence will either (i) impair or impede their ability to protect any such interest, or (ii) subject any parties already in the action to "double, multiple, or otherwise inconsistent obligations."

Having decided this, the Court reviews the defendants' argument for joining employers and insurers.

2. Employers and Insurers

The defendants also argue that employers and insurers must be joined. In making this argument, the defendants suggest that failing to join such parties would require them to defend similar "direct action" suits brought by either employers seeking to recover their contributions to the trust funds or by insurers seeking to recover premiums or benefits paid to Fund participants.

After reviewing these arguments, the Court finds that the defendants misconstrue the specific nature of Plaintiff Funds' claims and the relationship or interest, if any, employers or insurers have with the subject of

Plaintiff Funds' action against the defendants. First, the Funds' relationship with employer contributors is limited to contractual arrangements wherein the Funds and employers negotiate, either directly or through union contacts, participant benefits to be available to individual employees or participants. These arrangements are governed by ERISA.

By law, assets of employee benefit plans are held in trust and employers are not obligated on the benefits provided by the Funds. Rather, employers participating in such arrangements are only required, by contract, to pay the negotiated contribution or term. In this regard, the Court agrees with the plaintiffs that "the fiduciary requirements of ERISA specifically insulate the trust from the employer's interest." Accordingly, the Court does not find the absent employers to be "necessary parties" such to require their joinder in this action.

Insurers are likewise not necessary parties to this action. First, the defendants fail to show sufficient evidence that the plaintiffs or any of the Fund participants have insurance policies that are affected by this case. Second, the defendants fail to persuade the Court that even if such insurance relationships exist, that the carrier or provider would have an interest in the economic losses allegedly sustained by the trust funds. Further, the Court is not persuaded that even if an insurer had an interest in this action, that the claims, if any, would not lie against the Funds as opposed to the defendants. Although insurers may have independent damages claims against the defendants, there is little evidence suggesting that insurers would have interest in the particular economic losses sustained by Plaintiff Funds. Accordingly, the Court likewise does not find insurers to be "necessary parties" such to require their joinder in this action.

As to the defendants' arguments regarding the risk of double or multiple obligations, the Court finds that such risk would significantly be obviated by the single satisfaction rule. In [an earlier opinion], the Court stated the following:

> [T]he single satisfaction rule would allow defendants to seek credit for amounts paid plaintiffs in antitrust and RICO litigation in later personal injury litigation by beneficiaries. The payment by defendants of a judgment or settlement would give defendants a defense of satisfaction in any other suit in which an injured smoker/trust beneficiary might seek to recover any of the costs sought here. Defendants would not have to pay for the same medical cost damages twice.

This rule would also apply to any potential judgment obtained by either employers or insurers.

* * * [T]he Court concludes that employers or insurers are not parties with an "interest relating to the subject" of this action. The Court also finds insufficient evidence showing that such employers or insurers are "so situated that the disposition" of this action in their absence will either (i) impair or impede their ability to protect any such interest, or (ii) subject any parties already in the action to "double, multiple, or otherwise inconsistent obligations."

***

IV. Conclusion

***

Accordingly, the Court denies the defendants' motion in the alternative to dismiss this cause pursuant to Rule 12(b)(7) and Rule 19 for failure to join necessary or indispensable parties.

KESCOLI V. BABBITT

United States Court of Appeals, Ninth Circuit, 1996.
101 F.3d 1304.

Before THOMPSON, KLEINFELD, and TASHIMA, CIRCUIT JUDGES.

THOMPSON, CIRCUIT JUDGE.

Peabody Western Coal Company (Peabody) conducts coal mining operations at the Kayenta/Black Mesa mining complex pursuant to lease agreements entered into with the Navajo Nation and the Hopi Tribe. The United States Department of the Interior Office of Surface Mining (OSM) issued a permit to Peabody, which contained eighteen special conditions, governing Peabody's mining activities under the lease agreements at the Kayenta mine complex. Peabody challenged the majority of the special conditions. The present dispute arises out of the modification of special condition one through a settlement agreement entered into among Peabody, the OSM, the Navajo Nation, and the Hopi Tribe.

Maxine Kescoli, an enrolled member of the Navajo Nation, opposes the settlement of special condition one because she believes the condition, as modified by the settlement, does not guarantee adequate protection of sacred burial sites. After an Administrative Law Judge (ALJ) and the Interior Board of Land Appeals (IBLA) approved the settlement, Kescoli brought this action in the district court, naming as defendants the Secretary of the Interior, the OSM, and the IBLA. Kescoli sought a declaration that the modified condition was invalid.

The district court determined that Peabody was a necessary party, and that the Navajo Nation and the Hopi Tribe were necessary and indispensable parties that could not be joined due to their sovereign immunity. The court then dismissed the action under Federal Rule of Civil Procedure 19(b). We * * * affirm.

FACTS

In approximately 1970, Peabody began its coal mining operations at the Kayenta/Black Mesa mine complexes. Although the mine complexes are located on the Navajo Nation's reservation, the Navajo Nation and the Hopi Tribe are joint owners of some of the subsurface minerals.

In 1984, the OSM issued new regulations governing the permitting of mining operations on Native American lands. The new regulations required permits for all mining operations, but allowed existing mining operations to continue while awaiting action on permit applications.

In 1984, Peabody submitted a permit application for the Kayenta/Black Mesa mining complexes. Between 1985 and early 1990, the OSM was considering the application and preparing an environmental impact statement (EIS) addressing the Kayenta/Black Mesa mining operation. The EIS recommended approval of Peabody's permit application, subject to special conditions, to ensure compliance with the Surface Mining Control and Reclamation Act (SMCRA) and other federal laws.

In July 1990, the OSM issued permit AZ–0001C. This permit was limited to the Kayenta mine. The OSM reserved action on the Black Mesa mine. The permit included eighteen special conditions. At dispute in the present appeal is special condition one, which originally provided:

> Within 30 days of permit issuance, [Peabody] shall submit to OSM a description of measures, in addition to those proposed in the permit application package as it applies to the Kayenta Mine (PAP/KM), that [Peabody] will take to mitigate impacts on sacred and ceremonial sites. Such measures shall include: (1) verification, and mitigation of impacts where necessary, of the sacred and ceremonial resources identified in OSM's "Black Mesa–Kayenta Mine Final Socioeconomic Technical Report;" (2) coordination with any sacred site advisory committee formed by the Hopi or Navajo Tribe for exchanging information regarding sacred site concerns; and (3) means to resolve disputes between [Peabody] and the Tribes regarding sacred and ceremonial sites.

In August 1990, Peabody challenged thirteen of the special conditions, including special condition one, and filed a request for review. The ALJ permitted the Navajo Nation, the Hopi Tribe, and Kescoli to intervene.

After several hearings and after the parties had reached agreement on nine of the special conditions, the ALJ asked the parties to continue to pursue a settlement of the remaining conditions. After extensive negotiations, Peabody, the OSM, the Navajo Nation, and the Hopi Tribe reached an agreement on special condition one.

As modified by the settlement, special condition one: (1) adopts procedures to identify concerns about the impact of mining on religious and ceremonial locations; (2) addresses methods by which the Navajo Nation, the Hopi Tribe, and individual tribal members can communicate their concerns to Peabody, assuring that those communications will be kept confidential; (3) imposes an obligation on Peabody to meet annually with the Navajo Nation, the Hopi Tribe, and the OSM "to review the progress of the mining operation and future mining plans in order to keep the tribes informed concerning the anticipated schedule of areas to be disturbed;" and (4) imposes an obligation on the OSM to evaluate the procedures used to protect the religious sites at the end of the five-year permit to determine if revisions are needed.

Kescoli opposes the modification to condition one. She argues the original condition adequately protected burial sites, but the modified condition does not. Specifically, she argues the modified condition will permit Peabody to mine within 100 feet of a burial site, in violation of the SMCRA.

In 1992, the ALJ approved the settlement, addressing special condition one. The ALJ determined the settlement satisfied the concerns underlying the original condition and "more adequately addresse[d]" the OSM's desire to improve communications between Peabody and the Tribes, and the Tribes' desire for confidentiality and regular review of Peabody's mining operations. With regard to mining near burial sites, the ALJ determined that Kescoli could not challenge whether the permit adequately protects burial sites because the proceeding was limited to a challenge to the special conditions rather than to the issuance of the permit.

Kescoli then filed a petition for review with the IBLA. The IBLA affirmed the ALJ's approval of the settlement of special condition one. The IBLA found the settlement agreement to be "fair, adequate, reasonable" and not in violation of the SMCRA. Specifically, the IBLA found that the modified condition did not diminish Peabody's mitigation obligations and that federal law and the Navajo Burial Policy provide "ample protection for the known burials sacred to Kescoli." The IBLA denied Kescoli's request for reconsideration.

Kescoli then filed a petition for review in the district court. That court dismissed Kescoli's petition, because it determined the Navajo Nation and the Hopi Tribe were necessary and indispensable parties who could not be joined due to their sovereign immunity. Kescoli appeals.

DISCUSSION

* * *

B. Joinder

1. Standard of Review

The joinder determination is "a practical one and fact specific." We generally review for an abuse of discretion the district court's joinder determinations under Rule 19. However, if the district court's decision that an absent party's interest would be impaired involves a legal determination, we review *de novo* that determination.

Whether an action should be dismissed under Rule 19 involves a two-part analysis. First, the district court must determine whether the absent party is a "necessary" party. If the absent party is necessary and cannot be joined, the court next must determine whether the party is "indispensable." Because Peabody can be joined in the action, our review is limited to whether the Navajo Nation and the Hopi Tribe are necessary and indispensable parties.

2. Necessary Party

* * *

In this action, Kescoli seeks to invalidate the settlement of special condition one and to reinstate the original condition or to obtain a remand to the ALJ so the parties can renegotiate the condition and agree upon a condition which would provide greater protection for burial sites. The district court determined that Peabody, the Navajo Nation, and the Hopi Tribe have an interest in the litigation by virtue of their lease agreements. The district court reasoned:

The court assumes that the Navajo Nation and Hopi Tribes entered into the settlement on Special Condition One because they felt it struck a proper balance between sacred and burial site protection and economic gain. If Ms. Kescoli prevailed in obtaining the relief she requests, this balance would be disturbed.

The district court did not err in determining that the Navajo Nation and the Hopi Tribe are necessary parties. The settlement of special condition one affected the conditions under which Peabody may mine at the Kayenta complex and, thus, could affect Peabody's mining operations under the lease agreements. In turn, this could affect the amount of royalties received by the Navajo Nation and the Hopi Tribe and employment opportunities for their members.

Further, the Navajo Nation and the Hopi Tribe, by virtue of their sovereign capacity, have an interest in determining what is in their best interests by striking an appropriate balance between receiving royalties from the mining and the protection of their sacred sites. In her action, Kescoli challenges the balance struck by the Navajo Nation and the Hopi Tribe.

* * *

Kescoli's action could affect the Navajo Nation's and the Hopi Tribe's interests in their lease agreements and the ability to obtain the bargained-for royalties and jobs. Kescoli's action would directly affect the parties' settlement agreement and indirectly affect the parties' lease agreements by challenging the conditions under which Peabody may mine at the Kayenta complex. Her action is not limited to merely requiring the OSM to comply with procedural obligations in the future.

3. Sovereign Immunity

Because the Navajo Nation and the Hopi Tribe are necessary parties, the next question is whether they can be joined in the action. The sovereign immunity of the Navajo Nation and the Hopi Tribe, conceded by the parties, prevents them from being joined involuntarily unless they waive their immunity. Any waiver must be unequivocal and may not be implied.

Contrary to Kescoli's implication, the Navajo Nation and the Hopi Tribe did not waive their immunity by intervening in the administrative proceedings before the ALJ and the IBLA. "[A] tribe's participation in an administrative proceeding does not waive tribal immunity in an action filed by another party seeking review of the agency's decision." The district court, therefore, did not err in determining the Navajo Nation and the Hopi Tribe could not feasibly be joined in the action.

4. Indispensable Party

The Navajo Nation and the Hopi Tribe are indispensable parties if, "in equity and good conscience," the district court should not allow the action to proceed in their absence. Fed. R. Civ. P. 19(b). To make this determination, the district court balances four factors:

(1) prejudice to any party or to the absent party;

(2) whether relief can be shaped to lessen prejudice;

(3) whether an adequate remedy, even if not complete, can be awarded without the absent party; and

SEC. A   MISCELLANEOUS AGGREGATION DEVICES   1039

(4) whether there exists an alternative forum.

If no alternative forum exists, the district court should be "extra cautious" before dismissing an action.

The district court determined that, although the factors were not clearly in favor of dismissal, the concern for the protection of tribal sovereignty warranted dismissal. The district court did not abuse its discretion in making this determination.

With regard to the first factor, as discussed above, the Navajo Nation and the Hopi Tribe have an interest in the litigation by virtue of their lease and settlement agreements. Thus, the first factor weighs in favor of dismissal.

With regard to the second factor, the district court correctly determined that potential prejudice to the Navajo Nation and Hopi Tribe could not be effectively minimized because relief for Kescoli could not be effectively shaped, in their absence, to avoid prejudice to their interests.

Although the third and fourth factors may favor allowing Kescoli to proceed with her action, we have "recognized that a plaintiff's interest in litigating a claim may be outweighed by a tribe's interest in maintaining its sovereign immunity." If the necessary party is immune from suit, there may be "very little need for balancing Rule 19(b) factors because immunity itself may be viewed as the compelling factor."

Based on the need to protect tribal sovereignty and because the factors do not clearly weigh in favor of allowing Kescoli to proceed with her action, the district court correctly determined that the Navajo Nation and the Hopi Tribe are indispensable parties.

5.   Public Rights Exception

Kescoli argues she should be permitted to continue with her action because it falls within the "public rights" exception. Under this exception, even if the Navajo Nation and the Hopi Tribe are necessary parties, they are not deemed indispensable and, consequently, dismissal is not warranted.

The contours of the public rights exception have not been clearly defined. Generally, however, the litigation must transcend the private interests of the litigants and seek to vindicate a public right. Further, although the litigation may adversely affect the absent parties' interests, the litigation must not "destroy the legal entitlements of the absent parties." The present litigation does not satisfy either criterion.

As the district court determined, Kescoli's claim "is a private one focused on the merits of her dispute rather than on vindicating a larger public interest." Although Kescoli purports to represent others who believe the burial sites should receive maximum protection, the essence of her dispute is her disagreement with the Tribal leaders over what is in the best interests of the Navajo Nation and the Hopi Tribe. She believes additional protection for the burial sites is necessary. The Navajo Nation and the Hopi Tribe, however, by agreeing to the settlement have decided this protection is sufficient and the settlement agreement should be implemented so that they will receive the desired royalties. Kescoli's action is essentially private in nature, limited to a disagreement over the appropriate direction the Navajo Nation and the Hopi Tribe should take in relation to the mining.

Further, if the action proceeded in the absence of the Navajo Nation and the Hopi Tribe, the rights of their members under the lease agreements could be significantly affected.

The litigation also threatens the Navajo Nation's and the Hopi Tribe's sovereignty by attempting to disrupt their ability to govern themselves and to determine what is in their best interests in balancing potential harm caused by the mining operations against the benefits of the royalty payments. * * * [T]he present litigation is not limited to ensuring an agency's future compliance with statutory procedures and is not one in which the risk of prejudice to the Navajo Nation and the Hopi Tribe is nonexistent or minimal.

In view of the essentially private nature of the present litigation and the significant threat to the Navajo Nation's and the Hopi Tribe's interests, the application of the public rights exception is not appropriate.

AFFIRMED.

* * *

NOTES AND QUESTIONS

1. The need for compulsory joinder first arose in equity to address inefficiencies arising from litigation involving only some of the interested persons. *See, e.g., Provident Tradesmens Bank & Trust Co. v. Patterson*, 390 U.S. 102, 120 (1968) (describing history of compulsory joinder). The purpose of Rule 19 has not changed since that time: "Rule 19 is designed to protect the interests of absent parties, as well as those ordered before the court, from multiple litigation, inconsistent judicial determinations or the impairment of interests or rights." *CP Nat'l Corp. v. Bonneville Power Admin.*, 928 F.2d 905, 911 (9th Cir. 1991). Were those goals advanced in *Iron Workers*? In *Kescoli*?

2. Compulsory joinder under Rule 19(a)(1)(B)(i) is similar to Rule 23(b)(1)(B): both are designed to protect absentee parties. Likewise, compulsory joinder under Rule 19(a)(1)(B)(ii) is similar to Rule 23(b)(1)(A): both are designed to avoid subjecting defendants to incompatible standards of conduct. *See* Chapter 3(A) (discussing Rules 23(b)(1)(A) and 23(b)(1)(B)). In the MDL context, Rule 23 protections for absent class members apply whenever class actions are a part of the consolidation process. *See* Chapter 12. What about for non-class cases that are consolidated in an MDL? Are there any procedural safeguards to protect parties in individual cases, whose attorneys may not be playing a significant role in the MDL? Should there be?

3. Was *Iron Workers* correctly decided? Does the court explain under what circumstances, if any, joinder is necessary to prevent double recovery? Should the risk of double recovery or inconsistent obligations ever be a reason for finding a party to be necessary or indispensable? Should the answer depend on whether suits by absent entities have in fact already been filed elsewhere?

4. *Kescoli* holds that the question of whether a party is indispensable should generally be reviewed under an abuse of discretion standard. Is deference to the trial court warranted?

5. Courts consider the factual circumstances on a case-by-case basis when determining if a party is "necessary" and "indispensable." *See, e.g., SEC v. Bilzerian,* 378 F.3d 1100, 1107–08 (D.C. Cir. 2004) (because assignee merely stepped into shoes of assignor, assignee's presence was not needed for complete relief and assignee was not necessary); *Disabled Rights Action Comm. v. Las Vegas Events, Inc.,* 375 F.3d 861, 878–83 (9th Cir. 2004) (state university system was not necessary party where parties operating university-owned arena that was subject of lawsuit could provide meaningful relief); *Dixon v. Edwards,* 290 F.3d 699, 713–14 (4th Cir. 2002) (Diocese was not a necessary party where bishop sued priest to nullify a contract and regain control of church property, and complete relief could be achieved without Diocese, who consented to bishop's representing its interests); *Central Tools, Inc. v. Mitutoyo Corp.,* 381 F. Supp. 2d 71 (D.R.I. 2005) (patent owner who retained substantial rights in patent was necessary and indispensable party in dispute over patent validity and noninfringement between competitor and licensee).

6. Should the *Kescoli* court have been more cautious before upholding dismissal? What weight did the *Kescoli* appellate court give to each of the four indispensable-party factors?

7. The list of four factors in Rule 19(b) is neither exhaustive nor rigid. *See, e.g., Wichita & Affiliated Tribes of Okla. v. Hodel,* 788 F.2d 765, 774 (D.C. Cir. 1986). Courts use these factors and others to guide their analysis of what equity and good conscience require. Some courts have concluded that the fourth factor is the "perhaps the most important." *Sac and Fox Nation of Mo. v. Norton,* 240 F.3d 1250, 1260 (10th Cir. 2001) (stating that the "absence of an alternative forum * * * weigh[s] heavily, if not conclusively against dismissal").

8. The *Kescoli* court found that joinder was not feasible because the Navajo Nation and Hopi Tribe had sovereign immunity from suit. Several commentators have addressed this issue. *See, e.g.,* Matthew L. M. Fletcher, *The Comparative Rights of Indispensable Sovereigns,* 40 Gonz. L. Rev. 1 (2005); Note, *Compulsory Party Joinder and Tribal Sovereign Immunity: A Proposal to Modify Federal Courts' Application of Rule 19 to Cases Involving Absent Tribes As "Necessary" Parties,* 56 Okla. L. Rev. 931 (2003). Likewise, joinder is not feasible if the court lacks personal jurisdiction over a party sought to be joined, or lacks subject-matter jurisdiction over the claims brought by or against the party joined. *See, e.g.,* James W. Moore, *Moore's Federal Rules Pamphlet* §§ 19.4[c][2], 19.5 at 269–73 (2010).

9. The *Kescoli* court rejected the plaintiff's argument that the case fell within the "public rights" exception to joinder. Under that exception, even if the absentees are necessary parties, they are not deemed indispensable, and thus the case will not be dismissed. As one court explained:

> In public rights cases, what is at stake by definition are constitutional, national statutory or national administrative issues. Almost by the nature of the issues tendered by such litigation, the number of persons who will be affected as a practical matter is very large, and almost certainly a substantial number of those persons cannot be served in one district. To hold that such persons nevertheless must be joined or the case dismissed "would effectively preclude such litigation against the government." Rule 19 provides as a factor in considering the court's response to a joinder motion the issue of "whether the plaintiff will have an adequate remedy if the action is dismissed

> for nonjoinder." Clearly, the "public interest exception" is the effectuation of this provision.
>
> Yet another source, however, justifies the exception. The rules themselves provide that "[t]hey shall be construed to secure the just, speedy and inexpensive determination of every action." Fed. R. Civ. P. 1. Surely justice cannot be done if public interest litigation is precluded by virtue of the requirements of joinder. Inevitably, the joinder of the large number of persons who could potentially be affected by public interest litigation, even if possible, is not feasible and certainly is not inexpensive. In sum, then, the public interest exception is supported by both Rule 19 itself and Rule 1, and just makes good sense.

Sierra Club v. Watt, 608 F. Supp. 305, 324–25 (E.D. Cal. 1985); *see also Nat'l Licorice Co. v. NLRB*, 309 U.S. 350, 363 (1940). As the *Kescoli* court noted, the contours of the exception have not been well-defined. Did the district and appellate courts in *Kescoli* err in refusing to apply the public interest exception? Is the public interest exception reminiscent of any class action doctrine?

10. The old labels associated with compulsory joinder were "necessary" and "indispensable" parties. "Necessary" parties were "[p]ersons having an interest in the controversy, and who ought to be made parties, in order that the court may act on that rule which requires it to decide on, and finally determine the entire controversy, and do complete justice, by adjusting all the rights involved in it." *Shields v. Barrow*, 58 U.S. (17 How.) 130, 139 (1854), *quoted in Provident Tradesmens Bank & Trust Co. v. Patterson*, 390 U.S. 102, 124 (1968). "Indispensable" parties were "persons who not only have an interest in the controversy, but an interest of such a nature that a final decree cannot be made without either affecting that interest, or leaving the controversy in such a condition that its final termination may be wholly inconsistent with equity and good conscience." *Shields*, 58 U.S. at 139 (*quoted in Provident*, 390 U.S. at 124). Is the terminology used in the current Rule 19 clearer than the "necessary" and "indispensable" party labels? Note that even today, the terms "necessary" and "indispensable" parties are regularly used for the sake of simplicity, as the authors have done in this text.

11. Although the issue is normally raised by the parties, the absence of parties required by Rule 19 may be raised by a court *sua sponte*. Fed. R. Civ. P. 19, Advisory Committee Notes; *see also CP Nat'l Corp. v. Bonneville Power Admin.*, 928 F.2d 905, 911 (9th Cir. 1991). Should courts be allowed to raise the issue if the parties do not object? Or should it be entirely up to the parties to raise any potential Rule 19 issues?

12. In cases in which the plaintiff sues to have a statute, rule, or procedure changed, "complete relief" may require that the court join the party with power to make the change. For example, in *Cunningham v. Municipality of Metro. Seattle*, 751 F. Supp. 885, 896 (W.D. Wash. 1990), the court found that the method for selecting members of the Municipality of Metropolitan Seattle violated the "one person, one vote" rule. Because the method could be changed only by an act of the state legislature, complete relief could not be provided without joining the state as a necessary party. Similarly, in *CP National, supra*, 928 F.2d at 911–12, the Bonneville Power Administration (BPA) denied CP National's application for an increase in its average system cost rate for provision of electric power. CP National then sought review of this rate determination before the Federal Energy Regulatory Commission (FERC), which affirmed. On appeal directly to the Ninth Circuit, that court joined the BPA as

a necessary party because the BPA, not FERC, actually made rate determinations, meaning that the plaintiffs would have to sue the BPA for relief regardless of the outcome of their suit against FERC. Thus, complete relief could not be provided without the presence of the BPA. Does this mean that a party challenging the constitutionality of a statute must attempt to join the legislative body that enacted the statute? *Cf. McFarland v. Folsom*, 854 F. Supp. 862, 876–78 (M.D. Ala. 1994) (joinder of legislature that passed statutes governing unlawful practice of law and establishing board of bar examiners, but which had no authority over admission to the bar, was not proper in suit against state supreme court challenging state's bar examination and admissions process). In the same vein, most courts have concluded that, in general, federal and state agencies administering federal environmental laws are not necessary parties in citizen enforcement suits. *Ass'n to Protect Hammersley, Eld, and Totten Inlets v. Taylor Res., Inc.*, 299 F.3d 1007, 1014 (9th Cir. 2002); *The Wilderness Soc'y v. Kane Cnty., Utah*, 581 F.3d 1198, 1218 (10th Cir. 2009).

13. The *Kescoli* court notes that courts should be "extra cautious" before dismissing a case for failure to join an indispensable party if no alternative forum exists. Why is such caution warranted? Is there anything a court can do short of dismissing the case? Possible approaches, such as modifying the nature of relief sought, are discussed in Jack H. Friedenthal, Mary K. Kane & Arthur R. Miller, *Civil Procedure* § 6.5, at 363 (4th ed. 2005). *See also DPR Constr., Inc. v. IKEA Prop., Inc.*, 2005 WL 1667778, at * 4 (E.D. Va. 2005) (although district court concluded that architect was necessary and indispensable party in contract dispute between construction company and corporation, court transferred rather than dismissed case); *Askew v. Sheriff of Cook Cnty., Ill.*, 568 F.3d 632, 635–36 (7th Cir. 2009) (vacating and remanding decision because district court did not apply necessary caution in dismissing parties).

14. In *Temple v. Synthes Corp.*, 498 U.S. 5 (1990), the Supreme Court addressed whether potential joint tortfeasors are indispensable parties under Rule 19(b). Temple underwent surgery to have a plate and screw device implanted in his spine. After the device's screws broke off in his back, he sued Synthes, the manufacturer, in federal court. Separately, in state court, he sued the doctor who performed the surgery and the hospital in which the surgery was performed. Synthes moved to dismiss the federal suit for failure to join necessary parties. The district court ordered Temple to join the doctor and hospital, and when he refused, the court dismissed the case. The court of appeals affirmed, finding that the district court did not abuse its discretion. The Supreme Court summarily reversed, holding that "[i]t has long been the rule that it is not necessary for all joint tortfeasors to be named as defendants in a single lawsuit." *Id.* at 7. What arguments can be made that Temple should have sued all of the defendants in one proceeding?

15. For an interesting Rule 19 case involving a contention that the state of New York was a necessary party, *see, e.g., Am. Trucking Ass'n, Inc. v. N.Y. State Thruway Authority*, 795 F.3d 351, 354, 356, 359–60 (2d Cir. 2015) (concluding that, in a suit challenging the New York Thruway Authority's tolls as excessive, the state was not a necessary party and could protect its interests without joining the suit; the Thruway was an autonomous public benefit corporation and not an arm of the state).

b. **Compulsory Joinder in Class Actions**

SHIMKUS V. GERSTEN CO.[†]
United States Court of Appeals, Ninth Circuit, 1987.
816 F.2d 1318.

Before WRIGHT, SNEED, and KOZINSKI, CIRCUIT JUDGES.

WRIGHT, SENIOR CIRCUIT JUDGE.

This is an action to remedy housing discrimination under Title VIII of the Civil Rights Act of 1968. 42 U.S.C. § 3601 et seq. (1982). The Act prohibits, *inter alia*, discrimination against any person on the basis of race, color, religion, sex, or national origin in the rental of housing.

In this appeal we are confronted with a consent decree entered for private litigants that conflicts with a consent order previously entered for the government. Both judgments were intended to remedy the discrimination.

The question is whether the district court, in entering the private consent decree, erred in ignoring the rights of non-black minorities under Title VIII and, if so, what the proper remedy should be. We hold that these rights were ignored. The court should join the non-black minorities as additional parties and modify the consent decree to provide for their interests.

FACTS

In April 1983, Robert Shimkus filed a class action against the Gersten Companies, a property management business, claiming that Gersten violated, *inter alia*, Title VIII * * * by discriminating against blacks in selecting tenants at six of its apartment complexes. A week later, the United States also filed a discrimination suit against Gersten. The two cases were assigned to the same judge but were not consolidated.

The *Shimkus* class was composed only of blacks and did not include other minorities. The government did represent the interests of all minorities, black and non-black [including East Indians, Afghans, Iranians, Indians, Pakistanis, Hispanics, and Asians.]

In January 1984, the court entered a consent order between the government and Gersten. It enjoins Gersten from discriminating against any person on the basis of race, color, or national origin. It also identifies about 100 minority housing applicants who will receive priority status for the next available apartment units. Finally, it requires Gersten to (1) teach its employees their duties under the Federal Housing Act and the order; (2) publicize its non-discrimination policy in its advertising and on stationery, forms, and pamphlets; (3) advertise its apartment vacancies in newspapers circulated in the local black community; and (4) notify certain fair housing authorities of its non-discrimination policy. The *Shimkus* plaintiffs were not parties to the order.

That order remained in effect without modification for 18 months and met with the approval of all parties.

[†] For purposes of clarity, we have conformed the citations in this opinion to the 2007 version of Rule 19. [Ed.]

In February 1985, the *Shimkus* plaintiffs and Gersten submitted a consent decree in the other case for court approval (the *Shimkus* Decree). The government, upon receiving notice of the proposed Decree, successfully moved to intervene and objected to some provisions. The district court rejected these contentions, approved the *Shimkus* Decree, and entered it as a final judgment on July 23, 1985.

The Decree enjoins six Gersten apartment complexes from discriminating against any black applicant on the basis of race and requires those developments to give black applicants preferential consideration for available apartments according to an affirmative action plan. The plan requires each development to achieve a percentage of black residency that reflects the percentage of black applicants.

Specifically, the plan requires Gersten to fill vacant apartment units with qualified black applicants at a rate equal to the percentage of blacks in the applicant pool, and to augment this rate by the lesser of (1) 15% of the total applicant pool, or (2) the percentage of black applicants. If, at one development, the percentage of black residents drops below the percentage of black applicants for a six-month period (where not excused for any of the three reasons listed below), that development will be required to increase correspondingly the number of black residents in the next six-month period.

This affirmative action plan is to last a maximum of four and a half years. It will be suspended if, at the end of any six-month period, the percentage of black tenants in a targeted development equals the percentage of blacks in that complex's applicant pool. If these ratios are maintained for a full year, the *Shimkus* Decree will be terminated for that complex. If the ratios are not maintained, the Decree will be reinstated.

These black residency requirements are not absolute. Notwithstanding the level of black residency at a targeted development, Gersten will be deemed in compliance with the Decree if (1) Gersten extends *bona fide* offers to the requisite number of black applicants; (2) there is a shortage of qualified black applicants; or (3) the numbers of black applicants relative to available apartment units, or the requirements of federal housing subsidies, make it impossible to achieve the Decree's objectives.

The *Shimkus* Decree states explicitly that it supersedes the government order to the extent they conflict.

* * *

DISCUSSION

The government argues that the *Shimkus* Decree is improper because it conflicts with and, in effect, modifies the government order. The conflict lies in the Decree's affirmative action housing plan. It essentially requires Gersten to grant any available apartment units to qualified blacks until the targets are reached. But it does not impose upon Gersten similar requirements as to non-black minorities. Therefore, the government contends, the plan grants plaintiffs preferential relief at the expense of non-black minorities and others covered by the government order. Black applicants may displace non-black minorities who were also discriminated against by Gersten, if necessary to meet the plan's black residency targets. The government order, by contrast, provides relief for *all* minorities.

Because the *Shimkus* Decree supersedes the government order to the extent they conflict, the government order is effectively modified. This modification, says the government, is unnecessary and improper.

We disagree that it is improper. When the government brings a discrimination action against a party resulting in a consent order, private parties, not in privity with the order, are not bound by its terms and may bring their own suit against the defendant.

We agree, however, that the affirmative action plan *does* work an inequity upon the minorities not included in the *Shimkus* class and, hence, not protected by the Decree. The Decree, by providing relief in the form of objective residency requirements, and limiting that relief to blacks, effectively imposes an additional burden on non-black minorities. Those persons who qualified for units in one of the targeted apartment developments will lose them to qualified blacks until that development has satisfied the requirements of the plan, even though that development previously discriminated against *both* minority groups.

We find persuasive the reasoning applied in *Williams v. City of New Orleans*, 729 F.2d 1554 (5th Cir. 1984) (*en banc*). *Williams* was a Title VII action involving a consent decree providing relief for blacks in the form of an affirmative action quota. After considering the interests of all affected parties, the appeals court affirmed the district court's rejection of the affirmative action quota in part because it would impose undue hardship upon non-black minorities.

The quota in *Williams* required the New Orleans Police Department to promote black and white officers "on a one-to-one ratio until blacks constituted 50% of the NOPD. . . ." By requiring the NOPD to allot a specified percentage of its promotions to blacks, "the quota would create separate promotional tracks," and require non-black minorities to compete for fewer positions.

This is precisely our concern here. Although the *Shimkus* Decree's affirmative action plan is far less rigid than the quota used in *Williams*, the plan allots a specified percentage of vacant units to qualified blacks. The non-black minorities not only lose these units to blacks, but they must also compete with whites for the reduced number of vacancies.

In *Williams*, the non-black minorities intervened and represented their interests as parties. Here, the non-black minorities did not intervene. Their interests were represented, at best, indirectly by the government. The question then is not whether the affirmative action plan is valid, but is rather whether the non-black minorities should have been joined as necessary parties under Federal Rule of Civil Procedure 19(a).

We recognize that Rule 19(d) provides an "exception" for class actions. It states that Rule 19 is "subject to the provisions of Rule 23." Some courts have held that this language precludes the use of Rule 19 in class action proceedings.

We hold that Rule 19(d) simply requires us to respect the language of Rule 23, but allows joinder to the extent its use does not conflict with Rule

23's *provisions*. The *Shimkus* class was properly certified, although it would have been more economical if the class had included non-black minorities. The joinder that we consider is one of classes, rather than individuals. This minimizes the number of named parties before the court and preserves the usefulness of the class action device.

It is the peculiar circumstances of this case that move us to take this unusual step. Here, we find consideration of joinder appropriate because (1) not just blacks, but numerous classes of minorities, have suffered housing discrimination by Gersten; (2) the relief obtained by blacks will affect adversely the interests of non-black minorities who likewise suffer discrimination; and (3) these non-black minorities were not directly represented in the action.

* * *

A Court of Appeals may invoke Rule 19 *sua sponte* * * *.

Under Rule [19(a)(1)(B)(i)], these non-black minorities clearly have an interest relating to the subject of this action: remedying housing discrimination in Gersten apartments. The disposition of this action without their joinder clearly impairs *and* impedes their ability to protect that interest. The *Shimkus* Decree not only imposes an unfair burden on those minority persons but would require them to bring another federal action seeking [a] consent decree to avoid those burdens. This is not as simple as *Shimkus* seems to assert. The *Shimkus* plaintiffs would likely oppose an order that would provide equal relief to all discriminatees because it would deprive them of their advantage relative to other minorities. It would be ironic if a decree to remedy discrimination effectively pitted one minority group against another.

Rule [19(a)(1)(B)(ii)] also favors joinder of the non-black minorities. Without their joinder, Gersten is clearly "subject to a substantial risk of incurring double, multiple, or inconsistent obligations." Gersten would have to defend each subsequent minority class action. Each additional consent decree would increase Gersten's obligations to provide apartment units to minority applicants. Inconsistencies between decrees may well arise as they already have.

Although not a factor specified in Rule 19(a), judicial economy favors joining the non-black minorities. The *Shimkus* plaintiffs urged at oral argument that other minorities, including Hispanics, Koreans, Vietnamese and other Asians should each be required to bring an independent action against Gersten. If that were to happen, the court would be burdened, Gersten would have to defend multiple suits, and separate decrees would invite controversies between the several groups of minorities. We find this proposition somewhat outrageous.

The court in *Williams* said as much: "The purpose behind examining a proposed consent decree's effect on third parties is to protect the rights of those parties as well as to eliminate the need for subsequent lawsuits."

The Fifth Circuit's recognition [in *Williams*] of the need to consider the interests of all parties affected by an affirmative action plan, and of doing so in the same litigation, favors our decision here to require joinder.

CONCLUSION

The court abused its discretion in issuing the *Shimkus* Decree without joining as necessary parties the non-black minorities against whom Gersten discriminated. We remand that the court may determine which non-black minority classes suffered Gersten's discrimination and should be joined. The *Shimkus* Decree should be modified to provide relief to all identifiable discriminatee classes commensurate with the injury borne by each class.

NOTES AND QUESTIONS

1. What is the meaning of Rule 19(d)'s "exception of" class actions? Did the *Shimkus* court interpret that exception correctly? More generally, were the "non-black minorities" in fact necessary parties who should have been joined? For a discussion of the relationship between Rules 19 and 23, see Comment, *Compulsory Joinder of Classes Under Rule 19*, 58 U. Chi. L. Rev. 1453, 1455 (1991) (arguing that "joinder of necessary classes would facilitate protection of third parties and efficient and equitable resolution of disputes," especially in situations where defendant may be exposed to inconsistent obligations or standards of conduct).

2. Rule 19(d) states that it is subject to the provisions of Rule 23, but does not mention Rule 23.1 and Rule 23.2, governing derivative actions by shareholders and actions relating to unincorporated associations, respectively. Commentators have concluded that similar reasons exist for not imposing joinder requirements on derivative actions and actions relating to unincorporated associations, and therefore, Rule 19(d) should extend to Rules 23.1 and 23.2. See Charles A. Wright, Arthur R. Miller & Mary K. Kane, 7 *Federal Practice and Procedure* § 1626, at 388 (3d ed. 2005) (characterizing exclusion of Rules 23.1 and 23.2 as a drafting "oversight").

3. Should the *Shimkus* court have raised the joinder issue *sua sponte*? Or should the other minorities have been required to intervene under Rule 24 (*see* Part A(5) of this chapter) if they had wanted to protect their interests, as the "non-black minorities" did in *Williams*?

4. For a related case discussing compulsory joinder and intervention, see *Martin v. Wilks*, 490 U.S. 755 (1989) (set forth later in this chapter).

5. If an individual is a necessary party under Rule 19(a)(1)(B)(i) does that person have a right to intervene under Rule 24(a)(2)? The Third Circuit considered this question in *Liberty Mutual Insurance Co. v. Treesdale, Inc.*, 419 F.3d 216 (3d Cir. 2005):

> Appellants argue that they are necessary parties under Fed. R. Civ. P. 19(a) [now 19(a)(1)(B)(i)] and are therefore entitled to intervene as of right under Fed. R. Civ. P. 24(a)(2). Admittedly, the advisory committee's notes to the 1996 amendments to Rule 24 state that if a person should be joined under Rule 19, he/she should also be entitled to intervene under Rule 24. The note explains:
>
>> Intervention of right is here seen to be a kind of counterpoint to Rule 19(a)[(1)(B)(i)] on joinder of persons needed for a just adjudication: where, upon motion of a party in an action, an absentee should be joined so that he may protect his interest which as a

practical matter may be substantially impaired by the disposition of the action, he ought to have a right to intervene in the action on his own motion.

There is, however, a difference between Rule 19 and Rule 24. Although both Rules speak of the applicant's ability to protect an interest, Rule 24 contains an additional element, *i.e.*, the adequacy of representation. Rule 24(a)(2) [then provided]: "Upon timely application anyone shall be permitted to intervene in an action . . . when . . . the applicant is so situated that the disposition of the action may as a practical matter impair or impede the applicant's ability to protect that interest, *unless the applicant's interest is adequately represented by existing parties.*" (Emphasis added by Third Circuit). Rule 19 does not invite inquiry into the adequacy of representation. It is therefore illogical to conclude that a party who meets the joinder requirements of Rule 19(a)[(1)(B)(i)] automatically qualifies to intervene as of right under Rule 24(a)(2). That interpretation would read the "adequacy of representation" requirement out of Rule 24(a)(2) by creating a backdoor into the litigation though the less restrictive inquiry of Rule 19(a)[(1)(B)(i)].

419 F.3d at 230. Which approach is correct: that of the Advisory Committee or that of the Third Circuit?

6. On the broader issue of compulsory joinder as an aggregation device, the American Law Institute (ALI) has noted that compulsory joinder has only limited value:

Courts frequently conclude that although the absentees should be joined to adjudicate the dispute completely, if their joinder is impossible, the suit may proceed without them. * * * For this reason, in cases in which potential plaintiffs or defendants are dispersed widely and do not want to combine their actions, the operation of Rule 19 often does not result in consolidation.

American Law Institute, *Complex Litigation: Statutory Recommendations and Analysis* 25 (1994).

3. IMPLEADER

Impleader is a device that allows existing parties to a case to bring in a third party who may be liable for all or some of the damages. Like class actions and MDL, impleader is designed to promote efficiency by facilitating the resolution of multiple parties' claims before one judge. Indeed, the two devices often work in conjunction: defendants in class actions sometimes bring in third parties who may be liable in whole or part to the defendants for all or part of the class claims against the defendants. The following materials address some of the key issues that have arisen under Rule 14.

FED. R. CIV. P. 14: THIRD-PARTY PRACTICE

(a) When a Defending Party May Bring in a Third Party.

(1) Timing of the Summons and Complaint. A defending party may, as third-party plaintiff, serve a summons and complaint on a nonparty who is or may be liable to it for all or part of the claim against it. But the third-party plaintiff must, by motion, obtain the court's leave if it files the third-party complaint more than 14 days after serving its original answer.

(2) Third-Party Defendant's Claims and Defenses. The person served with the summons and third-party complaint—the "third-party defendant":

(A) must assert any defense against the third-party plaintiff's claim under Rule 12;

(B) must assert any counterclaim against the third-party plaintiff under Rule 13(a), and may assert any counterclaim against the third-party plaintiff under Rule 13(b) or any crossclaim against another third-party defendant under Rule 13(g);

(C) may assert against the plaintiff any defense that the third-party plaintiff has to the plaintiff's claim; and

(D) may also assert against the plaintiff any claim arising out of the transaction or occurrence that is the subject matter of the plaintiff's claims against the third-party plaintiff.

(3) Plaintiff's Claims Against a Third-Party Defendant. The plaintiff may assert against the third-party defendant any claim arising out of the transaction or occurrence that is the subject matter of the plaintiff's claim against the third-party plaintiff. The third-party defendant must then assert any defense under Rule 12 and any counterclaim under Rule 13(a), and may assert any counterclaim under Rule 13(b) or any crossclaim under Rule 13(g).

(4) Motion to Strike, Sever, or Try Separately. Any party may move to strike the third-party claim, to sever it, or to try it separately.

(5) Third-Party Defendant's Claim Against a Nonparty. A third-party defendant may proceed under this rule against a nonparty who is or may be liable to the third-party defendant for all or part of any claim against it.

* * *

(b) When a Plaintiff May Bring in a Third Party. When a claim is asserted against a plaintiff, the plaintiff may bring in a third party if this rule would allow a defendant to do so.

* * *

One commentator has succinctly described the purpose of Rule 14 as follows:

When A sues B, there is often a third party, C, who may ultimately be liable to B for all or some part of the damages which A might recover. This liability over [*i.e.*, conditional or derivative liability] may be based on such legal relationships as those which arise from a contract of indemnity for loss or liability or a right to contribution from a joint tortfeasor. If it were necessary for B to institute a separate action to recover reimbursement from C, the issue of B's liability to A would often have to be relitigated between B and C, since C, not a party to the original litigation, would generally not be bound by the prior determination. Even if B could obtain a wholly consistent result against C, the courts would have been burdened by two trials and B might have been seriously handicapped by having to satisfy A's judgment long before his recovery over from C. To avoid this situation in the federal courts, rule 14(a) provides for impleader. * * *

Note, *Developments in the Law: Multiparty Litigation in the Federal Courts*, 71 Harv. L. Rev. 874, 906 (1958). Two other authors have summarized the main contexts in which impleader typically arises:

> The heart of impleader is the requirement that the claim supporting it be based on secondary or derivative liability. That is, the third-party plaintiff must seek reimbursement from the third-party defendant for all or part of the former's liability to plaintiff. It is not enough that the impleader claim arose out of the same transaction or occurrence as the original plaintiff's claim; the impleader must, in addition, be contingent or derivative.
>
> While the third-party plaintiff's liability is established by a judgment for plaintiff against the third-party plaintiff, the existence of the contingent or derivative liability is a separate question. The answer to it is not supplied by Rule 14, which merely provides the procedure by which such a duty is asserted as an impleader claim. Instead, the answer must be found in the applicable substantive law. Four common theories of contingent or derivative liability are indemnity, subrogation, contribution and warranty. Their precise elements vary somewhat from jurisdiction to jurisdiction.
>
> A right to *indemnification* either arises out of an express contractual provision whereby one party agrees to indemnify (or "hold harmless") another for certain liabilities, or by implication. A right to indemnification will be implied when a person without fault is held legally liable for damages caused by the fault of another.
>
> *Subrogation* is the succession of one person to the rights of another. "Subrogees are generally joint tortfeasors or innocent insurers who have compensated the insured for an injury resulting from the negligence of a third-party." An insurer sued by its insured on an insurance policy may therefore implead the negligent third party on a subrogation theory to the extent that the insurer is or may be liable to its insured on the policy.
>
> The right of *contribution* typically arises among joint tortfeasors, two or more persons who are jointly or severally liable in tort for the same injury.

Finally, a *warranty*, in the impleader context, is an express or implied statement or representation typically made by a seller to a buyer or others in the chain of product distribution regarding the character of or title to the product.

Gene R. Shreve & Peter Raven–Hansen, *Understanding Civil Procedure* § 9.06, at 297–98 (4th ed. 2009).

TIESLER V. MARTIN PAINT STORES, INC.
United States District Court, Eastern District of Pennsylvania, 1977.
76 F.R.D. 640.

MCGLYNN, DISTRICT JUDGE.

This is an action for personal injuries resulting from an explosion of a can of denatured alcohol which showered the minor plaintiff with burning liquid. Plaintiff seeks damages from Martin Paint Stores (Martin) for allegedly failing to comply with the rules and orders of the Consumer Product Safety Commission (CPSC) in labeling and packaging the alcohol, which failure proximately caused the minor plaintiff's injuries. In addition plaintiffs allege Martin's breach of implied warranty, negligence and liability under § 402A, Restatement of Torts.

* * * Subsequently the defendant Martin, pursuant to Rule 14 of the Federal Rules of Civil Procedure, impleaded [minor] Joseph Keller as a third-party defendant claiming that his negligent use of the product was the proximate cause of the plaintiff's injuries.

Presently before the court is a motion to dismiss the third-party complaint because it is not related to the allegations against the original defendants and is based on ordinary negligence principles. * * * For the reasons set forth below, the court finds that the third-party defendant, Joseph Keller, was properly joined as a party to this action and thus the motion to dismiss the third-party complaint is denied. * * *

Whether Joseph Keller may be impleaded is controlled by the language of Federal Rule of Civil Procedure 14(a) which provides that a defendant may implead a person not a party to the action "who is or may be liable to [it] for all or part of the [claim against it]." The use of the word "claim" in Rule 14 avoids the narrow concepts of "cause of action" and instead employs the idea of the claim as a group of operative facts giving occasion for judicial action. The purpose of Rule 14 is to effectively dispose of the entire related litigation in the suit which is properly before the court and, for jurisdictional purposes, such a claim is ancillary to the main action so the inclusion of a third-party claim is justified though it does not of itself meet the diversity test or raise a federal question.

In seeking to have the third-party complaint dismissed, the movant relies on the rule that an entirely separate and independent claim cannot be maintained against a third party under Rule 14, even though it does arise out of the same general set of facts as the main claim. Impleader is proper and the claim not separate or independent if the third party's liability is in some way derivative of the outcome of the main claim in that the defendant seeks to hold the third party secondarily liable to him or to pass on to the third party all or part of the liability asserted against the defendant. It is immaterial that the liability of the third party is not identical to or rests on a different theory than that underlying plaintiff's claim.

Thus, it is not permissible to bring in a person as a third-party defendant simply because he is or may be liable to the plaintiff. Third party practice is permitted only where the defendant can show that if he is found liable to plaintiff, the third party will be liable to him. However, the Rule is not limited to situations in which the third-party defendant would automatically be liable for all or part of plaintiff's claim. Rather, the complaint should be allowed to stand, even if recovery is not certain, if under some construction of facts which might be adduced at trial, recovery would be possible.

The Rule creates no substantive rights and does not enlarge, abridge or modify the substantive rights of any litigant. But the impleader rule does require that the defendant have a substantive basis for his claim against the third party. The defendant in the present case claims that the third party is a joint tortfeasor and is jointly or severally liable in tort for the same accident and injury to the plaintiff. The right of contribution among joint tortfeasors is one of substantive law and since the parties to the action are residents of Pennsylvania and the accident occurred here, it is Pennsylvania law which governs. The Pennsylvania Statute provides for contribution among joint tortfeasors, and it may well be that as the facts are developed, the case in so far as it involves general tort and negligence principles, would be one for contribution under the statute. Martin may substantively claim that if it is found to have been negligent, the third-party defendant, Joseph Keller, is or may be found to be liable to him. Therefore, the motion to dismiss the third-party complaint is denied.

* * *

NOTES AND QUESTIONS

1. *Tiesler* sets forth the principle that impleader is appropriate only if the third party's liability is dependent upon the outcome of the suit by the plaintiff against the defendant. Courts use various approaches to determine whether the third-party claim depends sufficiently on the outcome of the original claim. For example, some courts look at the similarity between the duties owed to the plaintiff and the duties owed to the third-party plaintiff. *See, e.g., Foulke v. Dugan,* 212 F.R.D. 265, 270–71 (E.D. Pa. 2002) (defendant's third-party complaint asserting right to contribution improperly impleaded third-party defendant where they were not joint tortfeasors, but instead alleged "separate and distinct causes of action committed by different persons, owing different duties to the plaintiff, at clearly severable times"); *William S. v. Gill,* 536 F. Supp. 505, 514 (N.D. Ill. 1982) (school officials who were sued for failure to provide services to handicapped children were permitted to implead state agencies who were contractually obliged to provide those services in state schools).

Other courts consider whether the events at issue in the original claim are sufficiently linked with the events underlying the third-party claim. *See, e.g., Mattes v. ABC Plastics, Inc.,* 323 F.3d 695, 698–99 (8th Cir. 2003) (impleader not proper where plaintiff's claim was based on default under real estate lease and third-party claim failed to put forth coherent legal theory of how guarantor of loan could be liable under indemnity theory); *Klotz v. Superior Elect. Prods. Corp.*, 498 F. Supp. 1099, 1100–01 (E.D. Pa. 1980) (plaintiff alleged that she had contracted trichinosis from pork sausage that did not cook properly on electric cooker manufactured by defendant; defendant not allowed to implead Wilkes College based on theory that plaintiff had contracted trichinosis after eating pork sausage one day earlier at Wilkes College cafeteria).

Still other courts consider the similarity in the evidence required to prove the original and the third-party claims. *See, e.g., Marseilles Hydro Power, LLC v. Marseilles Land & Water Co.*, 299 F.3d 643 (7th Cir. 2002) (district court erred in prohibiting defendant canal company from filing third-party complaint against plaintiff power company, which may have contributed to collapse of canal wall, where plaintiff power company originally sued canal company for breaching its contractual duty to repair canal wall); *Robbins v. Yamaha Motor Corp.*, 98 F.R.D. 36, 38 (M.D. Pa.1983) (in motorcycle driver's action for damages from collision with car, defendant car manufacturer not permitted to implead automobile driver, because claim against manufacturer, which concerned crashworthiness, necessitated different proof from claim against driver, which concerned negligence).

Which approach is most consistent with the text of Rule 14? With Rule 14's purposes? Should courts instead allow impleader as long as a claim arises out of the same general facts as the original action, even though the outcome of the impleader action does not depend on the outcome of the original action?

2. What efficiencies are achieved by Rule 14? *See, e.g., LASA Per L'Industria Del Marmo Societa Per Azioni v. Alexander*, 414 F.2d 143, 146 (6th Cir. 1969) (purpose of impleader is "to avoid circuity of action and to dispose of the entire subject matter arising from one set of facts in one action"). Does impleader achieve the efficiencies noted in *Alexander*? If so, should impleader be *mandatory* rather than *permissive* when the requirements of Rule 14 are met? Why did the drafters opt for a discretionary approach? In light of the permissive nature of impleader, what tactical considerations should come into play in the decision whether to implead?

3. Why does Rule 14 require leave of court to implead once 14 days after the service of an answer has passed? The Advisory Committee Notes to the 1963 Amendment to Rule 14 stated:

> In dispensing with leave of court for an impleader filed not later than 10 [now 14] days after serving the answer, but retaining the leave requirement for impleaders sought to be effected thereafter, the amended subdivision takes a moderate position on the lines urged by some commentators. Other commentators would dispense with the requirement of leave regardless of the time when impleader is effected, and would rely on subsequent action by the court to dismiss the impleader if it would unduly delay or complicate the litigation or could be otherwise objectionable.

Should leave be dispensed with regardless of when the impleader is filed? Should leave be required in all cases? What factors should a court apply in deciding whether to grant leave to implead? In *McCurdy v. Wedgewood Capital Mgmt. Co.*, 1999 WL 554590 (E.D. Pa. 1999), the court identified the following factors when determining whether to grant a motion for impleader:

(1) the timeliness of the motion;

(2) whether the filing of the third party complaint will introduce an unrelated controversy or will unduly complicate the case to the prejudice of the plaintiff;

(3) whether the third party complaint will avoid circuity of action and settle related matters in one law suit; and

(4) whether the evidence, witnesses, and legal issues will be substantially the same in the defendant's third party action and plaintiff's action.

Id. at *1. *See also, e.g., Delco Wire & Cable Co. v. Keystone Roofing Co.*, 80 F.R.D. 428, 430 (E.D. Pa. 1978) (factors include "excusability of defendant's delay in moving" and "potential prejudice to the plaintiff and also to the proposed third-party defendant").

4. Rule 14(a) states that a defendant may serve a summons and complaint upon a third party without leave of court within 14 days of serving its "original answer." This has led courts to ask what constitutes the "original answer" under Rule 14(a). Courts are divided. *United Nat'l Ins. Corp. v. Jefferson Downs Corp.*, 220 F.R.D. 456, 457–58 (M.D. La. 2003) (describing various approaches). Some courts contend that a literal approach should be used, *i.e.*, the answer to the original complaint should trigger the 14-day period. *See, e.g., Guarantee Co. of N. Am. v. Pinto*, 208 F.R.D. 470, 473 (D. Mass. 2002). Others take the opposite view, contending that the answer to the most recently amended complaint should govern. *See, e.g., Nelson v. Quimby Island Reclamation Dist. Facilities Corp.*, 491 F. Supp. 1364, 1387 (N.D. Cal. 1980). Still other courts take a middle approach, concluding that only those amended complaints that put forth new legal theories that trigger the need for impleader should restart the 14-day deadline. *See, e.g., United Nat'l Ins. Corp. v. Jefferson Downs Corp.*, 220 F.R.D. 456, 458 (M.D. La. 2003); *Reynolds v. Rick's Mushroom Serv., Inc.*, 2003 WL 22741335, at *3–4 (E.D. Pa. 2003). Which approach is the most defensible?

5. Originally, Rule 14 allowed impleader of individuals liable to the plaintiff as well as impleader of those liable to the defendant. *See* Fed. R. Civ. P. 14, Advisory Committee Notes to 1946 Amendment. Rule 14 was amended in 1946 to delete the former form of impleader. Nonetheless, courts have occasionally allowed impleader of third-party defendants to lessen the liability of the defendant to the plaintiff in cases in which several parties may have caused the plaintiff's injury. For instance, in *Robinson v. U–Haul Co.*, 785 F. Supp. 1378 (D. Alaska 1992), Robinson sued U–Haul for personal injuries sustained in an accident in which the tow dolly she had rented from U–Haul allegedly failed to operate properly. To determine U–Haul's liability, the district court applied Alaska's procedural rules and an Alaskan statute concerning apportionment of damages among joint tortfeasors. In so doing, the district court decided that to enable the trier of fact to accurately allocate fault to each party, U–Haul could implead any persons liable to the plaintiff whom plaintiff chose not to sue. Although U–Haul would not be entitled to recover from any third-party defendants joined in this manner, it would benefit from the joinder. *See id.* at 1380–81 n.4. In *Carriere v. Cominco Alaska, Inc.*, 823 F. Supp. 680, 691 (D. Alaska 1993), the district court criticized *Robinson* and denied the defendant's motion to file a third-party complaint against all entities or individuals that were potential concurrent tortfeasors:

[T]he undersigned is not persuaded that a benefit to the defendant/third-party plaintiff because of a broader spreading of fault under the procedures contemplated by * * * *Robinson* is the equivalent in any sense of the assertion of a claim by a third-party plaintiff against someone who "is or may be liable to [him] for all or part of the plaintiff's claim against the third-party plaintiff." * * * This court concludes that [*Robinson*] * * * takes inappropriate liberties with * * * Federal Civil Rule 14(a).

Which court's approach is more consistent with the text of Rule 14? With the policies underlying impleader?

6. When a defendant becomes a non-party by settling with the plaintiff, may a non-settling co-defendant implead the one that settled? *See generally* 3 Moore's Federal Practice, § 14.09 (Matthew Bender 3d ed. 2010) (recognizing possibility of a dismissed defendant being "impleaded by any remaining defendants"); *Bank of the W. v. Estate of Leo*, 231 F.R.D. 386 (D. Ariz. 2005) ("A non-settling defendant may bring a third-party complaint against a settling defendant."). By permitting impleader under these circumstances, is settlement discouraged?

7. In one case in which the defendant moved to implead a class of third-party defendants, the court denied impleader because of potential confusion. *See In re "Agent Orange" Prod. Liab. Litig.*, 544 F. Supp. 808, 811 (E.D.N.Y. 1982) (denying impleader of seven defendants who supplied defendant Uniroyal with component chemicals used to manufacture Agent Orange on ground that impleader would not save time and expense and might confuse already complex litigation). Should a court be permitted to reject an otherwise proper third-party complaint solely on the ground that it makes the litigation more complex?

8. Numerous cases hold that Rule 14 should be liberally construed in favor of impleader because the Rule is designed to reduce multiplicity of litigation. *See, e.g., Lehman v. Revolution Portfolio L.L.C.*, 166 F.3d 389, 395 (1st Cir. 1999); *FDIC v. Loube*, 134 F.R.D. 270, 272 (N.D. Cal. 1991); *but see, e.g., Hewlett–Packard Co. v. Intelco Med. Sys., Inc.*, 1991 WL 70883 (N.D. Ill. 1991) (applying strict construction). Is a liberal construction appropriate? Is there any argument in support of the proposition that Rule 14 should be strictly construed?

9. The party seeking to utilize impleader must establish that the court has subject matter jurisdiction over any claims against the third-party defendant. Nonetheless, "[i]t is well settled that supplemental jurisdiction exists over a properly brought third-party complaint." *Grimes v. Mazda N. Am. Operations*, 355 F.3d 566, 572 (6th Cir. 2004); *accord, e.g., King Fisher Marine Serv., Inc. v. 21st Phoenix Corp.*, 893 F.2d 1155, 1161 (10th Cir. 1990); 6 Charles A. Wright, Arthur R. Miller & Mary K. Kane, *Federal Practice and Procedure* § 1444, at 377 (3d ed. 2010) ("[T]he cases on point almost all hold that defendant's claim against a third-party defendant is within the ancillary jurisdiction of the federal courts."). Under 28 U.S.C. § 1367 (*see* Chapter 7(B)), supplemental jurisdiction is permitted over claims by *defendants* against impleaded third parties when the claims are "so related" to the original claims as to form part of the same case or controversy, *see* 28 U.S.C. § 1367(a), but supplemental jurisdiction is not permitted over claims by *plaintiffs* against impleaded third parties. *See* 28 U.S.C. § 1367(b); *see, e.g., Town of Gordon v. Great Am. Ins. Co.*, 331 F. Supp. 2d 1357, 1359–60 (M.D. Ala. 2004) (noting courts' uniformity on this issue). Under this language, if a defendant impleads a third party in a

diversity case, section 1367(a) allows supplemental jurisdiction over such a claim. By contrast, a plaintiff who attempts to assert a claim against the impleaded party cannot rely on supplemental jurisdiction. *See, e.g., Air Liquide Am., L.P. v. Process Serv. Corp.*, 2004 WL 325143, at *4 (E.D. La. 2004).

Similarly, if a defendant asserts a counterclaim against a plaintiff, and plaintiff attempts to implead a third party in connection with the counterclaim, section 1367(b) would appear to prohibit the invocation of supplemental jurisdiction. Although courts have generally applied the statute as written, some have questioned the fairness of the distinctions drawn by section 1367. *See, e.g., Chase Manhattan Bank v. Aldridge*, 906 F. Supp. 866 (S.D.N.Y. 1995); *cf. Exxon Mobil Corp. v. Allapattah Servs., Inc.*, 545 U.S. 546 (2005) (*see* Chapter 7(B)) (discussing supplemental jurisdiction under Rules 20 and 23).

10. Rule 14 permits claims beyond those brought by a third-party defendant. In fact, the courts have even considered fifth- and sixth-party claims. *See, e.g., Philippine Am. Life Ins. v. Raytheon Aircraft Co.*, 2003 WL 23484637 (D. Kan. 2003) (fourth- and fifth-party impleader claims were proper). Subsequent party claims work like third-party claims. *Bevemet Metals, Ltda. v. Gallie Corp.*, 3 F.R.D. 352 (S.D.N.Y. 1942) (fifth- and sixth-party claims permitted under Rule 14(a), but claims severed for purpose of trial). *See* 6 Charles A. Wright, Arthur R. Miller & Mary K. Kane, *Federal Practice and Procedure* § 1461 (3d ed. 2010).

11. Under Rule 14, once the defendant (*i.e.*, third-party plaintiff) has properly impleaded a third-party defendant, the third-party plaintiff may raise any other claims it has against the third-party defendant, subject to the rule on joinder of claims, Fed. R. Civ. P. 18(a). *See, e.g., Schwab v. Erie Lackawanna R.R. Co.*, 438 F.2d 62 (3d Cir. 1971). Thus, the defendant/third-party plaintiff may implead the third-party defendant for damages that are greater than those claimed by the plaintiff against the defendant/third-party plaintiff, when the claim for additional damages by the defendant/third-party plaintiff arises out of the same transaction or occurrence as the original claim. *See id.* at 68–71. For an analysis of the *Schwab* approach and other alternatives, *see King Fisher Marine Serv., Inc. v. Phoenix Corp.*, 893 F.2d 1155, 1166–72 (10th Cir. 1990) (surveying various approaches and adopting *Schwab*).

12. One limitation on impleader is that it "is not suitable when the defendant believes that someone other than himself is responsible for the breach of legal duty giving rise to plaintiff's claim." Jack H. Friedenthal, Mary K. Kane & Arthur R. Miller, *Civil Procedure* § 6.9, at 382 (4th ed. 2005). Thus, "[w]hen a third party's conduct furnishes a complete defense against the defendant's liability, the defendant may raise that conduct defensively in the answer but may not use it as a foundation for impleader." *Id.* at 382–83. Is this limitation sensible? Or should impleader be allowed in such circumstances?

13. Under Rule 14(a), the third-party defendant may assert any defenses that it has against the third-party plaintiff. For example, the third-party defendant may make a Fed. R. Civ. P. 12(b)(6) motion if the third-party complaint fails to state a claim upon which the third-party defendant could be liable to the third-party plaintiff. The third-party defendant may also assert against the original plaintiff most of the defenses that the third-party plaintiff (the original defendant) has against the original plaintiff. For example, if the statute of limitations has run on the plaintiff's claim against the original defendant, the third-party could raise the limitations period as a defense, even if the original

defendant failed to do so. 6 Charles A. Wright, Arthur R. Miller & Mary K. Kane, *Federal Practice and Procedure* § 1457, at 517–19 (3d ed. 2010). The third-party defendant, however, may not raise the original defendant's *personal* defenses, such as lack of personal jurisdiction over the original defendant, lack of venue over the original action, or improper service of process. *Id.*; *see also id.* § 1457 at 518 n.12. Why are third-party defendants allowed to raise some defenses and not others?

14. Various limitations hamper the use of Rule 14 as a device for party aggregation. Most importantly, impleader must satisfy the requirements of Rule 14, such as showing that the third-party claim is dependent on the outcome of the suit by the plaintiff against the original defendant. In addition, there must also be sufficiency of process, personal jurisdiction over the third-party defendant, and subject matter jurisdiction over the third-party claim (although, as noted above, supplemental jurisdiction is sometimes available). Moreover, impleader is discretionary, not mandatory. Significantly, the 1994 ALI *Complex Litigation* project, which discusses various aggregation devices, does not even address impleader in that discussion. *See generally* American Law Institute, *Complex Litigation: Statutory Recommendations and Analysis* (1994). Is impleader an important device for party aggregation?

4. INTERPLEADER

Interpleader is an equitable device that enables a party facing multiple (and possibly conflicting) claims regarding a fund or *res* to resolve these disputes in a single pleading. As revealed below, interpleader shares many characteristics of a limited fund class action. There are two types of federal interpleader: Rule 22 interpleader and statutory interpleader. Both are considered in the following materials.

FED. R. CIV. P. 22: INTERPLEADER

(a) Grounds.

> **(1) By a Plaintiff.** Persons with claims that may expose a plaintiff to double or multiple liability may be joined as defendants and required to interplead. Joinder for interpleader is proper even though:
>
>> (A) the claims of the several claimants, or the titles on which their claims depend, lack a common origin or are adverse and independent rather than identical; or
>>
>> (B) the plaintiff denies liability in whole or in part to any or all of the claimants.
>
> **(2) By a Defendant.** A defendant exposed to similar liability may seek interpleader through a cross claim or counterclaim.

(b) Relation to Other Rules and Statutes. This rule supplements—and does not limit—the joinder of parties allowed by Rule 20. The remedy this rule provides is in addition to—and does not supersede or limit—the remedy provided by 28 U.S.C. §§ 1335 [statutory interpleader], 1397 [addressing venue in statutory interpleader or actions in the nature of interpleader], and 2361 [addressing service of process in statutory interpleader and actions in the nature of interpleader].

FEDERAL INTERPLEADER ACT
28 U.S.C. § 1335.

(a) The district courts shall have original jurisdiction of any civil action of interpleader or in the nature of interpleader filed by any person, firm, or corporation, association, or society having in his or its custody or possession money or property of the value of $500 or more, or having issued a note, bond, certificate, policy of insurance or other instrument of value or amount of $500 or more, or providing for the delivery or payment or the loan of money or property of such amount or value, or being under any obligation written or unwritten to the amount of $500 or more, if

(1) Two or more adverse claimants, of diverse citizenship as defined in subsection (a) or (d) of section 1332 of this title, are claiming or may claim to be entitled to such money or property, or to any one or more of the benefits arising by virtue of any note, bond, certificate, policy or other instrument, or arising by virtue of any such obligation; and if

(2) The plaintiff has deposited such money or property or has paid the amount of the loan or other value of such instrument or the amount due under such obligation into the registry of the court, there to abide the judgment of the court, or has given bond payable to the clerk of the court in such amount and with such surety as the court or judge may deem proper, conditioned upon the compliance by the plaintiff with the future order or judgment of the court with respect to the subject matter of the controversy.

(b) Such an action may be entertained although the titles or claims of the conflicting claimants do not have a common origin, or are not identical, but are adverse to and independent of one another.

STATE FARM FIRE & CASUALTY CO. v. TASHIRE
Supreme Court of the United States, 1967.
386 U.S. 523.

JUSTICE FORTAS delivered the opinion of the Court.

Early one September morning in 1964, a Greyhound bus proceeding northward through Shasta County, California, collided with a south-bound pickup truck. Two of the passengers aboard the bus were killed. Thirty-three others were injured, as were the bus driver, the driver of the truck and its lone passenger. One of the dead and 10 of the injured passengers were Canadians; the rest of the individuals involved were citizens of five American States. The ensuing litigation led to the present case, which raises important questions concerning administration of the interpleader remedy in the federal courts.

The litigation began when four of the injured passengers filed suit in California state courts, seeking damages in excess of $1,000,000. Named as defendants were Greyhound Lines, Inc., a California corporation; Theron Nauta, the bus driver; Ellis Clark, who drove the truck; and Kenneth Glasgow, the passenger in the truck who was apparently its owner as well. Each of the individual defendants was a citizen and resident of Oregon.

Before these cases could come to trial and before other suits were filed in California or elsewhere, petitioner State Farm Fire & Casualty Company, an Illinois corporation, brought this action in the nature of interpleader in the United States District Court for the District of Oregon.

In its complaint State Farm asserted that at the time of the Shasta County collision it had in force an insurance policy with respect to Ellis Clark, driver of the truck, providing for bodily injury liability up to $10,000 per person and $20,000 per occurrence and for legal representation of Clark in actions covered by the policy. It asserted that actions already filed in California and others which it anticipated would be filed far exceeded in aggregate damages sought the amount of its maximum liability under the policy. Accordingly, it paid into court the sum of $20,000 and asked the court (1) to require all claimants to establish their claims against Clark and his insurer in this single proceeding and in no other, and (2) to discharge State Farm from all further obligations under its policy—including its duty to defend Clark in lawsuits arising from the accident. Alternatively, State Farm expressed its conviction that the policy issued to Clark excluded from coverage accidents resulting from his operation of a truck which belonged to another and was being used in the business of another. The complaint, therefore, requested that the court decree that the insurer owed no duty to Clark and was not liable on the policy, and it asked the court to refund the $20,000 deposit.

Joined as defendants were Clark, Glasgow, Nauta, Greyhound Lines, and each of the prospective claimants. Jurisdiction was predicated upon 28 U.S.C. § 1335, the federal interpleader statute, and upon general diversity of citizenship, there being diversity between two or more of the claimants to the fund and between State Farm and all of the named defendants.

An order issued, requiring the defendants to show cause why they should not be restrained from filing or prosecuting "any proceeding in any state or United States Court affecting the property or obligation involved in this interpleader action, and specifically against the plaintiff and the defendant Ellis D. Clark." Personal service was effected on each of the American defendants, and registered mail was employed to reach the 11 Canadian claimants. Defendants Nauta, Greyhound, and several of the injured passengers responded, contending that the policy did cover this accident and advancing various arguments for the position that interpleader was either impermissible or inappropriate in the present circumstances. Greyhound, however, soon switched sides and moved that the court broaden any injunction to include Nauta and Greyhound among those who could not be sued except within the confines of the interpleader proceeding.

When a temporary injunction along the lines sought by State Farm was issued by the United States District Court for the District of Oregon, the present respondents moved to dismiss the action and, in the alternative, for a change of venue—to the Northern District of California, in which district the collision had occurred. After a hearing, the court declined to dissolve the temporary injunction, but continued the motion for a change of venue. The injunction was later broadened to include the protection sought by Greyhound, but modified to permit the filing—although not the prosecution—of suits. The injunction, therefore, provided that all suits against Clark, State Farm, Greyhound, and Nauta be prosecuted in the interpleader proceeding.

On interlocutory appeal, the Court of Appeals for the Ninth Circuit reversed. The court found it unnecessary to reach respondents' contentions relating to service of process and the scope of the injunction, for it concluded that interpleader was not available in the circumstances of this case. It held that in States like Oregon which do not permit "direct action" suits against insurance companies until judgments are obtained against the insured, the insurance companies may not invoke federal interpleader until the claims against the insured, the alleged tortfeasor, have been reduced to judgment. Until that is done, said the court, claimants with unliquidated tort claims are not "claimants" within the meaning of § 1335, nor are they "persons having claims against the plaintiff" within the meaning of Rule 22 * * *. In accord with that view, it directed dissolution of the temporary injunction and dismissal of the action. Because the Court of Appeals' decision on this point conflicts with those of other federal courts, and concerns a matter of significance to the administration of federal interpleader, we granted *certiorari*. Although we reverse the decision of the Court of Appeals upon the jurisdictional question, we direct a substantial modification of the District Court's injunction for reasons which will appear.

I.

Before considering the issues presented by the petition for *certiorari*, we find it necessary to dispose of a question neither raised by the parties nor passed upon by the courts below. Since the matter concerns our jurisdiction, we raise it on our own motion. The interpleader statute, 28 U.S.C. § 1335 applies where there are "Two or more adverse claimants, of diverse citizenship. . . ." This provision has been uniformly construed to require only "minimal diversity," that is, diversity of citizenship between two or more claimants, without regard to the circumstance that other rival claimants may be co-citizens. The language of the statute, the legislative purpose broadly to remedy the problems posed by multiple claimants to a single fund, and the consistent judicial interpretation tacitly accepted by Congress, persuade us that the statute requires no more. There remains, however, the question whether such a statutory construction is consistent with Article III of our Constitution, which extends the federal judicial power to "Controversies . . . between Citizens of different States . . . and between a State, or the Citizens thereof, and foreign States, Citizens or Subjects." In *Strawbridge v. Curtiss*, 7 U.S. (3 Cranch) 267 (1806), this Court held that the diversity of citizenship statute required "complete diversity": where co-citizens appeared on both sides of a dispute, jurisdiction was lost. But Chief Justice Marshall there purported to construe only "The words of the act of congress," not the Constitution itself. And in a variety of contexts this Court and the lower courts have concluded that Article III poses no obstacle to the legislative extension of federal jurisdiction, founded on diversity, so long as any two adverse parties are not co-citizens. Accordingly, we conclude that the present case is properly in the federal courts.

II.

We do not agree with the Court of Appeals that, in the absence of a state law or contractual provision for "direct action" suits against the insurance company, the company must wait until persons asserting claims against its insured have reduced those claims to judgment before seeking to invoke the benefits of federal interpleader. That may have been a tenable position under the 1926 and 1936 interpleader statutes. These statutes did not carry forward the language in the 1917 Act authorizing interpleader where adverse claimants "may claim" benefits as well as where they "are claiming" them. In 1948, however, in the revision of the Judicial Code, the "may claim" language was restored. Until the decision below, every court confronted by the question has concluded that the 1948 revision removed whatever requirement there might previously have been that the insurance company wait until at least two claimants reduced their claims to judgments. The commentators are in accord.

Considerations of judicial administration demonstrate the soundness of this view which, in any event, seems compelled by the language of the present statute, which is remedial and to be liberally construed. Were an insurance company required to await reduction of claims to judgment, the first claimant to obtain such a judgment or to negotiate a settlement might appropriate all or a disproportionate slice of the fund before his fellow claimants were able to establish their claims. The difficulties such a race to judgment pose for the insurer, and the unfairness which may result to some claimants, were among the principal evils the interpleader device was intended to remedy.

III.

The fact that State Farm had properly invoked the interpleader jurisdiction under § 1335 did not entitle it to an order both enjoining prosecution of suits against it outside the confines of the interpleader proceeding and also extending such protection to its insured, the alleged tortfeasor. Still less was Greyhound Lines entitled to have that order expanded so as to protect itself and its driver, also alleged to be tortfeasors, from suits brought by its passengers in various state or federal courts. Here, the scope of the litigation, in terms of parties and claims, was vastly more extensive than the confines of the "fund," the deposited proceeds of the insurance policy. In these circumstances, the mere existence of such a fund cannot, by use of interpleader, be employed to accomplish purposes that exceed the needs of orderly contest with respect to the fund.

There are situations, of a type not present here, where the effect of interpleader is to confine the total litigation to a single forum and proceeding. One such case is where a stakeholder, faced with rival claims to the fund itself, acknowledges—or denies—his liability to one or the other of the claimants. In this situation, the fund itself is the target of the claimants. It marks the outer limits of the controversy. It is, therefore, reasonable and sensible that interpleader, in discharge of its office to protect the fund, should also protect the stakeholder from vexatious and multiple litigation. In this context, the suits sought to be enjoined are squarely within the language of 28 U.S.C. § 2361 * * *.

But the present case is another matter. Here, an accident has happened. Thirty-five passengers or their representatives have claims which they wish to press against a variety of defendants: the bus company, its driver, the owner of the truck, and the truck driver. The circumstance that one of the prospective defendants happens to have an insurance policy is a fortuitous event which should not of itself shape the nature of the ensuing litigation. For example, a resident of California, injured in California aboard a bus owned by a California corporation should not be forced to sue that corporation anywhere but in California simply because another prospective defendant carried an insurance policy. And an insurance company whose maximum interest in the case cannot exceed $20,000 and who in fact asserts that it has no interest at all, should not be allowed to determine that dozens of tort plaintiffs must be compelled to press their claims—even those claims which are not against the insured and which in no event could be satisfied out of the meager insurance fund—in a single forum of the insurance company's choosing. There is nothing in the statutory scheme, and very little in the judicial and academic commentary upon that scheme, which requires that the tail be allowed to wag the dog in this fashion.

State Farm's interest in this case, which is the fulcrum of the interpleader procedure, is confined to its $20,000 fund. That interest receives full vindication when the court restrains claimants from seeking to enforce against the insurance company any judgment obtained against its insured, except in the interpleader proceeding itself. To the extent that the District Court sought to control claimants' lawsuits against the insured and other alleged tortfeasors, it exceeded the powers granted to it by the statutory scheme.

We recognize, of course, that our view of interpleader means that it cannot be used to solve all the vexing problems of multiparty litigation arising out of a mass tort. But interpleader was never intended to perform such a function, to be an all-purpose "bill of peace." Had it been so intended, careful provision would necessarily have been made to insure that a party with little or no interest in the outcome of a complex controversy should not strip truly interested parties of substantial rights—such as the right to choose the forum in which to establish their claims, subject to generally applicable rules of jurisdiction, venue, service of process, removal, and change of venue. None of the legislative and academic sponsors of a modern federal interpleader device viewed their accomplishment as a "bill of peace," capable of sweeping dozens of lawsuits out of the various state and federal courts in which they were brought and into a single interpleader proceeding. * * *

In light of the evidence that federal interpleader was not intended to serve the function of a "bill of peace" in the context of multiparty litigation arising out of a mass tort, of the anomalous power which such a construction of the statute would give the stakeholder, and of the thrust of the statute and the purpose it was intended to serve, we hold that the interpleader statute did not authorize the injunction entered in the present case. Upon remand, the injunction is to be modified consistently with this opinion.

* * *

[Dissenting opinion by JUSTICE DOUGLAS is omitted.]

6247 ATLAS CORP. v. MARINE INS. CO.
United States District Court, Southern District of New York, 1994.
155 F.R.D. 454.

SWEET, DISTRICT JUDGE.

[Plaintiff Atlas, a dealer in precious stones, metals, and jewelry, claimed that more than $6 million worth of jewelry and other valuables was stolen from the company on June 25, 1991. According to Atlas, about $3,005,000 of the loss consisted of valuables consigned by 37 "memoholders." Another 18 "memoholders" sought in excess of $1,000,000. Atlas had insurance coverage totaling $3,100,000, and sought recovery of approximately that amount against the defendants, various insurance companies. Defendants denied liability, claiming that the loss was fraudulent and that Atlas breached the terms of the insurance policies. In addition, defendants sought to interplead the memoholders into the case under Rule 22. Although some memoholders agreed to intervention, others did not, and were prosecuting their own suit or suits in New York state court against Atlas and various insurance entities.]

DISCUSSION

* * *

II. The Defendants May Assert Defensive Interpleader Pursuant to Rule 22

A. The Legal Standards of Rule 22 Interpleader

"Rooted in equity, interpleader is a handy tool to protect a stakeholder from multiple liability and the vexation of defending multiple claims to the same fund." There are two forms of interpleader: rule interpleader, as set forth in the Federal Rule of Civil Procedure 22; and statutory interpleader, as set forth in 28 U.S.C. § 1335.

Rule 22 of the Federal Rules of Civil Procedure provide[d] in relevant part [that] "[p]ersons having claims against the plaintiff may be joined as defendants and required to interplead when their claims are such that the plaintiff is or may be exposed to double or multiple liability. . . . *A defendant exposed to similar liability may obtain such interpleader by way of cross-claim or counterclaim.*"

Rule interpleader requires subject matter jurisdiction based either upon a general federal question or diversity of citizenship, as provided in 28 U.S.C. §§ 1331, 1332, between the stakeholder and the claimants, and an amount of controversy that exceeds $50,000 [now $75,000]. Under Rule 22, there is no requirement to deposit the "stake" in question with the Court. A defendant seeking to institute Rule 22 interpleader is merely required to have a nexus with a party in the case.

Alternately, statutory interpleader enables a party with "money or property of the value of $500 or more" to invoke interpleader when "two or more adverse claimants, of diverse citizenship . . . are claiming or may claim to be entitled to such money or property" and the "plaintiff has deposited such money or property . . . into the registry of the court." 28 U.S.C. § 1335. Thus, statutory interpleader relaxes the diversity jurisdictional requirements in exchange for the somewhat onerous requirement of depositing the stake with the Court.

Both rule and statutory interpleader are viewed as a "remedial joinder device" originally designed to protect a stakeholder in an action—who is unsure as to which party has the right to relief or liability over a common fund—by joining absent parties or claimants, in the form of a counter or cross claim, into one single action. The Supreme Court, in its definitive opinion on the subject of interpleader, *State Farm & Casualty Co. v. Tashire*, 386 U.S. 523 (1967), has emphasized that interpleader is a "remedial" device to be "liberally construed" * * *.

* * *

The objectives of interpleader, then, are to be viewed in "harmony with the flexible joinder provisions of the federal rules [of civil procedure], and many decisions hold that . . . [interpleader is] remedial in character and should be applied liberally. Thus, the trend, both with regard to statutory revision and judicial interpretation, has been directed toward increasing the availability of interpleader and eliminating those technical restraints on the device that are not founded on adequate policy considerations."

Finally, under the prevailing doctrine of both statutory and rule interpleader, the stakeholder is relieved from the obligation of determining which litigant has a superior claim and forces the claimants to the fund to "contest what essentially is a controversy between them without embroiling" the stakeholder into the action. As such, Rule 22 is "designed to insulate a stakeholder from contradictory judgments and multiple liability and to relieve a stakeholder from having to determine which claim among several is meritorious."

The three general requirements for the assertion of defensive interpleader are as follows: (1) the defendant "stakeholder" must legitimately fear multiple litigation directed against the fund; (2) two or more of the claimants must be adverse to each other; and (3) the defendant must frame a defensive interpleader by way of a cross-claim or counter-claim.

B. Defendants Legitimately Fear Multiple Litigation

[The court first determined that the correct standard for assessing whether interpleader is appropriate is whether "a shareholder legitimately fears multiple [liability] directed against a single fund, regardless of the merits of the competing claims."]

As provided by Rule 22, interpleader is available when a stakeholder is or may be exposed to "double or multiple liability." One of the seminal interpleader cases notes that:

> The key to [this] clause . . . is in the words "may be." The danger need not be immediate; any possibility of having to pay more than is justly due, no matter how improbable or remote, will suffice. At least, it is settled that an insurer with limited contractual liability

who faces claims in excess of his policy limits is "exposed" within the intendment of Rule 22. . . .

Pan Am. Fire & Casualty Co. v. Revere, 188 F. Supp. 474, 480 (E.D.La.1960).

The quintessential interpleader case is one in which an insurer is faced with rival claims which exceed the amount held in a limited fund. * * *

* * *

The Defendants contend that a refusal to interplead the additional memoholders will unnecessarily subject them to duplicative and wasteful litigation. Atlas has alleged that more than $[6.1] million worth of jewelry and valuables was stolen on the date of the loss. Atlas claims that approximately $[3.005] million of the loss consists of goods consigned to Atlas by 37 memoholders. Another 18 memoholders, as of yet unrecognized by Atlas, are claiming in excess of $1,000,000 under the fund. Atlas has refused to agree to these demands and asserts that the memoholders are not entitled to any of the policy proceeds. Thus, Atlas alone is making a claim for $3,078,572 against the $[3.1] million policy limit.

The Defendants argue that if they are ultimately found liable to Atlas * * * then they would be forced to exhaust the $[3.1] million fund without addressing the non-party memoholders' claims. Alternately, according to the Defendants, should they prevail over Atlas, the current non-party memoholders could return and attempt to relitigate the same issues on the theory that they were not parties to the original action, and thus not bound by the determination.

The Defendants are correct in their analysis that they run a substantial risk of multiple litigation from the various claimants. Accordingly, as it is evident that the Defendants legitimately fear multiple litigation arising from the limited fund, the Defendants have thus established that they may be exposed to double or multiple liability as required by Rule 22.

Parenthetically, [certain memoholders] assert that it is improper to interplead prospective claimants in the absence of a formal action against the stakeholder. However, Rule 22 interpleader is available to join prospective claimants even if they have not yet brought a formal demand against the stakeholder.

The language of Rule 22 specifically provides for interpleader when a stakeholder "may be exposed to double or multiple liability." Fed. R. Civ. P. Rule 22[(a)](1). In addition, the case law consistently supports the notion that interpleader may be utilized even if some of the alleged claims have not yet been asserted.

Should the Defendants be found liable to Atlas * * *, it is apparent that the absent memoholders will initiate actions, claiming their rights and asserting that the Defendants are bound by such a liability determination. Alternately, if the Defendants prevail against Atlas * * *, the absent memoholders are likely to seek to relitigate the exact same issue on the theory that they are not collaterally estopped by an action in which they were not parties. Accordingly, in the interest of equity, interpleader lies notwithstanding the prospective nature of the absent memoholders' claims.

C. Two or More of the Claimants Are Adverse to Each Other

The second requirement for rule interpleader is that two or more of the claimants to the fund must be adverse to one another. For example, as explained in *Trowbridge v. Prudential Ins. Co.*, 322 F. Supp. 190 (S.D.N.Y. 1971):

> if "A" was holding a particular picture for "B," and "B" then disappeared leaving behind "C" and "D," each of whom claimed that "B" owed the picture to him, "A" could interplead "C" and "D" because a decision on the merits in favor of one of the claimants would necessarily dictate a determination that the other was not legally entitled to recovery of the picture from "A."

One court has noted that the level of adversity is directly proportional to the number of claimants to the stake:

> [I]t has been urged that the action is not proper because the claimants do not have claims adverse to each other. It might, by the same reasoning be said that 100 persons adrift in the ocean with but one small lifeboat in sight were not adverse to each other. We fear, however, that the concept of non-adversity would dwindle in direct proportion to the number of swimmers reaching the boat.

Commercial Union Ins. Co. v. Adams, 231 F. Supp. 860, 863 (S.D.Ind.1964) (granting interpleader).

Here, Atlas * * * [has] adverse interests to the memoholders. Atlas, for example, does not even recognize 18 of the memoholders and challenges the sums claimed by several of the memoholders it does recognize. Additionally, the Defendants may be seen as adverse claimants for the purposes of Rule 22 since the Defendants are denying liability to Atlas * * * as well as liability to all the other claimant-memoholders.

Accordingly, the adversity requirement for interpleader is met in this case.

D. Jurisdiction is Proper

Under Rule 22, the jurisdictional amount in controversy must exceed the federal requirements of $50,000 [now $75,000]. However, "where adverse claims are asserted to a fund which exceeds the jurisdictional amount, the court is given jurisdiction to adjudicate the rights of all parties, including claimants whose individual claims are less than the jurisdictional amount."

In this case, the jurisdictional amount in controversy is $3,100,000 as the total fund is the subject matter of the action. Accordingly, it is irrelevant that some of the memoholders' individual claims are for less than the jurisdictional amount as only the total amount of the claims must be over [the amount necessary to] establish federal jurisdiction.

Rule interpleader does not provide an independent jurisdictional basis outside of 28 U.S.C. § 1332, which provides for actions between citizens of different states or between citizens of a state and citizens or subjects of a foreign state. As a result, in order to assert rule interpleader, a traditional basis for subject matter jurisdiction must exist.

Jurisdiction exists under Rule 22 when the citizenship of the stakeholder is diverse from that of all of the claimants, even if all the claimants share the same citizenship. Likewise, courts in the Second Circuit have found jurisdiction based on the diversity of citizenship between the stakeholder and the claimants. In a case, such as this, where the stakeholder is aligned against all of the claimants, and the stakeholder denies liability in whole or in part, the stakeholder's citizenship may be considered for diversity purposes.

Accordingly, the stakeholder Defendants have sufficiently established the requisite jurisdictional amount and, as they are citizens of a foreign state, they have established jurisdictional diversity from the claimants.

Conclusion

For the reasons set forth above, the Defendants' motion for an order of interpleader, pursuant to Fed. R. Civ. P. 22, is granted. * * *

NOTES AND QUESTIONS

1. Does the Court's analysis in *Tashire* withstand scrutiny? Is it supported by the purposes of interpleader as described in the case?

2. In order for an interpleader action to be valid, notice must be provided to potential claimants. In *Jefferson–Pilot Ins. Co. v. Short*, 346 F. Supp. 2d 825 (M.D.N.C. 2004), an insurer brought an interpleader action to determine whether the insured's wife or daughter was the beneficiary of his life insurance policy. The insurance company and daughter filed a proposed consent judgment, agreeing that she would receive the entire payment. The district court refused to sign the consent judgment because the record did not reflect whether the insured's wife had ever received the summons and complaint in the interpleader action (and if she did, whether the documents made clear she needed to take responsive action). Why is notice necessary? How, if at all, does the ruling in *Jefferson–Pilot Ins. Co.* differ from notice requirements under Rule 23?

3. Both *Tashire* and *Atlas* address diversity in the interpleader context. How does the determination of diversity differ as between statutory interpleader and rule interpleader? Why did the Supreme Court in *Tashire* raise the issue of jurisdiction *sua sponte*?

4. Under rule interpleader, the court has diversity jurisdiction when each stakeholder is diverse from each claimant. When a stakeholder is dismissed, a district court retains jurisdiction over the suit between the claimants, even if they are non-diverse. The fact that the claimants are not diverse does not divest the district court of its jurisdiction. *Leimbach v. Allen*, 976 F.2d 912, 916–17 (4th Cir. 1992).

5. Courts may assert jurisdiction over an interpleader suit either by statute or rule. Even when a complaint asserts the wrong source for federal jurisdiction, interpleader is often permitted if an alternative ground for jurisdiction exists. *See, e.g., Asbestos Workers Local No. 23 Pension Fund ex rel. Norcross v. United States*, 303 F. Supp. 2d 551, 555–56 (M.D.Pa. 2004) (where pension benefit fund brought statutory interpleader action against beneficiary and IRS, but sufficient diversity of citizenship did not exist because one claimant was a federal government agency, court construed the action as rule interpleader, which permitted jurisdiction premised on a federal statute); *International Painters & Allied Trades Indus. Pension Fund v. Calabro*, 312 F. Supp.

2d 697, 699 n.1 (E.D.Pa. 2004) (where plaintiffs attempted to bring a statutory interpleader action, but adverse claimants were not diverse, court treated the action as rule interpleader).

6. In *Atlas*, the defendants used rule interpleader to join the additional memoholders. Were there other procedural devices that the defendants could have used to resolve their liability to the claimants? (It should be noted that the *Atlas* court rejected the argument that the absent memoholders should be joined under Rule 19).

7. How strong must a stakeholder's fear of multiple liability be to satisfy the requirement for interpleader? Courts have said the fear must be "bona fide," *Allegheny Child Care Acad. v. Klein*, 2003 WL 23112776, at *1 (W.D. Pa. 2003), but the cases tend to be very fact-specific. *See, e.g., Bierman v. Marcus*, 246 F.2d 200, 203 (3d Cir. 1957) (interpleader denied where plaintiffs impleaded corporation in which they were sole stockholders and over which they had total control, thereby knowing that corporation could not assert a claim against them for unpaid purchase money without their consent); *Public Sch. Ret. Sys. of Missouri v. United States*, 227 F.R.D. 502, 504 (W.D. Mo. 2005) (where administrator of pension fund would be immune from suit if it complied with an Internal Revenue Service levy imposed on taxpayer, interpleader would not be necessary to protect administrator from multiple liability); *National Accident Ins. Underwriters, Inc. v. Citibank, FSB*, 333 F. Supp. 2d 720, 726 (N.D. Ill. 2004) (where check payee and intervenor filed mutually exclusive claims against Citibank and alleged converted funds claims in same lawsuit, Citibank was not in jeopardy of double or multiple liability, thereby making its interpleader action improper). Should the courts take a liberal or strict approach when determining the risk of multiple exposure? Which approach is more faithful to the goals of interpleader?

8. As Rule 22 suggests, the plaintiff usually initiates interpleader proceedings. As *Atlas* illustrates, however, the defendant may commence interpleader proceedings by bringing cross-claims or counterclaims against claimants. *See* Fed. R. Civ. P. 22. Why didn't plaintiff Atlas itself seek interpleader?

9. There are two types of interpleader: "true" or "traditional" interpleader and an action "in the nature of interpleader." True interpleader involves a plaintiff stakeholder who has no interest in the disposition of the fund. The stakeholder is dismissed once the court determines interpleader is appropriate, leaving the claimants to fight over the distribution of the fund. *See, e.g., Jackson Nat'l Life Ins. Co. v. Cabrera*, 48 F. App'x 618, 619–20 (9th Cir. 2002) (unpublished) (dismissal of insurance company from interpleader action was proper after company deposited death benefit and past interest with court, thereby extinguishing its obligations under the policy).

The interpleader standard has been liberalized with the development of the action "in the nature of interpleader." *Homestead Title of Pinellas, Inc. v. United States*, 2005 WL 1221865, at *3 (M.D. Fla. 2005). This type of action involves a plaintiff stakeholder who, like the other claimants, has an interest in the subject matter of the dispute. *See, e.g., Heller Fin., Inc. v. Prudential Ins. Co. of Am.*, 371 F.3d 944, 945 (7th Cir. 2004) (Posner, J.) ("Although [lender] is not a neutral stakeholder, neutrality is not required for a suit 'in the nature of interpleader' authorized by the federal interpleader statute"); *Fresh Am. Corp. v. Wal–Mart Stores, Inc.*, 393 F. Supp. 2d 411 (N.D. Tex. 2005). In all other respects, the action is like traditional interpleader. *See, e.g., Hussain v. Boston Old Colony Ins. Co.*, 311 F.3d 623, 631 (5th Cir. 2002).

10. In addition to using interpleader to adjudicate rival claims to the stake, a stakeholder may use interpleader to adjudicate underlying issues that will determine the claims to the stake. For example, interpleader may be used to determine the domicile of a decedent, when several states have attempted to impose death taxes on the decedent's estate. *See, e.g., Lummis v. White*, 629 F.2d 397, 400–01 (5th Cir. 1980), *rev'd on other grounds*, 457 U.S. 85 (1982).

11. The court in *Atlas* noted that statutory interpleader requires that the stakeholder deposit the stake with the court, while rule interpleader does not. *Compare* 28 U.S.C. §§ 1335, 1397, and 2361, *with* Rule 22. Is this distinction significant? The two forms of interpleader also differ in other ways, including:

- Venue: Whereas statutory interpleader may be brought in any district in which any claimant resides (28 U.S.C. § 1397), rule interpleader based upon diversity of citizenship may be brought, pursuant to the general venue statute (28 U.S.C. § 1391(a)), only in a district in which (i) a defendant resides (if all are in the same state), (ii) a substantial part of the events at issue occurred (or a substantial part of the property is situated), or (iii) any defendant is subject to personal jurisdiction (if there is no other district where the suit may be brought).

- Service of Process: Although a plaintiff may employ nationwide service of process under statutory interpleader (28 U.S.C. § 2361), service of process under Rule 22 is governed by Fed. R. Civ. P. 4.

- Subject Matter Jurisdiction. *See supra* note 5.

12. Interpleader is equitable in nature. Therefore, even when the stakeholder has met the requirements of 28 U.S.C. § 1335, discharge of the stakeholder may be delayed or denied if there are serious charges that the stakeholder commenced the action in bad faith. *See, e.g., Mendez v. Teacher's Ins. & Annuity Assoc. & Coll. Ret. Equities Fund*, 982 F.2d 783, 787 (2d Cir. 1992) (delay in commencing interpleader unreasonable); *see also Truck-a-Tune, Inc. v. Re*, 856 F. Supp. 77, 79 (D.Conn. 1993), *aff'd*, 23 F.3d 60 (2d Cir. 1994) (doctrine of unclean hands may bar stakeholder from successfully invoking interpleader).

13. Federal interpleader is not meant to provide a means of forum shopping for litigants who cannot achieve consolidation of claims in state court or whose goal is to obtain personal jurisdiction over a plaintiff that would not otherwise be subject to jurisdiction. *See, e.g., Wausau Ins. Cos. v. Gifford*, 954 F.2d 1098, 1101 (5th Cir. 1992) (where six insurers brought interpleader action to resolve various homeowners' claims against insured developer, court rejected interpleader suit, noting "[i]t does not provide a method of forum shopping for parties disappointed with the outcome of their consolidation motions in state court."); *Indianapolis Colts v. Mayor and City Council of Balt.*, 733 F.2d 484, 486–88 (7th Cir. 1984) (concluding that Baltimore football club improperly brought interpleader action to take advantage of interpleader statute's nationwide service of process over City of Indiana, and criticizing such "forum shopping" as antithetical to the statute's purpose). Moreover, some courts have concluded that where a state forum would be more appropriate, the courts should abstain from adjudicating interpleader actions. *See, e.g., Am.*

Airlines, Inc. v. Block, 905 F.2d 12, 14–15 (2d Cir. 1990) (while district court had subject matter jurisdiction over interpleader action involving matrimonial issues, court should have refrained from exercising jurisdiction where state court could have provided full and fair relief); *Fin. Guar. Ins. Co. v. City of Fayetteville*, 749 F. Supp. 934, 945 (W.D. Ark. 1990) (where prior state court action was capable of providing an adequate remedy, court should be wary of permitting litigants to manufacture federal jurisdiction through interpleader).

14. Interpleader may be used in conjunction with Rule 23 when the claimants to the stake meet all the requirements for a class action. *See, e.g., United States Trust Co. v. Alpert*, 10 F. Supp. 2d 290 (S.D.N.Y. 1998), *aff'd*, 168 F.3d 630 (2d Cir. 1999). In what circumstances might class action claimants satisfy the requirements for interpleader?

15. For a complicated interpleader case involving funds seized by the United States from a bank account held by a British Virgin Islands entity, *see United States v. Federative Republic of Brazil*, 784 F.3d 86 (2d Cir. 2014). Events leading to the interpleader action included 15 years of criminal and civil litigation in the United States, Brazil, the Cayman Islands, and the British Virgin Islands.

16. With respect to interpleader's ability to serve as a party-aggregation device, the Supreme Court in *Tashire* indicated that the rule is of limited use. Similarly, the American Law Institute has observed:

> interpleader generally is limited to claims to specific property and does not operate on a sufficiently large scale to be important in most complex multiparty, multiforum actions. It is not a representative action because all of the claimants are expected to appear as parties. Thus, the device generally is less suitable than the class action for suits involving large numbers of claimants.

American Law Institute, *Complex Litigation: Statutory Recommendations and Analysis* 34 (1994).

5. INTERVENTION

Intervention allows nonparties in certain circumstances to inject themselves into a suit and become parties. There are two forms of intervention—intervention of right and permissive intervention. The former is more difficult to satisfy, but the successful applicant is assured a critical role. The role of a permissive intervenor is frequently more limited.

One theme that pervades intervention law—as in class action law—is whether existing representation is adequate. When existing representation is adequate in the intervention context, the need to allow nonparties to enter a case is eliminated, or at least dramatically reduced.

FED. R. CIV. P. 24: INTERVENTION

(a) Intervention of Right. On timely motion, the court must permit anyone to intervene who:

> (1) is given an unconditional right to intervene by a federal statute; or

(2) claims an interest relating to the property or transaction that is the subject of the action, and is so situated that disposing of the action may as a practical matter impair or impede the movant's ability to protect its interest, unless existing parties adequately represent that interest.

(b) Permissive Intervention.

(1) In General. On timely motion, the court may permit anyone to intervene who:

(A) is given a conditional right to intervene by a federal statute; or

(B) has a claim or defense that shares with the main action a common question of law or fact.

(2) By a Government Officer or Agency. On timely motion, the court may permit a federal or state governmental officer or agency to intervene if a party's claim or defense is based on:

(A) a statute or executive order administered by the officer or agency; or

(B) any regulation, order, requirement, or agreement issued or made under the statute or executive order.

(3) Delay or Prejudice. In exercising its discretion, the court must consider whether the intervention will unduly delay or prejudice the adjudication of the original parties' rights.

(c) Notice and Pleading Required. A motion to intervene must be served on the parties as provided in Rule 5. The motion must state the grounds for intervention and be accompanied by a pleading that sets out the claim or defense for which intervention is sought.

a. General Concepts

JOHNSON V. CITY OF DALLAS
United States District Court, Northern District of Texas, 1994.
155 F.R.D. 581.

KENDALL, DISTRICT JUDGE.

NOW before the Court are the Motion to Intervene * * * and the response to that motion. * * * [T]he Court concludes that the motion should be, and hereby is, DENIED. However, Movants are granted leave to appear as *amici*, as noted below.

I.

This case concerns the constitutionality of various city ordinances enacted, enforced or both, allegedly to remove homeless persons from public view in the City of Dallas. Plaintiffs are themselves homeless, and they seek to represent a class of homeless persons. Defendants include the City of Dallas, the Dallas Police Department and members of the Dallas City Council. Plaintiffs attack, among other things, a city ordinance that would prohibit sleeping in public, as well as the proposed eviction of a homeless encampment under certain interstate highway bridges on the east side of Dallas' central business district. After a hearing * * *, the Court granted Plaintiffs' application for a temporary restraining order, which prevented the City from enforcing certain ordinances and evicting persons living under the bridges, and scheduled a hearing * * * on Plaintiffs' motion for preliminary injunction. Not long after the TRO hearing, Movants filed their motion to intervene.

The parties seeking intervention are various business and home-owners associations. * * * Movants argue that they are entitled to intervention as of right. Failing that, they argue that they should be allowed to intervene permissively. * * *

II.

A party seeking to intervene as of right must satisfy four requirements: (1) The application must be timely; (2) the applicant must have an interest relating to the property or transaction that is the subject of the action; (3) the applicant must be so situated that the disposition of the action may, as a practical matter, impair or impede its ability to protect its interest; and (4) the applicant's interest must be inadequately represented by the existing parties to the suit. If one seeking to intervene does not satisfy all of these requirements, intervention as of right is not possible. The inquiry regarding intervention of right is flexible, focusing on the particular facts and circumstances surrounding each application. Further, intervention of right must be measured by a practical rather than technical yardstick.

* * * [B]ecause Movants seek intervention on the heels of the case's filing, the Court concludes that they are clearly timely. * * * Plaintiffs filed the suit on May 18, and Movants filed their motion to intervene on May 25.

To satisfy the next requirement for intervention as of right, one must demonstrate an interest in the subject matter of the action. That interest must be "direct, substantial, [and] legally protectable." The interest prong of the analysis is primarily a practical guide to disposing of lawsuits by involving as many apparently concerned persons as is compatible with efficiency and due process. The thrust of Movants' argument on the issue of interest is straightforward: They worry that the Court's granting of Plaintiffs' motion for preliminary injunction will adversely affect their economic interest. They state that

> the Associations represent the interests that would be most adversely affected were the preliminary injunction granted. The conduct at issue here affects the willingness of customers to patronize the businesses that are members of the Associations, and thus has a direct economic impact on the Associations. The criminal conduct and health risks that are increased due to a concentration of the homeless on the border of downtown Dallas also pose a direct risk to the employees and patrons of the business members of the Associations as well as to the residents represented by various of the Associations.

Elsewhere, Movants note that "to the extent the illegal conduct of the Plaintiffs and members of the purported plaintiff class exacts a cost from the community, it is the members of the Associations and their customers and tenants who bear that cost. Consequently, the Associations' intervention in this case is both right and proper."

After careful consideration, the Court determines that Movants construe the interest requirement far too broadly and fail to demonstrate a sufficient interest in the case to warrant intervention under Rule 24(a). Under Movants' conception of the interest requirement, the number of those allowed to intervene of right would be virtually unbounded. Reasonable, persuasive arguments would not be difficult to fashion tending to demonstrate an adverse economic impact on all manner of banks, malls, restaurants and other merchants should the Court grant Plaintiffs' motion for preliminary injunction. * * * [T]he interest prong of the analysis is primarily a pragmatic guide to disposing of lawsuits by involving apparently concerned persons but tempering that involvement with concerns of efficiency and due process. Movants' unworkable take on the interest prong would read efficiency out of the inquiry. Nor have Movants made any showing that they are due some sort of process. Movants also voice concern with the enforcement of criminal and sanitation laws. Who in the whole city would not have an interest in such enforcement and therefore [a] right to intervene under Movants' formulation?

* * *

* * * Rule 24(a) requires Movants to be so situated that the disposition of the action may, as a practical matter, impair or impede their ability to protect their interests. On this point, Movants simply parrot the requirement and maintain that they have met it. * * * Indeed, Movants' own motion shows that they can address, and have been addressing, their concerns without the necessity of their intervening in this suit. On this prong of the analysis, then, the Court concludes that Movants have failed to demonstrate their entitlement to intervene.

The final requirement for intervention as a matter of right is that the movant's interest must be inadequately represented by the existing parties to the suit. Although the movant has the burden of demonstrating inadequate representation, this burden has been described as "minimal." The existence of the City in this suit may implicate a different perspective on this burden, however:

> There is a suggestion in the cases that where, as here, the existing representative in the suit is the government, there is a presumption of adequate representation which may be overcome by the intervenor only upon a showing of adversity of interest, the representative's collusion with the opposing party, or nonfeasance by the representative.

Texas v. United States Dep't of Energy, 754 F.2d 550, 553 (5th Cir. 1985). In any event, the Court concludes that any interest that Movants might have in the constitutionality of the ordinances at issue will be adequately addressed by able counsel for the City. The Court further notes that the City, like states and the federal government, is well experienced in litigating constitutional issues. For the foregoing reasons, the Court concludes that Movants have failed their burden under this final prong of the analysis, as well as under Rule 24(a) as a whole. Intervention as of right must therefore be denied.

III.

Next the Court turns to Movants' contention that permissive intervention is appropriate. An analysis concerning permissive intervention encompasses a two-stage process: First, the court must decide whether the movant's claim or defense and the main action have questions of law or fact in common. Second, if the first stage is met, the court must exercise its discretion in deciding whether intervention should be allowed. Assuming that Movants have demonstrated a common question of law or fact, the Court concludes that permissive intervention should be denied because the movants' interests are coextensive with the Defendants'—demonstrating constitutionality of the ordinances involved—and movants' interests are therefore adequately being represented by the defendants. Also, the intrusion of Movants into this litigation would do little more than needlessly increase costs and delay disposition of the case.

Additionally, the Court fails to understand what Movants could contribute to the case by way of evidentiary offerings that the defendants will not seek to make. Although Movants' express concerns that their business will continue to decrease if the encampment is allowed to maintain its current location, the Court also fails to understand how a third party's economic interest impacts an analysis of the constitutionality of city ordinances * * *. In short, it seems that economic considerations will be largely irrelevant to constitutional analysis in this case. The issues involved are primarily legal, and for that reason, as well as those discussed above, the Court concludes that Movants could adequately voice whatever concerns to the Court they have by appearing as *amici* rather than as intervenors. Although the Court hereby grants Movants leave to appear as *amici* for the sole purpose of filing briefs in relation to the injunctive relief that Plaintiffs seek, their motion is otherwise denied.

MAUSOLF V. BABBITT
United States Court of Appeals, Eighth Circuit, 1996.
85 F.3d 1295.

Before RICHARD S. ARNOLD, CHIEF JUDGE, WOLLMAN and MORRIS SHEPPARD ARNOLD, CIRCUIT JUDGES.

RICHARD S. ARNOLD, CHIEF JUDGE.

The plaintiffs—three snowmobile enthusiasts and the Minnesota United Snowmobilers Association (collectively, "the Snowmobilers")—sued the Secretary of the Interior and other defendants ("the Government"), seeking to enjoin the enforcement of restrictions on snowmobiling in Voyageurs National Park. The Voyageurs Region National Park Association and other conservation groups (collectively, "the Association") moved to intervene under Fed. R. Civ. P. 24. The Association claimed an interest in the vigorous enforcement of the restrictions and expressed concern that the Government might settle with the Snowmobilers or back away from the rules. The District Court denied the motion, concluding that the Government adequately represented the Association's interests.

We reverse.

* * *

I.

Voyageurs National Park is a watery maze of over 30 lakes and 900 islands along the border between northern Minnesota and Canada. * * * Most of the Park is quite remote, and accessible only by water. Voyageurs is renowned for its fishing and boating, and visitors often see bald eagles and grey wolves in the wild. Voyageurs has also long been a popular destination for snowmobilers, who have, over the years, used both the Park's frozen lake surfaces and—more controversially—certain overland trails. This case is the latest in a series of disputes over the use and management of the Park.

Some background information will make this case easier to understand. In 1991, after several years of study, the National Park Service issued final regulations, based on a series of environmental-and wildlife-impact reports, allowing snowmobiling on practically all the Park's lake surfaces and also on certain trails and portage routes. The Association then sued, claiming that the regulations, and the Department of the Interior's failure to submit a "wilderness recommendation" for the Park to the President, were illegal. The District Court ordered the Secretary of the Interior to make a "wilderness recommendation" within a year, but refused to enjoin snowmobiling in the Park's Kabetogama Peninsula.

Accordingly, in August 1991, the National Park Service proposed a wilderness plan which would have significantly reduced overland snowmobiling, but allowed it on major lakes, a few designated portage trails, and the Chain of Lakes Trail. The Park Service then asked the Fish and Wildlife Service for its "biological opinion" about the effect, if any, snowmobiling could have on grey wolves, bald eagles, and other animals in the Park. In March 1992, Fish and Wildlife concluded that the Park Service's plan would not threaten animals' survival or habitats. Nonetheless, Fish and Wildlife directed the Park Service to close specified trails, lakeshores, and lakes to snowmobiles and other motor vehicles. So, in December 1992, Park officials issued an order, without giving notice or inviting interested parties to comment, closing 16 of the Park's lake bays and certain shoreline areas to winter motorized access. This order, which was renewed in 1993 and 1994, dramatically reduced the area available for snowmobiling.

These new regulations angered many past and potential Park visitors, including the Snowmobilers, who could no longer enjoy some of the Park's more beautiful and remote areas. The Snowmobilers sued the Government in January 1994, claiming that Fish and Wildlife's biological opinion did not support closing so much of the Park, and that the regulations were therefore arbitrary and capricious. According to the Snowmobilers, not only had the Government turned an abrupt and unexplained "about face," it had also failed to consider the best available scientific and commercial information before imposing the new restrictions. The Association then moved to intervene so it could vindicate its interest in restricting snowmobiling in the Park and in making sure the new regulations were strictly enforced.

The Association contended that for years the Government illegally—and over the Association's objections—permitted unrestricted snowmobiling in the Park and refused to implement proper wilderness-protection measures. The Association asserts that the Government cannot be trusted to protect the Association's interests because of its alleged history of siding with the Snowmobilers.

The District Court conceded that the Association had a recognized interest which might be impaired by the disposition of the case. The Court noted, however, that, under the *parens patriae* doctrine, government entities are presumed to represent the interests of all their citizens. Would-be intervenors can rebut this "presumption of adequate representation" only by identifying their "local and individual interests not shared by the general citizenry." The District Court was not persuaded that the Government would unduly subordinate the Association's interests to more general, national interests, and, therefore, denied intervention as of right under Rule 24(a). The District Court also refused to exercise its discretion to allow permissive intervention under Rule 24(b), fearing that the Association might delay the case with additional discovery and further joinder of issues and parties. However, recognizing the potential benefits of the Association's collective knowledge and perspective, the Court allowed the Association to participate as *amicus curiae* and to file a memorandum addressing the parties' cross-motions for summary judgment. The District Court confirmed the Magistrate Judge's order, and the Association appealed. We reverse.

II.

The Snowmobilers contend that the Association may not intervene as of right because it lacks Article III standing. The Magistrate Judge concluded, and the District Judge agreed, that "[t]he question of standing ... is irrelevant to our determination of whether the Association may intervene as of right." The District Court said that even if the Association did not have standing to sue, it could still intervene under Rule 24(a) if it had a "recognized interest in the subject of the litigation."

A.

Rule 24(a) says nothing about standing. To intervene as of right, an applicant must (1) have a recognized interest in the subject matter of the litigation that (2) might be impaired by the disposition of the case and that (3) will not be adequately protected by the existing parties. As the District Court observed, the Supreme Court has not yet decided whether a would-be intervenor must have Article III standing.

The courts of appeals have taken diverse, sometimes "anomalous," approaches. By way of illustration, at least one circuit has held that Article III standing *is* required to intervene, *see, e.g., Building and Const. Trades Dept., AFL–CIO v. Reich*, 40 F.3d 1275, 1282 (D.C. Cir. 1994); another has stated that, while Article III standing is not required, it is "relevant" to identifying the "interest" required for intervention under Rule 24, *see, e.g., Chiles v. Thornburgh*, 865 F.2d 1197, 1213 (11th Cir. 1989); others have concluded that standing is not required for intervention, *see, e.g., United States Postal Service v. Brennan*, 579 F.2d 188, 190 (2d Cir. 1978); *Associated Builders & Contractors v. Perry*, 16 F.3d 688, 690 (6th Cir. 1994);

Yniguez v. State of Arizona, 939 F.2d 727, 731 (9th Cir. 1991); and still another has suggested that Rule 24 requires an interest even "greater than the interest sufficient to satisfy the standing requirement." *See, e.g., United States v. 36.96 Acres of Land*, 754 F.2d 855, 859 (7th Cir. 1985). Our Court has not yet taken a firm position in this debate, although we have, in some cases, decided intervention issues without discussing Article III standing.

The Association urges us to adopt the "majority view," and to hold that standing is not required for intervention. It contends that "[i]ntervention is not a means for beginning a lawsuit, but a mechanism that allows all parties with an interest to participate in an existing lawsuit." Because the lawsuit's original parties have created the "case" or "controversy" required by Article III, the Association argues, there is no reason to require a would-be intervenor, who satisfies Rule 24(a)'s requirements, to have standing.
* * *

We are not so sure as the Association that there is a "majority view" on this question—indeed, our survey of the cases reveals considerable diversity of views, not consensus. But even if the Association's position *did* represent the majority view, we would still disagree with it. We conclude that the Constitution requires that prospective intervenors have Article III standing to litigate their claims in federal court.

B.

* * *

The Association's position is that once an Article III case or controversy is underway, anybody who satisfies Rule 24's requirements may then join in. As long as the original parties are involved, the Association insists, the lawsuit remains within the scope of the federal "judicial power." We disagree. In our view, an Article III case or controversy, once joined by intervenors who lack standing, is—put bluntly—no longer an Article III case or controversy. An Article III case or controversy is one where all parties have standing, and a would-be intervenor, because he seeks to participate as a party, must have standing as well. The Supreme Court has made it very clear that "[t]hose who do not possess Art. III standing may not litigate as suitors in the courts of the United States." Because an intervenor seeks to become a "suitor," and asks the court to "decide the merits of the dispute," he must not only satisfy the requirements of Rule 24, he must also have Article III standing.

* * *

III.

Having decided that those wishing to intervene in federal court must have Article III standing, we must now determine whether the Association passes this test. We think it does. In *Lujan v. Defenders of Wildlife*, 564 U.S. 555 (1992), the Supreme Court held that the "irreducible constitutional minimum of standing" required by Article III has three elements: First, the would-be litigant must have suffered an "injury in fact"; that is, an "invasion of a legally protected interest which is (a) concrete and particularized . . . and (b) actual or imminent, not conjectural or hypothetical. . . ." *Lujan*, 504 U.S. at 560. Second, the would-be litigant must establish a causal connection between the alleged injury and the conduct being challenged. Third, he must show that the injury is likely to be redressed by a favorable decision. * * *

* * *

The alleged injuries in *Lujan* were far more speculative than those alleged here. In this case, the Association has submitted affidavits from several of its members stating that they have visited the Park in the past, that they plan to do so in the near and identifiable future, and that they will be injured directly if the restrictions on snowmobiling are lifted. Jennifer Hunt, Executive Director of the Voyageurs Region National Park Association, swore that she visits the Park at least twice a year, and described specific, imminent, future trips she had planned. She described her activities in the Park and how she thinks she would be affected if the restrictions on snowmobiling were lifted. Joe Kotnik, another member, submitted a similarly detailed affidavit. These members claim that snowmobiling will threaten the Park's eagles and wolves and detract from their enjoyment of the Park's tranquility and beauty. The Association has alleged concrete, imminent, and redressable injuries in fact, which are neither "conjectural" nor "hypothetical."

* * *

IV.

Because the Association has standing, the District Court could have granted the motion to intervene. We must now decide whether it should have. The District Court denied the motion for intervention as of right and for permissive intervention, and instead permitted the Association to participate as *amicus curiae*. The District Court reasoned that the Association's interests were adequately protected by the Government, and that, if permitted to intervene, the Association would likely prejudice the rights of the original parties by delaying the case with additional discovery. We review the District Court's denial of the Association's motion to intervene as of right *de novo*. Because we conclude that the Association should have been allowed to intervene as of right, we need not discuss whether the District Court abused its discretion by not granting permissive intervention.

We agree with the District Court that the Association has an interest in preventing unrestricted snowmobiling and in vindicating a conservationist vision for the Park. The Association has consistently demonstrated its interest in the Park's well-being (as it sees it) and has worked hard over the years, in various proceedings, to protect that interest. We also agree with the District Court's conclusion that the Association's interests might suffer if the Government were to lose this case, or to settle it against the Association's interests. The only question left for us to consider, then, is whether the District Court correctly held that Association's interests were adequately protected by the Government.

Usually, Rule 24(a)'s third criterion is easy to satisfy, and the would-be intervenor faces a "minimal burden" of showing that its interests are not adequately represented by the parties. But when one of the parties is an arm or agency of the government, and the case concerns a matter of "sovereign interest," the bar is raised, because *in such cases* the government is "presumed to represent the interests of all its citizens." We emphasize that the *parens patriae* presumption applies "in such cases" because it does *not* necessarily apply in all cases to which the government is a party. After all, when the proposed intervenors' concern is not a matter of "sovereign interest," there is no reason to think the government will represent it.

Here, however, we agree with the District Court that the Association's conservation interests *are* concerns that the Government, as *parens patriae*, is charged with protecting, and that the presumption of adequate representation therefore applies in this case. This presumption may be rebutted, though, when a would-be intervenor makes a strong showing of inadequate representation. That is, the presumption of adequate representation may be "rebutted by a showing that the applicant's interest cannot be subsumed within the shared interest of the citizens. . . ."

The Association has rebutted the *parens patriae* presumption in this case. Its concerns about the Government's enthusiasm for defending the snowmobiling restrictions are not grounded, as the Snowmobilers charge, in a nebulous and paranoid "distrust of government," but in the well-documented history of this particular case and controversy. The Association sued the Government in an earlier case concerning snowmobiling in the Park precisely because it thought the Government was not adequately representing the Association's interests. In fact, this earlier lawsuit is probably the reason for the current regulations. It is unquestioned that, in the past, the Government has waived and failed to enforce regulations against snowmobile use in the Park. The Government also "breached [its] obligation under the Voyageurs National Park Act to make a wilderness recommendation within four years of . . . the park's establishment." *Voyageurs Regional National Park Association v. Lujan*, 1991 WL 343370, at *11 (D. Minn. 1991), *aff'd*, 966 F.2d 424 (8th Cir. 1992).

The Snowmobilers insist that the Government, like the Association, is interested in protecting wildlife and in upholding environmental regulations. This is true; it does not, however, answer the Association's objection that this interest is not adequately represented by the Government in this case. Unlike the Association, the Government is "obliged to represent . . . all of its citizens." When managing and regulating public lands, to avoid what economists call the "tragedy of the commons," the Government must inevitably favor certain uses over others. The Park was established for both recreational and conservationist purposes. These purposes will sometimes, unavoidably, conflict, and even the Government cannot always adequately represent conflicting interests at the same time. In this case, the Government's interest in promoting recreational activity and tourism in the Park, an interest many citizens share, may be adverse to the Association's conservation interests, interests also shared by many.

V.

In conclusion: The Constitution requires that Rule 24 intervenors have Article III standing; the Association has standing; and it has rebutted any presumption that the Government will adequately represent its interests in this litigation. Therefore, the District Court should have allowed the Association to intervene as of right. The District Court's order denying intervention is reversed. The District Court is directed to enter an order granting the Association's motion for leave to intervene as of right.

WOLLMAN, CIRCUIT JUDGE, concurring and dissenting.

I concur in all of the court's opinion except the holding that a party seeking to intervene must have Article III standing. On that issue, I agree with the arguments advanced by the Association, as so well restated in the court's opinion.

MORRIS SHEPPARD ARNOLD, CIRCUIT JUDGE, dissenting.

I concur in all of the court's opinion except the holding that the presumption that the government is acting as *parens patriae* has been rebutted.

In order to qualify as one of the "very rare cases in which a member of the public is allowed to intervene in an action in which the United States ... represents the public interest," the Association must make "a very strong showing of inadequate representation." The Association asserts that the government's prior failures to embrace its view of the proper emphasis to place on conservation suffice to make that showing, but I do not think that they do. Although the Association and the government have differed over the issues relevant to this case in the past, the government has more recently demonstrated a strong inclination to champion the Association's environmental concerns. In fact, as the court itself observes, the Snowmobilers initiated this case because the government's snowmobiling limitations were *more restrictive* than those proposed in the 1991 wilderness plan, even though the Fish and Wildlife Service concluded that the wilderness plan posed no threat whatever to Park wildlife. The Association points to no specific evidence that the government has not diligently defended the relevant restrictions, or that it is likely to become irresolute in this respect in the future. In such circumstances, I cannot conclude that the Association has made a showing, much less a "very strong showing" of inadequate representation by the government.

In fact, the present interests of the government and the Association are essentially identical, both tactically and substantively. Both seek the continued enforcement of the snowmobiling restrictions. By doing so, both seek to prevent snowmobiling in large areas of the Park, thereby preserving the Park's tranquility and going the extra mile to protect Park wildlife. It is true that conservation is but one of a panoply of interests that the government is obliged to represent. But the fact that government is charged with representing the interests of all citizens, and that some citizens do not share the Association's zeal for conservation, is not enough to overcome the presumption of adequate representation. If it were, the *parens patriae* doctrine would serve no useful purpose, because it would be rebutted in virtually every case. It is important to understand that the government is not obliged to be as zealous about conservation as the Association is. It is merely obliged to be properly solicitous of conservation as one use among the many competing uses to which parks can be put. There is simply insufficient evidence in this record to rebut the presumption of proper governmental solicitousness.

I therefore respectfully dissent.

NOTES AND QUESTIONS

1. In *Johnson*, what policy considerations influenced the judge's discretionary determination to deny permissive intervention? Is the court's analysis convincing?

2. Did the majority in *Mausolf* properly hold that the Association was entitled to intervene as of right? How strong are the arguments to the contrary by Judge Morris Arnold (brother of Richard Arnold, the author of the majority opinion)?

3. Of the various approaches to standing discussed in *Mausolf*, which approach is most persuasive? Commentators are divided on the issue. *Compare, e.g.*, Note, *On the Outside Seeking In: Must Intervenors Demonstrate Standing to Join a Lawsuit?*, 52 Duke L.J. 455 (2002) (arguing that prospective intervenor should only have to satisfy Article III standing, in addition to Rule 24(a) criteria, where he has or could be subject to a legal claim, as opposed to where he "merely seeks to protect an interest that might be impaired by the outcome of a lawsuit"), *with* Note, *Rule 24(a) Intervention of Right: Why the Federal Courts Should Require Standing to Intervene*, 36 Loy. L.A. L. Rev. 527 (2002) (arguing that prospective intervenor should have to meet Article III standing, particularly in public law cases, in order to promote judicial efficiency and to prevent public interest groups from asserting their positions when they otherwise would be prohibited from litigating because of their lack of standing). *See generally* Carl Tobias, *Standing to Intervene*, 1991 Wis. L. Rev. 415 (in-depth analysis of issue); *Sokaogon Chippewa Cmty. v. Babbitt*, 214 F.3d 941, 946 (7th Cir. 2000) (noting continuing conflict among the circuits regarding whether Article III standing is required for intervention).

Despite the confusion among the circuits over whether a non-party must have standing to intervene, the courts are clear that an intervenor must have Article III standing to continue litigating where the original plaintiff with standing fails to do so. *See Mangual v. Rotger–Sabat*, 317 F.3d 45, 61–62 (1st Cir. 2003).

4. What is the difference between status as an intervenor and status as *amicus curiae*? Note that courts, as in *Johnson*, may deny a movant status as an intervenor but grant status as *amicus curiae*. In addition, courts may grant intervention for a limited purpose, such as participating in certain discovery. *See, e.g., Fidelity Bankers Life Ins. Co. v. Wedco, Inc.*, 102 F.R.D. 41 (D. Nev. 1984). *See also Maine v. Dir., U.S. Fish and Wildlife Serv.*, 262 F.3d 13, 14 (1st Cir. 2001) (noting, in holding that district court did not abuse its discretion in denying request of conservation group to intervene in an Endangered Species Act case, that the group had been given "amicus plus" status, *i.e.*, the right to submit briefs, a limited right to call and cross-examine witnesses, and a right to be served with all documents and orders served on parties); *Verizon New England v. Maine Pub. Utils. Comm'n*, 229 F.R.D. 335, 338 (D. Me. 2005) (describing "amicus curiae plus" as where movants seek to call their own witnesses and cross-examine the parties' witnesses).

5. In *Johnson*, there was no question that the timeliness requirement for intervention had been satisfied. In other cases, however, the issue is more complicated. In *Sierra Club v. Espy*, 18 F.3d 1202, 1205 (5th Cir. 1994), the court identified criteria for analyzing the timeliness of an intervention motion:

Determining the timeliness of a motion to intervene entails consideration of four factors: (1) The length of time during which the would-be intervenor actually knew or reasonably should have known of its interest in the case before it petitioned for leave to intervene; (2) the extent of the prejudice that the existing parties to the litigation may suffer as a result of the would-be intervenor's failure to apply for intervention as soon as it knew or reasonably should have known of its interest in the case; (3) the extent of the prejudice that the would-be intervenor may suffer if intervention is denied; and (4) the existence of unusual circumstances militating either for or against a determination that the application is timely.

Are these factors helpful in deciding the timeliness issue? Under Rule 24, is the timeliness analysis the same for intervention as of right as for permissive intervention? Should the considerations be the same?

6. What constitutes an interest sufficient to justify intervention as of right? Given its fact-specific nature, this determination has given courts difficulty. *See generally* Tobias, *supra*, 1991 Wis. L. Rev. at 434. In fact, although the text of Rule 24 arguably suggests that the court exercises its discretion only in determining motions for permissive intervention, the contextual analysis required by Rule 24(a) strongly suggests that courts also exercise substantial discretion in deciding motions for intervention as of right. *See id.*; *cf. Security Ins. Co. of Hartford v. Schipporeit, Inc.*, 69 F.3d 1377, 1381 (7th Cir. 1995) ("Whether an applicant has an interest sufficient to warrant intervention as a matter of right is a highly fact-specific determination, making comparison to other cases of limited value."). In general, a "significant protectable interest" justifying intervention is an interest that is protectable under law, such as contractual rights or federal pollution permits. *Ranchers Cattlemen Action Legal Fund United Stockgrowers of Am. v. U.S.D.A.*, 143 F. App'x 751, 753–54 (9th Cir. 2005) (unpublished) (citing published cases). A purely economic expectancy or economic interest, on the other hand, is not a legally protected interest for purposes of intervention. *Id.* (Ninth Circuit denied intervention to butchers' group in suit by ranchers' group against USDA concerning beef importation policies because butchers' group did not have a significant protectable interest, but rather a mere economic expectancy).

7. As *Johnson* indicates, courts hold that Rule 24(a) is to be construed flexibly. *See also Forest Conservation Council v. U.S. Forest Serv.*, 66 F.3d 1489, 1493 (9th Cir. 1995). Is there a plausible argument for taking a restrictive view of intervention?

8. In *Donnelly v. Glickman*, 159 F.3d 405 (9th Cir. 1998), female employees of the United States Forest Service brought a Title VII class action to challenge an allegedly hostile work environment. Male employees of the Forest Service sought to intervene to challenge alleged discrimination against male employees. The Ninth Circuit ruled as follows:

> The district court denied intervention in the liability phase of plaintiffs' class action on the grounds that the proposed intervenors lacked a significant protectable interest in plaintiffs' action and that denying intervention would not impair the interests of the proposed intervenors. * * *

The proposed intervenors argue that their independent claims for gender-based discrimination give them a significant protectable interest in plaintiffs' class action. An applicant has a "significant protectable interest" in an action if (1) it asserts an interest that is protected under some law, and (2) there is a "relationship" between its legally protected interest and the plaintiff's claims.

The proposed intervenors' independent claims of gender-based discrimination undeniably are covered by Title VII. However, their claims of discrimination against male employees are unrelated to plaintiffs' particular claims of "hostile-work-environment" discrimination against female employees. It is not enough that both groups assert discrimination claims against the same defendants.

An applicant generally satisfies the "relationship" requirement only if the resolution of the plaintiff's claim actually will affect the applicant.

Plaintiffs' action focuses exclusively on whether the Forest Service in Region 5 subjected female employees to a hostile work environment. Resolution of plaintiffs' action, therefore, will not affect the proposed intervenors' claims that the Forest Service subjected male employees to discriminatory treatment. Thus, the proposed intervenors do not have a "significant protectable interest" in the liability phase of plaintiffs' action.

Id. at 409–10. Is the *Donnelly* court's approach consistent with the text and policies of Rule 24? Compare *Donnelly* to a district court's holding that undocumented aliens and Hispanic American organizations have a property interest in the educational benefit of in-state tuition, thus permitting them to intervene as of right in a suit challenging the constitutionality of a law giving undocumented aliens in-state college tuition rates. *See Day v. Sebelius*, 227 F.R.D. 668, 673–74 (D. Kan. 2005) ("[u]nless and until it is ultimately decided that [the law] is unconstitutional, the law is in force and, as such, is sufficient to confer a legally protectable interest in the proposed intervenors").

9. A private party's interest in an abuse-free judicial system does not by itself warrant intervention. *See, e.g., New York News, Inc. v. Kheel*, 972 F.2d 482 (2d Cir. 1992) (district court did not abuse its discretion in denying intervention as of right or permissive intervention to nonparty who sought Rule 11 sanctions against plaintiffs for allegedly baseless allegations against him in complaint). By contrast, the government's prosecutorial and investigative interest may warrant its intervention in a related civil suit. *See, e.g., Bureerong v. Uvawas*, 167 F.R.D. 83, 86 (C.D. Cal. 1996) (in civil suit by immigrants against defendants for alleged false imprisonment and involuntary servitude in garment factory, government had substantial protectable interest in ensuring that civil discovery was not used to circumvent more limited discovery available in related criminal case).

10. Courts have often found that a movant who claims an interest in the confidentiality of its own records may intervene to protect that interest. *See, e.g., Yorkshire v. IRS*, 26 F.3d 942, 945–46 (9th Cir. 1994) (when parent company and its subsidiary file joint tax returns, parent company has right to intervene in Freedom of Information Act claim against its subsidiary to protect confidentiality of its own tax returns); *Blum v. Schlegel*, 150 F.R.D. 38, 38–39 (W.D.N.Y. 1993) (law professor may intervene in lawsuit filed by another law professor to protect confidentiality of her own tenure review file). *But see SEC*

v. *Dresser Indus., Inc.*, 628 F.2d 1368, 1390 (D.C. Cir. 1980) (corporate employee not permitted to intervene to protect his own confidentiality interest in corporate documents because employee's interests were adequately represented by corporation).

11. For intervention as of right, Rule 24(a) requires consideration of whether the original parties will adequately represent the applicant's interest. In *Johnson*, the court found that, because the applicants' interests were coextensive with the defendants' interests, the defendants would adequately represent the applicants' interests. How is Rule 24(a)'s adequacy of representation inquiry similar to, or different from, the adequacy inquiry under Rule 23(a)(4)? Although, under the terms of Rule 24(b), an adequacy analysis is not required for permissive intervention, the *Johnson* case illustrates that such an analysis is part of the judge's exercise of discretion in deciding motions for permissive intervention. Should an adequacy inquiry be added to the text of Rule 24(b)?

12. *Johnson* and *Mausolf* raise the important issue of how the presumption of adequate representation is overcome in the context of *parens patriae* actions. For additional authorities, *see, e.g., Day v. Sebelius*, 227 F.R.D. 668, 674–75 (D. Kan. 2005) (where intervenors' private interests diverged from the public interest of the government defendants, the presumption of adequate representation was rebutted); *Kitzmiller v. Dover Area Sch. Dist.*, 229 F.R.D. 463 (M.D. Pa. 2005) (presumption of adequate representation remained where publisher's interests were adequately represented by defendant school district because both shared common goal of demonstrating that intelligent design was not religious).

13. Federal courts must have an independent basis for subject matter jurisdiction over claims asserted by or against intervenors. When there is federal question jurisdiction over the original claims, the court may have supplemental jurisdiction over claims brought by or against an intervenor. *See* 28 U.S.C. § 1367(a). In a diversity action, however, the supplemental jurisdiction statute does not provide supplemental jurisdiction over either claims brought by non-diverse persons seeking to intervene as plaintiffs or claims made by plaintiffs against non-diverse intervenors. *See* 28 U.S.C. § 1367(b) (*see* Chapter 7(B)); *Liberty Mut. Group v. Hillman's Sheet Metal & Certified Welding, Inc.*, 168 F.R.D. 90, 91 (D. Me. 1996).

14. Recall that the Supreme Court in *Wal–Mart Stores, Inc. v. Dukes*, 564 U.S. 338 (2011), adopted a restrictive definition of commonality under Rule 23(a)(2). *See* Chapter 2. How, if at all, should *Dukes* impact the analysis of "common question[s]" under Rule 24(b)(1)(B)?

b. Intervention in Class Actions

WOOLEN V. SURTRAN TAXICABS, INC.
United States Court of Appeals, Fifth Circuit, 1982.
684 F.2d 324.

Before BROWN, GOLDBERG and POLITZ, CIRCUIT JUDGES.

BROWN, CIRCUIT JUDGE.

This case presents us with both unique facts and issues within the context of an antitrust class action challenging the Dallas/Fort Worth airport's restriction of solicitation of taxicab passengers to limited holders of permits. The controversy surrounding the antitrust claim which forms the merits of this case pales in comparison to this donnybrook between two factions of plaintiffs, the Woolen/Campisi (Campisi) group and the Whorton group. The loser in the first round, the *Whorton* plaintiffs, sought exclusion from the class suit filed by the *Campisi* plaintiffs, or intervention in that suit, alleging inadequate representation and imposition of a class attorney antagonistic to their interests. The District Court denied intervention, certified the class as a F.R.Civ.P. 23(b)(2) suit, and thus in practical effect denied exclusion. Unfortunately, although too frequently true, a ruling in the District Court made to avoid delay has itself engendered more delay. * * * Because the District Court's findings on the issue of intervention are not adequate, we reverse and remand.

A Touch Of Class

The underlying litigation in which the *Whorton* plaintiffs seek to intervene or from which they seek to be excluded is an antitrust action stemming from the establishment by the cities of Dallas and Fort Worth of the D/FW Surtran System to provide ground transportation for the D/FW airport. Surtran apparently accepted competitive bids for the privilege of picking up passengers at the airport. The winning bid was submitted by Yellow Cab of Dallas, Inc. and Fort Worth Cab and Baggage Company, who together formed Surtran Taxicabs, Inc., which contracted with Surtran System to pick up taxicab passengers at the airport for transportation to points in the ten counties surrounding the airport. The contract between Surtran System and Surtran Taxicabs set the rates to be charged, and provided that Surtran System would be paid seventy-five cents per trip plus fifty percent of all profits above a five percent operating profit. Both Dallas and Fort Worth adopted ordinances providing that only holders of permits issued by the airport board may provide ground transportation from the airport. The effect of these ordinances was that only Surtran Taxicabs, as the sole holder of a permit, could pick up taxi passengers at the airport.

On May 22, 1978, plaintiffs John Woolen, Jack Stephens, and John D. Campisi, individually and on behalf of a class of taxi drivers, filed suit against Surtran Taxicabs, the City of Dallas, City of Fort Worth, and three surrounding cities. The *Campisi* class action suit alleged that the arrangement between the cities and Surtran Taxicabs violated the Sherman Act by both restraining trade and creating a monopoly, in violation of Sections 1 and 2 of the Act, 15 U.S.C. §§ 1, 2. The initial complaint sought both injunctive relief and treble damages on behalf of taxicab drivers who held permits to operate cabs within the ten-county region surrounding the airport. Two weeks later, * * * the *Campisi* plaintiffs amended their complaint to add Yellow Cab as a defendant and to add approximately 50 additional named representatives as class members, including the Dallas Taxicab Association. On that same day, the *Whorton* plaintiffs filed over 200 requests for exclusion from the *Campisi* suit, alleging that they would not be represented adequately and that the suit would not be prosecuted vigorously since at least two of the three named members of the *Woolen* class suit were members of the Dallas Taxicab Association, a nonprofit association of taxicab drivers operating in Dallas and formed by Yellow Cab Co., itself a defendant in this lawsuit. Ten days later, the *Whorton* plaintiffs filed a separate suit naming over 200 individual plaintiffs, but not in the form of a class action, seeking to recover treble damages for the antitrust violations.

On June 29, 1978, the *Campisi* plaintiffs filed a motion to consolidate their action with the *Whorton* plaintiffs and to designate the Campisi's attorney, Tom Thomas, as lead counsel. In November 1978, the defendants' subsequent motion to dismiss was denied by the District Court. In December 1978, the *Campisi* plaintiffs moved for class certification to represent a class of all licensed taxicab drivers in the ten county area, a class estimated to be between 2000 and 2500 persons. The class included Woolen and 50 other named plaintiffs as well as the Dallas Taxicab Association. The motion requested certification under Rule 23(b)(2) and (b)(3). In February 1979, the *Campisi* and *Whorton* cases were consolidated for purposes of discovery and a hearing to determine class certification was set for late April and subsequently rescheduled for May 1979. In May 1979 the case was reassigned to another District Judge.

Trying to Get to the Head of the Class

In August 1979, four of the *Whorton* plaintiffs filed a motion to intervene in the *Campisi* case under Rule 24(a)(2), alleging that they had an interest in the transaction, were so situated that the disposition of the action might impair or impede their ability to protect that interest, and were not adequately represented by existing parties.

In October 1979, the four *Whorton* plaintiffs seeking to intervene filed "Requested Findings of Fact and Conclusions of Law in Opposition to Class Certification," alleging that the *Campisi* case should not be certified as a class action. The filing of this opposition is one of the more graphic examples of the antagonism and conflict between the *Campisi* and *Whorton* groups. The relations between the *Campisi* and *Whorton* plaintiffs continued to deteriorate for the next year as the attorneys for both groups were less than cooperative in discovery attempts.

According to the docket sheet, on October 9, 1979, after a hearing, the motion to intervene was granted. The record does not include a copy of the District Judge's order granting the motion and no reference is made to the granting of this motion in the subsequent December 1980 denial of the motion to intervene. In late October 1979, the District Judge held a hearing on class certification. Fourteen months later, on December 31, 1980, the District Judge filed an order certifying the *Campisi* suit as a 23(b)(2) class action and finding the *Campisi* plaintiffs adequate representatives for purposes of the class action. The class was defined as all taxicab operators who held permits to operate taxicabs issued by the municipalities located within the ten county area. Campisi's attorney * * * was appointed lead class action counsel. In addition, the District Judge denied the motion of the four *Whorton* plaintiffs to intervene. Although the District Judge did not rule on the motion for exclusion from the class suit[] filed by the *Whorton* plaintiffs[,] the practical effect of certification under (b)(2) was to deny the right to opt out to these class members. From this December 31, 1980 order the *Whorton* plaintiffs appeal.

United We Fall, Divided We Stand

Why, one might wonder, would two groups of taxicab drivers whom one would expect to be aligned against one common set of defendants, instead attempt to keep the other from active participation in the lawsuit? Each set of plaintiffs has tried to inhibit discovery by the other set. The *Campisi* group has worked to keep the *Whorton* group from intervening while the *Whorton* group has been busy trying to defeat the certification of the *Campisi* group. What we have in the final analysis is two factions of plaintiffs, each seeking to be represented by the attorney of their choice, and each seeking to get through the courtroom door first. While the underlying claim is the same, the *Campisi* plaintiffs seek injunctive relief as evident from their initial motion for certification. The *Whorton* group, on the other hand, is concerned primarily with damages.

Tax(i)ation Without Representation

In this appeal, the *Whorton* plaintiffs basically argue that the District Judge's order of December 31, 1980 results in their being locked into a class action in which they are not adequately represented, in which their interests are antagonistic to other members of the class, and in which they have no desire to participate unless they are allowed representation by the attorney of their choice. They assert that the class action device has been abused to preempt their claim through a sham class action filed by the *Campisi* group * * *. Through certification under Rule 23(b)(2), they fear that their claims for damages may eventually be lost should the *Campisi* class action fail on the merits or settle. To support these claims, the *Whorton* plaintiffs allege a pattern of delays, less than diligent prosecution by *Campisi* and the class attorney, antagonism between the two groups of plaintiffs, and conflicts of interest, both within the class and between *Campisi* and the defendants. For instance, they allege that the Dallas Taxicab Association, certified to represent the drivers, has members from only one of the ten counties, and was originally formed by Yellow Cab, one of the defendants, for the purpose of helping Yellow Cab drivers. Thus, the *Whorton* plaintiffs contend that the representation is inadequate. In addition, they allege that three of the four named *Campisi* plaintiffs are members of the Dallas Taxicab Association. Not only are there connections between the class representatives and defendant Yellow Cab, but, according to the *Whorton* group, there are connections between Campisi's lawyer and Yellow Cab. The *Whorton* plaintiffs charge that Campisi's attorney chose certification as a (b)(2) class action and included the denial of the request for intervention, without any specific request by the court, an assertion substantiated in a letter to the District Judge from the attorney for the defendants. Through a series of statements and examples, the *Whorton* plaintiffs attempt to demonstrate inadequate representation by class members and their counsel and to create the implication that the *Campisi* representatives are likely to compromise the *Whorton* claims for damages because of the connections between the *Campisi* plaintiffs and the defendants. While several examples are given of the inadequacy of representation, both by the named class representatives and their attorney, we find it unnecessary to provide more than the bare outline so far sketched.

In this appeal, the *Whorton* plaintiffs raise several issues. First they contend that they have an absolute right to intervene under F.R.Civ.P.

24(a)(2) because their interest is not adequately represented. Second, they maintain that the District Judge's order of December 31, 1980 was an abuse of discretion by eliminating the representation of the *Whorton* plaintiffs, including those 200 who originally requested exclusion from the *Campisi* suit. This abuse is demonstrated by certifying a class action with no opportunity to opt out or without any subclasses, denying exclusion to the 200 drivers, denying intervention to the [four] representatives of these 200 drivers,[7] staying the individual damage actions of these drivers, and imposing antagonistic class representation and counsel on these drivers through mandatory inclusion in the class action.

* * *

Let's All Join In

[The court initially held that the order denying intervention as of right was appealable.]

* * * [T]he notion of adequacy of representation sufficient to satisfy the prerequisites for a class action under Rule 23(a)(4) [is not] necessarily equivalent to the adequacy of representation contemplated by Rule 24 within the context of intervention of right. In the Advisory Committee's note to the 1966 amendment to Rule 24(a), the Committee indicated that the rule, as amended, no longer contained the prior requirement that as a condition of intervention an applicant be bound. Rather, "[a] class member who claims that his 'representative' does not adequately represent him, and is able to establish that proposition with sufficient probability, should not be put to the risk of having a judgment entered in the action which by its terms extends to him, and be obliged to test the validity of the judgment as applied to his interest by a later collateral attack. Rather he should, as a general rule, be entitled to intervene in the action."

From this statement it is clear that the Committee contemplated that one who was already a class member could intervene in a lawsuit. It is also apparent that the notion of adequacy for purposes of Rule 23(a)(4) is one having more concern with the *res judicata* effects of a judgment on absent members of a class. Without adequate representation a judgment cannot bind those absent class members. Rule 24(a), as amended, specifically drops the requirement that a party is or may be bound by a judgment, substituting instead a practical test, requiring only that the disposition of the action "*may* as a *practical* matter impair or impede his ability to protect that interest,. . . ." As revised, the Rule clearly leaves room for a situation where one's interest may be impaired by inadequate representation without necessarily requiring a *res judicata* effect. One therefore could intervene, claiming inadequacy of representation, without necessarily claiming that he will be precluded by the other action. This would appear to establish a lower threshold or showing of inadequacy for purposes of intervention as opposed to class action certification. The adequacy of representation in Rule 23(a)(4) is that essential to due process under *Hansberry v. Lee*, 311

---

[7] Although the *Whorton* plaintiffs claim to represent some 200 drivers, the motion for intervention was filed by four of the plaintiffs in the *Whorton* suit. The *Whorton* suit, although including approximately 200 plaintiffs, was not originally filed as a class action but rather as a multiple joinder case.

U.S. 32 (1940), before absent class members can be bound. The problem of intervention within a class action would appear to arise most likely in a class certified under 23(b)(1) or (b)(2), rather than under a class certified under 23(b)(3). A class member who does not consider that he is being represented adequately has the option in a (b)(3) action to opt out under 23(c)(2) or to enter an appearance through counsel of his choosing. Should he choose to opt out of the lawsuit, the plaintiff would not be bound. The concept of intervention within a class certified under 23(b)(2) balances the more likely impairment of the individual's interest since he is unable to opt out of this class. Also by allowing intervention, subsequent collateral attacks on the due process preclusive effect of a judgment are avoided.

Members of classes have been allowed to intervene, often within the context of desegregation or Title VII suits. For example, in *Calhoun v. Cook*, 487 F.2d 680, 683 (5th Cir. 1973), we indicated that school children members of a class would have a right to intervene if their interests were not adequately represented by existing parties in a school desegregation suit. We have also indicated that in the context of school desegregation suits, the proper vehicle for parents claiming inadequate representation is through intervention, rather than through the filing of another lawsuit. Within the context of Title VII cases, we have allowed members of a class to intervene to challenge both settlement offers concerning back pay and subsequent dismissals.

* * * [W]e now consider whether the *Whorton* plaintiffs are entitled to intervene of right. If they have no such right, we must dismiss.

Rule 24(a)(2) establishes three conditions which must be met for intervention of right. The applicant must (1) claim "an interest relating to the property or transaction which is the subject of the action"; (2) be "so situated that the disposition of the action may as a practical matter impair or impede his ability to protect that interest"; and (3) his interest is not adequately represented by existing parties. In this case the *Whorton* plaintiffs have claimed an interest in the transaction which is the subject of the action, that is, in the alleged antitrust violations. However, the interest is not identical to that of the *Campisi* plaintiffs, who have clearly indicated that at this point their interest is in injunctive relief, while that of the *Whorton* plaintiffs is in damages. The *Whorton* plaintiffs have alleged that the disposition of the *Campisi* class action *may as a practical matter* impair their ability to protect their interest. Should the *Campisi* plaintiffs fail on the liability issue in the class action, at least as a practical matter, the *Whorton* plaintiffs' ability to recover may be impaired. It is possible that any judgment on the issue of liability in the *Campisi* (b)(2) class action may be binding on the *Whorton* plaintiffs in a separate action unless they can demonstrate in a subsequent or collateral attack that they were inadequately represented and thus denied due process. Finally, the *Whorton* plaintiffs have alleged that their interest is not adequately represented by the existing parties. They contend that neither the class representatives nor their attorney adequately presents their position and have failed to protect their interest. On the basis of the pleadings and motions before the District Court, it is clear that the *Whorton* plaintiffs are "without a friend in this litigation." The *Whorton* plaintiffs have alleged that the *Campisi* plaintiffs have attempted to hamper their discovery, have encouraged burdensome damage interrogatories against the *Whorton* plaintiffs, and have abandoned any interest in the damage claims. From proceedings in this Court, it is clear that the *Campisi* plaintiffs, through opposing the motion of intervention and subsequent appeal, are not aligned with the *Whorton* plaintiffs.

The District Court held a hearing on the question of class certification at which the intervenors were allowed to participate. In its order of December 31, 1980, the District Court denied intervention. This order, entitled "Order Certifying Class Action," while containing findings of fact and conclusions of law, made no specific findings or conclusions as to the issue of intervention. This Court, in reviewing motions to intervene in school desegregation suits, has required the District Court to conduct an evidentiary hearing and to enter findings based upon an adequate record. In this case the District Court has provided no indication of why it denied intervention of right and we are thus unable to tell whether the action was based on the proper considerations or perhaps based on some incorrect assumptions such as that class members may not intervene in a class suit. In the order certifying the *Campisi* class, the District Judge made findings of fact that the class representatives would fairly and adequately protect the interest of the class. The first of the subfindings is that "there is no significant antagonism or conflict between the class action representatives and the class." This finding is perhaps the only relevant one to the issue of intervention and it is not clear whether at the time the District Court was considering the intervenors as members of the class. If so, this finding is clearly erroneous since the antagonism between the *Whorton* plaintiffs who, at least as defined by the District Court, are members of the class, and the class action representatives is too blatant to be ignored. For example, the *Whorton* plaintiffs had earlier attempted to defeat certification. Based on the filings in this case and the hearing, the District Court could not possibly find no antagonism. However, we think that given the lack of findings of fact specifically relating to the issue of intervention, in this case where the credibility of the parties, both the *Campisi* representatives and the *Whorton* plaintiffs, is so essential, this action should be remanded to the District Court to consider again the right to intervene under Rule 24(a)(2) so that this Court is provided with an adequate record on the merits of intervention of right, should this Court need to consider again the right to intervene.

* * *

NOTES AND QUESTIONS

1. As analyzed in *Woolen*, what is the difference between the adequacy inquiry under Rule 23(a)(4) and that under Rule 24(a)(2)? How do these inquiries differ from the considerations that an MDL judge addresses in selecting lead counsel and counsel for the steering committee? *See* Chapter 12(D).

2. Did the court reach the right decision in remanding the case? Why didn't it simply reverse the denial of intervention as an abuse of discretion? What additional factfinding did the Fifth Circuit anticipate that the district court would make on remand?

3. Should a right to intervene be liberally granted when members of a class action claim inadequate representation? Is there a *constitutional* right to intervene in a class action?

4. Was the *Woolen* court correct in observing that the need for intervention is more acute in (b)(1) and (b)(2) class actions because opt-out rights exist under (b)(3)? Isn't it possible that a class member would not want to opt out but would still want to ensure that representation of the class was adequate?

5. In a portion of the opinion not reproduced, the *Woolen* court suggested that one alternative available to the district court on remand was to consolidate the *Whorton* and *Campisi* cases for a joint trial. (Consolidation is discussed later in this chapter.) Under that approach, each group would be represented by its own counsel, and the Fifth Circuit noted that this would eliminate later claims of inadequate counsel.

6. Professor Edward Brunet contends that intervention by third parties in class actions can in some cases enhance fairness and efficiency, but in other cases can impede the progress of a case:

> A successful intervenor is, by definition, connected to the existing lawsuit. Providing the intervenor a voice in the suit seemingly advances participation or right-to-be heard values. In this way, fairness is furthered by procedures that allow third-party intervention.
>
> At the same time, intervention can improve litigation efficiency. If we define litigation efficiency in terms of reaching an accurate decision, intervenors have the potential to enhance the quality of judicial decision making by introducing valuable information into a case. Courts, like any decision makers, need information to decide disputes. Assuming that a judge can efficiently process the information proffered by an intervenor, intervention should improve judicial accuracy.
>
> The assumption that new information provided by intervenors is beneficial, however, may not be realistic. Intervenors are sometimes imitators, who do little more than free ride off the evidence already in a case. Intervenors can also delay and add to the cost of litigation. In addition, the information put forth by the intervenor could confuse a court or make the case unmanageable. In such a case, the informational input of the intervenor exceeds the optimal scale economies of the trial judge. When this occurs, the court should have the discretion to deny the counterproductive intervention petition.

Edward Brunet, *Class Action Objectors: Extortionist Free Riders or Fairness Guarantors*, 2003 U.Chi. Legal F. 403, 416 (2003). Are Professor Brunet's concerns valid? Does Rule 24 provide a vehicle to balance these competing harms and benefits of intervention?

PROBLEM

Rick Kurkland experienced serious side effects—including dizziness, blurry vision, and severe ear aches—from Meitlan Corp.'s pain medication (Reliever), which he had taken for arthritis. Most recently, he has noticed partial hearing loss in his left ear, which he believes was caused by Reliever. A class action suit was filed by someone else allegedly harmed by Reliever, but seeking relief only for those who suffered blurry vision or dizziness. Because he believes his injuries are much more extensive, Kurkland opted out of the class and filed his own case (assigned to the same judge).

He is now concerned that, if the class action goes poorly, it could severely impact his own case. Indeed, the judge has announced that he would be inclined to issue the same legal rulings on related issues in both cases. Would Kurkland have a valid basis to intervene in the class action? Under what theory? If not, what should he do? How would one oppose Kurkland's attempt to intervene?

c. Mandatory Intervention?

MARTIN V. WILKS
Supreme Court of the United States, 1989.

490 U.S. 755.

CHIEF JUSTICE REHNQUIST delivered the opinion of the Court.

A group of white firefighters sued the city of Birmingham, Alabama (City), and the Jefferson County Personnel Board (Board) alleging that they were being denied promotions in favor of less qualified black firefighters. They claimed that the City and the Board were making promotion decisions on the basis of race in reliance on certain consent decrees, and that these decisions constituted impermissible racial discrimination in violation of the Constitution and federal statutes. The District Court held that the white firefighters were precluded from challenging employment decisions taken pursuant to the decrees, even though these firefighters had not been parties to the proceedings in which the decrees were entered. We think this holding contravenes the general rule that a person cannot be deprived of his legal rights in a proceeding to which he is not a party.

The litigation in which the consent decrees were entered began in 1974, when the Ensley Branch of the National Association for the Advancement of Colored People and seven black individuals filed separate class-action complaints against the City and the Board. They alleged that both had engaged in racially discriminatory hiring and promotion practices in various public service jobs in violation of Title VII of the Civil Rights Act of 1964, 42 U.S.C. § 2000e *et seq.*, and other federal law. After a bench trial on some issues, but before judgment, the parties entered into two consent decrees, one between the black individuals and the City and the other between them and the Board. These proposed decrees set forth an extensive remedial scheme, including long-term and interim annual goals for the hiring of blacks as firefighters. The decrees also provided for goals for promotion of blacks within the fire department.

The District Court entered an order provisionally approving the decrees and directing publication of notice of the upcoming fairness hearings. Notice of the hearings, with a reference to the general nature of the decrees, was published in two local newspapers. At that hearing, the Birmingham Firefighters Association (BFA) appeared and filed objections as *amicus curiae*. After the hearing, but before final approval of the decrees, the BFA and two of its members also moved to intervene on the ground that the decrees would adversely affect their rights. The District Court denied the motions as untimely and approved the decrees. Seven white firefighters, all members of the BFA, then filed a complaint against the City and the

Board seeking injunctive relief against enforcement of the decrees. The seven argued that the decrees would operate to illegally discriminate against them; the District Court denied relief.

Both the denial of intervention and the denial of injunctive relief were affirmed on appeal. * * *

A new group of white firefighters, the *Wilks* respondents, then brought suit against the City and the Board in District Court. They too alleged that, because of their race, they were being denied promotions in favor of less qualified blacks in violation of federal law. The Board and the City admitted to making race-conscious employment decisions, but argued that the decisions were unassailable because they were made pursuant to the consent decrees. A group of black individuals, the *Martin* petitioners, were allowed to intervene in their individual capacities to defend the decrees.

The defendants moved to dismiss the reverse discrimination cases as impermissible collateral attacks on the consent decrees. The District Court [granted the motion after holding a trial].

On appeal, the Eleventh Circuit reversed. * * *

We granted *certiorari*, and now affirm the Eleventh Circuit's judgment. All agree that "[i]t is a principle of general application in Anglo–American jurisprudence that one is not bound by a judgment *in personam* in a litigation in which he is not designated as a party or to which he has not been made a party by service of process." *Hansberry v. Lee*, 311 U.S. 32, 40 (1940). *See, e.g., Parklane Hosiery Co. v. Shore*, 439 U.S. 322, 327, n.7 (1979); *Blonder–Tongue Laboratories, Inc. v. University Foundation*, 402 U.S. 313, 328–29 (1971); *Zenith Radio Corp. v. Hazeltine Research, Inc.*, 395 U.S. 100, 110 (1969). This rule is part of our "deep-rooted historic tradition that everyone should have his own day in court." A judgment or decree among parties to a lawsuit resolves issues as among them, but it does not conclude the rights of strangers to those proceedings.[2]

Petitioners argue that, because respondents failed to timely intervene in the initial proceedings, their current challenge to actions taken under the consent decree constitutes an impermissible "collateral attack." They argue that respondents were aware that the underlying suit might affect them, and if they chose to pass up an opportunity to intervene, they should not be permitted to later litigate the issues in a new action. The position has sufficient appeal to have commanded the approval of the great majority of the Federal Courts of Appeals, but we agree with the contrary view expressed by the Court of Appeals for the Eleventh Circuit in these cases.

We begin with the words of Justice Brandeis in *Chase National Bank v. Norwalk*, 291 U.S. 431, 441 (1934):

> The law does not impose upon any person absolutely entitled to a hearing the burden of voluntary intervention in a suit to which he

---

[2] We have recognized an exception to the general rule when, in certain limited circumstances, a person, although not a party, has his interests adequately represented by someone with the same interests who is a party. Additionally, where a special remedial scheme exists expressly foreclosing successive litigation by nonlitigants, as for example in bankruptcy or probate, legal proceedings may terminate preexisting rights if the scheme is otherwise consistent with due process. Neither of these exceptions, however, applies in these cases.

is a stranger.... Unless duly summoned to appear in a legal proceeding, a person not a privy may rest assured that a judgment recovered therein will not affect his legal rights.

While these words were written before the adoption of the Federal Rules of Civil Procedure, we think the Rules incorporate the same principle; a party seeking a judgment binding on another cannot obligate that person to intervene; he must be joined. Against the background of permissive intervention set forth in *Chase National Bank*, the drafters cast Rule 24, governing intervention, in permissive terms. *See* [Rule] 24(a) (intervention as of right); [Rule] 24(b) (permissive intervention). They determined that the concern for finality and completeness of judgments would be "better [served] by mandatory joinder procedures." Accordingly, Rule 19(a) provides for mandatory joinder in circumstances where a judgment rendered in the absence of a person may "leave ... persons already parties subject to a substantial risk of incurring ... inconsistent obligations...." Rule 19(b) sets forth the factors to be considered by a court in deciding whether to allow an action to proceed in the absence of an interested party.

Joinder as a party, rather than knowledge of a lawsuit and an opportunity to intervene, is the method by which potential parties are subjected to the jurisdiction of the court and bound by a judgment or decree. The parties to a lawsuit presumably know better than anyone else the nature and scope of relief sought in the action, and at whose expense such relief might be granted. It makes sense, therefore, to place on them a burden of bringing in additional parties where such a step is indicated, rather than placing on potential additional parties a duty to intervene when they acquire knowledge of the lawsuit. The linchpin of the "impermissible collateral attack" doctrine—the attribution of preclusive effect to a failure to intervene—is therefore quite inconsistent with Rule 19 and Rule 24.

* * *

Petitioners contend that a different result should be reached because the need to join affected parties will be burdensome and ultimately discouraging to civil rights litigation. Potential adverse claimants may be numerous and difficult to identify; if they are not joined, the possibility for inconsistent judgments exists. Judicial resources will be needlessly consumed in relitigation of the same question.

Even if we were wholly persuaded by these arguments as a matter of policy, acceptance of them would require a rewriting rather than an interpretation of the relevant Rules. But we are not persuaded that their acceptance would lead to a more satisfactory method of handling cases like these. It must be remembered that the alternatives are a duty to intervene based on knowledge, on the one hand, and some form of joinder, as the Rules presently provide, on the other. No one can seriously contend that an employer might successfully defend against a Title VII claim by one group of employees on the ground that its actions were required by an earlier decree entered in a suit brought against it by another, if the later group did not have adequate notice or knowledge of the earlier suit.

The difficulties petitioners foresee in identifying those who could be adversely affected by a decree granting broad remedial relief are undoubtedly present, but they arise from the nature of the relief sought and not because of any choice between mandatory intervention and joinder. Rule 19's provisions for joining interested parties are designed to accommodate the sort of complexities that may arise from a decree affecting numerous people in various ways. We doubt that a mandatory intervention rule would be any less awkward. As mentioned, plaintiffs who seek the aid of the courts to alter existing employment policies, or the employer who might be subject to conflicting decrees, are best able to bear the burden of designating those who would be adversely affected if plaintiffs prevail; these parties will generally have a better understanding of the scope of likely relief than employees who are not named but might be affected. Petitioners' alternative does not eliminate the need for, or difficulty of, identifying persons who, because of their interests, should be included in a lawsuit. It merely shifts that responsibility to less able shoulders.

Nor do we think that the system of joinder called for by the Rules is likely to produce more relitigation of issues than the converse rule. The breadth of a lawsuit and concomitant relief may be at least partially shaped in advance through Rule 19 to avoid needless clashes with future litigation. And even under a regime of mandatory intervention, parties who did not have adequate knowledge of the suit would relitigate issues. Additional questions about the adequacy and timeliness of knowledge would inevitably crop up. We think that the system of joinder presently contemplated by the Rules best serves the many interests involved in the run of litigated cases, including cases like the present ones.

Petitioners also urge that the congressional policy favoring voluntary settlement of employment discrimination claims * * * also supports the "impermissible collateral attack" doctrine. But once again it is essential to note just what is meant by "voluntary settlement." A voluntary settlement in the form of a consent decree between one group of employees and their employer cannot possibly "settle," voluntarily or otherwise, the conflicting claims of another group of employees who do not join in the agreement. * * *

Insofar as the argument is bottomed on the idea that it may be easier to settle claims among a disparate group of affected persons if they are all before the court, joinder bids fair to accomplish that result as well as a regime of mandatory intervention.

For the foregoing reasons we affirm the decision of the Court of Appeals for the Eleventh Circuit. * * *

JUSTICE STEVENS, with whom JUSTICES BRENNAN, MARSHALL, and BLACKMUN join, dissenting.

As a matter of law there is a vast difference between persons who are actual parties to litigation and persons who merely have the kind of interest that may as a practical matter be impaired by the outcome of a case. Persons in the first category have a right to participate in a trial and to appeal from an adverse judgment; depending on whether they win or lose, their legal rights may be enhanced or impaired. Persons in the latter category have a right to intervene in the action in a timely fashion, or they may be joined as parties against their will. But if they remain on the sidelines, they may be harmed as a practical matter even though their legal rights are unaffected. One of the disadvantages of sideline-sitting is that the bystander has no right to appeal from a judgment no matter how harmful it may be.

In these cases the Court quite rightly concludes that the white firefighters who brought the second series of Title VII cases could not be deprived of their legal rights in the first series of cases because they had neither intervened nor been joined as parties. The consent decrees obviously could not deprive them of any contractual rights, such as seniority, or accrued vacation pay, or of any other legal rights, such as the right to have their employer comply with federal statutes like Title VII. There is no reason, however, why the consent decrees might not produce changes in conditions at the white firefighters' place of employment that, as a practical matter, may have a serious effect on their opportunities for employment or promotion even though they are not bound by the decrees in any legal sense. The fact that one of the effects of a decree is to curtail the job opportunities of nonparties does not mean that the nonparties have been deprived of legal rights or that they have standing to appeal from that decree without becoming parties.

Persons who have no right to appeal from a final judgment—either because the time to appeal has elapsed or because they never became parties to the case—may nevertheless collaterally attack a judgment on certain narrow grounds. If the court had no jurisdiction over the subject matter, or if the judgment is the product of corruption, duress, fraud, collusion, or mistake, under limited circumstances it may be set aside in an appropriate collateral proceeding. This rule not only applies to parties to the original action, but also allows interested third parties collaterally to attack judgments. In both civil and criminal cases, however, the grounds that may be invoked to support a collateral attack are much more limited than those that may be asserted as error on direct appeal. Thus, a person who can foresee that a lawsuit is likely to have a practical impact on his interests may pay a heavy price if he elects to sit on the sidelines instead of intervening and taking the risk that his legal rights will be impaired.

In these cases there is no dispute about the fact that respondents are not parties to the consent decrees. It follows as a matter of course that they are not bound by those decrees. Those judgments could not, and did not, deprive them of any legal rights. The judgments did, however, have a practical impact on respondents' opportunities for advancement in their profession. For that reason, respondents had standing to challenge the validity of the decrees, but the grounds that they may advance in support of a collateral challenge are much more limited than would be allowed if they were parties prosecuting a direct appeal.

NOTES AND QUESTIONS

1. Did the majority strike the right balance in its interpretation of Rules 19 and 24 in *Martin*? What is the thrust of Justice Stevens's dissent?

2. Civil rights advocates were concerned that *Martin* would subject long-standing consent decrees to collateral attack through reverse discrimination claims, and that the rules set forth in *Martin* regarding challenges to consent decrees would inhibit voluntary settlements of Title VII cases. *See, e.g.,* Samuel Issacharoff, *When Substance Mandates Procedure:* Martin v. Wilks *and the Rights of Vested Incumbents in Civil Rights Consent Decrees*, 77 Cornell L. Rev. 189, 192–93 (1992) (summarizing concerns of civil rights community). Section 108 of the Civil Rights Act of 1991 legislatively overruled *Martin* in cases involving any "employment practice that implements and is within the scope of a litigated or consent judgment or order that resolves a claim of employment discrimination under the Constitution or Federal civil rights laws." Specifically, Section 108 provides, subject to certain exceptions, that:

> (A) Notwithstanding any other provision of law, * * * an employment practice that implements and is within the scope of a litigated or consent judgment or order that resolves a claim of employment discrimination under the Constitution or Federal civil rights laws may not be challenged under the circumstances described in subparagraph (B).
>
> (B) A practice described in subparagraph (A) may not be challenged in a claim under the Constitution or Federal civil rights laws—
>
>> (i) by a person who, prior to the entry of the judgment or order described in subparagraph (A), had—
>>
>>> (I) actual notice of the proposed judgment or order sufficient to apprise such person that such judgment or order might adversely affect the interests and legal rights of such person and that an opportunity was available to present objections to such judgment or order by a future date certain; and
>>>
>>> (II) a reasonable opportunity to present objections to such judgment or order; or
>>
>> (ii) by a person whose interests were adequately represented by another person who had previously challenged the judgment or order on the same legal grounds and with a similar factual situation, unless there has been an intervening change in law or fact.

42 U.S.C. § 2000e–2(n)(1). Does this legislative provision comport with due process?

3. Although *Martin* was overruled in the context of certain actions involving employment discrimination consent decrees, its analysis of Rules 19 and 24 still has vitality beyond that context. *See, e.g., Kourtis v. Cameron*, 419 F.3d 989 (9th Cir. 2005) (applying *Martin* in copyright case).

4. Rejecting any broad theory of "virtual representation" under which one party could be precluded from relitigating what another party with closely aligned interests had already litigated, the Supreme Court in 2008 established a framework for determining when nonparty preclusion is warranted. In *Taylor v. Sturgell*, 553 U.S. 880 (2008), the Court identified six recognized exceptions to the rule against nonparty preclusion as set forth in *Martin*:

> First, "[a] person who agrees to be bound by the determination of issues in an action between others is bound in accordance with the terms of his agreement." For example, "if separate actions involving the same transaction are brought by different plaintiffs against the same defendant, all the parties to all the actions may agree that the

question of the defendant's liability will be definitely determined, one way or the other, in a 'test case.' "

Second, nonparty preclusion may be justified based on a variety of pre-existing "substantive legal relationship[s]" between the person to be bound and a party to the judgment. Qualifying relationships include, but are not limited to, preceding and succeeding owners of property, bailee and bailor, and assignee and assignor. * * *

Third, we have confirmed that, "in certain limited circumstances," a nonparty may be bound by a judgment because she was "adequately represented by someone with the same interests who [wa]s a party" to the suit. Representative suits with preclusive effect on nonparties include properly conducted class actions and suits brought by trustees, guardians, and other fiduciaries.

Fourth, a nonparty is bound by a judgment if she "assume[d] control" over the litigation in which that judgment was rendered. Because such a person has had "the opportunity to present proofs and argument," he has already "had his day in court" even though he was not a formal party to the litigation.

Fifth, a party bound by a judgment may not avoid its preclusive force by religating through a proxy. Preclusion is thus in order when a person who did not participate in a litigation later brings suit as the designed representative of a person who was a party to the prior adjudication. And although our decisions have not addressed the issue directly, it also seems clear that preclusion is appropriate when a nonparty later brings suit as an agent for a party who is bound by a judgment.

Sixth, in certain circumstances a special statutory scheme may "expressly foreclos[e] successive litigation by nonlitigants ... if the scheme is otherwise consistent with due process." Examples of such schemes include bankruptcy and probate proceedings and *quo warranto* actions or other suits that, "under [the governing] law, [may] be brought only on behalf of the public at large."

Id. at 2172–73. Are each of these exceptions warranted under the *Martin* framework?

5. With respect to its ability to serve as a mass aggregation device, intervention is of relatively limited use. The American Law Institute has observed that, "[a]s is true of the other existing party joinder devices, intervention ordinarily is too narrow to be helpful in the type of large-scale actions that lie at the core of the complex litigation problem." American Law Institute, *Complex Litigation: Statutory Recommendations and Analysis* 26 (1994).

6. CONSOLIDATION

Consolidation under Rule 42 is a device that allows for a joint trial or hearing when multiple actions pending before a particular court involve one or more common questions of law or fact. These requirements are considerably easier to satisfy than those for a (b)(3) class action, where the common questions must predominate over any individual questions. Indeed, even the MDL standard is more rigorous; consolidation under the MDL statute requires a common question of fact, whereas Rule 42 permits consolidation even if the sole common question is one of *law*. At the same time, Rule 42 is not toothless; courts have imposed limits on consolidation under Rule 42 when a joint trial or hearing would result in unfairness or jury confusion.

FED. R. CIV. P. 42: CONSOLIDATION; SEPARATE TRIALS

(a) Consolidation. If actions before the court involve a common question of law or fact, the court may:

> (1) join for hearing or trial any or all matters at issue in the actions;
>
> (2) consolidate the actions; or
>
> (3) issue any other orders to avoid unnecessary cost or delay.

(b) Separate Trials. For convenience, to avoid prejudice, or to expedite and economize, the court may order a separate trial of one or more separate issues, claims, crossclaims, counterclaims, or third-party claims. When ordering a separate trial, the court must preserve any federal right to a jury trial.

DAYBROOK FISHERIES, INC. v. AM. MARINE CONSTR., INC.

United States District Court, Eastern District of Louisiana, 1998.

1998 WL 748586.

PORTEOUS, DISTRICT JUDGE.

[ON MOTION TO CONSOLIDATE]

Pool Company, a Texas corporation authorized to and doing business in Louisiana, is suing American Marine Construction, Inc., *et al.* (hereinafter "AMC"). On or about April 27, 1997, the POOL RANGER IV capsized in the Gulf of Mexico * * * while the vessel was under charter to and being operated by AMC. [T]his resulted in the total loss of the POOL RANGER IV (hereinafter "PR"). The plaintiff is suing AMC because PR was under the exclusive possession and control of AMC due to a charter party entitled "Time Charter," dated February 14, 1995. The plaintiff claims that under this charter AMC is responsible for any damage or destruction to PR. The plaintiff contends that in the Time Charter AMC agreed to

> defend, indemnify, and hold Pool Company (hereinafter "PC") and its successors harmless from and against, and to reimburse PC upon demand for any expenditures incurred by PC with respect to: any and all liabilities, obligations, losses, damages, penalties, fees, claims, actions, suits, costs, expenses and disbursements (including, without limitation, the reasonable legal fees and expenses reasonably incurred) of whatever kind and nature which PC may incur during the charter period as a consequence of or in any way relating to or arising out of the possession, use, operation, subchartering, condition, maintenance or repair, or storage, or removal of the PR under the Time Charter, including, among other things, any sums which PC shall become liable to pay for the removal or destruction of the wreck or obstruction in the event of the PR becoming a wreck or obstruction to navigation.

The plaintiff further avers that the capsizing of the PR on April 27, 1997 was caused by AMC's negligence. The plaintiff also seeks * * * damages [and recovery] of outstanding receivables owed under the Time Charter, $1 million in the remaining hull machinery policy * * *.

In [another] action [proposed for consolidation with Pool Company's suit,] * * * Daybrook and Highlands are suing for damages relating to the sinking of the Daybrook Fisheries vessel F/V Celia M (hereinafter "Celia"). On or about October 21, 1997, the Celia was navigating in the vicinity of the wreck of PR when it struck a leg of the PR that was submerged five feet below the water line.

The common issues of fact are: (1) the cause for the capsizing of the PR and any negligence on the part of the defendants and any unseaworthiness on the part of the vessel; (2) the terms, conditions, and allocation of liability provided for by the charter party; (3) who is responsible for the wreck and whose responsibility it was to mark and/or remove the wreck; (4) the question of indemnity and contribution between or among the owners and charters of the PR.

The preceding issues are common to the two causes of action and bear directly on the rights of all parties hereto to recover or to be exonerated from responsibility. The issues of the two cases are common both in fact and in law. Furthermore, jurisdiction in these cases is premised by the parties under the admiralty and maritime jurisdiction which as recognized in the comment to Rule 42 is conducive to consolidation * * *.

II. ANALYSIS

A. Consolidation

* * *

The Fifth Circuit suggests that FRCP 42(a) should be used to expedite trial and eliminate unnecessary repetition and confusion. *Miller v. USPS*, 729 F.2d 1033, 1035 (5th Cir. 1984). However, the Fifth Circuit stated that,

> Consolidation does not so completely merge the two cases as to deprive a party of any substantial rights that he may have had if the actions had proceeded separately, for the two suits retain their separate identities and each requires the entry of a separate judgment.

[*Id.*] at 1035.

Courts have broad discretion on whether or not to consolidate where there are common questions of law and fact and where consolidation would save time and money. As Wright and Miller point out: "It is for the court to weigh the saving of time and effort that consolidation would produce against any inconvenience, delay, or expense that it would cause." 9 Wright & Miller, *Federal Practice and Procedure*, § 2383 at 439 (2d ed. 1995). * * *

In the instant case the rights of the defendants will not be adversely affected by consolidating the two cases. Both accidents result from the same series of events, the capsizing of the PR and the failure of removing the wreck from navigable waters. Thus, common issues of fact exist between the two cases. Furthermore, common issues of law exist in both cases because in both instances the party that is responsible for the resulting damages will be determined by interpreting the Time Charter contract and indemnity agreement. Therefore, * * * if the present motion of consolidation * * * is granted, no one will be prejudiced by combining the claims and their consolidation will avoid unnecessary costs and delay.

Since consolidation pursuant to FRCP 42(a) is discretionary, this Court rules that such action is warranted and beneficial. The cases at hand have common issues of fact and law which are pending before the Court and consolidating the actions will not prejudice the parties and will avoid unnecessary costs and delay.

* * *

MALCOLM V. NAT'L GYPSUM CO.
United States Court of Appeals, Second Circuit, 1993.

995 F.2d 346.

Before TIMBERS, WALKER, and McLAUGHLIN, CIRCUIT JUDGES.

McLAUGHLIN, CIRCUIT JUDGE.

Keene Corporation appeals from a final judgment of the United States District Courts for the Eastern and Southern Districts of New York * * * awarding plaintiff Roberta Kranz, as the executrix of the estate of Lee Lewis, $226,038.49 for personal injury, wrongful death, and loss of consortium. The claims arose from Lewis's exposure to asbestos products manufactured by Keene's subsidiary, the Baldwin–Ehret–Hill Company ("BEH"). For the reasons stated below, we reverse and remand for a new trial.

BACKGROUND

The Explosion Of Asbestos Litigation

[The court discussed the challenges to the federal courts presented by asbestos litigation.]

In New York, the Chief Judges of the Second Circuit, the Southern District, and the Eastern District transferred all [asbestos] cases filed in either district to the district judge in this action for purposes of discovery. * * * Eventually, the cases approached the Rubicon of either settling or going to trial. To facilitate settlements and provide for manageable trials, the cases were "subdivided by the location in which the plaintiff suffered primary exposure."

The Consolidation Here

In the instant action, 600 cases were consolidated. The thread upon which all 600 cases hung was that each plaintiff had been exposed to asbestos in one or more of over 40 power-generating stations, or "powerhouses" as they are called, in New York State.

Forty-eight were selected from the 600 cases for trial on a reverse-bifurcated basis, *i.e.* damages to be tried first and then liability. The damages trial began on April 1, 1991. Each of the 48 plaintiffs had named as defendants between 14 and 42 manufacturers or distributors of asbestos-containing products. Of these, 25 appeared at trial as direct defendants. Several of the defendants impleaded third-party defendants. For example, on March 18, 1991, 13 days before the trial began, Judge Sifton allowed defendant Owens–Corning Fiberglas Corporation to implead over 200 companies. Some of the third-party defendants, in turn, impleaded fourth-party defendants.

During the four-month damages trial, evidence of the debilitating diseases and/or deaths of all 48 plaintiffs was presented to the jury. Often, the plaintiffs themselves would testify to the devastating consequences suffered as a result of asbestos-related disease. * * * A parade of medical doctors testified on the etiologies and pathologies of the asbestos-related diseases suffered by each of the plaintiffs. Economists testified concerning the present value of past and future income streams, and the dollar value of ordinary household services.

In addition, detailed testimony for each victim was necessary concerning his degree of impairment, specific medical history, emotional state, and medical prognosis. Further complicating matters, the jury had to sift through each victim's medical history to determine whether factors other than asbestos, such as smoking, were responsible, in whole or part, for his physical complaints. * * *

After four months of such evidence, the jury returned verdicts for 45 of the plaintiffs for an aggregate of over $94 million. * * *

The liability portion of the trial began on September 11, 1991. During this phase, the jury was presented with a dizzying amount of evidence regarding each victim's work history. Where a victim, like Lewis, had died before trial, the sites where he had worked during his career, the types of asbestos-containing products with which he had been involved, and the identity of the manufacturers or distributors of the asbestos products to which he may have been exposed were reconstructed through the testimony of family members and co-workers.

* * *

After three months, plaintiffs rested on December 4, 1991. For the next three months, the defendants presented their case. The district court and the lawyers valiantly attempted to maintain the identity of each claim throughout the trial. The jury was instructed on several occasions to consider each case separately and each juror was given a notebook for this purpose. Thanks to the effective settlement techniques of the district judge and a special master, only two plaintiffs remained by the time the jury rendered its liability verdict. It concluded that appellant Keene Corporation was 9% liable for the Kranz–Lewis damages.

Following the verdict, Keene moved for judgment as a matter of law, a new trial, or other post-verdict relief, contending, *inter alia*, that the district court's decision to consolidate the 48 cases for trial constituted prejudicial error. The district judge rejected this argument without extended discussion, and * * * entered a judgment for Kranz against Keene for $226,038.29.

DISCUSSION

Addressing the complaints of hundreds of thousands of severely injured asbestos plaintiffs, while safeguarding the rights of the defendants, all the while searching for equitable resolutions in each case, is a herculean task. Many of the asbestos victims suffered exposure for decades and at many different worksites. Finding an appropriate forum to resolve all these claims with minimal delay is the goal. Faced with this challenge, district judges throughout the country have reacted with commendable ingenuity. Pre-trial consolidation for the purposes of discovery, the appointment of special masters to expedite settlement, and, especially, the liberal use of consolidated trials have ameliorated what might otherwise be a sclerotic backlog of cases.

* * *

* * * As we recently noted,

> Consolidation of tort actions sharing common questions of law and fact is commonplace. This is true of asbestos-related personal injury cases as well.
>
> The trial court has broad discretion to determine whether consolidation is appropriate. In the exercise of discretion, courts have taken the view that considerations of judicial economy favor consolidation. However, the discretion to consolidate is not unfettered. Considerations of convenience and economy must yield to a paramount concern for a fair and impartial trial.

Johnson v. Celotex Corp., 899 F.2d 1281, 1284–85 (2d Cir. 1990). In *Johnson*, we noted that a court considering a consolidation must consider:

> [W]hether the specific risks of prejudice and possible confusion [are] overborne by the risk of inconsistent adjudications of common factual and legal issues, the burden on parties, witnesses, and available judicial resources posed by multiple lawsuits, the length of time required to conclude multiple suits as against a single one, and the relative expense to all concerned of the single-trial, multiple-trial alternatives.

The benefits of efficiency can never be purchased at the cost of fairness. As we recently stated:

> [W]e are mindful of the dangers of a streamlined trial process in which testimony must be curtailed and jurors must assimilate vast amounts of information. The systemic urge to aggregate litigation must not be allowed to trump our dedication to individual justice, and we must take care that each individual plaintiff's— and defendant's—cause not be lost in the shadow of a towering mass litigation.

In re Brooklyn Navy Yard Asbestos Litig., 971 F.2d 831, 853 (2d Cir. 1992).

To strike the appropriate balance as to consolidation *vel non*, "[c]ourts in the Southern and Eastern Districts of New York have used [a standard set of] criteria . . . as a guideline in determining whether to consolidate asbestos exposure cases." These criteria include: "(1) common worksite; (2) similar occupation; (3) similar time of exposure; (4) type of disease; (5)

whether plaintiffs were living or deceased; (6) status of discovery in each case; (7) whether all plaintiffs were represented by the same counsel; and (8) type of cancer alleged. . . ." As in *Johnson*, we again conclude that the test furnishes a useful guideline to evaluate consolidation of asbestos cases.

(1) Worksite

Plaintiffs did not all work at the same worksite. Rather, their only worksite similarity was that each was alleged to have suffered some part of his asbestos exposure at one or more of over 40 power-generating plants throughout New York State. * * *

* * * [T]he record contains evidence of over 250 worksites. Thus, not only was there no common worksite in this case, but any contention that there was a common type of worksite must be viewed with a skeptical eye.

(2) Similar Occupation

This inquiry is significant because a worker's exposure to asbestos must depend mainly on his occupation. For example, insulators, who actually applied the asbestos, suffered from direct asbestos exposure, whereas sheet-metal workers * * * suffered from asbestos exposure in a bystander capacity. The occupations of the plaintiffs in this case ranged from plumbers to machinists to carpenters to boilermakers to sheet-metal workers.

(3) Times of Exposure

The third factor similarly does not support a finding of commonality. The time frame that the jury was required to consider was enormous: a period involving exposures in intervals that began as early as the 1940's and ended as late as the 1970's. While some plaintiffs suffered asbestos exposure over periods of up to 30 years, others had much shorter periods of exposure, undercutting the benefit of efficiency, and increasing the likelihood of prejudice, particularly concerning "state-of-the-art" evidence.

(4) Disease Type

Not all plaintiffs alleged the same type of disease. Rather, of the 48 plaintiffs, 28 suffered from asbestosis, 10 suffered from lung cancer, and 10 from mesothelioma. The significance of this disparity is obvious. When the plaintiffs suffer from the same disease, the economy derived by not rehashing the etiology and pathology of the particular disease will be great, while the concomitant prejudice will be minimal. Here, by contrast, the jury was required to hear testimony about three different diseases. The opportunity for prejudice is particularly troubling where, as here, asbestosis sufferers, who may under certain circumstances expect close to a normal life spans, are paired for trial with those suffering from terminal cancers, such as mesothelioma and lung cancer.

(5) The Living & The Dead

Some victims in this case were still living during trial. Others had already died. * * * The significance of this factor is evident. *In re Joint E. & S. Asbestos Litig.*, 125 F.R.D. 60, 65–66 (E. & S.D.N.Y. 1989) ("[T]he presence of wrongful death claims and personal injury actions in a consolidated trial is somewhat troublesome. . . . [T]he dead plaintiffs may present the jury with a powerful demonstration of the fate that awaits those claimants who are still living.").

(6) Discovery Status

Keene does not argue that any of the 48 cases was not ready for trial. We note however, the absence of any express finding of readiness in the district court's decision rejecting a challenge to consolidation. Query: were the 200 third-party defendants that were impleaded two weeks before the trial ready for the trial?

(7) Counsel

Plaintiffs were represented by five law firms, each of which played an active role throughout the trial.

(8) Cancer

Two different types of cancer were alleged: lung cancer, and mesothelioma, a cancer of the lining of the wall of the chest. Each required distinct testimony regarding its etiology, pathology, and consequences.

In addition to the foregoing eight factors, courts contemplating consolidation must also take into account the number of cases affected. Here, the maelstrom of facts, figures, and witnesses, with 48 plaintiffs, 25 direct defendants, numerous third-and-fourth party defendants, and evidence regarding culpable non-parties and over 250 worksites throughout the world was likely to lead to jury confusion.

* * *

We are concerned that the jury's ability to focus on [the distinction between direct and bystander exposure applicable to different defendants] may have been compromised in this case. While the evidence regarding Lewis's exposure to Keene's products was vague, minimal, and heavily circumstantial when compared to the extensive evidence regarding the products of defendant Owens–Corning Fiberglas, the jury apportioned an equal 9% liability to each defendant. This is hard to explain. We conclude that under the unique circumstances of this case, there is an unacceptably strong chance that the equal apportionment of liability amounted to the jury throwing up its hands in the face of a torrent of evidence.

* * *

We do not wish to be understood as condemning all consolidations of asbestos cases. Our holding today is narrow and amounts to little more than a caution that it is possible to go too far in the interests of expediency and to sacrifice basic fairness in the process. * * *

Accordingly, the judgment of the district court is reversed, and the matter remanded for a new trial.

WALKER, CIRCUIT JUDGE, dissenting.

* * *

* * * I agree that trial courts should not employ consolidated trials where they pose substantial risks of prejudice, and that to do so when the risks are manifest and prejudice results amounts to an abuse of the considerable discretion the law accords to trial courts in deciding whether to consolidate. However, by overturning the consolidated trial here, where indisputably substantial common issues of fact and law prevailed, without a substantial showing of prejudice, I think the majority errs, while sending the wrong message to courts faced with the difficult task of administering such claims in a manner that is fair to all parties involved. * * *

* * *

NOTES AND QUESTIONS

1. *Daybrook Fisheries* is an example of a simple case in which consolidation proved useful. *Malcolm*, by contrast, was far more complicated. Both cases share a common focus on whether defendants' rights would be prejudiced. Between these two extremes, there is considerable room for judicial discretion. Is there a respectable argument that consolidation was appropriate in *Malcolm*? Or that consolidation was *inappropriate* in *Daybrook Fisheries*?

2. The district court in *Malcolm* attempted to manage asbestos litigation through consolidation. Are courts up to this task? Or is management of asbestos litigation better left to legislative (or executive) bodies?

3. Because most of the defendants in *Malcolm* had settled after the damages determination, could one argue that the appellate court's ruling had little effect in remedying the perceived unfairness of the trial structure adopted by the district court?

4. If the *Malcolm* court was writing to establish broad legal principles, why did it emphasize that the context was unique?

5. In *In re Repetitive Stress Injury Litigation*, 11 F.3d 368, 371 (2d Cir. 1993), plaintiffs were individuals who brought 44 lawsuits alleging injuries from "repetitive stress" arising from the use of equipment manufactured or distributed by the defendants. The "repetitive stress injuries" ("RSI") included "carpel tunnel" syndrome (a medical condition affecting the hands and wrists) and a variety of other ailments (such as rotator cuff tears, lumbrosacal sprains, degenerative disc disease, cervical sprain, muscle spasms, "trigger finger," neck pain, and/or back pain). Defendants were companies that manufactured, and in some cases distributed, various types of equipment, including keyboards, keypunches, alpha-numeric machines, video display terminals, cash registers, supermarket workstations, stenographic machines, and computer "mouse" devices. Each plaintiff alleged that a device of this sort caused his or her injury. Defendants argued that the claimed injuries did not have a single cause, and could result from hereditary factors, vascular disorders, obesity, metabolic disorders, high blood cholesterol levels, connective tissue disorders, primary pulmonary hypertension, or prior trauma. Reversing the consolidation of such lawsuits, the Second Circuit stated:

> When entering the consolidation orders, the district court contemplated the subdividing of discovery or other proceedings and even the severance of some cases as the litigation proceeds. Because the question of whether there are common issues of law or fact in these cases is open, there is no doubt some discovery that is applicable to a group of, or all, cases. The district judges' approach, however, reverses the proper process. The burden is on the party seeking aggregation to show common issues of law or fact; the burden is not on the party opposing aggregation to show divergences. This is so even in

the case of the so-called mass tort, where a shifting of this burden is likely to render the label mass tort into a self-fulfilling prophecy.

We emphasize, however, that we see nothing wrong with assigning all RSI cases in a district to a single district judge who may order that particular proceedings or certain discovery requests relate to defined groups of RSI cases or, when appropriate, all the RSI cases in the district. Our differences with the district court are more than philosophical. The burden is on the party seeking aggregation of discovery or other proceedings to show common factual or legal issues warranting it. A party may not use aggregation as a method of increasing the costs of its adversaries—whether plaintiffs or defendants—by forcing them to participate in discovery or other proceedings that are irrelevant to their case. It may be that such increased costs would make settlement easier to achieve, but that would occur only at the cost of elemental fairness.

Id. at 374. Should the Second Circuit have reversed the district court? What arguments, if any, can be advanced in *favor* of consolidation in *Repetitive Stress*?

6. Consolidation may be appropriate even when joinder is not proper. For example, in *Stanford v. Tennessee Valley Auth*, 18 F.R.D. 152, 154 (M.D.Tenn. 1955), plaintiffs sued two defendants for damage to their property resulting from the emission of gas fumes from defendants' nearby chemical plants. Because the defendants' plants were separately owned and operated, and because the plants were located at different distances from the plaintiffs' property, the court held that the defendants' actions could not be part of the same series of transactions or occurrences for purposes of permissive joinder. The plaintiffs, however, had presented common questions of law or fact, *i.e.*, whether the fumes could cause the property damage in question, and whether there were devices or processes available which would mitigate the damages caused. Therefore, the court ordered a joint trial pursuant to Rule 42.

Defendants asserted that they would be prejudiced by a common trial because of the difficulty in determining each company's respective responsibility for the plaintiffs' damages. The court conceded this possibility, but noted that the difficulty in determining the nature and extent of each company's responsibility for plaintiffs' damages would also plague the jury if the claims were tried separately. Given the efficiencies associated with a joint trial of claims that would involve many of the same witnesses and evidence, the court ordered that the claims be tried together before the same jury, but that they be severed for all other purposes, noting that:

> A joint trial has many advantages, including a saving of trial time, as well as a saving of expense not only to the Government but to the parties. Doubtless in a large measure, the trial of both claims will involve the use of the same witnesses and the same evidence. Upon the whole case, the Court feels that the ends of justice will be met by a joint trial of the claims.

Id. at 155. Does it make sense that a case not qualifying for joinder would be consolidated for trial?

7. As *Malcolm* illustrates, there are fairness limitations upon the use of consolidation as an aggregation device. The device is also limited because it applies only to cases pending within the same court.

8. In *Johnson v. Manhattan Ry. Co.*, 289 U.S. 479 (1933), the Supreme Court stated that "consolidation is permitted as a matter of convenience and economy in administration, but does not merge the suits into a single cause, or change the rights of the parties, or make those who are parties in one suit parties in another." *Id.* at 496–97. Thus, jurisdictional requirements must be met for each case. *See, e.g., In re Cmty. Bank of N. Va.*, 418 F.3d 277, 298 (3d Cir. 2005) (each consolidated case must independently satisfy subject matter jurisdiction); *Wright v. Dougherty Cnty., Ga.*, 358 F.3d 1352, 1356 (11th Cir. 2004) (each case must meet standing requirements); *Intown Props. Mgmt., Inc. v. Wheaton Van Lines, Inc.*, 271 F.3d 164, 168 (4th Cir. 2001) (each consolidated case must satisfy statute of limitations).

Professor Joan Steinman argues that despite the Supreme Court's cautionary statements in *Johnson*, courts have not followed—and should not always follow—such a restrictive approach. Joan Steinman, *The Effects of Case Consolidation on the Procedural Rights of Litigants: What They Are, What They Might Be Part 1: Justiciability and Jurisdiction (Original and Appellate)*, 42 UCLA L. Rev. 717 (1995). She argues that a consolidated action should create a single civil action, change the rights of the parties, and make them parties to an action that includes all components of the consolidation; this would lead to increased fairness, greater efficiency, and more accurate expectations. *Id.*

9. Recall from Chapter 2 that the Supreme Court adopted a restrictive approach to common questions under Rule 23(a)(2) in *Wal–Mart Stores, Inc. v. Dukes*, 564 U.S. 338 (2011). How, if at all, should that decision impact the analysis of common questions under Rule 42(a)? How about for transfer by the MDL Panel?

10. For a useful discussion of consolidation, including historical background, case law, policy issues, and reform proposals, *see* Richard L. Marcus, *Confronting the Consolidation Conundrum*, 1995 BYU L. Rev. 879. For comparisons of consolidations and class actions, *see* Elizabeth J. Cabraser, *The Class Action Counterreformation*, 57 Stan. L. Rev. 1475, 1496–99 (2005); Charles Silver, *Comparing Class Actions and Consolidations*, 10 Rev. Litig. 495 (1991).

B. ADDITIONAL AGGREGATION DEVICES

In addition to the above-described devices, all of which are contained in the Federal Rules of Civil Procedure, several other aggregation devices exist. This section focuses on transfers under 28 U.S.C. § 1404, aggregation under the bankruptcy code, and aggregation of individual claims for settlement (and constraints under the aggregate settlement rule).

1. TRANSFERS UNDER 28 U.S.C. § 1404

As noted in the prior subsection, the statute controlling change of venue—28 U.S.C. § 1404—is itself an aggregation device. Nonetheless, it has significant limitations. Consider the following case.

HOFFMAN v. BLASKI
Supreme Court of the United States, 1960.

363 U.S. 335.

JUSTICE WHITTAKER delivered the opinion of the Court.

To relieve against [the perceived] harshness of dismissal, under the doctrine of *forum non conveniens*, of an action brought in an inconvenient [forum when other legally available forums exist], Congress, in 1948, enacted 28 U.S.C. § 1404(a), which provides:

"§ 1404. Change of venue.

"(a) For the convenience of parties and witnesses, in the interest of justice, a district court may transfer any civil action to any other district or division where it might have been brought."

The instant cases present the question whether a District Court, in which a civil action has been properly brought, is empowered by § 1404(a) to transfer the action, on the motion of the defendant, to a district in which the plaintiff did not have a *right* to bring it.

Respondents, Blaski and others, residents of Illinois, brought this patent infringement action in the United States District Court for the Northern District of Texas against one Howell and a Texas corporation controlled by him, alleging that the defendants are residents of, and maintain their only place of business in, the City of Dallas, in the Northern District of Texas, where they are infringing respondents' patents. After being served with process and filing their answer, the defendants moved, under § 1404(a), to transfer the action to the United States District Court for the Northern District of Illinois.[9] Respondents objected to the transfer on the ground that, inasmuch as the defendants did not reside, maintain a place of business, or infringe the patents in, and could not have been served with process in, the Illinois district, the courts of that district lacked venue over the action and ability to command jurisdiction over the defendants; that therefore that district was not a forum in which the respondents had a right to bring the action, and, hence, the court was without power to transfer it to that district. Without mentioning that objection or the question it raised, the District Court found that "the motion should be granted for the convenience of the parties and witnesses in the interest of justice," and ordered the case transferred to the Illinois district. Thereupon, respondents moved in the Fifth Circuit for leave to file a petition for a writ of mandamus directing the vacation of that order. That court, holding that "[t]he purposes for which § 1404(a) was enacted would be unduly circumscribed if a transfer could not be made 'in the interest of justice' to a district where the defendants not only waive venue but to which they seek the transfer," denied the motion.

---

[9] The asserted basis of the motion was that trial of the action in the Illinois District Court would be more convenient to the parties and witnesses and in the interest of justice because several actions involving the validity of these patents were then pending in that court, and that pretrial and discovery steps taken in those actions had developed a substantial amount of evidence that would be relevant and useful in this action.

Defendants also stated in the motion that, if and when the case be so transferred, they would waive all objections to the venue of the Illinois District Court over the action and would enter their appearance in the action in that court.

* * *

[The Seventh Circuit reversed on the ground that the Illinois district was not a place where the case "might have been brought" as required by section 1404(a).]

* * *

Petitioners' "thesis" and sole claim is that § 1404(a), being remedial, should be broadly construed, and, when so construed, the phrase "where it might have been brought" should be held to relate not only to the time of the bringing of the action, but also to the time of the transfer; and that "if at such time the transferee forum has the power to adjudicate the issues of the action, it is a forum in which the action might *then* have been brought." They argue that in the interim between the bringing of the action and the filing of a motion to transfer it, the defendants may move their residence to, or, if corporations, may begin the transaction of business in, some other district, and, if such is done, the phrase "where it might have been brought" should be construed to empower the District Court to transfer the action, on motion of the defendants, to such other district; and that, similarly, if, as here, the defendants move to transfer the action to some other district and consent to submit to the jurisdiction of such other district, the latter district should be held one "in which the action might *then* have been brought."

We do not agree. We do not think the § 1404(a) phrase "where it might have been brought" can be interpreted to mean, as petitioners' theory would require, "where it may now be rebrought, with defendants' consent." This Court has said, in a different context, that § 1404(a) is "unambiguous, direct [and] clear," *Ex parte Collett*, 337 U.S. 55, 58 (1949), and that "the unequivocal words of § 1404(a) and the legislative history * * * [establish] that Congress indeed meant what it said." *United States v. National City Lines, Inc.*, 337 U.S. 78, 84 (1949).

It is not to be doubted that the transferee courts, like every District Court, had jurisdiction to entertain actions of the character involved, but it is obvious that they did not acquire jurisdiction over these particular actions when they were brought in the transferor courts. The transferee courts could have acquired jurisdiction over these actions only if properly brought in those courts, or if validly transferred thereto under § 1404(a). Of course, venue, like jurisdiction over the person, may be waived. A defendant, properly served with process by a court having subject matter jurisdiction, waives venue by failing seasonably to assert it, or even simply by making default. But the power of a District Court under § 1404(a) to transfer an action to another district is made to depend not upon the wish or waiver of the defendant but, rather, upon whether the transferee district was one in which the action "might have been brought" by the plaintiff.

The thesis urged by petitioners would not only do violence to the plain words of § 1404(a), but would also inject gross discrimination. That thesis, if adopted, would empower a District Court, upon a finding of convenience, to transfer an action to any district desired by the *defendants* and in which they were willing to waive their statutory defenses as to venue and jurisdiction over their persons, regardless of the fact that such transferee district was not one in which the action "might have been brought" by the plaintiff. Conversely, that thesis would not permit the court, upon motion of the *plaintiffs* and a like showing of convenience, to transfer the action to the same district, without the consent and waiver of venue and personal jurisdiction defenses by the defendants. Nothing in § 1404(a), or in its legislative history, suggests such a unilateral objective and we should not, under the guise of interpretation, ascribe to Congress any such discriminatory purpose.

* * *

Inasmuch as the respondents (plaintiffs) did not have a right to bring these actions in the respective transferee districts, it follows that the judgments of the Court of Appeals were correct and must be

Affirmed.

[Concurring opinion by JUSTICE STEWART is omitted.]

JUSTICE FRANKFURTER, with whom JUSTICE HARLAN and JUSTICE BRENNAN join, dissenting.

* * *

One would have to be singularly unmindful of the treachery and versatility of our language to deny that as a mere matter of English the words "where it might have been brought" may carry more than one meaning. * * * [T]he English of the phrase surely does not tell whether the defendant's actual or potential waiver or failure to raise such objections is to be taken into account in determining whether a district is one in which the action "might have been brought," or whether the phrase refers only to those districts where the plaintiff "might have brought" the action even over a timely objection on the part of the defendant, that is, where he had "a right" to bring it.

* * *

* * * At the crux of the business, as I see it, is the realization that we are concerned here not with a question of a limitation upon the power of a federal court but with the place in which that court may exercise its power. We are dealing, that is, not with the jurisdiction of the federal courts, which is beyond the power of litigants to confer, but with the locality of a lawsuit, the rules regulating which are designed mainly for the convenience of the litigants. * * *

* * *

* * * The transferee court in this case plainly had and has jurisdiction to adjudicate this action with the defendant's acquiescence. As the defendant, whose privilege it is to object to the place of trial, has moved for transfer, and has acquiesced to going forward with the litigation in the transferee court, it would appear presumptively, unless there are strong considerations otherwise, that there is no impediment to effecting the transfer so long as "convenience" and "justice" dictate that it be made. It does not counsel otherwise that here the plaintiff is to be sent to a venue to which he objects, whereas ordinarily, when the defendant waives his privilege to object to the place of trial, it is to acquiesce in the plaintiff's choice of forum.

This would be a powerful argument if, under § 1404(a), a transfer were to be made whenever requested by the defendant. Such is not the case, and this bears emphasis. A transfer can be made under § 1404(a) to a place where the action "might have been brought" only when "convenience" and "justice" so dictate, not whenever the defendant so moves. A legitimate objection by the plaintiff to proceeding in the transferee forum will presumably be reflected in a decision that the interest of justice does not require the transfer, and so it becomes irrelevant that the proposed place of transfer is deemed one where the action "might have been brought." If the plaintiff's objection to proceedings in the transferee court is not consonant with the interests of justice, a good reason is wanting why the transfer should not be made.

On the other hand, the Court's view restricts transfer, when concededly warranted in the interest of justice, to protect no legitimate interest on the part of the plaintiff. * * *

NOTES AND QUESTIONS

1. Is the *Hoffman* majority correct in concluding that the plain language of the venue statute forecloses the result advocated by the defendant in this action? Or is Justice Frankfurter correct in concluding that the language is sufficiently malleable to permit the district court's approach?

2. Which view—the majority or the dissent—would permit the venue statute to be the most robust party-aggregation device possible? Why?

3. In *In Re Joint Eastern & Southern Districts Asbestos Litigation*, 769 F. Supp. 85 (E.D.N.Y. 1991), the district judge transferred numerous asbestos cases under section 1404(a) from the Southern District of New York to the Eastern District of New York, where other asbestos cases were pending before the same judge (who was designated by the court of appeals to hear asbestos cases in both districts). The court found that transfer would promote convenience and efficiency by "avoid[ing] needless duplication in proof and decreas[ing] wasteful expenditures of time, energy and money." *Id.* at 88. Does that case suggest that section 1404(a) could be a significant vehicle for party aggregation?

4. Despite the Supreme Court's effort to set forth a simple and clear meaning of Section 1404(a)'s "where it might have been brought" requirement, *Hoffman* has received significant criticism. Consider the following:

> * * * [There are] two problems with the *Hoffman* rule. First, the actual rule adopted in *Hoffman* seems unnecessary. *Hoffman* prevents a transfer to a district where a defendant lacks contacts. But with the exception of the occasional bizarre case such as *Hoffman*, it is difficult to understand why a defendant would seek a transfer to a forum where she lacked any contacts. Even if a defendant did file such a strange motion, litigation in the alternative district probably would not facilitate "the convenience of the parties and witnesses." * * * Regardless of the *Hoffman* rule, a district court should deny such a transfer motion, because the alternative forum would be no more convenient than the district where the plaintiff first filed suit.
>
> Second, the decision in *Hoffman* focuses on the wrong party. *Hoffman* protects the defendant against a transfer to an inconvenient

forum. But the defendant does not need this protection where the defendant himself is seeking the transfer. * * *

> Instead, the party who may suffer prejudice from a section 1404 transfer is the plaintiff—the party opposing the defendant's motion. * * * [T]he *Hoffman* rule provides no protection to a plaintiff opposing a defendant's motion to transfer. A plaintiff's lack of contacts with a state in no way prevents a transfer to a court in that state.

David E. Steinberg, *The Motion to Transfer and the Interests of Justice*, 66 Notre Dame L. Rev. 443, 457–62 (1990). Are these criticisms of *Hoffman* justified?

5. The Federal Courts Jurisdiction and Venue Clarification Act of 2011, Public Law No. 112-63, amended 28 U.S.C. § 1404 to permit transfer "to any district or division to which all parties have consented." This partially abrogates *Hoffman* by authorizing transfer to a district in which the action could *not* have been brought initially, so long as *all* parties to the transfer consent. How, if at all, does this change in Section 1404 affect its viability as a potential aggregation device?

6. Some commentators are critical of the broad discretion district courts have in determining whether a Section 1404(a) change of venue is appropriate. One commentator contends that "[t]his seemingly straightforward statute has spawned a bewildering amount of litigation" and created tremendous frustration among the district courts. Note, *"Adrift on an Unchartered Sea": A Survey of Section 1404(a) Transfer in the Federal System*, 67 N.Y.U. L. Rev. 612, 614–15 (1992). The author contends that "[t]his unchecked district court discretion has resulted in several problems" including: (i) defendants overusing the transfer motion because of its unchecked scope; (ii) courts inconsistently weighing the factors applicable to transfer, resulting in unpredictability; and (iii) parties using transfer solely for strategic reasons because of undefined standards. Another commentator concludes that the lack of uniform standards governing transfers has encouraged defendants to seek unwarranted transfers unrelated to the "interests of justice," creating delay and court congestion. David E. Steinberg, *The Motion to Transfer and the Interests of Justice*, 66 Notre Dame L. Rev. 443, 444 (1990). The commentator concludes that instead of the "current bouillabaisse of factors used to resolve transfer motions[,]" courts should consider only the location of relevant witnesses and documents; transfer a case only to a forum where plaintiff has minimum contacts; and transfer to a court if specified in a valid forum selection clause. *Id.*

7. For a humorous approach to transfer, consider the order in *Republic of Bolivia v. Philip Morris Cos.*, 39 F. Supp. 2d 1008 (S.D.Tex. 1999):

> This is one of at least six similar actions brought by foreign governments in various courts throughout the United States. The governments of Guatemala, Panama, Nicaragua, Thailand, Venezuela, and Bolivia have filed suit in the geographically diverse locales of Washington, D.C., Puerto Rico, Texas, Louisiana, and Florida, in both state and federal courts. Why none of these countries seems to have a court system their own governments have confidence in is a mystery to this Court. Moreover, given the tremendous number of United States jurisdictions encompassing fascinating and exotic places, the Court can hardly imagine why the Republic of Bolivia elected to file suit in the veritable hinterlands of Brazoria County, Texas. The Court seriously doubts whether Brazoria County has ever seen a live

Bolivian ... even on the Discovery Channel. Though only here by removal, this humble Court by the sea is certainly flattered by what must be the worldwide renown of rural Texas courts for dispensing justice with unparalleled fairness and alacrity, apparently in common discussion even on the mountain peaks of Bolivia! Still, the Court would be remiss in accepting an obligation for which it truly does not have the necessary resources. Only one judge presides in the Galveston Division—which currently has before it over seven hundred cases and annual civil filings exceeding such number—and that judge is presently burdened with a significant personal situation which diminishes its ability to always give the attention it would like to all of its daunting docket obligations, despite genuinely heroic efforts to do so. And, while Galveston is indeed an international seaport, the capacity of this Court to address the complex and sophisticated issues of international law and foreign relations presented by this case is dwarfed by that of its esteemed colleagues in the District of Columbia who deftly address such awesome tasks as a matter of course. Indeed, this Court, while doing its very best to address the more prosaic matters routinely before it, cannot think of a Bench better versed and more capable of handling precisely this type of case, which requires a high level of expertise in international matters. In fact, proceedings brought by the Republic of Guatemala are currently well underway in that Court in a related action, and there is a request now before the Judicial Panel on Multidistrict Litigation to transfer to the United States District Court for the District of Columbia all six tobacco actions brought by foreign governments, ostensibly for consolidated treatment. Such a Bench, well-populated with genuinely renowned intellects, can certainly better bear and share the burden of multidistrict litigation than this single judge division, where the judge moves his lips when he reads. ...

Regardless of, and having nothing to do with, the outcome of Defendants' request for transfer and consolidation, it is the Court's opinion that the District of Columbia, located in this Nation's capital, is a much more logical venue for the parties and witnesses in this action because, among other things, Plaintiff has an embassy in Washington, D.C., and thus a physical presence and governmental representatives there, whereas there isn't even a Bolivian restaurant anywhere near here! Although the jurisdiction of this Court boasts no similar foreign offices, a somewhat dated globe is within its possession. While the Court does not therefrom profess to understand all of the political subtleties of the geographical transmogrifications ongoing in Eastern Europe, the Court is virtually certain that Bolivia is not within the four counties over which this Court presides, even though the words Bolivia and Brazoria are a lot alike and caused some real, initial confusion until the Court conferred with its law clerks. Thus, it is readily apparent, even from an outdated globe such as that possessed by this Court, that Bolivia, a hemisphere away, ain't in south-central Texas, and that, at the very least, the District of Columbia is a more appropriate venue (though Bolivia isn't located there either). Furthermore, as this Judicial District bears no significant relationship to any of the matters at issue, and the judge of this

Court simply loves cigars, the Plaintiff can be expected to suffer neither harm nor prejudice by a transfer to Washington, D.C., a Bench better able to rise to the smoky challenges presented by this case, despite the alleged and historic presence there of countless "smoke-filled" rooms. Consequently, pursuant to 28 U.S.C. § 1404(a), for the convenience of parties and witnesses, and in the interest of justice, this case is hereby TRANSFERRED to the United States District Court for the District of Columbia.

Id. at 1009–10.

8. The Multiparty, Multiforum Trial Jurisdiction Act of 2002 provides for federal jurisdiction in a narrow category of mass accident cases, such as airplane and train crash cases, in which traditional diversity rules would have required the cases to be heard in state court. The Act gives federal district courts "original jurisdiction of any civil action involving minimal diversity between adverse parties that arises from a single accident, where at least 75 natural persons have died in the accident at a discrete location" if one of three circumstances exist: (1) "a defendant resides in a state and a substantial part of the accident took place in another state or other location" (even if the defendant is also a resident of the state in which the accident occurred); (2) "any two defendants reside in different States"; or (3) "substantial parts of the accident took place in different states." 28 U.S.C. § 1369(a). *See, e.g., Passa v. Derderian,* 308 F. Supp. 2d 43 (D.R.I. 2004) (upholding removal of cases alleging state tort law claims as result of nightclub fire that killed 100 and injured over 200). "Minimal diversity" is defined as existing "if any party is a citizen of a State and any adverse party is a citizen of another state, a citizen or subject of a foreign state, or a foreign state * * *." The Act also permits removal from state court of cases that could have been brought originally in federal court under section 1369. 28 U.S.C. § 1441(e). When a district court presides over an action as a result of the Act, it "shall promptly notify the judicial panel on multidistrict litigation of the pendency of the action." *Id.* § 1369(e). This information will enable the MDL panel, when appropriate, to consolidate the cases for pretrial purposes before a single judge.

The Act limits jurisdiction of the district courts, however, by requiring them to "abstain from hearing any civil action" covered by the Act in which "the substantial majority of all plaintiffs are citizens of a single state of which the primary defendants are also citizens" if "the claims asserted will be governed primarily by the laws of that State." *Id.* § 1369(b). *See, e.g., Wallace v. Louisiana Citizens Property Ins. Co.,* 444 F.3d 697, 701–02 (5th Cir. 2006) (finding that abstention under section 1369(b) applies only to cases in which section 1369(a) was basis for original jurisdiction, as opposed to cases removed from state court under 28 U.S.C. § 1441(e)(1)(B)). The Act does not define certain key terms, such as "substantial part of the accident," "primary defendants," or "governed primarily" by the laws of a particular state. Some of these terms are also used in CAFA. *See* Chapter 7(B)(3)(b).

2. BANKRUPTCY

Bankruptcy serves as a means to aggregate cases. Although the complexities of the Bankruptcy Code are beyond the scope of this text, the following materials provide a brief overview. Among the topics addressed are pre-packaged bankruptcies and the use of bankruptcy to aggregate claims against parties other than the debtor.

a. General Framework

W. HOMER DRAKE, JR. & CHRISTOPHER S. STRICKLAND, CHAPTER 11 REORGANIZATIONS
Thomson/West (2d ed. 2002) § 1:7.

* * *

Under the present day Code, bankruptcy courts have * * * comprehensive jurisdiction to hear all controversies arising under, arising in, or related to cases under the Bankruptcy Code. * * * [T]he several provisions of the Bankruptcy Code serve to funnel all matters pertaining to the estate into the bankruptcy court, as the forum deemed most suitable for deciding those matters touching upon a given bankruptcy case.

Procedurally speaking, a voluntary Chapter 11 case is commenced by the filing of a petition by an eligible debtor; an involuntary case may be commenced whenever a sufficient group of creditors can show that specific circumstances exist. Upon filing, the Code provides for an automatic stay of all litigation and creditor action against the debtor or the property of the estate. Property of the estate is defined broadly under the Code to include all property of the debtor, wherever located, and all legal and equitable rights or interests that the debtor might hold. At the request of any party, the stay may be terminated or modified, if cause is established for such relief or the debtor is shown to lack either equity in or need for the property at issue.

Once a case has been commenced, the debtor has the right to continue possession of its property and operate its business until and unless the court orders otherwise. The court appoints a committee of unsecured creditors soon after filing, and the Code presumes that this committee will oversee the debtor in the reorganization process. * * *

* * *

A [debtor] has the initial and exclusive right to file a plan for a period of 120 days after filing, subject to court modification. Upon the appointment of a trustee or the expiration of the time for filing a plan, the debtor forfeits its exclusive opportunity, and other parties in interest may file competing plans of reorganization. Irrespective of who files it, the plan may provide for the restructuring of debt and equity interests * * * but it must comply with certain restrictions set forth under the Code.

Before any creditors' acceptance of the plan may be solicited, the proponent must file a disclosure statement setting forth the information necessary to evaluate the plan's merit. Upon court approval of the disclosure statement's adequacy, both it and a copy of the plan must be submitted to each creditor for review. A solicitation process thereafter ensues, with the proponent negotiating among the creditor body to obtain the necessary votes in support of its plan.

Following the completion of these steps, the court conducts a hearing with regard to confirmation of the plan. A reorganization plan only will be confirmed if certain preconditions have been satisfied, including the

Court's finding that at least one class of creditors accepts the plan and that it is in the best interests of creditors. The latter requirement essentially mandates that creditors must receive more under the plan than they would take in liquidation. If this criterion is met, and if other preconditions are satisfied, the plan may be confirmed. Classes which are not impaired are deemed to have accepted the plan, and those classes which receive nothing under the plan are deemed to have rejected it.

* * *

b. Aggregation of Claims Against a Debtor: Overview of Legal Concepts

A prominent federal district court judge and his co-authors have taken a skeptical view on bankruptcy as an aggregation device:

> The bankruptcy process * * * aggregates claims. Because a bankruptcy filing stays all litigation against the bankrupt [11 U.S.C. §§ 105, 362], it permits a comprehensive resolution of all the claims, including those pending in state courts. But this opportunity becomes available only when a defendant (or its creditor) files for bankruptcy. Additionally, when the bankrupt is only one of several defendants, a bankruptcy proceeding involving only that defendant will not result in significant aggregation. The bankruptcy process, which was not intended to supersede conventional adjudication, has only limited utility for the comprehensive and orderly resolution of large-scale litigation.

William W. Schwarzer, Alan Hirsch & Edward Sussman, *A Proposal to Amend the Multidistrict Litigation Statute to Permit Discovery Coordination of Large-Scale Litigation Pending in State and Federal Courts*, 73 Tex. L. Rev. 1529, 1535 (1995).

Consider, by contrast, the following more optimistic view of bankruptcy as an aggregation device.

RALPH R. MABEY & PETER A. ZISSER, IMPROVING TREATMENT OF FUTURE CLAIMS: THE UNFINISHED BUSINESS LEFT BY THE MANVILLE AMENDMENTS
69 Am. Bankr. L.J. 487, 489–94 (1995).

While a class action commenced in federal district court may aggregate lawsuits in one trial court, that nonbankruptcy court faces major obstacles in gathering or controlling state lawsuits: the court (i) lacks personal jurisdiction over unwilling plaintiffs, (ii) is arguably unable to enjoin proceedings pending in other courts, and (iii) does not now have removal jurisdiction from state to federal court absent complete diversity. Bankruptcy courts face none of these obstacles for a number of reasons.

First, the Judicial Code provides that all personal injury tort and wrongful death claims against a debtor must be tried in the federal district court in which the debtor's bankruptcy case is pending—even those lawsuits first commenced in state court.[8] Further, unlike a state or federal

---

[8] Lawsuits commenced in state court may be removed to federal court. 28 U.S.C. § 1452 (1994). More importantly, Judicial Code § 157(b)(5) provides:

court in which a class action is commenced, Congress has provided the bankruptcy court with personal jurisdiction over all parties who assert an interest in the debtor.[9] In addition, the bankruptcy court can enjoin the commencement or continuation of actions in both state and federal courts that may have an impact on the estate. * * *

* * *

Under Federal Rule of Civil Procedure 23(b), a class action cannot be certified unless strict requirements are met as to numerosity and commonality of legal and factual issues, as class action certification will restrict or eliminate the litigant's individual right to a trial. Under the Bankruptcy Clause, however, Congress has enacted a more flexible procedure. The majority of litigants may vote to bind all "substantially similar" claims to participate in a limited fund;[18] at the same time, each litigant may preserve its individual right to liquidate its claim by jury trial and participate *pro rata* in the fund based upon its jury award.[19] Thus, since the individual's opportunity to liquidate the tort claim is preserved, most factual or legal issues need not be held in common by the bankruptcy class. Further, the requirement of numerosity is not present.

Coupled with this flexibility is the Bankruptcy Code's attention to detailed standards of procedure and substance aimed at protecting the rights of claimants—protections generally not found in a class action. For example, the Code requires that a plan of reorganization cannot be confirmed unless stringent statutory standards are satisfied. Where statutory majorities do not favor the plan, additional standards are imposed. Even then, the plan cannot be confirmed over the objection of one dissenting creditor who would receive more in a Chapter 7 liquidation of the debtor than the reorganization provides. Further, counsel appointed by the court and charged with representing the interests of creditors, and a legal representative for future claimants if one is appointed, are compensated out of the estate, subject to review by the court, and need not rely on a contingency fee.

The participants in a class action under Rule 23(b) may not be so protected. Dissenting creditors do not have the option to insist on liquidation

---

The district court shall order that personal injury tort and wrongful death claims shall be tried in the district court in which the bankruptcy case is pending, or in the district court in the district in which the claim arose, as determined by the district court in which the bankruptcy case is pending.* * *

[9] Section 1334(e) of the Judicial Code provides that "[t]he district court in which a case under title 11 is commenced or is pending shall have exclusive jurisdiction of all of the property, wherever located, of the debtor as of the commencement of such case, and of property of the estate." 28 U.S.C. § 1334(e) (1994). The legislative history of this section shows that Congress intended to confer both *in personam* and *in rem* jurisdiction on the district court (and by reference, the bankruptcy court).

[18] Under Code § 1122(a), claims may be classified in the same class only if they are "substantially similar," 11 U.S.C. § 1122(a) (1994), meaning they must have the same "legal character or effect" in relation to the debtor's assets.

[19] Judicial Code § 1411(b) provides, in pertinent part, that "this chapter and title 11 do not affect any right to trial by jury that an individual has under applicable nonbankruptcy law with regard to a personal injury or wrongful death tort claim." 28 U.S.C. § 1411(b) (1994). Personal injury and wrongful death claims may be tried in the district court in the district where the bankruptcy case is pending or, if that district court so orders, in the district court where the claim arose. *Id.* § 157(b)(5).

even if they would receive more if the debtor were liquidated rather than under the class action settlement. Further, counsel representing classes or subclasses in a class action are usually compensated only if a settlement is reached, with such compensation generally based on a percentage of the settlement. This creates a built-in incentive to settle, notwithstanding the merits of the claims and may result in fees which bear little relation to the amount of work performed or the time spent in performing such work.

Chapter 11 of the Bankruptcy Code, with support from the Judicial Code and the Bankruptcy Clause, vests a court with far more power to deal with the problems of overwhelming tort litigation than can be found elsewhere. At the same time, Chapter 11 articulates important procedural safeguards not elsewhere collected. In sum, Chapter 11 provides the best framework for resolving present and future mass tort claims against a debtor company in financial distress. * * *

* * *

NOTES AND QUESTIONS

1. Why is Judge Schwarzer skeptical about the use of bankruptcy as an aggregation device? Does the Mabey and Zisser article suggest that Judge Schwarzer may have been unduly pessimistic?

2. One commentator has noted that, in light of *Ortiz v. Fibreboard Corp.*, 527 U.S. 815 (1999), "many corporate defendants have filed for bankruptcy under Chapter 11." Kathryn E. Spier, *Settlement With Multiple Plaintiffs: The Role of Insolvency*, 18 J.L. Econ. & Org. 295, 318 (2002). According to the author:

> As with limited-fund class actions, Chapter 11 has the benefit of establishing a mandatory class, avoiding the problems of opt-outs * * *, but has several added advantages for the defendant. Of importance is that filing for bankruptcy does not require the defendant to ascertain the value of the limited fund at the time of filing (in this case the corporate assets) and does not require proof that the claims would necessarily exhaust the assets. Second, a defendant may be able to achieve coordination between cases that would fail the Rule 23 similarity test: a contract suit and an employment discrimination claim, for example. Finally, cases from multiple jurisdictions would be consolidated under the same federal bankruptcy court.

Id. From a policy standpoint, is this shift from class actions to bankruptcy a positive development? Who benefits from this shift? Who, if anyone, is harmed?

c. Aggregation of Claims Against a Debtor: Mass Tort Litigation

Is Chapter 11 bankruptcy an effective aggregation tool in the area of mass tort litigation involving future claims?

ALAN N. RESNICK, BANKRUPTCY AS A VEHICLE FOR RESOLVING ENTERPRISE-THREATENING MASS TORT LIABILITY

148 U. Pa. L. Rev. 2045, 2045–68 (2000).

* * *

A difficult challenge facing the American judicial system is providing for the fair and efficient resolution of litigation arising from mass tort liability. * * * The most difficult cases are those involving "long-tail" mass torts, such as those relating to asbestos, where there is a long latency period between a person's use or exposure to a harmful product and the first manifestation of harm. * * * Given the thousands of future claimants who will first discover their injuries in decades to come, long-tail mass torts place an enormous burden on the defendant company and the judiciary. The high costs of litigation threaten both adequate compensation for the vast number of victims and the survival of the defendant's business.

* * * When a defendant company is faced with mass tort liability that threatens the viability of the enterprise, * * * it is likely to seek protection under the federal bankruptcy laws. Johns–Manville Corp., Celotex Corp., Eagle–Picher Industries, Inc., Keene Corp., and at least a dozen other asbestos manufacturers deluged with thousands of personal injury claims; A.H. Robins Co. facing potentially devastating Dalkon Shield personal injury claims; Dow Corning Corp. under an onslaught of breast implant litigation; and other companies—all expecting countless future claimants who have not yet manifested any injury—have sought protection under Chapter 11 of the Bankruptcy Code within the past twenty years.

* * *

* * * Ideally, class actions, multidistrict litigation, alternative dispute resolution, and other vehicles for resolving mass tort liability will continue to improve as mechanisms for dealing with mass tort cases. When other mechanisms fail or are likely to be ineffective, and survival of the enterprise is threatened, however, companies with otherwise viable businesses will seek protection under the federal bankruptcy laws. * * *

* * *

Traditional tort litigation and nonbankruptcy collective proceedings, including class actions, are designed to grant plaintiffs appropriate relief for their injuries without regard to the financial condition of the defendant. * * *

In contrast, * * * [t]he protection of the business enterprise by preserving its going concern value, thereby maximizing value for distribution to creditors, is central to the reorganization process.

The use of bankruptcy to protect a business whose viability is threatened by mass tort liability is not foreign to the[] underlying goals of the Bankruptcy Code. When a company has committed tortious conduct on a massive scale affecting thousands of victims, including those who have not yet manifested injury, all constituents would be disadvantaged by the destruction or termination of the business if it is otherwise viable. Those claimants whose injuries are manifested subsequent to the termination of the defendant business will have nowhere to turn for compensation. Despite its allegedly wrongful conduct, it will not benefit anyone to kill the goose that is laying the golden eggs. Rather, a plan devoting the future profits of the company, at least in part, to the compensation of present and future claimants offers the greatest likelihood that they will be compensated for their injuries. Bankruptcy's goal of providing equal treatment among similarly situated creditors also coincides with the difficult challenge of treating present claimants no better and no worse than unknown future claimants in mass tort cases.

* * *

When a company facing mass tort liability files a bankruptcy petition, it is typical for numerous personal injury and wrongful death tort actions to be pending in state and federal courts throughout the United States. Section 157(b)(5) of Title 28 provides that such claims shall be tried in the district court where the bankruptcy case is pending or in the district court where the claim arose, as determined by the district court where the bankruptcy case is pending. * * * [T]he laws governing jurisdiction in the bankruptcy context all point to bringing mass tort litigation into one court.

When a bankruptcy petition is filed, an automatic stay prevents the continuation of litigation against the debtor in any tribunal. The automatic stay has nationwide effect and is a powerful way to halt immediately all actions, including mass tort lawsuits pending in state and other federal courts. * * *

* * *

* * * [A] company beginning to face a deluge of mass tort litigation may seek Chapter 11 protection before its capital markets and trade credit disappear or the business is otherwise damaged.

The absence of an insolvency test for eligibility is * * * attractive because proving insolvency, which requires the valuation of all assets and liabilities, is a very difficult, subjective process, resulting in expensive and time-consuming litigation when the debtor is a large, complex corporation.

The ability to seek bankruptcy protection earlier, rather than later, can be contrasted with the more limited access to a non-opt-out "limited fund" class action under Rule 23(b)(1)(B). In *Ortiz v. Fibreboard Corp.* [527 U.S. 815 (1999)], the Supreme Court reversed a $1.535 billion class action settlement in part because the parties failed to show that the assets available for distribution to tort victims, including insurance proceeds, were, in fact, a limited fund that would be insufficient to pay claims in full. Although the Court commented that "we need not decide here how close to insolvency a limited fund defendant must be brought as a condition of class certification," it is clear that insufficiency of assets must be demonstrated. This would require a valuation of assets and estimation of liabilities to show at least near insolvency.

An important goal in resolving mass tort liability that affects future claimants is assuring that present tort claimants with manifested injuries and causes of action do not exhaust the defendant's assets before future claimants manifest injuries. Similarly, future claimants who will manifest injuries in the short term must not exhaust available assets if exhaustion will result in fewer assets being available for those with longer latency periods. These problems may be addressed by both attempting to estimate the number and amount of future claims, and by putting aside sufficient funds to compensate future claimants as injuries mature. The Bankruptcy Code, with its provisions for acceleration, estimation, and classification of claims that have not yet ripened into matured causes of action, provides an appropriate framework for dealing with these problems.

* * *

The requirements that a Chapter 11 plan place virtually all creditors in classes, that members of each class be similarly situated, and that the plan treat class members equally with others in the same class gives a Chapter 11 case the appearance, in structure, of a class action with multiple non-opt-out classes. The classification of claims under a Chapter 11 plan differs significantly, however, from the creation of a class for Rule 23 class action purposes.

Under the Bankruptcy Code, the "substantially similar" requirement in 1122(a) is far less restrictive than the four threshold requirements applicable to class actions under Rule 23. * * * [C]laims placed in a Chapter 11 class usually will satisfy the "substantially similar" requirement if they are of equal rank in distribution.

* * *

Although the Bankruptcy Code does not expressly provide for it, bankruptcy courts have appointed legal representatives to represent classes of future claimants in mass tort cases. If the bankruptcy court applies the same standards for appointment and disclosure that are applicable to creditors' committees and their counsel, conflicts of interest criticized by the Supreme Court in *Ortiz* could be avoided.

* * *

JOSEPH F. RICE & NANCY WORTH DAVIS, THE FUTURE OF MASS TORT CLAIMS: COMPARISON OF SETTLEMENT CLASS ACTION TO BANKRUPTCY TREATMENT OF MASS TORT CLAIMS

50 S.C. L. Rev. 405, 451–57, 460–61 (1999).

* * *

Comparison of Settlement Class Action and Chapter 11 Bankruptcy

A. *The Structure of Settlement Class Action and Chapter 11*

* * *

While settlement class action and Chapter 11 are similar in many respects, the differences between them bear attention. [For example, w]here Rule 23(b)(3) settlement class actions provide a voluntary settlement process from which dissenters may opt-out, bankruptcy is a mandatory process in which no form of "opt-out" is provided. "No opt-out" class actions under Rule 23(b)(1)(B) are also mandatory proceedings in which claimants are bound by the settlement with no direct recourse to a jury trial as is available to a Rule 23(b)(3) class. * * * The bankruptcy process allows removal of the tort claimant's case from its chosen forum through the application of the court's "related to" jurisdiction under 28 U.S.C. § 157, but in the settlement class action arena, the forum of choice is maintained.

From the mass tort claimant's perspective, the major differences between settlement class action and bankruptcy are the delays and high transaction costs inherent in the bankruptcy litigation process. The protection of the debtor and its codefendants through the extension of the automatic stay, indefinite extensions of the exclusive period, transfer of related cases to the bankruptcy court, and the court's reluctance to lift the automatic stay all serve to remove any pressure to negotiate a plan of reorganization. Without leverage to force serious settlement discussions, mass tort claimants are at a disadvantage in the bankruptcy process.

Because the settlement class action begins with a settlement, it provides the claimant and the defendant company with certainty as to the economic impact of the resolution of claims on each party. In a traditional Chapter 11 bankruptcy, the parties have no certainty at the commencement of the case as to how each will ultimately be treated. * * *

B. *Treatment of Future Claims*

One of the most vexing problems facing those seeking a global resolution of mass tort claims is the treatment of unknown and future claims which threaten to unravel attempts at permanent solutions. The Bankruptcy Code is flawed as a mechanism for resolving future mass torts claims: the definition of "claim" does not extend to future claimants. In essence, future claimants in bankruptcy enjoy a *de facto* opt-out by definition leaving the reorganized debtor open to successor liability. * * * If future claims are not effectively disposed of in Chapter 11, successive bankruptcies are needed to resolve latent claims as they mature and become "claims" within the meaning of § 101(5) of the Bankruptcy Code. In practice, the jurisdiction of the bankruptcy court over future claimants is eroding if it ever existed. Asbestos trust funds * * * are increasingly found to be inadequate. Where claims are impaired, courts are finding that future claimants' due process rights of notice and hearing are not met. The Supreme Court's concerns about due process requirements as expressed in *Amchem* [*Products, Inc. v. Windsor*, 521 U.S. 591 (1997),] are equally applicable [to] future claimants in a Chapter 11 reorganization. Where there is no effective notice to creditors, there is no discharge of claims through the bankruptcy process.

The focus of concern regarding treatment of future claims is the right to due process: the right to notice and an opportunity to be heard before property is taken or a claim is impaired. * * *

In settlement class actions the definition of the class determines the extent of the court's jurisdiction. In bankruptcy it is the definition of "claim" found in the Bankruptcy Code that sets the goalposts. * * * At this time, it is uncertain whether either settlement class action or bankruptcy has resolved the problem of providing due process notice to future claimants. Both employ the same forms of protection for future claimants: the appointment of a representative for the interests of future claimants, the establishment of trusts from which future claimants may seek recourse, and the remedy of injunctions channeling future claimants to the trust and away from the debtor or defendant companies. In the context of bankruptcy, these mechanisms are being challenged. In the settlement class action context, the Supreme Court is questioning the effectiveness of notice in cases that have employed all these protections for future claimants. * * *

C. Comparison of Representation in Settlement Class Action and Bankruptcy

In bankruptcy, mass tort claimants may be represented by members of a creditors' or claimants' committee who are appointed by the U.S. Trustee's office. There is no inquiry into the "representativeness" of members of creditors' and claimants' committees unless there is an objection to committee membership by a party in interest. In a settlement class action, representatives of the class undergo extensive qualification and court scrutiny prior to certification of the class. The criteria for certification of [a] class action, including representativeness, is strictly enforced in a settlement class action. Tort claimants have greater assurance of fair representation in a settlement class action.

D. Comparison of the Approval Processes

* * * The court, acting as a fiduciary in both (b)(3) and (b)(1) class actions, scrutinizes the agreement on behalf of class members and determines whether the agreement is fair to the class. In Chapter 11 reorganization the court presides over litigated matters in the reorganization process, such as the estimation of claims, although it is absent from the negotiation of the plan of reorganization. The bankruptcy court decides the issue of the fairness and feasibility of the plan of reorganization when a plan is presented for confirmation. The court does not scrutinize the process that leads to the formation of the plan. * * * If approved by those creditors who vote, the court's inquiry into the "fairness" of the plan is limited in scope. The bankruptcy court does not act as a fiduciary for claimants. If the creditors do not agree on a plan, it may be forced on them or "crammed down" over their objections. In that case, the bankruptcy court must determine if the plan is "fair and equitable." A "fairness" test is not applied in a Chapter 11 plan confirmation unless a "cramdown" is attempted. The plan of reorganization that is reached through negotiation in a bankruptcy does not receive the scrutiny of the negotiations and the settlement that the class action settlement receives.

E. Comparison of Settlement Class Action Valuation and Bankruptcy Estimation

* * *

Both settlement class action and Chapter 11 reorganization, if used properly, hold promise for resolution of mass tort claims. Neither should be discarded due to prevailing biases favoring one solution over the other. Each should be allowed to evolve so that mass tort claimants have choices available to them for the fair and equitable compensation of their injuries.

NOTES AND QUESTIONS

1. What are the advantages of bankruptcy over a class action as an aggregation tool for mass tort litigation involving future claims?

2. What arguments can be made for a class action settlement over bankruptcy?

d. Prepackaged Bankruptcies

MARL D. PLEVIN, ROBERT T. EBERT & LESLIE A. EPLEY, PRE-PACKAGED ASBESTOS BANKRUPTCIES: A FLAWED SOLUTION
44 S. Tex. L. Rev. 883, 884–88, 907–913, 923 (2003).

I. Introduction

"Pre-packaged" bankruptcies, or "pre-packs," are the latest thing in the world of litigation relating to asbestos-related bodily injury claims. The use of pre-packs is seen by some as a quick, cheap way out of a fast-rising tide of asbestos claims that are paralyzing both companies and the legal system, because the debtor is able to take advantage of the special "asbestos trust" and "channeling injunction" provisions of the Bankruptcy Code with only a short stay in Chapter 11.

At its core, a pre-pack is a plan of reorganization that is negotiated and voted on before the company actually files its bankruptcy petition. Although the Bankruptcy Code has long contained provisions that have allowed pre-packs to be successfully used in non-asbestos bankruptcies, only recently have they become commonplace in the asbestos context. Like many things in the field of asbestos litigation, however, what works seamlessly elsewhere encounters obstacles when transported to the asbestos area. In particular, asbestos bankruptcy pre-packs have not yet delivered on their promise of a quick, painless, and ultimately successful tour through bankruptcy court. * * *

* * *

II. How Do Conventional Chapter 11 Cases and Pre-Packaged Bankruptcy Cases Differ?

A. The Conventional Chapter 11 Process

The traditional or conventional Chapter 11 process involves many required steps that can frequently take years to complete. In a conventional Chapter 11 case, a debtor files in order to begin the process of negotiating with its creditors over a plan of reorganization. The filing of the Chapter 11 petition operates as an automatic stay of all lawsuits against the debtor and all efforts to collect on any pre-petition obligation of the debtor. The purpose of the stay is to provide the debtor with breathing room during which plan negotiations can take precedence.

Plan negotiations typically are conducted primarily between the debtor and one or more official committees appointed shortly after the filing of debtor's bankruptcy petition, although any party in interest may seek to participate in negotiations. The committees are permitted to engage professionals to represent them in court and in the negotiations, and the fees of such professionals are paid by the estate, subject to the approval of the bankruptcy court. The debtor has a 120-day period, beginning from the date the petition is filed, during which it has an exclusive right to file a plan, and a 180-day exclusive period to solicit acceptances of the plan. These exclusivity periods may be, and frequently are, extended, particularly in complex cases.

Once the debtor reaches agreement with its major constituencies on a plan that appears to have the necessary support to be confirmed, the plan will be filed with the bankruptcy court. The debtor may not solicit acceptances of the proposed plan, however, until the bankruptcy court, after notice and a hearing, approves a disclosure statement that is designed to provide persons voting on the plan with "adequate information" to make an informed judgment whether to vote in favor of or against the plan. In complex cases generally, and in asbestos bankruptcy cases in particular, disclosure statements are frequently several hundred pages long, containing a detailed description of the debtor's history, the reasons it filed for bankruptcy, a summary of the plan, and other required elements.

Once the disclosure statement is approved, it is mailed, together with the plan and ballots to be used in accepting or rejecting the plan, to those entitled to vote on the plan. In addition, notice is typically published in national, regional, and/or local newspapers, as appropriate. If it appears, after the votes have been tabulated, that the various classes have voted in favor of the plan, the bankruptcy court, after notice, will hold a hearing on whether to confirm the plan. Any party in interest may file an objection to confirmation of a plan. Whether or not an objection is filed, the bankruptcy court must review the plan to ensure that it meets the statutory requirements for confirmation. If it does, the plan will be confirmed.

It is not atypical for plans in conventional (*i.e.*, non-pre-packaged) asbestos bankruptcy Chapter 11 cases to not be confirmed until many years after commencement of the bankruptcy case. For example, in one of the earliest asbestos bankruptcy cases, Johns-Manville Corporation, the plan was confirmed six years after the bankruptcy case was commenced. * * *

B. The Chapter 11 Process in "Pre-Packaged" Cases

Pre-packaged asbestos bankruptcy cases, in contrast, proceed on a more expedited schedule. One defining difference between conventional cases and pre-packs is that in a pre-packaged case, plan negotiations, distribution of disclosure statements, and voting all take place before the bankruptcy case is filed. As a result, a debtor in a pre-packaged bankruptcy typically files along with its petition, a plan and disclosure statement. The court will then frequently hold a single hearing to determine the adequacy of the pre-petition disclosure and whether the plan should be confirmed. Depending on the court's calendar, it is theoretically possible for a pre-packaged bankruptcy to go from petition to confirmation in as few as 30 to 45 days. A faster trip through bankruptcy court means both lower bankruptcy-case professional fees and less business disruption.

There are, of course, risks to a debtor who chooses to proceed via a pre-packaged bankruptcy rather than a conventional one. If, for example, the bankruptcy court finds the disclosure statement inadequate in some respect, the debtor will have to amend and redistribute the disclosure statement, and re-solicit plan acceptances, resulting in potentially lengthy delays in confirmation. A second concern is that it is more likely than in a conventional case that all persons asserting claims were not properly solicited and given an opportunity to vote. In conventional Chapter 11 cases, the debtor typically gives notice of the bankruptcy case, and of the right to vote, by publication, in addition to direct notice to known claimants. By contrast, in a pre-packaged bankruptcy, it is possible for the debtor to overlook giving notice to potential claimants. If the debtor did not solicit claimants who have the right to vote on the pre-packaged plan, the debtor must give them an opportunity to vote; otherwise the claimants may be able to successfully challenge the plan on appeal.

A third concern is that parties in interest who were not included in the pre-petition plan negotiations, and whose interests are therefore not reflected in the proposed plan, may delay or derail confirmation by objecting to the plan, thereby depriving the debtor of some or all of the anticipated benefits of the pre-pack. * * *

* * *

IV. The Problems with Pre-Packaged Asbestos Bankruptcies

The pre-packaged asbestos bankruptcies that have been filed so far pervert and distort the purposes of Section 524(g) of the Bankruptcy Code. [11 U.S.C. §524(g)(1).] This results from a variety of factors, including the following:

> (1) The plan negotiations take place in secret, with the result that a select group of claimants whose lawyers know about the negotiations receive favorable treatment relative to the interests of other similarly situated claimants;
>
> (2) The Future Claimants' Representative is presented with a stacked deck, and is therefore unable adequately to represent the interests of future claimants;
>
> (3) The debtor is frequently negotiating with someone else's money, and has no incentive to cut a deal that protects the assets of those funding the plan; and
>
> (4) Conflicts of interest are rife in the process.

There is a reason that it takes years for the parties to reach agreement in "conventional," non-pre-packaged asbestos bankruptcies: all parties are present during the negotiations, all are vigorously advancing the conflicting interests of their respective constituencies, the negotiations themselves are complex, and it takes a long time to reach an agreement in such circumstances. The reason it takes far less time to reach deals in pre-packaged cases is that most of the checks and balances in the plan process are absent, and provisions of the Bankruptcy Code designed to protect the rights of parties in interest are typically honored only in the breach. Courts should refuse to confirm plans that result from such skewed negotiations.

A. The Interests of the Parties in an Asbestos Bankruptcy

An asbestos defendant that is contemplating filing for bankruptcy to resolve its asbestos liability problems has two primary concerns: (i) it wants to solve its asbestos liability problem at the lowest possible net financial cost to the company; and (ii) it wishes to maintain as much of the existing equity interests as possible for current shareholders, particularly where the company is both a healthy enterprise apart from asbestos concerns and is a subsidiary of a company that would like to capture as much as possible of the prospective debtor's future profits for its own benefit. The parent company, which may or may not become a debtor, wants to eliminate any asbestos-related "overhang" or "drag" on its stock price by seeing that it, its subsidiary the prospective debtor, and all of the parent's other subsidiaries and affiliates become "asbestos-free" through use of the Bankruptcy Code.

The asbestos claimants' interests are also clear: they want as much of the debtor's cash and stock as they can obtain. In a conventional, non-prepackaged asbestos bankruptcy case, the claimants are represented in negotiations with the debtor by two separate entities, the official committee of asbestos claimants (which represents current claimants), and the Future Claimants' Representative (who represents future claimants). While both the committee and the Future Claimants' Representative have a common interest in forcing the debtor to contribute as much cash and stock as possible, once that goal is achieved they have opposing interests concerning how such consideration is divided between the current and future claimants. In essence, they are playing a zero-sum game: each dollar or share of stock allocated to the future claimants is at the expense of the current claimants, and vice versa.

In these negotiations, each party can look to various provisions of the Bankruptcy Code that give it some leverage. The current asbestos claimants must be satisfied because no channeling injunction may be issued unless a supermajority of 75 percent of voting asbestos claimants vote in favor of the plan. These claimants and the future claimants' representative together can insist that the debtor and its parent company must give them at least 50% of the equity interests in the debtor. They can demand additional consideration as a basis for agreeing to include the debtor's parent and affiliates within the protection of the channeling injunction. The debtor's parent company or other owners will negotiate to keep at least 49.9 percent of their equity stakes, but accomplishing that goal will require that they provide other consideration satisfactory to the asbestos claimants. In short, all of the debtor's assets (and, to a large extent, those of its affiliates) are in play in the negotiations. The debtor has some leverage too: its exclusive right to file a plan, which is commonly extended for periods amounting to years.

In a conventional bankruptcy case, the official committee of asbestos claimants is appointed by the U.S. Trustee and, like all official committees, has fiduciary duties to all of its constituents. Thus, every asbestos claimant, regardless of who their personal lawyer is, is assured that his or her interests will be fully represented during the plan negotiations, without any favoritism or discrimination. Because the negotiations commence after the case is filed, the court-appointed future claimants' representative—another fiduciary—is able to participate in the negotiations from the outset, without having his or her hands tied by previously-agreed to deals.

In many of the recent large "conventional" asbestos bankruptcies, insurance coverage has not been a core concern of debtors or claimants, because insurance has long since been exhausted or settled. Where such issues do exist however, insurers have the ability to participate in the bankruptcy case in a meaningful way where their interests are affected.

Very little of the foregoing model is reflected in the recent pre-packaged asbestos bankruptcies. Instead, pre-packaged bankruptcies have so far proven to be a world unto themselves, turning many of the rules and requirements of the Bankruptcy Code on their head.

B. Secret Negotiations

In a conventional asbestos bankruptcy case, the debtor negotiates in the open with both an official committee of asbestos claimants appointed by the U.S. Trustee in the bankruptcy case, and a court-appointed Future Claimants' Representative. This is not true in an asbestos pre-pack. Instead of negotiating under the spotlight of a public bankruptcy court proceeding, the negotiations typically take place in secret. And instead of negotiating with an official committee and a court appointee, the prospective debtor hand-picks its negotiation partner (usually, someone who is thought to control a large block of asbestos claimants). Sometimes in a pre-pack, the prospective debtor (or its affiliates) take steps, which would never be permitted in a bankruptcy case, that are designed to make its negotiating partner beholden to it. * * *

* * *

The now-common structure used in asbestos pre-packs—a pre-petition trust that pays a subset of current claimants nearly full value for their claims, followed by a post-petition trust that pays other current claimants and future claimants a much smaller percentage of their claims, with significantly more stringent qualifying requirements—financially benefits the lawyers for the preferred claimants, since they typically receive, as contingent fee payments, as much as 40 cents of each dollar paid to their claimants. Because their clients get paid more, and sooner, than other claimants, these lawyers personally benefit when the plan is structured in such a fashion. If the plan treated all claimants the same, paying all current claimants through the mechanism of a post-petition trust, the lawyers for the current claimants would make less money—even assuming the bankruptcy court or the trust made no effort to restrict the portion of a trust beneficiary's payment that could be paid as a contingent fee. This, as much as anything, explains why asbestos pre-packs are structured in such a byzantine fashion that is so different than any "conventional" asbestos bankruptcy case.

C. Favorable Treatment for Certain Current Claimants

Similarly situated claimants in pre-packs generally do not receive similar treatment despite the fact one of the hallmarks of the Bankruptcy Code is the requirement that "a plan shall . . . provide the same treatment for each claim or interest of a particular class. . . ." [11 U.S.C. § 1123(a)(4).]

This unequal treatment manifests itself in several ways. First, as suggested above, there is typically a large discrepancy between what is paid to claimants who qualify for payment under the pre-petition trust and those who must look solely to the post-petition trust. * * *

Second, even those claimants lucky enough to be paid by the pre-petition trust, in whole or in part, are not treated equally. * * * Although outside of bankruptcy the litigation results obtained by otherwise similarly-situated claimants often vary based on a wide variety of subjective factors (including the skill and reputation of each claimant's lawyer), this is not an acceptable result in a bankruptcy context where similar claimants are to be treated similarly. In this sense, the pre-petition trust, created with knowledge of an imminent bankruptcy filing, circumvents the policy and provisions of the Bankruptcy Code.

Yet another difference in treatment of similarly-situated claimants is that those entitled to be paid by the pre-petition trust also enjoy the benefit of a far less stringent evaluation to determine entitlement to compensation. * * *

Why are a select group of current claimants given preferential treatment? The answer is obvious: to induce them to vote in favor of the pre-packaged plan in large enough numbers to meet the 75% "supermajority" requirement in Section 524(g). Those lawyers who control large "inventories" of asbestos claims, as they sometimes impersonally and inelegantly refer to their clientele, must have their demands satisfied, or they will vote against the plan (as they typically assert they can do, without client consultation, in reliance on broad powers of attorney granted at the outset of the representation). The lawyers with the largest number of clients, who can therefore deliver the most votes, therefore have the power and leverage to negotiate the highest "matrix values" for their clients. Naturally, those lawyers who control fewer votes have less ability to negotiate high matrix values. The result is that the amount a claimant recovers varies based not on the merit of his or her claim but, instead, on the identity of his or her counsel.

Why not pay all the current claimants at the highest matrix values? Presumably all attorneys for current claimants would agree on that as an ideal, but it is not achievable in a world of limited funding availability, since considerable value must be set aside for payment of future claimants and those current claimants who, for one reason or another, do not participate in the pre-petition trust. * * *

* * *

D. The Future Claimants' Representative Has Only a Limited Ability to Negotiate Plan Terms

In a "conventional" asbestos bankruptcy, the court-appointed Future Claimants' Representative is involved in the plan negotiations from the outset. His ability to negotiate favorable terms on behalf of his constituents is a function of: (i) his skill as a negotiator and that of his lawyers, and (ii) the leverage afforded by the provisions of the Bankruptcy Code to insist that at least 50% of the stock of the debtor and others is made available for payment of such claims.[145] All of the assets of the debtor and its affiliates are on the negotiating table for discussion. As a historical matter, in many "conventional" asbestos bankruptcies the claimants have ended up with majority ownership of the company. That way, the profits thrown off by the company once it is freed from asbestos liability, and any increase in the value of the company's stock, benefit the claimants the company allegedly harmed.

In pre-packs, however, the hands of the person chosen by the debtor to negotiate plan terms on behalf of future claimants are tied by the terms of the deal already negotiated by the debtor and its hand-selected negotiating partner. * * *

Moreover, in undertaking the pre-petition negotiations the prospective future claimants' representative only has access to such information as the debtor elects to provide. This is also unlike the case in a "conventional" bankruptcy, where the court-appointed Future Claimants' Representative can, if necessary, use the discovery devices made available by the Bankruptcy Rules to compel disclosure of information. Without such devices, even expensive "due diligence" efforts can fall short. * * *

Finally, there is the reality that the prospective debtor is the one who selected and is paying the person assigned the role of negotiating the pre-pack on behalf of future claimants. The prospective debtor is also the one paying the professionals retained by the prospective future claimants' representative. While this appears on its face to be similar to what would happen in the bankruptcy case—where the court-appointed Future Claimants' Representative and his or her professionals would be paid by the estate, subject to the supervision of the bankruptcy court—it is actually not the same, because there is no judicial scrutiny of the fees, and the prospective debtor has a measure of control that it does not have once a bankruptcy case is actually commenced. Further, because the person representing future claimants is not a court appointee when the negotiations are taking place, the debtor has the ability to terminate him or her if the negotiations get too tough. And while it is common for the debtor in a pre-pack to ask the court to appoint the pre-petition prospective future claimants' representative as the Future Claimants' Representative in the bankruptcy case, the appointment is close to meaningless, since the terms of the plan are already set.

It is perhaps the most notable feature of the recent asbestos pre-packs that ownership of the debtors has remained entirely with their parent companies. Not only is this contrary to what happens in most conventional asbestos pre-packs, it is arguably contrary to what Congress intended when it enacted Section 524(g) of the Bankruptcy Code: that in exchange for a broad channeling injunction making a debtor forever "asbestos free," the company should be required to both contribute at least 50% of its equity to the claimants and to make future payments to the trust, including dividends. The fact that pre-packaged and conventional asbestos bankruptcies have such discrepant outcomes is strong evidence that pre-packs fail to serve the interests of future claimants.

* * *

F. The Settlements Comprising Pre-Packs Typically Violate Insurer Rights in Ways that Jeopardize the Recoveries of Future Claimants

The manner in which pre-packs are negotiated jeopardizes the very insurance coverage proceeds that the future claimants largely depend on for payment of their claims.

Insurance policies typically contain provisions that, among other things, grant an insurer the right to control (or associate in) the defense and settlement of any claims it is called upon to pay. Under such provisions, settlements are not binding on (*i.e.*, need not be reimbursed by) the insurer if the insurer did not consent to the settlement in writing. A pre-pack is, of course, a settlement among the prospective debtor, the person(s) negotiating on behalf of current claimants, and the prospective future claimants' representative. If the insurers do not consent to the settlement, it may not be binding on them and insurance proceeds may not be available to pay claims submitted as part of such a settlement. Since in most pre-packs the future claimants are largely dependent on insurance funding for payment of their claims, the fact that insurers typically are excluded from pre-pack negotiations threatens to result in the future claimants being paid nothing on their claims, even as current claimants get paid nearly in full.

* * *

V. Conclusion

Companies facing tens of thousands of asbestos claims may view pre-pack bankruptcies as a panacea, in that they seem to provide a mechanism for quick and inexpensive relief from the asbestos litigation nightmare. However, experience has shown that this is not the case because such bankruptcies have drawn vigorous objections by persons claiming that pre-packaged asbestos bankruptcies, as currently practiced, violate the Bankruptcy Code and Rules, improperly treat some claimants more favorably than others, and disregard the contractual rights of the insurers expected to fund the payments under the plan. * * *

SAMUEL ISSACHAROFF, PRIVATE CLAIMS, AGGREGATE RIGHTS
2008 Sup. Ct. Rev. 183, 208–11 (2008).

* * *

* * * The most significant class action cases of the last decade were *Amchem Products v. Windsor* [521 U.S. 591 (1997)] and *Ortiz v. Fibreboard* [527 U.S. 815 (1999)], the two attempts to use class action settlement procedures to close out asbestos liabilities for not only current claimants but future ones as well. While there are many reasons to be skeptical of the way these work-out deals were structured and negotiated, the Court's response was to ratchet up the formalism of the rules to curtail what it termed the "adventuresome" use of the class device. As a result, class actions seemed to drop out of the available set of tools for attempting to settle most mass torts, absent some extraordinary willingness of a settling defendant to allow some form of future claims to return to the tort system.

Perhaps naively, the Court in the asbestos cases may have thought that it was restoring the primacy of what Justice Souter in *Ortiz* would term the "day-in-court ideal" of individual claimants represented by individual attorneys proceeding to trial. That account cannot withstand the realities of plummeting rates of cases actually being tried to judgment, nor the emergence of a raft of alternative mechanisms outside Article III courts that bundle claims in efforts to achieve closure. While most of the responses are private aggregations of claims portfolios through the plaintiffs' bar, other pathways have developed. In asbestos, a statutory option has emerged, offering an alternative to the perceived disutility of the class action device in contested mass torts.

Thus it is noteworthy that the most important post-*Amchem* judicial developments on the proper considerations for the resolution of mass harms come not through the processes of litigation in Article III courts, but through a specific exception for asbestos bankruptcies under Section 524(g) of the Bankruptcy Code. Rather than the formalized processes of class actions, Section 524(g) places a premium on private work-outs of mass torts * * * and offers the finality of bankruptcy protection for properly consummated private settlements. A debtor seeking bankruptcy protection for asbestos liabilities may proceed through a "pre-packaged" bankruptcy (known in the trade as "pre-packs") by showing that the plan is supported by a majority of the affected claimants, representing two-thirds of the amounts claimed against the debtor. The real work is done by the requirement that the reorganization be supported by 75 percent of the debtor's asbestos claimants in order for the debtor to be able to get a "channeling injunction"—the bankruptcy procedure that forecloses any claim against the debtor not obtained ("channeled through") the bankruptcy court. The channeling injunction is critical because it provides protection against claims made not only by present claimants (including the minority who might oppose the reorganization), but by future claimants as well.

To the untutored eye, the 524(g) workout looks strikingly similar to the efforts to obtain a judicial imprimatur for work-outs of present and future claims, as were struck down in *Amchem* and *Ortiz*. For good reason, as it appears that way to the tutored eye as well. The practical effect is that an agreement broadly supported by present claimants can be used to cram down the claims not only of dissenting plaintiffs, but of future claimants as well. The bankruptcy work-out includes a Future Claimants Representative who assumes a fiduciary responsibility. But the major difference is that the statutory scheme substitutes an Article I judge for an Article III judge, hardly a stirring form of enhanced protection for the due process interests that are at stake.

Because Section 524(g) provided a more welcoming port for judicially supervised and judicially enforced private settlement, the locus of asbestos work-outs shifted there following *Amchem* and *Ortiz*. Perhaps not surprisingly, the most significant mass tort "class action" case following *Amchem* and *Ortiz* emerges not from the overly formalized class action context but from the more flexible procedures of bankruptcy. In *In re Combustion Engineering*, [391 F.3d 190 (3d Cir. 2004)], the Third Circuit had to apply to a complicated pre-pack what the *Amchem* Court defined as the "structural assurance of fair and adequate representation for the diverse groups and individuals affected." At immediate issue in *Combustion Engineering* was a multitiered payment scheme that created a private pre-petition trust for the bulk of the payout to present claimants and what was in effect a diminished corpus to serve as the bankruptcy estate for satisfying future claimants. The two were linked because the approval of the bankruptcy trust was the predicate for the realization of the pre-petition trust and, accordingly, present claimants had a strong incentive to vote for the plan in order to get the benefits of the second trust.

Examining the disputed reorganization as a bankruptcy case, Judge Scirica was able to recapture the essential equitable inquiry that was obscured by the procedural formalism of *Amchem* and *Ortiz*[:] * * * "Equality of distribution among creditors is a central policy of the Bankruptcy Code." [*Combustion Engineering*, quoting *Begier v. IRS*, 496 U.S. 53, 58 (1990)]. The [Third Circuit] looked to the class action asbestos cases for the controlling principles of equity and concluded, "[t]hough *Ortiz* was decided under [Rule] 23(b)(1)(B), the Court's requirement of fair treatment for all claimants—a principle at the core of equity—also applies in the context of this case." As applied to the case, the proposed resolution failed, not because of any formal requirements of Rule 23 or any hypothesized need to return to the premise of the "day-in-court" ideal, but because the concerns of equity were sufficient to strike down a plan that gave preferential treatment to a group of voting claimants at the expense of those neither present nor voting.

* * *

NOTES & QUESTIONS

1. What are the pros and cons of pre-packaged bankruptcies?

2. Why do pre-packaged bankruptcies sometimes raise issues similar to those raised in *Amchem* and *Ortiz*?

3. For further discussions of pre-packaged bankruptcies and *Combustion Engineering*, see., e.g., Troy A. McKenzie, *The Mass Tort Bankruptcy: A Pre-History*, 5 J. Tort L. 59 (2012); Kenneth Pasquale, *Combustion Engineering: Setting Limits on Pre-Packaged Asbestos Bankruptcies*, 24-Feb. Am. Bankr. Inst. J. 36 (2005).

e. Aggregation of Related Claims Against Other Parties

The above articles focused primarily on bankruptcy as a device for aggregating claims asserted against the debtor by numerous parties. This subsection describes bankruptcy as a device to aggregate claims asserted against other parties in related litigation.

IN RE DOW CORNING CORP.
United States Court of Appeals, Sixth Circuit, 1996.

86 F.3d 482.

Before MARTIN and BATCHELDER, CIRCUIT JUDGES, and WISEMAN, DISTRICT JUDGE [(M.D. Tenn.), by designation].

MARTIN, CIRCUIT JUDGE.

This is an appeal to determine the subject matter jurisdiction of federal district courts, sitting as bankruptcy courts, over proceedings "related to" a case filed under Chapter 11 of the Bankruptcy Code, and the ability of federal district courts to transfer such proceedings to the district court in which the bankruptcy case is pending. The principal issue presented is whether the district court erred, as a matter of law, in its determination that claims for compensatory and punitive damages asserted in tens of thousands of actions against numerous nondebtor manufacturers and suppliers of silicone gel breast implants could have no conceivable effect upon, and therefore were not related to, the bankruptcy estate of The Dow Corning Corporation. The district court held that it did not have "related to" jurisdiction over those claims pursuant to 28 U.S.C. § 1334(b) and concluded that they could not be transferred to it pursuant to 28 U.S.C. § 157(b)(5). For the following reasons, we REVERSE and REMAND for further proceedings consistent with this opinion.

I.

Until it ceased their manufacture in 1992, Dow Corning was the predominant producer of silicone gel breast implants, accounting for nearly 50% of the entire market. In addition, Dow Corning supplied silicone raw materials to other manufacturers of silicone gel breast implants. In recent years, tens of thousands of implant recipients have sued Dow Corning, claiming to have been injured by autoimmune reactions to the silicone in their implants. Dow Chemical Company, Corning Incorporated, Minnesota Mining and Manufacturing Company, Baxter Healthcare Corporation and Baxter International Incorporated, and Bristol–Myers Squibb Company and Medical Engineering Corporation are other manufacturers and suppliers of silicone gel-filled implants, and are codefendants with Dow Corning in a large number of personal injury actions.

On June 25, 1992, prior to Dow Corning's filing of its Chapter 11 petition, the Federal Judicial Panel on Multidistrict Litigation ordered the consolidation of all breast implant actions pending in federal courts for coordinated pretrial proceedings, and transferred those actions to Chief Judge Pointer of the Northern District of Alabama. On September 1, 1994, Chief Judge Pointer certified a class for settlement purposes only, and approved a complex agreement between members of the class and certain defendants that contemplated the creation of a $4.25 billion fund to cover, among other things, the costs of treatment and other expenses incurred by breast implant recipients. Each class member was given the opportunity to opt out of the class and to pursue her individual claims separately. Several thousand plaintiffs opted out of the settlement class, while approximately 440,000 elected to register for inclusion in the Global Settlement.

Due to the litigation burden imposed by what is one of the world's largest mass tort litigations, and the threatened consequences of the thousands of product liability claims arising from its manufacture and sale of silicone breast implants and silicone gel, Dow Corning filed a petition for reorganization under Chapter 11 of the Bankruptcy Code on May 15, 1995, in the United States District Court for the Eastern District of Michigan. * * * As a result of Dow Corning's Chapter 11 filing, all breast implant claims against it were automatically stayed pursuant to 11 U.S.C. § 362(a).

Claims against Dow Corning's two shareholders, Dow Chemical and Corning Incorporated, and the other nondebtor defendants were not stayed. Dow Chemical, Corning Incorporated, Minnesota Mining, Baxter and Bristol–Myers Squibb subsequently removed many opt-out claims in which those companies were named defendants with Dow Corning from state to federal court pursuant to 28 U.S.C. § 1452(a) [*see* n. 8 of Mabey & Zisser excerpt in Section (B)(2)(b) of this chapter].

On June 12, 1995, Dow Corning filed a motion pursuant to 28 U.S.C. § 157(b)(5) [*see* n. 19 of Mabey & Zisser excerpt in Section (B)(2)(b) of this chapter] to transfer to the Eastern District of Michigan opt-out breast implant claims pending against it and its shareholders, Dow Chemical and Corning Incorporated. Dow Corning's motion covered claims that had been removed to federal court and were pending in the multidistrict forum, as well as claims pending in state courts which were in the process of being removed to federal courts pursuant to 28 U.S.C. § 1452(a). Dow Corning envisioned its transfer motion as the first step in ensuring a feasible plan of reorganization, and indicated that it would seek to have the transferred actions consolidated for a threshold jury trial on the issue of whether silicone gel breast implants cause the diseases claimed. Dow Chemical and Corning Incorporated joined in Dow Corning's motion.

On June 14, 1995, Minnesota Mining, Baxter, and Bristol–Myers Squibb also moved, pursuant to Section 157(b)(5), to transfer to the Eastern District of Michigan the opt-out cases in which those manufacturers were named as defendants with Dow Corning. In their Section 157(b)(5) motions, Minnesota Mining, Baxter, and Bristol–Myers Squibb also asked the district court to order that the claims at issue be transferred to the district court in which the bankruptcy case is pending so that the court could conduct a consolidated trial on the issue of causation.

On September 12, 1995, the district court issued two opinions and companion orders regarding the Section 157(b)(5) transfer motions. With respect to opt-out breast implant cases pending against Dow Corning, the district court asserted jurisdiction under Section 1334(b) and permitted transfer pursuant to Section 157(b)(5). The district court, however, denied the remainder of the transfer motions on the ground that, as a matter of law, it lacked subject matter jurisdiction over the claims sought to be transferred because they were not "related to" Dow Corning's bankruptcy proceeding pursuant to 28 U.S.C. § 1334(b). * * *

Dow Corning, Dow Chemical, Corning Incorporated, Minnesota Mining, Baxter, and Bristol–Myers Squibb subsequently filed appeals seeking review of the district court's partial denial of their motions to transfer. Those appeals were consolidated on October 10, 1995, and we are now faced with a complex set of questions pertaining to the scope of a district court's jurisdiction when it sits in bankruptcy, and its power to fix venue for the trial of wrongful death and personal injury tort claims that are "related to" a bankruptcy proceeding. * * * Realizing that we cannot satisfy all competing interests perfectly, our primary goal is to establish a mechanism for resolving the claims at issue in the most fair and equitable manner possible. In seeking to achieve that goal, we are called upon to balance four different, and frequently competing, interests: those of the individuals who have brought and will bring breast implant claims; Dow Corning's interests with regard to its attempt to formulate a successful reorganization plan; Dow Chemical and Corning Incorporated's interests as shareholders of Dow Corning; and the judicial system's interest in allocating its limited resources effectively and efficiently.

* * *

III.

The first issue to be resolved is whether the district court has subject matter jurisdiction over breast implant claims pending not only against the debtor, Dow Corning, but also over certain claims pending against the nondebtor defendants. The nondebtor defendants argue that such jurisdiction exists pursuant to 28 U.S.C. § 1334(b) or, alternatively, 28 U.S.C. § 1367(a). We review the district court's jurisdictional ruling *de novo*.

Section 1334 grants jurisdiction to district courts in bankruptcy cases and proceedings as follows:

> (a) Except as provided in subsection (b) of this section, the district court shall have original and exclusive jurisdiction of all cases under title 11.
>
> (b) Notwithstanding any Act of Congress that confers exclusive jurisdiction on a court or courts other than the district courts, the district courts shall have original but not exclusive jurisdiction of all civil proceedings arising under title 11, or arising in or *related to cases under title 11*. [This subsection of section 1334 has been modified somewhat, but not in any way material to the decision here. –Ed.]

28 U.S.C. § 1334.

In addressing the extent of a district court's bankruptcy jurisdiction under Section 1334(b) over civil proceedings "related to" cases under title 11, we start with the premise that the "emphatic terms in which the jurisdictional grant is described in the legislative history, and the extraordinarily broad wording of the grant itself, leave us with no doubt that Congress intended to grant to the district courts broad jurisdiction in bankruptcy cases." Although "situations may arise where an extremely tenuous connection to the estate would not satisfy the jurisdictional requirement" of Section 1334(b), Congressional intent was "to grant comprehensive jurisdiction to the bankruptcy courts so that they might deal efficiently and expeditiously with all matters connected with the bankruptcy estate." *Celotex Corp. v. Edwards*, 514 U.S. 300, 308 (1995).

The definition of a "related" proceeding under Section 1334(b) was first articulated by the Third Circuit in *Pacor, Inc. v. Higgins*, 743 F.2d 984 (3d Cir. 1984). As stated in that case, the "usual articulation of the test for determining whether a civil proceeding is related to bankruptcy is whether the outcome of that proceeding could conceivably have any effect on the estate being administered in bankruptcy." An action is "related to bankruptcy if the outcome could alter the debtor's rights, liabilities, options, or freedom of action (either positively or negatively) and which in any way impacts upon the handling and administration of the bankrupt estate." A proceeding "need not necessarily be against the debtor or against the debtor's property" to satisfy the requirements for "related to" jurisdiction. However, "the mere fact that there may be common issues of fact between a civil proceeding and a controversy involving the bankruptcy estate does not bring the matter within the scope of section [1334(b)]." Instead, "there must be some nexus between the 'related' civil proceeding and the title 11 case."

Our Circuit adopted the *Pacor* test for determining whether a civil proceeding is "related to" a bankruptcy proceeding under Section 1334(b). * * * The majority of our sister circuits have likewise adopted the *Pacor* test for "related to" jurisdiction. According to the Supreme Court, the Second and Seventh Circuits have adopted slightly different tests for determining whether Section 1334(b) jurisdiction exists. *Celotex*, 514 U.S. at 308 n.6.

In addition, the Supreme Court * * * cited *Pacor* with approval in addressing the broad scope of the jurisdictional grant in Section 1334(b). * * * With these standards in mind, we turn to an examination of whether subject matter jurisdiction exists pursuant to Section 1334(b) over joint claims pending against Dow Corning and the various non-debtor defendants.

* * *

* * * We believe two * * * theories support a finding that the district court has "related to" jurisdiction over the claims at issue, and address them in turn.

1. Claims for Contribution and Indemnification

Dow Corning, Dow Chemical and Corning Incorporated argue that the district court erred in its determination that "related to" jurisdiction does not exist over certain breast implant claims asserted against Dow Chemical and Corning Incorporated because, in addition to the claims asserted by the personal injury claimants, Dow Chemical and Corning Incorporated have asserted cross-claims against each other and Dow Corning in the underlying litigation, which will have an effect on the bankruptcy estate. Minnesota Mining, Baxter, and Bristol–Myers Squibb argue that, despite the fact that they have not yet filed contribution and indemnification claims or proofs of claim relating to implant litigation in Dow Corning's bankruptcy case, they have contingent claims for contribution and indemnification that will have a conceivable effect on the bankruptcy proceedings. Minnesota Mining, Baxter, and Bristol–Myers Squibb therefore argue that the breast implant claims covered by their section 157(b)(5) motions will give rise to thousands of claims against Dow Corning for indemnification and contribution. In addition, the nondebtor defendants claim that Dow Corning may itself have claims against them for contribution and indemnification under theories of joint and several liability. The companies argue that these claims need to be resolved as part of Dow Corning's bankruptcy proceedings and reorganization plan, and certainly will affect the debtor's rights, liabilities, options, and freedom of action in the administration of its estate.

* * * [T]he district court rejected this basis for "related to" jurisdiction and held that the possibility of contribution or indemnification should only

be regarded as relevant if and when judgments are actually entered against the nondebtors. * * *

* * *

* * * [W]e believe the district court has "related to" subject matter jurisdiction over the breast implant claims pending against the nondebtor defendants in this case. Thousands of suits asserted against Dow Corning include claims against the nondebtors, and the nature of the claims asserted establishes that Dow Corning and the various nondebtor defendants are closely related with regard to the pending breast implant litigation. Dow Chemical and Corning Incorporated have already asserted cross-claims against each other and Dow Corning in the underlying litigation, and the other nondebtor defendants have asserted repeatedly throughout their briefs, motions, and oral arguments that they intend to file claims for contribution and indemnification against Dow Corning, and we have no reason to doubt the veracity of those assertions at this time.

We find that it is not necessary for the appellees first to prevail on their claims against the nondebtor defendants, and for those companies to establish joint and several liability on Dow Corning's part, before the civil actions pending against the nondebtors may be viewed as conceivably impacting Dow Corning's bankruptcy proceedings. The claims currently pending against the nondebtors give rise to contingent claims against Dow Corning which unquestionably could ripen into fixed claims. The potential for Dow Corning's being held liable to the nondebtors in claims for contribution and indemnification, or vice versa, suffices to establish a conceivable impact on the estate in bankruptcy. Claims for indemnification and contribution, whether asserted against or by Dow Corning, obviously would affect the size of the estate and the length of time the bankruptcy proceedings will be pending, as well as Dow Corning's ability to resolve its liabilities and proceed with reorganization. * * *

Cognizant of the fact that "related to" jurisdiction cannot be limitless and concerned about granting benefits of the automatic stay in bankruptcy to solvent codefendants, we nevertheless believe the possibility of contribution or indemnification liability in this case is far from attenuated. We conclude that Section 1334(b) jurisdiction exists over the actions pending against Dow Chemical, Corning Incorporated, Minnesota Mining, Baxter, and Bristol–Myers Squibb that are the subject of the companies' section 157(b)(5) motions.

2. Joint Insurance

[The court also held that "related to" jurisdiction existed as to claims pending against the shareholders of Dow Corning—Dow Chemical and Corning Incorporated—because the three companies shared joint insurance policies, which together provided over $1 billion in coverage. Dow Corning's interest in the policies was one of the largest assets of its bankruptcy estate. The court found that the threat posed to those insurance policies if claims pending against Dow Chemical and Corning Incorporated were permitted to go forward in a separate manner supported "related to" jurisdiction.]

IV.

We next address the power of the district court, sitting in bankruptcy, to fix the venue for the trial of personal injury tort and wrongful death claims asserted in non-bankruptcy forums pursuant to 28 U.S.C. § 157(b)(5). Section 157(b)(5) provides:

> The district court shall order that personal injury tort and wrongful death claims shall be tried in the district court in which the bankruptcy case is pending, or in the district court in the district in which the claim arose, as determined by the district court in which the bankruptcy case is pending.

The purpose of Section 157(b)(5) is "to centralize the administration of the estate and to eliminate the 'multiplicity of forums for the adjudication of parts of a bankruptcy case.'" Centralization of claims increases the debtor's odds of developing a reasonable plan of reorganization which will "work a rehabilitation of the debtor and at the same time assure fair and non-preferential resolution of the . . . claims."

It has been established that a "bankrupt debtor who is a defendant in a personal injury action may move under section 157(b)(5) to transfer the case to one of two venues: (1) the district where the bankruptcy is proceeding; or (2) the district where the claim arose." The question for our consideration is whether Section 157(b)(5) allows for the transfer of personal injury and wrongful death claims pending against nondebtor defendants who have been sued with a debtor under claims of joint and several liability.

* * *

We [hold] that section 157(b)(5) should be read to allow a district court to fix venue for cases pending against nondebtor defendants which are "related to" a debtor's bankruptcy proceedings pursuant to Section 1334(b). This approach will further the prompt, fair, and complete resolution of all claims "related to" bankruptcy proceedings, and harmonize Section 1334(b)'s broad jurisdictional grant with the oft-stated goal of centralizing the administration of a bankruptcy estate.

V.

Finally, a Section 157(b)(5) motion "requires an abstention analysis." The abstention provisions of 28 U.S.C. § 1334(c) qualify Section 1334(b)'s broad grant of jurisdiction. It is for the district court to "determine in each individual case whether hearing it would promote or impair efficient and fair adjudication of bankruptcy cases."

Section 1334 provides for two types of abstention: discretionary abstention under 28 U.S.C. § 1334(c)(1) and mandatory abstention under 28 U.S.C. § 1334(c)(2). Section 1334(c)(1) provides:

> Nothing in this section prevents a district court in the interest of justice, or in the interest of comity with State courts or respect for State law, from abstaining from hearing a particular proceeding arising under title 11 or arising in or related to a case under title 11.

Section 1334(c)(2) states in relevant part:

> Upon timely motion of a party in a proceeding based upon a State law claim or State law cause of action, related to a case under title 11 but not arising under title 11 or arising in a case under title 11, with respect to which an action could not have been commenced in a court of the United States absent jurisdiction under this section, the district court shall abstain from hearing such proceeding if an action is commenced, and can be timely adjudicated, in a State forum of appropriate jurisdiction.

For mandatory abstention to apply, a proceeding must: (1) be based on a state law claim or cause of action; (2) lack a federal jurisdictional basis absent the bankruptcy; (3) be commenced in a state forum of appropriate jurisdiction; (4) be capable of timely adjudication; and (5) be a non-core proceeding. Non-core proceedings under Section 157(b)(2)(B) (*i.e.* liquidation of personal injury tort or wrongful death case) are not subject to section 1334(c)(2)'s mandatory abstention provisions pursuant to 28 U.S.C. § 157(b)(4).

The district court in this case determined that Section 157(b)(4) rendered exempt from the mandatory abstention requirement all personal injury tort claims pending solely against Dow Corning, and decided not to abstain discretionarily with regard to those claims at this time. Because the district court found that it did not have subject matter jurisdiction over the claims pending against the nondebtor defendants, it did not address the abstention issue in detail and merely incorporated by reference its analysis of the abstention issue pertaining to claims pending solely against Dow Corning. It also remains to be fully determined whether the abstention exception in Section 157(b)(4) applies to claims pending against nondebtor defendants and, if not, whether the factors calling for mandatory exemption under Section 1334(c)(2) have been met. The district court did not directly address these matters, and we refrain from addressing them in the first instance. Because we believe the district court is in a better position to make the necessary abstention determinations, as to both mandatory and discretionary abstention, we remand the case to the district court for further proceedings on this issue.

VI.

We REVERSE the district court's determination that it lacked subject matter jurisdiction over the tort claims pending against the nondebtor defendants and that it did not have the power to transfer those claims pursuant to section 157(b)(5). In addition, we REMAND this case to the district court for further proceedings on the issue of section 1334(c) abstention.

NOTES AND QUESTIONS

1. On remand, the *Dow Corning* district court held that the cases against the nondebtors were subject to mandatory abstention under 28 U.S.C. § 1334(c)(2), and, alternately, to discretionary abstention under 28 U.S.C. § 1334(c)(1). *See In re Dow Corning Corp.*, 1996 WL 511646 (E.D. Mich. 1996), *rev'd*, 113 F.3d 565 (6th Cir. 1997). It therefore refused to transfer the cases against the nondebtors to the Eastern District of Michigan. The Sixth Circuit granted a writ of mandamus and reversed, ordering the district court to transfer all claims against the nondebtors who were Dow Corning shareholders

(Dow Chemical and Corning Incorporated) and to evaluate each claim *individually* to determine whether mandatory abstention applied. *See In re Dow Corning Corp.*, 113 F.3d 565 (6th Cir. 1997). The Sixth Circuit reasoned that it made no sense to transfer claims against Dow Corning but not its shareholders, since the claims against the shareholders were identical to the claims against Dow Corning—the shareholders had never manufactured silicone-implant products and were named only because of their association with Dow Corning.

2. *Dow Corning* discusses the split among circuits for determining whether a civil action is sufficiently "related to" a bankruptcy proceeding to warrant the bankruptcy court's assertion of jurisdiction. *See* Jonathan M. Petts, William H. Hildbold & Ji Hun Kim, *Recent Developments in Related-To Jurisdiction Under* Pacor, 29 Am. Bankr. Inst. L. Rev. 22, 66–67 (2010) (noting that "*Pacor* has been adopted by nine of the 11 federal circuits").

3. In addition to *Dow Corning*, other courts have occasionally relied upon "related to" jurisdiction to aggregate cases involving nondebtor codefendants. One significant case, relied upon heavily by the *Dow Corning* court in a portion of the opinion not excerpted above, was *A.H. Robins Co. v. Piccinin*, 788 F.2d 994 (4th Cir. 1986). A.H. Robins, the debtor, filed a petition for bankruptcy after extensive personal injury litigation involving the Dalkon Shield intrauterine device. At the time of the filing, more than 5,000 suits had been filed. Many of those suits named other codefendants as well, including A.H. Robins' insurer and certain individuals (among them, the developer of the device), who were entitled by law or contract to indemnification from A.H. Robins. When A.H. Robins filed its petition, plaintiffs in a number of the suits sought to sever A.H. Robins from the codefendants so that plaintiffs could continue to pursue the codefendants despite the automatic stay relating to A.H. Robins under 11 U.S.C. § 362(a). A.H. Robins sought an injunction to restrain the prosecution of the actions against the codefendants. The district court stayed the codefendant cases and ultimately transferred them pursuant to 11 U.S.C. § 1334(b) to the Eastern District of Virginia, where A.H. Robins had filed for bankruptcy. The Fourth Circuit affirmed, noting that proceedings against codefendants of a debtor could be stayed if "unusual circumstances" existed. 788 F.2d at 999. Because the codefendants at issue either were entitled to indemnification from A.H. Robins or, in the instance of its insurers, had issued insurance policies that constituted property of A.H. Robins' estate, the court found that "unusual circumstances" were present. In those situations, a judgment against the third-party defendant would in effect be a judgment or finding against the debtor (*id.* at 1004) or an impermissible attempt to exercise control over property of the estate (*id.* at 1001–02).

4. One critic of the *Dow Corning* approach to "related to" jurisdiction has argued:

> Allowing a transfer of cases pending against nondebtor codefendants to the district court where the debtor's bankruptcy is proceeding can be a powerful delaying tactic. Such a transfer effectively blocks trial dates in federal and state courts around the country and potentially places thousands of cases on the docket of the district court where the bankruptcy case is proceeding. The transfer also relieves the pressure on the nondebtor codefendants to negotiate settlements with tort claimants by buying them months or years of delay. * * * Furthermore, * * * [b]y transferring the cases, the nondebtor codefendants

can force a plaintiff to litigate in a forum far away from where he or she resides.

Note, *Why Bankruptcy "Related To" Jurisdiction Should Not Reach Mass Tort Nondebtor Codefendants*, 73 N.Y.U. L. Rev. 1627, 1645 (1998). Are these concerns valid?

5. How significant is "related to" jurisdiction as an aggregation device? Can it be utilized frequently? Is it a limited doctrine even within the bankruptcy context? Will it likely affect many cases? What advantages does it have over other aggregation devices? What, if any, disadvantages does it have?

f. Attempted Use of Other Aggregation Devices to Escape Bankruptcy Jurisdiction

The discussion of bankruptcy thus far has addressed situations in which bankruptcy may serve as an aggregation device. Bankruptcy may also serve to preclude the use of *other* aggregation devices. As noted in Chapter 3(A)(2), in *Ortiz v. Fibreboard Corp.*, 527 U.S. 815 (1999), the Supreme Court raised, but did not decide, whether the use of a limited-fund class under Rule 23(b)(1)(B) may violate the bankruptcy laws. The following case provides an example of a court holding that an attempted use of a (b)(1)(B) class was an improper attempt to circumvent the Bankruptcy Code.

IN RE JOINT E. AND S. DIST. ASBESTOS LITIG.
United States Court of Appeals, Second Circuit, 1993.

14 F.3d 726.

Before WINTER and VAN GRAAFEILAND, CIRCUIT JUDGES, and POLLACK, DISTRICT JUDGE [(S.D.N.Y.), by designation].

WINTER, CIRCUIT JUDGE.

[In 1968, Keene Corporation purchased a manufacturer of asbestos-containing insulation products. As a result, beginning in 1977, Keene became embroiled in about 190,000 asbestos personal injury claims. Although it had settled about half of those claims, about 2000 new claims continued to be filed against it each month. Its net assets were about $51 million as of May 1993. At that time, Keene brought a "Verified Class Action Complaint in Connection with Settlement" under Rule 23(b)(1)(B), naming as individual defendants the people who had asserted asbestos claims against it, along with a mandatory class of present and future asbestos claimants. The complaint sought "court assistance, as provided by Rule 23(b)(1)(B), to negotiate and eventually approve a settlement that fairly resolves the claims with the limited funds Keene has available." The complaint further noted that "[c]ertification of the Class for settlement purposes [would] avoid a potential bankruptcy of Keene by allowing [the claims] to come to a successful and final resolution in an expeditious and fair manner with a minimum of transaction costs." The complaint sought a declaratory judgment that Keene was not liable to the defendants for asbestos-related injury. The district court found that a limited fund existed and certified a defendant class under Rule 23(b)(1)(B). The court enjoined Keene and all class members from continuing or starting any asbestos-related cases against Keene, except for cases already in trial. On appeal, the Second Circuit held that the complaint failed to allege a case or controversy under Article III of the Constitution. It held that Keene's request for a declaration of nonliability was "transparently pretextual," because it knew that such relief would never be granted. The court then turned to whether the proposed complaint was an attempt to evade the Bankruptcy Code.]

* * * [I]t is clear that the complaint is an attempt to compel an adjustment of Keene's creditors' rights outside the Bankruptcy Code and is defended almost entirely by the argument that a mandatory class settlement of present or future asbestos claims would be better for all parties than a bankruptcy proceeding. Indeed, the process contemplated by Keene mirrors a bankruptcy proceeding. The finding of a limited fund corresponds to a finding of insolvency. The preliminary injunction serves much the same function as the automatic stay under Section 362(a) of the Bankruptcy Code, 11 U.S.C. § 362(a) (1988). The proposed mandatory class settlement mirrors a reorganization plan and "cramdown" [forcing dissenting creditors to accept a plan that is fair, reasonable, and not discriminatory], *see* 11 U.S.C. § 1123, 1129(b).

Keene's argument is self-defeating, however, because it is a self-evident evasion of the exclusive legal system established by Congress for debtors to seek relief. The adoption of Keene's position would surely lead to further evasion of the Bankruptcy Code as other debtors sought relief in mandatory class actions. Keene argues that such a precedent would be limited to situations, like Keene's, of mass torts in which some plaintiffs are not known at the time of the accident. We are dubious that a limit to unknown plaintiffs is feasible. Under the limited fund theory espoused here, a class representative for a large number of trade creditors might be appointed to seek a settlement on their behalf where a company was deemed to be a limited fund because of insolvency. The argument that the company and its creditors would all be better off in such an action than in bankruptcy would be as plausible in a case involving a large number of contract creditors as it is here. Breach of warranty cases involving numerous purchasers might also fall within the theory.

Moreover, even if limited to so-called mass torts with yet unknown plaintiffs, Keene's theory would cover a large number of cases. The use of aggregative techniques and inventive legal theories are causing mass torts to become rather routine. Certainly the theory pressed here would apply to many products liability cases.

Evasion of bankruptcy is also not without costs or other perils. The injunction in the instant matter has already prevented execution of final judgments on supersedeas bonds and funds in escrow that are not Keene's assets. Moreover, class members in cases such as this would have no say in the conduct of the court-appointed class representatives and, unlike creditors in bankruptcy, are not able to vote on a settlement. For them, it would be "cram-down" from start to finish. Finally, unlike a lawyer for a creditors' committee, the class representatives in matters like the present one may not be compensated unless a settlement is reached, a situation fraught with danger to the rights of plaintiffs.

Keene argues passionately that bankruptcy will be a more costly route for the defendant class than this mandatory class action. It may be that the amount distributed to the class in a Keene bankruptcy will be less than in a settlement in the instant class action. Indeed, Keene has suggested that a trial be held on that issue. However, the function of federal courts is not to conduct trials over whether a statutory scheme should be ignored because a more efficient mechanism can be fashioned by judges.

* * *

CONCLUSION

For these reasons, we vacate the order and preliminary injunction issued by the district court and order dismissal of the complaint for lack of subject matter jurisdiction. * * *

NOTES AND QUESTIONS

1. Was the Second Circuit correct in refusing to allow Keene to go forward with its Rule 23(b)(1)(B) action?

2. Note that the Supreme Court in *Ortiz* cited a different Second Circuit case, *In re Drexel Burnham Lambert Group,* 960 F.2d 285, 292 (2d Cir. 1992), for the proposition that "there is no inherent conflict between a limited fund class action under Rule 23(b)(1)(B) and the Bankruptcy Code * * *." *Ortiz,* 527 U.S. at 860 n.34. In *Drexel,* the district court had certified a class under Rule 23(b)(1)(B) in connection with Drexel's transactions in "junk bonds." Drexel entered into a $350 million settlement to resolve a civil suit by the Securities and Exchange Commission (SEC). The funds were to be used to pay the victims of the junk bond transactions. Before paying $150 million of that settlement, however, Drexel filed a Chapter 11 bankruptcy petition. The SEC filed a bankruptcy claim, as did numerous other claimants, including 850 claimants seeking a portion of the SEC settlement fund. The district court withdrew the securities claim from the bankruptcy court under a bankruptcy provision that allows such action when U.S. laws regulating commerce are affected. Various groups of claimants reached a settlement whereby the 850 claimants would be certified as a Rule 23(b)(1)(B) class. The district court certified the class and approved the settlement, and the Second Circuit affirmed.

The Second Circuit found that "[a] succession of individual actions to determine Drexel's liability on each claim would involve costly litigation, thereby depleting Drexel's already limited resources." *Drexel,* 960 F.2d at 291. While noting that "a mandatory class action will not be appropriate in most bankruptcy cases," the court reasoned that, absent a class here, even though Drexel's assets would not be distributed on a "first come, first served" basis because Drexel was in bankruptcy, "some members of the class might attempt to maintain costly individual actions in the hope and, perhaps the belief that their claims are more meritorious than the claims of other class members." *Id.* at 292. As a result, the court concluded that a mandatory class was "necessary * * * to prevent claimants with such motivations from unfairly diminishing the eventual recovery of other class members." *Id.*

Can *Drexel* be reconciled with *Joint Eastern & Southern*? When should a mandatory class be allowed in the case of a company that is either in bankruptcy or threatened with bankruptcy?

3. In light of the materials in the above subsections, consider more broadly whether bankruptcy in fact has much utility as an aggregation device.

After a careful analysis of the issue, the American Law Institute concluded as follows:

> In complex litigation in which a defendant's assets are insufficient to cover its debts, the use of the federal bankruptcy law may operate in a fashion similar to the limited fund class action or interpleader in that the debtor's assets will be treated as a common pool to be distributed among classes of creditors, with *pro rata* distribution within the classes. Nonetheless, resort to bankruptcy cannot be seen as providing a viable or attractive solution for the vast majority of complex cases. Although it offers some advantages for those cases in which the defendant's financial position clearly is deficient, bankruptcy is not available in those complex settings in which matters are not so dire. Further, although the use of specialized judges, *see* 28 U.S.C. § 1334, is justified in the classic bankruptcy setting, as is the exclusive control given to the court where the debtor or its assets is located, *see* 28 U.S.C. §§ 1408, 1409, expansions of bankruptcy jurisdiction to accommodate a broader range of cases does not seem justified. Thus, the alteration of bankruptcy procedures to handle complex, dispersed litigation does not provide a viable * * * solution [for handling dispersed multi-party litigation].

American Law Institute, *Complex Litigation: Statutory Recommendations and Analysis* 35–36 (1994). Is the ALI's pessimistic conclusion justified?

C. POTENTIAL NEW DIRECTIONS: AGGREGATE SETTLEMENT WITHOUT THE CLASS MECHANISM

Parties in aggregate litigation often want to resolve their disputes by settlement. Sometimes, as discussed in Chapter 8, aggregate settlements arise in putative class actions, and often those settlements utilize class action procedures described in that chapter.

On other occasions, however, parties want to settle without using the class action mechanism, either because that mechanism is unavailable (*e.g.*, because of predominance/superiority issues) or because it would be otherwise unattractive (because of cost or timing). Such multiparty settlements have traditionally had to contend with what has come to be called the aggregate settlement rule, which (as described below) limits the ability of attorneys to settle claims of numerous clients at once.

Increasingly, however, especially given the wave of MDL cases involving non-class claims, academics and courts have addressed whether the rules relating to aggregate settlements should be modified. In 2010, the American Law Institute adopted proposed rules that would fundamentally alter the aggregate settlement rule. The materials in this section introduce the subject and explore some of the competing views.

Charles Silver & Lynn A. Baker, Mass Lawsuits and the Aggregate Settlement Rule
32 Wake Forest L. Rev. 773, 734–36 (1997).

* * *

Rule 1.8(g) of the Model Rules of Professional Conduct is known as the aggregate settlement rule. The portion of the rule relating to civil actions provides:

> A lawyer who represents two or more clients shall not participate in making an aggregate settlement of the claims of or against the clients * * * unless each client consents after consultation, including disclosure of the existence and nature of all the claims * * * involved and of the participation of each person in the settlement.

On its face and as interpreted in the few pertinent decisions to date, the Rule imposes three requirements on lawyers seeking to settle lawsuits in which they represent multiple clients: (1) disclosure of all settlement terms to all clients, including disclosure to each of what other plaintiffs are to receive or other defendants are to pay; (2) unanimous consent by all clients to all settlement terms; and (3) a prohibition on agreements to waive requirements (1) or (2) even with the clients' unanimous consent.

These requirements have been on the books for years. Model Rule 1.8(g) carries forward Disciplinary Rule (DR) 5–106 of the Model Code of Professional Responsibility "almost verbatim." The Restatement of the Law Governing Lawyers appears to continue the chain unbroken by endorsing the aggregate settlement rule in its current formulation. The continuity across the three sets of rules suggests broad agreement that the rule works well. This is probably because the rule does work well in most multiple-client representations, where the number of jointly represented clients, although greater than one, is nonetheless small. When the case is one in which a couple of people injured in an automobile accident are represented by the same attorney, the benefits of the rule may well exceed its costs.

When the number of clients is large, however, the costs of the rule may be much greater. Today, one can easily find mass lawsuits, which are not class actions, in which hundreds, thousands, and even tens of thousands of clients sue as a group. Many mass lawsuits involve defective products, but large claimant groups also form in the aftermath of fires and explosions, airplane crashes, toxic releases, and other catastrophes that expose large numbers of persons to risks. Injunctive cases involving exposure to common nuisances or patterns of discrimination can also involve numerous clients. Even legal malpractice can generate a mass lawsuit. Whatever their sources, these massive proceedings may seek remedies involving millions or billions of dollars, often from numerous defendants who are sued on different theories and who, if found to have violated the law, would likely be required to contribute different amounts. Because the stakes are so large and the issues so complex, settlement is both more urgent and more difficult in mass lawsuits than in other litigation, and the aggregate settlement rule is a complication that often gets in the way. One must therefore ask whether Rule 1.8(g) imposes costs that outweigh its benefits and, if so, how the rule should be changed to accommodate today's mass lawsuits.

NOTES AND QUESTIONS

1. What is the purpose of the aggregate settlement rule? What are the potential benefits and drawbacks of the rule?

2. In response to perceived shortcomings with the aggregate settlement rule, courts and commentators have adopted competing approaches. Consider, for example, the proposal set forth below, adopted in 2010 by the American Law Institute, along with a critique of that proposal by two commentators.

PRINCIPLES OF THE LAW OF AGGREGATE LITIGATION
American Law Institute, 2010.

§ 3.17 Circumstances Required for Aggregate Settlements to Be Binding

(a) A lawyer or group of lawyers who represent two or more claimants on a non-class basis may settle the claims of those claimants on an aggregate basis provided that each claimant gives informed consent in writing. Informed consent requires that each claimant be able to review the settlements of all other persons subject to the aggregate settlement or the formula by which the settlement will be divided among all claimants. Further, informed consent requires that the total financial interest of claimants' counsel be disclosed to each claimant.

(b) In lieu of the requirements set forth in subsection (a), individual claimants may, before the receipt of a proposed settlement offer, enter into an agreement in writing through shared counsel allowing each participating claimant to be bound by a substantial-majority vote of all claimants concerning an aggregate-settlement proposal (or, if the settlement significantly distinguishes among different categories of claimants, a separate substantial-majority vote of each category of claimants). An agreement under this subsection must meet each of the following requirements:

> (1) The power to approve a settlement offer must at all times rest with the claimants collectively and may under no circumstances be assigned to claimants' counsel. Claimants may exercise their collective decision-making power to approve a settlement through the selection of an independent agent other than counsel.
>
> (2) The agreement among the claimants may occur at the time the lawyer-client relationship is formed or thereafter, but only if all participating claimants give informed consent. Informed consent requires that the claimants' lawyer fully disclose all the terms of the agreement to the claimants to facilitate informed decision making regarding:
>
>> (A) Whether to enter into the settlement agreement;
>>
>> (B) Whether to subsequently challenge the fairness of the settlement agreement under subsections (d) or (e);
>>
>> (C) Whether to subsequently challenge the compliance of the settlement agreement with the requirements set forth in subsections (b) and (c); and

(D) The desirability of seeking, along with a reasonable opportunity to seek, the advice of independent legal counsel.

(3) The agreement must specify the procedures by which all participating claimants are to approve a settlement offer. The agreement may also specify the manner of allocating the proceeds of a settlement among the claimants or may provide for future development of an appropriate allocation mechanism.

(4) Before claimants enter into the agreement, their lawyer or group of lawyers must explain to all claimants that the mechanism under subsection (a) is available as an alternative means of settling an aggregate lawsuit under this Section. A lawyer or group of lawyers may not terminate an existing relationship solely because the claimant declines to enter into an agreement under subsection (b) and the lawyer must so inform the client. A lawyer who is simultaneously representing claimants proceeding under subsection (a) and claimants proceeding under subsection (b) must notify the subsection (a) claimants that they continue to exercise independent control over their cases and that they may refuse an offered settlement after its terms are disclosed.

(c) An agreement pursuant to subsection (b) is permissible only in cases involving a substantial amount in controversy, a large number of claimants, and when the agreement requires approval by a substantial majority of claimants, with the foregoing minimum criteria to be determined by the applicable legislative or rulemaking body.

(d) The enforceability of an agreement under subsection (b) should depend on whether, based on all facts and circumstances, the agreement is fair and reasonable from a procedural standpoint. Facts and circumstances to be considered include the timing of the agreement, the sophistication of the claimants, the information disclosed to the claimants, whether the terms of the settlement were reviewed by a neutral or special master * * *, whether the claimants have some prior common relationship, and whether the claims of the claimants are similar.

(e) In addition to the requirements of subsection (d), the enforceability of a settlement approved through an agreement under subsection (b) should depend on whether, under all the facts and circumstances, the settlement is substantively fair and reasonable. Facts and circumstances to be considered include the costs, risks, probability of success, and delays in achieving a verdict; whether the claimants are treated equitably (relative to each other) based on their facts and circumstances; and whether particular claimants are disadvantaged by the settlement considered as a whole.

(f) Responsibility for compliance with the prerequisites for the enforceability of an agreement under subsection (b) rests with the claimants' lawyer.

* * *

§ 3.18 Limited Judicial Review for Non–Class Aggregate Settlements

(a) Any claimant who is subject to a settlement entered into pursuant to § 3.17(b) is entitled, within the time period set by the legislature or rulemaking body, to challenge the settlement on the grounds that the settlement does not satisfy some or all of the requirements of § 3.17(b) and § 3.17(c), or is not procedurally and substantively fair and reasonable pursuant to § 3.17(d) and § 3.17(e). Such a challenge may be brought in the court in which the claimant's case is or was pending or, if no case is or was pending, in any court of competent jurisdiction.

(b) Any claimant who contests the amount of his or her share of a settlement approved under § 3.17(b)–(e) is entitled, within the time period set by the legislative or rulemaking body, to challenge the fairness of the settlement. Such a challenge may be brought in the court in which the case is or was pending or, if no case is or was pending, in any court of competent jurisdiction.

(c) The right to challenge the settlement under subsections (a) and (b) of this Section is nonwaivable.

(d) A claimant's lawyer who negotiates a settlement that a court later determines to be unenforceable under § 3.17(b)–(e) may be required to pay the reasonable attorneys' fees and costs incurred by the challenging claimant.

PRINCIPLES OF THE LAW OF AGGREGATE LITIGATION
American Law Institute, 2010.

Comment [to Section 3.17]: * * *

b. *Alternative to aggregate-settlement rule.* Subsection (b) provides an alternative to the aggregate-settlement rule as a vehicle for finalizing aggregate non-class settlements. Subsection (b) departs from the current aggregate-settlement rule by providing that a waiver of individual approval may be valid and binding provided that it is knowingly and voluntarily made, is in writing, is signed by the claimants after full disclosure, and vests decisionmaking power in the claimants either collectively or through some preestablished voting structure.

Waivers of important rights are valid in a variety of areas, including the most cherished of constitutional rights [such as a criminal defendant's right to jury trial, right to confront adverse witnesses, and right to require the state to prove its case beyond a reasonable doubt]. Subsection (b) rejects the view that individual decisionmaking over the settlement of a claim is so critical that it cannot be subject to a contractual waiver in favor of decisionmaking governed by substantial-majority vote. To that end, subsection (b) proposes a contractual-waiver mechanism for settling aggregate cases, while subsection (a) reaffirms that the aggregate-settlement rule remains the default mechanism for aggregate settlement.

Although an aggregate settlement may be binding on a claimant, the claimant remains free to terminate the attorney-client relationship. Subsection (b) does not change existing law governing a claimant's right to pursue malpractice or breach-of-fiduciary-duty claims against his attorney. Further, subsection (f) emphasizes that the risk of improper inducement into an aggregate settlement falls with claimants' counsel.

Current law prohibits waiving individual-claimant settlement decisionmaking, thereby empowering individual holdout claimants to exercise control over a proposed settlement and to demand premiums in exchange for approval. Moreover, in many instances, multiple claimants derive substantial benefits from joint representation by one lawyer or law firm, particularly one with expertise and stature in the particular area of law in which the claimant's claims arise. To the extent that reasonable aggregate settlements—achieved after good-faith, arm's-length negotiations and independent review—cannot go forward because one claimant (or a small number of claimants) objects, the other claimants lose the benefit of the collective representation. Indeed, there are numerous reported cases invalidating collective settlements for noncompliance with the aggregate-settlement rule. Even the threat of such a holdout may cause the defendant to withhold the premium associated with complete peace, thereby inuring to the detriment of all the represented claimants. Subsection (b) sets out an alternative mechanism for settling an aggregate lawsuit in certain circumstances, provided that specific safeguards, as described in subsections (b) through (e), are in place.

* * *

HOWARD M. ERICHSON & BENJAMIN C. ZIPURSKY, CONSENT VERSUS CLOSURE
96 Cornell L. Rev. 265, 293, 299, 301, 304, 306 (2011).

The ALI proposal would allow clients to consent at the outset of a representation to be bound by an aggregate settlement based on a supermajority vote. Put differently, the proposal is that lawyers be permitted to have their clients empower them, in advance, to negotiate binding settlements on their behalf as part of a collective resolution of claims. The difficulties in the *Vioxx* settlement agreement, and those like it, are not finessed but are plainly addressed by disclosure and consent at the front end of the lawyer-client relationship. Indeed, the ALI Reporters pointed to the ethical difficulties of the *Vioxx* settlement as a reason to support the advance consent proposal.

* * *

The report on the *Principles of the Law of Aggregate Litigation* acknowledges that the advance-consent proposal runs contrary to current law on aggregate settlements but argues that the law ought to be changed to facilitate comprehensive settlements of mass disputes. The solution it offers is both creative and attractive, and successive drafts have toned down some of its objectionable features. The proposal builds in certain safeguards to increase the likelihood of a fair settlement. Moreover, the advance-consent approach is transparent and non-coercive, particularly in comparison to approaches that mass tort lawyers currently employ to engineer comprehensive deals. * * * Ultimately, however, the ALI proposal suffers from the same problem as the *Vioxx* settlement: it shifts too much settlement power from the claimants to their lawyers.

* * *

Some of the problems with the ALI proposal echo the most basic concern about the *Vioxx* settlement. The ethical concerns about the *Vioxx* settlement largely boil down to this: when claimants consented to the settlement, their consent was inauthentic because they could not rely on independent advice from counsel and because the prospect of losing their lawyer left them with no real choice. For informed consent to be authentic, the client must understand the choice and it must be non-coercive. The ALI advance-consent proposal raises similar concerns about the authenticity of client consent. Rather than eliminating the problem of informed consent, the proposal frontloads the problem. It raises questions about whether clients, at the time they sign retainer agreements, can understand the implications of waiving their control over the settlement. There is reason to suspect that, if the ALI proposal became law, virtually every mass tort lawyer would include boilerplate advance-consent language in the retainer agreement, and virtually every client would sign it. Would clients understand what they are signing? Even if so, would they have any realistic alternative?

* * *

Doubtful as we are about the prospects of authentic client consent under the ALI proposal, the proposal is subject to an even more fundamental problem. Even if the problems of sophistication and adhesion could be overcome, advance consent should not be permitted because the conflicts inherent in most aggregate settlements are nonconsentable in advance. In other words, assuming a sophisticated client who fully understands the advance-consent mechanism, whose lawyer provides full disclosure of its advantages and disadvantages, and who has realistic alternatives, the client should not be permitted to waive in advance the right to accept or reject a settlement.

* * *

* * * [A]ggregate settlements appear poorly suited for advance consent to conflicts. Not only are plaintiffs in mass litigation less sophisticated on the whole than the typical corporate client, but the conflicts in aggregate settlements are devilishly hard to describe before the settlement terms exist. The terms and conditions of mass settlements vary widely and raise too many different sorts of conflicts, both client-client and lawyer-client. In other words, even if all clients had the sophistication to understand the idea of advance consent to aggregate settlement, whether such consent can ever suffice is questionable given that the conflicts inherent in an aggregate settlement cannot be accurately perceived until the contours of the settlement are known.

NOTES AND QUESTIONS

1. What are the differences between the *Vioxx* approach and the approach advocated in the ALI *Principles*? Is the ALI approach an improvement over the *Vioxx* approach? If so, how? Alternatively, is the *Vioxx* approach better? If so, how?

2. Professors Erichson and Zipursky express concern that lawyers would include boilerplate advance-consent language in their retention agreements if the ALI proposal were adopted. What provisions in the ALI proposal, if any, speak to that concern?

3. Some commentators are more sanguine than Professors Erichson and Zipursky about advance-consent waivers. *See, e.g.*, Note, *Consent Waivers in Non–Class Aggregate Settlements: Respecting Risk Preference in a Transactional Adjudication Model*, 22 Geo. J. Legal Ethics 677, 678 (2009) (arguing that "non-class aggregate settlements are not so unique that consent waivers are ethically unacceptable").

D. AFTERWORD

Having studied various party-aggregation tools available both under the Federal Rules of Civil Procedure and beyond those rules, return to the themes described in Chapter 1. How have those themes played out in the context of each device studied? Do the materials in this casebook resolve any of the tensions identified in those themes?

Reflect on two final excerpts—one from 1958, the other from some four decades later. The first focuses on the potential unfairness of mass litigation; the second, written by one of the Reporters for the Advisory Committee on the Federal Rules of Civil Procedure, addresses the persistent problem of adequate representation. In light of the materials set forth below, and against the backdrop of other materials studied in this casebook, consider what conclusions may be drawn about the future of party aggregation in the federal courts, whether in the class action and MDL contexts, or beyond.

DEVELOPMENTS IN THE LAW: MULTIPARTY LITIGATION IN THE FEDERAL COURTS
71 Harv. L. Rev. 874, 877–78 (1958).

There are a number of specific procedural devices which enable the federal courts to entertain multiparty suits. Two types of potential advantages resulting from the use of these devices are readily apparent. First, the multiparty suit can eliminate unfairness by preventing inconsistent verdicts, by protecting persons who are not original parties but whose rights will in some way be affected, and by making possible actions that, as a practical matter, could not otherwise be brought. Second, the multiparty suit may promote the convenience of the court and of the parties by permitting the adjudication in one action of all claims involving the same or related parties or involving common issues of fact or law. * * *

The mass trial, however, may not always result in convenience. The number of claims and parties involved and the volume of evidence introduced may cause the action to be so complex that the trial becomes unmanageable, and is prejudicial to the interests of the parties. There are, of course, a number of ways in which the trial judge can seek to prevent such a result. The pretrial conference, stipulations of parties as to matters of fact, acceptance by all parties of concise summaries of voluminous evidentiary material, utilization of special verdicts or verdicts with interrogatories to help clarify the issues for a jury, and, if necessary, separate trials and severance may keep the multiparty action under control. It is clear that in deciding to what extent the scope of the trial is to be enlarged, the trial court, when it has discretion, must weigh the desirability of having a single suit against the possibility that that suit cannot properly be managed.

Assuming, however, that a multiparty suit will promote convenience, the question arises whether convenience alone is a sufficient basis for enlarging the scope of the trial. The assumption underlying the current procedural devices, which facilitate the creation of the mass trial, seems to be that the mass trial is desirable if it promotes convenience, in the sense of reduced cost and time. Such an assumption, however, may fail to take into account historic institutional concepts of the effective and fair course of litigation. For example, to the extent that an original party loses control of the prosecution of his claim to more powerful litigants whose judgments as to the handling of evidence, cross-examination, the making of motions, or even the addition of further parties are opposed to his own, he may be deprived of significant components of his day in court. Furthermore, there may be introduced into the case a wealth of new material which may be irrelevant to the claims of the original parties and yet, because of apparent interrelations with matters that are relevant, may affect the results of those claims by confusing the trier of fact.

The development during the past century of multiparty practice has tended to free it from limitations on size and to vest increasing discretion in the trial court to admit additional parties and claims. This movement, which originated as a reaction to restraints which were genuinely arbitrary and even harmful, has advanced so far as to warrant a re-examination of the need for and the advisability of mass trials based primarily on the desire for speed and lowered cost. For example, arguments that federal jurisdiction be expanded in order to permit actions of increased scope assume that there are available soundly articulated standards under which the court's discretion to enlarge the action may be exercised. Such an assumption seems well founded when a party is added to avoid the possibility of inconsistent judgments which could produce double liability, or to avoid severely affecting the interest of an absentee by an action in which his interest, although adequately represented by those present, could best be protected by him. But when the primary interest asserted for the addition of parties is the reduction of cost or time, the courts have not adequately articulated the standards by which they have determined whether the plaintiff's interest in retaining control of an adversary proceeding concerning the issues he presents is outweighed by the need for "speedy and inexpensive" litigation.

* * *

EDWARD H. COOPER, THE (CLOUDY) FUTURE OF CLASS ACTIONS
40 Ariz. L. Rev. 923, 925–26 (1998).

* * * [M]any alternative means of aggregation can be substituted for class treatment. The choice is not between a single class suit and a stand-alone action for each individual class member. Voluntary joinder, intervention, consolidation of initially separate actions, joint trials, interpleader, consolidated pretrial, coordination among judges and courts with respect to proceedings that otherwise remain separate, and smaller class actions are among the alternatives. Even test cases and nonmutual preclusion should be considered in the array. * * * All alternatives must be appraised in determining the suitability of class treatment in any particular case.

For all the number of alternatives, however, there is a deeper reality. The more people who are to be caught up in a judgment, whether by settlement or trial, the more the problems and procedures will come to resemble those of class actions. So long as we retain any semblance of our adversary system, no more than a few lawyers can effectively plan and control a litigation. Although it is tempting to add that no more than a few parties can enjoy meaningful participation in working with the lawyers, that formulation seems too optimistic. As the number of persons caught up increases, it becomes increasingly difficult to arrange, or even to tolerate, meaningful control by a small sample. Whether called clients, parties, representatives, steering committees, or anything else, nonlawyers cannot meaningfully conceive of the scope of the interests, potential conflicts, and issues involved. Nor should nonlawyers fairly be asked to typify, much less meaningfully to represent, others. Even if it could be arranged for all parties to participate—as if all 100 plaintiffs in 100 consolidated actions acted as a committee to instruct counsel—the participation would be quite different from the relationship between one client and one lawyer. And, barring unbelievable unanimity of views, in the end the judgment of some must prevail over the judgments of others.

The problems that can be found in the class action setting, in short, will appear whatever means of aggregation are used. The forms may be different, and some forms may afford greater conceptual solace than others. But the core problems will be substantially the same. Class action procedure relies on aggregation by representation, subject to safeguards designed to ensure adequate representation. The question is whether these safeguards are effective in the only sense that is meaningful—whether they provide a substitute for individual participation that is both intrinsically satisfactory and superior to alternative means of aggregation or individual litigation. It may be that the central advantage of Rule 23 is that we have become accustomed to it. The fact that we have become accustomed to it also may be its central disadvantage—it is too easy to believe that because we are doing it, we must be doing it well.

* * *

APPENDIX A:
FEDERAL RULE OF CIVIL PROCEDURE 23

(a) Prerequisites. One or more members of a class may sue or be sued as representative parties on behalf of all members only if:

(1) the class is so numerous that joinder of all members is impracticable;

(2) there are questions of law or fact common to the class;

(3) the claims or defenses of the representative parties are typical of the claims or defenses of the class; and

(4) the representative parties will fairly and adequately protect the interests of the class.

(b) Types of Class Actions. A class action may be maintained if Rule 23(a) is satisfied and if:

(1) prosecuting separate actions by or against individual class members would create a risk of:

(A) inconsistent or varying adjudications with respect to individual class members that would establish incompatible standards of conduct for the party opposing the class; or

(B) adjudications with respect to individual class members that, as a practical matter, would be dispositive of the interests of the other members not parties to the individual adjudications or would substantially impair or impede their ability to protect their interests;

(2) the party opposing the class has acted or refused to act on grounds that apply generally to the class, so that final injunctive relief or corresponding declaratory relief is appropriate respecting the class as a whole; or

(3) the court finds that the questions of law or fact common to class members predominate over any questions affecting only individual members, and that a class action is superior to other available methods for fairly and efficiently adjudicating the controversy. The matters pertinent to these findings include:

(A) the class members' interests in individually controlling the prosecution or defense of separate actions;

(B) the extent and nature of any litigation concerning the controversy already begun by or against class members;

(C) the desirability or undesirability of concentrating the litigation of the claims in the particular forum; and

(D) the likely difficulties in managing a class action.

(c) Certification Order; Notice to Class Members; Judgment; Issues Classes; Subclasses.

(1) Certification Order.

(A) Time to Issue. At an early practicable time after a person sues or is sued as a class representative, the court must determine by order whether to certify the action as a class action.

(B) Defining the Class; Appointing Class Counsel. An order thatcertifies a class action must define the class and the class claims, issues, or defenses, and must appoint class counsel under Rule 23(g).

(C) Altering or Amending the Order. An order that grants or denies class certification may be altered or amended before final judgment.

(2) Notice.

(A) For (b)(1) or (b)(2) Classes. For any class certified under Rule23(b)(1) or (b)(2), the court may direct appropriate notice to the class.

(B) For (b)(3) Classes. For any class certified under Rule 23(b)(3), the court must direct to class members the best notice that is practicable under the circumstances, including individual notice to all members who can be identified through reasonable effort. The notice must clearly and concisely state in plain, easily understood language:

(i) the nature of the action;

(ii) the definition of the class certified;

(iii) the class claims, issues, or defenses;

(iv) that a class member may enter an appearance through an attorney if the member so desires;

(v) that the court will exclude from the class any member who requests exclusion;

(vi) the time and manner for requesting exclusion; and

(vii) the binding effect of a class judgment on members under Rule 23(c)(3).

(3) Judgment. Whether or not favorable to the class, the judgment in a class action must:

(A) for any class certified under Rule 23(b)(1) or (b)(2), include and describe those whom the court finds to be class members; and

(B) for any class certified under Rule 23(b)(3), include and specify or describe those to whom the Rule 23(c)(2) notice was directed, who have not requested exclusion, and whom the court finds to be class members.

(4) Particular Issues. When appropriate, an action may be brought or maintained as a class action with respect to particular issues.

(5) Subclasses. When appropriate, a class may be divided into subclasses that are each treated as a class under this rule.

(d) Conducting the Action.

(1) In General. In conducting an action under this rule, the court may issue orders that:

(A) determine the course of proceedings or prescribe measures to prevent undue repetition or complication in presenting evidence or argument;

(B) require—to protect class members and fairly conduct the action—giving appropriate notice to some or all class members of:

(i) any step in the action;

(ii) the proposed extent of the judgment; or

(iii) the members' opportunity to signify whether they consider the representation fair and adequate, to intervene and present claims or defenses, or to otherwise come into the action;

(C) impose conditions on the representative parties or on intervenors;

(D) require that the pleadings be amended to eliminate allegations about representation of absent persons and that the action proceed accordingly; or

(E) deal with similar procedural matters.

(2) *Combining and Amending Orders.* An order under Rule 23(d)(1) maybe altered or amended from time to time and may be combined with an order under Rule 16.

(e) Settlement, Voluntary Dismissal, or Compromise. The claims, issues, or defenses of a certified class may be settled, voluntarily dismissed, or compromised only with the court's approval. The following procedures apply to a proposed settlement, voluntary dismissal, or compromise:

(1) The court must direct notice in a reasonable manner to all class members who would be bound by the proposal.

(2) If the proposal would bind class members, the court may approve it only after a hearing and on finding that it is fair, reasonable, and adequate.

(3) The parties seeking approval must file a statement identifying any agreement made in connection with the proposal.

(4) If the class action was previously certified under Rule 23(b)(3), the court may refuse to approve a settlement unless it affords a new opportunity to request exclusion to individual class members who had an earlier opportunity to request exclusion but did not do so.

(5) Any class member may object to the proposal if it requires court approval under this subdivision (e); the objection may be withdrawn only with the court's approval.

(f) Appeals. A court of appeals may permit an appeal from an order granting or denying class-action certification under this rule if a petition for permission to appeal is filed with the circuit clerk within 14 days after the order is entered. An appeal does not stay proceedings in the district court unless the district judge or the court of appeals so orders.

(g) Class Counsel.

(1) *Appointing Class Counsel.* Unless a statute provides otherwise, a court that certifies a class must appoint class counsel. In appointing class counsel, the court:

(A) must consider:

(i) the work counsel has done in identifying or investigating potential claims in the action;

(ii) counsel's experience in handling class actions, other complex litigation, and the types of claims asserted in the action;

(iii) counsel's knowledge of the applicable law; and

(iv) the resources that counsel will commit to representing the class;

(B) may consider any other matter pertinent to counsel's ability to fairly and adequately represent the interests of the class;

(C) may order potential class counsel to provide information on any subject pertinent to the appointment and to propose terms for attorney's fees and nontaxable costs;

(D) may include in the appointing order provisions about the award of attorney's fees or nontaxable costs under Rule 23(h); and (E) may make further orders in connection with the appointment.

(2) Standard for Appointing Class Counsel. When one applicant seeks appointment as class counsel, the court may appoint that applicant only if the applicant is adequate under Rule 23(g)(1) and (4). If more than one adequate applicant seeks appointment, the court must appoint the applicant best able to represent the interests of the class.

(3) Interim Counsel. The court may designate interim counsel to act on behalf of a putative class before determining whether to certify the action as a class action.

(4) Duty of Class Counsel. Class counsel must fairly and adequately represent the interests of the class.

(h) Attorney's Fees and Nontaxable Costs. In a certified class action, the court may award reasonable attorney's fees and nontaxable costs that are authorized by law or by the parties' agreement. The following procedures apply:

(1) A claim for an award must be made by motion under Rule 54(d)(2), subject to the provisions of this subdivision (h), at a time the court sets. Notice of the motion must be served on all parties and, for motions by class counsel, directed to class members in a reasonable manner.

(2) A class member, or a party from whom payment is sought, may object to the motion.

(3) The court may hold a hearing and must find the facts and state its legal conclusions under Rule 52(a).

(4) The court may refer issues related to the amount of the award to a special master or a magistrate judge, as provided in Rule 54(d)(2)(D).

APPENDIX B:
CLASS ACTION FAIRNESS ACT OF 2005

AN ACT To amend the procedures that apply to consideration of interstate class actions to assure fairer outcomes for class members and defendants, and for other purposes.

Be it enacted by the Senate and House of Representatives of the United States of America in Congress assembled,

SECTION 1. SHORT TITLE; REFERENCE; TABLE OF CONTENTS.

   (a) SHORT TITLE.—This Act may be cited as the "Class Action Fairness Act of 2005".

   (b) REFERENCE.—Whenever in this Act reference is made to an amendment to, or repeal of, a section or other provision, the reference shall be considered to be made to a section or other provision of title 28, United States Code.

   (c) TABLE OF CONTENTS.—The table of contents for this Act is as follows:

   Sec. 1. Short title; reference; table of contents.

   Sec. 2. Findings and purposes.

   Sec. 3. Consumer class action bill of rights and improved procedures for interstate class actions.

   Sec. 4. Federal district court jurisdiction for interstate class actions.

   Sec. 5. Removal of interstate class actions to Federal district court.

   Sec. 6. Report on class action settlements.

   Sec. 7. Enactment of Judicial Conference recommendations.

   Sec. 8. Rulemaking authority of Supreme Court and Judicial Conference.

   Sec. 9. Effective date.

SEC. 2. FINDINGS AND PURPOSES.

(a) FINDINGS.—Congress finds the following:

(1) Class action lawsuits are an important and valuable part of the legal system when they permit the fair and efficient resolution of legitimate claims of numerous parties by allowing the claims to be aggregated into a single action against a defendant that has allegedly caused harm.

(2) Over the past decade, there have been abuses of the class action device that have—

(A) harmed class members with legitimate claims and defendants that have acted responsibly;

(B) adversely affected interstate commerce; and

(C) undermined public respect for our judicial system.

(3) Class members often receive little or no benefit from class actions, and are sometimes harmed, such as where—

(A) counsel are awarded large fees, while leaving class members with coupons or other awards of little or no value;

(B) unjustified awards are made to certain plaintiffs at the expense of other class members; and

(C) confusing notices are published that prevent class members from being able to fully understand and effectively exercise their rights.

(4) Abuses in class actions undermine the national judicial system, the free flow of interstate commerce and the concept of diversity jurisdiction as intended by the framers of the United States Constitution, in that State and local courts are—

(A) keeping cases of national importance out of Federal court

(B) sometimes acting in ways that demonstrate bias against out-of-State defendants, and

(C) making judgments that impose their view of the law on other States and bind the rights of the residents of those States.

(b) PURPOSES.—The purposes of this Act are to—

(1) assure fair and prompt recoveries for class members with legitimate claims;

(2) restore the intent of the framers of the United States Constitution by providing for Federal court consideration of interstate cases of national importance under diversity jurisdiction; and

(3) benefit society by encouraging innovation and lowering consumer prices.

SEC. 3. CONSUMER CLASS ACTION BILL OF RIGHTS AND IMPROVED PROCEDURES FOR INTERSTATE CLASS ACTIONS.

(a) IN GENERAL.—Part V is amended by inserting after chapter 113 the following:

"CHAPTER 114—CLASS ACTIONS

"Sec.

"1711. Definitions.

"1712. Coupon settlements.

"1713. Protection against loss by class members.

"1714. Protection against discrimination based on geographic location.

"1715. Notifications to appropriate Federal and State officials.

§ 1711. Definitions

"In this chapter:

"(1) CLASS.—The term 'class' means all of the class members in a class action.

"(2) CLASS ACTION.—The term 'class action' means any civil action filed in a district court of the United States under rule 23 of the Federal Rules of Civil Procedure or any civil action that is removed to a district court of the United States that was originally filed under a State statute or rule of judicial procedure authorizing an action to be brought by 1 or more representatives as a class action.

"(3) CLASS COUNSEL.—The term 'class counsel' means the persons who serve as the attorneys for the class members in a proposed or certified class action.

"(4) CLASS MEMBERS.—The term 'class members' means the persons (named or unnamed) who fall within the definition of the proposed or certified class in a class action.

"(5) PLAINTIFF CLASS ACTION.—The term 'plaintiff class action' means a class action in which class members are plaintiffs.

"(6) PROPOSED SETTLEMENT.—The term 'proposed settlement' means an agreement regarding a class action that is subject to court approval and that, if approved, would be binding on some or all class members.

§ 1712. Coupon settlements

"(a) CONTINGENT FEES IN COUPON SETTLEMENTS.—If a proposed settlement in a class action provides for a recovery of coupons to a class member, the portion of any attorney's fee award to class counsel that is attributable to the award of the coupons shall be based on the value to class members of the coupons that are redeemed.

"(b) OTHER ATTORNEY'S FEE AWARDS IN COUPON SETTLEMENTS.—

"(1) IN GENERAL.—If a proposed settlement in a class action provides for a recovery of coupons to class members, and a portion of the recovery of the coupons is not used to determine the attorney's fee to be paid to class counsel, any attorney's fee award shall be based upon the amount of time class counsel reasonably expended working on the action.

"(2) COURT APPROVAL.—Any attorney's fee under this subsection shall be subject to approval by the court and shall include an appropriate attorney's fee, if any, for obtaining equitable relief, including an injunction, if applicable. Nothing in this subsection shall be construed to prohibit application of a lodestar with a multiplier method of determining attorney's fees.

"(c) ATTORNEY'S FEE AWARDS CALCULATED ON A MIXED BASIS

IN COUPON SETTLEMENTS.—If a proposed settlement in a class action provides for an award of coupons to class members and also provides for equitable relief, including injunctive relief—

"(1) that portion of the attorney's fee to be paid to class counsel that is based upon a portion of the recovery of the coupons shall be calculated in accordance with subsection (a); and

"(2) that portion of the attorney's fee to be paid to class counsel that is not based upon a portion of the recovery of the coupons shall be calculated in accordance with subsection (b).

"(d) SETTLEMENT VALUATION EXPERTISE.—In a class action involving the awarding of coupons, the court may, in its discretion upon the motion of a party, receive expert testimony from a witness qualified to provide information on the actual value to the class members of the coupons that are redeemed.

"(e) JUDICIAL SCRUTINY OF COUPON SETTLEMENTS.—In a proposed settlement under which class members would be awarded coupons, the court may approve the proposed settlement only after a hearing to determine whether, and making a written finding that, the settlement is fair, reasonable, and adequate for class members. The court, in its discretion, may also require that a proposed settlement agreement provide for the distribution of a portion of the value of unclaimed coupons to 1 or more charitable or governmental organizations, as agreed to by the parties. The distribution and redemption of any proceeds under this subsection shall not be used to calculate attorneys' fees under this section.

§ 1713. Protection against loss by class members

"The court may approve a proposed settlement under which any class member is obligated to pay sums to class counsel that would result in a net loss to the class member only if the court makes a written finding that nonmonetary benefits to the class member substantially outweigh the monetary loss.

§ 1714. Protection against discrimination based on geographic location

"The court may not approve a proposed settlement that provides for the payment of greater sums to some class members than to others solely on the basis that the class members to whom the greater sums are to be paid are located in closer geographic proximity to the court.

§ 1715. Notifications to appropriate Federal and State officials

"(a) DEFINITIONS.—

"(1) APPROPRIATE FEDERAL OFFICIAL.—In this section, the term appropriate Federal official' means—

"(A) the Attorney General of the United States; or

"(B) in any case in which the defendant is a Federal depository institution, a State depository institution, a depository institution holding company, a foreign bank, or a nondepository institution subsidiary of the foregoing (as such terms are defined in section 3 of the Federal Deposit Insurance Act (12 U.S.C. 1813)), the person who has the primary Federal regulatory or supervisory responsibility with respect to the defendant, if some or all of the matters alleged in the class action are subject to regulation or supervision by that person.

"(2) APPROPRIATE STATE OFFICIAL.—In this section, the term 'appropriate State official' means the person in the State who has the primary regulatory or supervisory responsibility with respect to the defendant, or who licenses or otherwise authorizes the defendant to conduct business in the State, if some or all of the matters alleged in the class action are subject to regulation by that person. If there is no primary regulator, supervisor, or licensing authority, or the matters alleged in the class action are not subject to regulation or supervision by that person, then the appropriate State official shall be the State attorney general.

"(b) IN GENERAL.—Not later than 10 days after a proposed settlement of a class action is filed in court, each defendant that is participating in the proposed settlement shall serve upon the appropriate State official of each State in which a class member resides and the appropriate Federal official, a notice of the proposed settlement consisting of—

"(1) a copy of the complaint and any materials filed with the complaint and any amended complaints (except such materials shall not be required to be served if such materials are made electronically available through the Internet and such service includes notice of how to electronically access such material);

"(2) notice of any scheduled judicial hearing in the class action;

"(3) any proposed or final notification to class members of—

"(A)(i) the members' rights to request exclusion from the class action; or

"(ii) if no right to request exclusion exists, a statement that no such right exists; and

"(B) a proposed settlement of a class action;

"(4) any proposed or final class action settlement;

"(5) any settlement or other agreement contemporaneously made between class counsel and counsel for the defendants;

"(6) any final judgment or notice of dismissal;

"(7)(A) if feasible, the names of class members who reside in each State and the estimated proportionate share of the claims of such members to the entire settlement to that State's appropriate State official; or

"(B) if the provision of information under subparagraph (A) is not feasible, a reasonable estimate of the number of class members residing in each State and the estimated proportionate share of the claims of such members to the entire settlement; and

"(8) any written judicial opinion relating to the materials described under subparagraphs (3) through (6).

"(c) DEPOSITORY INSTITUTIONS NOTIFICATION.—

"(1) FEDERAL AND OTHER DEPOSITORY INSTITUTIONS.—In any case in which the defendant is a Federal depository institution, a depository institution holding company, a foreign bank, or a nondepository institution subsidiary of the foregoing, the notice requirements of this section are satisfied by serving the notice required under subsection (b) upon the person who has the primary Federal regulatory or supervisory responsibility with respect to the defendant, if some or all of the matters alleged in the class action are subject to regulation or supervision by that person.

"(2) STATE DEPOSITORY INSTITUTIONS.—In any case in which the defendant is a State depository institution (as that term is defined in section 3 of the Federal Deposit Insurance Act (12 U.S.C. 1813)), the notice requirements of this section are satisfied by serving the notice required under subsection (b) upon the State bank supervisor (as that term is defined in section 3 of the Federal Deposit Insurance Act (12 U.S.C. 1813)) of the State in which the defendant is incorporated or chartered, if some or all of the matters alleged in the class action are subject to regulation or supervision by that person, and upon the appropriate Federal official.

"(d) FINAL APPROVAL.—An order giving final approval of a proposed settlement may not be issued earlier than 90 days after the later of the dates on which the appropriate Federal official and the appropriate State official are served with the notice required under subsection (b).

"(e) NONCOMPLIANCE IF NOTICE NOT PROVIDED.—

"(1) IN GENERAL.—A class member may refuse to comply with and may choose not to be bound by a settlement agreement or consent decree in a class action if the class member demonstrates that the notice required under subsection (b) has not been provided.

"(2) LIMITATION.—A class member may not refuse to comply with or to be bound by a settlement agreement or consent decree under paragraph (1) if the notice required under subsection (b) was directed to the appropriate Federal official and to either the State attorney general or the person that has primary regulatory, supervisory, or licensing authority over the defendant.

"(3) APPLICATION OF RIGHTS.—The rights created by this subsection shall apply only to class members or any person acting on a class member's behalf, and shall not be construed to limit any other rights affecting a class member's participation in the settlement. "(f) RULE OF CONSTRUCTION.—Nothing in this section shall be construed to expand the authority of, or impose any obligations, duties, or responsibilities upon, Federal or State officials."

(b) TECHNICAL AND CONFORMING AMENDMENT.—The table of chapters for part V is amended by inserting after the item relating to chapter 113 the following:

"114. Class Actions 1711".

SEC. 4. FEDERAL DISTRICT COURT JURISDICTION FOR INTERSTATE CLASS ACTIONS.

(a) APPLICATION OF FEDERAL DIVERSITY JURISDICTION.—Section 1332 is amended—

(1) by redesignating subsection (d) as subsection (e); and

(2) by inserting after subsection (c) the following:

"(d)(1) In this subsection—

"(A) the term 'class' means all of the class members in a class action;

"(B) the term 'class action' means any civil action filed under rule 23 of the Federal Rules of Civil Procedure or similar State statute or rule of judicial procedure authorizing an action to be brought by 1 or more representative persons as a class action;

"(C) the term 'class certification order' means an order issued by a court approving the treatment of some or all aspects of a civil action as a class action; and

"(D) the term 'class members' means the persons (named or unnamed) who fall within the definition of the proposed or certified class in a class action.

"(2) The district courts shall have original jurisdiction of any civil action in which the matter in controversy exceeds the sum or value of $5,000,000, exclusive of interest and costs, and is a class action in which—

"(A) any member of a class of plaintiffs is a citizen of a State different from any defendant;

"(B) any member of a class of plaintiffs is a foreign state or a citizen or subject of a foreign state and any defendant is a citizen of a State; or

"(C) any member of a class of plaintiffs is a citizen of a State and any defendant is a foreign state or a citizen or subject of a foreign state.

"(3) A district court may, in the interests of justice and looking at the totality of the circumstances, decline to exercise jurisdiction under paragraph (2) over a class action in which greater than one-third but less than two-thirds of the members of all proposed plaintiff classes in the aggregate and the primary defendants are citizens of the State in which the action was originally filed based on consideration of—

"(A) whether the claims asserted involve matters of national or interstate interest;

"(B) whether the claims asserted will be governed by laws of the State in which the action was originally filed or by the laws of other States;

"(C) whether the class action has been pleaded in a manner that seeks to avoid Federal jurisdiction;

"(D) whether the action was brought in a forum with a distinct nexus with the class members, the alleged harm, or the defendants;

"(E) whether the number of citizens of the State in which the action was originally filed in all proposed plaintiff classes in the aggregate is substantially larger than the number of citizens from any other State, and the citizenship of the other members of the proposed class is dispersed among a substantial number of States; and

"(F) whether, during the 3-year period preceding the filing of that class action, 1 or more other class actions asserting the same or similar claims on behalf of the same or other persons have been filed.

"(4) A district court shall decline to exercise jurisdiction under paragraph (2)—

"(A)(i) over a class action in which—

"(I) greater than two-thirds of the members of all proposed plaintiff classes in the aggregate are citizens of the State in which the action was originally filed; "(II) at least 1 defendant is a defendant—

"(aa) from whom significant relief is sought by members of the plaintiff class;

"(bb) whose alleged conduct forms a significant basis for the claims asserted by the proposed plaintiff class; and

"(cc) who is a citizen of the State in which the action was originally filed; and

"(III) principal injuries resulting from the alleged conduct or any related conduct of each defendant were incurred in the State in which the action was originally filed; and

"(ii) during the 3-year period preceding the filing of that class action, no other class action has been filed asserting the same or similar factual allegations against any of the defendants on behalf of the same or other persons; or

"(B) two-thirds or more of the members of all proposed plaintiff classes in the aggregate and the primary defendants, are citizens of the State in which the action was originally filed

"(5) Paragraphs (2) through (4) shall not apply to any class action in which—

"(A) the primary defendants are States, State officials, or other governmental entities against whom the district court may be foreclosed from ordering relief; or

"(B) the number of members of all proposed plaintiff classes in the aggregate is less than 100.

"(6) In any class action, the claims of the individual class members shall be aggregated to determine whether the matter in controversy exceeds the sum or value of $5,000,000, exclusive of interest and costs.

"(7) Citizenship of the members of the proposed plaintiff classes shall be determined for purposes of paragraphs (2) through (6) as of the date of filing of the complaint or amended complaint, or, if the case stated by the initial pleading is not subject to Federal jurisdiction, as of the date of service by plaintiffs of an amended pleading, motion, or other paper, indicating the existence of Federal jurisdiction.

"(8) This subsection shall apply to any class action before or after the entry of a class certification order by the court with respect to that action.

"(9) Paragraph (2) shall not apply to any class action that solely involves a claim—

"(A) concerning a covered security as defined under 16(f)(3) of the Securities Act of 1933 (15 U.S.C. 78p(f)(3)) and section 28(f)(5)(E) of the Securities Exchange Act of 1934 (15 U.S.C. 78bb(f)(5)(E));

"(B) that relates to the internal affairs or governance of a corporation or other form of business enterprise and that arises under or by virtue of the laws of the State in which such corporation or business enterprise is incorporated or organized; or

"(C) that relates to the rights, duties (including fiduciary duties), and obligations relating to or created by or pursuant to any security (as defined under section 2(a)(1) of the Securities Act of 1933 (15 U.S.C. 77b(a)(1)) and the regulations issued thereunder).

"(10) For purposes of this subsection and section 1453, an unincorporated association shall be deemed to be a citizen of the State where it has its principal place of business and the State under whose laws it is organized.

"(11)(A) For purposes of this subsection and section 1453, a mass action shall be deemed to be a class action removable under paragraphs (2) through (10) if it otherwise meets the provisions of those paragraphs.

> "(B)(i) As used in subparagraph (A), the term 'mass action' means any civil action (except a civil action within the scope of section 17 11(2)) in which monetary relief claims of 100 or more persons are proposed to be tried jointly on the ground that the plaintiffs' claims involve common questions of law or fact, except that jurisdiction shall exist only over those plaintiffs whose claims in a mass action satisfy the jurisdictional amount requirements under subsection (a).
>
> "(ii) As used in subparagraph (A), the term 'mass action' shall not include any civil action in which—
>
>> "(I) all of the claims in the action arise from an event or occurrence in the State in which the action was filed, and that allegedly resulted in injuries in that State or in States contiguous to that State;
>>
>> "(II) the claims are joined upon motion of a defendant;
>>
>> "(III) all of the claims in the action are asserted on behalf of the general public (and not on behalf of individual claimants or members of a purported class) pursuant to a State statute specifically authorizing such action; or
>>
>> "(IV) the claims have been consolidated or coordinated solely for pretrial proceedings.

"(C)(i) Any action(s) removed to Federal court pursuant to this subsection shall not thereafter be transferred to any other court pursuant to section 1407, or the rules promulgated thereunder, unless a majority of the plaintiffs in the action request transfer pursuant to section 1407. "(ii) This subparagraph will not apply—

"(I) to cases certified pursuant to rule 23 of the Federal Rules of Civil Procedure; or

"(II) if plaintiffs propose that the action proceed as a class action pursuant to rule 23 of the Federal Rules of Civil Procedure.

"(D) The limitations periods on any claims asserted in a mass action that is removed to Federal court pursuant to this subsection shall be deemed tolled during the period that the action is pending in Federal court.".

(b) CONFORMING AMENDMENTS.—

(1) Section 1335(a)(1) is amended by inserting "subsection (a) or (d) of" before "section 1332".

(2) Section 1603(b)(3) is amended by striking "(d)" and inserting "(e)".

SEC. 5. REMOVAL OF INTERSTATE CLASS ACTIONS TO FEDERAL DISTRICT COURT.

(a) IN GENERAL.—Chapter 89 is amended by adding after section 1452 the following:

" 1453. Removal of class actions

"(a) DEFINITIONS.—In this section, the terms 'class', 'class action', 'class certification order', and 'class member' shall have the meanings given such terms under section 1332(d)(l).

"(b) IN GENERAL.—A class action may be removed to a district court of the United States in accordance with section 1446 (except that the 1-year limitation under section 1446(b) shall not apply), without regard to whether any defendant is a citizen of the State in which the action is brought, except that such action may be removed by any defendant without the consent of all defendants.

"(c) REVIEW OF REMAND ORDERS.—

"(1) IN GENERAL.—Section 1447 shall apply to any removal of a case under this section, except that notwithstanding section 1447(d), a court of appeals may accept an appeal from an order of a district court granting or denying a motion to remand a class action to the State court from which it was removed if application is made to the court of appeals not less than 7 days after entry of the order.

"(2) TIME PERIOD FOR JUDGMENT.—If the court of appeals accepts an appeal under paragraph (1), the court shall complete all action on such appeal, including rendering judgment, not later than 60 days after the date on which such appeal was filed, unless an extension is granted under paragraph (3).

"(3) EXTENSION OF TIME PERIOD.—The court of appeals may grant an extension of the 60-day period described in paragraph (2) if—

"(A) all parties to the proceeding agree to such extension, for any period of time; or

"(B) such extension is for good cause shown and in the interests of justice, for a period not to exceed 10 days.

"(4) DENIAL OF APPEAL.—If a final judgment on the appeal under paragraph (1) is not issued before the end of the period described in paragraph (2), including any extension under paragraph (3), the appeal shall be denied.

"(d) EXCEPTION.—This section shall not apply to any class action that solely involves—

"(1) a claim concerning a covered security as defined under section 16(f)(3) of the Securities Act of 1933 (15 U.S.C. 78p(f)(3)) and section 28(f)(5)(E) of the Securities Exchange Act of 1934 (15 U.S.C. 78bb(f)(5)(E));

"(2) a claim that relates to the internal affairs or governance of a corporation or other form of business enterprise and arises under or by virtue of the laws of the State in which such corporation or business enterprise is incorporated or organized;

"(3) a claim that relates to the rights, duties (including fiduciary duties), and obligations relating to or created by or pursuant to any security (as defined under section 2(a)(1) of the Securities Act of 1933 (15 U.S.C. 77b(a)(1)) and the regulations issued thereunder).".

(b) TECHNICAL AND CONFORMING AMENDMENTS.—The table of sections for chapter 89 is amended by adding after the item relating to section 1452 the following:

"1453. Removal of class actions.".

SEC. 6. REPORT ON CLASS ACTION SETTLEMENTS.

(a) IN GENERAL.—Not later than 12 months after the date of enactment of this Act, the Judicial Conference of the United States, with the assistance of the Director of the Federal Judicial Center and the Director of the Administrative Office of the United States Courts, shall prepare and transmit to the Committees on the Judiciary of the Senate and the House of Representatives a report on class action settlements.

(b) CONTENT.—The report under subsection (a) shall contain—

(1) recommendations on the best practices that courts can use to ensure that proposed class action settlements are fair to the class members that the settlements are supposed to benefit;

(2) recommendations on the best practices that courts can use to ensure that—

(A) the fees and expenses awarded to counsel in connection with a class action settlement appropriately reflect the extent to which counsel succeeded in obtaining full redress for the injuries alleged and the time, expense, and risk that counsel devoted to the litigation; and

(B) the class members on whose behalf the settlement is proposed are the primary beneficiaries of the settlement; and

(3) the actions that the Judicial Conference of the United States has taken and intends to take toward having the Federal judiciary implement any or all of the recommendations contained in the report.

(c) AUTHORITY OF FEDERAL COURTS.—Nothing in this section shall be construed to alter the authority of the Federal courts to supervise attorneys' fees.

SEC. 7. ENACTMENT OF JUDICIAL CONFERENCE RECOMMENDATIONS.

Notwithstanding any other provision of law, the amendments to rule 23 of the Federal Rules of Civil Procedure, which are set forth in the order entered by the Supreme Court of the United States on March 27, 2003, shall take effect on the date of enactment of this Act or on December 1, 2003 (as specified in that order), whichever occurs first.

SEC. 8. RULEMAKING AUTHORITY OF SUPREME COURT AND JUDICIAL CONFERENCE.

Nothing in this Act shall restrict in any way the authority of the Judicial Conference and the Supreme Court to propose and prescribe general rules of practice and procedure under chapter 131 of title 28, United States Code.

SEC. 9. EFFECTIVE DATE.

The amendments made by this Act shall apply to any civil action commenced on or after the date of enactment of this Act.

Approved February 18, 2005.

INDEX

References are to Pages

ADEQUACY OF REPRESENTATION
Generally, 115–158
Ability to finance the class action, 143
Adequacy of counsel, 147–155
Adequacy of *pro se* litigants, 157–158
Attacks on adequacy standard, 143–147
Attorney conflicts of interest, 153, 156
Conflicts of interest, 135–142
Defendant class actions, special issues relating to, 893–895, 897, 900–905
Future claimants, 36, 140, 749, 755–764
Honesty, character, and credibility, 128–135
Knowledge of the case, 123–128
Membership in the class, 54–58
Omitting or deleting claims to make certification more viable, 142–143
Reform issues, 143–147,
Reverse auction and, 154
Rule 23(g), 155–157
Settlement certification, 550–565
Third-party funding and, 649–657

ADVISORY COMMITTEE ON CIVIL RULES
Generally, 2, 12–30

AGGREGATE PROOF
See Trial Issues; Extrapolation and Statistical Proof

ALTERNATIVE DISPUTE RESOLUTION
Generally, 529, 668–696
Mass tort reform and, 783

ANTI-INJUNCTION ACT
Requirements, 492–502

APPELLATE REVIEW
Generally, 697–722
Appeal from certification decision, 697–709
Appeal from final judgment, 709–714
Appeal from settlement, 714–719
Appeal under Rule 23(f), 697–709
Intervention for purposes of appeal, 709–714
Standard of review, 719–722

APPOINTMENT OF CLASS COUNSEL
Generally, 28, 115–122, 155–157

ARBITRATION AND CLASS ACTIONS
Generally, 675–696

ASCERTAINABILITY
Generally, 44–54

ASSOCIATIONS
See Unincorporated Associations

ATTORNEYS' FEES
Generally, 579–605, 632–649
Lodestar method, 633–648
Percentage method of calculation, 634–648
Rule 23(h), 634–635, 645–649

BANKRUPTCY
Generally, 1116–1147
As an aggregation device, 1118–1147
Aggregation of claims against a debtor, 1118–1126
Mass tort litigation and, 1120–1126
Pre-packaged bankruptcies, 1126–1133
"Related to" jurisdiction, 1136–1144

BILATERAL CLASSES
Generally, 903–905

CERTIFICATION DECISION
See Class Certification Decision

CHOICE OF LAW
Choice-of-law analysis, 407–430
Due process limits, 407–414
Federal common law, 428–429

CLASS ACTION FAIRNESS ACT OF 2005
Generally, 27–30
Jurisdictional Provisions, 448–449
Settlement Provisions, 606–608

CLASS CERTIFICATION DECISION
Generally, 266–293
Appeal of, 697–709
Burden of proof, 268–269
Certification of specific issues, 298–302
Conditional certification, 296–298
Court's obligation to rule, 293–296
Decertification, 349, 387–389
Expert testimony, 269, 281–293
For settlement purposes, 307, 550–565
Inquiry into merits, propriety of, 269–281
Partial certification and bifurcation, 299–307
Timing of certification decision, 266–269
Use of subclasses, 302–307

CLASS CERTIFICATION DISCOVERY
See Discovery

CLASS DEFINITION
See Definition of Class

COLLATERAL ESTOPPEL
See Issue and Claim Preclusion

COMMONALITY
Generally, 86–103
Number of common legal or factual issues, 101

COMMUNICATION WITH CLASS MEMBERS
After class certification, 396–398
Before filing of class action, 389–390
Between filing and class certification, 390–396
Ethics of, 389–398
Use of Rule 23(d) to regulate, 347–350, 379–381

COMPETING CLASS ACTIONS
Generally, 502–503

COMPULSORY JOINDER
See Joinder

CONSOLIDATION
Generally, 1099–1109
As an aggregation device, 1099–1109
Considerations in evaluating whether to consolidate, 1107–1109

DEFENDANT CLASSES
Generally, 889–915
Adequacy of representation, 900–903
Bilateral classes, 903–905
Juridical link, 889–900
Notice, 896–898
Personal jurisdiction, 898–899
Statute of limitations, 899–900
Typicality, 902–904
Under Rule 23(b)(1)(A), 914–915
Under Rule 23(b)(1)(B), 914–915
Under Rule 23(b)(2), 905–915
Under Rule 23(b)(3), 890–891, 914–915

DEFINITION OF A CLASS
Generally, 35–54
Ascertainability, 44–54
Strategic considerations, 257

DISCOVERY
Class versus merits discovery, 312–315
Deferral of certification pending discovery, 268
Limitations on scope of class certification discovery, 315–326
Merits discovery, 312–315
Names of absent class members, 326–331
Pre-certification discovery, 307–335
Pre-certification discovery directed at absent class members, 326–331
Third-party funding and, 316–317, 649–657

DISMISSAL OF CLASS CLAIMS PRIOR TO CERTIFICATION
Generally, 605–606

DIVERSITY JURISDICTION IN CLASS ACTIONS
Determining citizenship for diversity purposes, 449–451
Establishing jurisdictional amount for diversity actions, 444–449
Under Class Action Fairness Act of 2005, 452–463

DUE PROCESS
Appearance and, 480–483
Notice and, 371, 373–374, 377–378, 477–480
Opt-Out rights and, 377–378, 477–480
"*Shutts*" problems, 477–483
Trial structure and, 359–369

EMPLOYMENT DISCRIMINATION ACTIONS
Generally, 783–836
Administrative Enforcement, 796–797
Age discrimination cases, 785, 813–836
Applicability of Rule 23 requirements in age discrimination cases, 813–822
Cases under 42 U.S.C. § 1981, 784, 808–809
Collective actions not governed by Rule 23, 813–822
Disability cases, 784
Fair Labor Standards Act, 785
Notice in age discrimination cases, 813–821
Pattern-or-practice cases, 803–807
Res Judicata issues, 807–813
Rule 23(b)(2) and, 800–803
Title VII, 785–796

EQUITY RULE 38
Generally, 17–19

EQUITY RULE 48
Generally, 17–19

ETHICAL ISSUES IN CLASS ACTIONS
Advancing costs of litigation, 143
Communications with class members, 389–398
Conflicts of interest, 135–142, 153, 472 535–544
Settlement dynamics and, 535–550

FEDERAL CONTROL OVER STATE COURTS
Binding effect on state court settlements of exclusively federal claims, 511–522

FEDERAL/STATE COORDINATION
Generally, 1004–1013
Competing class actions, 502–503
Reform proposals, 1008–1013

FULL FAITH AND CREDIT
Generally, 508–522

HISTORY
Class actions, 16–29
Early group litigation, 16–19

"HYBRID" CLASSES
Defined, 20–21
Under original Rule 23, 20–22

IMPLEADER
Generally, 1049–1058
Assertion of defenses, 1050, 1057–1058
Circumstances in which allowed, 1049–1054
Supplemental jurisdiction and, 1056–1058
When leave of court required, 1054–1055

INJUNCTIVE AND DECLARATORY RELIEF
Generally, 614–623

INTERPLEADER
Generally, 1058–1071
As an aggregation device, 1071
Diversity jurisdiction requirements for rule interpleader, 1064–1068
Diversity jurisdiction requirements for statutory interpleader, 1059–1063, 1068–1069
Rule interpleader, 1058, 1064–1071
Statutory interpleader, 1059–1063, 1068–1071

INTERVENTION
Generally, 1071–1099
Amicus participation, 1072–1075, 1082
As an aggregation device, 1098–1099
Intervention as of right, 1071–1084
Intervention in class actions, 1085–1092
Mandatory intervention, 1093–1099
Permissive intervention, 1071–1072, 1075–1084
Standing, 1077–1079, 1082

Supplemental jurisdiction and, 1085

INTERVENTION OF RIGHT
See Intervention

ISSUE AND CLAIM PRECLUSION
Claim preclusion (*res judicata*), 463–483
Class members who may not be bound by a prior adjudication, 469–480
Collateral estoppel effect of prior denial of class certification, 492–502
Competing class actions, 502–503
Issue preclusion (collateral estoppel), 483–502
Limitations when seeking only declaratory or injunctive relief, 473–477
"*Shutts*" problems, 477–483

JOINDER
Compulsory joinder, 1027–1049
Misjoinder, 1017–1023
Permissive joinder, 1015–1027
Public rights exception to compulsory joinder, 1039–1041
Supplemental jurisdiction and, 1025–1026

JUDICIAL CONTROL OF PROCEEDINGS
Generally, 339–350

"LIMITED FUND" CASES
Generally, 171–190
Stare decisis effect insufficient to satisfy, 190
Punitive damages, 188–189
Requirements for, 172–190

LOCAL RULES ON CLASS ACTIONS
Generally, 264–265

MANAGEABILITY
Generally, 247–251

MASS TORTS
Generally, 36, 165–171, 194–195, 228–229, 301–302, 347, 352–358, 428–429, 725–783, 956–957, 973–976, 1005–1008
Choice of law, 407–430
Defined, 725–726
Exposure-only claimants, 755–764
Historical overview, 735–749
Judicial trends, 737–751
Legislative inertia in reform, 779–783
"Mature v. immature," 742–751
Medical monitoring, 165–171, 194–195
Predominance in Rule 23(b)(3) classes, 742–747
Problems of classwide proof, 764–778
Reform proposals, 781–783
Settlement of, 538–542, 564
Trial of, 352–358

MEDICAL MONITORING
Under Rule 23(b)(1)(A), 165–171
Under Rule 23(b)(2), 194–195

MOOTNESS
Generally, 58–69
"Pick-offs" of class representatives with offers of judgment, 63–69

MULTIDISTRICT LITIGATION
Generally, 953–1013
Administration and resolution of MDL cases, 973–976
Bellwether trials in MDL proceedings, 987–992
Coordination of federal and state claims, 1004–1013
Policy and reform issues, 992–1000
Remand and trial issues, 976–987
Selection of the transferee court, 969–972
Self assignment for trial, 979–983
Settlement and, 973–976
Standards and best practices, 1000–1001
Standards for transfer, 960–969
Statistics, 953–954
Volkswagen Clean Diesel case study, 1001–1003

MULTI-JURISDICTIONAL CLASS ACTIONS
Choice of law and, 414–430
Due process constraints, 407–413
General considerations, 399–406
Standards for certifying, 402–406

NATIONWIDE CLASS ACTIONS
See Multi-Jurisdictional Class Actions

NON-CLASS AGGREGATE SETTLEMENTS
Generally, 1147–1154

NOTICE
Generally, 371–389
Defendant class actions, 889–896
Form and content of class certification notice, 371, 378–384, 386
In Rule 23(b)(1) and 23(b)(2) actions, 386–387
Of decertification, 387–389
Scope of requirement in Rule 23(b)(3) cases, 372–376
Timing of class certification notice, 378–384
Who pays cost of notice, 378–383

NUMEROSITY
Generally, 73–86
Applicability to subclasses, 306–307
Factors other than sheer numbers, 79–86
Size of the potential class, 73–86

OPT-OUT RIGHTS
In Rule 23(b)(1) classes, 386–387
In Rule 23(b)(2) classes, 386–387
In Rule 23(b)(3) classes, 371–376
Second Opt-Out, 578–579

ORDERS CONTROLLING CLASS PROCEEDINGS
Generally, 339–350

OVERLAPPING CLASS ACTIONS
See Competing Class Actions

PERMISSIVE INTERVENTION
See Intervention

PERMISSIVE JOINDER
See Joinder

PERSONAL JURISDICTION ISSUES IN CLASS ACTIONS
Generally, 407–429

POLICY AND REFORM ISSUES
Blackmail, class actions as, 30–33, 266–292
Federal legislation, 27–31
Mass torts proposals, 779–783
Proposals for federal/state coordination, 504–528
Securities class action reform, 862–871
Whether Rule 23 is trans-substantive, 4–6, 723–725

PREDOMINANCE OF COMMON ISSUES
Antitrust class actions and, 217–219
"*Basic*" presumption and, 837–844
Core analysis, 212–219
Choice of law and, 229, 423–430
Damages calculation impacting, 229–231
Fraud claims and reliance issues, 219–228
Individualized defenses, 229
Mass torts and, 228–229
Under Rule 23(b)(2), 194–197
Under Rule 23(b)(3), 212–231
"*Ute*" presumption and, 853–854

PREDOMINANCE OF NON-MONETARY RELIEF OVER DAMAGES
Generally, 197–207

REMEDIES
Generally, 614–632
Damages, 623–625
Equitable relief, 614–623
Fluid recovery (or "*cy pres*"), 548–549, 614, 625–632

REPRESENTATIVES
Adequacy of, 123–142
Threshold requirement of, 5, 115–158

RES JUDICATA
See Issue and Claim Preclusion

RIGHT TO PARTICIPATE IN CLASS ACTIONS
Generally, 482–483

ROOKER-FELDMAN DOCTRINE
Generally, 522–528

RULE 14
Generally, 1049–1058

RULE 19
Generally, 1027–1049

RULE 20
Generally, 1015–1027

RULE 21
Generally, 348, 1017–1023, 1026

RULE 22
Generally, 1058–1071

RULE 23
Generally, 1–951
1938 version, 19–23
1966 version, 23–30
Perspectives and themes, 1–16
Recurring questions, 4–7
Threshold requirements, 35–69

RULE 23(a)
Rule 23(a)(1) (numerosity) requirements, 73–86
Rule 23(a)(2) (commonality) requirements, 86–103
Rule 23(a)(3) (typicality) requirements, 103–115
Rule 23(a)(4) (adequacy of representation) requirements, 115–158

RULE 23(b)
Defendant classes, 889–915
Inconsistent or varying adjudications, 159–171
Medical monitoring under, 165–171, 194–195
Necessity doctrine, 207–211
Notice and opt-out rights, 371–389
Predominance in Rule 23(b)(3) classes, 212–231
Predominance issues in fraud cases, 837–854
Predominance issues in personal injury cases, 228–229
Right to appear, 385–387
Rule 23(b)(1)(A) classes, 159–171
Rule 23(b)(1)(B) classes, 171–190
Rule 23(b)(2) classes, 190–211
Rule 23(b)(3) classes, 211–251
Superiority in Rule 23(b)(3) classes, 231–251

RULE 23(c)
Generally, 266–293, 371–389
Certification of specific issues, 298–302
Form and content of notice under, 371, 378–384, 386
Notice in (b)(1) and (b)(2) classes, 386–387
Paying for notice, 378–383
Permitting opt-outs, 371–387
Requiring notice in Rule 23(b)(3) classes, 372–376
Right to appear in Rule 23(b)(3) class actions, 385–386
Subclasses, 302–307
Timing of notice under, 378–384
Timing of certification decision, 266–269

RULE 23(d)
Generally, 347–350
Notices of decertification, 387–389
Permitting notice in Rule 23(b)(1) or 23(b)(2) classes, 386–387
Permitting opt-out in Rule 23(b)(1) or 23(b)(2) classes, 386–387
Rule 23(d)(1), 347–350

RULE 23(e)
Generally, 28, 529–535, 543–546, 555–649
Second Opt-Out, 578–579
Side Agreements, 28, 543–544, 635

RULE 23(f)
Generally, 697–709

RULE 23(g)
Generally, 155–157

RULE 23(h)
Generally, 634–635, 645–649

RULE 23.1
See Shareholder Derivative Suits

RULE 23.2
See Unincorporated Associations

RULE 24
Generally, 1071–1099

RULE 42
Generally, 1099–1109

RULES ENABLING ACT
Class actions and, 6, 177, 365–369

SECOND OPT-OUT
Generally, 578–579

SECURITIES FRAUD CLASS ACTIONS
Generally, 836–888
Elements of a Rule 10b–5 claim, 837–844
Fraud-created-the-market, 856
Fraud-on-the-market, 840–862
Lead counsel, 878–885
Lead plaintiff, 866–878
Loss causation and class certification, 857–862
Materiality of the misrepresented or omitted fact, 837–857
Post-Reform Act federal removal legislation, 885–888
Presumption of reliance for omissions, 853–854
Reform legislation, 862–866
Reliance issues, 837–857
Shareholder derivative suits, 915–941

SETTLEMENTS
Generally, 529–614
Attorney-client conflicts, 601–605
Attorney conflicts of interest, 538–544
Class Action Fairness Act and, 606–608
Considerations in approving, 565–600
Discovery, 576–577
Fairness Assessment, 579–600
Fairness hearing, 577
Government notification of, 534, 606–607
Interested participants, 529–535
Intra-class conflicts, 535–538
Judge's role, 544–550
Non-class aggregate settlements, 1147–1154
Notice, 566–576
Pre-certification, 605–606
Proposed rule changes and, 608–610
Second Opt-Out, 578–579
Settlement certification, 550–565
Shareholder derivative suits, 939–940
Side agreements, 543–544, 635

SEVENTH AMENDMENT
Generally, 351–359, 764–773
Bifurcated trials and the reexamination clause, 205, 351–359
In employment cases, 356–359

SHAREHOLDER DERIVATIVE SUITS
Generally, 915–941
Adequate representation, 932–939
Contemporaneous ownership requirement, 920–925
Demand requirement, 925–932
Derivative injury requirement, 916–920
Requirements in common with Rule 23, 932–941
Settlement, 939–940

SIDE AGREEMENTS
Generally, 28, 543–544, 635

"SPURIOUS" CLASS ACTIONS
Defined, 20–22
Replaced by Rule 23(b)(3) classes, 23–27
Under original version of Rule 23, 19–23

STANDING
Generally, 57, 70–72

STATE-COURT CLASS ACTIONS
Generally, 7, 257, 260, 407–414
Class Action Fairness Act's impact on, 399, 442–443, 451–463

STATUTE OF LIMITATIONS ISSUES
Defendant class actions, 899–900
Tolling, 431–432

STRATEGIC ISSUES IN CLASS ACTIONS
Defendant's perspective, 259–263
Local rules, 264–265
Plaintiff's perspective, 253–259

SUBCLASSES
Generally, 35–43, 302–307

SUMMARY JUDGMENT MOTIONS IN CLASS ACTIONS
Generally, 344–347

SUPERIORITY
Generally, 231–251
Alternatives to class treatment, 232–233
Desirability of concentrating litigation in particular forum, 244–247
Enumerated factors under Rule 23(b)(3), 233–251
Extent and nature of pending litigation, 241–244
In Rule 23(b)(3) class actions, 233–251
Interest in individual control of litigation, 237–241
Manageability issues, 247–251

SUPPLEMENTAL JURISDICTION
Class actions, 443–449,
Impleader, 1056–1058
Intervention, 1085
Joinder, 1025–1026

THIRD-PARTY FUNDING
Generally, 649–657

THRESHOLD REQUIREMENTS
Generally, 35–69
Ascertainability, 44–54
Definable class, 35–54
Live controversy, 58–69
Representative's membership in class, 54–58
Standing issues, 70–72

TRANSFERS FOR THE CONVENIENCE OF PARTIES AND WITNESSES, AND IN THE INTERESTS OF JUSTICE
See Multidistrict Litigation

TRIAL ISSUES
Extrapolation and statistical proof, 359–369
Seventh Amendment, 351–359

Trial structure, 350–369

"TRUE" CLASS ACTIONS
Defined, 20–22
Under original version of Rule 23, 19–23

TYPICALITY
Generally, 103–115
Challenges raised by defendants, 103–104
Conspiracy or juridical link, 892–893, 897–898
Factual disparities defeating, 107–114
Recovery against only one of several defendants, 903–905
Reform, 114–115
Unique defenses to, 109–114

UNINCORPORATED ASSOCIATIONS
Generally, 941–951
Applicability of Rule 23 requirements, 948–951
Applicability of Rule 23.1 to jural entities, 944–948
Diversity jurisdiction issues, 942–948
Limitations on qualifying organization, 947–948
Prior existence of organization, 948

VENUE CHANGE UNDER 28 U.S.C. § 1404
As an aggregation device, 1109–1116

VIRTUAL REPRESENTATION
Rejection of broad theory of, 498, 1098–1099